Philips'
New World
ATLAS

Philips'
New World
ATLAS

GEORGE PHILIP

LONDON MELBOURNE MILWAUKEE

Edited by

B.M. Willett, B.A., Cartographic Editor, George Philip and Son Ltd

D. Gaylard, Assistant Cartographic Editor, George Philip Printers Ltd

G. Atkinson, B.A., J. Downs, B.A., N. Harris, B.A., Helen McCourt, B.Sc., Elizabeth Prince-Smith, B.Sc., and R.D. Smith, B.Sc.

Consultant Cartographer

Harold Fullard, M.Sc.

Maps and illustrations prepared by the cartographic staffs of
George Philip Printers Ltd
Fairey Surveys Ltd
and Ronald Parker Associates

Prepared under the direction of A.G. Poynter, M.A., Director of Cartography

Acknowledgements

The illustrations in *The Universe, Earth and Man* have been provided by the following: Air India, Australian Information Service, Brazilian Embassy, London, British Aircraft Corporation, British Airways, British Leyland, British Petroleum, British Rail, British Steel Corporation, British Tourist Authority, Central Electricity Generating Board, D. Chanter, Danish Embassy, London, Egypt Air, Fiat (England) Ltd., Finnish Tourist Bureau, Freightliners Ltd., H. Fullard, M. H. Fullard, Gas Council Exploration Ltd., Commander H. R. Hatfield/Astro Books, H. Hawes, Israeli Govt. Tourist Office, Japan Air Lines, Lufthansa, M.A.T. Transport Ltd., Meteorological Office, London, Moroccan Tourist Office, N.A.S.A. (Space Frontiers), National Coal Board, London, National Maritime Museum, London, Offshore Co, Pan American World Airways, Royal Astronomical Society, London, Shell International Petroleum Co. Ltd., Swan Hunter Group, Ltd., Swiss National Tourist Office, B. M. Willett, Woodmansterne Ltd.

Third Edition 1980

British Library Cataloguing in Publication Data

Philips' new world atlas. – 3rd ed.
1. Atlases, British
I. New world atlas
912 G1019

ISBN 0 540 05358 9

Preface

Philips' **New World Atlas** has been specially planned to meet the need for an atlas of convenient size and yet of sufficient proportions to provide adequate maps for normal reference purposes. This is essentially an atlas that a busy person requires in our modern world changed as it is by the increasingly rapid means of communications, the development of new organizations of many kinds and the ever faster pace of international events brought to our television screens every night by satellite.

An overall view of the earth in space, the composition of the earth and its surrounding atmosphere open the Atlas by diagrams, charts, tables and illustrations, followed by physical, demographic, economic and political maps. Further regional maps, designed for detailed reference, have an emphasis on the inclusion of a large number of place names on a physical background which also includes political and administrative divisions.

The style of colouring takes advantage of new developments in cartographic design and map production. Lighter yet cleaner layer colours have made possible the inclusion of a hill shading to bring out clearly the character of the landscape without impairing the detail of names, settlements and communications. The opportunity of new reproduction was also taken to revise topographical and cultural details from the new surveys of recent years, and to express measures in metric form.

Attention is drawn to the policy adopted where there are rival claims to territory: international boundaries are drawn to show the *de facto* situation. This does not denote international recognition of these boundaries: it shows the states which are administering the areas on either side of the line.

Spellings of names are in the forms given in the latest official lists. Generally, they agree with the rules of the Permanent Committee on Geographical Names and the United States Board on Geographical Names. This index contains approximately 45,000 entries.

HAROLD FULLARD

Contents I

THE UNIVERSE, EARTH AND MAN

1 Chart of the Stars
2-3 The Solar System
4 The Earth
5 The Moon
6-7 Time
8-9 The Atmosphere and Clouds
10-11 Climate and Weather
12-13 The Earth from Space
14-15 The Evolution of the Continents
16-17 The Unstable Earth
18-19 The Making of Landscape
20-21 The Earth: Physical Dimensions
22-23 Distances
24-25 Water Resources and Vegetation
26-27 Population
28 Language
29 Religion
30-31 The Growth of Cities
32-33 Food Resources: Vegetable
34 Food Resources: Animal
35 Nutrition
36-37 Mineral Resources I
38-39 Mineral Resources II
40-41 Fuel and Energy
42 Occupations
43 Industry
44-45 Transport
46-47 Trade
48 Wealth

The Himalayas from Apollo 7, taken at an altitude of 130 nautical miles. Mount Everest (8,848 m, 29,021 ft) is in the lower centre. The lake-studded highlands of Tibet appear in the upper right. *(Nasa, B. Coleman Ltd)*

WORLD MAPS 1-128

1	**General Reference**	
1	**The World** – Physical	1:150M
2-3	**The World** – Political	1:80M
4-5	**The Polar Regions**	1:35M
6-7	**The Atlantic Ocean** Equatorial Scale	1:50M

EUROPE

8-9	**Europe** Physical	1:17½M
	European Organisations	1:40M
10	**Europe** Political	1:20M
11	**The British Isles** Political	1:4M
12-13	**England and Wales**	1:2M
14	**Scotland**	1:2M
15	**Ireland**	1:2M
16	**The Netherlands, Belgium and Luxembourg**	1:2½M
17	**France**	1:5M
18-19	**Northern France**	1:2½M
20-21	**Southern France**	1:2½M

Contents 3

EUROPE CONTINUED

22-23	Central Europe	1:5M
24-25	Germany and Switzerland	1:2½M
26-27	Austria, Czechoslovakia and Hungary	1:2½M
28	Poland	1:2½M
29	Spain and Portugal	1:5M
30-31	Western Spain and Portugal	1:2½M
32-33	Eastern Spain	1:2½M
34-35	The Mediterranean Lands	1:10M
36-37	Italy and the Balkan States	1:5M
	Malta	1:1M
38-39	Northern Italy and Western Yugoslavia	1:2½M
40-41	Southern Italy	1:2½M
42-43	Eastern Yugoslavia and Bulgaria	1:2½M
44-45	Greece and Albania	1:2½M
46	Rumania	1:2½M
47	Southern Norway	1:2½M
48-49	Denmark and Southern Sweden	1:2½M
50-51	Scandinavia and the Baltic Lands	1:5M
	Iceland	1:5M
52-53	The U.S.S.R. in Europe	1:10M
54-55	European Russia Central	1:5M
56-57	European Russia South	1:5M

Sunset behind San Maria della Salute, Venice, Italy. *(N. Devore, B. Coleman Ltd)*

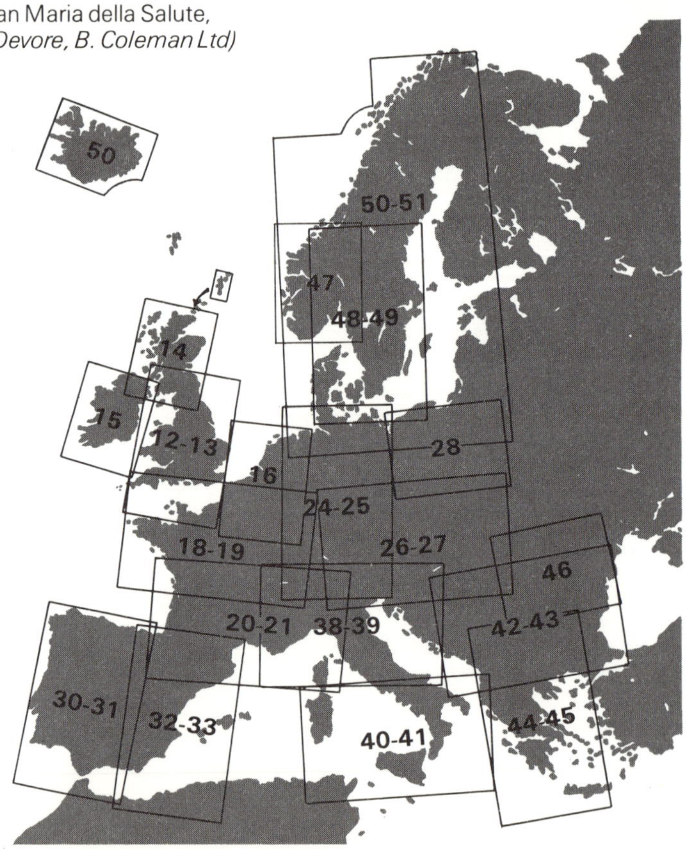

Grand Lac, Cambodia.*(M. P. Kahl, B. Coleman Ltd)*

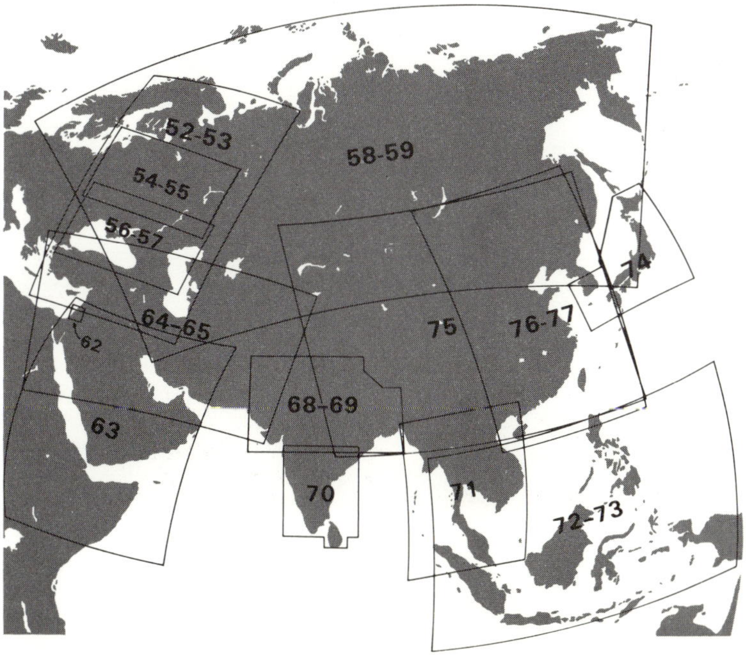

ASIA

58-59	**The Union of Soviet Socialist Republics**	1:20M
60	**Asia** Physical	1:50M
61	**Asia** Political	1:50M
62	**Israel and West Jordan**	1:1M
63	**Arabia and The Horn of Africa**	1:15M
64-65	**The Near and Middle East**	1:10M
66-67	**South Asia**	1:10M
68-69	**The Indo-Gangetic Plain**	1:6M
	S. Asia – Irrigation	1:40M
70	**Southern India and Sri Lanka**	1:6M
71	**Mainland South-East Asia**	1:10M
	Malaya & Singapore	1:6M
72-73	**The East Indies**	1:12½M
	Java & Madura	1:7½M
74	**Japan**	1:10M
	Southern Japan	1:5M
75	**China**	1:20M
76-77	**Eastern China and Korea**	1:10M

Contents 5

AFRICA

78	**Africa** Physical	1:40M
79	**Africa** Political	1:40M
80-81	**Northern Africa**	1:15M
82-83	**North-West Africa**	1:8M
84-85	**West Africa**	1:8M
86-87	**The Nile Valley**	1:8M
	The Nile Delta	1:4M
88-89	**Central and South Africa**	1:15M
90-91	**East Africa**	1:8M
92-93	**Southern Africa**	1:8M
	Madagascar	1:8M

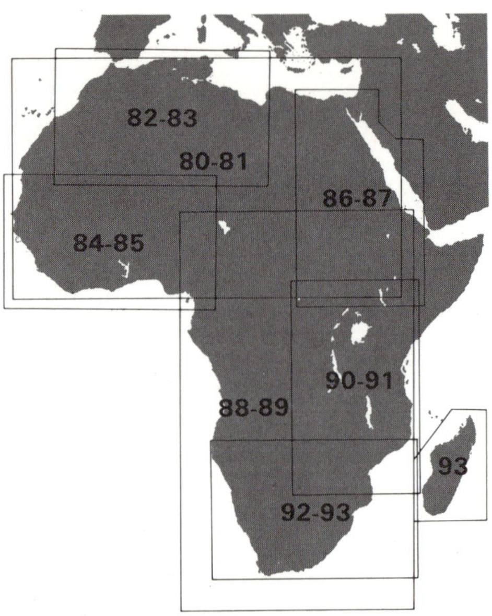

Fishermen in a dug-out canoe near Shakawe, Botswana *(G. D. Plage, B. Coleman Ltd)*

AUSTRALASIA

94-95	**The Pacific Ocean**	
	Equatorial Scale	1:60M
96-97	**Australia**	1:12M
	Australasia – Physical	1:80M
98-99	**Eastern Australia**	1:7½M
	Papua New Guinea	1:12M
100	**South-East Australia**	1:4½M
101	**New Zealand**	1:6M
	Samoa	1:12M
	Fiji and Tonga	1:12M
	New Zealand and Dependencies	1:60M

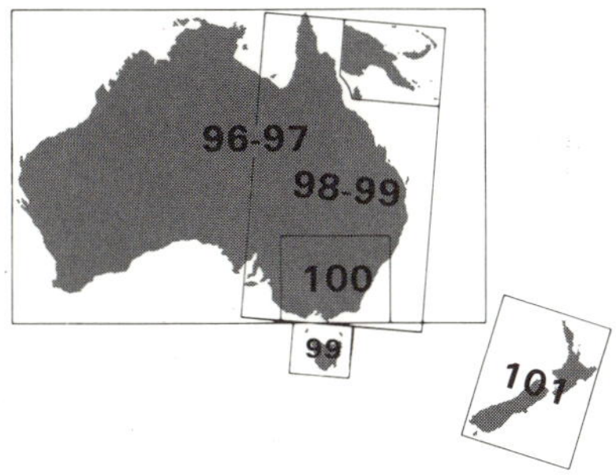

Sydney opera house and Sydney harbour bridge, New South Wales, Australia.
(F. Prenzel, B. Coleman Ltd)

Contents 7

THE AMERICAS

102-3	**North America**	
	Physical	1:30M
	Political	1:70M
104-5	**Canada**	1:15M
	Alaska	1:30M
106-7	**Eastern Canada**	1:7M
108-9	**Western Canada**	1:7M
110-11	**The United States**	1:12M
	Hawaii	1:10M
112-13	**North-Eastern United States**	1:2½M
114-15	**The Eastern United States**	1:6M
116-17	**The Middle United States**	1:6M
118-19	**The Western United States**	1:6M
120	**Mexico**	1:2M
	Panama Canal	1:1M
121	**The West Indies**	1:12M
	Bermuda	1:1M
	Leeward Is.	1:8M
	Windward Is.	1:8M
	Trinidad and Tobago	1:8M
	Jamaica	1:8M
122	**South America** Physical	1:30M
123	**South America** Political	1:30M
124-25	**Central South America**	1:8M
126-27	**South America** North	1:16M
128	**South America** South	1:16M

INDEX

Arizona, USA, on the Mexican border.
(M. P. L. Fogden, B. Coleman Ltd)

Chart of the Stars

Northern Stars

Stars of the Middle Heavens

Southern Stars

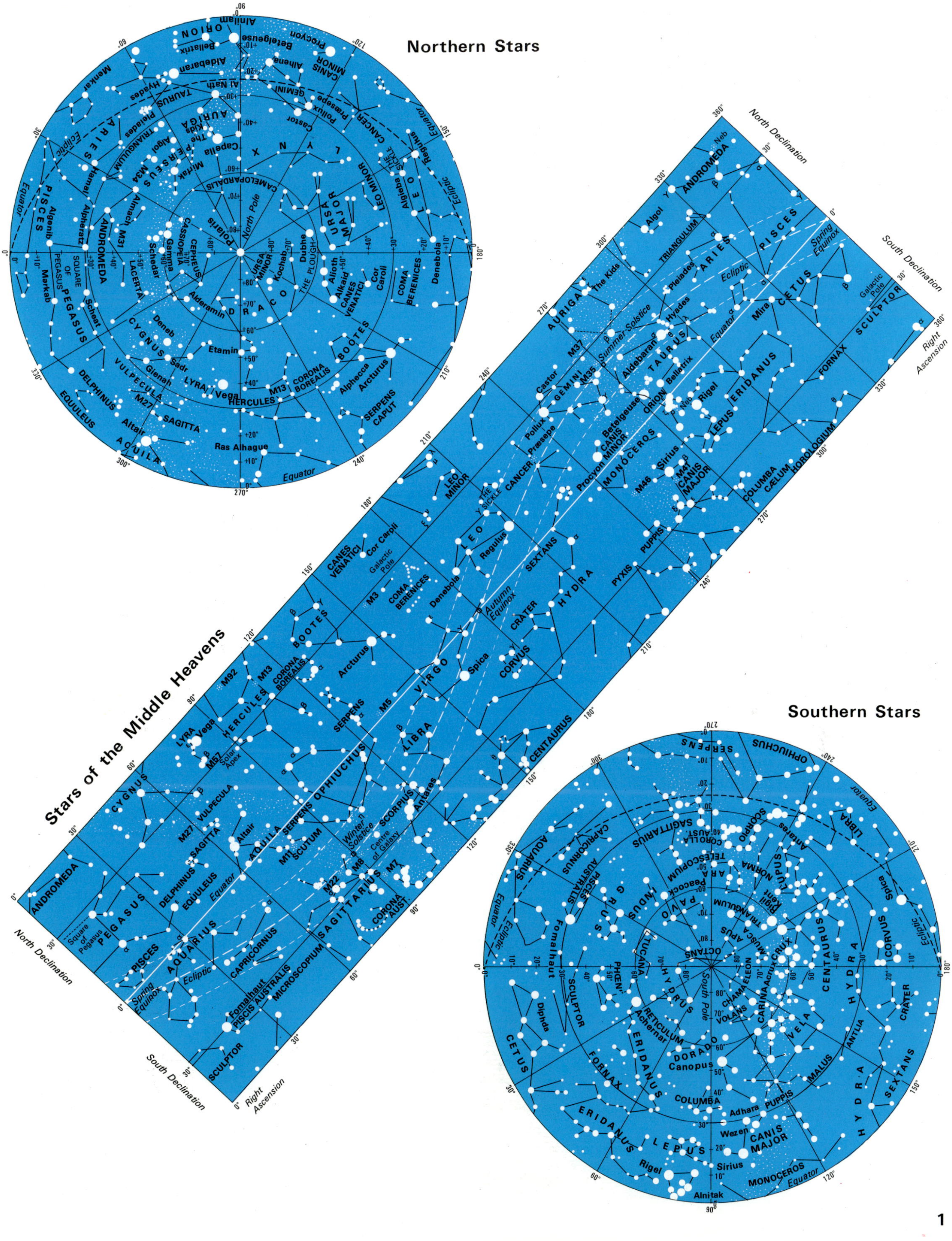

The Solar System

The Solar System is a minute part of one of the innumerable galaxies that make up the universe. Our Galaxy is represented in the drawing to the right and The Solar System (S) lies near the plane of spiral-shaped galaxy, but 27 000 light-years from the centre. The System consists of the Sun at the centre with planets, moons, asteroids, comets, meteors, meteorites, dust and gases revolving around it. It is calculated to be at least 4 700 million years old.

The Solar System can be considered in two parts: the Inner Region planets- Mercury, Venus, Earth and Mars - all small and solid, the Outer Region planets - Jupiter, Saturn, Uranus and Neptune - all gigantic in size, and on the edge of the system the smaller Pluto.

Our galaxy

Inner region planets

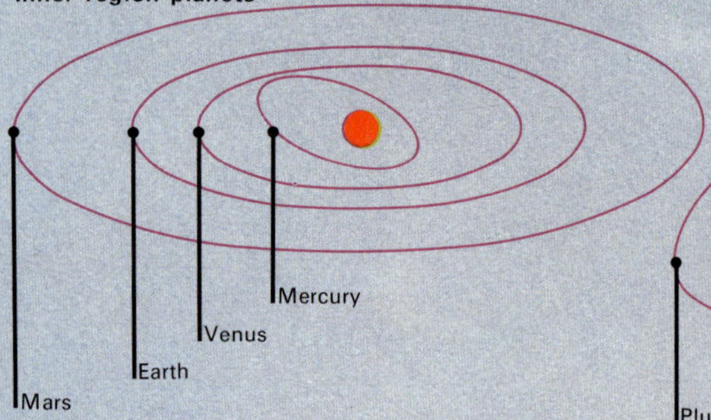

Outer region planets

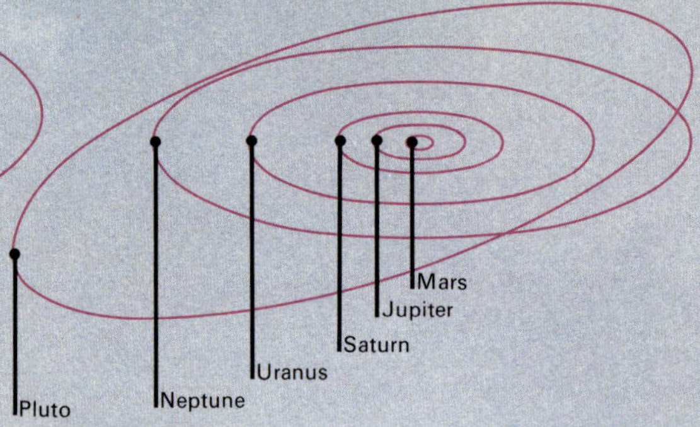

The planets

All planets revolve round the Sun in the same direction, and mostly in the same plane. Their orbits are shown (left) - they are not perfectly circular paths.

The table below summarizes the dimensions and movements of the Sun and planets.

The Sun

The Sun has an interior with temperatures believed to be of several million °C brought about by continuous thermo-nuclear fusions of hydrogen into helium. This immense energy is transferred by radiation into surrounding layers of gas the outer surface of which is called the chromosphere. From this "surface" with a temperature of many thousands °C "flames" (solar prominences) leap out into the diffuse corona which can best be seen at times of total eclipse (see photo right). The bright surface of the Sun, the photosphere, is calculated to have a temperature of about 6 000 °C, and when viewed through a telescope has a mottled appearance, the darker patches being called sunspots - the sites of large disturbances of the surface.

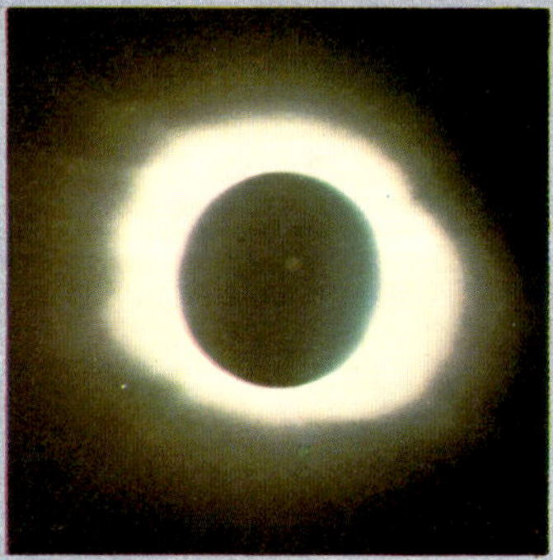

Total eclipse of the sun

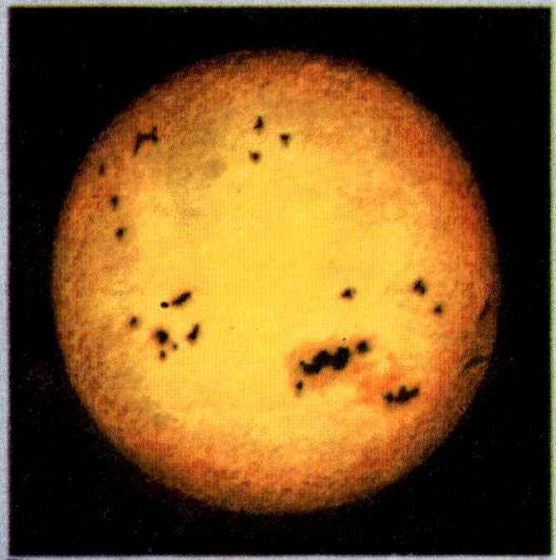

The sun's surface

	Equatorial diameter in km	Mass (earth=1)	Mean distance from sun in millions km	Mean radii of orbit (earth=1)	Orbital inclination	Mean sidereal period (days)	Mean period of rotation on axis (days)	Number of satellites
Sun	1 392 000	332 946	—	—	—	—	25·38	—
Mercury	4 878	0·05	57·9	0·38	7°	87·9	58·6	0
Venus	12 104	0·81	108·2	0·72	3°23′	224·7	243	0
Earth	12 756	1·00	149·6	1·00	—	365·2	0·99	1
Mars	6 794	0·10	227·9	1·52	1°50′	686·9	1·02	2
Jupiter	142 800	317·9	778·3	5·20	1°18′	4332·5	0·41	14 ?
Saturn	120 000	95·1	1 427	9·53	2°29′	10759·2	0·42	11
Uranus	52 000	14·5	2 869	19·17	0°46′	30684·8	0·45	5
Neptune	48 400	17·2	4 496	30·05	1°46′	60190·5	0·67	2
Pluto	3 000 ?	0·001	5 900	39·43	17°1′	91628·6	6·38	1 ?

The Sun's diameter is 109 times greater than that of the Earth.

Mercury is the nearest planet to the Sun. It is composed mostly of high density metals and probably has an atmosphere of heavy inert gases.

Venus is similar in size to the Earth, and probably in composition. It is, however, much hotter and has a dense atmosphere of carbon dioxide which obscures our view of its surface.

Earth is the largest of the inner planets. It has a dense iron-nickel core surrounded by layers of silicate rock. The surface is approximately $\frac{3}{8}$ land and $\frac{5}{8}$ water, and the lower atmosphere consists of a mixture of nitrogen, oxygen and other gases supplemented by water vapour. With this atmosphere and surface temperatures usually between −50°C and +40°C, life is possible.

Mars, smaller than the Earth, has a noticeably red appearance. Photographs taken by the Mariner probes show clearly the cratered surface and polar ice caps, probably made from frozen carbon dioxide.

The Asteroids orbit the Sun mainly between Mars and Jupiter. They consist of thousands of bodies of varying sizes with diameters ranging from yards to hundreds of miles.

Jupiter is the largest planet of the Solar System. Photographs taken by Voyager I and II have revealed an equatorial ring system and shown the distinctive Great Red Spot and rotating cloud belts in great detail.

Saturn, the second largest planet consists of hydrogen, helium and other gases. The equatorial rings are composed of small ice particles.

Uranus is extremely remote but just visible to the naked eye and has a greenish appearance. A faint equatorial ring system was discovered in 1977. The planet's axis is tilted through 98° from its orbital plane, therefore it revolves in a retrograde manner.

Neptune, yet more remote than Uranus and larger. It is composed of gases and has a bluish green appearance when seen in a telescope. As with Uranus, little detail can be observed on its surface.

Pluto. No details are known of its composition or surface. The existence of this planet was firstly surmised in a computed hypothesis, which was tested by repeated searches by large telescopes until in 1930 the planet was found. Latest evidence seems to suggest that Pluto has one satellite, provisionally named Charon.

The Earth

Seasons, Equinoxes and Solstices

The Earth revolves around the Sun once a year and rotates daily on its axis, which is inclined at 66½° to the orbital plane and always points into space in the same direction. At midsummer (N.) the North Pole tilts towards the Sun, six months later it points away and half way between the axis is at right angles to the direction of the Sun (right).

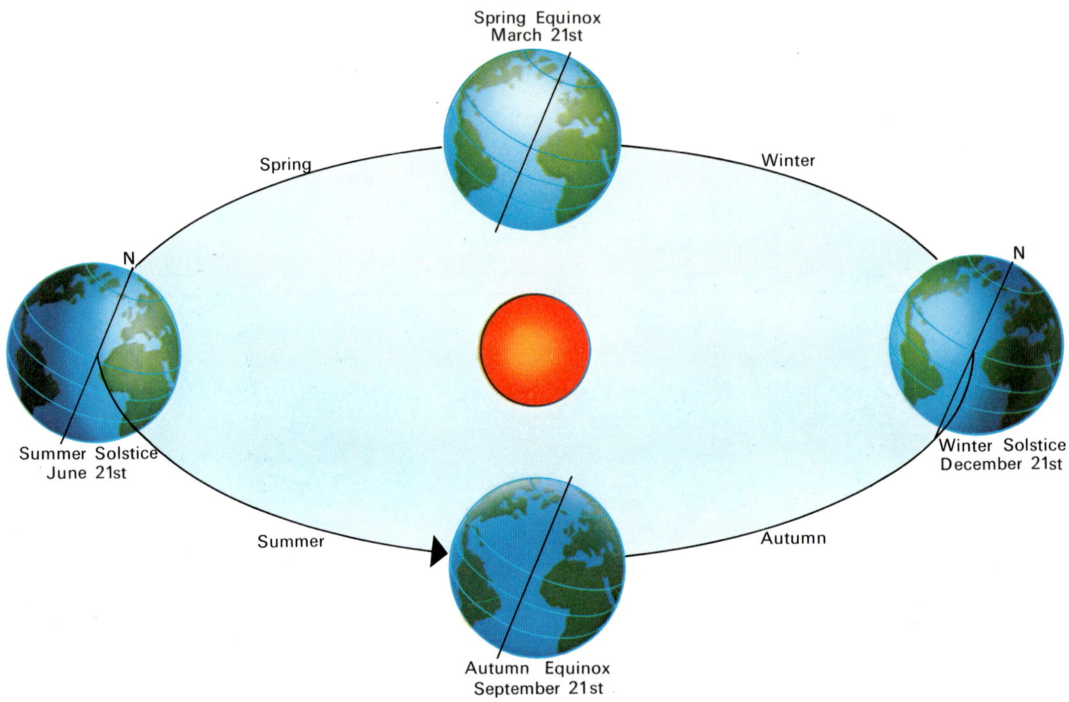

Earth data

Maximum distance from the Sun (Aphelion) 152 007 016 km
Minimum distance from the Sun (Perihelion) 147 000 830 km
Obliquity of the ecliptic 23° 27′ 08″
Length of year - tropical (equinox to equinox) 365.24 days
Length of year - sidereal (fixed star to fixed star) 365.26 days
Length of day - mean solar day 24h 03m 56s
Length of day - mean sidereal day 23h 56m 04s

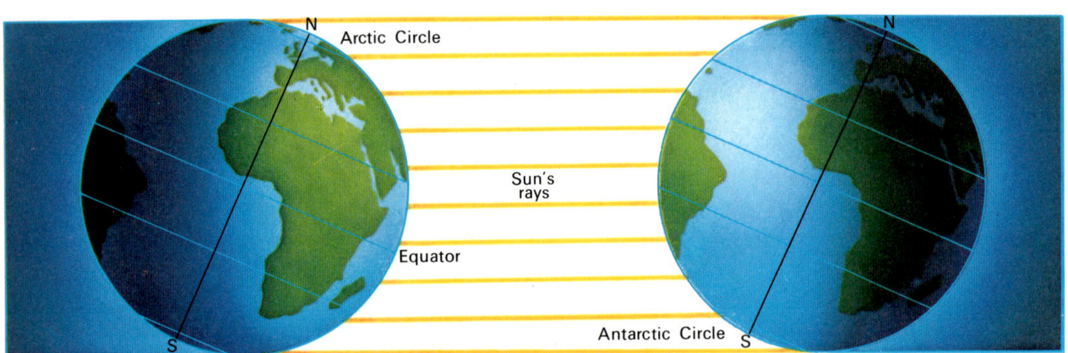

Length of day and night

At the summer solstice in the northern hemisphere, the Arctic has total daylight and the Antarctic total darkness. The opposite occurs at the winter solstice. At the equator, the length of day and night are almost equal all the year, at 30° the length of day varies from about 14 hours to 10 hours and at 50° from about 16 hours to 8 hours.

Apparent path of the Sun

The diagrams (right) illustrate the apparent path of the Sun at A the equator, B in mid latitudes say 45°N, C at the Arctic Circle 66½° and D at the North Pole where there is six months continuous daylight and six months continuous night

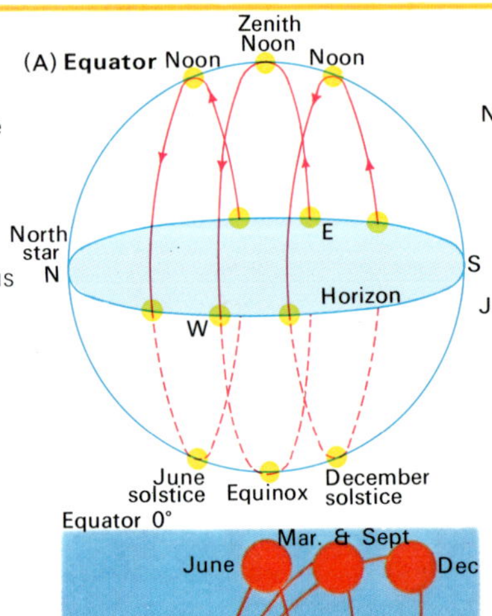

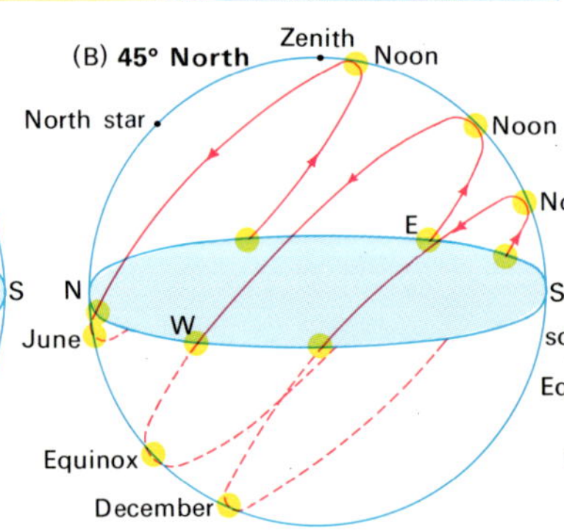

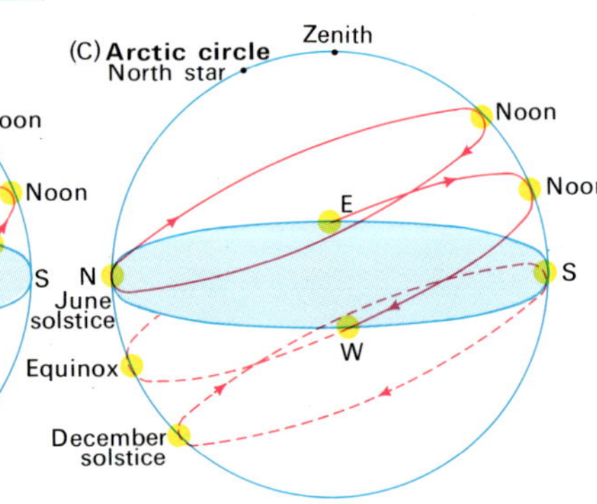

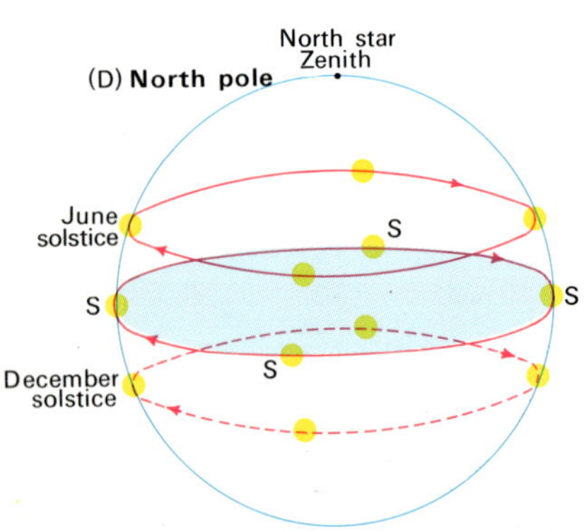

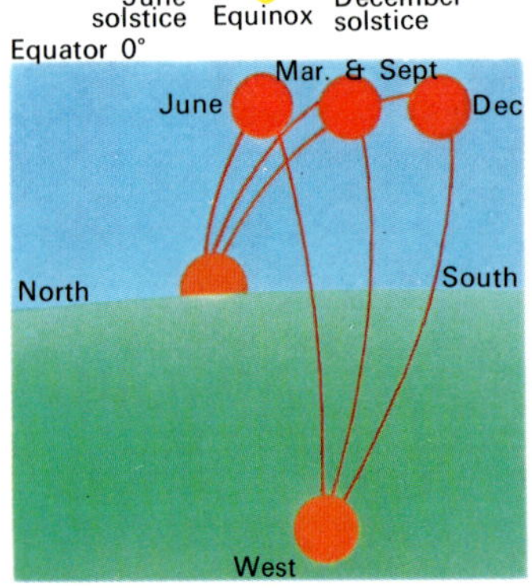

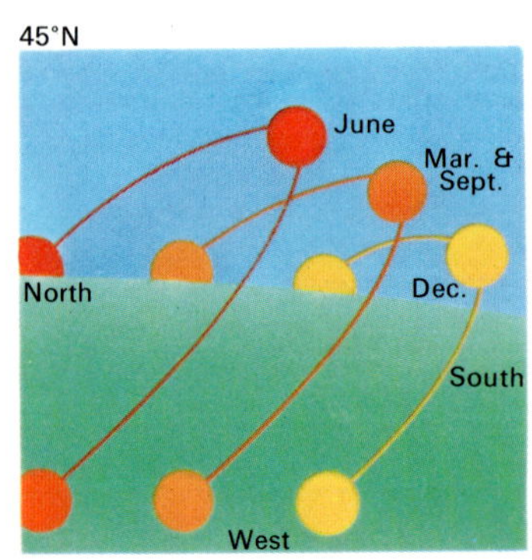

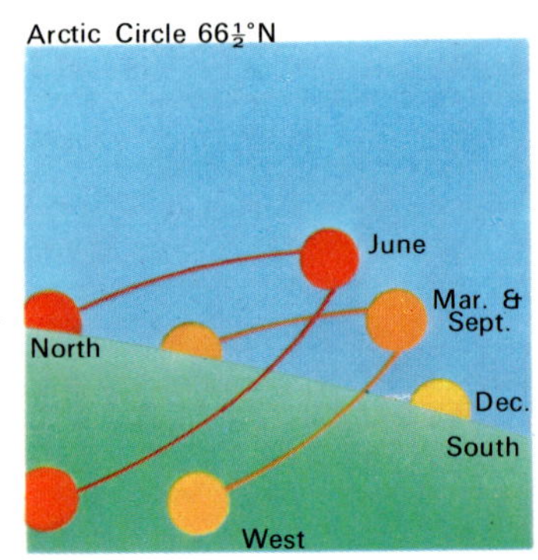

The Moon

The Moon rotates slowly making one complete turn on its axis in just over 27 days. This is the same as its period of revolution around the Earth and thus it always presents the same hemisphere ('face') to us. Surveys and photographs from space-craft have now added greatly to our knowledge of the Moon, and, for the first time, views of the hidden hemisphere.

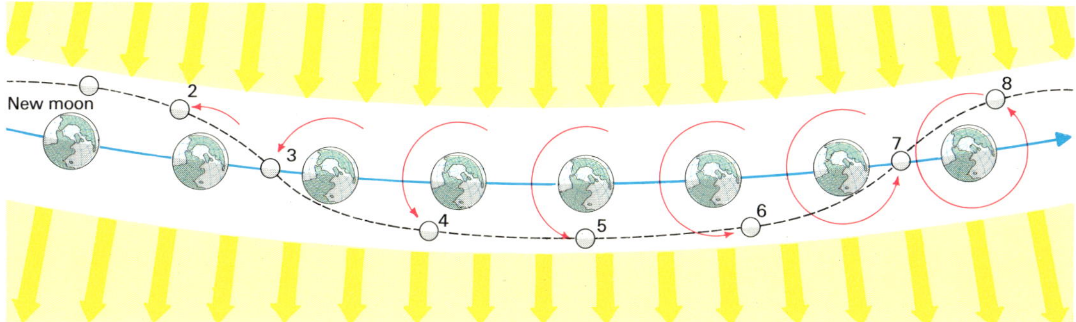

Crescent moon (2) | Half moon, first quarter (3) | Gibbous moon (4) | Full moon (5) | The waning moon (6) | Half moon, last quarter (7) | The old moon (8)

Phases of the Moon

The interval between one full Moon and the next is approximately $29\frac{1}{2}$ days - thus there is one new Moon and one full Moon every month. The diagrams and photographs (right) show how the apparent changes in shape of the Moon from new to full arise from its changing position in relation to the Earth and both to the fixed direction of the Sun's rays.

Moon data

Distance from Earth 356 410 km to 406 685 km
Mean diameter 3 473 km
Mass approx. $\frac{1}{81}$ of that of Earth
Surface gravity $\frac{1}{6}$ of that of Earth
Atmosphere - none, hence no clouds, no weather, no sound.
Diurnal range of temperature at the Equator +200°C

Landings on the Moon

Left are shown the landing sites of the U.S. Apollo programme.

Apollo 11 Sea of Tranquility (1°N 23°E) 1969
Apollo 12 Ocean of Storms (3°S 24°W) 1969
Apollo 14 Fra Mauro (4°S 17°W) 1971
Apollo 15 Hadley Rill (25°N 4°E) 1971
Apollo 16 Descartes (9°S 15°E) 1972
Apollo 17 Sea of Serenity (20°N 31°E) 1972

Eclipses of Sun and Moon

When the Moon passes between Sun and Earth it causes a partial eclipse of the Sun *(right 1)* if the Earth passes through the Moon's outer shadow *(P)*, or a total eclipse *(right 2)*, if the inner cone shadow crosses the Earth's surface.

In a lunar eclipse, the Earth's shadow crosses the Moon and gives either total or partial eclipses.

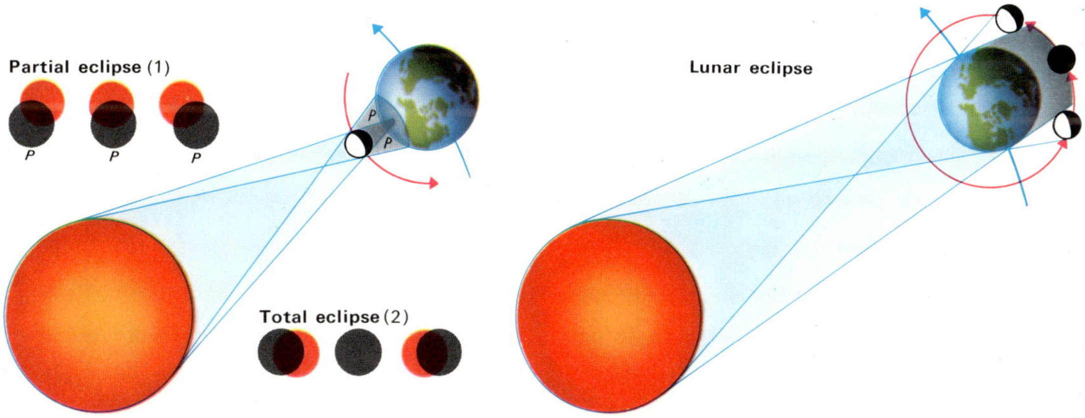

Tides

Ocean water moves around the Earth under the gravitational pull of the Moon, and, less strongly, that of the Sun. When solar and lunar forces pull together - near new and full Moon - high spring tides result. When solar and lunar forces are not combined - near Moon's first and third quarters - low neap tides occur.

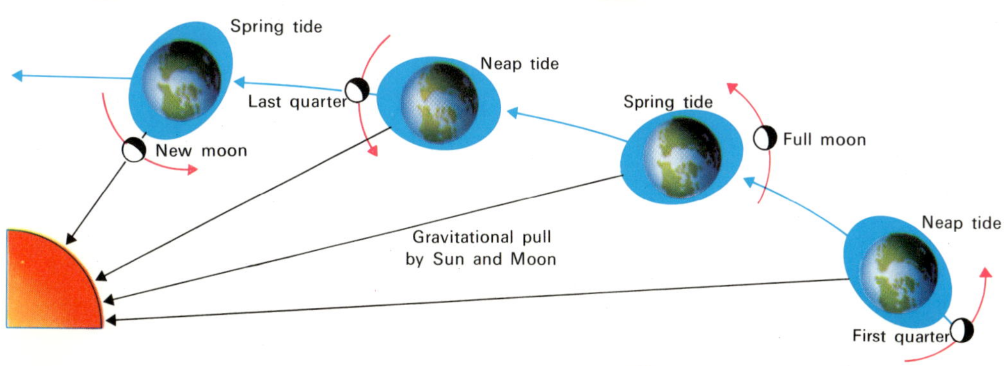

Time

Time measurement
The basic unit of time measurement is the day, one rotation of the earth on its axis. The subdivision of the day into hours and minutes is arbitrary and simply for our convenience. Our present calendar is based on the solar year of $365\frac{1}{4}$ days, the time taken for the earth to orbit the sun. A month was anciently based on the interval from new moon to new moon, approximately $29\frac{1}{2}$ days - and early calendars were entirely lunar.

Rotation of the Earth

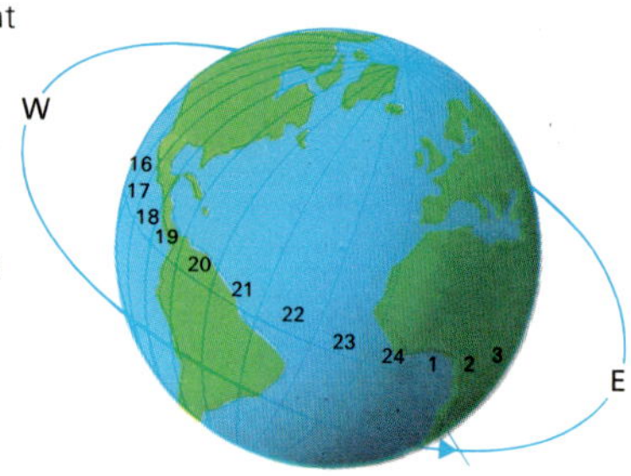

Greenwich Observatory

Prime Meridian

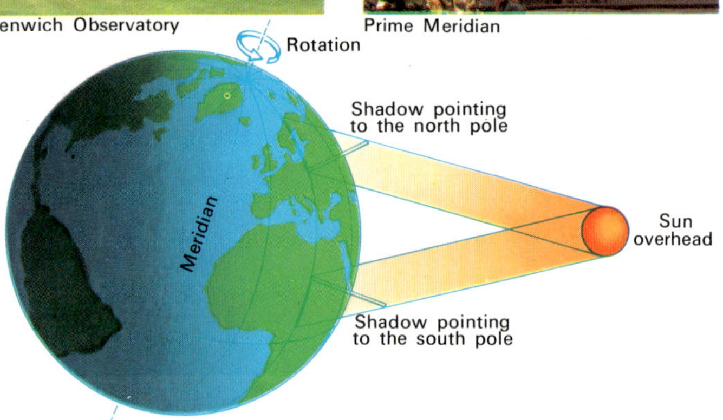

The International Date Line
When it is 12 noon at the Greenwich meridian, 180° east it is midnight of the same day while 180° west the day is only just beginning. To overcome this the International Date Line was established, approximately following the 180° meridian. Thus, for example, if one travelled eastwards from Japan (140° East) to Samoa (170° West) one would pass from Sunday night into Sunday morning.

Time zones
The world is divided into 24 time zones, each centred on meridians at 15° intervals which is the longitudinal distance the sun appears to travel every hour. The meridian running through Greenwich passes through the middle of the first zone. Successive zones to the east of Greenwich zone are ahead of Greenwich time by one hour for every 15° of longitude, while zones to the west are behind by one hour.

Night and day
As the earth rotates from west to east the sun appears to rise in the east and set in the west: when the sun is setting in Shanghai on the directly opposite side of the earth New York is just emerging into sunlight. Noon, when the sun is directly overhead, is coincident at all places on the same meridian with shadows pointing directly towards the poles.

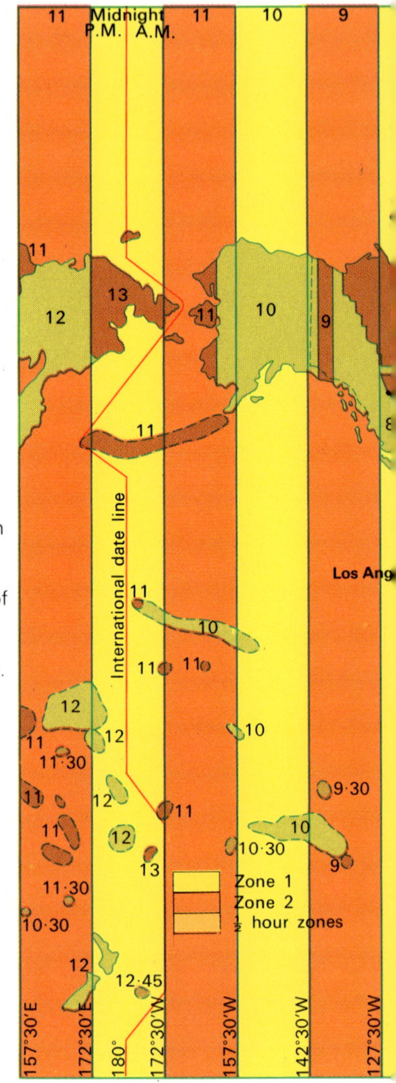

Solar time
The time taken for the earth to complete one rotation about its own axis is constant and defines a day but the speed of the earth along its orbit around the sun is inconstant. The length of day, or 'apparent solar day', as defined by the apparent successive transits of the sun is irregular because the earth must complete more than one rotation before the sun returns to the same meridian.

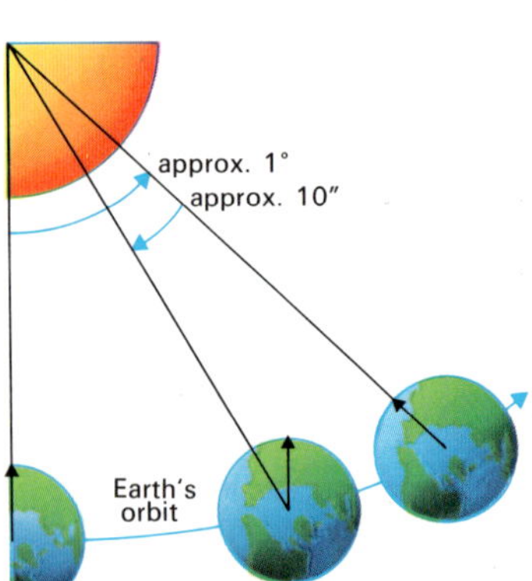

Sidereal time
The constant sidereal day is defined as the interval between two successive apparent transits of a star, or the first point of Aries, across the same meridian. If the sun is at the equinox and overhead at a meridian on one day, then the next day the sun will be to the east by approximately 1°; thus the sun will not cross the meridian until about 4 minutes after the sidereal noon.

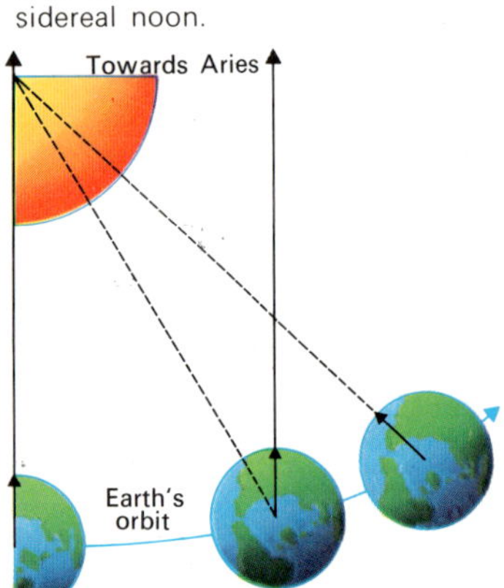

Astronomical clock, Delhi

Sundials
The earliest record of sundials dates back to 741 BC but they undoubtedly existed as early as 2000 BC although probably only as an upright stick or obelisk. A sundial marks the progress of the sun across the sky by casting the shadow of a central style or gnomon on the base. The base, generally made of stone, is delineated to represent the hours between sunrise and sunset.

Kendall's chronometer

Chronometers
With the increase of sea traffic in the 18th century and the need for accurate navigation clockmakers were faced with an intriguing problem. Harrison, an English carpenter, won a British award for designing a clock which was accurate at sea to one tenth of a second per day. He compensated for the effect of temperature changes by incorporating bi-metallic strips connected to thin wires and circular balance wheels.

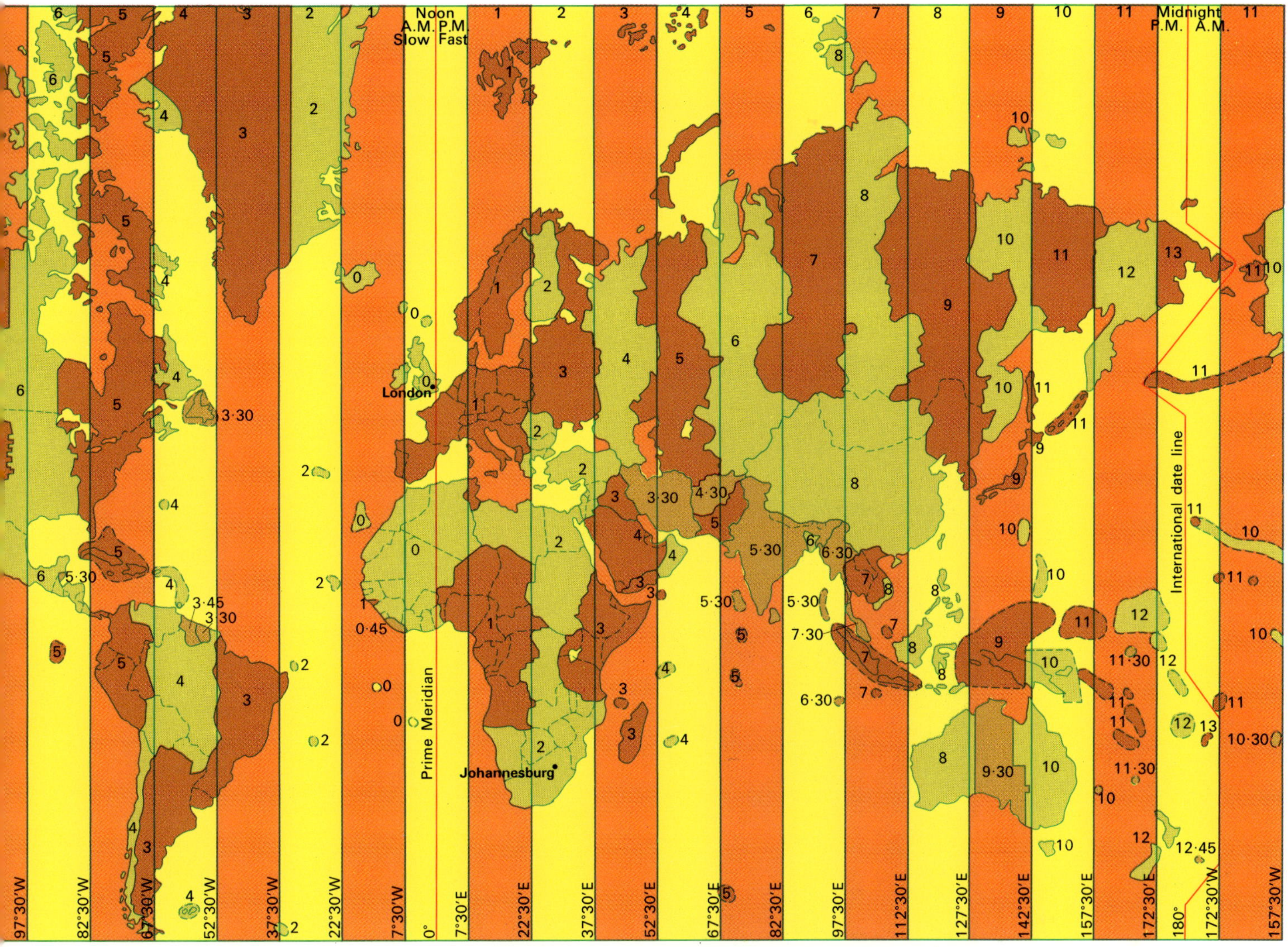

Progress of the accuracy of timekeepers

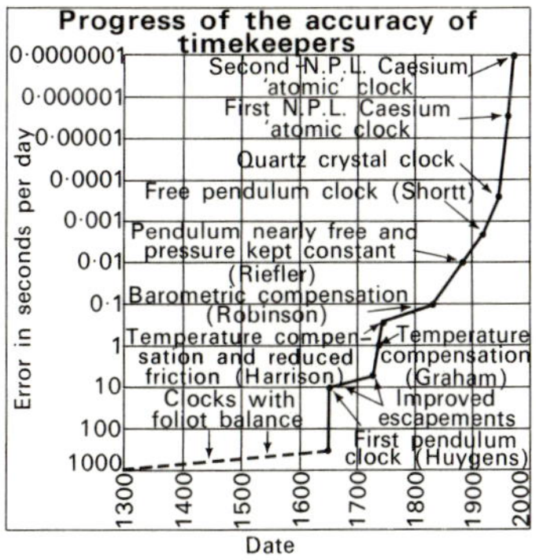

Vibration of quartz ring

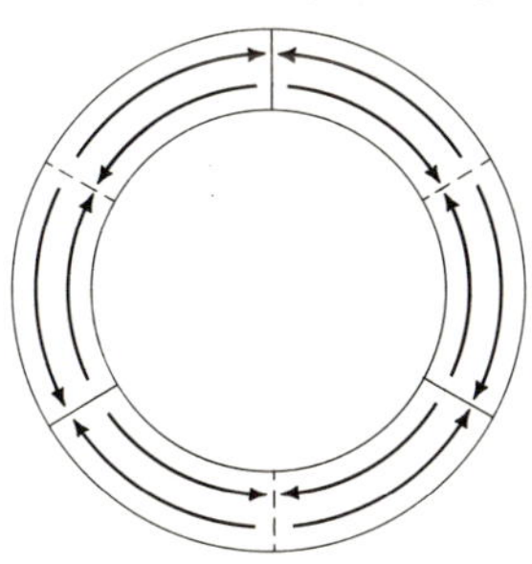

Time difference when travelling by air

London-Los Angeles (8780 km) (5456 miles)													
G.M.T.	1600	1700	1800	1900	2000	2100	2200	2300	2400	0100	0200	0300	0400
Pacific time	0800	0900	1000	1100	1200	1300	1400	1500	1600	1700	1800	1900	2000
In flight routine	Take off		Refreshments		Dinner	Motion picture					Refreshments		Landing
London routine	Afternoon tea				Dinner		Supper	Bed time	Sleep →				
Los Angeles routine	Breakfast		Morning coffee		Lunch				Afternoon tea			Dinner	

London-Johannesburg (9055 km)(5627 miles)														
G.M.T.	1800	1900	2000	2100	2200	2300	2400	0100	0200	0300	0400	0500	0600	0700
S.A. time	2000	2100	2200	2300	2400	0100	0200	0300	0400	0500	0600	0700	0800	0900
In flight routine	Take off		Dinner	Motion picture	←			Rest period	→		Breakfast			Landing
London routine		Dinner			Supper	Bed time			Sleep →					
Jo'burg routine			Supper	Bed time					Sleep →				Breakfast	

Chronographs

The invention of the chronograph by Charles Wheatstone in 1842 made it possible to record intervals of time to an accuracy of one sixtieth of a second. The simplest form of chronograph is the stop-watch. This was developed to a revolving drum and stylus and later electrical signals. A recent development is the cathode ray tube capable of recording to less than one ten-thousanth of a second.

Quartz crystal clocks

The quartz crystal clock, designed originally in America in 1929, can measure small units of time and radio frequencies. The connection between quartz clocks and the natural vibrations of atoms and molecules mean that the unchanging frequencies emitted by atoms can be used to control the oscillator which controls the quartz clock. A more recent version of the atomic clock is accurate to one second in 300 years.

International date line

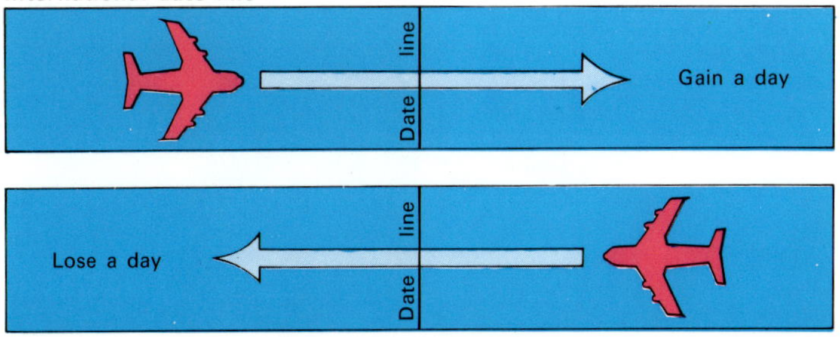

The Atmosphere and Clouds

Earth's thin coating *(right)*
The atmosphere is a blanket of protective gases around the earth providing insulation against otherwise extreme alternations in temperature. The gravitational pull increases the density nearer the earth's surface so that 5/6ths of the atmospheric mass is in the first 15 kms. It is a very thin layer in comparison with the earth's diameter of 12 680 kms., like the cellulose coating on a globe.

Exosphere*(1)*
The exosphere merges with the interplanetary medium and although there is no definite boundary with the ionosphere it starts at a height of about 600 kms. The rarified air mainly consists of a small amount of atomic oxygen up to 600 kms. and equal proportions of hydrogen and helium with hydrogen predominating above 2 400 kms.

Ionosphere*(2)*
Air particles of the ionosphere are electrically charged by the sun's radiation and congregate in four main layers, D, E, F1 and F2, which can reflect radio waves. Aurorae, caused by charged particles deflected by the earth's magnetic field towards the poles, occur between 65 and 965 kms. above the earth. It is mainly in the lower ionosphere that meteors from outer space burn up as they meet increased air resistance.

Stratosphere*(3)*
A thin layer of ozone contained within the stratosphere absorbs ultra-violet light and in the process gives off heat. The temperature ranges from about -55°C at the tropopause to about -60°C in the upper part, known as the mesosphere, with a rise to about 2°C just above the ozone layer. This portion of the atmosphere is separated from the lower layer by the tropopause.

Troposphere*(4)*
The earth's weather conditions are limited to this layer which is relatively thin, extending upwards to about 8 kms. at the poles and 15 kms. at the equator. It contains about 85% of the total atmospheric mass and almost all the water vapour. Air temperature falls steadily with increased height at about 1°C for every 100 metres above sea level.

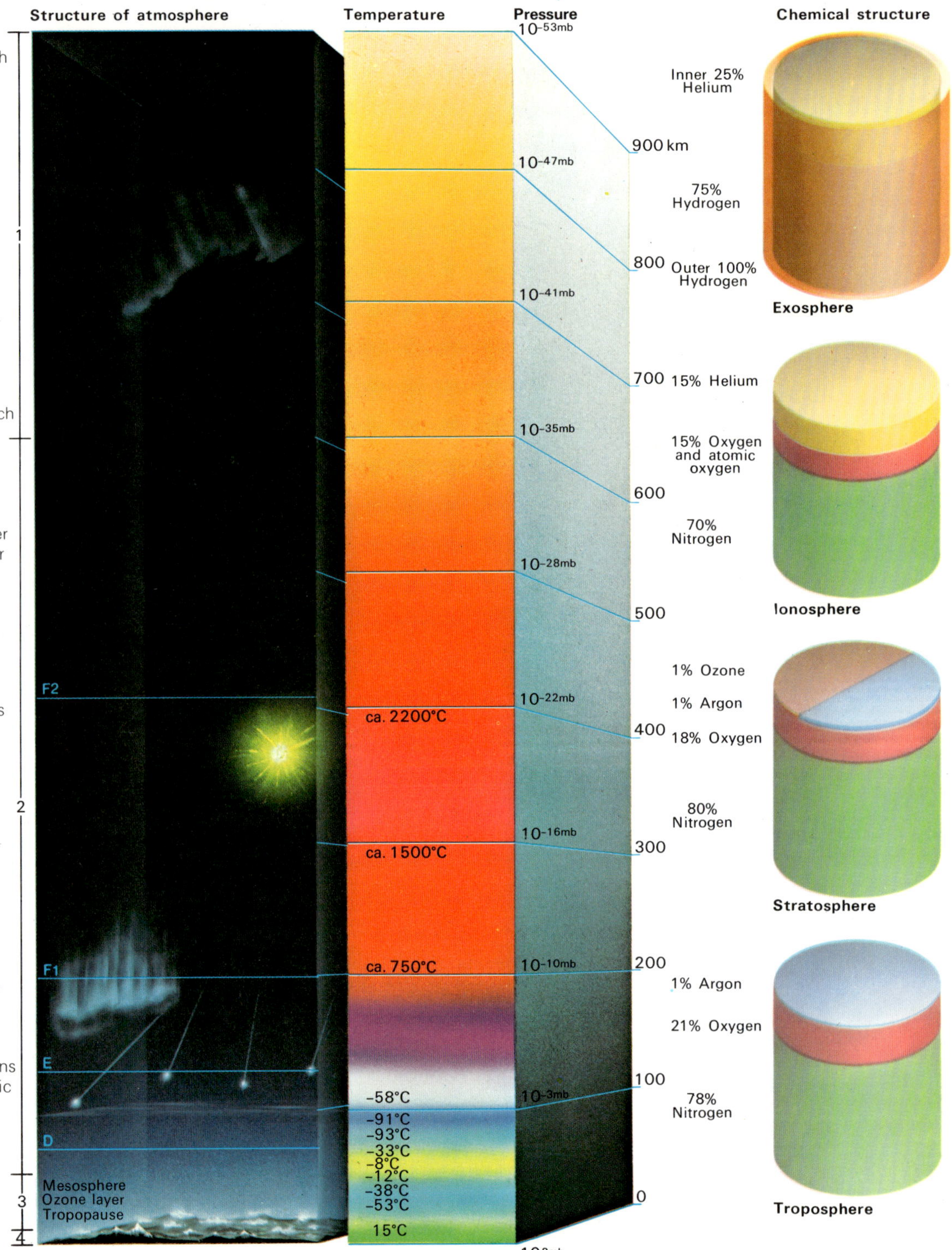

Pacific Ocean
Cloud patterns over the Pacific show the paths of prevailing winds.

Circulation of the air

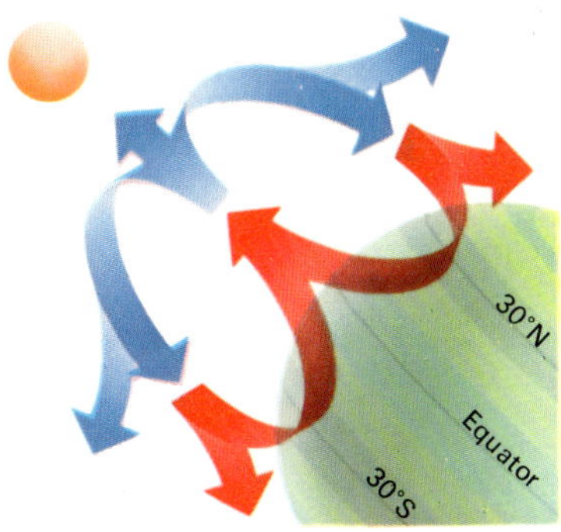

Circulation of the air
Owing to high temperatures in equatorial regions the air near the ground is heated, expands and rises producing a low pressure belt. It cools, causing rain, spreads out then sinks again about latitudes 30° north and south forming high pressure belts.

High and low pressure belts are areas of comparative calm but between them, blowing from high to low pressure, are the prevailing winds. These are deflected to the right in the northern hemisphere and to the left in the southern hemisphere (Corolis effect). The circulations appear in three distinct belts with a seasonal movement north and south following the overhead sun.

Cloud types

Clouds form when damp air is cooled, usually by rising. This may happen in three ways: when a wind rises to cross hills or mountains; when a mass of air rises over, or is pushed up by another mass of denser air; when local heating of the ground causes convection currents.

Cirrus *(1)* are detached clouds composed of microscopic ice crystals which gleam white in the sun resembling hair or feathers. They are found at heights of 6 000 to 12 000 metres.

Cirrostratus *(2)* are a whitish veil of cloud made up of ice crystals through which the sun can be seen often producing a halo of bright light.

Cirrocumulus *(3)* is another high altitude cloud formed by turbulence between layers moving in different directions.

Altostratus *(4)* is a grey or bluish striated, fibrous or uniform sheet of cloud producing light drizzle.

Altocumulus *(5)* is a thicker and fluffier version of cirro cumulus, it is a white and grey patchy sheet of cloud.

Nimbostratus *(6)* is a dark grey layer of cloud obscuring the sun and causing almost continuous rain or snow.

Cumulus *(7)* are detached heaped up, dense low clouds. The sunlit parts are brilliant white while the base is relatively dark and flat.

Stratus *(8)* forms dull overcast skies associated with depressions and occurs at low altitudes up to 1500 metres.

Cumulonimbus *(9)* are heavy and dense clouds associated with storms and rain. They have flat bases and a fluffy outline extending up to great altitudes.

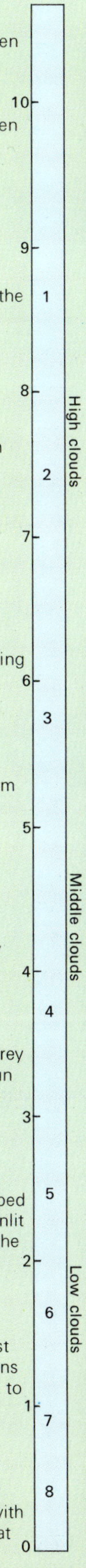

1 Cirrus

2 Cirrostratus

3 Cirrocumulus

4 Altostratus

5 Altocumulus

6 Nimbostratus

7 Cumulus

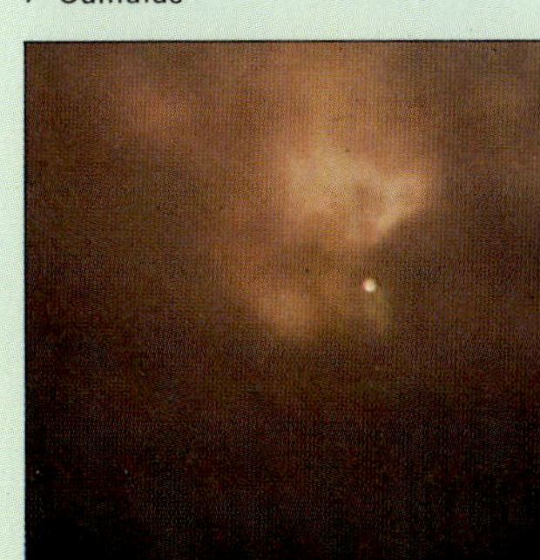
8 Stratus

9 Cumulonimbus

Climate and Weather

All weather occurs over the earth's surface in the lowest level of the atmosphere, the troposphere. Weather has been defined as the condition of the atmosphere at any place at a specific time with respect to the various elements: temperature, sunshine, pressure, winds, clouds, fog, precipitation. Climate, on the other hand, is the average of weather elements over previous months and years.

Climate graphs *right*
Each graph typifies the kind of climatic conditions one would experience in the region to which it is related by colour to the map. The scale refers to degrees Celsius for temperature and millimetres for rainfall, shown by bars. The graphs show average observations based over long periods of time, the study of which also compares the prime factors for vegetation differences.

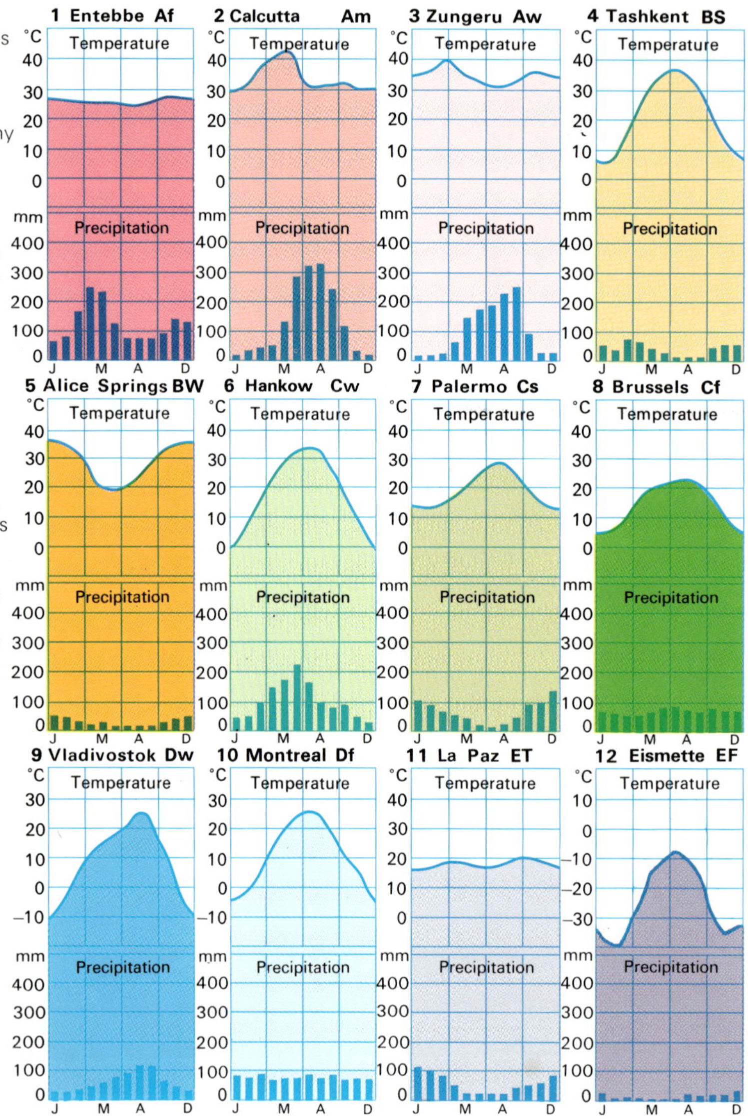

Development of a depression *below*
In an equilibrium front between cold and warm air masses (i) a wave disturbance develops as cold air undercuts the warm air (ii). This deflects the air flow and as the disturbance progresses a definite cyclonic circulation with warm and cold fronts is created (iii). The cold front moves more rapidly than the warm front eventually overtaking it, and occlusion occurs as the warm air is pinched out (iv).

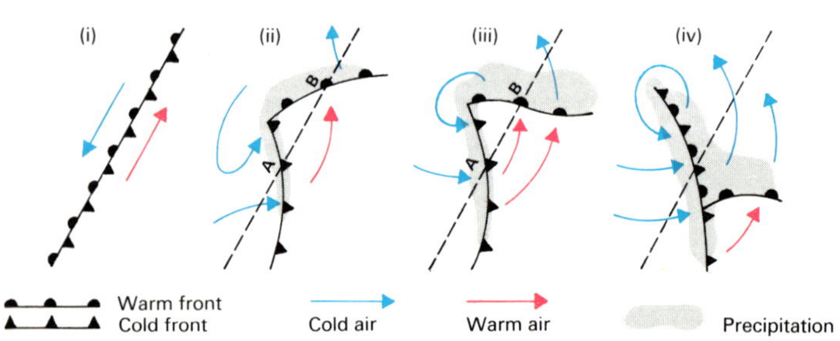

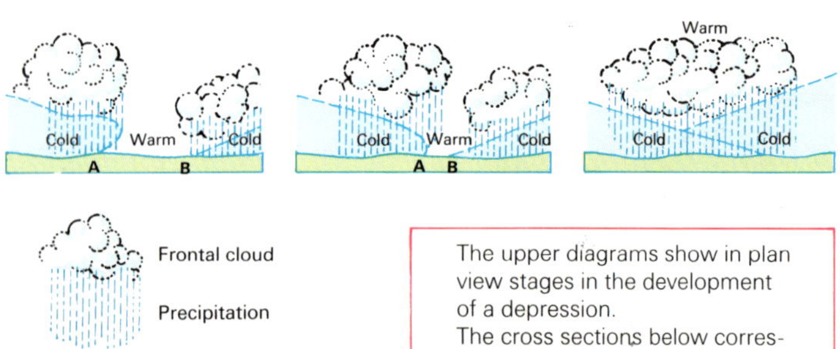

The upper diagrams show in plan view stages in the development of a depression.
The cross sections below correspond to stages (ii) to (iv).

Kinds of precipitation

Rain The condensation of water vapour on microscopic particles of dust, sulphur, soot or ice in the atmosphere forms water particles. These combine until they are heavy enough to fall as rain.

Hail Water particles, carried to a great height, freeze into ice particles which fall and become coated with fresh moisture. They are swept up again and refrozen. This may happen several times before falling as hail-stones.

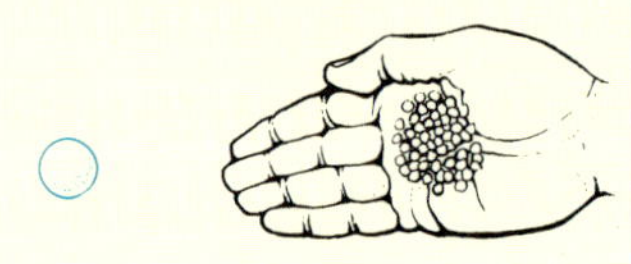

Frost Hoar, the most common type of frost, is precipitated instead of dew when water vapour changes directly into ice crystals on the surface of ground objects which have cooled below freezing point.

Snow is the precipitation of ice in the form of flakes, or clusters, of basically hexagonal ice crystals. They are formed by the condensation of water vapour directly into ice.

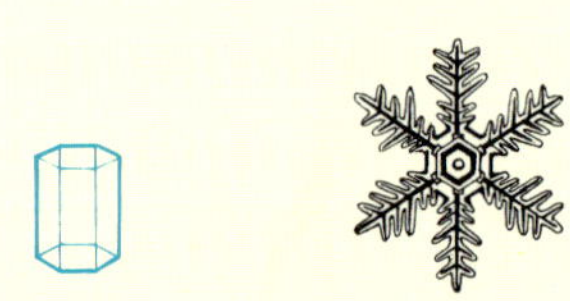

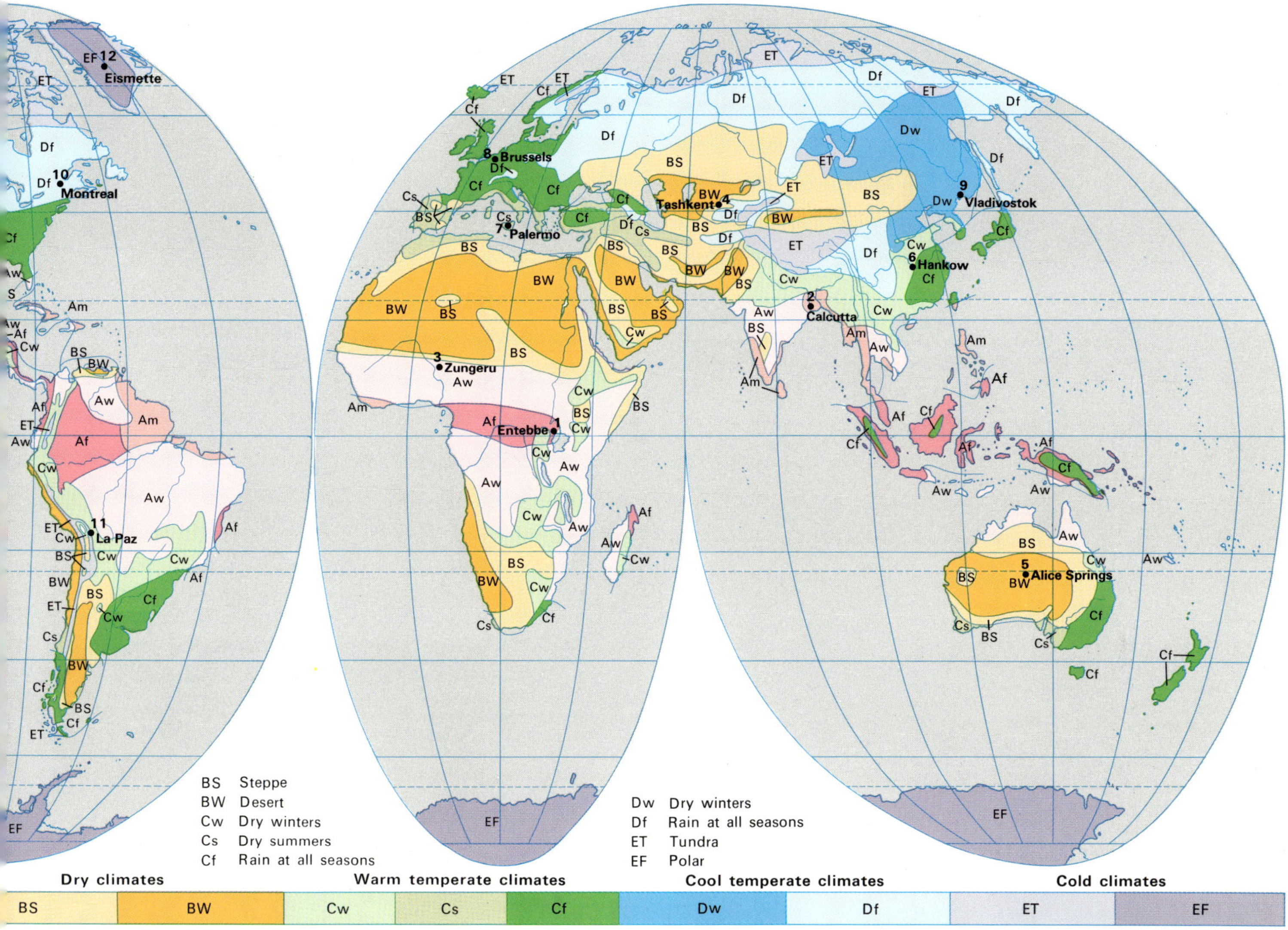

Tropical storm tracks *below*
A tropical cyclone, or storm, is designated as having winds of gale force (60 kph) but less than hurricane force (120 kph). It is a homogenous air mass with upward spiralling air currents around a windless centre, or eye. An average of 65 tropical storms occur each year, over 50% of which reach hurricane force. They originate mainly during the summer over tropical oceans.

Extremes of climate & weather *right*
Tropical high temperatures and polar low temperatures combined with wind systems, altitude and unequal rainfall distribution result in the extremes of tropical rain forests, inland deserts and frozen polar wastes. Fluctuations in the limits of these extreme zones and extremes of weather result in occasional catastrophic heat-waves and drought, floods and storms, frost and snow.

Hurricane devastation

Hot desert

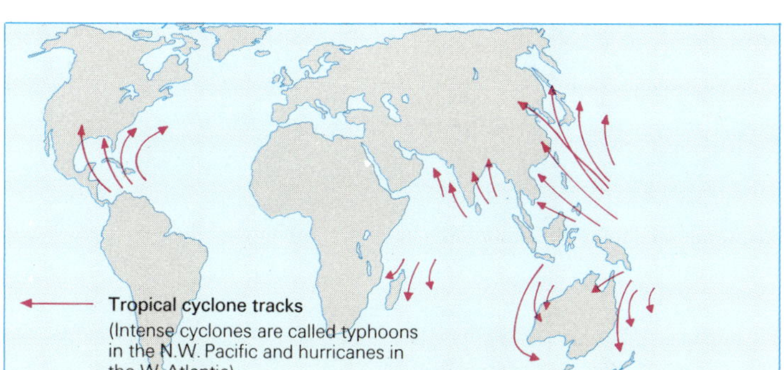

Tornado

Arctic dwellings

The Earth from Space

Mount Etna, Sicily *left*
Etna is at the top of the photograph, the Plain of Catania in the centre and the Mediterranean to the right. This is an infra-red photograph; vegetation shows as red, water as blue/black and urban areas as grey. The recent lava flows, as yet with no vegetation, show up as blue/black unlike the cultivated slopes which are red and red/pink.

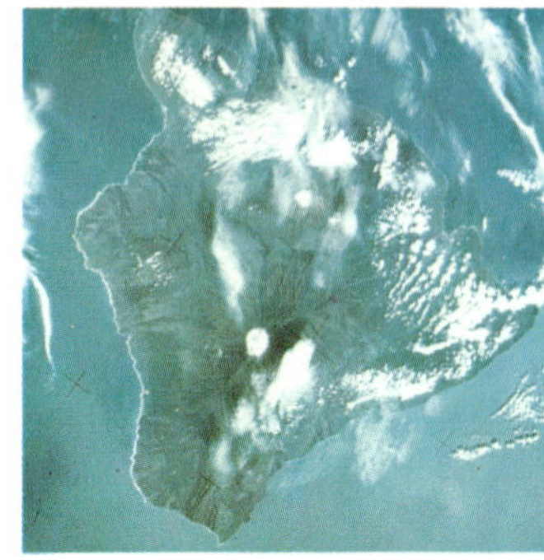

Hawaii, Pacific Ocean *above*
This is a photograph of Hawaii, the largest of the Hawaiian Islands in the Central Pacific. North is at the top of the photograph. The snowcapped craters of the volcanoes Mauna Kea (dormant) in the north centre and Mauna Loa (active) in the south centre of the photograph can be seen. The chief town, Hilo, is on the north east coast.

River Brahmaputra, India *left*
A view looking westwards down the Brahmaputra with the Himalayas on the right and the Khasi Hills of Assam to the left.

Szechwan, China *right*
The River Tachin in the mountainous region of Szechwan, Central China. The lightish blue area in the river valley in the north east of the photograph is a village and its related cultivation.

New York, U.S.A. *left*
This infra-red photograph shows the western end of Long Island and the entrance to the Hudson River. Vegetation appears as red, water as blue/black and the metropolitan areas of New York, through the cloud cover, as grey.

The Great Barrier Reef, Australia *right*
The Great Barrier Reef and the Queensland coast from Cape Melville to Cape Flattery. The smoke from a number of forest fires can be seen in the centre of the photograph.

Eastern Himalayas, Asia
above left
A view from Apollo IX looking north-westwards over the snowcapped, sunlit mountain peaks and the head waters of the Mekong, Salween, Irrawaddy and, in the distance, with its distinctive loop, the Brahmaputra.

Atacama Desert, Chile
above right
This view looking eastwards from the Pacific over the Mejillones peninsula with the city of Antofagasta in the southern bay of that peninsula. Inland the desert and salt-pans of Atacama, and beyond, the Andes.

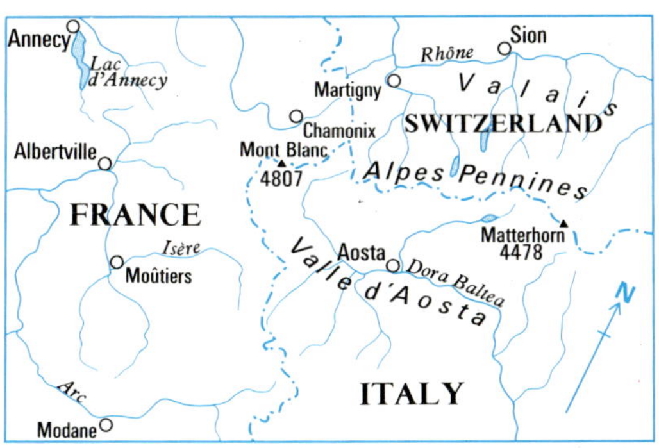

The Alps, Europe *right*
This vertical photograph shows the snow-covered mountains and glaciers of the Alps along the Swiss-Italian-French border. Mont Blanc and the Matterhorn are shown and, in the north, the Valley of the Rhône is seen making its sharp right-hand bend near Martigny. In the south the head waters of the Dora Baltea flow towards the Po and, in the north-west, the Lac d'Annecy can be seen.

The Evolution of the Continents

The origin of the earth is still open to much conjecture although the most widely accepted theory is that it was formed from a solar cloud consisting mainly of hydrogen. Under gravitation the cloud condensed and shrank to form our planets orbiting around the sun. Gravitation forced the lighter elements to the surface of the earth where they cooled to form a crust while the inner material remained hot and molten. Earth's first rocks formed over 3500 million years ago but since then the surface has been constantly altered.

Until comparatively recently the view that the primary units of the earth had remained essentially fixed throughout geological time was regarded as common sense, although the concept of moving continents has been traced back to references in the Bible of a break up of the land after Noah's floods. The continental drift theory was first developed by Antonio Snider in 1858 but probably the most important single advocate was Alfred Wegener who, in 1915, published evidence from geology, climatology and biology. His conclusions are very similar to those reached by current research although he was wrong about the speed of break-up.

The measurement of fossil magnetism found in rocks has probably proved the most influential evidence. While originally these drift theories were openly mocked, now they are considered standard doctrine.

The jigsaw
As knowledge of the shape and structure of the earth's surface grew, several of the early geographers noticed the great similarity in shape of the coasts bordering the Atlantic. It was this remarkable similarity which led to the first detailed geological and structural comparisons. Even more accurate fits can be made by placing the edges of the continental shelves in juxtaposition.

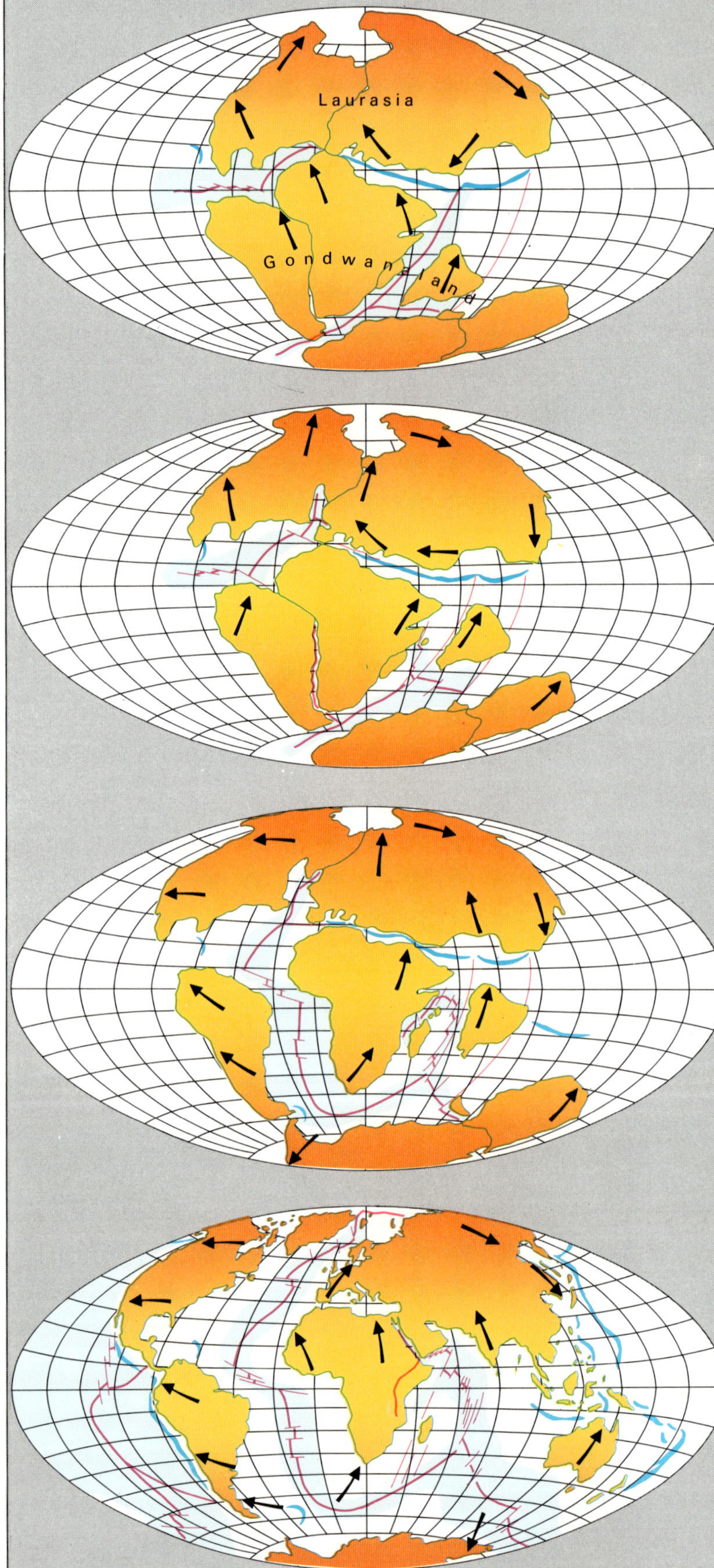

180 million years ago.
The original Pangaea land mass had split into two major continental groups. The southern group, Gondwanaland, had itself started to break up, India and Antarctica-Australia becoming isolated. A rift had begun to appear between South America and Africa and, in the East, Africa was closing up the Tethys Sea.

135 million years ago.
Both Gondwanaland and Laurasia continued to drift northwards but the widening of the splits in the North Atlantic and Indian Oceans persisted. The South Atlantic rift continued to lengthen and a further perpendicular rift appeared which will eventually separate Greenland from North America. India continues heading northward towards Asia.

65 million years ago.
South America, completely separated from Africa, moved quickly north and westwards. Madagascar broke free from Africa but, as yet, there is no sign of the Red Sea Rift which will split Africa from the Arabian Peninsula. The Mediterranean sea is recognizable. In the south, Australia is still connected to Antarctica.

Today.
India has moved northwards and is colliding with Asia, crumpling up the sediments to form the folded mountain range of the Himalayas. South America has rotated and moved west to connect with North America. Australia has separated from Antarctica.

Trench
Rift
New Ocean Floor
Zones of slippage

(After Dietz & Holden, Sci. Am. 1970)

Plate tectonics
The original debate about continental drift was only a prelude to a more radical idea; plate tectonics. The basic theory is that the earth's crust is made up of a series of rigid plates which float on a soft layer of the mantle and are moved about by convection currents in the earth's interior. These plates converge and diverge along margins marked by earthquakes, volcanoes and other seismic activity. Plates diverge from mid-ocean ridges where molten lava pushes upwards and forces the plates apart at a rate of up to 30mm. a year. Converging plates form either a trench, where the oceanic plate sinks below the lighter continental rock, or mountain ranges where two continents collide. This explains the paradox that while there have always been oceans none of the present oceans contain sediments more than 150 million years old.

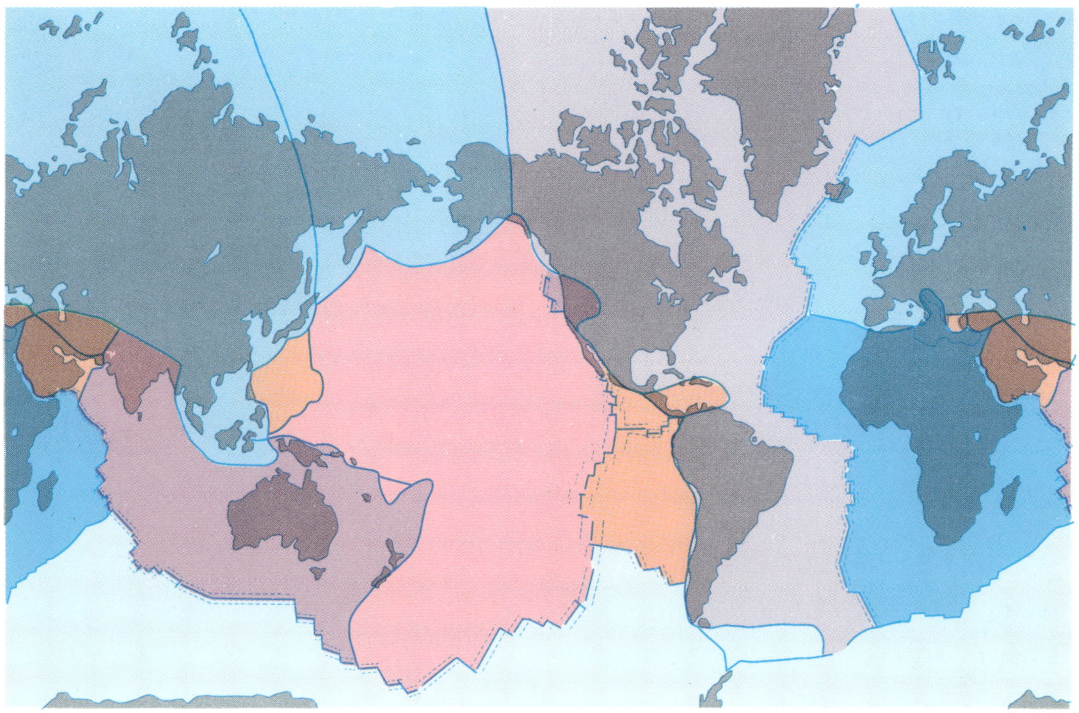

Trench boundary
The present explanation for the comparative youth of the ocean floors is that where an ocean and a continent meet the ocean plate dips under the less dense continental plate at an angle of approximately 45°. All previous crust is then ingested by downward convection currents. In the Japanese trench this occurs at a rate of about 120mm. a year.

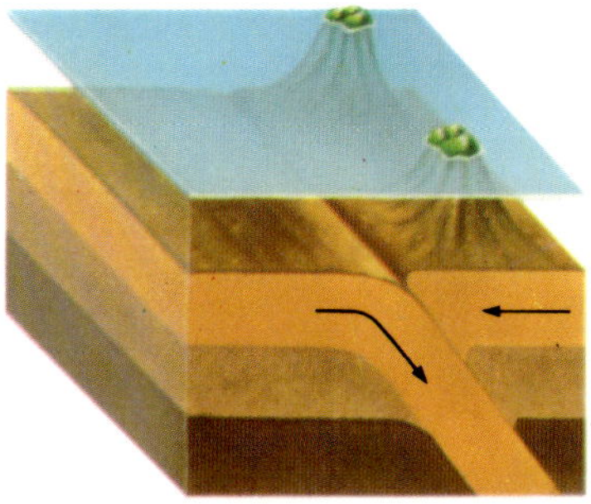

Transform fault
The recent identification of the transform, or transverse, fault proved to be one of the crucial preliminaries to the investigation of plate tectonics. They occur when two plates slip alongside each other without parting or approaching to any great extent. They complete the outline of the plates delineated by the ridges and trenches and demonstrate large scale movements of parts of the earth's surface

Ridge boundary
Ocean rises or crests are basically made up from basaltic lavas for although no gap can exist between plates, one plate can ease itself away from another. In that case hot, molten rock instantly rises from below to fill in the incipient rift and forms a ridge. These ridges trace a line almost exactly through the centre of the major oceans.

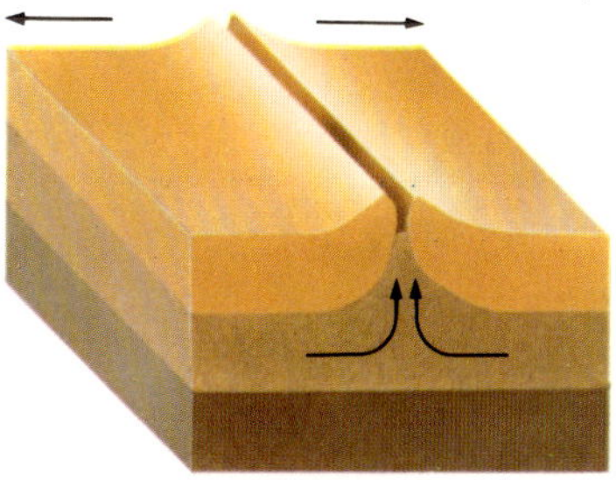

Destruction of ocean plates.
As the ocean plate sinks below the continental plate some of the sediment on its surface is scraped off and piled up on the landward side. This sediment is later incorporated in a folded mountain range which usually appears on the edge of the continent, such as the Andes. Similarly if two continents collide the sediments are squeezed up into new mountains.

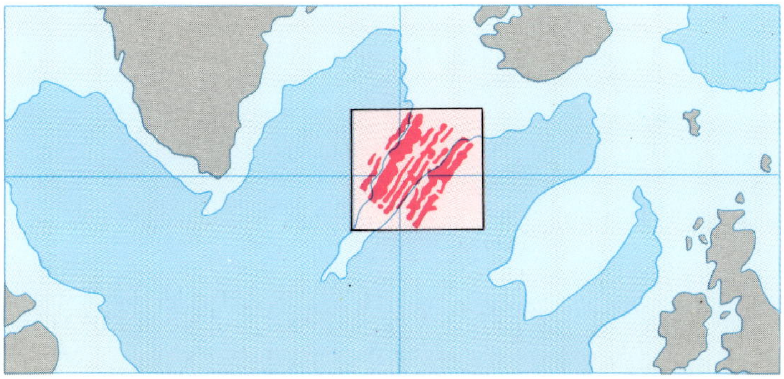

Sea floor spreading
Reversals in the earth's magnetic field have occured throughout history. As new rock emerges at the ocean ridges it cools and is magnetised in the direction of the prevailing magnetic field. By mapping the magnetic patterns either side of the ridge a symmetrical stripey pattern of alternating fields can be observed (see inset area in diagram). As the dates of the last few reversals are known the rate of spreading can be calculated.

The Unstable Earth

The earth's surface is slowly but continually being rearranged. Some changes such as erosion and deposition are extremely slow but they upset the balance which causes other more abrupt changes often originating deep within the earth's interior. The constant movements vary in intensity, often with stresses building up to a climax such as a particularly violent volcanic eruption or earthquake.

The crust *(below and right)*
The outer layer or crust of the earth consists of a comparatively low density, brittle material varying from 5 to 50 kilometres deep beneath the continents. Under this is a layer of rock consisting predominately of silica and aluminium; hence it is called 'sial'. Extending under the ocean floors and below the sial is a basaltic layer known as 'sima', consisting mainly of silica and magnesium.

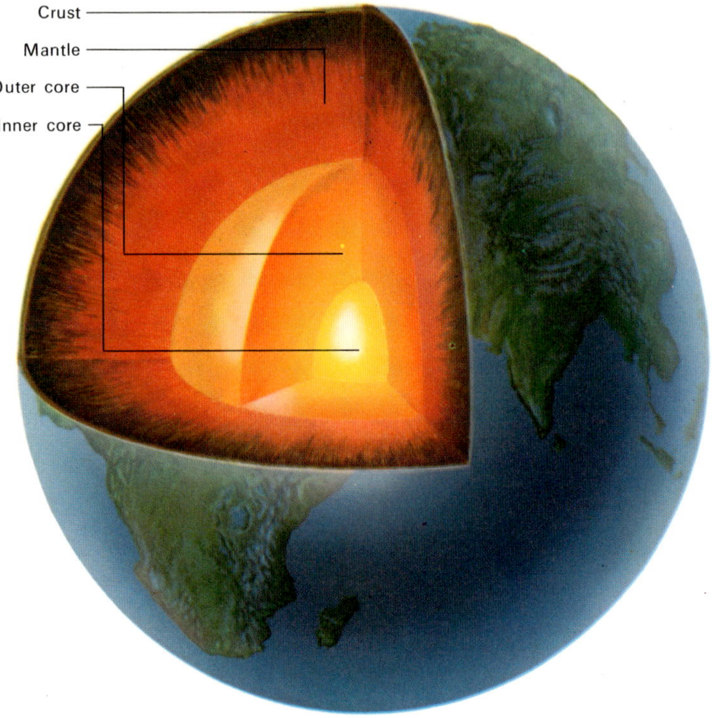

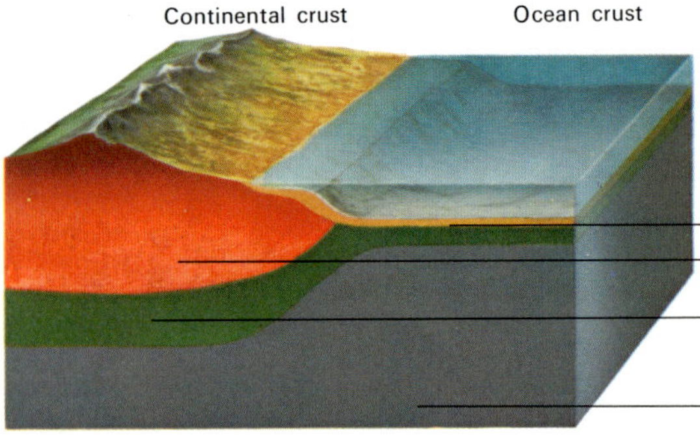

Volcanoes *(right, below and far right)*
Volcanoes occur when hot liquefied rock beneath the crust reaches the surface as lava. An accumulation of ash and cinders around a vent forms a cone. Successive layers of thin lava flows form an acid lava volcano while thick lava flows form a basic lava volcano. A caldera forms when a particularly violent eruption blows off the top of an already existing cone.

The mantle *(above)*
Immediately below the crust, at the mohorovicic discontinuity line, there is a distinct change in density and chemical properties. This is the mantle - made up of iron and magnesium silicates - with temperatures reaching 1 600°C. The rigid upper mantle extends down to a depth of about 1 000 km., below which is the more viscous lower mantle which is about 1 900 km. thick.

The core *(above)*
The outer core, approximately 2 100 km. thick, consists of molten iron and nickel at 2 000°C to 5 000°C possibly separated from the less dense mantle by an oxidised shell. About 5 000 km. below the surface is the liquid transition zone, below which is the solid inner core, a sphere of 2 740 km. diameter where rock is three times as dense as in the crust.

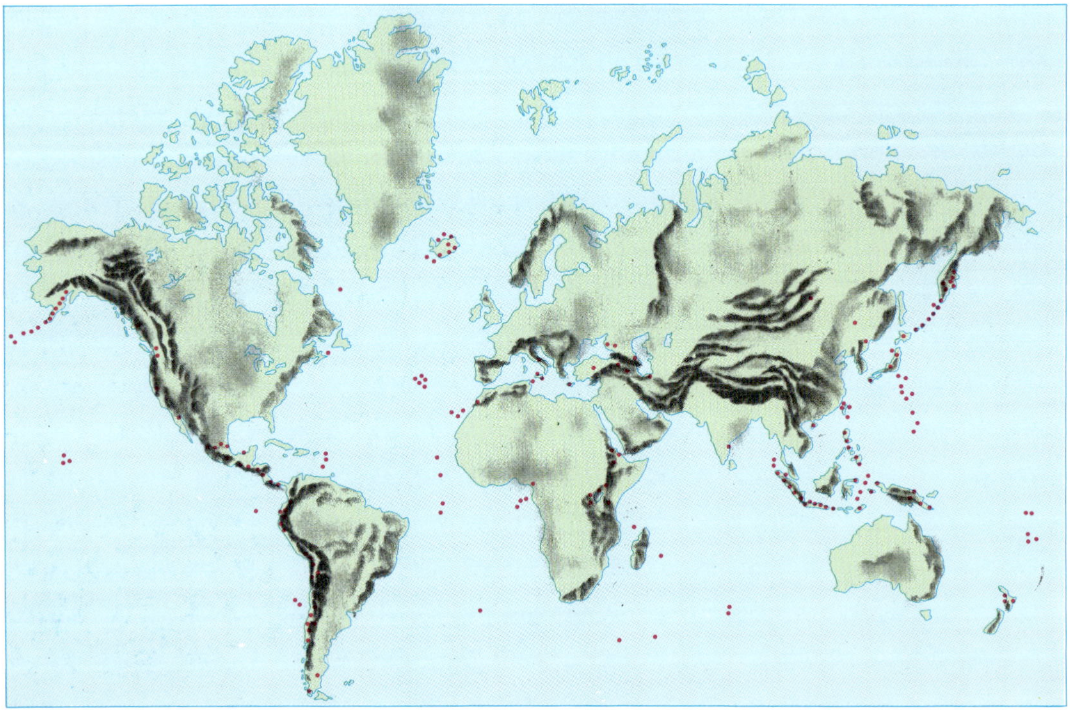

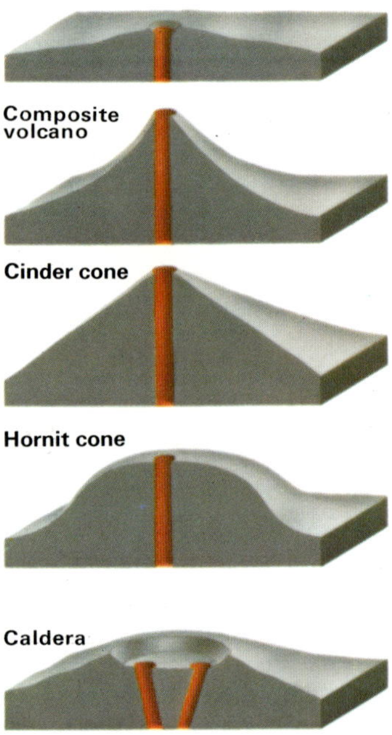

Major earthquakes in the last 100 years	numbers killed
1896 Japan (tsunami)	22 000
1906 San Francisco	destroyed
1906 Chile, Valparaiso	22 000
1908 Italy, Messina	77 000
1915 Italy, Avezzano	30 000
1920 China, Kansu	180 000
1923 Japan, Tokyo	143 000
1927 China, Nan-Shan	200 000
1931 Nicaragua, Managua	destroyed
1932 China, Kansu	70 000
1934 India, Bihar-Nepal	10 700
1935 India, Quetta	60 000
1939 Chile, Chillan	20 000
1939/40 Turkey, Erzincan	30 000
1960 Morocco, Agadir	12 000
1962 N.W. Iran	10 000
1966 U.S.S.R., Tashkent	destroyed
1968 Northeastern Iran	12 000
1970 N. Peru	66 800
1972 Nicaragua, Managua	7 000
1974 N. Pakistan	10 000
1976 Guatemala	22 778
1976 China, Taugshan	650 000
1976 Philippines, Mindanao	8 000
1977 Rumania, Bucharest	1 500
1978 Iran, Tabas, etc.	26 000

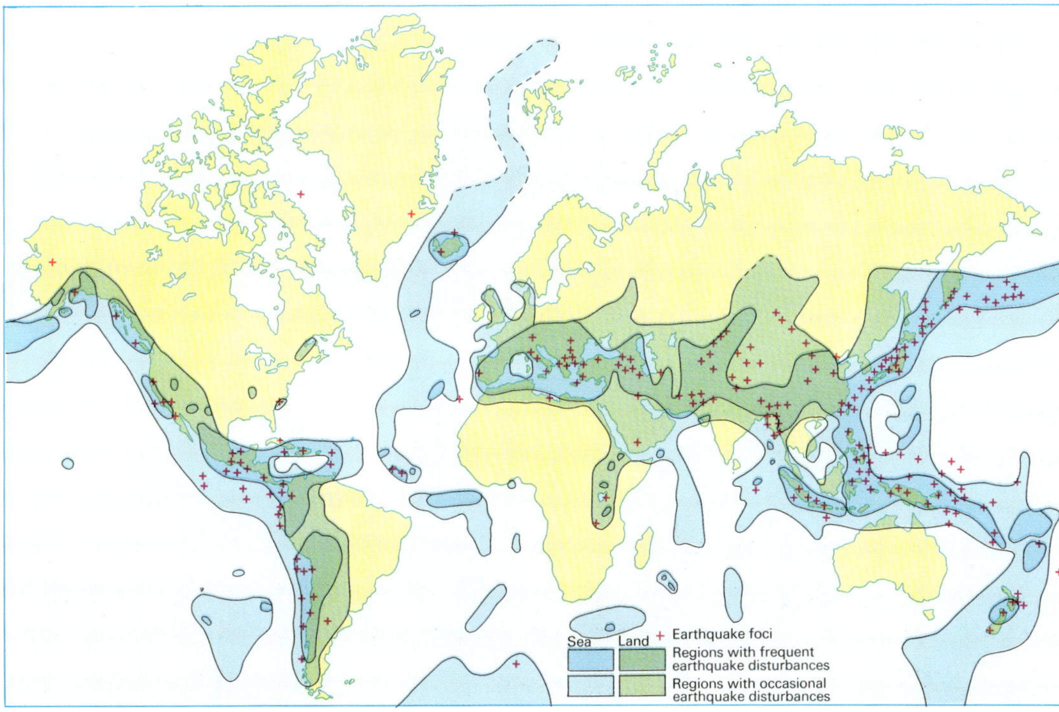

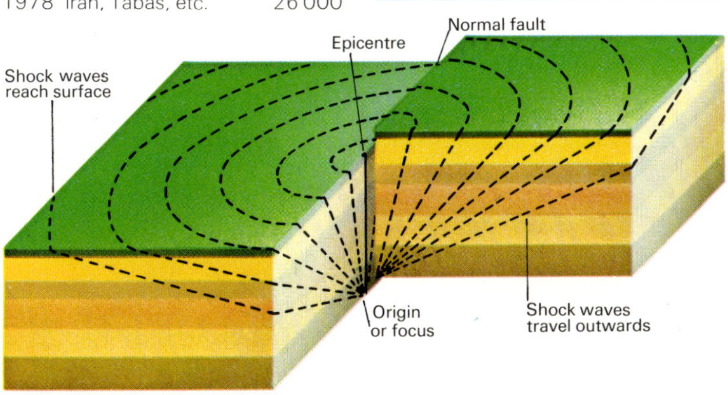

Earthquakes *(right and above)*
Earthquakes are a series of rapid vibrations originating from the slipping or faulting of parts of the earth's crust when stresses within build up to breaking point. They usually happen at depths varying from 8-30 km. Severe earthquakes cause extensive damage when they take place in populated areas destroying structures and severing communications. Most loss of life occurs due to secondary causes i.e. falling masonry, fires or tsunami waves.

Alaskan earthquake, 1964

Seismic Waves *(right)*
The shock waves sent out from the epicentre of an earthquake are of three main kinds each with distinct properties. Primary (P) waves are compressional waves which can be transmitted through both solids and liquids and therefore pass through the earth's liquid core. Secondary (S) waves are shear waves and can only pass through solids. They cannot pass through the core and are reflected at the core-mantle boundary taking a concave course back to the surface. The core also refracts the P waves causing them to alter course, and the net effect of this reflection and refraction is the production of a shadow zone at a certain distance from the epicentre, free from P and S waves. Due to their different properties P waves travel about 1·7 times faster than S waves. The third main kind of wave is a long (L) wave, a slow wave which travels along the earth's surface, its motion being either horizontal or vertical.

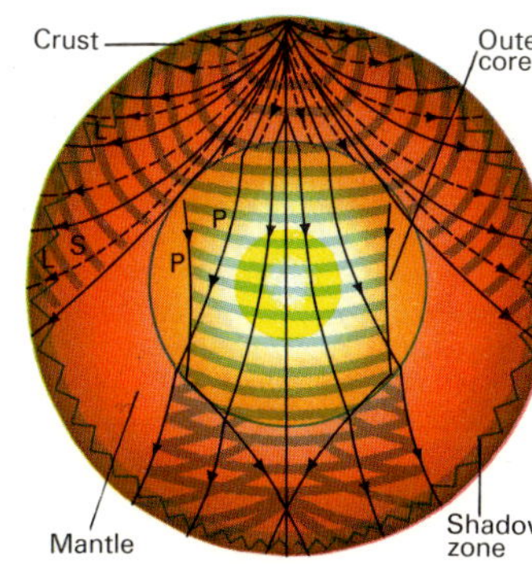

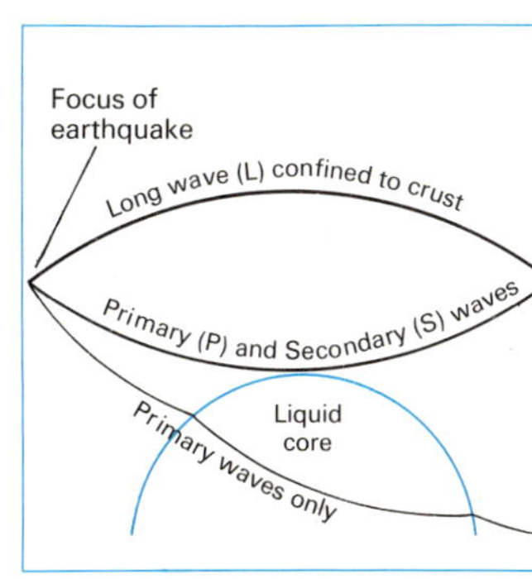

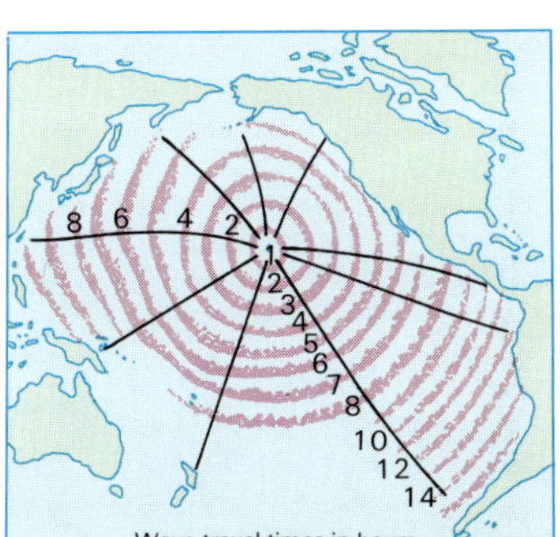

Tsunami waves *(left)*
A sudden slump in the ocean bed during an earthquake forms a trough in the water surface subsequently followed by a crest and smaller waves. A more marked change of level in the sea bed can form a crest, the start of a Tsunami which travels up to 60 kph with waves up to 60 metres high. Seismographic detectors continuously record earthquake shocks and warn of the Tsunami which may follow it.

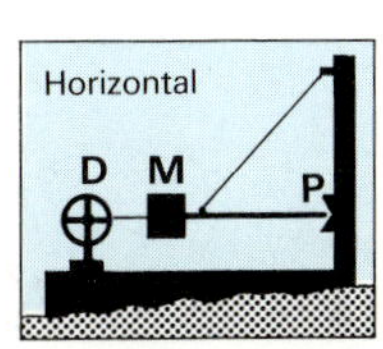

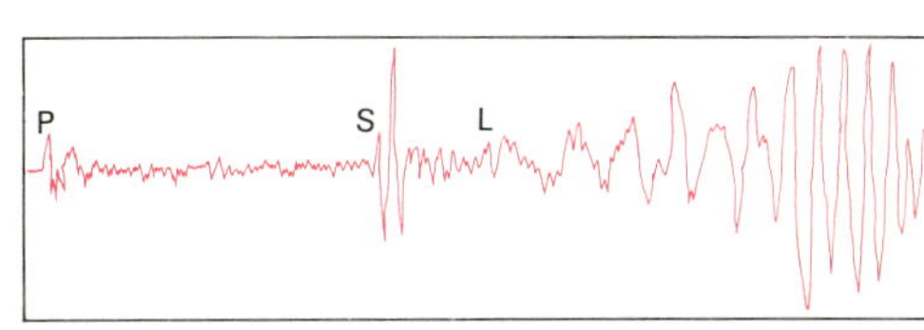

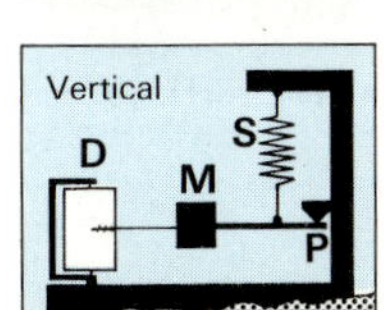

Principles of seismographs (left)
M = Mass
D = Drum
P = Pivot
S = Spring

Seismographs are delicate instruments capable of detecting and recording vibrations due to earthquakes thousands of miles away. P waves cause the first tremors. S the second, and L the main shock.

The Making of Landscape

The making of landscape

The major forces which shape our land would seem to act very slowly in comparison with man's average life span but in geological terms the erosion of rock is in fact very fast. Land goes through a cycle of transformation. It is broken up by earthquakes and other earth movements, temperature changes, water, wind and ice. Rock debris is then transported by water, wind and glaciers and deposited on lowlands and on the sea floor. Here it builds up and by the pressure of its own weight is converted into new rock strata. These in turn can be uplifted either gently as plains or plateaux or more irregularly to form mountains. In either case the new higher land is eroded and the cycle recommences.

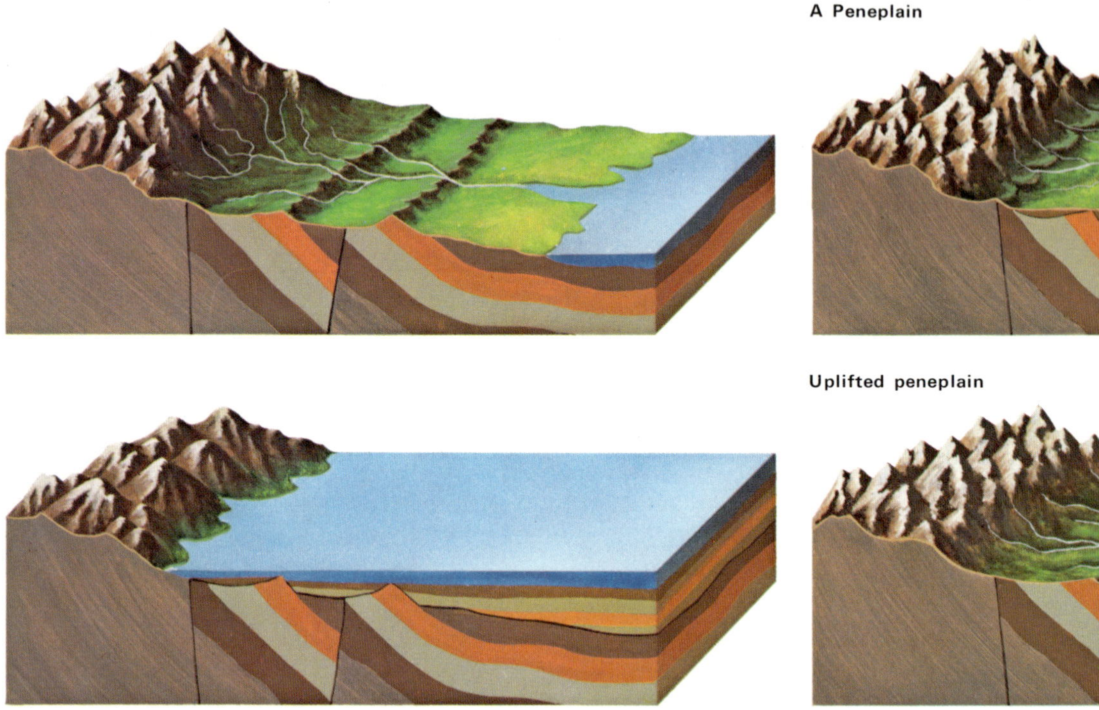

Rivers

Rivers shape the land by three basic processes: erosion, transportation and deposition. A youthful river flows fast eroding downwards quickly to form a narrow valley (1). As it matures it deposits some debris and erodes laterally to widen the valley (2). In its last stage it meanders across a wide flat flood plain depositing fine particles of alluvium (3).

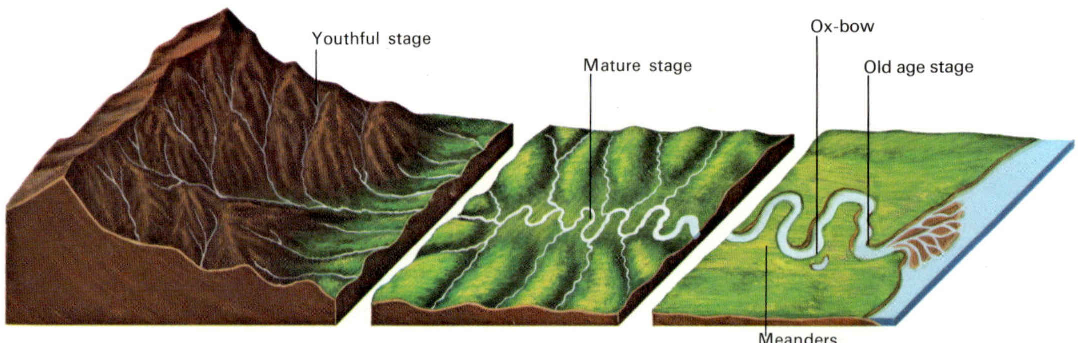

Underground water

Water enters porous and permeable rocks from the surface moving downward until it reaches a layer of impermeable rock. Joints in underground rock, such as limestone, are eroded to form underground caves and caverns. When the roof of a cave collapses a gorge is formed. Surface entrances to joints are often widened to form vertical openings called swallow holes.

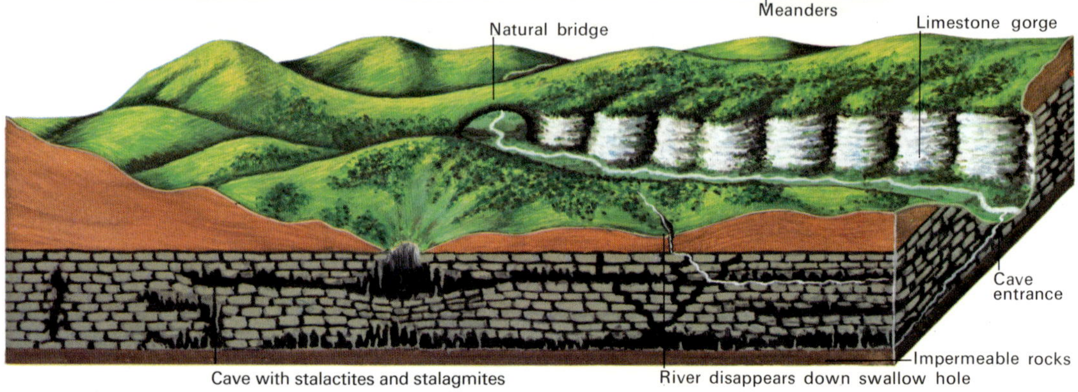

Wind

Wind action is particularly powerful in arid and semi-arid regions where rock waste produced by weathering is used as an abrasive tool by the wind. The rate of erosion varies with the characteristics of the rock which can cause weird shapes and effects (right). Desert sand can also be accumulated by the wind to form barchan dunes (far right) which slowly travel forward, horns first.

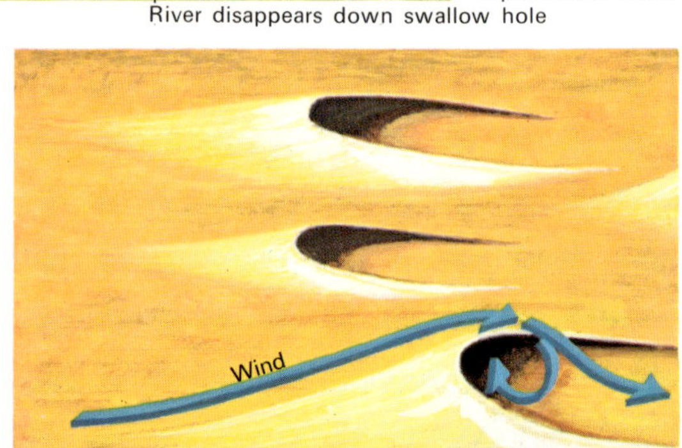

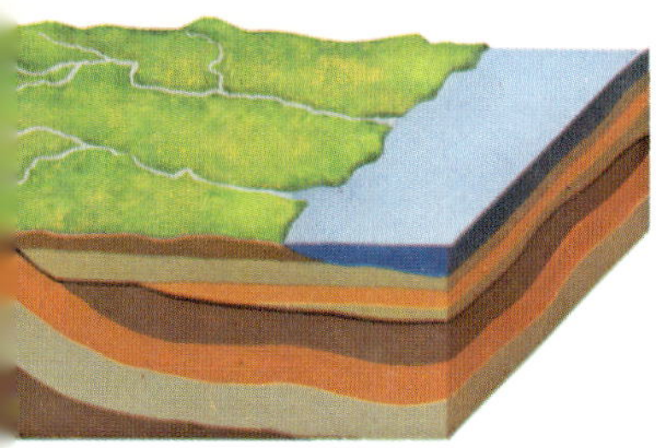

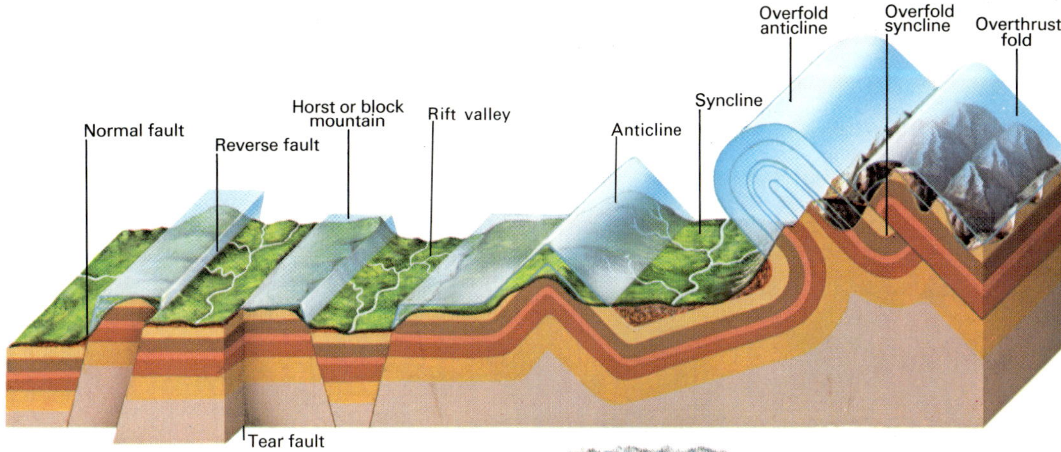

Folding and faulting

A vertical displacement in the earth's crust is called a fault or reverse fault; lateral displacement is a tear fault. An uplifted block is called a horst, the reverse of which is a rift valley. Compressed horizontal layers of sedimentary rock fold to form mountains. Those layers which bend up form an anticline, those bending down form a syncline: continued pressure forms an overfold.

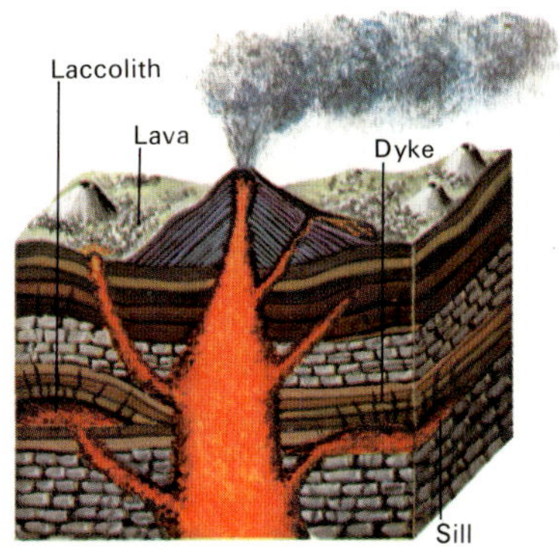

Volcanic activity

When pressure on rocks below the earth's crust is released the normally semi-solid hot rock becomes liquid magma. The magma forces its way into cracks of the crust and may either reach the surface where it forms volcanoes or it may collect in the crust as sills dykes or lacoliths. When magma reaches the surface it cools to form lava.

Waves

Coasts are continually changing, some retreat under wave erosion while others advance with wave deposition. These actions combined form steep cliffs and wave cut platforms. Eroded debris is in turn deposited as a terrace. As the water becomes shallower the erosive power of the waves decreases and gradually the cliff disappears. Wave action can also create other features (far right).

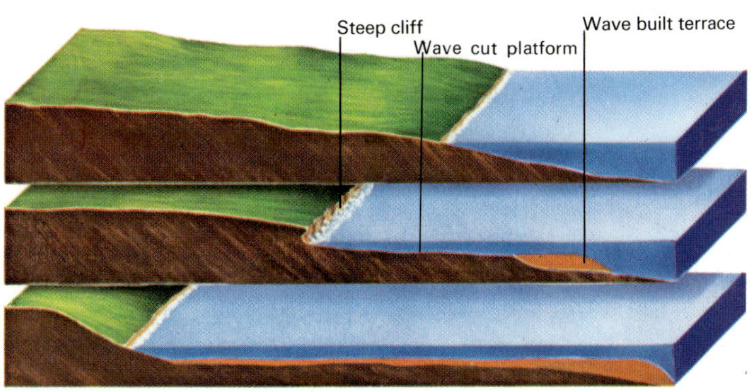

Ice

These diagrams *(right)* show how a glaciated valley may have formed. The glacier deepens, straightens and widens the river valley whose interlocking spurs become truncated or cut off. Intervalley divides are frost shattered to form sharp aretes and pyramidal peaks. Hanging valleys mark the entry of tributary rivers and eroded rocks form medial moraine. Terminal moraine is deposited as the glacier retreats.

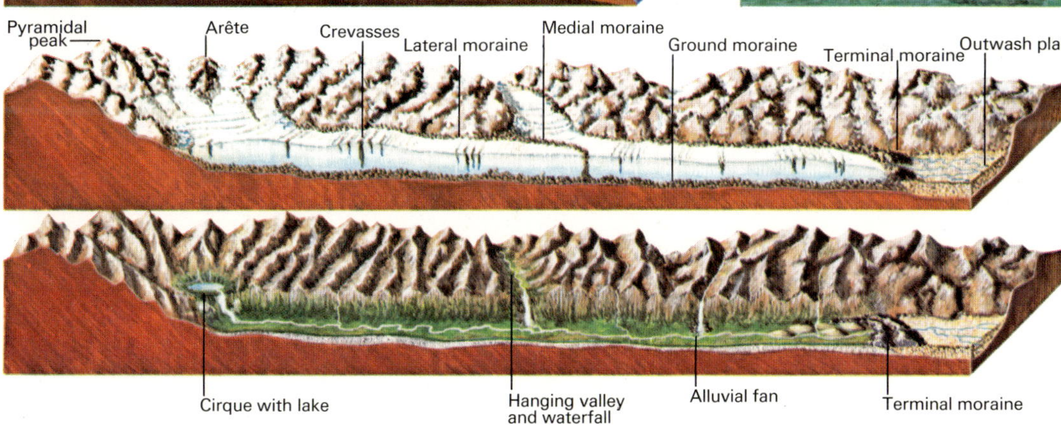

Subsidence and uplift

As the land surface is eroded it may eventually become a level plain - a peneplain, broken only by low hills, remnants of previous mountains. In turn this peneplain may be uplifted to form a plateau with steep edges. At the coast the uplifted wave platform becomes a coastal plain and in the rejuvenated rivers downward erosion once more predominates.

The Earth: Physical Dimensions

Its surface

Highest point on the earth's surface: Mt. Everest, Tibet - Nepal boundary	8 848 m
Lowest point on the earth's surface: The Dead Sea, Jordan below sea level	395 m
Greatest ocean depth,: Challenger Deep, Mariana Trench	11 022 m
Average height of land	840 m
Average depth of seas and oceans	3 808 m

The Figure of Earth

An imaginary sea-level surface is considered and called a geoid. By measuring at different places the angles from plumb lines to a fixed star there have been many determinations of the shape of parts of the geoid which is found to be an oblate spheriod with its axis along the axis of rotation of the earth. Observations from satellites have now given a new method of more accurate determinations of the figure of the earth and its local irregularities.

Land and Sea Hemispheres.

About 85% of the total land area is contained in the hemisphere centred on a point between Paris and Brussels.

Dimensions

Superficial area	510 000 000 km^2
Land surface	149 000 000 km^2
Land surface as % of total area	29·2 %
Water surface	361 000 000 km^2
Water surface as % of total area	70·8 %
Equatorial circumference	40 077 km
Meridional circumference	40 009 km
Equatorial diameter	12 756·8 km
Polar diameter	12 713·8 km
Equatorial radius	6 378·4 km
Polar radius	6 356·9 km
Volume of the Earth	1 083 230 x 10^6 km^3
Mass of the Earth	5·9 x 10^{21} tonnes

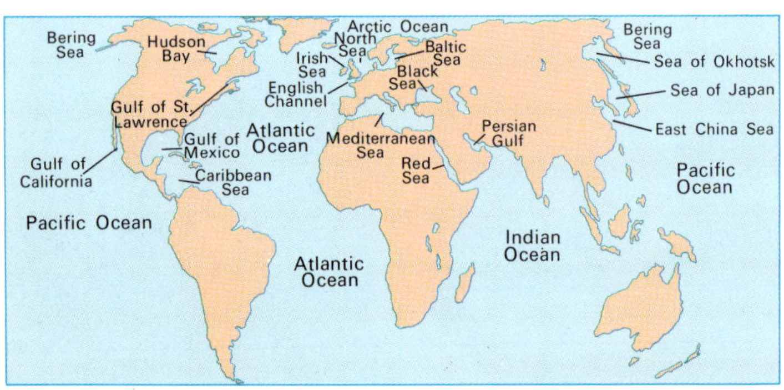

Oceans and Seas
Area in 1000 km²

Pacific Ocean	165 721
Atlantic Ocean	81 660
Indian Ocean	73 442
Arctic Ocean	14 351
Mediterranean Sea	2 966
Bering Sea	2 274
Caribbean Sea	1 942
Mexico, Gulf of	1 813
Okhotsk, Sea of	1 528
East China Sea	1 248
Hudson Bay	1 230
Japan, Sea of	1 049
North Sea	575
Black Sea	448
Red Sea	440
Baltic Sea	422
Persian Gulf	238
St. Lawrence, Gulf of	236
English Channel & Irish Sea	179
California, Gulf of	161

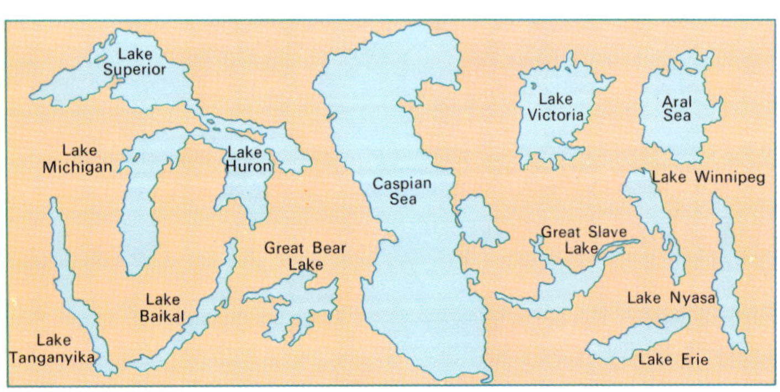

Lakes and Inland Seas
Areas in 1000 km²

Caspian Sea, Asia	424·2
Lake Superior, N.America	82·4
Lake Victoria, Africa	69·5
Aral Sea (Salt), Asia	63·8
Lake Huron, N.America	59·6
Lake Michigan, N.America	58·0
Lake Tanganyika, Africa	32·9
Lake Baikal, Asia	31·5
Great Bear Lake, N.America	31·1
Great Slave Lake, N.America	28·9
Lake Nyasa, Africa	28·5
Lake Erie, N.America	25·7
Lake Winnipeg, N.America	24·3
Lake Chad, Africa	20·7
Lake Ontario, N.America	19·5
Lake Ladoga, Europe	18·4
Lake Balkhash, Asia	17·3
Lake Maracaibo, S.America	16·3
Lake Onega, Europe	9·8
Lake Eyre (Salt), Australia	9·6
Lake Turkana (Salt), Africa	9·1
Lake Titicaca, S.America	8·3
Lake Nicaragua, C.America	8·0
Lake Athabasca, N.America	7·9
Reindeer Lake, N.America	6·3
Issyk-Kul, Asia	6·2
Lake Torrens (Salt), Australia	6·1
Koko Nor (Salt), Asia	6·0
Lake Urmia, Asia	6·0
Vänern, Europe	5·6

Longest rivers	km.
Nile, Africa	6 690
Amazon, S.America	6 280
Mississipi - Missouri, N.America	6 270
Yangtze, Asia	4 990
Zaïre, Africa	4 670
Amur, Asia	4 410
Hwang Ho (Yellow), Asia	4 350
Lena, Asia	4 260
Mekong, Asia	4 180
Niger, Africa	4 180
Mackenzie, N.America	4 040
Ob, Asia	4 000
Yenisei, Asia	3 800

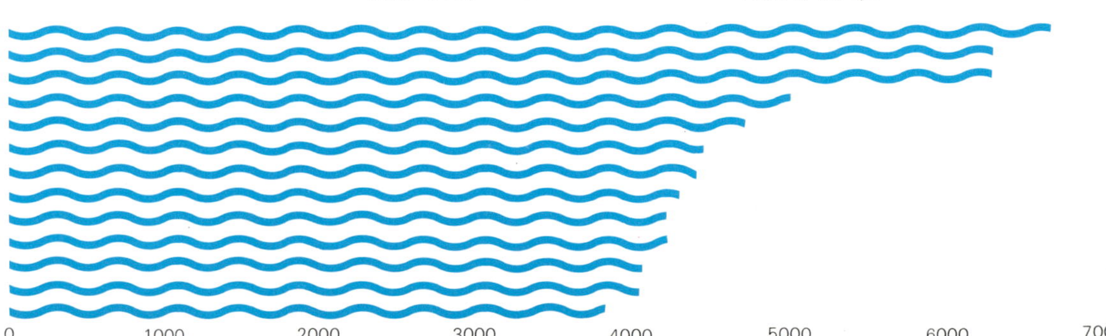

The Highest Mountains and the Greatest Depths.

Mount Everest defied the world's greatest mountaineers for 32 years and claimed the lives of many men. Not until 1920 was permission granted by the Dalai Lama to attempt the mountain, and the first successful ascent came in 1953. Since then the summit has been reached several times. The world's highest peaks have now been climbed but there are many as yet unexplored peaks in the Himalayas some of which may be over 7 600 m.

The greatest trenches are the Puerto Rico deep (9 200m). The Tonga (10 822 m) and Mindanao (10 497 m) trenches and the Mariana Trench (11 022 m) in the Pacific. The trenches represent less than 2% of the total area of the sea-bed but are of great interest as lines of structural weakness in the Earth's crust and as areas of frequent earthquakes.

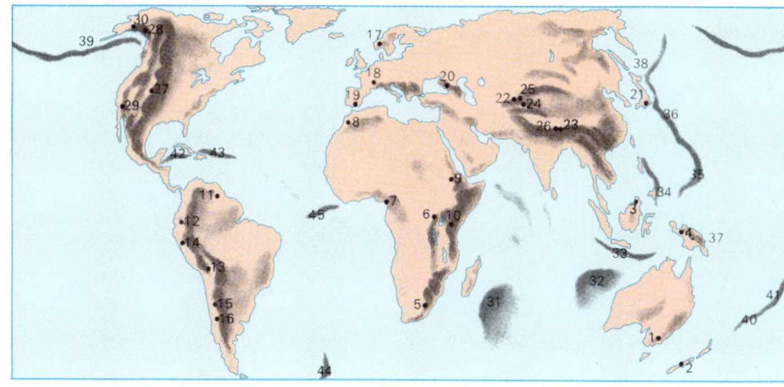

High mountains

Mountain heights in metres

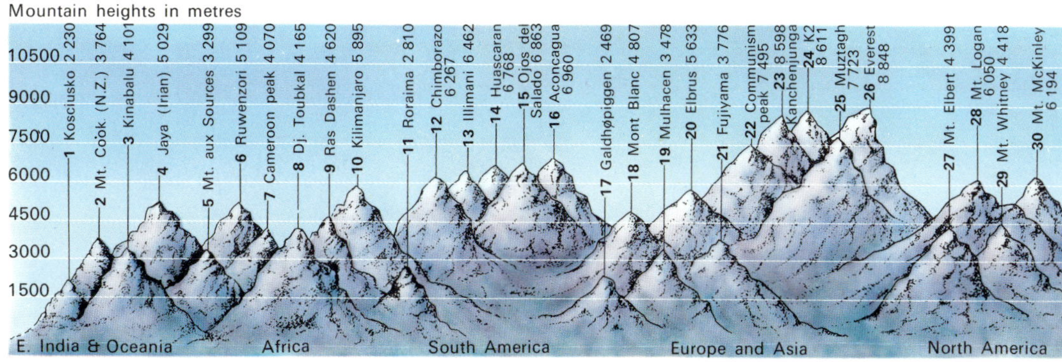

Bathyscaphe

Ocean depths in metres

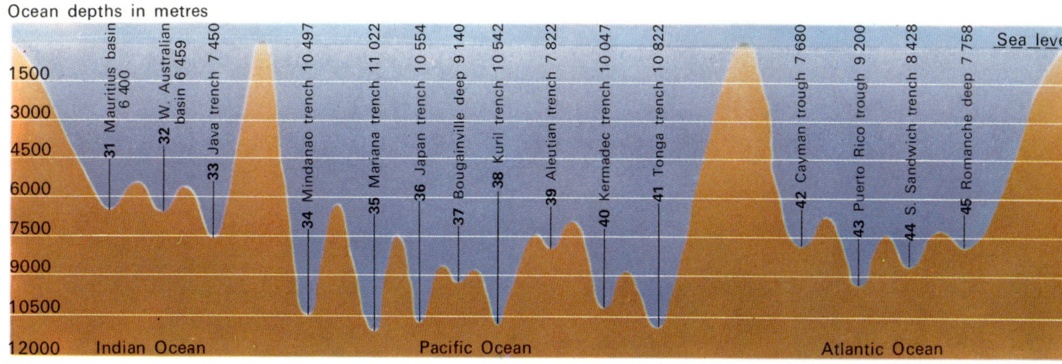

Waterfall

Notable Waterfalls heights in metres

Angel, Venezuela	980
Tugela, S. Africa	853
Mongefossen, Norway	774
Yosemite, California	738
Mardalsfossen, Norway	655
Cuquenan, Venezuela	610
Sutherland, N.Z.	579
Reichenbach, Switzerland	548
Wollomombi, Australia	518
Ribbon, California	491
Gavarnie, France	422
Tyssefallene, Norway	414
Krimml, Austria	370
King George VI, Guyana	366
Silver Strand, California	356
Geissbach, Switzerland	350
Staubbach, Switzerland	299
Trümmelbach, Switzerland	290
Chirombo, Zambia	268
Livingstone, Zaïre	259
King Edward VIII, Guyana	256
Gersoppa, India	253
Vettifossen Norway	250
Kalambo, Zambia	240
Kaieteur, Guyana	226
Maletsunyane, Lesotho	192
Terui, Italy	180
Murchison, Uganda	122
Victoria, Zimbabwe-Zambia	107
Cauvery, India	97
Stanley, Zaïre	61
Niagara, N.America	51
Schaffhausen, Switzerland	30

Dam

Notable Dams heights in metres

Africa

Cabora Bassa, Zambezi R.	168
Akosombo Main Dam, Volta R.	141
Kariba, Zambezi R.	128
Aswan High Dam, Nile R.	110

Asia

Nurek, Vakhsh R., U.S.S.R.	317
Bhakra, Sutlej R., India	226
Kurobegawa, Kurobe R. , Jap.	186
Charvak, Chirchik R., U.S.S.R.	168
Okutadami, Tadami R., Jap.	157
Bhumiphol, Ping R., Thai.	154

Australasia

Warragamba, N.S.W., Australia	137
Eucumbene, N.S.W., Australia	116

Europe

Grande Dixence, Switz.	284
Vajont, Vajont, R., Italy	261
Mauvoisin, Drance R., Switz.	237
Contra, Verzasca R., Switz.	230
Luzzone, Brenno R., Switz.	208
Tignes, Isère R., France	180
Amir Kabir, Karadj R., U.S.S.R.	180
Vidraru, Arges R., Rum.	165
Kremasta, Acheloos R., Greece	165

North America

Oroville, Feather R.,	235
Hoover, Colorado R.,	221
Glen Canyon, Colorado R.,	216
Daniel Johnson, Can.	214
New Bullards Bar, N. Yuba R.	194
Mossyrock, Cowlitz R.,	184
Shasta, Sacramento R.,	183
W.A.C. Bennett, Canada.	183
Don Pedro, Tuolumne R.,	178
Hungry Horse, Flathead R.,	172
Grand Coulee, Columbia R.,	168

Central and South America

Guri, Caroni R., Venezuela.	106

Distances

Kms	Berlin	Bombay	Buenos Aires	Cairo	Calcutta	Caracas	Chicago	Copenhagen	Darwin	Hong Kong	Honolulu	Johannesburg	Lagos	Lisbon	
Berlin		3907	7400	1795	4370	5241	4402	222	8044	5440	7310	5511	3230	1436	5
Bombay	6288		9275	2706	1034	9024	8048	3990	4510	2683	8024	4334	4730	4982	44
Buenos Aires	11909	14925		7341	10268	3167	5599	7498	9130	11481	7558	5025	4919	5964	69
Cairo	2890	4355	11814		3541	6340	6127	1992	7216	5064	8838	3894	2432	2358	21
Calcutta	7033	1664	16524	5699		9609	7978	4395	3758	1653	7048	5256	5727	5639	49
Caracas	8435	14522	5096	10203	15464		2502	5215	11221	10166	6009	6847	4810	4044	46
Chicago	7084	12953	9011	3206	12839	4027		4250	9361	7783	4247	8689	5973	3992	39
Copenhagen	357	6422	12067	9860	7072	8392	6840		8017	5388	7088	5732	3436	1540	5
Darwin	12946	7257	14693	11612	6047	18059	15065	12903		2654	5369	6611	8837	9391	86
Hong Kong	8754	4317	18478	8150	2659	16360	12526	8671	4271		5543	6669	7360	6853	59
Honolulu	11764	12914	12164	14223	11343	9670	6836	11407	8640	8921		11934	10133	7821	72
Johannesburg	8870	6974	8088	6267	8459	11019	13984	9225	10639	10732	19206		2799	5089	56
Lagos	5198	7612	7916	3915	9216	7741	9612	5530	14222	11845	16308	4505		2360	3
Lisbon	2311	8018	9600	3794	9075	6501	6424	2478	15114	11028	12587	8191	3799		
London	928	7190	11131	3508	7961	7507	6356	952	13848	9623	11632	9071	5017	1588	
Los Angeles	9311	14000	9852	12200	13120	5812	2804	9003	12695	11639	4117	16676	12414	9122	8
Mexico City	9732	15656	7389	12372	15280	3586	2726	9514	14631	14122	6085	14585	11071	8676	8
Moscow	1610	5031	13477	2902	5534	9938	8000	1561	11350	7144	11323	9161	6254	3906	2
Nairobi	6370	4532	10402	3536	6179	11544	12883	6706	10415	8776	17282	2927	3807	6461	6
New York	6385	12541	8526	9020	12747	3430	1145	6188	16047	12950	7980	12841	8477	5422	5
Paris	876	7010	11051	3210	7858	7625	6650	1026	13812	9630	11968	8732	4714	1454	
Peking	7822	4757	19268	7544	3269	14399	10603	7202	6011	1963	8160	11710	11457	9668	8
Reykjavik	2385	8335	11437	5266	8687	6915	4757	2103	13892	9681	9787	10938	6718	2948	1
Rio de Janeiro	10025	13409	1953	9896	15073	4546	8547	10211	16011	17704	13342	7113	6035	7734	9
Rome	1180	6175	11151	2133	7219	8363	7739	1531	13265	9284	12916	7743	4039	1861	1
Singapore	9944	3914	15879	8267	2897	18359	15078	9969	3349	2599	10816	8660	11145	11886	10
Sydney	16096	10160	11800	14418	9138	15343	14875	16042	3150	7374	8168	11040	15519	18178	16
Tokyo	8924	6742	18362	9571	5141	14164	10137	8696	5431	2874	6202	13547	13480	11149	9
Toronto	6497	12488	9093	9233	12661	3873	700	6265	15498	12569	7465	13374	8948	5737	5
Wellington	18140	12370	9981	16524	11354	13122	13451	17961	5325	9427	7513	11761	16050	19575	18

	Mexico City	Moscow	Nairobi	New York	Paris	Peking	Reykjavik	Rio de Janeiro	Rome	Singapore	Sydney	Tokyo	Toronto	Wellington	
35	6047	1000	3958	3967	545	4860	1482	6230	734	6179	10002	5545	4037	11272	Berlin
00	9728	3126	2816	7793	4356	2956	5179	8332	3837	2432	6313	4189	7760	7686	Bombay
22	4591	8374	6463	5298	6867	11972	7106	1214	6929	9867	7332	11410	5650	6202	Buenos Aires
30	7687	1803	2197	5605	1994	4688	3272	6149	1325	5137	8959	5947	5737	10268	Cairo
52	9494	3438	3839	7921	4883	2031	5398	9366	4486	1800	5678	3195	7805	7055	Calcutta
2	2228	6175	7173	2131	4738	8947	4297	2825	5196	11407	9534	8801	2406	8154	Caracas
2	1694	4971	8005	711	4132	6588	2956	5311	4809	9369	9243	6299	435	8358	Chicago
4	5912	970	4167	3845	638	4475	1306	6345	951	6195	9968	5403	3892	11160	Copenhagen
8	9091	7053	6472	9971	8582	3735	8632	9948	8243	2081	1957	3375	9630	3309	Darwin
32	8775	4439	5453	8047	5984	1220	6015	11001	5769	1615	4582	1786	7810	5857	Hong Kong
58	3781	7036	10739	4958	7437	5070	6081	8290	8026	6721	5075	3854	4638	4669	Honolulu
52	9063	5692	1818	7979	5426	7276	6797	4420	4811	5381	6860	8418	8310	7308	Johannesburg
3	6879	3886	2366	5268	2929	7119	4175	3750	2510	6925	9643	8376	5560	9973	Lagos
38	5391	2427	4015	3369	903	6007	1832	4805	1157	7385	11295	6928	3565	12163	Lisbon
2	5552	1552	4237	3463	212	5057	1172	5778	889	6743	10558	5942	3545	11691	London
	1549	6070	9659	2446	5645	6251	4310	6310	6331	8776	7502	5475	2170	6719	Los Angeles
		6664	9207	2090	5717	7742	4635	4780	6365	10321	8058	7024	2018	6897	Mexico City
			3942	4666	1545	3600	2053	7184	1477	5237	9008	4651	4637	10283	Moscow
				7358	4029	5727	5395	5548	3350	4635	7552	6996	7570	8490	Nairobi
					3626	6828	2613	4832	4280	9531	9935	6741	356	8951	New York
93						5106	1384	5708	687	6671	10539	6038	3738	11798	Paris
59	10724						4897	10773	5049	2783	5561	1304	6557	6700	Peking
44	14818	6344						6135	2048	7155	10325	5469	2600	10725	Reykjavik
36	3364	7510	11842						5725	9763	8389	11551	5180	7367	Rio de Janeiro
35	9200	2486	6485	5836						6229	10143	6127	4399	11523	Rome
50	12460	5794	9216	10988	8217						3915	3306	9350	5298	Singapore
36	7460	3304	8683	4206	2228	7882						4861	9800	1383	Sydney
55	7693	11562	8928	7777	9187	17338	9874						6410	5762	Tokyo
88	10243	2376	5391	6888	1105	8126	3297	9214						8820	Toronto
23	16610	8428	7460	15339	10737	4478	11514	15712	10025						Wellington
73	12969	14497	12153	15989	16962	8949	16617	13501	16324	6300					
11	11304	7485	11260	10849	9718	2099	8802	18589	9861	5321	7823				
92	3247	7462	12183	574	6015	10552	4184	8336	7080	15047	15772	10316			
14	11100	16549	13664	14405	18987	10782	17260	11855	18545	8526	2226	9273	14194		

Miles

Water Resources and Vegetation

Water resources and vegetation

Fresh water is essential for life on earth and in some parts of the world it is a most precious commodity. On the other hand it is very easy for industrialised temperate states to take its existence for granted, and man's increasing demand may only be met finally by the desalination of earth's 1250 million cubic kilometres of salt water. 70% of the earth's fresh water exists as ice.

The hydrological cycle

Water is continually being absorbed into the atmosphere as vapour from oceans, lakes, rivers and vegetation transpiration. On cooling the vapour either condenses or freezes and falls as rain, hail or snow. Most precipitation falls over the sea but one quarter falls over the land of which half evaporates again soon after falling while the rest flows back into the oceans.

Distribution of water

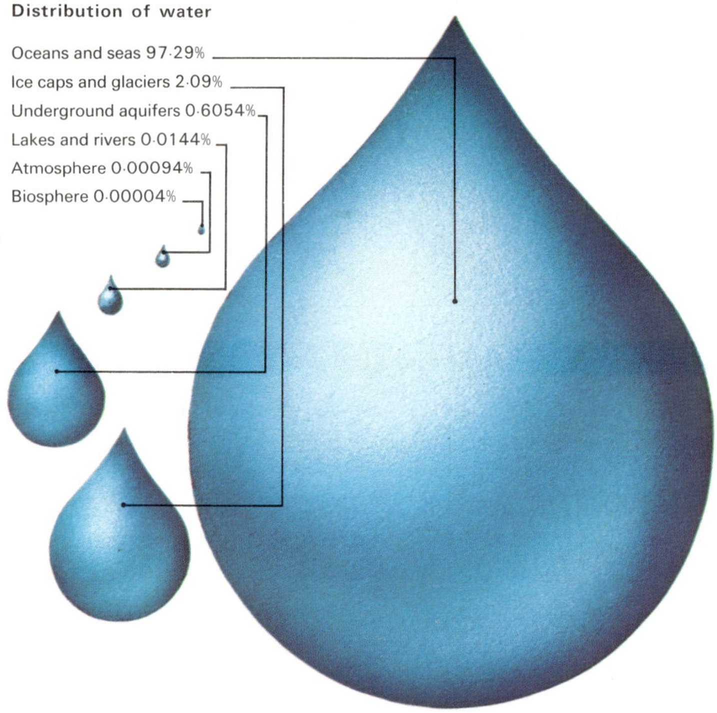

Tundra

Mediterranean scrub

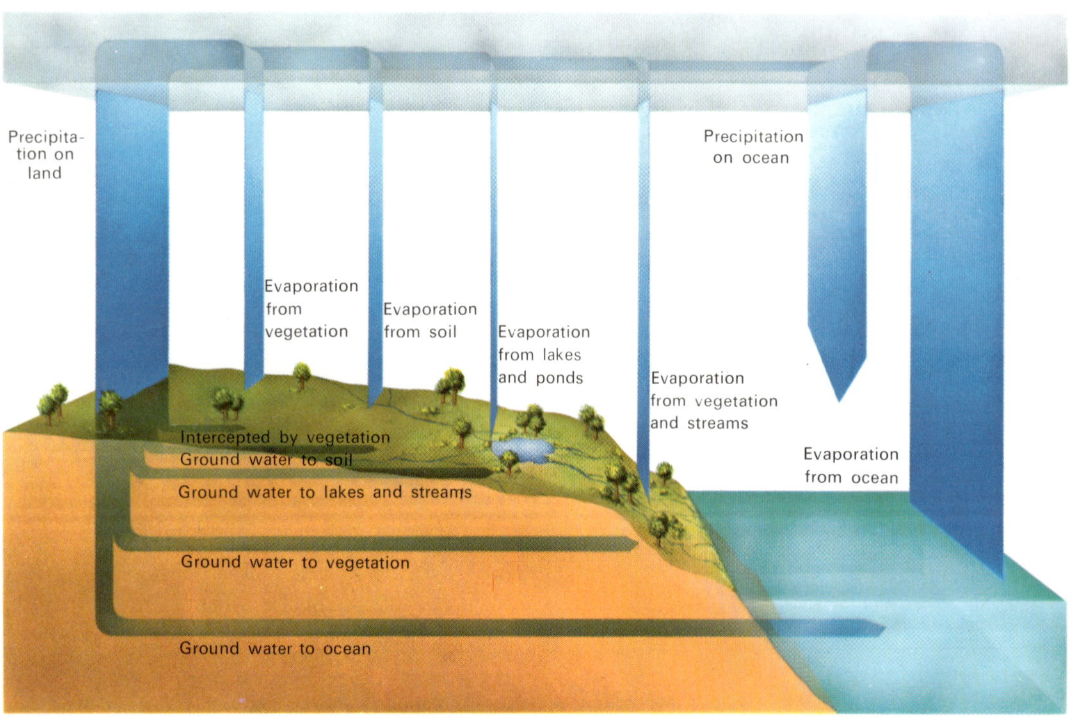

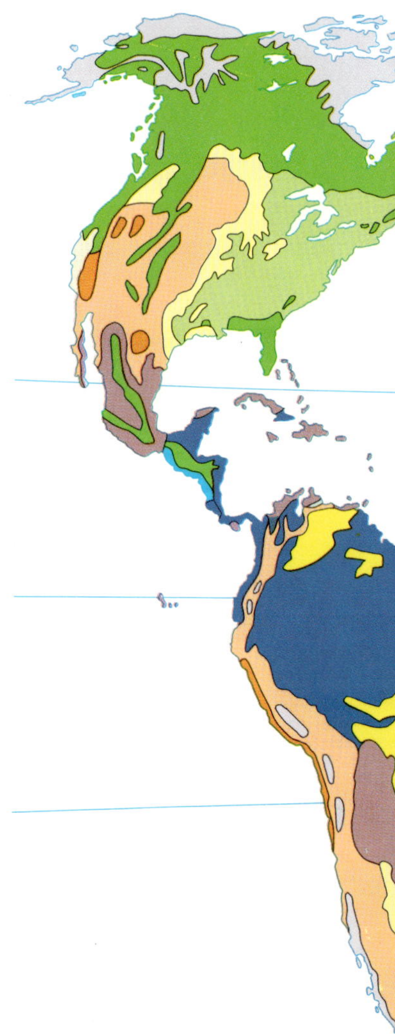

Domestic consumption of water

An area's level of industrialisation, climate and standard of living are all major influences in the consumption of water. On average Europe consumes 636 litres per head each day of which 180 litres is used domestically. In the U.S.A. domestic consumption is slightly higher at 270 litres per day. The graph (right) represents domestic consumption in the U.K. in 1970.

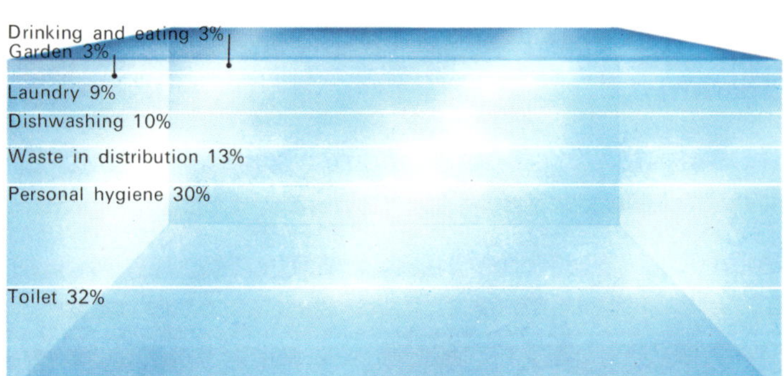

Coniferous forest

Broad-leaved forest

Tropical rain forest

Monsoon forest

Grassland

Savanna

Semidesert

Desert

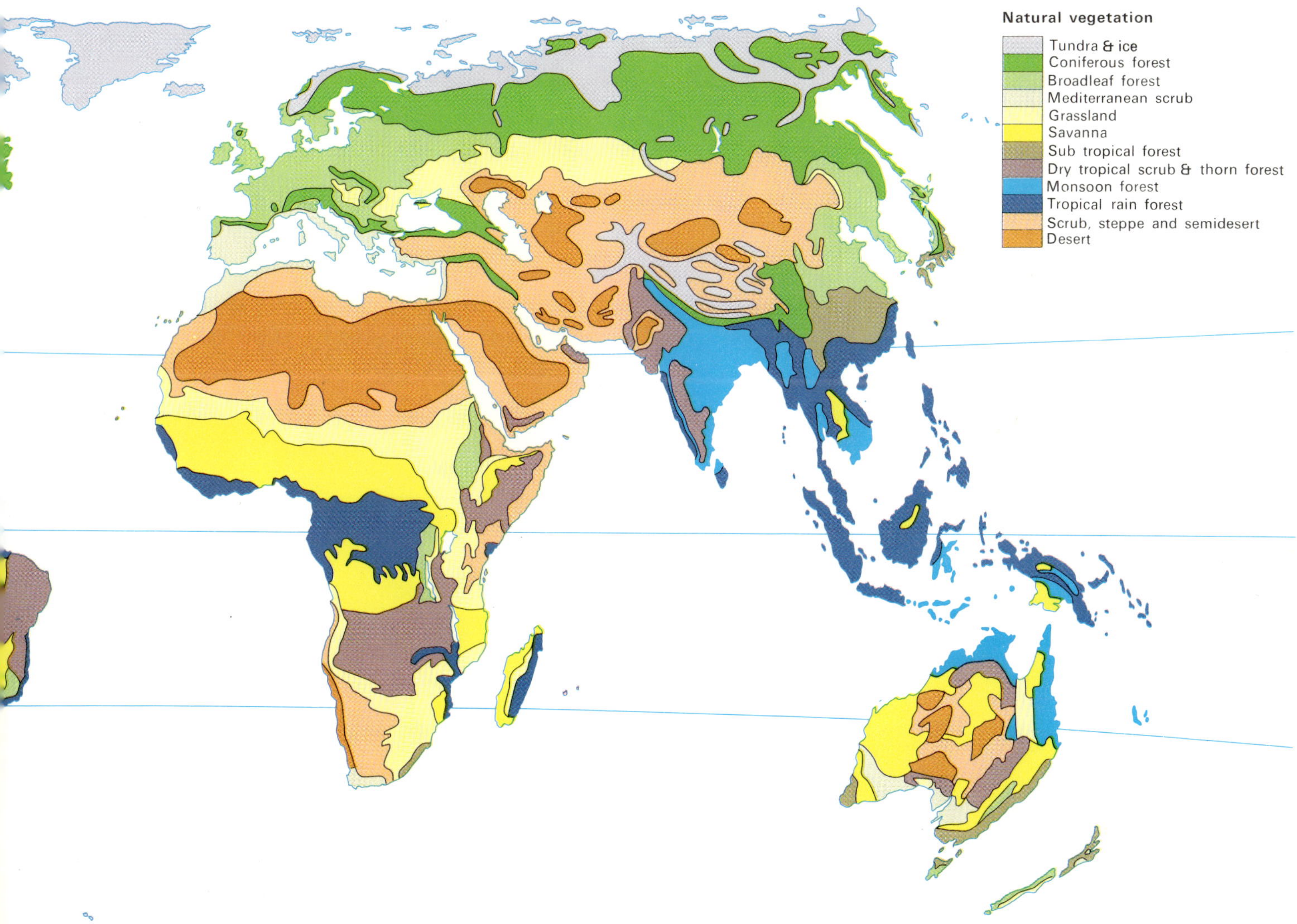

Population

Population distribution
(right and lower right)
People have always been unevenly distributed in the world. Europe has for centuries contained nearly 20% of the world's population but after the 16-19th century explorations and consequent migrations this proportion has rapidly reduced. In 1750 the Americas had 2% of the world's total: in 2000 AD they are expected to contain 16%.

The most densely populated regions are in India, China and Europe where the average density is between 100 and 200 per square km. although there are pockets of extremely high density elsewhere. In contrast Australia has only 1·5 people per square km. The countries in the lower map have been redrawn to make their areas proportional to their populations.

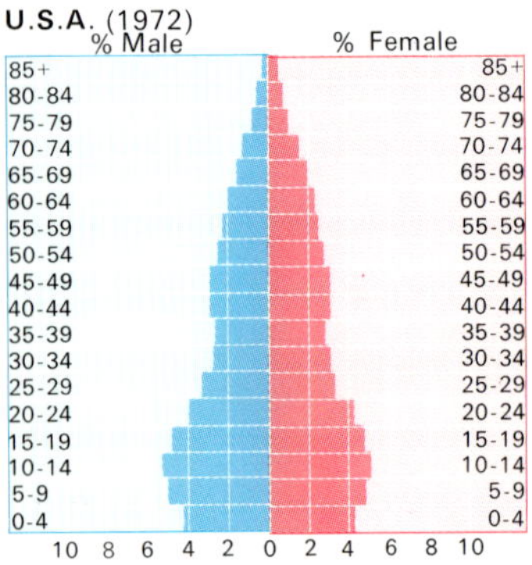

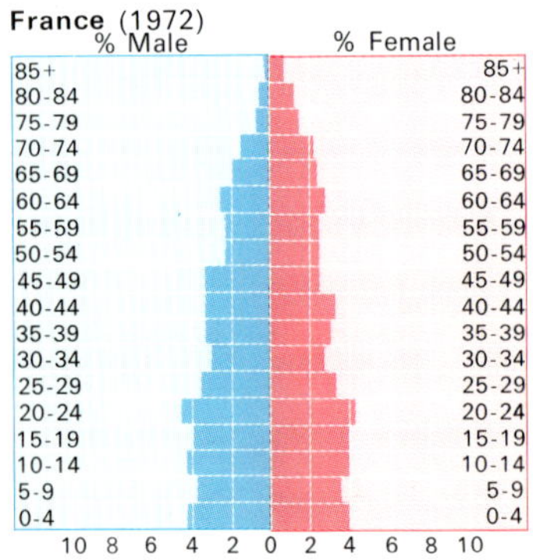

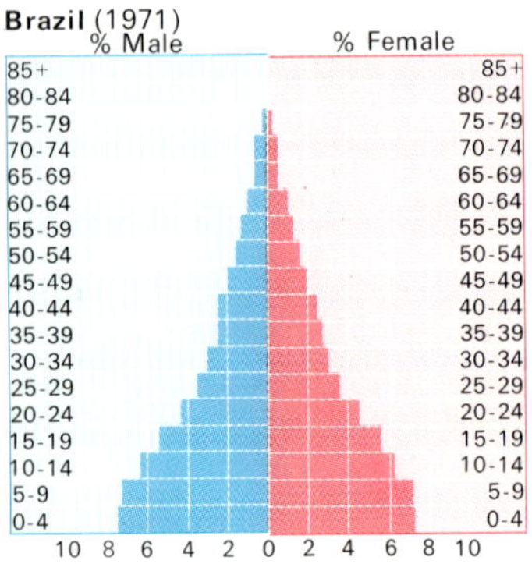

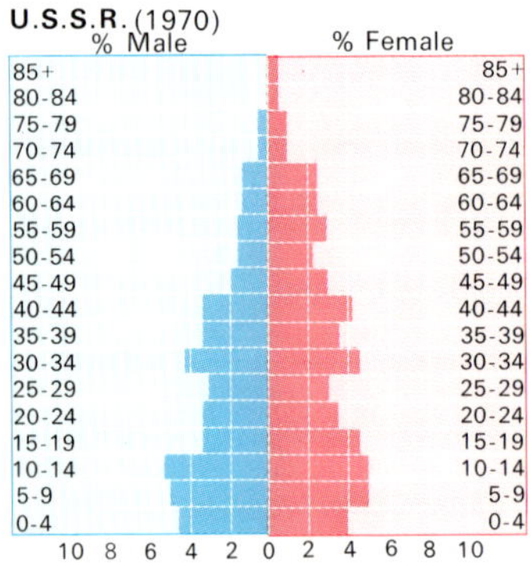

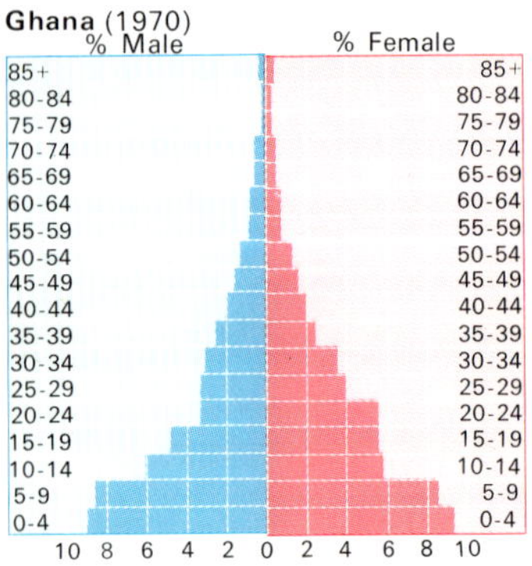

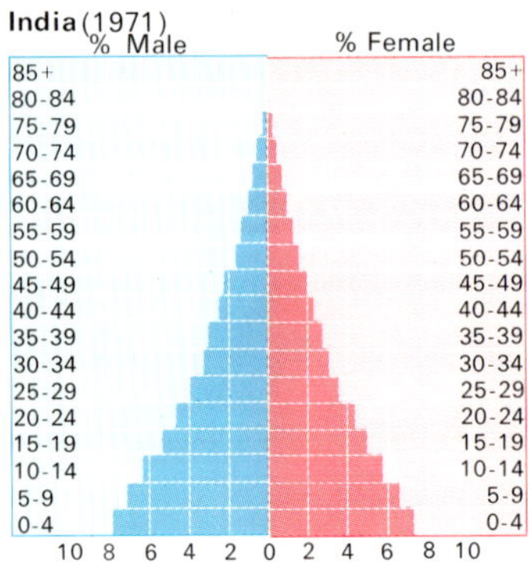

Age distribution
France shows many demographic features characteristic of European countries. Birth and death rates have declined with a moderate population growth - there are nearly as many old as young. In contrast, India and several other countries have few old and many young because of the high death rates and even higher birth rates. It is this excess that is responsible for the world's population explosion.

World population increase
Until comparatively recently there was little increase in the population of the world. About 6000 BC it is thought that there were about 200 million people and in the following 7000years an increase of just over 100 million. In the 1800's there were about 1000 million; at present there are over 3500 million and by the year 2000 if present trends continue there would be at least 7000 million.

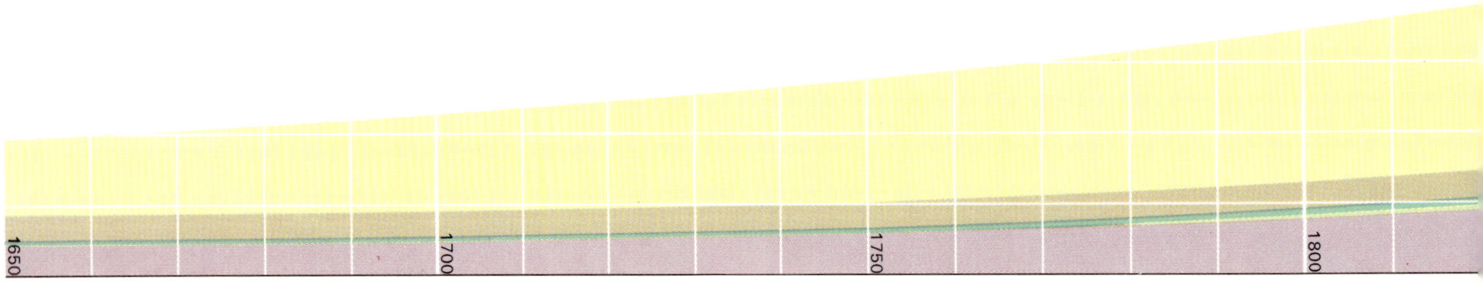

World population distribution

Population in 2000AD	
North America	296 000 000
South America	625 000 000
Europe inc. USSR	861 000 000
Asia	3 757 000 000
Africa	834 000 000
Oceania	33 000 000

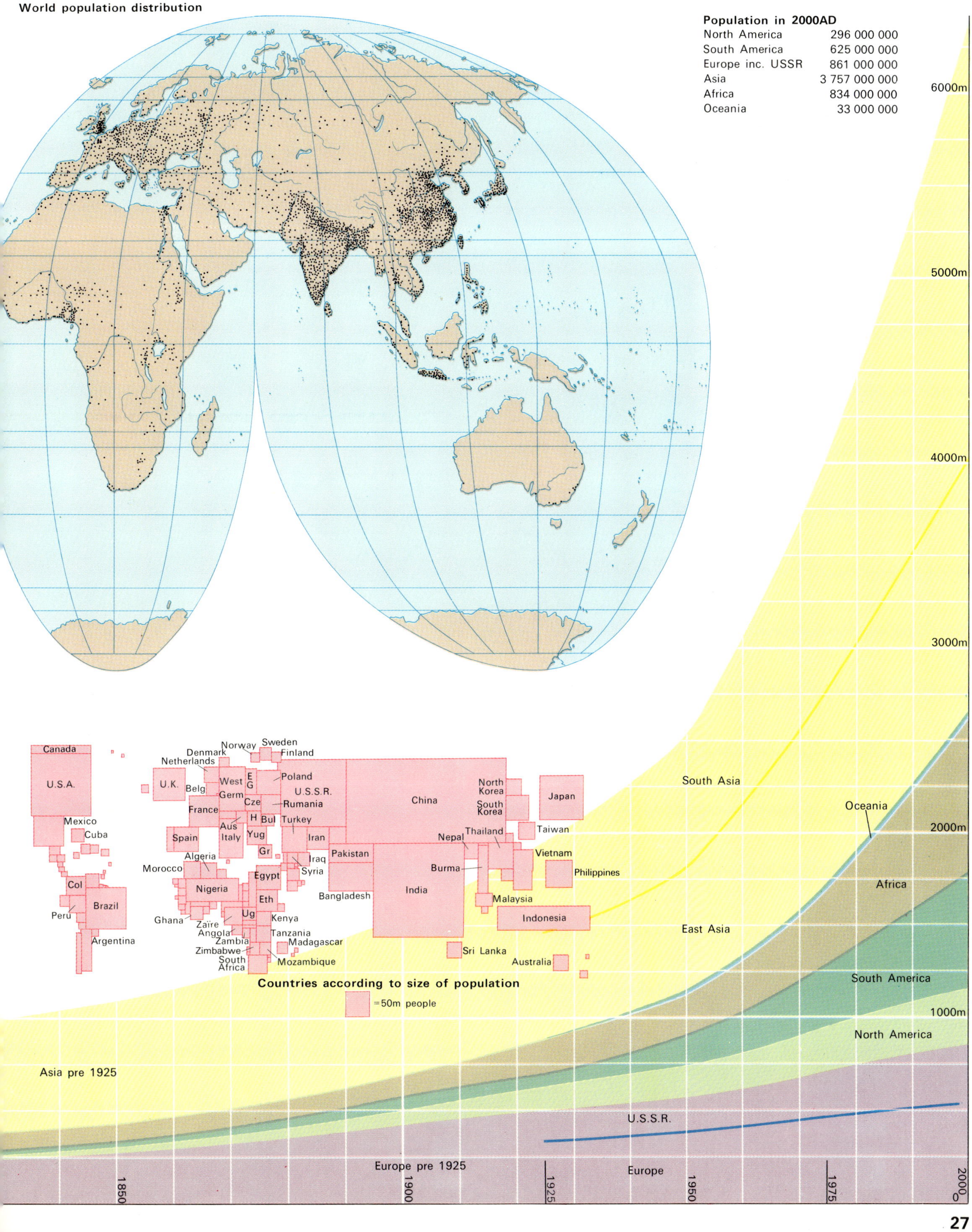

Language

Languages may be blamed partly for the division and lack of understanding between nations. While a common language binds countries together it in turn isolates them from other countries and groups. Thus beliefs, ideas and inventions remain exclusive to these groups and different cultures develop.

There are thousands of different languages and dialects spoken today. This can cause strife even within the one country, such as India, where different dialects are enough to break down the country into distinct groups.

As a result of colonization and the spread of internationally accepted languages, many countries have superimposed a completely unrelated language in order to combine isolated national groups and to facilitate international understanding, for example Spanish in South America, English in India.

Related languages

Certain languages showing marked similarities are thought to have developed from common parent languages for example Latin. After the retreat of the Roman Empire wherever Latin had been firmly established it remained as the new nation's language. With no unifying centre divergent development took place and Latin evolved into new languages.

Calligraphy

Writing was originally by a series of pictures, and these gradually developed in styles which were influenced by the tools generally used. Carved alphabets, such as that used by the Sumerians, tended to be angular, while those painted or written tended to be curved, as in Egyptian hieroglyphics development of which can be followed through the West Semitic, Greek and Latin alphabets to our own.

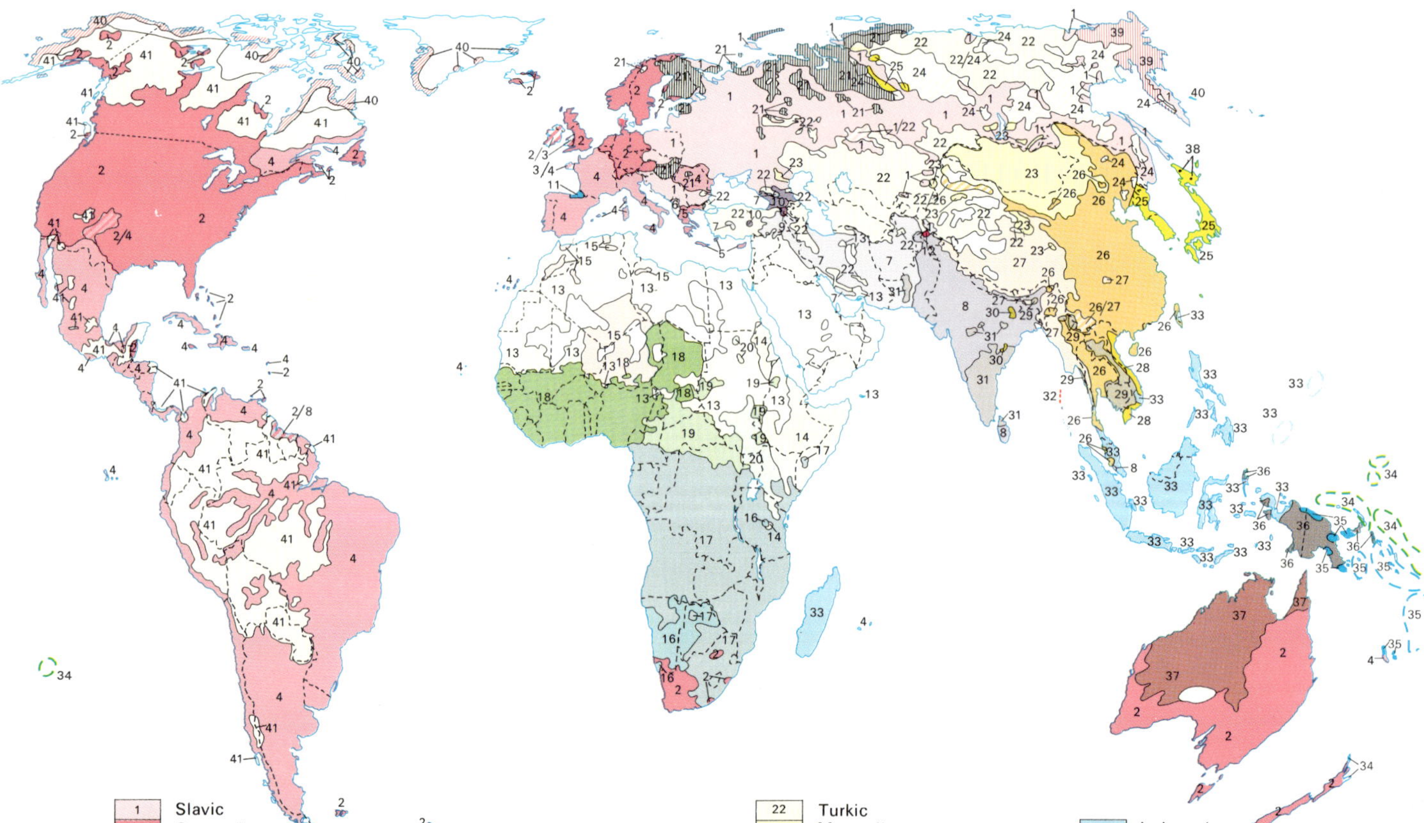

1 Slavic
2 Germanic
3 Celtic
4 Romance
5 Greek
6 Albanian
7 Iranian
8 Indo-Aryan
9 Armenian

10 Caucasian
11 Basque
12 Burushaskis

13 Semitic
14 Kushit
15 Berber

16 Khoisan
17 Bantu
18 Sudanese
19 E & C Sudan
20 Nilotic

21 Ural

22 Turkic
23 Mongolian
24 Tungus-Manchu
25 Japanese/Korean

26 Sinitic and other
27 Tibeto-Burman
28 Vietnamese

29 Mon-Khmer
30 Munda
31 Dravidian
32 Andamanese

33 Indonesian
34 Polynesian
35 Melanesian

36 Papuan
37 Australian Abor.
•38• Ainu
39 Paleoasiatic
40 Eskimo-Aleut
41 Amerindian

sparsely settled areas

Religion

Throughout history man has had beliefs in supernatural powers based on the forces of nature which have developed into worship of a god and some cases gods.

Hinduism honours many gods and goddesses which are all manifestations of the one divine spirit, Brahma, and incorporates beliefs such as reincarnation, worship of cattle and the caste system.

Buddhism, an offshoot of Hinduism, was founded in north east India by Gautama Buddha (563-483 BC) who taught that spiritual and moral discipline were essential to achieve supreme peace.

Confucianism is a mixture of Buddhism and Confucius' teachings which were elaborated to provide a moral basis for the political structure of Imperial China and to cover the already existing forms of ancestor worship.

Judaism dates back to c. 13th century B.C. The Jews were expelled from the Holy Land in AD70 and only reinstated in Palestine in 1948.

Christian monastery

Islam, founded in Mecca by Muhammad (570-632 AD) spread across Asia and Africa and in its retreat left isolated pockets of adherent communities.

Christianity was founded by Jesus of Nazareth in the 1st century AD The Papal authority, established in the 4th century, was rejected by Eastern churches in the 11th century. Later several other divisions developed eg. Roman Catholicism, Protestantism.

Jewish holy place

Hindu temple

Mohammedan mosque

Buddhist temple

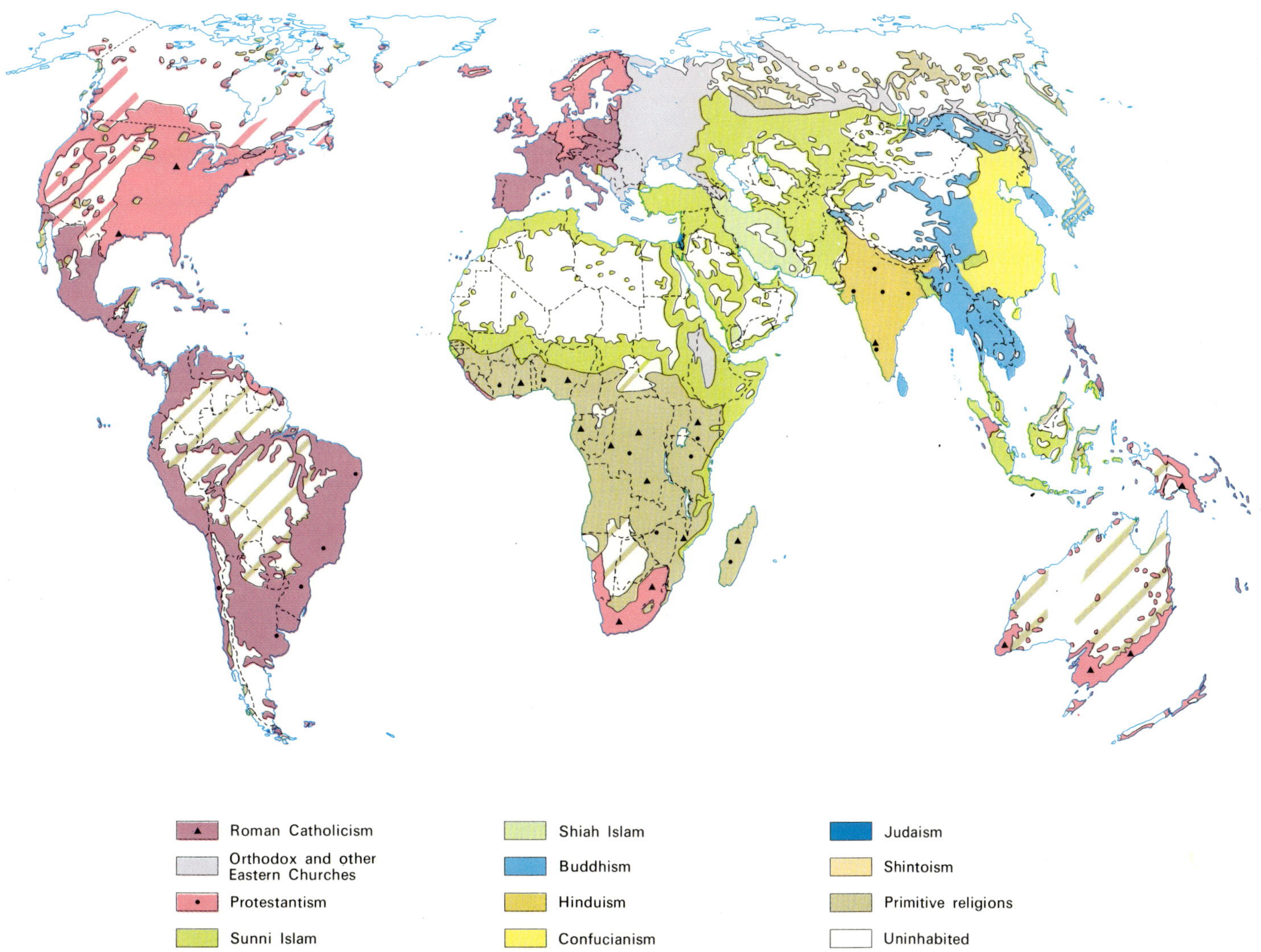

The Growth of Cities

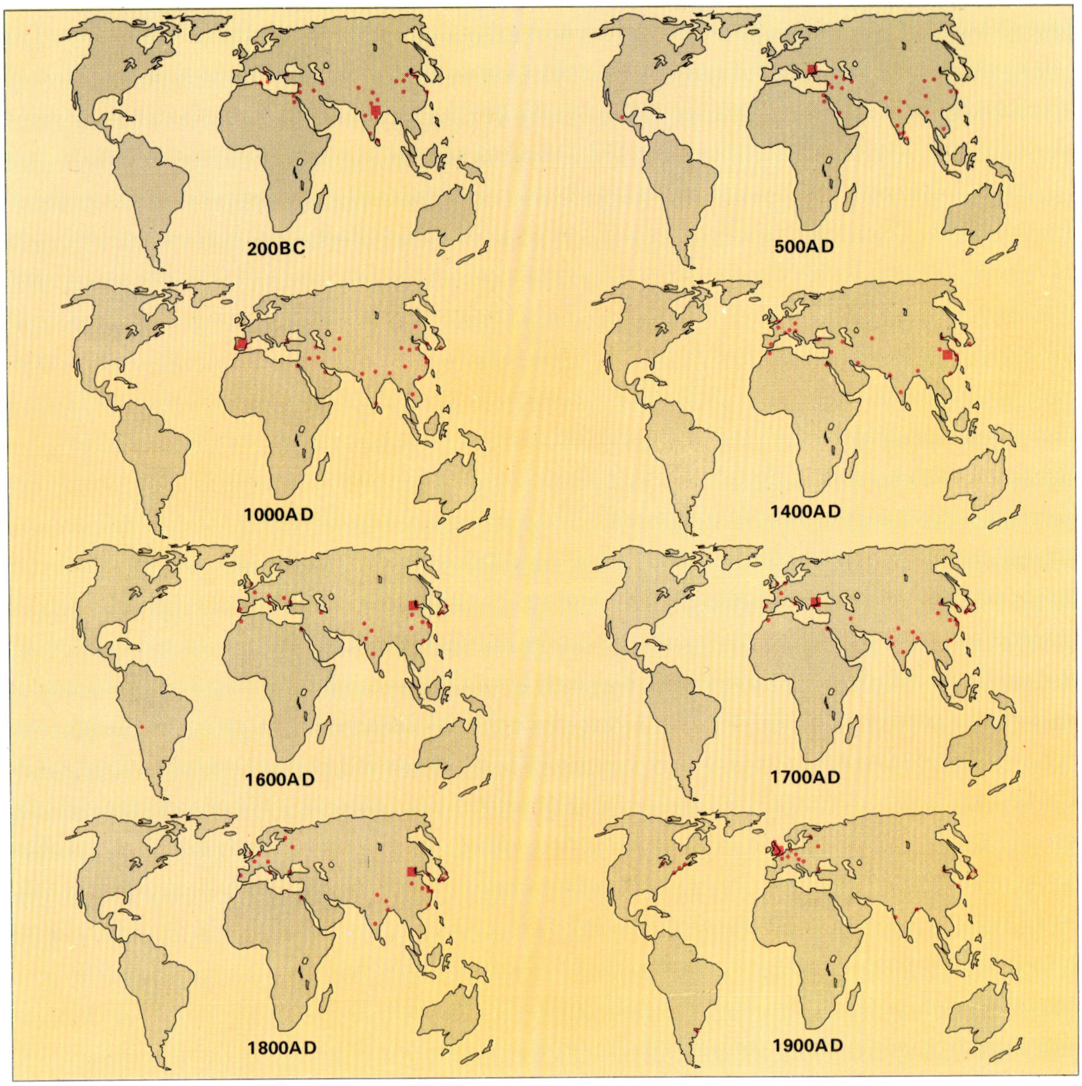

Cities through history

The evolution of the semi-permanent Neolithic settlements into a city took from 5000 until 3500 BC. Efficient communications and exchange systems were developed as population densities increased as high as 30 000 to 50 000 per square kilometre in 2000BC in Egypt and Babylonia, compared with New York City today at 10 000.

- ■ The largest city in the world
- • The twenty five largest cities in the world

Sao Paulo

Increase in urbanisation

The increase in urbanisation is a result primarily of better sanitation and health resulting in the growth of population and secondarily to the movement of man off the land into industry and service occupations in the cities. Generally the most highly developed industrial nations are the most intensely urbanised although exceptions such as Norway and Switzerland show that rural industrialisation can exist.

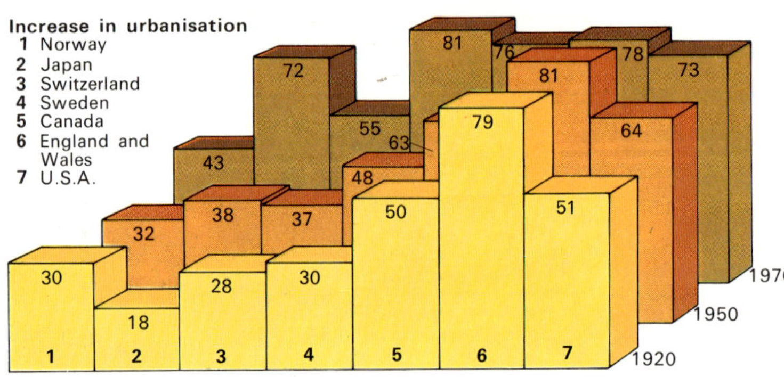

Metropolitan areas

A metropolitan area can be defined as a central city linked with surrounding communities by continuous built-up areas controlled by one municipal government. With improved communications the neighbouring communities generally continue to provide the city's work-force. The graph (right) compares the total populations of the world's ten largest cities.

City populations

1	New York	16 679 000
2	Mexico City	11 943 000
3	Tokyo	11 684 000
4	Shanghai	10 820 000
5	Los Angeles	10 350 000
6	Paris	9 863 000
7	Buenos Aires	8 435 000
8	Moscow	8 011 000
9	Peking	7 570 000
10	Sao Paulo	7 199 000

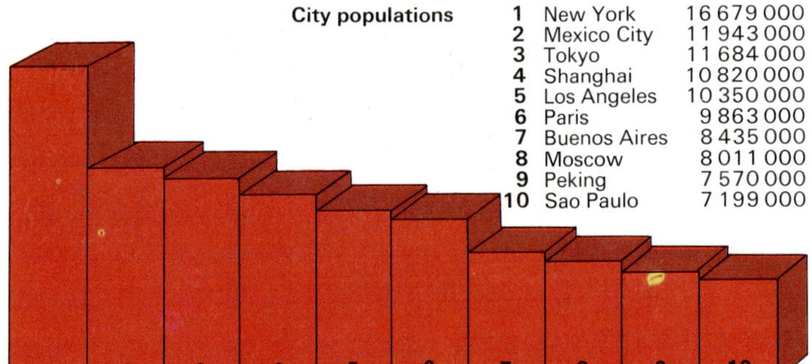

Major cities

Normally these are not only major centres of population and wealth but also of political power and trade. They are the sites of international airports and characteristically are great ports from which imported goods are distributed using the roads and railways which focus on the city. Their staple trades and industries are varied and flexible and depend on design and fashion rather than raw material production.

w York
Sydney
Tokyo
Moscow
Hong Kong
Bombay
London
Cairo
Rio de Janeiro
Rome
Cities over 5 000 000 inhabitants
2 000 000-5 000 000 inhabitants
1 000 000-2 000 000 inhabitants
250 000-1 000 000 inhabitants

Food Resources: Vegetable

Cocoa, tea , coffee
These tropical or sub-tropical crops are grown mainly for export to the economically advanced countries. Tea and coffee are the world's principal beverages. Cocoa is used more in the manufacture of chocolate.

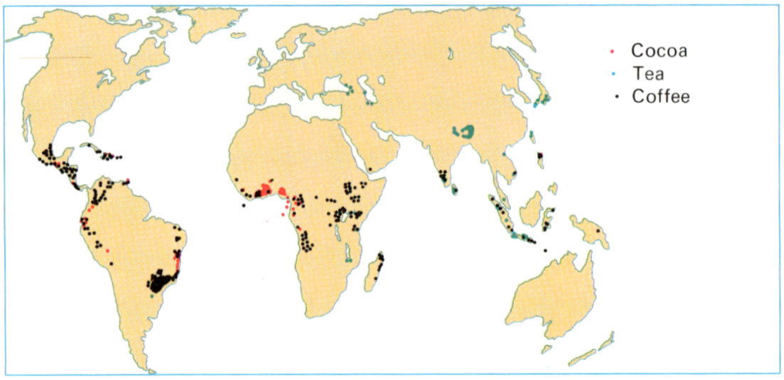

Sugar beet, sugar cane
Cane Sugar - a tropical crop - accounts for the bulk of the sugar entering into international trade. Beet Sugar, on the other hand, demands a temperate climate and is produced primarily for domestic consumption.

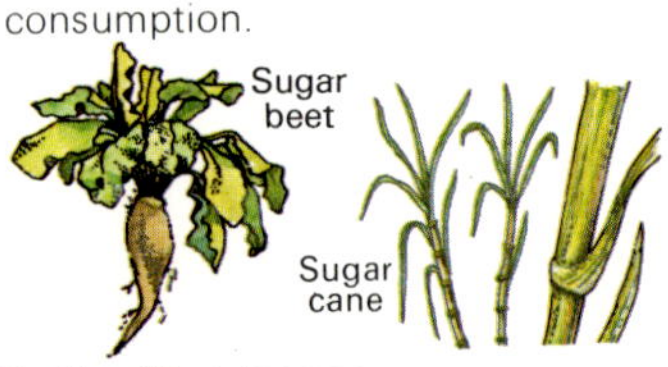

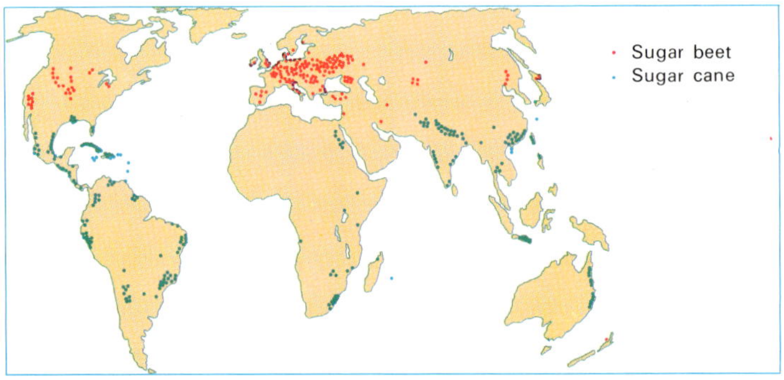

Cereals
Cereals include those members of the grain family with starchy edible seeds - wheat, maize, barley, oats, rye, rice, millets and sorghums.

Cereals and potatoes (not a cereal but starch-producing) are the principal source of food for our modern civilisations because of their high yield in bulk and food value per unit of land and labour required. They are also easy to store and transport, and provide food also for animals producing meat, fat, milk and eggs. Wheat is the principal bread grain of the temperate regions in which potatoes are the next most important food source. Rice is the principal cereal in the hotter, humid regions, especially in Asia. Oats, barley and maize are grown mainly for animal feed; millets and sorghums as main subsistence crops in Africa and India.

Fruit million tonnes

Wine

Fruit, wine
With the improvements in canning, drying and freezing, and in transport and marketing, the international trade and consumption of deciduous and soft fruits, citrus fruits and tropical fruits has greatly increased. Recent developments in the use of the peel will give added value to some of the fruit crops.

Over 80% of grapes are grown for wine and over a half in countries bordering the Mediterranean.

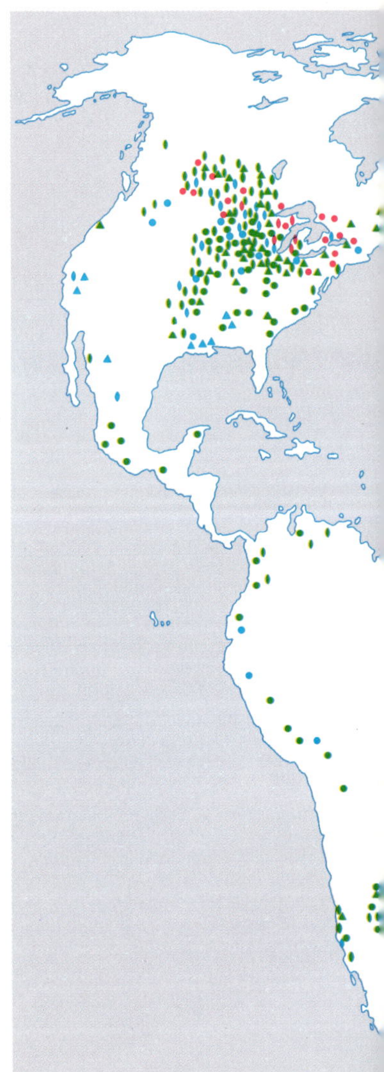

Vegetable oilseeds and oils
Despite the increasing use of synthetic chemical products and animal and marine fats, vegetable oils extracted from these crops grow in quantity, value and importance. Food is the major use- in margarine and cooking fats.

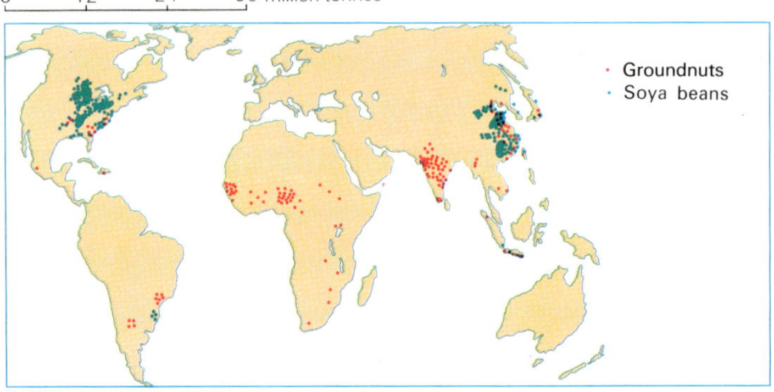

Groundnuts are also a valuable subsistence crop and the meal is used as animal feed. Soya-bean meal is a growing source of protein for humans and animals. The Mediterranean lands are the prime source of olive oil.

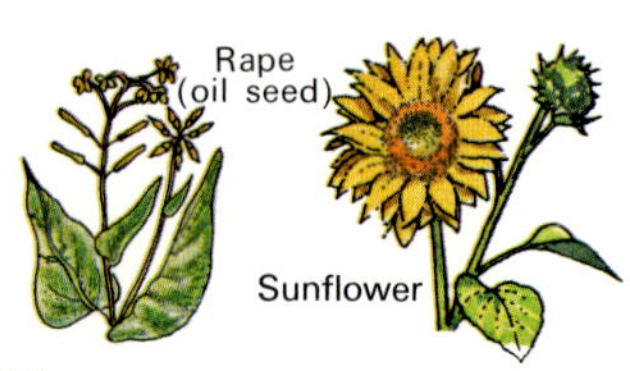

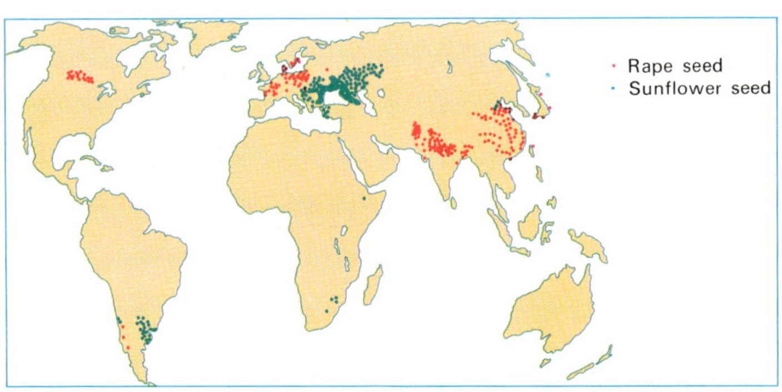

Maize (or Corn)

Needs plenty of sunshine, summer rain or irrigation and frost free for 6 months. Important as animal feed and for human food in Africa, Latin America and as a vegetable and breakfast cereal.

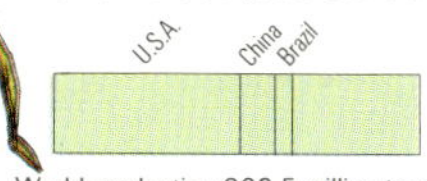

World production 362·5 million tonnes

Barley

Has the widest range of cultivation requiring only 8 weeks between seed time and harvest. Used mainly as animal-feed and by the malting industry.

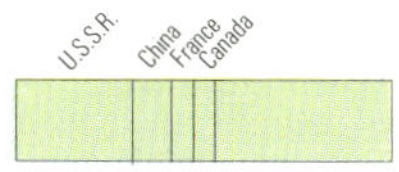

World production 188·6 million tonnes

Oats

Widely grown in temperate regions with the limit fixed by early autumn frosts. Mainly fed to cattle. The best quality oats are used for oatmeal, porridge and breakfast foods.

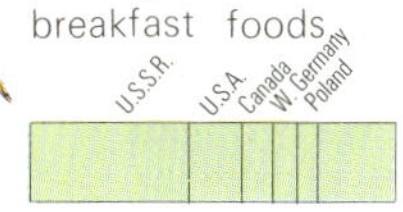

World production 51·4 million tonnes

Rice

Needs plains or terraces which can be flooded and abundant water in the growing season. The staple food of half the human race. In the husk, it is known as paddy.

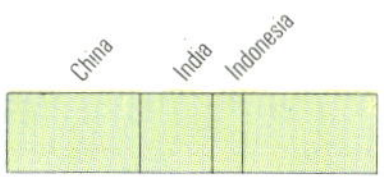

World production 378·6 million tonnes

Wheat

The most important grain crop in the temperate regions though it is also grown in a variety of climates e.g. in Monsoon lands as a winter crop.

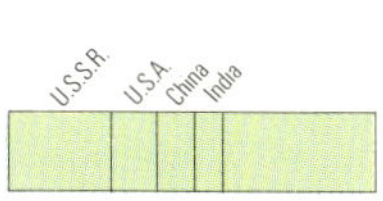

World production 437·2 million tonnes

Rye

The hardiest of cereals and more resistant to cold, pests and disease than wheat. An important foodstuff in Central and E. Europe and the U.S.S.R.

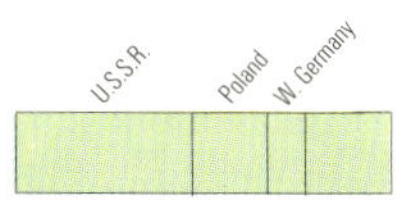

World production 29·5 million tonnes

Millets

The name given to a number of related members of the grass family, of which sorghum is one of the most important. They provide nutritious grain.

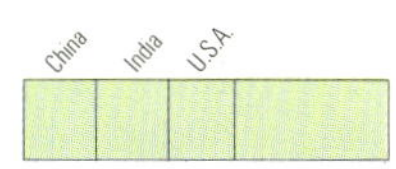

World production 101·7 million tonnes

Potato

An important food crop though less nutritious weight for weight than grain crops. World production is over 300 million tonnes.

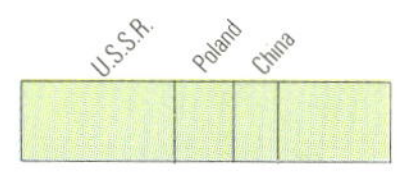

World production 302·8 million tonnes

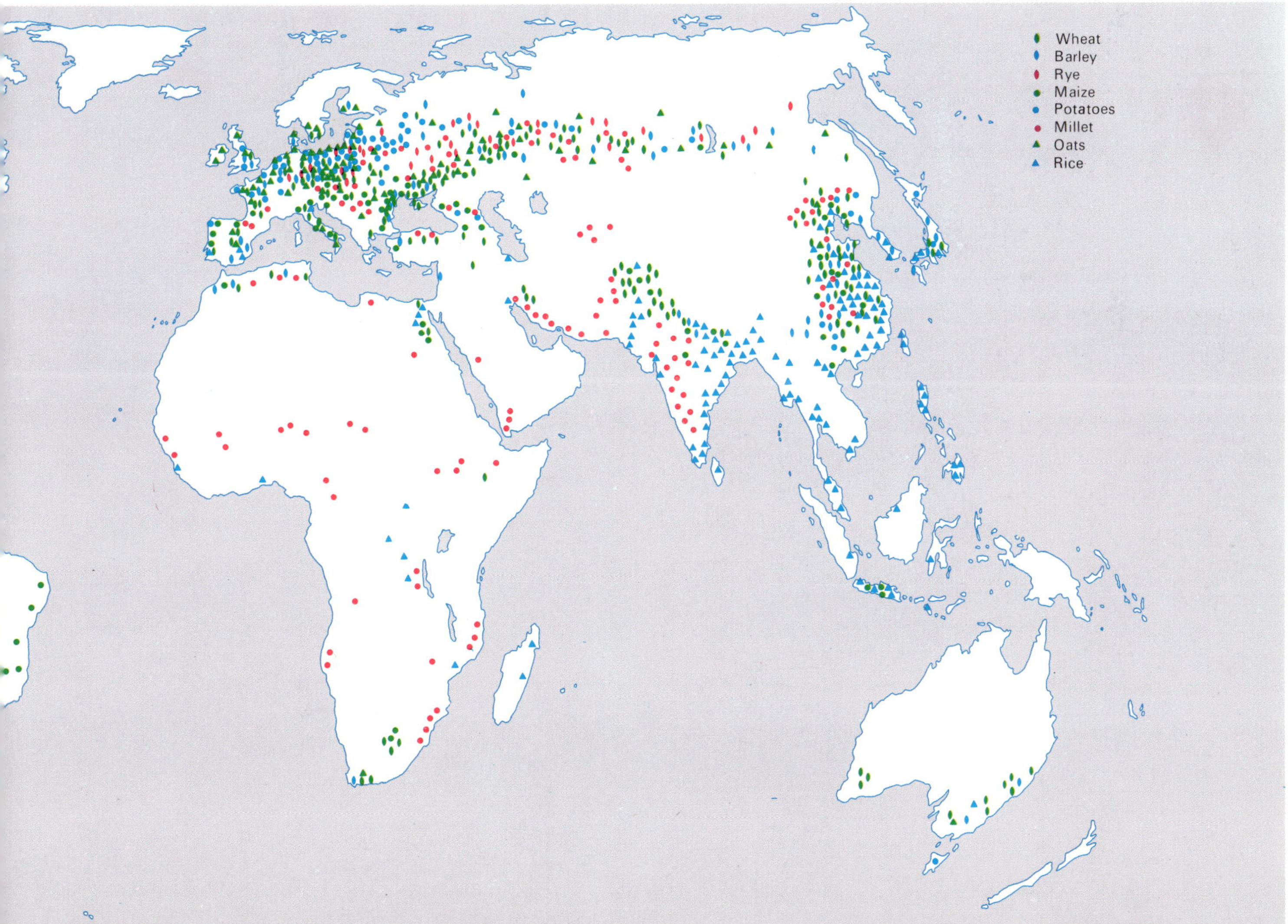

Food Resources: Animal

Food resources: Animal
Meat, milk and allied foods are prime protein-providers and are also sources of essential vitamins. Meat is mainly a product of continental and savannah grasslands and the cool west coasts, particularly in Europe. Milk and cheese, eggs and fish - though found in some quantity throughout the world - are primarily a product of the temperate zones.

Beef cattle

Australia, New Zealand and Argentina provide the major part of international beef exports. Western U.S.A. and Europe have considerable production of beef for their local high demand.

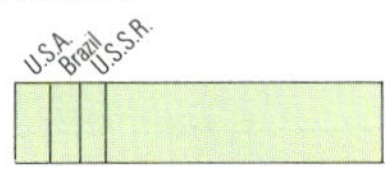

World production 1 005·8 million head

Dairy Cattle

The need of herds for a rich diet and for nearby markets result in dairying being characteristic of densely-populated areas of the temperate zones - U.S.A., N.W. Europe, N. Zealand and S.E. Australia.

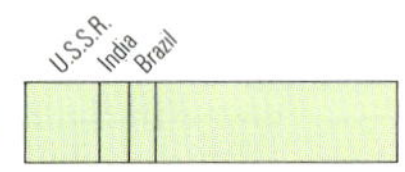

World production 206·2 million head

Cheese

The principal producers are the U.S.A., India, W. Europe, U.S.S.R., and New Zealand and principal exporters Netherlands, New Zealand, Denmark and France.

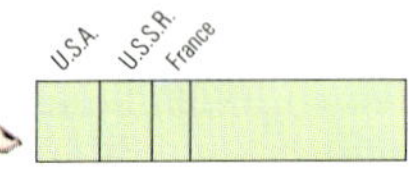

World production 10·6 million tonnes

Sheep

Raised mostly for wool and meat, the skins and cheese from their milk are important products in some countries. The merino yields a fine wool and crossbreds are best for meat.

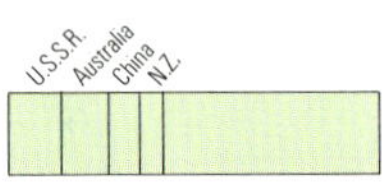

World production 1 055·0 million head

Pigs

Can be reared in most climates from monsoon to cool temperate. They are abundant in China, the corn belt of the U.S.A. N.W. and C. Europe, Brazil and U.S.S.R.

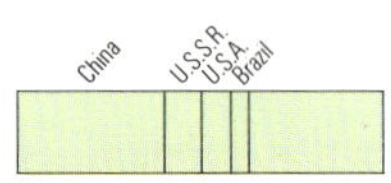

World production 732·4 million head

Fish

Commercial fishing requires large shoals of fish of one species within reach of markets. Freshwater fishing is also important. A rich source of protein, fish will become an increasingly valuable food source.

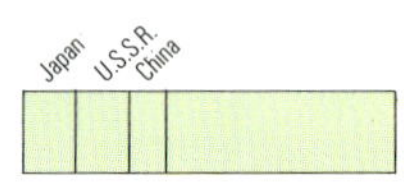

World production 73·5 million tonnes

Butter (includes Ghee)

The biggest producers are U.S.S.R., India, France and West Germany

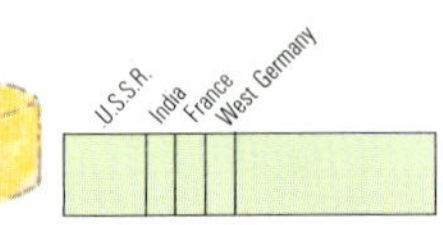

World production 7·03 million tonnes

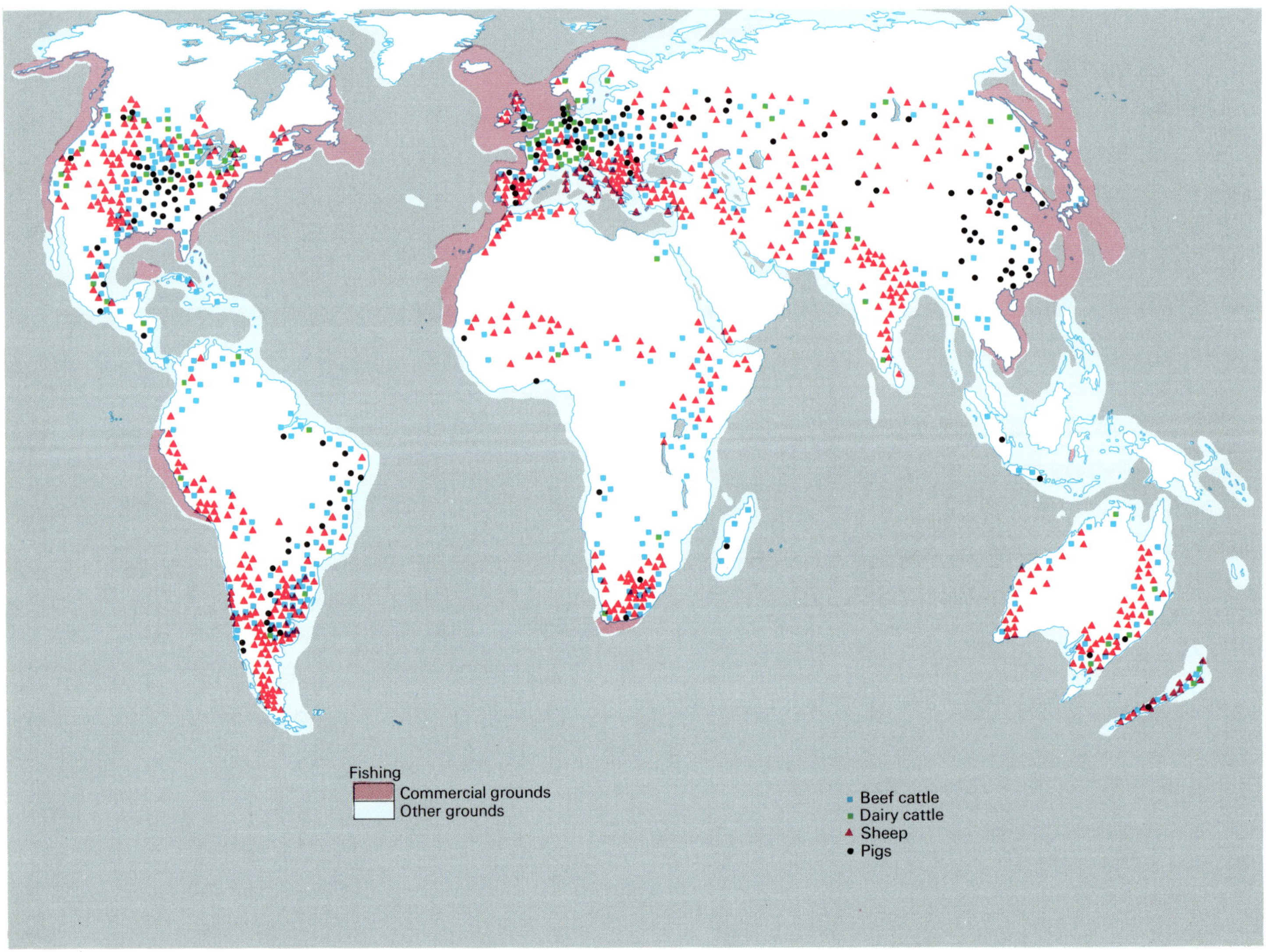

Nutrition

Foodstuffs fall, nutritionally, into three groups - providers of energy, protein and vitamins. Cereals and oil-seeds provide energy and second-class protein'; milk, meat and allied foods provide protein and vitamins, fruit and vegetables provide vitamins, especially Vitamin C, and some energy. To avoid malnutrition, a minimum level of these three groups of foodstuffs is required: the maps and diagrams show how unfortunately widespread are low standards of nutrition and even malnutrition.

Comparison of daily diets

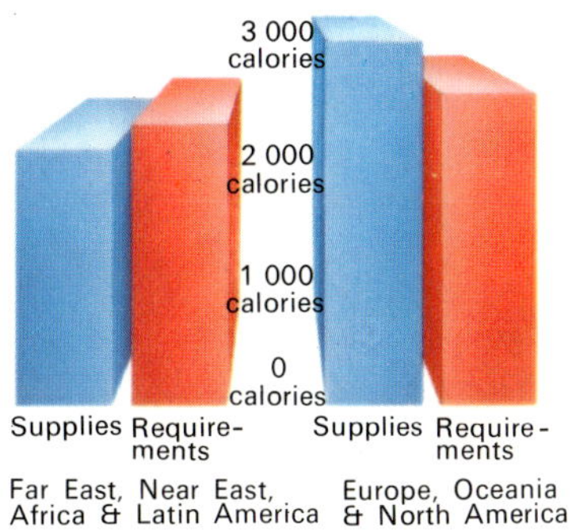

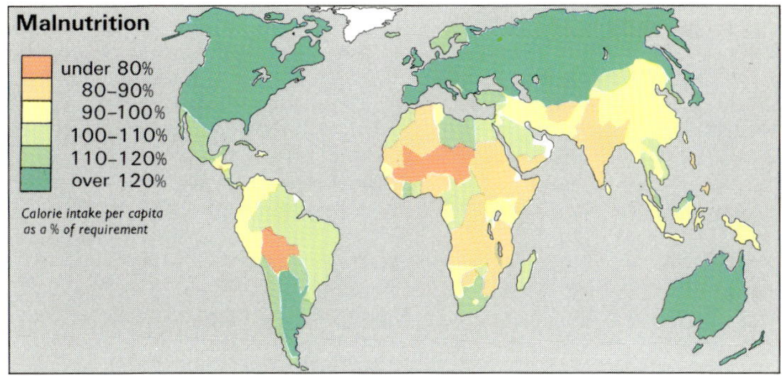

Proportions of calories

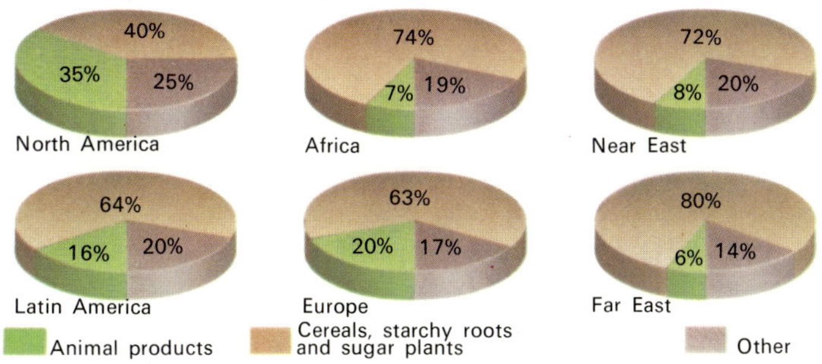

People and tractors engaged in agriculture

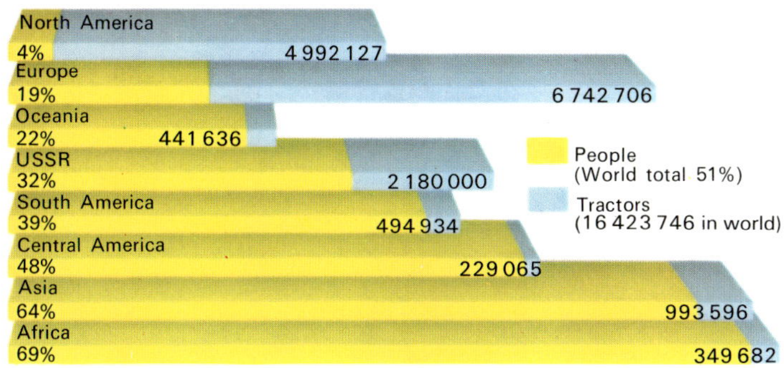

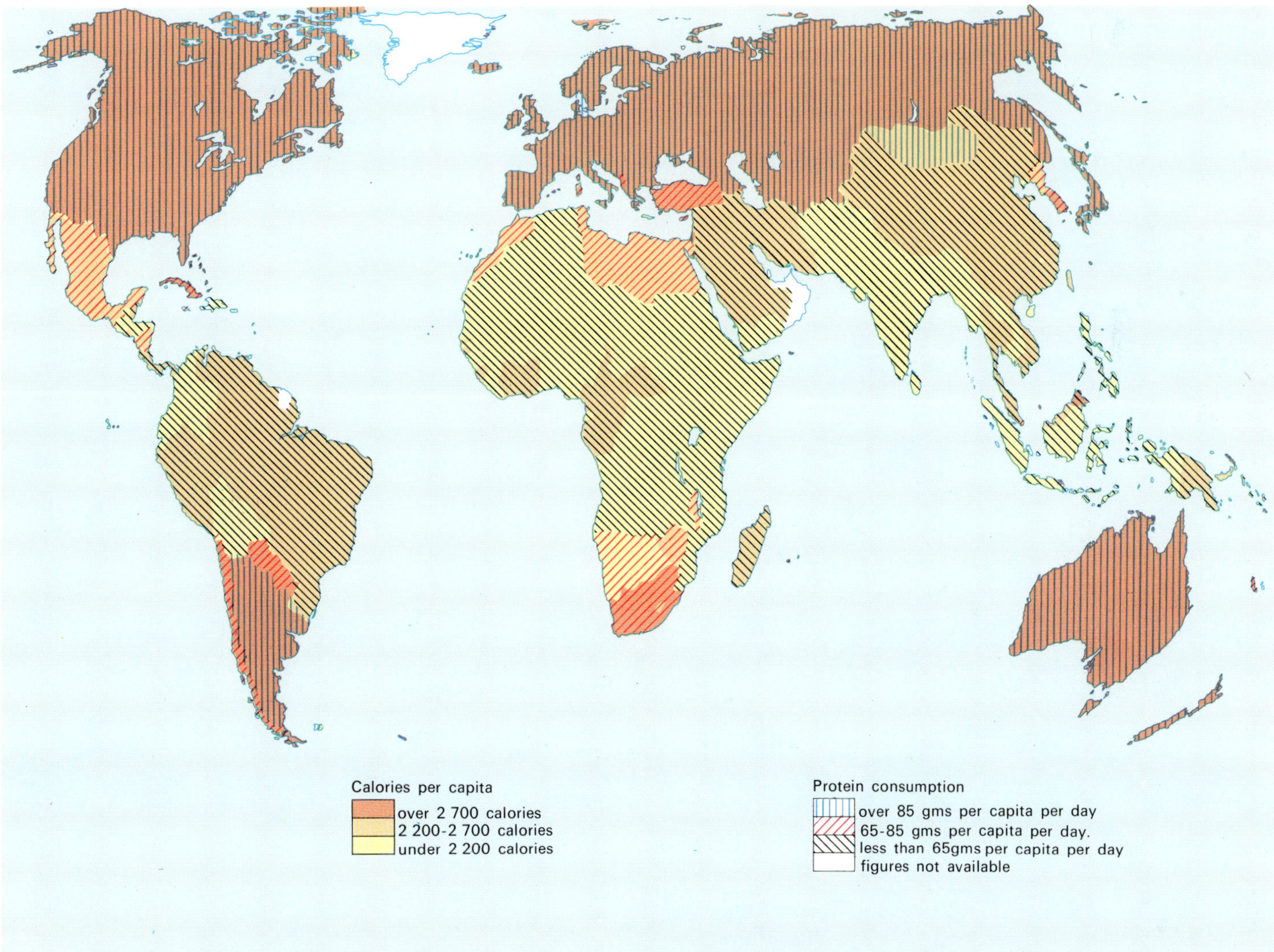

Mineral Resources I

Primitive man used iron for tools and vessels and its use extended gradually until iron, and later steel, became the backbone of the Modern World with the Industrial Revolution in the late 18th Century. At first, local ores were used, whereas today richer iron ores in huge deposits have been discovered and are mined on a large scale, often far away from the areas where they are used; for example, in Western Australia, Northern Sweden, Venezuela and Liberia. Iron smelting plants are today increasingly located at coastal sites, where the large ore carriers can easily discharge their cargo.

Steel is refined iron with the addition of other minerals, ferro-alloys, giving to the steel their own special properties; for example, resistance to corrosion (chromium, nickel, cobalt), hardness (tungsten, vanadium), elasticity (molybdenum), magnetic properties (cobalt), high tensile strength (manganese) and high ductility (molybdenum).

Production of Ferro-alloy metals

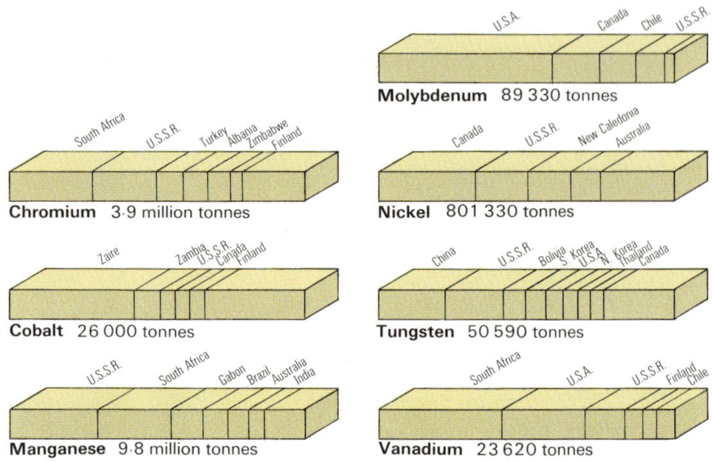

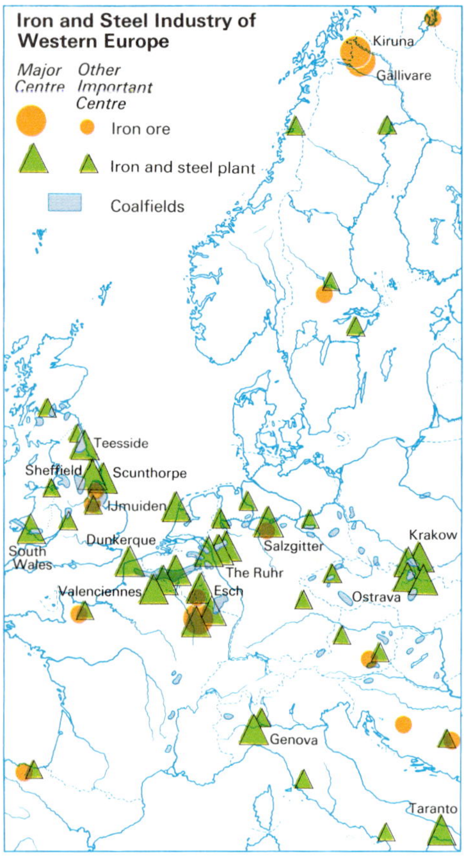

Sources of Iron ore imported into Western Europe
million tonnes

Imports from ▼	Austria	Belgium-Lux	France	Italy	Netherlands	Spain	U.K.	W. Germany
Algeria		0.7		0.2			0·1	
Australia		1·6	2·2	1·5	0·6	0·7	1·0	5·2
Brazil	1·2	1·4	4·3	3·2	1·1	1·3	3.0	1.0
Canada	0·3	0·2	0.9	1.8	2·1	0·4	3·2	4·5
India								0·3
Liberia	0·3	0·8	2·1	3·1	1·1	1·0	0·3	6·8
Mauritania		1·0	2.5	1.2		0·6	1·1	0·9
U.S.S.R.	0·4			0·7	0·1		0·3	0·1
Venezuela		0·5	0·4	1.7		0.7	0·3	1·3
Others (World)		0·2	1·1	0·8			1·7	2·5
France		10·4						1·6
Norway		0·5					1.2	1.4
Spain			0·1		2·5		0·1	1·1
Sweden		4·1	1·7		1·5		3·2	4·3
Total Imports	2·2	21.4	15.3	14·2	9·0	4·7	15·5	31·0
Home produced ore	3·4	1·6	36·6	0·5		7·8	3.7	2·5

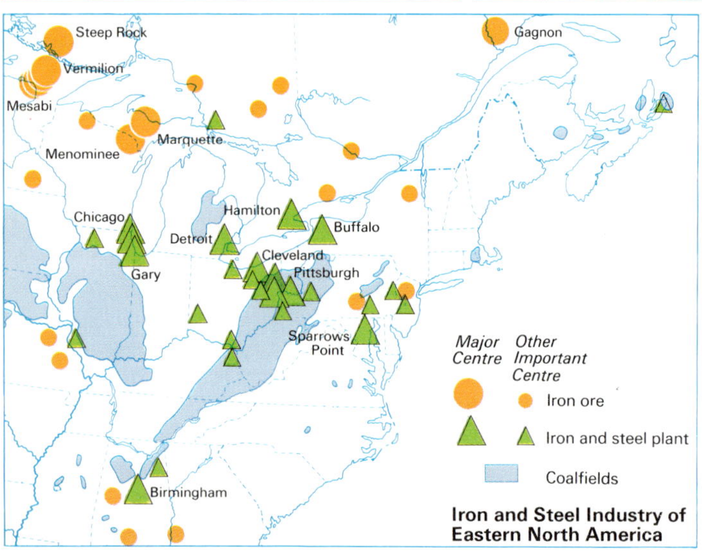

Iron and Steel Industry of Eastern North America

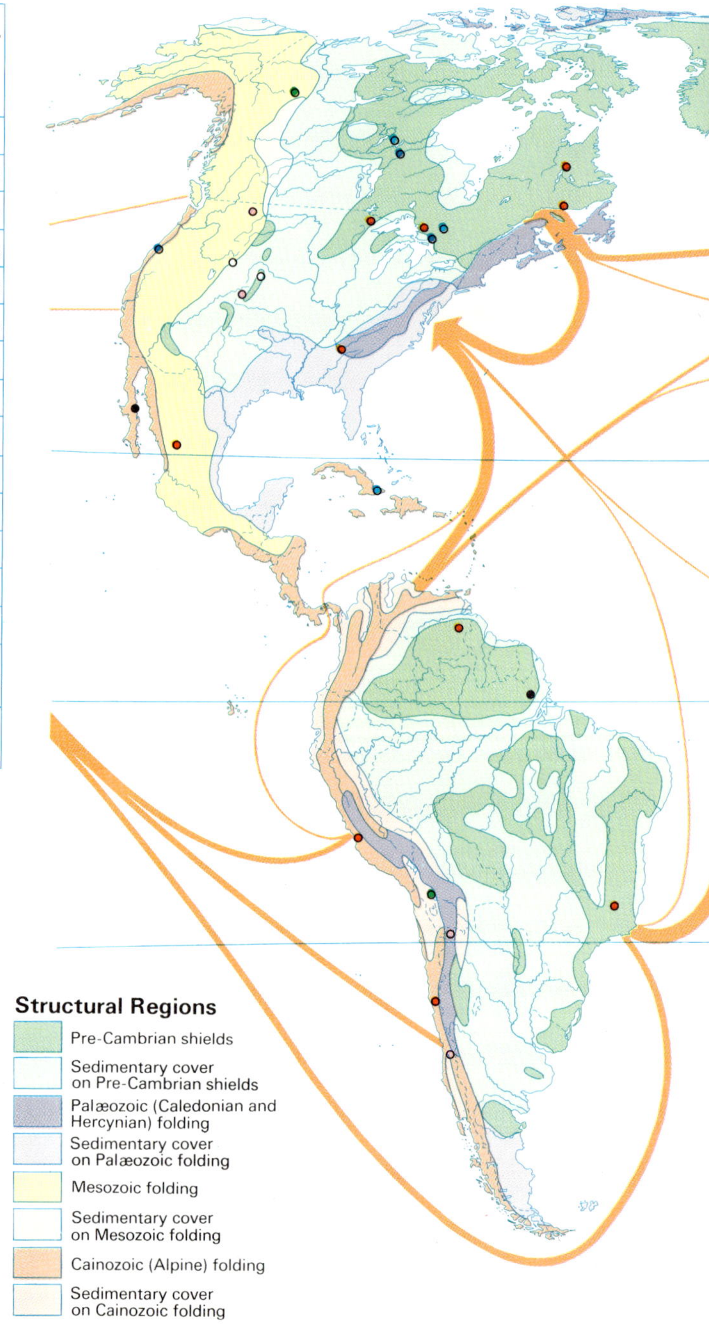

World production of Pig iron and Ferro-alloys

Total World production 504 million tonnes

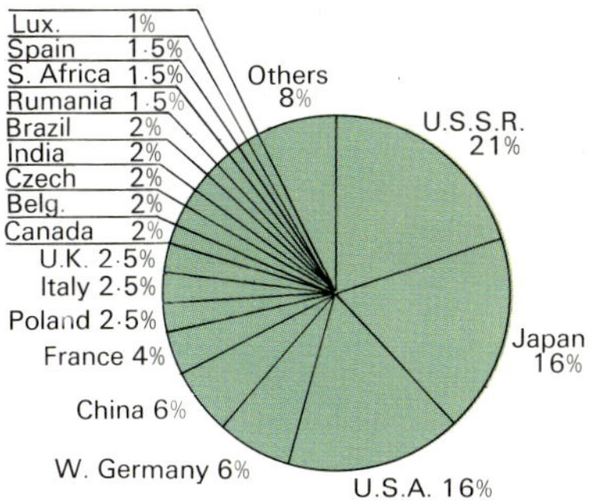

Growth of World production of Pig iron and Ferro-alloys

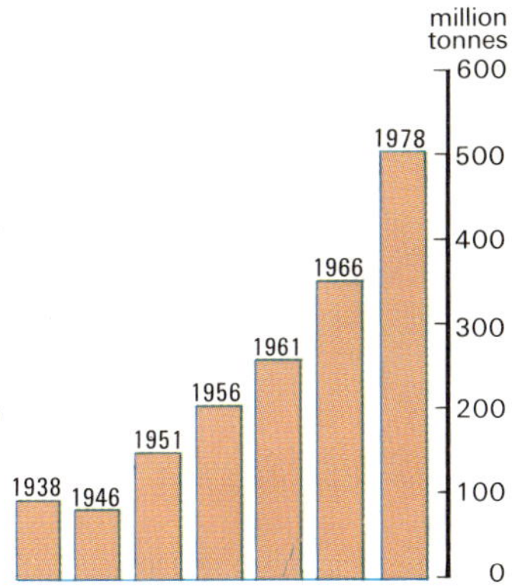

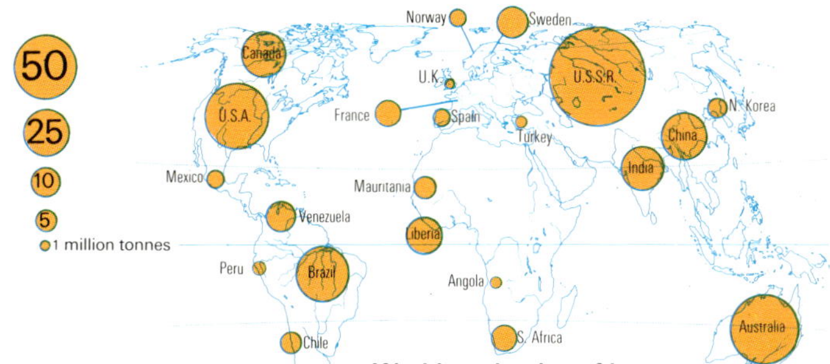

World production of Iron ore (Fe content)

Total World production 492 million tonnes

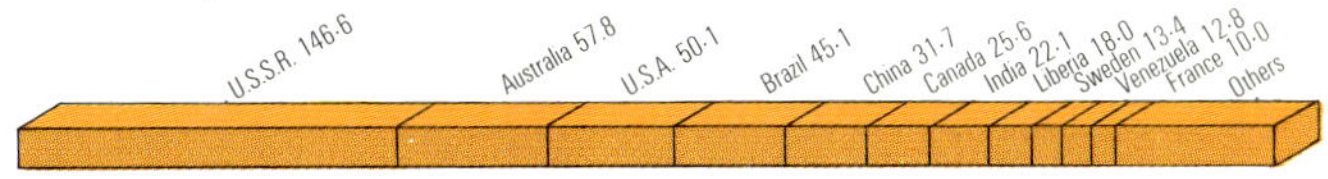

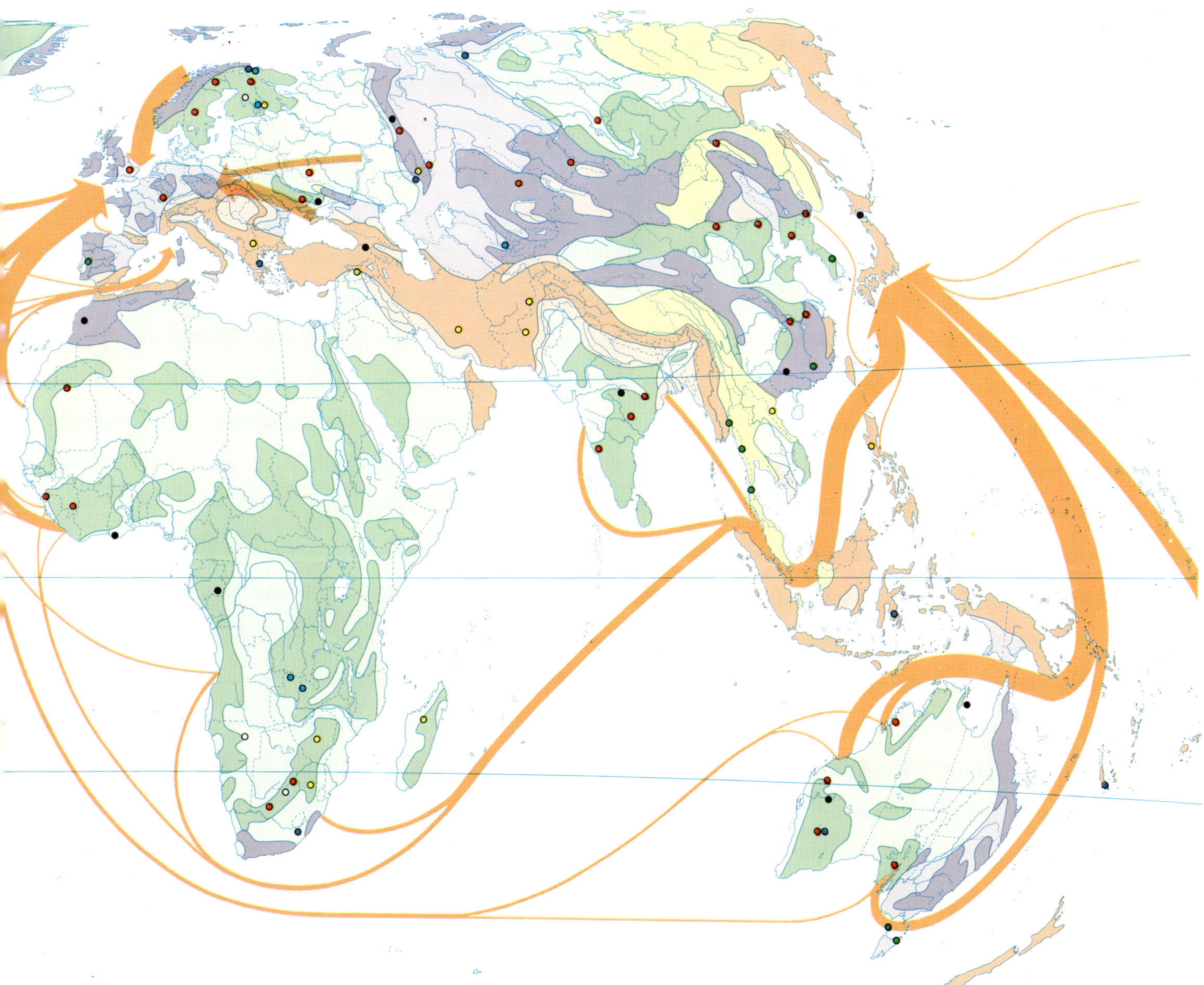

Principal Sources of Iron ore and ferro-alloys

- Iron
- Chrome
- Cobalt
- Manganese
- Molybdenum
- Nickel
- Tungsten
- Vanadium
- Iron ore trade flow

Mineral Resources II

Antimony – imparts hardness when alloyed to other metals, especially lead.
Uses: type metal, pigments to paints, glass and enamels, fireproofing of textiles

World production 69 163 tonnes

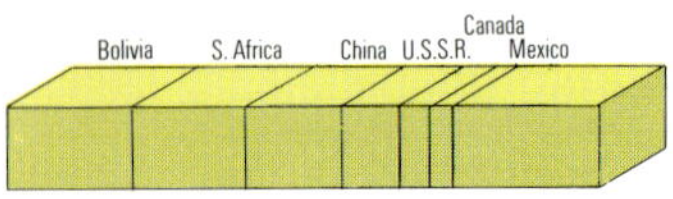

Lead – heavy, soft, malleable, acid resistant.
Uses: storage batteries, sheeting and piping, cable covering, ammunition, type metal, weights, additive to petrol.

World production 3·59 million tonnes

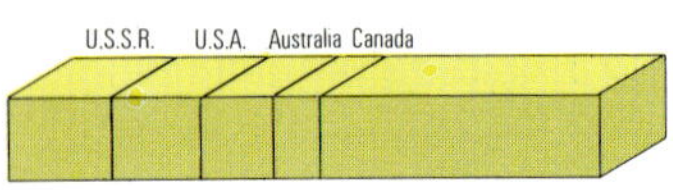

Tin – resistant to attacks by organic acids, malleable.
Uses: canning, foils, as an alloy to other metals (brass and bronze).

World production 224 600 tonnes

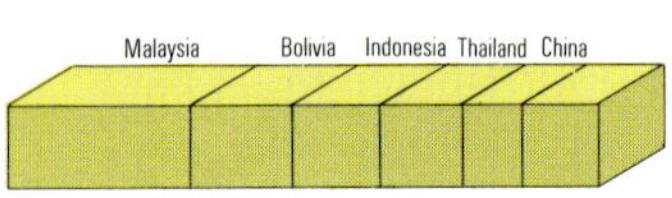

Aluminium – light, resists corrosion, good conductor.
Uses: aircraft, road and rail vehicles, domestic utensils, cables, makes highly tensile and light alloys.

World production 85·0 million tonnes (of Bauxite)

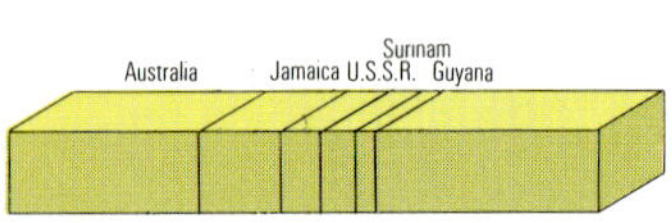

Gold – untarnishable and resistant to corrosion, highly ductile and malleable, good conductor. The pure metal is soft and it is alloyed to give it hardness.
Uses: bullion, coins, jewellery, gold-leaf, electronics.

World production 1 411 tonnes

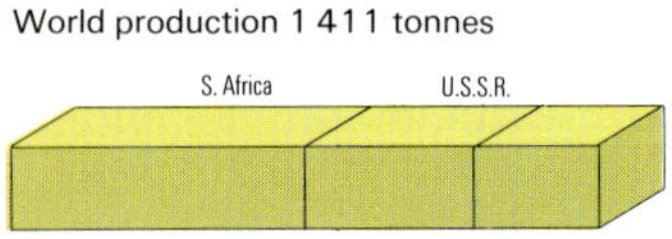

Copper – excellent conductor of electricity and heat, durable, resistant to corrosion, strong and ductile.
Uses: wire, tubing, brass (with zinc and tin), bronze (with tin), (compounds) – dyeing.

World production 8·03 million tonnes

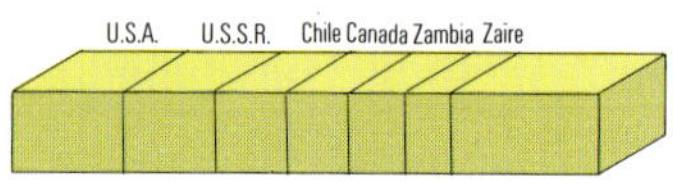

Mercury – the only liquid metal, excellent conductor of electricity
Uses: thermometers, electrical industry, gold and silver ore extraction, (compounds) – drugs, pigments, chemicals, dentistry.

World production 7 111 tonnes

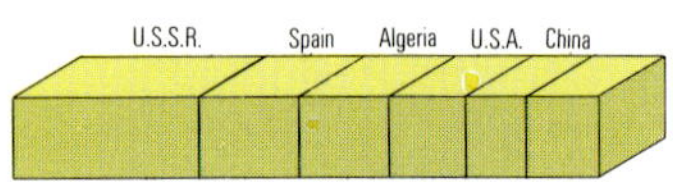

Zinc – hard metal, low corrosion factor.
Uses: brass (with copper and tin), galvanising, diecasting, medicines, paints and dyes.

World production 6·29 million tonnes

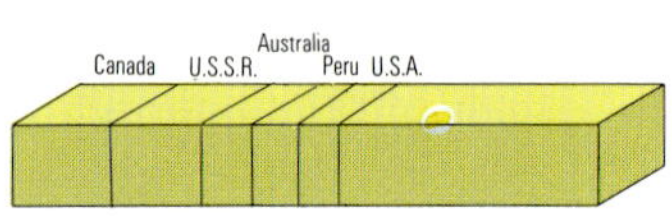

Diamonds – very hard and resistant to chemical attack, high lustre, very rare.
Uses: jewellery, cutting and abrading other materials.

World production 39·8 million carats

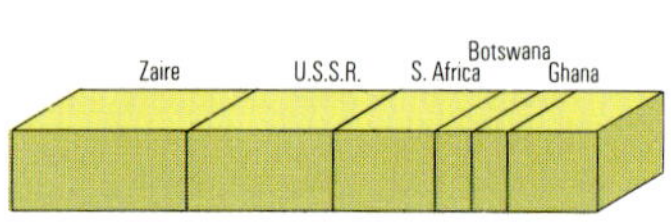

Silver – ductile and malleable, a soft metal and must be alloyed for use in coinage.
Uses: coins, jewellery, photography, electronics, medicines.

World production 10 550 tonnes

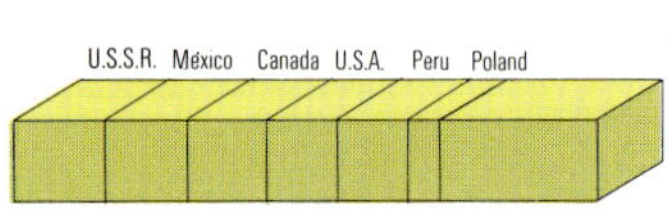

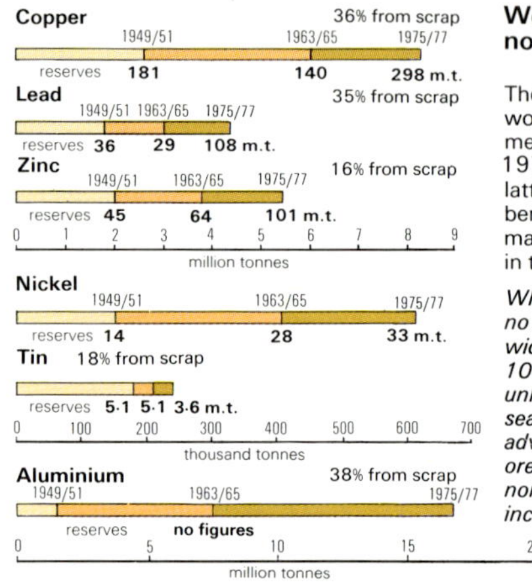

World consumption of non-ferrous metals

These diagrams show the average yearly world consumption of certain refined metals for 1949/51, 1963/65 and 1975/77and also the percentage of the latter produced from scrap. The figures beneath each diagram show estimates made in 1950, 1964 and1977 of reserves in the Western World.

While indicating that the reserves are by no means infinite the figures show how widely these estimates have differed over 10 years and take no account of unknown reserves, particularly in the sea-bed, nor the increasing economic advantages related to mining low content ores with advances in mining technology, nor exploiting more hazardous areas with increasing metal prices.

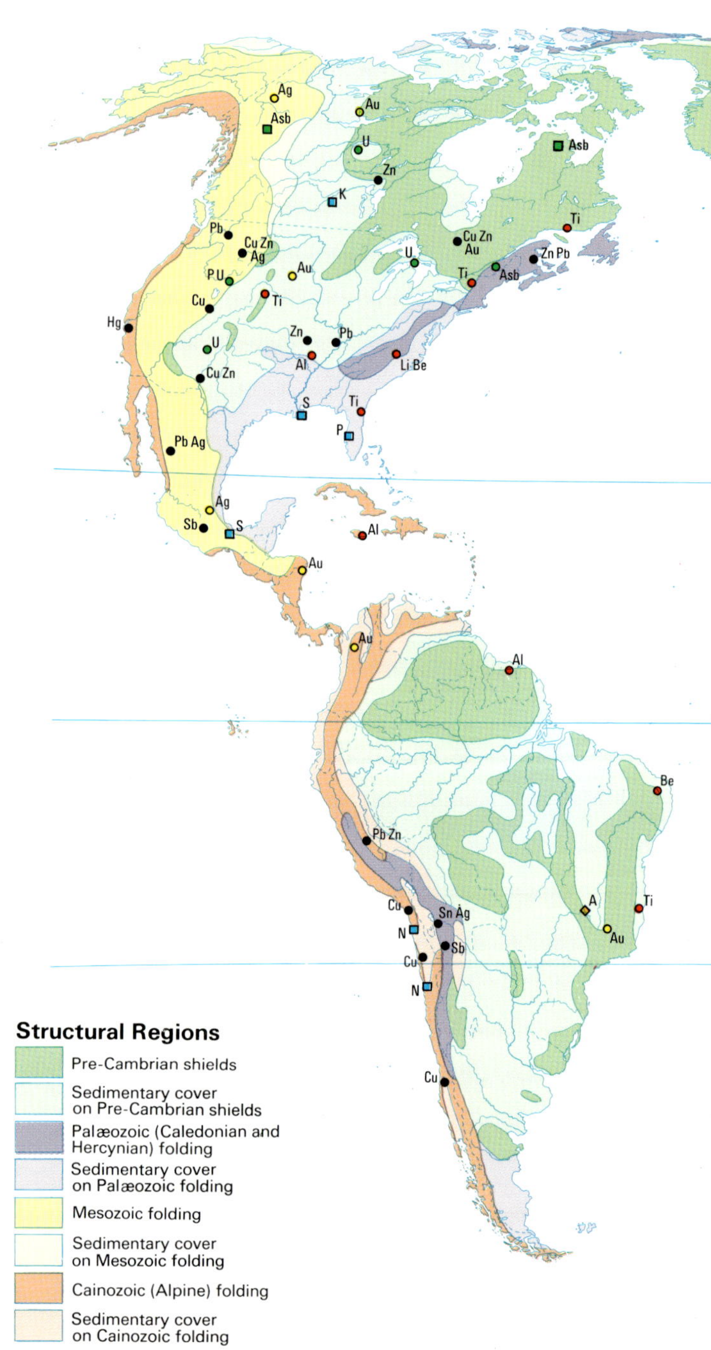

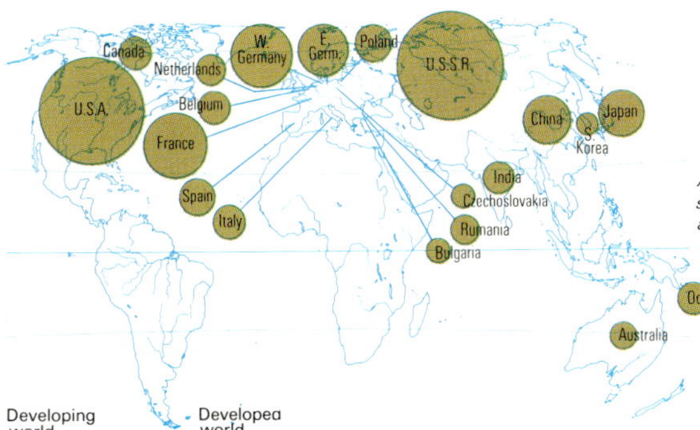

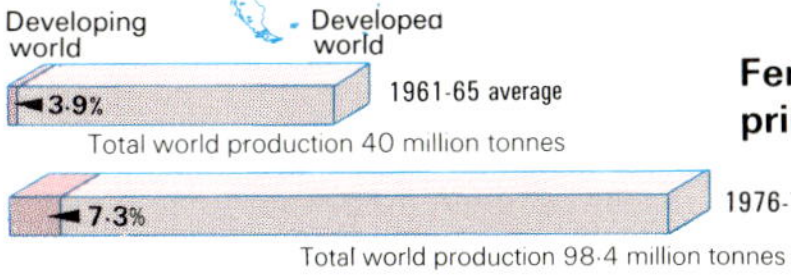

Fertilizers— principal producers

million tonnes

Artificial Fertilizers are produced from the minerals sodium nitrate, potassium, salt, phosphate and potash, and as by-products of other industries.

Tonnes of fertilizer per 1000 hectares of arable land

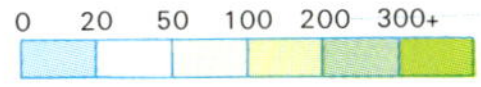

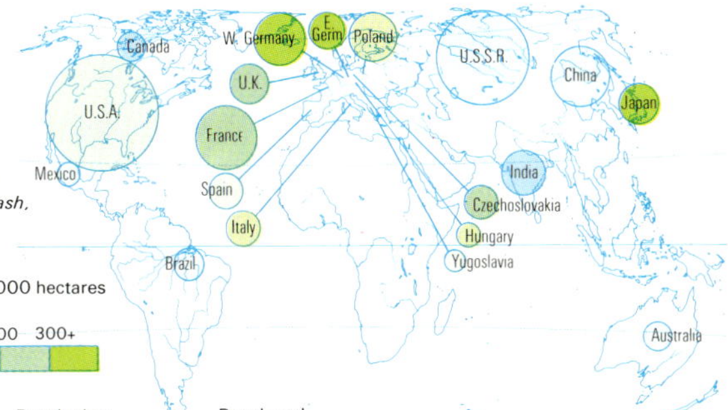

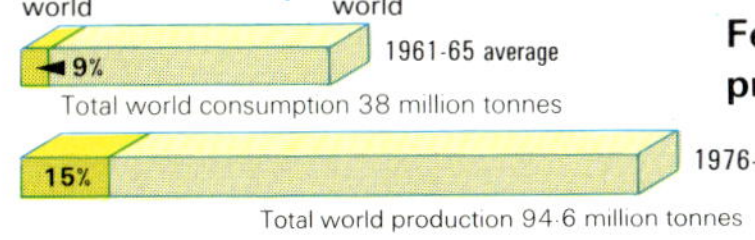

Fertilizers— principal consumers

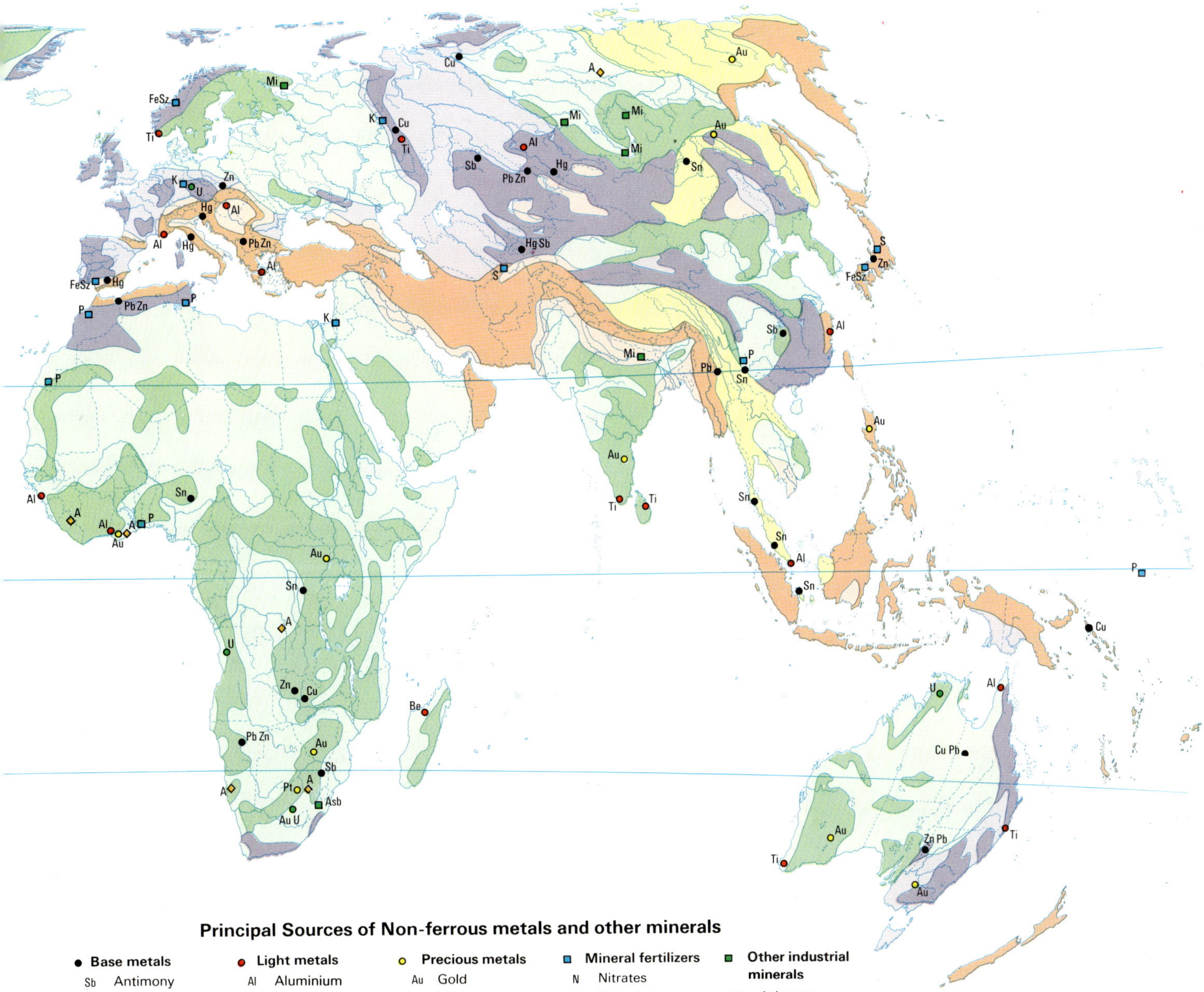

Principal Sources of Non-ferrous metals and other minerals

● Base metals
- Sb Antimony
- Cu Copper
- Pb Lead
- Hg Mercury
- Sn Tin
- Zn Zinc

● Light metals
- Al Aluminium
- Be Beryllium
- Li Lithium
- Ti Titanium

● Rare metals
- U Uranium

○ Precious metals
- Au Gold
- Pt Platinum
- Ag Silver

◇ Precious stones
- A Diamonds

■ Mineral fertilizers
- N Nitrates
- P Phosphates
- K Potash
- S Sulphur
- FeSz Pyrites

■ Other industrial minerals
- Asb Asbestos
- Mi Mica

Fuel and Energy

Coal
Coal is the result of the accumulation of vegetation over millions of years. Later under pressure from overlying sediments, it is hardened through four stages: peat, lignite, bituminous coal, and finally anthracite. Once the most important source of power, coal's importance now lies in the production of electricity and as a raw material in the production of plastics, heavy chemicals and disinfectants.

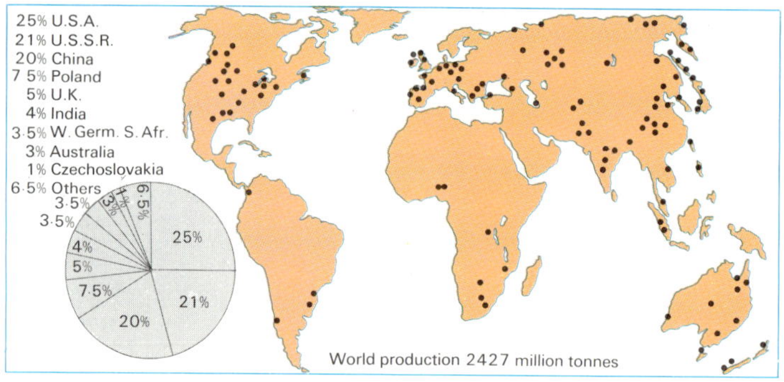

Coal mine

Oil
Oil is derived from the remains of marine animals and plants, probably as a result of pressure, heat and chemical action. It is a complex mixture of hydrocarbons which are refined to extract the various constituents. These include products such as gasolene, kerosene and heavy fuel oils. Oil is rapidly replacing coal because of easier handling and reduced pollution.

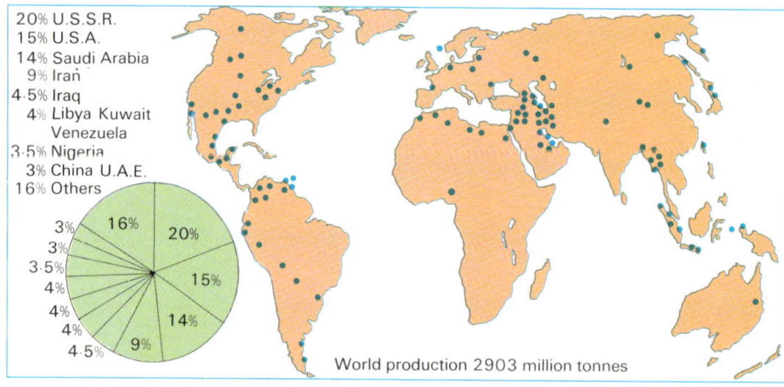

Oil derrick

Natural gas
Since the early 1960's natural gas (methane) has become one of the largest single sources of energy. By liquefaction its volume can be reduced to 1/600 of that of gas and hence is easily transported. It is often found directly above oil reserves and because it is both cheaper than coal gas and less polluting it has great potential.

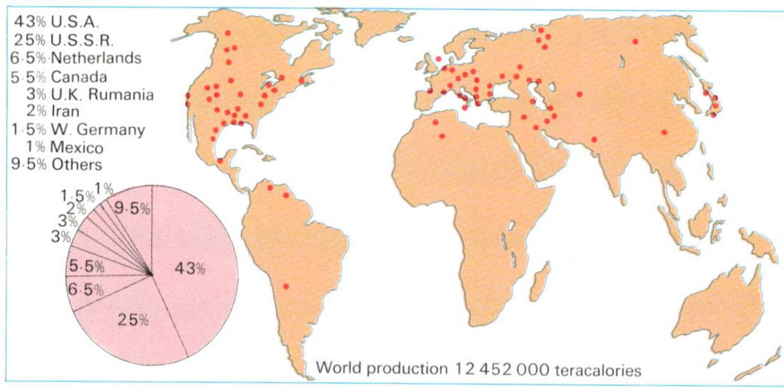

North sea gas rig

Water
Hydro-electric power stations use water to drive turbines which in turn generate electricity. The ideal site is one in which a consistently large volume of water falls a considerable height, hence sources of H.E.P. are found mainly in mountainous areas. Potential sources of hydro-electricity using waves or tides are yet to be exploited widely.

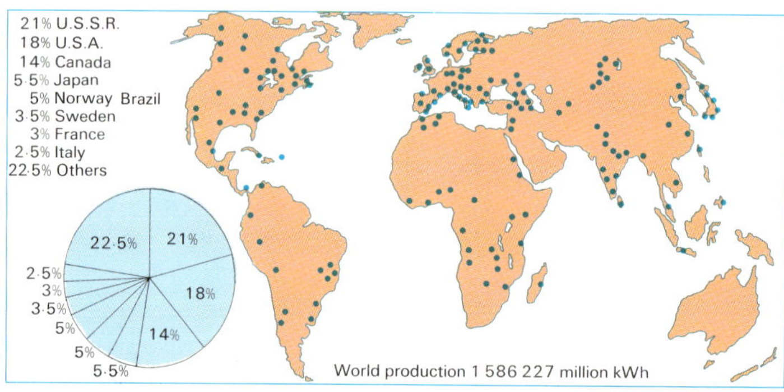

Water power

Nuclear energy
The first source of nuclear power was developed in Britain in 1956. Energy is obtained from heat generated by the reaction from splitting atoms of certain elements, of which uranium and plutonium are the most important. Although the initial installation costs are very high the actual running costs are low because of the slow consumption of fuel.

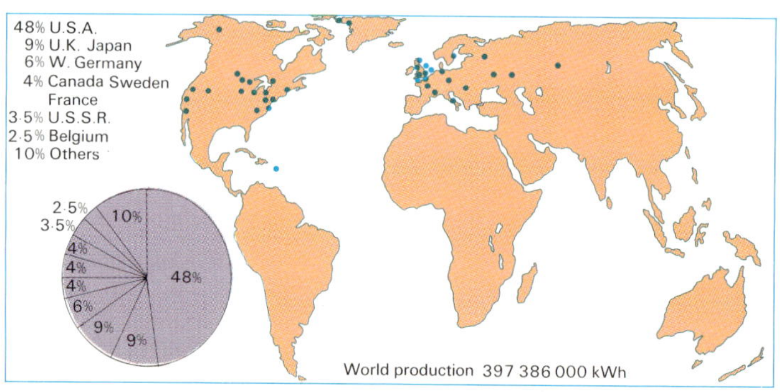

Nuclear power station

In a short space of time these two diagrams can change markedly; there can be a cut-back in supply owing to internal political change (Iran), or in consumption by vigorous government action (U.S.A.). The production of North Sea oil has changed the balance of oil trade in the U.K. and Norway but it is very costly to extract, relatively short-lived and is small on a world scale.

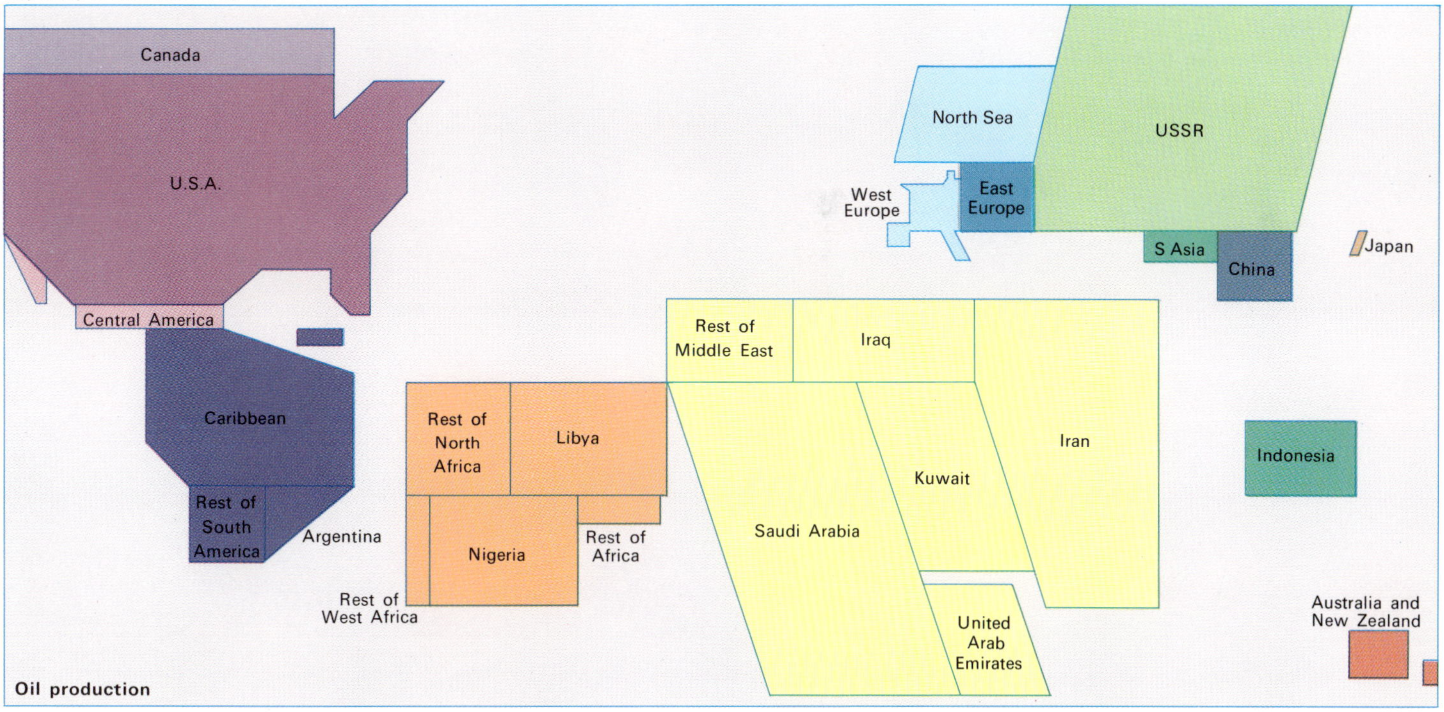

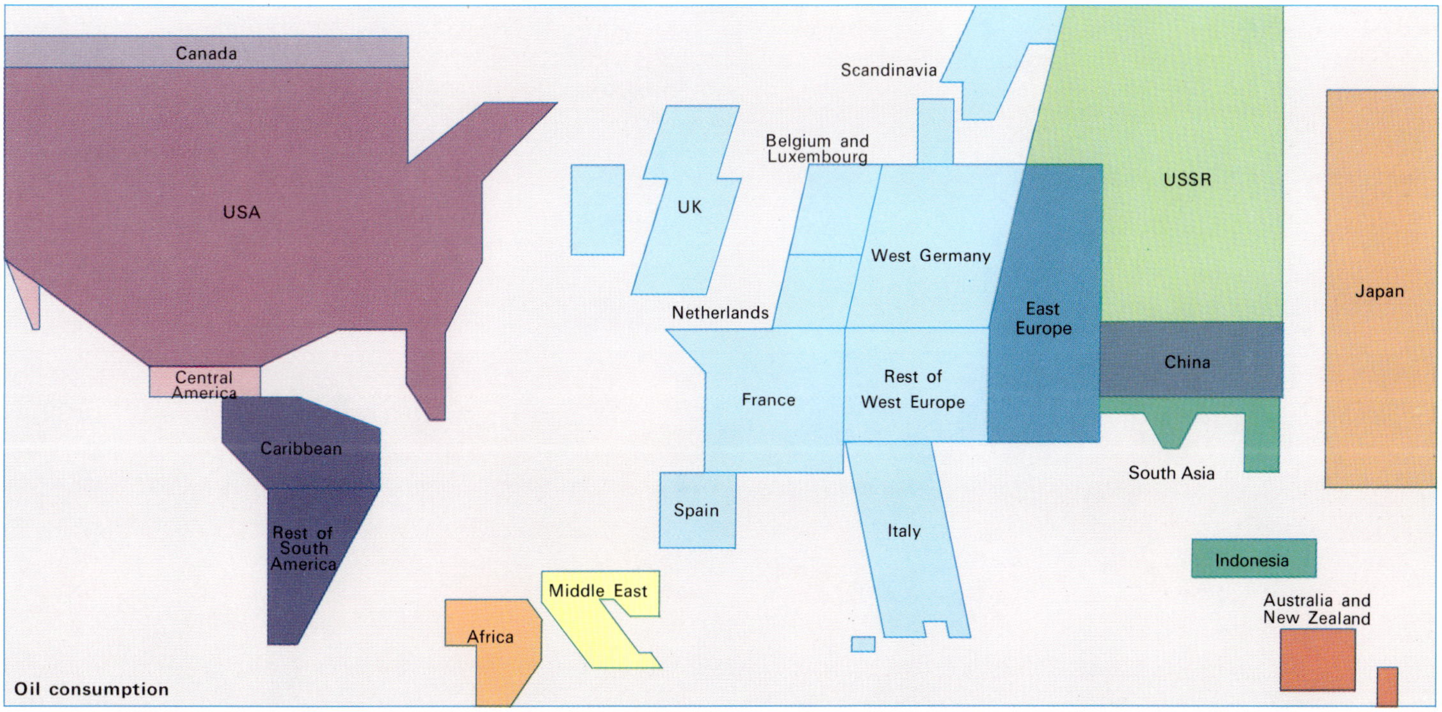

Oil's new super-powers *above* When countries are scaled according to their production and consumption of oil they take on new dimensions. At present, large supplies of oil are concentrated in a few countries of the Caribbean, the Middle East and North Africa, except for the vast indigenous supplies of the U.S.A. and U.S.S.R. The Middle East, with 58% of the world's reserves, produces 35% of the world's supply and yet consumes less than 3%. The U.S.A. despite its great production, has a deficiency of nearly 415 million tons a year, consuming 30% of the world's total. The U.S.S.R., with 11% of world reserves, produces 19% of world output and consumes 13%. Soviet production continues to grow annually although at a decreased rate since the mid-1970's. Japan, one of the largest oil importers, increased its consumption by 440% during the period 1963-73. Since then, total imports have decreased slightly.

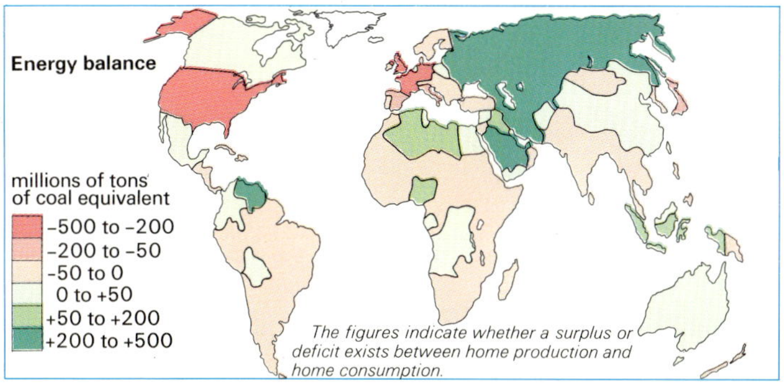

The figures indicate whether a surplus or deficit exists between home production and home consumption.

Occupations

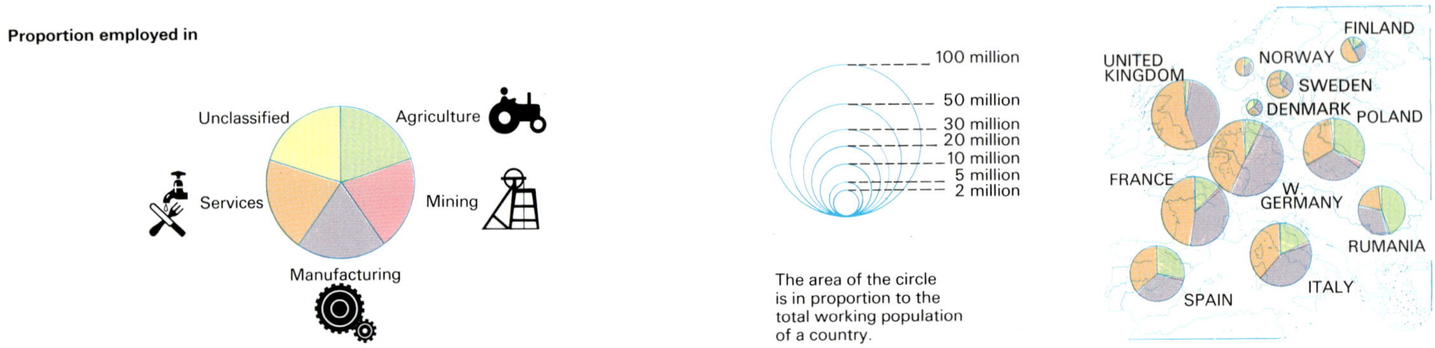

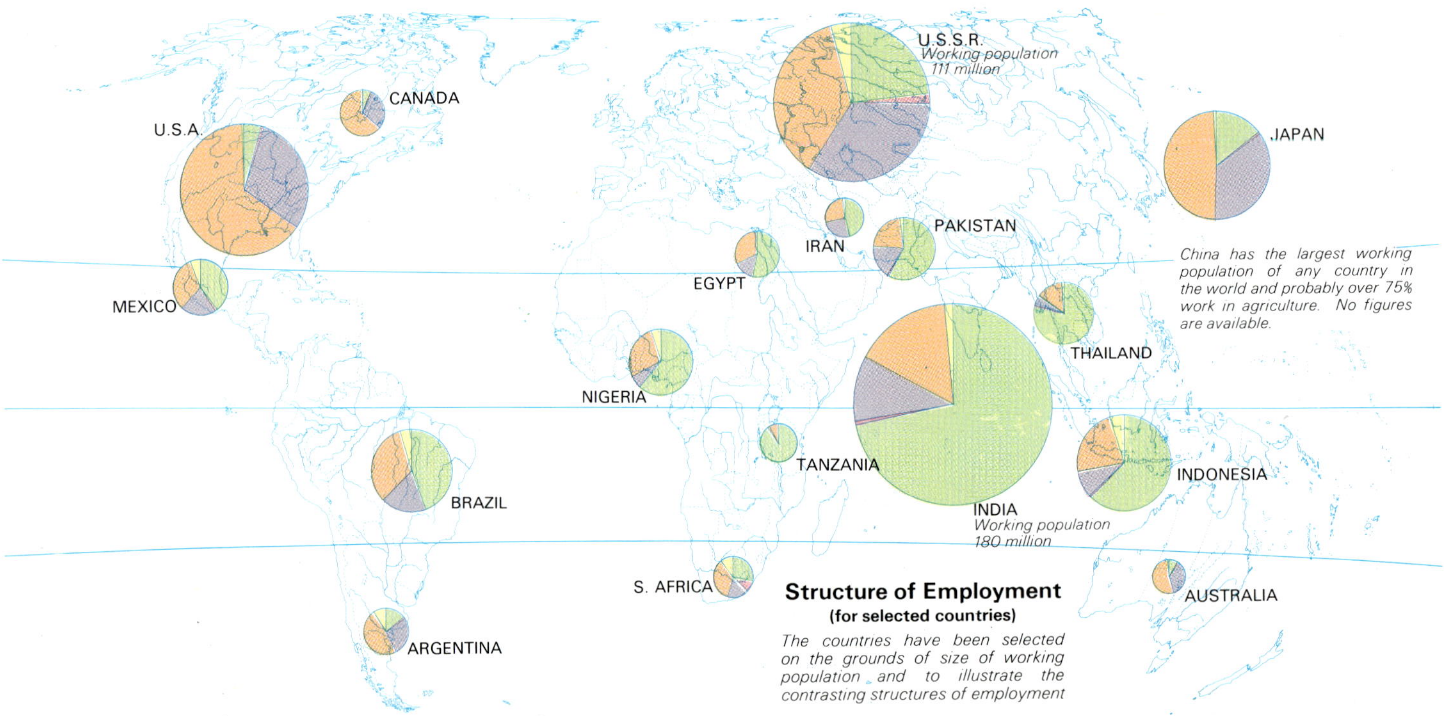

Structure of Employment
(for selected countries)

The countries have been selected on the grounds of size of working population and to illustrate the contrasting structures of employment

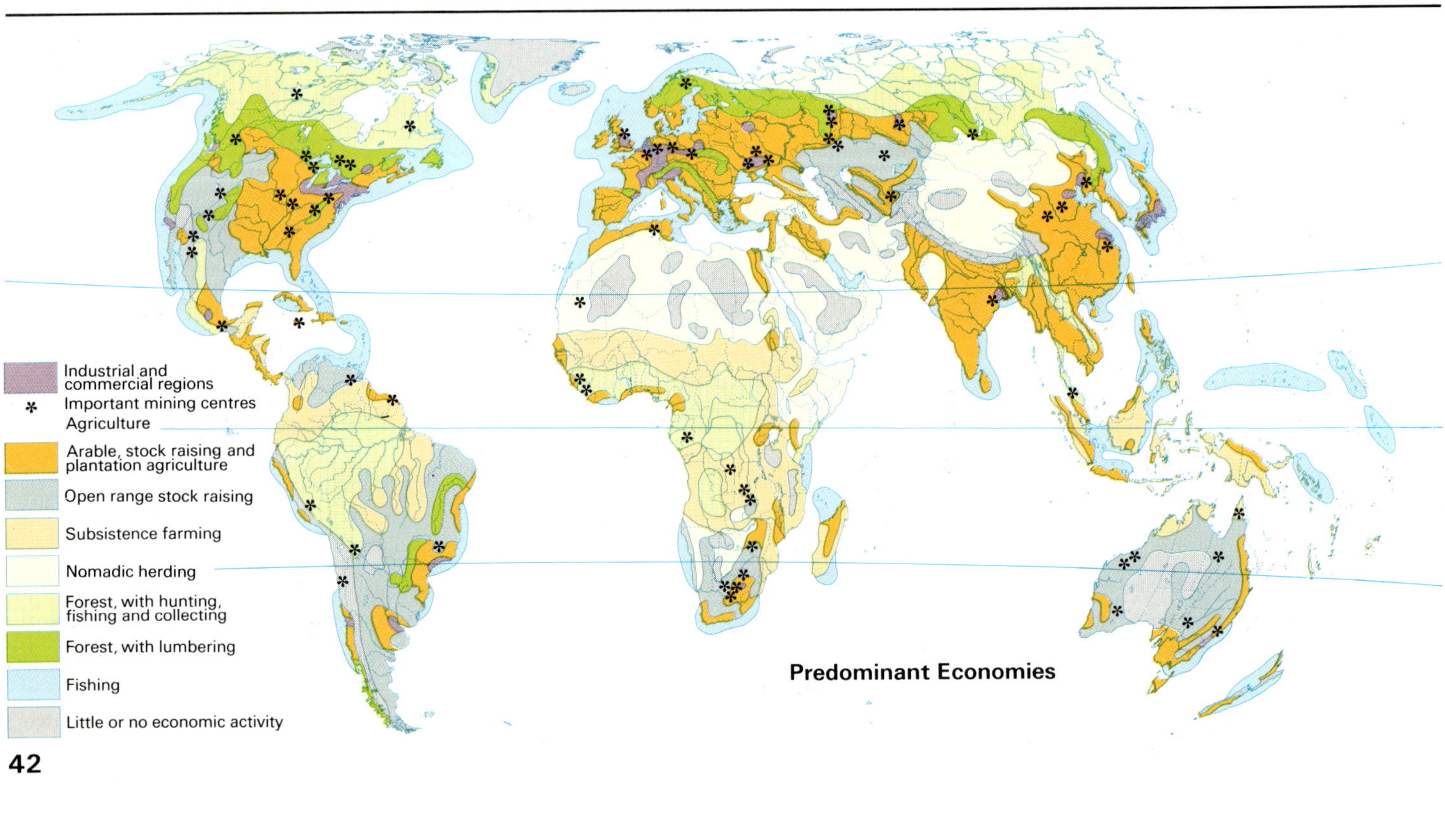

Predominant Economies

Industry

Casting steel ingots

World Steel production

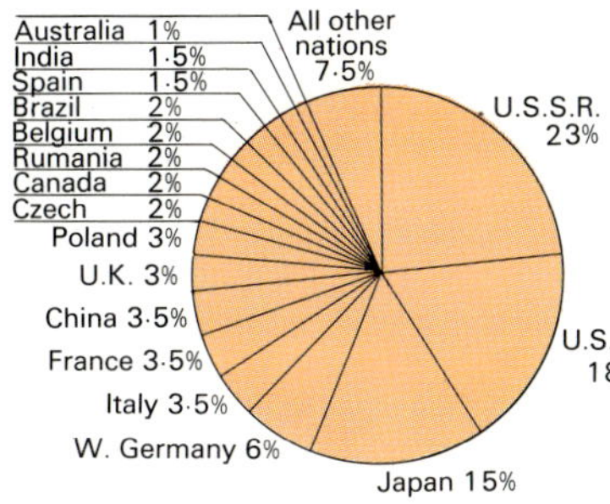

Growth of World Steel production

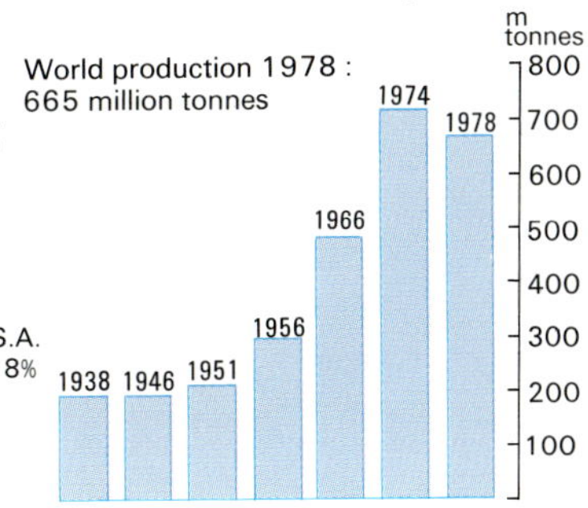

World Steel production per capita

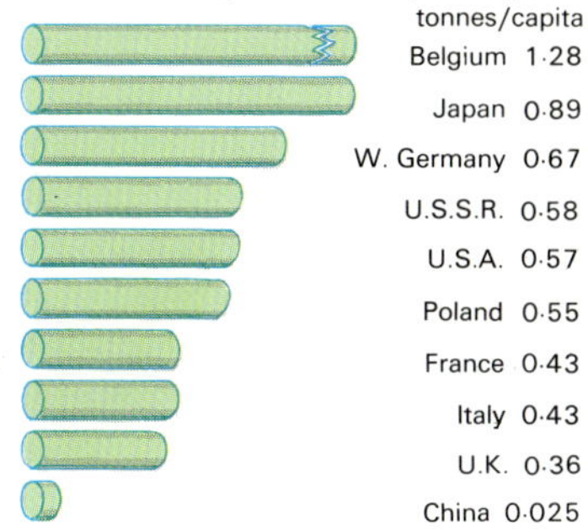

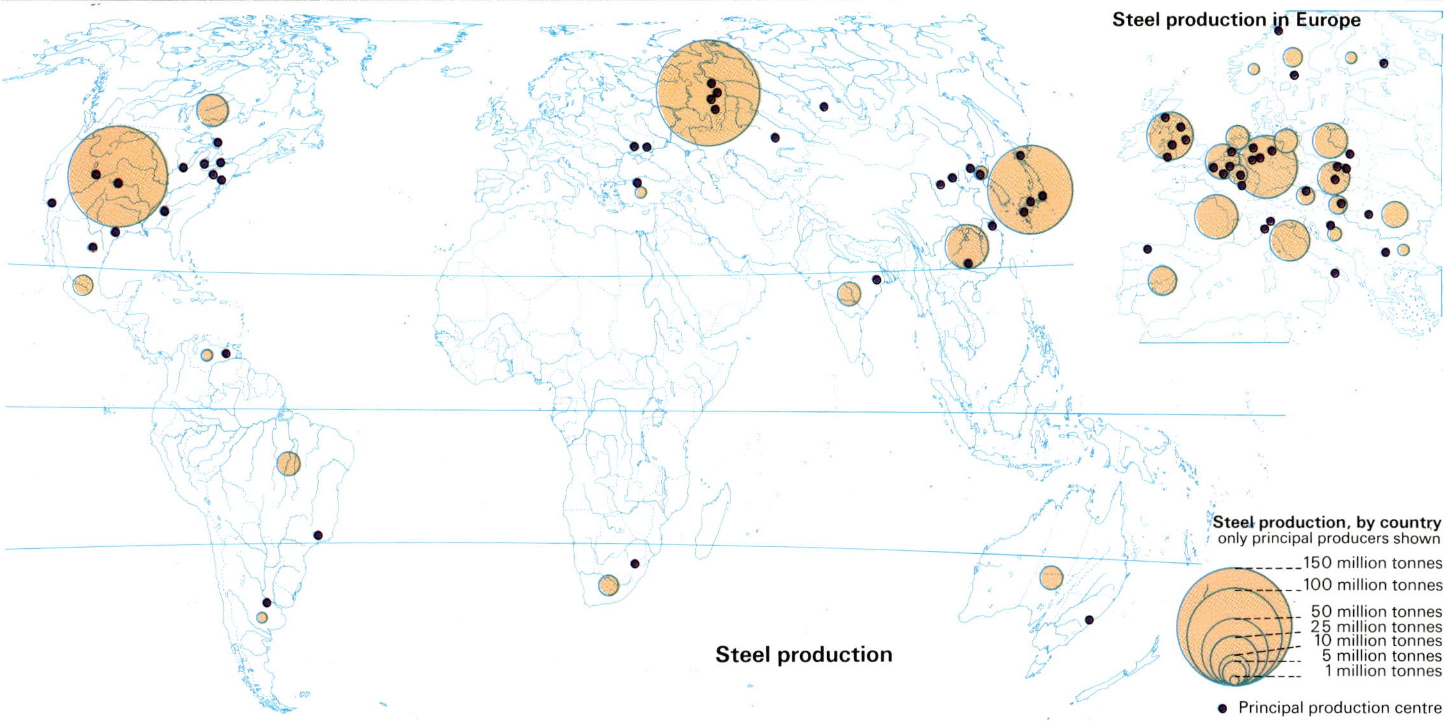

Steel production

Manufacturing industry

Transport

Shipyards

Shipbuilding

tonnage launched in thousand gross registered tons

Japan	4801
Sweden	1305
U.S.A.	913
U.K.	814
Poland	679
France	644
Spain	643
W. Germ.	599
S. Korea	402
Denmark	399
Finland	293
Belgium	266

• Principal shipbuilding centres

Europe

Japan

Concorde and Boeing 747

Aircraft Industry

In 1978 there were approximately 10 000 civil passenger airliners in service. This diagram shows where they were built.

Trade in Aircraft and Aircraft Engines

million U.S. $

Exports	Aircraft	Engines	Imports	Aircraft	Engines
U.S.A.	5893	789	W. Germ.	1218	136
France	995	262	U.K.	651	543
W. Germ.	915	227	U.S.A.	604	132
U.K.	861	721	France	472	278
Canada	303		Canada	264	149
Neth.	288	836	Neth.	210	132
Italy	279	88	Japan	201	151

• Principal aircraft manufacturing centres

Motor vehicles

Production thousand units	Exports million U.S. $	Imports million U.S. $
U.S.A. 12840	11916	17529
Japan 9240	14291	360
W. Germ. 4200	16567	5109
France 4152	7728	3846
U.S.S.R. 2066		
Canada 1907	8817	9598
Italy 1658	3928	2465
U.K. 1608	4667	3637
Spain 1139	897	389

Locomotive works

Railway vehicles

Exports million U.S. $		Imports million U.S. $	
Japan	496·9	Brazil	151·8
France	353·9	Mexico	95·3
W. Germany	329·3	U.S.A.	81·7
U.S.A.	306·0	S. Korea	69·6
U.K.	78·6	S. Africa	67·5
Italy	62·6	Egypt	53·0
Yugoslavia	57·5	W. Germany	52·7
Canada	48·5	Yugoslavia	52·2
S. Korea	41·7	Netherlands	48·1
Sweden	37·7	Sweden	44·4
Belg.-Lux.	27·8	U.K.	40·5
Switzerland	37·5	Belg.-Lux.	33·6
Spain	18·5	France	30·3
		Italy	30·0

• Principal locomotive building centres

Car assembly line

Europe

• Principal motor vehicle plants

Merchant Shipping

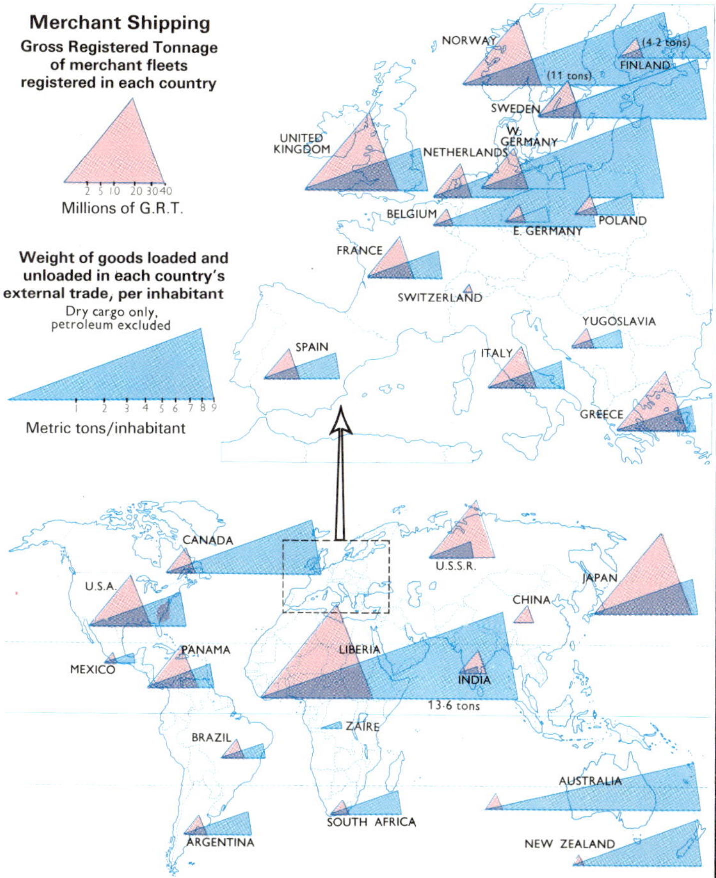

Density of Transport Networks

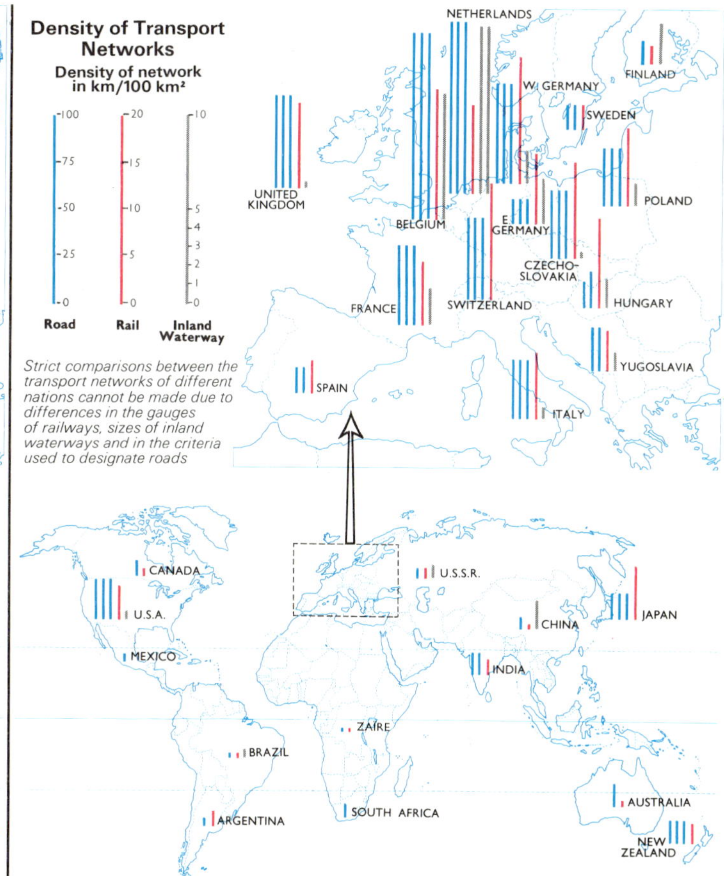

Motor Vehicles and Passenger Transport

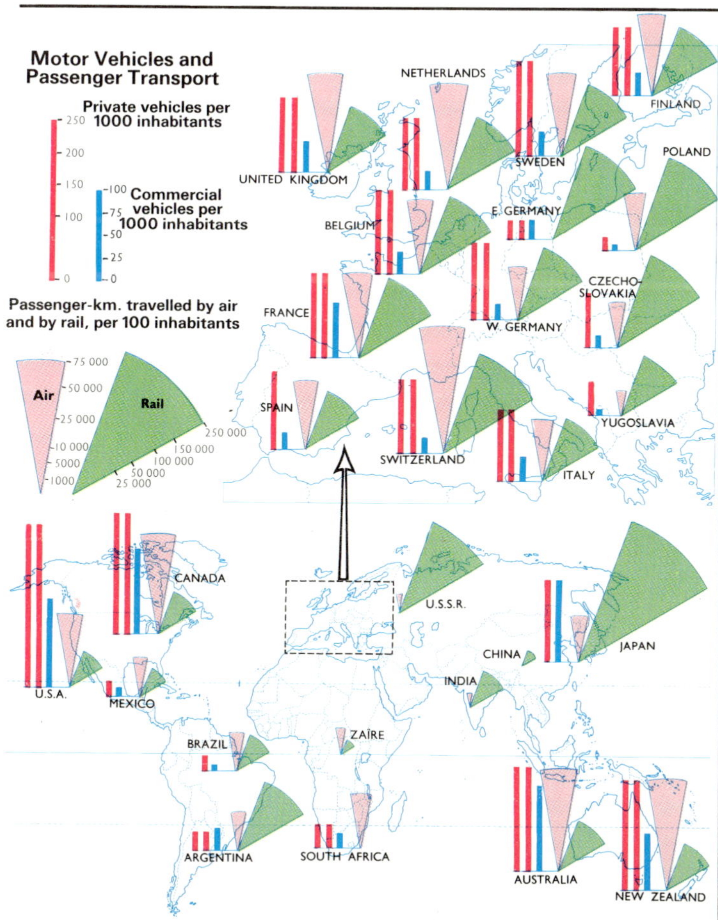

Freight Carried

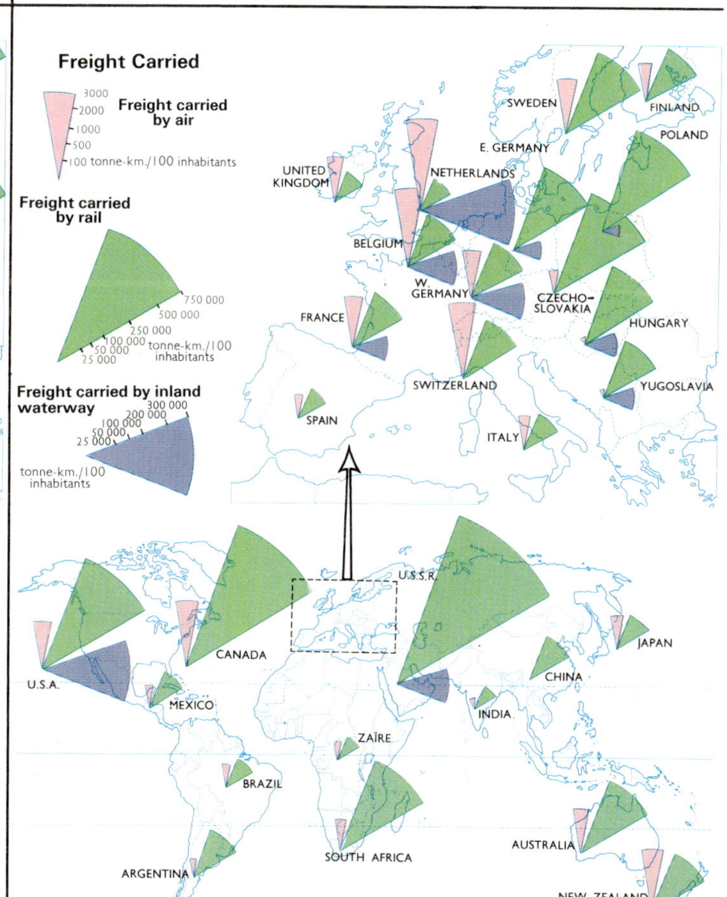

Trade

Road container lorry.

Oil tanker.

Airfreight.

Road/rail container depot.

The Trade of Europe

The semi-circles on this map are at the same scale as those on the World map below. See the legend to the latter.

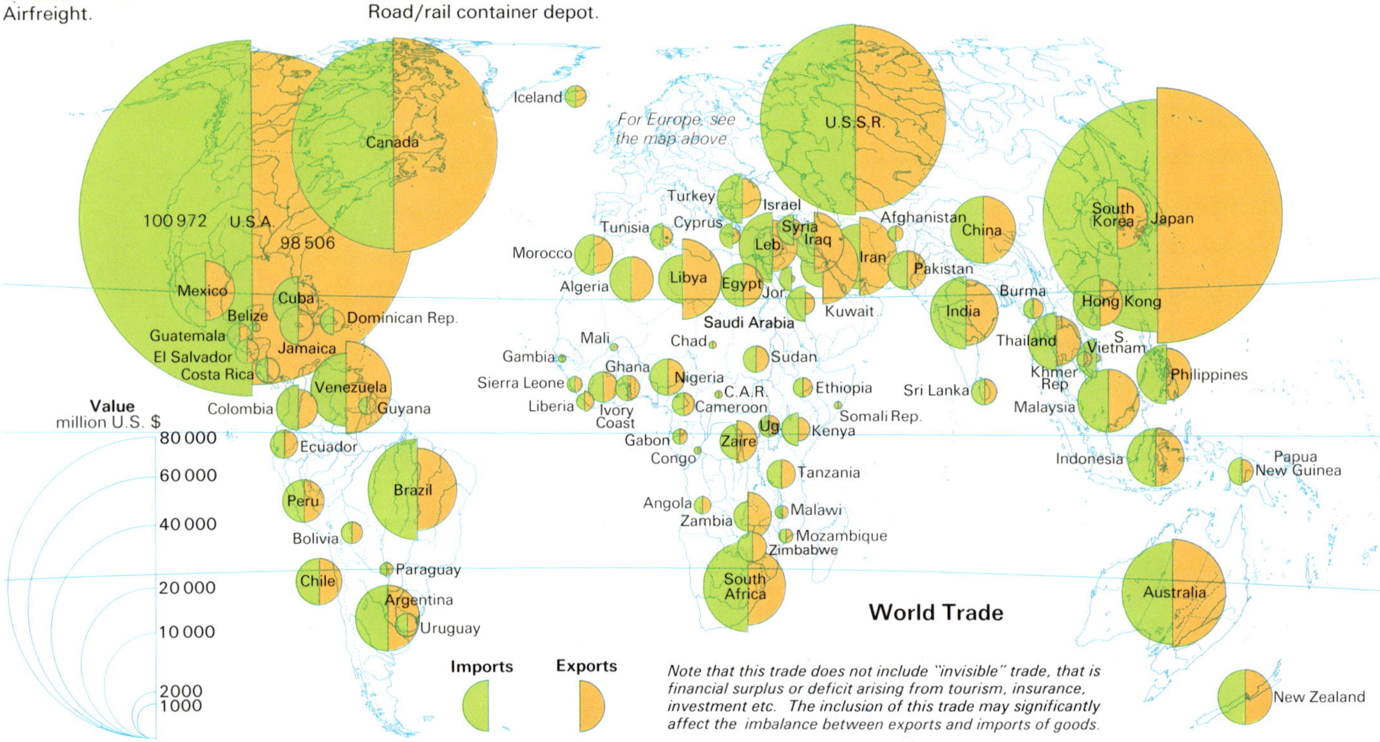

Note that this trade does not include "invisible" trade, that is financial surplus or deficit arising from tourism, insurance, investment etc. The inclusion of this trade may significantly affect the imbalance between exports and imports of goods.

These diagrams show the destination of exports from each of the regions of the World.

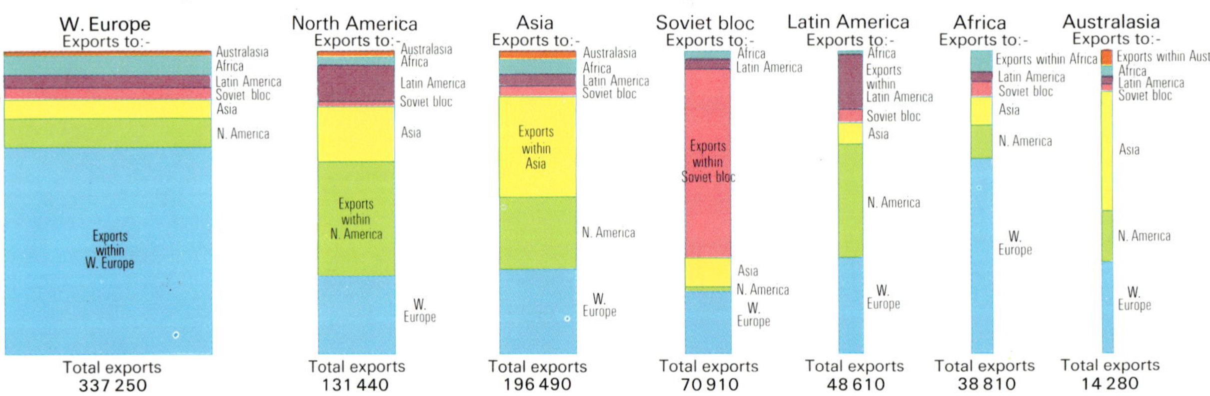

= 20 000 million U.S. $

The total exports are in million U.S. $

Imports

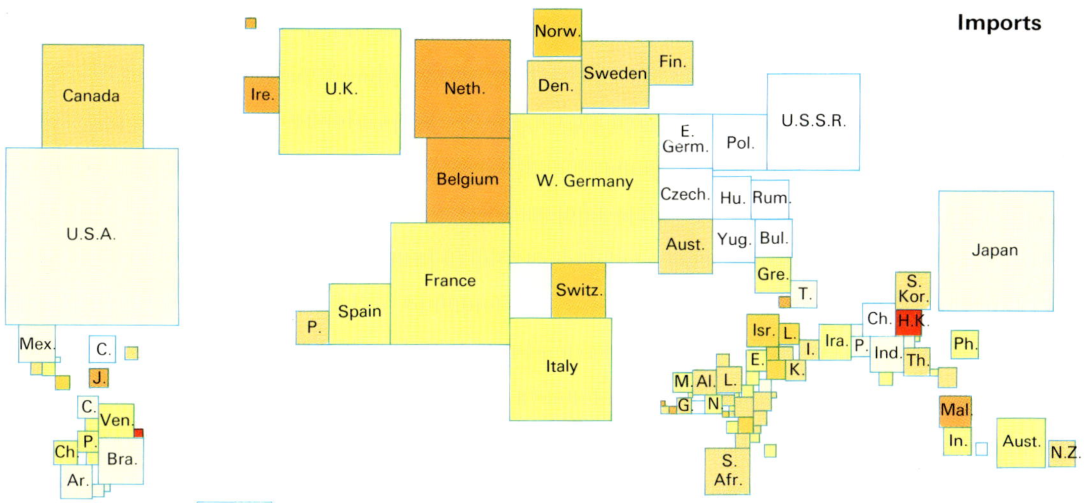

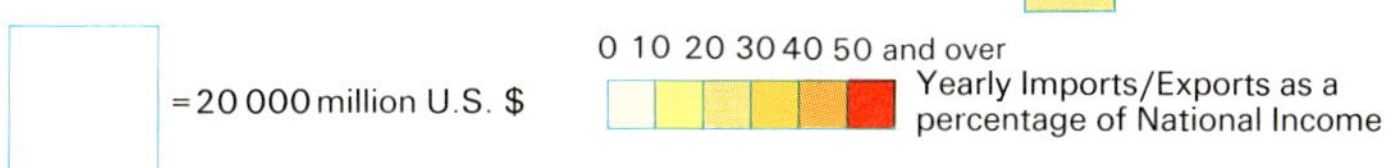

Exports

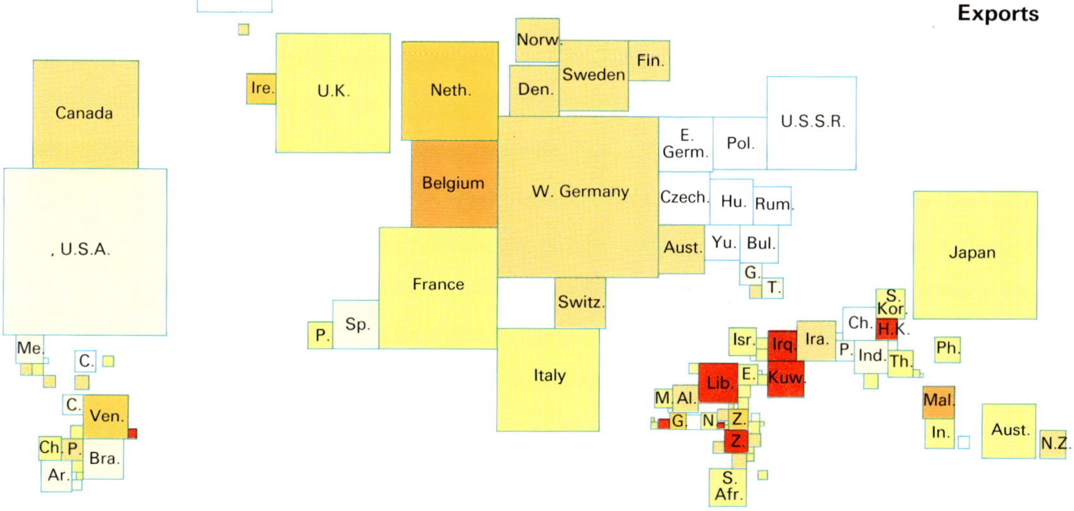

Trade and National Income *left*

The area of a square is proportional to the value of a country's imports/exports and the colour denotes the value of the imports/exports as a percentage of the National Income.

The principal Food Importing and Exporting countries

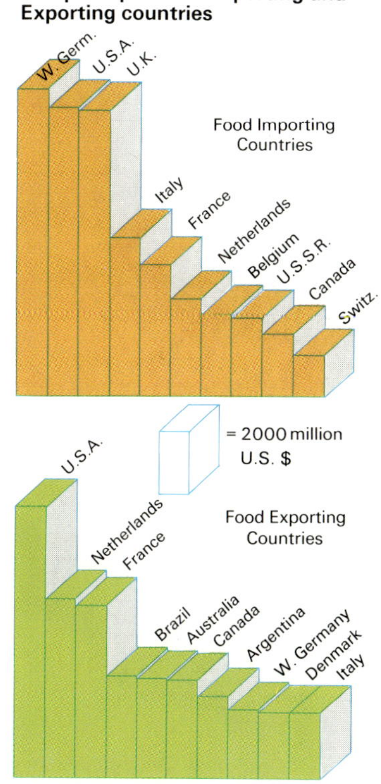

Trade of U.S.A.

U.S.A. imports goods to the value of 100 972 million U.S. $ from:

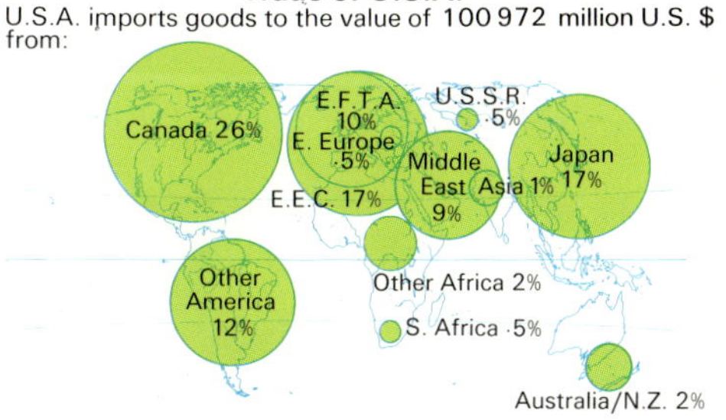

The percentage shows the contribution of the particular region to the total of exports or imports

U.S.A. exports goods to the value of 98 506 million U.S. $ to:

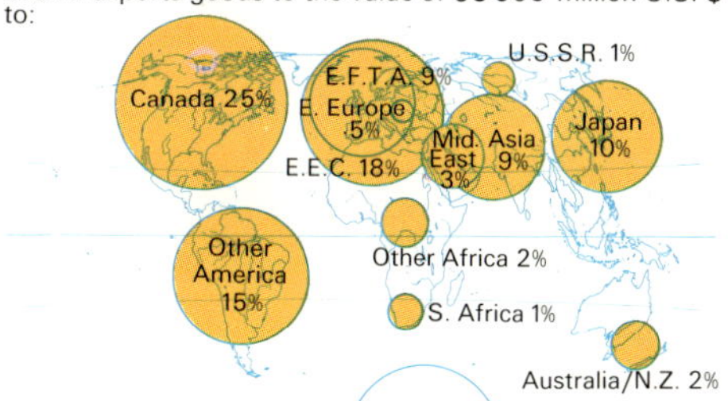

Trade of Japan

Japan imports goods to the value of 62 094 million U.S. $ from:

Japan exports goods to the value of 55 538 million U.S. $ to:

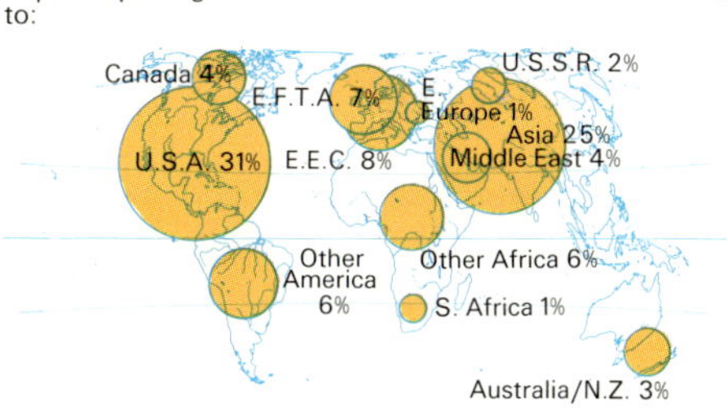

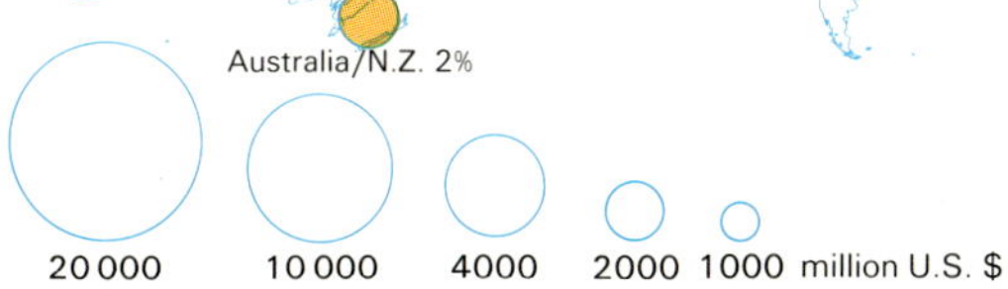

Container ports. These two maps show the location of ports which have purpose-built container handling facilities.

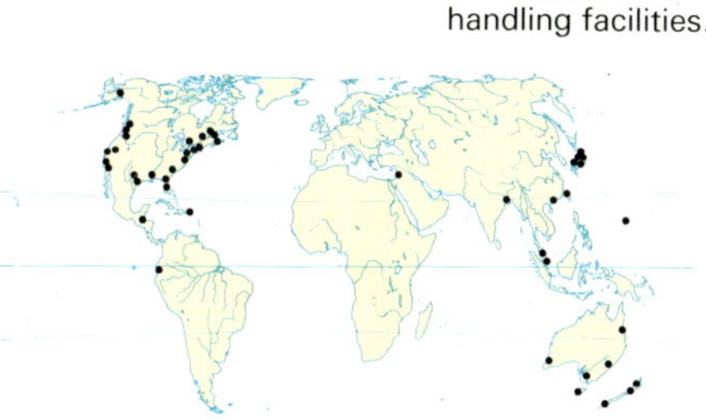

Wealth

The living standard of a few highly developed, urbanised, industrialised countries is a complete contrast to the conditions of the vast majority of economically undeveloped, agrarian states. It is this contrast which divides mankind into rich and poor, well fed and hungry. The developing world is still an overwhelmingly agricultural world: over 70% of all its people live off the land and yet the output from that land remains pitifully low. Many Africans, South Americans and Asians struggle with the soil but the bad years occur only too frequently and they seldom have anything left over to save. The need for foreign capital then arises.

National Income *see right*

The gap between developing and developed worlds is in fact widening eg. in 1938 the incomes for the United States and India were in the proportions of 1:15; now they are 1:35.

Islands *see map right*

a Antilles	h Mauritius
b Martinique	j Solomon
c Barbados	k New Hebrides
d Cape Verde	l Fiji
e Bahrein	m New Caledonia
f Comoro	n Tonga
g Reunion	

Incomes per capita in U.S. dollars

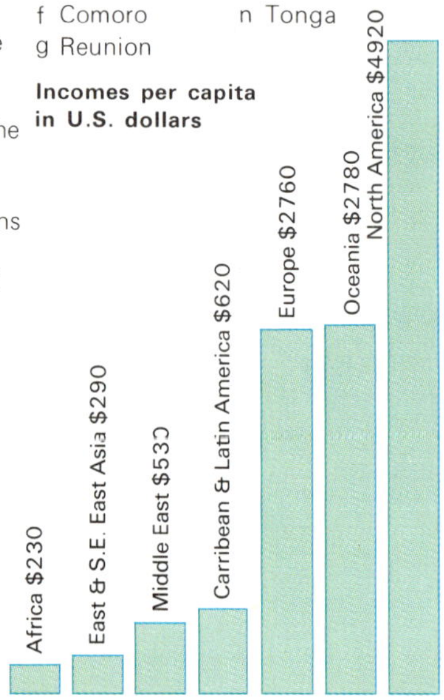

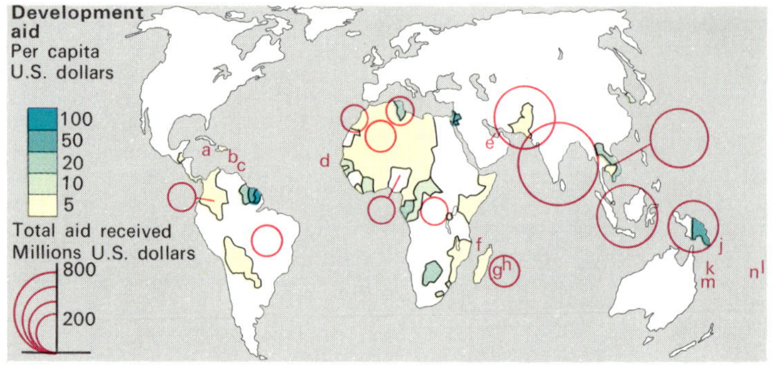

Development aid

The provision of foreign aid, defined as assistance on concessional terms for promoting development, is today an accepted, though controversial aspect of the economic policies of most advanced countries towards less developed countries. Aid for development is based not merely on economic considerations but also on social, political and historical factors. The most important international committee set up after the war was that of the U.N.; practically all aid however has been given bi-laterally direct from an industrialised country to an under-developed country. Although aid increased during the 1950's the donated proportion of industrialised countries GNP has diminished from 0·5 to 0·4%. Less developed countries share of world trade also decreased and increased population invalidated any progress made.

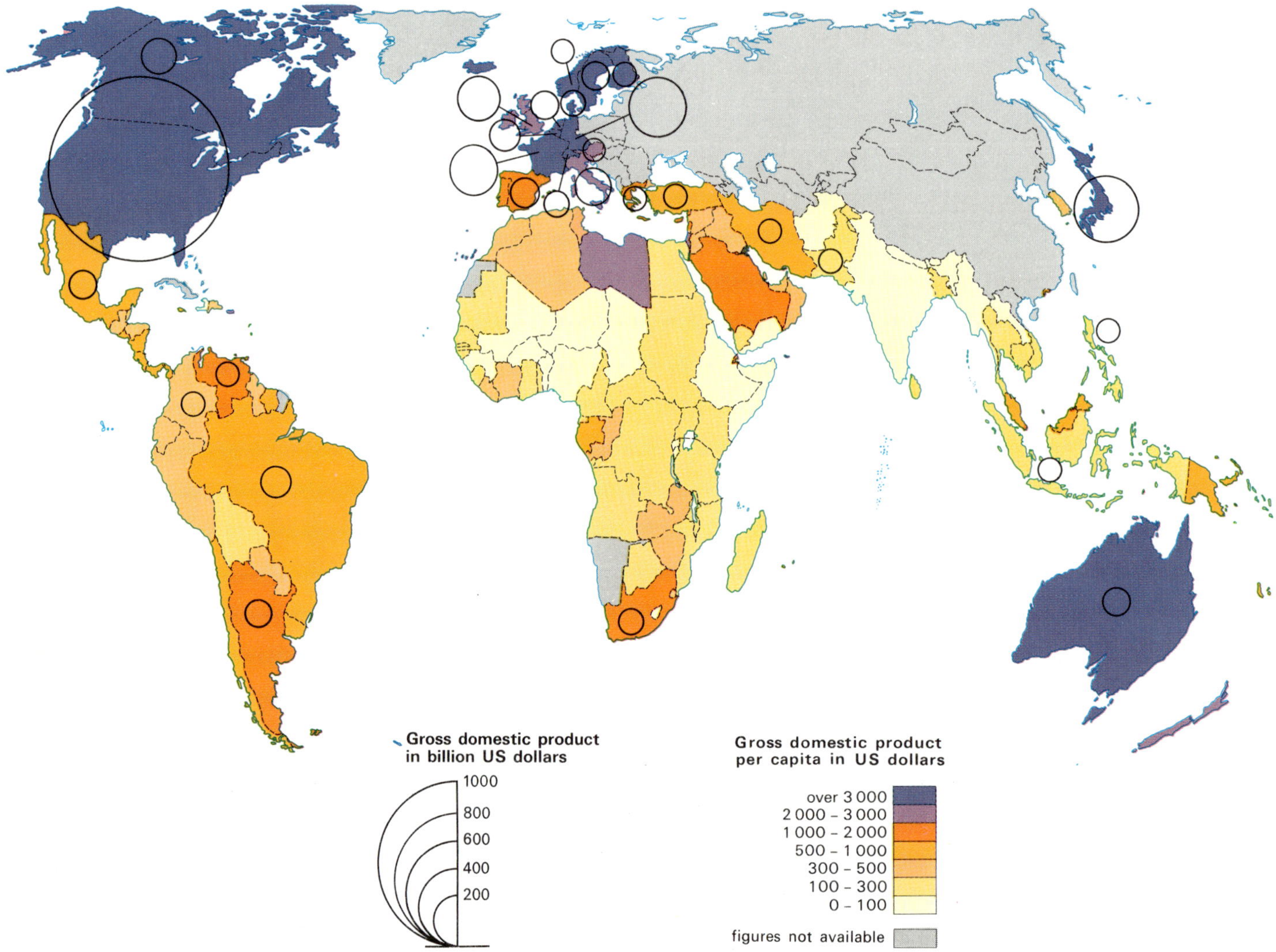

GENERAL REFERENCE

Abbreviations of measures used — ft Feet; mm {Millimetres / Millimeters; cm {Centimetres / Centimeters; m {Metres / Meters; Km {Kilometres / Kilometers; mb Millibars

City and Town symbols in order of size

∴ Sites of Archæological or Historical Importance

International Boundaries

International Boundaries (Undemarcated or Undefined)

Internal Boundaries

Principal Roads

Tracks, Seasonal and other Roads

Road Tunnels

Principal Railways

Other Railways

Railways under construction

Railway Tunnels

Principal Canals

Principal Oil Pipelines

Principal Air Routes

Principal Airports

3386 Principal Shipping Routes (Distances in Nautical Miles)

Perennial Streams

Seasonal Streams

Seasonal Lakes, Salt Flats

Swamps, Marshes

Wells in Desert

Permanent Ice

Passes

▲ 8848 Height above sea-level
▼ 8050 Depth below sea-level
1134 Height of lake-level
in metres

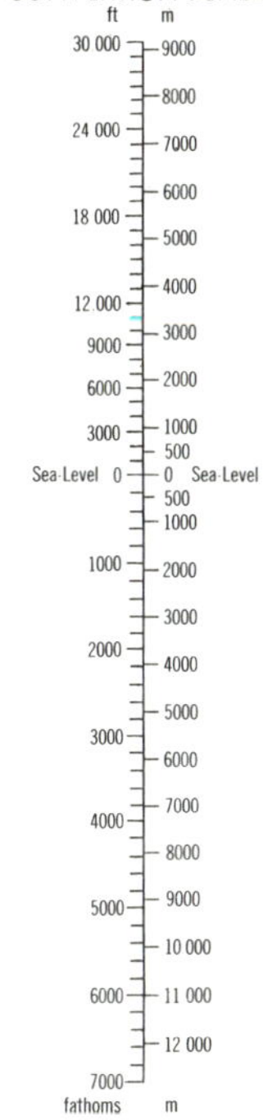

THE WORLD

Physical

1:150 000 000

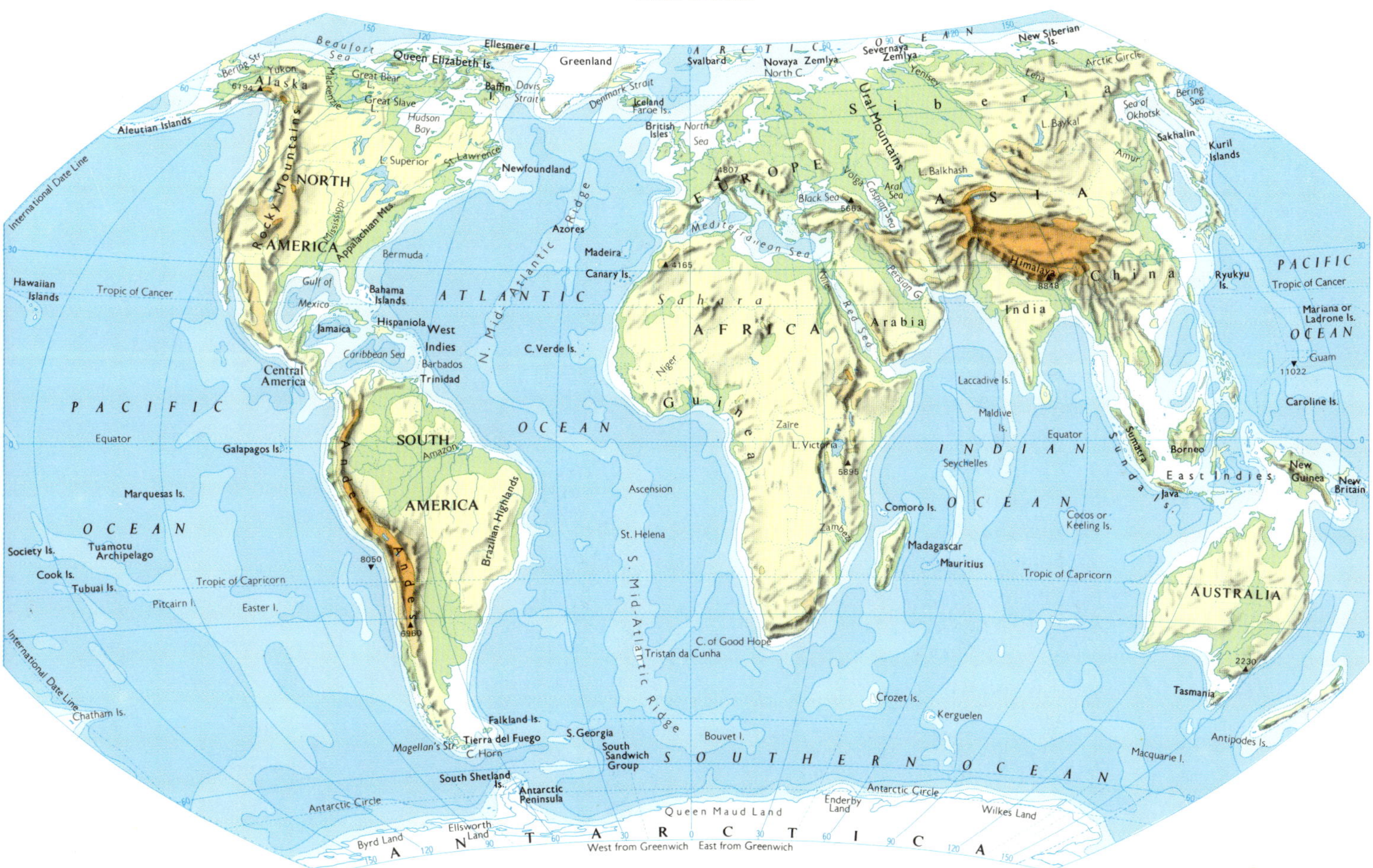

Projection: Hammer Equal Area

Projection: *Hammer Equal Area*

ARCTIC OCEAN
Franz Joseph Ld.
Severnaya Zemlya
New Siberian Is.
Laptev Sea
East Siberian Sea
Barents Sea
Kara Sea
Novaya Zemlya
Arctic Circle
Murmansk
Arkhangelsk
UNION OF SOVIET SOCIALIST REPUBLICS
RUSSIAN SOVIET FEDERAL SOCIALIST REPUBLIC
Siberia
Bering Sea
Sea of Okhotsk
Kamchatka
Sakhalin
Kuril Islands
Helsinki
Leningrad
Stockholm
Moskva
Gorkiy
Kazan
Sverdlovsk
Novosibirsk
Omsk
Chelyabinsk
Kuybyshev
Novokuznetsk
Barnaul
Irkutsk
Ulan Ude
Chita
Khabarovsk
Vladivostok
Minsk
Kiyev
Kharkov
Donetsk
Volgograd
Rostov
Astrakhan
Baku
Tbilisi
Black Sea
Caspian Sea
Aral Sea
KAZAKHSTAN
UZBEKISTAN
TURKMENISTAN
KIRGIZIA
Alma Ata
Tashkent
Samarkand
Dushanbe
Karaganda
L. Balkhash
Baltic Sea
Warszawa
Berlin
Praha
Wien
Budapest
Bucuresti
Beograd
Milano
Roma
Napoli
Barcelona
Sardinia
Sicily
Athinai
Istanbul
Ankara
TURKEY
Izmir
Mediterranean Sea
Crete
CYPRUS
Tunis
Tarabulus
LIBYA
Libyan Desert
EGYPT
El Iskandariya
El Qahira
Tel Aviv-Yafo
Bayrut
Dimashq
Amman
Baghdad
Tehran
IRAN (PERSIA)
Esfahan
Shiraz
Mashhad
AFGHANISTAN
Kabul
Rawalpindi
Srinagar
Lahore
PAKISTAN
Karachi
Persian Gulf
SAUDI ARABIA
Ar Riyad
Makkah
Al Madinah
U.A.E.
QATAR
BAHRAIN
KUWAIT
IRAQ
OMAN
SOUTH YEMEN
YEMEN
Red Sea
G. of Aden
Socotra (South Yemen)
Arabian Sea
INDIA
Delhi
Agra
Kanpur
Lucknow
Varanasi
NEPAL
Kathmandu
Calcutta
Dacca
Ahmadabad
Bombay
Pune
Nagpur
Hyderabad
Madras
Bangalore
Tiruchchirappalli
Colombo
SRI LANKA (CEYLON)
Bay of Bengal
Lakshadweep Is. (India)
Andaman Is. (India)
Nicobar Is. (India)
MALDIVE IS.
MONGOLIA
Ulaanbaatar
CHINA
Urumqi
Xizang (Tibet)
Lhasa
Harbin
Changchun
Shenyang
Qiqihar
Beijing
Tianjin
Taiyuan
Jinan
Lüda
Qingdao
Xi'an
Lanzhou
Nanjing
Wuhan
Shanghai
Chengdu
Chongqing
Changsha
Kunming
Guangzhou
Hong Kong
Fuzhou
Taibei
TAIWAN
East China Sea
South China Sea
Sea of Japan
Söul
Pusan
JAPAN
Tōkyō
Yokohama
Nagoya
Kyōto
Kōbe
Ōsaka
Kitakyūshū
Sapporo
Hakodate
Sendai
PACIFIC OCEAN
Tropic of Cancer
BURMA
Rangoon
Mandalay
THAILAND (SIAM)
Bangkok
Vientiane
Hanoi
Hainan
VIET-NAM
Hué
CAMBODIA
Phnom Penh
Phanh Bho Ho Chi Minh (Saigon)
G. of Siam
MALAYSIA
Kuala Lumpur
Singapore
George Town
Medan
SABAH
BRUNEI
SARAWAK
Borneo
PHILIPPINES
Manila
Quezon City
Cebu
Mariana or Ladrone Is.
Guam (U.S.)
Wake I. (U.S.)
Marshall Is.
Caroline Is.
(U.S. Trust Territory)
KIRIBATI
Nauru
INDONESIA
Sumatra
Sulawesi
Moluccas
Jakarta
Bandung
Surabaya
Ujung Pandang
Banjarmasin
Palembang
Sunda Islands
Irian Jaya
PAPUA NEW GUINEA
New Ireland
New Britain
Solomon Is.
Timor
Timor Sea
Arafura Sea
Torres Str.
INDIAN OCEAN
Equator
SEYCHELLES
Chagos Arch. (Br.)
Diego Garcia (Br.)
Cocos (Keeling) Is. (Australia)
Christmas I. (Australia)
Amsterdam (Fr.)
St. Paul (Fr.)
Kerguelen (Fr.)
Crozet Is. (Fr.)
Heard I. (Australia)
McDonald I. (Australia)
Pr. Edward Is (South Africa)
Tropic of Capricorn
AUSTRALIA
WESTERN AUSTRALIA
NORTHERN TERRITORY
QUEENSLAND
SOUTH AUSTRALIA
NEW SOUTH WALES
VICTORIA
TASMANIA
Darwin
Cairns
Townsville
Rockhampton
Brisbane
Newcastle
Sydney
Canberra
Melbourne
Adelaide
Perth
Kalgoorlie
Geraldton
Alice Springs
L. Eyre
Great Australian Bight
Bass Str.
Hobart
Tasman Sea
NEW ZEALAND
North I.
South I.
Auckland
Wellington
Christchurch
Dunedin
New Caledonia (Fr.)
New Hebrides
Fiji Is.
Norfolk I. (Australia)
Lord Howe I. (Australia)
AFRICA
NIGER
CHAD
SUDAN
Omdurman
El Khartum
ETHIOPIA
Addis Abeba
DJIBOUTI
SOMALI REP.
Muqdisho (Mogadishu)
KENYA
Nairobi
UGANDA
Kampala
TANZANIA
Dar es Salaam
Zanzibar
NIGERIA
Kano
Ibadan
CAMEROON
CENTRAL AFRICA
GABON
CONGO
ZAIRE
Kinshasa
Brazzaville
Cabinda
Luanda
ANGOLA
ZAMBIA
Lusaka
Malawi
ZIMBABWE
Salisbury
MOZAMBIQUE
Mozambique Chan.
MADAGASCAR
Antananarivo
COMOROS
MAURITIUS
Réunion (Fr.)
NAMIBIA
BOTSWANA
Kalahari
Pretoria
Johannesburg
SOUTH AFRICA
Durban
East London
Port Elizabeth
Cape Town
C. of Good Hope
C. Agulhas
Maputo (Lourenço Marques)
SOUTHERN OCEAN
König Haakon VII Sea
Antarctic Circle
Enderby Land
Wilkes Land
AUSTRALIAN DEPENDENCY
TERRE ADÉLIE
S. Magnetic Pole 1976
Ross Sea
Balleny Is.
Macquarie I. (Australia)
Campbell I. (N.Z.)
Auckland I. (N.Z.)
Antipodes Is.
Bounty Is.
East from Greenwich

Projection: Zenithal Equidistant

ANTARCTIC REGIONS

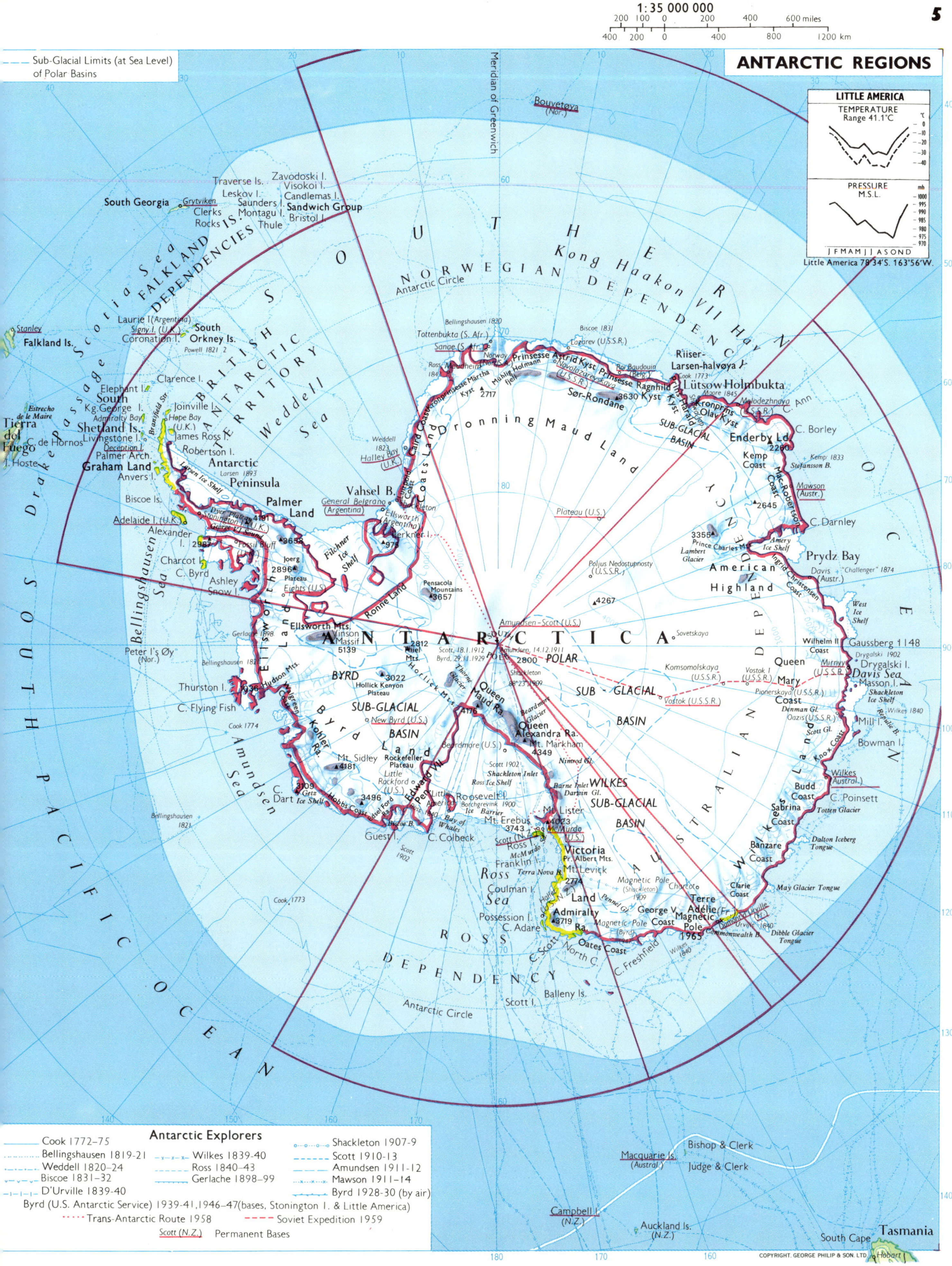

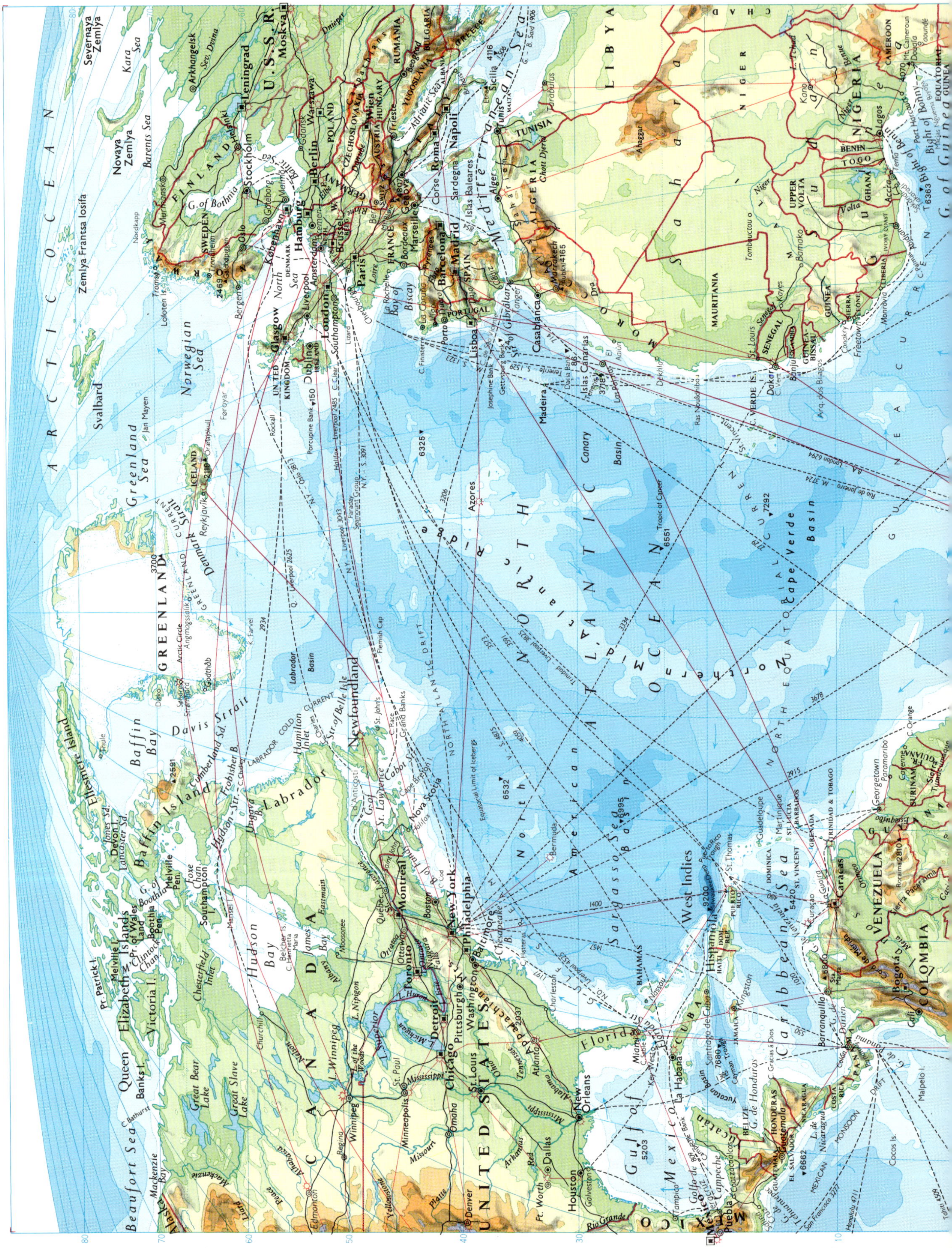
ARCTIC OCEAN
Svalbard
Greenland Sea
Norwegian Sea
Barents Sea
Kara Sea
Novaya Zemlya
Zemlya Frantsa Iosifa
Severnaya Zemlya
GREENLAND
ICELAND
Reykjavik
Denmark Strait
Baffin Bay
Davis Strait
Baffin Island
Ellesmere Island
Hudson Bay
Labrador
Newfoundland
CANADA
UNITED STATES
Beaufort Sea
Queen Elizabeth Islands
Great Bear Lake
Great Slave Lake
NORTH ATLANTIC OCEAN
Mid-Atlantic Ridge
North American Basin
Sargasso Sea
Bermuda
Azores
Madeira
Islas Canarias
Canary Basin
Cape Verde Basin
C. VERDE IS.
Tropic of Cancer
West Indies
Caribbean Sea
Gulf of Mexico
MEXICO
CUBA
BAHAMAS
Hispaniola
VENEZUELA
COLOMBIA
Sahara
LIBYA
NIGER
NIGERIA
MAURITANIA
SENEGAL
ALGERIA
TUNISIA
SPAIN
PORTUGAL
FRANCE
UNITED KINGDOM
U.S.S.R.
FINLAND
SWEDEN
POLAND
Mediterranean Sea
Bay of Biscay
North Sea
London
Paris
Madrid
Lisboa
Dublin
Glasgow
Hamburg
Berlin
Stockholm
Leningrad
Moskva
Casablanca
Dakar
New York
Philadelphia
Montreal
Toronto
Chicago
Detroit
Houston
New Orleans
Caracas
Bogotá
G. of Guinea
Bight of Benin
Bight of Bonny

SOUTH ATLANTIC OCEAN
PACIFIC OCEAN
SOUTHERN OCEAN
BRAZIL
BOLIVIA
PERU
ARGENTINA
CHILE
PARAGUAY
URUGUAY
ECUADOR
NAMIBIA
SOUTH AFRICA
ANGOLA
CONGO
Brazzaville
FALKLAND IS.
FALKLAND IS. DEPENDENCIES
BRITISH ANTARCTIC TERRITORY
Dronning Maud Land
Coats Land
Weddell Sea
Graham Land
Palmer Land
Antarctic Peninsula
Ellsworth Land
Byrd Land
Ross Sea
Enderby Land
Scotia Sea
Drake Passage
Tierra del Fuego
Falkland Is. (Islas Malvinas)
South Georgia
South Sandwich Is.
South Orkney Is.
South Shetland Is.
Argentine Basin
Brazil Basin
Angola Basin
Cape Basin
Agulhas Basin
Atlantic Indian Ridge
Southern Mid-Atlantic Ridge
Chile Rise
South East Pacific Basin
Antarctic (Southern Pacific) Basin
BENGUELA COLD CURRENT
PERUVIAN COLD CURRENT
SOUTH EQUATORIAL CURRENT
WEST WIND DRIFT
CAPE HORN CURRENT
Rio de Janeiro
São Paulo
Belo Horizonte
Brasília
Salvador
Recife
Fortaleza
Belém
Manaus
Pôrto Alegre
Montevideo
Buenos Aires
Rosario
Córdoba
Santiago
Valparaíso
Concepción
Asunción
La Paz
Lima
Guayaquil
Cape Town
Luanda
Benguela
Walvis Bay
Tropic of Capricorn
Antarctic Circle
Equatorial Limit of Icebergs
St. Helena
Ascension
Tristan da Cunha
Gough I.
Bouvetøya
Trindade
Martin Vaz
Arch. de Juan Fernández
Mato Grosso
Pampas
Patagonia
Río de la Plata
Estrecho de Magallanes
Direction of Currents
Principal Shipping Routes (Distances in Nautical Miles)
Principal Air Routes
Projection: Mollweide
COPYRIGHT GEORGE PHILIP & SON LTD.
m
ft

Projection: Bonne.

1:17 500 000

100 0 100 200 300 400 500 miles

100 0 200 400 600 800 km

1:20 000 000

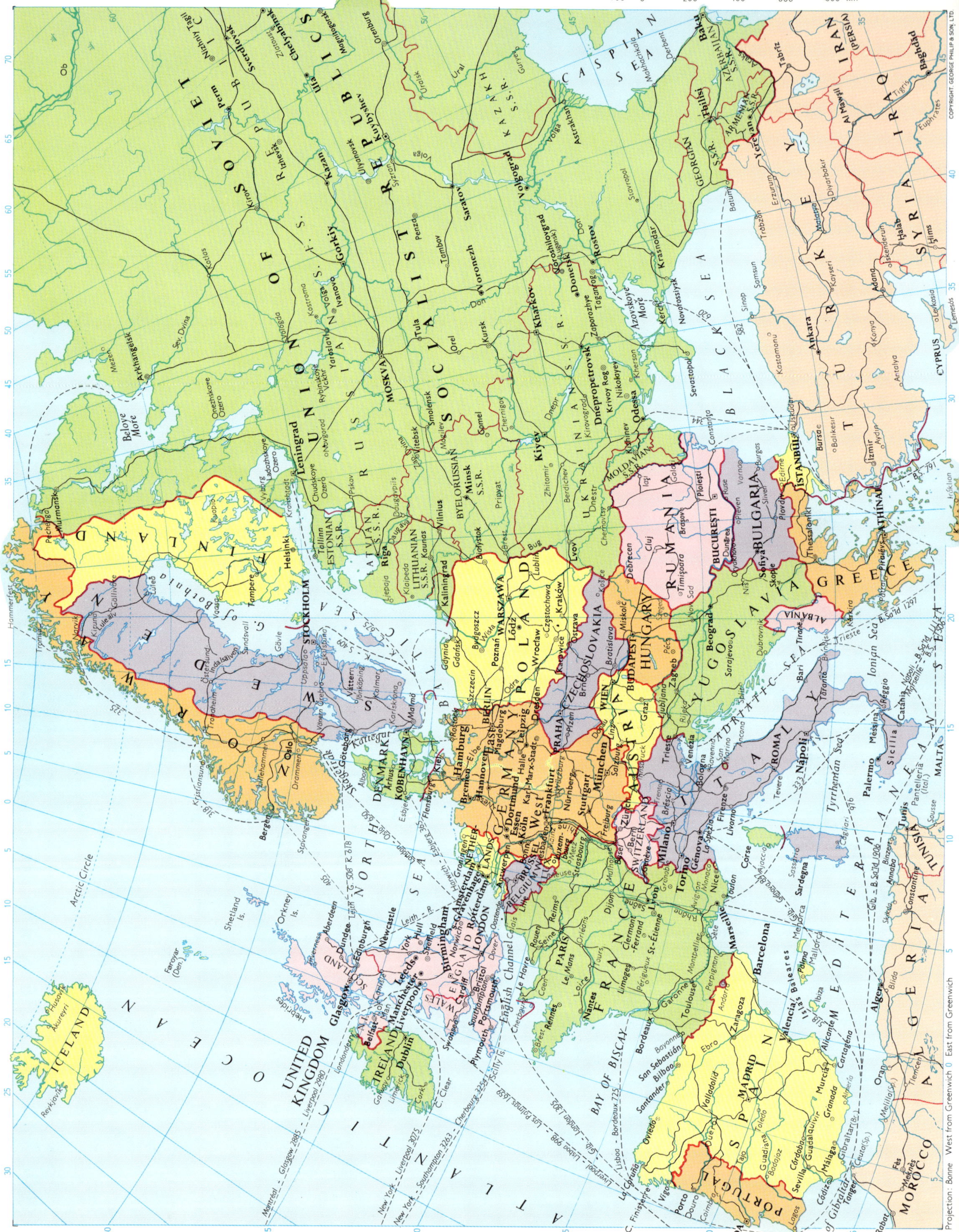

100 0 100 200 300 400 500 miles
100 0 200 400 600 800 km
UNION OF SOVIET SOCIALIST REPUBLICS
R.S.F.S.R.
MOSKVA
Leningrad
Gorkiy
Kazan
Kuybyshev
Volgograd
Saratov
Rostov
Voronezh
Kharkov
Kiyev
Odessa
Dnepropetrovsk
Donetsk
Minsk
BYELORUSSIAN S.S.R.
UKRAINIAN S.S.R.
MOLDAVIAN S.S.R.
ESTONIAN S.S.R.
LATVIAN S.S.R.
LITHUANIAN S.S.R.
Tallinn
Riga
Vilnius
Kaunas
Kaliningrad
GEORGIAN S.S.R.
ARMENIAN S.S.R.
AZERBAIJAN S.S.R.
KAZAKH S.S.R.
Tbilisi
Yerevan
Baku
CASPIAN SEA
BLACK SEA
FINLAND
Helsinki
SWEDEN
STOCKHOLM
NORWAY
Oslo
Bergen
DENMARK
KØBENHAVN
POLAND
WARSZAWA
GERMANY
BERLIN
Hamburg
München
Frankfurt
CZECHOSLOVAKIA
PRAHA
AUSTRIA
WIEN
HUNGARY
BUDAPEST
RUMANIA
BUCUREŞTI
BULGARIA
Sofiya
YUGOSLAVIA
Beograd
ALBANIA
Tiranë
GREECE
ATHINAI
TURKEY
Ankara
İstanbul
SYRIA
IRAQ
IRAN (PERSIA)
Baghdad
CYPRUS
ITALY
ROMA
Milano
Napoli
SWITZERLAND
Bern
NETHERLANDS
Amsterdam
BELGIUM
BRUXELLES
FRANCE
PARIS
Lyon
Marseille
SPAIN
MADRID
Barcelona
PORTUGAL
LISBOA
UNITED KINGDOM
LONDON
Birmingham
Manchester
Glasgow
Edinburgh
IRELAND
Dublin
ICELAND
Reykjavík
MOROCCO
ALGERIA
Alger
TUNISIA
Tunis
MALTA
Sicilia
Sardegna
Corse
NORTH SEA
BALTIC SEA
ATLANTIC OCEAN
MEDITERRANEAN SEA
ADRIATIC SEA
Tyrrhenian Sea
Ionian Sea
BAY OF BISCAY
English Channel
Arctic Circle
Projection: Bonne West from Greenwich 0 East from Greenwich
COPYRIGHT GEORGE PHILIP & SON, LTD.

1: 4 000 000

20 0 20 40 60 miles

20 0 20 40 60 80 km

Projection: Conical with two standard parallels

West from Greenwich 0 East from Greenwich

NORTH SEA
IRISH SEA
North Channel
SCOTLAND
Southern Uplands
Pennines
Cheviot Hills
Cumbrian Mts.
N. York Moors
NORTHUMBERLAND
DURHAM
CLEVELAND
TYNE & WEAR
CUMBRIA
NORTH YORKSHIRE
WEST YORKSHIRE
SOUTH YORKSHIRE
HUMBERSIDE
LANCASHIRE
GREATER MANCHESTER
MERSEYSIDE
CHESHIRE
DERBY
NOTTS
LINCOLN
STAFFORD
CLWYD
GWYNEDD
ISLE OF MAN
Anglesey
Edinburgh
Glasgow
Newcastle
Sunderland
Middlesbrough
Carlisle
Leeds
Bradford
York
Hull
Liverpool
Manchester
Sheffield
Nottingham
Derby
Lincoln
Blackpool
Preston
Douglas
Belfast
The Wash
Morecambe Bay
Solway Firth
Firth of Forth
Firth of Clyde

1:2 000 000

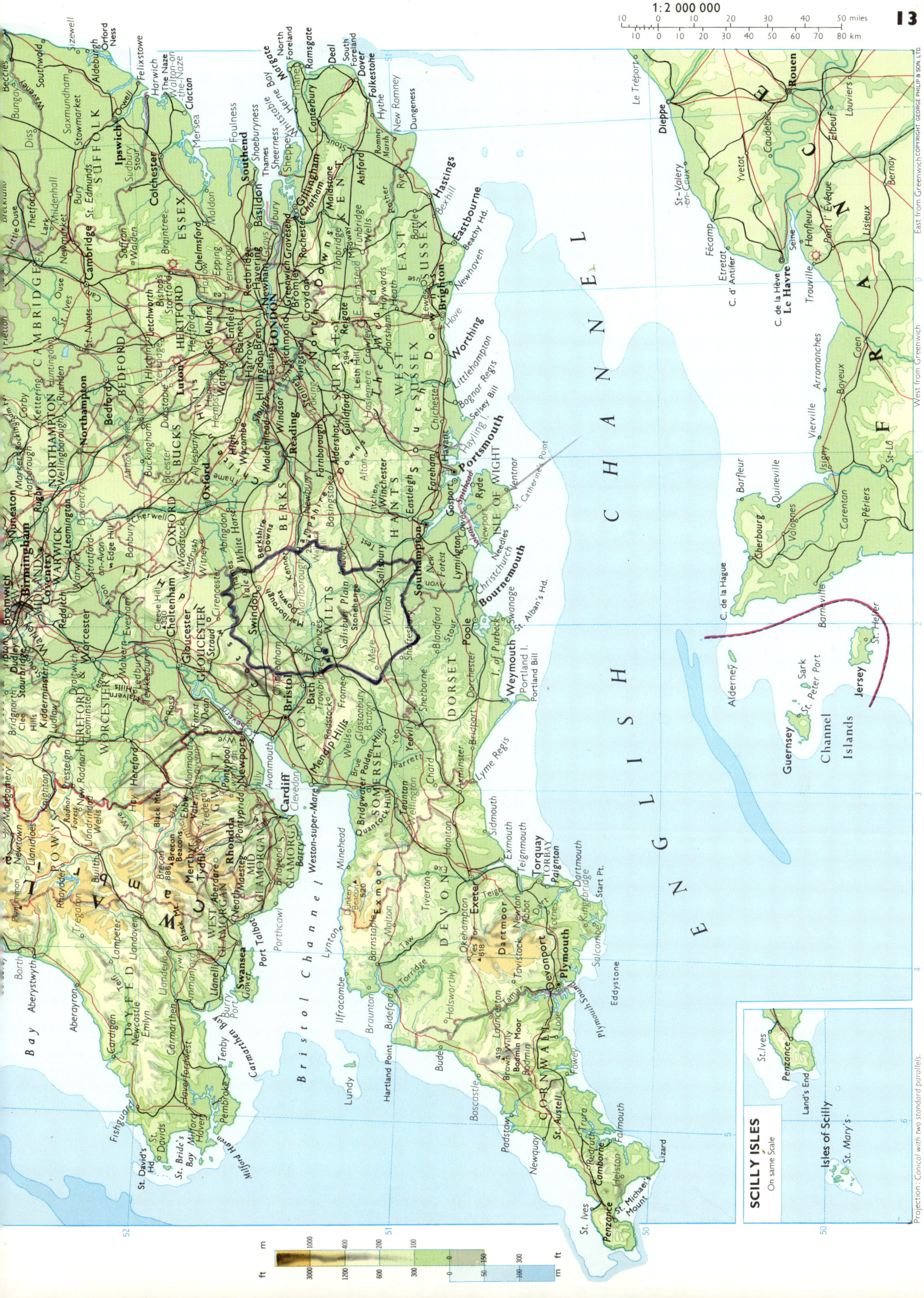
10 0 10 20 30 40 50 miles
10 0 10 20 30 40 50 60 70 80 km
ENGLISH CHANNEL
Bristol Channel
FRANCE
Channel Islands
Jersey
Guernsey
Alderney
Sark
St. Peter Port
St. Helier
SCILLY ISLES
On same Scale
Isles of Scilly
St. Mary's
Land's End
Penzance
St. Ives
CORNWALL
DEVON
SOMERSET
DORSET
AVON
WILTS
HANTS
ISLE OF WIGHT
WEST SUSSEX
EAST SUSSEX
SURREY
KENT
ESSEX
SUFFOLK
HERTFORD
BEDFORD
BUCKS
OXFORD
BERKS
GLOUCESTER
WORCESTER
HEREFORD
WARWICK
NORTHAMPTON
CAMBRIDGE
POWYS
DYFED
GWENT
MID GLAMORGAN
WEST GLAMORGAN
SOUTH GLAMORGAN
LONDON
Birmingham
Coventry
Bristol
Cardiff
Swansea
Newport
Plymouth
Exeter
Torquay
Southampton
Portsmouth
Bournemouth
Poole
Weymouth
Brighton
Worthing
Eastbourne
Hastings
Dover
Folkestone
Canterbury
Margate
Ramsgate
Ipswich
Colchester
Southend
Chelmsford
Cambridge
Northampton
Bedford
Luton
Oxford
Reading
Swindon
Salisbury
Gloucester
Cheltenham
Worcester
Hereford
Cherbourg
Le Havre
Rouen
Dieppe
Caen
Honfleur
Lisieux
Bayeux
Fécamp
Barfleur
Carentan
C. de la Hague
Dartmoor
Exmoor
Salisbury Plain
Mendip Hills
Lundy
Eddystone
Lizard
Start Pt.
Portland Bill
St. Alban's Hd.
Beachy Hd.
Dungeness
North Foreland
South Foreland
Projection: Conical with two standard parallels.
East from Greenwich
West from Greenwich
COPYRIGHT GEORGE PHILIP & SON, LTD.
m 1000 400 200 100 0 50 100
ft 3000 1200 600 300 0 150 300

Projection: *Conical with two standard parallels.*

1:2 000 000

10 0 10 20 30 40 50 miles

10 0 10 20 30 40 50 60 70 80 km

Projection: *Conical with two standard parallels.*

West from Greenwich

1:2 500 000

Projection: Conical with two standard parallels

East from Greenwich

1:5 000 000

20 10 0 20 40 60 80 100 miles

40 20 0 40 80 120 160 km

Projection: *Conical with two standard parallels* — West from Greenwich — East from Greenwich

1:2 500 000

10 0 10 20 30 40 50 miles

10 0 10 20 30 40 50 60 70 80 km

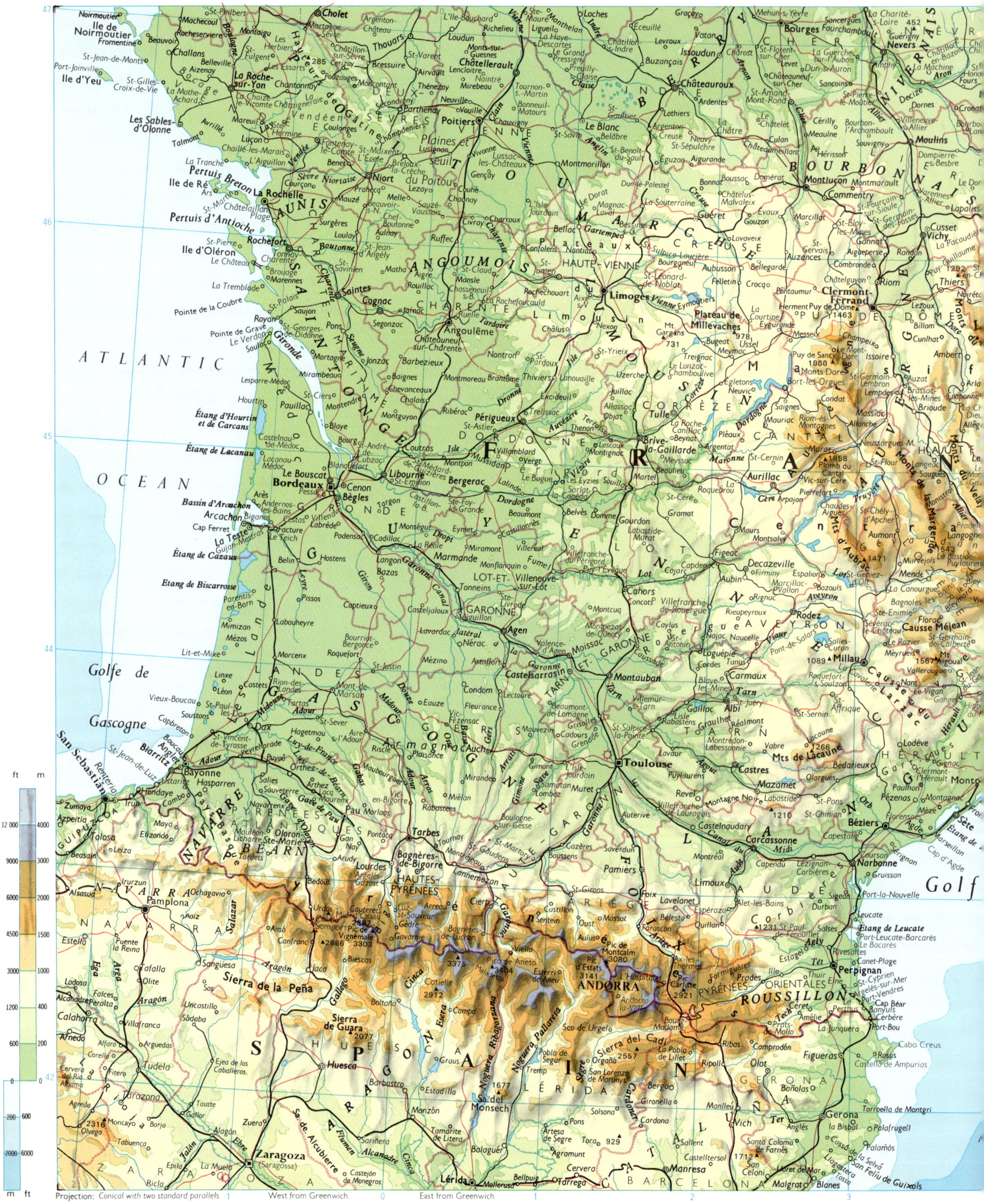

Projection: *Conical with two standard parallels* 1 West from Greenwich 0 East from Greenwich 1 2 3

1:2 500 000

SWITZERLAND
ITALY
CORSICA
LIGURIAN SEA
Golfo di Génova
MEDITERRANEAN SEA
G. du Lion
ILES D'HYÈRES
Côte d'Azur
ALPES-DE-HAUTE-PROVENCE
HAUTE-CORSE
CORSE DU SUD
MILANO
TORINO
GENOVA
MARSEILLE
LYON
Genève
Lausanne
Bern
Luzern
Nice
Toulon
Grenoble
Avignon
Aix-en-Provence
Ajaccio
Bastia
Livorno
La Spezia
Bergamo
Brescia
Parma
Cremona
Pavia
Novara
Alessandria
Asti
Cuneo
Savona
San Remo
Monaco
Cannes
Chambéry
Annecy
Valence
Lac Léman
Elba
Capraia
Gorgona

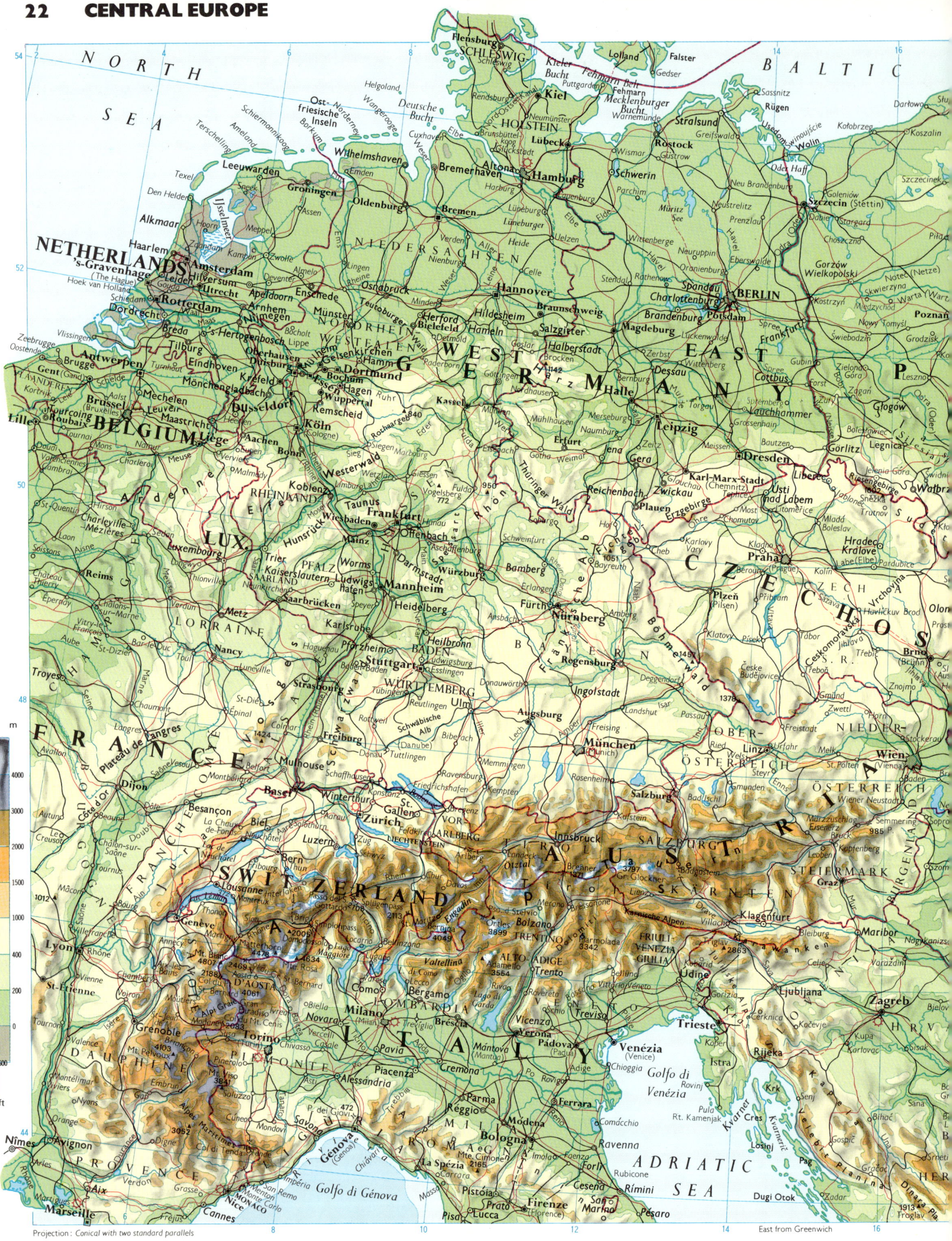

Projection: Conical with two standard parallels

East from Greenwich

1:5 000 000

50 0 50 100 miles

50 0 50 100 150 km

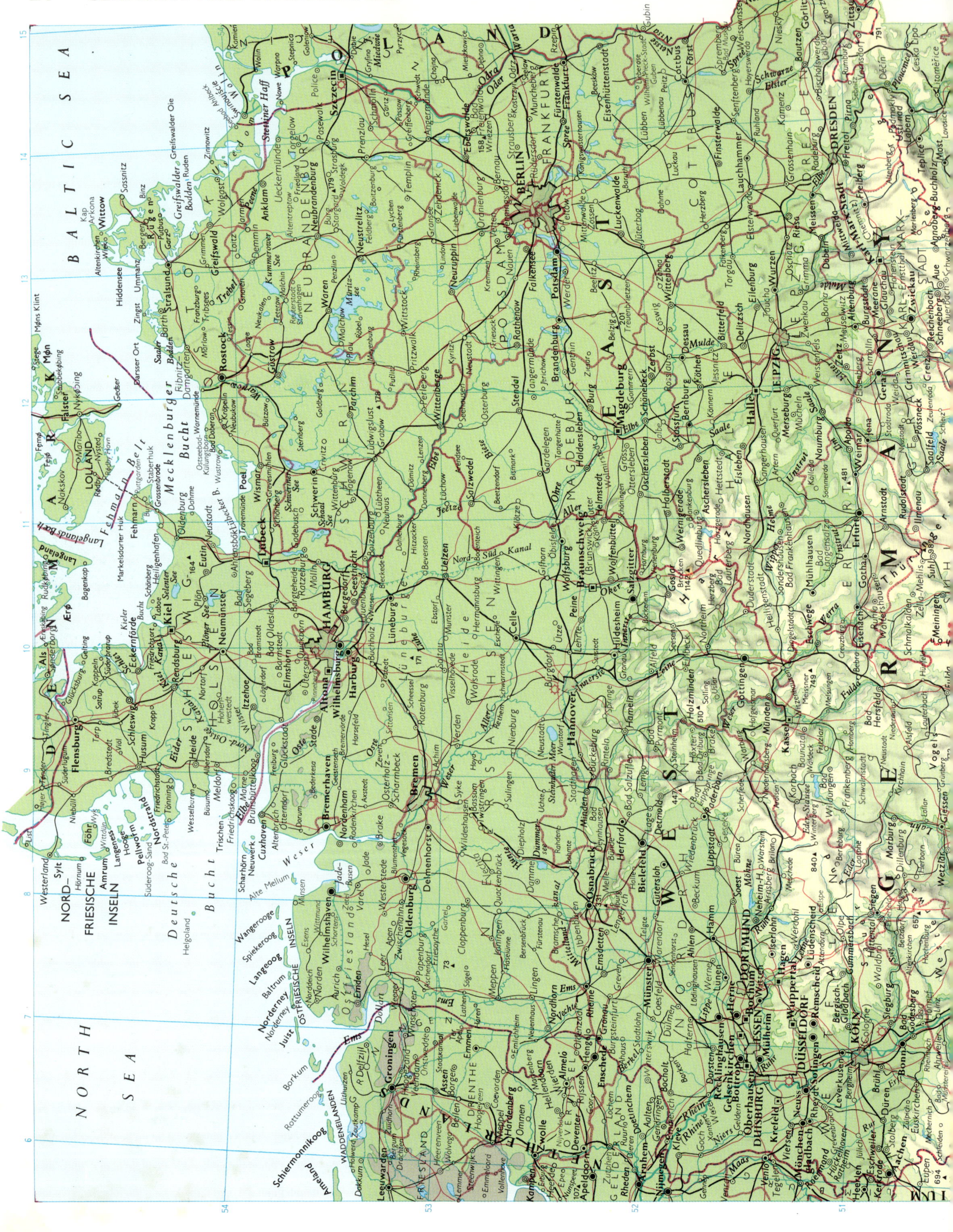
BALTIC SEA
NORTH SEA
DENMARK
POLAND
LOLLAND
NORD-FRIESISCHE INSELN
OSTFRIESISCHE INSELN
Deutsche Bucht
Mecklenburger Bucht
Fehmarn Belt
Stettiner Haff
BERLIN
HAMBURG
Bremen
Bremerhaven
Hannover
Kiel
Lübeck
Rostock
Stralsund
Greifswald
Schwerin
Wismar
Magdeburg
Potsdam
Brandenburg
FRANKFURT
Frankfurt
Szczecin
Cottbus
Dresden
Leipzig
Halle
Erfurt
Weimar
Jena
Gera
Zwickau
Karl-Marx-Stadt
Göttingen
Kassel
Braunschweig
Wolfsburg
Osnabrück
Münster
Bielefeld
Dortmund
Essen
Duisburg
Düsseldorf
Köln
Bonn
Aachen
Wuppertal
Oldenburg
Wilhelmshaven
Emden
Groningen
Leeuwarden
Flensburg
Rügen
Fehmarn
Elbe
Weser
Ems
Oder
Spree
Saale
Rhein
Mittelland Kanal
HARZ
Lüneburger Heide
Thüringer Wald

1:2 500 000

10 0 10 20 30 40 50 miles
10 0 10 20 30 40 50 60 70 80 km

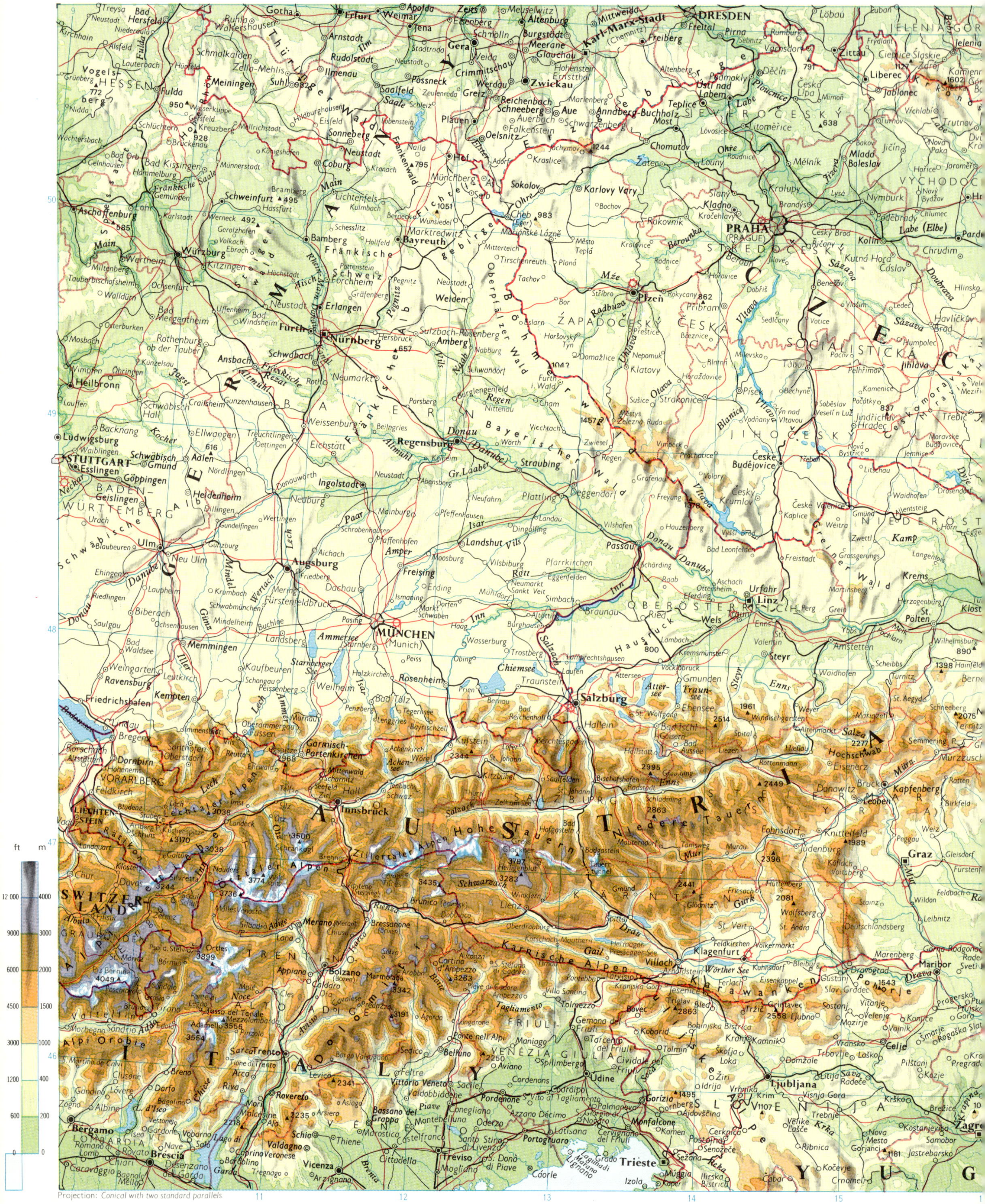

Projection: Conical with two standard parallels

1:2 500 000

10 0 10 20 30 40 50 miles

10 0 10 20 30 40 50 60 70 80 km

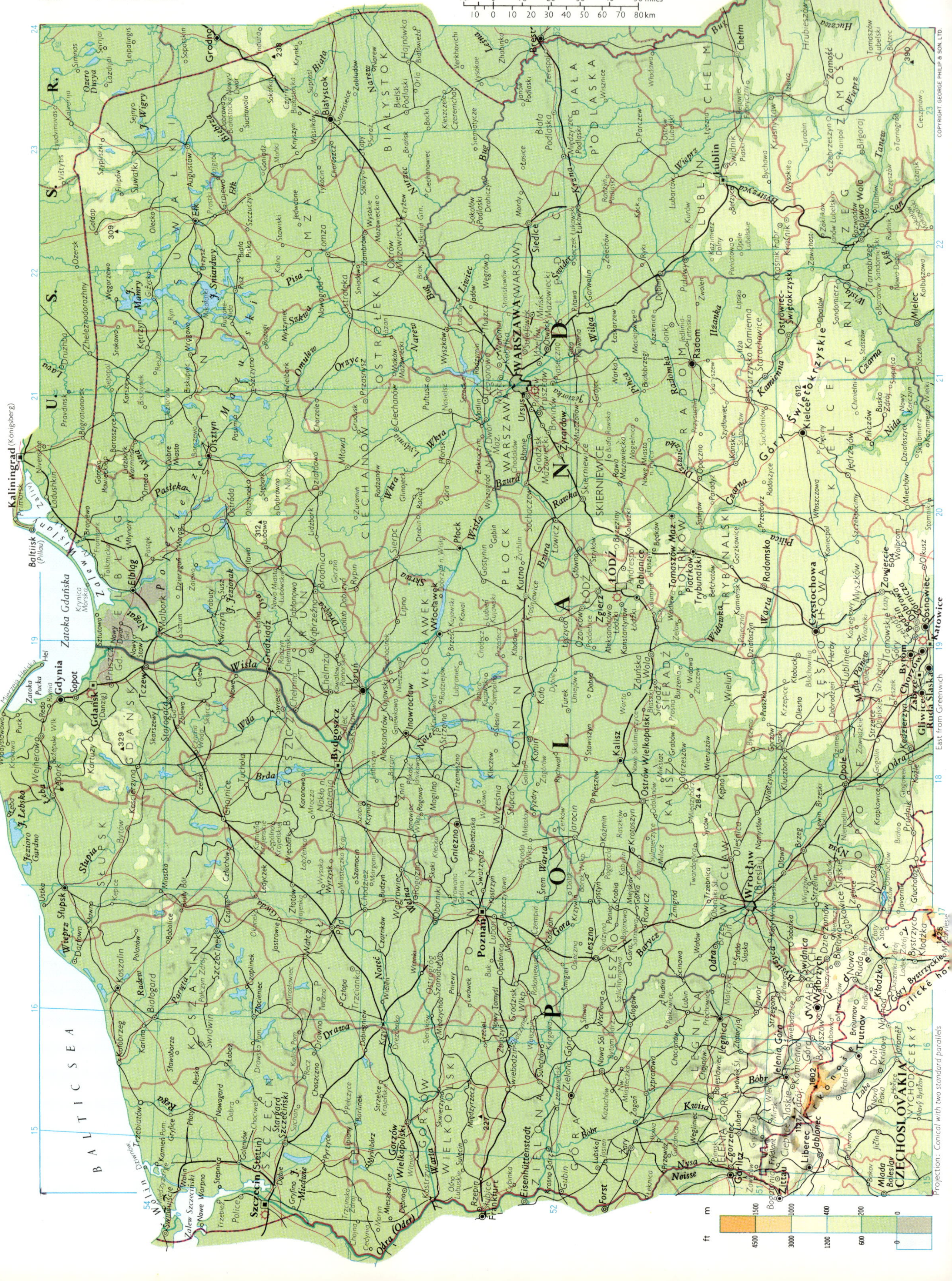

1:2 500 000
10 0 10 20 30 40 50 miles
10 0 10 20 30 40 50 60 70 80 km
BALTIC SEA
U. S. S. R.
P O L A N D
CZECHOSLOVAKIA
Kaliningrad (Königsberg)
Baltiysk (Pillau)
Zatoka Gdańska
Gdańsk (Danzig)
Gdynia
Sopot
Elbląg
Olsztyn
Białystok
Grodno
Brest
Chełm
Lublin
Zamość
Warszawa (Warsaw)
Łódź
Radom
Kielce
Częstochowa
Katowice
Kraków
Wrocław (Breslau)
Opole
Poznań
Bydgoszcz
Toruń
Płock
Włocławek
Szczecin (Stettin)
Koszalin
Słupsk
Gorzów Wielkopolski
Zielona Góra
Legnica
Wałbrzych
Jelenia Góra
Kalisz
Konin
Leszno
Piła
Suwałki
Łomża
Ostrołęka
Ciechanów
Siedlce
Biała Podlaska
Skierniewice
Piotrków Trybunalski
Sieradz
Tarnobrzeg
Krosno
Frankfurt
Eisenhüttenstadt
Forst
Görlitz
Zittau
Liberec
Wisła
Odra (Oder)
Warta
Bug
Narew
Nysa
Neisse
East from Greenwich
Projection: Conical with two standard parallels
COPYRIGHT GEORGE PHILIP & SON, LTD
m 1500 1000 400 200 0
ft 4500 3000 1200 600 0

1:5 000 000

50 0 50 100 miles

50 0 50 100 150 km

BAY OF BISCAY
ATLANTIC OCEAN
San Sebastián
Bilbao
Santander
Vitoria
Logroño
Burgos
Gijón
Oviedo
León
Palencia
Valladolid
Segovia
Ávila
Madrid
Guadalajara
Alcalá de Henares
Aranjuez
Salamanca
Zamora
Lugo
La Coruña (Corunna)
El Ferrol
Santiago de Compostela
Pontevedra
Vigo
Orense
Bragança
Vila Real
Braga
Porto (Oporto)
Vila Nova de Gaia
Aveiro
Viseu
Guarda
Coimbra
Figueira da Foz
Plasencia
Talavera de la Reina
Duero
Douro
Miño
Ebro
Tajo
Pisuerga
Esla
Tormes
Sierra de Gredos
Sierra de Guadarrama
Picos de Europa
Montes de León
Sierra de Gata
Serra da Estrela
Cabo Finisterre
Cabo Ortegal
Monte Redondo

1:2 500 000

10 0 10 20 30 40 50 miles

10 0 10 20 30 40 50 60 70 80 km

BAY OF BISCAY
Golfe de Gascogne
Santander
Bilbao
San Sebastián
Bayonne
Biarritz
Pamplona
Vitoria
Logroño
Burgos
Soria
Zaragoza (Saragossa)
Huesca
Lérida
Tarragona
BARCELONA
Gerona
Perpignan
Narbonne
Carcassonne
Toulouse
Tarbes
Lourdes
ANDORRA
ROUSSILLON
PYRÉNÉES
NAVARRA
ARAGÓN
CATALUÑA
GASCOGNE
BÉARN
Teruel
Cuenca
Guadalajara
Alcalá de Henares
MADRID
Aranjuez
Castellón de la Plana
Menorca (Minorca)
Mallorca (Majorca)
Golfo de San Jorge
Montes Universales
Sierra de la Demanda
Sa. del Moncayo
Mts. del Maestrazgo
Ebro
Duero

1:2 500 000

10 0 10 20 30 40 50 miles

10 0 10 20 30 40 50 60 70 80 km

Projection: Conical with two standard parallels. West from Greenwich 0 East from Greenwich

1:10 000 000

50 0 50 100 150 200 miles

50 0 100 200 300 km

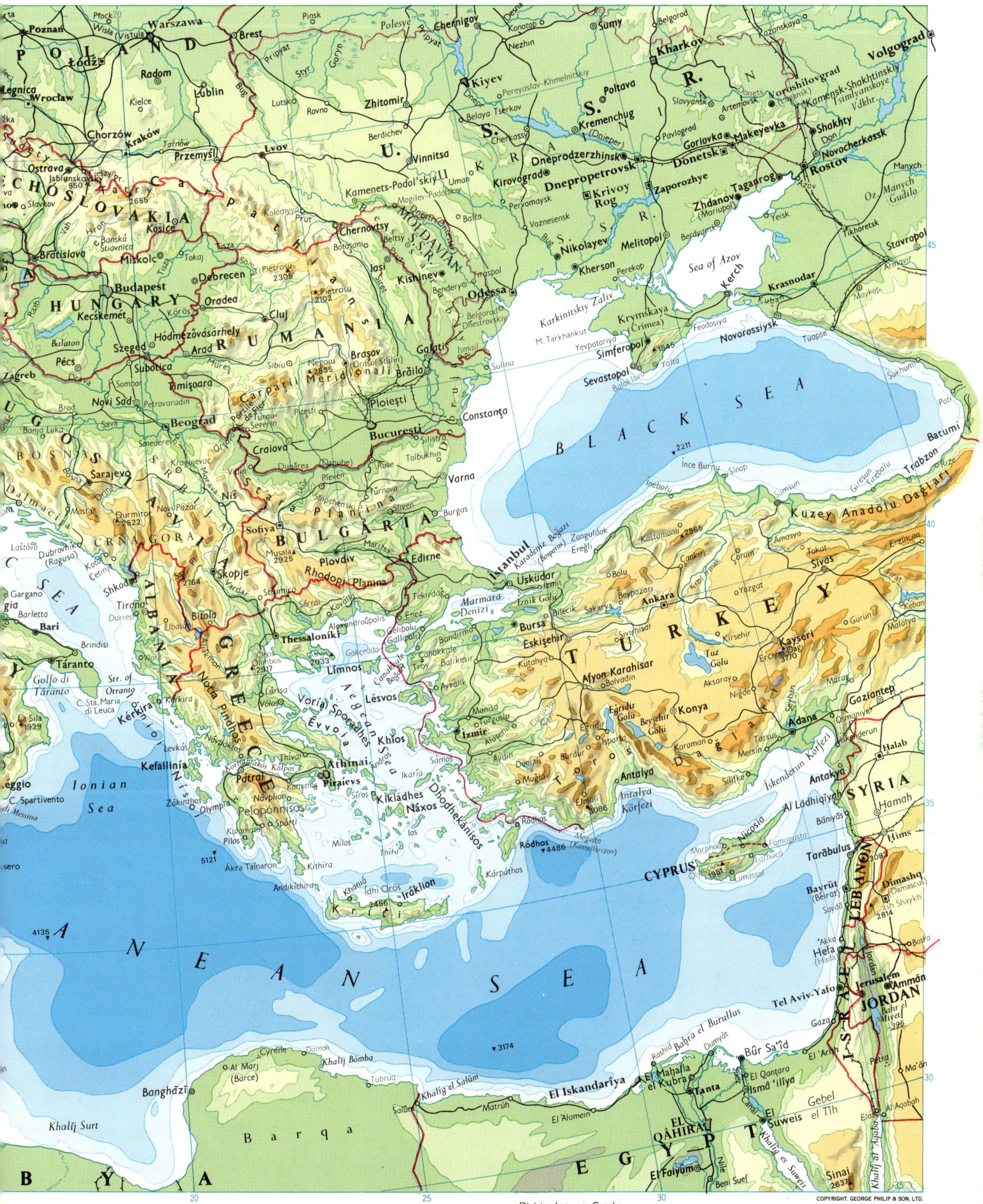

Division between Greeks and Turks in Cyprus; Turks to the north.

Projection: Conical with two standard parallels

1:5 000 000

50 0 50 100 miles

50 0 50 100 150 km

SWITZERLAND
FRANCE
LIGURIAN SEA
Golfo di Génova
CORSE
(CORSICA)
Riviera
Côte d'Azur
MILANO
TORINO
GENOVA (Genoa)
Grenoble
Lyon
Genève
Lausanne
Bern
Luzern
Marseille (Marseilles)
Toulon
Nice
Cannes
Monaco
Sanremo
La Spezia
Parma
Piacenza
Cremona
Brescia
Bergamo
Novara
Vercelli
Pavia
Asti
Alessandria
Cúneo
Savona
Livorno (Leghorn)
Pisa
Bastia
Ajaccio
Elba
Capraia
Gorgona
Pianosa
Montecristo
Giglio
ILES D'HYERES
Arles
Avignon
Aix-en-Provence
Valence
Chambéry
Annecy
Lac Léman (L. Geneva)
Lago Maggiore
L. di Como
Lago di Garda
Aosta
Vosges
Alpes-Maritimes
Alpes-de-Haute-Provence
Haute-Corse
Corse-du-Sud
Arcipelago Toscano
ft
m
12 000
9000
6000
4500
3000
1200
600
0
4000
3000
2000
1500
1000
400
200
200
2000
6000
Projectión: Conical with two standard parallels
East from Greenwich

Innsbruck
Hohe Tauern
Niedere Tauern
Zillertaler Alpen
Salzach
Graz
Judenburg
Mur
Klagenfurt
Villach
Wörther See
Karnische Alpen
Karawanken
Gurk
Drava
Maribor
Bolzano
Bressanone
Belluno
Feltre
Vittorio Veneto
Pordenone
Udine
Gorízia
Monfalcone
Trieste
G. di Trieste
Ljubljana
Kranj
Celje
Zagreb
Varaždin
Nagykanizsa
HUNGARY
Balaton
Zalaegerszeg
Keszthely
Szentgotthárd
Bjelovar
Karlovac
Sisak
Kupa
Sava
Una
Bihać
Banja Luka
Vicenza
Padova (Padua)
Treviso
Mestre
Venézia (Venice)
Laguna Veneta
Golfo di Venézia
Chióggia
Rovigo
Adria
Porto Tolle
Foci del Po
Ferrara
Valli di Comácchio
Ravenna
Lugo
Imola
Faenza
Forlì
Cesena
Cesenático
Rímini
Riccione
SAN MARINO
Pésaro
Fano
Senigállia
Ancona
Osimo
Porto Recanati
Civitanova Marche
Macerata
Fermo
Porto San Giórgio
S. Benedetto del Tronto
Giulianova
Roseto degli Abruzzi
Pescara
Chieti
Francavilla al Mare
Ortona
Vasto
Térmoli
Urbino
Perugia
L. Trasimeno
Assisi
Foligno
Spoleto
Terni
Orvieto
Arezzo
Viterbo
L. di Bolsena
L. di Vico
L. di Bracciano
Civitavécchia
ROMA (ROME)
Tívoli
Rieti
L'Aquila
Avezzano
Sulmona
Gran Sasso d'Italia
ABRUZZI
UMBRIA
MARCHE
MOLISE
Koper
Piran
Umag
Poreč
Rovinj
Pula
Rt. Kamenjak
Istra
Opatija
Rijeka (Fiume)
Krk
Cres
Lošinj
Rab
Pag
Kvarner
Kvarnerić
Velebitski Kanal
Velebit Planina
Velika Kapela
Mala Kapela
Gospić
Zadar
Dugi Otok
Kornat
Šibenik
Split
Trogir
Brač
Hvar
Šolta
Vis
Korčula
Lastovo
Mljet
Pelješac
Makarska
Dinara Planina
Knin
Drniš
HERCEGOVINA
BOSNA
JUGOSLAVIA
DALMACIJA
ADRIATIC SEA
Palagruža
Pianosa
Tremiti
L. di Lésina
L. di Varano
Vieste
Monte Sant'Ángelo
Testa del Gargano
Conca del Fúcino
Metauro
Tevere (Tiber)
Po

Iles Sanguinaires
G.d'Ajaccio
C.di Muro
Petreto
Taravo
L'Incudine
2136
Zonza
Levie
Solenzara
Favone
CORSE
CORSICA
G. de Valinco
Propriano
Sartène
Porto-Vecchio
CORSE-DU-SUD
Iles Cerbicales
Bonifacio
I. de Cavallo
Bouches de Bonifacio
Santa Teresa Gallura
Maddalena
La Maddalena
Caprera
Costa Smeralda
Asinara
Punta dello Scorno
Golfo dell' Asinara
Coghinas
Tempio Pausania
Calangianus
Golfo Aranci
G. di Ólbia
Tavolara
Ólbia
M. Limbara
1362
Porto Tórres
Sorso
Sennori
Sássari
Ósilo
C. dell'Argentiera
Oschiri
L. di Coghinas
Tanaunella
Posada
Fertilia
Ittiri
Ozieri
Alghero
Pattada
Buddusò
Villanova Monteleone
Siniscola
C. Comino
1259
Bonorva
Tirso
Bitti
Orune
Bosa
Temo
Nùoro
Dorgali
Macomer
Oliena
SARDEGNA
Golfo di Orosei
Ghilarza
L. del Tirso
Fonni
C. Mannu
Sorgono
Monti del Gennargentu
1834
Baunei
C. di Monte Santu
Tyrrhenian Sea
3719
Cabras
Oristano
SARDEGNA
Laconi
Golfo di Oristano
M. Arci
812
Arborea
Arbatax
Lanusei
Terralba
Jerzu
Mandas
SARDINIA
S. Gavino Monreale
Sanluri
Gúspini
Arbus
Gonnosfanádiga
Senorbì
Flumendosa
C. Pécora
Fluminimaggiore
1236
M. Linas
Villacidro
Serramanna
S. Vito
Villaputzu
Muravera
Iglésias
Cixerri
Sestu
Dolianova
Pta. Serpeddi
1069
Sinnai
Selárgius
Quartu Sant'Elena
Assemini
Portoscuso
Gonnesa
Siliqua
C. Ferrato
Carloforte
Carbonia
1116
Cagliari
Golfo di Cágliari
San Pietro
Sant'Antíoco
Santadi
Serpentara
C. Carbonara
Porto Botte
Pula
Teulada
G. di Palmas
C. Spartivento
TYRRHENIAN SEA
3589
Vatican City
ROMA
(Rome)
Tìvoli
Subiaco
Trosacco
Conca del Fucino
Fregene
Tevere (Tiber)
Palestrina
Valmontone
Anagni
Alatri
Veroli
Sora
Lido di Ostia (Lido di Roma)
Frascati
Velletri
Ferentino
Isola del Liri
Arpino
Prática di Mare
Albano Laziale
Cori
Frosinone
Aprilia
Cisterna di Latina
Ceccano
Ceprano
Latina
Sezze
Priverno
Cassino
Sonnino
Anzio
Nettuno
Fondi
1533
Liri
Pontinia
Formia
Terracina
Sabáudia
Monte Circeo
541
Gaeta
Minturno
Garigliano
Golfo di Gaeta
Mondragone
Zannone
Palmarola
Ponza
283
Ìsole Ponziane
Ventotene
Ìschia
788
Ustica
C. San Vito
Castellammare del Golfo
G. di Castellammare
Terrasini
Favarotta
C. Gallo
PALERMO
Bagheria
Monreale
Carini
Levanzo
Trápani
1110
Érice
Partinico
Misilmeri
Maréttimo
Ìsole Égadi
Alcamo
S. Giuseppe Iato
Favignana
Stagnone
Paceco
Calatafimi
Camporeale
Marineo
Salemi
Corleone
1613
Marsala
Gibellina
Lercara
Castelvetrano
Partanna
Bisacquino
Prizzi
Mazara del Vallo
Sambuca di Sicilia
Campobello di Mazara
Belice
Menfi
Burgio
Mussomeli
Sciacca
Caltabellotta
Ribera
Platani
Racalmuto
Sicilian Channel
Cattólica Eraclea
Raffadali
Siculiana
Porto Empédocle
Agrigento
Favara
Naro
Palma di Montechiaro
Campobello di Licata
Iles de la Galite
C. Serrat
Bizerte (Binzert)
C. Blanc
Cani
Menzel-Bourguiba
Plane
Zembra
Golfe de Tunis
C. Bon
El Kala
ALGERIA
Tabarka
Mateur
Tébourba
TUNIS
Halq el Oued
Kelibia
Menzel-Temime
Bou Salem
Béja
Medjerda
Soliman
Pantelleria
836
Pantelleria (It.)
TUNISIA
Téboursouk
Nabeul
Zaghouan
Hammamet
Mellègue
1319
MEDITE
ft m
9000 3000
6000 2000
4500 1500
3000 1000
1200 400
600 200
0 37 0
200 600
2000 6000
4000 12 000
m ft
Projection: Conical with two standard parallels
8 9 10 11 12 13
41 40 39 38
East from Greenwich

1:2 500 000

10 0 10 20 30 40 50 miles

10 0 10 20 30 40 50 60 70 80 km

HUNGARY
YUGOSLAVIA
ALBANIA
ADRIATIC SEA
Beograd (Belgrade)
Sarajevo
Skopje
Titograd
Tiranë (Tirana)
Novi Sad
Szeged
Timişoara
Niš
Priština
Zagreb
Dubrovnik
Durrës (Durazzo)
Ohridsko Jezero (L. Ohrid)
Prepansko Jezero (L. Prespa)
Skadarsko Jezero
Danube
ft m
9000 3000
6000 2000
4500 1500
3000 1000
1200 400
600 200
0 0
200 600
2000 6000
m ft
Projection: Conical with two standard parallels
East from Greenwich

1:2 500 000

10 0 10 20 30 40 50 miles

10 0 10 20 30 40 50 60 70 80 km

BULGARIA
YUGOSLAVIA
ALBANIA
Sofiya
Skopje
Thessaloníki
Tiranë
Plovdiv
Stara Zagora
Pleven
Niš
Priština
Kumanovo
Prilep
Bitola
Ohrid
Korçë
Durrës
Vlorë (Valona)
Kérkira
Lárisa
Kaválla
Sérrai
Drámi
Edirne
Thásos
Límnos
Samothráki
Áyios Evstrátios
Thermaïkós Kólpos
Thrakikón Pélagos
Sinyitikós Kólpos
Toronaíos Kólpos
Strimonikós Kólpos
Saros Körfezi
Çanakkale Boğazı
Gökçeada
Stara Planina
Rodopi
Sredna Gora
Rila
Pirin
Kopaonik
Ohridsko Jezero
Prespansko Jezero
Vardar
Strimón
Maritsa
Iskŭr
Dunav

1:2 500 000
miles
km
Continuation Eastwards on same scale
Projection: Conical with two standard parallels
East from Greenwich
COPYRIGHT GEORGE PHILIP & SON, LTD.
SEA OF CRETE
(Sea of Candia)
KIKLÁDHES
(CYCLADES)
DHODHEKÁNISOS
(DODECANESE)
ATHÍNAI
(ATHENS)
Piraiévs
Kríti
Iráklion
Khaniá
Rhodos
Rhodes
Kárpathos
Kos
Sámos
Khíos
Ikaría
Ándros
Tínos
Míkonos
Náxos
Páros
Mílos
Thíra
Kíthira
Zákinthos
Kefallinía
Itháki
Levkás
Pátrai
Kórinthos
Pelopónnisos
Corinth Canal
Saronikós Kólpos
Korinthiakós Kólpos
Argolikós Kólpos
Lakonikós Kólpos
Messiniakós Kólpos
Kiparissiakós Kólpos
Taíyetos Óros
Párnon Óros
Stenón Kásos
Stenón Karpáthos
Kerme Körfezi
Mandalya Körfezi
Kuşadası Körfezi
Stenón Kásos
ft
m

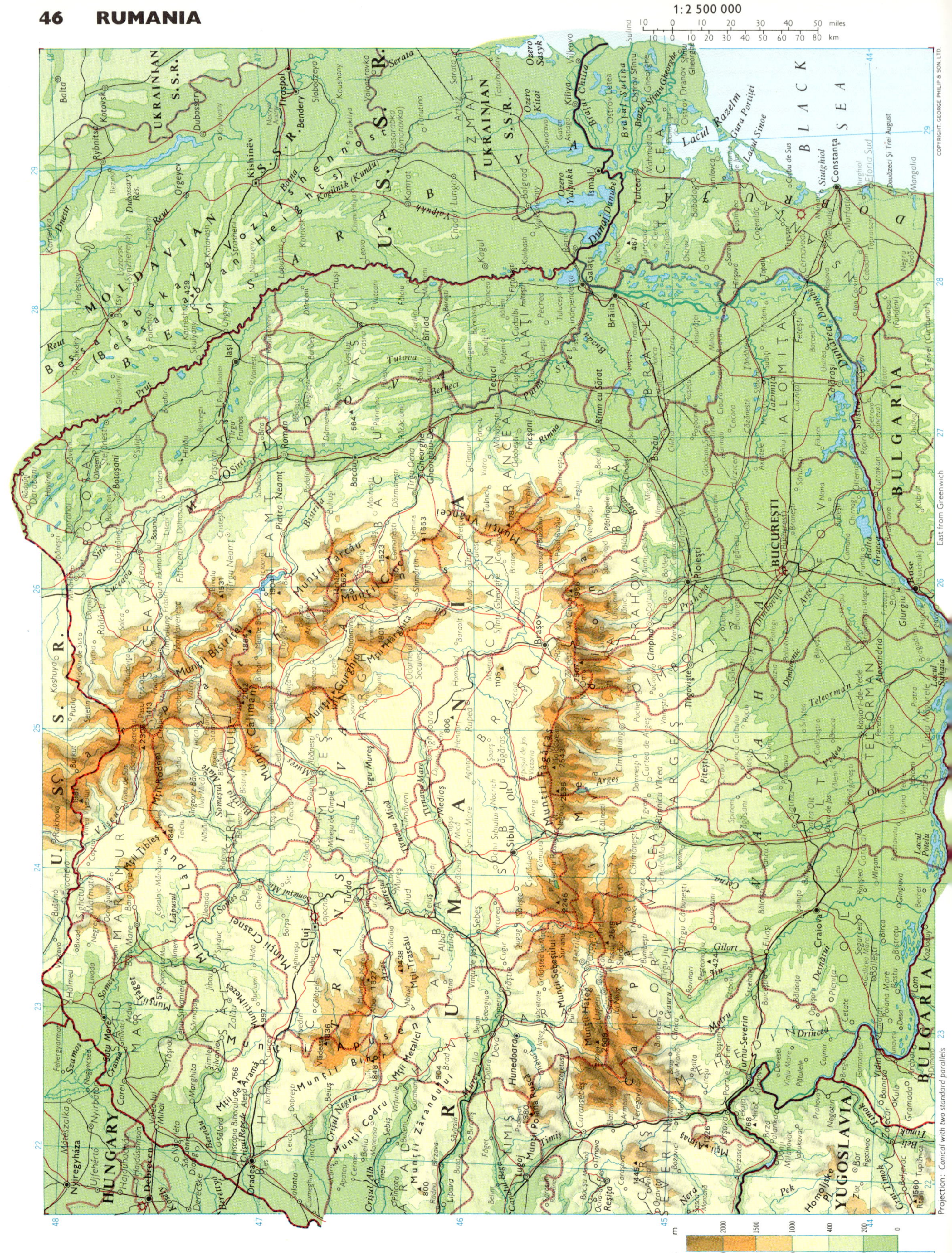
1:2 500 000
miles
km
COPYRIGHT GEORGE PHILIP & SON, LTD.
Projection: Conical with two standard parallels
East from Greenwich
m
ft
UKRAINIAN S.S.R.
MOLDAVIA
BESSARABIA
U.S.S.R.
BLACK SEA
HUNGARY
YUGOSLAVIA
BULGARIA
RUMANIA
TRANSILVANIA
MUNTENIA
DOBROGEA
OLTENIA
BUCUREŞTI
Kishinëv
Tiraspol
Bendery
Izmail
Galaţi
Brăila
Tulcea
Constanţa
Iaşi
Botoşani
Suceava
Piatra Neamţ
Bacău
Roman
Vaslui
Bîrlad
Focşani
Buzău
Ploieşti
Braşov
Sibiu
Cluj
Tîrgu Mureş
Mediaş
Alba Iulia
Deva
Hunedoara
Oradea
Arad
Timişoara
Reşiţa
Turnu-Severin
Craiova
Piteşti
Tîrgovişte
Giurgiu
Alexandria
Călăraşi
Slobozia
Satu Mare
Baia Mare
Debrecen
Nyíregyháza
Lacul Razelm
Dunărea
Prut
Siret
Mureş
Olt
Munţii Rodnei
Munţii Bistriţei
Munţii Călimani
Munţii Harghita
Munţii Făgăraş
Munţii Apuseni
Munţii Retezat

1:2 500 000

10 0 10 20 30 40 50 miles

10 0 10 20 30 40 50 60 70 80 km

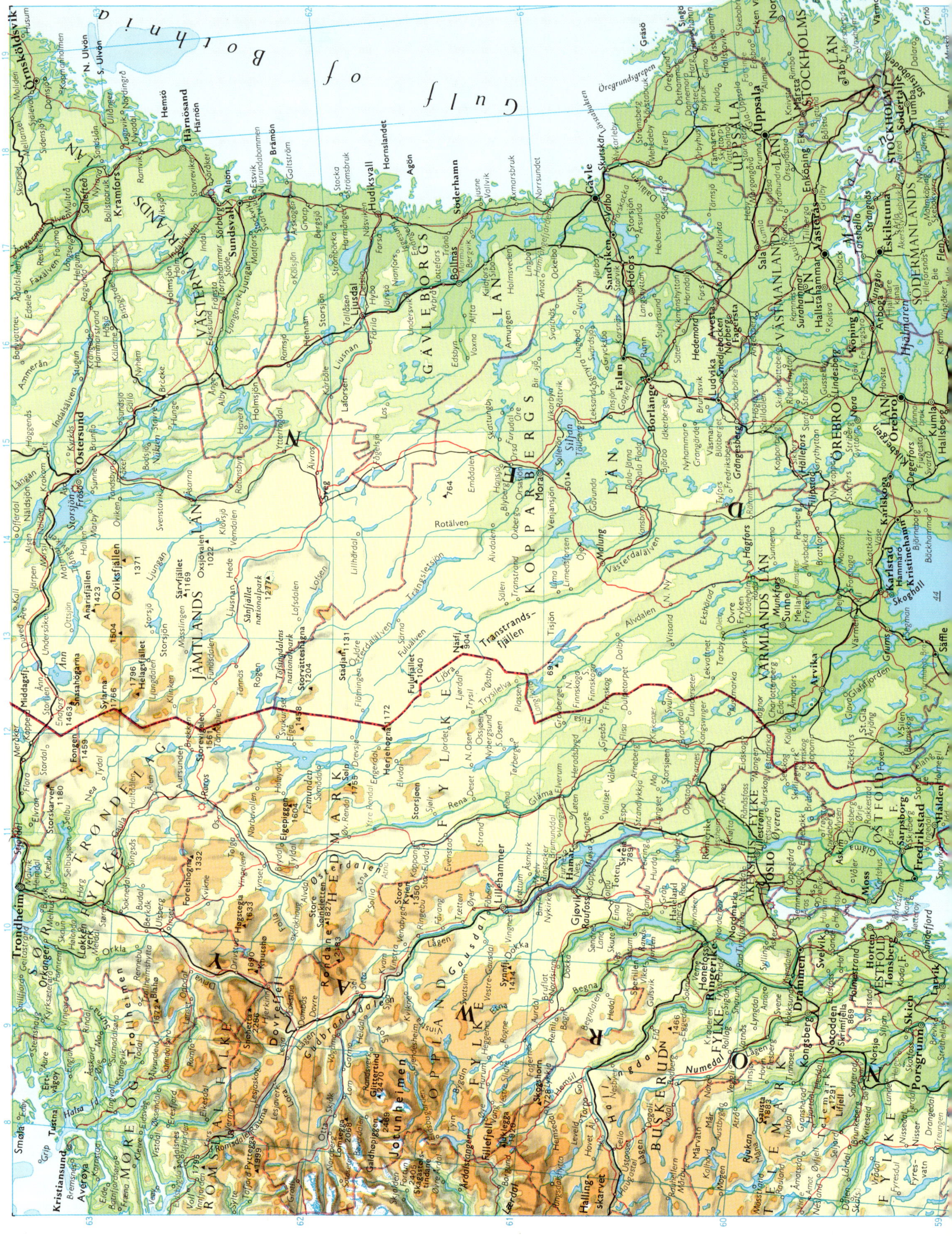
Gulf of Bothnia
GÄVLEBORGS LÄN
KOPPARBERGS LÄN
JÄMTLANDS LÄN
VÄRMLANDS LÄN
HEDMARK FYLKE
OPPLAND FYLKE
BUSKERUD
TELEMARK
SØR-TRØNDELAG FYLKE
MØRE OG ROMSDAL FYLKE
Trondheim
Östersund
Sundsvall
Gävle
Uppsala
Stockholm
Västerås
Örebro
Karlstad
Oslo
Drammen
Lillehammer
Hamar
Jotunheimen

1:2 500 000

10 0 10 20 30 40 50 miles

10 0 10 20 30 40 50 60 70 80 km

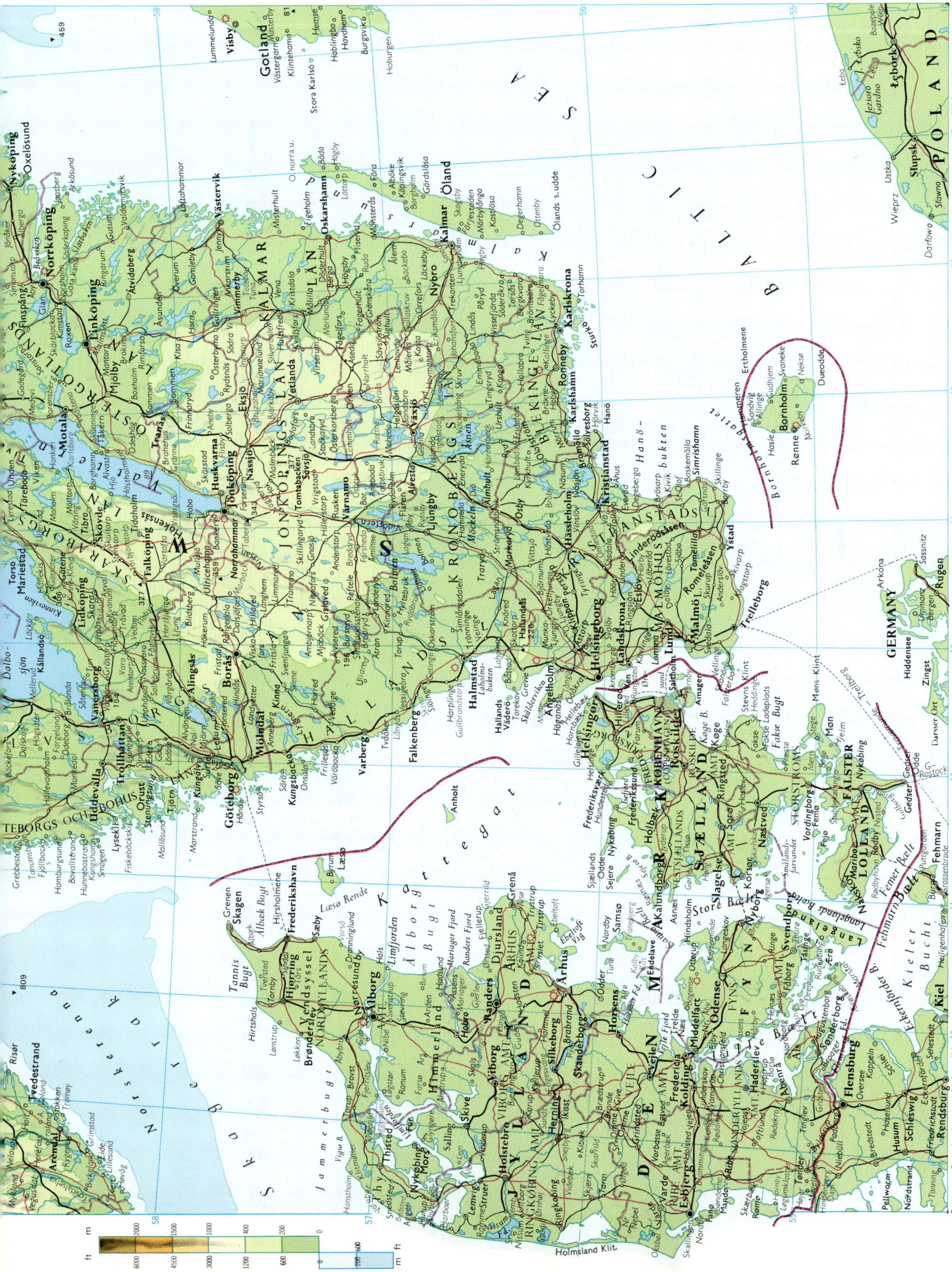

NORWEGIAN SEA
ICELAND
on the same scale as general map
West from Greenwich
Arctic Circle
Vatnajökull
Hofsjökull
Langjökull
Reykjavík
Keflavík
Hafnarfjördur
Akranes
Akureyri
Húsavík
Siglufjördur
Saudárkrókur
Seydisfjördur
Faxaflói
Húnaflói
Vestmannaeyjar
Surtsey
Hekla 1491
Lofoten
Vesterålen
Vestfjorden
Tromsø
Narvik
Bodø
Mo
Mosjøen
Namsos
Steinkjer
Levanger
Trondheim
Kristiansund
Molde
Ålesund
Hitra
Smøla
Frøya
Hammerfest
Nordkapp
Vadsø
Kirkenes
Inari
Kiruna
Gällivare
Luleå
Boden
Piteå
Skellefteå
Umeå
Lycksele
Örnsköldsvik
Härnösand
Östersund
Haparanda
Tornio
Kemi
Oulu
Rovaniemi
Kajaani
Iisalmi
Kuopio
Jyväskylä
Vaasa
Jakobstad
Kokkola
Hailuoto
Kebnekaise 2117
Sarektjåkkå 2090
Storsjön
Storavan
Uddjaur
Storuman
Malgomaj
Lofoten
Moskenstraumen
Torneträsk
Stora Lulevatten
LAPPI
LAPPLAND
NORRBOTTEN
VÄSTERBOTTEN
JÄMTLAND
OULU
KUOPIO
VAASA
KESKI-SUOMEN
FINNMARK
TROMS
NORDLAND
N. TRØNDELAG
SØR-TRØNDELAG
MØRE OG ROMSDAL
GULF OF BOTHNIA
Kvarken
Lopphavet
Varangerfjorden
Tanafjorden
Laksefjorden
Porsangen

1:5 000 000

20 10 0 20 40 60 80 100 miles

40 20 0 40 80 120 160 km

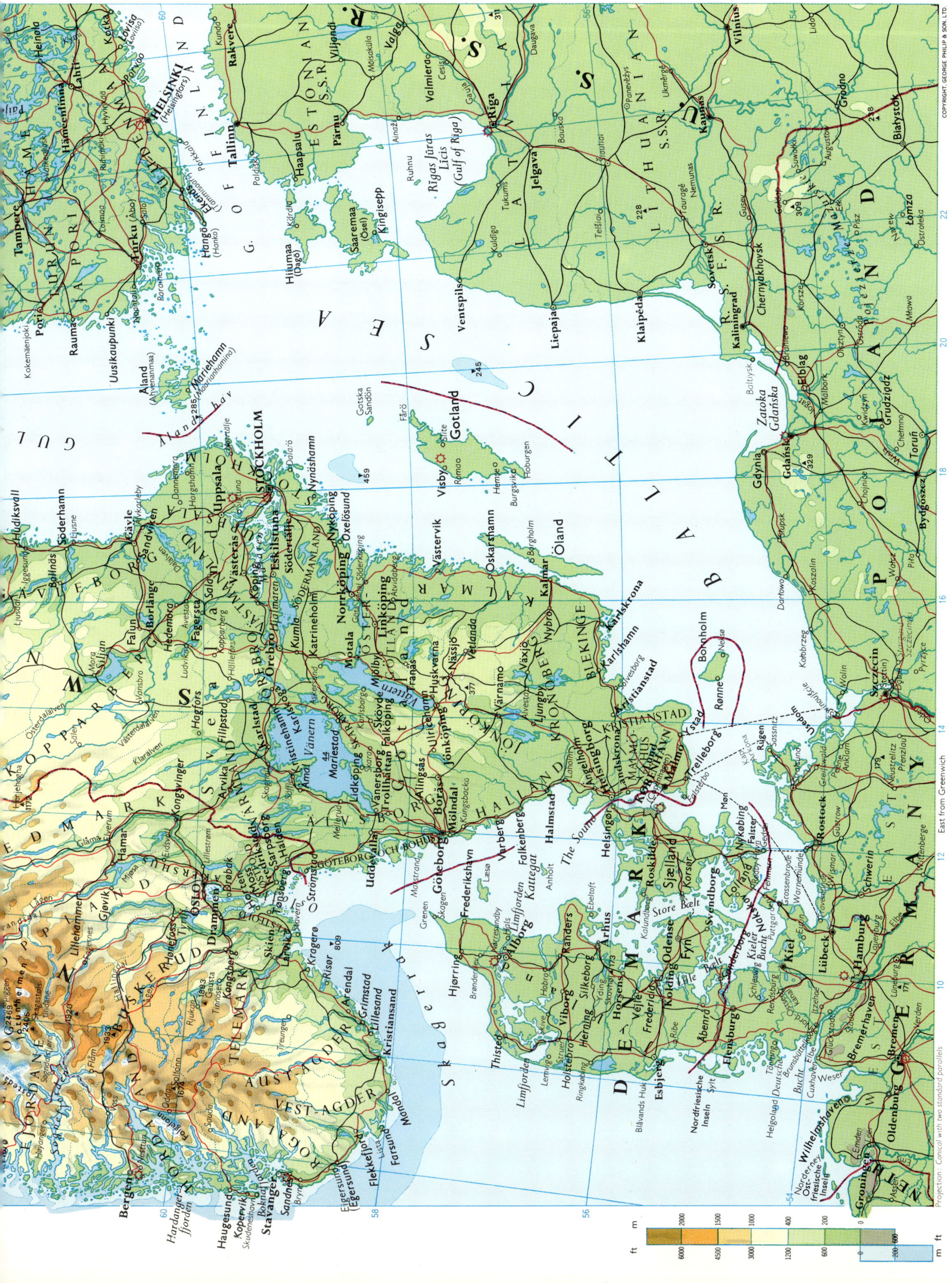

Timanskiy Kryazh
Bolshezemelskaya Tundra
Malozemelskaya Tundra
Kolguyev
P-ov. Kanin
Cheshskaya Guba
Pechorskaya Guba
Kolskiy Poluostrov
Beloye More (White Sea)
Onezhskaya Guba
Dvinskaya Guba
Kandalakshskiy Zaliv
Arkhangelsk (Archangel)
Murmansk
Syktyvkar
Kirov
Perm
SVERDLOVSK
Ufa
Kazan
Gorkiy
Kuybyshev
Orenburg
Penza
Ryazan
Tula
Kaluga
Bryansk
Smolensk
Vitebsk
Minsk
Vilnius
Kaunas
Riga
Tallinn
Helsinki
Stockholm
LENINGRAD
MOSKVA (Moscow)
Yaroslavl
Vologda
Kostroma
Ivanovo
Vladimir
Kalinin
Novgorod
Pskov
Petrozavodsk
Ladozhskoye Ozero
Onezhskoye Ozero
Rybinskoye Vdkhr.
Gulf of Bothnia
G. of Finland
FINLAND
SWEDEN
NORWAY
POLAND
WARSZAWA (Warsaw)
Kaliningrad (Königsberg)
ESTONIAN S.S.R.
LATVIAN S.S.R.
LITHUANIAN S.S.R.
BYELORUSSIAN S.S.R. (WHITE RUSSIA)
KARELIAN A.S.S.R.
RUSSIAN SOVIET FEDERAL SOCIALIST REPUBLIC
Severnyye Uvaly
Valdayskaya Vozvyshennost
Ural Mts.
Polesye (Pripet Marshes)
Lapland

1:10 000 000

100 50 0 50 100 150 200 miles

100 0 100 200 300 km

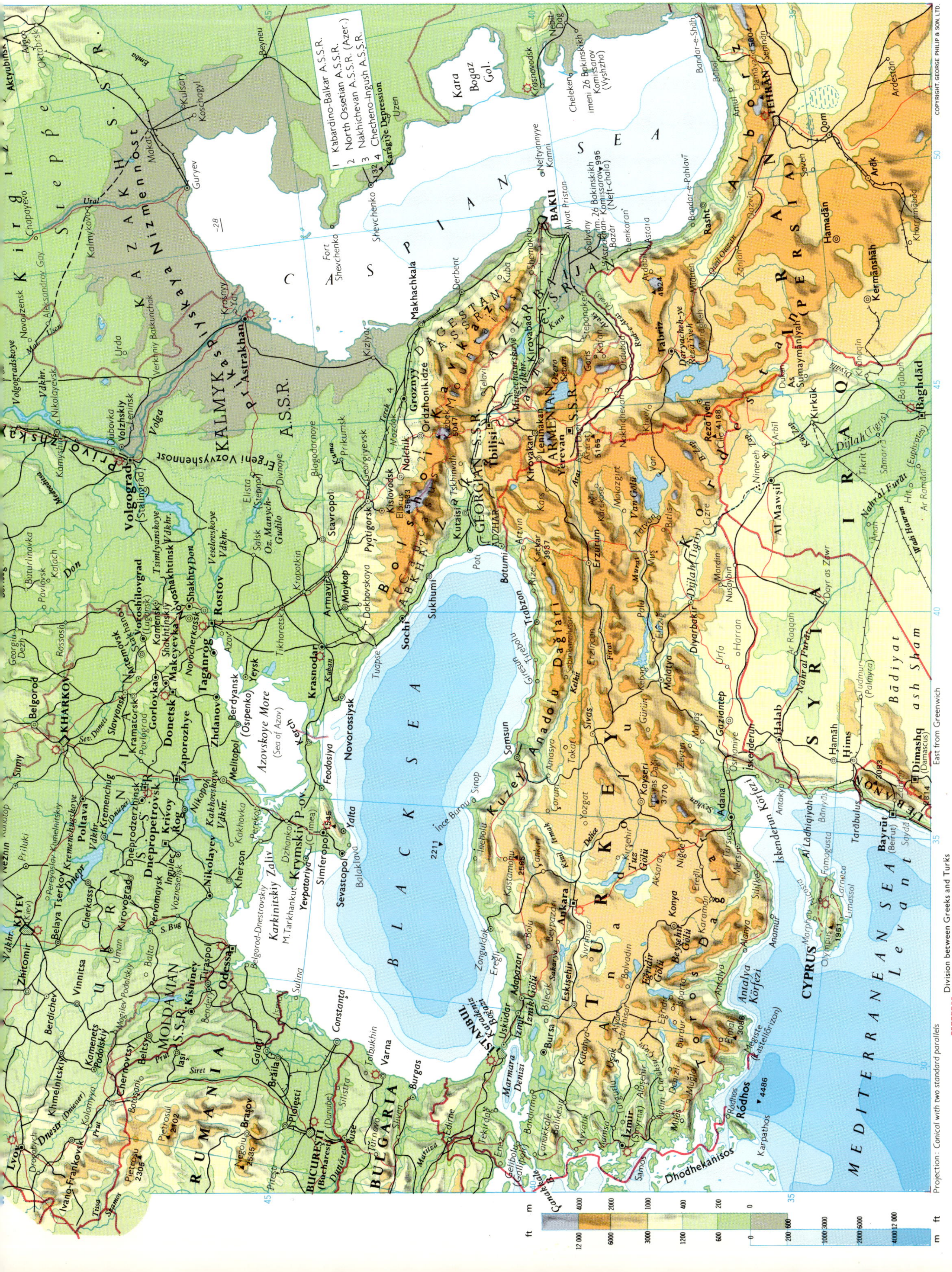

Projection: Conical with two standard parallels

East from Greenwich

1:5 000 000

50 0 50 100 miles
50 0 50 100 150 km

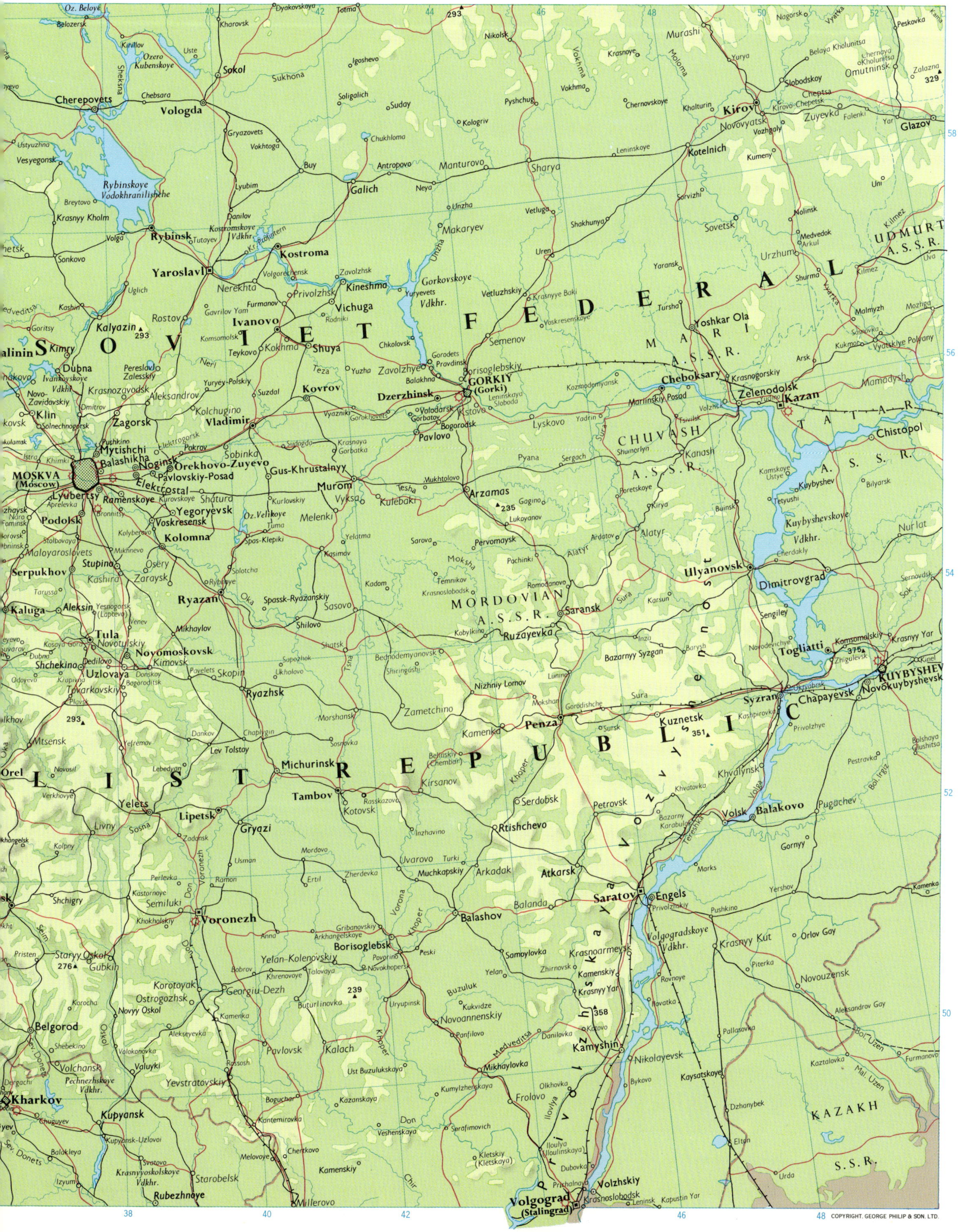

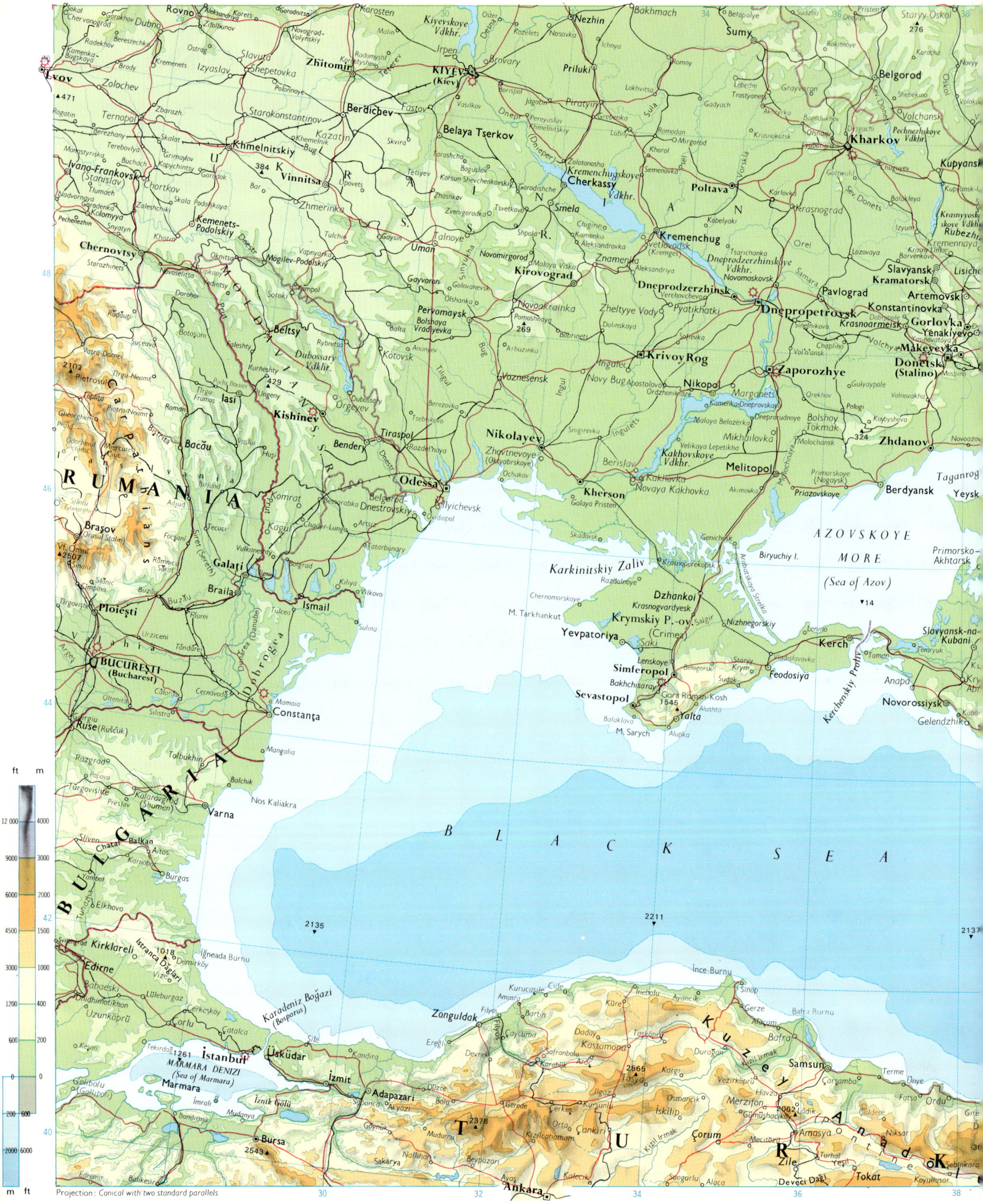

Projection: Conical with two standard parallels

1:5 000 000

50 0 50 100 miles

50 0 50 100 150 km

East from Greenwich 40 42 44 46 48

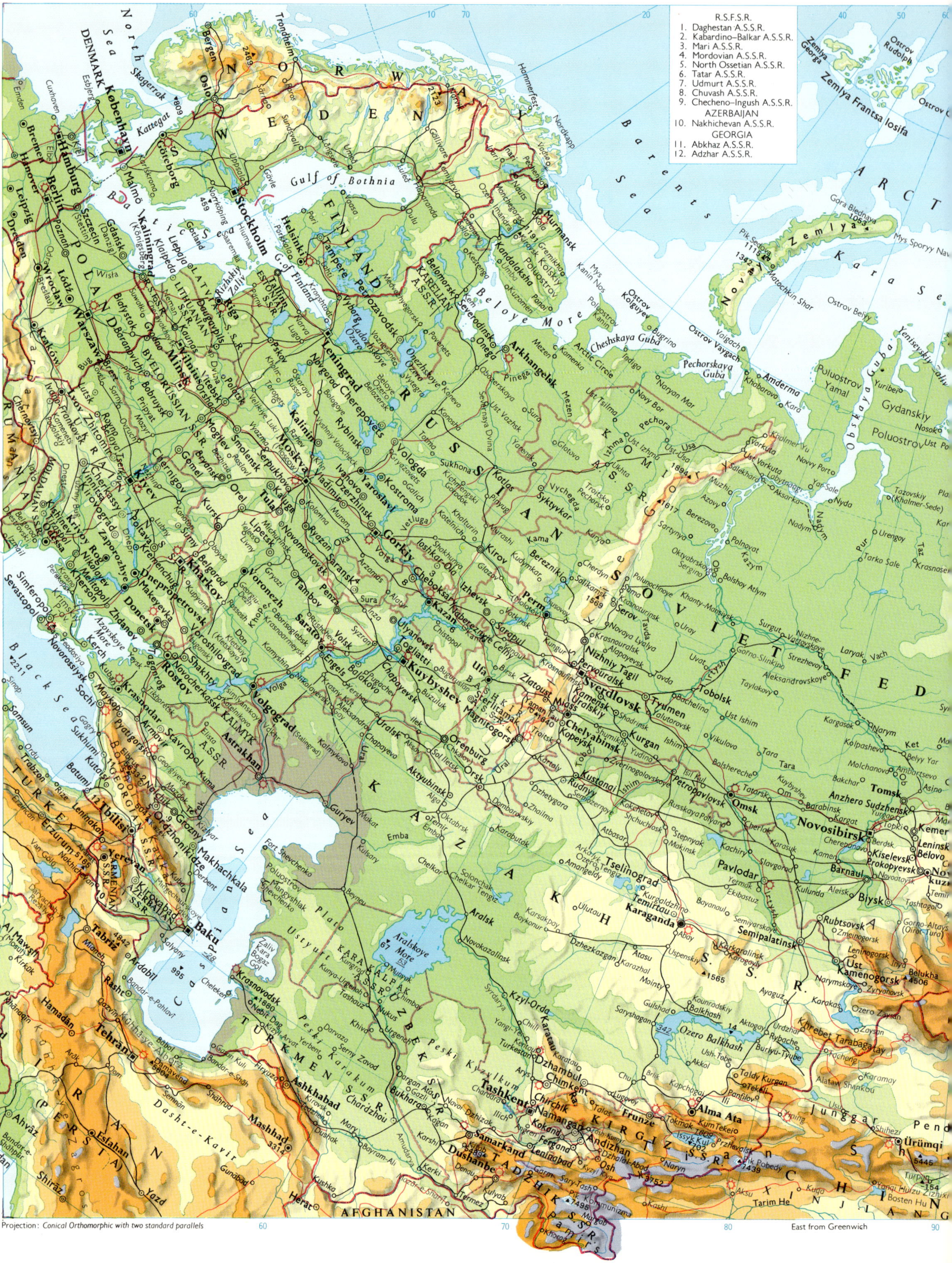

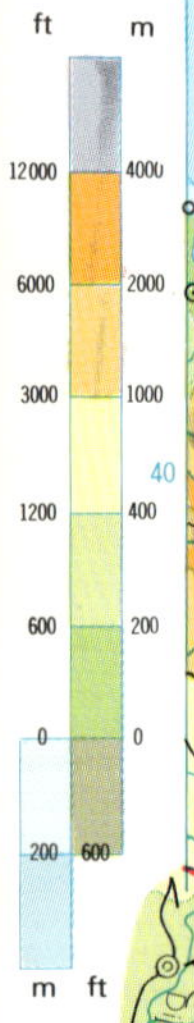

Projection: *Conical Orthomorphic with two standard parallels*

East from Greenwich

1:20 000 000
miles
km
Severnaya Zemlya
Ostrov Komsomolets
Ostrov Oktyabrskoy Revolyutsii
Ostrov Bolshevik
Proliv Vilkitskogo
Laptev Sea
OCEAN
Novosibirskiye Ostrova
Ostrov Kotelnyy
Ostrov Faddeyevskiy
Ostrov Novaya Sibir
Ostrova Delong
East Siberian Sea
Ostrov Vrangelya
Chukotskoye More
Mys Dezhneva (East C.)
St. Lawrence I. (U.S.A.)
Anadyrskiy Zaliv
Chukotskiy Khrebet
Koryakskiy Khrebet
Bering Sea
Poluostrov Taymyr
Gory Byrranga
Tiksi
Khatanga
Nordvik
Verkhoyanskiy Khrebet
Khrebet Cherskogo
Verkhoyansk
Srednekolymsk
Magadan
Sea of Okhotsk
Poluostrov Kamchatka
Petropavlovsk-Kamchatskiy
Arctic Circle
YAKUT A.S.S.R.
REPUBLIC
Yakutsk
Vilyuysk
Olekminsk
Okhotsk
Sakhalin
Stanovoy Khrebet
Khrebet Dzhugdzur
Krasnoyarsk
Bratsk
Nizhneudinsk
Kirensk
Irkutsk
Angarsk
Ulan Ude
Chita
Blagoveshchensk
Komsomolsk
Khabarovsk
Vladivostok
Hokkaido
Sapporo
Hakodate
Honshū
Sea of Japan
Harbin
Qiqihar
Jilin
Changchun
Shenyang
Anshan
Fushun
Lüda
Beijing
Baotou
P'yongyang
Soul
Pusan
MONGOLIA
Ulaanbaatar (Ulan Bator)
GOBI
Hangayn Nuruu
Hentiyn Nuruu
Da Hinggan Ling
Sikhote Alin
Boundaries of U.S.S.R.
Boundaries of S.S.R.
Boundaries of A.S.S.R.

1: 50 000 000

250 0 250 500 750 1000 miles

250 0 500 1000 1500 km

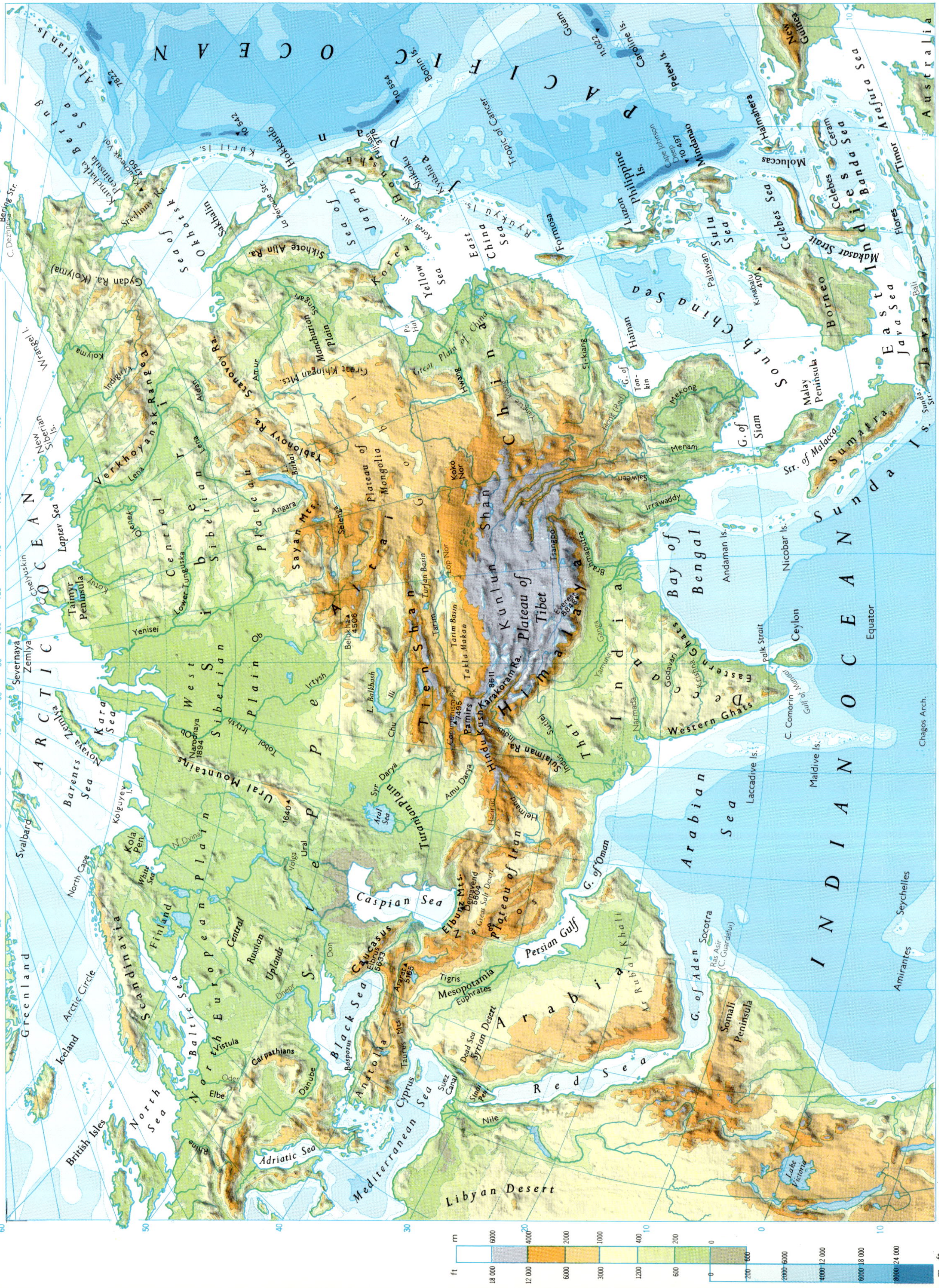

1:50 000 000

250 0 250 500 750 1000 miles

250 0 500 1000 1500 km

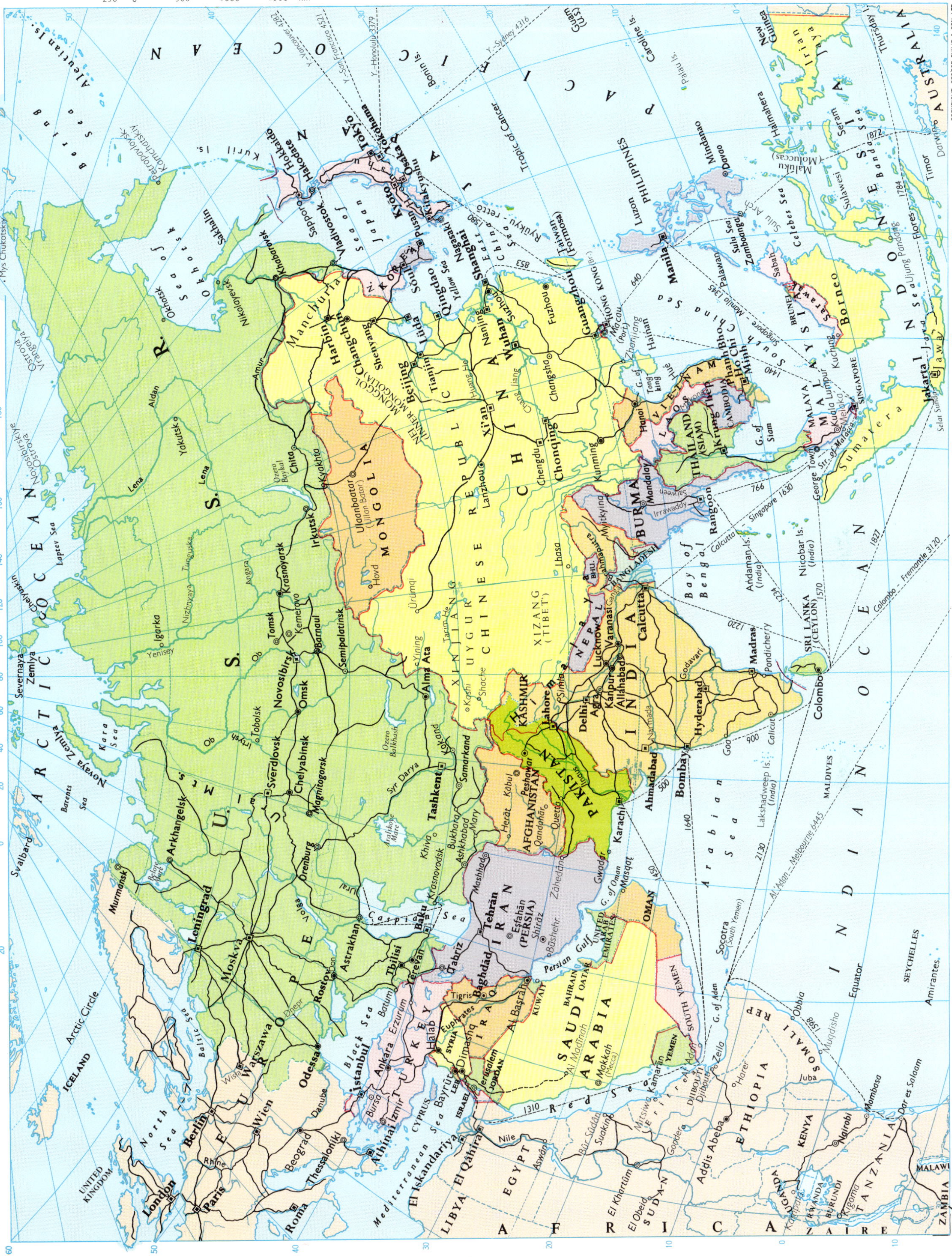

1:1 000 000

Projection: *Conical with two standard parallels*

East from Greenwich

1:15 000 000

100 0 100 200 300 400 miles

100 0 100 200 300 400 500 600 km

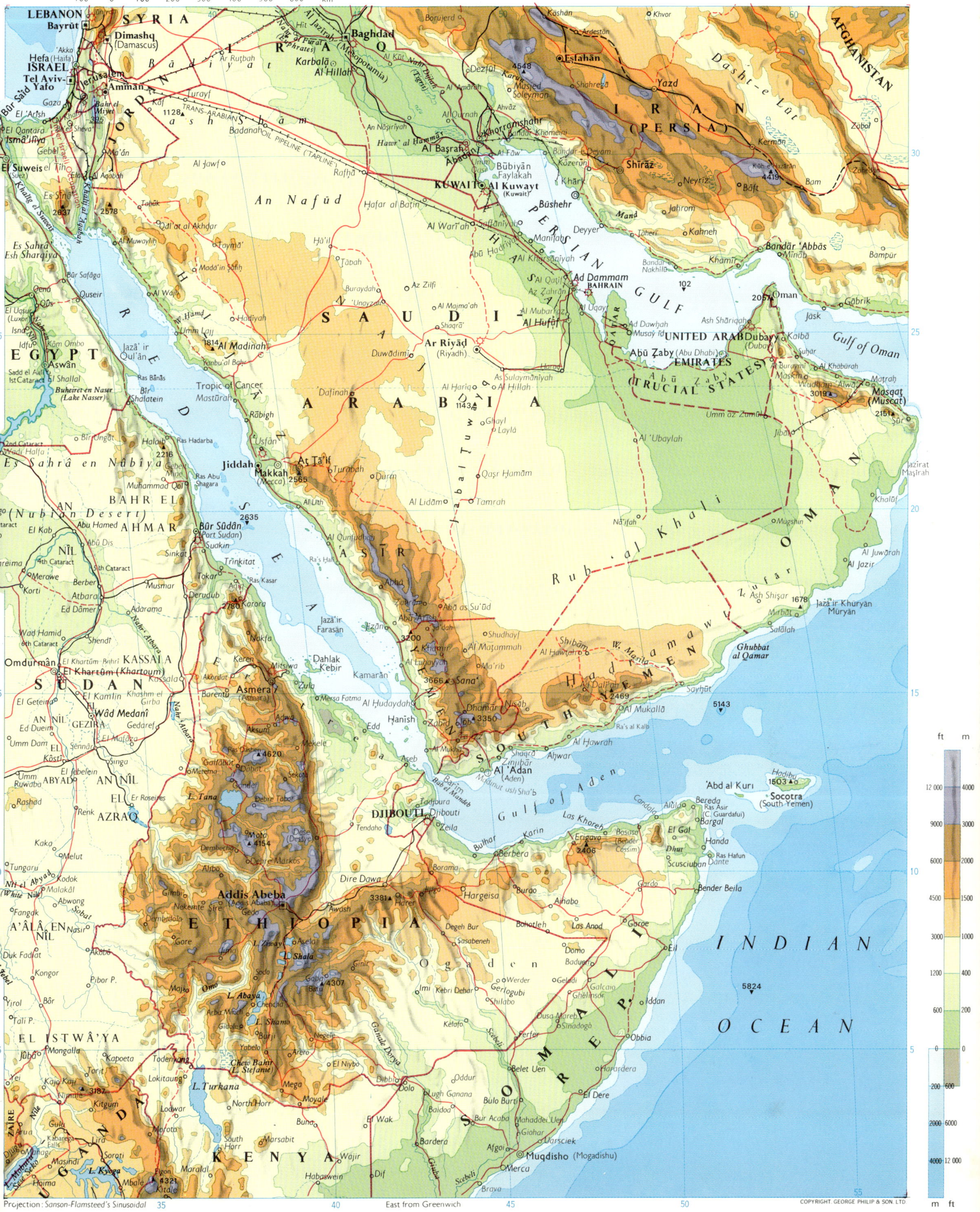

Projection: *Conical Orthomorphic with two standard parallels*

Division between Greeks and Turks in Cyprus; Turks to the North.

1:10 000 000

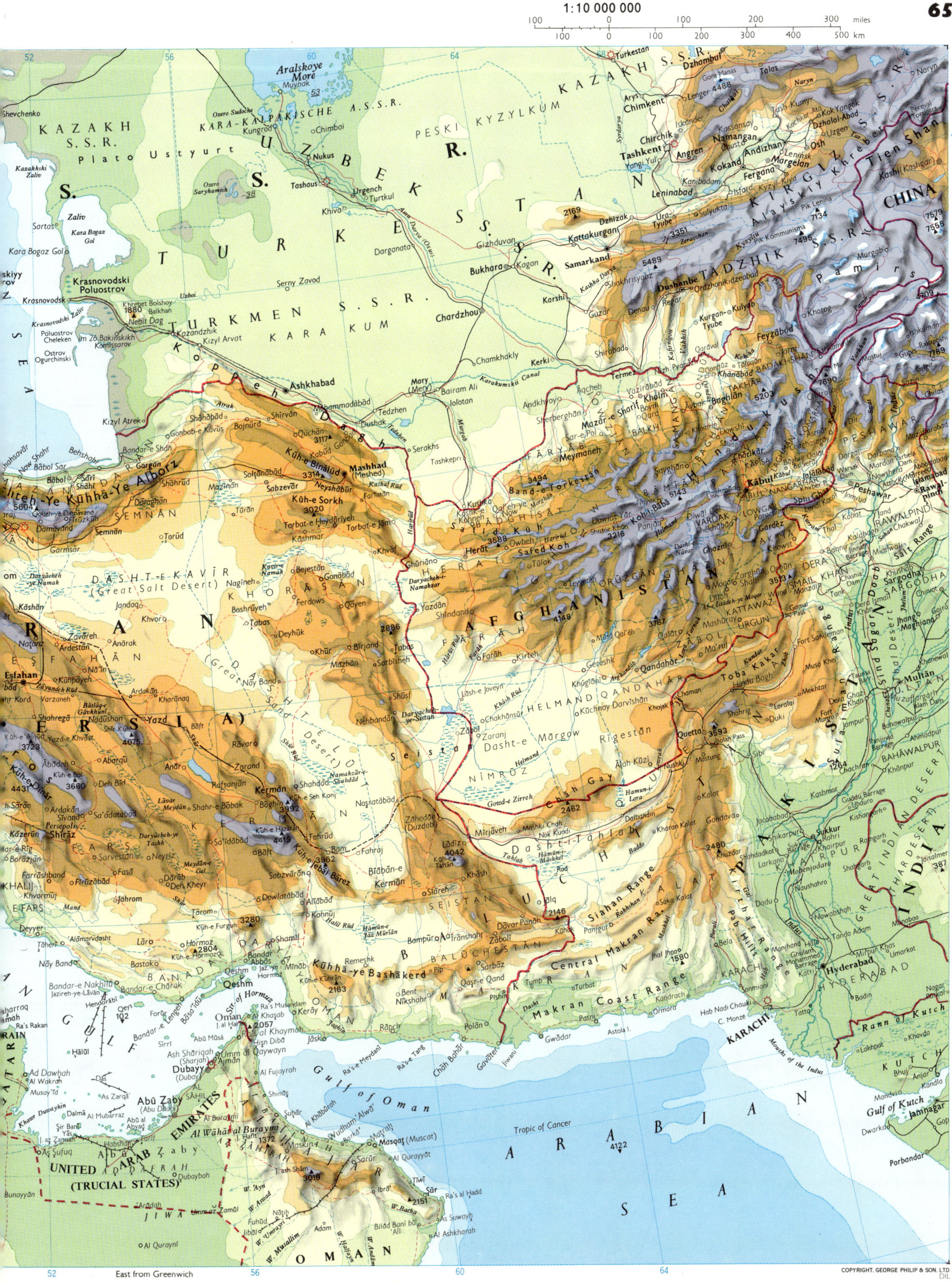
KAZAKH S.S.R.
Plato Ustyurt
Aralskoye More
KARA-KALPAKISCHE A.S.S.R.
PESKI KYZYLKUM
UZBEK S.S.R.
TURKMEN S.S.R.
KARA KUM
TADZHIK S.S.R.
KIRGIZ S.S.R.
CHINA
Tien Shan
Pamirs
Tashkent
Samarkand
Bukhara
Dushanbe
Krasnovodsk
Ashkhabad
Mary (Merv)
Kopet Dagh
Mashhad (Meshed)
DASHT-E-KAVĪR (Great Salt Desert)
DASHT-E LŪT (Great Sand Desert)
KHORĀSĀN
IRAN
Eşfahan
Yazd
Kermān
Shīrāz
Tehran
AFGHANISTAN
Kābul
Herāt
Qandahār
HINDU KUSH
Kōh-i-Baba
Dasht-e Mārgow
Rīgestān
PAKISTAN
Peshawar
Islamabad
Rawalpindi
Quetta
Karachi
Hyderabad
Multān
Sukkur
INDIA
THAR (GREAT INDIAN DESERT)
BALUCHESTĀN
Central Makran Range
Makran Coast Range
Siahan Range
Gulf of Oman
Str. of Hormuz
Masqat (Muscat)
OMAN
UNITED ARAB EMIRATES (TRUCIAL STATES)
Dubayy
Abū Zaby
ARABIAN SEA
Tropic of Cancer
Gulf of Kutch
Rann of Kutch
Mouths of the Indus
East from Greenwich

Projection: Conical with two standard parallels

1:10 000 000

50 0 50 100 150 200 miles

50 0 50 100 150 200 250 300 km

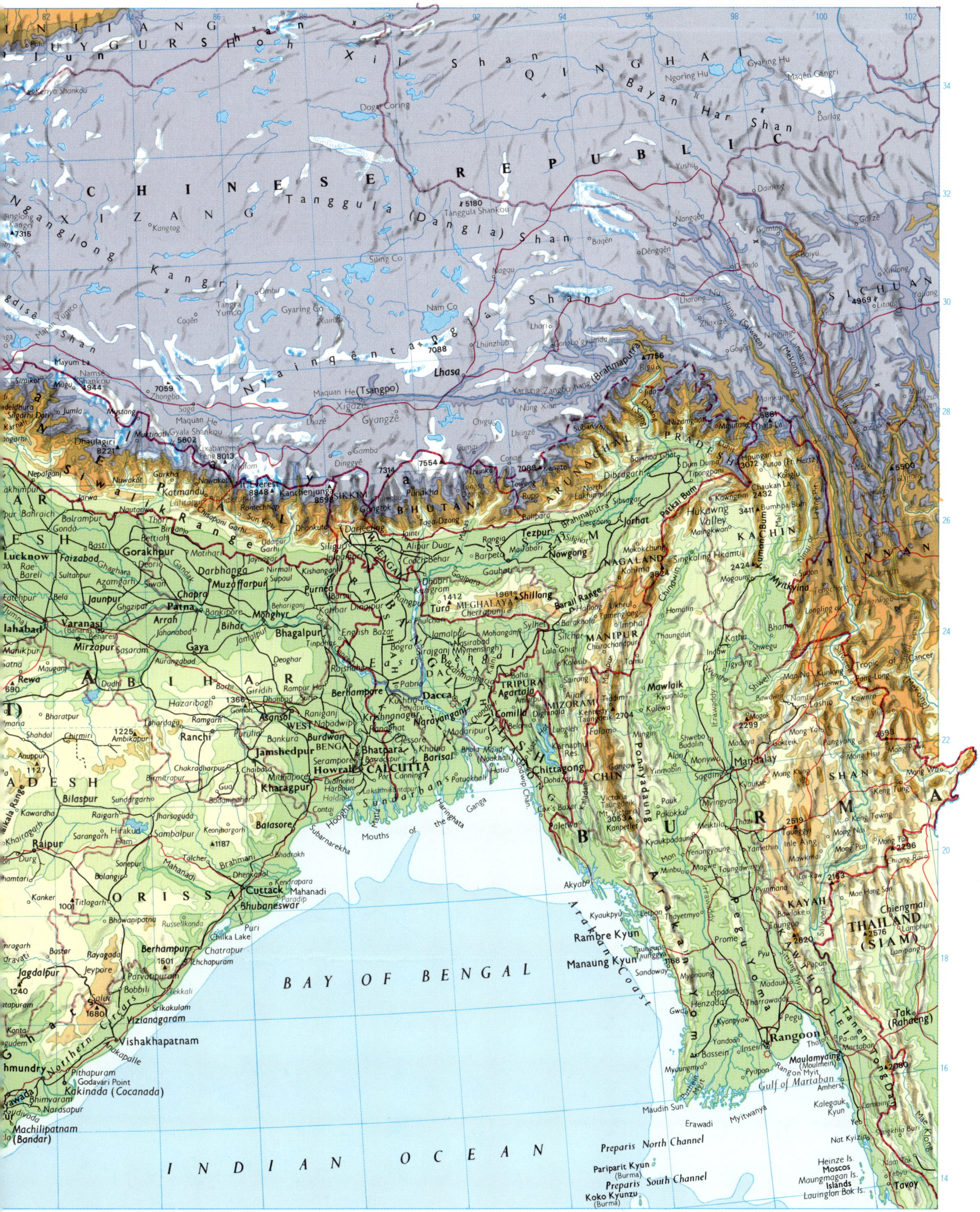

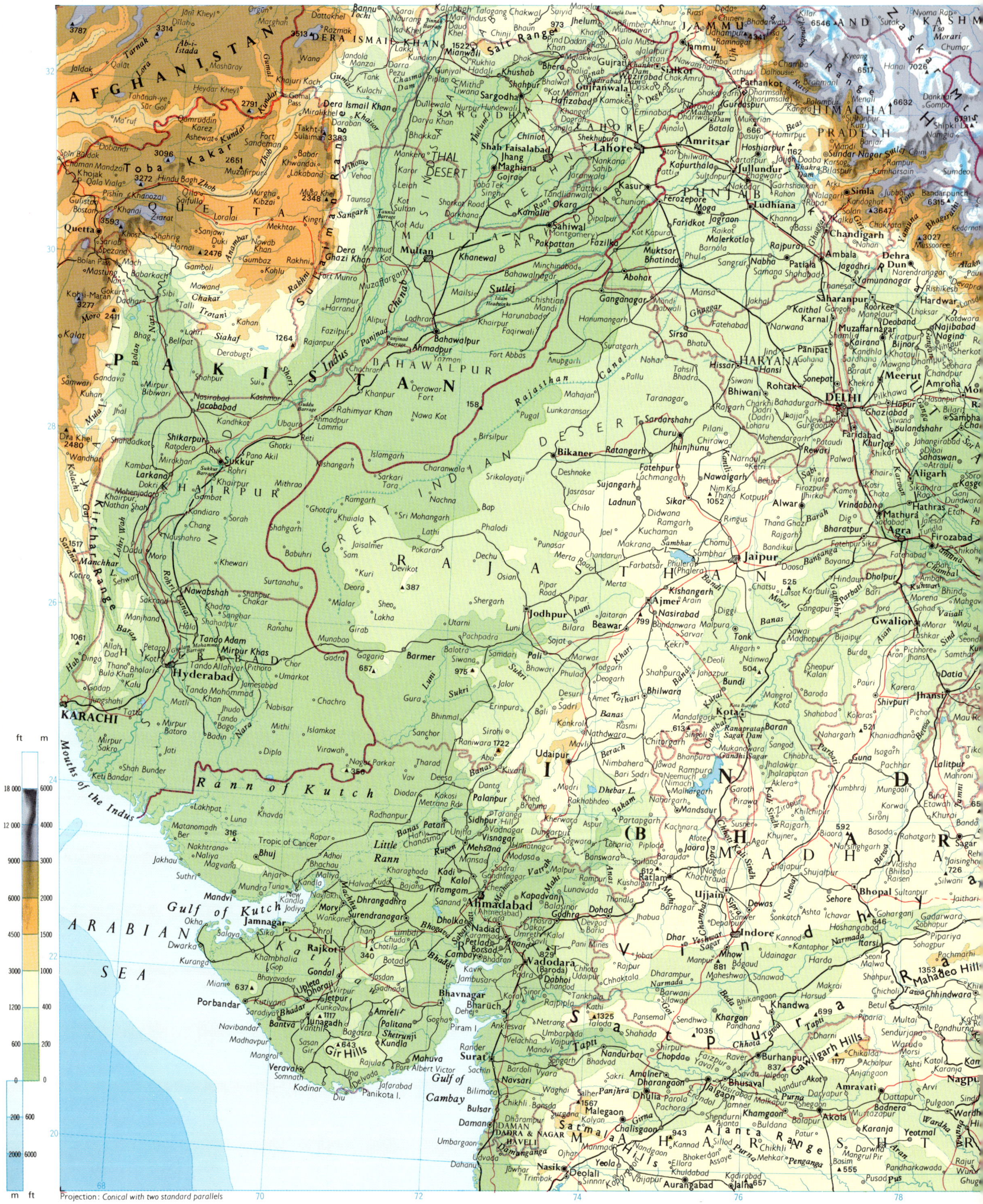
AFGHANISTAN
PAKISTAN
JAMMU AND KASHMIR
HIMACHAL PRADESH
PUNJAB
HARYANA
RAJASTHAN
MADHYA PRADESH
GUJARAT
MAHARASHTRA
UTTAR PRADESH
THAR DESERT
GREAT INDIAN DESERT
BAHAWALPUR
KHAIRPUR
QUETTA
Toba Kakar Range
Sulaiman Range
Kirthar Range
Salt Range
Aravalli Range
Satpura Range
Vindhya Range
Ajanta Range
Gir Hills
Rann of Kutch
Little Rann
Gulf of Kutch
Gulf of Cambay
ARABIAN SEA
Mouths of the Indus
Tropic of Cancer
Indus
Sutlej
Chenab
Ravi
Jhelum
Luni
Narmada
Tapti
Chambal
Yamuna
Ganga
KARACHI
Hyderabad
Sukkur
Multan
Lahore
Amritsar
Ludhiana
Chandigarh
Simla
Dehra Dun
DELHI
Agra
Gwalior
Jaipur
Ajmer
Jodhpur
Bikaner
Udaipur
Kota
Bhilwara
Ujjain
Indore
Bhopal
Ahmadabad
Vadodara (Baroda)
Surat
Rajkot
Jamnagar
Bhavnagar
Porbandar
Bhuj
Nasik
Malegaon
Dhule
Jalgaon
Aurangabad
Akola
Amravati
Dera Ismail Khan
Dera Ghazi Khan
Bahawalpur
Sargodha
Gujranwala
Sialkot
Jammu
Shah Faisalabad
Sahiwal
Jacobabad
Larkana
Kalat
Rohtak
Meerut
Saharanpur
Aligarh
Jhansi
Sagar
Ratlam
Mandsaur
Dewas
Khandwa
Burhanpur
Nagpur
DAMAN
DADRA & NAGAR HAVELI
Projection: Conical with two standard parallels
68
70
72
74
76
78
ft
m
18 000
12 000
9000
6000
4500
3000
1200
600
200
2000
400
1000
1500
2000
3000
4000
6000

1:6 000 000

50 0 50 100 150 miles

50 0 50 100 150 200 250 km

1:6 000 000

50 0 50 100 150 miles

50 0 50 100 150 200 250 km

Projection: Conical with two standard parallels

East from Greenwich

1:10 000 000
50 0 50 100 150 200 miles
50 0 100 200 300 km
CHINA
BURMA
SHAN
KAYAH
KAWTHOOLEI
THAILAND (SIAM)
LAOS
VIETNAM
CAMBODIA
INDIA
BANGLADESH
CHIN
Mandalay
Rangoon
Bassein
Akyab
Maulamyaing
Chiengmai
Luang Prabang
Vientiane
Hanoi
Haiphong
Hoa Binh
Vinh
Hué
Da Nang (Tourane)
Krung Thep (Bangkok)
Thonburi
Nakhon Ratchasima (Khorat)
Phnom Penh
Phanh Bho Ho Chi Minh (Saigon)
Can Tho
Nanning
Beihai
Hainan Dao
Gulf of Tongking
Gulf of Martaban
Gulf of Siam
ANDAMAN SEA
SOUTH CHINA SEA
Andaman Islands (India)
North Andaman
Middle Andaman
South Andaman
Little Andaman
Coco Channel
Preparis North Channel
Preparis South Channel
Duncan Passage
Ritchies Archipelago
Myeik Kyunzu (Mergui Archipelago)
Kho Khot Kra (Isthmus of Kra)
Phuket
Kota Baharu
George Town
Pulau Pinang
Kuala Lumpur
Kuala Terengganu
Kuantan
Melaka
Johor Baharu
SINGAPORE
MALAYA
SUMATERA
INDONESIA
Strait of Malacca
Kepulauan Natuna Besar
Kepulauan Anambas
Kepulauan Natuna Selatan
Kepulauan Tambelan
Côn Dao
MALAYA AND SINGAPORE
1:6 000 000
50 0 50 miles
50 0 50 km
Alor Setar
Butterworth
Ipoh
Kelang
Seremban
Kuala Kedah
Sungei Patani
Taiping
Telok Anson
KEDAH
PERAK
KELANTAN
TERENGGANU
PAHANG
SELANGOR
MELAKA
JOHOR
Projection: Conical with two standard parallels
East from Greenwich
COPYRIGHT, GEORGE PHILIP & SON, LTD.
ft m
9000 3000
6000 2000
4500 1500
3000 1000
1200 400
600 200
0 0
200 600
2000 6000

Projection: *Mercator*

East from Greenwich

1:12 500 000
100 0 100 200 300 miles
100 0 100 200 300 400 500 km
JAVA AND MADURA
1:7 500 000
50 0 50 100 150 200 miles
50 0 50 100 150 200 250 300 km
Jakarta
Bandung
Semarang
Surabaya
Madura
Yogyakarta
Surakarta
Malang
Bali
LUZON
Manila
Manila Bay
Polillo Islands
Catanduanes
Mindoro
Samar
Leyte
Cebu
Negros
Bohol
Mindanao
Zamboanga
Davao
Sulu Arch.
SULU SEA
CELEBES SEA
Mindanao Trench
10 497
9540
PACIFIC OCEAN
Yap Islands
Palau Islands
Babelthuap
Caroline Islands
(U.S. Trust Territory of the Pacific Islands)
Equator
Kepulauan Talaud
Kepulauan Sangihe
MOLUCCA SEA
Morotai
Halmahera
Ternate
Manado
Teluk Tomini
SULAWESI (CELEBES)
Kepulauan Sula
Buru
Seram (Ceram)
SERAM SEA
BANDA SEA
7440
Waigeo
Misool
Jazirah Doberai (Vogelkop)
Manokwari
Kepulauan Schouten
Yapen
Teluk Cenderawasih
IRIAN JAYA
Pegunungan Sudirman
Pegunungan Jayawijaya
Jayapura (Hollandia)
PAPUA NEW GUINEA
Merauke
Kepulauan Aru
Kepulauan Kai
Kepulauan Tanimbar
MALUKU
ARAFURA SEA
FLORES SEA
Flores
Sumba
Sawu Sea
TIMOR
NUSA TENGGARA TIMUR
Kupang
Alor
Wetar

SEA OF JAPAN
PACIFIC OCEAN
Sea of Okhotsk
SOUTH KOREA
HOKKAIDŌ
TŌHOKU
KANTŌ
CHŪBU
KINKI
CHŪGOKU
SHIKOKU
KYŪSHŪ
Oki-Shotō
Tokyo
Yokohama
Kawasaki
Nagoya
Kyōto
Ōsaka
Kōbe
Hiroshima
Kitakyūshū
Fukuoka
Sapporo
Sendai
Niigata
Nagasaki
Kagoshima
Ōsumi-Kaikyō
Tane-ga-Shima
Yaku-Shima
Tokara-Kaikyō
Nansei-Shoto
Amami-Ō-Shima
Toku-no-Shima
Tsugaru-Kaikyō
Korea-Kaikyō
Bungo-Suidō
Kii-Suidō
East from Greenwich
1:5 000 000
Projection: Conical with two standard parallels
1:10 000 000
Projection: Bonne
Continuation Southwards on same scale
ft m
9000 3000
6000 2000
4500 1500
3000 1000
1200 400
600 200
0 0
200 600
2000 6000
4000 12 000
6000 18 000
8000 24 000
m ft
REFERENCE TO PREFECTURES
HOKKAIDŌ DISTRICT
1 Hokkaidō
TŌHOKU DISTRICT
2 Aomori
3 Akita
4 Iwate
5 Yamagata
6 Miyagi
7 Fukushima
CHŪBU DISTRICT
8 Niigata
9 Ishikawa
10 Toyama
11 Fukui
12 Gifu
13 Nagano
14 Yamanashi
15 Aichi
16 Shizuoka
KANTŌ DISTRICT
17 Gumma
18 Tochigi
19 Saitama
20 Ibaraki
21 Tōkyō
22 Chiba
23 Kanagawa
KINKI DISTRICT
24 Hyogo
25 Kyōto
26 Shiga
27 Ōsaka
28 Nara
29 Mie
30 Wakayama
CHŪGOKU DISTRICT
31 Tottori
32 Okayama
33 Shimane
34 Hiroshima
35 Yamaguchi
SHIKOKU DISTRICT
36 Kagawa
37 Tokushima
38 Ehime
39 Kōchi
KYŪSHŪ DISTRICT
40 Fukuoka
41 Saga
42 Nagasaki
43 Kumamoto
44 Ōita
45 Miyazaki
46 Kagoshima

1:20 000 000

100 0 100 200 300 400 miles

100 0 100 200 300 400 500 600 km

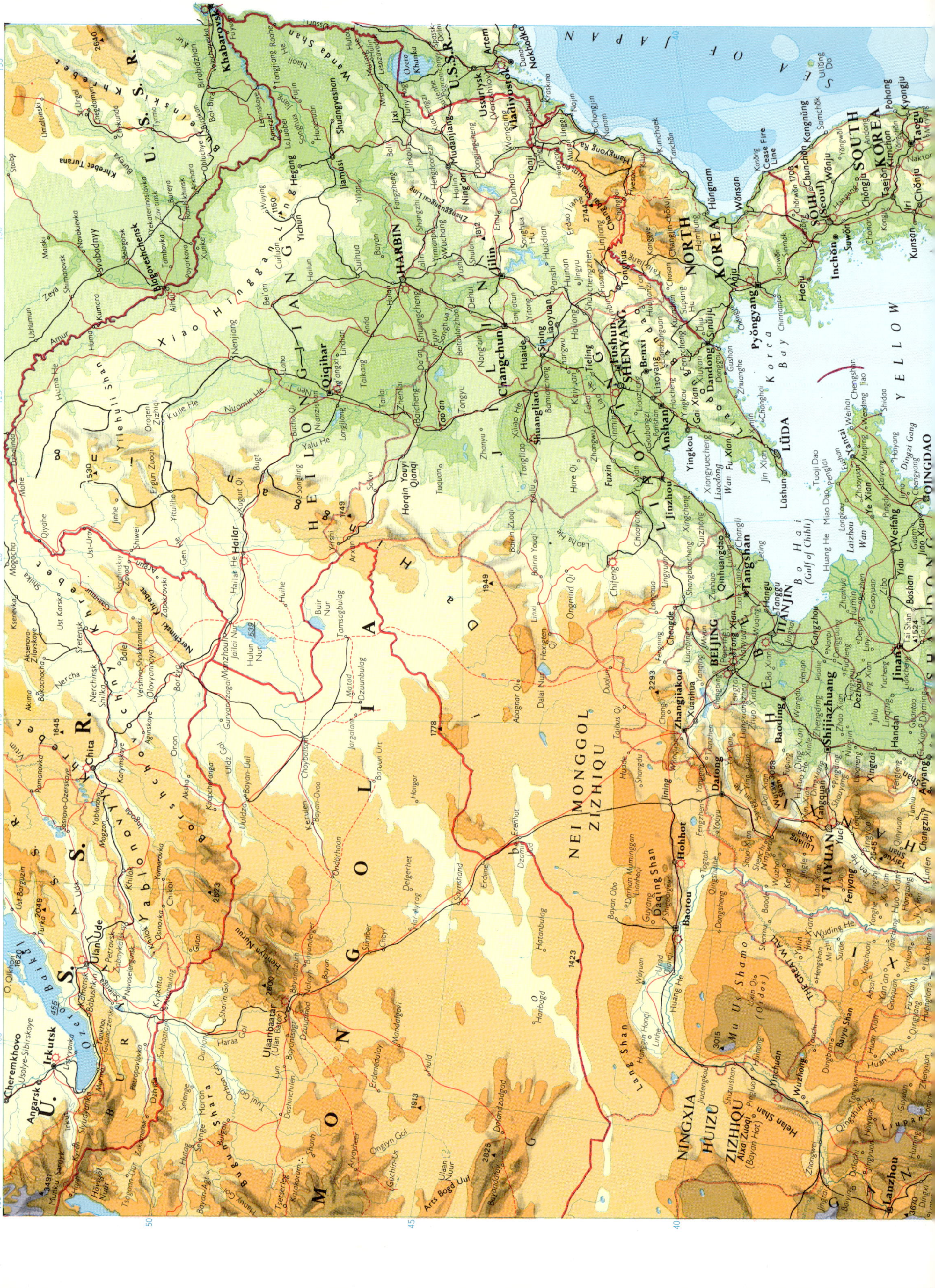
U.S.S.R.
MONGOLIA
NEI MONGGOL ZIZHIQU
HEILONGJIANG
JILIN
LIAONING
NORTH KOREA
SOUTH KOREA
SEA OF JAPAN
YELLOW
Korea Bay
Bo Hai (Gulf of Chihli)
NINGXIA HUIZU ZIZHIQU
HARBIN
Qiqihar
Changchun
SHENYANG
LÜDA
BEIJING
TIANJIN
Shijiazhuang
TAIYUAN
Hohhot
Baotou
Datong
Jinan
QINGDAO
Lanzhou
Yinchuan
Pyŏngyang
SŎUL (Seoul)
Vladivostok
Khabarovsk
Blagoveshchensk
Chita
Ulan-Ude
Irkutsk
Ulaanbaatar (Ulan Bator)
Oz. Baykal
Mu Us Shamo (Ordos)
Xiao Hinggan Ling
Da Hinggan Ling
Yablonovyy Khrebet
Lang Shan
Daqing Shan
Helan Shan
THE GREAT WALL

1:10 000 000

50 0 50 100 150 200 250 miles

50 0 50 100 150 200 250 300 350 400 km

1:40 000 000
200 0 200 400 600 800 1000 miles
200 0 200 400 600 800 1000 1200 1400 1600 km

Projection: Zenithal Equidistant. West from Greenwich 0 East from Greenwich

1:40 000 000

200 0 200 400 600 800 1000 miles

200 0 200 400 600 800 1000 1200 1400 1600 km

Projection: *Zenithal Equidistant.* West from Greenwich 0 East from Greenwich

NORTH ATLANTIC
OCEAN
SPAIN
Málaga
Almería
Cádiz
Str. of Gibraltar
Gibraltar (Br.)
Ceuta (Sp.)
Tanger
Tétouan
Melilla (Sp.)
Oran
Mostaganem
Alger (Algiers)
Tizi-Ouzou
Bejaïa
Skikda
Annaba
Constantine
Sétif
Batna
Biskra
Blida
Médéa
Larache
Kenitra (Port Lyautey)
Salé
Rabat
Casablanca
El Jadida
Settat
Khouribga
Meknès
Fes
Oujda
Tlemcen
Sidi-Bel-Abbès
Saïda
Tiaret
Djelfa
Laghouat
Béchar
Safi
Essaouira
Marrakech
Agadir
Ouarzazate
Madeira (Port.)
Funchal
Pto. Santo
Islas Canarias (Sp.)
La Palma
Tenerife
Gomera
Hierro
Gran Canaria
Las Palmas
Sta. Cruz
Lanzarote
Fuerteventura
Arrecife
Puerto del Rosario
Tarfaya (Villa Bens)
El Aaiún
Semara
Bu Craa
C. Bojador
Dakhla
Western Sahara
MOROCCO
Tindouf
Ghardaïa
Ouargla
Hassi Messaoud
Touggourt
El Oued
El Goléa
In Salah
Timimoun
Adrar
Reggane
Plateau du Tademait
ALGERIA
Ahaggar
Tamanrasset
Djanet
Illizi
Bordj Omar Driss
Tanezrouft
Adrar des Iforhas
Sahara
Chech
Erg
El Djouf
MAURITANIA
Nouâdhibou (Port Etienne)
Atâr
Chinguetti
Akjoujt
Nouakchott
Zouérate
Tidjikja
Tichit
Néma
St. Louis
Dakar
Thiès
Kaolack
SENEGAL
GAMBIA
Banjul
Ziguinchor
GUINEA-BISSAU
Bissau
Arquipélago dos Bijagós
Fouta Djalon
GUINEA
Conakry
SIERRA LEONE
Freetown
LIBERIA
Monrovia
IVORY COAST
Abidjan
Bouaké
MALI
Tombouctou
Gao
Mopti
Ségou
Bamako
Kayes
Kidal
Taoudenni
UPPER VOLTA
Ouagadougou
Bobo-Dioulasso
GHANA
Lake Volta
Kumasi
Accra
Sekondi-Takoradi
TOGO
Lomé
BENIN
Cotonou
Porto-Novo
Abeokuta
Ibadan
Lagos
Bight of Benin
NIGER
Niamey
Aïr (Azbine)
Agadez
Zinder
NIGERIA
Kano
Katsina
Zaria
Kaduna
Sokoto
Ilorin
Oshogbo
Benin City
Onitsha
Enugu
Aba
Port Harcourt
Calabar
Macias Nguema Biyoga
Douala
TUNISIA
Projection: Sanson Flamsteed's Sinusoidal
West from Greenwich
East from Greenwich

1:15 000 000

100 0 100 200 300 400 miles

100 0 100 200 300 400 500 600 km

Projection: Lambert's Equivalent Azimuthal

1:8 000 000
50 0 50 100 150 200 miles
50 0 50 100 150 200 250 300 km
MEDITERRANEAN SEA
SICILY
CATANIA
Siracusa
Caltanissetta
Agrigento
Marsala
Ragusa
C. Passero
C. Spartivento
Etna 3340
Pantelleria (Italian)
Linosa I.
Lampione I.
Lampedusa
Gozo
Valletta
MALTA
Bizerte (Binzert)
TUNIS
Menzel-Bourguiba
Halq el Oued
Kelibia
C. Bon
Nabeul
Hammamet
G. de Hammamet
Sousse
Monastir
Moknine
Kairouan
Mahdia
Sfax
Iles Kerkenna
G. de Gabès
Gabès
Djerba I.
Zarzis
Médenine
Tataouine
Ben Gardane
Bahiret el Bibane
TUNISIA
Kebili
Douz
Gafsa
Tozeur
Nefta
Chott el Fedjadj
Chott Djerid
Bejaia
Djidjelli
Skikda
Annaba
CONSTANTINE
Sétif
Batna
Biskra
Tébessa
Khenchela
Bordj bou Arreridj
El Eulma
Guelma
Souk Ahras
M'sila
Bou Saâda
Chott el Hodna
Monts du Zab
Chott Melrhir
El Meghaier
Touggourt
El Oued
Ouled Djellal
Ouargla
Hassi Messaoud
Guerrara
Grand Erg Oriental
Ghudāmis
Al Hammādah al Hamrā'
Plateau du Tinrhert
Idehan Ubari
Idehan Marzūq
Tarābulus (Tripoli)
Zuwārah
Sabrātah
Az Zāwiyah
Al 'Azīzīyah
Gharyān
Tarhūnah
Al Khums
Leptis Magna (Labdah)
Zlītan
Misrātah
Jabal Nafūsah
Nālūt
Yafran
Jādū
Mizdah
Banī Walīd
Khalīj Surt (Gulf of Sidra)
Surt
Banghāzī (Benghazi)
Ajdābiyah
Marsá Brega
Tūkrah
GHARYĀN
AL KHUMS
MISRĀTAH
SABHAH
AWBĀRĪ
BANGHĀZĪ
LIBYA
Sabhah (Sebha)
Marzūq
Brach
Wādī ash Shāṭi'
Al Jufrah
Hūn
Waddān
Jabal as Sawdā'
Al Harūj al Aswad
Zillah
Ramlat Zaltan
Tmassah
Waw al Kabīr
Al Qaṭrūn
Tropic of Cancer
ALGERIA
In Amenas
Illizi
Djanet
Tassili-n-Ajjer
Adrar 2254
Erg d'Admer
Ahaggar
Tamanrasset
Assekrem
Mt. Tahat 2918
Erg Tin Merzouga
Ghat
NIGER
Plateau du Djado
Djado
Chirfa
Séguédine
Bilma
Massif de Terazit
Ténéré
Hamada Manguéni
Toummo
Passe de Korizo
Tibesti
CHAD
Pic Toussidé 3265
Bardai
Zouar
Tarso Emissi 3150
Emi Koussi 3415
Massif 2286
Sarīr Tibasti

MAURITANIA
SENEGAL
GAMBIA
GUINEA-BISSAU
GUINEA
SIERRA LEONE
LIBERIA
IVORY COAST
Nouakchott
DAKAR
Banjul
Bissau
Conakry
Freetown
Monrovia
Bamako
Abidjan
St. Louis
Kaolack
Ziguinchor
Kayes
Ségou
Sikasso
Bobo-Dioulasso
Korhogo
Bouaké
Kankan
Labé
Mopti
Tombouctou (Timbuktu)
Akjoujt
Rosso
Kaédi
Kiffa
Néma
Oualâta
Tidjikja
Thiès
Rufisque
Tambacounda
Kédougou
Nioro du Sahel
Koulikoro
Bo
Kenema
Makeni
Buchanan
Harper
Yamoussoukro
Daloa
Man
Odienné
Grand Bassam
San-Pédro
Fouta Djalon
Archipélago dos Bijagós
Îles de Los
Grain Coast
Ivory Coast
Trarza
Tagânt
Aoukâr
Hôd
Ijâfene
El Mreyyé
Massif de l'Assaba
C. Vert
C. Palmas
C. Mount
Cape Three Points
NORTHERN
EASTERN
SOUTHERN
WESTERN
Niger
Bani
Volta Noire
Gambia
Casamance
Sassandra
Bandama
Comoé
Cavally
Sénégal
Faleme
Bafing
6363
1948
1752
1504
1537
ft
m
12 000
9000
6000
4500
3000
1200
600
4000
3000
2000
1500
1000
400
200
0
200
2000
4000
6000
600
6000
12 000
18 000
15
10
5

1:8 000 000

50 0 50 100 150 200 miles

50 0 50 100 150 200 250 300 km

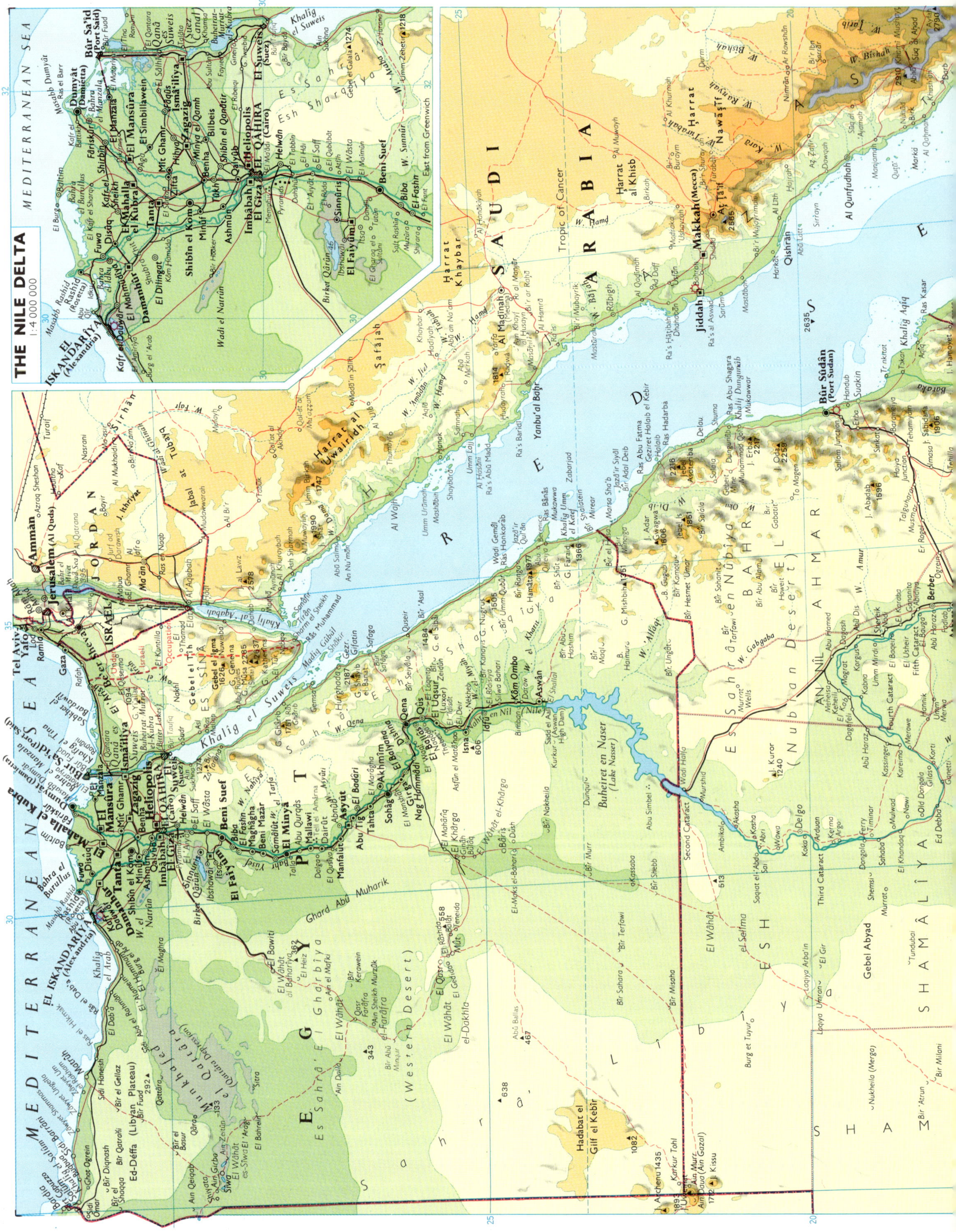
THE NILE DELTA
1:4 000 000
MEDITERRANEAN SEA
EL ISKANDARÎYA (Alexandria)
Bûr Sa'îd (Port Said)
Dumyât (Damietta)
Rashîd (Rosetta)
EL QÂHIRA (Cairo)
Heliopolis
El Gîza
El Mansûra
Tanta
Zagazig
Ismâ'iliya
El Suweis (Suez)
Beni Suef
El Faiyûm
East from Greenwich
JORDAN
Ammân
Jerusalem (Al Quds)
ISRAEL
Tel Aviv-Yafo
SAUDI ARABIA
Tropic of Cancer
Jiddah
Makkah (Mecca)
Al Madînah
RED SEA
Khalîg el Suweis
Khalîg el 'Aqaba
EGYPT
Es Sahrâ' el Gharbîya (Western Desert)
Es Sahrâ' en Nûbîya (Nubian Desert)
Buheiret en Naser (Lake Nasser)
Aswân
Luxor
Qena
Asyût
El Minya
Sohâg
Bûr Sûdân (Port Sudan)
Wadi Halfa
Second Cataract
Third Cataract
Fourth Cataract
Fifth Cataract
Berber
Gebel Abyad
Hadabat el Gilf el Kebir
El Wâhât el Khârga
El Wâhât el Dakhla
Munkhafad el Qattara (Qattara Depression)
Mersa Matruh

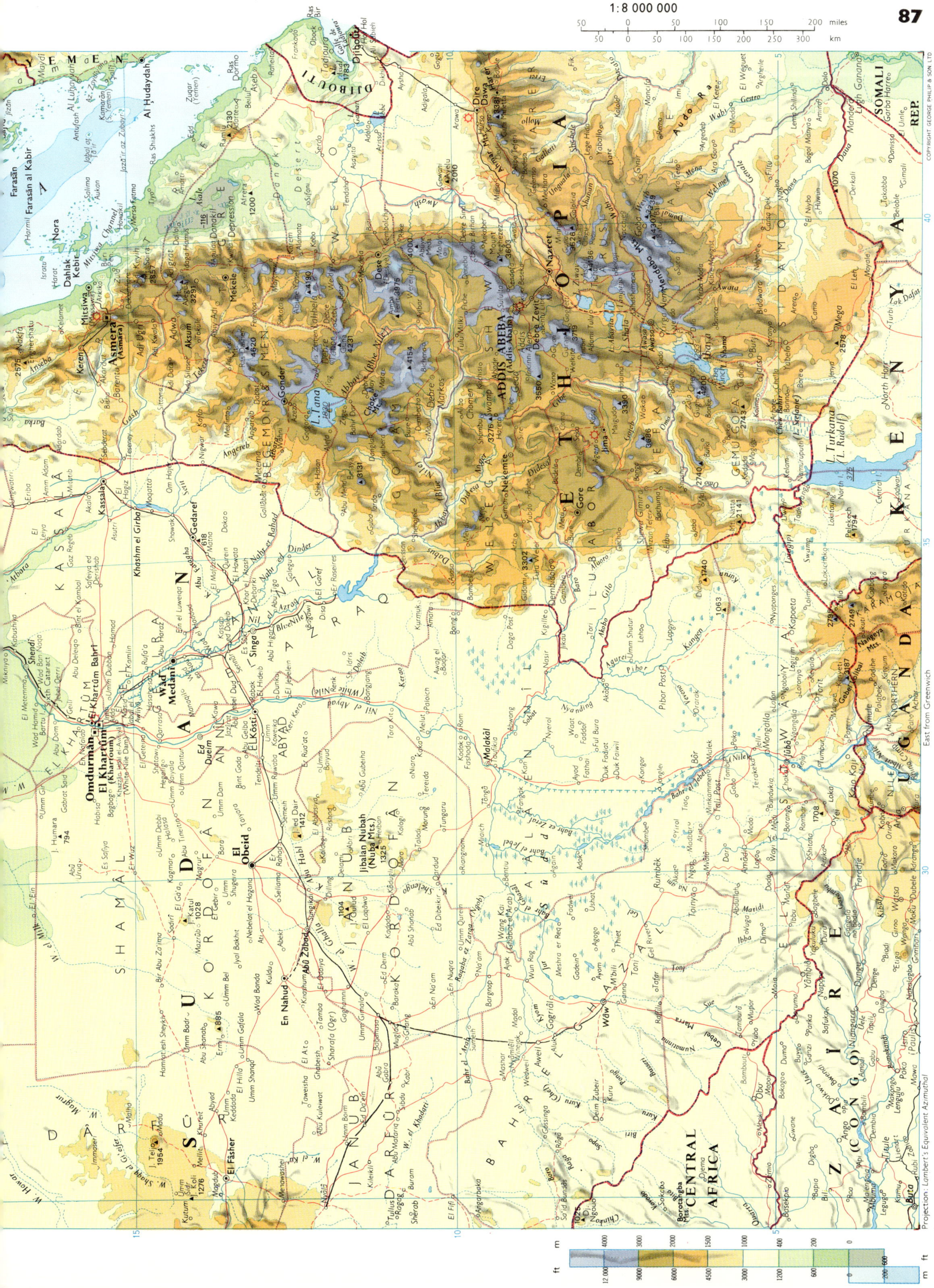
1:8 000 000
miles
km
ETHIOPIA
ADDIS ABEBA (Addis Abeba)
Asmera (Asmara)
DJIBOUTI
Djibouti
YEMEN
SOMALI REP.
KENYA
UGANDA
ZAÏRE (CONGO)
CENTRAL AFRICA
El Khartûm (Khartoum)
Omdurman
El Obeid
Kassala
Wad Medani
Gonder
L. Tana
L. Turkana (L. Rudolf)
Dire Dawa
Harer
Nazret
Mitsiwa
Wâw
En Nahud
El Fâsher
Projection: Lambert's Equivalent Azimuthal
East from Greenwich
COPYRIGHT GEORGE PHILIP & SON, LTD

ETHIOPIA
Addis Abeba
Asmera
KENYA
Nairobi
Mombasa
TANZANIA
Dar-es-Salaam
Zanzibar I.
Pemba I.
Mafia I.
UGANDA
Kampala
L. Victoria
RWANDA
BURUNDI
L. Tanganyika
SUDAN
El Khartûm
Omdurmân
Wad Medani
El Obeid
CHAD
Ndjamena
Lac Tchad
NIGER
NIGERIA
Kano
CAMEROON
Yaoundé
Douala
CENTRAL AFRICAN REPUBLIC
Bangui
ZAIRE
Kinshasa
Kisangani
Mbandaka
Kananga
Mbuji-Mayi
Kikwit
Matadi
GABON
Libreville
Port Gentil
CONGO
Brazzaville
Pointe Noire
CABINDA
EQUATORIAL GUINEA
Mbini
Luanda
Equator

1:15 000 000

100 0 100 200 300 400 miles
100 0 100 200 300 400 500 600 km

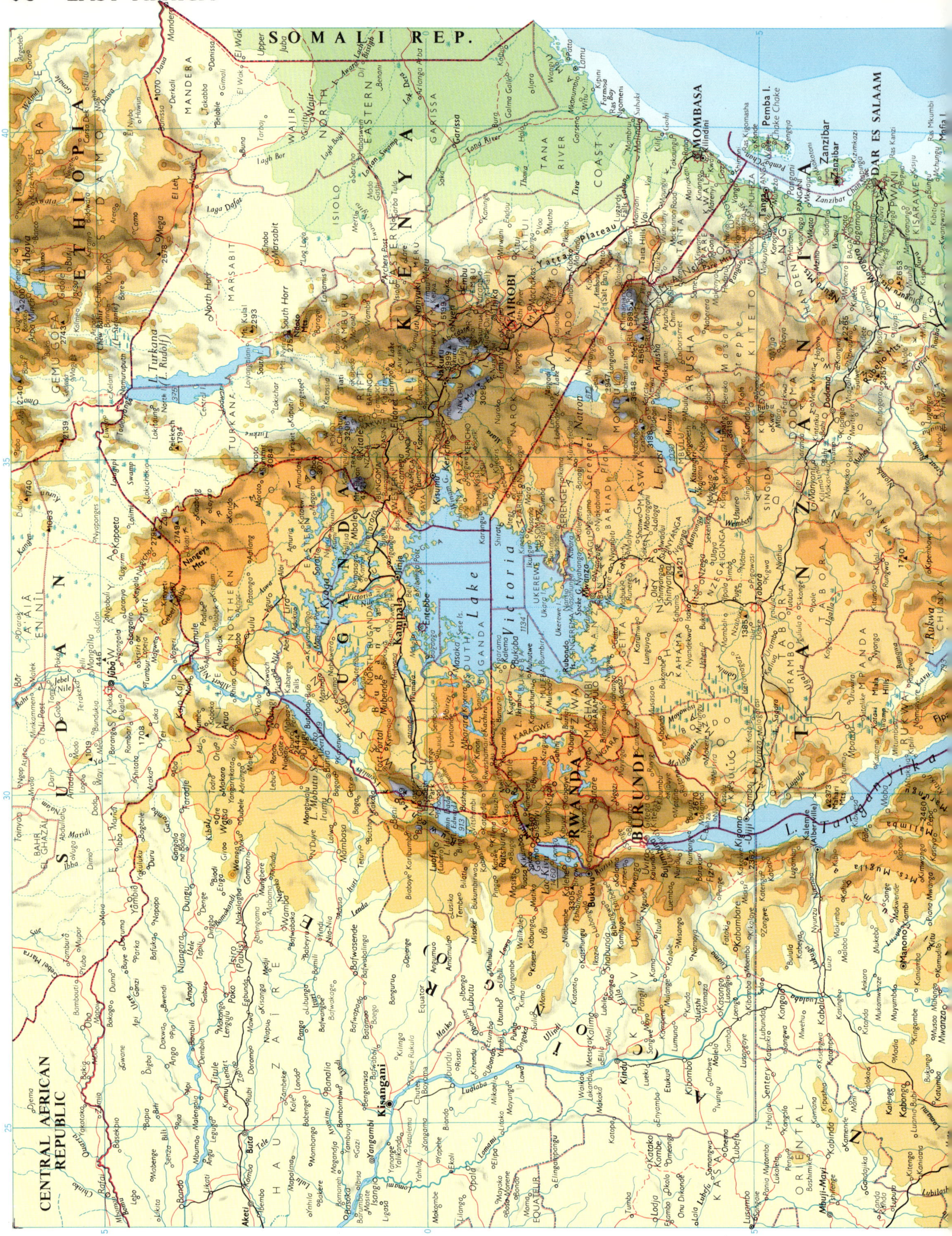
SOMALI REP.
ETHIOPIA
KENYA
UGANDA
TANZANIA
RWANDA
BURUNDI
SUDAN
ZAIRE
CENTRAL AFRICAN REPUBLIC
NAIROBI
MOMBASA
DAR ES SALAAM
Zanzibar
Pemba I.
Kampala
Kisangani
Lake Victoria
L. Turkana (L. Rudolf)
L. Tanganyika
L. Mobutu Sese Seko
L. Rukwa
Juba
Entebbe
Tanga
Bukavu

1:8 000 000

50 0 50 100 150 200 miles

50 0 100 200 300 km

Projection: Lambert's Equivalent Azimuthal

East from Greenwich

5615 Principal Shipping Routes (Distances in Nautical Miles)

Principal Air Routes

Boundaries of the artesian basins

1:12 000 000
miles
km
AUSTRALASIA
POLITICAL
1:80 000 000
INDONESIA
PAPUA NEW GUINEA
IRIAN JAYA
AUSTRALIA
WESTERN AUSTRALIA
NORTHERN TERRITORY
QUEENSLAND
SOUTH AUSTRALIA
NEW SOUTH WALES
VICTORIA
TASMANIA
NEW ZEALAND
INDIAN OCEAN
PACIFIC OCEAN
SOUTHERN OCEAN
Tasman Sea
Tropic of Capricorn
International Date Line
Perth
Adelaide
Melbourne
Canberra
Sydney
Brisbane
Hobart
Auckland
Wellington
Christchurch
Dunedin
Darwin
CORAL SEA ISLANDS TERRITORY
Coral Sea Basin
Great Barrier Reef
PACIFIC OCEAN
QUEENSLAND
NEW SOUTH WALES
VICTORIA
Gulf of Carpentaria
Cape York Peninsula
Great Dividing Range
Great Artesian Basin
Selwyn Range
Murray River Basin
Murray
Darling
Murrumbidgee
Lachlan
Flinders
Mitchell
Gilbert
Diamantina
Warrego
Thursday I.
Banks I.
Prince of Wales I.
C. York
Newcastle B.
Endeavour Str.
Groote Eylandt
Wellesley Is.
Mornington I.
Cairns
Townsville
Mackay
Rockhampton
Gladstone
Bundaberg
Maryborough
Fraser I.
Toowoomba
Gold Coast
Moreton I.
Bourke
Broken Hill
Dubbo
Newcastle
SYDNEY
Wollongong
Canberra
Albury
Bendigo
Ballarat
Geelong
MELBOURNE
Adelaide
Mt. Isa
Cloncurry
Longreach
Charleville
Roma
Mt. Kosciusko
2230
Australian Alps
Gippsland
Bass Strait
King I.
Flinders I.
Furneaux Group
TASMANIA
Launceston
Hobart
on same scale
COPYRIGHT. GEORGE PHILIP & SON. LTD

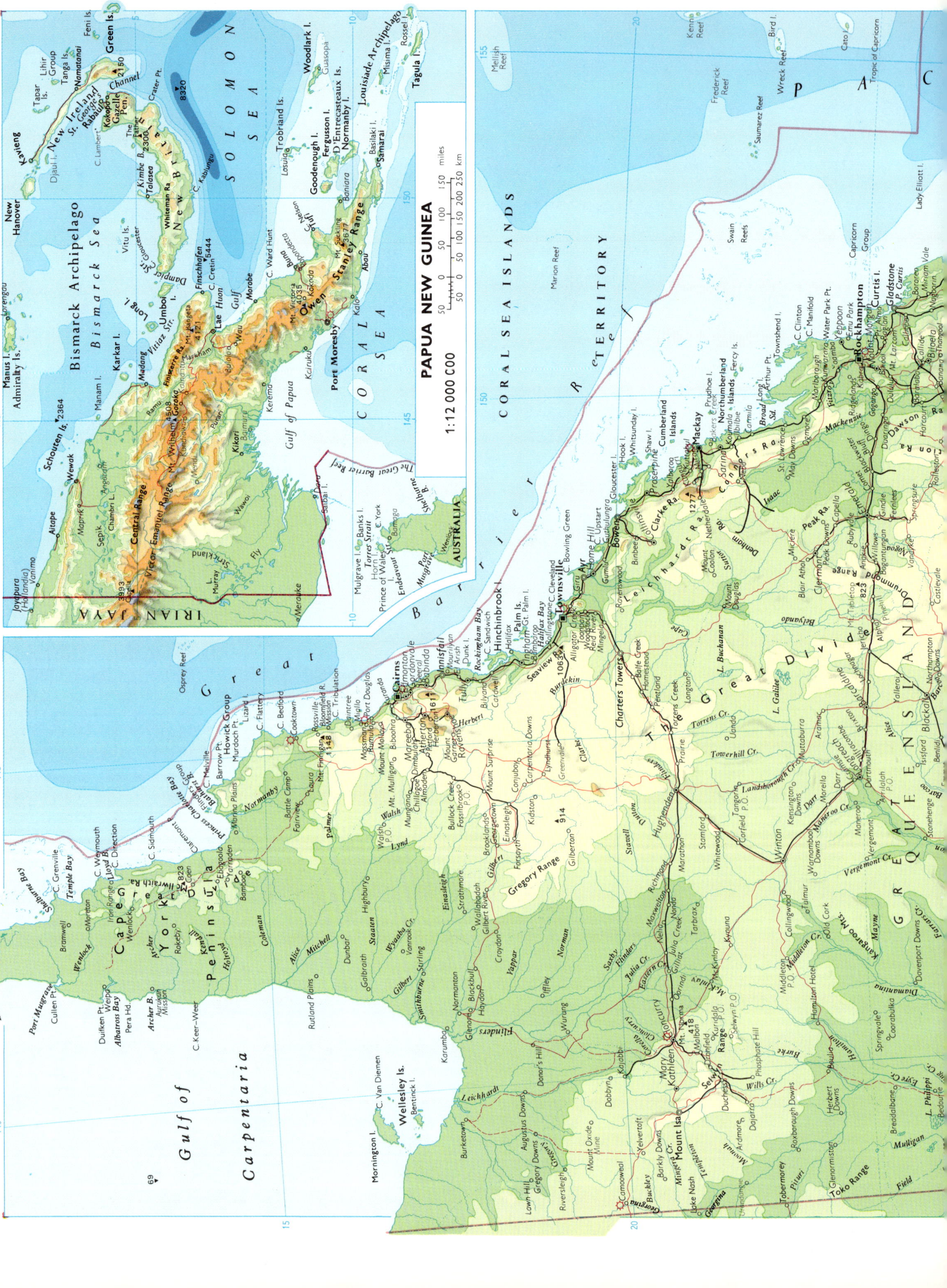

PAPUA NEW GUINEA
1:12 000 000
miles
km
Bismarck Archipelago
Bismarck Sea
SOLOMON SEA
CORAL SEA
Gulf of Papua
Port Moresby
Owen Stanley Range
Central Range
Victor Emanuel Range
New Britain
New Ireland
IRIAN JAYA
AUSTRALIA
The Great Barrier Reef
CORAL SEA ISLANDS TERRITORY
Great Barrier Reef
Gulf of Carpentaria
Cape York Peninsula
QUEENSLAND
Great Dividing Range
Cairns
Townsville
Mackay
Rockhampton
Gladstone
Mount Isa
Charters Towers
Hughenden
Winton
Cloncurry
Bowen
Cooktown
Innisfail
Hinchinbrook I.
Wellesley Is.
Mornington I.
Capricorn Group
Swain Reefs
Cumberland Islands
Northumberland Islands
Tropic of Capricorn

1:7 500 000

NEW SOUTH WALES
SOUTH AUSTRALIA
TASMANIA
Tasman Sea
Bass Strait
PACIFIC OCEAN
Great Dividing Range
SYDNEY
CANBERRA
MELBOURNE
BRISBANE
ADELAIDE
Hobart
Newcastle
Wollongong
Broken Hill
Continuation Southwards
East from Greenwich
Projection: Bonne
COPYRIGHT GEORGE PHILIP & SON, LTD

1: 4 500 000

TASMAN SEA
NEW SOUTH WALES
VICTORIA
AUSTRALIAN CAPITAL TERRITORY
SOUTH AUSTRALIA
SYDNEY
Canberra
MELBOURNE
Newcastle
Wollongong
Geelong
Ballarat
Bendigo
Albury
Wagga Wagga
Broken Hill
Mildura
Dubbo
Orange
Bathurst
Goulburn
Warrnambool
Hamilton
Horsham
East from Greenwich
Projection: Albers' Equal Area with two standard parallels
COPYRIGHT GEORGE PHILIP & SON, LTD.

1:6 000 000
20 0 20 40 60 80 100 miles
20 0 40 80 120 160 km

ARCTIC OCEAN
ATLANTIC
PACIFIC
Greenland
Greenland Sea
Iceland
Denmark Strait
Davis Strait
Baffin Bay
Baffin Island
Cumberland Sound
Frobisher Bay
Hudson Strait
Hudson Bay
James Bay
Foxe Basin
Foxe Channel
Southampton I.
Melville Pen.
Boothia Pen.
Gulf of Boothia
Ungava Peninsula
Labrador
Laurentian Plateau
Hamilton Inlet
Belle Isle Strait
Newfoundland
Gulf of St Lawrence
Nova Scotia
Bay of Fundy
Ellesmere I.
Kane Basin
Nares Str.
Axel Heiberg Land
Sverdrup Is.
Queen Elizabeth Islands
Parry Is.
Melville I.
Devon I.
Lancaster Sound
Prince of Wales I.
Victoria I.
Banks I.
M'Clure Strait
Melville Sound
Beaufort Sea
Mackenzie Mts.
Great Bear L.
Great Slave L.
Athabasca
Reindeer L.
Churchill
Nelson
Lake Winnipeg
Winnipeg
Regina
Edmonton
Calgary
Selkirk Mts
Rocky Mountains
Great Plains
Coast Mountains
Alexander Archipelago
Queen Charlotte Islands
Queen Charlotte Sound
Vancouver I.
Juan de Fuca Strait
Vancouver
Seattle
Portland
Coast Range
Sierra Nevada
Great Basin
Great Salt Lake
Wasatch Mountains
Colorado Plateau
Grand Canyon
Death Valley
Los Angeles
San Francisco
Sacramento
Denver
Llano Estacado
Dallas
Ozark Plateau
Kansas City
St Louis
Memphis
Minneapolis
Chicago
Detroit
Toronto
L. Superior
L. Michigan
L. Huron
L. Erie
L. Ontario
Niagara Falls
Hamilton
Ottawa
Montreal
Quebec
Appalachian Mts
Allegheny Mts
Cumberland Plateau
Blue Ridge
Atlanta
Washington
Philadelphia
New York
Chesapeake Bay
C. Hatteras
Bermuda
Alaska
Alaska Range
Mt. McKinley 6194
Brooks Range
Yukon
Gulf of Alaska
Alaska Pen.
Kodiak I.
Bering Strait
Bering Sea
St. Lawrence I.
Nunivak I.
Wrangel I.
C. Barrow
Aleutian Islands
Asia
Mendocino Seascarp
Murray Seascarp

1:30 000 000

100 0 100 200 300 400 500 600 700 miles

100 0 200 400 600 800 1000 km

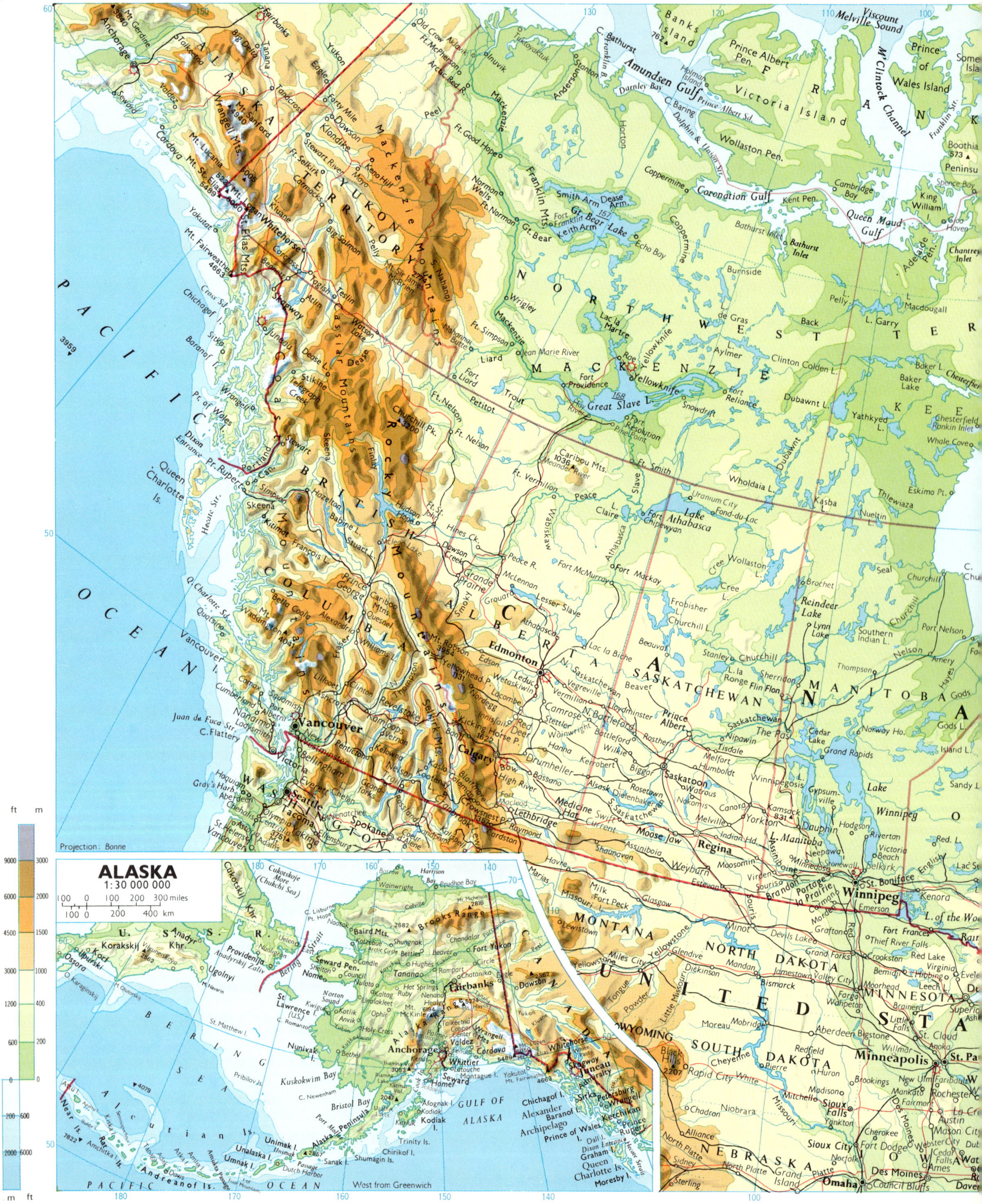
PACIFIC OCEAN
ALASKA
YUKON TERRITORY
NORTHWEST TERRITORIES
MACKENZIE
BRITISH COLUMBIA
ALBERTA
SASKATCHEWAN
MANITOBA
WASHINGTON
MONTANA
NORTH DAKOTA
SOUTH DAKOTA
WYOMING
NEBRASKA
MINNESOTA
UNITED STATES
Mackenzie Mountains
Rocky Mountains
Coast Mountains
Cassiar Mountains
Banks Island
Victoria Island
Prince of Wales Island
Amundsen Gulf
Coronation Gulf
Queen Maud Gulf
Viscount Melville Sound
M'Clintock Channel
Great Bear Lake
Great Slave L.
Lake Athabasca
Reindeer Lake
Lake Winnipeg
Queen Charlotte Is.
Vancouver
Victoria
Seattle
Spokane
Edmonton
Calgary
Regina
Saskatoon
Winnipeg
Minneapolis
Fairbanks
Anchorage
Whitehorse
Yellowknife
Juneau
Prince Rupert
Prince George
Kamloops
Lethbridge
Medicine Hat
Moose Jaw
Brandon
Bismarck
Omaha
Des Moines
Sioux Falls
Mt. Robson 3954
Mt. Logan 6050
Mt. Fairweather 4663
Projection: Bonne
ALASKA
1:30 000 000
100 0 100 200 300 miles
100 0 200 400 km
Brooks Range
BERING SEA
Bering Str.
Aleutian Is.
GULF OF ALASKA
Kodiak I.
Alaska Peninsula
Bristol Bay
Nome
Kuskokwim Bay
Fort Yukon
Dawson
Valdez
Seward
West from Greenwich
ft m
9000 3000
6000 2000
4500 1500
3000 1000
1200 400
600 200
0 0
200 600
2000 6000
m ft

1:15 000 000

100 50 0 100 200 300 400 miles

100 0 100 200 300 400 500 600 km

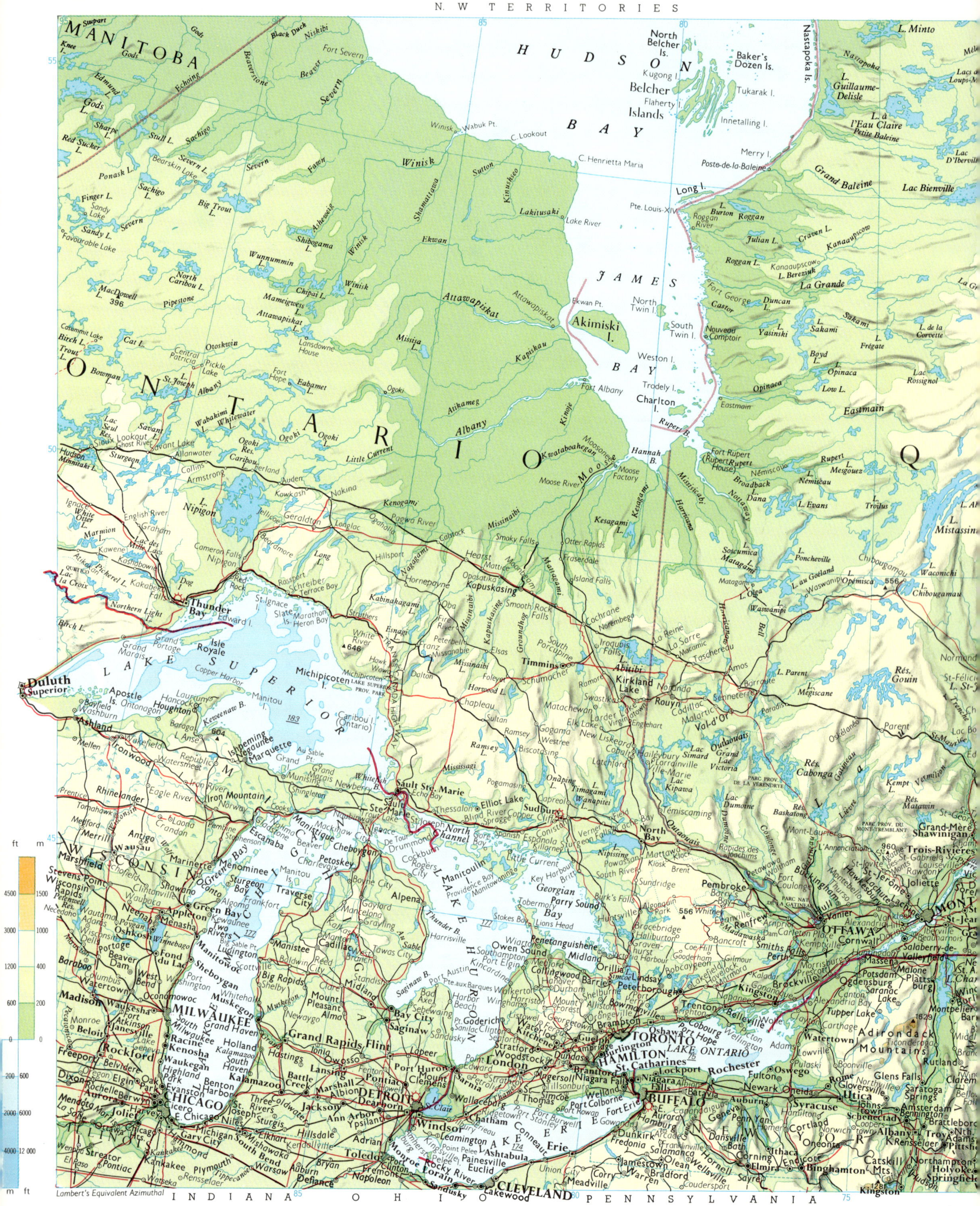
N. W TERRITORIES
HUDSON BAY
JAMES BAY
MANITOBA
ONTARIO
Q
North Belcher Is.
Belcher Islands
Baker's Dozen Is.
Akimiski I.
Charlton I.
C. Henrietta Maria
Long I.
Winisk
Attawapiskat
Albany
Moosonee
Moose Factory
Fort Severn
Big Trout L.
Lake Nipigon
Thunder Bay
LAKE SUPERIOR
Isle Royale
Duluth
Superior
Sault Ste. Marie
Marquette
Michipicoten
Kapuskasing
Timmins
Kirkland Lake
Rouyn
Val-d'Or
Sudbury
North Bay
Elliot Lake
LAKE HURON
Georgian Bay
Manitoulin I.
LAKE MICHIGAN
WISCONSIN
Green Bay
MILWAUKEE
CHICAGO
Madison
Rockford
Gary
Grand Rapids
Lansing
Flint
Saginaw
DETROIT
Windsor
Toledo
LAKE ERIE
CLEVELAND
Erie
London
HAMILTON
TORONTO
LAKE ONTARIO
St. Catharines
BUFFALO
Rochester
Syracuse
Kingston
Pembroke
OTTAWA
Cornwall
Trois-Rivières
Chibougamau
Mistassini
Rés. Gouin
Adirondack Mountains
Utica
Albany
Binghamton
Catskill Mts.
INDIANA
OHIO
PENNSYLVANIA
Lambert's Equivalent Azimuthal
ft
m

1:7 000 000

50 0 50 100 150 200 miles
50 0 50 100 150 200 250 300 km

YUKON TERRITORY
NORTHWEST TERRITORIES
BRITISH COLUMBIA
ALBERTA
ALASKA
WASHINGTON
IDAHO
PACIFIC OCEAN
QUEEN CHARLOTTE ISLANDS
VANCOUVER ISLAND
GREAT SLAVE LAKE
Yellowknife
Whitehorse
Fort Nelson
Fort St. John
Dawson Creek
Grande Prairie
Prince Rupert
Prince George
Kamloops
Vernon
Kelowna
Penticton
VANCOUVER
Victoria
SEATTLE
Bellingham
EDMONTON
Red Deer
Calgary
Lethbridge
Medicine Hat
Peace River
Hay River
Fort Simpson
Fort Providence
Fort Resolution
Fort Smith
Kitimat
Williams Lake
Quesnel
Nelson
Cranbrook
Kimberley
Revelstoke
Banff
Jasper
Coast Mountains
Skeena Mountains
Cariboo Mountains
Selkirk Mountains
Rocky Mountains
Mackenzie
Liard
Peace
Fraser
Mt. Robson 3954
Horn Mts.
Caribou Mts.
Birch Mountains
Buffalo Head Hills
Projection: Lambert's Equivalent Azimuthal
West from Greenwich
ft m
12 000 4000
9000 3000
6000 2000
4500 1500
3000 1000
1200 400
600 200
0 0
200 600
2000 6000
m ft

1:7 000 000

50 0 50 100 150 200 miles

50 0 50 100 150 200 250 300 km

Projection: Albers' Equal Area with two standard parallels

West from Greenwich

1:12 000 000

50 0 50 100 150 200 250 300 miles

50 0 50 100 150 200 250 300 350 400 450 km

Interstate Highways (U.S.A.), Superhighways (Canada)

Interstate Highways and Superhighways under Construction

1:2 500 000

10 0 10 20 30 40 50 60 miles

10 0 10 20 30 40 50 60 70 80 90 km

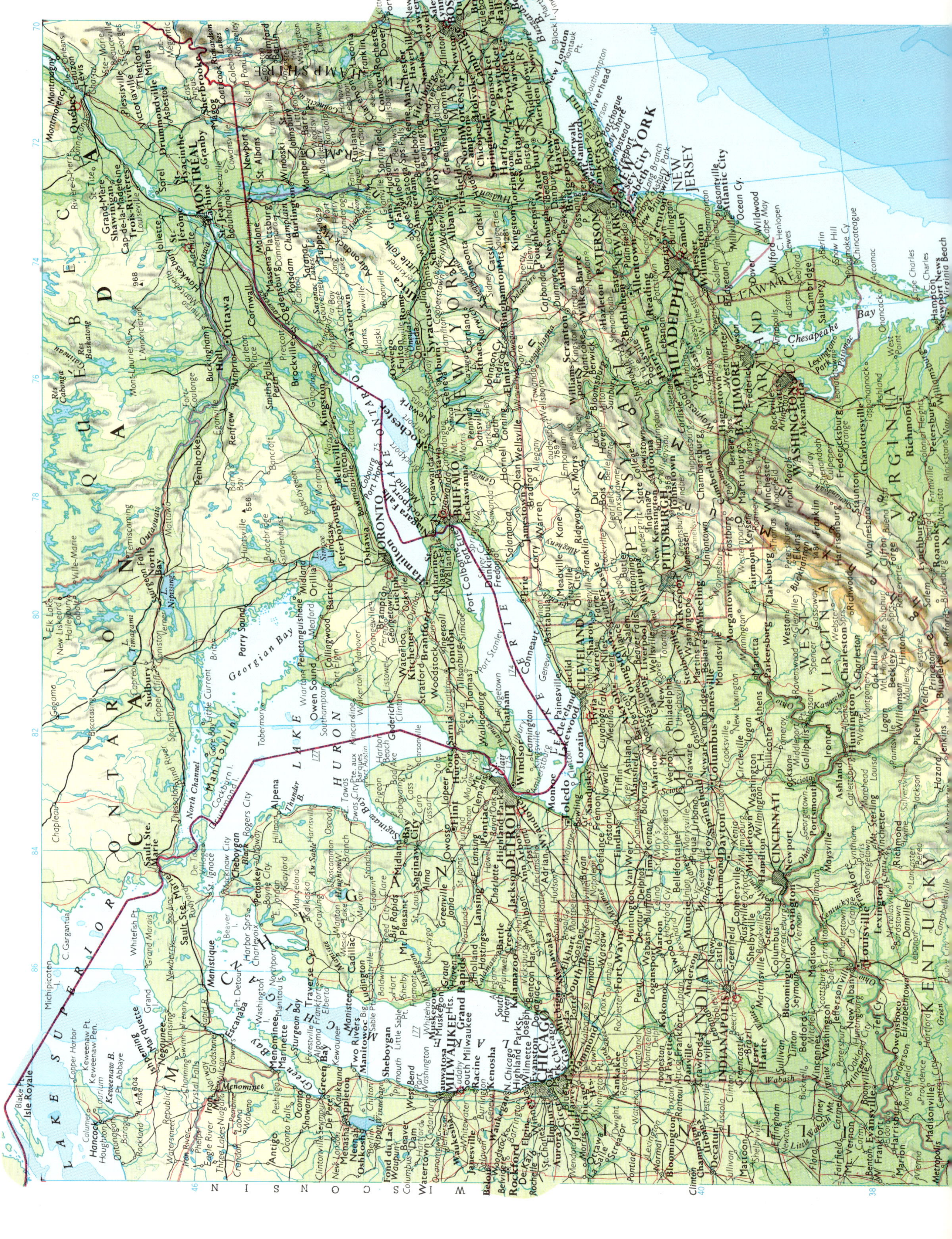
LAKE SUPERIOR
LAKE MICHIGAN
LAKE HURON
Georgian Bay
LAKE ERIE
LAKE ONTARIO
ONTARIO
QUEBEC
WISCONSIN
MICHIGAN
ILLINOIS
INDIANA
OHIO
KENTUCKY
WEST VIRGINIA
VIRGINIA
PENNSYLVANIA
NEW YORK
NEW JERSEY
MARYLAND
DELAWARE
Chesapeake Bay
CHICAGO
MILWAUKEE
DETROIT
TORONTO
BUFFALO
CLEVELAND
PITTSBURGH
CINCINNATI
INDIANAPOLIS
PHILADELPHIA
BALTIMORE
WASHINGTON D.C.
NEW YORK
BOSTON
MONTREAL
Ottawa
Quebec

1:6 000 000

50 0 50 100 miles
50 0 50 100 150 km

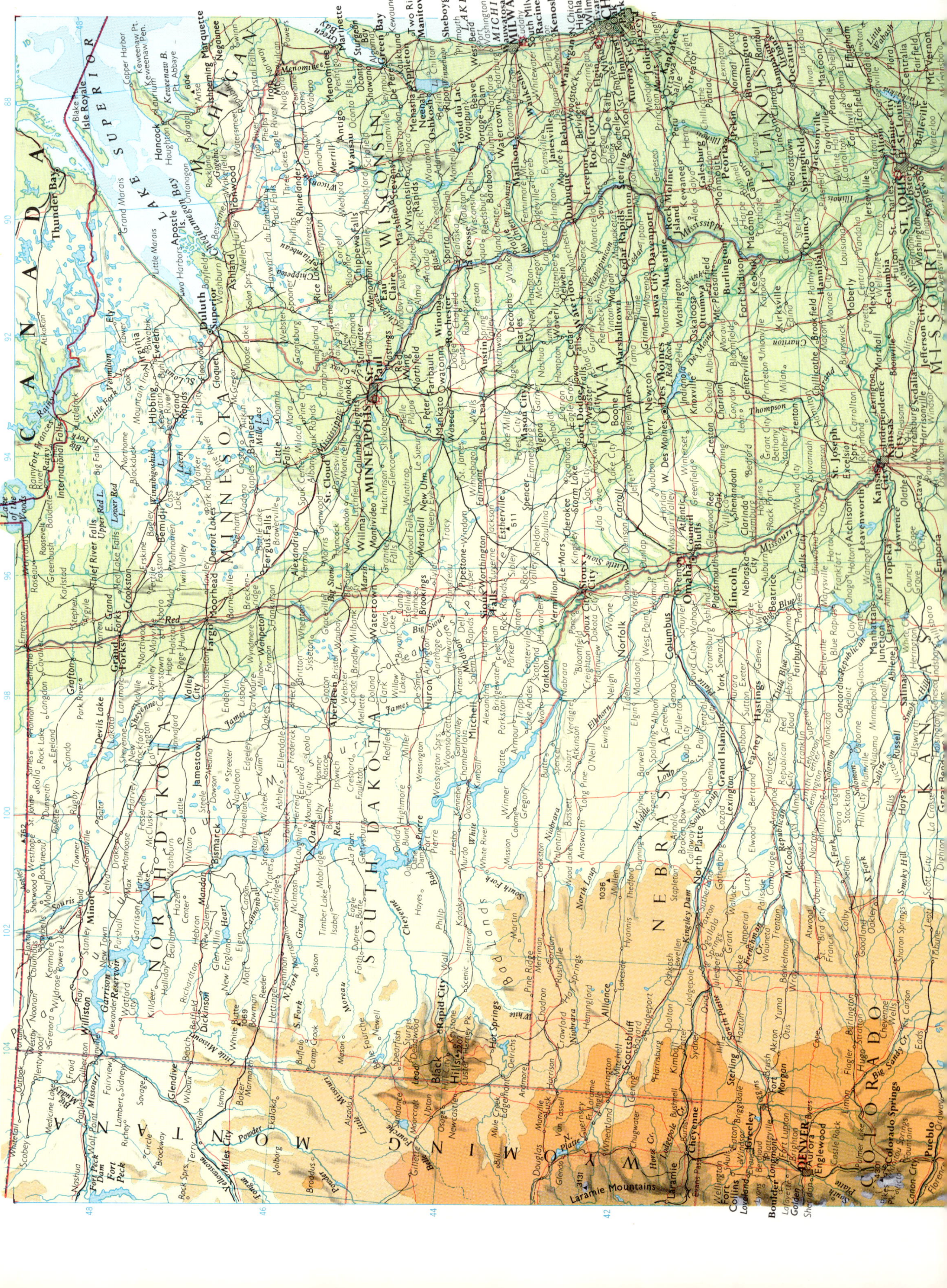
CANADA
LAKE SUPERIOR
MICHIGAN
LAKE MICHIGAN
WISCONSIN
MINNESOTA
NORTH DAKOTA
SOUTH DAKOTA
IOWA
ILLINOIS
MISSOURI
NEBRASKA
KANSAS
COLORADO
WYOMING
MONTANA
CHICAGO
MILWAUKEE
MINNEAPOLIS
ST. LOUIS
DENVER
Laramie Mountains
Bad Lands

1:6 000 000

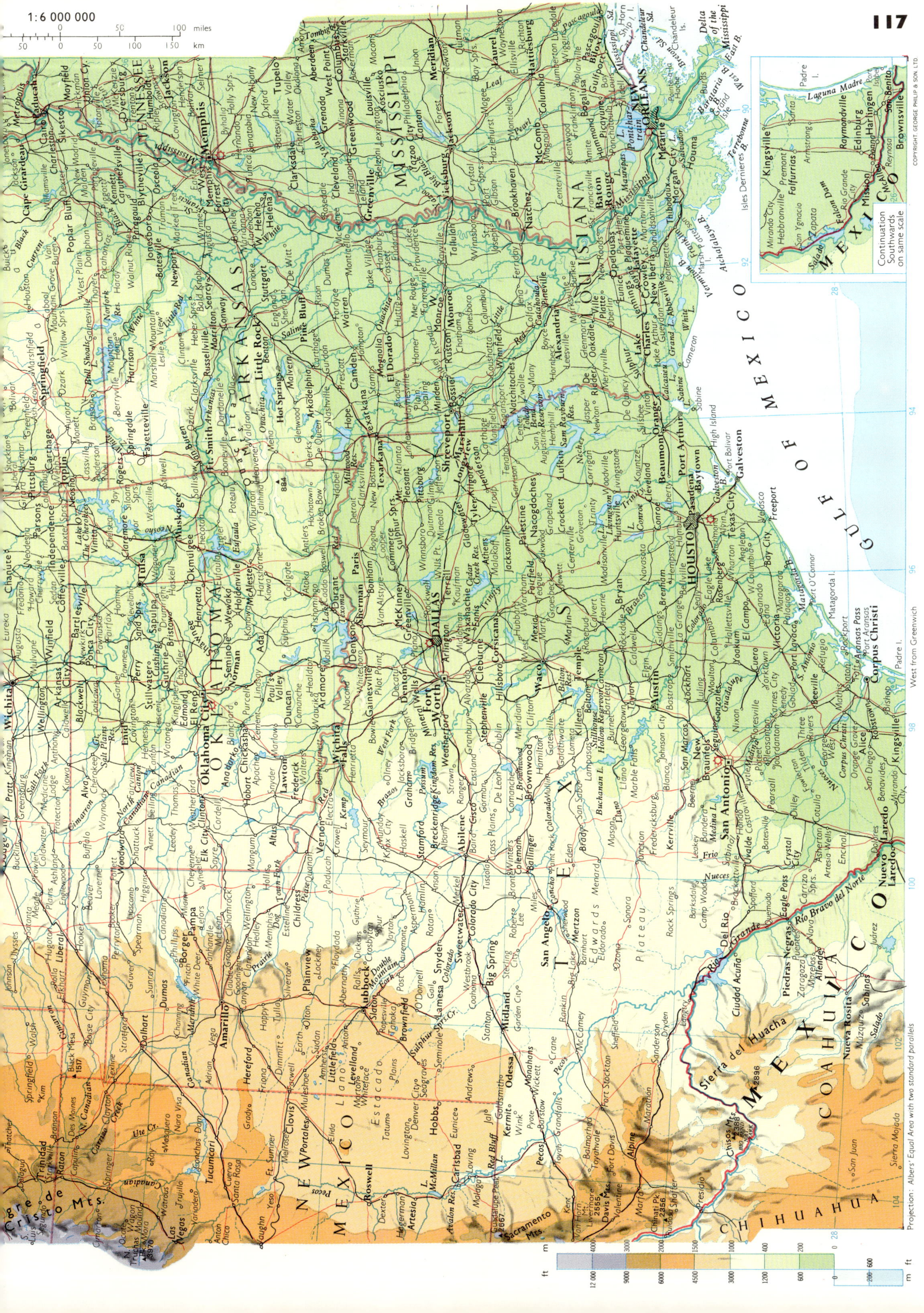

OKLAHOMA
ARKANSAS
MISSISSIPPI
LOUISIANA
TEXAS
NEW MEXICO
MEXICO
COAHUILA
CHIHUAHUA
GULF OF MEXICO
Dallas
Fort Worth
Houston
San Antonio
New Orleans
Oklahoma City
Tulsa
Little Rock
Memphis
Shreveport
Baton Rouge
Jackson
Austin
Corpus Christi
Galveston
Amarillo
Lubbock
Wichita
Springfield
Sierra del Huacha
Sacramento Mts.
Sangre de Cristo Mts.
Llano Estacado
Edwards Plateau
Rio Bravo del Norte
Rio Grande
Mississippi
Continuation Southwards on same scale
West from Greenwich
Projection: Albers' Equal Area with two standard parallels
COPYRIGHT GEORGE PHILIP & SON, LTD

1:6 000 000

50 0 50 100 miles

50 0 50 100 150 km

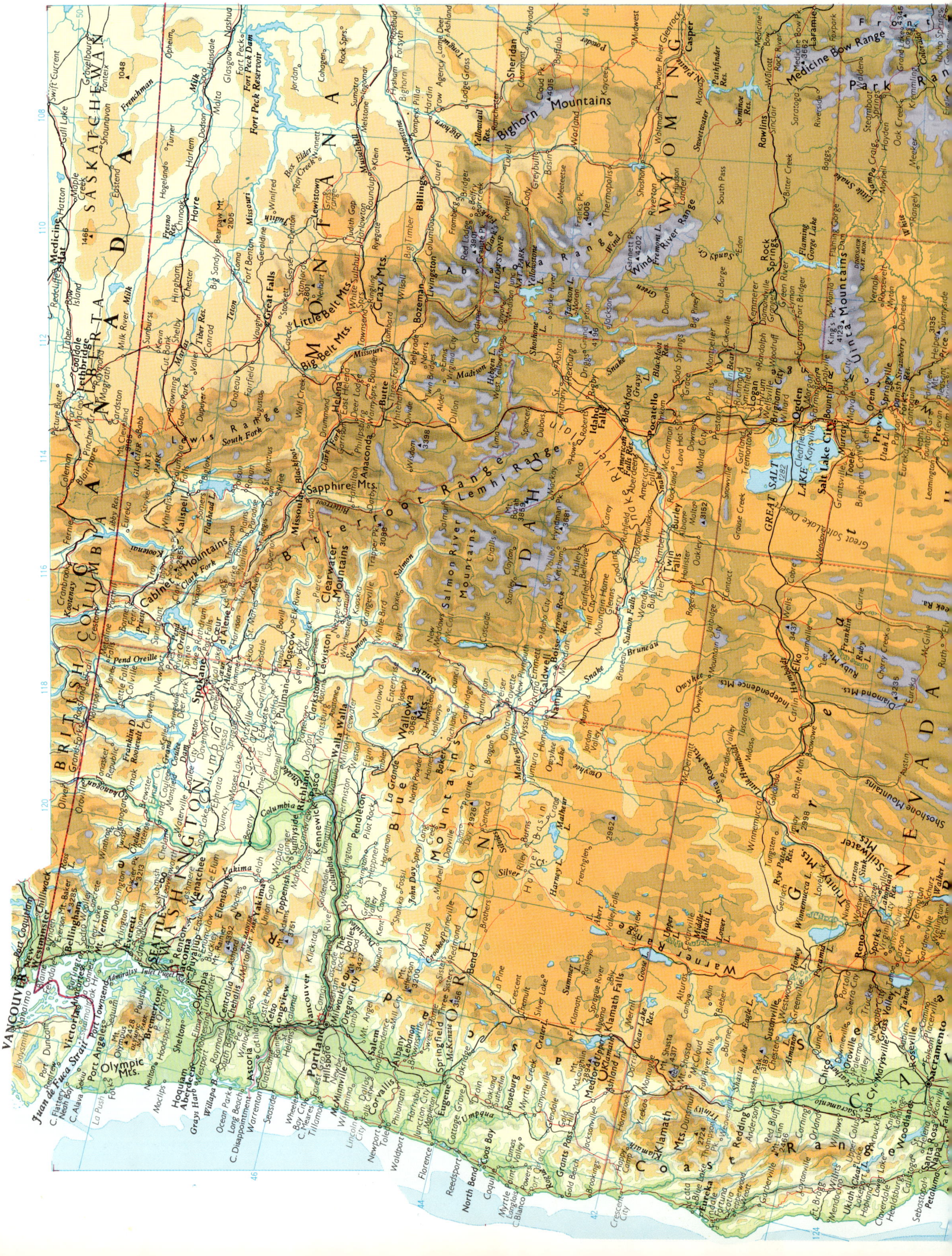

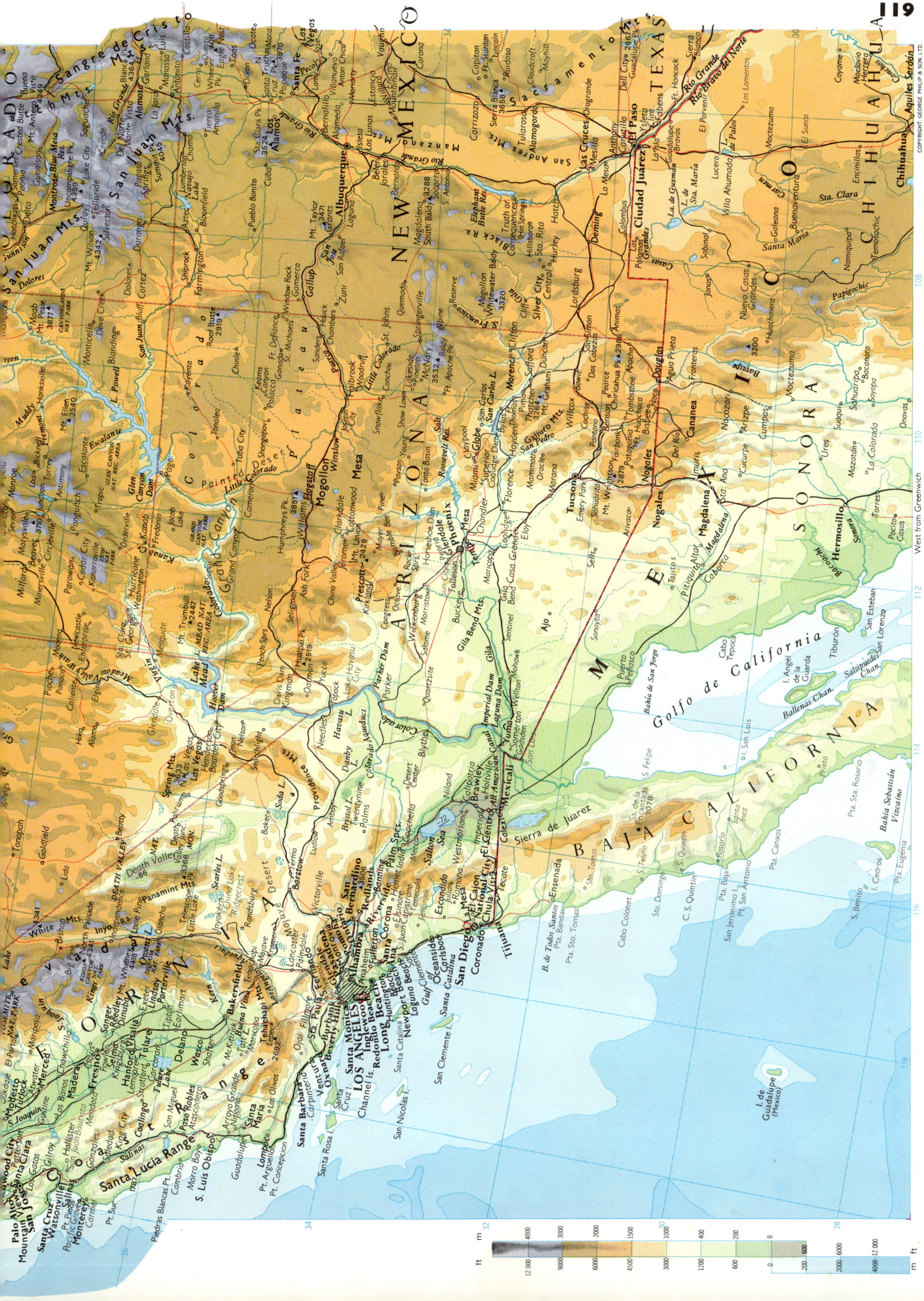
NEW MEXICO
ARIZONA
TEXAS
CHIHUAHUA
SONORA
BAJA CALIFORNIA
MEXICO
COLORADO
Golfo de California
Colorado Plateau
Grand Canyon
Albuquerque
Santa Fe
El Paso
Ciudad Juárez
Tucson
Phoenix
Hermosillo
Chihuahua
LOS ANGELES
San Diego
Tijuana
Mexicali
Bakersfield
Fresno
Las Vegas
Sierra de Juarez
San Juan Mts.
Sangre de Cristo Mts.
Sacramento Mts.
Death Valley
Mojave Desert
Santa Lucia Range
I. de Guadalupe (Mexico)
Isla Angel de la Guarda
Tiburón
West from Greenwich
COPYRIGHT, GEORGE PHILIP & SON, LTD
m
ft

1:12 000 000

100 0 100 200 miles

100 0 100 200 300 km

m	ft
4000	12 000
3000	9000
2000	6000
1500	4500
1000	3000
400	1200
200	600
0	0
200	600
2000	6000
4000	12 000

1:12 000 000

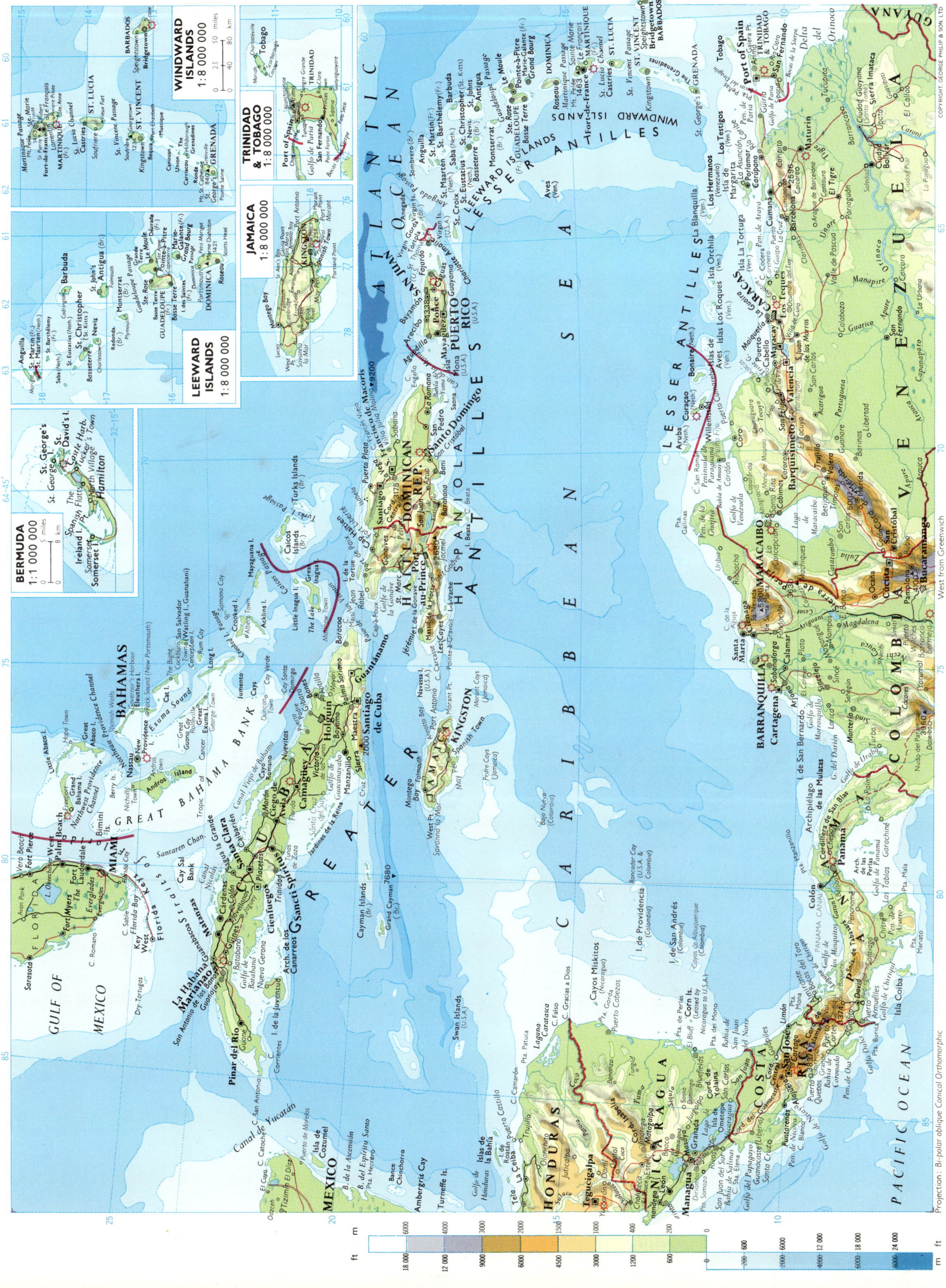
100 0 100 200 miles
100 0 100 200 300 km
BERMUDA 1:1 000 000
LEEWARD ISLANDS 1:8 000 000
WINDWARD ISLANDS 1:8 000 000
JAMAICA 1:8 000 000
TRINIDAD & TOBAGO 1:8 000 000
ATLANTIC OCEAN
CARIBBEAN SEA
PACIFIC OCEAN
GULF OF MEXICO
GREATER ANTILLES
LESSER ANTILLES
LEEWARD ISLANDS
WINDWARD ISLANDS
BAHAMAS
GREAT BAHAMA BANK
CUBA
JAMAICA
HAITI
DOMINICAN REP.
HISPANIOLA
PUERTO RICO
VENEZUELA
COLOMBIA
PANAMA
COSTA RICA
NICARAGUA
HONDURAS
MEXICO
La Habana
Santiago de Cuba
KINGSTON
Port-au-Prince
Santo Domingo
SAN JUAN
CARACAS
MARACAIBO
BARRANQUILLA
Port of Spain
Panama
Managua
San José
Tegucigalpa
MIAMI
Nassau
Projection: Bi-polar oblique Conical Orthomorphic
West from Greenwich
COPYRIGHT GEORGE PHILIP & SON LTD.
m 6000 4000 3000 2000 1500 1000 400 200 0
ft 18 000 12 000 9000 6000 4500 3000 1200 600 0
200 2000 4000 6000 8000 m
600 6000 12 000 18 000 24 000 ft

1:30 000 000

100 0 100 200 300 400 500 miles
100 0 200 400 600 800 km

Projection: Lambert's Equivalent Azimuthal

1:30 000 000

100 0 100 200 300 400 500 miles

100 0 200 400 600 800 km

Projection: *Lambert's Equivalent Azimuthal*

Projection: Lambert's Equivalent Azimuthal

1:8 000 000
50 0 50 100 150 miles
50 0 50 100 150 200 km
BELO HORIZONTE
Lima
Itabirito
Vitória
Vila Velha
Guarapari
Cachoeiro de Itapemirim
CAMPOS
Cabo de São Tomé
Macaé
Cabo Frio
NITERÓI
RIO DE JANEIRO
SÃO GONÇALO
DUQUE DE CAXIAS
Nova Iguaçu
Petrópolis
Nova Friburgo
RIO DE JANEIRO
Juiz de Fora
Barbacena
São João del Rei
Congonhas
Cons. Lafaiete
Ouro Prêto
Ponte Nova
Ubá
Muriaé
Leopoldina
Itaperuna
Guarus
Volta Redonda
Barra do Pirai
Barra Mansa
Taubaté
S. J. dos Campos
Jacareí
Mogi das Cruzes
SANTO ANDRÉ
SÃO PAULO
SANTOS
São Vicente
Guarujá
Ilha de São Sebastião
Angra dos Reis
Ilha Grande
Tropic of Capricorn
Três Lagoas
Andradina
Araçatuba
Birigui
Mirassol
S. José do Rio Prêto
Catanduva
Olímpia
Bebedouro
Ribeirão Prêto
Franca
Passos
Jaboticabal
Araraquara
São Carlos
Rio Claro
Limeira
Piracicaba
CAMPINAS
Americana
Jundiaí
Sorocaba
Itu
Bauru
Marília
Presidente Prudente
Lins
Penápolis
Tupã
Assis
Ourinhos
Avaré
Botucatu
Tatuí
Itapetininga
Poços de Caldas
Pouso Alegre
Varginha
Três Corações
Lavras
Itajubá
Guaxupé
Alfenas
SÃO PAULO
Três Pontas
Três Rios
MATO GROSSO DO SUL
Ponta Porã
Pedro Juan Caballero
Dourados
Paranavaí
Londrina
Maringá
Apucarana
Arapongas
Cornélio Procópio
Cianorte
Cruzeiro do Oeste
Guaíra
PARANÁ
BRAZIL
Cascavel
Ponta Grossa
Castro
Guarapuava
Irati
CURITIBA
Paranaguá
Antonina
Iguape
Ilha Comprida
Ilha do Cardoso
Foz do Iguaçu
Iguaçu Falls
União da Vitória
Rio Negro
Mafra
São Francisco do Sul
Joinvile
Itajaí
Blumenau
Brusque
SANTA CATARINA
Caçador
Joaçaba
Chapecó
Lajes
Ilha de Santa Catarina
Florianópolis
Tubarão
Laguna
Cabo Santa Marta Grande
Criciúma
Araranguá
MISIONES
Posadas
Encarnación
Oberá
Erechim
Passo Fundo
Santo Ângelo
Santa Rosa
Cruz Alta
Caràzinho
Vacaria
Bento Gonçalves
Caxias do Sul
Nôvo Hamburgo
Taquara
São Leopoldo
PÔRTO ALEGRE
Osório
RIO GRANDE DO SUL
Santa Maria
Santa Cruz do Sul
Montenegro
Santiago
Alegrete
Cachoeira do Sul
Rio Pardo
São Gabriel
Santana do Livramento
Rivera
Dom Pedrito
Bagé
Camaquã
Canguçu
Pelotas
Lagoa dos Patos
Mostardas
Rio Grande
URUGUAY
Tacuarembó
Melo
Jaguarão
Lagoa Mirim
Lagoa Mangueira
Santa Vitória do Palmar
Treinta y Tres
José Batlle y Ordóñez
Minas
Rocha
San Carlos
Maldonado
MONTEVIDEO
ATLANTIC OCEAN
5304
55
West from Greenwich
50
45
40

NICARAGUA
COSTA RICA
PANAMA
COLOMBIA
VENEZUELA
ECUADOR
PERU
BOLIVIA
GUYANA
TRINIDAD & TOBAGO
GRENADA
ARGENTINA
PARAGU
RORAIMA
RONDÔNIA
A M A Z O N A S
A C R E
P A C I F I C O C E A N
Equator
Cocos Ridge
Milne Edwards Trench
Peru - Chile Trench
Krümmel Trench
Managua
Granada
Bluefields
San José
Panamá
Barranquilla
Cartagena
Maracaibo
CARACAS
Valencia
Barquisimeto
Port of Spain
Ciudad Guayana
Ciudad Bolívar
Medellín
BOGOTÁ
Cali
Cúcuta
Bucaramanga
Quito
Guayaquil
Cuenca
Iquitos
Manaus
Trujillo
Chimbote
LIMA
Callao
Huancayo
Cuzco
Arequipa
La Paz
Cochabamba
Santa Cruz
Oruro
Sucre
Potosí
Porto Velho
Rio Branco
Arica
Iquique
Tocopilla
L. Titicaca
L. Poopó
Sierra Pacaraima
Mt. Roraima
Orinoco
Negro
Solimões (Amazonas)
Amazonas (Amazon)
Madeira
Purus
Juruá
Japurá
Putumayo
Marañón
Ucayali
Cotopaxi 5896
Chimborazo 6267
Huascarán 6768
6384
6550
6462
6520
5230
5215
5750
4646
4100
5007
2810
2585
2285
6369
6866
5970
ft m
18 000 6000
12 000 4000
9000 3000
6000 2000
4500 1500
3000 1000
1200 400
600 200
0 0
200 600
2000 6000
4000 12 000
6000 18 000
8000 24 000
m ft
Projection: Sanson-Flamsteed's Sinusoidal
80
75
70
65
60
West

1:16 000 000

100 0 100 200 300 400 500 miles

100 0 100 200 300 400 500 600 700 800 km

1:16 000 000

100 50 0 100 200 300 miles

100 0 100 200 300 400 km

Projection: Sanson-Flamsteed's Sinusoidal

80 75 70 65 60 West from Greenwich 55 50 45 40 35

INDEX

The number printed in bold type against each entry indicates the map page where the feature can be found. This is followed by its geographical coordinates. The first coordinate indicates latitude, i.e. distance north or south of the Equator. The second coordinate indicates longitude, i.e. distance east or west of the meridian of Greenwich in England (shown as 0° longitude). Both latitude and longitude are measured in degrees and minutes (with 60 minutes in a degree), and appear on the map as horizontal and vertical gridlines respectively. Thus the entry for Paris in France reads.

Paris, France **19** 48 50 N 2 20 E

This entry indicates that Paris is on page 19, at latitude 48 degrees 50 minutes north (approximately five-sixths of the distance between horizontal gridlines 48 and 49, marked on either side of the page) and at longitude 2 degrees 20 minutes east (approximately one-third of the distance between vertical gridlines 2 and 3, marked at top and bottom of the page). Paris can be found where lines extended from these two points cross on the page. The geographical coordinates are sometimes only approximate but are close enough for the place to be located. Rivers have been indexed to their mouth or confluence.

An open square □ signifies that the name refers to an administrative subdivision of a country while a solid square ■ follows the name of a country. An arrow ⤳ follows the name of a river.

The alphabetical order of names composed of two or more words is governed primarily by the first word and then by the second. This rule applies even if the second word is a description or its abbreviation, R.,L.,I. for example. Names composed of a proper name (Gibraltar) and a description (Strait of) are positioned alphabetically by the proper name.

If the same place name occurs twice or more times in the index and all are in the same country, each is followed by the name of the administrative subdivision in which it is located. The names are placed in the alphabetical order of the subdivisions. If the same place name occurs twice or more in the index and the places are in different countries they will be followed by their country names, the latter governing the alphabetical order. In a mixture of these situations the primary order is fixed by the alphabetical sequence of the countries and the secondary order by that of the country subdivisions.

Abbreviations used in the index:

A. R.–Autonomous Region
A. S. S. R.–Autonomous Soviet Socialist Republic
Afghan.–Afghanistan
Afr.–Africa
Ala.–Alabama
Alas.–Alaska
Alg.–Algeria
Alta.–Alberta
Amer.–America
And. P.–Andhra Pradesh
Arch.–Archipelago
Argent.–Argentina
Ariz.–Arizona
Ark.–Arkansas
Atl. Oc. – Atlantic Ocean
Austral. – Australia
B. – Baie, Bahía, Bay, Bucht, Bugt
B.A. – Buenos Aires
B.C. – British Columbia
Bangla. – Bangladesh
Barr. – Barrage
Bay. – Bayern
Belg. – Belgium
Berks. – Berkshire
Bol. – Bolshoi
Boliv. – Bolivia
Bots. – Botswana
Br. – British
Bri. – Bridge
Bt. – Bight
Bucks. – Buckinghamshire
Bulg. – Bulgaria
C. – Cabo, Cap, Cape, Coast
C. Prov. – Cape Province
Calif. – California
Camb. – Cambodia
Cambs. – Cambridgeshire
Can. – Canada
Cent. – Central
Chan. – Channel
Co. – Country
Colomb. – Colombia
Colo. – Colorado
Conn. – Connecticut
Cord. – Cordillera
Cr. – Creek
Cumb. – Cumbria
Czech. – Czechoslovakia
D.C. – District of Columbia
Del. – Delaware
Dep. – Dependency
Derby. – Derbyshire
Des. – Desert
Dist. – District
Dj. – Djebel
Dumf. & Gall. – Dumfries and Galloway
E. – East
Eng. – England
Fed. – Federal, Federation
Fla. – Florida
For. – Forest
Fr. – France, French
Fs. – Falls
Ft. – Fort
G. – Golfe, Golfo, Gulf, Guba
Ga. – Georgia
Ger. – Germany
Glam. – Glamorgan
Glos. – Gloucestershire
Gr. – Grande, Great, Greater, Group
H.K. – Hong Kong
H.P. – Himachal Pradesh
Hants. – Hampshire
Harb. – Harbor, Harbour
Hd. – Head
Here. & Worcs. – Hereford and Worcester
Herts. – Hertfordshire
Hts. – Heights
Hung. – Hungary
I.o.M. – Isle of Man
I.(s). – Île, Ilha, Insel, Isla, Island, Isle
Id. – Idaho
Ill. – Illinois
Ind. – Indiana
Ind. Oc. – Indian Ocean
Indon. – Indonesia
J. – Jabal, Jabel, Jazira
Junc. – Junction
K. – Kap, Kapp
K. – Kuala
Kal. – Kalmyk A.S.S.R.
Kans. – Kansas
Kep. – Kepulauan
Ky. – Kentucky
L. – Lac, Lacul, Lago, Lagoa, Lake, Limni, Loch, Lough
La. – Lousiana
Lancs. – Lancashire
Leb. – Lebanon
Leics. – Leicestershire
Lim. – Limerick
Lincs. – Lincolnshire
Lit. – Little
Lr. – Lower
Mad. P. – Madhya Pradesh
Madag. – Madagascar
Malay. – Malaysia
Man. – Manitoba
Manch. – Manchester
Maran. – Maranhão
Mass. – Massachusetts
Md. – Maryland
Me. – Maine
Mend. – Mendoza
Mér. – Méridionale
Mich. – Michigan
Mid. – Middle
Minn. – Minnesota
Miss. – Mississippi
Mo. – Missouri
Mong. – Mongolia
Mont. – Montana
Moroc. – Morocco
Mozam. – Mozambique
Mt.(e). – Mont, Monte, Monti, Montaña, Mountain
Mys. – Mysore
N. – Nord, Norte, North, Northern, Nouveau
N.B. – New Brunswick
N.C. – North Carolina
N.D. – North Dakota
N.H. – New Hampshire
N.I. – North Island
N.J. – New Jersey
N. Mex. – New Mexico
N.S. – Nova Scotia
N.S.W. – New South Wales
N.T. – Northern Territory
N.W.T. – North West Territory
N.Y. – New York
N.Z. – New Zealand
Nat. – National
Nat.Park. – National Park
Nebr. – Nebraska
Neth. – Netherlands
Nev. – Nevada
Newf. – Newfoundland
Nic. – Nicaragua
Northants. – Northamptonshire
Northumb. – Northumberland
Notts. – Nottinghamshire
O. – Oued, ouadi
Occ. – Occidentale
O.F.S. – Orange Free State
Okla. – Oklahoma
Ont. – Ontario
Or. – Orientale
Oreg. – Oregon
Os. – Ostrov
Oxon. – Oxfordshire
Oz. – Ozero
P. – Pass, Passo, Pasul, Pulau
P.E.I. – Prince Edward Island
P.N.G. – Papua New Guinea
P.O. – Post Office
P. Rico.–Puerto Rico
Pa. – Pennsylvania
Pac. Oc. – Pacific Ocean
Pak. – Pakistan
Parag. – Paraguay
Pass. – Passage
Pen. – Peninsula, Peninsule
Phil. – Philippines
Pk. – Peak
Plat. – Plateau
P-ov. – Poluostrov
Port. – Portugal, Portuguese
Prom. – Promontory
Prov. – Province, Provincial
Pt. – Point
Pta. – Ponta, Punta
Pte. – Pointe
Qué. – Québec
Queens. – Queensland
R. – Rio, River
R.I. – Rhode Island
R.S.F.S.R. – Russian Soviet Federal Socialist Republic
Ra.(s). – Range(s)
Raj. – Rajasthan
Reg. – Region
Rep. – Republic
Res. – Reserve, Reservoir
Rhld. – Pfz. – Rheinland–Pfalz
S. – San, South
S. Afr. – South Africa
S. Austral. – South Australia
S.C. – South Carolina
S.D. – South Dakota
S.-Holst. – Schleswig-Holstein
S.I. – South Island
S. Leone–Sierra Leone
S.S.R. – Soviet Socialist Republic
Sa. – Serra, Sierra
Sard. – Sardinia
Sask. – Saskatchewan
Scot. – Scotland
Sd. – Sound
Sept. – Septentrionale
Sev. – Severnaja
Sib. – Siberia
Som. – Somerset
Span. – Spanish
Sprs. – Springs
St. – Saint
Sta. – Santa, Station
Staffs. – Staffordshire
Ste. – Sainte
Sto. – Santo
Str. – Strait, Stretto
Switz. – Switzerland
T.O. – Telegraph Office
Tas. – Tasmania
Tenn. – Tennessee
Terr. – Territory
Tex. – Texas
Tg. – Tanjung
Thai. – Thailand
Tipp. – Tipperary
Trans. – Transvaal
U.K. – United Kingdom
U.S.A. – United States of America
U.S.S.R. – Union of Soviet Socialist Republics
Ukr. – Ukraine
Ut.P. – Uttar Pradesh
Utd. – United
V. – Vorota
Va. – Virginia
Vdkhr. – Vodokhranilishche
Venez. – Venezuela
Vic. – Victoria
Viet. – Vietnam
Vol. – Volcano
Vt. – Vermont
W. – Wadi, West
W.A. – Western Australia
W. Isles–Western Isles
W. Va. – West Virginia
Wash. – Washington
Wilts. – Wiltshire
Wis. – Wisconsin
Wlkp. – Wielkopolski
Wyo. – Wyoming
Yorks. – Yorkshire
Yug. – Yugoslavia
Zap. – Zapadnaja
Zimb. – Zimbabwe

A

Aachen 24 50 47N 6 4 E
Aâlâ en Nîl □ 87 8 50N 29 55 E
Aalen 25 48 49N 10 6 E
Aalsmeer 16 52 17N 4 43 E
Aalst 16 50 56N 4 2 E
Aalten 16 51 56N 6 35 E
Aarau 25 47 23N 8 4 E
Aarberg 25 47 2N 7 16 E
Aare → 25 47 33N 8 14 E
Aargau □ 25 47 26N 8 10 E
Aarschot 16 50 59N 4 49 E
Aba, Nigeria 85 5 10N 7 19 E
Aba, Zaïre 90 3 58N 30 17 E
Âbâ, Jazîrat 87 13 30N 32 31 E
Âbâdân 64 30 22N 48 20 E
Abade, Ethiopia 87 9 22N 38 3 E
Abade, Iran 65 31 8N 52 40 E
Abadin 30 43 21N 7 29W
Abadla 82 31 2N 2 45W
Abaetetuba 127 1 40 S 48 50W
Abagnar Qi 76 43 52N 116 2 E
Abai 125 25 58 S 55 54W
Abak 85 4 58N 7 50 E
Abakaliki 85 6 22N 8 2 E
Abakan 59 53 40N 91 10 E
Abal Nam 86 25 20N 38 37 E
Abalemma 85 16 12N 7 50 E
Abanilla 33 38 12N 1 3W
Abano Terme 39 45 22N 11 46 E
Abarán 33 38 12N 1 23W
Abarqû 65 31 10N 53 20 E
'Abasân 62 31 19N 34 21 E
Abashiri 74 44 0N 144 15 E
Abashiri-Wan 74 44 0N 144 30 E
Abau 98 10 11 S 148 46 E
Abaújszántó 27 48 16N 21 12 E
Abay 58 49 38N 72 53 E
Abaya L. 87 6 30N 37 50 E
Abaza 58 52 39N 90 6 E
Abbadia San Salvatore 39 42 53N 11 40 E
Abbay (Nîl el Azraq) → 87 15 38N 32 31 E
Abbaye, Pt. 114 46 58N 88 4W
Abbé, L. 87 11 8N 41 47 E
Abbeville, France 19 50 6N 1 49 E
Abbeville, La., U.S.A. 117 30 0N 92 7W
Abbeville, S.C., U.S.A. 115 34 12N 82 21W
Abbiategrasso 38 45 23N 8 55 E
Abbieglassie 99 27 15 S 147 28 E
Abbotsford, B.C., Can. 108 49 5N 122 20W
Abbotsford, Qué., Can. 113 45 25N 72 53W
Abbotsford, U.S.A. 116 44 55N 90 20W
Abbottabad 66 34 10N 73 15 E
Abd al Kûrî 63 12 5N 52 20 E
Abéché 81 13 50N 20 35 E
Abejar 32 41 48N 2 47W
Abekr 87 12 45N 28 50 E
Abêlessa 82 22 58N 4 47 E
Abengourou 84 6 42N 3 27W
Åbenrå 49 55 3N 9 25 E
Abensberg 25 48 49N 11 51 E
Abeokuta 85 7 3N 3 19 E
Aber 90 2 12N 32 25 E
Aberaeron 13 52 15N 4 16W
Aberayron = Aberaeron 13 52 15N 4 16W
Abercorn 99 25 12 S 151 5 E
Abercorn = Mbala 91 8 46 S 31 17 E
Abercrombie → 100 33 54 S 149 8 E
Aberdare 13 51 43N 3 27W
Aberdare Ra. 90 0 15 S 36 50 E
Aberdeen, Austral. 99 32 9 S 150 56 E
Aberdeen, Can. 109 52 20N 106 8W
Aberdeen, S. Afr. 92 32 28 S 24 2 E
Aberdeen, U.K. 14 57 9N 2 6W
Aberdeen, Ala., U.S.A. 115 33 49N 88 33W
Aberdeen, Idaho, U.S.A. 118 42 57N 112 50W
Aberdeen, S.D., U.S.A. 116 45 30N 98 30W
Aberdeen, Wash., U.S.A. 118 47 0N 123 50W
Aberdovey 13 52 33N 4 3W
Aberfeldy 14 56 37N 3 50W
Abergaria-a-Velha 30 40 41N 8 32W
Abergavenny 13 51 49N 3 1W
Abernathy 117 33 49N 101 49W
Abert L. 118 42 40N 120 8W
Aberystwyth 13 52 25N 4 6W
Abha 86 18 0N 42 34 E
Abhayapuri 69 26 24N 90 38 E
Abidiya 86 18 18N 34 3 E
Abidjan 84 5 26N 3 58W
Abilene, Kans., U.S.A. 116 39 0N 97 16W
Abilene, Texas, U.S.A. 117 32 22N 99 40W
Abingdon, U.K. 13 51 40N 1 17W
Abingdon, Ill., U.S.A. 116 40 53N 90 23W
Abingdon, Va., U.S.A. 115 36 46N 81 56W
Abitau → 109 59 53N 109 3W
Abitau L. 109 60 27N 107 15W
Abitibi L. 106 48 40N 79 40W
Abiy Adi 87 13 39N 39 3 E
Abkhaz A.S.S.R. □ 57 43 0N 41 0 E
Abkit 59 64 10N 157 10 E
Abnûb 86 27 18N 31 4 E
Åbo 51 60 28N 22 15 E
Abo, Massif d' 83 21 41N 16 8 E
Abocho 85 7 35N 6 56 E
Abohar 68 30 10N 74 10 E
Aboisso 84 5 30N 3 5W
Aboméy 85 7 10N 2 5 E
Abondance 21 46 18N 6 42 E
Abong-Mbang 88 4 0N 13 8 E
Abonnema 85 4 41N 6 49 E
Abony 27 47 12N 20 3 E
Aboso 84 5 23N 1 57W
Abou-Deïa 81 11 20N 19 20 E
Aboyne 14 57 4N 2 48W
Abra Pampa 124 22 43 S 65 42W
Abrantes 31 39 24N 8 7W
Abraveses 30 40 41N 7 55W
Abreojos, Pta. 120 26 50N 113 40W
Abreschviller 19 48 39N 7 6 E
Abrets, Les 21 45 32N 5 35 E
Abri, Esh Shimâliya, Sudan 86 20 50N 30 27 E
Abri, Janub Kordofân, Sudan 87 11 40N 30 21 E
Abrud 46 46 19N 23 5 E
Abruzzi □ 39 42 15N 14 0 E
Absaroka Ra. 118 44 40N 110 0W
Abû al Khaşîb 64 30 25N 48 0 E
Abû 'Alî 64 27 20N 49 27 E
Abu 'Arîsh 63 16 53N 42 48 E
Abû Ballas 86 24 26N 27 36 E
Abu Deleiq 87 15 57N 33 48 E
Abû Dhabî 65 24 28N 54 36 E
Abû Dîs 62 31 47N 35 16 E
Abû Dis 86 19 12N 33 38 E
Abû Dom 87 16 18N 32 25 E
Abû Gabra 87 11 2N 26 50 E
Abû Ghaush 62 31 48N 35 6 E
Abû Gubeiha 87 11 30N 31 15 E
Abu Habl, Khawr → 87 12 37N 31 0 E
Abu Hamed 86 19 32N 33 13 E
Abu Haraz 87 14 35N 33 30 E
Abû Haraz 86 19 8N 32 18 E
Abû Higar 87 12 50N 33 59 E
Abû Kamâl 64 34 30N 41 0 E
Abû Madd, Ra's 64 24 50N 37 7 E
Abû Markhah 64 25 4N 38 22 E
Abu Qir 86 31 18N 30 0 E
Abu Qireiya 86 24 5N 35 28 E
Abu Qurqâs 86 28 1N 30 44 E
Abû Rudies 86 29 0N 33 15 E
Abu Salama 86 27 10N 35 51 E
Abû Simbel 86 22 18N 31 40 E
Abu Tig 86 27 4N 31 15 E
Abu Tiga 87 12 47N 34 12 E
Abû Zabad 87 12 25N 29 10 E
Abû Zâbî 65 24 28N 54 22 E
Abuja 85 9 16N 7 2 E
Abukuma-Gawa → 74 38 06N 140 52 E
Abunâ 126 9 40 S 65 20W
Abunâ → 126 9 41 S 65 20W
Aburo, Mt. 90 2 4N 30 53 E
Abut Hd. 101 43 7 S 170 15 E
Abwong 87 9 2N 32 14 E
Åby 49 58 40N 16 10 E
Aby, Lagune 84 5 15N 3 14W
Acámbaro 120 20 0N 100 40W
Acanthus 44 40 27N 23 47 E
Acaponeta 120 22 30N 105 20W
Acapulco 120 16 51N 99 56W
Acatlán 120 18 10N 98 3W
Acayucan 120 17 59N 94 58W
Accéglio 38 44 28N 6 59 E
Accomac 114 37 43N 75 40W
Accra 85 5 35N 0 6W
Accrington 12 53 46N 2 22W
Acebal 124 33 20 S 60 50W
Aceh □ 72 4 15N 97 30 E
Acerenza 41 40 50N 15 58 E
Acerra 41 40 57N 14 22 E
Aceuchal 31 38 39N 6 30W
Achalpur 68 21 22N 77 32 E
Achenkirch 26 47 32N 11 45 E
Achensee 26 47 26N 11 45 E
Acher 68 23 10N 72 32 E
Achern 25 48 37N 8 5 E
Achill 15 53 56N 9 55W
Achill Hd. 15 53 59N 10 15W
Achill I. 15 53 58N 10 5W
Achill Sound 15 53 53N 9 55W
Achim 24 53 1N 9 2 E
Achinsk 59 56 20N 90 20 E
Achol 87 6 35N 31 32 E
Acireale 41 37 37N 15 9 E
Ackerman 117 33 20N 89 8W
Acklins I. 121 22 30N 74 0W
Acland, Mt. 97 24 50 S 148 20 E
Acme 108 51 33N 113 30W
Aconcagua □, Argent. 124 32 50 S 70 0W
Aconcagua □, Chile 124 32 15 S 70 30W
Aconcagua, Cerro 124 32 39 S 70 0W
Aconquija, Mt. 124 27 0 S 66 0W
Açores, Is. dos = Azores 6 38 44N 29 0W
Acquapendente 39 42 45N 11 50 E
Acquasanta 39 42 46N 13 24 E
Acquaviva delle Fonti 41 40 53N 16 50 E
Acqui 38 44 40N 8 28 E
Acre = 'Akko 62 32 55N 35 4 E
Acre □ 126 9 1 S 71 0W
Acre → 126 8 45 S 67 22W
Acri 41 39 29N 16 23 E
Acs 27 47 42N 18 0 E
Actium 44 38 57N 20 45 E
Acton 112 43 38N 80 3W
Ad Dahnâ 64 24 30N 48 10 E
Ad Dammâm 64 26 20N 50 5 E
Ad Dâr al Ḥamrâ' 64 27 20N 37 45 E
Ad Dawhah 65 25 15N 51 35 E
Ad Dilam 64 23 55N 47 10 E
Ada, Ghana 85 5 44N 0 40 E
Ada, Minn., U.S.A. 116 47 20N 96 30W
Ada, Okla., U.S.A. 117 34 50N 96 45W
Ada, Yugo. 42 45 49N 20 9 E
Adaja → 30 41 32N 4 52W
Ådalslinden 48 63 27N 16 55 E
Adam 65 22 15N 57 28 E
Adamaoua, Massif de l' 85 7 20N 12 20 E
Adamawa Highlands = Adamaoua, Massif de l' 85 7 20N 12 20 E
Adamello, Mt. 38 46 10N 10 34 E
Adami Tulu 87 7 53N 38 41 E
Adaminaby 99 36 0 S 148 45 E
Adams, Mass., U.S.A. 113 42 38N 73 8W
Adams, N.Y., U.S.A. 114 43 50N 76 3W
Adams, Wis., U.S.A. 116 43 59N 89 50W
Adam's Bridge 70 9 15N 79 40 E
Adams Center 113 43 51N 76 1W
Adams L. 108 51 10N 119 40W
Adams, Mt. 118 46 10N 121 28W
Adam's Peak 70 6 48N 80 30 E
Adamuz 31 38 2N 4 32W
Adana 64 37 0N 35 16 E
Adanero 30 40 56N 4 36W
Adapazarı 64 40 48N 30 25 E
Adarama 87 17 10N 34 52 E
Adare, C. 5 71 0 S 171 0 E
Adaut 73 8 8 S 131 7 E
Adavale 97 25 52 S 144 32 E
Adda → 38 45 8N 9 53 E
Addis Ababa = Addis Abeba 87 9 2N 38 42 E
Addis Abeba 87 9 2N 38 42 E
Addis Alem 87 9 0N 38 17 E
Addison 112 42 9N 77 15W
Adebour 85 13 17N 11 50 E
Adel 115 31 10N 83 28W
Adelaide, Austral. 97 34 52 S 138 30 E
Adelaide, Madag. 93 32 42 S 26 20 E
Adelaide I. 5 67 15 S 68 30W
Adelaide Pen. 104 68 15N 97 30W
Adélie, Terre 5 68 0 S 140 0 E
Ademuz 32 40 5N 1 13W
Aden = Al 'Adan 63 12 45N 45 12 E
Aden, G. of 63 13 0N 50 0 E
Adendorp 92 32 25 S 24 30 E
Adgz 82 30 47N 6 30W
Adhoi 68 23 26N 70 32 E
Adi 73 4 15 S 133 30 E
Adi Daro 87 14 20N 38 14 E
Adi Keyih 87 14 51N 39 22 E
Adi Kwala 87 14 38N 38 48 E
Adi Ugri 87 14 58N 38 48 E
Adieu, C. 96 32 0 S 132 10 E
Adigala 87 10 24N 42 15 E
Adige → 39 45 9N 12 20 E
Adigrat 87 14 20N 39 26 E
Adilabad 70 19 33N 78 20 E
Adin 118 41 10N 121 0W
Adin Khel 65 32 45N 68 5 E
Adirampattinam 70 10 28N 79 20 E
Adirondack Mts. 114 44 0N 74 15W
Adjim 83 33 47N 10 50 E
Adjohon 85 6 41N 2 32 E
Adjud 46 46 7N 27 10 E
Adjumani 90 3 20N 31 50 E
Adlavik Is. 107 55 2N 57 45W
Adler 57 43 28N 39 52 E
Admer 83 20 21N 5 27 E
Admer, Erg d' 83 24 0N 9 5 E
Admiralty B. 5 62 0 S 59 0W
Admiralty G. 96 14 20 S 125 55 E
Admiralty I. 104 57 40N 134 35W
Admiralty Inlet 118 48 0N 122 40W
Admiralty Is. 94 2 0 S 147 0 E
Admiralty Ra. 5 72 0 S 164 0 E
Ado 85 6 36N 2 56 E
Ado Ekiti 85 7 38N 5 12 E
Adok 87 8 10N 30 20 E
Adola 87 11 14N 41 44 E
Adonara 73 8 15 S 123 5 E
Adoni 70 15 33N 77 18W
Adony 27 47 6N 18 52 E
Adour → 20 43 32N 1 32W
Adra, India 69 23 30N 86 42 E
Adra, Spain 33 36 43N 3 3W
Adrano 41 37 40N 14 49 E
Adrar 82 27 51N 0 11W
Adré 81 13 40N 22 20 E
Adrī 83 27 32N 13 2 E
Ádria 39 45 4N 12 3 E
Adrian, Mich., U.S.A. 114 41 55N 84 0W
Adrian, Tex., U.S.A. 117 35 19N 102 37W
Adriatic Sea 34 43 0N 16 0 E
Adua 73 1 45 S 129 50 E
Adur 70 9 8N 76 40 E
Adwa 87 14 15N 38 52 E
Adzhar A.S.S.R. □ 57 42 0N 42 0 E
Adzopé 84 6 7N 3 49W
Ægean Sea 35 37 0N 25 0 E
Æolian Is. = Eólie 41 38 30N 14 50 E
Aerht'ai Shan 75 46 40N 92 45 E
Ærø 49 54 52N 10 25 E
Ærøskøbing 49 54 53N 10 24 E
Aëtós 45 37 15N 21 50 E
Afafi, Massif d' 83 22 11N 15 10 E
Afándou 45 36 18N 28 12 E
Afarag, Erg 82 23 50N 2 47 E
Affreville = Khemis Miliania 82 36 11N 2 14 E
Afghanistan ■ 65 33 0N 65 0 E
Afgoi 63 2 7N 44 59 E
'Afif 64 23 53N 42 56 E
Afikpo 85 5 53N 7 54 E
Aflisses, O. → 82 28 40N 0 50 E
Aflou 82 34 7N 2 3 E
Afognak I. 104 58 10N 152 50W
Afragola 41 40 54N 14 15 E
Afrera 87 13 16N 41 5 E
Africa 78 10 0N 20 0 E
Afton 113 42 14N 75 31W
Aftout 82 26 50N 3 45W
Afuá 127 0 15 S 50 20W
Afula 62 32 37N 35 17 E
Afyonkarahisar 64 38 45N 30 33 E
Aga 86 30 55N 31 10 E
Agadès = Agadez 85 16 58N 7 59 E
Agadez 85 16 58N 7 59 E
Agadir 82 30 28N 9 35W
Agano → 74 37 57N 139 8 E
Agapa 59 71 27N 89 15 E
Agar 68 23 40N 76 2 E
Agaro 87 7 50N 36 38 E
Agartala 67 23 50N 91 23 E
Agâş 46 46 28N 26 15 E
Agassiz 108 49 14N 121 46W
Agats 73 5 33 S 138 0 E
Agattu I. 104 52 25N 172 30 E
Agbélouvé 85 6 35N 1 14 E
Agboville 84 5 55N 4 15W
Agdam 57 40 0N 46 58 E
Agdash 57 40 44N 47 22 E
Agde 20 43 19N 3 28 E
Agde, C. d' 20 43 16N 3 28 E
Agdzhabedi 57 40 5N 47 27 E
Agen 20 44 12N 0 38 E
Ager Tay 83 20 0N 17 41 E
Agersø 49 55 13N 11 12 E
Ageyevo 55 54 10N 36 27 E
Agger 49 56 47N 8 13 E
Aggius 40 40 56N 9 4 E
Aghil Mts. 69 36 0N 77 0 E
Aginskoye 59 51 6N 114 32 E
Agira 41 37 40N 14 30 E
Agly → 20 42 46N 3 3 E
Agnibilékrou 84 7 10N 3 11W
Agnita 46 45 59N 24 40 E
Agnone 41 41 49N 14 20 E
Agofie 85 8 27N 0 15 E
Agogna → 38 45 4N 8 52 E
Agogo 87 7 50N 28 45 E
Agon 18 49 2N 1 34W
Agön 48 61 34N 17 23 E
Agordo 39 46 18N 12 2 E
Agout → 20 43 47N 1 41 E
Agra 68 27 17N 77 58 E
Agramunt 32 41 48N 1 6 E
Agreda 32 41 51N 1 55W
Agri → 41 40 13N 16 44 E
Ağri Daği 64 39 50N 44 15 E
Ağri Karakose 64 39 44N 43 3 E
Agrigento 40 37 19N 13 33 E
Agrinion 45 38 37N 21 27 E
Agrópoli 41 40 23N 14 59 E
Água Clara 127 20 25 S 52 45W
Agua Prieta 120 31 20N 109 32W
Aguadas 126 5 40N 75 38W
Aguadilla 121 18 27N 67 10W
Aguanish 107 50 14N 62 2W
Aguanus → 107 50 13N 62 5W
Aguapey → 124 29 7 S 56 36W
Aguaray Guazú → 124 24 47 S 57 19W
Aguarico → 126 0 59 S 75 11W
Aguas → 32 41 20N 0 30W
Aguas Blancas 124 24 15 S 69 55W
Aguas Calientes, Sierra de 124 25 26 S 66 40W
Aguascalientes 120 21 53N 102 12W
Aguascalientes □ 120 22 0N 102 20W
Agudo 31 38 59N 4 52W
Águeda 30 40 34N 8 27W
Agueda → 30 41 2N 6 56W
Aguié 85 13 31N 7 46 E
Aguilafuente 30 41 13N 4 7W
Aguilar 31 37 31N 4 40W
Aguilar de Campóo 30 42 47N 4 15W
Aguilares 124 27 26 S 65 35W
Aguilas 33 37 23N 1 35W
Agulaa 87 13 40N 39 40 E
Agulhas, Kaap 92 34 52 S 20 0 E
Agung 72 8 20 S 115 28 E
'Agur 62 31 42N 34 55 E
Agur 90 2 28N 32 55 E
Agusan → 73 9 0N 125 30 E
Agvali 57 42 36N 46 8 E
Aha Mts. 92 19 45 S 21 0 E
Ahaggar 83 23 0N 6 30 E
Ahamansu 85 7 38N 0 35 E
Ahar 64 38 35N 47 0 E
Ahaus 24 52 4N 7 1 E
Ahelledjem 83 26 37N 6 58 E
Ahipara B. 101 35 5 S 173 5 E
Ahiri 70 19 30N 80 0 E
Ahlen 24 51 45N 7 52 E
Ahmadabad (Ahmedabad) 68 23 0N 72 40 E
Ahmadnagar (Ahmednagar) 70 19 7N 74 46 E
Ahmadpur 68 29 12N 71 10 E
Ahmar Mts. 87 9 20N 41 15 E
Ahoada 85 5 8N 6 36 E
Ahr → 24 50 33N 7 17 E
Ahrensbök 24 54 0N 10 34 E
Ahrweiler 24 50 31N 7 3 E
Aḥsā', Wāḥat al 64 25 50N 49 0 E
Ahuachapán 120 13 54N 89 52W
Åhus 49 55 56N 14 18 E
Ahvâz 64 31 20N 48 40 E
Ahvenanmaa = Åland 51 60 15N 20 0 E
Ahwar 63 13 30N 46 40 E
Ahzar 85 15 30N 3 20 E
Aichach 25 48 28N 11 9 E
Aichi □ 74 35 0N 137 15 E
Aidone 41 37 26N 14 26 E
Aiello Cálabro 41 39 6N 16 12 E
Aigle 25 46 18N 6 58 E
Aigle, L' 18 48 46N 0 38 E
Aignay-le-Duc 19 47 40N 4 43 E
Aigre 20 45 54N 0 1 E
Aigua 125 34 13 S 54 46W
Aigueperse 20 46 3N 3 13 E
Aigues-Mortes 21 43 35N 4 12 E
Aigues-Mortes, G. d' 21 43 31N 4 3 E
Aiguilles 21 44 47N 6 51 E
Aiguillon 20 44 18N 0 21 E
Aiguillon, L' 20 46 20N 1 16W
Aigurande 20 46 27N 1 49 E
Aihui 75 50 10N 127 30 E
Aija 126 9 50 S 77 45W
Aijal 67 23 40N 92 44 E
Aiken 115 33 34N 81 50W
Aillant-sur-Tholon 19 47 52N 3 20 E
Aillik 107 55 11N 59 18W
Ailly-sur-Noye 19 49 45N 2 20 E
Ailsa Craig 14 55 15N 5 7W
'Ailûn 62 32 18N 35 47 E
Aim 59 59 0N 133 55 E
Aimere 73 8 45 S 121 3 E
Aimogasta 124 28 33 S 66 50W
Aimorés 127 19 30 S 41 4W
Ain □ 21 46 5N 5 20 E
Ain → 21 45 45N 5 11 E
Ain Banaiyan 65 23 0N 51 0 E
Aïn Beïda 83 35 50N 7 29 E
Aïn ben Khellil 82 33 15N 0 49W
Aïn Ben Tili 82 25 59N 9 27W
Aïn Beni Mathar 82 34 1N 2 0W
Aïn Benian 82 36 48N 2 55 E
Ain Dalla 86 27 20N 27 23 E
Ain Dar 64 25 55N 49 10 E
Ain el Mafki 86 27 30N 28 15 E

Aïn Galakka 81 18 10N 18 30 E
Ain Girba 86 29 20N 25 14 E
Aïn M'lila 83 36 2N 6 35 E
Ain Qeiqab 86 29 42N 24 55 E
Aïn-Sefra 82 32 47N 0 37W
Ain Sheikh Murzûk 86 26 47N 27 45 E
Ain Sukhna 86 29 32N 32 20 E
Aïn Tédelès 82 36 0N 0 21 E
Aïn-Témouchent 82 35 16N 1 8W
Aïn Touta 83 35 26N 5 54 E
Ain Zeitûn 86 29 10N 25 48 E
Aïn Zorah 82 34 37N 3 32W
Ainabo 63 9 0N 46 25 E
Ainaži 54 57 50N 24 24 E
Aínos Óros 45 38 10N 20 35 E
Ainsworth 116 42 33N 99 52W
Aïr 85 18 30N 8 0 E
Airaines 19 49 58N 1 55 E
Airdrie 14 55 53N 3 57W
Aire 19 50 37N 2 22 E
Aire →, France 19 49 18N 4 55 E
Aire →, U.K. 12 53 42N 0 55W
Aire, I. del 32 39 48N 4 16 E
Aire-sur-l'Adour 20 43 42N 0 15W
Airvault 18 46 50N 0 8W
Aisch → 25 49 46N 11 1 E
Aisne □ 19 49 42N 3 40 E
Aisne → 19 49 26N 2 50 E
Aitana, Sierra de 33 38 35N 0 24W
Aitape 98 3 11 S 142 22 E
Aitkin 116 46 32N 93 43W
Aitolía Kai Akarnanía □ 45 38 45N 21 18 E
Aitolikón 45 38 26N 21 21 E
Aiud 46 46 19N 23 44 E
Aix-en-Provence 21 43 32N 5 27 E
Aix-la-Chapelle = Aachen 24 50 47N 6 4 E
Aix-les-Bains 21 45 41N 5 53 E
Aix-sur-Vienne 20 45 48N 1 8 E
Aiyansh 108 55 17N 129 2W
Áiyina 45 37 45N 23 26 E
Aiyínion 44 40 28N 22 28 E
Aiyion 45 38 15N 22 5 E
Aizenay 18 46 44N 1 38W
Aizpute 54 56 43N 21 40 E
Ajaccio 21 41 55N 8 40 E
Ajaccio, G. d' 21 41 52N 8 40 E
Ajanta Ra. 70 20 28N 75 50 E
Ajax 112 43 50N 79 1W
Ajdâbiyah 83 30 54N 20 4 E
Ajdovščina 39 45 54N 13 54 E
Ajibar 87 10 35N 38 36 E
Ajka 27 47 4N 17 31 E
'Ajmân 65 25 25N 55 30 E
Ajmer 68 26 28N 74 37 E
Ajo 119 32 18N 112 54W
Ajok 87 9 15N 28 28 E
Ak Dağ 64 36 30N 30 0 E
Akaba 85 8 10N 1 2 E
Akabli 82 26 49N 1 31 E
Akaki Beseka 87 8 55N 38 45 E
Akala 87 15 39N 36 13 E
Akaroa 101 43 49 S 172 59 E
Akasha 86 21 10N 30 32 E
Akashi 74 34 45N 135 0 E
Akbou 83 36 31N 4 31 E
Akelamo 73 1 35N 129 40 E
Åkernes 47 58 45N 7 30 E
Akershus fylke □ 47 60 0N 11 10 E
Akeru → 70 17 25N 80 0 E
Aketi 88 2 38N 23 47 E
Akhaïa □ 45 38 5N 21 45 E
Akhalkalaki 57 41 27N 43 25 E
Akhaltsikhe 57 41 40N 43 0 E
Akharnaí 45 38 5N 23 44 E
Akhelóös → 45 38 36N 21 14 E
Akhendria 45 34 58N 25 16 E
Akhéron → 44 39 20N 20 29 E
Akhisar 64 38 56N 27 48 E
Akhladhókambos 45 37 31N 22 35 E
Akhmîm 86 26 31N 31 47 E
Akhtopol 43 42 6N 27 56 E
Akhtubinsk (Petropavlovskiy) 57 48 13N 46 7 E
Akhty 57 41 30N 47 45 E
Akhtyrka 54 50 25N 35 0 E
Akimiski I. 106 52 50N 81 30W
Akimovka 56 46 44N 35 0 E
Åkirkeby 49 55 4N 14 55 E
Akita 74 39 45N 140 7 E
Akita □ 74 39 40N 140 30 E
Akjoujt 84 19 45N 14 15W
Akka 82 29 22N 8 9W
'Akko 62 32 55N 35 4 E
Akkol 58 45 0N 75 39 E
Akköy 45 37 30N 27 18 E
Aklampa 85 8 15N 2 10 E
Aklavik 104 68 12N 135 0W
Akmonte 31 37 13N 6 38W
Aknoul 82 34 40N 3 55W
Ako 85 10 19N 10 48 E
Akobo → 87 7 48N 33 3 E
Akola 68 20 42N 77 2 E
Akonolinga 85 3 50N 12 18 E
Akordat 87 15 30N 37 40 E
Akosombo Dam 85 6 20N 0 5 E
Akot, India 68 21 10N 77 10 E
Akot, Sudan 87 6 31N 30 9 E
Akpatok I. 105 60 25N 68 8W
Akranes 50 64 19N 21 58W
Åkrehamn 47 59 15N 5 10 E
Akreïjit 84 18 19N 9 11W
Akrítas Venétiko, Ákra 45 36 43N 21 54 E
Akron, Colo., U.S.A. 116 40 13N 103 15W
Akron, Ohio, U.S.A. 114 41 7N 81 31W
Akrotíri, Ákra 44 40 26N 25 27 E
Aksai Chih 69 35 15N 79 55 E
Aksaray 64 38 25N 34 2 E
Aksarka 58 66 31N 67 50 E
Aksay 52 51 11N 53 0 E
Akşehir 64 38 18N 31 30 E
Aksenovo Zilovskoye 59 53 20N 117 40 E
Akstafa 57 41 7N 45 27 E
Aksu 75 41 5N 80 10 E
Aksum 87 14 5N 38 40 E
Aktogay 58 46 57N 79 40 E
Aktyubinsk 53 50 17N 57 10 E
Aku 85 6 40N 7 18 E
Akure 85 7 15N 5 5 E
Akureyri 50 65 40N 18 6W
Akusha 57 42 18N 47 30 E
Al Abyār 83 32 9N 20 29 E
Al 'Adan 63 12 45N 45 0 E
Al Amādā03yah 64 37 5N 43 30 E
Al Amārah 64 31 55N 47 15 E
Al 'Aqabah 62 29 31N 35 0 E
Al 'Aramah 64 25 30N 46 0 E
Al Ashkhara 65 21 50N 59 30 E
Al 'Ayzarīyah (Bethany) 62 31 47N 35 15 E
Al 'Azīzīyah 83 32 30N 13 1 E
Al Badī' 64 22 0N 46 35 E
Al Barkāt 83 24 56N 10 14 E
Al Başrah 64 30 30N 47 50 E
Al Bāzūrīyah 62 33 15N 35 16 E
Al Bīrah 62 31 55N 35 12 E
Al Bu'ayrāt 83 31 24N 15 44 E
Al Buqay'ah 62 32 15N 35 30 E
Al Dīwaniyah 64 32 0N 45 0 E
Al Fallūjah 64 33 20N 43 55 E
Al Fāw 64 30 0N 48 30 E
Al Fujayrah 65 25 7N 56 18 E
Al Ghatghat 64 24 40N 46 15 E
Al Hābah 64 27 10N 47 0 E
Al Haddār 64 21 58N 45 57 E
Al Ḩadīthah 64 34 0N 41 13 E
Al Hāmad 64 31 30N 39 30 E
Al Ḩamar 64 22 23N 46 6 E
Al Hamādah al Ḩamrā' 83 29 30N 12 0 E
Al Hamrā 64 24 2N 38 55 E
Al Ḩarīq 64 23 29N 46 27 E
Al Harīr, W. → 62 32 44N 35 59 E
Al Harūj al Aswad 83 27 0N 17 10 E
Al Ḩasakah 64 36 35N 40 45 E
Al Ḩawīyah 64 24 40N 49 15 E
Al Ḩawrah 63 13 50N 47 35 E
Al Ḩawţah 63 16 5N 48 20 E
Al Ḩayy 64 32 5N 46 5 E
Al Ḩillah, Iraq 64 32 30N 44 25 E
Al Ḩillah, Si. Arab. 64 23 35N 46 50 E
Al Hindīyah 64 32 30N 44 10 E
Al Ḩişnn 62 32 29N 35 52 E
Al Hoceïma 82 35 8N 3 58W
Al Ḩudaydah 63 14 50N 43 0 E
Al Ḩufrah, Awbārī, Libya 83 25 32N 14 1 E
Al Ḩufrah, Misrātah, Libya 83 29 5N 18 3 E
Al Hūfuf 64 25 25N 49 45 E
Al Ḩulwah 64 23 24N 46 48 E
Al Husayyāt 83 30 24N 20 37 E
Al 'Idwah 64 27 15N 42 35 E
Al Irq 81 29 5N 21 35 E
Al Ittihad = Madīnat ash Sha'b 63 12 50N 45 0 E
Al Jāfūrah 64 25 0N 50 15 E
Al Jaghbūb 81 29 42N 24 38 E
Al Jahrah 64 29 25N 47 40 E
Al Jalāmīd 64 31 20N 39 45 E
Al Jawf, Libya 81 24 10N 23 24 E
Al Jawf, Si. Arab. 64 29 55N 39 40 E
Al Jazir 63 18 30N 56 31 E
Al Jazirah, Libya 81 26 10N 21 20 E
Al Jazirah, Si. Arab. 64 33 30N 44 0 E
Al Jubayl 64 27 0N 49 50 E
Al Jubaylah 64 24 55N 46 25 E
Al Junaynah 81 13 27N 22 45 E
Al Juwārah 63 19 0N 57 13 E
Al Khābūrah 65 23 57N 57 5 E
Al Khalīl = Hebron 62 31 32N 35 6 E
Al Khalūf 63 20 30N 58 13 E
Al Kharfah 64 22 0N 46 35 E
Al Kharj 64 24 0N 47 0 E
Al Khufayfīyah 64 24 50N 44 35 E
Al Khums 83 32 40N 14 17 E
Al Khums □ 83 31 20N 14 10 E
Al Khurmah 64 21 58N 42 3 E
Al Kufrah 81 24 17N 23 15 E
Al Kūt 64 32 30N 46 0 E
Al Kuwayt 64 29 30N 47 30 E
Al Lādhiqīyah 64 35 30N 35 45 E
Al Lidām 63 20 33N 44 45 E
Al Līth 86 20 9N 40 15 E
Al Lubban 62 32 9N 35 14 E
Al Luḩayyah 63 15 45N 42 40 E
Al Madīnah 64 24 35N 39 52 E
Al-Mafraq 62 32 17N 36 14 E
Al Majma'ah 64 25 57N 45 22 E
Al Manāmāh 65 26 10N 50 30 E
Al Marj 81 32 25N 20 30 E
Al Maşīrah 63 20 25N 58 50 E
Al Matamma 63 16 10N 44 30 E
Al Mawşil 64 36 15N 43 5 E
Al Mazra 62 31 16N 35 31 E
Al Midhnab 64 25 50N 44 18 E
Al Miqdādīyah 64 34 0N 45 0 E
Al Mish'āb 64 28 12N 48 36 E
Al Mubarraz 64 25 30N 49 40 E
Al Muḩarraq 65 26 15N 50 40 E
Al Mukallā 63 14 33N 49 2 E
Al Mukhā 63 13 18N 43 15 E
Al Musayyib 64 32 40N 44 25 E
Al Mustajiddah 64 26 30N 41 50 E
Al Muwayliḩ 64 27 40N 35 30 E
Al Qaddāḩīyah 83 31 15N 15 9 E
Al Qadīmah 64 22 20N 39 13 E
Al Qāmishli 64 37 10N 41 10 E
Al Qaryah ash Sharqīyah 83 30 28N 13 40 E
Al Qaşabát 83 32 39N 14 1 E
Al Qaţīf 64 26 35N 50 0 E
Al Qaţrūn 83 24 56N 15 3 E
Al Quaisūmah 64 28 10N 46 20 E
Al Quds 62 31 47N 35 10 E
Al Qunfidha 86 19 3N 41 4 E
Al Quraiyat 65 23 17N 58 53 E
Al Qurnah 64 31 1N 47 25 E
Al 'Ulá 64 26 35N 38 0 E
Al Uqaylah ash Sharqīgah 83 30 12N 19 10 E
Al Uqayr 64 25 40N 50 15 E
Al 'Uthmānīyahyah 64 25 5N 49 22 E
Al 'Uwaynid 64 24 50N 46 0 E
Al' 'Uwayqīlah ash Sharqīgah 64 30 30N 42 10 E
Al 'Uyūn 64 26 30N 43 50 E
Al Wajh 86 26 10N 36 30 E
Al Wakrah 65 25 10N 51 40 E
Al Wari'āh 64 27 51N 47 25 E
Al Wātīyah 83 32 28N 11 57 E
Al Yāmūn 62 32 29N 35 14 E
Ala 38 45 46N 11 0 E
Alabama □ 115 33 0N 87 0W
Alabama → 115 31 8N 87 57W
Alaçati 45 38 16N 26 23 E
Alaejos 30 41 18N 5 13W
Alagna Valsésia 38 45 51N 7 56 E
Alagoa Grande 127 7 3 S 35 35W
Alagoas □ 127 9 0 S 36 0W
Alagoinhas 127 12 7 S 38 20W
Alagón 32 41 46N 1 12W
Alagón → 31 39 44N 6 53W
Alajuela 121 10 2N 84 8W
Alakamisy 93 21 19 S 47 14 E
Alakurtti 52 67 0N 30 30 E
Alameda, Spain 31 37 12N 4 39W
Alameda, Idaho, U.S.A. 118 43 2N 112 30W
Alameda, N. Mex., U.S.A. 119 35 10N 106 43W
Alamitos, Sierra de los 120 37 21N 115 10W
Alamo 119 36 21N 115 10W
Alamogordo 119 32 59N 106 0W
Alamos 120 27 0N 109 0W
Alamosa 119 37 30N 106 0W
Åland 51 60 15N 20 0 E
Aland 70 17 36N 76 35 E
Alandroal 31 38 41N 7 24W
Alandur 70 13 0N 80 15 E
Alange, Presa de 31 38 45N 6 18W
Alanis 31 38 3N 5 43W
Alanya 64 36 38N 32 0 E
Alaotra, Farihin' 93 17 30 S 48 30 E
Alapayevsk 58 57 52N 61 42 E
Alar del Rey 30 42 38N 4 20W
Alaraz 30 40 45N 5 17W
Alaşehir 53 38 23N 28 30 E
Alaska □ 104 65 0N 150 0W
Alaska, G. of 104 58 0N 145 0W
Alaska Highway 108 60 0N 130 0W
Alaska Pen. 104 56 0N 160 0W
Alaska Range 104 62 50N 151 0W
Alássio 38 44 1N 8 10 E
Alataw Shankou 75 45 5N 81 57 E
Alatri 40 41 44N 13 21 E
Alatyr 55 54 45N 46 35 E
Alatyr → 55 54 52N 46 36 E
Alausi 126 2 0 S 78 50W
Álava □ 32 42 48N 2 28W
Alava, C. 118 48 10N 124 40W
Alaverdi 57 41 15N 44 37 E
Alawoona 99 34 45 S 140 30 E
Alayor 32 39 57N 4 8 E
Alazan → 57 41 5N 46 40 E
Alba 38 44 41N 8 1 E
Alba □ 46 46 10N 23 30 E
Alba de Tormes 30 40 50N 5 30W
Alba Iulia 46 46 8N 23 39 E
Albac 46 46 28N 23 1 E
Albacete 33 39 0N 1 50W
Albacete □ 33 38 50N 2 0W
Albacutya, L. 99 35 45 S 141 58 E
Ålbæk 49 57 36N 10 25 E
Ålbæk Bucht 49 57 35N 10 40 E
Albaida 33 38 51N 0 31W
Albalate de las Nogueras 32 40 22N 2 18W
Albalate del Arzobispo 32 41 6N 0 31W
Albania ■ 44 41 0N 20 0 E
Albano Laziale 40 41 44N 12 40 E
Albany, Austral. 96 35 1 S 117 58 E
Albany, Ga., U.S.A. 115 31 40N 84 10W
Albany, Minn., U.S.A. 116 45 37N 94 38W
Albany, N.Y., U.S.A. 114 42 35N 73 47W
Albany, Oreg., U.S.A. 118 44 41N 123 0W
Albany, Tex., U.S.A. 117 32 45N 99 20W
Albany → 106 52 17N 81 31W
Albardón 124 31 20 S 68 30W
Albarracín 32 40 25N 1 26W
Albarracín, Sierra de 32 40 30N 1 30W
Albatross B. 97 12 45 S 141 30 E
Albegna → 39 42 30N 11 11 E
Albemarle 115 35 27N 80 15W
Albemarle Sd. 115 36 0N 76 30W
Albenga 38 44 3N 8 12 E
Alberche → 30 39 58N 4 46W
Alberdi 124 26 14 S 58 20W
Alberes, Mts. 32 42 28N 2 56 E
Alberique 33 39 7N 0 31W
Albersdorf 24 54 8N 9 19 E
Albert 19 50 0N 2 38 E
Albert Canyon 108 51 8N 117 41W
Albert L. 99 35 30 S 139 10 E
Albert, L. = Mobutu Sese Seko, L. 90 1 30N 31 0 E
Albert Lea 116 43 32N 93 20W
Albert Nile → 90 3 36N 32 2 E
Alberta □ 108 54 40N 115 0W
Alberti 124 35 1 S 60 16W
Albertinia 92 34 11 S 21 34 E
Albertirsa 27 47 14N 19 37 E
Alberton 107 46 50N 64 0W
Albertville 21 45 40N 6 22 E
Albertville = Kalemie 90 5 55 S 29 9 E
Alberz, Reshteh-Ye Kūhhā-Ye 65 36 0N 52 0 E
Albi 20 43 56N 2 9 E
Albia 116 41 0N 92 50W
Albina 127 5 37N 54 15W
Albina, Ponta 92 15 52 S 11 44 E
Albino 38 45 47N 9 48 E
Albion, Idaho, U.S.A. 118 42 21N 113 37W
Albion, Mich., U.S.A. 114 42 15N 84 45W
Albion, Nebr., U.S.A. 116 41 47N 98 0W
Albion, Pa., U.S.A. 112 41 53N 80 21W
Albocácer 32 40 21N 0 1 E
Alböke 49 56 57N 16 47 E
Alborán 31 35 57N 3 0W
Alborea 33 39 17N 1 24W
Ålborg 49 57 2N 9 54 E
Ålborg B. 49 56 50N 10 35 E
Albox 33 37 23N 2 8W
Albreda 108 52 35N 119 10W
Albuera, La 31 38 45N 6 49W
Albufeira 31 37 5N 8 15W
Albula → 25 46 38N 9 30 E
Albuñol 33 36 48N 3 11W
Albuquerque 119 35 5N 106 47W
Albuquerque, Cayos de 121 12 10N 81 50W
Alburg 113 44 58N 73 19W
Alburno, Mte. 41 40 32N 15 15 E
Alburquerque 31 39 15N 6 59W
Albury 97 36 3 S 146 56 E
Alby 48 62 30N 15 28 E
Alcácer do Sal 31 38 22N 8 33W
Alcaçovas 31 38 23N 8 9W
Alcalá de Chisvert 32 40 19N 0 13 E
Alcalá de Guadaira 31 37 20N 5 50W
Alcalá de Henares 32 40 28N 3 22W
Alcalá de los Gazules 31 36 29N 5 43W
Alcalá la Real 31 37 27N 3 57W
Alcamo 40 37 59N 12 55 E
Alcanadre 32 42 24N 2 7W
Alcanadre → 32 41 43N 0 12W
Alcanar 32 40 33N 0 28 E
Alcanede 31 39 25N 8 49W
Alcanena 31 39 27N 8 40W
Alcañices 30 41 41N 6 21W
Alcaníz 32 41 2N 0 8W
Alcântara 127 2 20 S 44 30W
Alcántara 31 39 41N 6 57W
Alcantara L. 109 60 57N 108 9W
Alcantarilla 33 37 59N 1 12W
Alcaracejos 31 38 24N 4 58W
Alcaraz 33 38 40N 2 29W
Alcaraz, Sierra de 33 38 40N 2 20W
Alcarria, La 32 40 31N 2 45W
Alcaudete 31 37 35N 4 5W
Alcázar de San Juan 33 39 24N 3 12W
Alcira 33 39 9N 0 30W
Alcoa 115 35 50N 84 0W
Alcobaça 31 39 32N 9 0W
Alcobendas 32 40 32N 3 38W
Alcolea del Pinar 32 41 2N 2 28W
Alcora 32 40 5N 0 14W
Alcoutim 31 37 25N 7 28W
Alcova 118 42 37N 106 52W
Alcoy 33 38 43N 0 30W
Alcubierre, Sierra de 32 41 45N 0 22W
Alcublas 32 39 48N 0 43W
Alcudia 32 39 51N 3 7 E
Alcudia, B. de 32 39 47N 3 15 E
Alcudia, Sierra de la 31 38 34N 4 30W
Aldabra Is. 3 9 22 S 46 28 E
Aldan 59 58 40N 125 30 E
Aldan → 59 63 28N 129 35 E
Aldeburgh 13 52 9N 1 35 E
Aldeia Nova 31 37 55N 7 24W
Alder 118 45 27N 112 3W
Alderney 18 49 42N 2 12W
Aldershot 13 51 15N 0 43W
Aldersyde 108 50 40N 113 53W
Aledo 116 41 10N 90 50W
Alefa 87 11 55N 36 55 E
Aleg 84 17 3N 13 55W
Alegre 125 20 50 S 41 30W
Alegrete 125 29 40 S 56 0W
Aleisk 58 52 40N 83 0 E
Alejandro Selkirk, I. 95 33 50 S 80 15W
Aleksandriya, Ukraine S.S.R., U.S.S.R. 54 50 37N 26 19 E
Aleksandriya, Ukraine S.S.R., U.S.S.R. 56 48 42N 33 3 E
Aleksandriyskaya 57 43 59N 47 0 E
Aleksandrov 55 56 23N 38 44 E
Aleksandrovac, Srbija, Yugo. 42 44 28N 21 13 E
Aleksandrovac, Srbija, Yugo. 42 43 28N 21 3 E
Aleksandrovka 56 48 55N 32 20 E
Aleksandrovo 43 43 14N 24 51 E
Aleksandrovsk-Sakhaliniskiy 59 50 50N 142 20 E
Aleksandrovskiy Zavod 59 50 40N 117 50 E
Aleksandrovskoye 58 60 35N 77 50 E
Aleksandrów Kujawski 28 52 53N 18 43 E
Aleksandrów Łódźki 28 51 49N 19 17 E
Alekseyevka 55 50 43N 38 40 E
Aleksin 55 54 31N 37 9 E
Aleksinac 42 43 31N 21 42 E
Além Paraíba 125 21 52 S 42 41W
Alemania, Argent. 124 25 40 S 65 30W
Alemania, Chile 124 25 10 S 69 55W
Ålen 47 62 51N 11 17 E
Alençon 18 48 27N 0 4 E
Alenuihaha Chan. 110 20 25N 156 0W
Aleppo = Ḩalab 64 36 10N 37 15 E
Aléria 21 42 5N 9 26 E
Alert Bay 108 50 30N 126 55W
Alès 21 44 9N 4 5 E
Aleşd 46 47 3N 22 22 E
Alessándria 38 44 54N 8 37 E
Ålestrup 49 56 42N 9 29 E
Ålesund 47 62 28N 6 12 E
Alet-les-Bains 20 43 0N 2 14 E
Aleutian Is. 104 52 0N 175 0W
Aleutian Trench 94 48 0N 180 0
Alexander 116 47 51N 103 40W
Alexander Arch. 104 57 0N 135 0W
Alexander B. 92 28 36 S 16 33 E
Alexander City 115 32 58N 85 57W
Alexander I. 5 69 0 S 70 0W
Alexandra, Austral. 99 37 8 S 145 40 E
Alexandra, N.Z. 101 45 14 S 169 25 E
Alexandra Falls 108 60 29N 116 18W
Alexandria, B.C., Can. 108 52 35N 122 27W
Alexandria, Ont., Can. 106 45 19N 74 38W
Alexandria, Romania 46 43 57N 25 24 E
Alexandria, S. Afr. 92 33 38 S 26 28 E
Alexandria, Ind., U.S.A. 114 40 18N 85 40W
Alexandria, La., U.S.A. 117 31 20N 92 30W
Alexandria, Minn., U.S.A. 116 45 50N 95 20W
Alexandria, S.D., U.S.A. 116 43 40N 97 45W
Alexandria, Va., U.S.A. 114 38 47N 77 1W

Alexandria = El Iskandarîya	**86**	31 0N	30 0 E
Alexandria Bay	**114**	44 20N	75 52W
Alexandrina, L.	**97**	35 25 S	139 10 E
Alexandroúpolis	**44**	40 50N	25 54 E
Alexis →	**107**	52 33N	56 8W
Alexis Creek	**108**	52 10N	123 20W
Alfambra	**32**	40 33N	1 5W
Alfândega da Fé	**30**	41 20N	6 59W
Alfaro	**32**	42 10N	1 50W
Alfatar	**43**	43 59N	27 13 E
Alfeld	**24**	52 0N	9 49 E
Alfenas	**125**	21 20 S	46 10W
Alfiós →	**45**	37 40N	21 33 E
Alfonsine	**39**	44 30N	12 1 E
Alford	**14**	57 13N	2 42W
Alfred, Me., U.S.A.	**113**	43 28N	70 40W
Alfred, N.Y., U.S.A.	**112**	42 15N	77 45W
Alfreton	**12**	53 6N	1 22W
Alfta	**48**	61 21N	16 4 E
Alga	**58**	49 53N	57 20 E
Algaba, La	**31**	37 27N	6 1W
Algar	**31**	36 40N	5 39W
Ålgård	**47**	58 46N	5 53 E
Algarinejo	**31**	37 19N	4 9W
Algarve	**31**	36 58N	8 20W
Algeciras	**31**	36 9N	5 28W
Algemesí	**33**	39 11N	0 27W
Alger	**82**	36 42N	3 8 E
Algeria ■	**82**	35 10N	3 11 E
Alghero	**40**	40 34N	8 20 E
Algiers = Alger	**82**	36 42N	3 8 E
Algoabaai	**92**	33 50 S	25 45 E
Algodonales	**31**	36 54N	5 24W
Algodor →	**30**	39 55N	3 53W
Algoma, Oreg., U.S.A.	**118**	42 25N	121 54W
Algoma, Wis., U.S.A.	**114**	44 35N	87 27W
Algona	**116**	43 4N	94 14W
Algonac	**112**	42 37N	82 32W
Alhama de Almería	**33**	36 57N	2 34W
Alhama de Aragón	**32**	41 18N	1 54W
Alhama de Granada	**31**	37 0N	3 59W
Alhama de Murcia	**33**	37 51N	1 25W
Alhambra, Spain	**33**	38 54N	3 4W
Alhambra, U.S.A.	**119**	34 2N	118 10W
Alhaurín el Grande	**31**	36 39N	4 41W
Alhucemas = Al-Hoceïma	**82**	35 8N	3 58W
'Alī al Gharbī	**64**	32 30N	46 45 E
Ali Bayramly	**57**	39 59N	48 52 E
Ali Sabieh	**87**	11 10N	42 44 E
Ália	**40**	37 47N	13 42 E
'Alīābād	**65**	28 10N	57 35 E
Aliaga	**32**	40 40N	0 42W
Aliákmon →	**44**	40 30N	22 36 E
Alibag	**70**	18 38N	72 56 E
Alibo	**87**	9 52N	37 5 E
Alibunar	**42**	45 5N	20 57 E
Alicante	**33**	38 23N	0 30W
Alicante □	**33**	38 30N	0 37W
Alice, S. Afr.	**92**	32 48 S	26 55 E
Alice, U.S.A.	**117**	27 47N	98 1W
Alice →, Queens., Austral.	**98**	24 2 S	144 50 E
Alice →, Queens., Austral.	**98**	15 35 S	142 20 E
Alice Arm	**108**	55 29N	129 31W
Alice, Punta dell'	**41**	39 23N	17 10 E
Alice Springs	**96**	23 40 S	133 50 E
Alicedale	**92**	33 15 S	26 4 E
Aliceville	**115**	33 9N	88 10W
Alick Cr. →	**98**	20 55 S	142 20 E
Alicudi, I.	**41**	38 33N	14 20 E
Alida	**109**	49 25N	101 55W
Aligarh, Raj., India	**68**	25 55N	76 15 E
Aligarh, Ut. P., India	**68**	27 55N	78 10 E
Alīgūdarz	**64**	33 25N	49 45 E
Alijó	**30**	41 16N	7 27W
Alimena	**41**	37 42N	14 4 E
Alimnía	**45**	36 16N	27 43 E
Alingsås	**49**	57 56N	12 31 E
Alipur	**68**	29 25N	70 55 E
Alipur Duar	**69**	26 30N	89 35 E
Aliquippa	**114**	40 38N	80 18W
Aliste →	**30**	41 34N	5 58W
Alitus	**54**	54 24N	24 3 E
Alivérion	**45**	38 24N	24 2 E
Aliwal North	**92**	30 45 S	26 45 E
Alix	**108**	52 24N	113 11W
Aljezur	**31**	37 18N	8 49W
Aljustrel	**31**	37 55N	8 10W
Alkamari	**85**	13 27N	11 10 E
Alkmaar	**16**	52 37N	4 45 E
All American Canal	**119**	32 45N	115 0W
Allada	**85**	6 41N	2 9 E
Allah Dad	**68**	25 38N	67 34 E
Allahabad	**69**	25 25N	81 58 E
Allakh-Yun	**59**	60 50N	137 5 E
Allal Tazi	**82**	34 30N	6 20W
Allan	**109**	51 53N	106 4W
Allanche	**20**	45 14N	2 57 E
Allanmyo	**67**	19 30N	95 17 E
Allanridge	**92**	27 45 S	26 40 E
Allanwater	**106**	50 14N	90 10W
Allaqi, Wadi →	**86**	23 7N	32 47 E
Allariz	**30**	42 11N	7 50W
Allassac	**20**	45 15N	1 29 E
Allegan	**114**	42 32N	85 52W
Allegany	**112**	42 6N	78 30W
Allegheny →	**114**	40 27N	80 0W
Allegheny Mts.	**114**	38 0N	80 0W
Allegheny Res.	**112**	42 0N	78 55W
Allègre	**20**	45 12N	3 41 E
Allen, Bog of	**15**	53 15N	7 0W
Allen, L.	**15**	54 12N	8 5W
Allenby (Hussein) Bridge	**62**	31 53N	35 33 E
Allende	**120**	28 20N	100 50W
Allentown	**114**	40 36N	75 30W
Allentsteig	**26**	48 41N	15 20 E
Alleppey	**70**	9 30N	76 28 E
Aller →	**24**	52 57N	9 10 E
Allevard	**21**	45 24N	6 5 E
Alliance, Nebr., U.S.A.	**116**	42 10N	102 50W
Alliance, Ohio, U.S.A.	**114**	40 53N	81 7W
Allier □	**20**	46 25N	3 0 E
Allier →	**19**	46 57N	3 4 E
Allingåbro	**49**	56 28N	10 20 E
Allinge	**49**	55 17N	14 50 E
Alliston	**106**	44 9N	79 52W
Alloa	**14**	56 7N	3 49W
Allos	**21**	44 15N	6 38 E
Alma, Can.	**107**	48 35N	71 40W
Alma, Ga., U.S.A.	**115**	31 33N	82 28W
Alma, Kans., U.S.A.	**116**	39 1N	96 22W
Alma, Mich., U.S.A.	**114**	43 25N	84 40W
Alma, Nebr., U.S.A.	**116**	40 10N	99 25W
Alma, Wis., U.S.A.	**116**	44 19N	91 54W
'Almā ash Sha'b	**62**	33 7N	35 9 E
Alma Ata	**58**	43 15N	76 57 E
Almada	**31**	38 40N	9 9W
Almaden	**98**	17 22 S	144 40 E
Almadén	**31**	38 49N	4 52W
Almagro	**31**	38 50N	3 45W
Almanor, L.	**118**	40 15N	121 11W
Almansa	**33**	38 51N	1 5W
Almanza	**30**	42 39N	5 3W
Almanzor, Pico de	**30**	40 15N	5 18W
Almanzora →	**33**	37 14N	1 46W
Almarcha, La	**32**	39 41N	2 24W
Almaş, Mţii.	**46**	44 49N	22 12 E
Almazán	**32**	41 30N	2 30W
Almazora	**32**	39 57N	0 3W
Almeirim, Brazil	**127**	1 30 S	52 34W
Almeirim, Port.	**31**	39 12N	8 37W
Almelo	**16**	52 22N	6 42 E
Almenar	**32**	41 43N	2 12W
Almenara	**32**	39 46N	0 14W
Almenara, Sierra de	**33**	37 34N	1 32W
Almendralejo	**31**	38 41N	6 26W
Almería	**33**	36 52N	2 27W
Almería □	**33**	37 20N	2 20W
Almería, G. de	**33**	36 41N	2 28W
Almirante	**14**	9 10N	82 30W
Almiropótamos	**45**	38 16N	24 11 E
Almirós	**45**	39 11N	22 45 E
Almodôvar	**31**	37 31N	8 2W
Almodóvar del Campo	**31**	38 43N	4 10W
Almogia	**31**	36 50N	4 32W
Almonaster la Real	**31**	37 52N	6 48W
Almont	**112**	42 53N	83 2W
Almonte	**113**	45 14N	76 12W
Almonte →	**31**	39 41N	6 28W
Almora	**69**	29 38N	79 40 E
Almoradi	**33**	38 7N	0 46W
Almorox	**30**	40 14N	4 24W
Almoustarat	**85**	17 35N	0 8 E
Älmult	**49**	56 33N	14 8 E
Almuñécar	**31**	36 43N	3 41W
Almunia de Doña Godina, La	**32**	41 29N	1 23W
Alnif	**82**	31 10N	5 8W
Alnwick	**12**	55 25N	1 42W
Aloi	**90**	2 16N	33 10 E
Alonsa	**109**	50 50N	99 0W
Alor	**73**	8 15 S	124 30 E
Alor Setar	**71**	6 7N	100 22 E
Alora	**31**	36 49N	4 46W
Alosno	**31**	37 33N	7 7W
Alougoum	**82**	30 17N	6 56W
Alpedrinha	**30**	40 6N	7 27W
Alpena	**114**	45 6N	83 24W
Alpes-de-Haute-Provence □	**21**	44 8N	6 10 E
Alpes-Maritimes □	**21**	43 55N	7 10 E
Alpha	**97**	23 39 S	146 37 E
Alpi Apuane	**38**	44 7N	10 14 E
Alpi Lepontine	**25**	46 22N	8 27 E
Alpi Orobie	**38**	46 7N	10 0 E
Alpi Retiche	**25**	46 30N	10 0 E
Alpiarça	**31**	39 15N	8 35W
Alpine, Ariz., U.S.A.	**119**	33 57N	109 4W
Alpine, Tex., U.S.A.	**117**	30 25N	103 35W
Alps	**22**	47 0N	8 0 E
Alpujarras, Las	**33**	36 55N	3 20W
Alrø	**49**	55 52N	10 5 E
Alsace	**19**	48 15N	7 25 E
Alsask	**109**	51 21N	109 59W
Alsásua	**32**	42 54N	2 10W
Alsen	**48**	63 23N	13 56 E
Alsfeld	**24**	50 44N	9 19 E
Alsónémedi	**27**	47 20N	19 15 E
Alsten	**50**	65 58N	12 40 E
Alta	**50**	69 57N	23 10 E
Alta Gracia	**124**	31 40 S	64 30W
Alta Lake	**108**	50 10N	123 0W
Alta, Sierra	**32**	40 31N	1 30W
Altaelva →	**50**	69 46N	23 45 E
Altafjorden	**50**	70 5N	23 5 E
Altagracia	**126**	10 45N	71 30W
Altai = Aerhatai Shan	**75**	46 40N	92 45 E
Altamaha →	**115**	31 19N	81 17W
Altamira, Brazil	**127**	3 12 S	52 10W
Altamira, Chile	**124**	25 47 S	69 51W
Altamira, Cuevas de	**30**	43 20N	4 5W
Altamont	**113**	42 43N	74 3W
Altamura	**41**	40 50N	16 33 E
Altanbulag	**75**	50 16N	106 30 E
Altar	**120**	30 40N	111 50W
Altata	**120**	24 30N	108 0W
Altavista	**114**	37 9N	79 22W
Altay	**75**	47 48N	88 10 E
Altdorf	**25**	46 52N	8 36 E
Alte Mellum	**24**	53 45N	8 6 E
Altea	**33**	38 38N	0 2W
Altenberg	**24**	50 46N	13 47 E
Altenbruch	**24**	53 48N	8 44 E
Altenburg	**24**	50 59N	12 28 E
Altenkirchen, Germ., E.	**24**	54 38N	13 20 E
Altenkirchen, Germ., W.	**24**	50 41N	7 38 E
Altenmarkt	**26**	47 43N	14 39 E
Altenteptow	**24**	53 42N	13 15 E
Alter do Chão	**31**	39 12N	7 40W
Altkirch	**19**	47 37N	7 15 E
Altmühl →	**25**	48 54N	11 54 E
Alto Adige = Trentino-Alto Adige	**38**	46 30N	11 0 E
Alto Araguaia	**127**	17 15 S	53 20W
Alto Chindio	**91**	16 19 S	35 25 E
Alto Cuchumatanes = Cuchumatanes, Sa. de los	**120**	15 30N	91 10W
Alto del Inca	**124**	24 10 S	68 10W
Alto Ligonha	**91**	15 30 S	38 11 E
Alto Molocue	**91**	15 50 S	37 35 E
Alto Paraná □	**125**	25 0 S	54 50W
Alton, Can.	**112**	43 54N	80 5W
Alton, U.S.A.	**116**	38 55N	90 5W
Alton Downs	**99**	26 7 S	138 57 E
Altona, Austral.	**100**	37 51 S	144 50 E
Altona, Ger.	**24**	53 32N	9 56 E
Altoona	**114**	40 32N	78 24W
Altopáscio	**38**	43 50N	10 40 E
Altötting	**25**	48 14N	12 41 E
Altstätten	**25**	47 22N	9 33 E
Altun Shan	**75**	38 30N	88 0 E
Alturas	**118**	41 36N	120 37W
Altus	**117**	34 30N	99 25W
Alucra	**57**	40 22N	38 47 E
Aluksne	**54**	57 24N	27 3 E
Alùla	**63**	11 50N	50 45 E
Alupka	**56**	44 23N	34 2 E
Alushta	**56**	44 40N	34 25 E
Alusi	**73**	7 35 S	131 40 E
Alustante	**32**	40 36N	1 40W
Alva	**117**	36 50N	98 50W
Alvaiázere	**30**	39 49N	8 23W
Älvängen	**49**	57 58N	12 8 E
Alvarado, Mexico	**120**	18 40N	95 50W
Alvarado, U.S.A.	**117**	32 25N	97 15W
Alvaro Obregón, Presa	**120**	27 55N	109 52W
Alvdal	**47**	62 6N	10 37 E
Alvear	**124**	29 5 S	56 30W
Alverca	**31**	38 56N	9 1W
Alvesta	**49**	56 54N	14 35 E
Alvie	**99**	38 14 S	143 30 E
Alvin	**117**	29 23N	95 12W
Alvinston	**113**	42 49N	81 52W
Alvito	**31**	38 15N	8 0W
Älvros	**48**	62 3N	14 38 E
Älvsborgs län □	**49**	58 30N	12 30 E
Älvsbyn	**50**	65 40N	21 0 E
Älvsered	**49**	57 14N	12 51 E
Alwar	**68**	27 38N	76 34 E
Alwaye	**70**	10 8N	76 24 E
Alxa Zuoqi	**76**	38 50N	105 40 E
Alyangula	**97**	13 55 S	136 30 E
Alyaskitovyy	**59**	64 45N	141 30 E
Alyata	**57**	39 58N	49 25 E
Alyth	**14**	56 38N	3 15W
Alzada	**116**	45 3N	104 22W
Alzano Lombardo	**38**	45 44N	9 43 E
Alzey	**25**	49 48N	8 4 E
Am Dam	**81**	12 40N	20 35 E
Am Géréda	**81**	12 53N	21 14 E
Am-Timan	**81**	11 0N	20 10 E
Amadeus, L.	**96**	24 54 S	131 0 E
Amâdi	**87**	5 29N	30 25 E
Amadi	**90**	3 40N	26 40 E
Amadjuak	**105**	64 0N	72 39W
Amadjuak L.	**105**	65 0N	71 8W
Amadora	**31**	38 45N	9 13W
Amagasaki	**74**	34 42N	135 20 E
Amager	**49**	55 37N	12 35 E
Amakusa-Shotō	**74**	32 15N	130 10 E
Åmål	**48**	59 3N	12 42 E
Amalapuram	**70**	16 35N	81 55 E
Amalfi	**41**	40 39N	14 34 E
Amaliás	**45**	37 47N	21 22 E
Amalner	**68**	21 5N	75 5 E
Amambaí	**125**	23 5 S	55 13W
Amambaí →	**125**	23 22 S	53 56W
Amambay □	**125**	23 0 S	56 0W
Amambay, Cordillera de	**125**	23 0 S	55 45W
Amándola	**39**	42 59N	13 21 E
Amangeldy	**58**	50 10N	65 10 E
Amantea	**41**	39 8N	16 3 E
Amapá	**127**	2 5N	50 50W
Amapá □	**127**	1 40N	52 0W
Amara	**87**	10 25N	34 10 E
Amarante, Brazil	**127**	6 14 S	42 50W
Amarante, Port.	**30**	41 16N	8 5W
Amaranth	**109**	50 36N	98 43W
Amaravati →	**70**	11 0N	78 15 E
Amareleja	**31**	38 12N	7 13W
Amargosa	**127**	13 2 S	39 36W
Amarillo	**117**	35 14N	101 46W
Amaro, Mt.	**39**	42 5N	14 6 E
Amarpur	**69**	25 5N	87 0 E
Amasra	**64**	41 45N	32 30 E
Amassama	**85**	5 1N	6 2 E
Amasya	**64**	40 40N	35 50 E
Amatikulu	**93**	29 3 S	31 33 E
Amatitlán	**120**	14 29N	90 38W
Amatrice	**39**	42 38N	13 16 E
Amazon = Amazonas →	**127**	0 5 S	50 0W
Amazonas □	**126**	4 0 S	62 0W
Amazonas →	**127**	0 5 S	50 0W
Ambad	**70**	19 38N	75 50 E
Ambahakily	**93**	21 36 S	43 41 E
Ambala	**68**	30 23N	76 56 E
Ambalangoda	**70**	6 15N	80 5 E
Ambalapuzha	**70**	9 25N	76 25 E
Ambalavao	**93**	21 50 S	46 56 E
Ambam	**88**	2 20N	11 15 E
Ambanja	**93**	13 40 S	48 27 E
Ambarchik	**59**	69 40N	162 20 E
Ambarijeby	**93**	14 56 S	47 41 E
Ambarnath	**70**	19 12N	73 22 E
Ambaro, Helodranon'	**93**	13 23 S	48 38 E
Ambartsevo	**58**	57 30N	83 52 E
Ambasamudram	**70**	8 43N	77 25 E
Ambato	**126**	1 5 S	78 42W
Ambato Boeny	**93**	16 28 S	46 43 E
Ambato, Sierra de	**124**	28 25 S	66 10W
Ambatofinandrahana	**93**	20 33 S	46 48 E
Ambatolampy	**93**	19 20 S	47 35 E
Ambatondrazaka	**93**	17 55 S	48 28 E
Ambatosoratra	**93**	17 37 S	48 31 E
Ambenja	**93**	15 17 S	46 58 E
Amberg	**25**	49 25N	11 52 E
Ambergris Cay	**120**	18 0N	88 0W
Ambérieu-en-Bugey	**21**	45 57N	5 20 E
Amberley	**101**	43 9 S	172 44 E
Ambert	**20**	45 33N	3 44 E
Ambidédi	**84**	14 35N	11 47W
Ambikapur	**69**	23 15N	83 15 E
Ambikol	**86**	21 20N	30 50 E
Ambinanindrano	**93**	20 5 S	48 23 E
Ambjörnarp	**49**	57 25N	13 17 E
Ambleside	**12**	54 26N	2 58W
Ambo, Ethiopia	**87**	12 20N	37 30 E
Ambo, Peru	**126**	10 5 S	76 10W
Ambodifototra	**93**	16 59 S	49 52 E
Ambodilazana	**93**	18 6 S	49 10 E
Ambohimahasoa	**93**	21 7 S	47 13 E
Ambohimanga	**93**	20 52 S	47 36 E
Ambon	**73**	3 35 S	128 20 E
Amboseli L.	**90**	2 40 S	37 10 E
Ambositra	**93**	20 31 S	47 25 E
Ambovombé	**93**	25 11 S	46 5 E
Amboy	**119**	34 33N	115 51W
Amboyna I.	**72**	7 50N	112 50 E
Ambridge	**112**	40 36N	80 15W
Ambriz	**88**	7 48 S	13 8 E
Ambur	**70**	12 48N	78 43 E
Amby	**99**	26 30 S	148 11 E
Amchitka I.	**104**	51 30N	179 0W
Amderma	**58**	69 45N	61 30 E
Ameca	**120**	20 30N	104 0W
Ameca →	**120**	20 40N	105 15W
Amecameca	**120**	19 7N	98 46W
Ameland	**16**	53 27N	5 45 E
Amélia	**39**	42 34N	12 25 E
Amélie-les-Bains-Palalda	**20**	42 29N	2 41 E
Amen	**59**	68 45N	180 0 E
Amendolaro	**41**	39 58N	16 34 E
American Falls	**118**	42 46N	112 56W
American Falls Res.	**118**	43 0N	112 50W
American Highland	**5**	73 0 S	75 0 E
American Samoa	**101**	14 20 S	170 40W
Americana	**125**	22 45 S	47 20W
Americus	**115**	32 0N	84 10W
Amersfoort, Neth.	**16**	52 9N	5 23 E
Amersfoort, S. Afr.	**93**	26 59 S	29 53 E
Amery	**109**	56 34N	94 3W
Amery Ice Shelf	**5**	69 30 S	72 0 E
Ames	**116**	42 0N	93 40W
Amesbury	**113**	42 50N	70 52W
Amesdale	**109**	50 2N	92 55W
Amfíklia	**45**	38 38N	22 35 E
Amfilokhía	**45**	38 52N	21 9 E
Amfípolis	**44**	40 48N	23 52 E
Ámfissa	**45**	38 32N	22 22 E
Amga	**59**	60 50N	132 0 E
Amga →	**59**	62 38N	134 32 E
Amgu	**59**	45 45N	137 15 E
Amgun →	**59**	52 56N	139 38 E
Amherst, Burma	**67**	16 2N	97 20 E
Amherst, Can.	**107**	45 48N	64 8W
Amherst, Mass., U.S.A.	**113**	42 21N	72 30W
Amherst, Ohio, U.S.A.	**112**	41 23N	82 15W
Amherst, Tex., U.S.A.	**117**	34 0N	102 24W
Amherst I.	**113**	44 8N	76 43W
Amherstburg	**106**	42 6N	83 6W
Amiata, Mte.	**39**	42 54N	11 40 E
Amiens	**19**	49 54N	2 16 E
Amigdhalokefáli	**45**	35 23N	23 30 E
Amindaion	**44**	40 42N	21 42 E
Amirante Is.	**3**	6 0 S	53 0 E
Amisk L.	**109**	54 35N	102 15W
Amite	**117**	30 47N	90 31W
Amizmiz	**82**	31 12N	8 15W
Åmli	**47**	58 45N	8 32 E
Amlwch	**12**	53 24N	4 21W
Amm Adam	**87**	16 20N	36 1 E
'Ammān	**62**	31 57N	35 52 E
Ammanford	**13**	51 48N	4 0W
Ammerån	**48**	63 9N	16 13 E
Ammerån →	**48**	63 9N	16 13 E
Ammersee	**25**	48 0N	11 7 E
Ammi'ad	**62**	32 55N	35 32 E
Amnéville	**19**	49 16N	6 9 E
Amorebieta	**32**	43 13N	2 44W
Amorgós	**45**	36 50N	25 57 E
Amory	**115**	33 59N	88 29W
Amos	**106**	48 35N	78 5W
Åmot, Buskerud, Norway	**47**	59 54N	9 54 E
Åmot, Telemark, Norway	**47**	59 34N	8 0 E
Åmotsdal	**47**	59 37N	8 26 E
Amour, Djebel	**82**	33 42N	1 37 E
Amoy = Xiamen	**76**	24 25N	118 4 E
Ampanihy	**93**	24 40 S	44 45 E
Ampasindava, Helodranon'	**93**	13 40 S	48 15 E
Ampasindava, Saikanosy	**93**	13 42 S	47 55W
Amper	**85**	9 25N	9 40 E
Amper →	**25**	48 30N	11 57 E
Ampère	**83**	35 44N	5 27 E
Ampezzo	**39**	46 25N	12 48 E
Amposta	**32**	40 43N	0 34 E
Ampotaka	**93**	25 3 S	44 41 E
Ampoza	**93**	22 20 S	44 44 E
Amqa	**62**	32 59N	35 10 E
Amqui	**107**	48 28N	67 27W
Amraoti	**68**	20 55N	77 45 E
Amreli	**68**	21 35N	71 17 E
Amrenene el Kasba	**82**	22 10N	0 30 E
Amritsar	**68**	31 35N	74 57 E
Amroha	**68**	28 53N	78 30 E
Amrum	**24**	54 37N	8 21 E
Amsel	**83**	22 47N	5 29 E
Amsterdam, Neth.	**16**	52 23N	4 54 E
Amsterdam, U.S.A.	**114**	42 58N	74 10W
Amsterdam, I.	**3**	37 30 S	77 30 E
Amstetten	**26**	48 7N	14 51 E
Amudarya →	**58**	43 40N	59 0 E
Amund Ringnes I.	**4**	78 20N	96 25W
Amundsen Gulf	**104**	71 0N	124 0W
Amundsen Sea	**5**	72 0 S	115 0W
Amungen	**48**	61 10N	15 40 E
Amuntai	**72**	2 28 S	115 25 E
Amur →	**59**	52 56N	141 10 E
Amurang	**73**	1 5N	124 40 E
Amuri Pass	**101**	42 31 S	172 11 E
Amurrio	**32**	43 3N	3 0W
Amursk	**59**	50 14N	136 54 E

Amurzet **59** 47 50N 131 5 E
Amusco **30** 42 10N 4 28W
Amvrakikós Kólpos **45** 39 0N 20 55 E
Amvrosiyevka **57** 47 43N 38 30 E
Amzeglouf **82** 26 50N 0 1 E
An Nafūd **64** 28 15N 41 0 E
An Najaf **64** 32 3N 44 15 E
An Nāqūrah **62** 33 7N 35 8 E
An Nāşirīyah **64** 31 0N 46 15 E
An Nawfaliyah **83** 30 54N 17 58 E
An Nhon (Binh Dinh) **71** 13 55N 109 7 E
An Nîl □ **86** 19 30N 33 0 E
An Nîl el Abyad □ **87** 14 0N 32 15 E
An Nîl el Azraq □ **87** 12 30N 34 30 E
An Nu'ayrīyah **64** 27 30N 48 30 E
An Uaimh **15** 53 39N 6 40W
Ána-Sira **47** 58 17N 6 25 E
Anabar → **59** 73 8N 113 36 E
'Anabtā **62** 32 19N 35 7 E
Anaconda **118** 46 7N 113 0W
Anacortes **118** 48 30N 122 40W
Anadarko **117** 35 4N 98 15W
Anadia **30** 40 26N 8 27W
Anadolu **64** 38 0N 30 0 E
Anadyr **59** 64 35N 177 20 E
Anadyr → **59** 64 55N 176 5 E
Anadyrskiy Zaliv **59** 64 0N 180 0 E
Anáfi **45** 36 22N 25 48 E
Anafópoulo **45** 36 17N 25 50 E
Anagni **40** 41 44N 13 8 E
'Ānah **64** 34 25N 42 0 E
Anahim Lake **108** 52 28N 125 18W
Anáhuac **120** 27 14N 100 9W
Anai Mudi, Mt. **70** 10 12N 77 4 E
Anaimalai Hills **70** 10 20N 76 40 E
Anakapalle **70** 17 42N 83 06 E
Anakie **98** 23 32 S 147 45 E
Anaklia **57** 42 22N 41 35 E
Analalava **93** 14 35 S 48 0 E
Anambar → **68** 30 15N 68 50 E
Anambas, Kepulauan **72** 3 20N 106 30 E
Anamoose **116** 47 55N 100 20W
Anamosa **116** 42 7N 91 30W
Anamur **64** 36 8N 32 58 E
Anan **74** 33 54N 134 40 E
Anand **68** 22 32N 72 59 E
Anandpur **69** 21 16N 86 13 E
Anánes **45** 36 33N 24 9 E
Anantapur **70** 14 39N 77 42 E
Anantnag **69** 33 45N 75 10 E
Ananyev **56** 47 44N 29 47 E
Anapa **56** 44 55N 37 25 E
Anápolis **127** 16 15 S 48 50W
Anâr **65** 30 55N 55 13 E
Anārak **65** 33 25N 53 40 E
Anatolia = Anadolu **64** 38 0N 30 0 E
Anatone **118** 46 9N 117 4W
Añatuya **124** 28 20 S 62 50W
Anaunethad L. **109** 60 55N 104 25W
Anaye **81** 19 15N 12 50 E
Ancenis **18** 47 21N 1 10W
Anchorage **104** 61 10N 149 50W
Ancião **30** 39 56N 8 27W
Ancohuma, Nevada **126** 16 0 S 68 50W
Ancón **126** 11 50 S 77 10W
Ancona **39** 43 37N 13 30 E
Ancud **128** 42 0 S 73 50W
Ancud, G. de **128** 42 0 S 73 0W
Anda **76** 46 24N 125 19 E
Andacollo, Argent. **124** 37 10 S 70 42W
Andacollo, Chile **124** 30 5 S 71 10W
Andalgalá **124** 27 40 S 66 30W
Åndalsnes **47** 62 35N 7 43 E
Andalucía **31** 37 35N 5 0W
Andalusia **115** 31 19N 86 30W
Andalusia = Andalucía **31** 37 35N 5 0W
Andaman Is. **71** 12 30N 92 30 E
Andaman Sea **72** 13 0N 96 0 E
Andaman Str. **71** 12 15N 92 20 E
Andara **92** 18 2 S 21 9 E
Andelot **19** 48 15N 5 18 E
Andelys, Les **18** 49 15N 1 25 E
Andenne **16** 50 30N 5 5 E
Andéranboukane **85** 15 26N 3 2 E
Andermatt **25** 46 38N 8 35 E
Andernach **24** 50 24N 7 25 E
Andernos-les-Bains **20** 44 44N 1 6W
Anderslöv **49** 55 26N 13 19 E
Anderson, Calif., U.S.A. **118** 40 30N 122 19W
Anderson, Ind., U.S.A. **114** 40 5N 85 40W
Anderson, Mo., U.S.A. **117** 36 43N 94 29W
Anderson, S.C., U.S.A. **115** 34 32N 82 40W
Anderson → **104** 69 42N 129 0W
Anderson, Mt. **93** 25 5 S 30 42 E
Anderstorp **49** 57 19N 13 39 E
Andes **126** 5 40N 75 53W
Andes, Cord de los **126** 20 0 S 68 0W
Andfjorden **50** 69 10N 16 20 E
Andhra, L. **70** 18 54N 73 32 E
Andhra Pradesh □ **70** 16 0N 79 0 E
Andikíthira **45** 35 52N 23 15 E
Andímilos **45** 36 47N 24 12 E
Andíparos **45** 37 0N 25 3 E
Andípaxoi **45** 39 9N 20 13 E
Andípsara **45** 38 30N 25 29 E
Andirrion **45** 38 24N 21 46 E
Andizhan **58** 41 10N 72 0 E
Andkhvoy **65** 36 52N 65 8 E
Andol **70** 17 51N 78 4 E
Andong **76** 36 40N 128 43 E
Andorra ■ **32** 42 30N 1 30 E
Andorra La Vella **32** 42 31N 1 32 E
Andover, U.K. **13** 51 13N 1 29W
Andover, N.Y., U.S.A. **112** 42 11N 77 48W
Andover, Ohio, U.S.A. **112** 41 35N 80 35W
Andrahary, Mt. **93** 13 37 S 49 17 E
Andraitx **32** 39 39N 2 25 E
Andramasina **93** 19 11 S 47 35 E
Andranopasy **93** 21 17 S 43 44 E
Andreanof Is. **104** 52 0N 178 0W
Andreapol **54** 56 40N 32 17 E
Andrespol **28** 51 45N 19 34 E
Andrews, S.C., U.S.A. **115** 33 29N 79 30W
Andrews, Tex., U.S.A. **117** 32 18N 102 33W
Ándria **41** 41 13N 16 17 E
Andriba **93** 17 30 S 46 58 E
Andrijevica **42** 42 45N 19 48 E
Andrítsaina **45** 37 29N 21 52 E
Androka **93** 24 58 S 44 2 E
Ándros **45** 37 50N 24 57 E
Andros I. **121** 24 30N 78 0W
Andros Town **121** 24 43N 77 47W
Andrychów **27** 49 51N 19 18 E
Andújar **31** 38 3N 4 5W
Aneby **49** 57 48N 14 49 E
Anegada I. **121** 18 45N 64 20W
Anegada Passage **121** 18 15N 63 45W
Anécho **85** 6 12N 1 34 E
Anergane **82** 31 4N 7 14W
Aneto, Pico de **32** 42 37N 0 40 E
Ang Thong **71** 14 35N 100 31 E
Angamos, Punta **124** 23 1 S 70 32W
Ang'angxi **75** 47 10N 123 48 E
Angara → **59** 58 30N 97 0 E
Angarab **87** 13 11N 37 7 E
Angarsk **59** 52 30N 104 0 E
Angaston **99** 34 30 S 139 8 E
Ånge **48** 62 31N 15 35 E
Angel de la Guarda **120** 29 30N 113 30W
Angeles **73** 15 9N 120 33 E
Ängelholm **49** 56 15N 12 58 E
Angellala **99** 26 24 S 146 54 E
Angels Camp **119** 38 8N 120 30W
Ängelsberg **48** 59 58N 16 0 E
Anger → **87** 9 37N 36 6 E
Angereb → **87** 13 45N 36 40 E
Ångermanälven → **48** 62 40N 18 0 E
Angermünde **24** 53 1N 14 0 E
Angers, Can. **113** 45 31N 75 29W
Angers, France **18** 47 30N 0 35W
Angerville **19** 48 19N 2 0 E
Ängesån → **50** 66 50N 22 15 E
Anghiari **39** 43 32N 12 3 E
Angikuni L. **109** 62 0N 100 0W
Angkor **71** 13 22N 103 50 E
Anglés **32** 41 57N 2 38 E
Anglesey **12** 53 17N 4 20W
Anglet **20** 43 29N 1 31W
Angleton **117** 29 12N 95 23W
Anglin → **20** 46 42N 0 52 E
Anglure **19** 48 35N 3 50 E
Angmagssalik **4** 65 40N 37 20W
Ango **90** 4 10N 26 5 E
Angoche **91** 16 8 S 40 0 E
Angoche, I. **91** 16 20 S 39 50 E
Angol **124** 37 56 S 72 45W
Angola, Ind., U.S.A. **114** 41 40N 85 0W
Angola, N.Y., U.S.A. **112** 42 38N 79 2W
Angola ■ **89** 12 0 S 18 0 E
Angoon **108** 57 40N 134 40W
Angoram **98** 4 4 S 144 4 E
Angoulême **20** 45 39N 0 10 E
Angoumois **20** 45 50N 0 25 E
Angra dos Reis **125** 23 0 S 44 10W
Angren **58** 41 1N 70 12 E
Angu **90** 3 25N 24 28 E
Anguilla **121** 18 14N 63 5W
Angus, Braes of **14** 56 51N 3 10W
Anhanduí → **125** 21 46 S 52 9W
Anholt **49** 56 42N 11 33 E
Anhua **77** 28 23N 111 12 E
Anhui □ **75** 32 0N 117 0 E
Anhwei □ = Anhui □ **75** 32 0N 117 0 E
Ánidhros **45** 36 38N 25 43 E
Anie **85** 7 42N 1 8 E
Animas **119** 31 58N 108 58W
Ånimskog **49** 58 53N 12 35 E
Anin **71** 15 36N 97 50 E
Anina **42** 45 6N 21 51 E
Anivorano **93** 18 44 S 48 58 E
Anjangaon **68** 21 10N 77 20 E
Anjar **68** 23 6N 70 10 E
Anjidiv I. **70** 14 40N 74 10 E
Anjou **18** 47 20N 0 15W
Anjozorobe **93** 18 22 S 47 52 E
Anju **76** 39 36N 125 40 E
Anka **85** 12 13N 5 58 E
Ankang **75** 32 40N 109 1 E
Ankara **64** 40 0N 32 54 E
Ankaramena **93** 21 57 S 46 39 E
Ankazoabo **93** 22 18 S 44 31 E
Ankazobe **93** 18 20 S 47 10 E
Ankisabe **93** 19 17 S 46 29 E
Anklam **24** 53 48N 13 40 E
Anklesvar **68** 21 38N 73 3 E
Ankober **87** 9 35N 39 40 E
Ankoro **90** 6 45 S 26 55 E
Anlu **77** 31 15N 113 45 E
Ånn **48** 63 19N 12 34 E
Ann Arbor **114** 42 17N 83 45W
Ann C., Antarct. **5** 66 30 S 50 30 E
Ann C., U.S.A. **114** 42 39N 70 37W
Anna, U.S.A. **117** 37 28N 89 10W
Anna, U.S.S.R. **55** 51 28N 40 23 E
Annaba **83** 36 50N 7 46 E
Annaberg-Buchholz **24** 50 34N 12 58 E
Annalee → **15** 54 3N 7 15W
Annam = Trung-Phan **71** 16 30N 107 30 E
Annamitique, Chaîne **71** 17 0N 106 0 E
Annan **14** 55 0N 3 17W
Annan → **14** 54 58N 3 18W
Annapolis **114** 38 95N 76 30W
Annapolis Royal **107** 44 44N 65 32W
Annapurna **69** 28 34N 83 50 E
Anneberg **49** 57 32N 12 6 E
Annecy **21** 45 55N 6 8 E
Annecy, L. d' **21** 45 52N 6 10 E
Annemasse **21** 46 12N 6 16 E
Anning **75** 24 55N 102 26 E
Anniston **115** 33 45N 85 50W
Annobón = Pagalu **79** 1 25S 5 35 E
Annonay **21** 45 15N 4 40 E
Annonciation, L' **106** 46 25N 74 55W
Annot **21** 43 58N 6 38 E
Annotto Bay **121** 18 17N 77 3W
Annuello **99** 34 53 S 142 55 E
Annville **113** 40 18N 76 32W
Annweiler **25** 49 12N 7 58 E
Áno Arkhánai **45** 35 16N 25 11 E
Áno Porróia **44** 41 17N 23 2 E
Áno Viánnos **45** 35 2N 25 21 E
Anoka **116** 45 10N 93 26W
Anorotsangana **93** 13 56 S 47 55 E
Anqing **75** 30 30N 117 3 E
Anren **77** 26 43N 113 18 E
Ansāb **64** 29 11N 44 43 E
Ansai **76** 36 50N 109 20 E
Ansbach **25** 49 17N 10 34 E
Anse au Loup, L' **107** 51 32N 56 50W
Anse, L' **106** 46 47N 88 28W
Anseba → **87** 16 0N 38 30 E
Anshan **76** 41 5N 122 58 E
Anshun **75** 26 18N 105 57 E
Ansirabe **93** 19 55 S 47 2 E
Ansley **116** 41 19N 99 24W
Ansó **32** 42 51N 0 48W
Anson **117** 32 46N 99 54W
Anson B. **96** 13 20 S 130 6 E
Ansongo **85** 15 25N 0 35 E
Ansonia **113** 41 21N 73 6W
Anstruther **14** 56 14N 2 40W
Ansudu **73** 2 11 S 139 22 E
Antabamba **126** 14 40 S 73 0W
Antakya **64** 36 14N 36 10 E
Antalaha **93** 14 57 S 50 20 E
Antalya **64** 36 52N 30 45 E
Antalya Körfezi **64** 36 15N 31 30 E
Antananarivo **93** 18 55 S 47 31 E
Antananarivo □ **93** 19 0 S 47 0 E
Antanimbaribe **93** 21 30 S 44 48 E
Antarctic Pen. **5** 67 0 S 60 0W
Antarctica **5** 90 0 S 0 0
Antelope **91** 21 2 S 28 31 E
Antequera, Parag. **124** 24 8 S 57 7W
Antequera, Spain **31** 37 5N 4 33W
Antero Mt. **119** 38 45N 106 15W
Anthemoús **44** 40 31N 23 15 E
Anthony, Kans., U.S.A. **117** 37 8N 98 2W
Anthony, N. Mex., U.S.A. **119** 32 1N 106 37W
Anti Atlas, Mts. **82** 30 0N 8 30W
Antibes **21** 43 34N 7 6 E
Antibes, C. d' **21** 43 31N 7 7 E
Anticosti, Î. d' **107** 49 30N 63 0W
Antifer, C. d' **18** 49 41N 0 10 E
Antigo **116** 45 8N 89 5W
Antigonish **107** 45 38N 61 58W
Antigua, Guat. **120** 14 34N 90 41W
Antigua, W. Indies **121** 17 0N 61 50W
Antilla **121** 20 40N 75 50W
Antimony **119** 38 7N 112 0W
Antioch **118** 38 7N 121 45W
Antioche, Pertuis d' **20** 46 6N 1 20W
Antioquia **126** 6 40N 75 55W
Antipodes Is. **94** 49 45 S 178 40 E
Antler **116** 48 58N 101 18W
Antler → **109** 49 8N 101 0W
Antlers **117** 34 15N 95 35W
Antofagasta **124** 23 50 S 70 30W
Antofagasta □ **124** 24 0 S 69 0W
Antofagasta de la Sierra **124** 26 5 S 67 20W
Antofalla **124** 25 30 S 68 5W
Antofalla, Salar de **124** 25 40 S 67 45W
Anton **117** 33 49N 102 5W
Anton Chico **119** 35 12N 105 5W
Antongila, Helodrano **93** 15 30 S 49 50 E
Antonibé **93** 15 7 S 47 24 E
Antonibé, Presqu'île d' **93** 14 55 S 47 20 E
Antonina **125** 25 26 S 48 42W
Antonito **119** 37 4N 106 1W
Antonovo **57** 49 25N 51 42 E
Antrain **18** 48 28N 1 30W
Antrim **15** 54 43N 6 13W
Antrim □ **15** 54 55N 6 20W
Antrim, Mts. of **15** 54 57N 6 8W
Antrodoco **39** 42 25N 13 4 E
Antropovo **55** 58 26N 42 51 E
Antsalova **93** 18 40 S 44 37 E
Antsiranana **93** 12 25 S 49 20 E
Antsohihy **93** 14 50 S 47 59 E
Antwerp **113** 44 12N 75 36W
Antwerp = Antwerpen **16** 51 13N 4 25 E
Antwerpen **16** 51 13N 4 25 E
Antwerpen □ **16** 51 15N 4 40 E
Anupgarh **68** 29 10N 73 10 E
Anuradhapura **70** 8 22N 80 28 E
Anvers = Antwerpen **16** 51 13N 4 25 E
Anvers I. **5** 64 30 S 63 40W
Anvik **104** 62 37N 160 20W
Anxi, Fujian, China **77** 25 2N 118 12 E
Anxi, Gansu, China **75** 40 30N 95 43 E
Anxious B. **96** 33 24 S 134 45 E
Anyama **84** 5 30N 4 3W
Anyang **76** 36 5N 114 21 E
Anyer-Lor **73** 6 6 S 105 56 E
Anyi, Jiangxi, China **77** 28 49N 115 25 E
Anyi, Shanxi, China **77** 35 2N 111 2 E
Anyuan **77** 25 9N 115 21 E
'Anzah **62** 32 22N 35 12 E
Anzhero-Sudzhensk **58** 56 10N 86 0 E
Anzio **40** 41 28N 12 37 E
Aoiz **32** 42 46N 1 22W
Aomori **74** 40 45N 140 45 E
Aomori □ **74** 40 45N 140 40 E
Aonla **68** 28 16N 79 11 E
Aoreora **82** 28 51N 10 53W
Aosta **38** 45 43N 7 20 E
Aoudéras **85** 17 45N 8 20 E
Aouinet Torkoz **82** 28 31N 9 46W
Aoukar **82** 23 50N 2 45W
Aouker **84** 17 40N 10 0W
Aoulef el Arab **82** 26 55N 1 2 E
Apa → **124** 22 6 S 58 2W
Apache, Ariz., U.S.A. **119** 31 46N 109 6W
Apache, Okla., U.S.A. **117** 34 53N 98 22W
Apalachee B. **115** 30 0N 84 0W
Apalachicola **115** 29 40N 85 0W
Apapa **85** 6 25N 3 25 E
Apaporis → **126** 1 23 S 69 25W
Aparri **73** 18 22N 121 38 E
Apateu **46** 46 36N 21 47 E
Apatin **42** 45 40N 19 0 E
Apàtity **52** 67 34N 33 22 E
Apatzingán **120** 19 0N 102 20W
Apeldoorn **16** 52 13N 5 57 E
Apen **24** 53 12N 7 47 E
Apenam **72** 8 35 S 116 13 E
Apennines **9** 44 20N 10 20 E
Apia **101** 13 50 S 171 50W
Apiacás, Serra dos **126** 9 50 S 57 0W
Apizaco **120** 19 26N 98 9W
Aplao **126** 16 0 S 72 40W
Apo, Mt. **73** 6 53N 125 14 E
Apolda **24** 51 1N 11 30 E
Apollo Bay **100** 38 45 S 143 40 E
Apollonia **45** 36 58N 24 43 E
Apollonia = Marsá Susah **81** 32 52N 21 59 E
Apolo **126** 14 30 S 68 30W
Apostle Is. **116** 47 0N 90 30W
Apóstoles **125** 28 0 S 56 0W
Apostolovo **56** 47 39N 33 39 E
Apoteri **126** 4 2N 58 32W
Appalachian Mts. **114** 38 0N 80 0W
Appalachicola → **115** 29 40N 85 0W
Appennini **41** 41 0N 15 0 E
Appennino Ligure **38** 44 30N 9 0 E
Appenzell-Ausser Rhoden □ **25** 47 23N 9 23 E
Appenzell-Inner Rhoden □ **25** 47 20N 9 25 E
Appiano **39** 46 27N 11 17 E
Apple Hill **113** 45 13N 74 46W
Appleby **12** 54 35N 2 29W
Appleton **114** 44 17N 88 25W
Approuague **127** 4 20N 52 0W
Aprelevka, U.S.S.R. **55** 55 33N 37 4 E
Aprelevka, U.S.S.R. **55** 55 34N 37 4 E
Apricena **41** 41 47N 15 25 E
Aprigliano **41** 39 17N 16 19 E
Aprília **40** 41 38N 12 38 E
Apsheronsk **57** 44 28N 39 42 E
Apt **21** 43 53N 5 24 E
Apucarana **125** 23 55 S 51 33W
Apulia = Púglia **41** 41 0N 16 30 E
Apure → **126** 7 37N 66 25W
Apurimac → **126** 12 17 S 73 56W
Apuseni, Munţii **46** 46 30N 22 45 E
Aqabah = Al 'Aqabah **86** 29 13N 35 0 E
'Aqabah, Khalīj al **64** 28 15N 33 20 E
Āqcheh **65** 37 0N 66 5 E
Aqiq **86** 18 14N 38 12 E
Aqîq, Khalîg **86** 18 20N 38 10 E
Aqrabā **62** 32 9N 35 20 E
Aqrah **64** 36 46N 43 45 E
Aquidauana **127** 20 30 S 55 50W
Aquila, L' **39** 42 21N 13 24 E
Aquiles Serdán **120** 28 37N 105 54W
Ar Rachidiya **82** 31 58N 4 20W
Ar Rafid **62** 32 57N 35 52 E
Ar Ramādī **64** 33 25N 43 20 E
Ar Raml **83** 26 45N 19 40 E
Ar Ramthā **62** 32 34N 36 0 E
Ar Raqqah **64** 36 0N 38 55 E
Ar Rass **64** 25 50N 43 40 E
Ar Rifā'ī **64** 31 50N 46 10 E
Ar Riyāḍ **64** 24 41N 46 42 E
Ar Rummān **62** 32 9N 35 48 E
Ar Ruţbah **64** 33 0N 40 15 E
Ar Ruwayḍah **64** 23 40N 44 40 E
Arab, Bahr el → **87** 9 50N 29 0 E
Arab, Khalîg el **86** 30 55N 29 0 E
Arab, Shatt al **64** 30 0N 48 31 E
Arabatskaya Strelka **56** 45 40N 35 0 E
Arabba **39** 46 30N 11 51 E
Arabia **60** 25 0N 45 0 E
Arabian Sea **60** 16 0N 65 0 E
Arac **64** 41 15N 33 21 E
Aracaju **127** 10 55 S 37 4W
Aracataca **126** 10 38N 74 9W
Aracati **127** 4 30 S 37 44W
Araçatuba **125** 21 10 S 50 30W
Aracena **31** 37 53N 6 38W
Aracena, Sierra de **31** 37 50N 6 50W
Araçuai **127** 16 52 S 42 4W
'Arad **62** 31 15N 35 12 E
Arad **42** 46 10N 21 20 E
Arad □ **42** 46 20N 22 0 E
Arada **81** 15 0N 20 20 E
Aradu Nou **42** 46 8N 21 20 E
Arafura Sea **73** 9 0 S 135 0 E
Aragats **57** 40 30N 44 15 E
Aragón **32** 41 25N 1 0W
Aragón → **32** 42 13N 1 44W
Aragona **40** 37 24N 13 36 E
Araguacema **127** 8 50 S 49 20W
Araguaia → **127** 5 21 S 48 41W
Araguari **127** 18 38 S 48 11W
Araguari → **127** 1 15N 49 55W
Arak **82** 25 20N 3 45 E
Arāk **64** 34 0N 49 40 E
Arakan Coast **67** 19 0N 94 0 E
Arakan Yoma **67** 20 0N 94 40 E
Arákhova **45** 38 28N 22 35 E
Araks = Aras, Rūd-e → **64** 39 10N 47 10 E
Aral Sea = Aralskoye More **58** 44 30N 60 0 E
Aralsk **58** 46 50N 61 20 E
Aralskoye More **58** 44 30N 60 0 E
Aramā, Mţii. de **46** 47 10N 22 30 E
Aramac **97** 22 58 S 145 14 E
Arambagh **69** 22 53N 87 48 E
Aran I. **15** 55 0N 8 30W
Aran Is. **15** 53 5N 9 42W
Aranda de Duero **32** 41 39N 3 42W
Aranđelovac **42** 44 18N 20 27 E
Aranjuez **30** 40 1N 3 40W
Aranos **92** 24 9 S 19 7 E
Aransas Pass **117** 27 55N 97 9W
Araouane **84** 18 55N 3 30W
Arapahoe **116** 40 22N 99 53W
Arapey Grande → **124** 30 55 S 57 49W
Arapkir **64** 39 5N 38 30 E

Arapongas 125 23 29 S 51 28 W
Araranguá 125 29 0 S 49 30 W
Araraquara 127 21 50 S 48 0 W
Ararás, Serra das 125 25 0 S 53 10 W
Ararat 97 37 16 S 143 0 E
Ararat, Mt. = Ağri Daği 64 39 50 N 44 15 E
Araria 69 26 9 N 87 33 E
Araripe, Chapada do 127 7 20 S 40 0 W
Araruama, Lagoa de 125 22 53 S 42 12 W
Aras, Rūd-e → 64 39 10 N 47 10 E
Arauca 126 7 0 N 70 40 W
Arauca → 126 7 24 N 66 35 W
Arauco 124 37 16 S 73 25 W
Arauco □ 124 37 40 S 73 25 W
Arawa 87 9 57 N 41 58 E
Araxá 127 19 35 S 46 55 W
Araya, Pen. de 126 10 40 N 64 0 W
Arba Minch 87 6 0 N 37 30 E
Arbatax 40 39 57 N 9 42 E
Arbaza 59 52 40 N 92 30 E
Arbīl 64 36 15 N 44 5 E
Arboga 48 59 24 N 15 52 E
Arbois 19 46 55 N 5 46 E
Arbore 87 5 3 N 36 50 E
Arborea 40 39 46 N 8 34 E
Arborfield 109 53 6 N 103 39 W
Arborg 109 50 54 N 97 13 W
Arbrå 48 61 28 N 16 22 E
Arbresle, L' 21 45 50 N 4 26 E
Arbroath 14 56 34 N 2 35 W
Arbuckle 118 39 3 N 122 2 W
Arbus 40 39 30 N 8 33 E
Arbuzinka 56 47 0 N 31 59 E
Arc 19 47 28 N 5 34 E
Arc → 21 45 34 N 6 12 E
Arcachon 20 44 40 N 1 10 W
Arcachon, Bassin d' 20 44 42 N 1 10 W
Arcade 112 42 34 N 78 25 W
Arcadia, Fla., U.S.A. 115 27 20 N 81 50 W
Arcadia, La., U.S.A. 117 32 34 N 92 53 W
Arcadia, Nebr., U.S.A. 116 41 29 N 99 4 W
Arcadia, Pa., U.S.A. 112 40 46 N 78 54 W
Arcadia, Wis., U.S.A. 116 44 13 N 91 29 W
Arcata 118 40 55 N 124 4 W
Arcévia 39 43 29 N 12 58 E
Archangel = Arkhangelsk 52 64 40 N 41 0 E
Archar 42 43 50 N 22 54 E
Archbald 113 41 30 N 75 31 W
Archena 33 38 9 N 1 16 W
Archer → 97 13 28 S 141 41 E
Archer B. 98 13 20 S 141 30 E
Archers Post 90 0 35 N 37 35 E
Archidona 31 37 6 N 4 22 W
Arci, Monte 40 39 47 N 8 44 E
Arcidosso 39 42 51 N 11 30 E
Arcila = Asilah 82 35 29 N 6 0 W
Arcis-sur-Aube 19 48 32 N 4 10 E
Arco, Italy 38 45 55 N 10 54 E
Arco, U.S.A. 118 43 45 N 113 16 W
Arcola 109 49 40 N 102 30 W
Arcos 32 41 12 N 2 16 W
Arcos de los Frontera 31 36 45 N 5 49 W
Arcos de Valdevez 30 41 55 N 8 22 W
Arcot 70 12 53 N 79 20 E
Arcoverde 127 8 25 S 37 4 W
Arcs, Les 21 43 27 N 6 29 E
Arctic Bay 105 73 1 N 85 7 W
Arctic Ocean 4 78 0 N 160 0 W
Arctic Red River 104 67 15 N 134 0 W
Arda →, Bulg. 43 41 40 N 26 29 E
Arda →, Italy 38 44 53 N 9 52 E
Ardabīl 64 38 15 N 48 18 E
Ardahan 64 41 7 N 42 41 E
Ardakān 65 30 20 N 52 5 E
Årdal, Aust-Agder, Norway 47 58 42 N 7 48 E
Årdal, Rogaland, Norway 47 59 9 N 6 13 E
Ardales 31 36 53 N 4 51 W
Årdalstangen 47 61 14 N 7 43 E
Ardatov 55 54 51 N 46 15 E
Ardea 44 40 58 N 22 3 E
Ardèche □ 21 44 42 N 4 16 E
Ardèche → 21 44 16 N 4 39 E
Ardee 15 53 51 N 6 32 W
Arden 112 44 43 N 76 56 W
Arden Stby. 49 56 46 N 9 52 E
Ardennes 16 50 0 N 5 10 E
Ardennes □ 19 49 35 N 4 40 E
Ardentes 19 46 45 N 1 50 E
Ardestān 65 33 20 N 52 25 E
Ardgour 14 56 45 N 5 25 W
Ardhas → 44 41 36 N 26 25 E
Ardila → 31 38 12 N 7 28 W
Ardino 43 41 34 N 25 9 E
Ardjuno 73 7 49 S 112 34 E
Ardlethan 99 34 22 S 146 53 E
Ardmore, Austral. 98 21 39 S 139 11 E
Ardmore, Okla., U.S.A. 117 34 10 N 97 5 W
Ardmore, Pa., U.S.A. 113 39 58 N 75 18 W
Ardmore, S.D., U.S.A. 116 43 0 N 103 40 W
Ardnacrusha 15 52 43 N 8 38 W
Ardnamurchan, Pt. of 14 56 44 N 6 14 W
Ardore Marina 41 38 11 N 16 10 E
Ardres 19 50 50 N 2 0 E
Ardrossan, Austral. 99 34 26 S 137 53 E
Ardrossan, U.K. 14 55 39 N 4 50 W
Ards □ 15 54 35 N 5 30 W
Ards Pen. 15 54 30 N 5 25 W
Ardud 46 47 37 N 22 52 E
Ardunac 57 41 8 N 42 5 E
Åre 48 63 22 N 13 15 E
Arecibo 121 18 29 N 66 42 W
Areia Branca 127 5 0 S 37 0 W
Aremark 47 59 15 N 11 42 E
Arenas 30 43 17 N 4 50 W
Arenas de San Pedro 30 40 12 N 5 5 W
Arendal 47 58 28 N 8 46 E
Arendsee 24 52 52 N 11 27 E
Arenys de Mar 32 41 35 N 2 33 E
Arenzano 38 44 24 N 8 40 E
Areópolis 45 36 40 N 22 22 E
Arequipa 126 16 20 S 71 30 W
Arero 87 4 41 N 38 50 E
Arès 20 44 47 N 1 8 W
Arévalo 30 41 3 N 4 43 W
Arezzo 39 43 28 N 11 50 E
Arga → 32 42 18 N 1 47 W
Argalastí 44 39 13 N 23 13 E
Argamasilla de Alba 33 39 8 N 3 5 W
Arganda 32 40 19 N 3 26 W
Arganil 30 40 13 N 8 3 W
Argelès-Gazost 20 43 0 N 0 6 W
Argelès-sur-Mer 20 42 34 N 3 1 E
Argens → 21 43 24 N 6 44 E
Argent-sur-Sauldre 19 47 33 N 2 25 E
Argenta, Can. 108 50 20 N 116 55 W
Argenta, Italy 39 44 37 N 11 50 E
Argentan 18 48 45 N 0 1 W
Argentário, Mte. 39 42 23 N 11 11 E
Argentat 20 45 6 N 1 56 E
Argentera 38 44 23 N 6 58 E
Argentera, Monte del 38 44 12 N 7 5 E
Argenteuil 19 48 57 N 2 14 E
Argentia 107 47 18 N 53 58 W
Argentiera, C. dell' 40 40 44 N 8 8 E
Argentière, L' 21 44 47 N 6 33 E
Argentina ■ 128 35 0 S 66 0 W
Argentino, L. 128 50 10 S 73 0 W
Argenton-Château 18 46 59 N 0 27 W
Argenton-sur-Creuse 20 46 36 N 1 30 E
Argeş □ 46 45 0 N 24 45 E
Argeş → 46 44 30 N 25 50 E
Arghandab → 66 31 30 N 64 15 E
Argo 86 19 28 N 30 30 E
Argolikós Kólpos 45 37 20 N 22 52 E
Argolís □ 45 37 38 N 22 50 E
Argonne 19 49 0 N 5 20 E
Árgos 45 37 40 N 22 43 E
Árgos Orestikón 44 40 27 N 21 26 E
Argostólion 45 38 12 N 20 33 E
Arguedas 32 42 11 N 1 36 W
Arguello, Pt. 119 34 34 N 120 40 W
Argun → 59 53 20 N 121 28 E
Argungu 85 12 40 N 4 31 E
Argyle 116 48 23 N 96 49 W
Argyrádhes 44 39 27 N 19 58 E
Århus 49 56 8 N 10 11 E
Århus Amtskommune □ 49 56 15 N 10 15 E
Ariamsvlei 92 28 9 S 19 51 E
Ariana 83 36 52 N 10 12 E
Ariano Irpino 41 41 10 N 15 4 E
Ariano nel Polèsine 39 44 56 N 12 5 E
Aribinda 85 14 17 N 0 52 W
Arica, Chile 126 18 32 S 70 20 W
Arica, Colomb. 126 2 0 S 71 50 W
Arid, C. 96 34 1 S 123 10 E
Aridh 64 25 0 N 46 0 E
Ariège □ 20 42 56 N 1 30 E
Ariège → 20 43 30 N 1 25 E
Arieş → 46 46 24 N 23 20 E
Arilje 42 43 44 N 20 7 E
Arima 121 10 38 N 61 17 W
Arinos → 126 10 25 S 58 20 W
Ario de Rosales 120 19 12 N 102 0 W
Aripuanã 126 9 25 S 60 30 W
Aripuanã → 126 5 7 S 60 25 W
Ariquemes 126 9 55 S 63 6 W
Arisaig 14 56 55 N 5 50 W
Arîsh, W. el → 86 31 9 N 33 49 E
Arissa 87 11 10 N 41 35 E
Aristazabal I. 108 52 40 N 129 10 W
Arivaca 119 31 37 N 111 25 W
Arivonimamo 93 19 1 S 47 11 E
Ariyalur 70 11 8 N 79 8 E
Ariza 74 41 19 N 2 3 W
Arizaro, Salar de 124 24 40 S 67 50 W
Arizona 124 35 45 S 65 25 W
Arizona □ 119 34 20 N 111 30 W
Arizpe 120 30 20 N 110 11 W
Årjäng 48 59 24 N 12 8 E
Arjeplog 50 66 3 N 18 2 E
Arjona, Colomb. 126 10 14 N 75 22 W
Arjona, Spain 31 37 56 N 4 4 W
Arka 59 60 15 N 142 0 E
Arkadak 55 51 58 N 43 19 E
Arkadelphia 117 34 5 N 93 0 W
Arkadhia □ 45 37 30 N 22 20 E
Arkaig, L. 14 56 58 N 5 10 W
Arkalyk 58 50 13 N 66 50 E
Arkansas □ 117 35 0 N 92 30 W
Arkansas → 117 33 48 N 91 4 W
Arkansas City 117 37 4 N 97 3 W
Arkathos → 44 39 20 N 21 4 E
Arkhángelos 45 36 13 N 28 7 E
Arkhangelsk 52 64 40 N 41 0 E
Arkhangelskoye 55 51 32 N 40 58 E
Arkiko 87 15 33 N 39 30 E
Arklow 15 52 48 N 6 10 W
Árkoi 45 37 24 N 26 44 E
Arkona, Kap 24 54 41 N 13 26 E
Arkonam 70 13 7 N 79 43 E
Arkösund 49 58 29 N 16 56 E
Arkoúdhi 45 38 33 N 20 43 E
Arkticheskiy, Mys 59 81 10 N 95 0 E
Arkul 55 57 17 N 50 3 E
Arlanc 20 45 25 N 3 42 E
Arlanza → 30 42 6 N 4 9 W
Arlanzón → 30 42 3 N 4 17 W
Arlberg Pass 25 47 9 N 10 12 E
Arlee 118 47 10 N 114 4 W
Arles 21 43 41 N 4 40 E
Arlington, S. Afr. 93 28 1 S 27 53 E
Arlington, Oreg., U.S.A. 118 45 48 N 120 6 W
Arlington, S.D., U.S.A. 116 44 25 N 97 4 W
Arlington, Va., U.S.A. 114 38 52 N 77 5 W
Arlington, Wash., U.S.A. 118 48 11 N 122 4 W
Arlon 16 49 42 N 5 49 E
Arlöv 49 55 38 N 13 5 E
Arly 85 11 35 N 1 28 E
Armagh 15 54 22 N 6 40 W
Armagh □ 15 54 18 N 6 37 W
Armagnac 20 43 44 N 0 10 E
Armançon → 19 47 59 N 3 30 E
Armavir 57 45 2 N 41 7 E
Armenia 126 4 35 N 75 45 W
Armenian S.S.R. □ 57 40 0 N 44 0 E
Armeniş 46 45 13 N 22 17 E
Armentières 19 50 40 N 2 50 E
Armidale 97 30 30 S 151 40 E
Armour 116 43 20 N 98 25 W
Armstrong, B.C., Can. 108 50 25 N 119 10 W
Armstrong, Ont., Can. 106 50 18 N 89 4 W
Armstrong, U.S.A. 117 26 59 N 97 48 W
Armur 70 18 48 N 78 16 E
Arnaia 44 40 30 N 23 40 E
Arnaouti, C. 64 35 0 N 32 20 E
Arnarfjörður 50 65 48 N 23 40 W
Arnaud → 105 60 0 N 70 0 W
Arnay-le-Duc 19 47 10 N 4 27 E
Arnedillo 32 42 13 N 2 14 W
Arnedo 32 42 12 N 2 5 W
Árnes 50 66 1 N 21 31 W
Årnes 47 60 7 N 11 28 E
Arnett 117 36 9 N 99 44 W
Arnhem 16 51 58 N 5 55 E
Arnhem B. 96 12 20 S 136 10 E
Arnhem, C. 97 12 20 S 137 30 E
Arnhem Land 96 13 10 S 134 30 E
Arni 70 12 43 N 79 19 E
Árnissa 44 40 47 N 21 49 E
Arno → 38 43 41 N 10 17 E
Arnold, Nebr., U.S.A. 116 41 29 N 100 10 W
Arnold, Pa., U.S.A. 112 40 36 N 79 44 W
Arnoldstein 26 46 33 N 13 43 E
Arnon → 19 47 13 N 2 1 E
Arnot 109 55 56 N 96 41 W
Arnøy 50 70 9 N 20 40 E
Arnprior 106 45 26 N 76 21 W
Arnsberg 24 51 25 N 8 2 E
Arnstadt 24 50 50 N 10 56 E
Aroab 92 26 41 S 19 39 E
Aroánia Óri 45 37 56 N 22 12 E
Aroche 31 37 56 N 6 57 W
Arolsen 24 51 23 N 9 1 E
Aron → 19 46 50 N 3 27 E
Arona 38 45 45 N 8 32 E
Arosa, Ria de → 30 42 28 N 8 57 W
Arpajon, Cantal, France 20 44 54 N 2 28 E
Arpajon, Essonne, France 19 48 37 N 2 12 E
Arpino 40 41 40 N 13 35 E
Arrabury 99 26 45 S 141 0 E
Arrah 69 25 35 N 84 32 E
Arraiján 120 8 56 N 79 36 W
Arraiolos 31 38 44 N 7 59 W
Arran 14 55 34 N 5 12 W
Arrandale 108 54 57 N 130 0 W
Arras 19 50 17 N 2 46 E
Arrats → 20 44 6 N 0 52 E
Arreau 20 42 54 N 0 22 E
Arrecife 80 28 57 N 13 37 W
Arrecifes 124 34 06 S 60 9 W
Arrée, Mts. d' 18 48 26 N 3 55 W
Arriaga 120 21 55 N 101 23 W
Arrilalah P.O. 98 23 43 S 143 54 E
Arromanches-les-Bains 18 49 20 N 0 38 W
Arronches 31 39 8 N 7 16 W
Arros, R 20 43 40 N 0 2 W
Arrou 18 48 6 N 1 8 E
Arrow, L. 15 54 3 N 8 20 W
Arrow Rock Res. 118 43 45 N 115 50 W
Arrowhead 108 50 40 N 117 55 W
Arrowtown 101 44 57 S 168 50 E
Arroyo de la Luz 31 39 30 N 6 38 W
Arroyo Grande 119 35 9 N 120 32 W
Ärs 49 56 48 N 9 30 E
Ars 20 46 13 N 1 30 W
Ars-sur-Moselle 19 49 5 N 6 4 E
Arsenault L. 109 55 6 N 108 32 W
Arsiero 39 45 49 N 11 22 E
Arsikere 70 13 15 N 76 15 E
Arsk 55 56 10 N 49 50 E
Árta 45 39 8 N 21 2 E
Artá 32 39 41 N 3 21 E
Árta □ 44 39 15 N 21 5 E
Arteaga 120 18 50 N 102 20 W
Arteijo 30 43 19 N 8 29 W
Artem, Ostrov 57 40 28 N 50 20 E
Artemovsk, R.S.F.S.R., U.S.S.R. 59 54 45 N 93 35 E
Artemovsk, Ukraine S.S.R., U.S.S.R. 56 48 35 N 38 0 E
Artemovski 57 47 45 N 40 16 E
Artenay 19 48 5 N 1 50 E
Artern 24 51 22 N 11 18 E
Artesa de Segre 32 41 54 N 1 3 E
Artesia 117 32 55 N 104 25 W
Artesia Wells 117 28 17 N 99 18 W
Artesian 116 44 2 N 97 54 W
Arthez-de-Béarn 20 43 29 N 0 38 W
Arthington 84 6 35 N 10 45 W
Arthur → 99 41 2 S 144 40 E
Arthur Pt. 98 22 7 S 150 3 E
Arthur's Pass 101 42 54 S 171 35 E
Artigas 124 30 20 S 56 30 W
Artik 57 40 38 N 43 58 E
Artillery L. 109 63 9 N 107 52 W
Artois 19 50 20 N 2 30 E
Artotina 45 38 42 N 22 2 E
Artsiz 56 46 4 N 29 26 E
Artvin 64 41 14 N 41 44 E
Aru, Kepulauan 73 6 0 S 134 30 E
Aru Meru □ 90 3 20 S 36 50 E
Arua 90 3 1 N 30 58 E
Aruanã 127 14 54 S 51 10 W
Aruba 121 12 30 N 70 0 W
Arudy 20 43 7 N 0 28 W
Arun → 69 26 55 N 87 10 E
Arunachal Pradesh □ 67 28 0 N 95 0 E
Aruppukottai 70 9 31 N 78 8 E
Arusha 90 3 20 S 36 40 E
Arusha □ 90 4 0 S 36 30 E
Arusha Chini 90 3 32 S 37 20 E
Arusi □ 87 7 45 N 39 00 E
Aruvi → 70 8 48 N 79 53 E
Aruwimi → 90 1 13 N 23 36 E
Arvada 118 44 43 N 106 6 W
Arvakalu 70 8 20 N 79 58 E
Arvayheer 75 46 15 N 102 48 E
Arve → 21 46 11 N 6 8 E
Arvi 68 20 59 N 78 16 E
Arvida 107 48 25 N 71 14 W
Arvidsjaur 50 65 35 N 19 10 E
Arvika 48 59 40 N 12 36 E
Arxan 75 47 11 N 119 57 E
Arys 58 42 26 N 68 48 E
Arzachena 40 41 5 N 9 27 E
Arzamas 55 55 27 N 43 55 E
Arzew 82 35 50 N 0 23 W
Arzgir 57 45 18 N 44 23 E
Arzignano 39 45 30 N 11 20 E
Aš 26 50 13 N 12 12 E
'As Saffānīyah 64 28 5 N 48 50 E
Aş Şāfī 62 31 2 N 35 28 E
As Salt 62 32 2 N 35 43 E
As Samāwah 64 31 15 N 45 15 E
As Samū' 62 31 24 N 35 4 E
As Sanamayn 62 33 3 N 36 10 E
As Sulaymānīyah 64 24 9 N 47 18 E
As Sulţan 83 31 4 N 17 8 E
As Sumaymānīyah 64 35 35 N 45 29 E
As Summān 64 25 0 N 47 0 E
As Suwaih 65 22 10 N 59 33 E
As Suwaydā' 64 32 40 N 36 30 E
Aş Şuwayrah 64 32 55 N 45 0 E
Asab 92 25 30 S 18 0 E
Asaba 85 6 12 N 6 38 E
Asafo 84 6 20 N 2 40 W
Asahigawa 74 43 46 N 142 22 E
Asale, L. 87 14 0 N 40 20 E
Asamankese 85 5 50 N 0 40 W
Asansol 69 23 40 N 87 1 E
Åsarna 48 62 39 N 14 22 E
Asbe Teferi 87 9 4 N 40 49 E
Asbesberge 92 29 0 S 23 0 E
Asbestos 107 45 47 N 71 58 W
Asbury Park 114 40 15 N 74 1 W
Ascensión, B. de la 120 19 50 N 87 20 W
Ascension I. 7 8 0 S 14 15 W
Aschach 26 48 22 N 14 2 E
Aschaffenburg 25 49 58 N 9 8 E
Aschendorf 24 53 2 N 7 22 E
Aschersleben 24 51 45 N 11 28 E
Asciano 39 43 14 N 11 32 E
Áscoli Piceno 39 42 51 N 13 34 E
Áscoli Satriano 41 41 11 N 15 32 E
Ascope 126 7 46 S 79 8 W
Ascotán 124 21 45 S 68 17 W
Aseb 87 13 0 N 42 40 E
Åseda 49 57 10 N 15 20 E
Asedjrad 82 24 51 N 1 29 E
Asela 87 8 0 N 39 0 E
Asenovgrad 43 42 1 N 24 51 E
Aseral 47 58 37 N 7 25 E
Asfeld 19 49 27 N 4 5 E
Asfûn el Matâ'na 86 25 26 N 32 30 E
Åsgårdstrand 47 59 22 N 10 27 E
Ash Fork 119 35 14 N 112 32 W
Ash Grove 117 37 21 N 93 36 W
Ash Shām, Bādiyat 64 32 0 N 40 0 E
Ash Shāmīyah 64 31 55 N 44 35 E
Ash Shāriqah 65 25 23 N 55 26 E
Ash Shaţrah 64 31 30 N 46 10 E
Ash Shu'aybah 64 27 53 N 42 43 E
Ash Shu'bah 64 28 54 N 44 44 E
Ash Shūnah ash Shamālīyah 62 32 37 N 35 34 E
Asha 52 55 0 N 57 16 E
Ashaira 86 21 40 N 40 40 E
Ashanti □ 85 7 30 N 1 30 W
Ashburn 115 31 42 N 83 40 W
Ashburton 101 43 53 S 171 48 E
Ashburton → 96 21 40 S 114 56 E
Ashby-de-la-Zouch 12 52 45 N 1 29 W
Ashcroft 108 50 40 N 121 20 W
Ashdod 62 31 49 N 34 35 E
Ashdot Yaaqov 62 32 39 N 35 35 E
Asheboro 115 35 43 N 79 46 W
Asherton 117 28 25 N 99 43 W
Asheville 115 35 39 N 82 30 W
Asheweig → 106 54 17 N 87 12 W
Ashford, Austral. 99 29 15 S 151 3 E
Ashford, U.K. 13 51 8 N 0 53 E
Ashford, U.S.A. 118 46 45 N 122 2 W
Ashikaga 74 36 28 N 139 29 E
Ashizuri-Zaki 74 32 44 N 133 0 E
Ashkhabad 58 38 0 N 57 50 E
Ashland, Kans., U.S.A. 117 37 13 N 99 43 W
Ashland, Ky., U.S.A. 114 38 25 N 82 40 W
Ashland, Me., U.S.A. 107 46 34 N 68 26 W
Ashland, Mont., U.S.A. 118 45 41 N 106 12 W
Ashland, Nebr., U.S.A. 116 41 5 N 96 27 W
Ashland, Ohio, U.S.A. 114 40 52 N 82 20 W
Ashland, Oreg., U.S.A. 118 42 10 N 122 38 W
Ashland, Pa., U.S.A. 113 40 45 N 76 22 W
Ashland, Va., U.S.A. 114 37 46 N 77 30 W
Ashland, Wis., U.S.A. 116 46 40 N 90 52 W
Ashley, N.D., U.S.A. 116 46 3 N 99 23 W
Ashley, Pa., U.S.A. 113 41 12 N 75 55 W
Ashley Snow I. 5 73 35 S 77 6 W
Ashmont 108 54 7 N 111 35 W
Ashmore Reef 96 12 14 S 123 5 E
Ashmûn 86 30 18 N 30 55 E
Ashq'elon 62 31 42 N 34 35 E
Ashtabula 114 41 52 N 80 50 W
Ashti 70 18 50 N 75 15 E
Ashton, S. Afr. 92 33 50 S 20 5 E
Ashton, U.S.A. 118 44 6 N 111 30 W
Ashton-under-Lyne 12 53 30 N 2 8 W
Ashuanipi, L. 107 52 45 N 66 15 W
Asia 60 45 0 N 75 0 E
Asia, Kepulauan 73 1 0 N 131 13 E
Asiago 39 45 52 N 11 30 E
Asifabad 70 19 20 N 79 24 E
Asike 73 6 39 S 140 24 E
Asilah 82 35 29 N 6 0 W
Asinara, G. dell' 40 41 0 N 8 30 E
Asinara I. 40 41 5 N 8 15 E
Asino 58 57 0 N 86 0 E
'Asīr □ 63 18 40 N 42 30 E
Asir, Ras 63 11 55 N 51 10 E
Aska 70 19 2 N 84 42 E

Asker 47 59 50N 10 26 E
Askersund 49 58 53N 14 55 E
Askim 47 59 35N 11 10 E
Askja 50 65 3N 16 48W
Asl 86 29 33N 32 44 E
Asmâr 65 35 10N 71 27 E
Asmera (Asmara) 87 15 19N 38 55 E
Asnæs 49 55 40N 11 0 E
Asni 82 31 17N 7 58W
Aso 74 33 0N 131 5 E
Asola 38 45 12N 10 25 E
Asoteriba, Jebel 86 21 51N 36 30 E
Asotin 118 46 20N 117 3W
Aspe 33 38 20N 0 40W
Aspen 119 39 12N 106 56W
Aspermont 117 33 11N 100 15W
Aspiring, Mt. 101 44 23 S 168 46 E
Aspres 21 44 32N 5 44 E
Aspromonte 41 38 10N 16 0 E
Aspur 68 23 58N 74 7 E
Asquith 109 52 8N 107 13W
Assa 82 28 35N 9 6W
Assâba 84 16 10N 11 45W
Assam □ 67 26 0N 93 0 E
Assamakka 85 19 21N 5 38 E
Asse 16 50 24N 4 10 E
Assekrem 83 23 16N 5 49 E
Assémini 40 39 18N 9 0 E
Assen 16 53 0N 6 35 E
Assens, Fyn, Denmark 49 56 41N 10 3 E
Assens, Fyn, Denmark 49 55 16N 9 55 E
Assini 84 5 9N 3 17W
Assiniboia 109 49 40N 105 59W
Assiniboine → 109 49 53N 97 8W
Assis 125 22 40 S 50 20W
Assisi 39 43 4N 12 36 E
Ássos 45 38 22N 20 33 E
Assus 44 39 32N 26 22 E
Assynt, L. 14 58 25N 5 15W
Astaffort 20 44 4N 0 40 E
Astakidha 45 35 53N 26 50 E
Astara 53 38 30N 48 50 E
Asti 38 44 54N 8 11 E
Astipálaia 45 36 32N 26 22 E
Astorga 30 42 29N 6 8W
Astoria 118 46 16N 123 50W
Åstorp 49 56 6N 12 55 E
Astrakhan 57 46 25N 48 5 E
Astrakhan-Bazâr 53 39 14N 48 30 E
Astudillo 30 42 12N 4 22W
Asturias 30 43 15N 6 0W
Asunción 124 25 10 S 57 30W
Asunción, La 126 11 2N 63 53W
Asutri 87 15 25N 35 45 E
Aswa → 90 3 43N 31 55 E
Aswad, Ras al 86 21 20N 39 0 E
Aswân 86 24 4N 32 57 E
Aswân High Dam = Sadd el Aali 86 24 5N 32 54 E
Asyût 86 27 11N 31 4 E
Asyûti, Wadi → 86 27 11N 31 16 E
Aszód 27 47 39N 19 28 E
At Țafilah 64 30 45N 35 30 E
At Ta'if 86 21 5N 40 27 E
Aț Țur 62 31 47N 35 14 E
Aț Țurrah 62 32 39N 35 59 E
Atacama □ 124 27 30 S 70 0W
Atacama, Desierto de 124 24 0 S 69 20W
Atacama, Salar de 124 23 30N 68 20W
Atakor 83 23 27N 5 31 E
Atakpamé 85 7 31N 1 13 E
Atalándi 45 38 39N 22 58 E
Atalaya 126 10 45 S 73 50W
Atami 74 35 5N 139 4 E
Atapupu 73 9 0 S 124 51 E
Atâr 80 20 30N 13 5W
Atara 59 63 10N 129 10 E
Ataram, Erg n- 82 23 57N 2 0 E
Atarfe 31 37 13N 3 40W
Atascadero 119 35 32N 120 44W
Atasu 58 48 30N 71 0 E
Atauro 73 8 10 S 125 30 E
Atbara 86 17 42N 33 59 E
'Atbara → 86 17 40N 33 56 E
Atbasar 58 51 48N 68 20 E
Atchafalaya B. 117 29 30N 91 20W
Atchison 116 39 40N 95 10W
Atebubu 85 7 47N 1 0W
Ateca 32 41 20N 1 49W
Aterno → 39 42 11N 13 51 E
Atesine, Alpi 38 46 55N 11 30 E
Atessa 39 42 5N 14 27 E
Ath 16 50 38N 3 47 E
Ath Thāmāmi 64 27 45N 44 45 E
Athabasca 108 54 45N 113 20W
Athabasca → 109 58 40N 110 50W
Athabasca, L. 109 59 15N 109 15W
Athboy 15 53 37N 6 55W
Athenry 15 53 18N 8 45W
Athens, Can. 113 44 38N 75 57W
Athens, Ala., U.S.A. 115 34 49N 86 58W
Athens, Ga., U.S.A. 115 33 56N 83 24W
Athens, N.Y., U.S.A. 113 42 15N 73 48W
Athens, Ohio, U.S.A. 114 39 25N 82 6W
Athens, Pa., U.S.A. 113 41 57N 76 36W
Athens, Tenn., U.S.A. 115 35 45N 84 38W
Athens, Tex., U.S.A. 117 32 11N 95 48W
Athens = Athinai 45 37 58N 23 46 E
Atherley 112 44 37N 79 20W
Atherton 97 17 17 S 145 30 E
Athiéme 85 6 37N 1 40 E
Athínai 45 37 58N 23 46 E
Athlone 15 53 26N 7 57W
Athni 70 16 44N 75 6 E
Atholl, Forest of 14 56 51N 3 50W
Atholville 107 47 59N 66 43W
Áthos, Mt. 44 40 9N 24 22 E
Athy 15 53 0N 7 0W
Ati, Chad 81 13 13N 18 20 E
Ati, Sudan 87 13 5N 29 2 E
Atiak 90 3 12N 32 2 E
Atico 126 16 14 S 73 40W
Atienza 32 41 12N 2 52W
Atikokan 106 48 45N 91 37W
Atikonak L. 107 52 40N 64 32W
Atka 59 60 50N 151 48 E
Atkarsk 55 51 55N 45 2 E
Atkinson 116 42 35N 98 59W
Atlanta, Ga., U.S.A. 115 33 50N 84 24W
Atlanta, Tex., U.S.A. 117 33 7N 94 8W
Atlantic 116 41 25N 95 0W
Atlantic City 114 39 25N 74 25W
Atlantic Ocean 6 0 0 20 0W
Atlin 104 59 31N 133 41W
Atlin, L. 108 59 26N 133 45W
'Atlit 62 32 42N 34 56 E
Atløy 47 61 21N 4 58 E
Atmakur 70 14 37N 79 40 E
Atmore 115 31 2N 87 30W
Atna → 47 61 44N 10 49 E
Atoka 117 34 22N 96 10W
Átokos 45 38 28N 20 49 E
Atouguia 31 39 20N 9 20W
Atoyac → 120 16 30N 97 31W
Atrak → 65 37 50N 57 0 E
Ätran 49 57 7N 12 57 E
Atrauli 68 28 2N 78 20 E
Atri 39 42 35N 14 0 E
Atsbi 87 13 52N 39 50 E
Atsoum, Mts. 85 6 41N 12 57 E
Attalla 115 34 2N 86 5W
Attawapiskat 106 52 56N 82 24W
Attawapiskat → 106 52 57N 82 18W
Attawapiskat, L. 106 52 18N 87 54W
Attendorn 24 51 8N 7 54 E
Attersee 26 47 55N 13 32 E
Attica 114 40 20N 87 15W
Attichy 19 49 25N 3 3 E
Attigny 19 49 28N 4 35 E
Attikamagen L. 107 55 0N 66 30W
Attikí □ 45 38 10N 23 40 E
'Attīl 62 32 23N 35 4 E
Attleboro 114 41 56N 71 18W
Attock 66 33 52N 72 20 E
Attopeu 71 14 48N 106 50 E
Attur 70 11 35N 78 30 E
Atuel → 124 36 17 S 66 50W
Åtvidaberg 49 58 12N 16 0 E
Atwater 119 37 21N 120 37W
Atwood, Can. 112 43 40N 81 1W
Atwood, U.S.A. 116 39 52N 101 3W
Au Sable → 114 44 25N 83 20W
Au Sable Pt. 106 46 40N 86 10W
Aubagne 21 43 17N 5 37 E
Aube □ 19 48 15N 4 0 E
Aube → 19 48 34N 3 43 E
Aubenas 21 44 37N 4 24 E
Aubenton 19 49 50N 4 12 E
Aubigny-sur-Nère 19 47 30N 2 24 E
Aubin 20 44 33N 2 15 E
Aubrac, Mts. d' 20 44 38N 2 58 E
Auburn, Ala., U.S.A. 115 32 37N 85 30W
Auburn, Calif., U.S.A. 118 38 53N 121 4W
Auburn, Ind., U.S.A. 114 41 20N 85 0W
Auburn, N.Y., U.S.A. 114 42 57N 76 39W
Auburn, Nebr., U.S.A. 116 40 25N 95 50W
Auburn Range 99 25 15 S 150 30 E
Auburndale 115 28 5N 81 45W
Aubusson 20 45 57N 2 11 E
Auch 20 43 39N 0 36 E
Auchel 19 50 30N 2 29 E
Auchi 85 7 6N 6 13 E
Auckland 101 36 52 S 174 46 E
Auckland Is. 94 50 40 S 166 5 E
Aude □ 20 43 8N 2 28 E
Aude → 20 43 13N 3 14 E
Auden 106 50 14N 87 53W
Auderville 18 49 43N 1 57W
Audierne 18 48 1N 4 34W
Audincourt 19 47 30N 6 50 E
Audo Ra. 87 6 20N 41 50 E
Audubon 116 41 43N 94 56W
Aue 24 50 34N 12 43 E
Auerbach 24 50 30N 12 25 E
Auffay 18 49 43N 1 07 E
Augathella 97 25 48 S 146 35 E
Augrabies Falls 92 28 35 S 20 20 E
Augsburg 25 48 22N 10 54 E
Augusta, Italy 41 37 14N 15 12 E
Augusta, Ark., U.S.A. 117 35 17N 91 25W
Augusta, Ga., U.S.A. 115 33 29N 81 59W
Augusta, Kans., U.S.A. 117 37 40N 97 0W
Augusta, Me., U.S.A. 107 44 20N 69 46W
Augusta, Mont., U.S.A. 118 47 30N 112 29W
Augusta, Wis., U.S.A. 116 44 41N 91 8W
Augustenborg 49 54 57N 9 53 E
Augusto Cardosa 91 12 40 S 34 50 E
Augustów 28 53 51N 23 00 E
Augustus Downs 98 18 35 S 139 55 E
Augustus, Mt. 96 24 20 S 116 50 E
Aukan 87 15 29N 40 50 E
Aulla 38 44 12N 10 0 E
Aulnay 20 46 2N 0 22W
Aulne → 18 48 17N 4 16W
Aulnoye 19 50 12N 3 50 E
Ault 116 40 40N 104 42W
Ault-Onival 18 50 5N 1 29 E
Aulus-les-Bains 20 42 49N 1 19 E
Aumale 19 49 46N 1 46 E
Aumont-Aubrac 20 44 43N 3 17 E
Auna 85 10 9N 4 42 E
Aundh 70 17 33N 74 23 E
Aunis 20 46 5N 0 50W
Auponhia 73 1 58 S 125 27 E
Aups 21 43 37N 6 15 E
Auraiya 69 26 28N 79 33 E
Aurangabad, Bihar, India 69 24 45N 84 18 E
Aurangabad, Maharashtra, India 70 19 50N 75 23 E
Auray 18 47 40N 3 0W
Aurès 83 35 8N 6 30 E
Aurich 24 53 28N 7 30 E
Aurillac 20 44 55N 2 26 E
Aurlandsvangen 47 60 55N 7 12 E
Auronza 39 46 33N 12 27 E
Aurora, Can. 112 44 0N 79 28W
Aurora, S. Afr. 92 32 40 S 18 29 E
Aurora, Colo., U.S.A. 116 39 44N 104 55W
Aurora, Ill., U.S.A. 114 41 42N 88 12W
Aurora, Mo., U.S.A. 117 36 58N 93 42W
Aurora, Nebr., U.S.A. 116 40 55N 98 0W
Aurora, Ohio, U.S.A. 112 41 21N 81 20W
Aurskog 47 59 55N 11 26 E
Aurukun Mission 98 13 20 S 141 45 E
Aus 92 26 35 S 16 12 E
Aust-Agder fylke □ 47 58 55N 7 40 E
Austad 47 58 58N 7 37 E
Austerlitz = Slavkov 27 49 10N 16 52 E
Austevoll 47 60 5N 5 13 E
Austin, Minn., U.S.A. 116 43 37N 92 59W
Austin, Nev., U.S.A. 118 39 30N 117 1W
Austin, Pa., U.S.A. 112 41 40N 78 7W
Austin, Tex., U.S.A. 117 30 20N 97 45W
Austin, L. 96 27 40 S 118 0 E
Austral Downs 97 20 30 S 137 45 E
Austral Is. = Tubuai Is. 95 23 0 S 150 0W
Austral Seamount Chain 95 24 0 S 150 0W
Australia ■ 94 23 0 S 135 0 E
Australian Alps 97 36 30 S 148 30 E
Australian Cap. Terr. □ 97 35 30 S 149 0 E
Australian Dependency □ 5 73 0 S 90 0 E
Austria ■ 26 47 0N 14 0 E
Austvågøy 50 68 20N 14 40 E
Auterive 20 43 21N 1 29 E
Authie → 19 50 22N 1 38 E
Authon 18 48 12N 0 55 E
Autlán 120 19 40N 104 30W
Autun 19 46 58N 4 17 E
Auvergne 20 45 20N 3 15 E
Auvézére → 20 45 12N 0 50 E
Auxerre 19 47 48N 3 32 E
Auxi-le-Château 19 50 15N 2 8 E
Auxonne 19 47 10N 5 20 E
Auzances 20 46 2N 2 30 E
Auzat 20 45 27N 3 19 E
Avallon 19 47 30N 3 53 E
Avalon Pen. 107 47 30N 53 20W
Avalon Res. 117 32 30N 104 30W
Avanigadda 70 16 0N 80 56 E
Avaré 125 23 4 S 48 58W
Ávas 44 40 57N 25 56 E
Aveiro, Brazil 127 3 10 S 55 5W
Aveiro, Port. 30 40 37N 8 38W
Aveiro □ 30 40 40N 8 35W
Avej 64 35 40N 49 15 E
Avellaneda 124 34 50 S 58 10W
Avellino 41 40 54N 14 46 E
Averøya 47 63 0N 7 35 E
Aversa 41 40 58N 14 11 E
Avery 118 47 22N 115 56W
Aves, I. de 121 15 45N 63 55W
Aves, Is. de 121 12 0N 67 30W
Avesnes-sur-Helpe 19 50 8N 3 55 E
Avesta 48 60 9N 16 10 E
Aveyron □ 20 44 22N 2 45 E
Aveyron → 20 44 7N 1 5 E
Avezzano 39 42 2N 13 24 E
Avgó 45 35 33N 25 37 E
Aviá Terai 124 26 45 S 60 50W
Aviano 39 46 3N 12 35 E
Avigliana 38 45 7N 7 13 E
Avigliano 41 40 44N 15 41 E
Avignon 21 43 57N 4 50 E
Ávila 30 40 39N 4 43W
Ávila □ 30 40 30N 5 0W
Ávila, Sierra de 30 40 40N 5 0W
Avilés 30 43 35N 5 57W
Avionárion 45 38 31N 24 8 E
Avisio → 39 46 7N 11 5 E
Aviz 31 39 4N 7 53W
Avize 19 48 59N 4 0 E
Avoca, Austral. 100 37 5 S 143 26 E
Avoca, Ireland 15 52 52N 6 13W
Avoca, U.S.A. 112 42 24N 77 25W
Avoca → 100 35 40 S 143 43 E
Avola, Can. 108 51 45N 119 19W
Avola, Italy 41 36 56N 15 7 E
Avon, N.Y., U.S.A. 112 43 0N 77 42W
Avon, S.D., U.S.A. 116 43 0N 98 3W
Avon □ 13 51 30N 2 40W
Avon →, Avon, U.K. 13 51 30N 2 43W
Avon →, Hants., U.K. 13 50 44N 1 45W
Avon →, Warwick, U.K. 13 52 0N 2 9W
Avon Downs 97 19 58 S 137 25 E
Avon, Îles 97 19 37 S 158 17 E
Avon Lake 112 41 28N 82 3W
Avondale 91 17 43 S 30 58 E
Avonlea 109 50 0N 105 0W
Avonmore 113 45 10N 74 58W
Avonmouth 13 51 30N 2 42W
Avramov 43 42 45N 26 38 E
Avranches 18 48 40N 1 20W
Avre → 18 48 47N 1 22 E
Avrig 46 45 43N 24 21 E
Avrillé 20 46 28N 1 28W
Avtovac 42 43 9N 18 35 E
Awag el Baqar 87 10 10N 33 10 E
'Awālī 65 26 0N 50 30 E
Awarja → 70 17 5N 76 15 E
'Awartā 62 32 10N 35 17 E
Awasa, L. 87 7 0N 38 30 E
Awash 87 9 1N 40 10 E
Awash → 87 11 45N 41 5 E
Awaso 84 6 15N 2 22W
Awatere → 101 41 37 S 174 10 E
Awbārī 83 26 46N 12 57 E
Awbārī □ 83 26 35N 12 46 E
Awe, L. 14 56 15N 5 15W
Aweil 87 8 42N 27 20 E
Awgu 85 6 4N 7 24 E
Awjilah 81 29 8N 21 7 E
Ax-les-Thermes 20 42 44N 1 50 E
Axarfjörður 50 66 15N 16 45W
Axel Heiberg I. 4 80 0N 90 0W
Axim 84 4 51N 2 15W
Axintele 46 44 37N 26 47 E
Axiós → 44 40 57N 22 35 E
Axmarsbruk 48 61 3N 17 10 E
Axminster 13 50 47N 3 1W
Axstedt 24 53 26N 8 43 E
Axvall 49 58 23N 13 34 E
Ay 19 49 3N 4 0 E
Ayabaca 126 4 40 S 79 53W
Ayabe 74 35 20N 135 20 E
Ayacucho, Argent. 124 37 5 S 58 20W
Ayacucho, Peru 126 13 0 S 74 0W
Ayaguz 58 48 10N 80 0 E
Ayakudi 70 10 28N 77 56 E
Ayamonte 31 37 12N 7 24W
Ayan 59 56 30N 138 16 E
Ayancık 56 41 57N 34 18 E
Ayas 56 40 10N 32 14 E
Ayaviri 126 14 50 S 70 35W
Aybaq 65 36 15N 68 5 E
Ayenngré 85 8 40N 1 1 E
Ayeritam 71 5 24N 100 15 E
Ayer's Cliff 113 45 10N 72 3W
Ayers Rock 96 25 23 S 131 5 E
Aygues → 21 44 7N 4 43 E
Ayiá 44 39 43N 22 45 E
Ayía Ánna 45 38 52N 23 24 E
Ayía Marína 45 35 27N 26 53 E
Ayía Marína 45 37 11N 26 48 E
Ayía Paraskeví 44 39 14N 26 16 E
Ayía Rouméli 45 35 14N 23 58 E
Ayiássos 45 39 5N 26 23 E
Áyion Óros 44 40 25N 24 6 E
Áyios Andréas 45 37 21N 22 45 E
Áyios Evstrátios 44 39 34N 24 58 E
Áyios Evstrátios 44 39 30N 25 0 E
Áyios Ioannis, Ákra 45 35 20N 25 40 E
Áyios Kírikos 45 37 34N 26 17 E
Áyios Matthaíos 44 39 30N 19 47 E
Áyios Míronos 45 35 15N 25 1 E
Áyios Nikólaos 45 35 11N 25 41 E
Áyios Pétros 45 38 38N 20 33 E
Áyios Yeóryios 45 37 28N 23 57 E
Aykathonisi 45 37 28N 27 0 E
Aykin 52 62 15N 49 56 E
Aylesbury 13 51 48N 0 49W
Aylmer 112 42 46N 80 59W
Aylmer L. 104 64 0N 110 8W
'Ayn al Mubārak 64 24 10N 38 10 E
'Ayn 'Arīk 62 31 54N 35 8 E
'Ayn Zaqqūt 83 29 0N 19 30 E
Ayn Zhālah 64 36 45N 42 35 E
Ayna 33 38 34N 2 3W
Ayolas 124 27 10 S 56 59W
Ayom 87 7 49N 28 23 E
Ayon, Ostrov 59 69 50N 169 0 E
Ayora 33 39 3N 1 3W
Ayr, Austral. 97 19 35 S 147 25 E
Ayr, U.K. 14 55 28N 4 37W
Ayr → 14 55 29N 4 40W
Ayre, Pt. of 12 54 27N 4 21W
Aysha 87 10 50N 42 23 E
Aytos 43 42 42N 27 16 E
Aytoska Planina 43 42 45N 27 30 E
Ayu, Kepulauan 73 0 35N 131 5 E
Ayutla 120 16 58N 99 17W
Ayvalık 64 39 20N 26 46 E
Az Zāhirīyah 62 31 25N 34 58 E
Az Zahrān 64 26 10N 50 7 E
Az Zarqā 62 32 5N 36 4 E
Az Zāwiyah 83 32 52N 12 56 E
Az-Zilfī 64 26 12N 44 52 E
Az Zubayr 64 30 20N 47 50 E
Azambuja 31 39 4N 8 51W
Azamgarh 69 26 5N 83 13 E
Azaouak, Vallée de l' 85 15 50N 3 20 E
Āzārbāijān □ 64 37 0N 44 30 E
Azare 85 11 55N 10 10 E
Azay-le-Rideau 18 47 16N 0 30 E
Azazga 83 36 48N 4 22 E
Azbine = Aïr 85 18 0N 8 0 E
Azeffoun 83 36 51N 4 26 E
Azemmour 82 33 20N 9 20W
Azerbaijan S.S.R. □ 57 40 20N 48 0 E
Azezo 87 12 28N 37 15 E
Azilal, Beni Mallal 82 32 0N 6 30W
Azimganj 69 24 14N 88 16 E
Aznalcóllar 31 37 32N 6 17W
Azogues 126 2 35 S 78 0W
Azor 62 32 2N 34 48 E
Azores 6 38 44N 29 0W
Azov 57 47 3N 39 25 E
Azov Sea = Azovskoye More 56 46 0N 36 30 E
Azovskoye More 56 46 0N 36 30 E
Azovy 58 64 55N 64 35 E
Azpeitia 32 43 12N 2 19W
Azrou 82 33 28N 5 19W
Aztec 119 36 54N 108 0W
Azúa de Compostela 121 18 25N 70 44W
Azuaga 31 38 16N 5 39W
Azuara 32 41 15N 0 53W
Azuer → 31 39 8N 3 36W
Azuero, Pen. de 121 7 30N 80 30W
Azul 124 36 42 S 59 43W
Azzaba 83 36 48N 7 6 E
Azzano Décimo 39 45 53N 12 46 E

B

Ba Don 71 17 45N 106 26 E
Ba Ngoi = Cam Lam 71 11 50N 109 10 E
Ba Xian 76 39 8N 116 22 E
Baa 73 10 50 S 123 0 E
Baamonde 30 43 7N 7 44W
Baarle Nassau 16 51 27N 4 56 E
Baarn 16 52 12N 5 17 E
Báb el Māndeb 63 12 35N 43 25 E
Baba 43 42 44N 23 59 E
Baba Burnu 44 39 29N 26 2 E
Baba dag 57 41 0N 48 19W
Babadag 46 44 53N 28 44 E
Babaeski 43 41 26N 27 6 E
Babahoyo 126 1 40 S 79 30W
Babana 85 10 31N 3 46 E

Babar, Alg. **83** 35 10N 7 6 E
Babar, Indon. **73** 8 0S 129 30 E
Babar, Pak. **68** 31 7N 69 32 E
Babarkach **68** 29 45N 68 0 E
Babayevo **55** 59 24N 35 55 E
Babb **118** 48 56N 113 27W
Babenhausen **25** 49 57N 8 56 E
Babia Gora **27** 49 38N 19 38 E
Babile **87** 9 16N 42 11 E
Babinda **98** 17 20S 145 56 E
Babine **108** 55 22N 126 37W
Babine → **108** 55 45N 127 44W
Babine L. **108** 54 48N 126 0W
Babo **73** 2 30S 133 30 E
Babócsa **27** 46 2N 17 21 E
Bābol **65** 36 40N 52 50 E
Bābol Sar **65** 36 45N 52 45 E
Baborówo Kietrz **27** 50 7N 18 1 E
Baboua **88** 5 49N 14 58 E
Babuna **42** 41 30N 21 40 E
Babura **85** 12 51N 8 59 E
Babušnica **42** 43 7N 22 27 E
Babuyan Chan. **73** 19 10N 122 0 E
Babylon, Iraq **64** 32 40N 44 30 E
Babylon, U.S.A. **113** 40 42N 73 20W
Bač **42** 45 29N 19 17 E
Bac Kan **71** 22 5N 105 50 E
Bac Ninh **71** 21 13N 106 4 E
Bac Phan **71** 22 0N 105 0 E
Bac Quang **71** 22 30N 104 48 E
Bacabal **127** 4 15S 44 45W
Bacan, Kepulauan **73** 0 35S 127 30 E
Bacan, Pulau **73** 0 50S 127 30 E
Bacarès, Le **20** 42 47N 3 3 E
Bacarra **73** 18 15N 120 37 E
Bacau **73** 8 27S 126 27 E
Bacău **46** 46 35N 26 55 E
Bacău □ **46** 46 30N 26 45 E
Baccarat **19** 48 28N 6 42 E
Bacchus Marsh **100** 37 43S 144 27 E
Bacerac **120** 30 18N 108 50W
Băceşti **46** 46 50N 27 11 E
Bacharach **25** 50 3N 7 46 E
Bachelina **58** 57 45N 67 20 E
Bachuma **87** 6 48N 35 53 E
Bačina **42** 43 42N 21 23 E
Back → **104** 65 10N 104 0W
Bačka Palanka **42** 45 17N 19 27 E
Bačka Topola **42** 45 49N 19 39 E
Bäckefors **49** 58 48N 12 9 E
Bački Petrovac **42** 45 29N 19 32 E
Backnang **25** 48 57N 9 26 E
Backstairs Passage **97** 35 40S 138 5 E
Bacolod **73** 10 40N 122 57 E
Bacqueville **18** 49 47N 1 0 E
Bacs-Kiskun □ **27** 46 43N 19 30 E
Bácsalmás **27** 46 8N 19 17 E
Bad → **116** 44 22N 100 22W
Bad Aussee **26** 47 43N 13 45 E
Bad Axe **106** 43 48N 82 59W
Bad Bergzabern **25** 49 6N 8 0 E
Bad Bramstedt **24** 53 56N 9 53 E
Bad Doberan **24** 54 6N 11 55 E
Bad Driburg **24** 51 44N 9 0 E
Bad Ems **25** 50 22N 7 44 E
Bad Frankenhausen **24** 51 21N 11 3 E
Bad Freienwalde **24** 52 47N 14 3 E
Bad Godesberg **24** 50 41N 7 4 E
Bad Hersfeld **24** 50 52N 9 42 E
Bad Hofgastein **26** 47 17N 13 6 E
Bad Homburg **25** 50 17N 8 33 E
Bad Honnef **24** 50 39N 7 13 E
Bad Ischl **26** 47 44N 13 38 E
Bad Kissingen **25** 50 11N 10 5 E
Bad Kreuznach **25** 49 47N 7 47 E
Bad Lands **116** 43 40N 102 10W
Bad Langensalza **24** 51 6N 10 40 E
Bad Lauterberg **24** 51 38N 10 29 E
Bad Leonfelden **26** 48 31N 14 18 E
Bad Lippspringe **24** 51 47N 8 46 E
Bad Mergentheim **25** 49 29N 9 47 E
Bad Münstereifel **24** 50 33N 6 46 E
Bad Muskau **24** 51 33N 14 43 E
Bad Nauheim **25** 50 24N 8 45 E
Bad Oeynhausen **24** 52 16N 8 45 E
Bad Oldesloe **24** 53 48N 10 22 E
Bad Orb **25** 50 16N 9 21 E
Bad Pyrmont **24** 51 59N 9 15 E
Bad Reichenhall **25** 47 44N 12 53 E
Bad St.-Peter **24** 54 23N 8 32 E
Bad Salzuflen **24** 52 8N 8 44 E
Bad Segeberg **24** 53 58N 10 16 E
Bad Tölz **25** 47 43N 11 34 E
Bad Waldsee **25** 47 56N 9 46 E
Bad Wildungen **24** 51 7N 9 10 E
Bad Wimpfen **25** 49 12N 9 10 E
Bad Windsheim **25** 49 29N 10 25 E
Badagara **70** 11 35N 75 40 E
Badagri **85** 6 25N 2 55 E
Badajoz **31** 38 50N 6 59W
Badajoz □ **31** 38 40N 6 30W
Badakhshan □ **65** 36 30N 71 0 E
Badalona **32** 41 26N 2 15 E
Badalzai **66** 29 50N 65 35 E
Badampahar **69** 22 10N 86 10 E
Badanah **64** 30 58N 41 30 E
Badas **72** 4 33N 114 25 E
Badas, Kepulauan **72** 0 45N 107 5 E
Baddo → **66** 28 0N 64 20 E
Bade **73** 7 10S 139 35 E
Baden, Austria **27** 48 1N 16 13 E
Baden, Can. **112** 43 14N 80 40W
Baden, Switz. **25** 47 28N 8 18 E
Baden-Baden **25** 48 45N 8 15 E
Baden-Württemberg □ **25** 48 40N 9 0 E
Badgastein **26** 47 7N 13 9 E
Badger **107** 49 0N 56 4W
Bādghīsāt □ **65** 35 0N 63 0 E
Badia Polèsine **39** 45 6N 11 30 E
Badin **68** 24 38N 68 54 E
Badnera **68** 20 48N 77 44 E
Badogo **84** 11 2N 8 13W
Badong **77** 31 1N 110 23 E
Badrinath **69** 30 45N 79 30 E
Baduen **63** 7 15N 47 40 E
Badulla **70** 7 1N 81 7 E
Baena **31** 37 37N 4 20W
Baeza **33** 37 57N 3 25W
Bafa Gölü **45** 37 30N 27 29 E
Bafang **85** 5 9N 10 11 E
Bafatá **84** 12 8N 14 40W
Baffin B. **4** 72 0N 64 0W
Baffin I. **105** 68 0N 75 0W
Bafia **88** 4 40N 11 10 E
Bafilo **85** 9 22N 1 22 E
Bafing → **84** 13 49N 10 50W
Bafoulabé **84** 13 50N 10 55W
Bafoussam **85** 5 28N 10 25 E
Bafra **56** 41 34N 35 54 E
Bafra, C. **56** 41 44N 35 58 E
Bāft, Esfahān, Iran **65** 31 40N 55 25 E
Bāft, Kermān, Iran **65** 29 15N 56 38 E
Bafut **85** 6 6N 10 2 E
Bafwasende **90** 1 3N 27 5 E
Bagalkot **70** 16 10N 75 40 E
Bagamoyo **90** 6 28S 38 55 E
Bagamoyo □ **90** 6 20S 38 30 E
Baganga **73** 7 34N 126 33 E
Bagansiapiapi **72** 2 12N 100 50 E
Bagasra **68** 21 30N 71 0 E
Bagawi **87** 12 20N 34 18 E
Bagdarin **59** 54 26N 113 36 E
Bagé **125** 31 20S 54 15W
Bagenalstown = Muine Bheag **15** 52 42N 6 57W
Baggs **118** 41 8N 107 46W
Baghdād **64** 33 20N 44 30 E
Bagherhat **69** 22 40N 89 47 E
Bagheria **40** 38 5N 13 30 E
Bāghīn **65** 30 12N 56 45 E
Baghlān **65** 36 12N 69 0 E
Baghlān □ **65** 36 0N 68 30 E
Bagley **116** 47 30N 95 22W
Bagnacavallo **39** 44 25N 11 58 E
Bagnara Cálabra **41** 38 16N 15 49 E
Bagnères-de-Bigorre **20** 43 5N 0 9 E
Bagnères-de-Luchon **20** 42 47N 0 38 E
Bagni di Lucca **38** 44 1N 10 37 E
Bagno di Romagna **39** 43 50N 11 59 E
Bagnoles-de-l'Orne **18** 48 32N 0 25W
Bagnoli di Sopra **39** 45 13N 11 55 E
Bagnolo Mella **38** 45 27N 10 14 E
Bagnols-les-Bains **20** 44 30N 3 40 E
Bagnols-sur-Cèze **21** 44 10N 4 36 E
Bagnorégio **39** 42 38N 12 7 E
Bagolino **38** 45 49N 10 28 E
Bagotville **107** 48 22N 70 54W
Bagrdan **42** 44 5N 21 11 E
Baguio **73** 16 26N 120 34 E
Bahabón de Esgueva **32** 41 52N 3 43W
Bahadurgarh **68** 28 40N 76 57 E
Bahama, Canal Viejo de **121** 22 10N 77 30W
Bahamas ■ **121** 24 0N 75 0W
Baharîya, El Wâhât al **86** 28 0N 28 50 E
Bahau **71** 2 48N 102 26 E
Bahawalnagar **68** 30 0N 73 15 E
Bahawalpur **68** 29 24N 71 40 E
Bahawalpur □ **68** 29 5N 71 3 E
Baheri **69** 28 45N 79 34 E
Bahi **90** 5 58S 35 21 E
Bahi Swamp **90** 6 10S 35 0 E
Bahia = Salvador **127** 13 0S 38 30W
Bahia □ **127** 12 0S 42 0W
Bahía Blanca **124** 38 35S 62 13W
Bahía de Caráquez **126** 0 40S 80 27W
Bahía, Islas de la **121** 16 45N 86 15W
Bahía Laura **128** 48 10S 66 30W
Bahía Negra **126** 20 5S 58 5W
Bahir Dar **87** 11 37N 37 10 E
Bahmer **82** 27 32N 0 10W
Bahönye **27** 46 25N 17 28 E
Bahr Aouk → **88** 8 40N 19 0 E
Bahr el Ahmar □ **86** 20 0N 35 0 E
Bahr el Ghazâl □ **87** 7 0N 28 0 E
Bahr el Jebel → **87** 7 30N 30 30 E
Bahr Salamat → **81** 9 20N 18 0 E
Bahr Yûsef → **86** 28 25N 30 35 E
Bahra el Burullus **86** 31 28N 30 48 E
Bahraich **69** 27 38N 81 37 E
Bahrain ■ **65** 26 0N 50 35 E
Bai **84** 13 35N 3 28W
Baia Mare **46** 47 40N 23 35 E
Baia-Sprie **46** 47 41N 23 43 E
Baïbokoum **81** 7 46N 15 43 E
Baicheng **76** 45 38N 122 42 E
Băicoi **46** 45 3N 25 52 E
Baidoa **63** 3 8N 43 30 E
Baie Comeau **107** 49 12N 68 10W
Baie-St-Paul **107** 47 28N 70 32W
Baie Trinité **107** 49 25N 67 20W
Baie Verte **107** 49 55N 56 12W
Baignes **20** 45 23N 0 25W
Baigneux-les-Juifs **19** 47 31N 4 39 E
Ba'ījī **64** 35 0N 43 30 E
Baikal, L. = Baykal, Oz. **59** 53 0N 108 0 E
Bailadila, Mt. **70** 18 43N 81 15 E
Baile Atha Cliath = Dublin **15** 53 20N 6 18W
Bailei **87** 6 44N 40 18 E
Bailén **31** 38 8N 3 48W
Băileşti **46** 44 01N 23 20 E
Bailhongal **70** 15 55N 74 53 E
Bailleul **19** 50 44N 2 41 E
Bailundo **89** 12 10S 15 50 E
Baimuru **98** 7 35S 144 51 E
Bain-de-Bretagne **18** 47 50N 1 40W
Bainbridge, Ga., U.S.A. **115** 30 53N 84 34W
Bainbridge, N.Y., U.S.A. **113** 42 17N 75 29W
Baing **73** 10 14S 120 34 E
Bainville **116** 48 8N 104 10W
Bā'ir **64** 30 45N 36 55 E
Baird **117** 32 25N 99 25W
Baird Mts. **104** 67 10N 160 15W
Bairin Youqi **76** 43 30N 118 35 E
Bairin Zuoqi **76** 43 58N 119 15 E
Bairnsdale **97** 37 48S 147 36 E
Baise → **20** 44 17N 0 18 E
Baissa **85** 7 14N 10 38 E
Baitadi **69** 29 35N 80 25 E
Baiyin **76** 36 45N 104 14 E
Baiyu Shan **76** 37 15N 107 30 E
Baiyuda **86** 17 35N 32 07 E
Baja **27** 46 12N 18 59 E
Baja California **120** 31 10N 115 12W
Baja, Pta. **120** 29 50N 116 0W
Bajah, Wadi → **86** 23 14N 39 20 E
Bajana **68** 23 7N 71 49 E
Bajimba, Mt. **99** 29 17S 152 6 E
Bajina Bašta **42** 43 58N 19 35 E
Bajmok **42** 45 57N 19 24 E
Bajo Nuevo **121** 15 40N 78 50W
Bajoga **85** 10 57N 11 20 E
Bajool **98** 23 40S 150 35 E
Bak **27** 46 43N 16 51 E
Bakala **88** 6 15N 20 20 E
Bakar **39** 45 18N 14 32 E
Bakchav **58** 57 1N 82 5 E
Bakel **84** 14 56N 12 20W
Baker, Calif., U.S.A. **119** 35 16N 116 8W
Baker, Mont., U.S.A. **116** 46 22N 104 12W
Baker, Nev., U.S.A. **118** 38 59N 114 7W
Baker, Oreg., U.S.A. **118** 44 50N 117 55W
Baker I. **94** 0 10N 176 35W
Baker, L. **104** 64 0N 96 0W
Baker Lake **104** 64 20N 96 3W
Baker Mt. **118** 48 50N 121 49W
Baker's Dozen Is. **106** 56 45N 78 45W
Bakersfield, Calif., U.S.A. **119** 35 25N 119 0W
Bakersfield, Vt., U.S.A. **113** 44 46N 72 48W
Bakhchisaray **56** 44 40N 33 45 E
Bakhmach **54** 51 10N 32 45 E
Bakhtīārī □ **64** 32 0N 49 0 E
Bakinskikh Komissarov, im 26 **64** 39 20N 49 15 E
Bakırköy **43** 40 59N 28 53 E
Bakkafjörður **50** 66 2N 14 48W
Bakkagerði **50** 65 31N 13 49W
Bakony → **27** 47 35N 17 54 E
Bakony Forest = Bakony Hegység **27** 47 10N 17 30 E
Bakony Hegység **27** 47 10N 17 30 E
Bakori **85** 11 34N 7 25 E
Bakouma **88** 5 40N 22 56 E
Bakov **26** 50 27N 14 55 E
Baku **57** 40 25N 49 45 E
Bala **112** 45 1N 79 37W
Bal'ā **62** 32 20N 35 6 E
Bala, L. = Tegid, L. **12** 52 53N 3 38W
Balabac I. **72** 8 0N 117 0 E
Balabac, Str. **72** 7 53N 117 5 E
Balabakk **64** 34 0N 36 10 E
Balabalangan, Kepulauan **72** 2 20S 117 30 E
Bălăciţa **46** 44 23N 23 8 E
Balaghat **69** 21 49N 80 12 E
Balaghat Ra. **70** 18 50N 76 30 E
Balaguer **32** 41 50N 0 50 E
Balakhna **55** 56 25N 43 32 E
Balaklava, Austral. **99** 34 7S 138 22 E
Balaklava, U.S.S.R. **56** 44 30N 33 30 E
Balakleya **56** 49 28N 36 55 E
Balakovo **55** 52 4N 47 55 E
Balanda **55** 51 30N 44 40 E
Balangir **69** 20 43N 83 35 E
Balapur **68** 20 40N 76 45 E
Balashikha **55** 55 49N 37 59 E
Balashov **55** 51 30N 43 10 E
Balasinor **68** 22 57N 73 23 E
Balasore **69** 21 35N 87 3 E
Balassagyarmat **27** 48 4N 19 15 E
Balât **86** 25 36N 29 19 E
Balaton **27** 46 50N 17 40 E
Balatonfüred **27** 46 58N 17 54 E
Balatonszentgyörgy **27** 46 41N 17 19 E
Balazote **33** 38 54N 2 09W
Balboa **120** 9 0N 79 30W
Balboa Hill **120** 9 6N 79 44W
Balbriggan **15** 53 35N 6 10W
Balcarce **124** 38 0S 58 10W
Balcarres **109** 50 50N 103 35W
Balchik **43** 43 28N 28 11 E
Balclutha **101** 46 15S 169 45 E
Bald Knob **117** 35 20N 91 35W
Baldock L. **109** 56 33N 97 57W
Baldwin, Fla., U.S.A. **115** 30 15N 82 10W
Baldwin, Mich., U.S.A. **114** 43 54N 85 53W
Baldwinsville **114** 43 10N 76 19W
Bale **39** 45 4N 13 46 E
Bale □ **87** 6 20N 41 30 E
Baleares □ **32** 39 30N 3 0 E
Baleares, Islas **32** 39 30N 3 0 E
Balearic Is. = Baleares, Islas **32** 39 30N 3 0 E
Băleni **46** 45 48N 27 51 E
Baler **73** 15 46N 121 34 E
Balfe's Creek **98** 20 12S 145 55 E
Balfour **93** 26 38S 28 35 E
Balfouriyya **62** 32 38N 35 18 E
Bali, Camer. **85** 5 54N 10 0 E
Bali, Indon. **72** 8 20S 115 0 E
Bali □ **72** 8 20S 115 0 E
Bali, Selat **73** 8 30S 114 35 E
Baligród **27** 49 20N 22 17 E
Balikesir **64** 39 35N 27 58 E
Balikpapan **72** 1 10S 116 55 E
Balimbing **73** 5 10N 120 3 E
Baling **71** 5 41N 100 55 E
Balipara **67** 26 50N 92 45 E
Baliza **127** 16 0S 52 20W
Balkan Mts. = Stara Planina **43** 43 15N 23 0 E
Balkan Pen. **9** 42 0N 22 0 E
Balkh **65** 36 44N 66 47 E
Balkh □ **65** 36 30N 67 0 E
Balkhash **58** 46 50N 74 50 E
Balkhash, Ozero **58** 46 0N 74 50 E
Ballachulish **14** 56 40N 5 10W
Balladoran **100** 31 52S 148 39 E
Ballarat **97** 37 33S 143 50 E
Ballard, L. **96** 29 20S 120 10 E
Ballarpur **70** 19 50N 79 23 E
Ballater **14** 57 2N 3 2W
Ballenas, Canal de las **120** 29 10N 113 45W
Balleny Is. **5** 66 30S 163 0 E
Ballia **69** 25 46N 84 12 E
Ballina, Austral. **97** 28 50S 153 31 E
Ballina, Mayo, Ireland **15** 54 7N 9 10W
Ballina, Tipp., Ireland **15** 52 49N 8 27W
Ballinasloe **15** 53 20N 8 12W
Ballinger **117** 31 45N 99 58W
Ballinrobe **15** 53 36N 9 13W
Ballinskelligs B. **15** 51 46N 10 11W
Ballon **18** 48 10N 0 14 E
Ballycastle **15** 55 12N 6 15W
Ballymena **15** 54 53N 6 18W
Ballymena □ **15** 54 53N 6 18W
Ballymoney **15** 55 5N 6 30W
Ballymoney □ **15** 55 5N 6 23W
Ballyshannon **15** 54 30N 8 10W
Balmaceda **128** 46 0S 71 50W
Balmazújváros **27** 47 37N 21 21 E
Balmoral, Austral. **99** 37 15S 141 48 E
Balmoral, U.K. **14** 57 3N 3 13W
Balmorhea **117** 31 2N 103 41W
Balonne → **97** 28 47S 147 56 E
Balrampur **69** 27 30N 82 20 E
Balranald **97** 34 38S 143 33 E
Balş **46** 44 22N 24 5 E
Balsas → **120** 17 55N 102 10W
Bålsta **48** 59 35N 17 30 E
Balston Spa **113** 43 0N 73 52W
Balta, Romania **46** 44 54N 22 38 E
Balta, U.S.A. **116** 48 12N 100 7W
Balta, R.S.F.S.R., U.S.S.R. **57** 42 58N 44 32 E
Balta, Ukraine S.S.R., U.S.S.R. **56** 48 2N 29 45 E
Baltanás **30** 41 56N 4 15W
Baltic Sea **51** 56 0N 20 0 E
Baltîm **86** 31 35N 31 10 E
Baltimore, Ireland **15** 51 29N 9 22W
Baltimore, U.S.A. **114** 39 18N 76 37W
Baltrum **24** 53 43N 7 25 E
Baluchistan □ **65** 27 30N 65 0 E
Balurghat **69** 25 15N 88 44 E
Balygychan **59** 63 56N 154 12 E
Bam **65** 29 7N 58 14 E
Bama **85** 11 33N 13 41 E
Bamako **84** 12 34N 7 55W
Bamba **85** 17 5N 1 24W
Bambari **88** 5 40N 20 35 E
Bamberg, Ger. **25** 49 54N 10 53 E
Bamberg, U.S.A. **115** 33 19N 81 1W
Bambesi **87** 9 45N 34 40 E
Bambey **84** 14 42N 16 28W
Bambili **90** 3 40N 26 0 E
Bamboo **98** 14 34S 143 20 E
Bamenda **85** 5 57N 10 11 E
Bamfield **108** 48 45N 125 10W
Bāmīān □ **65** 35 0N 67 0 E
Bamiancheng **76** 43 15N 124 2 E
Bamkin **85** 6 3N 11 27 E
Bampūr **65** 27 15N 60 21 E
Ban Aranyaprathet **71** 13 41N 102 30 E
Ban Ban **71** 19 31N 103 30 E
Ban Bua Chum **71** 15 11N 101 12 E
Ban Houei Sai **71** 20 22N 100 32 E
Ban Khe Bo **71** 19 10N 104 39 E
Ban Khun Yuam **71** 18 49N 97 57 E
Ban Me Thuot **71** 12 40N 108 3 E
Ban Phai **71** 16 4N 102 44 E
Ban Thateng **71** 15 25N 106 27 E
Baña, Punta de la **32** 40 33N 0 40 E
Banaba **94** 0 45S 169 50 E
Banadar Daryay Oman □ **65** 27 30N 56 0 E
Banalia **90** 1 32N 25 5 E
Banam **71** 11 20N 105 17 E
Banamba **84** 13 29N 7 22W
Banana **98** 24 28S 150 8 E
Bananal, I. do **127** 11 30S 50 30W
Banaras = Varanasi **69** 25 22N 83 8 E
Banas →, Gujarat, India **68** 23 45N 71 25 E
Banas →, Madhya Pradesh, India **69** 24 15N 81 30 E
Bânâs, Ras. **86** 23 57N 35 50 E
Banbridge **15** 54 21N 6 17W
Banbridge □ **15** 54 21N 6 16W
Banbury **13** 52 4N 1 21W
Banchory **14** 57 3N 2 30W
Bancroft **106** 45 3N 77 51W
Band **43** 46 30N 24 25 E
Band-e Torkestān **65** 35 30N 64 0 E
Banda **68** 25 30N 80 26 E
Banda Aceh **72** 5 35N 95 20 E
Banda Banda, Mt. **99** 31 10S 152 28 E
Banda Elat **73** 5 40S 133 5 E
Banda, Kepulauan **73** 4 37S 129 50 E
Banda, La **124** 27 45S 64 10W
Banda Sea **73** 6 0S 130 0 E
Bandama → **84** 6 32N 5 30W
Bandanaira **73** 4 32S 129 54 E
Bandanwara **68** 26 9N 74 38 E
Bandar = Machilipatnam **70** 16 12N 81 12 E
Bandār 'Abbās **65** 27 15N 56 15 E
Bandar-e Būshehr **65** 28 55N 50 55 E
Bandar-e Chārak **65** 26 45N 54 20 E
Bandar-e Deylam **64** 30 5N 50 10 E
Bandar-e Lengeh **65** 26 35N 54 58 E
Bandar-e Ma'shur **64** 30 35N 49 10 E
Bandar-e Nakhīlū **65** 26 58N 53 30 E
Bandar-e Rīg **65** 29 30N 50 45 E
Bandar-e Shāh **65** 37 0N 54 10 E
Bandar-e Shāhpūr **64** 30 30N 49 5 E
Bandar-i-Pahlavī **64** 37 30N 49 30 E
Bandar Seri Begawan **72** 4 52N 115 0 E
Bandawe **91** 11 58S 34 5 E
Bande **30** 42 3N 7 58W
Bandeira, Pico da **125** 20 26S 41 47W
Bandera, Argent. **124** 28 55S 62 20W
Bandera, U.S.A. **117** 29 45N 99 3W
Banderas, Bahía de **120** 20 40N 105 30W
Bandia → **70** 19 2N 80 28 E
Bandiagara **84** 14 12N 3 29W
Bandırma **64** 40 20N 28 0 E
Bandon **15** 51 44N 8 45W
Bandon → **15** 51 40N 8 41W
Bandula **91** 19 0S 33 7 E

Bandundu 88 3 15 S 17 22 E
Bandung 73 6 54 S 107 36 E
Băneasa 46 45 56N 27 55 E
Bañeres 33 38 44N 0 38W
Banes 121 21 0N 75 42W
Bañeza, La 30 42 17N 5 54W
Banff, Can. 108 51 10N 115 34W
Banff, U.K. 14 57 40N 2 32W
Banff Nat. Park 108 51 30N 116 15W
Banfora 84 10 40N 4 40W
Bang Hieng → 71 16 10N 105 10 E
Bang Lamung 71 13 3N 100 56 E
Bang Saphan 71 11 14N 99 28 E
Bangala Dam 91 21 7 S 31 25 E
Bangalore 70 12 59N 77 40 E
Bangante 85 5 8N 10 32 E
Bangaon 69 23 0N 88 47 E
Bangassou 88 4 55N 23 7 E
Bangeta, Mt. 98 6 21 S 147 3 E
Banggai 73 1 40 S 123 30 E
Banggi, P. 72 7 17N 117 12 E
Banghāzī 83 32 11N 20 3 E
Banghāzi □ 83 32 7N 20 4 E
Bangil 73 7 36 S 112 50 E
Bangjang 87 11 23N 32 41 E
Bangka, Pulau, Sulawesi, Indon. 73 1 50N 125 5 E
Bangka, Pulau, Sumatera, Indon. 72 2 0 S 105 50 E
Bangka, Selat 72 2 30 S 105 30 E
Bangkalan 73 7 2 S 112 46 E
Bangkinang 72 0 18N 101 5 E
Bangko 72 2 5 S 102 9 E
Bangkok = Krung Thep 71 13 45N 100 35 E
Bangladesh ■ 67 24 0N 90 0 E
Bangolo 84 7 1N 7 29W
Bangor, N. Ireland, U.K. 15 54 40N 5 40W
Bangor, Wales, U.K. 12 53 13N 4 9W
Bangor, Me., U.S.A. 107 44 48N 68 42W
Bangor, Pa., U.S.A. 113 40 51N 75 13W
Bangued 73 17 40N 120 37 E
Bangui 88 4 23N 18 35 E
Banguru 90 0 30N 27 10 E
Bangweulu, L. 91 11 0 S 30 0 E
Bangweulu Swamp 91 11 20 S 30 15 E
Bani 121 18 16N 70 22W
Bani → 84 14 30N 4 12W
Bani Bangou 85 15 3N 2 42 E
Bani, Djebel 82 29 16N 8 0W
Banī Na'īm 62 31 31N 35 10 E
Banī Suhaylah 62 31 21N 34 19 E
Bania 84 9 4N 3 6W
Baniara 98 9 44 S 149 54 E
Banīnah 83 32 0N 20 12 E
Bāniyās 64 35 10N 36 0 E
Banja Luka 42 44 49N 17 11 E
Banjar 73 7 24 S 108 30 E
Banjarmasin 72 3 20 S 114 35 E
Banjarnegara 73 7 24 S 109 42 E
Banjul 84 13 28N 16 40W
Bankeryd 49 57 53N 14 6 E
Banket 91 17 27 S 30 19 E
Bankilaré 85 14 35N 0 44 E
Bankipore 69 25 35N 85 10 E
Banks I., B.C., Can. 108 53 20N 130 0W
Banks I., N.W.T., Can. 4 73 15N 121 30W
Banks I., P.N.G. 97 10 10 S 142 15 E
Banks Pen. 101 43 45 S 173 15 E
Banks Str. 99 40 40 S 148 10 E
Bankura 69 23 11N 87 18 E
Bankya 42 42 43N 23 8 E
Bann →, Down, U.K. 15 54 30N 6 31W
Bann →, Londonderry, U.K. 15 55 10N 6 34W
Bannalec 18 47 57N 3 42W
Banning 119 33 58N 116 52W
Banningville = Bandundu 88 3 15 S 17 22 E
Bannockburn, Can. 112 44 39N 77 33W
Bannockburn, U.K. 14 56 5N 3 55W
Bannockburn, Zimb. 91 20 17 S 29 48 E
Bañolas 32 42 16N 2 44 E
Banon 21 44 2N 5 38 E
Baños de la Encina 31 38 10N 3 46W
Baños de Molgas 30 42 15N 7 40W
Bánovce 27 48 44N 18 16 E
Banská Bystrica 27 48 46N 19 14 E
Banská Štiavnica 27 48 25N 18 55 E
Bansko 43 41 52N 23 28 E
Banswara 68 23 32N 74 24 E
Banten 73 6 5 S 106 8 E
Bantry 15 51 40N 9 28W
Bantry, B. 15 51 35N 9 50W
Bantul 73 7 55 S 110 19 E
Bantva 68 21 29N 70 12 E
Bantval 70 12 55N 75 0 E
Banya 43 42 33N 24 50 E
Banyak, Kepulauan 72 2 10N 97 10 E
Banyo 85 6 52N 11 45 E
Banyuls 20 42 29N 3 8 E
Banyumas 73 7 32 S 109 18 E
Banyuwangi 73 8 13 S 114 21 E
Banzare Coast 5 68 0 S 125 0 E
Banzyville = Mobayi 88 4 15N 21 8 E
Baocheng 77 33 12N 106 56 E
Baode 76 39 1N 111 5 E
Baoding 76 38 50N 115 28 E
Baoji 77 34 20N 107 5 E
Baojing 77 28 45N 109 41 E
Baokang 77 31 54N 111 12 E
Baoshan 75 25 10N 99 5 E
Baotou 76 40 32N 110 2 E
Baoying 77 33 17N 119 20 E
Bap 68 27 23N 72 18 E
Bapatla 70 15 55N 80 30 E
Bapaume 19 50 7N 2 50 E
Bāqa el Gharbīyya 62 32 25N 35 2 E
Ba'qūbah 64 33 45N 44 50 E
Baquedano 124 23 20 S 69 52W
Bar, U.S.S.R. 56 49 4N 27 40 E
Bar, Yugo. 42 42 8N 19 8 E
Bar Harbor 107 44 15N 68 20W
Bar-le-Duc 19 48 47N 5 10 E
Bar-sur-Aube 19 48 14N 4 40 E
Bar-sur-Seine 19 48 7N 4 20 E
Barabai 72 2 32 S 115 34 E
Barabinsk 58 55 20N 78 20 E
Baraboo 116 43 28N 89 46W
Baracoa 121 20 20N 74 30W
Baradero 124 33 52 S 59 29W
Baraga 116 46 49N 88 29W
Barahona, Dom. Rep. 121 18 13N 71 7W
Barahona, Spain 32 41 17N 2 39W
Barail Range 67 25 15N 93 20 E
Baraka → 86 18 13N 37 35 E
Barakhola 67 25 0N 92 45 E
Barakot 69 21 33N 84 59 E
Barakula 99 26 30 S 150 33 E
Baralaba 98 24 13 S 149 50 E
Baralzon L. 109 60 0N 98 3W
Baramati 70 18 11N 74 33 E
Baramba 69 20 25N 85 23 E
Barameiya 86 18 32N 36 38 E
Baramula 69 34 15N 74 20 E
Baran 68 25 9N 76 40 E
Baranof I. 104 57 0N 135 10W
Baranovichi 54 53 10N 26 0 E
Baranów Sandomierski 28 50 29N 21 30 E
Baranya □ 27 46 0N 18 15 E
Barão de Melgaço 126 11 50 S 60 45W
Baraolt 46 46 5N 25 34 E
Barapasi 73 2 15 S 137 5 E
Barasat 69 22 46N 88 31 E
Barat Daya, Kepulauan 73 7 30 S 128 0 E
Barataria B. 117 29 15N 89 45W
Baraut 68 29 13N 77 7 E
Barbacena 125 21 15 S 43 56W
Barbacoas 126 1 45N 78 0W
Barbados ■ 121 13 0N 59 30W
Barban 39 45 5N 14 4 E
Barbastro 32 42 2N 0 5 E
Barbate 31 36 13N 5 56W
Barberino di Mugello 39 44 1N 11 15 E
Barberton, S. Afr. 93 25 42 S 31 2 E
Barberton, U.S.A. 114 41 0N 81 40W
Barbezieux 20 45 28N 0 9W
Barbigha 69 25 21N 85 47 E
Barbourville 115 36 57N 83 52W
Barbuda I. 121 17 30N 61 40W
Barca, La 120 20 20N 102 40W
Barcaldine 97 23 43 S 145 6 E
Barcarrota 31 38 31N 6 51W
Barcellona Pozzo di Gotto 41 38 8N 15 15 E
Barcelona, Spain 32 41 21N 2 10 E
Barcelona, Venez. 126 10 10N 64 40W
Barcelona □ 32 41 30N 2 0 E
Barcelonette 21 44 23N 6 40 E
Barcelos 126 1 0 S 63 0W
Barcin 28 52 52N 17 55 E
Barcoo → 97 25 30 S 142 50 E
Barcs 27 45 58N 17 28 E
Barczewo 28 53 50N 20 42 E
Barda 57 40 25N 47 10 E
Bardai 83 21 25N 17 0 E
Bardas Blancas 124 35 49 S 69 45W
Bardejov 27 49 18N 21 15 E
Bardera 63 2 20N 42 27 E
Bardi 38 44 38N 9 43 E
Bardi, Ra's 64 24 17N 37 31 E
Bardia 81 31 45N 25 0 E
Bardo 28 50 31N 16 42 E
Bardoli 68 21 12N 73 5 E
Bardolino 38 45 33N 10 43 E
Bardsey I. 12 52 46N 4 47W
Bardstown 114 37 50N 85 29W
Bareilly 69 28 22N 79 27 E
Barentin 18 49 33N 0 58 E
Barenton 18 48 38N 0 50W
Barents Sea 4 73 0N 39 0 E
Barentu 87 15 2N 37 35 E
Barfleur 18 49 40N 1 17W
Barga, China 75 30 40N 81 20 E
Barga, Italy 38 44 5N 10 30 E
Bargal 63 11 25N 51 0 E
Bargara 98 24 50 S 152 25 E
Barge 38 44 43N 7 19 E
Barge, La 118 42 12N 110 4W
Bargnop 87 9 32N 28 25 E
Bargteheide 24 53 42N 10 13 E
Barguzin 59 53 37N 109 37 E
Barh 69 25 29N 85 46 E
Barhaj 69 26 18N 83 44 E
Barham 100 35 36 S 144 8 E
Barhi 69 24 15N 85 25 E
Bari, India 68 26 39N 77 39 E
Bari, Italy 41 41 6N 16 52 E
Bari Doab 68 30 20N 73 0 E
Bariadi □ 90 2 45 S 34 40 E
Barīm 63 12 39N 43 25 E
Barinas 126 8 36N 70 15W
Baring C. 104 70 0N 117 30W
Baringo 90 0 47N 36 16 E
Baringo □ 90 0 55N 36 0 E
Baringo, L. 90 0 47N 36 16 E
Baripada 69 21 57N 86 45 E
Bârîs 86 24 42N 30 31 E
Barisal 69 22 45N 90 20 E
Barisan, Bukit 72 3 30 S 102 15 E
Barito → 72 4 0 S 114 50 E
Barjac 21 44 20N 4 22 E
Barjols 21 43 34N 6 2 E
Barjūj, Wadi → 83 25 26N 12 12 E
Bark L. 112 45 27N 77 51W
Barka = Baraka → 87 18 13N 37 35 E
Barkalı 65 23 40N 58 0 E
Barker 112 43 20N 78 35W
Barkley Sound 108 48 50N 125 10W
Barkly Downs 98 20 30 S 138 30 E
Barkly East 92 30 58 S 27 33 E
Barkly Tableland 97 17 50 S 136 40 E
Barkly West 92 28 5 S 24 31 E
Barkol, Wadi → 86 17 40N 32 0 E
Barksdale 117 29 47N 100 2W
Barlee, L. 96 29 15 S 119 30 E
Barlee Ra. 96 23 30 S 116 0 E
Barletta 41 41 20N 16 17 E
Barleur, Pointe de 18 49 42N 1 16W
Barlinek 28 53 0N 15 15 E
Barlow L. 109 62 00N 103 0W
Barmedman 99 34 9 S 147 21 E
Barmer 68 25 45N 71 20 E
Barmera 99 34 15 S 140 28 E
Barmouth 12 52 44N 4 3W
Barmstedt 24 53 47N 9 46 E
Barnagar 68 23 7N 75 19 E
Barnard Castle 12 54 33N 1 55W
Barnato 99 31 38 S 145 0 E
Barnaul 58 53 20N 83 40 E
Barne Inlet 5 80 15 S 160 0 E
Barnes 99 36 2 S 144 47 E
Barnesville 115 33 6N 84 9W
Barnet 13 51 37N 0 15W
Barneveld, Neth. 16 52 7N 5 36 E
Barneveld, U.S.A. 113 43 16N 75 14W
Barneville 18 49 23N 1 46W
Barney, Mt. 97 28 17 S 152 44 E
Barngo 99 25 3 S 147 20 E
Barnhart 117 31 10N 101 8W
Barnsley 12 53 33N 1 29W
Barnstaple 13 51 5N 4 3W
Barnsville 116 46 43N 96 28W
Baro 85 8 35N 6 18 E
Baro → 87 8 26N 33 13 E
Baroda 68 25 29N 76 35 E
Baroda = Vadodara 68 22 20N 73 10 E
Barpali 69 21 11N 83 35 E
Barqin 83 27 33N 13 34 E
Barques, Pte. aux 114 44 5N 82 55W
Barquinha 31 39 28N 8 25W
Barquísimeto 126 10 4N 69 19W
Barr 19 48 25N 7 28 E
Barra, Brazil 127 11 5 S 43 10W
Barra, U.K. 14 57 0N 7 30W
Barra do Corda 127 5 30 S 45 10W
Barra do Piraí 125 22 30 S 43 50W
Barra Falsa, Pta. da 93 22 58 S 35 37 E
Barra Hd. 14 56 47N 7 40W
Barra Mansa 125 22 35 S 44 12W
Barra, Sd. of 14 57 4N 7 25W
Barraba 99 30 21 S 150 35 E
Barrackpur 69 22 44N 88 30 E
Barrafranca 41 37 22N 14 10 E
Barranca, Lima, Peru 126 10 45 S 77 50W
Barranca, Loreto, Peru 126 4 50 S 76 50W
Barrancabermeja 126 7 0N 73 50W
Barrancas 126 8 55N 62 5W
Barrancos 31 38 10N 6 58W
Barranqueras 124 27 30 S 59 0W
Barranquilla 126 11 0N 74 50W
Barras 127 4 15 S 42 18W
Barraute 106 48 26N 77 38W
Barre 114 44 15N 72 30W
Barreal 124 31 33 S 69 28W
Barreiras 127 12 8 S 45 0W
Barreirinhas 127 2 30 S 42 50W
Barreiro 31 38 40N 9 6W
Barreiros 127 8 49 S 35 12W
Barrême 21 43 57N 6 23 E
Barren I. 71 12 17N 93 50 E
Barren, Nosy 93 18 25 S 43 40 E
Barretos 127 20 30 S 48 35W
Barrhead 108 54 10N 114 24W
Barrie 106 44 24N 79 40W
Barrier Ra. 97 31 0 S 141 30 E
Barrière 108 51 12N 120 7W
Barrington, Ill., U.S.A. 114 42 8N 88 5W
Barrington, R.I., U.S.A. 113 41 43N 71 20W
Barrington L. 109 56 55N 100 15W
Barrington Tops 97 32 6 S 151 28 E
Barrow 104 71 16N 156 50W
Barrow → 15 52 10N 6 57W
Barrow Creek T.O. 96 21 30 S 133 55 E
Barrow I. 96 20 45 S 115 20 E
Barrow-in-Furness 12 54 8N 3 15W
Barrow Pt. 98 14 20 S 144 40 E
Barrow Ra. 96 26 0 S 127 40 E
Barrow Str. 4 74 20N 95 0W
Barruecopardo 30 41 4N 6 40W
Barruelo 30 42 54N 4 17W
Barry 13 51 23N 3 19W
Barry's Bay 106 45 29N 77 41W
Barsalogho 85 13 25N 1 3W
Barsi 70 18 10N 75 50 E
Barsø 49 55 7N 9 33 E
Barstow, Calif., U.S.A. 119 34 58N 117 2W
Barstow, Tex., U.S.A. 117 31 28N 103 24W
Barth 24 54 20N 12 36 E
Bartica 126 6 25N 58 40W
Bartin 64 41 38N 32 21 E
Bartle Frere, Mt. 97 17 27 S 145 50 E
Bartlesville 117 36 50N 95 58W
Bartlett 117 30 46N 97 30W
Bartlett, L. 108 63 5N 118 20W
Bartolomeu Dias 91 21 10 S 35 8 E
Barton-upon-Humber 12 53 41N 0 27W
Bartoszyce 28 54 15N 20 55 E
Bartow 115 27 53N 81 49W
Barumba 90 1 3N 23 37 E
Baruth 24 52 3N 13 31 E
Barvenkovo 56 48 57N 37 0 E
Barwani 68 22 2N 74 57 E
Barycz → 28 51 42N 16 15 E
Barysh 55 53 39N 47 8 E
Bas-Rhin □ 19 48 40N 7 30 E
Başaid 42 45 38N 20 25 E
Bāsa'idū 65 26 35N 55 20 E
Basankusa 88 1 5N 19 50 E
Bascuñán, C. 124 28 52 S 71 35W
Basel (Basle) 25 47 35N 7 35 E
Basel-Stadt □ 25 47 35N 7 35 E
Baselland □ 25 47 26N 7 45 E
Basento → 41 40 21N 16 50 E
Bashkir A.S.S.R. □ 52 54 0N 57 0 E
Basilaki I. 98 10 35 S 151 0 E
Basilan 73 6 35N 122 0 E
Basilan Str. 73 6 50N 122 0 E
Basildon 13 51 34N 0 29 E
Basilicata □ 41 40 30N 16 0 E
Basim 70 20 3N 77 0 E
Basin 118 44 22N 108 2W
Basingstoke 13 51 15N 1 5W
Basirhat 69 22 40N 88 54 E
Baška 39 44 58N 14 45 E
Baskatong, Rés. 106 46 46N 75 50W
Baskerville C. 96 17 10 S 122 15 E
Basle = Basel 25 47 35N 7 35 E
Basmat 70 19 15N 77 12 E
Basoda 68 23 52N 77 54 E
Basoka 90 1 16N 23 40 E
Basongo 88 4 15 S 20 20 E
Basque Provinces = Vascongadas 32 42 50N 2 45W
Basra = Al Başrah 64 30 30N 47 50 E
Bass Rock 14 56 5N 2 40W
Bass Str. 97 39 15 S 146 30 E
Bassano 108 50 48N 112 20W
Bassano del Grappa 39 45 45N 11 45 E
Bassar 85 9 19N 0 57 E
Basse Santa-Su 84 13 13N 14 15W
Basse-Terre 121 16 0N 61 40W
Bassée, La 19 50 31N 2 49 E
Bassein 70 19 26N 72 48 E
Basseterre 121 17 17N 62 43W
Bassett, Nebr., U.S.A. 116 42 37N 99 30W
Bassett, Va., U.S.A. 115 36 48N 79 59W
Bassi 68 30 44N 76 21 E
Bassigny 19 48 0N 5 10 E
Bassikounou 84 15 55N 6 1W
Bassum 24 52 50N 8 42 E
Båstad 49 56 25N 12 51 E
Bastak 65 27 15N 54 25 E
Bastar 70 19 15N 81 40 E
Basti 69 26 52N 82 55 E
Bastia 21 42 40N 9 30 E
Bastia Umbra 39 43 4N 12 34 E
Bastide-Puylaurent, La 20 44 35N 3 55 E
Bastogne 16 50 1N 5 43 E
Bastrop 117 30 5N 97 22W
Basuto 92 19 50 S 26 25 E
Bat Yam 62 32 2N 34 44 E
Bata, Eq. Guin. 88 1 57N 9 50 E
Bata, Romania 46 46 1N 22 4 E
Bataan 73 14 40N 120 25 E
Batabanó 121 22 40N 82 20W
Batabanó, G. de 121 22 30N 82 30W
Batac 73 18 3N 120 34 E
Batagoy 59 67 38N 134 38 E
Batak 43 41 57N 24 12 E
Batakan 72 4 5 S 114 38 E
Batalha 31 39 40N 8 50W
Batama 90 0 58N 26 33 E
Batamay 59 63 30N 129 15 E
Batang, China 75 30 1N 99 0 E
Batang, Indon. 73 6 55 S 109 40 E
Batangafo 88 7 25N 18 20 E
Batangas 73 13 35N 121 10 E
Batanta 73 0 55 S 130 40 E
Batatais 125 20 54 S 47 37W
Batavia 114 43 0N 78 10W
Bataysk 57 47 3N 39 45 E
Batchelor 96 13 4 S 131 1 E
Bateman's B. 97 35 40 S 150 12 E
Batemans Bay 99 35 44 S 150 11 E
Batesburg 115 33 54N 81 32W
Batesville, Ark., U.S.A. 117 35 48N 91 40W
Batesville, Miss., U.S.A. 117 34 17N 89 58W
Batesville, Tex., U.S.A. 117 28 59N 99 38W
Bath, U.K. 13 51 22N 2 22W
Bath, Maine, U.S.A. 107 43 50N 69 49W
Bath, N.Y., U.S.A. 114 42 20N 77 17W
Bathgate 14 55 54N 3 38W
Bathurst, Austral. 97 33 25 S 149 31 E
Bathurst, Can. 107 47 37N 65 43W
Bathurst = Banjul 84 13 28N 16 40W
Bathurst B. 97 14 16 S 144 25 E
Bathurst, C. 104 70 34N 128 0W
Bathurst Harb. 99 43 15 S 146 10 E
Bathurst I., Austral. 96 11 30 S 130 10 E
Bathurst I., Can. 4 76 0N 100 30W
Bathurst In. 104 68 10N 108 50W
Bathurst Inlet 104 66 50N 108 1W
Batie 84 9 53N 2 53W
Batinah 65 24 0N 56 0 E
Batlow 99 35 31 S 148 9 E
Batman 64 37 55N 41 5 E
Batna 83 35 34N 6 15 E
Batočina 42 44 7N 21 5 E
Batoka 91 16 45 S 27 15 E
Baton Rouge 117 30 30N 91 5W
Batopilas 120 27 0N 107 45W
Batouri 88 4 30N 14 25 E
Battambang 71 13 7N 103 12 E
Batticaloa 70 7 43N 81 45 E
Battipáglia 41 40 38N 15 0 E
Battīr 62 31 44N 35 8 E
Battle, Can. 109 52 58N 110 52W
Battle, U.K. 13 50 55N 0 30 E
Battle → 109 52 43N 108 15W
Battle Camp 98 15 20 S 144 40 E
Battle Creek 114 42 20N 85 6W
Battle Harbour 107 52 16N 55 35W
Battle Lake 116 46 20N 95 43W
Battle Mountain 118 40 45N 117 0W
Battlefields 91 18 37 S 29 47 E
Battleford 109 52 45N 108 15W
Battonya 27 46 16N 21 3 E
Batu 87 6 55N 39 45 E
Batu Gajah 71 4 28N 101 3 E
Batu, Kepulauan 72 0 30 S 98 25 E
Batu Pahat 71 1 50N 102 56 E
Batuata 73 6 12 S 122 42 E
Batumi 57 41 30N 41 30 E
Baturaja 72 4 11 S 104 15 E
Baturité 127 4 28 S 38 45W
Bau 72 1 25N 110 9 E
Baubau 73 5 25 S 122 38 E
Bauchi 85 10 22N 9 48 E
Bauchi □ 85 10 30N 10 0 E
Baud 18 47 52N 3 1W
Baudette 116 48 46N 94 35W
Baugé 18 47 31N 0 8W
Baule-Escoublac, La 18 47 18N 2 23W
Baume-les-Dames 19 47 22N 6 22 E

Baunatal **24** 51 13N 9 25 E
Baunei **40** 40 2N 9 41 E
Bauru **125** 22 10 S 49 0W
Baús **127** 18 22 S 52 47W
Bauska **54** 56 24N 25 15 E
Bautzen **24** 51 11N 14 25 E
Baux, Les **21** 43 45N 4 51 E
Bavanište **42** 44 49N 20 53 E
Bavaria = Bayern □ **25** 49 7N 11 30 E
Båven **48** 59 0N 16 56 E
Bavi Sadri **68** 24 28N 74 30 E
Bavispe → **120** 29 30N 109 11W
Baw Baw, Mt. **100** 37 49 S 146 19 E
Bawdwin **67** 23 5N 97 20 E
Bawean **72** 5 46 S 112 35 E
Bawku **85** 11 3N 0 19W
Bawlake **67** 19 11N 97 21 E
Baxley **115** 31 43N 82 23W
Baxter Springs **117** 37 3N 94 45W
Bay Bulls **107** 47 19N 52 50W
Bay City, Mich., U.S.A. **114** 43 35N 83 51W
Bay City, Oreg., U.S.A. **118** 45 45N 123 58W
Bay City, Tex., U.S.A. **117** 28 59N 95 55W
Bay de Verde **107** 48 5N 52 54W
Bay, Laguna de **73** 14 20N 121 11 E
Bay Minette **115** 30 54N 87 43W
Bay St. Louis **117** 30 18N 89 22W
Bay Shore **114** 40 44N 73 15W
Bay Springs **117** 31 58N 89 18W
Bay View **101** 39 25 S 176 50 E
Baya **91** 11 53 S 27 25 E
Bayamo **121** 20 20N 76 40W
Bayamón **121** 18 24N 66 10W
Bayan **76** 46 5N 127 24 E
Bayan Har Shan **75** 34 0N 98 0 E
Bayan Hot = Alxa Zuoqi **76** 38 50N 105 40 E
Bayan Obo **76** 41 52N 109 59 E
Bayana **68** 26 55N 77 18 E
Bayanaul **58** 50 45N 75 45 E
Bayanhongor **75** 46 8N 102 43 E
Bayard **116** 41 48N 103 17W
Bayázeh **65** 33 30N 54 40 E
Baybay **73** 10 40N 124 55 E
Bayburt **64** 40 15N 40 20 E
Bayerischer Wald **25** 49 0N 13 0 E
Bayern □ **25** 49 7N 11 30 E
Bayeux **18** 49 17N 0 42W
Bayfield, Can. **112** 43 34N 81 42W
Bayfield, U.S.A. **116** 46 50N 90 48W
Baykal, Oz. **59** 53 0N 108 0 E
Baykit **59** 61 50N 95 50 E
Baykonur **58** 47 48N 65 50 E
Baymak **52** 52 36N 58 19 E
Baynes Mts. **92** 17 15 S 13 0 E
Bayombong **73** 16 30N 121 10 E
Bayon **19** 48 30N 6 20 E
Bayona **30** 42 6N 8 52W
Bayonne, France **20** 43 30N 1 28W
Bayonne, U.S.A. **113** 40 41N 74 7W
Bayovar **126** 5 50 S 81 0W
Baypore → **70** 11 10N 75 47 E
Bayram-Ali **58** 37 37N 62 10 E
Bayreuth **25** 49 56N 11 35 E
Bayrischzell **25** 47 39N 12 1 E
Bayrūt **64** 33 53N 35 31 E
Bayt Awlá **62** 31 37N 35 2 E
Bayt Fajjār **62** 31 38N 35 9 E
Bayt Fūrīk **62** 32 11N 35 20 E
Bayt Ḩānūn **62** 31 32N 34 32 E
Bayt Jālā **62** 31 43N 35 11 E
Bayt Lahm **62** 31 43N 35 12 E
Bayt Rīma **62** 32 2N 35 6 E
Bayt Sāḩūr **62** 31 42N 35 13 E
Bayt Ummar **62** 31 38N 35 7 E
Bayt 'ūr al Taḩtā **62** 31 54N 35 5 E
Baytīn **62** 31 56N 35 14 E
Baytown **117** 29 42N 94 57W
Baytūniyā **62** 31 54N 35 10 E
Bayzo **85** 13 52N 4 35 E
Baza **33** 37 30N 2 47W
Bazar Dyuzi **57** 41 12N 47 50 E
Bazarny Karabulak **55** 52 15N 46 20 E
Bazarnyy Syzgan **55** 53 45N 46 40 E
Bazartobe **57** 49 26N 51 45 E
Bazaruto, I. do **93** 21 40 S 35 28 E
Bazas **20** 44 27N 0 13W
Bazhong **77** 31 52N 106 46 E
Beach **116** 46 57N 103 58W
Beach City **112** 40 38N 81 35W
Beachport **99** 37 29 S 140 0 E
Beachy Head **13** 50 44N 0 16 E
Beacon **114** 41 32N 73 58W
Beaconia **109** 50 25N 96 31W
Beaconsfield **97** 41 11 S 146 48 E
Beagle, Canal **128** 55 0 S 68 30W
Bealanana **93** 14 33N 48 44 E
Beamsville **112** 43 12N 79 28W
Béar, C. **20** 42 31N 3 8 E
Bear I. **15** 51 38N 9 50W
Bear L., B.C., Can. **108** 56 10N 126 52W
Bear L., Man., Can. **109** 55 8N 96 0W
Bear L., U.S.A. **118** 42 0N 111 20W
Bearcreek **118** 45 11N 109 6W
Beardmore **106** 49 36N 87 57W
Beardmore Glacier **5** 84 30 S 170 0 E
Beardstown **116** 40 0N 90 25W
Béarn **20** 43 8N 0 36W
Bearpaw Mt. **118** 48 15N 109 30W
Bearskin Lake **106** 53 58N 91 2W
Beas de Segura **33** 38 15N 2 53W
Beasain **32** 43 3N 2 11W
Beata, C. **121** 17 40N 71 30W
Beatrice, U.S.A. **116** 40 20N 96 40W
Beatrice, Zimb. **91** 18 15 S 30 55 E
Beatrice, C. **97** 14 20 S 136 55 E
Beatton → **108** 56 15N 120 45W
Beatton River **108** 57 26N 121 20W
Beatty **119** 36 58N 116 46W
Beaucaire **21** 43 48N 4 39 E
Beauce, Plaine de la **19** 48 10N 1 45 E
Beauceville **107** 46 13N 70 46W
Beaudesert **99** 27 59 S 153 0 E
Beaufort, Austral. **100** 37 25 S 143 25 E
Beaufort, Malay. **72** 5 30N 115 40 E
Beaufort, N.C., U.S.A. **115** 34 45N 76 40W
Beaufort, S.C., U.S.A. **115** 32 25N 80 40W
Beaufort Sea **4** 72 0N 140 0W
Beaufort West **92** 32 18 S 22 36 E
Beaugency **19** 47 47N 1 38 E
Beauharnois **106** 45 20N 73 52W
Beaujeu **21** 46 10N 4 35 E
Beaulieu **20** 44 59N 1 50 E
Beaulieu → **108** 62 3N 113 11W
Beauly **14** 57 29N 4 27W
Beauly → **14** 57 26N 4 28W
Beaumaris **12** 53 16N 4 7W
Beaumetz-les-Loges **19** 50 15N 2 40 E
Beaumont, Dordogne, France **20** 44 45N 0 46 E
Beaumont, Sarthe, France **18** 48 13N 0 8 E
Beaumont, U.S.A. **117** 30 5N 94 8W
Beaumont-de-Lomagne **20** 43 53N 0 59 E
Beaumont-le-Roger **18** 49 4N 0 47 E
Beaumont-sur-Oise **19** 49 9N 2 17 E
Beaune **19** 47 2N 4 50 E
Beaune-la-Rolande **19** 48 4N 2 25 E
Beaupréau **18** 47 12N 1 00W
Beauséjour **109** 50 5N 96 35W
Beausset, Le **21** 43 10N 5 46 E
Beauvais **19** 49 25N 2 8 E
Beauval **109** 55 9N 107 37W
Beauvoir **18** 46 55N 2 1W
Beauvoir-sur-Niort **20** 46 12N 0 30W
Beaver, Alaska, U.S.A. **104** 66 20N 147 30W
Beaver, Okla., U.S.A. **117** 36 52N 100 31W
Beaver, Pa., U.S.A. **112** 40 40N 80 18W
Beaver, Utah, U.S.A. **119** 38 20N 112 45W
Beaver →, B.C., Can. **108** 59 52N 124 20W
Beaver →, Sask., Can. **109** 55 26N 107 45W
Beaver City **116** 40 13N 99 50W
Beaver Dam **116** 43 28N 88 50W
Beaver Falls **114** 40 44N 80 20W
Beaver I. **106** 45 40N 85 31W
Beaver, R **106** 55 55N 87 48W
Beaverhill L., Alta., Can. **108** 53 27N 112 32W
Beaverhill L., Man., Can. **109** 54 5N 94 50W
Beaverhill L., N.W.T., Can. **109** 63 2N 104 22W
Beaverlodge **108** 55 11N 119 29W
Beavermouth **108** 51 32N 117 23W
Beaverstone → **106** 54 59N 89 25W
Beaverton **112** 44 26N 79 9W
Beawar **68** 26 3N 74 18 E
Bebedouro **125** 21 0 S 48 25W
Beboa **93** 17 22 S 44 33 E
Bebra **24** 50 59N 9 48 E
Beccles **13** 52 27N 1 33 E
Bečej **42** 45 36N 20 3 E
Beceni **46** 45 23N 26 48 E
Becerreá **30** 42 51N 7 10W
Béchar **82** 31 38N 2 18W
Bechyně **26** 49 17N 14 29 E
Beckley **114** 37 50N 81 8W
Beckum **24** 51 46N 8 3 E
Bécon **18** 47 30N 0 50W
Bečva → **27** 49 31N 17 40 E
Bédar **33** 37 11N 1 59W
Bédarieux **20** 43 37N 3 10 E
Bédarrides **21** 44 2N 4 54 E
Beddouza, Ras **82** 32 33N 9 9W
Bedele **87** 8 31N 36 23 E
Bederkesa **24** 53 37N 8 50 E
Bedeso **87** 9 58N 40 52 E
Bedford, Can. **106** 45 7N 72 59W
Bedford, S. Afr. **92** 32 40 S 26 10 E
Bedford, U.K. **13** 52 8N 0 29W
Bedford, Ind., U.S.A. **114** 38 50N 86 30W
Bedford, Iowa, U.S.A. **116** 40 40N 94 41W
Bedford, Ohio, U.S.A. **114** 41 23N 81 32W
Bedford, Pa., U.S.A. **112** 40 1N 78 30W
Bedford, Va., U.S.A. **114** 37 25N 79 30W
Bedford □ **13** 52 4N 0 28W
Bedford, C. **97** 15 14 S 145 21 E
Będków **28** 51 36N 19 44 E
Bednja → **39** 46 12N 16 25 E
Bednodemyanovsk **55** 53 55N 43 15 E
Bedónia **38** 44 28N 9 36 E
Bedourie **97** 24 30 S 139 30 E
Bedous **20** 43 0N 0 36W
Będzin **28** 50 19N 19 7 E
Beech Grove **114** 39 40N 86 2W
Beechworth **99** 36 22 S 146 43 E
Beechy **109** 50 53N 107 24W
Beelitz **24** 52 14N 12 58 E
Beenleigh **99** 27 43 S 153 10 E
Be'er Sheva' **62** 31 15N 34 48 E
Be'er Sheva' → **62** 31 12N 34 40 E
Be'er Toviyya **62** 31 44N 34 42 E
Be'eri **62** 31 25N 34 30 E
Be'erotayim **62** 32 19N 34 59 E
Beersheba = Be'er Sheva' **62** 31 15N 34 48 E
Beeskow **24** 52 9N 14 14 E
Beeston **12** 52 55N 1 11W
Beetzendorf **24** 52 42N 11 6 E
Beeville **117** 28 27N 97 44W
Befale **88** 0 25N 20 45 E
Befotaka **93** 23 49 S 47 0 E
Bega **97** 36 41 S 149 51 E
Bega, Canalul **42** 45 37N 20 46 E
Bégard **18** 48 38N 3 18W
Begemdir & Simen □ **87** 12 55N 37 30 E
Bègles **20** 44 45N 0 35W
Begna → **47** 60 41N 10 0 E
Begonte **30** 43 10N 7 40W
Begu-Sarai **69** 25 24N 86 9 E
Behbehān **65** 30 30N 50 15 E
Behror **68** 27 51N 76 20 E
Behshahr **65** 36 45N 53 35 E
Bei Jiang → **75** 23 2N 112 58 E
Bei'an **75** 48 10N 126 20 E
Beibei **75** 29 47N 106 22 E
Beihai **75** 21 28N 109 6 E
Beijing **76** 39 55N 116 20 E
Beijing □ **76** 39 55N 116 20 E
Beilen **16** 52 52N 6 27 E
Beilngries **25** 49 1N 11 27 E
Beilpajah **99** 32 54 S 143 52 E
Beilul **87** 13 2N 42 20 E
Beira **91** 19 50 S 34 52 E
Beirut = Bayrūt **64** 33 53N 35 31 E
Beit Lāhiyah **62** 31 32N 34 30 E
Beitaolaizhao **76** 44 58N 125 58 E
Beitbridge **91** 22 12 S 30 0 E
Beiuş **46** 46 40N 22 21 E
Beizhen **76** 37 20N 118 2 E
Beja **31** 38 2N 7 53W
Béja **83** 36 43N 9 12 E
Beja □ **31** 37 55N 7 55W
Bejaia **83** 36 42N 5 2 E
Béjar **30** 40 23N 5 46W
Bejestān **65** 34 30N 58 5 E
Bekasi **73** 6 20 S 107 0 E
Békés **27** 46 47N 21 9 E
Békés □ **27** 46 45N 21 0 E
Békéscsaba **27** 46 40N 21 5 E
Bekily **93** 24 13 S 45 19 E
Bekoji **87** 7 40N 39 17 E
Bekok **71** 2 20N 103 7 E
Bekwai **85** 6 30N 1 34W
Bela, India **69** 25 50N 82 0 E
Bela, Pak. **66** 26 12N 66 20 E
Bela Crkva **42** 44 55N 21 27 E
Bela Palanka **42** 43 13N 22 17 E
Bela Vista, Brazil **124** 22 12 S 56 20W
Bela Vista, Mozam. **93** 26 10 S 32 44 E
Bélâbre **20** 46 34N 1 8 E
Belalcázar **31** 38 35N 5 10W
Belanovica **42** 44 15N 20 23 E
Belavenona **93** 24 50 S 47 4 E
Belawan **72** 3 33N 98 32 E
Belaya → **52** 56 0N 54 32 E
Belaya Glina **57** 46 5N 40 48 E
Belaya Kalitva **57** 48 13N 40 50 E
Belaya Kholunitsa **55** 58 41N 50 13 E
Belaya, Mt. **87** 11 25N 36 8 E
Belaya Tserkov **54** 49 45N 30 10 E
Belceşti **46** 47 19N 27 7 E
Bełchatów **28** 51 21N 19 22 E
Belcher, C. **4** 71 0N 161 0W
Belcher Is. **106** 56 15N 78 45W
Belchite **32** 41 18N 0 43W
Belebey **52** 54 7N 54 7 E
Belém (Pará) **127** 1 20 S 48 30W
Belén, Argent. **124** 27 40 S 67 5W
Belén, Parag. **124** 23 30 S 57 6W
Belen **119** 34 40N 106 50W
Belene **43** 43 39N 25 10 E
Bélesta **20** 42 55N 1 56 E
Belet Uen **63** 4 30N 45 5 E
Belev **55** 53 50N 36 5 E
Belfast, S. Afr. **93** 25 42 S 30 2 E
Belfast, U.K. **15** 54 35N 5 56W
Belfast, Maine, U.S.A. **107** 44 30N 69 0W
Belfast, N.Y., U.S.A. **112** 42 21N 78 9W
Belfast □ **15** 54 35N 5 56W
Belfast, L. **15** 54 40N 5 50W
Belfield **116** 46 54N 103 11W
Belfort **19** 47 38N 6 50 E
Belfort □ **19** 47 38N 6 52 E
Belfry **118** 45 10N 109 2W
Belgaum **70** 15 55N 74 35 E
Belgioioso **38** 45 9N 9 21 E
Belgium ■ **16** 50 30N 5 0 E
Belgorod **56** 50 35N 36 35 E
Belgorod-Dnestrovskiy **56** 46 11N 30 23 E
Belgrade **118** 45 50N 111 10W
Belgrade = Beograd **42** 44 50N 20 37 E
Belhaven **115** 35 34N 76 35W
Beli Drim → **42** 42 6N 20 25 E
Beli Manastir **42** 45 45N 18 36 E
Beli Timok → **42** 43 53N 22 14 E
Belice → **40** 37 35N 12 55 E
Belin **20** 44 30N 0 47W
Belinga **88** 1 10N 13 2 E
Belingwe **91** 20 29 S 29 57 E
Belingwe, N. **91** 20 37 S 29 55 E
Belinskiy (Chembar) **55** 53 0N 43 25 E
Belinţ **42** 45 48N 21 54 E
Belinyu **72** 1 35 S 105 50 E
Belitung, P. **72** 3 10 S 107 50 E
Beliu **46** 46 30N 22 0 E
Belize ■ **120** 17 0N 88 30W
Belize City **120** 17 25N 88 0W
Beljanica **42** 44 08N 21 43 E
Belkovskiy, Ostrov **59** 75 32N 135 44 E
Bell → **106** 49 48N 77 38W
Bell Bay **99** 41 6 S 146 53 E
Bell I. **107** 50 46N 55 35W
Bell-Irving → **108** 56 12N 129 5W
Bell Peninsula **105** 63 50N 82 0W
Bell Ville **124** 32 40 S 62 40W
Bella Bella **108** 52 10N 128 10W
Bella Coola **108** 52 25N 126 40W
Bella Unión **124** 30 15 S 57 40W
Bella Vista, Corrientes, Argent. **124** 28 33 S 59 0W
Bella Vista, Tucuman, Argent. **124** 27 10 S 65 25W
Bellac **20** 46 7N 1 3 E
Bellágio **38** 45 59N 9 15 E
Bellaire **114** 40 1N 80 46W
Bellary **70** 15 10N 76 56 E
Bellata **99** 29 53 S 149 46 E
Belle Fourche **116** 44 43N 103 52W
Belle Fourche → **116** 44 25N 102 19W
Belle Glade **115** 26 43N 80 38W
Belle-Île **18** 47 20N 3 10W
Belle Isle **107** 51 57N 55 25W
Belle-Isle-en-Terre **18** 48 33N 3 23W
Belle Isle, Str. of **107** 51 30N 56 30W
Belle, La **115** 26 45N 81 22W
Belle Plaine, Iowa, U.S.A. **116** 41 51N 92 18W
Belle Plaine, Minn., U.S.A. **116** 44 35N 93 48W
Belle Yella **84** 7 24N 10 0W
Belledonne **21** 45 30N 6 10 E
Belledune **107** 47 55N 65 50W
Bellefontaine **114** 40 20N 83 45W
Bellefonte **114** 40 56N 77 45W
Bellegarde, Ain, France **21** 46 4N 5 49 E
Bellegarde, Creuse, France **20** 45 59N 2 18 E
Bellegarde, Loiret, France **19** 48 0N 2 26 E
Bellême **18** 48 22N 0 34 E
Belleoram **107** 47 31N 55 25W
Belleville, Can. **106** 44 10N 77 23W
Belleville, Rhône, France **21** 46 7N 4 45 E
Belleville, Vendée, France **18** 46 48N 1 28W
Belleville, Ill., U.S.A. **116** 38 30N 90 0W
Belleville, Kans., U.S.A. **116** 39 51N 97 38W
Belleville, N.Y., U.S.A. **113** 43 46N 76 10W
Bellevue, Can. **108** 49 35N 114 22W
Bellevue, Idaho, U.S.A. **118** 43 25N 114 23W
Bellevue, Ohio, U.S.A. **112** 41 20N 82 48W
Bellevue, Pa., U.S.A. **112** 40 29N 80 3W
Belley **21** 45 46N 5 41 E
Bellin (Payne Bay) **105** 60 0N 70 0W
Bellingen **99** 30 25 S 152 50 E
Bellingham **118** 48 45N 122 27W
Bellingshausen Sea **5** 66 0 S 80 0W
Bellinzona **25** 46 11N 9 1 E
Bellona Reefs **97** 21 26 S 159 0 E
Bellows Falls **114** 43 10N 72 30W
Bellpat **68** 29 0N 68 5 E
Bellpuig **32** 41 37N 1 1 E
Belluno **39** 46 8N 12 13 E
Bellville **117** 29 58N 96 18W
Bellwood **112** 40 36N 78 21W
Belmar **113** 40 10N 74 2W
Bélmez **31** 38 17N 5 17W
Belmont, Austral. **99** 33 4 S 151 42 E
Belmont, Can. **112** 42 53N 81 5W
Belmont, U.S.A. **112** 42 14N 78 3W
Belmonte, Brazil **127** 16 0 S 39 0W
Belmonte, Port. **30** 40 21N 7 20W
Belmonte, Spain **32** 39 34N 2 43W
Belmopan **120** 17 18N 88 30W
Belmullet **15** 54 13N 9 58W
Belo Horizonte **127** 19 55 S 43 56W
Belo-sur-Mer **93** 20 42 S 44 0 E
Belo-Tsiribihina **93** 19 40 S 44 30 E
Belogorsk, R.S.F.S.R., U.S.S.R. **59** 51 0N 128 20 E
Belogorsk, Ukraine S.S.R., U.S.S.R. **56** 45 3N 34 35 E
Belogradchik **42** 43 53N 22 15 E
Belogradets **43** 43 22N 27 18 E
Beloha **93** 25 10 S 45 3 E
Beloit, Kans., U.S.A. **116** 39 32N 98 9W
Beloit, Wis., U.S.A. **116** 42 35N 89 0W
Belokorovichi **54** 51 7N 28 2 E
Belomorsk **52** 64 35N 34 30 E
Belonia **67** 23 15N 91 30 E
Belopolye **54** 51 14N 34 20 E
Beloretsk **52** 53 58N 58 24 E
Belovo **58** 54 30N 86 0 E
Beloye More **52** 66 30N 38 0 E
Beloye, Oz. **52** 60 10N 37 35 E
Beloye Ozero **57** 45 15N 46 50 E
Belozem **43** 42 12N 25 2 E
Belozersk **55** 60 0N 37 30 E
Belpasso **41** 37 37N 15 0 E
Belsito **40** 37 50N 13 47 E
Beltana **99** 30 48 S 138 25 E
Belterra **127** 2 45 S 55 0W
Beltinci **39** 46 37N 16 20 E
Belton, S.C., U.S.A. **115** 34 31N 82 39W
Belton, Tex., U.S.A. **117** 31 4N 97 30W
Belton Res. **117** 31 8N 97 32W
Beltsy **56** 47 48N 28 0 E
Belturbet **15** 54 6N 7 28W
Belukha **58** 49 50N 86 50 E
Beluran **72** 5 48N 117 35 E
Beluša **27** 49 5N 18 27 E
Belušić **42** 43 50N 21 10 E
Belvedere Marittimo **41** 39 37N 15 52 E
Belvès **20** 44 46N 1 0 E
Belvidere, Ill., U.S.A. **116** 42 15N 88 55W
Belvidere, N.J., U.S.A. **113** 40 48N 75 5W
Belvis de la Jara **31** 39 45N 4 57W
Belyando → **97** 21 38 S 146 50 E
Belyy **54** 55 48N 32 51 E
Belyy, Ostrov **58** 73 30N 71 0 E
Belyy Yar **58** 58 26N 84 39 E
Belzig **24** 52 8N 12 36 E
Belzoni **117** 33 12N 90 30W
Bełżyce **28** 51 11N 22 17 E
Bemaraha, Lembalemban' i **93** 18 40 S 44 45 E
Bemarivo **93** 21 45 S 44 45 E
Bemarivo → **93** 15 27 S 47 40 E
Bemavo **93** 21 33 S 45 25 E
Bembéréke **85** 10 11N 2 43 E
Bembesi **91** 20 0 S 28 58 E
Bembesi → **91** 18 57 S 27 47 E
Bembézar → **31** 37 45N 5 13W
Bemidji **116** 47 30N 94 50W
Ben 'Ammi **62** 33 0N 35 7 E
Ben Cruachan **14** 56 26N 5 8W
Ben Dearg **14** 57 47N 4 58W
Ben Gardane **83** 33 11N 11 11 E
Ben Hope **14** 58 24N 4 36W
Ben Lawers **14** 56 33N 4 13W
Ben Lomond, Austral. **97** 41 38 S 147 42 E
Ben Lomond, U.K. **14** 56 12N 4 39W
Ben Macdhui **14** 57 4N 3 40W
Ben Mhor **14** 57 16N 7 21W
Ben More, Central, U.K. **14** 56 23N 4 31W
Ben More, Strathclyde, U.K. **14** 56 26N 6 2W
Ben More Assynt **14** 58 7N 4 51W
Ben Nevis **14** 56 48N 5 0W
Ben Slimane **82** 33 38N 7 7W
Ben Vorlich **14** 56 22N 4 15W
Ben Wyvis **14** 57 40N 4 35W
Bena **85** 11 20N 5 50 E
Bena Dibele **88** 4 4 S 22 50 E
Benagalbón **31** 36 45N 4 15W
Benagerie **99** 31 25 S 140 22 E
Benahmed **82** 33 4N 7 9W
Benalla **97** 36 30 S 146 0 E
Benambra, Mt. **100** 36 31 S 147 34 E
Benamejí **31** 37 16N 4 33W
Benanee **99** 34 31 S 142 52 E
Benares = Varanasi **69** 25 22N 83 8 E
Bénat, C. **21** 43 5N 6 22 E
Benavente, Port. **31** 38 59N 8 49W

Benavente, Spain **30** 42 2N 5 43W
Benavides, Spain **30** 42 30N 5 54W
Benavides, U.S.A. **117** 27 35N 98 28W
Benbecula **14** 57 26N 7 21W
Bencubbin **96** 30 48 S 117 52 E
Bend **118** 44 2N 121 15W
Bendel □ **85** 6 0N 6 0 E
Bender Beila **63** 9 30N 50 48 E
Bendery **56** 46 50N 29 30 E
Bendigo **97** 36 40 S 144 15 E
Bendorf **24** 50 26N 7 34 E
Benē Beraq, Israel **62** 32 6N 34 51 E
Benē Beraq, Israel **62** 32 6N 34 51 E
Bénéna **84** 13 9N 4 17W
Benenitra **93** 23 27 S 45 5 E
Benešöv **26** 49 46N 14 41 E
Bénestroff **19** 48 54N 6 45 E
Benet **20** 46 22N 0 35W
Benevento **41** 41 7N 14 45 E
Benfeld **19** 48 22N 7 34 E
Benga **91** 16 11 S 33 40 E
Bengal, Bay of **60** 15 0N 90 0 E
Bengawan Solo → **73** 7 5 S 112 35 E
Bengbu **75** 32 58N 117 20 E
Benghazi = Banghāzī **83** 32 11N 20 3 E
Bengkalis **72** 1 30N 102 10 E
Bengkulu **72** 3 50 S 102 12 E
Bengkulu □ **72** 3 48 S 102 16 E
Bengough **109** 49 25N 105 10W
Benguela **89** 12 37 S 13 25 E
Benguerir **82** 32 16N 7 56W
Benguérua, I. **93** 21 58 S 35 28 E
Benha **86** 30 26N 31 8 E
Beni **90** 0 30N 29 27 E
Beni → **126** 10 23 S 65 24W
Beni Abbès **82** 30 5N 2 5W
Beni-Haoua **82** 36 30N 1 30 E
Beni Mazâr **86** 28 32N 30 44 E
Beni Mellal **82** 32 21N 6 21W
Beni Ounif **82** 32 0N 1 10W
Beni Saf **82** 35 17N 1 15W
Beni Suef **86** 29 5N 31 6 E
Beniah L. **108** 63 23N 112 17W
Benicarló **32** 40 23N 0 23 E
Benidorm **33** 38 33N 0 9W
Benidorm, Islote de **33** 38 31N 0 9W
Benin ■ **85** 10 0N 2 0 E
Benin, Bight of **85** 5 0N 3 0 E
Benin City **85** 6 20N 5 31 E
Benisa **33** 38 43N 0 03 E
Benjamin Aceval **124** 24 58 S 57 34W
Benjamin Constant **126** 4 40 S 70 15W
Benkelman **116** 40 7N 101 32W
Benkovac **39** 44 2N 15 37 E
Benlidi **98** 24 35 S 144 50 E
Bennett **108** 59 56N 134 53W
Bennett, Ostrov **59** 76 21N 148 56 E
Bennettsville **115** 34 38N 79 39W
Bennington **114** 42 52N 73 12W
Benoa **72** 8 50 S 115 20 E
Bénodet **18** 47 53N 4 7W
Benoni **93** 26 11 S 28 18 E
Benoud **82** 32 20N 0 16 E
Bensheim **25** 49 40N 8 38 E
Benson **119** 31 59N 110 19W
Bent **65** 26 20N 59 31 E
Benteng **73** 6 10 S 120 30 E
Bentinck I. **97** 17 3 S 139 35 E
Bentiu **87** 9 10N 29 55 E
Bento Gonçalves **125** 29 10 S 51 31W
Benton, Ark., U.S.A. **117** 34 30N 92 35W
Benton, Ill., U.S.A. **116** 38 0N 88 55W
Benton Harbor **114** 42 10N 86 28W
Bentong **71** 3 31N 101 55 E
Bentu Liben **87** 8 32N 38 21 E
Benue □ **85** 7 30N 7 30 E
Benue → **85** 7 48N 6 46 E
Benxi **76** 41 20N 123 48 E
Beo **73** 4 25N 126 50 E
Beograd **42** 44 50N 20 37 E
Beowawe **118** 40 35N 116 30W
Beppu **74** 33 15N 131 30 E
Berati **44** 40 43N 19 59 E
Berau, Teluk **73** 2 30 S 132 30 E
Berber **86** 18 0N 34 0 E
Berbera **63** 10 30N 45 2 E
Berbérati **88** 4 15N 15 40 E
Berberia, C. del **33** 38 39N 1 24 E
Berbice → **126** 6 20N 57 32W
Berceto **38** 44 30N 10 0 E
Berchtesgaden **25** 47 37N 12 58 E
Berck-sur-Mer **19** 50 25N 1 36 E
Berdichev **56** 49 57N 28 30 E
Berdsk **58** 54 47N 83 2 E
Berdyansk **56** 46 45N 36 50 E
Berea, Ky., U.S.A. **114** 37 35N 84 18W
Berea, Ohio, U.S.A. **112** 41 21N 81 50W
Berebere **73** 2 25N 128 45 E
Bereda **63** 11 45N 51 0 E
Berekum **84** 7 29N 2 34W
Berenice **86** 24 2N 35 25 E
Berens → **109** 52 25N 97 2W
Berens I. **109** 52 18N 97 18W
Berens River **109** 52 25N 97 0W
Berestechko **54** 50 22N 25 5 E
Bereşti **46** 46 6N 27 50 E
Beretău → **46** 46 59N 21 7 E
Berettyo → **27** 46 59N 21 7 E
Berettyóújfalu **27** 47 13N 21 33 E
Berevo, Majunga, Madag. **93** 17 14 S 44 17 E
Berevo, Tuléar, Madag. **93** 19 44 S 44 58 E
Bereza **54** 52 31N 24 51 E
Berezhany **54** 49 26N 24 58 E
Berezina → **54** 52 33N 30 14 E
Berezna **55** 51 35N 31 46 E
Berezniki **58** 59 24N 56 46 E
Berezovka **56** 47 14N 30 55 E
Berezovo **58** 64 0N 65 0 E
Berg **47** 59 10N 11 18 E
Berga, Spain **32** 42 6N 1 48 E
Berga, Sweden **49** 57 14N 16 3 E
Bergama **64** 39 8N 27 15 E
Bérgamo **38** 45 42N 9 40 E
Bergantiños **30** 43 20N 8 40W
Bergedorf **24** 53 28N 10 12 E
Bergen, Ger. **24** 54 24N 13 26 E
Bergen, Neth. **16** 52 40N 4 43 E
Bergen, Norway **47** 60 23N 5 20 E
Bergen, U.S.A. **112** 43 5N 77 56W
Bergen-op-Zoom **16** 51 30N 4 18 E
Bergerac **20** 44 51N 0 30 E
Bergheim **24** 50 57N 6 38 E
Bergisch-Gladbach **24** 50 59N 7 9 E
Bergkvara **49** 56 23N 16 5 E
Bergsjö **48** 61 59N 17 3 E
Bergues **19** 50 58N 2 24 E
Bergum **16** 53 13N 5 59 E
Bergvik **48** 61 16N 16 50 E
Berhala, Selat **72** 1 0 S 104 15 E
Berhampore **69** 24 2N 88 27 E
Berhampur **70** 19 15N 84 54 E
Berheci → **46** 46 7N 27 19 E
Bering Sea **94** 58 0N 167 0 E
Bering Str. **104** 66 0N 170 0W
Beringen **16** 51 3N 5 14 E
Beringovskiy **59** 63 3N 179 19 E
Berislav **56** 46 50N 33 30 E
Berisso **124** 34 56 S 57 50W
Berja **33** 36 50N 2 56W
Berkane **82** 34 52N 2 20W
Berkeley **13** 51 41N 2 28W
Berkeley Springs **114** 39 38N 78 12W
Berkner I. **5** 79 30 S 50 0W
Berkovitsa **43** 43 16N 23 8 E
Berkshire □ **13** 51 30N 1 20W
Berland → **108** 54 0N 116 50W
Berlanga **31** 38 17N 5 50W
Berleburg **24** 51 3N 8 22 E
Berlenga, Ilhas **31** 39 25N 9 30W
Berlin, Ger. **24** 52 32N 13 24 E
Berlin, Md., U.S.A. **114** 38 19N 75 12W
Berlin, N.H., U.S.A. **114** 44 29N 71 10W
Berlin, Wis., U.S.A. **114** 43 58N 88 55W
Berlin, E. □ **24** 52 30N 13 30 E
Berlin, W. □ **24** 52 30N 13 20 E
Bermeja, Sierra **31** 36 30N 5 11W
Bermejo →, Formosa, Argent. **124** 26 51 S 58 23W
Bermejo →, San Juan, Argent. **124** 32 30 S 67 30W
Bermeo **32** 43 25N 2 47W
Bermillo de Sayago **30** 41 22N 6 8W
Bermuda ■ **121** 32 45N 65 0W
Bern (Berne) **25** 46 57N 7 28 E
Bern (Berne) □ **25** 46 45N 7 40 E
Bernado **119** 34 30N 106 53W
Bernalda **41** 40 24N 16 44 E
Bernalillo **119** 35 17N 106 37W
Bernam → **71** 3 45N 101 5 E
Bernardo de Irigoyen **125** 26 15 S 53 40W
Bernasconi **124** 37 55 S 63 44W
Bernau, Germ., E. **24** 52 40N 13 35 E
Bernau, Germ., W. **25** 47 45N 12 20 E
Bernay **18** 49 5N 0 35 E
Bernburg **24** 51 40N 11 42 E
Berndorf **26** 47 59N 16 1 E
Berne = Bern **25** 46 57N 7 28 E
Berneck **25** 51 3N 11 40 E
Berner Alpen **25** 46 27N 7 35 E
Bernese Oberland = Oberland **25** 46 27N 7 35 E
Bernier I. **96** 24 50 S 113 12 E
Bernina, Piz **25** 46 20N 9 54 E
Bernkastel-Kues **25** 49 55N 7 04 E
Beror Hayil **62** 31 34N 34 38 E
Béroubouay **85** 10 34N 2 46 E
Beroun **26** 49 57N 14 5 E
Berounka → **26** 50 0N 13 47 E
Berovo **42** 41 38N 22 51 E
Berrahal **83** 36 54N 7 33 E
Berre, Étang de **21** 43 27N 5 5 E
Berrechid **82** 33 18N 7 36W
Berri **99** 34 14 S 140 35 E
Berriane **82** 32 50N 3 46 E
Berrigan **100** 35 38 S 145 49 E
Berrouaghia **82** 36 10N 2 53 E
Berry, Austral. **99** 34 46 S 150 43 E
Berry, France **19** 47 0N 2 0 E
Berry Is. **121** 25 40N 77 50W
Berryville **117** 36 23N 93 35W
Bersenbrück **24** 52 33N 7 56 E
Berthold **116** 48 19N 101 45W
Berthoud **116** 40 21N 105 5W
Bertincourt **19** 50 5N 2 58 E
Bertoua **88** 4 30N 13 45 E
Bertrand **116** 40 35N 99 38W
Berufjörður **50** 64 48N 14 29W
Berwick **114** 41 4N 76 17W
Berwick-upon-Tweed **12** 55 47N 2 0W
Berwyn Mts. **12** 52 54N 3 26W
Berzasca **42** 44 39N 21 58 E
Berzence **27** 46 12N 17 11 E
Besalampy **93** 16 43 S 44 29 E
Besançon **19** 47 15N 6 0 E
Besar **72** 2 40 S 116 0 E
Beserah **71** 3 50N 103 21 E
Beshenkovichi **54** 55 2N 29 29 E
Beška **42** 45 8N 20 6 E
Beskydy **27** 49 35N 18 40 E
Beslan **57** 43 15N 44 28 E
Besna Kobila **42** 42 31N 22 10 E
Besnard L. **109** 55 25N 106 0W
Besni **64** 37 41N 37 52 E
Besor, N. → **62** 31 28N 34 22 E
Beşparmak Dağı **45** 37 32N 27 30 E
Bessarabiya **46** 47 0N 28 10 E
Bessarabka **56** 46 21N 28 58 E
Bessèges **21** 44 18N 4 8 E
Bessemer, Ala., U.S.A. **115** 33 25N 86 57W
Bessemer, Mich., U.S.A. **116** 46 27N 90 0W
Bessin **18** 49 21N 1 0W
Bessines-sur-Gartempe **20** 46 6N 1 22 E
Bet Alfa **62** 32 31N 35 25 E
Bet Dagan **62** 32 1N 34 49 E
Bet Guvrin **62** 31 37N 34 54 E
Bet Ha'Emeq **62** 32 58N 35 8 E
Bet Hashitta **62** 32 31N 35 27 E
Bet Qeshet **62** 32 41N 35 21 E
Bet She'an **62** 32 30N 35 30 E
Bet Shemesh **62** 31 44N 35 0 E
Bet Tadjine, Djebel **82** 29 0N 3 30W
Bet Yosef **62** 32 34N 35 33 E
Betafo **93** 19 50 S 46 51 E
Betanzos **30** 43 15N 8 12W
Bétaré Oya **88** 5 40N 14 5 E
Bétera **32** 39 35N 0 28W
Bethal **93** 26 27 S 29 28 E
Bethanien **92** 26 31 S 17 8 E
Bethany, S. Afr. **92** 29 34 S 25 59 E
Bethany, U.S.A. **116** 40 18N 94 0W
Bethany = Al Ayzarīyah **62** 31 47N 35 15 E
Bethel, Alaska, U.S.A. **104** 60 50N 161 50W
Bethel, Pa., U.S.A. **112** 40 20N 80 2W
Bethel, Vt., U.S.A. **113** 43 50N 72 37W
Bethlehem, S. Afr. **93** 28 14 S 28 18 E
Bethlehem, U.S.A. **114** 40 39N 75 24W
Bethlehem = Bayt Lahm **62** 31 43N 35 12 E
Bethulie **92** 30 30 S 25 59 E
Béthune **19** 50 30N 2 38 E
Béthune → **18** 49 53N 1 9 E
Betioky **93** 23 48 S 44 20 E
Beton Bazoches **19** 48 42N 3 15 E
Betong, Malay. **72** 1 24N 111 31 E
Betong, Thai. **71** 5 45N 101 5 E
Betoota **99** 25 45 S 140 42 E
Betroka **93** 23 16 S 46 0 E
Betsiamites **107** 48 56N 68 40W
Betsiamites → **107** 48 56N 68 38W
Betsiboka → **93** 16 3 S 46 36 E
Betsjoeanaland **92** 26 30 S 22 30 E
Bettiah **69** 26 48N 84 33 E
Bèttola **38** 44 42N 9 32 E
Betul **68** 21 58N 77 59 E
Betzdorf **24** 50 47N 7 53 E
Beuca **46** 44 14N 24 56 E
Beuil **21** 44 6N 6 59 E
Beulah **116** 47 18N 101 47W
Bevensen **24** 53 5N 10 34 E
Beverley, Austral. **96** 32 9 S 116 56 E
Beverley, U.K. **12** 53 52N 0 26W
Beverly, Mass., U.S.A. **113** 42 32N 70 50W
Beverly, Wash., U.S.A. **118** 46 55N 119 59W
Beverly Hills **119** 34 4N 118 29W
Beverwijk **16** 52 28N 4 38 E
Bex **25** 46 15N 7 0 E
Beyin **84** 5 1N 2 41W
Beykoz **43** 41 8N 29 7 E
Beyla **84** 8 30N 8 38W
Beynat **20** 45 8N 1 44 E
Beyneu **58** 45 10N 55 3 E
Beypazarı **64** 40 10N 31 56 E
Beyşehir Gölü **64** 37 40N 31 45 E
Bezdan **42** 45 50N 18 57 E
Bezet **62** 33 4N 35 8 E
Bezhetsk **55** 57 47N 36 39 E
Bezhitsa **54** 53 19N 34 17 E
Béziers **20** 43 20N 3 12 E
Bezwada = Vijayawada **70** 16 31N 80 39 E
Bhadra → **70** 14 0N 75 20 E
Bhadrakh **69** 21 10N 86 30 E
Bhadravati **70** 13 49N 75 40 E
Bhagalpur **69** 25 10N 87 0 E
Bhaisa **70** 19 10N 77 58 E
Bhakkar **68** 31 40N 71 5 E
Bhakra Dam **68** 31 30N 76 45 E
Bhamo **67** 24 15N 97 15 E
Bhamragarh **70** 19 30N 80 40 E
Bhandara **69** 21 5N 79 42 E
Bhanrer Ra. **68** 23 40N 79 45 E
Bharatpur **68** 27 15N 77 30 E
Bharuch **68** 21 47N 73 0 E
Bhatghar L. **70** 18 10N 73 48 E
Bhatiapara Ghat **69** 23 13N 89 42 E
Bhatinda **68** 30 15N 74 57 E
Bhatkal **70** 13 58N 74 35 E
Bhatpara **69** 22 50N 88 25 E
Bhattiprolu **70** 16 7N 80 45 E
Bhaun **68** 32 55N 72 40 E
Bhaunagar = Bhavnagar **68** 21 45N 72 10 E
Bhavani **70** 11 27N 77 43 E
Bhavani → **70** 11 0N 78 15 E
Bhavnagar **68** 21 45N 72 10 E
Bhawanipatna **70** 19 55N 80 10 E
Bhera **68** 32 29N 72 57 E
Bhilsa = Vidisha **68** 23 28N 77 53 E
Bhilwara **68** 25 25N 74 38 E
Bhima → **70** 16 25N 77 17 E
Bhimavaram **70** 16 30N 81 30 E
Bhind **68** 26 30N 78 46 E
Bhir **70** 19 4N 75 46 E
Bhiwandi **70** 19 20N 73 0 E
Bhiwani **68** 28 50N 76 9 E
Bhola **69** 22 45N 90 35 E
Bhongir **70** 17 30N 78 56 E
Bhopal **68** 23 20N 77 30 E
Bhor **70** 18 12N 73 53 E
Bhubaneswar **69** 20 15N 85 50 E
Bhuj **68** 23 15N 69 49 E
Bhumibol Dam **72** 17 15N 98 58 E
Bhusaval **68** 21 3N 75 46 E
Bhutan ■ **69** 27 25N 90 30 E
Biafra, B. of = Bonny, Bight of **85** 3 30N 9 20 E
Biak **73** 1 10 S 136 6 E
Biała **28** 50 24N 17 40 E
Biała →, Białystok, Poland **28** 53 11N 23 4 E
Biała →, Tarnów, Poland **27** 50 3N 20 55 E
Biała Piska **28** 53 37N 22 5 E
Biała Podlaska **28** 52 4N 23 6 E
Biała Podlaska □ **28** 52 0N 23 0 E
Biała Rawska **28** 51 48N 20 29 E
Białobrzegi **28** 52 27N 21 3 E
Białogard **28** 54 2N 15 58 E
Białowieża **28** 52 41N 23 49 E
Biały Bór **28** 53 53N 16 51 E
Białystok **28** 53 10N 23 10 E
Białystok □ **28** 53 9N 23 10 E
Biancavilla **41** 37 39N 14 50 E
Biaro **73** 2 5N 125 26 E
Biarritz **20** 43 29N 1 33W
Biasca **25** 46 22N 8 58 E
Biba **86** 28 55N 31 0 E
Bibala **89** 14 44 S 13 24 E
Bibane, Bahiret el **83** 33 16N 11 13 E
Bibbiena **39** 43 43N 11 50 E
Bibby I. **109** 61 55N 93 0W
Biberach **25** 48 5N 9 49 E
Bibey → **30** 42 24N 7 13W
Bibiani **84** 6 30N 2 8W
Bibile **70** 7 10N 81 25 E
Biboohra **98** 16 56 S 145 25 E
Bibungwa **90** 2 40 S 28 15 E
Bic **107** 48 20N 68 41W
Bicaj **44** 42 0N 20 25 E
Bicaz **46** 46 53N 26 5 E
Biccari **41** 41 23N 15 12 E
Biche, La → **108** 59 57N 123 50W
Bichena **87** 10 28N 38 10 E
Bicknell, Ind., U.S.A. **114** 38 50N 87 20W
Bicknell, Utah, U.S.A. **119** 38 16N 111 35W
Bida **85** 9 3N 5 58 E
Bidar **70** 17 55N 77 35 E
Biddeford **107** 43 30N 70 28W
Biddiyā **62** 32 7N 35 4 E
Biddū **62** 31 50N 35 8 E
Biddwara **87** 5 11N 38 34 E
Bideford **13** 51 1N 4 13W
Bidor **71** 4 6N 101 15 E
Bié, Planalto de **89** 12 0 S 16 0 E
Bieber **118** 41 4N 121 6W
Biebrza → **28** 53 13N 22 25 E
Biecz **27** 49 44N 21 15 E
Biel (Bienne) **25** 47 8N 7 14 E
Bielawa **28** 50 43N 16 37 E
Bielé Karpaty **27** 49 5N 18 0 E
Bielefeld **24** 52 2N 8 31 E
Bielersee **25** 47 6N 7 5 E
Biella **38** 45 33N 8 3 E
Bielsk Podlaski **28** 52 47N 23 12 E
Bielsko-Biała **27** 49 50N 19 2 E
Bielsko-Biała □ **27** 49 45N 19 15 E
Bien Hoa **71** 10 57N 106 49 E
Bienfait **109** 49 10N 102 50W
Bienne = Biel **25** 47 8N 7 14 E
Bienvenida **31** 38 18N 6 12W
Bienville, L. **106** 55 5N 72 40W
Biescas **32** 42 37N 0 20W
Biese → **24** 52 53N 11 46 E
Biesiesfontein **92** 30 57 S 17 58 E
Bietigheim **25** 48 57N 9 8 E
Biferno → **41** 41 59N 15 2 E
Big → **107** 54 50N 58 55W
Big B. **107** 55 43N 60 35W
Big Beaver **109** 49 10N 105 10W
Big Belt Mts. **118** 46 50N 111 30W
Big Bend **93** 26 50 S 32 2 E
Big Bend Nat. Park **117** 29 15N 103 15W
Big Black → **117** 32 0N 91 5W
Big Blue → **116** 39 11N 96 40W
Big Cr. → **108** 51 42N 122 41W
Big Cypress Swamp **115** 26 12N 81 10W
Big Falls **116** 48 11N 93 48W
Big Fork → **116** 48 31N 93 43W
Big Horn **118** 46 11N 107 25W
Big Horn Mts. = Bighorn Mts. **118** 44 30N 107 30W
Big Lake **117** 31 12N 101 25W
Big Moose **113** 43 49N 74 58W
Big Muddy → **116** 48 8N 104 36W
Big Pine **119** 37 12N 118 17W
Big Piney **118** 42 32N 110 3W
Big Quill L. **109** 51 55N 104 50W
Big Rapids **114** 43 42N 85 27W
Big River **109** 53 50N 107 0W
Big Run **112** 40 57N 78 55W
Big Sable Pt. **114** 44 5N 86 30W
Big Sand L. **109** 57 45N 99 45W
Big Sandy **118** 48 12N 110 9W
Big Sandy Cr. → **116** 38 6N 102 29W
Big Sioux → **116** 42 30N 96 25W
Big Spring **117** 32 10N 101 25W
Big Springs **116** 41 4N 102 3W
Big Stone City **116** 45 20N 96 30W
Big Stone Gap **115** 36 52N 82 45W
Big Stone L. **116** 45 30N 96 35W
Big Trout L. **106** 53 40N 90 0W
Biganos **20** 44 39N 0 59W
Bigfork **118** 48 3N 114 2W
Biggar, Can. **109** 52 4N 108 0W
Biggar, U.K. **14** 55 38N 3 31W
Biggenden **99** 25 31 S 152 4 E
Bighorn → **118** 46 9N 107 28W
Bighorn Mts. **118** 44 30N 107 30W
Bignona **84** 12 52N 16 14W
Bigorre **20** 43 6N 0 5 E
Bigstone L. **109** 53 42N 95 44W
Bigtimber **118** 45 53N 110 0W
Bigwa **90** 7 10 S 39 10 E
Bihać **39** 44 49N 15 57 E
Bihar **69** 25 5N 85 40 E
Bihar □ **69** 25 0N 86 0 E
Biharamulo **90** 2 25 S 31 25 E
Biharamulo □ **90** 2 30 S 31 20 E
Biharkeresztes **27** 47 8N 21 44 E
Bihor □ **46** 47 0N 22 10 E
Bihor, Munţii **46** 46 29N 22 47 E
Bijagós, Arquipélago dos **84** 11 15N 16 10W
Bijaipur **68** 26 2N 77 20 E
Bijapur, Mad. P., India **70** 18 50N 80 50 E
Bijapur, Mysore, India **70** 16 50N 75 55 E
Bijār **64** 35 52N 47 35 E
Bijeljina **42** 44 46N 19 17 E
Bijelo Polje **42** 43 1N 19 45 E
Bijie **77** 27 20N 105 16 E
Bijnor **68** 29 27N 78 11 E
Bikaner **68** 28 2N 73 18 E
Bikapur **69** 26 30N 82 7 E
Bikin **59** 46 50N 134 20 E
Bikini Atoll **94** 12 0N 167 30 E
Bikoué **85** 3 55N 11 50 E
Bilād Banī Bū 'Ali **65** 22 0N 59 20 E
Bilara **68** 26 14N 73 53 E
Bilaspur, Mad. P., India **69** 22 2N 82 15 E

Bilaspur, Punjab, India 68 31 19N 76 50 E
Bilauk Taung dan 71 13 0N 99 0 E
Bilbao 32 43 16N 2 56W
Bilbeis 86 30 25N 31 34 E
Bilbor 46 47 6N 25 30 E
Bildudalur 50 65 41N 23 36W
Bileća 42 42 53N 18 27 E
Bilecik 64 40 5N 30 5 E
Biłgoraj 28 50 33N 22 42 E
Bilibino 59 68 3N 166 20 E
Bilibiza 91 12 30S 40 20 E
Bilir 59 65 40N 131 20 E
Bilishti 44 40 37N 21 2 E
Bill 116 43 18N 105 18W
Billabong Creek 100 35 5S 144 2 E
Billingham 12 54 36N 1 18W
Billings 118 45 43N 108 29W
Billingsfors 48 58 59N 12 15 E
Billiton Is = Belitung 72 3 10S 107 50 E
Billom 20 45 43N 3 20 E
Bilma 81 18 50N 13 30 E
Bilo Gora 42 45 53N 17 15 E
Biloela 97 24 24S 150 31 E
Biloxi 117 30 24N 88 53W
Bilpa Morea Claypan 99 25 0S 140 0 E
Biltine 81 14 40N 20 50 E
Bilyana 98 18 5S 145 50 E
Bilyarsk 55 54 58N 50 22 E
Bima 73 8 22S 118 49 E
Bimban 86 24 24N 32 54 E
Bimberi Peak 100 35 44S 148 51 E
Bimbila 85 8 54N 0 5 E
Bimbo 88 4 15N 18 33 E
Bimini Is. 121 25 42N 79 25W
Bin Xian 77 35 2N 108 4 E
Bina-Etawah 68 24 13N 78 14 E
Binalbagan 73 10 12N 122 50 E
Binalong 100 34 40S 148 39 E
Binalud, Kuh-e 65 36 30N 58 30 E
Binatang 72 2 10N 111 40 E
Binche 16 50 26N 4 10 E
Binda 99 27 52S 147 21 E
Bindle 99 27 40S 148 45 E
Bindura 91 17 18S 31 18 E
Bingara, N.S.W., Austral. 99 29 52S 150 36 E
Bingara, Queens., Austral. 99 28 10S 144 37 E
Bingen 25 49 57N 7 53 E
Bingerville 84 5 18N 3 49W
Bingham 107 45 5N 69 50W
Bingham Canyon 118 40 31N 112 10W
Binghamton 114 42 9N 75 54W
Bingöl 64 38 53N 40 29 E
Binh Dinh = An Nhon 71 13 55N 109 7 E
Binh Son 71 15 20N 108 40 E
Binjai 72 3 20N 98 30 E
Binnaway 99 31 28S 149 24 E
Binongko 73 5 55S 123 55 E
Binscarth 109 50 37N 101 17W
Bint Jubayl 62 33 8N 35 25 E
Bintan 72 1 0N 104 0 E
Bintulu 72 3 10N 113 0 E
Bintuni (Steenkool) 73 2 7S 133 32 E
Binyamina 62 32 32N 34 56 E
Binyang 77 23 12N 108 47 E
Binz 24 54 23N 13 37 E
Binzert = Bizerte 83 37 15N 9 50 E
Bio Bio □ 124 37 35S 72 0W
Biograd 39 43 56N 15 29 E
Biokovo 42 43 23N 17 0 E
Biougra 82 30 15N 9 14W
Biq'at Bet Netofa 62 32 49N 35 22 E
Bîr Abu Hashim 86 23 42N 34 6 E
Bîr Abu M'nqar 86 26 33N 27 33 E
Bîr Adal Deib 86 22 35N 36 10 E
Bi'r al Malfa 83 31 58N 15 18 E
Bir Aouine 83 32 25N 9 18 E
Bîr 'Asal 86 25 55N 34 20 E
Bir Autrun 81 18 15N 26 40 E
Bi'r Dhu'fân 83 31 59N 14 32 E
Bîr Diqnash 86 31 3N 25 23 E
Bir el Abbes 82 26 7N 6 9W
Bir el Ater 83 34 46N 8 3 E
Bîr el Basur 86 29 51N 25 49 E
Bîr el Gellaz 86 30 50N 26 40 E
Bîr el Shaqqa 86 30 54N 25 1 E
Bîr Fuad 86 30 35N 26 28 E
Bîr Haimur 86 22 45N 33 40 E
Bir Jdid 82 33 26N 8 0W
Bîr Kanayis 86 24 59N 33 15 E
Bîr Kerawein 86 27 10N 28 25 E
Bîr Lahrache 83 32 1N 8 12 E
Bîr Maql 86 23 7N 33 40 E
Bîr Misaha 86 22 13N 27 59 E
Bîr Mogrein 82 25 10N 11 25W
Bi'r Mubayrīk 64 23 22N 39 8 E
Bîr Murr 86 23 28N 30 10 E
Bi'r Nabālā 62 31 52N 35 12 E
Bîr Nakheila 86 24 1N 30 50 E
Bîr Qatrani 86 30 55N 26 10 E
Bîr Ranga 86 24 25N 35 15 E
Bir, Ras 87 12 0N 43 20 E
Bîr Sahara 86 22 54N 28 40 E
Bîr Seiyâla 86 26 10N 33 50 E
Bir Semguine 82 30 1N 5 39W
Bîr Shalatein 86 23 5N 35 25 E
Bîr Shebb 86 22 25N 29 40 E
Bîr Shût 86 23 50N 35 15 E
Bîr Terfawi 86 22 57N 28 55 E
Bîr Umm Qubûr 86 24 35N 34 2 E
Bîr Ungât 86 22 8N 33 48 E
Bîr Za'farâna 86 29 10N 32 40 E
Bîr Zāmūs 83 24 16N 15 6 E
Bi'r Zayt 62 31 59N 35 11 E
Bîr Zeidûn 86 25 45N 33 40 E
Bira 73 2 3S 132 2 E
Bîra 46 47 2N 27 3 E
Birak Sulaymān 62 31 42N 35 7 E
Biramféro 84 11 40N 9 10W
Birao 81 10 20N 22 47 E
Birawa 90 2 20S 28 48 E
Bîrca 46 43 59N 23 36 E
Birch Hills 109 52 59N 105 25W
Birch I. 109 52 26N 99 54W
Birch L., N.W.T., Can. 108 62 4N 116 33W
Birch L., Ont., Can. 106 51 23N 92 18W
Birch L., U.S.A. 106 47 48N 91 43W
Birch Mts. 108 57 30N 113 10W
Birch River 109 52 24N 101 6W
Birchip 99 35 56S 142 55 E
Birchiş 46 45 58N 22 9 E
Bird 109 56 30N 94 13W
Bird City 116 39 48N 101 33W
Bird I., Austral. 97 22 10S 155 28 E
Bird I., S. Afr. 92 32 3S 18 17 E
Bird I. = Aves, I. de 121 12 0N 67 30W
Birdlip 13 51 50N 2 7W
Birdsville 97 25 51S 139 20 E
Birdum 96 15 39S 133 13 E
Birecik 64 37 0N 38 0 E
Bireuen 72 5 14N 96 39 E
Birifo 84 13 30N 14 0W
Birigui 125 21 18S 50 16W
Birk 86 18 8N 41 30 E
Birka 86 22 11N 40 38 E
Birkenfeld 25 49 39N 7 11 E
Birkenhead 12 53 24N 3 1W
Birket Qârûn 86 29 30N 30 40 E
Birkfeld 26 47 21N 15 45 E
Birkhadem 82 36 43N 3 3 E
Bîrlad 46 46 15N 27 38 E
Birmingham, U.K. 13 52 30N 1 55W
Birmingham, U.S.A. 115 33 31N 86 50W
Birmitrapur 69 22 24N 84 46 E
Birni Ngaouré 85 13 5N 2 51 E
Birni Nkonni 85 13 55N 5 15 E
Birnin Gwari 85 11 0N 6 45 E
Birnin Kebbi 85 12 32N 4 12 E
Birnin Kudu 85 11 30N 9 29 E
Birobidzhan 59 48 50N 132 50 E
Birqīn 62 32 27N 35 15 E
Birr 15 53 7N 7 55W
Birrie → 99 29 43S 146 37 E
Birsilpur 68 28 11N 72 15 E
Birsk 52 55 25N 55 30 E
Birtin 46 46 59N 22 31 E
Birtle 109 50 30N 101 5W
Biryuchiy 56 46 10N 35 0 E
Birzai 54 56 11N 24 45 E
Bîrzava 46 46 7N 21 59 E
Bisa 73 1 15S 127 28 E
Bisáccia 41 41 0N 15 20 E
Bisacquino 40 37 42N 13 13 E
Bisalpur 69 28 14N 79 48 E
Bisbal, La 32 41 58N 3 2 E
Bisbee 119 31 30N 110 0W
Biscarrosse, Étang de 20 44 21N 1 10W
Biscay, B. of 6 45 0N 2 0W
Biscayne B. 115 25 40N 80 12W
Biscéglie 41 41 14N 16 30 E
Bischofshofen 26 47 26N 13 14 E
Bischofswerda 24 51 8N 14 11 E
Bischwiller 19 48 41N 7 50 E
Biscoe Bay 5 77 0S 152 0W
Biscoe I. 5 66 0S 67 0W
Biscostasing 106 47 18N 82 9W
Biševo 39 42 57N 16 3 E
Bisha 87 15 30N 37 31 E
Bisha, Wadi → 86 21 24N 43 26 E
Bishop, Calif., U.S.A. 119 37 20N 118 26W
Bishop, Tex., U.S.A. 117 27 35N 97 49W
Bishop Auckland 12 54 40N 1 40W
Bishop's Falls 107 49 2N 55 30W
Bishop's Stortford 13 51 52N 0 11 E
Bisignano 41 39 30N 16 17 E
Bisina, L. 90 1 38N 33 56 E
Biskra 83 34 50N 5 44 E
Biskupiec 28 53 53N 20 58 E
Bislig 73 8 15N 126 27 E
Bismarck 116 46 49N 100 49W
Bismarck Arch. 94 2 30S 150 0 E
Bismarck Sea 98 4 10S 146 50 E
Bismark 24 52 39N 11 31 E
Biso 90 1 44N 31 26 E
Bison 116 45 34N 102 28W
Bispfors 50 63 1N 16 37 E
Bispgården 48 63 2N 16 40 E
Bissagos = Bijagós, Arquipélago dos 84 11 15N 16 10W
Bissau 84 11 45N 15 45W
Bissett 109 51 2N 95 41W
Bissikrima 84 10 50N 10 58W
Bistcho L. 108 59 45N 118 50W
Bistreţu 46 43 54N 23 23 E
Bistrica = Ilirska-Bistrica 39 45 34N 14 14 E
Bistriţa 46 47 9N 24 35 E
Bistriţa → 46 46 30N 26 57 E
Bistriţa Năsăud □ 46 47 15N 24 30 E
Bistriţei, Munţii 46 47 15N 25 40 E
Biswan 69 27 29N 81 2 E
Bisztynek 28 54 8N 20 53 E
Bitam 88 2 5N 11 25 E
Bitburg 25 49 58N 6 32 E
Bitche 19 49 2N 7 25 E
Bitkine 81 11 59N 18 13 E
Bitlis 64 38 20N 42 3 E
Bitola (Bitolj) 42 41 5N 21 10 E
Bitonto 41 41 7N 16 40 E
Bitter Creek 118 41 39N 108 36W
Bitter L. = Buheirat-Murrat-el-Kubra 86 30 15N 32 40 E
Bitterfeld 24 51 36N 12 20 E
Bitterfontein 92 31 0S 18 32 E
Bitterroot → 118 46 52N 114 6W
Bitterroot Range 118 46 0N 114 20W
Bitti 40 40 29N 9 20 E
Bittou 85 11 17N 0 18W
Biu 85 10 40N 12 3 E
Bivolari 46 47 31N 27 27 E
Bivolu 46 47 16N 25 58 E
Biwa-Ko 74 35 15N 136 10 E
Biwabik 116 47 33N 92 19W
Bixad 46 47 56N 23 28 E
Biyang 77 32 38N 113 21 E
Biysk 58 52 40N 85 0 E
Bizana 93 30 50S 29 52 E
Bizerte (Binzert) 83 37 15N 9 50 E
Bjargtangar 50 65 30N 24 30W
Bjelasica 42 42 50N 19 40 E
Bjelašnica 42 43 43N 18 9 E
Bjelovar 42 45 56N 16 49 E
Bjerringbro 49 56 23N 9 39 E
Björbo 48 60 27N 14 44 E
Björneborg 48 59 14N 14 16 E
Bjørnøya 4 74 30N 19 0 E
Bjuv 49 56 5N 12 55 E
Blace 42 43 18N 21 17 E
Blachownia 28 50 49N 18 56 E
Black →, Can. 112 44 42N 79 19W
Black →, Ark., U.S.A. 117 35 38N 91 19W
Black →, N.Y., U.S.A. 113 43 59N 76 4W
Black →, Wis., U.S.A. 116 43 52N 91 22W
Black Diamond 108 50 45N 114 14W
Black Forest = Schwarzwald 25 48 0N 8 0 E
Black Hills 116 44 0N 103 50W
Black I. 109 51 12N 96 30W
Black L., Can. 109 59 12N 105 15W
Black L., U.S.A. 114 45 28N 84 15W
Black Mesa, Mt. 117 36 57N 102 55W
Black Mt. = Mynydd Du 13 51 45N 3 45W
Black Mts. 13 51 52N 3 5W
Black Range 119 33 30N 107 55W
Black River 121 18 0N 77 50W
Black River Falls 116 44 23N 90 52W
Black Sea 9 43 30N 35 0 E
Black Sugarloaf, Mt. 100 31 18S 151 35 E
Black Volta → 84 8 41N 1 33W
Black Warrior → 115 32 32N 87 51W
Blackall 97 24 25S 145 45 E
Blackball 101 42 22S 171 26 E
Blackbull 98 17 55S 141 45 E
Blackburn 12 53 44N 2 30W
Blackduck 116 47 43N 94 32W
Blackfoot 118 43 13N 112 12W
Blackfoot → 118 46 52N 113 53W
Blackfoot River Res. 118 43 0N 111 35W
Blackie 108 50 36N 113 37W
Blackpool 12 53 48N 3 3W
Blackriver 112 44 46N 83 17W
Blacks Harbour 107 45 3N 66 49W
Blacksburg 114 37 17N 80 23W
Blacksod B. 15 54 6N 10 0W
Blackstone 114 37 6N 78 0W
Blackstone → 108 61 5N 122 55W
Blackstone Ra. 96 26 00S 129 00 E
Blackville 107 46 44N 65 50W
Blackwater 98 23 35S 148 53 E
Blackwater →, Ireland 15 51 55N 7 50W
Blackwater →, U.K. 15 54 31N 6 35W
Blackwater Cr. → 99 25 56S 144 30 E
Blackwell 117 36 55N 97 20W
Blaenau Ffestiniog 12 53 0N 3 57W
Blagaj 42 43 16N 17 55 E
Blagodarnoye 57 45 7N 43 37 E
Blagoevgrad (Gorna Dzhumayo) 42 42 2N 23 5 E
Blagoveshchensk 59 50 20N 127 30 E
Blain 18 47 29N 1 45W
Blaine 118 48 59N 122 43W
Blaine Lake 109 52 51N 106 52W
Blainville 19 48 33N 6 23 E
Blair 116 41 38N 96 10W
Blair Athol 97 22 42S 147 31 E
Blair Atholl 14 56 46N 3 50W
Blairgowrie 14 56 36N 3 20W
Blairmore 108 49 40N 114 25W
Blairsville 112 40 27N 79 15W
Blaj 46 46 10N 23 57 E
Blake Pt. 116 48 12N 88 27W
Blakely 115 31 22N 85 0W
Blâmont 19 48 35N 6 50 E
Blanc, C. 83 37 15N 9 56 E
Blanc, Le 20 46 37N 1 3 E
Blanc, Mont 21 45 48N 6 50 E
Blanca, Bahía 128 39 10S 61 30W
Blanca Peak 119 37 35N 105 29W
Blanchard 117 35 8N 97 40W
Blanche L., S. Austral., Austral. 97 29 15S 139 40 E
Blanche L., W. Austral., Austral. 96 22 25S 123 17 E
Blanco, S. Afr. 92 33 55S 22 23 E
Blanco, U.S.A. 117 30 7N 98 30W
Blanco → 124 30 20S 68 42W
Blanco, C., C. Rica 121 9 34N 85 8W
Blanco, C., Spain 33 39 21N 2 51 E
Blanco, C., U.S.A. 118 42 50N 124 40W
Blanda → 50 65 20N 19 40W
Blandford Forum 13 50 52N 2 10W
Blanding 119 37 35N 109 30W
Blanes 32 41 40N 2 48 E
Blanice → 26 49 10N 14 5 E
Blankenberge 16 51 20N 3 9 E
Blankenburg 24 51 46N 10 56 E
Blanquefort 20 44 55N 0 38W
Blanquillo 125 32 53S 55 37W
Blansko 27 49 22N 16 40 E
Blantyre 91 15 45S 35 0 E
Blarney 15 51 57N 8 35W
Błaski 28 51 38N 18 30 E
Blatná 26 49 25N 13 52 E
Blatnitsa 43 43 41N 28 32 E
Blato 39 42 56N 16 48 E
Blaubeuren 25 48 24N 9 47 E
Blaydon 12 54 56N 1 47W
Blaye 20 45 8N 0 40W
Blaye-les-Mines 20 44 1N 2 8 E
Blayney 99 33 32S 149 14 E
Blaze, Pt. 96 12 56S 130 11 E
Błazowa 27 49 53N 22 7 E
Bleckede 24 53 18N 10 43 E
Bled 39 46 27N 14 7 E
Blednaya, Gora 58 76 20N 65 0 E
Bleiburg 26 46 35N 14 49 E
Blejeşti 46 44 19N 25 27 E
Blekinge län □ 49 56 20N 15 20 E
Blenheim, Can. 112 42 20N 82 0W
Blenheim, N.Z. 101 41 38S 173 57 E
Bléone → 21 44 5N 6 0 E
Bletchley 13 51 59N 0 44W
Bleymard, Le 20 44 30N 3 42 E
Blida 82 36 30N 2 49 E
Blidet Amor 83 32 59N 5 58 E
Blidö 48 59 37N 18 53 E
Blidsberg 49 57 56N 13 30 E
Bligh Sound 101 44 47S 167 32 E
Blind River 106 46 10N 82 58W
Blinishti 44 41 52N 19 58 E
Blitar 73 8 5S 112 11 E
Blitta 85 8 23N 1 6 E
Block I. 114 41 11N 71 35W
Block Island Sd. 113 41 17N 71 35W
Bloemfontein 92 29 6S 26 14 E
Bloemhof 92 27 38S 25 32 E
Blois 18 47 35N 1 20 E
Blomskog 48 59 16N 12 2 E
Blönduós 50 65 40N 20 12W
Błonie 28 52 12N 20 37 E
Bloodvein → 109 51 47N 96 43W
Bloody Foreland 15 55 10N 8 18W
Bloomer 116 45 8N 91 30W
Bloomfield, Can. 112 43 59N 77 14W
Bloomfield, Iowa, U.S.A. 116 40 44N 92 26W
Bloomfield, N. Mexico, U.S.A. 119 36 46N 107 59W
Bloomfield, Nebr., U.S.A. 116 42 38N 97 40W
Bloomfield River Mission 98 15 56S 145 22 E
Bloomington, Ill., U.S.A. 116 40 27N 89 0W
Bloomington, Ind., U.S.A. 114 39 10N 86 30W
Bloomsburg 114 41 0N 76 30W
Blora 73 6 57S 111 25 E
Blossburg 112 41 40N 77 4W
Blouberg 93 23 8S 29 0 E
Blountstown 115 30 28N 85 5W
Bludenz 26 47 10N 9 50 E
Blue Island 114 41 40N 87 40W
Blue Lake 118 40 53N 124 0W
Blue Mesa Res. 119 38 30N 107 15W
Blue Mts., Austral. 97 33 40S 150 0 E
Blue Mts., Ore., U.S.A. 118 45 15N 119 0W
Blue Mts., Pa., U.S.A. 114 40 30N 76 30W
Blue Mud B. 97 13 30S 136 0 E
Blue Nile = An Nîl el Azraq □ 87 12 30N 34 30 E
Blue Nile = Nîl el Azraq → 87 15 38N 32 31 E
Blue Rapids 116 39 41N 96 39W
Blue Ridge Mts. 115 36 30N 80 15W
Blue Stack Mts. 15 54 46N 8 5W
Blueberry → 108 56 45N 120 49W
Bluefield 114 37 18N 81 14W
Bluefields 121 12 20N 83 50W
Bluff, Austral. 98 23 35S 149 4 E
Bluff, N.Z. 101 46 37S 168 20 E
Bluff, U.S.A. 119 37 17N 109 33W
Bluffton 114 40 43N 85 9W
Blumenau 125 27 0S 49 0W
Blumenthal 24 53 5N 8 20 E
Blunt 116 44 32N 100 0W
Bly 118 42 23N 121 0W
Blyberg 48 61 9N 14 11 E
Blyth, Can. 112 43 44N 81 26W
Blyth, U.K. 12 55 8N 1 32W
Blythe 119 33 40N 114 33W
Blytheswood 112 42 8N 82 37W
Bø 47 59 25N 9 3 E
Bo 84 7 55N 11 50W
Bo Duc 71 11 58N 106 50 E
Bo Hai 76 39 0N 120 0 E
Bo Xian 77 33 50N 115 45 E
Boa Vista 126 2 48N 60 30W
Boaco 121 12 29N 85 35W
Boal 30 43 25N 6 49W
Boatman 99 27 16S 146 55 E
Bobai 77 22 17N 109 59 E
Bobbili 70 18 35N 83 30 E
Bòbbio 38 44 47N 9 22 E
Bobcaygeon 106 44 33N 78 33W
Böblingen 25 48 41N 9 1 E
Bobo-Dioulasso 84 11 8N 4 13W
Boboc 43 45 13N 26 59 E
Bobolice 28 53 58N 16 37 E
Boboshevo 42 42 9N 23 0 E
Bobov Dol 42 42 20N 23 0 E
Bóbr → 28 52 4N 15 4 E
Bobraomby, Tanjon' i 93 12 40S 49 10 E
Bobrinets 56 48 4N 32 5 E
Bobrov 55 51 5N 40 2 E
Bobruysk 54 53 10N 29 15 E
Bôca do Acre 126 8 50S 67 27W
Boca, La 120 8 56N 79 30W
Boca Raton 115 26 21N 80 5W
Bocaiúva 127 17 7S 43 49W
Bocanda 84 7 5N 4 31W
Bocaranga 88 7 0N 15 35 E
Bocas del Toro 121 9 15N 82 20W
Boceguillas 32 41 20N 3 39W
Bochnia 27 49 58N 20 27 E
Bocholt 24 51 50N 6 35 E
Bochov 26 50 9N 13 3 E
Bochum 24 51 28N 7 12 E
Bockenem 24 52 1N 10 8 E
Boćki 28 52 39N 23 3 E
Bocşa Montană 42 45 21N 21 47 E
Boda 88 4 19N 17 26 E
Böda 49 57 15N 17 3 E
Bodafors 49 57 48N 14 23 E
Bodaybo 59 57 50N 114 0 E
Boden 50 65 50N 21 42 E
Bodensee 25 47 35N 9 25 E
Bodenteich 24 52 49N 10 41 E
Bodhan 70 18 40N 77 44 E
Bodinayakkanur 70 10 2N 77 10 E
Bodinga 85 12 58N 5 10 E
Bodmin 13 50 28N 4 44W
Bodmin Moor 13 50 33N 4 36W
Bodrog → 27 48 15N 21 35 E
Bodrum 64 37 5N 27 30 E
Bödva → 27 48 19N 20 45 E
Boegoebergdam 92 29 7S 22 9 E
Boën 21 45 44N 4 0 E
Boende 88 0 24S 21 12 E
Boerne 117 29 48N 98 41W
Boffa 84 10 16N 14 3W
Bogalusa 117 30 50N 89 55W

Bogan → 97 29 59 S 146 17 E
Bogan Gate 99 33 7 S 147 49 E
Bogantungan 98 23 41 S 147 17 E
Bogata 117 33 26N 95 10W
Bogatić 42 44 51N 19 30 E
Bogenfels 92 27 25 S 15 25 E
Bogense 49 55 34N 10 5 E
Boggabilla 99 28 36 S 150 24 E
Boggabri 99 30 45 S 150 0 E
Boggeragh Mts. 15 52 2N 8 55W
Bognor Regis 13 50 47N 0 40W
Bogø 49 54 55N 12 2 E
Bogo 73 11 3N 124 0 E
Bogodukhov 54 50 9N 35 33 E
Bogong, Mt. 97 36 47 S 147 17 E
Bogor 73 6 36 S 106 48 E
Bogoroditsk 55 53 47N 38 8 E
Bogorodsk 55 56 4N 43 30 E
Bogorodskoye 59 52 22N 140 30 E
Bogoso 84 5 38N 2 3W
Bogota 126 4 34N 74 0W
Bogotol 58 56 15N 89 50 E
Bogra 69 24 51N 89 22 E
Boguchany 59 58 40N 97 30 E
Boguchar 57 49 55N 40 32 E
Bogué 84 16 45N 14 10W
Boguslav 56 49 47N 30 53 E
Boguszów 28 50 45N 16 12 E
Bohain 19 49 59N 3 28 E
Bohemia 26 50 0N 14 0 E
Bohemian Forest = Böhmerwald 25 49 30N 12 40 E
Bohena Cr. → 99 30 17 S 149 42 E
Bohinjska Bistrica 39 46 17N 14 1 E
Böhmerwald 25 49 30N 12 40 E
Bohmte 24 52 24N 8 20 E
Bohol 73 9 50N 124 10 E
Bohotleh 63 8 20N 46 25 E
Boi 85 9 35N 9 27 E
Boi, Pta. de 125 23 55 S 45 15W
Boiano 41 41 28N 14 29 E
Boileau, C. 96 17 40 S 122 7 E
Boinitsa 42 43 58N 22 32 E
Boise 118 43 43N 116 9W
Boise City 117 36 45N 102 30W
Boissevain 109 49 15N 100 5W
Boite → 39 46 5N 12 5 E
Boitzenburg 24 53 16N 13 36 E
Boizenburg 24 53 22N 10 42 E
Bojador C. 80 26 0N 14 30W
Bojana → 42 41 52N 19 22 E
Bojanowo 28 51 43N 16 42 E
Bojnūrd 65 37 30N 57 20 E
Bojonegoro 73 7 11 S 111 54 E
Boju 85 7 22N 7 55 E
Boka 42 45 22N 20 52 E
Boka Kotorska 42 42 23N 18 32 E
Bokala 84 8 31N 4 33W
Boké 84 10 56N 14 17W
Bokhara → 99 29 55 S 146 42 E
Bokkos 85 9 17N 9 1 E
Boknafjorden 47 59 14N 5 40 E
Bokoro 81 12 25N 17 14 E
Bokote 88 0 12 S 21 8 E
Bokpyin 71 11 18N 98 42 E
Boksitogorsk 54 59 32N 33 56 E
Bokungu 88 0 35 S 22 50 E
Bol, Chad 81 13 30N 15 0 E
Bol, Yugo. 39 43 18N 16 38 E
Bolama 84 11 30N 15 30W
Bolan Pass 66 29 50N 67 20 E
Bolaños → 120 21 14N 104 8W
Bolbec 18 49 30N 0 30 E
Boldeşti 46 45 3N 26 2 E
Bole, China 75 45 11N 81 37 E
Bole, Ethiopia 87 6 36N 37 20 E
Bolekhov 54 49 0N 24 0 E
Bolesławiec 28 51 17N 15 37 E
Bolgatanga 85 10 44N 0 53W
Bolgrad 56 45 40N 28 32 E
Boli, China 76 45 46N 130 31 E
Boli, Sudan 87 6 2N 28 48 E
Bolinao C. 73 16 23N 119 55 E
Bolívar, Argent. 124 36 15 S 60 53W
Bolívar, Colomb. 126 2 0N 77 0W
Bolivar, Mo., U.S.A. 117 37 38N 93 22W
Bolivar, Tenn., U.S.A. 117 35 14N 89 0W
Bolivia ■ 126 17 6 S 64 0W
Boljevac 42 43 51N 21 58 E
Bolkhov 55 53 25N 36 0 E
Bollène 21 44 18N 4 45 E
Bollnäs 48 61 21N 16 24 E
Bollon 99 28 2 S 147 29 E
Bollstabruk 48 63 1N 17 40 E
Bollullos 31 37 19N 6 32W
Bolmen 49 56 55N 13 40 E
Bolobo 88 2 6 S 16 20 E
Bologna 39 44 30N 11 20 E
Bologne 19 48 10N 5 8 E
Bologoye 54 57 55N 34 0 E
Bolomba 88 0 35N 19 0 E
Bolong 73 7 6N 122 16 E
Boloven, Cao Nguyen 71 15 10N 106 30 E
Bolpur 69 23 40N 87 45 E
Bolsena 39 42 40N 11 58 E
Bolsena, L. di 39 42 35N 11 55 E
Bolshaya Glushitsa 55 52 24N 50 29 E
Bolshaya Martynovka 57 47 12N 41 46 E
Bolshaya Vradiyevka 56 47 50N 30 40 E
Bolshereche 58 56 4N 74 45 E
Bolshevik, Ostrov 59 78 30N 102 0 E
Bolshezemelskaya Tundra 52 67 0N 56 0 E
Bolshoi Kavkas 57 42 50N 44 0 E
Bolshoy Anyuy → 59 68 30N 160 49 E
Bolshoy Atlym 58 62 25N 66 50 E
Bolshoy Begichev, Ostrov 59 74 20N 112 30 E
Bolshoy Lyakhovskiy, Ostrov 59 73 35N 142 0 E
Bolshoy Tokmak 56 47 16N 35 42 E
Bol'shoy Tyuters, Ostrov 54 59 51N 27 13 E
Bolsward 16 53 3N 5 32 E
Boltaña 32 42 28N 0 4 E
Boltigen 25 46 38N 7 24 E
Bolton, Can. 112 43 54N 79 45W
Bolton, U.K. 12 53 35N 2 26W
Bolu 64 40 45N 31 35 E
Bolvadin 64 38 45N 31 4 E
Bolzano (Bozen) 39 46 30N 11 20 E
Bom Despacho 127 19 43 S 45 15W
Bom Jesus da Lapa 127 13 15 S 43 25W
Boma 88 5 50 S 13 4 E
Bomaderry 99 34 52 S 150 37 E
Bombala 97 36 56 S 149 15 E
Bombarral 31 39 15N 9 9W
Bombay 70 18 55N 72 50 E
Bomboma 88 2 25N 18 55 E
Bombombwa 90 1 40N 25 40 E
Bomi Hills 84 7 1N 10 38W
Bomili 90 1 45N 27 5 E
Bomokandi → 90 3 39N 26 8 E
Bomongo 88 1 27N 18 21 E
Bomu → 88 4 40N 23 30 E
Bon C. 83 37 1N 11 2 E
Bonaire 121 12 10N 68 15W
Bonang 99 37 11 S 148 41 E
Bonanza 121 13 54N 84 35W
Bonaparte Archipelago 96 14 0 S 124 30 E
Boñar 30 42 52N 5 19W
Bonaventure 107 48 5N 65 32W
Bonavista 107 48 40N 53 5W
Bonavista, C. 107 48 42N 53 5W
Bondeno 39 44 53N 11 22 E
Bondo 88 3 55N 23 53 E
Bondoukou 84 8 2N 2 47W
Bondowoso 73 7 56 S 113 49 E
Bone Rate 73 7 25 S 121 5 E
Bone Rate, Kepulauan 73 6 30 S 121 10 E
Bone, Teluk 73 4 10 S 120 50 E
Bonefro 41 41 42N 14 55 E
Bo'ness 14 56 0N 3 38W
Bong Son = Hoai Nhon 71 14 28N 109 1 E
Bongandanga 88 1 24N 21 3 E
Bongor 81 10 35N 15 20 E
Bongouanou 84 6 42N 4 15W
Bonham 117 33 30N 96 10W
Bonifacio 21 41 24N 9 10 E
Bonifacio, Bouches de 40 41 12N 9 15 E
Bonin Is. 94 27 0N 142 0 E
Bonke 87 6 5N 37 16 E
Bonn 24 50 43N 7 6 E
Bonnat 20 46 20N 1 54 E
Bonne Terre 117 37 57N 90 33W
Bonners Ferry 118 48 38N 116 21W
Bonnétable 18 48 11N 0 25 E
Bonneuil-Matours 18 46 41N 0 34 E
Bonneval 18 48 11N 1 24 E
Bonneville 21 46 5N 6 24 E
Bonney, L. 99 37 50 S 140 20 E
Bonnie Rock 96 30 29 S 118 22 E
Bonny, France 19 47 34N 2 50 E
Bonny, Nigeria 85 4 25N 7 13 E
Bonny → 85 4 20N 7 10 E
Bonny, Bight of 88 3 30N 9 20 E
Bonnyville 109 54 20N 110 45W
Bonoi 73 1 45 S 137 41 E
Bonorva 40 40 25N 8 47 E
Bontang 72 0 10N 117 30 E
Bonthain 73 5 34 S 119 56 E
Bonthe 84 7 30N 12 33W
Bontoc 73 17 7N 120 58 E
Bonyeri 84 5 1N 2 46W
Bonyhád 27 46 18N 18 32 E
Booker 117 36 29N 100 30W
Boolaboolka, L. 99 32 38 S 143 10 E
Booligal 99 33 58 S 144 53 E
Boom 16 51 6N 4 20 E
Boonah 99 27 58 S 152 41 E
Boone, Iowa, U.S.A. 116 42 5N 93 53W
Boone, N.C., U.S.A. 115 36 14N 81 43W
Booneville, Ark., U.S.A. 117 35 10N 93 54W
Booneville, Miss., U.S.A. 115 34 39N 88 34W
Boonville, Ind., U.S.A. 114 38 3N 87 13W
Boonville, Mo., U.S.A. 116 38 57N 92 45W
Boonville, N.Y., U.S.A. 114 43 31N 75 20W
Boorindal 99 30 22 S 146 11 E
Boorowa 99 34 28 S 148 44 E
Boothia, Gulf of 105 71 0N 90 0W
Boothia Pen. 104 71 0N 94 0W
Bootle, Cumb., U.K. 12 54 17N 3 24W
Bootle, Merseyside, U.K. 12 53 28N 3 1W
Booué 88 0 5 S 11 55 E
Bopeechee 99 29 36 S 137 22 E
Bophuthatswana □ 92 26 0 S 26 0 E
Boppard 25 50 13N 7 36 E
Boquete 121 8 49N 82 27W
Bor 26 49 41N 12 45 E
Bôr 87 6 10N 31 40 E
Bor, Sweden 49 57 9N 14 10 E
Bor, Yugo. 42 44 8N 22 7 E
Borah, Mt. 118 44 19N 113 46W
Borama 63 9 55N 43 7 E
Borang 87 4 50N 30 59 E
Borås 49 57 43N 12 56 E
Borāzjān 65 29 22N 51 10 E
Borba, Brazil 126 4 12 S 59 34W
Borba, Port. 31 38 50N 7 26W
Borçka 57 41 25N 41 41 E
Bordeaux 20 44 50N 0 36W
Borden 107 46 18N 63 47W
Borden I. 4 78 30N 111 30W
Borders □ 14 55 35N 2 50W
Bordertown 97 36 19 S 140 45 E
Borðeyri 50 65 12N 21 6W
Bordighera 38 43 47N 7 40 E
Bordj bou Arreridj 83 36 4N 4 45 E
Bordj Bourguiba 83 32 12N 10 2 E
Bordj el Hobra 83 32 9N 4 51 E
Bordj Fly Ste. Marie 82 27 19N 2 32W
Bordj-in-Eker 83 24 9N 5 3 E
Bordj Menaiel 83 36 46N 3 43 E
Bordj Messouda 83 30 12N 9 25 E
Bordj Nili 82 33 28N 3 2 E
Bordj Omar Driss 83 28 10N 6 40 E
Bordj Zelfana 83 32 27N 4 15 E
Borek Wielkopolski 28 51 54N 17 11 E
Borensberg 49 58 34N 15 17 E
Borgarnes 50 64 32N 21 55W
Børgefjellet 50 65 20N 13 45 E
Borger, Neth. 16 52 54N 6 44 E
Borger, U.S.A. 117 35 40N 101 20W
Borghamn 49 58 23N 14 41 E
Borgholm 49 56 52N 16 39 E
Bórgia 41 38 50N 16 30 E
Borgo San Dalmazzo 38 44 19N 7 29 E
Borgo San Lorenzo 39 43 57N 11 21 E
Borgo Valsugano 39 46 3N 11 27 E
Borgomanero 38 45 41N 8 28 E
Borgonovo Val Tidone 38 45 1N 9 28 E
Borgorose 39 42 12N 13 14 E
Borgosésia 38 45 43N 8 17 E
Borgvattnet 48 63 26N 15 48 E
Borislav 54 49 18N 23 28 E
Borisoglebsk 55 51 27N 42 5 E
Borisoglebskiy 55 56 28N 43 59 E
Borisov 54 54 17N 28 28 E
Borispol 54 50 21N 30 59 E
Borja, Peru 126 4 20 S 77 40W
Borja, Spain 32 41 48N 1 34W
Borjas Blancas 32 41 31N 0 52 E
Borken 24 51 51N 6 52 E
Borkou 81 18 15N 18 50 E
Borkum 24 53 36N 6 42 E
Borlänge 48 60 29N 15 26 E
Borley, C. 5 66 15 S 52 30 E
Bormida → 38 44 23N 8 13 E
Bórmio 38 46 28N 10 22 E
Borna 24 51 8N 12 31 E
Borneo 72 1 0N 115 0 E
Bornholm 49 55 10N 15 0 E
Bornholmsgattet 49 55 15N 14 20 E
Borno □ 85 12 30N 12 30 E
Bornos 31 36 48N 5 42W
Bornu Yassa 85 12 14N 12 25 E
Borobudur 73 7 36 S 110 13 E
Borodino 54 55 31N 35 40 E
Borogontsy 59 62 42N 131 8 E
Boromo 84 11 45N 2 58W
Borongan 73 11 37N 125 26 E
Bororen 98 24 13 S 151 33 E
Borotangba Mts. 87 6 30N 25 0 E
Borovan 43 43 27N 23 45 E
Borovichi 54 58 25N 33 55 E
Borovsk 55 55 12N 36 24 E
Borrby 49 55 27N 14 10 E
Borriol 32 40 4N 0 4W
Borroloola 97 16 4 S 136 17 E
Borşa 46 47 41N 24 50 E
Borsod-Abaúj-Zemplén □ 27 48 20N 21 0 E
Bort-les-Orgues 20 45 24N 2 29 E
Borth 13 52 29N 4 3W
Borujerd 64 33 55N 48 50 E
Borzhomi 57 41 48N 43 28 E
Borzna 54 51 18N 32 26 E
Borzya 59 50 24N 116 31 E
Bosa 40 40 17N 8 32 E
Bosanska Brod 42 45 10N 18 0 E
Bosanska Dubica 39 45 10N 16 50 E
Bosanska Gradiška 42 45 10N 17 15 E
Bosanska Kostajnica 39 45 11N 16 33 E
Bosanska Krupa 39 44 53N 16 10 E
Bosanski Novi 39 45 2N 16 22 E
Bosanski Samac 42 45 3N 18 29 E
Bosansko Grahovo 39 44 12N 16 26 E
Bosansko Petrovac 39 44 35N 16 21 E
Bosaso 63 11 12N 49 18 E
Boscastle 13 50 42N 4 42W
Boscotrecase 41 40 46N 14 28 E
Bose 77 23 53N 106 35 E
Boshan 76 36 28N 117 49 E
Boshoek 92 25 30 S 27 9 E
Boshof 92 28 31 S 25 13 E
Boshrūyeh 65 33 50N 57 30 E
Bosilegrad 42 42 30N 22 27 E
Boskovice 27 49 29N 16 40 E
Bosna → 42 45 4N 18 29 E
Bosna i Hercegovina □ 42 44 0N 18 0 E
Bosnia = Bosna □ 42 44 0N 18 0 E
Bosnik 73 1 5 S 136 10 E
Bōsō-Hantō 74 35 20N 140 20 E
Bosobolo 88 4 15N 19 50 E
Bosporus = Karadeniz Boğazı 64 41 10N 29 10 E
Bossangoa 88 6 35N 17 30 E
Bossekop 50 69 57N 23 15 E
Bossembélé 81 5 25N 17 40 E
Bossier City 117 32 28N 93 48W
Bosso 85 13 43N 13 19 E
Bossut C. 96 18 42 S 121 35 E
Bosten Hu 75 41 55N 87 40 E
Boston, U.K. 12 52 59N 0 2W
Boston, U.S.A. 114 42 20N 71 0W
Boston Bar 108 49 52N 121 30W
Bosut → 42 45 20N 19 0 E
Boswell, Can. 108 49 28N 116 45W
Boswell, Okla., U.S.A. 117 34 1N 95 50W
Boswell, Pa., U.S.A. 112 40 9N 79 2W
Botad 68 22 15N 71 40 E
Botevgrad 43 42 55N 23 47 E
Bothaville 92 27 23 S 26 34 E
Bothnia, G. of 50 63 0N 20 0 E
Bothwell, Austral. 99 42 20 S 147 1 E
Bothwell, Can. 112 42 38N 81 52W
Boticas 30 41 41N 7 40W
Botletle → 92 20 10 S 23 15 E
Botoroaga 46 44 8N 25 32 E
Botoşani 46 47 42N 26 41 E
Botoşani □ 46 47 50N 26 50 E
Botro 84 7 51N 5 19W
Botswana ■ 92 22 0 S 24 0 E
Bottineau 116 48 49N 100 25W
Bottrop 24 51 34N 6 59 E
Botucatu 125 22 55 S 48 30W
Botwood 107 49 6N 55 23W
Bou Alam 82 33 50N 1 26 E
Bou Ali 82 27 11N 0 4W
Bou Djébéha 84 18 25N 2 45W
Bou Guema 82 28 49N 0 19 E
Bou Ismael 82 36 38N 2 42 E
Bou Izakarn 82 29 12N 9 46W
Bou Saâda 83 35 11N 4 9 E
Bou Salem 83 36 45N 9 2 E
Bouaké 84 7 40N 5 2W
Bouar 88 6 0N 15 40 E
Bouârfa 82 32 32N 1 58 E
Bouca 88 6 45N 18 25 E
Boucau 20 43 32N 1 29W
Bouches-du-Rhône □ 21 43 37N 5 2 E
Bouda 82 27 50N 0 27W
Boudenib 82 31 59N 3 31W
Boufarik 82 36 34N 2 58 E
Bougainville C. 96 13 57 S 126 4 E
Bougaroun, C. 83 37 6N 6 30 E
Bougie = Bejaia 83 36 42N 5 2 E
Bougouni 84 11 30N 7 20W
Bouillon 16 49 44N 5 3 E
Bouïra 83 36 20N 3 59 E
Boulder, Austral. 96 30 46 S 121 30 E
Boulder, Colo., U.S.A. 116 40 3N 105 10W
Boulder, Mont., U.S.A. 118 46 14N 112 4W
Boulder City 119 36 0N 114 50W
Boulder Dam = Hoover Dam 119 36 0N 114 45W
Bouli 84 15 17N 12 18W
Boulia 97 22 52 S 139 51 E
Bouligny 19 49 17N 5 45 E
Boulogne → 18 47 12N 1 47W
Boulogne-sur-Gesse 20 43 18N 0 38 E
Boulogne-sur-Mer 19 50 42N 1 36 E
Bouloire 18 47 58N 0 33 E
Boulsa 85 12 39N 0 34W
Boultoum 85 14 45N 10 25 E
Boumalne 82 31 25N 6 0W
Bouna 84 9 10N 3 0W
Boundiali 84 9 30N 6 20W
Bountiful 118 40 57N 111 58W
Bounty I. 94 48 0 S 178 30 E
Bourbon-Lancy 20 46 37N 3 45 E
Bourbon-l'Archambault 20 46 36N 3 4 E
Bourbonnais 20 46 28N 3 0 E
Bourbonne-les-Bains 19 47 59N 5 45 E
Bourem 85 17 0N 0 24W
Bourg 20 45 3N 0 34W
Bourg-Argental 21 45 18N 4 32 E
Bourg-de-Péage 21 45 2N 5 3 E
Bourg-en-Bresse 21 46 13N 5 12 E
Bourg-St.-Andéol 21 44 23N 4 39 E
Bourg-St.-Maurice 21 45 35N 6 46 E
Bourganeuf 20 45 57N 1 45 E
Bourges 19 47 9N 2 25 E
Bourget 113 45 26N 75 9W
Bourget, L. du 21 45 44N 5 52 E
Bourgneuf, B. de 18 47 3N 2 10W
Bourgneuf-en-Retz 18 47 2N 1 58W
Bourgneuf-la-Fôret, Le 18 48 10N 0 59W
Bourgogne 19 47 0N 4 30 E
Bourgoin-Jallieu 21 45 36N 5 17 E
Bourgueil 18 47 17N 0 10 E
Bourke 97 30 8 S 145 55 E
Bournemouth 13 50 43N 1 53W
Bourriot-Bergonce 20 44 7N 0 14W
Bouscat, Le 20 44 53N 0 32W
Boussac 20 46 22N 2 13 E
Boussens 20 43 12N 0 58 E
Bousso 81 10 34N 16 52 E
Boutilimit 84 17 45N 14 40W
Boutonne → 20 45 55N 0 43 E
Bouvet I. = Bouvetøya 7 54 26 S 3 24 E
Bouvetøya 7 54 26 S 3 24 E
Bouznika 82 33 46N 7 6W
Bouzonville 19 49 17N 6 32 E
Bova Marina 41 37 59N 15 56 E
Bovalino Marina 41 38 9N 16 10 E
Bovec 39 46 20N 13 33 E
Bovigny 16 50 12N 5 55 E
Bovill 118 46 58N 116 27W
Bovino 41 41 15N 15 20 E
Bow Island 108 49 50N 111 23W
Bowbells 116 48 47N 102 19W
Bowdle 116 45 30N 99 40W
Bowen 97 20 0 S 148 16 E
Bowen → 98 20 24 S 147 20 E
Bowen Mts. 99 37 0 S 148 0 E
Bowie, Ariz., U.S.A. 119 32 15N 109 30W
Bowie, Tex., U.S.A. 117 33 33N 97 50W
Bowland, Forest of 12 54 0N 2 30W
Bowling Green, Ky., U.S.A. 114 37 0N 86 25W
Bowling Green, Ohio, U.S.A. 114 41 22N 83 40W
Bowling Green, C. 97 19 19 S 147 25 E
Bowman 116 46 12N 103 21W
Bowman I. 5 65 0 S 104 0 E
Bowmans 99 34 10 S 138 17 E
Bowmanville 106 43 55N 78 41W
Bowmore 14 55 45N 6 18W
Bowral 97 34 26 S 150 27 E
Bowraville 99 30 37 S 152 52 E
Bowron → 108 54 3N 121 50W
Bowser L. 108 56 30N 129 30W
Bowsman 109 52 14N 101 12W
Bowwood 91 17 5 S 26 20 E
Boxelder Cr. → 118 47 20N 108 30W
Boxholm 49 58 12N 15 3 E
Boxtel 16 51 36N 5 20 E
Boyabat 56 41 28N 34 42 E
Boyce 117 31 25N 92 39W
Boyer → 108 58 27N 115 57W
Boyle 15 53 58N 8 19W
Boyne → 15 53 43N 6 15W
Boyne City 114 45 13N 85 1W
Boyni Qara 65 36 20N 67 0 E
Boynton Beach 115 26 31N 80 3W
Bozburun 45 36 43N 28 8 E
Bozcaada 44 39 49N 26 3 E
Bozeman 118 45 40N 111 0W
Bozen = Bolzano 39 46 30N 11 20 E
Božepole Wielkopolski 28 54 33N 17 56 E
Boževac 42 44 32N 21 24 E
Bozouls 20 44 28N 2 43 E
Bozoum 88 6 25N 16 35 E
Bozovici 46 44 56N 22 1 E
Bra 38 44 41N 7 50 E
Brabant □ 16 50 46N 4 30 E
Brabant L. 109 55 58N 103 43W

Brabrand	49	56 9N	10 7 E
Brač	39	43 20N	16 40 E
Bracadale, L.	14	57 20N	6 30W
Bracciano	39	42 6N	12 10 E
Bracciano, L. di	39	42 8N	12 11 E
Bracebridge	106	45 2N	79 19W
Brach	83	27 31N	14 20 E
Bracieux	19	47 30N	1 30 E
Bräcke	48	62 45N	15 26 E
Brackettville	117	29 21N	100 20W
Bracki Kanal	39	43 24N	16 40 E
Brad	46	46 10N	22 50 E
Brădano →	41	40 23N	16 51 E
Braddock	112	40 24N	79 51W
Bradenton	115	27 25N	82 35W
Bradford, Can.	112	44 7N	79 34W
Bradford, U.K.	12	53 47N	1 45W
Bradford, Pa., U.S.A.	114	41 58N	78 41W
Bradford, Vt., U.S.A.	113	43 59N	72 9W
Brădiceni	46	45 3N	23 4 E
Bradley, Ark., U.S.A.	117	33 7N	93 39W
Bradley, S.D., U.S.A.	116	45 10N	97 40W
Bradley Institute	91	17 7 S	31 25 E
Bradore Bay	107	51 27N	57 18W
Bradshaw	97	15 21 S	130 16 E
Brady	117	31 8N	99 25W
Brædstrup	49	55 58N	9 37 E
Braeside	113	45 28N	76 24W
Braga	30	41 35N	8 25W
Braga □	30	41 30N	8 30W
Bragado	124	35 2 S	60 27W
Bragança, Brazil	127	1 0 S	47 2W
Bragança, Port.	30	41 48N	6 50W
Bragança □	30	41 30N	6 45W
Bragança Paulista	125	22 55 S	46 32W
Brahmanbaria	69	23 58N	91 15 E
Brahmani →	69	20 39N	86 46 E
Brahmaputra →	67	24 2N	90 59 E
Braich-y-pwll	12	52 47N	4 46W
Braidwood	99	35 27 S	149 49 E
Brăila	46	45 19N	27 59 E
Brăila □	46	45 5N	27 30 E
Brainerd	116	46 20N	94 10W
Braintree, U.K.	13	51 53N	0 34 E
Braintree, U.S.A.	113	42 11N	71 0W
Brak →	92	29 35 S	22 55 E
Brake, Niedersachsen, Ger.	24	53 19N	8 30 E
Brake, Nordrhein, Ger.	24	51 43N	9 12 E
Bräkne-Hoby	49	56 14N	15 6 E
Brakwater	92	22 28 S	17 3 E
Brålanda	49	58 34N	12 21 E
Bralorne	108	50 50N	123 45W
Bramberg	25	50 6N	10 40 E
Bramminge	49	55 28N	8 42 E
Brämön	48	62 14N	17 40 E
Brampton	106	43 45N	79 45W
Bramsche	24	52 25N	7 58 E
Bramwell	98	12 8 S	142 37 E
Branco →	126	1 20 S	61 50W
Brande	49	55 57N	9 8 E
Brandenburg	24	52 24N	12 33 E
Brandfort	92	28 40 S	26 30 E
Brandon, Can.	109	49 50N	99 57W
Brandon, U.S.A.	113	43 48N	73 4W
Brandon B.	15	52 17N	10 8W
Brandon, Mt.	15	52 15N	10 15W
Brandsen	124	35 10 S	58 15W
Brandval	47	60 19N	12 1 E
Brandvlei	92	30 25 S	20 30 E
Brandýs	26	50 10N	14 40 E
Branford	113	41 15N	72 48W
Braniewo	28	54 25N	19 50 E
Bransfield Str.	5	63 0 S	59 0W
Brańsk	28	52 44N	22 51 E
Branson, Colo., U.S.A.	117	37 4N	103 53W
Branson, Mo., U.S.A.	117	36 40N	93 18W
Brantford	106	43 10N	80 15W
Brantôme	20	45 22N	0 39 E
Branxholme	99	37 52 S	141 49 E
Branzi	38	46 0N	9 46 E
Bras d'or, L.	107	45 50N	60 50W
Brasiléia	126	11 0 S	68 45W
Brasília	127	15 47 S	47 55 E
Braslav	54	55 38N	27 0 E
Braslovce	39	46 21N	15 3 E
Braşov	46	45 38N	25 35 E
Braşov □	46	45 45N	25 15 E
Brass	85	4 35N	6 14 E
Brass →	85	4 15N	6 13 E
Brassac-les-Mines	20	45 24N	3 20 E
Brasschaat	16	51 19N	4 27 E
Brassey, Barisan	72	5 0N	117 15 E
Brasstown Bald, Mt.	115	34 54N	83 45W
Bratislava	27	48 10N	17 7 E
Bratsigovo	43	42 1N	24 22 E
Bratsk	59	56 10N	101 30 E
Brattleboro	114	42 53N	72 37W
Braţul Chilia →	46	45 25N	29 20 E
Bratul Sfintu Gheorghe →	46	45 0N	29 20 E
Braţul Sulina →	46	45 10N	29 20 E
Bratunac	42	44 13N	19 21 E
Braunau	26	48 15N	13 3 E
Braunschweig	24	52 17N	10 28 E
Braunton	13	51 6N	4 9W
Brava	63	1 20N	44 8 E
Bråviken	48	58 38N	16 32 E
Bravo del Norte →	120	25 57N	97 9W
Brawley	119	32 58N	115 30W
Bray	15	53 12N	6 6W
Bray, Pays de	19	49 46N	1 26 E
Bray-sur-Seine	19	48 25N	3 14 E
Brazeau →	108	52 55N	115 14W
Brazil	114	39 32N	87 8W
Brazil ■	127	10 0 S	50 0W
Brazilian Highlands = Brasil, Planalto	122	18 0 S	46 30W
Brazo Sur →	124	25 21 S	57 42W
Brazos →	117	28 53N	95 23W
Brazzaville	88	4 9 S	15 12 E
Brčko	42	44 54N	18 46 E
Brda →	28	53 8N	18 8 E
Breadalbane, Austral.	98	23 50 S	139 35 E
Breadalbane, U.K.	14	56 30N	4 15W
Breaksea Sd.	101	45 35 S	166 35 E
Bream Bay	101	35 56 S	174 28 E
Bream Head	101	35 51 S	174 36 E
Breas	124	25 29 S	70 24W
Brebes	73	6 52 S	109 3 E
Brechin, Can.	112	44 32N	79 10W
Brechin, U.K.	14	56 44N	2 40W
Breckenridge, Colo., U.S.A.	118	39 30N	106 2W
Breckenridge, Minn., U.S.A.	116	46 20N	96 36W
Breckenridge, Tex., U.S.A.	117	32 48N	98 55W
Břeclav	27	48 46N	16 53 E
Brecon	13	51 57N	3 23W
Brecon Beacons	13	51 53N	3 27W
Breda	16	51 35N	4 45 E
Bredaryd	49	57 10N	13 45 E
Bredasdorp	92	34 33 S	20 2 E
Bredbo	99	35 58 S	149 10 E
Bredstedt	24	54 37N	8 59 E
Bregalnica →	42	41 43N	22 9 E
Bregenz	26	47 30N	9 45 E
Bregovo	42	44 9N	22 39 E
Bréhal	18	48 53N	1 30W
Bréhat, I. de	18	48 51N	3 0W
Breiðafjörður	50	65 15N	23 15W
Breil	21	43 56N	7 31 E
Breisach	25	48 2N	7 37 E
Brejo	127	3 41 S	42 47W
Brekke	47	61 1N	5 26 E
Breloux-la-Crèche	20	46 23N	0 19W
Bremangerlandet	47	61 51N	5 0 E
Bremen	24	53 4N	8 47 E
Bremen □	24	53 6N	8 46 E
Bremerhaven	24	53 34N	8 35 E
Bremerton	118	47 30N	122 38W
Bremervörde	24	53 28N	9 10 E
Bremnes	47	59 47N	5 8 E
Bremsnes	47	63 6N	7 40 E
Brenes	31	37 32N	5 54W
Brenham	117	30 5N	96 27W
Brenner Pass	26	47 0N	11 30 E
Breno	38	45 57N	10 20 E
Brent, Can.	106	46 2N	78 29W
Brent, U.K.	13	51 33N	0 18W
Brenta →	39	45 11N	12 18 E
Brentwood	13	51 37N	0 19 E
Bréscia	38	45 33N	10 13 E
Breskens	16	51 23N	3 33 E
Breslau = Wrocław	28	51 5N	17 5 E
Bresle →	18	50 4N	1 22 E
Bresles	19	49 25N	2 13 E
Bressanone	39	46 43N	11 40 E
Bressay I.	14	60 10N	1 5W
Bresse, La	19	48 0N	6 53 E
Bresse, Plaine de	19	46 50N	5 10 E
Bressuire	18	46 51N	0 30W
Brest, France	18	48 24N	4 31W
Brest, U.S.S.R.	54	52 10N	23 40 E
Bretagne	18	48 0N	3 0W
Bretçu	46	46 7N	26 18 E
Breteuil, Eur, France	18	48 50N	0 53 E
Breteuil, Oise, France	19	49 38N	2 18 E
Breton	108	53 7N	114 28W
Breton, Pertuis	20	46 17N	1 25W
Breton Sd.	117	29 40N	89 12W
Brett, C.	101	35 10 S	174 20 E
Bretten	25	49 2N	8 43 E
Brevard	115	35 19N	82 42W
Brevik	47	59 4N	9 42 E
Brewarrina	99	30 0 S	146 51 E
Brewer	107	44 43N	68 50W
Brewster, N.Y., U.S.A.	113	41 23N	73 37W
Brewster, Wash., U.S.A.	118	48 10N	119 51W
Brewster, Kap	4	70 7N	22 0W
Brewton	115	31 9N	87 2W
Breyten	93	26 16 S	30 0 E
Breytovo	55	58 18N	37 50 E
Brežice	39	45 54N	15 35 E
Brézina	82	33 4N	1 14 E
Březnice	26	49 32N	13 57 E
Breznik	42	42 44N	22 50 E
Brezno	27	48 50N	19 40 E
Brezovo	43	42 21N	25 5 E
Bria	88	6 30N	21 58 E
Briançon	21	44 54N	6 39 E
Briare	19	47 38N	2 45 E
Bribie I.	97	27 0 S	152 58 E
Bricon	19	48 5N	5 0 E
Bricquebec	18	49 28N	1 38W
Bridgehampton	113	40 56N	72 19W
Bridgend	13	51 30N	3 35W
Bridgeport, Calif., U.S.A.	119	38 14N	119 15W
Bridgeport, Conn., U.S.A.	114	41 12N	73 12W
Bridgeport, Nebr., U.S.A.	116	41 42N	103 10W
Bridgeport, Tex., U.S.A.	117	33 15N	97 45W
Bridger	118	45 20N	108 58W
Bridgeton	114	39 29N	75 10W
Bridgetown, Austral.	96	33 58 S	116 7 E
Bridgetown, Barbados	121	13 0N	59 30W
Bridgetown, Can.	107	44 55N	65 18W
Bridgewater, Can.	107	44 25N	64 31W
Bridgewater, Mass., U.S.A.	113	41 59N	70 56W
Bridgewater, S.D., U.S.A.	116	43 34N	97 29W
Bridgewater, C.	97	38 23 S	141 23 E
Bridgnorth	13	52 33N	2 25W
Bridgton	113	44 5N	70 41W
Bridgwater	13	51 7N	3 0W
Bridlington	12	54 6N	0 11W
Bridport, Austral.	99	40 59 S	147 23 E
Bridport, U.K.	13	50 43N	2 45W
Brie-Comte-Robert	19	48 40N	2 35 E
Brie, Plaine de la	19	48 35N	3 10 E
Briec	18	48 6N	4 0W
Brienne-le-Château	19	48 24N	4 30 E
Brienon	19	48 0N	3 35 E
Brienz	25	46 46N	8 2 E
Brienzersee	25	46 44N	7 53 E
Briey	19	49 14N	5 57 E
Brig	25	46 18N	7 59 E
Brigg	12	53 33N	0 30W
Briggsdale	116	40 40N	104 20W
Brigham City	118	41 30N	112 1W
Bright	99	36 42 S	146 56 E
Brighton, Austral.	99	35 5 S	138 30 E
Brighton, Can.	106	44 2N	77 44W
Brighton, U.K.	13	50 50N	0 9W
Brighton, U.S.A.	116	39 59N	104 50W
Brignogan-Plage	18	48 40N	4 20W
Brignoles	21	43 25N	6 5 E
Brihuega	32	40 45N	2 52W
Brikama	84	13 15N	16 45W
Brilliant, Can.	108	49 19N	117 38W
Brilliant, U.S.A.	112	40 15N	80 39W
Brilon	24	51 23N	8 32 E
Brindisi	41	40 39N	17 55 E
Brinje	39	45 0N	15 9 E
Brinkley	117	34 55N	91 15W
Brinkworth	99	33 42 S	138 26 E
Brion, I.	107	47 46N	61 26W
Brionne	18	49 11N	0 43 E
Brionski	39	44 55N	13 45 E
Brioude	20	45 18N	3 24 E
Briouze	18	48 42N	0 23W
Brisbane	97	27 25 S	153 2 E
Brisbane →	99	27 24 S	153 9 E
Brisighella	39	44 14N	11 46 E
Bristol, U.K.	13	51 26N	2 35W
Bristol, Conn., U.S.A.	114	41 44N	72 57W
Bristol, Pa., U.S.A.	113	40 6N	74 52W
Bristol, R.I., U.S.A.	113	41 40N	71 15W
Bristol, S.D., U.S.A.	116	45 25N	97 43W
Bristol, Tenn., U.S.A.	115	36 36N	82 11W
Bristol B.	104	58 0N	160 0W
Bristol Channel	13	51 18N	4 30W
Bristol I.	5	58 45 S	28 0W
Bristol L.	119	34 23N	116 50W
Bristow	117	35 55N	96 28W
British Antarctic Territory □	5	66 0 S	45 0W
British Columbia □	108	55 0N	125 15W
British Guiana = Guyana ■	126	5 0N	59 0W
British Honduras = Belize ■	120	17 0N	88 30W
British Isles	8	55 0N	4 0W
Brits	93	25 37 S	27 48 E
Britstown	92	30 37 S	23 30 E
Britt	106	45 46N	80 34W
Brittany = Bretagne	18	48 0N	3 0W
Britton	116	45 50N	97 47W
Brive-la-Gaillarde	20	45 10N	1 32 E
Briviesca	32	42 32N	3 19W
Brixton	98	23 32 S	144 57 E
Brlik	58	44 0N	74 5 E
Brno	27	49 10N	16 35 E
Bro	48	59 31N	17 38 E
Broach = Bharuch	68	21 47N	73 0 E
Broad →	115	33 59N	82 39W
Broad B.	14	58 14N	6 16W
Broad Haven	15	54 20N	9 55W
Broad Law	14	55 30N	3 22W
Broad Sd.	97	22 0 S	149 45 E
Broadford	100	37 14 S	145 4 E
Broads, The	12	52 45N	1 30 E
Broadsound Ra.	97	22 50 S	149 30 E
Broadus	116	45 28N	105 27W
Broadview	109	50 22N	102 35W
Broager	49	54 53N	9 40 E
Broaryd	49	57 7N	13 15 E
Brochet	109	57 53N	101 40W
Brochet, L.	109	58 36N	101 35W
Brock	109	51 26N	108 43W
Brocken	24	51 48N	10 40 E
Brockport	114	43 12N	77 56W
Brockton	113	42 8N	71 2W
Brockville	106	44 35N	75 41W
Brockway, Mont., U.S.A.	116	47 18N	105 46W
Brockway, Pa., U.S.A.	112	41 14N	78 48W
Brocton	112	42 25N	79 26W
Brod	42	41 35N	21 17 E
Brodarevo	42	43 14N	19 44 E
Brodeur Pen.	105	72 30N	88 10W
Brodick	14	55 34N	5 9W
Brodnica	28	53 15N	19 25 E
Brody	54	50 5N	25 10 E
Brogan	118	44 14N	117 32W
Broglie	18	49 0N	0 30 E
Brok	28	52 43N	21 52 E
Broken →	100	36 24 S	145 24 E
Broken Bay	100	33 30 S	151 15 E
Broken Bow, Nebr., U.S.A.	116	41 25N	99 35W
Broken Bow, Okla., U.S.A.	117	34 2N	94 43W
Broken Hill	97	31 58 S	141 29 E
Broken Hill = Kabwe	91	14 27 S	28 28 E
Brokind	49	58 13N	15 42 E
Bromfield	13	52 25N	2 45W
Bromley	13	51 20N	0 5 E
Bromölla	49	56 5N	14 28 E
Brønderslev	49	57 16N	9 57 E
Brong-Ahafo	84	7 50N	2 0W
Bronkhorstspruit	93	25 46 S	28 45 E
Bronnitsy	55	55 27N	38 10 E
Bronte, Italy	41	37 48N	14 49 E
Bronte, U.S.A.	117	31 54N	100 18W
Bronte Park	99	42 8 S	146 30 E
Brookfield	116	39 50N	93 4W
Brookhaven	117	31 40N	90 25W
Brookings, Oreg., U.S.A.	118	42 4N	124 10W
Brookings, S.D., U.S.A.	116	44 20N	96 45W
Brooklands	98	18 10 S	144 0 E
Brooklin	112	43 55N	78 55W
Brookmere	108	49 52N	120 53W
Brooks	108	50 35N	111 55W
Brooks B.	108	50 15N	127 55W
Brooks L.	109	61 55N	106 35W
Brooks Ra.	104	68 40N	147 0W
Brooksville	115	28 32N	82 21W
Brookton	96	32 22 S	117 1 E
Brookville	114	39 25N	85 0W
Brooloo	99	26 30 S	152 43 E
Broom, L.	14	57 55N	5 15W
Broome	96	18 0 S	122 15 E
Broons	18	48 20N	2 16W
Brora	14	58 0N	3 50W
Brora →	14	58 4N	3 52W
Brösarp	49	55 43N	14 6 E
Brosna →	15	53 8N	8 0W
Broşteni	46	47 14N	25 43 E
Brothers	118	43 56N	120 39W
Brøttum	47	61 2N	10 34 E
Brou	18	48 13N	1 11 E
Brouage	20	45 52N	1 4W
Broughton Island	105	67 33N	63 0W
Broughty Ferry	14	56 29N	2 50W
Broumov	27	50 35N	16 20 E
Brouwershaven	16	51 45N	3 55 E
Brovary	54	50 34N	30 48 E
Brovst	49	57 6N	9 31 E
Browerville	116	46 3N	94 50W
Brown Willy	13	50 35N	4 34W
Brownfield	117	33 10N	102 15W
Browning	118	48 35N	113 0W
Brownlee	109	50 43N	106 1W
Brownsville, Oreg., U.S.A.	118	44 29N	123 0W
Brownsville, Tenn., U.S.A.	117	35 35N	89 15W
Brownsville, Tex., U.S.A.	117	25 56N	97 25W
Brownwood	117	31 45N	99 0W
Brownwood, L.	117	31 51N	98 35W
Brozas	31	39 37N	6 47W
Bru	47	61 32N	5 11 E
Bruas	71	4 31N	100 46 E
Bruay-en-Artois	19	50 29N	2 33 E
Bruce, Mt.	96	22 37 S	118 8 E
Bruce Pen.	112	45 0N	81 30W
Bruche →	19	48 34N	7 43 E
Bruchsal	25	49 9N	8 39 E
Bruck an der Leitha	27	48 1N	16 47 E
Bruck an der Mur	26	47 24N	15 16 E
Brückenau	25	50 17N	9 48 E
Brue →	13	51 10N	2 59W
Bruges = Brugge	16	51 13N	3 13 E
Brugg	25	47 29N	8 11 E
Brugge	16	51 13N	3 13 E
Brühl	24	50 49N	6 51 E
Brûlé	108	53 15N	117 58W
Brûlon	18	47 58N	0 15W
Brumado	127	14 14 S	41 40W
Brumath	19	48 43N	7 40 E
Brumunddal	47	60 53N	10 56 E
Brundidge	115	31 43N	85 45W
Bruneau	118	42 57N	115 55W
Bruneau →	118	42 57N	115 58W
Brunei = Bandar Seri Begawan	72	4 52N	115 0 E
Brunei ■	72	4 50N	115 0 E
Brunflo	48	63 5N	14 50 E
Brunico	39	46 50N	11 55 E
Brunkeberg	47	59 26N	8 28 E
Brunna	48	59 52N	17 25 E
Brunnen	25	46 59N	8 37 E
Brunner	101	42 27 S	171 20 E
Brunner, L.	101	42 37 S	171 27 E
Brunnsvik	48	60 12N	15 8 E
Bruno	109	52 20N	105 30W
Brunsbüttelkoog	24	53 52N	9 13 E
Brunswick, Ga., U.S.A.	115	31 10N	81 30W
Brunswick, Md., U.S.A.	114	39 20N	77 38W
Brunswick, Me., U.S.A.	107	43 53N	69 50W
Brunswick, Mo., U.S.A.	116	39 26N	93 10W
Brunswick, Ohio, U.S.A.	112	41 15N	81 50W
Brunswick = Braunschweig	24	52 17N	10 28 E
Brunswick B.	96	15 15 S	124 50 E
Brunswick, Pen. de	128	53 30 S	71 30W
Bruntál	27	50 0N	17 27 E
Bruny I.	97	43 20 S	147 15 E
Brusartsi	42	43 40N	23 5 E
Brush	116	40 17N	103 33W
Brushton	113	44 50N	74 62W
Brusio	25	46 14N	10 8 E
Brusque	125	27 5 S	49 0W
Brussel	16	50 51N	4 21 E
Brussels, Can.	112	43 45N	81 25W
Brussels, Ont., Can.	112	43 44N	81 15W
Brussels = Bruxelles	16	50 51N	4 21 E
Bruthen	99	37 42 S	147 50 E
Bruxelles	16	50 51N	4 21 E
Bruyères	19	48 10N	6 40 E
Brwinów	28	52 9N	20 40 E
Bryagovo	43	41 58N	25 8 E
Bryan, Ohio, U.S.A.	114	41 30N	84 30W
Bryan, Texas, U.S.A.	117	30 40N	96 27W
Bryan, Mt.	99	33 30 S	139 0 E
Bryanka	57	48 32N	38 45 E
Bryansk	54	53 13N	34 25 E
Bryanskoye	57	44 20N	47 10 E
Bryant	116	44 35N	97 28W
Bryne	47	58 44N	5 38 E
Bryson City	115	35 28N	83 25W
Brza Palanka	42	44 28N	22 27 E
Brzava →	42	45 21N	20 45 E
Brzeg	28	50 52N	17 30 E
Brzeg Din	28	51 16N	16 41 E
Brześć Kujawski	28	52 36N	18 55 E
Brzesko	27	49 59N	20 34 E
Brzeszcze	27	49 59N	19 10 E
Brzeziny	28	51 49N	19 42 E
Brzozów	27	49 41N	22 3 E
Bū Athlah	83	30 9N	15 39 E
Bu Craa	80	26 45N	12 50W
Bua Yai	71	15 33N	102 26 E
Buabuq	86	31 29N	25 29 E
Buapinang	73	4 40 S	121 30 E
Buayan	73	6 3N	125 6 E
Buba	84	11 40N	14 59W
Bubanza	90	3 6 S	29 23 E
Bucak	64	37 28N	30 36 E
Bucaramanga	126	7 0N	73 0W
Bucchiánico	39	42 20N	14 10 E
Bucecea	46	47 47N	26 28 E
Buchach	54	49 5N	25 25 E
Buchan	14	57 32N	2 8W
Buchan Ness	14	57 29N	1 48W
Buchanan, Can.	109	51 40N	102 45W
Buchanan, Liberia	84	5 57N	10 2W
Buchanan, L., Queens., Austral.	98	21 35 S	145 52 E
Buchanan, L., W. Australia, Austral.	96	25 33 S	123 2 E
Buchanan, L., U.S.A.	117	30 50N	98 25W
Buchans	107	48 50N	56 52W
Bucharest = Bucureşti	46	44 27N	26 10 E

Buchholz 24 53 19N 9 51 E
Buchloe 25 48 3N 10 45 E
Bückeburg 24 52 16N 9 2 E
Buckeye 119 33 28N 112 40W
Buckhannon 114 39 2N 80 10W
Buckhaven 14 56 10N 3 2W
Buckie 14 57 40N 2 58W
Buckingham, Can. 106 45 37N 75 24W
Buckingham, U.K. 13 52 0N 0 59W
Buckingham □ 13 51 50N 0 55W
Buckingham B. 97 12 10 S 135 40 E
Buckingham Can. 70 14 0N 80 5 E
Buckinguy 99 31 3 S 147 30 E
Buckland Newton 13 50 45N 2 25W
Buckley 118 47 10N 122 2W
Bucklin 117 37 37N 99 40W
Bucquoy 19 50 9N 2 43 E
Buctouche 107 46 30N 64 45W
Bucureşti 46 44 27N 26 10 E
Bucyrus 114 40 48N 83 0W
Budafok 27 47 26N 19 2 E
Budalin 67 22 20N 95 10 E
Budapest 27 47 29N 19 5 E
Budaun 68 28 5N 79 10 E
Budd Coast 5 68 0 S 112 0 E
Buddusò 40 40 35N 9 18 E
Bude 13 50 49N 4 33W
Budeşti 46 44 13N 26 30 E
Budge Budge 69 22 30N 88 5 E
Búðareyri 50 65 2N 14 13W
Búðir 50 64 49N 23 23W
Budia 32 40 38N 2 46W
Budjala 88 2 50N 19 40 E
Búdrio 39 44 31N 11 31 E
Budva 42 42 17N 18 50 E
Budzyń 28 52 54N 16 59 E
Buea 85 4 10N 9 9 E
Buena Vista, Colo., U.S.A. 119 38 56N 106 6W
Buena Vista, Va., U.S.A. 114 37 47N 79 23W
Buena Vista L. 119 35 15N 119 21W
Buenaventura, Colomb. 126 3 53N 77 4W
Buenaventura, Mexico 120 29 50N 107 30W
Buendía, Pantano de 32 40 25N 2 43W
Buenos Aires 124 34 30 S 58 20W
Buenos Aires □ 124 36 30 S 60 0W
Buenos Aires, Lago 128 46 35 S 72 30W
Buffalo, Mo., U.S.A. 117 37 40N 93 5W
Buffalo, N.Y., U.S.A. 114 42 55N 78 50W
Buffalo, Okla., U.S.A. 117 36 55N 99 42W
Buffalo, S.D., U.S.A. 116 45 39N 103 31W
Buffalo, Wyo., U.S.A. 118 44 25N 106 50W
Buffalo → 108 60 5N 115 5W
Buffalo Head Hills 108 57 25N 115 55W
Buffalo L. 108 52 27N 112 54W
Buffalo Narrows 109 55 51N 108 29W
Buffels → 92 29 36 S 17 15 E
Buford 115 34 5N 84 0W
Bug →, Poland 28 52 31N 21 5 E
Bug →, U.S.S.R. 56 46 59N 31 58 E
Buga 126 4 0N 76 15W
Buganda □ 90 0 0N 31 30 E
Buganga 90 0 3 S 32 0 E
Bugeat 20 45 36N 1 55 E
Bugel, Tanjung 72 6 26 S 111 3 E
Bugojno 42 44 2N 17 25 E
Bugsuk 72 8 15N 117 15 E
Bugt 76 48 47N 121 56 E
Bugue, Le 20 44 55N 0 56 E
Bugulma 52 54 33N 52 48 E
Buguma 85 4 42N 6 55 E
Buguruslan 52 53 39N 52 26 E
Buhăeşti 46 46 47N 27 32 E
Buheirat-Murrat-el-Kubra 86 30 15N 32 40 E
Buhl, Idaho, U.S.A. 118 42 35N 114 54W
Buhl, Minn., U.S.A. 116 47 30N 92 46W
Buhuşi 46 46 41N 26 45 E
Buick 117 37 38N 91 2W
Builth Wells 13 52 10N 3 26W
Buinsk 55 55 0N 48 18 E
Buir Nur 75 47 50N 117 42 E
Buis-les-Baronnies 21 44 17N 5 16 E
Buitrago 30 41 0N 3 38W
Bujalance 31 37 54N 4 23W
Buján 30 42 59N 8 36W
Bujanovac 42 42 28N 21 44 E
Bujaraloz 32 41 29N 0 10W
Buje 39 45 24N 13 39 E
Bujumbura (Usumbura) 90 3 16 S 29 18 E
Bük 27 47 22N 16 45 E
Buk 28 52 21N 16 30 E
Bukachacha 59 52 55N 116 50 E
Bukama 91 9 10 S 25 50 E
Bukavu 90 2 20 S 28 52 E
Bukene 90 4 15 S 32 48 E
Bukhara 58 39 48N 64 25 E
Bukima 90 1 50 S 33 25 E
Bukittinggi 72 0 20 S 100 20 E
Bukkapatnam 70 14 14N 77 46 E
Bukoba 90 1 20 S 31 49 E
Bukoba □ 90 1 30 S 32 0 E
Bukowno 27 50 17N 19 35 E
Bukuru 85 9 42N 8 48 E
Bukuya 90 0 40N 31 52 E
Bula, Guin.-Biss. 84 12 7N 15 43W
Bula, Indon. 73 3 6 S 130 30 E
Bulan 73 12 40N 123 52 E
Bulandshahr 68 28 28N 77 51 E
Bûlâq 86 25 10N 30 38 E
Bulawayo 91 20 7 S 28 32 E
Buldana 68 20 30N 76 18 E
Bulgan 75 48 45N 103 34 E
Bulgaria ■ 43 42 35N 25 30 E
Bulgroo 99 25 47 S 143 58 E
Bulhar 63 10 25N 44 30 E
Buli, Teluk 73 1 5N 128 25 E
Buliluyan, C. 72 8 20N 117 15 E
Bulki 87 6 11N 36 31 E
Bulkley → 108 55 15N 127 40W
Bull Shoals L. 117 36 40N 93 5W
Bullaque → 31 38 59N 4 17W
Bullas 33 38 2N 1 40W
Bulle 25 46 37N 7 3 E
Buller, Mt. 100 37 10 S 146 28 E
Bullfinch 96 30 58 S 119 3 E
Bulli 99 34 15 S 150 57 E
Bullock Creek 98 17 43 S 144 31 E
Bulloo → 97 28 43 S 142 30 E
Bulloo Downs 99 28 31 S 142 57 E
Bulloo L. 99 28 43 S 142 25 E
Bulls 101 40 10 S 175 24 E
Bully-les-Mines 19 50 27N 2 44 E
Bulnes 124 36 42 S 72 19W
Bulo Burti 63 3 50N 45 33 E
Bulolo 98 7 10 S 146 40 E
Bulqiza 44 41 30N 20 21 E
Bulsar 68 20 40N 72 58 E
Bultfontein 92 28 18 S 26 10 E
Bulu Karakelong 73 4 35N 126 50 E
Bulukumba 73 5 33 S 120 11 E
Bulun 59 70 37N 127 30 E
Bumba 88 2 13N 22 30 E
Bumbiri I. 90 1 40 S 31 55 E
Bumble Bee 119 34 8N 112 18W
Bumhpa Bum 67 26 51N 97 14 E
Bumi → 91 17 0 S 28 20 E
Buna, Kenya 90 2 58N 39 30 E
Buna, P.N.G. 98 8 42 S 148 27 E
Bunazi 90 1 3 S 31 23 E
Bunbah, Khalīj 81 32 20N 23 15 E
Bunbury 96 33 20 S 115 35 E
Buncrana 15 55 8N 7 28W
Bundaberg 97 24 54 S 152 22 E
Bünde 24 52 11N 8 33 E
Bundi 68 25 30N 75 35 E
Bundoran 15 54 24N 8 17W
Bundukia 87 5 14N 30 55 E
Bundure 100 35 10 S 146 1 E
Bungendore 100 35 14 S 149 30 E
Bungo-Suidō 74 33 0N 132 15 E
Bungoma 90 0 34N 34 34 E
Bungu 90 7 35 S 39 0 E
Bungun Shara 75 49 0N 104 0 E
Bunia 90 1 35N 30 20 E
Bunji 69 35 45N 74 40 E
Bunju 72 3 35N 117 50 E
Bunkerville 119 36 47N 114 6W
Bunkie 117 31 1N 92 12W
Bunnell 115 29 28N 81 12W
Buñol 33 39 25N 0 47W
Buntok 72 1 40 S 114 58 E
Bununu 85 9 51N 9 32 E
Bununu Dass 85 10 0N 9 31 E
Bunza 85 12 8N 4 0 E
Buol 73 1 15N 121 32 E
Buorkhaya, Mys 59 71 50N 132 40 E
Buqayq 64 26 0N 49 45 E
Buqei'a 62 32 58N 35 20 E
Bur Acaba 63 3 12N 44 20 E
Bûr Fuad 86 31 15N 32 20 E
Bûr Safâga 86 26 43N 33 57 E
Bûr Sa'îd 86 31 16N 32 18 E
Bûr Sûdân 86 19 32N 37 9 E
Bûr Taufiq 86 29 54N 32 32 E
Bura 90 1 4 S 39 58 E
Buraimī, Al Wāhāt al 65 24 10N 55 43 E
Burao 63 9 32N 45 32 E
Buras 117 29 20N 89 33W
Buraydah 64 26 20N 44 8 E
Burbank 119 34 9N 118 23W
Burcher 99 33 30 S 147 16 E
Burdekin → 98 19 38 S 147 25 E
Burdett 108 49 50N 111 32W
Burdur 64 37 45N 30 22 E
Burdwan 69 23 14N 87 39 E
Bure 87 10 40N 37 4 E
Bure → 12 52 38N 1 45 E
Bureba, La 32 42 36N 3 24W
Büren 24 51 33N 8 34 E
Bureya → 59 49 27N 129 30 E
Burford 112 43 7N 80 27W
Burg, Magdeburg, Ger. 24 52 16N 11 50 E
Burg, Schleswig-Holstein, Ger. 24 54 25N 11 10 E
Burg el Arab 86 30 54N 29 32 E
Burg et Tuyur 86 20 55N 27 56 E
Burgas 43 42 33N 27 29 E
Burgaski Zaliv 43 42 30N 27 39 E
Burgdorf, Ger. 24 52 27N 10 0 E
Burgdorf, Switz. 25 47 3N 7 37 E
Burgenland □ 27 47 20N 16 20 E
Burgeo 107 47 37N 57 38W
Burgersdorp 92 31 0 S 26 20 E
Burghausen 25 48 10N 12 50 E
Búrgio 40 37 35N 13 18 E
Burglengenfeld 25 49 11N 12 2 E
Burgo de Osma 32 41 35N 3 4W
Burgohondo 30 40 26N 4 47W
Burgos 32 42 21N 3 41W
Burgos □ 32 42 21N 3 42W
Burgstädt 24 50 55N 12 49 E
Burgsteinfurt 24 52 9N 7 23 E
Burgsvik 49 57 3N 18 19 E
Burguillos del Cerro 31 38 23N 6 35W
Burgundy = Bourgogne 19 47 0N 4 30 E
Burhanpur 68 21 18N 76 14 E
Burhou 18 49 45N 2 15W
Buri Pen. 87 15 25N 39 55 E
Burias 73 12 55N 123 5 E
Burica, Pta. 121 8 3N 82 51W
Burigi, L. 90 2 2 S 31 22 E
Burin 107 47 1N 55 14W
Būrīn 62 32 11N 35 15 E
Buriram 71 15 0N 103 0 E
Burji 87 5 29N 37 51 E
Burkburnett 117 34 7N 98 35W
Burke 118 47 31N 115 56W
Burke → 98 23 12 S 139 33 E
Burketown 97 17 45 S 139 33 E
Burk's Falls 106 45 37N 79 24W
Burley 118 42 37N 113 55W
Burlington, Can. 112 43 18N 79 45W
Burlington, Colo., U.S.A. 116 39 21N 102 18W
Burlington, Iowa, U.S.A. 116 40 50N 91 5W
Burlington, Kans., U.S.A. 116 38 15N 95 47W
Burlington, N.C., U.S.A. 115 36 7N 79 27W
Burlington, N.J., U.S.A. 114 40 5N 74 50W
Burlington, Vt., U.S.A. 114 44 27N 73 14W
Burlington, Wash., U.S.A. 118 48 29N 122 19W
Burlington, Wis., U.S.A. 114 42 41N 88 18W
Burlyu-Tyube 58 46 30N 79 10 E
Burma ■ 67 21 0N 96 30 E
Burnaby I. 108 52 25N 131 19W
Burnet 117 30 45N 98 11W
Burnett → 97 24 45 S 152 23 E
Burney 118 40 56N 121 41W
Burnham 112 40 37N 77 34W
Burnie 97 41 4 S 145 56 E
Burnley 12 53 47N 2 15W
Burns, Oreg., U.S.A. 118 43 40N 119 4W
Burns, Wyo., U.S.A. 116 41 13N 104 18W
Burns Lake 108 54 20N 125 45W
Burnside → 104 66 51N 108 4W
Burnt River 112 44 41N 78 42W
Burntwood → 109 56 8N 96 34W
Burntwood L. 109 55 22N 100 26W
Burqā 62 32 18N 35 11 E
Burqān 64 29 0N 47 57 E
Burqin 75 47 43N 87 0 E
Burra 97 33 40 S 138 55 E
Burragorang, L. 100 33 52 S 150 37 E
Burreli 44 41 36N 20 1 E
Burrendong, L. 100 32 45 S 149 10 E
Burrewarra Pt. 100 35 50 S 150 15 E
Burriana 32 39 50N 0 4W
Burrinjuck Dam 100 35 0 S 148 34 E
Burrinjuck Res. 99 35 0 S 148 36 E
Burro, Serranías del 120 29 0N 102 0W
Burruyacú 124 26 30 S 64 40W
Burry Port 13 51 41N 4 17W
Bursa 64 40 15N 29 5 E
Burseryd 49 57 12N 13 17 E
Burstall 109 50 39N 109 54W
Burton L. 106 54 45N 78 20W
Burton-upon-Trent 12 52 48N 1 39W
Burtundy 99 33 45 S 142 15 E
Buru 73 3 30 S 126 30 E
Burullus, Bahra el 86 31 25N 31 0 E
Burundi ■ 90 3 15 S 30 0 E
Burung 72 0 24N 103 33 E
Bururi 90 3 57 S 29 37 E
Burutu 85 5 20N 5 29 E
Burwell 116 41 49N 99 8W
Bury 12 53 36N 2 19W
Bury St. Edmunds 13 52 15N 0 42 E
Buryat A.S.S.R. □ 59 53 0N 110 0 E
Buryn 54 51 13N 33 50 E
Burzenin 28 51 28N 18 47 E
Busalla 38 44 34N 8 58 E
Busango Swamp 91 14 15 S 25 45 E
Buşayyah 64 30 0N 46 10 E
Busca 38 44 31N 7 29 E
Bushati 44 41 58N 19 34 E
Bushell 109 59 31N 108 45W
Bushenyi 90 0 35 S 30 10 E
Bushnell, Ill., U.S.A. 116 40 32N 90 30W
Bushnell, Nebr., U.S.A. 116 41 18N 103 50W
Busia □ 90 0 25N 34 6 E
Busie 84 10 29N 2 22W
Businga 88 3 16N 20 59 E
Buskerud fylke □ 47 60 13N 9 0 E
Busko Zdrój 28 50 28N 20 42 E
Busoga □ 90 0 5N 33 30 E
Busovača 42 44 6N 17 53 E
Busra ash Shām 64 32 30N 36 25 E
Bussang 19 47 50N 6 50 E
Busselton 96 33 42 S 115 15 E
Busseto 38 44 59N 10 2 E
Bussum 16 52 16N 5 10 E
Bustard Hd. 97 24 0 S 151 48 E
Busto Arsizio 38 45 40N 8 50 E
Busto, C. 30 43 34N 6 28W
Busu-Djanoa 88 1 43N 21 23 E
Busuanga 73 12 10N 120 0 E
Büsum 24 54 7N 8 50 E
Buta 90 2 50N 24 53 E
Butare 90 2 31 S 29 52 E
Bute 14 55 48N 5 2W
Bute Inlet 108 50 40N 124 53W
Butemba 90 1 9N 31 37 E
Butembo 90 0 9N 29 18 E
Butera 41 37 10N 14 10 E
Butha Qi 75 48 0N 122 32 E
Butiaba 90 1 50N 31 20 E
Butler, Mo., U.S.A. 116 38 17N 94 18W
Butler, Pa., U.S.A. 114 40 52N 79 52W
Butom Odrzánski 28 51 44N 15 48 E
Butte, Mont., U.S.A. 118 46 0N 112 31W
Butte, Nebr., U.S.A. 116 42 56N 98 54W
Butterworth 71 5 24N 100 23 E
Button B. 109 58 45N 94 23W
Butuan 73 8 57N 125 33 E
Butuku-Luba 85 3 29N 8 33 E
Butung 73 5 0 S 122 45 E
Buturlinovka 55 50 50N 40 35 E
Butzbach 24 50 24N 8 40 E
Bützow 24 53 51N 11 59 E
Buxar 69 25 34N 83 58 E
Buxton, S. Afr. 92 27 38 S 24 42 E
Buxton, U.K. 12 53 16N 1 54W
Buxy 19 46 44N 4 40 E
Buy 55 58 28N 41 28 E
Buyaga 59 59 50N 127 0 E
Buynaksk 57 42 48N 47 7 E
Büyük Çekmece 43 41 2N 28 35 E
Büyük Kemikli Burun 44 40 20N 26 15 E
Buzançais 18 46 54N 1 25 E
Buzău 46 45 10N 26 50 E
Buzău □ 46 45 20N 26 30 E
Buzău → 46 45 10N 27 20 E
Buzău, Pasul 46 45 35N 26 12 E
Buzaymah 81 24 35N 22 2 E
Buzen 74 33 35N 131 5 E
Buzet 39 45 24N 13 58 E
Buzi → 91 19 50 S 34 43 E
Buziaş 42 45 38N 21 36 E
Buzuluk 52 52 48N 52 12 E
Buzuluk → 55 50 15N 42 7 E
Buzzards Bay 114 41 45N 70 38W
Bwana Mkubwe 91 13 8 S 28 38 E
Byala, Ruse, Bulg. 43 43 28N 25 44 E
Byala, Varna, Bulg. 43 42 53N 27 55 E
Byala Slatina 43 43 26N 23 55 E
Byandovan, Mys 57 39 45N 49 28 E
Bychawa 28 51 1N 22 36 E
Byczyna 28 51 7N 18 12 E
Bydgoszcz 28 53 10N 18 0 E
Bydgoszcz □ 28 53 16N 17 33 E
Byelorussian S.S.R. □ 54 53 30N 27 0 E
Byers 116 39 46N 104 13W
Byesville 112 39 56N 81 32W
Bygland 47 58 50N 7 48 E
Byglandsfjord 47 58 40N 7 50 E
Byglandsfjorden 47 58 44N 7 50 E
Byhalia 117 34 53N 89 41W
Bykhov 54 53 31N 30 14 E
Bykle 47 59 20N 7 22 E
Bykovo 57 49 50N 45 25 E
Bylas 119 33 11N 110 9W
Bylderup 49 54 57N 9 6 E
Bylot I. 105 73 13N 78 34W
Byrd, C. 5 69 38 S 76 7W
Byrd Land 5 79 30 S 125 0W
Byrd Sub-Glacial Basin 5 82 0 S 120 0W
Byrock 99 30 40 S 146 27 E
Byron, C. 97 28 38 S 153 40 E
Byrranga, Gory 59 75 0N 100 0 E
Byrum 49 57 16N 11 0 E
Byske 50 64 57N 21 11 E
Byske älv → 50 64 57N 21 13 E
Bystrzyca →, Lublin, Poland 28 51 21N 22 46 E
Bystrzyca →, Wrocław, Poland 28 51 12N 16 55 E
Bystrzyca Kłodzka 28 50 19N 16 39 E
Byten 54 52 50N 25 27 E
Bytom 28 50 25N 18 54 E
Bytów 28 54 10N 17 30 E
Byumba 90 1 35 S 30 4 E
Bzenec 27 48 58N 17 18 E
Bzura → 28 52 25N 20 15 E

C

Ca Mau = Quan Long 71 9 7N 105 8 E
Ca Mau, Mui = Bai Bung 71 8 35N 104 42 E
Caacupé 124 25 23 S 57 5W
Caála 89 12 46 S 15 30 E
Caamano Sd. 108 52 55N 129 25W
Caazapá 124 26 8 S 56 19W
Caazapá □ 125 26 10 S 56 0W
Caballeria, C. de 32 40 5N 4 5 E
Cabañaquinta 30 43 10N 5 38W
Cabanatuan 73 15 30N 120 58 E
Cabanes 32 40 9N 0 2 E
Cabano 107 47 40N 68 56W
Čabar 39 45 36N 14 39 E
Cabedelo 127 7 0 S 34 50W
Cabeza del Buey 31 38 44N 5 13W
Cabildo 124 32 30 S 71 5W
Cabimas 126 10 23N 71 25W
Cabinda 88 5 33 S 12 11 E
Cabinda □ 88 5 0 S 12 30 E
Cabinet Mts. 118 48 0N 115 30W
Cabo Blanco 128 47 15 S 65 47W
Cabo Frio 125 22 51 S 42 3W
Cabo Pantoja 126 1 0 S 75 10W
Cabonga, Réservoir 106 47 20N 76 40W
Cabool 117 37 10N 92 8W
Caboolture 99 27 5 S 152 58 E
Cabora Bassa Dam 91 15 20 S 32 50 E
Caborca (Heroica) 120 30 40N 112 10W
Cabot, Mt. 113 44 30N 71 25W
Cabot Strait 107 47 15N 59 40W
Cabra 31 37 30N 4 28W
Cabra del Santo Cristo 33 37 42N 3 16W
Cábras 40 39 57N 8 30 E
Cabrera, I. 33 39 8N 2 57 E
Cabrera, Sierra 30 42 12N 6 40W
Cabri 109 50 35N 108 25W
Cabriel → 33 39 14N 1 3W
Cacabelos 30 42 36N 6 44W
Čačak 42 43 54N 20 20 E
Cáceres, Brazil 126 16 5 S 57 40W
Cáceres, Spain 31 39 26N 6 23W
Cáceres □ 31 39 45N 6 0W
Cache Bay 106 46 22N 80 0W
Cachepo 31 37 20N 7 49W
Cachéu 84 12 14N 16 8W
Cachi 124 25 5 S 66 10W
Cachimbo, Serra do 127 9 30 S 55 0W
Cachoeira 127 12 30 S 39 0W
Cachoeira de Itapemirim 125 20 51 S 41 7W
Cachoeira do Sul 125 30 3 S 52 53W
Cachopo 31 37 20N 7 49W
Cacólo 88 10 9 S 19 21 E
Caconda 89 13 48 S 15 8 E
Cadarache, Barrage de 21 43 42N 5 47 E
Čadca 27 49 26N 18 45 E
Caddo 117 34 8N 96 18W
Cader Idris 12 52 43N 3 56W
Cadí, Sierra del 32 42 17N 1 42 E
Cadillac, Can. 106 48 14N 78 23W
Cadillac, France 20 44 38N 0 20W
Cadillac, U.S.A. 114 44 16N 85 25W
Cadiz 73 10 57N 123 15 E
Cádiz 31 36 30N 6 20W
Cadiz 112 40 13N 81 0W
Cádiz □ 31 36 36N 5 45W
Cádiz, G. de 31 36 40N 7 0W
Cadomin 108 53 2N 117 20W
Cadotte → 108 56 43N 117 10W
Cadours 20 43 44N 1 2 E
Caen 18 49 10N 0 22W
Caernarfon 12 53 8N 4 17W
Caernarfon B. 12 53 4N 4 40W
Caernarvon = Caernarfon 12 53 8N 4 17W
Caerphilly 13 51 34N 3 13W
Caesarea 62 32 30N 34 53 E
Caeté 127 19 55 S 43 40W

Caetité 127 13 50S 42 32W
Cafayate 124 26 2S 66 0W
Cafu 92 16 30S 15 8 E
Cagayan 73 9 39N 121 16 E
Cagayan → 73 18 25N 121 42 E
Cagayan de Oro 73 8 30N 124 40 E
Cagli 39 43 32N 12 38 E
Cágliari 40 39 15N 9 6 E
Cágliari, G. di 40 39 8N 9 10 E
Cagnano Varano 41 41 49N 15 47 E
Cagnes-sur-Mer 21 43 40N 7 9 E
Caguas 121 18 14N 66 4W
Caha Mts. 15 51 45N 9 40W
Cahama 92 16 17S 14 19 E
Caher 15 52 23N 7 56W
Cahersiveen 15 51 57N 10 13W
Cahore Pt. 15 52 34N 6 11W
Cahors 20 44 27N 1 27 E
Cahuapanas 126 5 15S 77 0W
Caianda 91 11 2S 23 31 E
Caibarién 121 22 30N 79 30W
Caicara 126 7 38N 66 10W
Caicó 127 6 20S 37 0W
Caicos Is. 121 21 40N 71 40W
Caicos Passage 121 22 45N 72 45W
Cainsville 112 43 9N 80 15W
Caird Coast 5 75 0S 25 0W
Cairn Gorm 14 57 7N 3 40W
Cairn Toul 14 57 3N 3 44W
Cairngorm Mts. 14 57 6N 3 42W
Cairns 97 16 57S 145 45 E
Cairo, Ga., U.S.A. 115 30 52N 84 12W
Cairo, Illinois, U.S.A. 117 37 0N 89 10W
Cairo = El Qâhira 86 30 1N 31 14 E
Cairo Montenotte 38 44 23N 8 16 E
Caithness, Ord of 14 58 9N 3 37W
Caiundo 89 15 50S 17 28 E
Caiza 126 20 2S 65 40W
Cajamarca 126 7 5S 78 28W
Cajarc 20 44 29N 1 50 E
Cajàzeiras 127 6 52S 38 30W
Čajetina 42 43 47N 19 42 E
Čajniče 42 43 34N 19 5 E
Çakirgol 57 40 33N 39 40 E
Čakovec 39 46 23N 16 26 E
Cala 31 37 59N 6 21W
Cala → 31 37 38N 6 5W
Cala Cadolar, Punta de 33 38 38N 1 35 E
Calabar 85 4 57N 8 20 E
Calábria □ 41 39 24N 16 30 E
Calaburras, Pta. de 31 36 30N 4 38W
Calaceite 32 41 1N 0 11 E
Calafat 46 43 58N 22 59 E
Calafate 128 50 19S 72 15W
Calahorra 32 42 18N 1 59W
Calais, France 19 50 57N 1 56 E
Calais, U.S.A. 107 45 11N 67 20W
Calais, Pas de 19 50 57N 1 20 E
Calalaste, Cord. de 124 25 0S 67 0W
Calama, Brazil 126 8 0S 62 50W
Calama, Chile 124 22 30S 68 55W
Calamar, Bolívar, Colomb. 126 10 15N 74 55W
Calamar, Vaupés, Colomb. 126 1 58N 72 32W
Calamian Group 73 11 50N 119 55 E
Calamocha 32 40 50N 1 17W
Calañas 31 37 40N 6 53W
Calanda 32 40 56N 0 15W
Calang 72 4 37N 95 37 E
Calangiánus 40 40 56N 9 12 E
Calapan 73 13 25N 121 7 E
Călăraşi 46 44 12N 27 20 E
Calasparra 33 38 14N 1 41W
Calatafimi 40 37 56N 12 50 E
Calatayud 32 41 20N 1 40W
Calauag 73 13 55N 122 15 E
Calavà, C. 41 38 11N 14 55 E
Calavite, Cape 73 13 26N 120 20 E
Calbayog 73 12 4N 124 38 E
Calbe 24 51 57N 11 47 E
Calca 126 13 22S 72 0W
Calcasieu L. 117 30 0N 93 17W
Calci 38 43 44N 10 31 E
Calcutta 69 22 36N 88 24 E
Caldaro 39 46 23N 11 15 E
Caldas da Rainha 31 39 24N 9 8W
Caldas de Reyes 30 42 36N 8 39W
Calder → 12 53 44N 1 21W
Caldera 124 27 5S 70 55W
Caldwell, Idaho, U.S.A. 118 43 45N 116 42W
Caldwell, Kans., U.S.A. 117 37 5N 97 37W
Caldwell, Texas, U.S.A. 117 30 30N 96 42W
Caledon 92 34 14S 19 26 E
Caledon → 92 30 31S 26 5 E
Caledon B. 97 12 45S 137 0 E
Caledonia, Can. 112 43 7N 79 58W
Caledonia, U.S.A. 112 42 57N 77 54W
Calella 32 41 37N 2 40 E
Calemba 92 16 0S 15 44 E
Calera, La 124 32 50S 71 10W
Calexico 119 32 40N 115 33W
Calf of Man 12 54 4N 4 48W
Calgary 108 51 0N 114 10W
Calhoun 115 34 30N 84 55W
Cali 126 3 25N 76 35W
Calicoan 73 10 59N 125 50 E
Calicut (Kozhikode) 70 11 15N 75 43 E
Caliente 119 37 36N 114 34W
California, Mo., U.S.A. 116 38 37N 92 30W
California, Pa., U.S.A. 112 40 5N 79 55W
California □ 119 37 25N 120 0W
California, Baja, T.N. □ 120 30 0N 115 0W
California, Baja, T.S. □ 120 25 50N 111 50W
California, Golfo de 120 27 0N 111 0W
California, Lr. = California, Baja 120 25 50N 111 50W
Călimăneşti 46 45 14N 24 20 E
Călimani, Munţii 46 47 12N 25 0 E
Călineşti 46 45 21N 24 18 E
Calingasta 124 31 15S 69 30W
Calipatria 119 33 8N 115 30W
Calistoga 118 38 36N 122 32W
Calitri 41 40 54N 15 25 E
Callabonna, L. 97 29 40S 140 5 E
Callac 18 48 25N 3 27W
Callan 15 52 33N 7 25W
Callander 14 56 15N 4 14W
Callao 126 12 0S 77 0W
Callaway 116 41 20N 99 56W
Callide 98 24 18S 150 28 E
Calling Lake 108 55 15N 113 12W
Callosa de Ensarriá. 33 38 40N 0 8W
Callosa de Segura 33 38 7N 0 53W
Calne 12 51 26N 2 0W
Calola 92 16 25S 17 48 E
Calore → 41 41 11N 14 28 E
Caloundra 99 26 45S 153 10 E
Calpe 33 38 39N 0 3 E
Calstock 106 49 47N 84 9W
Caltabellotta 40 37 36N 13 11 E
Caltagirone 41 37 13N 14 30 E
Caltanissetta 41 37 30N 14 3 E
Caluire-et-Cuire 21 45 49N 4 51 E
Calulo 88 10 1S 14 56 E
Calumet 114 47 14N 88 27W
Calunda 89 12 7S 23 36 E
Caluso 38 45 18N 7 52 E
Calvados □ 18 49 5N 0 15W
Calvert 117 30 59N 96 40W
Calvert I. 108 51 30N 128 0W
Calvinia 92 31 28S 19 45 E
Calw 25 48 43N 8 44 E
Calzada Almuradiel 33 38 32N 3 28W
Calzada de Calatrava 31 38 42N 3 46W
Cam → 13 52 21N 0 16 E
Cam Lam 71 11 54N 109 10 E
Cam Ranh 71 11 54N 109 12 E
Camabatela 88 8 20S 15 26 E
Camacupa 89 11 58S 17 22 E
Camagüey 121 21 20N 78 0W
Camaiore 38 43 57N 10 18 E
Camaná 126 16 30S 72 50W
Camaquã → 125 31 17S 51 47W
Camarat, C. 21 43 12N 6 41 E
Camaret 18 48 16N 4 37W
Camargo 126 20 38S 65 15 E
Camargue 21 43 34N 4 34 E
Camariñas 30 43 8N 9 12W
Camarón, C. 121 16 0N 85 0W
Camarones 128 44 50S 65 40W
Camas 118 45 35N 122 24W
Camas Valley 118 43 0N 123 46W
Cambados 30 42 31N 8 49W
Cambará 125 23 2S 50 5W
Cambay 68 22 23N 72 33 E
Cambay, G. of 68 20 45N 72 30 E
Cambil 33 37 40N 3 33W
Cambo-les-Bains 20 43 22N 1 23W
Cambodia ■ 71 12 15N 105 0 E
Camborne 13 50 13N 5 18W
Cambrai 19 50 11N 3 14 E
Cambria 119 35 39N 121 6W
Cambrian Mts. 13 52 25N 3 52W
Cambridge, Can. 106 43 23N 80 15W
Cambridge, N.Z. 101 37 54S 175 29 E
Cambridge, U.K. 13 52 13N 0 8 E
Cambridge, Idaho, U.S.A. 118 44 36N 116 40W
Cambridge, Mass., U.S.A. 114 42 20N 71 8W
Cambridge, Md., U.S.A. 114 38 33N 76 2W
Cambridge, Minn., U.S.A. 116 45 34N 93 15W
Cambridge, N.Y., U.S.A. 113 43 2N 73 22W
Cambridge, Nebr., U.S.A. 116 40 20N 100 12W
Cambridge, Ohio, U.S.A. 114 40 1N 81 35W
Cambridge Bay 104 69 10N 105 0W
Cambridge Gulf 96 14 55S 128 15 E
Cambridge Springs 112 41 47N 80 4W
Cambridgeshire □ 13 52 12N 0 7 E
Cambrils 32 41 8N 1 3 E
Cambuci 125 21 35S 41 55W
Camden, Ala., U.S.A. 115 31 59N 87 15W
Camden, Ark., U.S.A. 117 33 40N 92 50W
Camden, Me., U.S.A. 107 44 14N 69 6W
Camden, N.J., U.S.A. 114 39 57N 75 7W
Camden, S.C., U.S.A. 115 34 17N 80 34W
Camdenton 117 38 0N 92 45W
Camembert 18 48 53N 0 10 E
Cámeri 38 45 30N 8 40 E
Camerino 39 43 10N 13 4 E
Cameron, Ariz., U.S.A. 119 35 55N 111 31W
Cameron, La., U.S.A. 117 29 50N 93 18W
Cameron, Mo., U.S.A. 116 39 42N 94 14W
Cameron, Tex., U.S.A. 117 30 53N 97 0W
Cameron Falls 106 49 8N 88 19W
Cameron Highlands 71 4 27N 101 22 E
Cameron Hills 108 59 48N 118 0W
Cameroon ■ 88 6 0N 12 30 E
Camerota 41 40 2N 15 21 E
Cameroun → 85 4 0N 9 35 E
Cameroun, Mt. 88 4 13N 9 10 E
Cametá 127 2 12S 49 30W
Camiguin 73 8 55N 123 55 E
Caminha 30 41 50N 8 50W
Camino 118 38 47N 120 40W
Camira Creek 99 29 15S 152 58 E
Cammal 112 41 24N 77 28W
Camocim 127 2 55S 40 50W
Camogli 38 44 21N 9 9 E
Camooweal 97 19 56S 138 7 E
Camopi → 127 3 10N 52 20W
Camp Crook 116 45 36N 103 59W
Camp Wood 117 29 41N 100 0W
Campagna 41 40 40N 15 5 E
Campana 124 34 10S 58 55W
Campana, I. 128 48 20S 75 20W
Campanario 31 38 52N 5 36W
Campania □ 41 40 50N 14 45 E
Campbell 112 41 5N 80 36W
Campbell I. 94 52 30S 169 0 E
Campbell L. 109 63 14N 106 55W
Campbell River 108 50 5N 125 20W
Campbell Town 99 41 52S 147 30 E
Campbellford 112 44 18N 77 48W
Campbellsville 114 37 23N 85 21W
Campbellton 107 47 57N 66 43W
Campbelltown 99 34 4S 150 49 E
Campbeltown 14 55 25N 5 36W
Campeche 120 19 50N 90 32W
Campeche □ 120 19 50N 90 32W
Campeche, Bahía de 120 19 30N 93 0W
Camperdown 99 38 14S 143 9 E
Camperville 109 51 59N 100 9W
Campi Salentina 41 40 22N 18 2 E
Campidano 40 39 30N 8 40 E
Campillo de Altobuey 32 39 36N 1 49W
Campillo de Llerena 31 38 30N 5 50W
Campillos 31 37 4N 4 51W
Campina Grande 127 7 20S 35 47W
Campiña, La 31 37 45N 4 45W
Campinas 125 22 50S 47 0W
Campli 39 42 44N 13 40 E
Campo, Camer. 88 2 22N 9 50 E
Campo, Spain 32 42 25N 0 24 E
Campo Belo 127 20 52S 45 16W
Campo de Criptana 33 39 24N 3 7W
Campo de Gibraltar 31 36 15N 5 25W
Campo Formoso 127 10 30S 40 20W
Campo Grande 127 20 25S 54 40W
Campo Maíor 127 4 50S 42 12W
Campo Maior 31 38 59N 7 7W
Campo Túres 39 46 53N 11 55 E
Campoalegre 126 2 41N 75 20W
Campobasso 41 41 34N 14 40 E
Campobello di Licata 40 37 16N 13 55 E
Campobello di Mazara 40 37 38N 12 45 E
Campofelice 40 37 54N 13 53 E
Camporeale 40 37 53N 13 3 E
Campos 125 21 50S 41 20W
Campos Belos 127 13 10S 47 3W
Campos del Puerto 33 39 26N 3 1 E
Campos Novos 125 27 21S 51 50W
Camprodón 32 42 19N 2 23 E
Campuya → 126 1 40S 73 30W
Camrose 108 53 0N 112 50W
Camsell Portage 109 59 37N 109 15W
Can Tho 71 10 2N 105 46 E
Canaan 113 42 1N 73 20W
Canada ■ 104 60 0N 100 0W
Cañada de Gómez 124 32 40S 61 30W
Canadian 117 35 56N 100 25W
Canadian → 117 35 27N 95 3W
Canakkale 44 40 8N 26 30 E
Canakkale Boğazi 44 40 0N 26 0 E
Canal Flats 108 50 10N 115 48W
Canal latéral à la Garonne 20 44 25N 0 15 E
Canalejas 124 35 15S 66 34W
Canals, Argent. 124 33 35S 62 53W
Canals, Spain 33 38 58N 0 35W
Canandaigua 114 42 55N 77 18W
Cananea 120 31 0N 110 20W
Canarias, Islas 80 28 30N 16 0W
Canarreos, Arch. de los 121 21 35N 81 40W
Canary Is. = Canarias, Islas 80 29 30N 17 0W
Canaveral, C. 115 28 28N 80 31W
Cañaveras 32 40 27N 2 24W
Canavieiras 127 15 39S 39 0W
Canbelego 99 31 32S 146 18 E
Canberra 97 35 15S 149 8 E
Canby, Calif., U.S.A. 118 41 26N 120 58W
Canby, Minn., U.S.A. 116 44 44N 96 15W
Canby, Ore., U.S.A. 118 45 16N 122 42W
Cancale 18 48 40N 1 50W
Canche → 19 50 31N 1 39 E
Candala 63 11 30N 49 58 E
Candas 30 43 35N 5 45W
Candé 18 47 34N 1 0W
Candela 41 41 8N 15 31 E
Candelaria 125 27 29S 55 44W
Candelaria, Pta. de la 30 43 45N 8 0W
Candeleda 30 40 10N 5 14W
Candelo 99 36 47S 149 43 E
Candia = Iráklion 45 35 20N 25 12 E
Candia, Sea of = Crete, Sea of 45 36 0N 25 0 E
Candle L. 109 53 50N 105 18W
Candlemas I. 5 57 3S 26 40W
Cando 116 48 30N 99 14W
Canea = Khaniá 45 35 30N 24 4 E
Canelli 38 44 44N 8 18 E
Canelones 125 34 32S 56 17W
Canet-Plage 20 42 41N 3 2 E
Cañete, Chile 124 37 50S 73 30W
Cañete, Peru 126 13 8S 76 30W
Cañete, Spain 32 40 3N 1 54W
Cañete de las Torres 31 37 53N 4 19W
Canfranc 32 42 42N 0 31W
Cangas 30 42 16N 8 47W
Cangas de Narcea 30 43 10N 6 32W
Cangas de Onís 30 43 21N 5 8W
Canguaretama 127 6 20S 35 5W
Canguçu 125 31 22S 52 43W
Cangxi 77 31 47N 105 59 E
Cangzhou 76 38 19N 116 52 E
Cani, I. 83 36 21N 10 5 E
Canicattì 40 37 21N 13 50 E
Canicattini 41 37 1N 15 3 E
Canim Lake 108 51 47N 120 54W
Canipaan 72 8 33N 117 15 E
Canisteo 112 42 17N 77 37W
Canisteo → 112 42 15N 77 30W
Cañiza, La 30 42 13N 8 16W
Cañizal 30 41 12N 5 22W
Canjáyar 33 37 1N 2 44W
Cankırı 64 40 40N 33 37 E
Cankuzo 90 3 10S 30 31 E
Canmore 108 51 7N 115 18W
Cann River 99 37 35S 149 7 E
Canna 14 57 3N 6 33W
Cannanore 70 11 53N 75 27 E
Cannes 21 43 32N 7 0 E
Canning Basin 96 19 50S 124 0 E
Canning Town 69 22 23N 88 40 E
Cannington 112 44 20N 79 2W
Cannock 12 52 42N 2 2W
Cannon Ball → 116 46 20N 100 38W
Canoe L. 109 55 10N 108 15W
Canon City 116 38 27N 105 14W
Canora 109 51 40N 102 30W
Canosa di Púglia 41 41 13N 16 4 E
Canourgue, Le 20 44 26N 3 13 E
Canowindra 99 33 35S 148 38 E
Canso 107 45 20N 61 0W
Cantabria, Sierra de 32 42 40N 2 30W
Cantabrian Mts. = Cantábrica, Cordillera 30 43 0N 5 10W
Cantábrica, Cordillera 30 43 0N 5 10W
Cantal □ 20 45 4N 2 45 E
Cantanhede 30 40 20N 8 36W
Cantavieja 32 40 31N 0 25W
Čantavir 42 45 55N 19 46 E
Canterbury, Austral. 99 25 23S 141 53 E
Canterbury, U.K. 13 51 17N 1 5 E
Canterbury □ 101 43 45S 171 19 E
Canterbury Bight 101 44 16S 171 55 E
Canterbury Plains 101 43 55S 171 22 E
Cantillana 31 37 36N 5 50W
Canton, Ga., U.S.A. 115 34 13N 84 29W
Canton, Ill., U.S.A. 116 40 32N 90 0W
Canton, Mass., U.S.A. 113 42 8N 71 8W
Canton, Miss., U.S.A. 117 32 40N 90 1W
Canton, Mo., U.S.A. 116 40 10N 91 33W
Canton, N.Y., U.S.A. 114 44 32N 75 3W
Canton, Ohio, U.S.A. 114 40 47N 81 22W
Canton, Okla., U.S.A. 117 36 5N 98 36W
Canton, S.D., U.S.A. 116 43 20N 96 35W
Canton = Guangzhou 75 23 5N 113 10 E
Canton I. 94 2 50S 171 40W
Canton L. 117 36 12N 98 40W
Cantù 38 45 44N 9 8 E
Canudos 126 7 13S 58 5W
Canutama 126 6 30S 64 20W
Canutillo 119 31 58N 106 36W
Canyon, Texas, U.S.A. 117 35 0N 101 57W
Canyon, Wyo., U.S.A. 118 44 43N 110 36W
Canyonlands Nat. Park 119 38 25N 109 30W
Canyonville 118 42 55N 123 14W
Canzo 38 45 54N 9 18 E
Cao Xian 77 34 50N 115 35 E
Cáorle 39 45 36N 12 51 E
Cap-aux-Meules 107 47 23N 61 52W
Cap-Chat 107 49 6N 66 40W
Cap-de-la-Madeleine 106 46 22N 72 31W
Cap-Haïtien 121 19 40N 72 20W
Capa Stilo 41 38 25N 16 35 E
Capáccio 41 40 26N 15 4 E
Capaia 88 8 27S 20 13 E
Capanaparo → 126 7 1N 67 7W
Capbreton 20 43 39N 1 26W
Capdenac 20 44 34N 2 5 E
Cape → 98 20 49S 146 51 E
Cape Barren I. 97 40 25S 148 15 E
Cape Breton Highlands Nat. Park 107 46 50N 60 40W
Cape Breton I. 107 46 0N 60 30W
Cape Charles 114 37 15N 75 59W
Cape Coast 85 5 5N 1 15W
Cape Dorset 105 64 14N 76 32W
Cape Dyer 105 66 30N 61 22W
Cape Fear → 115 34 30N 78 25W
Cape Girardeau 117 37 20N 89 30W
Cape May 114 39 1N 74 53W
Cape Montague 107 46 5N 62 25W
Cape Palmas 84 4 25N 7 49W
Cape Province □ 92 32 0S 23 0 E
Cape Tormentine 107 46 8N 63 47W
Cape Town (Kaapstad) 92 33 55S 18 22 E
Cape Verde Is. ■ 6 17 10N 25 20W
Cape Vincent 113 44 9N 76 21W
Cape York Peninsula 97 12 0S 142 30 E
Capela 127 10 30S 37 0W
Capella 98 23 2S 148 1 E
Capella, Mt. 98 5 4S 141 8 E
Capelle, La 19 49 59N 3 50 E
Capendu 20 43 11N 2 31 E
Capernaum = Kefar Naḥum 62 32 54N 35 32 E
Capestang 20 43 20N 3 2 E
Capim → 127 1 40S 47 47W
Capitan 119 33 33N 105 41W
Capizzi 41 37 50N 14 26 E
Čapljina 42 43 10N 17 43 E
Capoche → 91 15 35S 33 0 E
Capraia 38 43 2N 9 50 E
Caprarola 39 42 21N 12 11 E
Capreol 106 46 43N 80 56W
Caprera 40 41 12N 9 28 E
Capri 41 40 34N 14 15 E
Capricorn, C. 97 23 30S 151 13 E
Capricorn Group 98 23 30S 151 55 E
Caprino Veronese 38 45 37N 10 47 E
Caprivi Strip 92 18 0S 23 0 E
Captainganj 69 26 55N 83 45 E
Captain's Flat 99 35 35S 149 27 E
Captieux 20 44 18N 0 16W
Cápua 41 41 7N 14 15 E
Capulin 117 36 48N 103 59W
Caquetá → 126 1 15S 69 15W
Caracal 46 44 8N 24 22 E
Caracas 126 10 30N 66 55W
Caracol 127 9 15S 43 22W
Caradoc 99 30 35S 143 5 E
Caráglio 38 44 25N 7 25 E
Carajás, Serra dos 127 6 0S 51 30W
Carangola 125 20 44S 42 5W
Caransebeş 46 45 28N 22 18 E
Carantec 18 48 40N 3 55W
Carapelle → 41 41 3N 15 55 E
Caraş Severin □ 42 45 10N 22 10 E
Caraşova 42 45 11N 21 51 E
Caratasca, Laguna 121 15 20N 83 40W
Caratinga 127 19 50S 42 10W
Caraúbas 127 5 43S 37 33W
Caravaca 33 38 8N 1 52W
Caravággio 38 45 30N 9 39 E
Caravelas 127 17 45S 39 15W
Caraveli 126 15 45S 73 25W
Caràzinho 125 28 16S 52 46W
Carballino 30 42 26N 8 5W
Carballo 30 43 13N 8 41W
Carberry 109 49 50N 99 25W
Carbia 30 42 48N 8 14W
Carbó 120 29 42N 110 58W
Carbon 108 51 30N 113 9W

Carbonara, C. 40 39 8N 9 30 E
Carbondale, Colo, U.S.A. 118 39 30N 107 10W
Carbondale, Ill., U.S.A. 117 37 45N 89 10W
Carbondale, Pa., U.S.A. 114 41 37N 75 30W
Carbonear 107 47 42N 53 13W
Carboneras 33 37 0N 1 53W
Carboneras de Guadazaón 32 39 54N 1 50W
Carbonia 40 39 10N 8 30 E
Carcabuey 31 37 27N 4 17W
Carcagente 33 39 8N 0 28W
Carcajou 108 57 47N 117 6W
Carcans, Étang d' 20 45 6N 1 7W
Carcasse, C. 121 18 30N 74 28W
Carcassonne 20 43 13N 2 20 E
Carche 33 38 26N 1 9W
Carcross 104 60 13N 134 45W
Cardamom Hills 70 9 30N 77 15 E
Cárdenas, Cuba 121 23 0N 81 30W
Cárdenas, San Luis Potosí, Mexico 120 22 0N 99 41W
Cárdenas, Tabasco, Mexico 120 17 59N 93 21W
Cardenete 32 39 46N 1 41W
Cardiff 13 51 28N 3 11W
Cardigan 13 52 6N 4 41W
Cardigan B. 13 52 30N 4 30W
Cardinal 113 44 47N 75 23W
Cardona, Spain 32 41 56N 1 40 E
Cardona, Uruguay 124 33 53 S 57 18W
Cardoner → 32 41 41N 1 51 E
Cardross 109 49 50N 105 40W
Cardston 108 49 15N 113 20W
Cardwell 98 18 14 S 146 2 E
Careen L. 109 57 0N 108 11W
Carei 46 47 40N 22 29 E
Careme 73 6 55 S 108 27 E
Carentan 18 49 19N 1 15W
Carey, Idaho, U.S.A. 118 43 19N 113 58W
Carey, Ohio, U.S.A. 114 40 58N 83 22W
Carey, L. 96 29 0 S 122 15 E
Carey L. 109 62 12N 102 55W
Careysburg 84 6 34N 10 30W
Cargados Garajos 3 17 0 S 59 0 E
Cargèse 21 42 7N 8 35 E
Carhaix-Plouguer 18 48 18N 3 36W
Carhué 124 37 10 S 62 50W
Caribbean Sea 121 15 0N 75 0W
Cariboo Mts. 108 53 0N 121 0W
Caribou 107 46 55N 68 0W
Caribou →, Man., Can. 109 59 20N 94 44W
Caribou →, N.W.T., Can. 108 61 27N 125 45W
Caribou I. 106 47 22N 85 49W
Caribou Is. 108 61 55N 113 15W
Caribou L., Man., Can. 109 59 21N 96 10W
Caribou L., Ont., Can. 106 50 25N 89 5W
Caribou Mts. 108 59 12N 115 40W
Carignan 19 49 38N 5 10 E
Carignano 38 44 55N 7 40 E
Carinda 99 30 28 S 147 41 E
Cariñena 32 41 20N 1 13W
Carinhanha 127 14 15 S 44 46W
Carini 40 38 9N 13 10 E
Carinola 40 41 11N 13 58 E
Carinthia □ = Kärnten 26 46 52N 13 30 E
Caripito 126 10 8N 63 6W
Caritianas 126 9 20 S 63 6W
Carlbrod = Dimitrovgrad 42 43 0N 22 48 E
Carlentini 41 37 15N 15 2 E
Carleton Place 106 45 8N 76 9W
Carletonville 92 26 23 S 27 22 E
Carlin 118 40 44N 116 5W
Carlingford, L. 15 54 0N 6 5W
Carlinville 116 39 20N 89 55W
Carlisle, U.K. 12 54 54N 2 55W
Carlisle, U.S.A. 114 40 12N 77 10W
Carlitte, Pic 20 42 35N 1 55 E
Carloforte 40 39 10N 8 18 E
Carlos Casares 124 35 32 S 61 20W
Carlos Tejedor 124 35 25 S 62 25W
Carlota, La 124 33 30 S 63 20W
Carlow 15 52 50N 6 58W
Carlow □ 15 52 43N 6 50W
Carlsbad, Calif., U.S.A. 119 33 11N 117 25W
Carlsbad, N. Mex., U.S.A. 117 32 20N 104 14W
Carlyle, Can. 109 49 40N 102 20W
Carlyle, U.S.A. 116 38 38N 89 23W
Carmacks 104 62 5N 136 16W
Carmagnola 38 44 50N 7 42 E
Carman 109 49 30N 98 0W
Carmangay 108 50 10N 113 10W
Carmanville 107 49 23N 54 19W
Carmarthen 13 51 52N 4 20W
Carmarthen B. 13 51 40N 4 30W
Carmaux 20 44 3N 2 10 E
Carmel 113 41 25N 73 38W
Carmel-by-the-Sea 119 36 38N 121 55W
Carmel Mt. 62 32 45N 35 3 E
Carmelo 124 34 0 S 58 20W
Carmen, Colomb. 126 9 43N 75 8W
Carmen, Parag. 125 27 13 S 56 12W
Carmen de Patagones 128 40 50 S 63 0W
Carmen, I. 120 26 0N 111 20W
Cármenes 30 42 58N 5 34W
Carmensa 124 35 15 S 67 40W
Carmi 114 38 6N 88 10W
Carmila 98 21 55 S 149 24 E
Carmona 31 37 28N 5 42W
Carnarvon, Queens., Austral. 98 24 48 S 147 45 E
Carnarvon, W. Austral., Austral. 96 24 51 S 113 42 E
Carnarvon, S. Afr. 92 30 56 S 22 8 E
Carnarvon Ra. 99 25 15 S 148 30 E
Carnaxide 31 38 43N 9 14W
Carndonagh 15 55 15N 7 16W
Carnduff 109 49 10N 101 50W
Carnegie 112 40 24N 80 4W
Carnegie, L. 96 26 5 S 122 30 E
Carnic Alps = Karnische Alpen 26 46 36N 13 0 E
Carnot 88 4 59N 15 56 E
Carnot B. 96 17 20 S 121 30 E
Carnsore Pt. 15 52 10N 6 20W
Caro 114 43 29N 83 27W
Carol City 115 25 5N 80 16W
Carolina, Brazil 127 7 10 S 47 30W
Carolina, S. Afr. 93 26 5 S 30 6 E
Carolina, La 31 38 17N 3 38W
Caroline I. 95 9 15 S 150 3W
Caroline Is. 94 8 0N 150 0 E
Caron 109 50 30N 105 50W
Caroni → 126 8 21N 62 43W
Carovigno 41 40 42N 17 40 E
Carpathians 46 49 50N 21 0 E
Carpaţii Meridionali 46 45 30N 25 0 E
Carpenédolo 38 45 22N 10 25 E
Carpentaria Downs 98 18 44 S 144 20 E
Carpentaria, G. of 97 14 0 S 139 0 E
Carpentras 21 44 3N 5 2 E
Carpi 38 44 47N 10 52 E
Carpino 41 41 50N 15 51 E
Carpinteria 119 34 25N 119 31W
Carpio 30 41 13N 5 7W
Carrabelle 115 29 52N 84 40W
Carrara 38 44 5N 10 7 E
Carrascosa del Campo 32 40 2N 2 45W
Carrauntohill, Mt. 15 52 0N 9 49W
Carrick-on-Shannon 15 53 57N 8 7W
Carrick-on-Suir 15 52 22N 7 30W
Carrickfergus 15 54 43N 5 50W
Carrickfergus □ 15 54 43N 5 49W
Carrickmacross 15 54 0N 6 43W
Carrieton 99 32 25 S 138 31 E
Carrington 116 47 30N 99 7W
Carrión → 30 41 53N 4 32W
Carrión de los Condes 30 42 20N 4 37W
Carrizal Bajo 124 28 5 S 71 20W
Carrizalillo 124 29 5 S 71 30W
Carrizo Cr. 117 36 30N 103 40W
Carrizo Springs 117 28 28N 99 50W
Carrizozo 119 33 40N 105 57W
Carroll 116 42 2N 94 55W
Carrollton, Ga., U.S.A. 115 33 36N 85 5W
Carrollton, Ill., U.S.A. 116 39 20N 90 25W
Carrollton, Ky., U.S.A. 114 38 40N 85 10W
Carrollton, Mo., U.S.A. 116 39 19N 93 24W
Carrollton, Ohio, U.S.A. 112 40 31N 81 9W
Carron → 14 57 30N 5 30W
Carron, L. 14 57 22N 5 35W
Carrot → 109 53 50N 101 17W
Carrot River 109 53 17N 103 35W
Carrouges 18 48 34N 0 10W
Carruthers 109 52 52N 109 16W
Çarşamba 64 41 15N 36 45 E
Carse of Gowrie 14 56 30N 3 10W
Carsoli 39 42 7N 13 3 E
Carson 116 46 27N 101 29W
Carson City 118 39 12N 119 46W
Carson Sink 118 39 50N 118 40W
Carsonville 114 43 25N 82 39W
Carstairs 14 55 42N 3 41W
Cartagena, Colomb. 126 10 25N 75 33W
Cartagena, Spain 33 37 38N 0 59W
Cartago, Colomb. 126 4 45N 75 55W
Cartago, C. Rica 121 9 50N 85 52W
Cartaxo 31 39 10N 8 47W
Cartaya 31 37 16N 7 9W
Carteret 18 49 23N 1 47W
Cartersville 115 34 11N 84 48W
Carterton 101 41 2 S 175 31 E
Carthage, Ark., U.S.A. 117 34 4N 92 32W
Carthage, Ill., U.S.A. 116 40 25N 91 10W
Carthage, Mo., U.S.A. 117 37 10N 94 20W
Carthage, N.Y., U.S.A. 114 43 59N 75 37W
Carthage, S.D., U.S.A. 116 44 14N 97 38W
Carthage, Texas, U.S.A. 117 32 8N 94 20W
Cartier I. 96 12 31 S 123 29 E
Cartwright 107 53 41N 56 58W
Caruaru 127 8 15 S 35 55W
Carúpano 126 10 39N 63 15W
Caruthersville 117 36 10N 89 40W
Carvin 19 50 30N 2 57 E
Carvoeiro 126 1 30 S 61 59W
Carvoeiro, Cabo 31 39 21N 9 24W
Casa Branca 31 38 29N 8 12W
Casa Grande 119 32 53N 111 51W
Casa Nova 127 9 25 S 41 5W
Casablanca, Chile 124 33 20 S 71 25W
Casablanca, Moroc. 82 33 36N 7 36W
Casacalenda 41 41 45N 14 50 E
Casal di Principe 41 41 0N 14 8 E
Casalbordino 39 42 10N 14 34 E
Casale Monferrato 38 45 8N 8 28 E
Casalmaggiore 38 44 59N 10 25 E
Casalpusterlengo 38 45 10N 9 40 E
Casamance → 84 12 33N 16 46W
Casamássima 41 40 58N 16 55 E
Casarano 41 40 0N 16 10 E
Casares 31 36 27N 5 16W
Casas Grandes 120 30 22N 108 0W
Casas Ibañez 33 39 17N 1 30W
Casasimarro 33 39 22N 2 3W
Casatejada 30 39 54N 5 40W
Casavieja 30 40 17N 4 46W
Cascade, Idaho, U.S.A. 118 44 30N 116 2W
Cascade, Mont., U.S.A. 118 47 16N 111 46W
Cascade Locks 118 45 44N 121 54W
Cascade Ra. 102 47 0N 121 30W
Cascais 31 38 41N 9 25W
Cáscina 38 43 40N 10 32 E
Caselle Torinese 38 45 12N 7 39 E
Caserta 41 41 5N 14 20 E
Cashel 15 52 31N 7 53W
Cashmere 118 47 31N 120 30W
Casiguran 73 16 22N 122 7 E
Casilda 124 33 10 S 61 10W
Casimcea 46 44 45N 28 23 E
Casino 97 28 52 S 153 3 E
Casiquiare → 126 2 1N 67 7W
Caslan 108 54 38N 112 31W
Čáslav 26 49 54N 15 22 E
Casma 126 9 30 S 78 20W
Casola Valsenio 39 44 12N 11 40 E
Cásoli 39 42 7N 14 18 E
Caspe 32 41 14N 0 1W
Casper 118 42 52N 106 20W
Caspian Sea 53 43 0N 50 0 E
Casquets 18 49 46N 2 15W
Cass City 114 43 34N 83 24W
Cass Lake 116 47 23N 94 38W
Cassá de la Selva 32 41 53N 2 52 E
Cassano Iónio 41 39 47N 16 20 E
Cassel 19 50 48N 2 30 E
Casselman 113 45 19N 75 5W
Casselton 116 47 0N 97 15W
Cassiar 108 59 16N 129 40W
Cassiar Mts. 108 59 30N 130 30W
Cassino 40 41 30N 13 50 E
Cassis 21 43 14N 5 32 E
Cassville 117 36 45N 93 52W
Cástagneto Carducci 38 43 9N 10 36 E
Castéggio 38 45 1N 9 8 E
Castejón de Monegros 32 41 37N 0 15W
Castel di Sangro 39 41 47N 14 6 E
Castel San Giovanni 38 45 4N 9 25 E
Castel San Pietro 39 44 23N 11 30 E
Castelbuono 41 37 56N 14 4 E
Casteldelfino 38 44 35N 7 4 E
Castelfiorentino 38 43 36N 10 58 E
Castelfranco Emília 38 44 37N 11 2 E
Castelfranco Véneto 39 45 40N 11 56 E
Casteljaloux 20 44 19N 0 6 E
Castellabate 41 40 18N 14 55 E
Castellammare del Golfo 40 38 2N 12 53 E
Castellammare di Stábia 41 40 47N 14 29 E
Castellammare, G. di 40 38 5N 12 55 E
Castellamonte 38 45 23N 7 42 E
Castellana Grotte 41 40 53N 17 10 E
Castellane 21 43 50N 6 31 E
Castellaneta 41 40 40N 16 57 E
Castellar de Santisteban 33 38 16N 3 8W
Castelleone 38 45 19N 9 47 E
Castelli 124 36 7 S 57 47W
Castelló de Ampurias 32 42 15N 3 4 E
Castellón □ 32 40 15N 0 5W
Castellón de la Plana 32 39 58N 0 3W
Castellote 32 40 48N 0 15W
Castellterçol 32 41 45N 2 8 E
Castelmáuro 41 41 50N 14 40 E
Castelnau-de-Médoc 20 45 2N 0 48W
Castelnaudary 20 43 20N 1 58 E
Castelnovo ne' Monti 38 44 27N 10 26 E
Castelnuovo di Val di Cécina 38 43 12N 10 54 E
Castelo 125 20 33 S 41 14 E
Castelo Branco 30 39 50N 7 31W
Castelo Branco □ 30 39 52N 7 45W
Castelo de Paiva 30 41 2N 8 16W
Castelo de Vide 31 39 25N 7 27W
Castelsarrasin 20 44 2N 1 7 E
Casteltérmini 40 37 32N 13 38 E
Castelvetrano 40 37 40N 12 46 E
Casterton 99 37 30 S 141 30 E
Castets 20 43 52N 1 6W
Castiglione del Lago 39 43 7N 12 3 E
Castiglione della Pescáia 38 42 46N 10 53 E
Castiglione della Stiviere 38 45 23N 10 30 E
Castiglione Fiorentino 39 43 20N 11 55 E
Castilblanco 31 39 17N 5 5W
Castilla La Nueva 31 39 45N 3 20W
Castilla La Vieja 30 41 55N 4 0W
Castilla, Playa de 31 37 0N 6 33W
Castille = Castilla 30 40 0N 3 30W
Castillon, Barrage de 21 43 53N 6 33 E
Castillon-en-Couserans 20 42 56N 1 1 E
Castillon-la-Bataille 20 44 51N 0 2W
Castillonès 20 44 39N 0 37 E
Castillos 125 34 12 S 53 52W
Castle Dale 118 39 11N 111 1W
Castle Douglas 14 54 57N 3 57W
Castle Harbour 121 32 17N 64 44W
Castle Point 101 40 54 S 176 15 E
Castle Rock, Colo., U.S.A. 116 39 26N 104 50W
Castle Rock, Wash., U.S.A. 118 46 20N 122 58W
Castlebar 15 53 52N 9 17W
Castleblaney 15 54 7N 6 44W
Castlegar 108 49 20N 117 40W
Castlegate 118 39 45N 110 57W
Castlemaine 97 37 2 S 144 12 E
Castlereagh 15 53 47N 8 30W
Castlereagh □ 15 54 33N 5 53W
Castlereagh → 97 30 12 S 147 32 E
Castlereagh B. 96 12 10 S 135 10 E
Castletown 12 54 4N 4 40W
Castletown Bearhaven 15 51 40N 9 54W
Castlevale 98 24 30 S 146 48 E
Castor 108 52 15N 111 50W
Castres 20 43 37N 2 13 E
Castries 121 14 0N 60 50W
Castril 33 37 48N 2 46W
Castro, Brazil 125 24 45 S 50 0W
Castro, Chile 128 42 30 S 73 50W
Castro Alves 127 12 46 S 39 33W
Castro del Río 31 37 41N 4 29W
Castro Marim 31 37 13N 7 26W
Castro Urdiales 32 43 23N 3 11W
Castro Verde 31 37 41N 8 4W
Castrojeriz 30 42 17N 4 9W
Castropol 30 43 32N 7 0W
Castroreale 41 38 5N 15 15 E
Castrovíllari 41 39 49N 16 11 E
Castroville 117 29 20N 98 53W
Castuera 31 38 43N 5 37W
Casummit Lake 106 51 29N 92 22W
Cat I., Bahamas 121 24 30N 75 30W
Cat I., U.S.A. 117 30 15N 89 7W
Cat L. 106 51 40N 91 50W
Čata 27 47 58N 18 38 E
Catacáos 126 5 20 S 80 45W
Cataguases 125 21 23 S 42 39W
Catahoula L. 117 31 30N 92 5W
Catalão 127 18 10 S 47 57W
Catalina 107 48 31N 53 4W
Catalonia = Cataluña 32 41 40N 1 15 E
Cataluña 32 41 40N 1 15 E
Catamarca 124 28 30 S 65 50W
Catamarca □ 124 27 0 S 65 50W
Catanduanes 73 13 50N 124 20 E
Catanduva 125 21 5 S 48 58W
Catánia 41 37 31N 15 4 E
Catánia, G. di 41 37 25N 15 8 E
Catanzaro 41 38 54N 16 38 E
Catarman 73 12 28N 124 35 E
Catastrophe C. 96 34 59 S 136 0 E
Cateau, Le 19 50 6N 3 30 E
Cateel 73 7 47N 126 24 E
Cathcart 92 32 18 S 27 10 E
Cathlamet 118 46 12N 123 23W
Catio 84 11 17N 15 15W
Cativa 120 9 21N 79 49W
Catlettsburg 114 38 23N 82 38W
Cato I. 97 23 15 S 155 32 E
Catoche, C. 120 21 40N 87 8W
Catral 33 38 10N 0 47W
Catria, Mt. 39 43 28N 12 42 E
Catrimani 126 0 27N 61 41W
Catskill 114 42 14N 73 52W
Catskill Mts. 114 42 15N 74 15W
Cattaraugus 112 42 22N 78 52W
Cattólica 39 43 58N 12 43 E
Cattólica Eraclea 40 37 27N 13 24 E
Catuala 92 16 25 S 19 2 E
Catur 91 13 45 S 35 30 E
Cauca → 126 8 54N 74 28W
Caucaia 127 3 40 S 38 35W
Caucasus Mts. = Bolshoi Kavkas 57 42 50N 44 0 E
Caudebec-en-Caux 18 49 30N 0 42 E
Caudete 33 38 42N 1 2W
Caudry 19 50 7N 3 22 E
Caulnes 18 48 18N 2 10W
Caulónia 41 38 23N 16 25 E
Caúngula 88 8 26 S 18 38 E
Cauquenes 124 36 0 S 72 22W
Caura → 126 7 38N 64 53W
Cauresi → 91 17 8 S 33 0 E
Causapscal 107 48 19N 67 12W
Caussade 20 44 10N 1 33 E
Cauterets 20 42 52N 0 8W
Caux, Pays de 18 49 38N 0 35 E
Cava dei Tirreni 41 40 42N 14 42 E
Cávado → 30 41 32N 8 48W
Cavaillon 21 43 50N 5 2 E
Cavalaire-sur-Mer 21 43 10N 6 33 E
Cavalerie, La 20 44 0N 3 10 E
Cavalese 39 46 17N 11 29 E
Cavalier 116 48 50N 97 39W
Cavallo, Île de 21 41 22N 9 16 E
Cavally → 84 4 22N 7 32W
Cavan 15 54 0N 7 22W
Cavan □ 15 53 58N 7 10W
Cavárzere 39 45 8N 12 6 E
Cave City 114 37 13N 85 57W
Cavendish 99 37 31 S 142 2 E
Caviana, I. 127 0 10N 50 10W
Cavite 73 14 29N 120 55 E
Cavour 38 44 47N 7 22 E
Cavtat 42 42 35N 18 13 E
Cawndilla, L. 99 32 30 S 142 15 E
Cawnpore = Kanpur 69 26 28N 80 20 E
Caxias 127 4 55 S 43 20W
Caxias do Sul 125 29 10 S 51 10W
Caxine, C. 82 35 56N 0 27W
Caxito 88 8 30 S 13 30 E
Cay Sal Bank 121 23 45N 80 0W
Cayambe 126 0 3N 78 8W
Cayce 115 33 59N 81 10W
Cayenne 127 5 0N 52 18W
Cayes, Les 121 18 15N 73 46W
Cayeux-sur-Mer 19 50 10N 1 30 E
Caylus 20 44 15N 1 47 E
Cayman Is. 121 19 40N 80 30W
Cayo 120 17 10N 89 0W
Cayo Romano 121 22 0N 78 0W
Cayuga, Can. 112 42 59N 79 50W
Cayuga, U.S.A. 113 42 54N 76 44W
Cayuga L. 114 42 45N 76 45W
Cazalla de la Sierra 31 37 56N 5 45W
Căzănești 46 44 36N 27 3 E
Cazaux et de Sanguinet, Étang de 20 44 29N 1 10W
Cazères 20 43 13N 1 5 E
Cazin 39 44 57N 15 57 E
Čazma 39 45 45N 16 39 E
Čazma → 39 45 35N 16 29 E
Cazombo 89 11 54 S 22 56 E
Cazorla 33 37 55N 3 2W
Cazorla, Sierra de 33 38 5N 2 55W
Cea → 30 42 0N 5 36W
Ceamurlia de Jos 43 44 43N 28 47 E
Ceanannus Mor 15 53 42N 6 53W
Ceará = Fortaleza 127 3 43 S 38 35W
Ceará □ 127 5 0 S 40 0W
Ceará Mirim 127 5 38 S 35 25W
Ceauru, L. 46 44 58N 23 11 E
Cebollar 124 29 10 S 66 35W
Cebollera, Sierra de 32 42 0N 2 30W
Cebreros 30 40 27N 4 28W
Cebu 73 10 18N 123 54 E
Ceccano 40 41 34N 13 18 E
Cece 27 46 46N 18 39 E
Cechi 84 6 15N 4 25W
Cecil Plains 99 27 30 S 151 11 E
Cécina 38 43 19N 10 33 E
Cécina → 38 43 19N 10 29 E
Ceclavin 30 39 50N 6 45W
Cedar → 116 41 17N 91 21W
Cedar City 119 37 41N 113 3W
Cedar Creek Res. 117 32 4N 96 5W
Cedar Falls 116 42 39N 92 29W
Cedar Key 115 29 9N 83 5W
Cedar L. 109 53 10N 100 0W
Cedar Rapids 116 42 0N 91 38W
Cedarburg 114 43 18N 87 55W
Cedartown 115 34 1N 85 15W
Cedarvale 108 55 1N 128 22W
Cedarville 118 41 37N 120 13W
Cedeira 30 43 39N 8 2W
Cedral 120 23 50N 100 42W
Cedrino → 40 40 23N 9 44 E
Cedro 127 6 34 S 39 3W
Cedros, I. de 120 28 10N 115 20W
Ceduna 96 32 7 S 133 46 E
Cedynia 28 52 53N 14 12 E
Cefalù 41 38 3N 14 1 E

EIL

Cega → 30 41 33N 4 46W
Cegléd 27 47 11N 19 47 E
Céglie Messápico 41 40 39N 17 31 E
Cehegín 33 38 6N 1 48W
Cehu-Silvaniei 46 47 24N 23 9 E
Ceiba, La 121 15 40N 86 50W
Ceica 46 46 53N 22 10 E
Ceira → 30 40 13N 8 16W
Cekhira 83 34 20N 10 5 E
Celano 39 42 6N 13 30 E
Celanova 30 42 9N 7 58W
Celaya 120 20 31N 100 37W
Celbridge 15 53 20N 6 33W
Celebes = Sulawesi 73 2 0 S 120 0 E
Celebes Sea 73 3 0N 123 0 E
Čelić 42 44 43N 18 47 E
Celina 114 40 32N 84 31W
Celje 39 46 16N 15 18 E
Celldömölk 27 47 16N 17 10 E
Celle 24 52 37N 10 4 E
Celorico da Beira 30 40 38N 7 24W
Cement 117 34 56N 98 8W
Cengong 77 27 13N 108 44 E
Cenis, Col du Mt. 21 45 15N 6 55 E
Ceno → 38 44 4N 10 5 E
Cenon 20 44 50N 0 33W
Centallo 38 44 30N 7 35 E
Center, N.D., U.S.A. 116 47 9N 101 17W
Center, Texas, U.S.A. 117 31 50N 94 10W
Centerfield 119 39 9N 111 56W
Centerville, Ala., U.S.A. 115 32 55N 87 7W
Centerville, Iowa, U.S.A. 116 40 45N 92 57W
Centerville, Miss., U.S.A. 117 31 10N 91 3W
Centerville, Pa., U.S.A. 112 40 3N 79 59W
Centerville, S.D., U.S.A. 116 43 10N 96 58W
Centerville, Tenn., U.S.A. 115 35 46N 87 29W
Centerville, Tex., U.S.A. 117 31 15N 95 56W
Cento 39 44 43N 11 16 E
Central 119 32 46N 108 9W
Central □, Kenya 90 0 30 S 37 30 E
Central □, Malawi 91 13 30 S 33 30 E
Central □, U.K. 14 56 10N 4 30W
Central □, Zambia 91 14 25 S 28 50 E
Central African Republic ■ 88 7 0N 20 0 E
Central City, Ky., U.S.A. 114 37 20N 87 7W
Central City, Nebr., U.S.A. 116 41 8N 98 0W
Central, Cordillera, Colomb. 126 5 0N 75 0W
Central, Cordillera, C. Rica 121 10 10N 84 5W
Central I. 90 3 30N 36 0 E
Central Islip 113 40 49N 73 13W
Central Makran Range 65 26 30N 64 15 E
Central Patricia 106 51 30N 90 9W
Central Ra. 98 5 0 S 143 0 E
Central Russian Uplands 9 54 0N 36 0 E
Central Siberian Plateau 59 65 0N 105 0 E
Centralia, Ill., U.S.A. 116 38 32N 89 5W
Centralia, Mo., U.S.A. 116 39 12N 92 6W
Centralia, Wash., U.S.A. 118 46 46N 122 59W
Centúripe 41 37 37N 14 41 E
Cephalonia = Kefallinía 45 38 15N 20 30 E
Čepin 42 45 32N 18 34 E
Ceprano 40 41 33N 13 30 E
Ceptura 46 45 1N 26 21 E
Cepu 73 7 12 S 111 31 E
Ceram = Seram 73 3 10 S 129 0 E
Ceram Sea = Seram Sea 73 2 30 S 128 30 E
Cerbère 20 42 26N 3 10 E
Cerbicales, Îles 21 41 33N 9 22 E
Cerbu 46 44 46N 24 46 E
Cercal 31 37 48N 8 40W
Cercemaggiore 41 41 27N 14 43 E
Cerdaña 32 42 22N 1 35 E
Cerdedo 30 42 33N 8 23W
Cère → 20 44 55N 1 49 E
Cerea 39 45 12N 11 13 E
Ceres, Argent. 124 29 55 S 61 55W
Ceres, Italy 38 45 19N 7 22 E
Ceres, S. Afr. 92 33 21 S 19 18 E
Céret 20 42 30N 2 42 E
Cerignola 41 41 17N 15 53 E
Cerigo = Kíthira 45 36 15N 23 0 E
Cérilly 20 46 37N 2 50 E
Cerisiers 19 48 8N 3 30 E
Cerizay 18 46 50N 0 40W
Çerkeş 64 40 49N 32 52 E
Cerknica 39 45 48N 14 21 E
Cermerno 42 43 35N 20 25 E
Cerna 46 45 4N 28 17 E
Cerna → 46 44 45N 24 0 E
Cernavodă 46 44 22N 28 3 E
Cernay 19 47 44N 7 10 E
Cernik 42 45 17N 17 22 E
Cerralvo 120 24 20N 109 45 E
Cerreto Sannita 41 41 17N 14 34 E
Cerritos 120 22 27N 100 20W
Cerro 119 36 47N 105 36W
Certaldo 38 43 32N 11 2 E
Cervaro → 41 41 30N 15 52 E
Cervera 32 41 40N 1 16 E
Cervera de Pisuerga 30 42 51N 4 30W
Cervera del Río Alhama 32 42 2N 1 58W
Cérvia 39 44 15N 12 20 E
Cervignano del Friuli 39 45 49N 13 20 E
Cervinara 41 41 2N 14 36 E
Cervione 21 42 20N 9 29 E
Cervo 30 43 40N 7 24W
Cesaro 41 37 50N 14 38 E
Cesena 39 44 9N 12 14 E
Cesenático 39 44 12N 12 22 E
Cēsis 54 57 17N 25 28 E
Česká Lípa 26 50 45N 14 30 E
Česka Socialistická Republika □ 26 49 30N 14 40 E
Česká Třebová 27 49 54N 16 27 E
České Budějovice 26 48 55N 14 25 E
České Velenice 26 48 45N 15 1 E
Ceskomoravská Vrchovina 26 49 30N 15 40 E
Český Brod 26 50 4N 14 52 E
Český Krumlov 26 48 43N 14 21 E
Český Těšin 27 49 45N 18 39 E
Çeşme 45 38 20N 26 23 E
Cessnock 97 32 50 S 151 21 E
Cestas 20 44 44N 0 41W
Cestos → 84 5 40N 9 10W
Cetate 46 44 7N 23 2 E
Cétin Grad 39 45 9N 15 45 E
Cetina → 39 43 26N 16 42 E
Cetinje 42 42 23N 18 59 E
Cetraro 41 39 30N 15 56 E
Ceuta 82 35 52N 5 18W
Ceva 38 44 23N 8 3 E
Cévennes 20 44 10N 3 50 E
Ceyhan 64 37 4N 35 47 E
Ceylon = Sri Lanka ■ 70 7 30N 80 50 E
Cèze → 21 44 13N 4 43 E
Cha Pa 71 22 20N 103 47 E
Chabeuil 21 44 54N 5 1 E
Chablais 21 46 20N 6 36 E
Chablis 19 47 47N 3 48 E
Chabounia 82 35 30N 2 38 E
Chacabuco 124 34 40 S 60 27W
Chachapoyas 126 6 15 S 77 50W
Chachro 68 25 5N 70 15 E
Chaco □ 124 26 30 S 61 0W
Chad ■ 81 15 0N 17 15 E
Chad, L. = Tchad, L. 81 13 30N 14 30 E
Chadan 59 51 17N 91 35 E
Chadileuvú → 124 37 46 S 66 0W
Chadiza 91 14 45 S 32 27 E
Chadron 116 42 50N 103 0W
Chadyr-Lunga 56 46 3N 28 51 E
Chagda 59 58 45N 130 38 E
Chagny 19 46 57N 4 45 E
Chagoda 54 59 10N 35 15 E
Chagos Arch. 60 6 0 S 72 0 E
Chágres → 120 9 10N 79 40W
Chāh Bahār 65 25 20N 60 40 E
Chāh Gay Hills 65 29 30N 64 0 E
Chaillé-les-Marais 20 46 25N 1 2W
Chaise-Dieu, La 20 45 20N 3 40 E
Chaize-le-Vicomte, La 18 46 40N 1 18W
Chaj Doab 68 32 15N 73 0 E
Chajari 124 30 42 S 58 0W
Chake Chake 90 5 15 S 39 45 E
Chakhansur 65 31 10N 62 0 E
Chakhansur □ 65 30 0N 62 0 E
Chakonipau, L. 107 56 18N 68 30W
Chakradharpur 69 22 45N 85 40 E
Chakwal 68 32 56N 72 53 E
Chala 126 15 48 S 74 20W
Chalais 20 45 16N 0 3 E
Chalakudi 70 10 18N 76 20 E
Chalcis = Khalkis 45 38 27N 23 42 E
Chaleur B. 107 47 55N 65 30W
Chalhuanca 126 14 15 S 73 15W
Chalindrey 19 47 48N 5 26 E
Chaling 77 26 58N 113 30 E
Chalisgaon 70 20 30N 75 10 E
Chalkar 57 50 35N 51 52 E
Chalkar Oz. 57 50 33N 51 45 E
Chalky Inlet 101 46 3 S 166 31 E
Challans 18 46 50N 1 52W
Challapata 126 18 53 S 66 50W
Challerange 19 49 18N 4 46 E
Challis 118 44 32N 114 25W
Chalna 69 22 36N 89 35 E
Chalon-sur-Saône 19 46 48N 4 50 E
Chalonnes 18 47 20N 0 45W
Châlons-sur-Marne 19 48 58N 4 20 E
Châlus 20 45 39N 0 58 E
Cham 25 49 12N 12 40 E
Chama 119 36 54N 106 35W
Chaman 66 30 58N 66 25 E
Chamarajnagar-Ramasamudram 70 11 52N 76 52 E
Chamartín de la Rosa 32 40 28N 3 40W
Chamba 68 32 35N 76 10 E
Chambal → 69 26 29N 79 15 E
Chamberlain 116 43 50N 99 21W
Chambers 119 35 13N 109 30W
Chambersburg 114 39 53N 77 41W
Chambéry 21 45 34N 5 55 E
Chambly 113 45 27N 73 17W
Chambois 18 48 48N 0 6 E
Chambon-Feugerolles, Le 21 45 24N 4 18 E
Chambord 107 48 25N 72 6W
Chambri L. 98 4 15 S 143 10 E
Chamical 124 30 22 S 66 27W
Chamonix 21 45 55N 6 51 E
Champa 69 22 2N 82 43 E
Champagne, Can. 108 60 49N 136 30W
Champagne, France 19 49 0N 4 40 E
Champagne, Plaine de 19 49 0N 4 30 E
Champagnole 19 46 45N 5 55 E
Champaign 114 40 8N 88 14W
Champaubert 19 48 50N 3 45 E
Champdeniers 20 46 29N 0 25W
Champeix 20 45 37N 3 8 E
Champion B. 96 28 44 S 114 36 E
Champlain, Can. 106 46 27N 72 24W
Champlain, U.S.A. 114 44 59N 73 27W
Champlain, L. 114 44 30N 73 20W
Champotón 120 19 20N 90 50W
Chamusca 31 39 21N 8 29W
Chañaral 124 26 23 S 70 40W
Chanasma 68 23 44N 72 5 E
Chandalar 104 67 30N 148 35W
Chandannagar 69 22 52N 88 24 E
Chandausi 68 28 27N 78 49 E
Chandeleur Is. 117 29 48N 88 51W
Chandeleur Sd. 117 29 58N 88 40W
Chandigarh 68 30 43N 76 47 E
Chandler, Can. 107 48 18N 64 46W
Chandler, Ariz., U.S.A. 119 33 20N 111 56W
Chandler, Okla., U.S.A. 117 35 43N 96 53W
Chandmani 75 45 22N 98 2 E
Chandpur, Bangla. 69 23 8N 90 45 E
Chandpur, India 68 29 8N 78 19 E
Chandrapur 70 19 57N 79 25 E
Chang 68 26 59N 68 30 E
Chang Jiang →, Jiangsu, China 75 31 48N 121 10 E
Chang Jiang →, Shanghai, China 75 31 35N 121 15 E
Changanacheri 70 9 25N 76 31 E
Changbai 76 41 25N 128 5 E
Changbai Shan 76 42 20N 129 0 E
Changchiak'ou = Zhangjiakou 76 40 48N 114 55 E
Ch'angchou = Changzhou 75 31 47N 119 58 E
Changchun 76 43 57N 125 17 E
Changde 75 29 4N 111 35 E
Changfeng 77 32 28N 117 10 E
Changhai = Shanghai 75 31 15N 121 26 E
Changjiang 75 19 20N 108 55 E
Changjin-chŏsuji 76 40 30N 127 15 E
Changle 77 25 59N 119 27 E
Changli 76 39 40N 119 13 E
Changning 77 26 28N 112 22 E
Changping 76 40 14N 116 12 E
Changsha 75 28 12N 113 0 E
Changshou 77 29 51N 107 8 E
Changshu 77 31 38N 120 43 E
Changshun 77 26 3N 106 25 E
Changtai 77 24 35N 117 42 E
Changting 75 25 50N 116 22 E
Changyang 77 30 30N 111 10 E
Changzhi 76 36 10N 113 6 E
Changzhou 75 31 47N 119 58 E
Chanhanga 92 16 0 S 14 8 E
Chanlar 57 40 25N 46 10 E
Channapatna 70 12 40N 77 15 E
Channel Is., U.K. 18 49 30N 2 40W
Channel Is., U.S.A. 119 33 55N 119 26W
Channel-Port aux Basques 107 47 30N 59 9W
Channing, Mich., U.S.A. 114 46 9N 88 1W
Channing, Tex., U.S.A. 117 35 45N 102 20W
Chantada 30 42 36N 7 46W
Chanthaburi 71 12 38N 102 12 E
Chantilly 19 49 12N 2 29 E
Chantonnay 18 46 40N 1 3W
Chantrey Inlet 104 67 48N 96 20W
Chanute 117 37 45N 95 25W
Chanza → 31 37 32N 7 30W
Chao Hu 77 31 30N 117 30 E
Chao Phraya → 71 13 32N 100 36 E
Chao'an 75 23 42N 116 32 E
Chaoyang, Guangdong, China 75 23 17N 116 30 E
Chaoyang, Liaoning, China 76 41 35N 120 22 E
Chapala 91 15 50 S 37 35 E
Chapala, Lago de 120 20 10N 103 20W
Chapayevo 57 50 25N 51 10 E
Chapayevsk 55 53 0N 49 40 E
Chapecó 125 27 14 S 52 41W
Chapel Hill 115 35 53N 79 3W
Chapelle-d'Angillon, La 19 47 21N 2 25 E
Chapelle-Glain, La 18 47 38N 1 11W
Chapleau 106 47 50N 83 24W
Chaplin 109 50 28N 106 40W
Chaplino 56 48 8N 36 15 E
Chaplygin 55 53 15N 40 0 E
Chapra 69 25 48N 84 44 E
Châr 80 21 32N 12 45 E
Chara 59 56 54N 118 20 E
Charadai 124 27 35 S 60 0W
Charagua 126 19 45 S 63 10W
Charaña 126 17 30 S 69 25W
Charata 124 27 13 S 61 14W
Charcas 120 23 10N 101 20W
Charcoal L. 109 58 49N 102 22W
Charcot I. 5 70 0 S 75 0W
Chard 13 50 52N 2 59W
Chardara 58 41 16N 67 59 E
Chardon 112 41 34N 81 17W
Chardzhou 58 39 6N 63 34 E
Charente 20 45 40N 0 5 E
Charente □ 20 45 50N 0 16 E
Charente → 20 45 57N 1 5W
Charente-Maritime □ 20 45 30N 0 35W
Charentsavan 57 40 35N 44 41 E
Chārīkār 65 35 0N 69 10 E
Charité, La 19 47 10N 3 0 E
Chariton → 116 39 19N 92 58W
Charkhari 69 25 24N 79 45 E
Charkhi Dadri 68 28 37N 76 17 E
Charleroi 16 50 24N 4 27 E
Charlerol 112 40 8N 79 54W
Charles, C. 114 37 10N 75 59W
Charles City 116 43 2N 92 41W
Charles L. 109 59 50N 110 33W
Charles Town 114 39 20N 77 50W
Charleston, Ill., U.S.A. 114 39 30N 88 10W
Charleston, Miss., U.S.A. 117 34 2N 90 3W
Charleston, Mo., U.S.A. 117 36 52N 89 20W
Charleston, S.C., U.S.A. 115 32 47N 79 56W
Charleston, W. Va., U.S.A. 114 38 24N 81 36W
Charleston Harb. 115 32 46N 79 55W
Charlestown, S. Afr. 93 27 26 S 29 53 E
Charlestown, U.S.A. 114 38 29N 85 40W
Charlesville 88 5 27 S 20 59 E
Charleville 97 26 24 S 146 15 E
Charleville = Rath Luirc 15 52 21N 8 40W
Charleville-Mézières 19 49 44N 4 40 E
Charlevoix 114 45 19N 85 14W
Charlieu 21 46 10N 4 10 E
Charlotte, Mich., U.S.A. 114 42 36N 84 48W
Charlotte, N.C., U.S.A. 115 35 16N 80 46W
Charlotte Amalie 121 18 22N 64 56W
Charlotte Harbor 115 26 58N 82 4W
Charlotte Waters 96 25 56 S 134 54 E
Charlottenberg 48 59 54N 12 17 E
Charlottesville 114 38 1N 78 30W
Charlottetown 107 46 14N 63 8W
Charlton, Austral. 99 36 16 S 143 24 E
Charlton, U.S.A. 116 40 59N 93 20W
Charlton I. 106 52 0N 79 20W
Charmes 19 48 22N 6 17 E
Charny 107 46 43N 71 15W
Charolles 21 46 27N 4 16 E
Charost 19 47 0N 2 7 E
Charouine 82 29 0N 0 15W
Charre 91 17 13 S 35 10 E
Charroux 20 46 9N 0 25 E
Charters Towers 97 20 5 S 146 13 E
Chartre, La 18 47 42N 0 34 E
Chartres 18 48 29N 1 30 E
Chascomús 124 35 30 S 58 0W
Chasefu 91 11 55 S 33 8 E
Chasovnya-Uchurskaya 59 57 15N 132 50 E
Chasseneuil-sur-Bonnieure 20 45 52N 0 29 E
Chata 68 27 42N 77 30 E
Châtaigneraie, La 18 46 38N 0 45W
Chatal Balkan = Udvoy Balkan 43 42 50N 26 50 E
Château-Chinon 19 47 4N 3 56 E
Château-du-Loir 18 47 40N 0 25 E
Château-Gontier 18 47 50N 0 48W
Château-la-Vallière 18 47 30N 0 20 E
Château-Landon 19 48 8N 2 40 E
Château, Le 20 45 52N 1 12W
Château-Porcien 19 49 31N 4 13 E
Château-Renault 18 47 36N 0 56 E
Château-Salins 19 48 50N 6 30 E
Château-Thierry 19 49 3N 3 20 E
Châteaubourg 18 48 7N 1 25W
Châteaubriant 18 47 43N 1 23W
Châteaudun 18 48 3N 1 20 E
Châteaugiron 18 48 3N 1 30W
Châteauguay 113 45 23N 73 45W
Châteaulin 18 48 11N 4 8W
Châteaumeillant 20 46 35N 2 12 E
Châteauneuf 18 48 35N 1 15 E
Châteauneuf-du-Faou 18 48 11N 3 50W
Châteauneuf-sur-Charente 20 45 36N 0 3W
Châteauneuf-sur-Cher 19 46 52N 2 18 E
Châteauneuf-sur-Loire 19 47 52N 2 13 E
Châteaurenard 21 43 53N 4 51 E
Châteauroux 19 46 50N 1 40 E
Châteaux-Arnoux 21 44 6N 6 0 E
Châtelaillon-Plage 20 46 5N 1 5W
Châtelaudren 18 48 33N 2 59W
Châtelet, Le, Cher, France 20 46 40N 2 20 E
Châtelet, Le, Seine-et-Marne, France 19 48 30N 2 47 E
Châtelguyon 20 45 55N 3 4 E
Châtellerault 18 46 50N 0 30 E
Châtelus-Malvaleix 20 46 18N 2 1 E
Chatfield 116 43 15N 91 58W
Chatham, N.B., Can. 107 47 2N 65 28W
Chatham, Ont., Can. 106 42 24N 82 11W
Chatham, U.K. 13 51 22N 0 32 E
Chatham, La., U.S.A. 117 32 22N 92 26W
Chatham, N.Y., U.S.A. 113 42 21N 73 32W
Chatham Is. 94 44 0 S 176 40W
Chatham Str. 108 57 0N 134 40W
Châtillon, Loiret, France 19 47 36N 2 44 E
Châtillon, Marne, France 19 49 5N 3 43 E
Chatillon 38 45 45N 7 40 E
Châtillon-Coligny 19 47 50N 2 51 E
Châtillon-en-Bazois 19 47 3N 3 39 E
Châtillon-en-Diois 21 44 41N 5 29 E
Châtillon-sur-Indre 18 46 59N 1 10 E
Châtillon-sur-Seine 19 47 50N 4 33 E
Châtillon-sur-Sèvre 18 46 56N 0 45W
Chatmohar 69 24 15N 89 15 E
Chatra 69 24 12N 84 56 E
Chatrapur 69 19 22N 85 2 E
Châtre, La 20 46 35N 1 59 E
Chats, L. des 113 45 30N 76 20W
Chatsworth, Can. 112 44 27N 80 54W
Chatsworth, Zimb. 91 19 38 S 31 13 E
Chattahoochee 115 30 43N 84 51W
Chattanooga 115 35 2N 85 17W
Chaudanne, Barrage de 21 43 51N 6 32 E
Chaudes-Aigues 20 44 51N 3 1 E
Chauffailles 21 46 13N 4 20 E
Chauk 67 20 53N 94 49 E
Chaukan La 67 27 0N 97 15 E
Chaulnes 19 49 48N 2 47 E
Chaumont, France 19 48 7N 5 8 E
Chaumont, U.S.A. 113 44 4N 76 9W
Chaumont-en-Vexin 19 49 16N 1 53 E
Chaumont-sur-Loire 18 47 29N 1 11 E
Chaunay 20 46 13N 0 9 E
Chauny 19 49 37N 3 12 E
Chausey, Îs. 18 48 52N 1 49W
Chaussin 19 46 59N 5 22 E
Chautauqua 112 42 17N 79 30W
Chauvigny 18 46 34N 0 39 E
Chauvin 109 52 45N 110 10W
Chaux-de-Fonds, La 25 47 7N 6 50 E
Chaves, Brazil 127 0 15 S 49 55W
Chaves, Port. 30 41 45N 7 32W
Chavuma 89 13 4 S 22 40 E
Chaykovskiy 52 56 47N 54 9 E
Chazelles-sur-Lyon 21 45 39N 4 22 E
Chazy 113 44 52N 73 28W
Cheb (Eger) 26 50 9N 12 28 E
Cheboksary 55 56 8N 47 12 E
Cheboygan 114 45 38N 84 29W
Chebsara 55 59 10N 38 59 E
Chech, Erg 82 25 0N 2 15W
Chechaouen 82 35 9N 5 15W
Chechen, Os. 57 43 59N 47 40 E
Checheno-Ingush A.S.S.R. □ 57 43 30N 45 29 E
Chęciny 28 50 46N 20 28 E
Checleset B. 108 50 5N 127 35W
Checotah 117 35 31N 95 30W
Chedabucto B. 107 45 25N 61 8W
Cheduba I. 67 18 45N 93 40 E
Cheepie 99 26 33 S 145 1 E
Chef-Boutonne 20 46 7N 0 4W
Chegdomyn 59 51 7N 133 1 E
Chegga 82 25 27N 5 40W
Chehalis 118 46 44N 122 59W
Cheiron 21 43 49N 6 58 E
Cheju Do 77 33 29N 126 34 E
Chekalin 55 54 10N 36 10 E
Chekiang = Zhejiang □ 75 29 0N 120 0 E
Chela, Sa. da 92 16 20 S 13 20 E
Chelan 118 47 49N 120 0W
Chelan, L. 108 48 5N 120 30W
Cheleken 53 39 26N 53 7 E
Chelforó 128 39 0 S 66 33W
Chéliff, O. → 82 36 0N 0 8 E
Chelkar 58 47 48N 59 39 E
Chelkar Tengiz, Solonchak 58 48 0N 62 30 E
Chellala Dahrania 82 33 2N 0 1 E
Chelles 19 48 52N 2 33 E
Chełm 28 51 8N 23 30 E
Chełm □ 28 51 15N 23 30 E
Chełmek 27 50 6N 19 16 E
Chełmno 28 53 20N 18 30 E
Chelmsford 13 51 44N 0 29 E

Chelmsford Dam 93 27 55 S 29 59 E
Chelmża 28 53 10N 18 39 E
Chelsea, Austral. 100 38 5 S 145 8 E
Chelsea, Can. 113 45 30N 75 47W
Chelsea, Okla., U.S.A. 117 36 35N 95 35W
Chelsea, Vt., U.S.A. 113 43 59N 72 27W
Cheltenham 13 51 55N 2 5W
Chelva 32 39 45N 1 0W
Chelyabinsk 58 55 10N 61 24 E
Chemainus 108 48 55N 123 42W
Chemillé 18 47 14N 0 45W
Chemnitz = Karl-Marx-Stadt 24 50 50N 12 55 E
Chemult 118 43 14N 121 47W
Chen, Gora 59 65 16N 141 50 E
Chen Xian 75 25 47N 113 1 E
Chenab → 68 30 23N 71 2 E
Chenachane, O. → 82 25 20N 3 20W
Chenango Forks 113 42 15N 75 51W
Chencha 87 6 15N 37 32 E
Chenchiang = Zhenjiang 75 32 12N 119 24 E
Cheney 118 47 29N 117 34W
Chengbu 77 26 18N 110 16 E
Chengcheng 77 35 8N 109 56 E
Chengde 76 40 59N 117 58 E
Chengdu 75 30 38N 104 2 E
Chenggu 77 33 10N 107 21 E
Chengjiang 75 24 39N 103 0 E
Ch'engtu = Chengdu 75 30 38N 104 2 E
Chengyang 76 36 18N 120 21 E
Chenxi 77 28 2N 110 12 E
Cheo Reo = Hau Bon 71 13 25N 108 28 E
Cheom Ksan 71 14 13N 104 56 E
Chepelare 43 41 44N 24 40 E
Chepén 126 7 15 S 79 23W
Chepes 124 31 20 S 66 35W
Chepo 121 9 10N 79 6W
Cheptsa → 55 58 36N 50 4 E
Cheptulil, Mt. 90 1 25N 35 35 E
Chequamegon B. 116 46 40N 90 30W
Cher □ 19 47 10N 2 30 E
Cher → 18 47 21N 0 29 E
Cheran 69 25 45N 90 44 E
Cherasco 38 44 39N 7 50 E
Cheraw 115 34 42N 79 54W
Cherbourg 18 49 39N 1 40W
Cherchell 82 36 35N 2 12 E
Cherdakly 55 54 25N 48 50 E
Cherdyn 52 60 24N 56 29 E
Cheremkhovo 59 53 8N 103 1 E
Cherepanovo 58 54 15N 83 30 E
Cherepovets 55 59 5N 37 55 E
Chergui, Chott ech 82 34 21N 0 25 E
Cherikov 54 53 32N 31 20 E
Cherkassy 56 49 27N 32 4 E
Cherkessk 57 44 15N 42 5 E
Cherlak 58 54 15N 74 55 E
Chernaya Kholunitsa 55 58 51N 51 52 E
Cherni 43 42 35N 23 18 E
Chernigov 54 51 28N 31 20 E
Chernikovsk 52 54 48N 56 8 E
Chernobyl 54 51 13N 30 15 E
Chernogorsk 59 53 49N 91 18 E
Chernomorskoye 56 45 31N 32 40 E
Chernovskoye 55 58 48N 47 20 E
Chernovtsy 56 48 15N 25 52 E
Chernoye 59 70 30N 89 10 E
Chernyakhovsk 54 54 36N 21 48 E
Chernyshkovskiy 57 48 30N 42 13 E
Chernyshovskiy 59 63 0N 112 30 E
Cherokee, Iowa, U.S.A. 116 42 40N 95 30W
Cherokee, Okla., U.S.A. 117 36 45N 98 25W
Cherokees, L. O'The 117 36 50N 95 12W
Cherquenco 128 38 35 S 72 0W
Cherrapunji 67 25 17N 91 47 E
Cherry Creek 118 39 50N 114 58W
Cherryvale 117 37 20N 95 33W
Cherskiy 59 68 45N 161 18 E
Cherskogo Khrebet 59 65 0N 143 0 E
Chertkovo 57 49 25N 40 19 E
Cherven 54 53 45N 28 28 E
Cherven-Bryag 43 43 17N 24 7 E
Chervonograd 54 50 25N 24 10 E
Cherwell → 13 51 46N 1 18W
Chesapeake 114 36 43N 76 15W
Chesapeake Bay 114 38 0N 76 12W
Cheshire □ 12 53 14N 2 30W
Cheshskaya Guba 52 67 20N 47 0 E
Cheslatta L. 108 53 49N 125 20W
Chesley 112 44 17N 81 5W
Chesne, Le 19 49 30N 4 45 E
Cheste 33 39 30N 0 41W
Chester, U.K. 12 53 12N 2 53W
Chester, Calif., U.S.A. 118 40 22N 121 14W
Chester, Ill., U.S.A. 117 37 58N 89 50W
Chester, Mont., U.S.A. 118 48 31N 111 0W
Chester, N.Y., U.S.A. 113 41 22N 74 16W
Chester, Pa., U.S.A. 114 39 54N 75 20W
Chester, S.C., U.S.A. 115 34 44N 81 13W
Chesterfield 12 53 14N 1 26W
Chesterfield, Îles 94 19 52 S 158 15 E
Chesterfield In. 104 63 25N 90 45W
Chesterfield Inlet 104 63 30N 90 45W
Chesterton Range 99 25 30 S 147 27 E
Chesterville 113 45 6N 75 14W
Chesuncook L. 107 46 0N 69 10W
Chetaibi 83 37 1N 7 20 E
Chéticamp 107 46 37N 60 59W
Chetumal 120 18 30N 88 20W
Chetumal, Bahía de 120 18 40N 88 10W
Chetwynd 108 55 45N 121 36W
Chevanceaux 20 45 18N 0 14W
Cheviot Hills 12 55 20N 2 30W
Cheviot Ra. 99 25 20 S 143 45 E
Cheviot, The 12 55 29N 2 8W
Chew Bahir 87 4 40N 36 50 E
Chewelah 118 48 17N 117 43W
Cheyenne, Okla., U.S.A. 117 35 35N 99 40W
Cheyenne, Wyo., U.S.A. 116 41 9N 104 49W
Cheyenne → 116 44 40N 101 15W
Cheyenne Wells 116 38 51N 102 10W
Cheylard, Le 21 44 55N 4 25 E
Chhabra 68 24 40N 76 54 E
Chhatarpur 69 24 55N 79 35 E
Chhindwara 68 22 2N 78 59 E
Chhlong 71 12 15N 105 58 E
Chi → 71 15 11N 104 43 E
Chiamis 73 7 20 S 108 21 E
Chiamussu = Jiamusi 75 46 40N 130 26 E
Chiang Mai 71 18 47N 98 59 E
Chiange 89 15 35 S 13 40 E
Chiapa → 120 16 42N 93 0W
Chiapas □ 120 17 0N 92 45W
Chiaramonte Gulfi 41 37 1N 14 41 E
Chiaravalle 39 43 38N 13 17 E
Chiaravalle Centrale 41 38 41N 16 25 E
Chiari 38 45 31N 9 55 E
Chiatura 57 42 15N 43 17 E
Chiávari 38 44 20N 9 20 E
Chiavenna 38 46 18N 9 23 E
Chiba 74 35 30N 140 7 E
Chiba □ 74 35 30N 140 20 E
Chibabava 93 20 17 S 33 35 E
Chibatu 73 7 6 S 107 59 E
Chibemba, Angola 89 15 48 S 14 8 E
Chibemba, Angola 92 16 20 S 15 20 E
Chibia 89 15 10 S 13 42 E
Chibougamau 106 49 56N 74 24W
Chibougamau L. 106 49 50N 74 20W
Chibuk 85 10 52N 12 50 E
Chic-Chocs, Mts. 107 48 55N 66 0W
Chicacole = Srikakulam 70 18 14N 84 4 E
Chicago 114 41 53N 87 40W
Chicago Heights 114 41 29N 87 37W
Chichagof I. 108 58 0N 136 0W
Chichaoua 82 31 32N 8 44W
Chichén Itzá 120 20 40N 88 32W
Chichester 13 50 50N 0 47W
Chichibu 74 36 5N 139 10 E
Ch'ich'ihaerh = Qiqihar 75 47 26N 124 0 E
Chickasha 117 35 0N 98 0W
Chiclana de la Frontera 31 36 26N 6 9W
Chiclayo 126 6 42 S 79 50W
Chico 118 39 45N 121 54W
Chico →, Chubut, Argent. 118 44 0 S 67 0W
Chico →, Santa Cruz, Argent. 128 50 0 S 68 30W
Chicomo 93 24 31 S 34 6 E
Chicopee 114 42 6N 72 37W
Chicoutimi 107 48 28N 71 5W
Chidambaram 70 11 20N 79 45 E
Chidenguele 93 24 55 S 34 11 E
Chidley C. 105 60 23N 64 26W
Chiede 92 17 15 S 16 22 E
Chiefs Pt. 112 44 41N 81 18W
Chiemsee 25 47 53N 12 27 E
Chiengi 91 8 45 S 29 10 E
Chienti → 39 43 18N 13 45 E
Chieri 38 45 0N 7 50 E
Chiers → 19 49 39N 5 0 E
Chiese → 38 45 8N 10 25 E
Chieti 39 42 22N 14 10 E
Chifeng 76 42 18N 118 58 E
Chigirin 56 49 4N 32 38 E
Chignecto B. 107 45 30N 64 40W
Chiguana 124 21 0 S 67 58W
Chihli, G. of = Bo Hai 76 39 0N 120 0 E
Chihuahua 120 28 40N 106 3W
Chihuahua □ 120 28 40N 106 3W
Chiili 58 44 20N 66 15 E
Chik Bollapur 70 13 25N 77 45 E
Chikhli 68 20 20N 76 18 E
Chikmagalur 70 13 15N 75 45 E
Chikodi 70 16 26N 74 38 E
Chikwawa 91 16 2 S 34 50 E
Chilako → 108 53 53N 122 57W
Chilanga 91 15 33 S 28 16 E
Chilapa 120 17 40N 99 11W
Chilas 69 35 25N 74 5 E
Chilcotin → 108 51 44N 122 23W
Childers 97 25 15 S 152 17 E
Childress 117 34 30N 100 15W
Chile ■ 128 35 0 S 72 0W
Chile Rise 95 38 0 S 92 0W
Chilecito 124 29 10 S 67 30W
Chilete 126 7 10 S 78 50W
Chililabombwe 91 12 18 S 27 43 E
Chilin = Jilin 76 43 55N 126 30 E
Chilka L. 69 19 40N 85 25 E
Chilko → 108 52 0N 123 40W
Chilko, L. 108 51 20N 124 10W
Chillagoe 97 17 7 S 144 33 E
Chillán 124 36 40 S 72 10W
Chillicothe, Ill., U.S.A. 116 40 55N 89 32W
Chillicothe, Mo., U.S.A. 116 39 45N 93 30W
Chillicothe, Ohio, U.S.A. 114 39 20N 82 58W
Chilliwack 108 49 10N 121 54W
Chilo 68 27 25N 73 32 E
Chiloane, I. 93 20 40 S 34 55 E
Chiloé, I. de 128 42 30 S 73 50W
Chilpancingo 120 17 30N 99 30W
Chiltern Hills 13 51 44N 0 42W
Chilton 114 44 1N 88 12W
Chiluage 88 9 30 S 21 50 E
Chilubula 91 10 14 S 30 51 E
Chilumba 91 10 28 S 34 12 E
Chilwa, L. 91 15 15 S 35 40 E
Chimacum 118 48 1N 122 46W
Chimay 16 50 3N 4 20 E
Chimbay 58 42 57N 59 47 E
Chimborazo 126 1 29 S 78 55W
Chimbote 126 9 0 S 78 35W
Chimishliya 46 46 34N 28 44 E
Chimkent 58 42 18N 69 36 E
Chimoio 91 19 4 S 33 30 E
Chimpembe 91 9 31 S 29 33 E
Chin □ 67 22 0N 93 0 E
Chin Ling Shan = Qinling Shandi 77 33 50N 108 10 E
China 120 25 40N 99 20W
China ■ 75 30 0N 110 0 E
Chinan = Jinan 76 36 38N 117 1 E
Chinandega 121 12 35N 87 12W
Chinati Pk. 117 30 0N 104 25W
Chincha Alta 126 13 25 S 76 7W
Chinchilla 99 26 45 S 150 38 E
Chinchilla de Monte Aragón 33 38 53N 1 40W
Chinchón 32 40 9N 3 26W
Chinchorro, Banco 120 18 35N 87 20W
Chinchou = Jinzhou 76 41 5N 121 3 E
Chincoteague 114 37 58N 75 21W
Chinde 91 18 35 S 36 30 E
Chindwin → 67 21 26N 95 15 E
Chinga 91 15 13 S 38 35 E
Chingleput 70 12 42N 79 58 E
Chingola 91 12 31 S 27 53 E
Chingole 91 13 4 S 34 17 E
Ch'ingtao = Qingdao 76 36 5N 120 20 E
Chinguetti 80 20 25N 12 24W
Chingune 93 20 33 S 35 0 E
Chinhae 76 35 9N 128 47 E
Chinhanguanine 93 25 21 S 32 30 E
Chiniot 68 31 45N 73 0 E
Chinju 76 35 12N 128 2 E
Chinle 119 36 14N 109 38W
Chinnamanur 70 9 50N 77 24 E
Chinnampo 76 38 52N 125 10 E
Chinnur 70 18 57N 79 49 E
Chino Valley 119 34 54N 112 28W
Chinon 18 47 10N 0 15 E
Chinook, Can. 109 51 28N 110 59W
Chinook, U.S.A. 118 48 35N 109 19W
Chinsali 91 10 30 S 32 2 E
Chintamani 70 13 26N 78 3 E
Chióggia 39 45 13N 12 15 E
Chíos = Khíos 45 38 27N 26 9 E
Chipai L. 106 52 56N 87 53W
Chipata 91 13 38 S 32 28 E
Chipatujah 73 7 45 S 108 0 E
Chipewyan L. 109 58 0N 98 27W
Chipinga 91 20 13 S 32 28 E
Chipiona 31 36 44N 6 26W
Chipley 115 30 45N 85 32W
Chiplun 70 17 31N 73 34 E
Chipman 107 46 6N 65 53W
Chipoka 91 13 57 S 34 28 E
Chippawa 112 43 5N 79 2W
Chippenham 13 51 27N 2 7W
Chippewa → 116 44 25N 92 10W
Chippewa Falls 116 44 55N 91 22W
Chiprovtsi 42 43 24N 22 52 E
Chiquián 126 10 10 S 77 0W
Chiquimula 120 14 51N 89 37W
Chiquinquira 126 5 37N 73 50W
Chir → 57 48 30N 43 0 E
Chirala 70 15 50N 80 26 E
Chiramba 91 16 55 S 34 39 E
Chirawa 68 28 14N 75 42 E
Chirayinkil 70 8 41N 76 49 E
Chirchik 58 41 29N 69 35 E
Chirfa 83 20 55N 12 22 E
Chiricahua Pk. 119 31 53N 109 14W
Chirikof I. 104 55 50N 155 40W
Chiriquí, Golfo de 121 8 0N 82 10W
Chiriquí, Lago de 121 9 10N 82 0W
Chiriquí, Vol. de 121 8 55N 82 35W
Chirivira Falls 91 21 10 S 32 12 E
Chirnogi 46 44 7N 26 32 E
Chirpan 43 42 10N 25 19 E
Chirripó Grande, Cerro 121 9 29N 83 29W
Chisamba 91 14 55 S 28 20 E
Chisholm 108 54 55N 114 10W
Chishtian Mandi 68 29 50N 72 55 E
Chisimaio 79 0 22 S 42 32 E
Chisimba Falls 91 10 12 S 30 56 E
Chisineu Criş 42 46 32N 21 37 E
Chisone → 38 44 49N 7 25 E
Chisos Mts. 117 29 20N 103 15W
Chistopol 55 55 25N 50 38 E
Chita 59 52 0N 113 35 E
Chitapur 70 17 10N 77 5 E
Chitembo 89 13 30 S 16 50 E
Chitipa 91 9 41 S 33 19 E
Chitokoloki 89 13 50 S 23 13 E
Chitorgarh 68 24 52N 74 38 E
Chitrakot 70 19 10N 81 40 E
Chitral 66 35 50N 71 56 E
Chitravati → 70 14 45N 78 15 E
Chitré 121 7 59N 80 27W
Chittagong 67 22 19N 91 48 E
Chittagong □ 67 24 5N 91 0 E
Chittoor 70 13 15N 79 5 E
Chittur 70 10 40N 76 45 E
Chiusa 39 46 38N 11 34 E
Chiusi 39 43 1N 11 58 E
Chiva 33 39 27N 0 41W
Chivasso 38 45 10N 7 52 E
Chivilcoy 124 34 55 S 60 0W
Chiwanda 91 11 23 S 34 55 E
Chizela 91 13 10 S 25 0 E
Chkalov = Orenburg 52 52 0N 55 5 E
Chkolovsk 55 56 50N 43 10 E
Chlumec 26 50 9N 15 29 E
Chmielnik 28 50 37N 20 43 E
Choba 90 2 30N 38 5 E
Chobe National Park 92 18 0 S 25 0 E
Chocianów 28 51 27N 15 55 E
Chociwel 28 53 29N 15 21 E
Chodaków 28 52 16N 20 18 E
Chodavaram 70 17 50N 82 57 E
Chodecz 28 52 24N 19 2 E
Chodziez 28 52 58N 16 58 E
Choele Choel 128 39 11 S 65 40W
Choisy-le-Roi 19 48 45N 2 24 E
Choix 120 26 40N 108 23W
Chojna 28 52 58N 14 25 E
Chojnice 28 53 42N 17 32 E
Chojnów 28 51 18N 15 58 E
Choke Mts. 87 11 18N 37 15 E
Chokurdakh 59 70 38N 147 55 E
Cholet 18 47 4N 0 52W
Choluteca 121 13 20N 87 14W
Choma 91 16 48 S 26 59 E
Chomen Swamp 87 9 20N 37 10 E
Chomu 68 27 15N 75 40 E
Chomutov 26 50 28N 13 23 E
Chon Buri 71 13 21N 101 1 E
Chonan 76 36 48N 127 9 E
Chone 126 0 40 S 80 0W
Chong'an 77 27 45N 118 0 E
Chongde 77 30 32N 120 26 E
Chongjin 76 41 47N 129 50 E
Chŏngju 76 39 40N 125 5 E
Chŏngju 76 36 39N 127 27 E
Chongli 76 40 58N 115 15 E
Chongqing 75 29 35N 106 25 E
Chongzuo 77 22 23N 107 20 E
Chŏnju 76 35 50N 127 4 E
Chonming Dao 77 31 40N 121 30 E
Chonos, Arch. de los 128 45 0 S 75 0W
Chopda 68 21 20N 75 15 E
Chopim → 125 25 35 S 53 5W
Chorley 12 53 39N 2 39W
Chorolque, Cerro 124 20 59 S 66 5W
Choroszcz 28 53 10N 22 59 E
Chorrera, La 120 8 50N 79 50W
Chortkov, U.S.S.R. 54 49 2N 25 46 E
Chortkov, U.S.S.R. 56 49 1N 25 42 E
Chŏrwŏn 76 38 15N 127 10 E
Chorzele 28 53 15N 20 55 E
Chorzów 28 50 18N 18 57 E
Chos-Malal 124 37 20 S 70 15W
Chosan 76 40 50N 125 47 E
Chōshi 74 35 45N 140 51 E
Choszczno 28 53 7N 15 25 E
Choteau 118 47 50N 112 10W
Chotila 68 22 23N 71 15 E
Chowchilla 119 37 11N 120 12W
Choybalsan 75 48 4N 114 30 E
Christchurch, N.Z. 101 43 33 S 172 47 E
Christchurch, U.K. 13 50 44N 1 33W
Christian I. 112 44 50N 80 12W
Christiana 92 27 52 S 25 8 E
Christiansfeld 49 55 21N 9 29 E
Christie B. 109 62 32N 111 10W
Christina → 109 56 40N 111 3W
Christmas I., Ind. Oc. 94 10 30 S 105 40 E
Christmas I., Pac. Oc. 95 1 58N 157 27W
Chrudim 26 49 58N 15 43 E
Chrzanów 27 50 10N 19 21 E
Chtimba 91 10 35 S 34 13 E
Chu 58 43 36N 73 42 E
Chu → 71 19 53N 105 45 E
Chu Chua 108 51 22N 120 10W
Ch'uanchou = Quanzhou 75 24 55N 118 34 E
Chūbu □ 74 36 45N 137 30 E
Chubut → 128 43 20 S 65 5W
Chuchi L. 108 55 12N 124 30W
Chudovo 54 59 10N 31 41 E
Chudskoye, Oz. 54 58 13N 27 30 E
Chūgoku □ 74 35 0N 133 0 E
Chūgoku-Sanchi 74 35 0N 133 0 E
Chuguyev 56 49 55N 36 45 E
Chugwater 116 41 48N 104 47W
Chukai 71 4 13N 103 25 E
Chukhloma 55 58 45N 42 40 E
Chukotskiy Khrebet 59 68 0N 175 0 E
Chukotskoye More 59 68 0N 175 0W
Chula Vista 119 32 39N 117 8W
Chulman 59 56 52N 124 52 E
Chulucanas 126 5 8 S 80 10W
Chulym → 58 57 43N 83 51 E
Chumbicha 124 29 0 S 66 10W
Chumerna 43 42 45N 25 55 E
Chumikan 59 54 40N 135 10 E
Chumphon 71 10 35N 99 14 E
Chumuare 91 14 31 S 31 50 E
Chuna → 59 57 47N 94 37 E
Chun'an 77 29 35N 119 3 E
Chunchŏn 76 37 58N 127 44 E
Chunga 91 15 0 S 26 2 E
Chungking = Chongqing 75 29 35N 106 25 E
Chunian 68 30 57N 74 0 E
Chunya 91 8 30 S 33 27 E
Chunya □ 90 7 48 S 33 0 E
Chuquibamba 126 15 47 S 72 44W
Chuquicamata 124 22 15 S 69 0W
Chuquisaca □ 126 23 30 S 63 30W
Chur 25 46 52N 9 32 E
Churachandpur 67 24 20N 93 40 E
Churchill 109 58 47N 94 11W
Churchill →, Man., Can. 109 58 47N 94 12W
Churchill →, Newf., Can. 107 53 19N 60 10W
Churchill, C. 109 58 46N 93 12W
Churchill Falls 107 53 36N 64 19W
Churchill L. 109 55 55N 108 20W
Churchill Pk. 108 58 10N 125 10W
Churu 68 28 20N 74 50 E
Chushal 69 33 40N 78 40 E
Chusovoy 52 58 15N 57 40 E
Chuvash A.S.S.R.□ 55 55 30N 47 0 E
Ci Xian 76 36 20N 114 25 E
Ciacova 42 45 35N 21 10 E
Cianjur 73 6 51 S 107 7 E
Cibadok 73 6 53 S 106 47 E
Cibatu 73 7 8 S 107 59 E
Cicero 114 41 48N 87 48W
Cidacos → 32 42 21N 1 38W
Cide 56 41 53N 33 1 E
Ciechanów 28 52 52N 20 38 E
Ciechanów □ 28 53 0N 20 30 E
Ciechanowiec 28 52 40N 22 31 E
Ciechocinek 28 52 53N 18 45 E
Ciego de Avila 121 21 50N 78 50W
Ciénaga 126 11 1N 74 15W
Cienfuegos 121 22 10N 80 30W
Cieplice Śląskie Zdrój 28 50 50N 15 40 E
Cierp 20 42 55N 0 40 E
Cíes, Islas 30 42 12N 8 55W
Cieszanów 28 50 14N 23 8 E
Cieszyn 27 49 45N 18 35 E
Cieza 33 38 17N 1 23W
Cifuentes 32 40 47N 2 37W
Cijara, Pantano de 31 39 18N 4 52W
Cijulang 73 7 42 S 108 27 E
Cikajang 73 7 25 S 107 48 E
Cikampek 73 6 23 S 107 28 E
Cilacap 73 7 43 S 109 0 E
Çıldır 57 41 10N 43 20 E
Cilician Gates P. 64 37 20N 34 52 E

Cîlnicu 46 44 54N 23 4 E
Cimahi 73 6 53S 107 33 E
Cimarron, Kans., U.S.A. 117 37 50N 100 20W
Cimarron, N. Mex., U.S.A. 117 36 30N 104 52W
Cimarron → 117 36 10N 96 17W
Cimone, Mte. 38 44 10N 10 40 E
Cîmpic Turzii 46 46 34N 23 53 E
Cîmpina 46 45 10N 25 45 E
Cîmpulung, Argeş, Romania 46 45 17N 25 3 E
Cîmpulung, Moldovenesc, Romania 46 47 32N 25 30 E
Cîmpuri 43 46 0N 26 50 E
Cinca → 32 41 26N 0 21 E
Cincer 42 43 55N 17 5 E
Cincinnati 114 39 10N 84 26W
Cîndeşti 46 45 15N 26 42 E
Ciney 16 50 18N 5 5 E
Cingoli 39 43 23N 13 10 E
Cinigiano 39 42 53N 11 23 E
Cinto, Mt. 21 42 24N 8 54 E
Ciorani 46 44 45N 26 25 E
Ciotat, La 21 43 12N 5 36 E
Čiovo 39 43 30N 16 17 E
Circeo, Monte 40 41 14N 13 3 E
Circle, Alaska, U.S.A. 104 65 50N 144 10W
Circle, Montana, U.S.A. 116 47 26N 105 35W
Circleville, Ohio, U.S.A. 114 39 35N 82 57W
Circleville, Utah, U.S.A. 119 38 12N 112 24W
Cirebon 73 6 45S 108 32 E
Cirencester 13 51 43N 1 59W
Cireşu 46 44 47N 22 31 E
Cirey-sur-Vezouze 19 48 35N 6 57 E
Ciriè 38 45 14N 7 35 E
Cirò 41 39 23N 17 3 E
Cisco 117 32 25N 99 0W
Cislău 46 45 14N 26 20 E
Cisna 27 49 12N 22 20 E
Cisnădie 46 45 42N 24 9 E
Cisterna di Latina 40 41 35N 12 50 E
Cisternino 41 40 45N 17 26 E
Citeli-Ckaro 57 41 33N 46 0 E
Citlaltépetl 120 19 0N 97 20W
Citrusdal 92 32 35S 19 0 E
Città della Pieve 39 42 57N 12 0 E
Città di Castello 39 43 27N 12 14 E
Città Sant' Angelo 39 42 32N 14 5 E
Cittadella 39 45 39N 11 48 E
Cittaducale 39 42 24N 12 58 E
Cittanova 41 38 22N 16 5 E
Ciuc, Munţii 46 46 25N 26 5 E
Ciucaş 46 45 31N 25 56 E
Ciudad Acuña 120 29 20N 100 58W
Ciudad Altamirano 120 18 20N 100 40W
Ciudad Bolívar 126 8 5N 63 36W
Ciudad Camargo 120 27 41N 105 10W
Ciudad de Valles 120 22 0N 99 0W
Ciudad del Carmen 120 18 38N 91 50W
Ciudad Delicias = Delicias 120 28 10N 105 30W
Ciudad Guayana 126 8 0N 62 30W
Ciudad Guerrero 120 28 33N 107 28W
Ciudad Guzmán 120 19 40N 103 30W
Ciudad Juárez 120 31 40N 106 28W
Ciudad Madero 120 22 19N 97 50W
Ciudad Mante 120 22 50N 99 0W
Ciudad Obregón 120 27 28N 109 59W
Ciudad Real 31 38 59N 3 55W
Ciudad Real □ 31 38 50N 4 0W
Ciudad Rodrigo 30 40 35N 6 32W
Ciudad Trujillo = Sto. Domingo 121 18 30N 70 0W
Ciudad Victoria 120 23 41N 99 9W
Ciudadela 32 40 0N 3 50 E
Ciulniţa 46 44 26N 27 22 E
Cividale del Friuli 39 46 6N 13 25 E
Cívita Castellana 39 42 18N 12 24 E
Civitanova Marche 39 43 18N 13 41 E
Civitavécchia 39 42 6N 11 46 E
Civitella del Tronto 39 42 48N 13 40 E
Civray 20 46 10N 0 17 E
Çivril 64 38 20N 29 43 E
Cixerri → 40 39 20N 8 40 E
Cizre 64 37 19N 42 10 E
Clacton-on-Sea 13 51 47N 1 10 E
Clain → 18 46 47N 0 33 E
Claire, L. 108 58 35N 112 5W
Clairemont 117 33 9N 100 44W
Clairton 112 40 18N 79 54W
Clairvaux-les-Lacs 21 46 35N 5 45 E
Claise → 18 46 56N 0 42 E
Clamecy 19 47 28N 3 30 E
Clanton 115 32 48N 86 36W
Clanwilliam 92 32 11S 18 52 E
Clara 15 53 20N 7 38W
Clare, Austral. 99 33 50S 138 37 E
Clare, U.S.A. 114 43 47N 84 45W
Clare □ 15 52 20N 9 0W
Clare → 15 53 22N 9 5W
Clare I. 15 53 48N 10 0W
Claremont 114 43 23N 72 20W
Claremont Pt. 98 14 1S 143 41 E
Claremore 117 36 40N 95 37W
Claremorris 15 53 45N 9 0W
Clarence →, Austral. 97 29 25S 153 22 E
Clarence →, N.Z. 101 42 10S 173 56 E
Clarence I. 5 61 10S 54 0W
Clarence, I. 128 54 0S 72 0W
Clarence Str., Austral. 96 12 0S 131 0 E
Clarence Str., U.S.A. 108 55 40N 132 10W
Clarendon, Ark., U.S.A. 117 34 41N 91 20W
Clarendon, Tex., U.S.A. 117 34 58N 100 54W
Clarenville 107 48 10N 54 1W
Claresholm 108 50 0N 113 33W
Clarie Coast 5 68 0S 135 0 E
Clarinda 116 40 45N 95 0W
Clarion, Iowa, U.S.A. 116 42 41N 93 46W
Clarion, Pa., U.S.A. 112 41 12N 79 22W
Clarion → 112 41 9N 79 41W
Clarion Fracture Zone 95 20 0N 120 0W
Clark 116 44 55N 97 45W
Clark Fork 118 48 9N 116 9W
Clark Fork → 118 48 9N 116 15W
Clark Hill Res. 115 33 45N 82 20W
Clark, Pt. 112 44 4N 81 45W
Clarkdale 119 34 53N 112 3W
Clarke City 107 50 12N 66 38W
Clarke, I. 97 40 32S 148 10 E
Clarke L. 109 54 24N 106 54W
Clarke Ra. 98 20 45S 148 20 E
Clark's Fork → 118 45 39N 108 43W
Clark's Harbour 107 43 25N 65 38W
Clarks Summit 113 41 31N 75 44W
Clarksburg 114 39 18N 80 21W
Clarksdale 117 34 12N 90 33W
Clarkston 118 46 28N 117 2W
Clarksville, Ark., U.S.A. 117 35 29N 93 27W
Clarksville, Tenn., U.S.A. 115 36 32N 87 20W
Clarksville, Tex., U.S.A. 117 33 37N 94 59W
Clatskanie 118 46 9N 123 12W
Claude 117 35 8N 101 22W
Claveria 73 18 37N 121 4 E
Clay Center 116 39 27N 97 9W
Clayette, La 21 46 17N 4 19 E
Claypool 119 33 27N 110 55W
Claysville 112 40 5N 80 25W
Clayton, Idaho, U.S.A. 118 44 12N 114 31W
Clayton, N. Mex., U.S.A. 117 36 30N 103 10W
Cle Elum 118 47 15N 120 57W
Clear L. 118 39 5N 122 47W
Clear, C. 15 51 26N 9 30W
Clear I. 15 51 26N 9 30W
Clear Lake, S.D., U.S.A. 116 44 48N 96 41W
Clear Lake, Wash., U.S.A. 118 48 27N 122 15W
Clear Lake Res. 118 41 55N 121 10W
Clearfield, Pa., U.S.A. 114 41 0N 78 27W
Clearfield, Utah, U.S.A. 118 41 10N 112 0W
Clearmont 118 44 43N 106 29W
Clearwater, Can. 108 51 38N 120 2W
Clearwater, U.S.A. 115 27 58N 82 45W
Clearwater →, Alta., Can. 108 52 22N 114 57W
Clearwater →, Alta., Can. 109 56 44N 111 23W
Clearwater Cr. 108 61 36N 125 30W
Clearwater, Mts. 118 46 20N 115 30W
Clearwater Prov. Park 109 54 0N 101 0W
Cleburne 117 32 18N 97 25W
Clécy 18 48 55N 0 29W
Cleethorpes 12 53 33N 0 2W
Cleeve Cloud 13 51 56N 2 0W
Clelles 21 44 50N 5 38 E
Clerks Rocks 5 56 0S 34 30W
Clermont, Austral. 97 22 49S 147 39 E
Clermont, France 19 49 23N 2 24 E
Clermont-en-Argonne 19 49 5N 5 4 E
Clermont-Ferrand 20 45 46N 3 4 E
Clermont-l'Hérault 20 43 38N 3 26 E
Clerval 19 47 25N 6 30 E
Clervaux 16 50 4N 6 2 E
Cléry-Saint-André 19 47 50N 1 46 E
Cles 38 46 21N 11 4 E
Cleveland, Austral. 99 27 30S 153 15 E
Cleveland, Miss., U.S.A. 117 33 43N 90 43W
Cleveland, Ohio, U.S.A. 114 41 28N 81 43W
Cleveland, Okla., U.S.A. 117 36 21N 96 33W
Cleveland, Tenn., U.S.A. 115 35 9N 84 52W
Cleveland, Tex., U.S.A. 117 30 18N 95 0W
Cleveland □ 12 54 35N 1 8 E
Cleveland, C. 97 19 11S 147 1 E
Cleveland Heights 112 41 32N 81 30W
Clevelândia 125 26 24S 52 23W
Clew B. 15 53 54N 9 50W
Clewiston 115 26 44N 80 50W
Clifden, Ireland 15 53 30N 10 2W
Clifden, N.Z. 101 46 1S 167 42 E
Cliff 119 33 0N 108 36W
Clifton, Austral. 99 27 59S 151 53 E
Clifton, Ariz., U.S.A. 119 33 8N 109 23W
Clifton, Tex., U.S.A. 117 31 46N 97 35W
Clifton Forge 114 37 49N 79 51W
Climax 109 49 10N 108 20W
Clinch → 115 36 0N 84 29W
Clingmans Dome 115 35 35N 83 30W
Clint 119 31 37N 106 11W
Clinton, B.C., Can. 108 51 6N 121 35W
Clinton, Ont., Can. 106 43 37N 81 32W
Clinton, N.Z. 101 46 12S 169 23 E
Clinton, Ark., U.S.A. 117 35 37N 92 30W
Clinton, Ill., U.S.A. 116 40 8N 89 0W
Clinton, Ind., U.S.A. 114 39 40N 87 22W
Clinton, Iowa, U.S.A. 116 41 50N 90 12W
Clinton, Mass., U.S.A. 114 42 26N 71 40W
Clinton, Mo., U.S.A. 116 38 20N 93 46W
Clinton, N.C., U.S.A. 115 35 5N 78 15W
Clinton, Okla., U.S.A. 117 35 30N 99 0W
Clinton, S.C., U.S.A. 115 34 30N 81 54W
Clinton, Tenn., U.S.A. 115 36 6N 84 10W
Clinton C. 98 22 30S 150 45 E
Clinton Colden L. 104 63 58N 107 27W
Clintonville 116 44 35N 88 46W
Clipperton Fracture Zone 95 19 0N 122 0W
Clipperton, I. 95 10 18N 109 13W
Clisson 18 47 5N 1 16W
Clive L. 108 63 13N 118 54W
Cloates, Pt. 96 22 43S 113 40 E
Clocolan 93 28 55S 27 34 E
Clodomira 124 27 35S 64 14W
Clonakilty 15 51 37N 8 53W
Clonakilty B. 15 51 33N 8 50W
Cloncurry 97 20 40S 140 28 E
Cloncurry → 98 18 37S 140 40 E
Clones 15 54 10N 7 13W
Clonmel 15 52 22N 7 42W
Cloppenburg 24 52 50N 8 3 E
Cloquet 116 46 40N 92 30W
Clorinda 124 25 16S 57 45W
Cloud Peak 118 44 23N 107 10W
Cloudcroft 119 33 0N 105 48W
Cloverdale 118 38 49N 123 0W
Clovis, Calif., U.S.A. 119 36 47N 119 45W
Clovis, N. Mex., U.S.A. 117 34 20N 103 10W
Cloyes 18 48 0N 1 14 E
Cluj 46 46 47N 23 38 E
Cluj □ 46 46 45N 23 30 E
Clunes 99 37 20S 143 45 E
Cluny 21 46 26N 4 38 E
Cluses 21 46 5N 6 35 E
Clusone 38 45 54N 9 58 E
Clutha → 101 46 20S 169 49 E
Clwyd □ 12 53 5N 3 20W
Clwyd → 12 53 20N 3 30W
Clyde, Can. 105 70 30N 68 30W
Clyde, N.Z. 101 45 12S 169 20 E
Clyde, U.S.A. 112 43 8N 76 52W
Clyde → 14 55 56N 4 29W
Clyde, Firth of 14 55 20N 5 0W
Clydebank 14 55 54N 4 25W
Clymer 112 42 3N 79 39W
Côa → 30 41 5N 7 6W
Coachella 119 33 44N 116 13W
Coahoma 117 32 17N 101 20W
Coahuayana → 120 18 41N 103 45W
Coahuila de Zaragoza □ 120 27 0N 103 0W
Coal → 108 59 39N 126 57W
Coalane 91 17 48S 37 2 E
Coalcomán 120 18 40N 103 10W
Coaldale 108 49 45N 112 35W
Coalgate 117 34 35N 96 13W
Coalinga 119 36 10N 120 21W
Coalville, U.K. 12 52 43N 1 21W
Coalville, U.S.A. 118 40 58N 111 24W
Coari 126 4 8S 63 7W
Coast □ 90 2 40S 39 45 E
Coast Mts. 108 55 0N 129 0W
Coast Ranges 102 41 0N 123 0W
Coastal Plains Basin 96 30 10S 115 30 E
Coatbridge 14 55 52N 4 2W
Coatepeque 120 14 46N 91 55W
Coatesville 114 39 59N 75 55W
Coaticook 107 45 10N 71 46W
Coats I. 105 62 30N 83 0W
Coats Land 5 77 0S 25 0W
Coatzacoalcos 120 18 7N 94 25W
Cobadin 46 44 5N 28 13 E
Cobalt 106 47 25N 79 42W
Cobán 120 15 30N 90 21W
Cobar 97 31 27S 145 48 E
Cóbh 15 51 50N 8 18W
Cobija 126 11 0S 68 50W
Cobleskill 114 42 40N 74 30W
Coboconk 112 44 39N 78 48W
Cobourg 106 43 58N 78 10W
Cobourg Pen. 96 11 20S 132 15 E
Cobram 99 35 54S 145 40 E
Cobre 118 41 6N 114 25W
Coburg 25 50 15N 10 58 E
Coca 30 41 13N 4 32W
Cocanada = Kakinada 70 16 50N 82 11 E
Cocentaina 33 38 45N 0 27W
Cocha, La 124 27 50S 65 40W
Cochabamba 126 17 26S 66 10W
Cochem 25 50 8N 7 7 E
Cochemane 91 17 0S 32 54 E
Cochin 70 9 59N 76 22 E
Cochin China = Nam-Phan 71 10 30N 106 0 E
Cochise 119 32 6N 109 58W
Cochran 115 32 25N 83 23W
Cochrane, Alta., Can. 108 51 11N 114 30W
Cochrane, Ont., Can. 106 49 0N 81 0W
Cochrane → 109 59 0N 103 40W
Cochrane, L. 128 47 10S 72 0W
Cockatoo I. 96 16 6S 123 37 E
Cockburn 99 32 5S 141 0 E
Cockburn, Canal 128 54 30S 72 0W
Cockburn I. 106 45 55N 83 22W
Coco → 121 15 0N 83 8W
Coco Chan. 71 13 50N 93 25 E
Coco Solo 120 9 22N 79 53W
Cocoa 115 28 22N 80 40W
Cocobeach 88 0 59N 9 34 E
Cocora 46 44 45N 27 3 E
Cocos I. 95 5 25N 87 55W
Cocos Is. 94 12 10S 96 55 E
Cod, C. 111 42 8N 70 10W
Codajás 126 3 55S 62 0W
Coderre 109 50 11N 106 31W
Codigoro 39 44 50N 12 5 E
Codó 127 4 30S 43 55W
Codogno 38 45 10N 9 42 E
Codróipo 39 45 57N 13 0 E
Codru, Munţii 46 46 30N 22 15 E
Cody 118 44 35N 109 0W
Coe Hill 106 44 52N 77 50W
Coelemu 124 36 30S 72 48W
Coen 97 13 52S 143 12 E
Coesfeld 24 51 56N 7 10 E
Coeur d'Alene 118 47 45N 116 51W
Cœur d'Alene L. 118 47 32N 116 48W
Coevorden 16 52 40N 6 44 E
Coffeyville 117 37 0N 95 40W
Coffs Harbour 97 30 16S 153 5 E
Cofrentes 33 39 13N 1 5W
Cogealac 46 44 36N 28 36 E
Coghinas → 40 40 55N 8 48 E
Coghinas, L. di 40 40 46N 9 3 E
Cognac 20 45 41N 0 20W
Cogne 38 45 37N 7 21 E
Cogolludo 32 40 59N 3 10W
Cohagen 118 47 2N 106 36W
Cohoes 114 42 47N 73 42W
Cohuna 99 35 45S 144 15 E
Coiba, I. 121 7 30N 81 40W
Coig → 128 51 0S 69 10W
Coihaique 128 45 30S 71 45W
Coimbatore 70 11 2N 76 59 E
Coimbra, Brazil 126 19 55S 57 48W
Coimbra, Port. 30 40 15N 8 27W
Coimbra □ 30 40 12N 8 25W
Coín 31 36 40N 4 48W
Cojimies 126 0 20N 80 0W
Cojocna 46 46 45N 23 50 E
Cojutepequé 120 13 41N 88 54W
Čoka 42 45 57N 20 12 E
Cokeville 118 42 4N 111 0W
Col di Tenda 38 44 7N 7 36 E
Colaba Pt. 70 18 54N 72 47 E
Colac 97 38 21S 143 35 E
Colachel 70 8 10N 77 15 E
Colares 31 38 48N 9 30W
Colbeck, C. 5 77 6S 157 48W
Colbinabbin 99 36 38S 144 48 E
Colborne 112 44 0N 77 53W
Colby 116 39 27N 101 2W
Colchagua □ 124 34 30S 71 0W
Colchester 13 51 54N 0 55 E
Coldstream 14 55 39N 2 14W
Coldwater, Can. 112 44 42N 79 40W
Coldwater, U.S.A. 117 37 18N 99 24W
Colebrook, Austral. 99 42 31S 147 21 E
Colebrook, U.S.A. 114 44 54N 71 29W
Coleman, Can. 108 49 40N 114 30W
Coleman, U.S.A. 117 31 52N 99 30W
Coleman → 97 15 6S 141 38 E
Colenso 93 28 44S 29 50 E
Coleraine, Austral. 99 37 36S 141 40 E
Coleraine, U.K. 15 55 8N 6 40 E
Coleraine □ 15 55 8N 6 40 E
Coleridge, L. 101 43 17S 171 30 E
Coleroon → 70 11 25N 79 50 E
Colesberg 92 30 45S 25 5 E
Colfax, La., U.S.A. 117 31 35N 92 39W
Colfax, Wash., U.S.A. 118 46 57N 117 28W
Colhué Huapi, L. 128 45 30S 69 0W
Cólico 38 46 8N 9 22 E
Coligny 93 26 17S 26 15 E
Colima 120 19 10N 103 40W
Colima □ 120 19 10N 103 40W
Colima, Nevado de 120 19 35N 103 45W
Colina 124 33 13S 70 45W
Colina do Norte 84 12 28N 15 0W
Colinas 127 6 0S 44 10W
Colinton 100 35 50S 149 10 E
Coll 14 56 40N 6 35W
Collaguasi 124 21 5S 68 45W
Collarada, Peña 32 42 43N 0 29W
Collarenebri 99 29 33S 148 34 E
Collbran 119 39 16N 107 58W
Colle di Val d'Elsa 39 43 25N 11 7 E
Colle Salvetti 38 43 34N 10 27 E
Colle Sannita 41 41 22N 14 48 E
Collécchio 38 44 45N 10 10 E
Colleen Bawn 91 21 0S 29 12 E
College Park 115 33 42N 84 27W
Collette 107 46 40N 65 30W
Collie 96 33 22S 116 8 E
Collier B. 96 16 10S 124 15 E
Colline Metallifere 38 43 10N 11 0 E
Collingwood, Austral. 98 22 20S 142 31 E
Collingwood, Can. 106 44 29N 80 13W
Collingwood, N.Z. 101 40 41S 172 40 E
Collins 106 50 17N 89 27W
Collinsville 97 20 30S 147 56 E
Collipulli 124 37 55S 72 30W
Collo 83 36 58N 6 37 E
Collonges 21 46 9N 5 52 E
Collooney 15 54 11N 8 28W
Colmar 19 48 5N 7 20 E
Colmars 21 44 11N 6 39 E
Colmenar 31 36 54N 4 20W
Colmenar de Oreja 32 40 6N 3 25W
Colmenar Viejo 30 40 39N 3 47W
Colne 12 53 51N 2 11W
Colo → 99 33 25S 150 52 E
Cologna Véneta 39 45 19N 11 21 E
Cologne = Köln 24 50 56N 9 58 E
Colomb-Béchar = Béchar 82 31 38N 2 18W
Colombey-les-Belles 19 48 32N 5 54 E
Colombey-les-Deux-Églises 19 48 13N 4 50 E
Colômbia 127 20 10S 48 40W
Colombia ■ 126 3 45N 73 0W
Colombo 70 6 56N 79 58 E
Colombus 119 31 54N 107 43W
Colome 116 43 20N 99 44W
Colón, Argent. 124 32 12S 58 10W
Colón, Cuba 121 22 42N 80 54W
Colón, Panama 120 9 20N 79 54W
Colonella 39 42 52N 13 50 E
Colonia 124 34 25S 57 50W
Colonia Dora 124 28 34S 62 59W
Colonial Hts. 114 37 19N 77 25W
Colonne, C. delle 41 39 2N 17 11 E
Colonsay, Can. 109 51 59N 105 52W
Colonsay, U.K. 14 56 4N 6 12W
Colorado □ 110 37 40N 106 0W
Colorado →, Argent. 128 39 50S 62 8W
Colorado →, Calif., U.S.A. 119 34 45N 114 40W
Colorado →, Tex., U.S.A. 117 28 36N 95 58W
Colorado City 117 32 25N 100 50W
Colorado Desert 110 34 20N 116 0W
Colorado, I. 120 9 12N 79 50W
Colorado Plateau 119 36 40N 110 30W
Colorado R. Aqueduct 119 34 17N 114 10W
Colorado Springs 116 38 55N 104 50W
Colorno 38 44 55N 10 21 E
Colton, N.Y., U.S.A. 113 44 34N 74 58W
Colton, Wash., U.S.A. 118 46 41N 117 6W
Columbia, La., U.S.A. 117 32 7N 92 5W
Columbia, Miss., U.S.A. 117 31 16N 89 50W
Columbia, Mo., U.S.A. 116 38 58N 92 20W
Columbia, Pa., U.S.A. 114 40 2N 76 30W
Columbia, S.C., U.S.A. 115 34 0N 81 0W
Columbia, Tenn., U.S.A. 115 35 40N 87 0W
Columbia → 118 46 15N 124 5W
Columbia Basin 118 47 30N 118 30W
Columbia, C. 4 83 0N 70 0W
Columbia City 114 41 8N 85 30W
Columbia, District of □ 114 38 55N 77 0W
Columbia Falls 118 48 25N 114 16W
Columbia Heights 116 45 5N 93 10W
Columbia, Mt. 108 52 8N 117 20W
Columbiana 112 40 53N 80 40W
Columbretes, Is. 32 39 50N 0 50 E
Columbus, Ga., U.S.A. 115 32 30N 84 58W
Columbus, Ind., U.S.A. 114 39 14N 85 55W
Columbus, Kans., U.S.A. 117 37 15N 94 30W
Columbus, Miss., U.S.A. 115 33 30N 88 26W
Columbus, Mont., U.S.A. 118 45 38N 109 14W
Columbus, N.D., U.S.A. 116 48 52N 102 48W
Columbus, Nebr., U.S.A. 116 41 30N 97 25W
Columbus, Ohio, U.S.A. 114 39 57N 83 1W
Columbus, Tex., U.S.A. 117 29 42N 96 33W
Columbus, Wis., U.S.A. 116 43 20N 89 2W

Colunga 30 43 29N 5 16W
Colusa 118 39 15N 122 1W
Colville 118 48 33N 117 54W
Colville → 104 70 25N 151 0W
Colville, C. 101 36 29 S 175 21 E
Colwyn Bay 12 53 17N 3 44W
Coma 87 8 29N 36 53 E
Comácchio 39 44 41N 12 10 E
Comallo 128 41 0 S 70 5W
Comana 46 44 10N 26 10 E
Comanche, Okla., U.S.A. 117 34 27N 97 58W
Comanche, Tex., U.S.A. 117 31 55N 98 35W
Comănești 46 46 25N 26 26 E
Combahee → 115 32 30N 80 31W
Combeaufontaine 19 47 38N 5 54 E
Comber 112 42 14N 82 33W
Comblain-au-Pont 16 50 29N 5 35 E
Combles 19 50 0N 2 50 E
Combourg 18 48 25N 1 46W
Combronde 20 45 58N 3 5 E
Comeragh Mts. 15 52 17N 7 35W
Comet 98 23 36 S 148 38 E
Comilla 69 23 28N 91 10 E
Comino, C. 40 40 28N 9 47 E
Comino I. 36 36 0N 14 20 E
Cómiso 41 36 57N 14 35 E
Comitán 120 16 18N 92 9W
Commentry 20 46 20N 2 46 E
Commerce, Ga., U.S.A. 115 34 10N 83 25W
Commerce, Tex., U.S.A. 117 33 15N 95 50W
Commercy 19 48 46N 5 34 E
Committee B. 105 68 30N 86 30W
Commonwealth B. 5 67 0 S 144 0 E
Commoron Cr. → 99 28 22 S 150 8 E
Communism Pk. = Kommunizma, Pic 65 38 40N 72 0 E
Como 38 45 48N 9 5 E
Como, L. di 38 46 5N 9 17 E
Comodoro Rivadavia 128 45 50 S 67 40W
Comorin, C. 70 8 3N 77 40 E
Comoriște 42 45 10N 21 35 E
Comoro Is. 3 12 10 S 44 15 E
Comox 108 49 42N 124 55W
Compiègne 19 49 24N 2 50 E
Compíglia Marittima 38 43 4N 10 37 E
Comporta 31 38 22N 8 46W
Comprida, I. 125 24 50 S 47 42W
Compton Downs 99 30 28 S 146 30 E
Côn Dao 71 8 45N 106 45 E
Conakry 84 9 29N 13 49W
Conara Junction 99 41 50 S 147 26 E
Concarneau 18 47 52N 3 56W
Conceição 91 18 47 S 36 7 E
Conceição da Barra 127 18 35 S 39 45W
Conceição do Araguaia 127 8 0 S 49 2W
Concepción, Argent. 124 27 20 S 65 35W
Concepción, Boliv. 126 16 15 S 62 8W
Concepción, Chile 124 36 50 S 73 0W
Concepción, Parag. 124 23 22 S 57 26W
Concepción □ 124 37 0 S 72 30W
Concepción → 120 30 32N 113 2W
Concepción del Oro 120 24 40N 101 30W
Concepción del Uruguay 124 32 35 S 58 20W
Concepción, L. 126 17 20 S 61 20W
Concepción, La = Ri-Aba 85 3 28N 8 40 E
Concepcion, Pt. 119 34 27N 120 27W
Concepción, Punta 120 26 55N 111 59W
Conception B. 92 23 55 S 14 22 E
Conception I. 121 23 52N 75 9W
Conception, Pt. 119 34 30N 120 34W
Concession 91 17 27 S 30 56 E
Conchas Dam 117 35 25N 104 10W
Conche 107 50 55N 55 58W
Conches 18 48 51N 2 43 E
Concho 119 34 32N 109 43W
Concho → 117 31 30N 99 45W
Conchos → 120 29 32N 104 25W
Concord, N.C., U.S.A. 115 35 28N 80 35W
Concord, N.H., U.S.A. 114 43 12N 71 30W
Concordia 124 31 20 S 58 2W
Concórdia 126 4 36 S 66 36W
Concordia 116 39 35N 97 40W
Concordia, La 120 16 8N 92 38W
Concots 20 44 26N 1 40 E
Concrete 118 48 35N 121 49W
Condamine → 97 27 7 S 149 48 E
Condat 20 45 21N 2 46 E
Condé 19 50 26N 3 34 E
Conde 116 45 13N 98 5W
Condé-sur-Noireau 18 48 51N 0 33W
Condeúba 127 14 52 S 42 0W
Condobolin 99 33 4 S 147 6 E
Condom 20 43 57N 0 22 E
Condon 118 45 15N 120 8W
Condove 38 45 8N 7 19 E
Conegliano 39 45 53N 12 18 E
Conejera, I. 33 39 11N 2 58 E
Conflans-en-Jarnisy 19 49 10N 5 52 E
Confolens 20 46 2N 0 40 E
Confuso → 124 25 9 S 57 34W
Congleton 12 53 10N 2 12W
Congo = Zaïre → 88 1 30N 28 0 E
Congo ■ 88 1 0 S 16 0 E
Congo Basin 78 0 10 S 24 30 E
Congonhas 125 20 30 S 43 52W
Congress 119 34 11N 112 56W
Conil 31 36 17N 6 10W
Coniston 106 46 29N 80 51W
Conjeevaram = Kanchipuram 70 12 52N 79 45 E
Conjuboy 98 18 35 S 144 35 E
Conklin 109 55 38N 111 5W
Conlea 99 30 7 S 144 35 E
Conn, L. 15 54 3N 9 15W
Connacht 15 53 23N 8 40W
Conneaut 114 41 55N 80 32W
Connecticut □ 114 41 40N 72 40W
Connecticut → 114 41 17N 72 21W
Connell 118 46 36N 118 51W
Connellsville 114 40 3N 79 32W
Connemara 15 53 29N 9 45W
Connemaugh → 112 40 38N 79 42W
Conner, La 118 48 22N 122 27W
Connerré 18 48 3N 0 30 E
Connersville 114 39 40N 85 10W
Connors Ra. 98 21 40 S 149 10 E
Conoble 99 32 55 S 144 33 E
Conon → 14 57 33N 4 28W
Cononaco → 126 1 32 S 75 35W
Cononbridge 14 57 32N 4 30W
Conquest 109 51 32N 107 14W
Conquet, Le 18 48 21N 4 46W
Conrad 118 48 11N 112 0W
Conran, C. 99 37 49 S 148 44 E
Conroe 117 30 15N 95 28W
Conselheiro Lafaiete 125 20 40 S 43 48W
Conshohocken 113 40 5N 75 18W
Consort 109 52 1N 110 46W
Constance = Konstanz 25 47 39N 9 10 E
Constance, L. = Bodensee 25 47 35N 9 25 E
Constanța 46 44 14N 28 38 E
Constanța □ 46 44 15N 28 15 E
Constantina 31 37 51N 5 40W
Constantine 83 36 25N 6 42 E
Constitución, Chile 124 35 20 S 72 30W
Constitución, Uruguay 124 42 0 S 57 50W
Consuegra 31 39 28N 3 36W
Consul 109 49 20N 109 30W
Contact 118 41 50N 114 56W
Contai 69 21 54N 87 46 E
Contamana 126 7 19 S 74 55W
Contarina 39 45 2N 12 13 E
Contas → 127 14 17 S 39 1W
Contes 21 43 49N 7 19 E
Contoocook 113 43 13N 71 45W
Contra Costa 93 25 9 S 33 30 E
Contres 18 47 24N 1 26 E
Contrexéville 19 48 6N 5 53 E
Conversano 41 40 57N 17 8 E
Conway, Ark., U.S.A. 117 35 5N 92 30W
Conway, N.H., U.S.A. 114 43 58N 71 8W
Conway, S.C., U.S.A. 115 33 49N 79 2W
Conway = Conwy 12 53 17N 3 50W
Conwy 12 53 17N 3 50W
Conwy → 12 53 18N 3 50W
Coober Pedy 96 29 1 S 134 43 E
Cooch Behar 69 26 22N 89 29 E
Cook 116 47 49N 92 39W
Cook, Bahía 128 55 10 S 70 0W
Cook Inlet 104 59 0N 151 0W
Cook Is. 95 17 0 S 160 0W
Cook, Mt. 101 43 36 S 170 9 E
Cook Strait 101 41 15 S 174 29 E
Cookeville 115 36 12N 85 30W
Cookhouse 92 32 44 S 25 47 E
Cookshire 113 45 25N 71 38W
Cookstown 15 54 40N 6 43W
Cookstown □ 15 54 40N 6 43W
Cooksville 112 43 36N 79 35W
Cooktown 97 15 30 S 145 16 E
Coolabah 99 31 1 S 146 43 E
Cooladdi 99 26 37 S 145 23 E
Coolah 99 31 48 S 149 41 E
Coolamon 99 34 46 S 147 8 E
Coolangatta 99 28 11 S 153 29 E
Coolgardie 96 30 55 S 121 8 E
Coolidge 119 33 1N 111 35W
Coolidge Dam 119 33 10N 110 30W
Cooma 97 36 12 S 149 8 E
Coonabarabran 99 31 14 S 149 18 E
Coonamble 97 30 56 S 148 27 E
Coondapoor 70 13 42N 74 40 E
Coongie 99 27 9 S 140 8 E
Coongoola 99 27 43 S 145 51 E
Cooninie, L. 99 26 4 S 139 59 E
Coonoor 70 11 21N 76 45 E
Cooper 117 33 20N 95 40W
Cooper → 115 33 0N 79 55W
Coopers Cr. → 97 28 29 S 137 46 E
Cooperstown, N.D., U.S.A. 116 47 30N 98 6W
Cooperstown, N.Y., U.S.A. 114 42 42N 74 57W
Coorabulka 98 23 41 S 140 20 E
Coorong, The 97 35 50 S 139 20 E
Cooroy 99 26 22 S 152 54 E
Coos Bay 118 43 26N 124 7W
Cootamundra 97 34 36 S 148 1 E
Cootehill 15 54 5N 7 5W
Cooyar 99 26 59 S 151 51 E
Cooyeana 98 24 29 S 138 45 E
Copahue Paso 124 37 49 S 71 8W
Copainalá 120 17 8N 93 11W
Cope 116 39 44N 102 50W
Cope, Cabo 33 37 26N 1 28W
Copenhagen = København 49 55 41N 12 34 E
Copertino 41 40 17N 18 2 E
Copiapó 124 27 30 S 70 20W
Copiapó → 124 27 19 S 70 56W
Copley 99 30 36 S 138 26 E
Copp L. 108 60 14N 114 40W
Copparo 39 44 52N 11 49 E
Copper Center 104 62 10N 145 25W
Copper Cliff 106 46 28N 81 4W
Copper Harbor 114 47 31N 87 55W
Copper Queen 91 17 29 S 29 18 E
Copperbelt □ 91 13 15 S 27 30 E
Coppermine 104 67 50N 115 5W
Coppermine → 104 67 49N 116 4W
Coquet → 12 55 18N 1 45W
Coquilhatville = Mbandaka 88 0 1N 18 18 E
Coquille 118 43 15N 124 12W
Coquimbo 124 30 0 S 71 20W
Coquimbo □ 124 31 0 S 71 0W
Corabia 46 43 48N 24 30 E
Coracora 126 15 5 S 73 45W
Coradi, Is. 41 40 27N 17 10 E
Coral Gables 115 25 45N 80 16W
Coral Harbour 105 64 8N 83 10W
Coral Sea 94 15 0 S 150 0 E
Coral Sea Islands Terr. 97 20 0 S 155 0 E
Corangamite, L. 100 38 0 S 143 30 E
Coraopolis 112 40 30N 80 10W
Corato 41 41 12N 16 22 E
Corbeil-Essonnes 19 48 36N 2 26 E
Corbie 19 49 54N 2 30 E
Corbières 20 42 55N 2 35 E
Corbigny 19 47 16N 3 40 E
Corbin 114 37 0N 84 3W
Corbones → 31 37 36N 5 39W
Corby 13 52 49N 0 31W
Corcoles → 33 39 40N 3 18W
Corcoran 119 36 6N 119 35W
Corcubión 30 42 56N 9 12W
Cordele 115 31 55N 83 49W
Cordell 117 35 18N 99 0W
Cordenons 39 45 59N 12 42 E
Cordes 20 44 5N 1 57 E
Córdoba, Argent. 124 31 20 S 64 10W
Córdoba, Mexico 120 18 50N 97 0W
Córdoba, Spain 31 37 50N 4 50W
Córdoba □, Argent. 124 31 22 S 64 15W
Córdoba □, Spain 31 38 5N 5 0W
Córdoba, Sierra de 124 31 10 S 64 25W
Cordon 73 16 42N 121 32 E
Cordova, Ala., U.S.A. 115 33 45N 87 12W
Cordova, Alaska, U.S.A. 104 60 36N 145 45W
Corella 32 42 7N 1 48W
Corella → 98 19 34 S 140 47 E
Corfield 98 21 40 S 143 21 E
Corfu = Kérkira 44 39 38N 19 50 E
Corgo 30 42 56N 7 25W
Cori 40 41 39N 12 53 E
Coria 30 40 0N 6 33W
Coricudgy, Mt. 100 32 51 S 150 24 E
Corigliano Cálabro 41 39 36N 16 31 E
Corinna 99 41 35 S 145 10 E
Corinth, Miss., U.S.A. 115 34 54N 88 30W
Corinth, N.Y., U.S.A. 113 43 15N 73 50W
Corinth = Kórinthos 45 38 19N 22 24 E
Corinth Canal 45 37 58N 23 0 E
Corinth, G. of = Korinthiakós 45 38 16N 22 30 E
Corinto, Brazil 127 18 20 S 44 30W
Corinto, Nic. 121 12 30N 87 10W
Corj □ 46 45 5N 23 25 E
Cork 15 51 54N 8 30W
Cork □ 15 51 50N 8 50W
Cork Harbour 15 51 46N 8 16W
Corlay 18 48 20N 3 5W
Corleone 40 37 48N 13 16 E
Corleto Perticara 41 40 23N 16 2 E
Çorlu 43 41 11N 27 49 E
Cormack L. 108 60 56N 121 37W
Cormóns 39 45 58N 13 29 E
Cormorant 109 54 14N 100 35W
Cormorant L. 109 54 15N 100 50W
Corn Is. = Maiz, Is. del 121 12 0N 83 0W
Cornélio Procópio 125 23 7 S 50 40W
Cornell 116 45 10N 91 8W
Corner Brook 107 48 57N 57 58W
Corner Inlet 97 38 45 S 146 20 E
Corniglio 38 44 29N 10 5 E
Corning, Ark., U.S.A. 117 36 27N 90 34W
Corning, Calif., U.S.A. 118 39 56N 122 9W
Corning, Iowa, U.S.A. 116 40 57N 94 40W
Corning, N.Y., U.S.A. 114 42 10N 77 3W
Corno, Monte 39 42 28N 13 34 E
Cornwall, Austral. 99 41 33 S 148 7 E
Cornwall, Can. 106 45 2N 74 44W
Cornwall □ 13 50 26N 4 40W
Cornwallis I. 4 75 8N 95 0W
Corny Pt. 99 34 55 S 137 0 E
Coro 126 11 25N 69 41W
Coroatá 127 4 8 S 44 0W
Corocoro 126 17 15 S 68 28W
Coroico 126 16 0 S 67 50W
Coromandel 101 36 45 S 175 31 E
Coromandel Coast 70 12 30N 81 0 E
Corona, Austral. 99 31 16 S 141 24 E
Corona, Calif., U.S.A. 119 33 49N 117 36W
Corona, N. Mex., U.S.A. 119 34 15N 105 32W
Coronada 119 32 45N 117 9W
Coronado, Bahía de 121 9 0N 83 40W
Coronation 108 52 5N 111 27W
Coronation Gulf 104 68 25N 110 0W
Coronation I., Antarct. 5 60 45 S 46 0W
Coronation I., U.S.A. 108 55 52N 134 20W
Coronda 124 31 58 S 60 56W
Coronel 124 37 0 S 73 10W
Coronel Bogado 124 27 11 S 56 18W
Coronel Dorrego 124 38 40 S 61 10W
Coronel Oviedo 124 25 24 S 56 30W
Coronel Pringles 124 38 0 S 61 30W
Coronel Suárez 124 37 30 S 61 52W
Coronel Vidal 124 37 28 S 57 45W
Çorovoda 44 40 31N 20 14 E
Corowa 99 35 58 S 146 21 E
Corozal, Belize 120 18 23N 88 23W
Corozal, Panama 120 8 59N 79 34W
Corps 21 44 50N 5 56 E
Corpus 125 27 10 S 55 30W
Corpus Christi 117 27 50N 97 28W
Corpus Christi L. 117 28 5N 97 54W
Corque 126 18 20 S 67 41W
Corral de Almaguer 32 39 45N 3 10W
Corréggio 38 44 46N 10 47 E
Correntes, C. das 93 24 6 S 35 34 E
Corrèze □ 20 45 20N 1 45 E
Correze → 20 45 10N 1 28 E
Corrib, L. 15 53 5N 9 10W
Corrientes 124 27 30 S 58 45W
Corrientes □ 124 28 0 S 57 0W
Corrientes →, Argent. 124 30 42 S 59 38W
Corrientes →, Peru 126 3 43 S 74 35W
Corrientes, C., Colomb. 126 5 30N 77 34W
Corrientes, C., Cuba 121 21 43N 84 30W
Corrientes, C., Mexico 120 20 25N 105 42W
Corrigan 117 31 0N 94 48W
Corry 114 41 55N 79 39W
Corse 21 42 0N 9 0 E
Corse, C. 21 43 1N 9 25 E
Corse-du-Sud □ 21 41 45N 9 0 E
Corsica = Corse 21 42 0N 9 0 E
Corsicana 117 32 5N 96 30W
Corté 21 42 19N 9 11 E
Corte do Pinto 31 37 42N 7 29W
Cortegana 31 37 52N 6 49W
Cortez 119 37 24N 108 35W
Cortina d'Ampezzo 39 46 32N 12 9 E
Cortland 114 42 35N 76 11W
Cortona 39 43 16N 12 0 E
Coruche 31 38 57N 8 30W
Çorum 64 40 30N 34 57 E
Corumbá 126 19 0 S 57 30W
Corumbá de Goiás 127 16 0 S 48 50W
Coruña, La 30 43 20N 8 25W
Coruña, La □ 30 43 10N 8 30W
Corund 46 46 30N 25 13 E
Corunna = La Coruña 30 43 20N 8 25W
Corvallis 118 44 36N 123 15W
Corvette, L. de la 106 53 25N 74 3W
Corydon 116 40 42N 93 22W
Cosalá 120 24 28N 106 40W
Cosamaloapan 120 18 23N 95 50W
Cosenza 41 39 17N 16 14 E
Coșereni 46 44 38N 26 35 E
Coshocton 114 40 17N 81 51W
Cosne-sur-Loire 19 47 24N 2 54 E
Cospeito 30 43 12N 7 34W
Cosquin 124 31 15 S 64 30W
Cossato 38 45 34N 8 10 E
Cossé-le-Vivien 18 47 57N 0 54W
Cosson → 19 47 30N 1 15 E
Costa Blanca 33 38 25N 0 10W
Costa Brava 32 41 30N 3 0 E
Costa del Sol 31 36 30N 4 30W
Costa Dorada 32 40 45N 1 15 E
Costa Rica ■ 121 10 0N 84 0W
Costa Smeralda 40 41 5N 9 35 E
Costigliole d'Asti 38 44 48N 8 11 E
Costilla 119 37 0N 105 30W
Coștiui 46 47 53N 24 2 E
Coswig 24 51 52N 12 31 E
Cotabato 73 7 14N 124 15 E
Cotagaita 124 20 45 S 65 40W
Côte d'Azur 21 43 25N 6 50 E
Côte d'Or 19 47 10N 4 50 E
Côte-d'Or □ 19 47 30N 4 50 E
Côte-St.-André, La 21 45 24N 5 15 E
Coteau des Prairies 116 44 30N 97 0W
Coteau du Missouri, Plat. du 116 47 0N 101 0W
Coteau Landing 113 45 15N 74 13W
Cotentin 18 49 30N 1 30W
Côtes de Meuse 19 49 15N 5 22 E
Côtes-du-Nord □ 18 48 25N 2 40W
Cotiella 32 42 31N 0 19 E
Cotina → 42 43 36N 18 50 E
Cotonou 85 6 20N 2 25 E
Cotopaxi, Vol. 126 0 40 S 78 30W
Cotronei 41 39 9N 16 45 E
Cotswold Hills 13 51 42N 2 10W
Cottage Grove 118 43 48N 123 2W
Cottbus 24 51 44N 14 20 E
Cottbus □ 24 51 43N 13 30 E
Cottonwood 119 34 48N 112 1W
Cotulla 117 28 26N 99 14W
Coubre, Pte. de la 20 45 42N 1 15W
Couches 19 46 53N 4 30 E
Couço 31 38 59N 8 17W
Coudersport 114 41 45N 77 40W
Couëron 18 47 13N 1 44W
Couesnon → 18 48 38N 1 32W
Couhe-Vérac 20 46 18N 0 12 E
Coulanges 19 47 30N 3 30 E
Coulee City 118 47 36N 119 18W
Coulman I. 5 73 35 S 170 0 E
Coulommiers 19 48 50N 3 3 E
Coulon → 21 43 51N 5 0 E
Coulonge → 106 45 52N 76 46W
Coulonges 20 46 28N 0 35W
Council, Alaska, U.S.A. 104 64 55N 163 45W
Council, Idaho, U.S.A. 118 44 44N 116 26W
Council Bluffs 116 41 20N 95 50W
Council Grove 116 38 41N 96 30W
Courantyne → 126 5 55N 57 5W
Courçon 20 46 15N 0 50W
Couronne, C. 21 43 19N 5 3 E
Cours 21 46 7N 4 19 E
Coursan 20 43 14N 3 4 E
Courseulles 18 49 20N 0 29W
Courtenay 108 49 45N 125 0W
Courtine, La 20 45 43N 2 16 E
Courtrai = Kortrijk 16 50 50N 3 17 E
Courtright 112 42 49N 82 28W
Courville 18 48 28N 1 15 E
Coushatta 117 32 0N 93 21W
Coutances 18 49 3N 1 28W
Couterne 18 48 30N 0 25W
Coutras 20 45 3N 0 8W
Coutts 108 49 0N 111 57W
Covarrubias 32 42 4N 3 31W
Covasna 46 45 50N 26 10 E
Covasna □ 46 45 50N 26 0 E
Coventry 13 52 25N 1 31W
Coventry L. 109 61 15N 106 15W
Covilhã 30 40 17N 7 31W
Covington, Ga., U.S.A. 115 33 36N 83 50W
Covington, Ky., U.S.A. 114 39 5N 84 30W
Covington, Okla., U.S.A. 117 36 21N 97 36W
Covington, Tenn., U.S.A. 117 35 34N 89 39W
Cowal, L. 97 33 40 S 147 25 E
Cowan 109 52 5N 100 45W
Cowan, L. 96 31 45 S 121 45 E
Cowan L. 109 54 0N 107 15W
Cowangie 99 35 12 S 141 26 E
Cowansville 113 45 14N 72 46W
Cowarie 99 27 45 S 138 15 E
Cowdenbeath 14 56 7N 3 20W
Cowes 13 50 45N 1 18W
Cowra 97 33 49 S 148 42 E
Coxim 127 18 30 S 54 55W
Cox's Bazar 67 21 26N 91 59 E
Cox's Cove 107 49 7N 58 5W
Coyuca de Benítez 120 17 1N 100 8W
Coyuca de Catalan 120 18 18N 100 41W
Cozad 116 40 55N 99 57W
Cozumel, Isla de 120 20 30N 86 40W
Craboon 99 32 3 S 149 30 E
Cracow 99 25 17 S 150 17 E
Cracow = Kraków 27 50 4N 19 57 E
Cradock 92 32 8 S 25 36 E

Craig, Alaska, U.S.A. **108** 55 30N 133 5W
Craig, Colo., U.S.A. **118** 40 32N 107 33W
Craigavon = Lurgan **15** 54 28N 6 20W
Craigmore **91** 20 28 S 32 50 E
Crailsheim **25** 49 7N 10 5 E
Craiova **46** 44 21N 23 48 E
Cramsie **98** 23 20 S 144 15 E
Cranberry Portage **109** 54 35N 101 23W
Cranbrook, Austral. **99** 42 0 S 148 5 E
Cranbrook, Can. **108** 49 30N 115 46W
Crandon **116** 45 32N 88 52W
Crane, Oregon, U.S.A. **118** 43 21N 118 39W
Crane, Texas, U.S.A. **117** 31 26N 102 27W
Cranston **113** 41 47N 71 27W
Craon **18** 47 50N 0 58W
Craonne **19** 49 27N 3 46 E
Craponne **20** 45 20N 3 51 E
Crasna **46** 46 32N 27 51 E
Crasna → **46** 47 44N 22 35 E
Crasnei, Munţii **46** 47 0N 23 20 E
Crater, L. **118** 42 55N 122 3W
Crater Pt. **98** 5 25 S 152 9 E
Crateús **127** 5 10 S 40 39W
Crati → **41** 39 41N 16 30 E
Crato, Brazil **127** 7 10 S 39 25W
Crato, Port. **31** 39 16N 7 39W
Crau **21** 43 32N 4 40 E
Crawford **116** 42 40N 103 25W
Crawfordsville **114** 40 2N 86 51W
Crawley **13** 51 7N 0 10W
Crazy Mts. **118** 46 14N 110 30W
Crean L. **109** 54 5N 106 9W
Crécy-en-Brie **19** 48 50N 2 53 E
Crécy-en-Ponthieu **19** 50 15N 1 53 E
Crediton **112** 43 17N 81 33W
Cree →, Can. **109** 58 57N 105 47W
Cree →, U.K. **14** 54 51N 4 24W
Cree L. **109** 57 30N 106 30W
Creede **119** 37 56N 106 59W
Creel **120** 27 45N 107 38W
Creighton **116** 42 30N 97 52W
Creil **19** 49 15N 2 34 E
Crema **38** 45 21N 9 40 E
Cremona **38** 45 8N 10 2 E
Crepaja **42** 45 1N 20 38 E
Crépy **19** 49 37N 3 32 E
Crépy-en-Valois **19** 49 14N 2 54 E
Cres **39** 44 58N 14 25 E
Cresbard **116** 45 13N 98 57W
Crescent, Okla., U.S.A. **117** 35 58N 97 36W
Crescent, Oreg., U.S.A. **118** 43 30N 121 37W
Crescent City **118** 41 45N 124 12W
Crescentino **38** 45 11N 8 7 E
Crespino **39** 44 59N 11 51 E
Crespo **124** 32 2 S 60 19W
Cressy **99** 38 2 S 143 40 E
Crest **21** 44 44N 5 2 E
Crested Butte **119** 38 57N 107 0W
Crestline **112** 40 46N 82 45W
Creston, Can. **108** 49 10N 116 31W
Creston, Iowa, U.S.A. **116** 41 0N 94 20W
Creston, Wash., U.S.A. **118** 47 47N 118 36W
Creston, Wyo., U.S.A. **118** 41 46N 107 50W
Crestview **115** 30 45N 86 35W
Crestwick **100** 37 25 S 143 58 E
Crete **116** 40 38N 96 58W
Crete = Kríti **45** 35 15N 25 0 E
Crete, La **108** 58 11N 116 24W
Crete, Sea of **45** 36 0N 25 0 E
Cretin, C. **98** 6 40 S 147 53 E
Creus, C. **32** 42 20N 3 19 E
Creuse □ **20** 46 0N 2 0 E
Creuse → **20** 47 0N 0 34 E
Creusot, Le **19** 46 50N 4 24 E
Creuzburg **24** 51 3N 10 15 E
Crevalcore **39** 44 41N 11 10 E
Crèvecœur-le-Grand **19** 49 37N 2 5 E
Crevillente **33** 38 12N 0 48W
Crewe **12** 53 6N 2 28W
Crib Point **99** 38 22 S 145 13 E
Criciúma **125** 28 40 S 49 23W
Crieff **14** 56 22N 3 50W
Crikvenica **39** 45 11N 14 40 E
Crimea = Krymskaya **56** 45 0N 34 0 E
Crimmitschau **24** 50 48N 12 23 E
Crinan **14** 56 6N 5 34W
Cristeşti **46** 47 15N 26 33 E
Cristóbal **120** 9 19N 79 54W
Crişul Alb → **42** 46 42N 21 17 E
Crişul Negru → **46** 46 38N 22 26 E
Crişul Repede → **46** 46 55N 20 59 E
Crivitz **24** 53 35N 11 39 E
Crna Gora **42** 42 10N 21 30 E
Crna Gora □ **42** 42 40N 19 20 E
Crna Reka → **42** 41 33N 21 59 E
Crna Trava **42** 42 49N 22 19 E
Crni Drim → **42** 41 17N 20 40 E
Crni Timok → **42** 43 53N 22 15 E
Črnoljeva Planina **42** 42 20N 21 0 E
Črnomelj **39** 45 33N 15 10 E
Croaghpatrick **15** 53 46N 9 40W
Croatia = Hrvatska □ **39** 45 20N 16 0 E
Crocker, Barisan **72** 5 40N 116 30 E
Crocker I. **96** 11 12 S 132 32 E
Crockett **117** 31 20N 95 30W
Crocodile = Krokodil → **93** 25 26 S 32 0 E
Crocodile Is. **96** 12 3 S 134 58 E
Crocq **20** 45 52N 2 21 E
Croisette, C. **21** 43 13N 5 20 E
Croisic, Le **18** 47 18N 2 30W
Croisic, Pte. du **18** 47 19N 2 31W
Croix, La, L. **106** 48 20N 92 15W
Cromarty, Can. **109** 58 3N 94 9W
Cromarty, U.K. **14** 57 40N 4 2W
Cromer **12** 52 56N 1 18 E
Cromwell **101** 45 3 S 169 14 E
Cronat **19** 46 43N 3 40 E
Cronulla **100** 34 3 S 151 8 E
Crooked →, Can. **108** 54 50N 122 54W
Crooked →, U.S.A. **118** 44 30N 121 16W
Crooked I. **121** 22 50N 74 10W
Crookston, Minn., U.S.A. **116** 47 50N 96 40W
Crookston, Nebr., U.S.A. **116** 42 56N 100 45W
Crooksville **114** 39 45N 82 8W
Crookwell **99** 34 28 S 149 24 E
Crosby, Minn., U.S.A. **116** 46 28N 93 57W
Crosby, N.D., U.S.A. **109** 48 55N 103 18W
Crosby, Pa., U.S.A. **112** 41 45N 78 23W
Crosbyton **117** 33 37N 101 12W
Cross → **85** 4 42N 8 21 E
Cross City **115** 29 35N 83 5W
Cross Fell **12** 54 44N 2 29W
Cross L. **109** 54 45N 97 30W
Cross Plains **117** 32 8N 99 7W
Cross River □ **85** 6 0N 8 0 E
Cross Sound **104** 58 20N 136 30W
Crosse, La, Kans., U.S.A. **116** 38 33N 99 20W
Crosse, La, Wis., U.S.A. **116** 43 48N 91 13W
Crossett **117** 33 10N 91 57W
Crossfield **108** 51 25N 114 0W
Crosshaven **15** 51 48N 8 19W
Croton-on-Hudson **113** 41 12N 73 55W
Crotone **41** 39 5N 17 6 E
Crow → **108** 59 41N 124 20W
Crow Agency **118** 45 40N 107 30W
Crow Hd. **15** 51 34N 10 9W
Crowell **117** 33 59N 99 45W
Crowley **117** 30 15N 92 20W
Crown Point **114** 41 24N 87 23W
Crows Nest **99** 27 16 S 152 4 E
Crowsnest Pass **108** 49 40N 114 40W
Croydon, Austral. **97** 18 13 S 142 14 E
Croydon, U.K. **13** 51 18N 0 5W
Crozet Is. **3** 46 27 S 52 0 E
Crozon **18** 48 15N 4 30W
Cruz Alta **125** 28 45 S 53 40W
Cruz, C. **121** 19 50N 77 50W
Cruz del Eje **124** 30 45 S 64 50W
Cruz, La **120** 23 55N 106 54W
Cruzeiro **125** 22 33 S 45 0W
Cruzeiro do Oeste **125** 23 46 S 53 4W
Cruzeiro do Sul **126** 7 35 S 72 35W
Cry L. **108** 58 45N 129 0W
Crystal Brook **99** 33 21 S 138 12 E
Crystal City, Mo., U.S.A. **116** 38 15N 90 23W
Crystal City, Tex., U.S.A. **117** 28 40N 99 50W
Crystal Falls **114** 46 9N 88 11W
Crystal River **115** 28 54N 82 35W
Crystal Springs **117** 31 59N 90 25W
Csongrád **27** 46 43N 20 12 E
Csongrád □ **27** 46 32N 20 15 E
Csorna **27** 47 38N 17 18 E
Csurgo **27** 46 16N 17 9 E
Cu Lao Hon **71** 10 54N 108 18 E
Cuácua → **91** 17 54 S 37 0 E
Cuamato **92** 17 2 S 15 7 E
Cuamba **91** 14 45 S 36 22 E
Cuando → **89** 14 0 S 19 30 E
Cuando Cubango □ **92** 16 25 S 20 0 E
Cuangar **92** 17 36 S 18 39 E
Cuarto → **124** 33 25 S 63 2W
Cuba, Port. **31** 38 10N 7 54W
Cuba, N. Mex., U.S.A. **119** 36 0N 107 0W
Cuba, N.Y., U.S.A. **112** 42 12N 78 18W
Cuba ■ **121** 22 0N 79 0W
Cubango → **92** 18 50 S 22 25 E
Cuchi **89** 14 37 S 16 58 E
Cúcuta **126** 7 54N 72 31W
Cudahy **114** 42 54N 87 50W
Cudalbi **46** 45 46N 27 41 E
Cuddalore **70** 11 46N 79 45 E
Cuddapah **70** 14 30N 78 47 E
Cuddapan, L. **99** 25 45 S 141 26 E
Cudgewa **99** 36 10 S 147 42 E
Cudillero **30** 43 33N 6 9W
Cue **96** 27 25 S 117 54 E
Cuéllar **30** 41 23N 4 21W
Cuenca, Ecuador **126** 2 50 S 79 9W
Cuenca, Spain **32** 40 5N 2 10W
Cuenca □ **32** 40 0N 2 0W
Cuenca, Serranía de **32** 39 55N 1 50W
Cuerda del Pozo, Pantano de la **32** 41 51N 2 44W
Cuernavaca **120** 18 50N 99 20W
Cuero **117** 29 5N 97 17W
Cuers **21** 43 14N 6 5 E
Cuervo **117** 35 5N 104 25W
Cuevas del Almanzora **33** 37 18N 1 58W
Cuevo **126** 20 15 S 63 30W
Cugir **46** 45 48N 23 25 E
Cuiabá **127** 15 30 S 56 0W
Cuiabá → **127** 17 5 S 56 36W
Cuillin Hills **14** 57 14N 6 15W
Cuillin Sd. **14** 57 4N 6 20W
Cuiluan **76** 47 51N 128 32 E
Cuima **89** 13 25 S 15 45 E
Cuiseaux **21** 46 30N 5 22 E
Cuito → **92** 18 1 S 20 48 E
Cuitzeo, L. de **120** 19 55N 101 5W
Cujmir **46** 44 13N 22 57 E
Culan **20** 46 34N 2 20 E
Culbertson **116** 48 9N 104 30W
Culcairn **99** 35 41 S 147 3 E
Culebra, Sierra de la **36** 41 55N 6 20W
Culgoa → **99** 29 56 S 146 20 E
Culiacán **120** 24 50N 107 23W
Culion **73** 11 54N 120 1 E
Cúllar de Baza **33** 37 35N 2 34W
Cullarin Range **99** 34 30 S 149 30 E
Cullen **14** 57 45N 2 50W
Cullen Pt. **98** 11 57 S 141 54 E
Cullera **33** 39 9N 0 17W
Cullman **115** 34 13N 86 50W
Culloden Moor **14** 57 29N 4 7W
Culoz **21** 45 47N 5 46 E
Culpeper **114** 38 29N 77 59W
Culuene → **127** 12 56 S 52 51W
Culver, Pt. **96** 32 54 S 124 43 E
Culverden **101** 42 47 S 172 49 E
Cumali **45** 36 42N 27 28 E
Cumaná **126** 10 30N 64 5W
Cumberland, B.C., Can. **108** 49 40N 125 0W
Cumberland, Qué., Can. **113** 45 30N 75 24W
Cumberland, Md., U.S.A. **114** 39 40N 78 43W
Cumberland, Wis., U.S.A. **116** 45 32N 92 3W
Cumberland → **115** 36 15N 87 0W
Cumberland I. **115** 30 52N 81 30W
Cumberland Is. **97** 20 35 S 149 10 E
Cumberland L. **109** 54 3N 102 18W
Cumberland Pen. **105** 67 0N 64 0W
Cumberland Plat. **115** 36 0N 84 30W
Cumberland Sd. **105** 65 30N 66 0W
Cumborah **99** 29 40 S 147 45 E
Cumbres Mayores **31** 38 4N 6 39W
Cumbria □ **12** 54 35N 2 55W
Cumbrian Mts. **12** 54 30N 3 0W
Cumbum **70** 15 40N 79 10 E
Cumnock, Austral. **99** 32 59 S 148 46 E
Cumnock, U.K. **14** 55 27N 4 18W
Cuncumén **124** 31 53 S 70 38W
Cunene → **92** 17 20 S 11 50 E
Cúneo **38** 44 23N 7 31 E
Cunillera, I. **33** 38 59N 1 13 E
Cunlhat **20** 45 38N 3 32 E
Cunnamulla **97** 28 2 S 145 38 E
Cuorgnè **38** 45 23N 7 39 E
Cupar, Can. **109** 50 57N 104 10W
Cupar, U.K. **14** 56 20N 3 0W
Cupica, Golfo de **126** 6 25N 77 30W
Ćuprija **42** 43 57N 21 26 E
Curaçao **121** 12 10N 69 0W
Curanilahue **124** 37 29 S 73 28W
Curaray → **126** 2 20 S 74 5W
Cure → **19** 47 40N 3 41 E
Curepto **124** 35 8 S 72 1W
Curiapo **126** 8 33N 61 5W
Curicó **124** 34 55 S 71 20W
Curicó □ **124** 34 50 S 71 15W
Curitiba **125** 25 20 S 49 10W
Currabubula **99** 31 16 S 150 44 E
Currais Novos **127** 6 13 S 36 30W
Curralinho **127** 1 45 S 49 46W
Currant **118** 38 51N 115 32W
Curraweena **99** 30 47 S 145 54 E
Currawilla **99** 25 10 S 141 20 E
Current → **117** 37 15N 91 10W
Currie, Austral. **99** 39 56 S 143 53 E
Currie, U.S.A. **118** 40 16N 114 45W
Currie, Mt. **93** 30 29 S 29 21 E
Currituck Sd. **115** 36 20N 75 50W
Currockbilly Mt. **100** 35 25 S 150 0 E
Curtea de Argeş **46** 45 12N 24 42 E
Curtis, Spain **30** 43 7N 8 4W
Curtis, U.S.A. **116** 40 41N 100 32W
Curtis I. **97** 23 35 S 151 10 E
Curuápanema → **127** 2 25 S 55 2W
Curuçá **127** 0 43 S 47 50W
Curuguaty **125** 24 31 S 55 42W
Çürüksu Çayi → **53** 37 27N 27 11 E
Curundu **120** 8 59N 79 38W
Curup **72** 4 26 S 102 13 E
Cururupu **127** 1 50 S 44 50W
Curuzú Cuatiá **124** 29 50 S 58 5W
Curvelo **127** 18 45 S 44 27W
Cushing **117** 35 59N 96 46W
Cushing, Mt. **108** 57 35N 126 57W
Cusihuiriáchic **120** 28 10N 106 50W
Cusna, Monte **38** 44 13N 10 25 E
Cusset **20** 46 8N 3 28 E
Custer **116** 43 45N 103 38W
Cut Bank **118** 48 40N 112 15W
Cuthbert **115** 31 47N 84 47W
Cutro **41** 39 1N 16 58 E
Cuttaburra → **99** 29 43 S 144 22 E
Cuttack **69** 20 25N 85 57 E
Cuvier, C. **96** 23 14 S 113 22 E
Cuvier I. **101** 36 27 S 175 50 E
Cuxhaven **24** 53 51N 8 41 E
Cuyahoga Falls **114** 41 8N 81 30W
Cuyo **73** 10 50N 121 5 E
Cuzco, Boliv. **126** 20 0 S 66 50W
Cuzco, Peru **126** 13 32 S 72 0W
Čvrsnica **42** 43 36N 17 35 E
Cwmbran **13** 51 39N 3 0W
Cyangugu **90** 2 29 S 28 54 E
Cybinka **28** 52 12N 14 46 E
Cyclades = Kikladhes **45** 37 20N 24 30 E
Cygnet **99** 43 8 S 147 1 E
Cynthiana **114** 38 23N 84 10W
Cypress Hills **109** 49 40N 109 30W
Cyprus ■ **64** 35 0N 33 0 E
Cyrenaica **81** 27 0N 23 0 E
Cyrene = Shaḥḥāt **81** 32 40N 21 35 E
Czaplinek **28** 53 34N 16 14 E
Czar **109** 52 27N 110 50W
Czarna →, Piotrkow Trybunalski, Poland **28** 51 18N 19 55 E
Czarna →, Tarnobrzeg, Poland **28** 50 3N 21 21 E
Czarna Woda **28** 53 51N 18 6 E
Czarne **28** 53 42N 16 58 E
Czarnków **28** 52 55N 16 38 E
Czechoslovakia ■ **27** 49 0N 17 0 E
Czechowice-Dziedzice **27** 49 54N 18 59 E
Czeladz **28** 50 16N 19 2 E
Czempiń **28** 52 9N 16 33 E
Czeremcha **28** 52 31N 23 21 E
Czersk **28** 53 46N 17 58 E
Czerwieńsk **28** 52 1N 15 13 E
Czerwionka **27** 50 7N 18 37 E
Częstochowa **28** 50 49N 19 7 E
Częstochowa □ **28** 50 45N 19 0 E
Człopa **28** 53 6N 16 6 E
Człuchów **28** 53 41N 17 22 E
Czyzew **28** 52 48N 22 19 E

D

Da → **71** 21 15N 105 20 E
Da Hinggan Ling **75** 48 0N 121 0 E
Da Lat **71** 11 56N 108 25 E
Da Nang **71** 16 4N 108 13 E
Da Qaidam **75** 37 50N 95 15 E
Da Yunhe, Jiangsu, China **77** 34 25N 120 5 E
Da Yunhe, Zhejiang, China **77** 30 45N 120 35 E
Da'an **76** 45 30N 124 7 E
Dab'a, Râs el **86** 31 3N 28 31 E
Daba Shan **75** 32 0N 109 0 E
Dabai **85** 11 25N 5 15 E
Dabakala **84** 8 15N 4 20W
Dabbūriya **62** 32 42N 35 22 E
Dabhoi **68** 22 10N 73 20 E
Dąbie, Poland **28** 53 27N 14 45 E
Dąbie, Poland **28** 52 5N 18 50 E
Dabo **72** 0 30 S 104 33 E
Dabola **84** 10 50N 11 5W
Dabou **84** 5 20N 4 23W
Daboya **85** 9 30N 1 20W
Dabrowa Górnicza **28** 50 15N 19 10 E
Dabrowa Tarnówska **27** 50 10N 20 59 E
Dąbrówno **28** 53 27N 20 2 E
Dabus → **87** 10 48N 35 10 E
Dacato → **87** 7 25N 42 40 E
Dacca **69** 23 43N 90 26 E
Dacca □ **69** 24 25N 90 25 E
Dachau **25** 48 16N 11 27 E
Dadanawa **126** 2 50N 59 30W
Daday **56** 41 28N 33 27 E
Dade City **115** 28 20N 82 12W
Dades, Oued → **82** 30 58N 6 44W
Dadiya **85** 9 35N 11 24 E
Dadra and Nagar Haveli □ **68** 20 5N 73 0 E
Dadri = Charkhi Dadri **68** 28 37N 76 17 E
Dadu **68** 26 45N 67 45 E
Dăeni **46** 44 51N 28 10 E
Daet **73** 14 2N 122 55 E
Dafang **77** 27 9N 105 39 E
Dagana **84** 16 30N 15 35W
Dagash **86** 19 19N 33 25 E
Dagestan A.S.S.R. □ **57** 42 30N 47 0 E
Dagestanskiye Ogni **57** 42 6N 48 12 E
Daghfeli **86** 19 18N 32 40 E
Dagö = Hiiumaa **54** 58 50N 22 45 E
Dagupan **73** 16 3N 120 20 E
Dahab **86** 28 30N 34 31 E
Dahlak Kebir **87** 15 50N 40 10 E
Dahlenburg **24** 53 11N 10 43 E
Dahlonega **115** 34 35N 83 59W
Dahme, Germ., E. **24** 51 51N 13 25 E
Dahme, Germ., W. **24** 54 13N 11 5 E
Dahomey = Benin ■ **85** 10 0N 2 0 E
Dahra **84** 15 22N 15 30W
Dahra, Massif de **82** 36 7N 1 21 E
Dai Shan **77** 30 25N 122 10 E
Dai Xian **76** 39 4N 112 58 E
Daimiel **33** 39 5N 3 35W
Daingean **15** 53 18N 7 15W
Daintree **98** 16 20 S 145 20 E
Daiō-Misaki **74** 34 15N 136 45 E
Dairût **86** 27 34N 30 43 E
Daitari **69** 21 10N 85 46 E
Dajarra **97** 21 42 S 139 30 E
Dakar **84** 14 34N 17 29W
Dakhla **80** 23 50N 15 53W
Dakhla, El Wâhât el- **86** 25 30N 28 50 E
Dakhovskaya **57** 44 13N 40 13 E
Dakingari **85** 11 37N 4 1 E
Dakor **68** 22 45N 73 11 E
Dakoro **85** 14 31N 6 46 E
Dakota City **116** 42 27N 96 28W
Đakovica **42** 42 22N 20 26 E
Đakovo **42** 45 19N 18 24 E
Dalaba **84** 10 42N 12 15W
Dalachi **76** 36 48N 105 0 E
Dalai Nur **76** 43 20N 116 45 E
Dalandzadgad **75** 43 27N 104 30 E
Dalbandin **65** 29 0N 64 23 E
Dalbeattie **14** 54 55N 3 50W
Dalbosjön **49** 58 40N 12 45 E
Dalby, Austral. **97** 27 10 S 151 17 E
Dalby, Sweden **49** 55 40N 13 22 E
Dale **47** 61 22N 5 23 E
Dalen **47** 59 26N 8 0 E
Dalga **86** 27 39N 30 41 E
Dalhart **117** 36 10N 102 30W
Dalhousie, Can. **107** 48 5N 66 26W
Dalhousie, India **68** 32 38N 76 0 E
Dali, Shaanxi, China **77** 34 48N 109 58 E
Dali, Yunnan, China **75** 25 40N 100 10 E
Daliang Shan **75** 28 0N 102 45 E
Dalias **33** 36 49N 2 52W
Dāliyat el Karmel **62** 32 43N 35 2 E
Dalj **42** 45 29N 18 59 E
Dalkeith **14** 55 54N 3 5W
Dall I. **108** 54 59N 133 25W
Dallarnil **99** 25 19 S 152 2 E
Dallas, Oregon, U.S.A. **118** 45 0N 123 15W
Dallas, Texas, U.S.A. **117** 32 50N 96 50W
Dallol **87** 14 14N 40 17 E
Dalmacija □ **42** 43 20N 17 0 E
Dalmatia = Dalmacija □ **42** 43 20N 17 0 E
Dalmellington **14** 55 20N 4 25W
Dalneretchensk **59** 45 50N 133 40 E
Daloa **84** 7 0N 6 30W
Dalrymple, Mt. **97** 21 1 S 148 39 E
Dalsjöfors **49** 57 46N 13 5 E
Dalskog **49** 58 44N 12 18 E
Dalton, Can. **166** 48 11N 84 1W
Dalton, Ga., U.S.A. **115** 34 47N 84 58W
Dalton, Mass., U.S.A. **113** 42 28N 73 11W
Dalton, Nebr., U.S.A. **116** 41 27N 103 0W
Dalton Iceberg Tongue **5** 66 15 S 121 30 E
Daltonganj **69** 24 0N 84 4 E
Dalvík **50** 65 58N 18 32W
Daly → **96** 13 35 S 130 19 E
Daly L. **109** 56 32N 105 39W
Daly Waters **96** 16 15 S 133 24 E
Dama, Wadi → **86** 27 12N 35 50 E
Daman **68** 20 25N 72 57 E
Daman □ **68** 20 25N 72 58 E
Damanhûr **86** 31 0N 30 30 E
Damar **73** 7 7 S 128 40 E
Damaraland **92** 21 0 S 17 0 E
Damascus = Dimashq **64** 33 30N 36 18 E
Damaturu **85** 11 45N 11 55 E
Damāvand **65** 35 47N 52 0 E
Damāvand, Qolleh-ye **65** 35 56N 52 10 E
Damba **88** 6 44 S 15 20 E

Dāmghān 65 36 10N 54 17 E
Dāmienesti 46 46 44N 27 1 E
Damietta = Dumyât 86 31 24N 31 48 E
Daming 76 36 15N 115 6 E
Dāmīya 62 32 6N 35 34 E
Dammarie 19 48 20N 1 30 E
Dammartin 19 49 3N 2 41 E
Damme 24 52 32N 8 12 E
Damodar → 69 23 17N 87 35 E
Damoh 69 23 50N 79 28 E
Damous 82 36 31N 1 42 E
Dampier 96 20 41 S 116 42 E
Dampier Arch. 96 20 38 S 116 32 E
Dampier Downs 96 18 24 S 123 5 E
Dampier, Selat 73 0 40 S 131 0 E
Dampier Str. 98 5 50 S 148 0 E
Damville 18 48 51N 1 5 E
Damvillers 19 49 20N 5 21 E
Dan-Gulbi 85 11 40N 6 15 E
Dan Xian 77 19 31N 109 33 E
Dana 73 11 0 S 122 52 E
Dana, Lac 106 50 53N 77 20W
Danakil Depression 87 12 45N 41 0 E
Danao 73 10 31N 124 1 E
Danbury 114 41 23N 73 29W
Danby L. 119 34 17N 115 0W
Dandeldhura 69 29 20N 80 35 E
Dandenong 99 38 0 S 145 15 E
Dandong 76 40 10N 124 20 E
Danforth 107 45 39N 67 57W
Danger Is. 95 10 53 S 165 49W
Danger Pt. 92 34 40 S 19 17 E
Dangla 87 11 18N 36 56 E
Dangora 85 11 30N 8 7 E
Dangshan 77 34 27N 116 22 E
Dangtu 77 31 32N 118 25 E
Dangyang 77 30 52N 111 44 E
Daniel 118 42 56N 110 2W
Daniel's Harbour 107 50 13N 57 35W
Danielskull 92 28 11 S 23 33 E
Danielson 113 41 50N 71 52W
Danilov 55 58 16N 40 13 E
Danilovgrad 42 42 38N 19 9 E
Danilovka 55 50 25N 44 12 E
Danissa 90 3 15N 40 58 E
Danja 85 11 21N 7 30 E
Dankalwa 85 11 52N 12 12 E
Dankama 85 13 20N 7 44 E
Dankov 55 53 20N 39 5 E
Danlí 121 14 4N 86 35W
Dannemora, Sweden 48 60 12N 17 51 E
Dannemora, U.S.A. 114 44 41N 73 44W
Dannenberg 24 53 7N 11 4 E
Dannevirke 101 40 12 S 176 8 E
Dannhauser 93 28 0 S 30 3 E
Danshui 77 25 12N 121 25 E
Dansville 114 42 32N 77 41W
Dantan 69 21 57N 87 20 E
Dante 63 10 25N 51 26 E
Danube → 43 45 20N 29 40 E
Danukandi 69 23 32N 90 43 E
Danvers 113 42 34N 70 55W
Danville, Ill., U.S.A. 114 40 10N 87 40W
Danville, Ky., U.S.A. 114 37 40N 84 45W
Danville, Va., U.S.A. 115 36 40N 79 20W
Danzhai 77 26 11N 107 48 E
Danzig = Gdańsk 28 54 22N 18 40 E
Dao 73 10 30N 121 57 E
Dão → 30 40 20N 8 11W
Dao Xian 77 25 36N 111 31 E
Daosa 68 26 52N 76 20 E
Daoud = Aïn Beida 83 35 44N 7 22 E
Daoulas 18 48 22N 4 17W
Dapong 85 10 55N 0 16 E
Daqing Shan 76 40 40N 111 0 E
Daqu Shan 77 30 25N 122 20 E
Dar al Hamrā, Ad 64 27 22N 37 43 E
Dar es Salaam 90 6 50 S 39 12 E
Dar'ā 62 32 36N 36 7 E
Dārāb 65 28 50N 54 30 E
Darabani 46 48 10N 26 39 E
Daraj 83 30 10N 10 28 E
Daravica 42 42 32N 20 8 E
Daraw 86 24 22N 32 51 E
Darazo 85 11 1N 10 24 E
Darband 66 34 20N 72 50 E
Darbhanga 69 26 15N 85 55 E
Darby 118 46 2N 114 7W
Darda 42 45 40N 18 41 E
Dardanelle 117 35 12N 93 9W
Dardanelles = Canakkale Boğazi 44 40 0N 26 0 E
Darfo 38 45 52N 10 11 E
Dargai 66 34 25N 71 55 E
Dargan Ata 58 40 29N 62 10 E
Dargaville 101 35 57 S 173 52 E
Darhan Muminggan Lianheqi 76 41 40N 110 28 E
Dari 87 5 48N 30 26 E
Darien 120 9 7N 79 46W
Darien, G. del 126 9 0N 77 0W
Darjeeling 69 27 3N 88 18 E
Dark Cove 107 48 47N 54 13W
Darling → 97 34 4 S 141 54 E
Darling Downs 99 27 30 S 150 30 E
Darling Ra. 96 32 30 S 116 0 E
Darlington, U.K. 12 54 33N 1 33W
Darlington, S.C., U.S.A. 115 34 18N 79 50W
Darlington, Wis., U.S.A. 116 42 43N 90 7W
Darlington Point 100 34 37 S 146 1 E
Darłowo 28 54 25N 16 25 E
Dărmăneşti 46 46 21N 26 33 E
Darmstadt 25 49 51N 8 40 E
Darnah 81 32 40N 22 35 E
Darnall 93 29 23 S 31 18 E
Darnétal 18 49 25N 1 10 E
Darney 19 48 5N 6 0 E
Darnick 100 32 48 S 143 38 E
Darnley B. 104 69 30N 123 30W
Darnley, C. 5 68 0 S 69 0 E
Daroca 32 41 9N 1 25W
Darr 98 23 13 S 144 7 E
Darr → 98 23 39 S 143 50 E
Darrington 118 48 14N 121 37W
Darror → 63 10 30N 50 0 E
Darsana 69 23 35N 88 48 E
Darsi 70 15 46N 79 44 E
Darsser Ort 24 54 29N 12 31 E
Dart → 13 50 24N 3 36W
Dart, C. 5 73 6 S 126 20W
Dartmoor 13 50 36N 4 0W
Dartmouth, Austral. 98 23 31 S 144 44 E
Dartmouth, Can. 107 44 40N 63 30W
Dartmouth, U.K. 13 50 21N 3 35W
Dartmouth, L. 99 26 4 S 145 18 E
Dartuch, C. 32 39 55N 3 49 E
Daru 98 9 3 S 143 13 E
Daruvar 42 45 35N 17 14 E
Darvaza 58 40 11N 58 24 E
Darwha 68 20 15N 77 45 E
Darwin 96 12 25 S 130 51 E
Darwin Glacier 5 79 53 S 159 0 E
Daryacheh-ye-Sistan 65 31 0N 61 0 E
Daryapur 68 20 55N 77 20 E
Das 65 25 20N 53 30 E
Dashkesan 57 40 40N 46 0 E
Dasht → 65 25 10N 61 40 E
Dasht-e Kavīr 65 34 30N 55 0 E
Dasht-e Lūt 65 31 30N 58 0 E
Dasht-e Mārgow 65 30 40N 62 30 E
Daska 68 32 20N 74 20 E
Dassa-Zoume 85 7 46N 2 14 E
Dasseneiland 92 33 25 S 18 3 E
Datça 45 36 46N 27 40 E
Datia 68 25 39N 78 27 E
Datian 77 25 40N 117 50 E
Datong, Anhui, China 77 30 48N 117 44 E
Datong, Shanxi, China 76 40 6N 113 18 E
Dattapur 68 20 45N 78 15 E
Datu Piang 73 7 2N 124 30 E
Datu, Tanjung 72 2 5N 109 39 E
Daugava → 54 57 4N 24 3 E
Daugavpils 54 55 53N 26 32 E
Daulatabad 70 19 57N 75 15 E
Daun 25 50 10N 6 53 E
Dauphin 109 51 9N 100 5W
Dauphin I. 115 30 16N 88 10W
Dauphin L. 109 51 20N 99 45W
Dauphiné 21 45 15N 5 25 E
Dauqa 86 19 30N 41 0 E
Daura, Borno, Nigeria 85 11 31N 11 24 E
Daura, Kaduna, Nigeria 85 13 2N 8 21 E
Davangere 70 14 25N 75 55 E
Davao 73 7 0N 125 40 E
Davao, G. of 73 6 30N 125 48 E
Dāvar Panāh 65 27 25N 62 15 E
Davenport, Iowa, U.S.A. 116 41 30N 90 40W
Davenport, Wash., U.S.A. 118 47 40N 118 5W
Davenport Downs 98 24 8 S 141 7 E
Davenport Ra. 96 20 28 S 134 0 E
David 121 8 30N 82 30W
David City 116 41 18N 97 10W
David Gorodok 54 52 4N 27 8 E
Davidson 109 51 16N 105 59W
Davis, Antarct. 5 68 34 S 77 55 E
Davis, U.S.A. 118 38 33N 121 44W
Davis Dam 119 35 11N 114 35W
Davis Inlet 107 55 50N 60 59W
Davis Mts. 117 30 42N 104 15W
Davis Sea 5 66 0 S 92 0 E
Davis Str. 105 65 0N 58 0W
Davos 25 46 48N 9 49 E
Davy L. 109 58 53N 108 18W
Dawa → 87 4 11N 42 6 E
Dawaki, Bauchi, Nigeria 85 9 25N 9 33 E
Dawaki, Kano, Nigeria 85 12 5N 8 23 E
Dawes Ra. 98 24 40 S 150 40 E
Dawson, Can. 104 64 10N 139 30W
Dawson, Ga., U.S.A. 115 31 45N 84 28W
Dawson, N.D., U.S.A. 116 46 56N 99 45W
Dawson → 97 23 25 S 149 45 E
Dawson Creek 108 55 45N 120 15W
Dawson, I. 128 53 50 S 70 50W
Dawson Inlet 109 61 50N 93 25W
Dawson Range 98 24 30 S 149 48 E
Dax 20 43 44N 1 3W
Daxian 75 31 15N 107 23 E
Daxin 77 22 50N 107 11 E
Daxue Shan 75 30 30N 101 30 E
Daye 77 30 6N 114 58 E
Daylesford 100 37 21 S 144 9 E
Dayong 77 29 11N 110 30 E
Dayr Abū Sa'īd 62 32 30N 35 42 E
Dayr al-Ghuṣūn 62 32 21N 35 4 E
Dayr az Zawr 64 35 20N 40 5 E
Dayr Dirwān 62 31 55N 35 15 E
Daysland 108 52 50N 112 20W
Dayton, Ohio, U.S.A. 114 39 45N 84 10W
Dayton, Pa., U.S.A. 112 40 54N 79 18W
Dayton, Tenn., U.S.A. 115 35 30N 85 1W
Dayton, Wash., U.S.A. 118 46 20N 118 10W
Daytona Beach 115 29 14N 81 0W
Dayu 77 25 24N 114 22 E
Dayville 118 44 33N 119 37W
Dazhu 77 30 41N 107 15 E
Dazu 77 29 40N 105 42 E
De Aar 92 30 39 S 24 0 E
De Funiak Springs 115 30 42N 86 10W
De Grey 96 20 12 S 119 12 E
De Land 115 29 1N 81 19W
De Leon 117 32 9N 98 35W
De Pere 114 44 28N 88 1W
De Queen 117 34 3N 94 24W
De Quincy 117 30 30N 93 27W
De Ridder 117 30 48N 93 15W
De Smet 116 44 25N 97 35W
De Soto 116 38 7N 90 33W
De Tour 114 45 59N 83 56W
De Witt 117 34 19N 91 20W
Dead Sea = Miyet, Bahr el 64 31 30N 35 30 E
Deadwood 116 44 23N 103 44W
Deadwood L. 108 59 10N 128 30W
Deakin 96 30 46 S 128 0 E
Deal 13 51 13N 1 25 E
Dealesville 92 28 41 S 25 44 E
Dean, Forest of 13 51 50N 2 35W
Deán Funes 124 30 20 S 64 20W
Dearborn 106 42 18N 83 15W
Dease → 108 59 56N 128 32W
Dease L. 108 58 40N 130 5W
Dease Lake 108 58 25N 130 6W
Death Valley 119 36 19N 116 52W
Death Valley Junc. 119 36 21N 116 30W
Death Valley Nat. Monument 119 36 30N 117 0W
Deauville 18 49 23N 0 2 E
Deba Habe 85 10 14N 11 20 E
Debaltsevo 56 48 22N 38 26 E
Debao 77 23 21N 106 46 E
Debar 42 41 31N 20 30 E
Debden 109 53 30N 106 50W
Debdou 82 33 59N 3 0W
Dębica 27 50 2N 21 25 E
Dęblin 28 51 34N 21 50 E
Debno 28 52 44N 14 41 E
Débo, L. 84 15 14N 4 15W
Debolt 108 55 12N 118 1W
Debrc 42 44 38N 19 53 E
Debre Birhan 87 9 41N 39 31 E
Debre Markos 87 10 20N 37 40 E
Debre May 87 11 20N 37 25 E
Debre Sina 87 9 51N 39 50 E
Debre Tabor 87 11 50N 38 26 E
Debre Zebit 87 11 48N 38 30 E
Debrecen 27 47 33N 21 42 E
Dečani 42 42 30N 20 10 E
Decatur, Ala., U.S.A. 115 34 35N 87 0W
Decatur, Ga., U.S.A. 115 33 47N 84 17W
Decatur, Ill., U.S.A. 116 39 50N 89 0W
Decatur, Ind , U.S.A. 114 40 50N 84 56W
Decatur, Texas, U.S.A. 117 33 15N 97 35W
Decazeville 20 44 34N 2 15 E
Deccan 70 18 0N 79 0 E
Deception I. 5 63 0 S 60 15W
Deception L. 109 56 33N 104 13W
Děčín 26 50 47N 14 12 E
Decize 19 46 50N 3 28 E
Deckerville 112 43 33N 82 46W
Decollatura 41 39 2N 16 21 E
Decorah 116 43 20N 91 50W
Deda 46 46 56N 24 50 E
Dedéagach = Alexandroúpotis 44 40 50N 25 54 E
Dedham 113 42 14N 71 10W
Dedilovo 55 53 59N 37 50 E
Dédougou 84 12 30N 3 25W
Deduru Oya 70 7 32N 79 50 E
Dedza 91 14 20 S 34 20 E
Dee →, Scot., U.K. 14 57 4N 2 7W
Dee →, Wales, U.K. 12 53 15N 3 7W
Deep B. 108 61 15N 116 35W
Deepdale 96 21 42 S 116 10 E
Deepwater 99 29 25 S 151 51 E
Deer → 109 58 23N 94 13W
Deer Lake, Newf., Can. 107 49 11N 57 27W
Deer Lake, Ontario, Can. 109 52 36N 94 20W
Deer Lodge 118 46 25N 112 40W
Deer Park 118 47 55N 117 21W
Deer River 116 47 21N 93 44W
Deeral 98 17 14 S 145 55 E
Deerdepoort 92 24 37 S 26 27 E
Deesa 68 24 18N 72 10 E
Deferiet 113 44 2N 75 41W
Defiance 114 41 20N 84 20W
Deganya 62 32 43N 35 34 E
Degebe → 31 38 13N 7 29W
Degeh Bur 63 8 11N 43 31 E
Degema 85 4 50N 6 48 E
Deggendorf 25 48 49N 12 59 E
Degloor 70 18 34N 77 33 E
Deh Bīd 65 30 39N 53 11 E
Deh Kheyr 65 28 45N 54 40 E
Dehibat 83 32 0N 10 47 E
Dehiwala 70 6 50N 79 51 E
Dehkareqan 64 37 43N 45 55 E
Dehra Dun 68 30 20N 78 4 E
Dehri 69 24 50N 84 15 E
Dehui 76 44 30N 125 40 E
Deinze 16 50 59N 3 32 E
Dej 46 47 10N 23 52 E
Deje 48 59 35N 13 29 E
Dekalb 116 41 55N 88 45W
Dekemhare 87 15 6N 39 0 E
Dekese 88 3 24 S 21 24 E
Del Norte 119 37 40N 106 27W
Del Rio 117 29 23N 100 50W
Delagua 117 37 21N 104 35W
Delai 86 17 21N 36 6 E
Delano 119 35 48N 119 13W
Delareyville 92 26 41 S 25 26 E
Delavan 116 42 40N 88 39W
Delaware 114 40 20N 83 0W
Delaware □ 114 39 0N 75 40W
Delaware → 114 39 20N 75 25W
Delčevo 42 41 58N 22 46 E
Delegate 99 37 4 S 148 56 E
Delémont 25 47 22N 7 20 E
Delft 16 52 1N 4 22 E
Delft I. 70 9 30N 79 40 E
Delfzijl 16 53 20N 6 55 E
Delgado, C. 91 10 45 S 40 40 E
Delgo 86 20 6N 30 40 E
Delhi, Can. 112 42 51N 80 30W
Delhi, India 68 28 38N 77 17 E
Delhi, U.S.A. 113 42 17N 74 56W
Deli Jovan 42 44 13N 22 9 E
Delia 108 51 38N 112 23W
Delice → 64 39 45N 34 15 E
Delicias 120 28 10N 105 30W
Delitzsch 24 51 32N 12 22 E
Dell City 119 31 58N 105 19W
Dell Rapids 116 43 53N 96 44W
Delle 19 47 30N 7 2 E
Dellys 83 36 57N 3 57 E
Delmar 113 42 37N 73 47W
Delmenhorst 24 53 3N 8 37 E
Delmiro Gouveia 127 9 24 S 38 6W
Delnice 39 45 23N 14 50 E
Delong, Ostrova 59 76 40N 149 20 E
Deloraine, Austral. 99 41 30 S 146 40 E
Deloraine, Can. 109 49 15N 100 29W
Delorme, L. 107 54 31N 69 52W
Delphi, Greece 45 38 28N 22 30 E
Delphi, U.S.A. 114 40 37N 86 40W
Delphos 114 40 51N 84 17W
Delportshoop 92 28 22 S 24 20 E
Delray Beach 115 26 27N 80 4W
Delsbo 48 61 48N 16 32 E
Delta, Colo., U.S.A. 119 38 44N 108 5W
Delta, Utah, U.S.A. 118 39 21N 112 29W
Delungra 99 29 39 S 150 51 E
Delvina 44 39 59N 20 4 E
Delvinákion 44 39 57N 20 32 E
Demanda, Sierra de la 32 42 15N 3 0W
Demba 88 5 28 S 22 15 E
Dembecha 87 10 32N 37 30 E
Dembi 87 8 5N 36 25 E
Dembia 90 3 33N 25 48 E
Dembidolo 87 8 34N 34 50 E
Demer → 16 50 57N 4 42 E
Demetrias 44 39 22N 23 1 E
Demidov 54 55 16N 31 30 E
Deming 119 32 10N 107 50W
Demini → 126 0 46 S 62 56W
Demmin 24 53 54N 13 2 E
Demnate 82 31 44N 6 59W
Demonte 38 44 18N 7 18 E
Demopolis 115 32 30N 87 48W
Dempo, Mt. 72 4 2 S 103 15 E
Demyansk 54 57 40N 32 27 E
Den Burg 16 53 3N 4 47 E
Den Haag = 's Gravenhage 16 52 7N 4 17 E
Den Helder 16 52 57N 4 45 E
Den Oever 16 52 56N 5 2 E
Denain 19 50 20N 3 22 E
Denau 58 38 16N 67 54 E
Denbigh 12 53 12N 3 26W
Dendang 72 3 7 S 107 56 E
Dendermonde 16 51 2N 4 5 E
Deneba 87 9 47N 39 10 E
Deng Xian 77 32 34N 112 4 E
Denge 85 12 52N 5 21 E
Dengi 85 9 25N 9 55 E
Denham 96 25 56 S 113 31 E
Denham Ra. 97 21 55 S 147 46 E
Denia 33 38 49N 0 8 E
Deniliquin 97 35 30 S 144 58 E
Denison, Iowa, U.S.A. 116 42 0N 95 18W
Denison, Texas, U.S.A. 117 33 50N 96 40W
Denison Range 97 28 30 S 136 5 E
Denizli 64 37 42N 29 2 E
Denman Glacier 5 66 45 S 99 25 E
Denmark 96 34 59 S 117 25 E
Denmark ■ 49 55 30N 9 0 E
Denmark Str. 6 66 0N 30 0W
Dennison 112 40 21N 81 21W
Denpasar 72 8 45 S 115 14 E
Denton, Mont., U.S.A. 118 47 25N 109 56W
Denton, Texas, U.S.A. 117 33 12N 97 10W
D'Entrecasteaux Is. 98 9 0 S 151 0 E
D'Entrecasteaux Pt. 96 34 50 S 115 57 E
Denu 85 6 4N 1 8 E
Denver 116 39 45N 105 0W
Denver City 117 32 58N 102 48W
Deoband 68 29 42N 77 43 E
Deobhog 70 19 53N 82 44 E
Deogarh 69 21 32N 84 45 E
Deoghar 69 24 30N 86 42 E
Deolali 70 19 58N 73 50 E
Deoli 68 25 50N 75 20 E
Deoria 69 26 31N 83 48 E
Deosai Mts. 69 35 40N 75 0 E
Depew 112 42 55N 78 43W
Deping 76 37 25N 116 58 E
Deposit 113 42 5N 75 23W
Deputatskiy 59 69 18N 139 54 E
Dêqên 75 28 34N 98 51 E
Deqing 77 23 8N 111 42 E
Dera Ghazi Khan 68 30 5N 70 43 E
Dera Ismail Khan 68 31 50N 70 50 E
Dera Ismail Khan □ 68 32 30N 70 0 E
Derbent 56 42 5N 48 4 E
Derby, Austral. 96 17 18 S 123 38 E
Derby, U.K. 12 52 55N 1 28W
Derby, Conn., U.S.A. 113 41 20N 73 5W
Derby, N.Y., U.S.A. 112 42 40N 78 59W
Derby □ 12 52 55N 1 28W
Derecske 27 47 20N 21 33 E
Derg → 15 54 42N 7 26W
Derg, L. 15 53 0N 8 20W
Dergachi 55 50 9N 36 11 E
Dergaon 67 26 45N 94 0 E
Dermantsi 43 43 8N 24 17 E
Dernieres Isles 117 29 0N 90 45W
Derryveagh Mts. 15 55 0N 8 40W
Derudub 86 17 31N 36 7 E
Derval 18 47 40N 1 41W
Dervéni 45 38 8N 22 25 E
Derventa 42 44 59N 17 55 E
Derwent 109 53 41N 110 58W
Derwent →, Derby, U.K. 12 52 53N 1 17W
Derwent →, N. Yorks., U.K. 12 53 45N 0 57W
Derwentwater, L. 12 54 35N 3 9W
Des Moines, Iowa, U.S.A. 116 41 35N 93 37W
Des Moines, N. Mex., U.S.A. 117 36 50N 103 51W
Des Moines → 116 40 23N 91 25W
Desaguadero →, Argent. 124 34 30 S 66 46W
Desaguadero →, Boliv. 126 18 24 S 67 5W
Deschaillons 107 46 32N 72 7W
Descharme → 109 56 51N 109 13W
Deschutes → 118 45 30N 121 0W
Dese 87 11 5N 39 40 E
Desenzano del Gardo 38 45 28N 10 32 E
Desert Center 119 33 45N 115 27W
Deskenatlata L. 108 60 55N 112 3W
Desna → 54 50 33N 30 32 E
Desnătui → 46 44 15N 23 27 E
Desolación, I. 128 53 0 S 74 0W
Despeñaperros, Paso 33 38 24N 3 30W
Despotovac 42 44 6N 21 30 E
Dessau 24 51 49N 12 15 E
Dessye = Dese 87 11 5N 39 40 E

D'Estrees B.	**99**	35 55 S	137 45 E
Desuri	**68**	25 18N	73 35 E
Desvrès	**19**	50 40N	1 48 E
Deta	**42**	45 24N	21 13 E
Detinja →	**42**	43 51N	19 45 E
Detmold	**24**	51 55N	8 50 E
Detour Pt.	**114**	45 37N	86 35W
Detroit, Mich., U.S.A.	**106**	42 23N	83 5W
Detroit, Tex., U.S.A.	**117**	33 40N	95 10W
Detroit Lakes	**116**	46 50N	95 50W
Dett	**91**	18 38 S	26 50 E
Deurne, Belg.	**16**	51 12N	4 24 E
Deurne, Neth.	**16**	51 27N	5 49 E
Deutsche Bucht	**24**	54 10N	7 51 E
Deutschlandsberg	**26**	46 49N	15 14 E
Deux-Sèvres □	**18**	46 35N	0 20W
Deva	**46**	45 53N	22 55 E
Devakottai	**70**	9 55N	78 45 E
Devaprayag	**68**	30 13N	78 35 E
Dévaványa	**27**	47 2N	20 59 E
Deveci Daği	**56**	40 10N	36 0 E
Devecser	**27**	47 6N	17 26 E
Deventer	**16**	52 15N	6 10 E
Deveron →	**14**	57 40N	2 31W
Devesel	**46**	44 28N	22 41 E
Devgad Baria	**68**	22 40N	73 55 E
Devgad, I.	**70**	14 48N	74 5 E
Devils Lake	**116**	48 5N	98 50W
Devils Paw	**108**	58 47N	134 0W
Devil's Pt.	**70**	9 26N	80 6 E
Devin	**43**	41 44N	24 24 E
Devizes	**13**	51 21N	2 0W
Devnya	**43**	43 13N	27 33 E
Devolii →	**44**	40 57N	20 15 E
Devon	**108**	53 24N	113 44W
Devon I.	**4**	75 10N	85 0W
Devonport, Austral.	**97**	41 10 S	146 22 E
Devonport, N.Z.	**101**	36 49 S	174 49 E
Devonport, U.K.	**13**	50 23N	4 11W
Devonshire □	**13**	50 50N	3 40W
Dewas	**68**	22 59N	76 3 E
Dewetsdorp	**92**	29 33 S	26 39 E
Dewsbury	**12**	53 42N	1 38W
Dexter, Mo., U.S.A.	**117**	36 50N	90 0W
Dexter, N. Mex., U.S.A.	**117**	33 15N	104 25W
Deyhūk	**65**	33 15N	57 30 E
Deyyer	**65**	27 55N	51 55 E
Dezadeash L.	**108**	60 28N	136 58W
Dezfūl	**64**	32 20N	48 30 E
Dezh Shāhpūr	**64**	35 30N	46 25 E
Dezhneva, Mys	**59**	66 5N	169 40W
Dezhou	**76**	37 26N	116 18 E
Dháfni	**45**	37 48N	22 1 E
Dhafra	**65**	23 20N	54 0 E
Dhahaban	**86**	21 58N	39 3 E
Dhahira	**65**	23 40N	57 0 E
Dhahiriya = Aẓ Ẓāhirīyah	**62**	31 25N	34 58 E
Dhahran = Aẓ Ẓahrān	**64**	26 18N	50 10 E
Dhamar	**63**	14 30N	44 20 E
Dhamási	**44**	39 43N	22 11 E
Dhampur	**68**	29 19N	78 33 E
Dhamtari	**69**	20 42N	81 35 E
Dhanbad	**69**	23 50N	86 30 E
Dhankuta	**69**	26 55N	87 40 E
Dhanora	**69**	20 20N	80 22 E
Dhar	**68**	22 35N	75 26 E
Dharampur, Gujarat, India	**70**	20 32N	73 17 E
Dharampur, Mad. P., India	**68**	22 13N	75 18 E
Dharapuram	**70**	10 45N	77 34 E
Dharmapuri	**70**	12 10N	78 10 E
Dharmavaram	**70**	14 29N	77 44 E
Dharmsala (Dharamsala)	**68**	32 16N	76 23 E
Dhaulagiri	**69**	28 39N	83 28 E
Dhebar, L.	**68**	24 10N	74 0 E
Dhenkanal	**69**	20 45N	85 35 E
Dhenoúsa	**45**	37 8N	25 48 E
Dheskáti	**44**	39 55N	21 49 E
Dhespotikó	**45**	36 57N	24 58 E
Dhestina	**45**	38 25N	22 31 E
Dhidhimótikhon	**44**	41 22N	26 29 E
Dhikti	**45**	35 8N	25 22 E
Dhilianáta	**45**	38 15N	20 34 E
Dhílos	**45**	37 23N	25 15 E
Dhimitsána	**45**	37 36N	22 3 E
Dhírfis	**45**	38 40N	23 54 E
Dhodhekánisos	**45**	36 35N	27 0 E
Dhokós	**45**	37 20N	23 20 E
Dholiana	**44**	39 54N	20 32 E
Dholka	**68**	22 44N	72 29 E
Dholpur	**68**	26 45N	77 59 E
Dhomokós	**45**	39 10N	22 18 E
Dhond	**70**	18 26N	74 40 E
Dhoraji	**68**	21 45N	70 37 E
Dhoxáton	**44**	41 9N	24 16 E
Dhragonísi	**45**	37 27N	25 29 E
Dhrangadhra	**68**	22 59N	71 31 E
Dhriopís	**45**	37 25N	24 35 E
Dhrol	**68**	22 33N	70 25 E
Dhubaibah	**65**	23 25N	54 35 E
Dhubri	**69**	26 2N	89 59 E
Dhula	**63**	15 10N	47 30 E
Dhulia	**68**	20 58N	74 50 E
Dhurm →	**86**	20 18N	42 53 E
Di Linh, Cao Nguyen	**71**	11 30N	108 0 E
Día	**45**	35 26N	25 13 E
Diablo Heights	**120**	8 58N	79 34W
Diafarabé	**84**	14 9N	4 57W
Diala	**84**	14 10N	10 0W
Dialakoro	**84**	12 18N	7 54W
Diallassagou	**84**	13 47N	3 41W
Diamante	**124**	32 5 S	60 40W
Diamante →	**124**	34 30 S	66 46W
Diamantina	**127**	18 17 S	43 40W
Diamantina →	**97**	26 45 S	139 10 E
Diamantino	**127**	14 30 S	56 30W
Diamond Harbour	**69**	22 11N	88 14 E
Diamond Mts.	**118**	40 0N	115 58W
Diamondville	**118**	41 51N	110 30W
Diancheng	**77**	21 30N	111 4 E
Diano Marina	**38**	43 55N	8 3 E
Dianra	**84**	8 45N	6 14W
Diapaga	**85**	12 5N	1 46 E
Diapangou	**85**	12 5N	0 10 E
Diariguila	**84**	10 35N	10 2W
Dibaya	**88**	6 30 S	22 57 E
Dibaya-Lubue	**88**	4 12 S	19 54 E
Dibbi	**87**	4 10N	41 52 E
Dibble Glacier Tongue	**5**	66 8 S	134 32 E
Dibete	**92**	23 45 S	26 32 E
Dibrugarh	**67**	27 29N	94 55 E
Dickinson	**116**	46 50N	102 48W
Dickson	**115**	36 5N	87 22W
Dickson City	**113**	41 29N	75 40W
Dickson (Dikson)	**58**	73 40N	80 5 E
Dicomano	**39**	43 53N	11 30 E
Didesa, W. →	**87**	10 2N	35 32 E
Didiéni	**84**	13 53N	8 6W
Didsbury	**108**	51 35N	114 10W
Didwana	**68**	27 23N	17 36 E
Die	**21**	44 47N	5 22 E
Diébougou	**84**	11 0N	3 15W
Diefenbaker L.	**109**	51 0N	106 55W
Diego Garcia	**3**	7 50 S	72 50 E
Diekirch	**16**	49 52N	6 10 E
Diélette	**18**	49 33N	1 52W
Diéma	**84**	14 32N	9 12W
Diémbéring	**84**	12 29N	16 47W
Dien Bien Phu	**71**	21 20N	103 0 E
Diepholz	**24**	52 37N	8 22 E
Dieppe	**18**	49 54N	1 4 E
Dieren	**16**	52 3N	6 6 E
Dierks	**117**	34 9N	94 0W
Diest	**16**	50 58N	5 4 E
Dieulefit	**21**	44 32N	5 4 E
Dieuze	**19**	48 49N	6 43 E
Differdange	**16**	49 31N	5 54 E
Dig	**68**	27 28N	77 20 E
Digba	**90**	4 25N	25 48 E
Digby	**107**	44 38N	65 50W
Digges	**109**	58 40N	94 0W
Digges Is.	**105**	62 40N	77 50W
Dighinala	**67**	23 15N	92 5 E
Dighton	**116**	38 30N	100 26W
Digne	**21**	44 5N	6 12 E
Digoin	**20**	46 29N	3 58 E
Digos	**73**	6 45N	125 20 E
Digranes	**50**	66 4N	14 44 E
Digras	**70**	20 6N	77 45 E
Digul →	**73**	7 7 S	138 42 E
Dihang →	**67**	27 48N	95 30 E
Dijlah, Nahr →	**64**	31 0N	47 25 E
Dijon	**19**	47 20N	5 0 E
Dikala	**87**	4 45N	31 28 E
Dikkil	**87**	11 8N	42 20 E
Dikomu di Kai	**92**	24 58 S	24 36 E
Diksmuide	**16**	51 2N	2 52 E
Dikwa	**85**	12 4N	13 30 E
Dila	**87**	6 21N	38 22 E
Dili	**73**	8 39 S	125 34 E
Dilizhan	**57**	40 46N	44 57 E
Dilj	**42**	45 29N	18 1 E
Dillenburg	**24**	50 44N	8 17 E
Dilley	**117**	28 40N	99 12W
Dilling	**87**	12 3N	29 35 E
Dillingen	**25**	48 32N	10 29 E
Dillon, Can.	**109**	55 56N	108 35W
Dillon, Mont., U.S.A.	**118**	45 9N	112 36W
Dillon, S.C., U.S.A.	**115**	34 26N	79 20W
Dillon →	**109**	55 56N	108 56W
Dilston	**99**	41 22 S	147 10 E
Dimashq	**64**	33 30N	36 18 E
Dimbokro	**84**	6 45N	4 46W
Dimboola	**99**	36 28 S	142 7 E
Dîmboviţa □	**46**	45 0N	25 30 E
Dîmboviţa →	**46**	44 14N	26 13 E
Dîmbovnic →	**46**	44 28N	25 18 E
Dimbulah	**98**	17 8 S	145 4 E
Dimitrovgrad, Bulg.	**43**	42 5N	25 35 E
Dimitrovgrad, U.S.S.R.	**55**	54 14N	49 39 E
Dimitrovgrad, Yugo.	**42**	43 0N	22 48 E
Dimitrovo = Pernik	**42**	42 35N	23 2 E
Dimmitt	**117**	34 36N	102 16W
Dimo	**87**	5 19N	29 10 E
Dimona	**62**	31 2N	35 1 E
Dimovo	**42**	43 43N	22 50 E
Dinagat	**73**	10 10N	125 40 E
Dinajpur	**69**	25 33N	88 43 E
Dinan	**18**	48 28N	2 2W
Dinant	**16**	50 16N	4 55 E
Dinapur	**69**	25 38N	85 5 E
Dinar	**64**	38 5N	30 15 E
Dinara Planina	**39**	43 50N	16 35 E
Dinard	**18**	48 38N	2 6W
Dinaric Alps = Dinara Planina	**9**	43 50N	16 35 E
Dinder, Nahr ed →	**87**	14 6N	33 40 E
Dindi →	**70**	16 24N	78 15 E
Dindigul	**70**	10 25N	78 0 E
Ding Xian	**76**	38 30N	114 59 E
Dingbian	**76**	37 35N	107 32 E
Dingelstädt	**24**	51 19N	10 19 E
Dinghai	**77**	30 1N	122 6 E
Dingle	**15**	52 9N	10 17W
Dingle B.	**15**	52 3N	10 20W
Dingmans Ferry	**113**	41 13N	74 55W
Dingnan	**77**	24 45N	115 0 E
Dingo	**98**	23 38 S	149 19 E
Dingolfing	**25**	48 38N	12 30 E
Dingtao	**77**	35 5N	115 35 E
Dinguiraye	**84**	11 18N	10 49W
Dingwall	**14**	57 36N	4 26W
Dingxi	**76**	35 30N	104 33 E
Dingxiang	**76**	38 30N	112 58 E
Dinokwe (Palla Road)	**92**	23 29 S	26 37 E
Dinosaur National Monument	**118**	40 30N	108 58W
Dinuba	**119**	36 31N	119 22W
Dio	**49**	56 37N	14 15 E
Diósgyör	**27**	48 7N	20 43 E
Diosig	**46**	47 18N	22 2 E
Diourbel	**84**	14 39N	16 12W
Diplo	**68**	24 35N	69 35 E
Dipolog	**73**	8 36N	123 20 E
Dipşa	**46**	46 58N	24 27 E
Dir	**66**	35 08N	71 59 E
Diré	**84**	16 20N	3 25W
Dire Dawa	**87**	9 35N	41 45 E
Direction, C.	**97**	12 51 S	143 32 E
Diriamba	**121**	11 51N	86 19W
Dirk Hartog I.	**96**	25 50 S	113 5 E
Dirranbandi	**97**	28 33 S	148 17 E
Disa	**87**	12 5N	34 15 E
Disappointment, C.	**118**	46 20N	124 0W
Disappointment L.	**96**	23 20 S	122 40 E
Disaster B.	**97**	37 15 S	150 0 E
Discovery B.	**97**	38 10 S	140 40 E
Disentis	**25**	46 42N	8 50 E
Dishna	**86**	26 9N	32 32 E
Disina	**85**	11 35N	9 50 E
Disko	**4**	69 45N	53 30W
Disko Bugt	**4**	69 10N	52 0W
Disna	**54**	55 32N	28 11 E
Disna →	**54**	55 34N	28 12 E
Distrito Federal □	**127**	15 45 S	47 45W
Disûq	**86**	31 8N	30 35 E
Diu	**68**	20 45N	70 58 E
Dives →	**18**	49 18N	0 7W
Dives-sur-Mer	**18**	49 18N	0 8W
Divi Pt.	**70**	15 59N	81 9 E
Divichi	**57**	41 15N	48 57 E
Divide	**118**	45 48N	112 47W
Divinópolis	**127**	20 10 S	44 54W
Divnoye	**57**	45 55N	43 21 E
Divo	**84**	5 48N	5 15W
Diwal Kol	**66**	34 23N	67 52 E
Dixie	**118**	45 37N	115 27W
Dixon, Ill., U.S.A.	**116**	41 50N	89 30W
Dixon, Mont., U.S.A.	**118**	47 19N	114 25W
Dixon, N. Mex., U.S.A.	**119**	36 15N	105 57W
Dixon Entrance	**108**	54 30N	132 0W
Dixonville	**108**	56 32N	117 40W
Diyarbakir	**64**	37 55N	40 18 E
Diz Chah	**65**	35 30N	55 30 E
Djado	**83**	21 4N	12 14 E
Djado, Plateau du	**83**	21 29N	12 21 E
Djakarta = Jakarta	**73**	6 9 S	106 49 E
Djamâa	**83**	33 32N	5 59 E
Djamba	**92**	16 45 S	13 58 E
Djambala	**88**	2 32 S	14 30 E
Djanet	**83**	24 35N	9 32 E
Djaul I.	**98**	2 58 S	150 57 E
Djawa = Jawa	**73**	7 0 S	110 0 E
Djebiniana	**83**	35 1N	11 0 E
Djelfa	**82**	34 40N	3 15 E
Djema	**90**	6 3N	25 15 E
Djendel	**82**	36 15N	2 25 E
Djeneïene	**83**	31 45N	10 9 E
Djenné	**84**	14 0N	4 30W
Djenoun, Garet el	**83**	25 4N	5 31 E
Djerba	**83**	33 52N	10 51 E
Djerba, Île de	**83**	33 56N	11 0 E
Djerid, Chott	**83**	33 42N	8 30 E
Djibo	**85**	14 9N	1 35W
Djibouti	**87**	11 30N	43 5 E
Djibouti ■	**63**	12 0N	43 0 E
Djolu	**88**	0 35N	22 5 E
Djorong	**72**	3 58 S	114 56 E
Djougou	**85**	9 40N	1 45 E
Djoum	**88**	2 41N	12 35 E
Djourab	**81**	16 40N	18 50 E
Djugu	**90**	1 55N	30 35 E
Djúpivogur	**50**	64 39N	14 17W
Djursholm	**48**	59 25N	18 6 E
Djursland	**49**	56 27N	10 45 E
Dmitriev-Lgovskiy	**54**	52 10N	35 0 E
Dmitriya Lapteva, Proliv	**59**	73 0N	140 0 E
Dmitrov	**55**	56 25N	37 32 E
Dmitrovsk-Orlovskiy	**54**	52 29N	35 10 E
Dneiper = Dnepr →	**56**	46 30N	32 18 E
Dnepr →	**56**	46 30N	32 18 E
Dneprodzerzhinsk	**56**	48 32N	34 37 E
Dneprodzerzhinskoye Vdkhr.	**56**	49 0N	34 0 E
Dnepropetrovsk	**56**	48 30N	35 0 E
Dneprorudnoye	**56**	47 21N	34 58 E
Dnestr →	**56**	46 18N	30 17 E
Dnestrovski = Belgorod	**56**	50 35N	36 35 E
Dniester = Dnestr →	**56**	46 18N	30 17 E
Dno	**54**	57 50N	29 58 E
Doba	**81**	8 40N	16 50 E
Dobbiaco	**39**	46 44N	12 13 E
Dobbyn	**97**	19 44 S	139 59 E
Dobczyce	**27**	49 52N	20 25 E
Döbeln	**24**	51 7N	13 10 E
Doberai, Jazirah	**73**	1 25 S	133 0 E
Dobiegniew	**28**	52 59N	15 45 E
Doblas	**124**	37 5 S	64 0W
Dobo	**73**	5 45 S	134 15 E
Doboj	**42**	44 46N	18 6 E
Dobra, Konin, Poland	**28**	51 55N	18 37 E
Dobra, Szczecin, Poland	**28**	53 34N	15 20 E
Dobra, Dîmbovita, Romania	**43**	44 52N	25 40 E
Dobra, Hunedoara, Romania	**46**	45 54N	22 36 E
Dobre Miasto	**28**	53 58N	20 26 E
Dobrinishta	**43**	41 49N	23 34 E
Dobřiš	**26**	49 46N	14 10 E
Dobrodzień	**28**	50 45N	18 25 E
Dobropole	**56**	48 25N	37 2 E
Dobruja	**46**	44 30N	28 15 E
Dobrush	**55**	52 28N	30 19 E
Dobrzyń nad Wisłą	**28**	52 39N	19 22 E
Dobtong	**87**	6 25N	31 40 E
Dodecanese = Dhodhekánisos	**45**	36 35N	27 0 E
Dodge Center	**116**	44 1N	92 50W
Dodge City	**117**	37 42N	100 0W
Dodge L.	**109**	59 50N	105 36W
Dodgeville	**116**	42 55N	90 8W
Dodo	**87**	5 10N	29 57 E
Dodola	**87**	6 59N	39 11 E
Dodoma	**90**	6 8 S	35 45 E
Dodoma □	**90**	6 0 S	36 0 E
Dodona	**44**	39 40N	20 46 E
Dodsland	**109**	51 50N	108 45W
Dodson	**118**	48 23N	108 16W
Doetinchem	**16**	51 59N	6 18 E
Doftana	**46**	45 11N	25 45 E
Dog Creek	**108**	51 35N	122 14W
Dog L., Man., Can.	**109**	51 2N	98 31W
Dog L., Ont., Can.	**106**	48 18N	89 30W
Doğanbey	**45**	37 40N	27 10 E
Dogliani	**38**	44 35N	7 55 E
Dogondoutchi	**85**	13 38N	4 2 E
Dogran	**68**	31 48N	73 35 E
Doguéraoua	**85**	14 0N	5 31 E
Dohad	**68**	22 50N	74 15 E
Dohazari	**67**	22 10N	92 5 E
Doi	**73**	2 14N	127 49 E
Doi Luang	**71**	18 30N	101 0 E
Doig →	**108**	56 25N	120 40W
Dois Irmãos, Sa.	**127**	9 0 S	42 30W
Dojransko Jezero	**42**	41 13N	22 44 E
Dokka	**47**	60 49N	10 7 E
Dokka →	**47**	61 7N	10 0 E
Dokkum	**16**	53 20N	5 59 E
Dokri	**68**	27 25N	68 7 E
Dol-de-Bretagne	**18**	48 34N	1 47W
Doland	**116**	44 55N	98 5W
Dolbeau	**107**	48 53N	72 18W
Dole	**19**	47 7N	5 31 E
Doleib, Wadi →	**87**	12 10N	33 15 E
Dolgellau	**12**	52 44N	3 53W
Dolgelley = Dolgellau	**12**	52 44N	3 53W
Dolginovo	**54**	54 39N	27 29 E
Dolianova	**40**	39 23N	9 11 E
Dolinskaya	**56**	48 6N	32 46 E
Dolj □	**46**	44 10N	23 30 E
Dollart	**16**	53 20N	7 10 E
Dolna Banya	**43**	42 18N	23 44 E
Dolni Dŭbnik	**43**	43 24N	24 26 E
Dolo, Ethiopia	**87**	4 11N	42 3 E
Dolo, Italy	**39**	45 25N	12 4 E
Dolomites = Dolomiti	**39**	46 30N	11 40 E
Dolomiti	**39**	46 30N	11 40 E
Dolores, Argent.	**124**	36 20 S	57 40W
Dolores, Uruguay	**124**	33 34 S	58 15W
Dolores, Colo., U.S.A.	**119**	37 30N	108 30W
Dolores, Tex., U.S.A.	**117**	27 40N	99 38W
Dolores →	**119**	38 49N	108 17W
Đolovo	**42**	44 55N	20 52 E
Dolphin and Union Str.	**104**	69 5N	114 45W
Dolphin C.	**128**	51 10 S	59 0W
Dolsk	**28**	51 59N	17 3 E
Dom Pedrito	**125**	31 0 S	54 40W
Doma	**85**	8 25N	8 18 E
Domasi	**91**	15 15 S	35 22 E
Domazlice	**26**	49 28N	13 0 E
Dombarovskiy	**58**	50 46N	59 32 E
Dombasle	**19**	48 38N	6 21 E
Dombes	**21**	46 3N	5 0 E
Dombóvár	**27**	46 21N	18 9 E
Dombrád	**27**	48 13N	21 54 E
Domburg	**16**	51 34N	3 30 E
Domel I. = Letsok-aw Kyun	**71**	11 30N	98 25 E
Domérat	**20**	46 21N	2 32 E
Domeyko	**124**	29 0 S	71 0W
Domeyko, Cordillera	**124**	24 30 S	69 0W
Domfront	**18**	48 37N	0 40W
Dominador	**124**	24 21 S	69 20W
Dominica ■	**121**	15 20N	61 20W
Dominican Rep. ■	**121**	19 0N	70 30W
Dömitz	**24**	53 9N	11 13 E
Domme	**20**	44 48N	1 12 E
Domo	**63**	7 50N	47 10 E
Domodóssola	**38**	46 6N	8 19 E
Dompaire	**19**	48 14N	6 14 E
Dompierre-sur-Besbre	**20**	46 31N	3 41 E
Dompim	**84**	5 10N	2 5W
Domrémy	**19**	48 26N	5 40 E
Domsjö	**48**	63 16N	18 41 E
Domville, Mt.	**99**	28 1 S	151 15 E
Domvraína	**45**	38 15N	22 59 E
Domžale	**39**	46 9N	14 35 E
Don →, India	**70**	16 20N	76 15 E
Don →, Eng., U.K.	**12**	53 41N	0 51W
Don →, Scot., U.K.	**14**	57 14N	2 5W
Don →, U.S.S.R.	**57**	47 4N	39 18 E
Don Benito	**31**	38 53N	5 51W
Don Martín, Presa de	**120**	27 30N	100 50W
Dona Ana	**91**	17 25 S	35 5 E
Donaghadee	**15**	54 38N	5 32W
Donald	**99**	36 23 S	143 0 E
Donalda	**108**	52 35N	112 34W
Donaldsonville	**117**	30 2N	91 0W
Donalsonville	**115**	31 3N	84 52W
Donau →	**23**	48 10N	17 0 E
Donaueschingen	**25**	47 57N	8 30 E
Donauwörth	**25**	48 42N	10 47 E
Donawitz	**26**	47 22N	15 4 E
Doncaster	**12**	53 31N	1 9W
Dondo, Angola	**88**	9 45 S	14 25 E
Dondo, Mozam.	**91**	19 33 S	34 46 E
Dondo, Teluk	**73**	0 29N	120 30 E
Dondra Head	**70**	5 55N	80 40 E
Donegal	**15**	54 39N	8 8W
Donegal □	**15**	54 53N	8 0W
Donegal B.	**15**	54 30N	8 35W
Donets →	**57**	47 33N	40 55 E
Donetsk	**56**	48 0N	37 45 E
Donga	**85**	7 45N	10 2 E
Dongara	**96**	29 14 S	114 57 E
Dongargarh	**69**	21 10N	80 40 E
Donges	**18**	47 18N	2 4W
Dongfang	**77**	18 50N	108 33 E
Donggala	**73**	0 30 S	119 40 E
Donggou	**76**	39 52N	124 10 E
Dongguan	**77**	22 58N	113 44 E
Dongguang	**76**	37 50N	116 30 E
Dongjingcheng	**76**	44 0N	129 10 E
Donglan	**77**	24 30N	107 21 E
Dongliu	**77**	30 13N	116 55 E
Dongola	**86**	19 9N	30 22 E
Dongou	**88**	2 0N	18 5 E
Dongping	**76**	35 55N	116 20 E
Dongshan	**77**	23 43N	117 30 E
Dongsheng	**76**	39 50N	110 0 E
Dongtai	**77**	32 51N	120 21 E
Dongting Hu	**75**	29 18N	112 45 E
Dongxing	**75**	21 34N	108 0 E
Dongyang	**77**	29 13N	120 15 E
Doniphan	**117**	36 40N	90 50W
Donja Stubica	**39**	45 59N	16 0 E

Donji Dušnik 42 43 12N 22 5 E
Donji Miholjac 42 45 45N 18 10 E
Donji Milanovac 42 44 28N 22 6 E
Donji Vakuf 42 44 8N 17 24 E
Donjon, Le 20 46 22N 3 48 E
Dønna 50 66 6N 12 30 E
Donna 117 26 12N 98 2W
Donnaconna 107 46 41N 71 41W
Donnelly's Crossing 101 35 42 S 173 38 E
Donora 112 40 11N 79 50W
Donor's Hills 98 18 42 S 140 33 E
Donskoy 55 53 55N 38 15 E
Donya Lendava 39 46 35N 16 25 E
Donzère-Mondragon 21 44 28N 4 43 E
Donzère-Mondragon, Barrage de 21 44 13N 4 42 E
Donzy 19 47 20N 3 6 E
Doon → 14 55 26N 4 41W
Dor (Tantūra) 62 32 37N 34 55 E
Dora Báltea → 38 45 11N 8 5 E
Dora, L. 96 22 0 S 123 0 E
Dora Riparia → 38 45 5N 7 44 E
Dorada, La 126 5 30N 74 40W
Doran L. 109 61 13N 108 6W
Dorat, Le 20 46 14N 1 5 E
Dorchester 13 50 42N 2 28W
Dorchester, C. 105 65 27N 77 27W
Dordogne □ 20 45 5N 0 40 E
Dordogne → 20 45 2N 0 36W
Dordrecht, Neth. 16 51 48N 4 39 E
Dordrecht, S. Afr. 92 31 20 S 27 3 E
Dore → 20 45 50N 3 35 E
Doré L. 109 54 46N 107 17W
Doré Lake 109 54 38N 107 36W
Dore, Mt. 20 45 32N 2 50 E
Dorfen 25 48 16N 12 10 E
Dorgali 40 40 18N 9 35 E
Dori 85 14 3N 0 2W
Doring → 92 31 54 S 18 39 E
Dorion 106 45 23N 74 3W
Dormaa-Ahenkro 84 7 15N 2 52W
Dormo, Ras 87 13 14N 42 35 E
Dornberg 39 55 45N 13 50 E
Dornbirn 26 47 25N 9 45 E
Dornes 19 46 48N 3 18 E
Dornoch 14 57 52N 4 0W
Dornoch Firth 14 57 52N 4 0W
Doro 85 16 9N 0 51W
Dorog 27 47 42N 18 45 E
Dorogobuzh 54 54 50N 33 18 E
Dorohoi 46 47 56N 26 30 E
Döröö Nuur 75 48 0N 93 0 E
Dorre I. 96 25 13 S 113 12 E
Dorrigo 99 30 20 S 152 44 E
Dorris 118 41 59N 121 58W
Dorset, Can. 112 45 14N 78 54W
Dorset, U.S.A. 112 41 4N 80 40W
Dorset □ 13 50 48N 2 25W
Dorsten 24 51 40N 6 55 E
Dortmund 24 51 32N 7 28 E
Dörtyol 64 36 52N 36 12 E
Dorum 24 53 40N 8 33 E
Doruma 90 4 42N 27 33 E
Dos Bahías, C. 128 44 58 S 65 32W
Dos Cabezas 119 32 10N 109 37W
Dos Hermanas 31 37 16N 5 55W
Dosso 85 13 0N 3 13 E
Dothan 115 31 10N 85 25W
Douai 19 50 21N 3 4 E
Douala 88 4 0N 9 45 E
Douaouir 82 20 45N 3 0W
Douarnenez 18 48 6N 4 21W
Douăzeci Şi Trei August 46 43 55N 28 40 E
Double Island Pt. 99 25 56 S 153 11 E
Doubrava → 26 49 40N 15 30 E
Doubs □ 19 47 10N 6 20 E
Doubs → 19 46 53N 5 1 E
Doubtful B. 96 34 15 S 119 28 E
Doubtful Sd. 101 45 20 S 166 49 E
Doubtless B. 101 34 55 S 173 26 E
Doudeville 18 49 43N 0 47 E
Doué 18 47 11N 0 20W
Douentza 84 14 58N 2 48W
Douglas, S. Afr. 92 29 4 S 23 46 E
Douglas, U.K. 12 54 9N 4 29W
Douglas, Alaska, U.S.A. 108 58 23N 134 24W
Douglas, Ariz., U.S.A. 119 31 21N 109 30W
Douglas, Ga., U.S.A. 115 31 32N 82 52W
Douglas, Wyo., U.S.A. 116 42 45N 105 20W
Douglastown 107 48 46N 64 24W
Douglasville 115 33 46N 84 43W
Douirat 82 33 2N 4 11W
Doukáton, Ákra 45 38 34N 20 30 E
Doulevant 19 48 22N 4 53 E
Doullens 19 50 10N 2 20 E
Doumé 88 4 15N 13 25 E
Douna 84 13 13N 6 0W
Dounreay 14 58 34N 3 44W
Dourados 125 22 9 S 54 50W
Dourados → 125 21 58 S 54 18W
Dourdan 19 48 30N 2 0 E
Douro → 30 41 8N 8 40W
Douvaine 21 46 19N 6 16 E
Douz 83 33 25N 9 0 E
Douze → 20 43 54N 0 30W
Dove → 12 52 51N 1 36W
Dove Creek 119 37 46N 108 59W
Dover, Austral. 99 43 18 S 147 2 E
Dover, U.K. 13 51 7N 1 19 E
Dover, Del., U.S.A. 114 39 10N 75 31W
Dover, N.H., U.S.A. 114 43 12N 70 51W
Dover, N.J., U.S.A. 113 40 53N 74 34W
Dover, Ohio, U.S.A. 114 40 32N 81 30W
Dover-Foxcroft 107 45 14N 69 14W
Dover Plains 113 41 43N 73 35W
Dover, Pt. 96 32 32 S 125 32 E
Dover, Str. of 18 51 0N 1 30 E
Dovey → 13 52 32N 4 0W
Dovrefjell 47 62 15N 9 33 E
Dowa 91 13 38 S 33 58 E
Dowagiac 114 42 0N 86 8W
Dowlat Yār 65 34 30N 65 45 E
Dowlatabad 65 28 20N 56 40W
Down □ 15 54 20N 6 0W
Downey 118 42 29N 112 3W
Downham Market 13 52 36N 0 22 E
Downieville 118 39 34N 120 50W
Downpatrick 15 54 20N 5 43W
Downpatrick Hd. 15 54 20N 9 21W
Dowshī 65 35 35N 68 43 E
Doylestown 113 40 21N 75 10W
Draa, C. 82 28 47N 11 0W
Draa, Oued → 82 30 29N 6 1W
Drac → 21 45 13N 5 41 E
Drachten 16 53 7N 6 5 E
Drăgănești 46 44 9N 24 32 E
Drăgănești-Viașca 46 44 5N 25 33 E
Dragaš 42 42 5N 20 35 E
Drăgășani 46 44 39N 24 17 E
Dragina 42 44 30N 19 25 E
Dragocvet 42 44 0N 21 15 E
Dragoman, Prokhod 42 43 0N 22 53 E
Dragonera, I. 32 39 35N 2 19 E
Dragovishtitsa (Perivol) 42 42 22N 22 39 E
Draguignan 21 43 30N 6 27 E
Drain 118 43 45N 123 17W
Drake, Austral. 99 28 55 S 152 25 E
Drake, U.S.A. 116 47 56N 100 21W
Drake Passage 5 58 0 S 68 0W
Drakensberg 93 31 0 S 28 0 E
Dráma 44 41 9N 24 10 E
Dráma □ 44 41 20N 24 0 E
Drammen 47 59 42N 10 12 E
Drangajökull 50 66 9N 22 15W
Drangedal 47 59 6N 9 3 E
Dranov, Ostrov 46 44 55N 29 30 E
Drau = Drava → 26 46 32N 14 58 E
Drava → 42 45 33N 18 55 E
Draveil 19 48 41N 2 25 E
Dravograd 39 46 36N 15 5 E
Drawa → 28 52 52N 15 59 E
Drawno 28 53 13N 15 46 E
Drawsko Pomorskie 28 53 35N 15 50 E
Drayton Valley 108 53 12N 114 58W
Dren 42 43 8N 20 44 E
Drenthe □ 16 52 52N 6 40 E
Dresden, Can. 112 42 35N 82 11W
Dresden, Ger. 24 51 2N 13 45 E
Dresden □ 24 51 12N 14 0 E
Dreux 18 48 44N 1 23 E
Drezdenko 28 52 50N 15 49 E
Driffield 12 54 0N 0 25W
Driftwood 112 41 22N 78 9W
Driggs 118 43 50N 111 8W
Drin i zi → 44 41 37N 20 28 E
Drina → 42 44 53N 19 21 E
Drincea → 46 44 20N 22 55 E
Drînceni 46 46 49N 28 10 E
Drini → 44 42 20N 20 0 E
Drinjača → 42 44 15N 19 8 E
Driva → 47 62 33N 9 38 E
Drivstua 47 62 26N 9 47 E
Drniš 39 43 51N 16 10 E
Drøbak 47 59 39N 10 39 E
Drobin 28 52 42N 19 58 E
Drogheda 15 53 45N 6 20W
Drogichin 54 52 15N 25 8 E
Drogobych 54 49 20N 23 30 E
Drohiczyn 28 52 24N 22 39 E
Droichead Nua 15 53 11N 6 50W
Droitwich 13 52 16N 2 10W
Drôme □ 21 44 38N 5 15 E
Drôme → 21 44 46N 4 46 E
Dromedary, C. 99 36 17 S 150 10 E
Dronero 38 44 29N 7 22 E
Dronfield 98 21 12 S 140 3 E
Dronne → 20 45 2N 0 9W
Dronning Maud Land 5 72 30 S 12 0 E
Dronninglund 49 57 10N 10 19 E
Dropt → 20 44 35N 0 6W
Drosendorf 26 48 52N 15 37 E
Drouzhba 43 43 15N 28 0 E
Drumbo 112 43 16N 80 35W
Drumheller 108 51 25N 112 40W
Drummond 118 46 40N 113 4W
Drummond I. 106 46 0N 83 40W
Drummond Ra. 97 23 45 S 147 10 E
Drummondville 106 45 55N 72 25W
Drumright 117 35 59N 96 38W
Druskininkai 54 54 3N 23 58 E
Drut → 54 53 3N 30 42 E
Druya 54 55 45N 27 28 E
Druzhina 59 68 14N 145 18 E
Drvar 39 44 21N 16 23 E
Drvenik 39 43 27N 16 3 E
Drwęca → 28 53 0N 18 42 E
Dry Tortugas 121 24 38N 82 55W
Dryanovo 43 42 59N 25 28 E
Dryden, Can. 109 49 47N 92 50W
Dryden, U.S.A. 117 30 3N 102 3W
Drygalski I. 5 66 0 S 92 0 E
Drysdale → 96 13 59 S 126 51 E
Drzewiczka → 28 51 36N 20 36 E
Dschang 85 5 32N 10 3 E
Du Bois 114 41 8N 78 46W
Du Quoin 116 38 0N 89 10W
Duanesburg 113 42 45N 74 11W
Duaringa 98 23 42 S 149 42 E
Ḑubā 64 27 10N 35 40 E
Dubai = Dubayy 65 25 18N 55 20 E
Dubawnt → 109 64 33N 100 6W
Dubawnt, L. 109 63 4N 101 42W
Dubayy 65 25 18N 55 20 E
Dubbo 97 32 11 S 148 35 E
Dubele 90 2 56N 29 35 E
Dubica 39 45 11N 16 48 E
Dublin, Ireland 15 53 20N 6 18W
Dublin, Ga., U.S.A. 115 32 30N 82 34W
Dublin, Tex., U.S.A. 117 32 0N 98 20W
Dublin □ 15 53 24N 6 20W
Dublin B. 15 53 18N 6 5W
Dubna, U.S.S.R. 55 54 8N 36 59 E
Dubna, U.S.S.R. 55 56 44N 37 10 E
Dubno 54 50 25N 25 45 E
Dubois 118 44 7N 112 9W
Dubossary 56 47 15N 29 10 E
Dubossasy Vdkhr. 56 47 30N 29 0 E
Dubovka 57 49 5N 44 50 E
Dubovskoye 57 47 28N 42 46 E
Dubrajpur 69 23 48N 87 25 E
Dubréka 84 9 46N 13 31W
Dubrovitsa 54 51 31N 26 35 E
Dubrovnik 42 42 39N 18 6 E
Dubrovskoye 59 58 55N 111 10 E
Dubuque 116 42 30N 90 41W
Duchang 77 29 18N 116 12 E
Duchesne 118 40 14N 110 22W
Duchess 97 21 20 S 139 50 E
Ducie I. 95 24 40 S 124 48W
Duck Lake 109 52 50N 106 16W
Duck Mt. Prov. Parks 109 51 45N 101 0W
Duderstadt 24 51 30N 10 15 E
Dudinka 59 69 30N 86 13 E
Dudley 13 52 30N 2 5W
Dudna → 70 19 17N 76 54 E
Dueñas 30 41 52N 4 33W
Dueodde 49 54 59N 15 4 E
Duero → 30 41 8N 8 40W
Duff Is. 94 9 53 S 167 8 E
Dufftown 14 57 26N 3 9W
Dugi 39 44 0N 15 0 E
Dugo Selo 39 45 51N 16 18 E
Duifken Pt. 97 12 33 S 141 38 E
Duisburg 24 51 27N 6 42 E
Duiwelskloof 93 23 42 S 30 10 E
Dukati 44 40 16N 19 32 E
Duke I. 108 54 50N 131 20W
Dukelsky průsmyk 27 49 25N 21 42 E
Dukhān 65 25 25N 50 50 E
Dukhovshchina 54 55 15N 32 27 E
Dukla 27 49 30N 21 35 E
Duku, Bauchi, Nigeria 85 10 43N 10 43 E
Duku, Sokoto, Nigeria 85 11 11N 4 55 E
Dulce → 124 30 32 S 62 33W
Dulce, Golfo 121 8 40N 83 20W
Dŭlgopol 43 43 3N 27 22 E
Dullewala 68 31 50N 71 25 E
Dülmen 24 51 49N 7 18 E
Dulovo 43 43 48N 27 9 E
Dululu 98 23 48 S 150 15 E
Duluth 116 46 48N 92 10W
Dum Dum 69 22 39N 88 33 E
Dum Duma 67 27 40N 95 40 E
Dum Hadjer 81 13 18N 19 41 E
Dumaguete 73 9 17N 123 15 E
Dumai 72 1 35N 101 28 E
Dumaran 73 10 33N 119 50 E
Dumaring 73 1 46N 118 10 E
Dumas, Ark., U.S.A. 117 33 52N 91 30W
Dumas, Tex., U.S.A. 117 35 50N 101 58W
Dumbarton 14 55 58N 4 35W
Dumbrăveni 46 46 14N 24 34 E
Dumfries 14 55 4N 3 37W
Dumfries & Galloway □ 14 55 0N 4 0W
Dumka 69 24 12N 87 15 E
Dümmersee 24 52 30N 8 21 E
Dumoine → 106 46 13N 77 51W
Dumoine L. 106 46 55N 77 55W
Dumraon 69 25 33N 84 8 E
Dumyât 86 31 24N 31 48 E
Dumyât, Masabb 86 31 28N 31 51 E
Dun Laoghaire 15 53 17N 6 9W
Dun-le-Palestel 20 46 18N 1 39 E
Dun-sur-Auron 19 46 53N 2 33 E
Duna → 27 45 51N 18 48 E
Dunaföldvár 27 46 50N 18 57 E
Dunaj → 27 48 5N 17 10 E
Dunajec → 27 50 15N 20 44 E
Dunajska Streda 27 48 0N 17 37 E
Dunapatai 27 46 39N 19 4 E
Dunărea → 46 45 30N 8 15 E
Dunaszekcsö 27 46 6N 18 45 E
Dunaújváros 27 47 0N 18 57 E
Dunav → 42 44 47N 21 20 E
Dunavtsi 42 43 57N 22 53 E
Dunback 101 45 23 S 170 36 E
Dunbar, Austral. 98 16 0 S 142 22 E
Dunbar, U.K. 14 56 0N 2 32W
Dunblane 14 56 10N 3 58W
Duncan, Can. 108 48 45N 123 40W
Duncan, Ariz., U.S.A. 119 32 46N 109 6W
Duncan, Okla., U.S.A. 117 34 25N 98 0W
Duncan L. 108 62 51N 113 58W
Duncan, L. 106 53 29N 77 58W
Duncan Pass. 71 11 0N 92 30 E
Duncan Town 121 22 15N 75 45W
Duncannon 112 40 23N 77 2W
Dundalk, Can. 112 44 10N 80 24W
Dundalk, Ireland 15 54 1N 6 25W
Dundalk Bay 15 53 55N 6 15W
Dundas 106 43 17N 79 59W
Dundas I. 108 54 30N 130 50W
Dundas, L. 96 32 35 S 121 50 E
Dundas Str. 96 11 15 S 131 35 E
Dundee, S. Afr. 93 28 11 S 30 15 E
Dundee, U.K. 14 56 29N 3 0W
Dundoo 99 27 40 S 144 37 E
Dundrum 15 54 17N 5 50W
Dundrum B. 15 54 12N 5 40W
Dundwara 68 27 48N 79 9 E
Dunedin, N.Z. 101 45 50 S 170 33 E
Dunedin, U.S.A. 115 28 1N 82 45W
Dunedin → 108 59 30N 124 5W
Dunfermline 14 56 5N 3 28W
Dungannon, Can. 112 43 51N 81 36W
Dungannon, U.K. 15 54 30N 6 47W
Dungannon □ 15 54 30N 6 55W
Dungarpur 68 23 52N 73 45 E
Dungarvan 15 52 6N 7 40W
Dungarvan Bay 15 52 5N 7 35W
Dungeness 13 50 54N 0 59 E
Dungo, L. do 92 17 15 S 19 0 E
Dungog 99 32 22 S 151 46 E
Dungu 90 3 40N 28 32 E
Dungunâb 86 21 10N 37 9 E
Dungunâb, Khalij 86 21 5N 37 12 E
Dunhinda Falls 70 7 5N 81 6 E
Dunhua 76 43 20N 128 14 E
Dunhuang 75 40 8N 94 36 E
Dunières 21 45 13N 4 20 E
Dunk I. 98 17 59 S 146 29 E
Dunkeld 14 56 34N 3 36W
Dunkerque 19 51 2N 2 20 E
Dunkery Beacon 13 51 15N 3 37W
Dunkirk 114 42 30N 79 18W
Dunkirk = Dunkerque 19 51 2N 2 20 E
Dunkuj 87 12 50N 32 49 E
Dunkwa, Central, Ghana 84 6 0N 1 47W
Dunkwa, Central, Ghana 85 5 30N 1 0W
Dunlap 116 41 50N 95 36W
Dunmanus B. 15 51 31N 9 50W
Dunmore 114 41 27N 75 38W
Dunmore Hd. 15 52 10N 10 35W
Dunn 115 35 18N 78 36W
Dunnellon 115 29 4N 82 28W
Dunnet Hd. 14 58 38N 3 22W
Dunning 116 41 52N 100 4W
Dunnville 112 42 54N 79 36W
Dunolly 99 36 51 S 143 44 E
Dunoon 14 55 57N 4 56W
Dunqul 86 23 26N 31 37 E
Duns 14 55 47N 2 20W
Dunseith 116 48 49N 100 2W
Dunsmuir 118 41 10N 122 18W
Dunstable 13 51 53N 0 31W
Dunstan Mts. 101 44 53 S 169 35 E
Dunster 108 53 8N 119 50W
Dunvegan L. 109 60 8N 107 10W
Duolun 76 42 12N 116 28 E
Dupree 116 45 4N 101 35W
Dupuyer 118 48 11N 112 31W
Duque de Caxias 125 22 45 S 43 19W
Duquesne 112 40 22N 79 55W
Dūrā 62 31 31N 35 1 E
Durack Range 96 16 50 S 127 40 E
Durance → 21 43 55N 4 45 E
Durand 114 42 54N 83 58W
Durango, Mexico 120 24 3N 104 39W
Durango, Spain 32 43 13N 2 40W
Durango, U.S.A. 119 37 16N 107 50W
Durango □ 120 25 0N 105 0W
Durant 117 34 0N 96 25W
Duratón → 30 41 37N 4 7W
Durazno 124 33 25 S 56 31W
Durazzo = Durrësi 44 41 19N 19 28 E
Durban, France 20 43 0N 2 49 E
Durban, S. Afr. 93 29 49 S 31 1 E
Dúrcal 31 37 0N 3 34W
Đurđevac 42 46 2N 17 3 E
Düren 24 50 48N 6 30 E
Durg 69 21 15N 81 22 E
Durgapur 69 23 30N 87 20 E
Durham, Can. 106 44 10N 80 49W
Durham, U.K. 12 54 47N 1 34W
Durham, U.S.A. 115 36 0N 78 55W
Durham □ 12 54 42N 1 45W
Durmitor 34 43 10N 19 0 E
Durness 14 58 34N 4 45W
Durrës 44 41 19N 19 28 E
Durrësi 44 41 19N 19 28 E
Durrie 99 25 40 S 140 15 E
Durtal 18 47 40N 0 18W
Duru 90 4 14N 28 50 E
D'Urville I. 101 40 50 S 173 55 E
D'Urville, Tanjung 73 1 28 S 137 54 E
Duryea 113 41 20N 75 45W
Dusa Mareb 63 5 30N 46 15 E
Dūsh 86 24 35N 30 41 E
Dushak 58 37 13N 60 1 E
Dushan 77 25 48N 107 30 E
Dushanbe 58 38 33N 68 48 E
Dusheti 57 42 10N 44 42 E
Dusky Sd. 101 45 47 S 166 30 E
Düsseldorf 24 51 15N 6 46 E
Duszniki-Zdrój 28 50 24N 16 24 E
Dutch Harbor 104 53 54N 166 35W
Duthe 92 23 58 S 23 46 E
Dutsan Wai 85 10 50N 8 10 E
Dutton 112 42 39N 81 30W
Dutton → 98 20 44 S 143 10 E
Duved 48 63 24N 12 55 E
Duvno 42 43 42N 17 13 E
Duwādimi 64 24 35N 44 15 E
Duyun 77 26 18N 107 29 E
Duzce 64 40 50N 31 10 E
Duzdab = Zāhedān 65 29 30N 60 50 E
Dve Mogili 43 43 35N 25 55 E
Dvina, Sev. 52 64 32N 40 30 E
Dvinsk = Daugavpils 54 55 53N 26 32 E
Dvinskaya Guba 52 65 0N 39 0 E
Dvor 39 45 4N 16 22 E
Dvorce 27 49 50N 17 34 E
Dvur Králové 26 50 27N 15 50 E
Dwarka 68 22 18N 69 8 E
Dwight, Can. 112 45 20N 79 1W
Dwight, U.S.A. 114 41 5N 88 25W
Dyakovskoya 55 60 5N 41 12 E
Dyatkovo 54 53 40N 34 27 E
Dyatlovo 54 53 28N 25 28 E
Dyer, C. 105 66 40N 61 0W
Dyer Plateau 5 70 45 S 65 30W
Dyersburg 117 36 2N 89 20W
Dyfed □ 13 52 0N 4 30W
Dyje → 27 48 37N 16 56 E
Dynevor Downs 99 28 10 S 144 20 E
Dynów 27 49 50N 22 11 E
Dysart 109 50 57N 104 2W
Dzamin Üüd 75 43 50N 111 58 E
Dzerzhinsk, Byelorussian S.S.R., U.S.S.R. 54 53 40N 27 1 E
Dzerzhinsk, R.S.F.S.R., U.S.S.R. 55 56 14N 43 30 E
Dzhalal-Abad 58 40 56N 73 0 E
Dzhalinda 59 53 26N 124 0 E
Dzhambeyty 57 50 15N 52 30 E
Dzhambul 58 42 54N 71 22 E
Dzhankoi 56 45 40N 34 20 E
Dzhanybek 57 49 25N 46 50 E
Dzhardzhan 59 68 10N 124 10 E
Dzhelinde 59 70 0N 114 20 E

Dzhetygara 58 52 11N 61 12 E
Dzhezkazgan 58 47 44N 67 40 E
Dzhikimde 59 59 1N 121 47 E
Dzhizak 58 40 6N 67 50 E
Dzhugdzur, Khrebet 59 57 30N 138 0 E
Dzhungarskiye Vorota 58 45 0N 82 0 E
Dzhvari 57 42 42N 42 4 E
Działdowo 28 53 15N 20 15 E
Działoszyce 28 50 22N 20 20 E
Działoszyn 28 51 6N 18 50 E
Dzierzgoń 28 53 58N 19 20 E
Dzierzoniów 28 50 45N 16 39 E
Dzioua 83 33 14N 5 14 E
Dziwnów 28 54 2N 14 45 E
Dzungarian Gate = Alataw Shankou 75 45 5N 81 57 E
Dzuumod 75 47 45N 106 58 E

E

Eabamet, L. 106 51 30N 87 46W
Eads 116 38 30N 102 46W
Eagle, Alaska, U.S.A. 104 64 44N 141 7W
Eagle, Colo., U.S.A. 118 39 39N 106 55W
Eagle → 107 53 36N 57 26W
Eagle Butt 116 45 1N 101 12W
Eagle Grove 116 42 37N 93 53W
Eagle L., Calif., U.S.A. 118 40 35N 120 50W
Eagle L., Me., U.S.A. 107 46 23N 69 22W
Eagle Lake 117 29 35N 96 21W
Eagle Nest 119 36 33N 105 13W
Eagle Pass 117 28 45N 100 35W
Eagle River 116 45 55N 89 17W
Eaglehawk 99 36 39 S 144 16 E
Ealing 13 51 30N 0 19W
Earl Grey 109 50 57N 104 43W
Earle 117 35 18N 90 26W
Earlimart 119 35 53N 119 16W
Earn → 14 56 20N 3 19W
Earn, L. 14 56 23N 4 14W
Earnslaw, Mt. 101 44 32 S 168 27 E
Earth 117 34 18N 102 30W
Easley 115 34 52N 82 35W
East Angus 107 45 30N 71 40W
East Aurora 112 42 46N 78 38W
East B. 117 29 2N 89 16W
East Bengal 67 24 0N 90 0 E
East Beskids = Vychodné Beskydy 27 49 30N 22 0 E
East Brady 112 40 59N 79 36W
East C. 101 37 42 S 178 35 E
East Chicago 114 41 40N 87 30W
East China Sea 75 30 5N 126 0 E
East Coulee 108 51 23N 112 27W
East Falkland 128 51 30 S 58 30W
East Grand Forks 116 47 55N 97 5W
East Greenwich 113 41 39N 71 27W
East Hartford 113 41 45N 72 39W
East Helena 118 46 37N 111 58W
East Indies 72 0 0 120 0 E
East Jordan 114 45 10N 85 7W
East Kilbride 14 55 46N 4 10W
East Lansing 114 42 44N 84 29W
East Liverpool 114 40 39N 80 35W
East London 93 33 0 S 27 55 E
East Orange 114 40 46N 74 13W
East Pacific Ridge 95 15 0 S 110 0W
East Pakistan = Bangladesh ■ 67 24 0N 90 0 E
East Palestine 112 40 50N 80 32W
East Pine 108 55 48N 120 12W
East Pt. 107 46 27N 61 58W
East Point 115 33 40N 84 28W
East Providence 113 41 48N 71 22W
East Retford 12 53 19N 0 55W
East St. Louis 116 38 37N 90 4W
East Schelde → = Oosterschelde 16 51 38N 3 40 E
East Siberian Sea 59 73 0N 160 0 E
East Stroudsburg 113 41 1N 75 11W
East Sussex □ 13 51 0N 0 20 E
East Tawas 114 44 17N 83 31W
Eastbourne, N.Z. 101 41 19 S 174 55 E
Eastbourne, U.K. 13 50 46N 0 18 E
Eastend 109 49 32N 108 50W
Easter I. 95 27 8 S 109 23W
Easter Islands 95 27 0 S 109 0W
Eastern □, Kenya 90 0 0 S 38 30 E
Eastern □, Uganda 90 1 50N 33 45 E
Eastern Cr. → 98 20 40 S 141 35 E
Eastern Ghats 70 14 0N 78 50 E
Eastern Province □ 84 8 15N 11 0W
Easterville 109 53 8N 99 49W
Easthampton 113 42 15N 72 41W
Eastland 117 32 26N 98 45W
Eastleigh 13 50 58N 1 21W
Eastmain → 106 52 27N 78 26W
Eastmain (East Main) 106 52 10N 78 30W
Eastman, Can. 113 45 18N 72 19W
Eastman, U.S.A. 115 32 13N 83 20W
Easton, Md., U.S.A. 114 38 47N 76 7W
Easton, Pa., U.S.A. 114 40 41N 75 15W
Easton, Wash., U.S.A. 118 47 14N 121 8W
Eastport 107 44 57N 67 0W
Eaton 116 40 35N 104 42W
Eatonia 109 51 13N 109 25W
Eatonton 115 33 22N 83 24W
Eatontown 113 40 18N 74 7W
Eau Claire, S.C., U.S.A. 115 34 5N 81 2W
Eau Claire, Wis., U.S.A. 116 44 46N 91 30W
Eauze 20 43 53N 0 7 E
Ebagoola 98 14 15 S 143 12 E
Eban 85 9 40N 4 50 E
Ebbw Vale 13 51 47N 3 12W
Ebeggui 83 26 2N 6 0 E
Ebensburg 112 40 29N 78 43W
Ebensee 26 47 48N 13 46 E
Eberbach 25 49 27N 8 59 E
Eberswalde 24 52 49N 13 50 E
Ebingen 25 48 13N 9 1 E
Eboli 41 40 39N 15 2 E
Ebolowa 88 2 55N 11 10 E
Ebrach 25 49 50N 10 30 E
Ébrié, Lagune 84 5 12N 4 26W
Ebro → 32 40 43N 0 54 E
Ebro, Pantano del 30 43 0N 3 58W
Ebstorf 24 53 2N 10 23 E
Eceabat 44 40 11N 26 21 E
Éceuillé 18 47 10N 1 19 E
Echelles, Les 21 45 27N 5 45 E
Echmiadzin 57 40 12N 44 19 E
Echo Bay 106 46 29N 84 4W
Echo Bay (Port Radium) 104 66 05N 117 55W
Echoing → 109 55 51N 92 5W
Echternach 16 49 49N 6 25 E
Echuca 100 36 10 S 144 20 E
Ecija 31 37 30N 5 10W
Eckernförde 24 54 26N 9 50 E
Écommoy 18 47 50N 0 17 E
Écos 19 49 9N 1 35 E
Écouché 18 48 42N 0 10W
Ecuador ■ 126 2 0 S 78 0W
Ed 49 58 55N 11 55 E
Ed Dabbura 86 17 40N 34 15 E
Ed Dâmer 86 17 27N 34 0 E
Ed Debba 86 18 0N 30 51 E
Ed-Déffa 86 30 40N 26 30 E
Ed Deim 87 10 10N 28 20 E
Ed Dueim 87 14 0N 32 10 E
Edam, Can. 109 53 11N 108 46W
Edam, Neth. 16 52 31N 5 3 E
Edapally 70 11 19N 78 3 E
Eday 14 59 11N 2 47W
Edd 87 14 0N 41 38 E
Eddrachillis B. 14 58 16N 5 10W
Eddystone 13 50 11N 4 16W
Eddystone Pt. 99 40 59 S 148 20 E
Ede, Neth. 16 52 4N 5 40 E
Ede, Nigeria 85 7 45N 4 29 E
Édea 88 3 51N 10 9 E
Edehon L. 109 60 25N 97 15W
Edekel, Adrar 83 23 56N 6 47 E
Eden, Austral. 99 37 3 S 149 55 E
Eden, N.C., U.S.A. 115 36 29N 79 53W
Eden, N.Y., U.S.A. 112 42 39N 78 55W
Eden, Tex., U.S.A. 117 31 16N 99 50W
Eden, Wyo., U.S.A. 118 42 2N 109 27W
Eden → 12 54 57N 3 2W
Eden L. 109 56 38N 100 15W
Edenburg 92 29 43 S 25 58 E
Edenderry 15 53 21N 7 3W
Edenton 115 36 5N 76 36W
Edenville 93 27 37 S 27 34 E
Eder → 24 51 15N 9 25 E
Ederstausee 24 51 11N 9 0 E
Edgar 116 40 25N 98 0W
Edgartown 113 41 22N 70 28W
Edge Hill 13 52 7N 1 28W
Edgefield 115 33 50N 81 59W
Edgeley 116 46 27N 98 41W
Edgemont 116 43 15N 103 53W
Edgeøya 4 77 45N 22 30 E
Edhessa 44 40 48N 22 5 E
Edievale 101 45 49 S 169 22 E
Edina, Liberia 84 6 0N 10 10W
Edina, U.S.A. 116 40 6N 92 10W
Edinburg 117 26 22N 98 10W
Edinburgh 14 55 57N 3 12W
Edirne 43 41 40N 26 34 E
Edithburgh 99 35 5 S 137 43 E
Edjeleh 83 28 38N 9 50 E
Edmeston 113 42 42N 75 15W
Edmond 117 35 37N 97 30W
Edmonds 118 47 47N 122 22W
Edmonton, Austral. 98 17 2 S 145 46 E
Edmonton, Can. 108 53 30N 113 30W
Edmund L. 109 54 45N 93 17W
Edmundston 107 47 23N 68 20W
Edna 117 29 0N 96 40W
Edna Bay 108 55 55N 133 40W
Edolo 38 46 10N 10 21 E
Edremit 64 39 34N 27 0 E
Edsbyn 48 61 23N 15 49 E
Edsel Ford Ra. 5 77 0 S 143 0W
Edsele 48 63 25N 16 32 E
Edson 108 53 35N 116 28W
Eduardo Castex 124 35 50 S 64 18W
Edward → 99 35 0 S 143 30 E
Edward I. 106 48 22N 88 37W
Edward, L. = Idi Amin Dada, L. 90 0 25 S 29 40 E
Edward VII Pen. 5 80 0 S 150 0W
Edwards Plat. 117 30 30N 101 5W
Edwardsville 113 41 15N 75 56W
Edzo 108 62 49N 116 4W
Eekloo 16 51 11N 3 33 E
Efe, Nahal 62 31 9N 35 13 E
Eferding 26 48 18N 14 1 E
Efferi 83 24 30N 9 28 E
Effingham 114 39 8N 88 30W
Eforie Sud 46 44 1N 28 37 E
Ega → 32 42 19N 1 55W
Égadi, Ísole 40 37 55N 12 16 E
Eganville 106 45 32N 77 5W
Egeland 116 48 42N 99 6W
Egenolf L. 109 59 3N 100 0W
Eger 27 47 53N 20 27 E
Eger → 27 47 38N 20 50 E
Egersund 47 58 26N 6 1 E
Egerton, Mt. 96 24 42 S 117 44 E
Egg L. 109 55 5N 105 30W
Eggenburg 26 48 38N 15 50 E
Eggenfelden 25 48 24N 12 46 E
Égletons 20 45 24N 2 3 E
Egmont, C. 101 39 16 S 173 45 E
Egmont, Mt. 101 39 17 S 174 5 E
Eğridir 64 37 52N 30 51 E
Eğridir Gölü 64 37 53N 30 50 E
Egtved 49 55 38N 9 18 E
Egume 85 7 30N 7 14 E
Éguzon 20 46 27N 1 33 E
Egvekinot 59 66 19N 179 50W
Egyek 27 47 39N 20 52 E
Egypt ■ 86 28 0N 31 0 E
Eha Amufu 85 6 30N 7 46 E
Ehime □ 74 33 30N 132 40 E
Ehingen 25 48 16N 9 43 E
Ehrwald 26 47 24N 10 56 E
Eibar 32 43 11N 2 28W
Eichstatt 25 48 53N 11 12 E
Eida 47 60 32N 6 43 E
Eider → 24 54 19N 8 58 E
Eidsvold 99 25 25 S 151 12 E
Eifel 25 50 10N 6 45 E
Eiffel Flats 91 18 20 S 30 0 E
Eigg 14 56 54N 6 10W
Eighty Mile Beach 96 19 30 S 120 40 E
Eil 63 8 0N 49 50 E
Eil, L. 14 56 50N 5 15W
Eildon, L. 99 37 10 S 146 0 E
Eileen L. 109 62 16N 107 37W
Eilenburg 24 51 28N 12 38 E
Ein el Luweiqa 87 14 5N 33 50 E
Einasleigh 97 18 32 S 144 5 E
Einasleigh → 98 17 30 S 142 17 E
Einbeck 24 51 48N 9 50 E
Eindhoven 16 51 26N 5 30 E
Einsiedeln 25 47 7N 8 46 E
Eiríksjökull 50 64 46N 20 24W
Eirunepé 126 6 35 S 69 53W
Eisenach 24 50 58N 10 18 E
Eisenberg 24 50 59N 11 50 E
Eisenerz 26 47 32N 14 54 E
Eisenhüttenstadt 24 52 9N 14 41 E
Eisenkappel 26 46 29N 14 36 E
Eisenstadt 27 47 51N 16 31 E
Eiserfeld 24 50 50N 7 59 E
Eisfeld 24 50 25N 10 54 E
Eisleben 24 51 31N 11 31 E
Ejby 49 55 25N 9 56 E
Eje, Sierra del 30 42 24N 6 54W
Ejea de los Caballeros 32 42 7N 1 9W
Ekalaka 116 45 55N 104 30W
Eket 85 4 38N 7 56 E
Eketahuna 101 40 38 S 175 43 E
Ekhínos 44 41 16N 25 1 E
Ekibastuz 58 51 50N 75 10 E
Ekimchan 59 53 0N 133 0W
Ekoli 90 0 23 S 24 13 E
Eksjö 49 57 40N 14 58W
Ekwan → 106 53 12N 82 15W
Ekwan Pt. 106 53 16N 82 7W
El Aaiún 80 27 9N 13 12W
El Aat 62 32 50N 35 45 E
El Abiodh-Sidi-Cheikh 82 32 53N 0 31 E
El Aïoun 82 34 33N 2 30W
El 'Aiyat 86 29 36N 31 15 E
El Alamein 86 30 48N 28 58 E
El 'Arag 86 28 40N 26 20 E
El Arahal 31 37 15N 5 33W
El Arba 82 36 37N 3 12 E
El Aricha 82 34 13N 1 10W
El Arīhā 62 31 52N 35 27 E
El Arish 98 17 35 S 146 1 E
El 'Arîsh 86 31 8N 33 50 E
El Arrouch 83 36 37N 6 53 E
El Asnam 82 36 10N 1 20 E
El Astillero 30 43 24N 3 49W
El Badâri 86 27 4N 31 25 E
El Bahrein 86 28 30N 26 25 E
El Ballâs 86 26 2N 32 43 E
El Balyana 86 26 10N 32 3 E
El Baqeir 86 18 40N 33 40 E
El Barco de Ávila 30 40 21N 5 31W
El Barco de Valdeorras 30 42 23N 7 0W
El Bauga 86 18 18N 33 52 E
El Bawiti 86 28 25N 28 45 E
El Bayadh 82 33 40N 1 1 E
El Bierzo 30 42 45N 6 30W
El Bluff 121 11 59N 83 40W
El Bonillo 33 38 57N 2 35W
El Cajon 119 32 49N 117 0W
El Callao 126 7 18N 61 50W
El Camp 32 41 5N 1 10 E
El Campo 117 29 10N 96 20W
El Castillo 31 37 41N 6 19W
El Centro 119 32 50N 115 40W
El Cerro, Boliv. 126 17 30 S 61 40W
El Cerro, Spain 31 37 45N 6 57W
El Coronil 31 37 5N 5 38W
El Cuy 128 39 55 S 68 25W
El Cuyo 120 21 30N 87 40W
El Dab'a 86 31 0N 28 27 E
El Deir 86 25 25N 32 20 E
El Dere 63 3 50N 47 8 E
El Dias 120 20 40N 87 20W
El Dilingat 86 30 50N 30 31 E
El Diviso 126 1 22N 78 14W
El Djem 83 35 18N 10 42 E
El Djouf 84 20 0N 11 30 E
El Dorado, Ark., U.S.A. 117 33 10N 92 40W
El Dorado, Kans., U.S.A. 117 37 55N 96 56W
El Dorado, Venez. 126 6 55N 61 37W
El Dorado Springs 117 37 54N 93 59W
El Eglab 82 26 20N 4 30W
El Escorial 30 40 35N 4 7W
El Eulma 83 36 9N 5 42 E
El Faiyûm 86 29 19N 30 50 E
El Fâsher 87 13 33N 25 26 E
El Fashn 86 28 50N 30 54 E
El Ferrol 30 43 29N 8 15W
El Fifi 87 10 4N 25 0 E
El Fuerte 120 26 30N 108 40W
El Gal 63 10 58N 50 20 E
El Gebir 87 13 40N 29 40 E
El Gedida 86 25 40N 28 30 E
El Geteina 87 14 50N 32 27 E
El Gezira □ 87 15 0N 33 0 E
El Gîza 86 30 0N 31 10 E
El Goléa 82 30 30N 2 50 E
El Guettar 83 34 5N 4 38 E
El Hadjira 83 32 36N 5 30 E
El Hagiz 87 15 15N 35 50 E
El Hajeb 82 33 43N 5 13W
El Hammam 86 30 52N 29 25 E
El Hank 82 24 30N 7 0W
El Harrache 80 36 45N 3 5 E
El Hawata 87 13 25N 34 42 E
El Heiz 86 27 50N 28 40 E
El 'Idisât 86 25 30N 32 35 E
El Iskandarîya 86 31 0N 30 0 E
El Istwâ'ya □ 87 5 0N 30 0 E
El Jadida 80 33 11N 8 17W
El Jebelein 81 12 40N 32 55 E
El Kab 86 19 27N 32 46 E
El Kala 83 36 50N 8 30 E
El Kalâa 82 32 4N 7 27W
El Kamlin 87 15 3N 33 11 E
El Kantara, Alg. 83 35 14N 5 45 E
El Kantara, Tunisia 83 33 45N 10 58 E
El Karaba 86 18 32N 33 41 E
El Kef 83 36 12N 8 47 E
El Khandaq 86 18 30N 30 30 E
El Khârga 86 25 30N 30 33 E
El Khartûm 87 15 31N 32 35 E
El Khartûm □ 87 16 0N 33 0 E
El Khartûm Bahrî 87 15 40N 32 31 E
El-Khroubs 83 36 10N 6 55 E
El Khureiba 86 28 3N 35 10 E
El Kseur 83 36 46N 4 49 E
El Ksiba 82 32 45N 6 1W
El Kuntilla 86 30 1N 34 45 E
El Laqâwa 81 11 25N 29 1 E
El Laqeita 86 25 50N 33 15 E
El Leiya 87 16 15N 35 28 E
El Mafâza 87 13 38N 34 30 E
El Mahalla el Kubra 86 31 0N 31 0 E
El Mahârîq 86 25 35N 30 35 E
El Mahmûdîya 86 31 10N 30 32 E
El Maiz 82 28 19N 0 9W
El-Maks el-Bahari 86 24 30N 30 40 E
El Manshâh 86 26 26N 31 50 E
El Mansour 82 27 47N 0 14W
El Mansûra 86 31 0N 31 19 E
El Manzala 86 31 10N 31 50 E
El Marâgha 86 26 35N 31 10 E
El Masid 87 15 15N 33 0 E
El Matariya 86 31 15N 32 0 E
El Meghaier 83 33 55N 5 58 E
El Meraguen 82 28 0N 0 7W
El Metemma 87 16 50N 33 10 E
El Milagro 124 30 59 S 65 59W
El Milia 83 36 51N 6 13 E
El Minyâ 86 28 7N 30 33 E
El Molar 32 40 42N 3 45W
El Mreyye 84 18 0N 6 0W
El Obeid 87 13 8N 30 10 E
El Odaiya 81 12 8N 28 12 E
El Oro 120 19 48N 100 8W
El Oro = Sta. María del Oro 120 25 50N 105 20W
El Oued 83 33 20N 6 58 E
El Palmito, Presa 120 25 40N 105 30W
El Panadés 32 41 10N 1 30 E
El Pardo 30 40 31N 3 47W
El Paso 119 31 50N 106 30W
El Pedernoso 33 39 29N 2 45W
El Pedroso 31 37 51N 5 45W
El Pobo de Dueñas 32 40 46N 1 39W
El Portal 119 37 44N 119 49W
El Prat de Llobregat 32 41 18N 2 3 E
El Progreso 120 15 26N 87 51W
El Provencio 33 39 23N 2 35W
El Pueblito 120 29 3N 105 4W
El Qâhira 86 30 1N 31 14 E
El Qantara 86 30 51N 32 20 E
El Qasr 86 25 44N 28 42 E
El Quseima 86 30 40N 34 15 E
El Qusîya 86 27 29N 30 44 E
El Râshda 86 25 36N 28 57 E
El Reno 117 35 30N 98 0W
El Ribero 30 42 30N 8 30W
El Rîdisiya 86 24 56N 32 51 E
El Ronquillo 31 37 44N 6 10W
El Rubio 31 37 22N 5 0W
El Saff 86 29 34N 31 16 E
El Salvador ■ 120 13 50N 89 0W
El Sancejo 31 37 4N 5 6W
El Sauce 121 13 0N 86 40W
El Shallal 86 24 0N 32 53 E
El Simbillawein 86 30 48N 31 13 E
El Suweis 86 29 58N 32 31 E
El Thamad 86 29 40N 34 28 E
El Tigre 126 8 44N 64 15W
El Tocuyo 126 9 47N 69 48W
El Tofo 124 29 22 S 71 18W
El Tránsito 124 28 52 S 70 17W
El Tûr 86 28 14N 33 36 E
El Turbio 128 51 45 S 72 5W
El Uqsur 86 25 41N 32 38 E
El Vado 32 41 2N 3 18W
El Vallés 32 41 35N 2 20 E
El Vigía 126 8 38N 71 39W
El Wak 90 2 49N 40 56 E
El Waqf 86 25 45N 32 15 E
El Wâsta 86 29 19N 31 12 E
El Weguet 87 5 28N 42 17 E
El Wuz 81 15 0N 30 7 E
Elafónisos 45 36 29N 22 56 E
Elamanchili = Yellamanchilli 70 17 26N 82 50 E
Elandsvlei 92 32 19 S 19 31 E
Élassa 45 35 18N 26 21 E
Elassón 44 39 53N 22 12 E
Elat 62 29 30N 34 56 E
Eláthia 45 38 37N 22 46 E
Elâzığ 64 38 37N 39 14 E
Elba, Italy 38 42 48N 10 15 E
Elba, U.S.A. 115 31 27N 86 4W
Elbasani 44 41 9N 20 9 E
Elbasani-Berati □ 44 40 58N 20 0 E
Elbe → 24 53 50N 9 0 E
Elbert, Mt. 119 39 5N 106 27W
Elberta 114 44 35N 86 14W
Elberton 115 34 7N 82 51W
Elbeuf 18 49 17N 1 2 E
Elbidtan 64 38 13N 37 12 E
Elbing = Elbląg 28 54 10N 19 25 E
Elbląg 28 54 10N 19 25 E
Elbląg □ 28 54 15N 19 30 E
Elbow 109 51 7N 106 35W

Elbrus 57 43 21N 42 30 E
Elburg 16 52 26N 5 50 E
Elburz Mts. = Alborz 65 36 0N 52 0 E
Elche 33 38 15N 0 42W
Elche de la Sierra 33 38 27N 2 3W
Elcho I. 97 11 55 S 135 45 E
Elda 33 38 29N 0 47W
Eldon 116 38 20N 92 38W
Eldora 116 42 20N 93 5W
Eldorado, Argent. 125 26 28 S 54 43W
Eldorado, Can. 109 59 35N 108 30W
Eldorado, Mexico 120 24 20N 107 22W
Eldorado, Ill., U.S.A. 114 37 50N 88 25W
Eldorado, Tex., U.S.A. 117 30 52N 100 35W
Eldoret 90 0 30N 35 17 E
Eldred 112 41 57N 78 24W
Electra 117 34 0N 99 0W
Elefantes → 93 24 10 S 32 40 E
Elektrogorsk 55 55 56N 38 50 E
Elektrostal 55 55 41N 38 32 E
Elele 85 5 5N 6 50 E
Elena 43 42 55N 25 53 E
Elephant Butte Res. 119 33 45N 107 30W
Elephant I. 5 61 0 S 55 0W
Elephant Pass 70 9 35N 80 25 E
Eleshnitsa 43 41 52N 23 36 E
Eleuthera 121 25 0N 76 20W
Elevsis 45 38 4N 23 26 E
Elevtheroúpolis 44 40 52N 24 20 E
Elgepiggen 47 62 10N 11 21 E
Elgeyo-Marakwet □ 90 0 45N 35 30 E
Elgin, N.B., Can. 107 45 48N 65 10W
Elgin, Ont., Can. 113 44 36N 76 13W
Elgin, U.K. 14 57 39N 3 20W
Elgin, Ill., U.S.A. 114 42 0N 88 20W
Elgin, N.D., U.S.A. 116 46 24N 101 46W
Elgin, Nebr., U.S.A. 116 41 58N 98 3W
Elgin, Nev., U.S.A. 119 37 21N 114 20W
Elgin, Oreg., U.S.A. 118 45 37N 118 0W
Elgin, Texas, U.S.A. 117 30 21N 97 22W
Elgon, Mt. 90 1 10N 34 30 E
Eliase 73 8 21 S 130 48 E
Elida 117 33 56N 103 41W
Elikón, Mt. 45 38 18N 22 45 E
Elin Pelin 43 42 40N 23 36 E
Elisabethville = Lubumbashi 91 11 40 S 27 28 E
Elista 57 46 16N 44 14 E
Elizabeth, Austral. 97 34 42 S 138 41 E
Elizabeth, U.S.A. 114 40 37N 74 12W
Elizabeth City 115 36 18N 76 16W
Elizabethton 115 36 20N 82 13W
Elizabethtown, Ky., U.S.A. 114 37 40N 85 54W
Elizabethtown, N.Y., U.S.A. 113 44 13N 73 36W
Elizabethtown, Pa., U.S.A. 113 40 8N 76 36W
Elizondo 32 43 12N 1 30W
Ełk 28 53 50N 22 21 E
Ełk → 28 53 41N 22 28 E
Elk City 117 35 25N 99 25W
Elk Island Nat. Park 108 53 35N 112 59W
Elk Lake 106 47 40N 80 25W
Elk Point 109 53 54N 110 55W
Elk River, Idaho, U.S.A. 118 46 50N 116 8W
Elk River, Minn., U.S.A. 116 45 17N 93 34W
Elkhart, Ind., U.S.A. 114 41 42N 85 55W
Elkhart, Kans., U.S.A. 117 37 3N 101 54W
Elkhorn 109 49 59N 101 14W
Elkhorn → 116 41 7N 98 15W
Elkhotovo 57 43 19N 44 15 E
Elkhovo 43 42 10N 26 40 E
Elkin 115 36 17N 80 50W
Elkins 114 38 53N 79 53W
Elko, Can. 108 49 20N 115 10W
Elko, U.S.A. 118 40 50N 115 50W
Ellef Ringnes I. 4 78 30N 102 2W
Ellen, Mt. 119 38 4N 110 56W
Ellendale 116 46 3N 98 30W
Ellensburg 118 47 0N 120 30W
Ellenville 114 41 42N 74 23W
Ellery, Mt. 99 37 28 S 148 47 E
Ellesmere I. 4 79 30N 80 0W
Ellesworth Land 5 76 0 S 89 0W
Ellice Is. = Tuvalu ■ 94 8 0 S 176 0 E
Ellinwood 116 38 27N 98 37W
Elliot 93 31 22 S 27 48 E
Elliot Lake 106 46 25N 82 35W
Ellis 116 39 0N 99 39W
Ellisville 117 31 38N 89 12W
Ellon 14 57 21N 2 5W
Ellore = Eluru 70 16 48N 81 8 E
Ells → 108 57 18N 111 40W
Ellsworth 116 38 47N 98 15W
Ellsworth Land 5 76 0 S 89 0W
Ellsworth Mts. 5 78 30 S 85 0W
Ellwangen 25 48 57N 10 9 E
Ellwood City 114 40 52N 80 19W
Elm 25 46 54N 9 10 E
Elma, Can. 109 49 52N 95 55W
Elma, U.S.A. 118 47 0N 123 30 E
Elmalı 64 36 44N 29 56 E
Elmhurst 114 41 52N 87 58W
Elmina 85 5 5N 1 21W
Elmira, Can. 112 43 36N 80 33W
Elmira, U.S.A. 114 42 8N 76 49W
Elmore 99 36 30 S 144 37 E
Elmshorn 24 53 44N 9 40 E
Elmvale 112 44 35N 79 52W
Elne 20 42 36N 2 58 E
Elora 112 43 41N 80 26W
Elos 45 36 46N 22 43 E
Eloy 119 32 46N 111 33W
Éloyes 19 48 6N 6 36 E
Elrose 109 51 12N 108 0W
Elsas 106 48 32N 82 55W
Elsinore, Cal., U.S.A. 119 33 40N 117 15W
Elsinore, Utah, U.S.A. 119 38 40N 112 2W
Elspe 24 51 10N 8 1 E
Elster → 24 51 25N 11 57 E
Elsterwerda 24 51 27N 13 32 E
Eltham 101 39 26 S 174 19 E
Elton 57 49 5N 46 52 E
Eluru 70 16 48N 81 8 E
Elvas 31 38 50N 7 10W
Elven 18 47 44N 2 36W
Elverum 47 60 53N 11 34 E
Elvo → 38 45 23N 8 21 E
Elvran 47 63 24N 11 3 E
Elwood, Ind., U.S.A. 114 40 20N 85 50W
Elwood, Nebr., U.S.A. 116 40 38N 99 51W
Ely, U.K. 13 52 24N 0 16 E
Ely, Minn., U.S.A. 116 47 54N 91 52W
Ely, Nev., U.S.A. 118 39 10N 114 50W
Elyashiv 62 32 23N 34 55 E
Elyria 114 41 22N 82 8W
Elyrus 45 35 15N 23 45 E
Elz → 25 48 21N 7 45 E
Emådalen 48 61 20N 14 44 E
Emba 58 48 50N 58 8 E
Emba → 58 45 25N 52 30 E
Embarcación 124 23 10 S 64 0W
Embarras Portage 109 58 27N 111 28W
Embóna 45 36 13N 27 51 E
Embrun 21 44 34N 6 30 E
Embu 90 0 32 S 37 38 E
Embu □ 90 0 30 S 37 35 E
Emden 24 53 22N 7 12 E
'Emeq Yizre'el 62 32 35N 35 12 E
Emerald 97 23 32 S 148 10 E
Emerson 109 49 0N 97 10W
Emery 119 38 59N 111 17W
Emery Park 119 32 10N 110 59W
Emi Koussi 83 20 0N 18 55 E
Emilia-Romagna □ 38 44 33N 10 40 E
Emilius, Mte. 38 45 41N 7 23 E
Eminabad 68 32 2N 74 8 E
Emine, Nos 43 42 40N 27 56 E
Emlenton 112 41 11N 79 41W
Emlichheim 24 52 37N 6 51 E
Emmaboda 49 56 37N 15 32 E
Emme → 25 47 0N 7 42 E
Emmeloord 16 52 44N 5 46 E
Emmen 16 52 48N 6 57 E
Emmendingen 25 48 7N 7 51 E
Emmental 25 47 0N 7 35 E
Emmerich 24 51 50N 6 12 E
Emmet 98 24 45 S 144 30 E
Emmetsburg 116 43 3N 94 40W
Emmett 118 43 51N 116 33W
Emöd 27 47 57N 20 47 E
Emona 43 42 43N 27 53 E
Empalme 120 28 1N 110 49W
Empangeni 93 28 50 S 31 52 E
Empedrado 124 28 0 S 58 46W
Emperor Seamount Chain 94 40 0N 170 0 E
Empoli 38 43 43N 10 57 E
Emporia, Kans., U.S.A. 116 38 25N 96 10W
Emporia, Va., U.S.A. 115 36 41N 77 32W
Emporium 114 41 30N 78 17W
Empress 109 50 57N 110 0W
Ems → 24 52 37N 9 26 E
Emsdale 112 45 32N 79 19W
Emsdetten 24 52 11N 7 31 E
Emu 76 43 40N 128 6 E
Emu Park 98 23 13 S 150 50 E
En Gedi 62 31 28N 35 25 E
En Gev 62 32 47N 35 38 E
En Harod 62 32 33N 35 22 E
'En Kerem 62 31 47N 35 6 E
En Nahud 87 12 45N 28 25 E
Enafors 48 63 17N 12 20 E
Enana 92 17 30 S 16 23 E
Enånger 48 61 30N 17 9 E
Enaratoli 73 3 55 S 136 21 E
Enard B. 14 58 5N 5 20W
Encantadas, Serra 125 30 40 S 53 0W
Encanto, C. 73 15 45N 121 38 E
Encarnación 125 27 15 S 55 50W
Encarnación de Diaz 120 21 30N 102 13W
Enchi 84 5 53N 2 48W
Encinal 117 28 3N 99 25W
Encino 119 34 38N 105 40W
Encounter B. 97 35 45 S 138 45 E
Endau 71 2 40N 103 38 E
Endau → 71 2 30N 103 30 E
Ende 73 8 45 S 121 40 E
Endeavour 109 52 10N 102 39W
Endeavour Str. 97 10 45 S 142 0 E
Endelave 49 55 46N 10 18 E
Enderbury I. 94 3 8 S 171 5W
Enderby 108 50 35N 119 10W
Enderby Land 5 66 0 S 53 0 E
Enderlin 116 46 37N 97 41W
Endicott, N.Y., U.S.A. 114 42 6N 76 2W
Endicott, Wash., U.S.A. 118 47 0N 117 45W
Endröd 27 46 55N 20 47 E
Enez 44 40 45N 26 5 E
Enfida 83 36 6N 10 28 E
Enfield 13 51 39N 0 4W
Engadin = Engiadina 25 46 51N 10 18 E
Engaño, C., Dom. Rep. 121 18 30N 68 20W
Engaño, C., Phil. 73 18 35N 122 23 E
Engelberg 25 46 48N 8 26 E
Engels 55 51 28N 46 6 E
Engemann L. 109 58 0N 106 55W
Enger 47 60 35N 10 20 E
Enggano 72 5 20 S 102 40 E
Enghien 16 50 37N 4 2 E
Engiadina 25 46 51N 10 18 E
Engil 82 33 12N 4 32W
Engkilili 72 1 3N 111 42 E
England 117 34 30N 91 58W
England □ 11 53 0N 2 0W
Englee 107 50 45N 56 5W
Englehart 106 47 49N 79 52W
Engler L. 109 59 8N 106 52W
Englewood, Colo., U.S.A. 116 39 40N 105 0W
Englewood, Kans., U.S.A. 117 37 7N 99 59W
Englewood, N.J., U.S.A. 113 40 54N 73 59W
English → 109 50 35N 93 30W
English Bazar 69 24 58N 88 10 E
English Channel 18 50 0N 2 0W
English River 106 49 14N 91 0W
Enid 117 36 26N 97 52W
Enipévs → 44 39 22N 22 17 E
Eniwetok 94 11 30N 162 15 E
Enkeldoorn 91 19 2 S 30 52 E
Enkhuizen 16 52 42N 5 17 E
Enköping 48 59 37N 17 4 E
Enna 41 37 34N 14 15 E
Ennadai 109 61 8N 100 53W
Ennadai L. 109 61 0N 101 0W
Ennedi 81 17 15N 22 0 E
Enngonia 99 29 21 S 145 50 E
Ennis, Ireland 15 52 51N 8 59W
Ennis, Mont., U.S.A. 118 45 20N 111 42W
Ennis, Texas, U.S.A. 117 32 15N 96 40W
Enniscorthy 15 52 30N 6 35W
Enniskillen 15 54 20N 7 40W
Ennistimon 15 52 56N 9 18W
Enns 26 48 12N 14 28 E
Enns → 26 48 14N 14 32 E
Enontekiö 50 68 23N 23 37 E
Enping 77 22 16N 112 21 E
Enriquillo, L. 121 18 20N 72 5W
Enschede 16 52 13N 6 53 E
Ensenada, Argent. 124 34 55 S 57 55W
Ensenada, Mexico 120 31 50N 116 50W
Enshi 77 30 18N 109 29 E
Ensisheim 19 47 50N 7 20 E
Entebbe 90 0 4N 32 28 E
Enterprise, Can. 108 60 47N 115 45W
Enterprise, Oreg., U.S.A. 118 45 30N 117 18W
Enterprise, Utah, U.S.A. 119 37 37N 113 36W
Entre Ríos, Boliv. 124 21 30 S 64 25W
Entre Ríos, Mozam. 91 14 57 S 37 20 E
Entre Ríos □ 124 30 30 S 58 30W
Entrecasteaux, Pt. d' 96 34 50 S 115 56 E
Entrepeñas, Pantano de 32 40 34N 2 42W
Enugu 85 6 20N 7 30 E
Enugu Ezike 85 7 0N 7 29 E
Enumclaw 118 47 12N 122 0W
Envermeières 18 49 54N 1 16 E
Envermeu 18 49 53N 1 15 E
Enz → 25 49 1N 9 6 E
Enza → 38 44 54N 10 31 E
Eólie, I. 41 38 30N 14 50 E
Epanomí 44 40 25N 22 59 E
Epe, Neth. 16 52 21N 5 59 E
Epe, Nigeria 85 6 36N 3 59 E
Épernay 19 49 3N 3 56 E
Épernon 19 48 35N 1 40 E
Ephesus, Turkey 45 37 50N 27 33 E
Ephesus, Turkey 64 38 0N 27 19 E
Ephraim 118 39 21N 111 37W
Ephrata 118 47 20N 119 32W
Epidaurus Limera 45 36 46N 23 0 E
Épila 32 41 36N 1 17W
Épinac-les-Mines 19 46 59N 4 31 E
Épinal 19 48 10N 6 27 E
Episcopia Bihorului 46 47 12N 21 55 E
Epitálion 45 37 37N 21 30 E
Epping 13 51 42N 0 8 E
Epukiro 92 21 40 S 19 9 E
Equatorial Guinea ■ 88 2 0 S 8 0 E
Er Rahad 87 12 45N 30 32 E
Er Rif 82 35 1N 4 1W
Er Roseires 87 11 55N 34 30 E
Er Yébigué 83 22 30N 17 30 E
Frandol 68 20 56N 75 20 E
Erāwadī Myit = Irrawaddy → 67 15 50N 95 6 E
Erba, Italy 38 45 49N 9 12 E
Erba, Sudan 86 19 5N 36 51 E
Ercha 59 69 45N 147 20 E
Erciyaş Dağı 64 38 30N 35 30 E
Erdao Jiang → 76 43 0N 127 0 E
Erding 25 48 18N 11 55 E
Erdre → 18 47 13N 1 32W
Erebus, Mt. 5 77 35 S 167 0 E
Erechim 125 27 35 S 52 15W
Ereğli, Turkey 64 41 15N 31 30 E
Ereğli, Turkey 64 37 31N 34 4 E
Erei, Monti 41 37 20N 14 20 E
Erenhot 76 43 48N 111 59 E
Eresma → 30 41 26N 40 45W
Eressós 45 39 11N 25 57 E
Erfenis Dam 92 28 30 S 26 50 E
Erfjord 47 59 20N 6 14 E
Erfoud 82 31 30N 4 15W
Erft → 24 51 11N 6 44 E
Erfurt 24 50 58N 11 2 E
Erfurt □ 24 51 10N 10 30 E
Ergani 64 38 17N 39 49 E
Ergene → 43 41 1N 26 22 E
Ergeni Vozyshennost 57 47 0N 44 0 E
Ergli 54 56 54N 25 38 E
Ergun Zuoqi 76 50 47N 121 31 E
Eria → 30 42 3N 5 44W
Eriba 87 16 40N 36 10 E
Eriboll, L. 14 58 28N 4 41W
Érice 40 38 4N 12 34 E
Erie 114 42 10N 80 7W
Erie Canal 112 43 15N 78 0W
Erie, L. 112 42 15N 81 0W
Erieau 112 42 16N 81 57W
Erigavo 63 10 35N 47 20 E
Erikoúsa 44 39 55N 19 14 E
Eriksdale 109 50 52N 98 7W
Erikslund 48 62 31N 15 54 E
Erimanthos 45 37 57N 21 50 E
Erimo-misaki 74 41 50N 143 15 E
Erithraí 45 38 13N 23 20 E
Eritrea □ 87 14 0N 41 0 E
Erjas → 31 39 40N 7 1W
Erlangen 25 49 35N 11 0 E
Ermelo, Neth. 16 52 18N 5 35 E
Ermelo, S. Afr. 93 26 31 S 29 59 E
Ermenak 64 36 38N 33 0 E
Ermióni 45 37 23N 23 15 E
Ermoúpolis = Síros 45 37 28N 24 57 E
Ernakulam = Cochin 70 9 59N 76 22 E
Erne → 15 54 30N 8 16W
Erne, Lough 15 54 26N 7 46W
Ernée 18 48 18N 0 56W
Ernstberg 25 50 14N 6 46 E
Erode 70 11 24N 77 45 E
Eromanga 99 26 40 S 143 11 E
Erongo 92 21 39 S 15 58 E
Erquy 18 48 38N 2 29W
Erquy, Cap d' 18 48 39N 2 29W
Erramala Hills 70 15 30N 78 15 E
Errer → 87 7 32N 42 35 E
Errigal, Mt. 15 55 2N 8 8W
Erris Hd. 15 54 19N 10 0W
Erseka 44 40 22N 20 40 E
Erskine 116 47 37N 96 0W
Erstein 19 48 25N 7 38 E
Ertil 55 51 55N 40 50 E
Ertvågøy 47 63 13N 8 26 E
Eruwa 85 7 33N 3 26 E
Ervy-le-Châtel 19 48 2N 3 55 E
Erwin 115 36 10N 82 28W
Erzgebirge 24 50 25N 13 0 E
Erzin 59 50 15N 95 10 E
Erzincan 64 39 46N 39 30 E
Erzurum 64 39 57N 41 15 E
Es Sahrâ' Esh Sharqîya 86 26 0N 33 30 E
Es Sînâ' 86 29 0N 34 0 E
Es Sûkî 87 13 20N 33 58 E
Esambo 90 3 48 S 23 30 E
Esan-Misaki 74 41 40N 141 10 E
Esbjerg 49 55 29N 8 29 E
Escalante 119 37 47N 111 37W
Escalante → 119 37 17N 110 53W
Escalón 120 26 46N 104 20W
Escalona 30 40 9N 4 29W
Escambia → 115 30 32N 87 15W
Escanaba 114 45 44N 87 5W
Esch-sur-Alzette 16 49 32N 6 0 E
Eschallens 25 46 39N 6 38 E
Eschede 24 52 44N 10 13 E
Eschwege 24 51 10N 10 3 E
Eschweiler 24 50 49N 6 14 E
Escobal 120 9 6N 80 1W
Escondido 119 33 9N 117 4W
Escuinapa 120 22 50N 105 50W
Escuintla 120 14 20N 90 48W
Eséka 85 3 41N 10 44 E
Esens 24 53 40N 7 35 E
Esera → 32 42 6N 0 15 E
Eşfahān 65 33 0N 53 0 E
Esgueva → 30 41 40N 4 43W
Esh Sham = Dimashq 64 33 30N 36 18 E
Esh Shamâlîya □ 86 19 0N 29 0 E
Eshowe 93 28 50 S 31 30 E
Eshta' ol 62 31 47N 35 0 E
Esiama 84 4 56N 2 25W
Esino → 39 43 39N 13 22 E
Esk →, Dumfries, U.K. 14 54 58N 3 4W
Esk →, N. Yorks., U.K. 12 54 27N 0 36W
Eskifjörður 50 65 3N 13 55W
Eskilstuna 48 59 22N 16 32 E
Eskimo Pt. 109 61 10N 94 15W
Eskişehir 64 39 50N 30 35 E
Esla → 30 41 29N 6 3W
Esla, Pantano del 30 41 29N 6 3W
Eslöv 49 55 50N 13 20 E
Esmeralda, La 124 22 16 S 62 33W
Esmeraldas 126 1 0N 79 40W
Espalion 20 44 32N 2 47 E
Espalmador, I. 33 38 47N 1 26 E
Espanola 106 46 15N 81 46W
Espardell, I. del 33 38 48N 1 29 E
Esparraguera 32 41 33N 1 52 E
Espejo 31 37 40N 4 34W
Esperance 96 33 45 S 121 55 E
Esperance B. 96 33 48 S 121 55 E
Esperanza 124 31 29 S 61 3W
Espéraza 20 42 56N 2 14 E
Espevær 47 59 35N 5 7 E
Espichel, C. 31 38 22N 9 16W
Espiel 31 38 11N 5 1W
Espigão, Serra do 125 26 35 S 50 30W
Espinal 126 4 9N 74 53W
Espinhaço, Serra do 127 17 30 S 43 30W
Espinho 30 41 1N 8 38W
Espinilho, Serra do 125 28 30 S 55 0W
Espinosa de los Monteros 30 43 5N 3 34W
Espírito Santo □ 127 20 0 S 40 45W
Espíritu Santo, B. del 120 19 15N 87 0W
Espíritu Santo, I. 120 24 30N 110 23W
Espluga de Francolí 32 41 24N 1 7 E
Espuña, Sierra 33 37 51N 1 35W
Espungabera 93 20 29 S 32 45 E
Esquel 128 42 55 S 71 20W
Esquina 124 30 0 S 59 30W
Essaouira (Mogador) 82 31 32N 9 48W
Essarts, Les 18 46 47N 1 12W
Essebie 90 2 58N 30 40 E
Essen, Belg. 16 51 28N 4 28 E
Essen, Ger. 24 51 28N 6 59 E
Essequibo → 126 6 50N 58 30W
Essex, Can. 112 42 10N 82 49W
Essex, U.S.A. 113 44 17N 73 21W
Essex □ 13 51 48N 0 30 E
Esslingen 25 48 43N 9 19 E
Essonne □ 19 48 30N 2 20 E
Essvik 48 62 18N 17 24 E
Estaca, Pta. del 30 43 46N 7 42W
Estadilla 32 42 4N 0 16 E
Estados, I. de Los 128 54 40 S 64 30W
Estagel 20 42 47N 2 40 E
Estância 127 11 16 S 37 26W
Estancia 119 34 50N 106 1W
Estarreja 30 40 45N 8 35W
Estats, Pic d' 32 42 40N 1 24 E
Estcourt 93 28 58 S 29 53 E
Este 39 45 12N 11 40 E
Esteban 30 43 33N 6 5W
Estelí 121 13 9N 86 22W
Estella 32 42 40N 2 0W
Estelline, S.D., U.S.A. 116 44 39N 96 52W
Estelline, Texas, U.S.A. 117 34 35N 100 27W
Estena → 31 39 23N 4 44W
Estepa 31 37 17N 4 52W
Estepona 31 36 24N 5 7W
Esterhazy 109 50 37N 102 5W
Esternay 19 48 44N 3 33 E
Esterri de Aneu 32 42 38N 1 5 E
Estevan 109 49 10N 102 59W

Estevan Group 108 53 3N 129 38W
Estherville 116 43 25N 94 50W
Estissac 19 48 16N 3 48 E
Eston 109 51 8N 108 40W
Estonian S.S.R. □ 54 58 30N 25 30 E
Estoril 31 38 42N 9 23W
Estouk 85 18 14N 1 2 E
Estrada, La 30 42 43N 8 27W
Estrêla, Serra da 30 40 10N 7 45W
Estrella 33 38 25N 3 35W
Estremoz 31 38 51N 7 39W
Estrondo, Serra do 127 7 20 S 48 0W
Esztergom 27 47 47N 18 44 E
Et Tîdra 84 19 45N 16 20W
Eṭ Ṭîra 62 32 14N 34 56 E
Étables-sur-Mer 18 48 38N 2 51W
Etah 68 27 35N 78 40 E
Étain 19 49 13N 5 38 E
Etamamu 107 50 18N 59 59W
Étampes 19 48 26N 2 10 E
Étang 19 46 52N 4 10 E
Etanga 92 17 55 S 13 00 E
Étaples 19 50 30N 1 39 E
Etawah 68 26 48N 79 6 E
Etawah → 115 34 20N 84 15W
Etawney L. 109 57 50N 96 50W
Eteh 85 7 2N 7 28 E
Ethel, Oued el → 82 28 31N 3 37W
Ethelbert 109 51 32N 100 25W
Ethiopia ■ 63 8 0N 40 0 E
Ethiopian Highlands 78 10 0N 37 0 E
Etive, L. 14 56 30N 5 12W
Etna, Mt. 41 37 45N 15 0 E
Etne 47 59 40N 5 56 E
Etoile 91 11 33 S 27 30 E
Etolin I. 108 56 5N 132 20W
Etosha Pan 92 18 40 S 16 30 E
Etowah 115 35 20N 84 30W
Étrépagny 18 49 18N 1 36 E
Étretat 18 49 42N 0 12 E
Étroits, Les 107 47 24N 68 54W
Etropole 43 42 50N 24 0 E
Ettlingen 25 48 58N 8 25 E
Ettrick Water 14 55 31N 2 55W
Etuku 90 3 42 S 25 45 E
Etzatlán 120 20 48N 104 5W
Eu 18 50 3N 1 26 E
Euabalong West 100 33 3 S 146 23 E
Euboea = Évvoia 45 38 40N 23 40 E
Eucla Basin 96 31 19 S 126 9 E
Euclid 114 41 32N 81 31W
Eucumbene, L. 99 36 2 S 148 40 E
Eudora 117 33 5N 91 17W
Eufaula, Ala., U.S.A. 115 31 55N 85 11W
Eufaula, Okla., U.S.A. 117 35 20N 95 33W
Eufaula, L. 117 35 15N 95 28W
Eugene 118 44 0N 123 8W
Eugenia, Punta 120 27 50N 115 5W
Eugowra 99 33 22 S 148 24 E
Eulo 99 28 10 S 145 3 E
Eunice, La., U.S.A. 117 30 35N 92 28W
Eunice, N. Mex., U.S.A. 117 32 30N 103 10W
Eupen 16 50 37N 6 3 E
Euphrates = Furāt, Nahr al → 64 31 0N 47 25 E
Eure □ 18 49 6N 1 0 E
Eure → 18 49 18N 1 12 E
Eure-et-Loir □ 18 48 22N 1 30 E
Eureka, Can. 4 80 0N 85 56W
Eureka, Calif., U.S.A. 118 40 50N 124 0W
Eureka, Kans., U.S.A. 117 37 50N 96 20W
Eureka, Mont., U.S.A. 118 48 53N 115 6W
Eureka, Nev., U.S.A. 118 39 32N 116 2W
Eureka, S.D., U.S.A. 116 45 49N 99 38W
Eureka, Utah, U.S.A. 118 40 0N 112 9W
Euroa 99 36 44 S 145 35 E
Europa, Picos de 30 43 10N 4 49W
Europa Pt. = Europa, Pta. de 31 36 3N 5 21W
Europa, Pta. de 31 36 3N 5 21W
Europe 8 50 0N 20 0 E
Europoort 16 51 57N 4 10 E
Euskirchen 24 50 40N 6 45 E
Eustis 115 28 54N 81 36W
Eutin 24 54 7N 10 38 E
Eutsuk L. 108 53 20N 126 45W
Eval 62 32 15N 35 15 E
Evale 92 16 33 S 15 44 E
Evanger 47 60 39N 6 7 E
Evans 116 40 25N 104 43W
Evans Head 99 29 7 S 153 27 E
Evans L. 106 50 50N 77 0W
Evans Mills 113 44 6N 75 48W
Evans Pass 116 41 0N 105 35W
Evanston, Ill., U.S.A. 114 42 0N 87 40W
Evanston, Wyo., U.S.A. 118 41 10N 111 0W
Evansville, Ind., U.S.A. 114 38 0N 87 35W
Evansville, Wis., U.S.A. 116 42 47N 89 18W
Évaux-les-Bains 20 46 12N 2 29 E
Eveleth 116 47 29N 92 46W
Even Yahuda 62 32 16N 34 53 E
Evensk 59 62 12N 159 30 E
Evenstad 47 61 25N 11 7 E
Everard, L. 96 31 30 S 135 0 E
Everard Ras. 96 27 5 S 132 28 E
Everest, Mt. 69 28 5N 86 58 E
Everett, Pa., U.S.A. 112 40 2N 78 24W
Everett, Wash., U.S.A. 118 48 0N 122 10W
Everglades, Fla., U.S.A. 115 26 0N 80 30W
Everglades, Fla., U.S.A. 115 25 52N 81 23W
Everglades Nat. Park. 115 25 27N 80 53W
Evergreen 115 31 28N 86 55W
Everson 118 48 57N 122 22W
Evesham 13 52 6N 1 57W
Evian-les-Bains 21 46 24N 6 35 E
Evinayong 88 1 26N 10 35 E
Évinos → 45 38 27N 21 40 E
Evisa 21 42 15N 8 48 E
Evje 47 58 36N 7 51 E
Évora 31 38 33N 7 57W
Évora □ 31 38 33N 7 50W
Évreux 18 49 0N 1 8 E
Evritania □ 45 39 5N 21 30 E
Évron 18 48 10N 0 24W
Évros □ 44 41 10N 26 0 E
Evrótas → 45 36 50N 22 40 E
Évvoia 45 38 30N 24 0 E
Évvoia □ 45 38 40N 23 40 E
Ewe, L. 14 57 49N 5 38W
Ewing 116 42 18N 98 22W
Ewo 88 0 48 S 14 45 E
Exaltación 126 13 10 S 65 20W
Excelsior Springs 116 39 20N 94 10W
Excideuil 20 45 20N 1 4 E
Exe → 13 50 38N 3 27W
Exeter, Can. 112 43 21N 81 29W
Exeter, U.K. 13 50 43N 3 31W
Exeter, Calif., U.S.A. 119 36 17N 119 9W
Exeter, N.H., U.S.A. 113 43 0N 70 58W
Exeter, Nebr., U.S.A. 116 40 43N 97 30W
Exmes 18 48 45N 0 10 E
Exmoor 13 51 10N 3 59W
Exmouth, Austral. 96 21 54 S 114 10 E
Exmouth, U.K. 13 50 37N 3 26W
Exmouth G. 96 22 15 S 114 15 E
Expedition Range 97 24 30 S 149 12 E
Extremadura 31 39 30N 6 5W
Exuma Sound 121 24 30N 76 20W
Eyasi, L. 90 3 30 S 35 0 E
Eyeberry L. 109 63 8N 104 43W
Eyemouth 14 55 53N 2 5W
Eygurande 20 45 40N 2 26 E
Eyjafjörður 50 66 15N 18 30W
Eymet 20 44 40N 0 25 E
Eymoutiers 20 45 40N 1 45 E
Eyrarbakki 50 63 52N 21 9W
Eyre 96 32 15 S 126 18 E
Eyre Cr. → 97 26 40 S 139 0 E
Eyre, L. 97 29 30 S 137 26 E
Eyre Mts. 101 45 25 S 168 25 E
Eyre (North), L. 97 28 30 S 137 20 E
Eyre Pen. 96 33 30 S 137 17 E
Eyre (South), L. 99 29 18 S 137 25 E
Eyzies, Les 20 44 56N 1 1 E
Ez Zeidab 86 17 25N 33 55 E
Ezcaray 32 42 19N 3 0W
Ezine 44 39 48N 26 12 E

F

Fabens 119 31 30N 106 8W
Fåborg 49 55 6N 10 15 E
Fabriano 39 43 20N 12 52 E
Făcăeni 46 44 32N 27 53 E
Facatativá 126 4 49N 74 22W
Fachi 80 18 6N 11 34 E
Facture 20 44 39N 0 58W
Fada 81 17 13N 21 34 E
Fada-n-Gourma 85 12 10N 0 30 E
Fadd 27 46 28N 18 49 E
Faddeyevskiy, Ostrov 59 76 0N 150 0 E
Fāḑilī 64 26 55N 49 10 E
Fadlab 86 17 42N 34 2 E
Faenza 39 44 17N 11 53 E
Fafa 85 15 22N 0 48 E
Fafe 30 41 27N 8 11W
Fagam 85 11 1N 10 1 E
Făgăras 46 45 48N 24 58 E
Făgăras, Munţii 46 45 40N 24 40 E
Fågelsjö 48 61 50N 14 35 E
Fagerhult 49 57 8N 15 40 E
Fagersta 48 60 1N 15 46 E
Făget 46 45 52N 22 10 E
Făget, Munţii 46 47 40N 23 10 E
Fagnano Castello 41 39 31N 16 4 E
Fagnano, L. 128 54 30 S 68 0W
Fagnières 19 48 58N 4 20 E
Fahraj 65 29 0N 59 0 E
Fahūd 65 22 18N 56 28 E
Fair Hd. 15 55 14N 6 10W
Fair Isle 11 59 30N 1 40W
Fairbank 119 31 44N 110 12W
Fairbanks 104 64 50N 147 50W
Fairbury 116 40 5N 97 5W
Fairfax 117 36 37N 96 45W
Fairfield, Austral. 100 33 53 S 150 57 E
Fairfield, Ala., U.S.A. 115 33 30N 87 0W
Fairfield, Calif., U.S.A. 118 38 14N 122 1W
Fairfield, Conn., U.S.A. 113 41 8N 73 16W
Fairfield, Idaho, U.S.A. 118 43 21N 114 46W
Fairfield, Ill., U.S.A. 114 38 20N 88 20W
Fairfield, Iowa, U.S.A. 116 41 0N 91 58W
Fairfield, Mont., U.S.A. 118 47 40N 112 0W
Fairfield, Texas, U.S.A. 117 31 40N 96 0W
Fairford 109 51 37N 98 38W
Fairhope 115 30 35N 87 50W
Fairlie 101 44 5 S 170 49 E
Fairmont, Minn., U.S.A. 116 43 37N 94 30W
Fairmont, W. Va., U.S.A. 114 39 29N 80 10W
Fairmont Hot Springs 108 50 20N 115 56W
Fairplay 119 39 9N 105 40W
Fairport, N.Y., U.S.A. 114 43 8N 77 29W
Fairport, Ohio, U.S.A. 112 41 45N 81 17W
Fairview, Austral. 98 15 31 S 144 17 E
Fairview, Can. 108 56 5N 118 25W
Fairview, N. Dak., U.S.A. 116 47 49N 104 7W
Fairview, Okla., U.S.A. 117 36 19N 98 30W
Fairview, Utah, U.S.A. 118 39 50N 111 0W
Fairweather, Mt. 104 58 55N 137 45W
Faith 116 45 2N 102 4W
Faizabad 69 26 45N 82 10 E
Faizpur 68 21 14N 75 49 E
Fajardo 121 18 20N 65 39W
Fakfak 73 3 0 S 132 15 E
Fakiya 43 42 10N 27 6 E
Fakobli 84 7 23N 7 23W
Fakse 49 55 15N 12 8 E
Fakse B. 49 55 11N 12 15 E
Fakse Ladeplads 49 55 11N 12 9 E
Faku 76 42 32N 123 21 E
Falaise 18 48 54N 0 12W
Falakrón Óros 44 41 15N 23 58 E
Falam 67 23 0N 93 45 E
Falces 32 42 24N 1 48W
Fălciu 46 46 17N 28 7 E
Falcon, C. 82 35 50N 0 50W
Falcon Dam 117 26 50N 99 20W
Falconara Marittima 39 43 37N 13 23 E
Falconer 112 42 7N 79 13W
Faléa 84 12 16N 11 17W
Falenki 55 58 22N 51 35 E
Faleshty 56 47 32N 27 44 E
Falfurrias 117 27 14N 98 8W
Falher 108 55 44N 117 15W
Falkenberg, Ger. 24 51 34N 13 13 E
Falkenberg, Sweden 49 56 54N 12 30 E
Falkensee 24 52 35N 13 6 E
Falkenstein 24 50 27N 12 24 E
Falkirk 14 56 0N 3 47W
Falkland Is. 128 51 30 S 59 0W
Falkland Is. Dependency □ 5 57 0 S 40 0W
Falkland Sd. 128 52 0 S 60 0W
Falkonéra 45 36 50N 23 52 E
Falköping 49 58 12N 13 33 E
Fall Brook 119 33 25N 117 12W
Fall River 114 41 45N 71 5W
Fall River Mills 118 41 1N 121 30W
Fallon, Mont., U.S.A. 116 46 52N 105 8W
Fallon, Nev., U.S.A. 118 39 31N 118 51W
Falls City, Nebr., U.S.A. 116 40 0N 95 40W
Falls City, Oreg., U.S.A. 118 44 54N 123 29W
Falls Creek 112 41 8N 78 49W
Falmouth, Jamaica 121 18 30N 77 40W
Falmouth, U.K. 13 50 9N 5 5W
Falmouth, U.S.A. 114 38 40N 84 20W
False Divi Pt. 70 15 43N 80 50 E
Falset 32 41 7N 0 50 E
Falso, C. 121 15 12N 83 21W
Falster 49 54 45N 11 55 E
Falsterbo 49 55 23N 12 50 E
Fălticeni 46 47 21N 26 20 E
Falun 48 60 37N 15 37 E
Famagusta 64 35 8N 33 55 E
Famatina, Sierra, de 124 27 30 S 68 0W
Family L. 109 51 54N 95 27W
Fan Xian 76 35 55N 115 38 E
Fana, Mali 84 13 0N 6 56W
Fana, Norway 47 60 16N 5 20 E
Fanárion 44 39 24N 21 47 E
Fandriana 93 20 14 S 47 21 E
Fang Xian 77 32 3N 110 40 E
Fangchang 77 31 5N 118 4 E
Fangcheng 77 33 18N 112 59 E
Fangliao 77 22 22N 120 38 E
Fangzheng 76 49 50N 128 48 E
Fani i Madh → 44 41 56N 20 16 E
Fanjiatun 76 43 40N 125 0 E
Fannich, L. 14 57 40N 5 0W
Fanning I. 95 3 51N 159 22W
Fanny Bay 108 49 27N 124 48W
Fanø 49 55 25N 8 25 E
Fano 39 43 50N 13 0 E
Fanshaw 108 57 11N 133 30W
Fao (Al Fāw) 64 30 0N 48 30 E
Faqirwali 68 29 27N 73 0 E
Fara in Sabina 39 42 13N 12 44 E
Faradje 90 3 50N 29 45 E
Faradofay 93 25 2 S 47 0 E
Farafangana 93 22 49 S 47 50 E
Farâfra, El Wâhât el- 86 27 15N 28 20 E
Farāh 65 32 20N 62 7 E
Farāh □ 65 32 25N 62 10 E
Farahalana 93 14 26 S 50 10 E
Faraid, Gebel 86 23 33N 35 19 E
Faramana 84 11 56N 4 45W
Faranah 84 10 3N 10 45W
Farasān, Jazā'ir 63 16 45N 41 55 E
Faratsiho 93 19 24 S 46 57 E
Fardes → 33 37 35N 3 0W
Fareham 13 50 52N 1 11W
Farewell, C. 101 40 29 S 172 43 E
Farewell C. = Farvel, K. 4 59 48N 43 55W
Fargo 116 46 52N 96 40W
Fari'a → 62 32 12N 35 27 E
Faribault 116 44 15N 93 19W
Faridkot 68 30 44N 74 45 E
Faridpur 69 23 15N 89 55 E
Fărila 48 61 48N 15 50 E
Farim 84 12 27N 15 9W
Farīmān 65 35 40N 59 49 E
Farina 99 30 3 S 138 15 E
Faringe 48 59 55N 18 7 E
Fâriskûr 86 31 20N 31 43 E
Farmakonisi 45 37 17N 27 8 E
Farmerville 117 32 48N 92 23W
Farmington, N. Mex., U.S.A. 119 36 45N 108 28W
Farmington, N.H., U.S.A. 113 43 25N 71 7W
Farmington, Utah, U.S.A. 118 41 0N 111 12W
Farmington → 113 41 51N 72 38W
Farmville 114 37 19N 78 22W
Farnborough 13 51 17N 0 46W
Farne Is. 12 55 38N 1 37W
Farnham 113 45 17N 72 59W
Faro, Brazil 127 2 10 S 56 39W
Faro, Port. 31 37 2N 7 55W
Faro □ 31 37 12N 8 10W
Faroe Is. 8 62 0N 7 0W
Farquhar, C. 96 23 50 S 113 36 E
Farrar → 14 57 30N 4 30W
Farrars, Cr. → 98 25 35 S 140 43 E
Farrāshband 65 28 57N 52 5 E
Farrell 114 41 13N 80 29W
Farrell Flat 99 33 48 S 138 48 E
Farrukhabad-cum-Fatehgarh 69 27 30N 79 32 E
Fars □ 65 29 30N 55 0 E
Fársala 44 39 17N 22 23 E
Farsø 49 56 46N 9 19 E
Farsund 47 58 5N 6 55 E
Fartak, Râs 64 28 5N 34 34 E
Fartura, Serra da 125 26 21 S 52 52W
Faru 85 12 48N 6 12 E
Farum 49 55 49N 12 21 E
Farvel, Kap 4 59 48N 43 55W
Farwell 117 34 25N 103 0W
Faryab □ 65 36 0N 65 0 E
Fasā 65 29 0N 53 39 E
Fasano 41 40 50N 17 20 E
Fashoda 87 9 50N 32 2 E
Fastnet Rock 15 51 22N 9 37W
Fastov 54 50 7N 29 57 E
Fatagar, Tanjung 73 2 46 S 131 57 E
Fatehgarh 69 27 25N 79 35 E
Fatehpur, Raj., India 68 28 0N 74 40 E
Fatehpur, Ut. P., India 69 25 56N 81 13 E
Fatesh 55 52 8N 35 57 E
Fatick 84 14 19N 16 27W
Fatima 107 47 24N 61 53W
Fátima 31 39 37N 8 39W
Fatoya 84 11 37N 9 10W
Faucille, Col de la 21 46 22N 6 2 E
Faucilles, Monts 19 48 5N 5 50 E
Faulkton 116 45 4N 99 8W
Faulquemont 19 49 3N 6 36 E
Fauquembergues 19 50 36N 2 5 E
Făurei 46 45 6N 27 19 E
Fauresmith 92 29 44 S 25 17 E
Fauske 50 67 17N 15 25 E
Fåvang 47 61 27N 10 11 E
Favara 40 37 19N 13 39 E
Favignana 40 37 56N 12 18 E
Favignana, I. 40 37 56N 12 18 E
Favone 21 41 47N 9 26 E
Favourable Lake 106 52 50N 93 39W
Fawn → 106 52 22N 88 20W
Faxaflói 50 64 29N 23 0W
Faya-Largeau 81 17 58N 19 6 E
Fayd 64 27 1N 42 52 E
Fayence 21 43 38N 6 42 E
Fayette, Ala., U.S.A. 115 33 40N 87 50W
Fayette, Mo., U.S.A. 116 39 10N 92 40W
Fayette, La 114 40 22N 86 52W
Fayetteville, Ark., U.S.A. 117 36 0N 94 5W
Fayetteville, N.C., U.S.A. 115 35 0N 78 58W
Fayetteville, Tenn., U.S.A. 115 35 8N 86 30W
Fayón 32 41 15N 0 20 E
Fazilka 68 30 27N 74 2 E
Fazilpur 68 29 18N 70 29 E
Fdérik 80 22 40N 12 45W
Feale → 15 52 26N 9 40W
Fear, C. 115 33 51N 78 0W
Feather → 118 38 47N 121 36W
Featherston 101 41 6 S 175 20 E
Featherstone 91 18 42 S 30 55 E
Fécamp 18 49 45N 0 22 E
Fedala = Mohammedia 82 33 44N 7 21W
Federación 124 31 0 S 57 55W
Fedjadj, Chott el 83 33 52N 9 14 E
Fedje 47 60 47N 4 43 E
Fehérgyarmat 27 48 0N 22 30 E
Fehmarn 24 54 26N 11 10 E
Fei Xian 77 35 18N 117 59 E
Feilding 101 40 13 S 175 35 E
Feira de Santana 127 12 15 S 38 57W
Fejér □ 27 47 9N 18 30 E
Fejø 49 54 55N 11 30 E
Fekete → 27 45 47N 18 15 E
Felanitx 33 39 28N 3 9 E
Feldbach 26 46 57N 15 52 E
Feldberg, Germ., E. 24 53 20N 13 26 E
Feldberg, Germ., W. 25 47 51N 7 58 E
Feldkirch 26 47 15N 9 37 E
Feldkirchen 26 46 44N 14 6 E
Felipe Carrillo Puerto 120 19 38N 88 3W
Felixstowe 13 51 58N 1 22 E
Felletin 20 45 53N 2 11 E
Feltre 39 46 1N 11 55 E
Femø 49 54 58N 11 53 E
Femunden 47 62 10N 11 53 E
Fen He → 76 35 36N 110 42 E
Fenelon Falls 112 44 32N 78 45W
Feneroa 87 13 5N 39 3 E
Feng Xian, Jiangsu, China 77 34 43N 116 35 E
Feng Xian, Shaanxi, China 77 33 54N 106 40 E
Fengári 44 40 25N 25 32 E
Fengcheng, Jiangxi, China 77 28 12N 115 48 E
Fengcheng, Liaoning, China 76 40 28N 124 5 E
Fengdu 77 29 55N 107 41 E
Fengfeng 76 36 28N 114 8 E
Fenghua 77 29 40N 121 25 E
Fenghuang 77 27 57N 109 29 E
Fengjie 75 31 5N 109 36 E
Fengkai 77 23 24N 111 30 E
Fengle 77 31 29N 112 29 E
Fengning 76 41 10N 116 33 E
Fengtai 76 39 50N 116 18 E
Fengxian 77 30 55N 121 26 E
Fengxiang 77 34 29N 107 25 E
Fengxin 77 28 41N 115 18 E
Fengyang 77 32 51N 117 29 E
Fengzhen 76 40 25N 113 2 E
Feni Is. 98 4 0 S 153 40 E
Fenit 15 52 17N 9 51W
Fennimore 116 42 58N 90 41W
Fenny 69 22 55N 91 32 E
Feno, C. de 21 41 58N 8 33 E
Fenoarivo Afovoany 93 18 26 S 46 34 E
Fenoarivo Atsinanana 93 17 22 S 49 25 E
Fens, The 12 52 45N 0 2 E
Fenton 114 42 47N 83 44W
Fenyang 76 37 18N 111 48 E
Feodosiya 56 45 2N 35 28 E
Fer, C. de 83 37 3N 7 10 E
Ferdow 65 33 58N 58 2 E
Fère-Champenoise 19 48 45N 4 0 E
Fère-en-Tardenois 19 49 10N 3 30 E
Fère, La 19 49 40N 3 20 E
Ferentino 40 41 42N 13 14 E
Ferfer 63 5 4N 45 9 E
Fergana 58 40 23N 71 19 E
Fergus 106 43 43N 80 24W
Fergus Falls 116 46 18N 96 7W
Fergusson I. 98 9 30 S 150 45 E
Fériana 83 34 59N 8 33 E
Feričanci 42 45 32N 18 0 E
Ferkane 83 34 37N 7 26 E
Ferkéssédougou 84 9 35N 5 6W
Ferlach 26 46 32N 14 18 E
Ferland 106 50 19N 88 27W

Ferlo, Vallée du 84 15 15N 14 15W
Fermanagh □ 15 54 21N 7 40W
Fermo 39 43 10N 13 42 E
Fermoselle 30 41 19N 6 27W
Fermoy 15 52 4N 8 18W
Fernán Nuñéz 31 37 40N 4 44W
Fernández 124 27 55 S 63 50W
Fernandina Beach 115 30 40N 81 30W
Fernando de Noronha 127 4 0 S 33 10W
Fernando Póo = Macias Nguema Biyoga 85 3 30N 8 40 E
Ferndale, Calif., U.S.A. 118 40 37N 124 12W
Ferndale, Wash., U.S.A. 118 48 51N 122 41W
Fernie 108 49 30N 115 5W
Fernlees 98 23 51 S 148 7 E
Fernley 118 39 36N 119 14W
Feroke 70 11 9N 75 46 E
Ferozepore 68 30 55N 74 40 E
Férrai 44 40 53N 26 10 E
Ferrandina 41 40 30N 16 28 E
Ferrara 39 44 50N 11 36 E
Ferrato, C. 40 39 18N 9 39 E
Ferreira do Alentejo 31 38 4N 8 6W
Ferreñafe 126 6 42 S 79 50W
Ferret, C. 20 44 38N 1 15W
Ferrette 19 47 30N 7 20 E
Ferriday 117 31 35N 91 33W
Ferrières 19 48 5N 2 48 E
Ferriete 38 44 40N 9 30 E
Ferron 119 39 3N 111 3W
Ferryland 107 47 2N 52 53W
Ferté-Bernard, La 18 48 10N 0 40 E
Ferté, La 19 48 57N 3 6 E
Ferté-Mace, La 18 48 35N 0 21W
Ferté-St.-Aubin, La 19 47 42N 1 57 E
Ferté-Vidame, La 18 48 37N 0 53 E
Fertile 116 47 31N 96 18W
Fertília 40 40 37N 8 13 E
Fertöszentmiklós 27 47 35N 16 53 E
Fès 82 34 0N 5 0W
Feshi 88 6 8 S 18 10 E
Fessenden 116 47 42N 99 38W
Feteşti 46 44 22N 27 51 E
Fethiye 64 36 36N 29 10 E
Fetlar 14 60 36N 0 52W
Feuilles → 105 58 47N 70 4W
Feurs 21 45 45N 4 13 E
Feyzābād 65 37 7N 70 33 E
Fezzan 81 27 0N 15 0 E
Ffestiniog 12 52 58N 3 56W
Fiambalá 124 27 45 S 67 37W
Fianarantsoa 93 21 26 S 47 5 E
Fianarantsoa □ 93 19 30 S 47 0 E
Fianga 81 9 55N 15 9 E
Fibiş 42 45 57N 21 26 E
Fichtelgebirge 25 50 10N 12 0 E
Ficksburg 93 28 51 S 27 53 E
Fidenza 38 44 51N 10 3 E
Field 106 46 31N 80 1W
Field → 98 23 48 S 138 0 E
Fieri 44 40 43N 19 33 E
Fife □ 14 56 13N 3 2W
Fife Ness 14 56 17N 2 35W
Fifth Cataract 86 18 22N 33 50 E
Figeac 20 44 37N 2 2 E
Figline Valdarno 39 43 37N 11 28 E
Figtree 91 20 22 S 28 20 E
Figueira Castelo Rodrigo 30 40 57N 6 58W
Figueira da Foz 30 40 7N 8 54W
Figueiró dos Vinhos 30 39 55N 8 16W
Figueras 32 42 18N 2 58 E
Figuig 82 32 5N 1 11W
Fihaonana 93 18 36 S 47 12 E
Fiherenana 93 18 29 S 48 24 E
Fiherenana → 93 23 19 S 43 37 E
Fiji ■ 101 17 20 S 179 0 E
Fika 85 11 15N 11 13 E
Filabres, Sierra de los 33 37 13N 2 20W
Filadélfia 41 38 47N 16 17 E
Fil'akovo 27 48 17N 19 50 E
Filchner Ice Shelf 5 78 0 S 60 0W
Filer 118 42 30N 114 35W
Filey 12 54 13N 0 18W
Filiaşi 46 44 32N 23 31 E
Filiátes 44 39 38N 20 16 E
Filiatrá 45 37 9N 21 35 E
Filicudi 41 38 35N 14 33 E
Filiourí → 44 41 15N 25 40 E
Filipów 28 54 11N 22 37 E
Filipstad 48 59 43N 14 9 E
Filisur 25 46 41N 9 40 E
Fillmore, Can. 109 49 50N 103 25W
Fillmore, Calif., U.S.A. 119 34 23N 118 58W
Fillmore, Utah, U.S.A. 119 38 58N 112 20W
Filottrano 39 43 28N 13 20 E
Filyos 56 41 34N 32 4 E
Filyos → 64 41 35N 32 10 E
Finale Ligure 38 44 10N 8 21 E
Finale nell' Emília 39 44 50N 11 18 E
Fiñana 33 37 10N 2 50W
Finch 113 45 11N 75 7W
Findhorn → 14 57 38N 3 38W
Findlay 114 41 0N 83 41W
Finger L. 109 53 33N 124 18W
Fingõe 91 15 12 S 31 50 E
Finike 64 36 21N 30 10 E
Finistère □ 18 48 20N 4 0W
Finisterre 30 42 54N 9 16W
Finisterre, C. 30 42 50N 9 19W
Finisterre Ra. 98 6 0 S 146 30 E
Finke → 96 27 0 S 136 10 E
Finland ■ 52 63 0N 27 0 E
Finland, G. of 52 60 0N 26 0 E
Finlay → 108 57 0N 125 10W
Finley, Austral. 99 35 38 S 145 35 E
Finley, U.S.A. 116 47 35N 97 50W
Finn → 15 54 50N 7 55W
Finnigan, Mt. 98 15 49 S 145 17 E
Finnmark fylke □ 50 69 30N 25 0 E
Finschhafen 98 6 33 S 147 50 E
Finse 47 60 36N 7 30 E
Finsteraarhorn 25 46 31N 8 10 E
Finsterwalde 24 51 37N 13 42 E
Finucane I. 96 20 19 S 118 30 E
Fiora → 39 42 20N 11 35 E
Fiorenzuola d'Arda 38 44 56N 9 54 E
Fīq 62 32 46N 35 41 E
Fire River 106 48 47N 83 21W
Firebag → 109 57 45N 111 21W
Firedrake L. 109 61 25N 104 30W
Firenze 39 43 47N 11 15 E
Firminy, Aveyron, France 20 44 32N 2 19 E
Firminy, Loire, France 21 45 23N 4 18 E
Firozabad 68 27 10N 78 25 E
Fīrūzābād 65 28 52N 52 35 E
Fīrūzkūh 65 35 50N 52 50 E
Firvale 108 52 27N 126 13W
Fish → 92 28 7 S 17 45 E
Fisher B. 109 51 35N 97 13W
Fishguard 13 51 59N 4 59W
Fishing L. 109 52 10N 95 24W
Fismes 19 49 20N 3 40 E
Fitchburg 114 42 35N 71 47W
Fitero 32 42 4N 1 52W
Fitjar 47 59 55N 5 17 E
Fitri, L. 81 12 50N 17 28 E
Fitz Roy 128 47 0 S 67 0W
Fitzgerald, Can. 108 59 51N 111 36W
Fitzgerald, U.S.A. 115 31 45N 83 16W
Fitzroy →, Queens., Austral. 98 23 32 S 150 52 E
Fitzroy →, W. Australia, Austral. 96 17 31 S 123 35 E
Fitzroy Crossing 96 18 9 S 125 38 E
Fitzwilliam I. 112 45 30N 81 45W
Fiume = Rijeka 39 45 20N 14 27 E
Fiumefreddo Brúzio 41 39 14N 16 4 E
Fivizzano 38 44 12N 10 11 E
Fizi 90 4 17 S 28 55 E
Fjæra 47 59 52N 6 22 E
Fjellerup 49 56 29N 10 34 E
Fjerritslev 49 57 5N 9 15 E
Fkih ben Salah 82 32 32N 6 45W
Flå, Buskerud, Norway 47 60 25N 9 28 E
Flå, Sør-Trøndelag, Norway 47 63 13N 10 18 E
Flagler 116 39 20N 103 4W
Flagstaff 119 35 10N 111 40W
Flaherty I. 106 56 15N 79 15W
Flambeau → 116 45 18N 91 15W
Flamborough Hd. 12 54 8N 0 4W
Flaming Gorge Dam 118 40 50N 109 46W
Flaming Gorge L. 118 41 15N 109 30W
Flamingo, Teluk 73 5 30 S 138 0 E
Flanders = Flandres 16 51 10N 3 15 E
Flandre Occidental □ 16 51 0N 3 0 E
Flandre Orientale □ 16 51 0N 4 0 E
Flandreau 116 44 5N 96 38W
Flandres, Plaines des 16 51 10N 3 15 E
Flannan Is. 11 58 9N 7 52W
Flåsjön 50 64 5N 15 40 E
Flat → 108 61 51N 128 0W
Flat River 117 37 50N 90 30W
Flatey, Barðastrandarsýsla, Iceland 50 66 10N 17 52W
Flatey, Suður-Þingeyjarsýsla, Iceland 50 65 22N 22 56W
Flathead L. 118 47 50N 114 0W
Flattery, C., Austral. 98 14 58 S 145 21 E
Flattery, C., U.S.A. 118 48 21N 124 43W
Flavy-le-Martel 19 49 43N 3 12 E
Flaxton 116 48 52N 102 24W
Flèche, La 18 47 42N 0 5W
Fleetwood 12 53 55N 3 1W
Flekkefjord 47 58 18N 6 39 E
Flemington 112 41 7N 77 28W
Flensborg Fjord 49 54 50N 9 40 E
Flensburg 24 54 46N 9 28 E
Flers 18 48 47N 0 33W
Flesherton 112 44 16N 80 33W
Flesko, Tanjung 73 0 29N 124 30 E
Fletton 13 52 34N 0 13W
Fleurance 20 43 52N 0 40 E
Fleurier 25 46 54N 6 35 E
Flin Flon 109 54 46N 101 53W
Flinders → 97 17 36 S 140 36 E
Flinders B. 96 34 19 S 115 19 E
Flinders Group 98 14 11 S 144 15 E
Flinders I. 97 40 0 S 148 0 E
Flinders Ranges 97 31 30 S 138 30 E
Flint, U.K. 12 53 15N 3 7W
Flint, U.S.A. 114 43 5N 83 40W
Flint → 115 30 52N 84 38W
Flint, I. 95 11 26 S 151 48W
Flinton 99 27 55 S 149 32 E
Fliseryd 49 57 6N 16 15 E
Flix 32 41 14N 0 32 E
Flixecourt 19 50 0N 2 5 E
Flodden 12 55 37N 2 8W
Floodwood 116 46 55N 92 55W
Flora, Norway 47 63 27N 11 22 E
Flora, U.S.A. 114 38 40N 88 30W
Florac 20 44 20N 3 37 E
Florala 115 31 0N 86 20W
Florence, Ala., U.S.A. 115 34 50N 87 40W
Florence, Ariz., U.S.A. 119 33 0N 111 25W
Florence, Colo., U.S.A. 116 38 26N 105 0W
Florence, Oreg., U.S.A. 118 44 0N 124 3W
Florence, S.C., U.S.A. 115 34 12N 79 44W
Florence = Firenze 39 43 47N 11 15 E
Florence, L. 99 28 53 S 138 9 E
Florennes 16 50 15N 4 35 E
Florensac 20 43 23N 3 28 E
Florenville 16 49 40N 5 19 E
Flores, Azores 8 39 13N 31 13W
Flores, Guat. 120 16 59N 89 50W
Flores, Indon. 73 8 35 S 121 0 E
Flores I. 108 49 20N 126 10W
Flores Sea 72 6 30 S 124 0 E
Floresville 117 29 10N 98 10W
Floriano 127 6 50 S 43 0W
Florianópolis 125 27 30 S 48 30W
Florida, Cuba 121 21 32N 78 14W
Florida, Uruguay 125 34 7 S 56 10W
Florida □ 115 28 30N 82 0W
Florida B. 121 25 0N 81 20W
Florida Keys 121 25 0N 80 40W
Florida, Straits of 121 25 0N 80 0W
Florídia 41 37 6N 15 9 E
Floridsdorf 27 48 14N 16 22 E
Flórina 44 40 48N 21 26 E
Flórina □ 44 40 45N 21 20 E
Florø 47 61 35N 5 1 E
Flower Sta. 113 45 10N 76 41W
Flower's Cove 107 51 14N 56 46W
Floydada 117 33 58N 101 18W
Fluk 73 1 42 S 127 44 E
Flumen → 32 41 43N 0 9W
Flumendosa → 40 39 26N 9 38 E
Fluminimaggiore 40 39 25N 8 30 E
Flushing = Vlissingen 16 51 26N 3 34 E
Fluviá → 32 42 12N 3 7 E
Fly → 94 8 25 S 143 0 E
Flying Fish, C. 5 72 6 S 102 29W
Foam Lake 109 51 40N 103 32W
Foča 42 43 31N 18 47 E
Focşani 46 45 41N 27 15 E
Fogang 77 23 52N 113 30 E
Foggaret el Arab 82 27 13N 2 49 E
Foggaret ez Zoua 82 27 20N 2 53 E
Fóggia 41 41 28N 15 31 E
Foggo 85 11 21N 9 57 E
Foglia → 39 43 55N 12 54 E
Fogo 107 49 43N 54 17W
Fogo I. 107 49 40N 54 5W
Fohnsdorf 26 47 12N 14 40 E
Föhr 24 54 40N 8 30 E
Foia 31 37 19N 8 37W
Foix 20 42 58N 1 38 E
Foix □ 20 43 0N 1 30 E
Fojnica 42 43 59N 17 51 E
Fokino 54 53 30N 34 22 E
Fokis □ 45 38 30N 22 15 E
Fokstua 47 62 7N 9 17 E
Folda, Nord-Trøndelag, Norway 50 64 41N 10 50 E
Folda, Nordland, Norway 50 67 38N 14 50 E
Földeák 27 46 19N 20 30 E
Folégandros 45 36 40N 24 55 E
Folette, La 115 36 23N 84 9W
Foleyet 106 48 15N 82 25W
Folgefonn 47 60 3N 6 23 E
Foligno 39 42 58N 12 40 E
Folkestone 13 51 5N 1 11 E
Folkston 115 30 55N 82 0W
Follett 117 36 30N 100 12W
Follónica 38 42 55N 10 45 E
Follónica, Golfo di 38 42 50N 10 40 E
Folsom 118 38 41N 121 7W
Fond-du-Lac 109 59 19N 107 12W
Fond du Lac 116 43 46N 88 26W
Fond-du-Lac → 109 59 17N 106 0W
Fonda 113 42 57N 74 23W
Fondi 40 41 21N 13 25 E
Fonfría 30 41 37N 6 9W
Fongen 47 63 11N 11 38 E
Fonni 40 40 5N 9 16 E
Fonsagrada 30 43 8N 7 4W
Fonseca, G. de 120 13 10N 87 40W
Fontaine-Française 19 47 32N 5 21 E
Fontainebleau 19 48 24N 2 40 E
Fontas → 108 58 14N 121 48W
Fonte Boa 126 2 33 S 66 0W
Fontem 85 5 32N 9 52 E
Fontenay-le-Comte 20 46 28N 0 48W
Fontur 50 66 23N 14 32W
Fonyód 27 46 44N 17 33 E
Foochow = Fuzhou 75 26 5N 119 16 E
Foping 77 33 41N 108 0 E
Foppiano 38 46 21N 8 24 E
Föra 49 57 1N 16 51 E
Forbach 19 49 10N 6 52 E
Forbes 97 33 22 S 148 0 E
Forbesganj 69 26 17N 87 18 E
Forcados 85 5 26N 5 26 E
Forcados → 85 5 25N 5 19 E
Forcall → 32 40 51N 0 16W
Forcalquier 21 43 58N 5 47 E
Forchheim 25 49 42N 11 4 E
Ford City 112 40 47N 79 31W
Førde 47 61 27N 5 53 E
Ford's Bridge 99 29 41 S 145 29 E
Fordyce 117 33 50N 92 20W
Forécariah 84 9 28N 13 10W
Forel, Mt. 4 66 52N 36 55W
Foremost 108 49 26N 111 34W
Forenza 41 40 50N 15 50 E
Forest, Can. 112 43 6N 82 0W
Forest, U.S.A. 117 32 21N 89 27W
Forest City, Iowa, U.S.A. 116 43 12N 93 39W
Forest City, N.C., U.S.A. 115 35 23N 81 50W
Forest City, Pa., U.S.A. 113 41 39N 75 29W
Forest Grove 118 45 31N 123 4W
Forestburg 108 52 35N 112 1W
Forestier Pen. 99 43 0 S 148 0 E
Forestville, Can. 107 48 48N 69 2W
Forestville, U.S.A. 114 44 41N 87 29W
Forez, Mts. du 20 45 40N 3 50 E
Forfar 14 56 40N 2 53W
Forges-les-Eaux 19 49 37N 1 30 E
Forks 118 47 56N 124 23W
Forlì 39 44 14N 12 2 E
Forman 116 46 9N 97 43W
Formazza 38 46 23N 8 26 E
Formby Pt. 12 53 33N 3 7W
Formentera 33 38 43N 1 27 E
Formentor, C. de 32 39 58N 3 13 E
Fórmia 40 41 15N 13 34 E
Formigine 38 44 37N 10 51 E
Formiguères 20 42 37N 2 5 E
Formosa 124 26 15 S 58 10W
Formosa = Taiwan ■ 75 24 0N 121 0 E
Formosa □ 124 25 0 S 60 0W
Formosa Bay 90 2 40 S 40 20 E
Formosa, Serra 127 12 0 S 55 0W
Fornells 32 40 3N 4 7 E
Fornos de Algodres 30 40 38N 7 32W
Fornovo di Taro 38 44 42N 10 7 E
Forres 14 57 37N 3 38W
Forrest 99 38 33 S 143 47 E
Forrest City 117 35 0N 90 50W
Fors 48 60 14N 16 20 E
Forsa 48 61 44N 16 55 E
Forsand 47 58 54N 6 5 E
Forsayth 97 18 33 S 143 34 E
Forserum 49 57 42N 14 30 E
Forshaga 48 59 33N 13 29 E
Forskacka 48 60 39N 16 54 E
Forsmo 48 63 16N 17 11 E
Forst 24 51 43N 14 37 E
Forster 99 32 12 S 152 31 E
Forsyth, Ga., U.S.A. 115 33 4N 83 55W
Forsyth, Mont., U.S.A. 118 46 14N 106 37W
Fort Albany 106 52 15N 81 35W
Fort Amador 120 8 56N 79 32W
Fort Apache 119 33 50N 110 0W
Fort Assiniboine 108 54 20N 114 45W
Fort Augustus 14 57 9N 4 40W
Fort Beaufort 92 32 46 S 26 40 E
Fort Benton 118 47 50N 110 40W
Fort Bragg 118 39 28N 123 50W
Fort Bridger 118 41 22N 110 20W
Fort Chimo 105 58 6N 68 15W
Fort Chipewyan 109 58 42N 111 8W
Fort Clayton 120 9 0N 79 35W
Fort Collins 116 40 30N 105 4W
Fort-Coulonge 106 45 50N 76 45W
Fort Davis, Panama 120 9 17N 79 56W
Fort Davis, U.S.A. 117 30 38N 103 53W
Fort-de-France 121 14 36N 61 2W
Fort de Possel = Possel 88 5 5N 19 10 E
Fort Defiance 119 35 47N 109 4W
Fort Dodge 116 42 29N 94 10W
Fort Edward 113 43 16N 73 35W
Fort Frances 109 48 36N 93 24W
Fort Franklin 104 65 10N 123 30W
Fort Garland 119 37 28N 105 30W
Fort George 106 53 50N 79 0W
Fort Good-Hope 104 66 14N 128 40W
Fort Hancock 119 31 19N 105 56W
Fort Hertz (Putao) 67 27 28N 97 30 E
Fort Hope 106 51 30N 88 0W
Fort Huachuca 119 31 32N 110 30W
Fort Jameson = Chipata 91 13 38 S 32 28 E
Fort Kent 107 47 12N 68 30W
Fort Klamath 118 42 45N 122 0W
Fort Lallemand 83 31 13N 6 17 E
Fort-Lamy = Ndjamena 81 12 4N 15 8 E
Fort Laramie 116 42 15N 104 30W
Fort Lauderdale 115 26 10N 80 5W
Fort Liard 108 60 14N 123 30W
Fort Liberté 121 19 42N 71 51W
Fort Lupton 116 40 8N 104 48W
Fort Mackay 108 57 12N 111 41W
Fort McKenzie 107 57 20N 69 0W
Fort Macleod 108 49 45N 113 30W
Fort MacMahon 82 29 43N 1 45 E
Fort McMurray 108 56 44N 111 7W
Fort McPherson 104 67 30N 134 55W
Fort Madison 116 40 39N 91 20W
Fort Meade 115 27 45N 81 45W
Fort Miribel 82 29 25N 2 55 E
Fort Morgan 116 40 10N 103 50W
Fort Myers 115 26 39N 81 51W
Fort Nelson 108 58 50N 122 44W
Fort Nelson → 108 59 32N 124 0W
Fort Norman 104 64 57N 125 30W
Fort Payne 115 34 25N 85 44W
Fort Peck 118 48 1N 106 30W
Fort Peck Dam 118 48 0N 106 38W
Fort Peck L. 118 47 40N 107 0W
Fort Pierce 115 27 29N 80 19W
Fort Pierre 116 44 25N 100 25W
Fort Pierre Bordes = Ti-n-Zaouatene 82 20 0N 2 55 E
Fort Plain 113 42 56N 74 39W
Fort Portal 90 0 40N 30 20 E
Fort Providence 108 61 3N 117 40W
Fort Qu'Appelle 109 50 45N 103 50W
Fort Randolph 120 9 23N 79 53W
Fort Resolution 108 61 10N 113 40W
Fort Rixon 91 20 2 S 29 17 E
Fort Roseberry = Mansa 91 11 10 S 28 50 E
Fort Rupert (Rupert House) 106 51 30N 78 40W
Fort Saint 83 30 19N 9 31 E
Fort St. James 108 54 30N 124 10W
Fort St. John 108 56 15N 120 50W
Fort Sandeman 68 31 20N 69 31 E
Fort Saskatchewan 108 53 40N 113 15W
Fort Scott 117 37 50N 94 40W
Fort Severn 106 56 0N 87 40W
Fort Sherman 120 9 22N 79 56W
Fort Shevchenko 57 43 40N 51 20 E
Fort-Sibut 88 5 46N 19 10 E
Fort Simpson 108 61 45N 121 15W
Fort Smith, Can. 108 60 0N 111 51W
Fort Smith, U.S.A. 117 35 25N 94 25W
Fort Stanton 119 33 33N 105 36W
Fort Stockton 117 30 54N 102 54W
Fort Sumner 117 34 24N 104 16W
Fort Thomas 119 33 2N 109 59W
Fort Trinquet = Bir Mogrein 80 25 10N 11 35W
Fort Valley 115 32 33N 83 52W
Fort Vermilion 108 58 24N 116 0W
Fort Victoria 91 20 8 S 30 49 E
Fort Walton Beach 115 30 25N 86 40W
Fort Wayne 114 41 5N 85 10W
Fort William 14 56 48N 5 8W
Fort Worth 117 32 45N 97 25W
Fort Yates 116 46 8N 100 38W
Fort Yukon 104 66 35N 145 20W
Fortaleza 127 3 45 S 38 35W
Forteau 107 51 28N 56 58W
Fortescue → 96 21 20 S 116 5 E
Forth, Firth of 14 56 5N 2 55W
Forthassa Rharbia 82 32 52N 1 18W
Fortore → 39 41 55N 15 17 E
Fortrose 14 57 35N 4 10W
Fortuna, Spain 33 38 11N 1 7W
Fortuna, Cal., U.S.A. 118 40 38N 124 8W
Fortuna, N.D., U.S.A. 116 48 55N 103 48W

Fortune B.	107	47 30N	55 22W
Forûr	65	26 20N	54 30 E
Fos	21	43 26N	4 56 E
Foshan	75	23 4N	113 5 E
Fossacesia	39	42 15N	14 30 E
Fossano	38	44 33N	7 40 E
Fossil	118	45 0N	120 9W
Fossilbrook P.O.	98	17 47 S	144 29 E
Fossombrone	39	43 41N	12 49 E
Fosston	116	47 33N	95 39W
Foster	113	45 17N	72 30W
Foster →	109	55 47N	105 49W
Fostoria	114	41 8N	83 25W
Fougamou	88	1 16 S	10 30 E
Fougères	18	48 21N	1 14W
Foul Pt.	70	8 35N	81 18 E
Foulness I.	13	51 36N	0 55 E
Foulness Pt.	13	51 36N	0 59 E
Foulpointe	93	17 41 S	49 31 E
Foum Assaka	82	29 8N	10 24W
Foum Zguid	82	30 2N	6 59W
Foumban	85	5 45N	10 50 E
Foundiougne	84	14 5N	16 32W
Fountain, Colo., U.S.A.	116	38 42N	104 40W
Fountain, Utah, U.S.A.	118	39 41N	111 37W
Fourchambault	19	47 0N	3 3 E
Fourchu	107	45 43N	60 17W
Fourmies	19	50 1N	4 2 E
Fournás	45	39 3N	21 52 E
Foúrnoi, Greece	45	37 36N	26 32 E
Foúrnoi, Greece	45	37 36N	26 28 E
Fours	19	46 50N	3 42 E
Fouta Djalon	84	11 20N	12 10W
Foux, Cap-à-	121	19 43N	73 27W
Foveaux Str.	101	46 42 S	168 10 E
Fowey	13	50 20N	4 39W
Fowler, Calif., U.S.A.	119	36 41N	119 41W
Fowler, Colo., U.S.A.	116	38 10N	104 0W
Fowler, Kans., U.S.A.	117	37 28N	100 7W
Fowlerton	117	28 26N	98 50W
Fownhope	13	52 0N	2 37W
Fox →	109	56 3N	93 18W
Fox Valley	109	50 30N	109 25W
Foxe Basin	105	68 30N	77 0W
Foxe Channel	105	66 0N	80 0W
Foxe Pen.	105	65 0N	76 0W
Foxen, L.	48	59 25N	11 55 E
Foxpark	118	41 4N	106 6W
Foxton	101	40 29 S	175 18 E
Foyle, Lough	15	55 6N	7 8W
Foynes	15	52 37N	9 5W
Foz	30	43 33N	7 20W
Fóz do Cunene	92	17 15 S	11 48 E
Foz do Gregório	126	6 47 S	70 44W
Foz do Iguaçu	125	25 30 S	54 30W
Frackville	113	40 46N	76 15W
Fraga	32	41 32N	0 21 E
Framingham	113	42 18N	71 26W
Frampol	28	50 41N	22 40 E
Franca	127	20 33 S	47 30W
Francavilla al Mare	39	42 25N	14 16 E
Francavilla Fontana	41	40 32N	17 35 E
France ■	17	47 0N	3 0 E
Frances	99	36 41 S	140 55 E
Frances →	108	60 16N	129 10W
Frances L.	108	61 23N	129 30W
Franceville	88	1 40 S	13 32 E
Franche-Comté	19	46 30N	5 50 E
Francisco I. Madero, Coahuila, Mexico	120	25 48N	103 18W
Francisco I. Madero, Durango, Mexico	120	24 32N	104 22W
Francofonte	41	37 13N	14 50 E
François, Can.	107	47 35N	56 45W
François, Mart.	121	14 38N	60 57W
François L.	108	54 0N	125 30W
Franeker	16	53 12N	5 33 E
Frankado	87	12 30N	43 12 E
Frankenberg	24	51 3N	8 47 E
Frankenthal	25	49 32N	8 21 E
Frankenwald	25	50 18N	11 36 E
Frankfort, Madag.	93	27 17 S	28 30 E
Frankfort, Ind., U.S.A.	114	40 20N	86 33W
Frankfort, Kans., U.S.A.	116	39 42N	96 26W
Frankfort, Ky., U.S.A.	114	38 12N	84 52W
Frankfort, Mich., U.S.A.	114	44 38N	86 14W
Frankfurt □	24	52 30N	14 0 E
Frankfurt am Main	25	50 7N	8 40 E
Frankfurt an der Oder	24	52 50N	14 31 E
Fränkische Alb	25	49 20N	11 30 E
Fränkische Rezal →	25	49 11N	11 1 E
Fränkische Saale →	25	50 30N	9 42 E
Fränkische Schweiz	25	49 45N	11 10 E
Franklin, Ky., U.S.A.	115	36 40N	86 30W
Franklin, La., U.S.A.	117	29 45N	91 30W
Franklin, Mass., U.S.A.	113	42 4N	71 23W
Franklin, N.H., U.S.A.	114	43 28N	71 39W
Franklin, N.J., U.S.A.	113	41 9N	74 38W
Franklin, Nebr., U.S.A.	116	40 9N	98 55W
Franklin, Pa., U.S.A.	114	41 22N	79 45W
Franklin, Tenn., U.S.A.	115	35 54N	86 53W
Franklin, Va., U.S.A.	115	36 40N	76 58W
Franklin, W. Va., U.S.A.	114	38 38N	79 21W
Franklin □	105	71 0N	99 0W
Franklin B.	104	69 45N	126 0W
Franklin D. Roosevelt L.	118	48 30N	118 16W
Franklin I.	5	76 10 S	168 30 E
Franklin, L.	118	40 20N	115 26W
Franklin Mts.	104	65 0N	125 0W
Franklin Str.	104	72 0N	96 0W
Franklinton	117	30 53N	90 10W
Franklinville	112	42 21N	78 28W
Franks Peak	118	43 50N	109 5W
Frankston	99	38 8 S	145 8 E
Fränsta	48	62 30N	16 11 E
Frantsa Josifa, Zemlya	58	82 0N	55 0 E
Franz	106	48 25N	84 30W
Franz Josef Land = Frantsa Josifa	58	79 0N	62 0 E
Franzburg	24	54 9N	12 52 E
Frascati	40	41 48N	12 41 E
Fraser →, B.C., Can.	108	49 7N	123 11W
Fraser →, Newf., Can.	107	56 39N	62 10W
Fraser I.	97	25 15 S	153 10 E
Fraser Lake	108	54 0N	124 50W
Fraserburg	92	31 55 S	21 30 E
Fraserburgh	14	57 41N	2 0W
Fraserdale	106	49 55N	81 37W
Frashëri	44	40 23N	20 26 E
Frasne	19	46 50N	6 10 E
Frauenfeld	25	47 34N	8 54 E
Fray Bentos	124	33 10 S	58 15W
Frechilla	30	42 8N	4 50W
Fredericia	49	55 34N	9 45 E
Frederick, Md., U.S.A.	114	39 25N	77 23W
Frederick, Okla., U.S.A.	117	34 22N	99 0W
Frederick, S.D., U.S.A.	116	45 55N	98 29W
Frederick Reef	97	20 58 S	154 23 E
Frederick Sd.	108	57 10N	134 0W
Fredericksburg, Tex., U.S.A.	117	30 17N	98 55W
Fredericksburg, Va., U.S.A.	114	38 16N	77 29W
Fredericktown	117	37 35N	90 15W
Fredericton	107	45 57N	66 40W
Fredericton Junc.	107	45 41N	66 40W
Frederikshavn	49	57 28N	10 31 E
Frederikssund	49	55 50N	12 3 E
Fredonia, Ariz., U.S.A.	119	36 59N	112 36W
Fredonia, Kans., U.S.A.	117	37 34N	95 50W
Fredonia, N.Y., U.S.A.	112	42 26N	79 20W
Fredrikstad	47	59 13N	10 57 E
Freehold	113	40 15N	74 18W
Freeland	113	41 3N	75 48W
Freeling, Mt.	96	22 35 S	133 06 E
Freels, C.	107	49 15N	53 30W
Freeman	116	43 25N	97 20W
Freeport, Bahamas	121	26 30N	78 47W
Freeport, Can.	107	44 15N	66 20W
Freeport, Ill., U.S.A.	116	42 18N	89 40W
Freeport, N.Y., U.S.A.	114	40 39N	73 35W
Freeport, Tex., U.S.A.	117	28 55N	95 22W
Freetown	84	8 30N	13 17W
Frégate, L.	106	53 15N	74 45W
Fregenal de la Sierra	31	38 10N	6 39W
Fregene	40	41 50N	12 12 E
Fregeneda, La	30	40 58N	6 54W
Fréhel, C.	18	48 40N	2 20W
Frei	47	63 4N	7 48 E
Freiberg	24	50 55N	13 20 E
Freibourg = Fribourg	25	46 49N	7 9 E
Freiburg, Baden, Ger.	25	48 0N	7 52 E
Freiburg, Niedersachsen, Ger.	24	53 49N	9 17 E
Freire	128	38 54 S	72 38W
Freirina	124	28 30 S	71 10W
Freising	25	48 24N	11 47 E
Freistadt	26	48 30N	14 30 E
Freital	24	51 0N	13 40 E
Fréjus	21	43 25N	6 44 E
Fremantle	96	32 7 S	115 47 E
Fremont, Mich., U.S.A.	114	43 29N	85 59W
Fremont, Nebr., U.S.A.	116	41 30N	96 30W
Fremont, Ohio, U.S.A.	114	41 20N	83 5W
Fremont →	119	38 15N	110 20W
Fremont, L.	118	43 0N	109 50W
French →	114	41 30N	80 2W
French Guiana ■	127	4 0N	53 0W
French I.	100	38 20 S	145 22 E
French Terr. of Afars & Issas = Djibouti ■	87	11 30N	42 15 E
Frenchglen	118	42 48N	119 0W
Frenchman →	118	48 24N	107 5W
Frenchman Butte	109	53 35N	109 38W
Frenchman Creek →	116	40 13N	100 50W
Frenda	82	35 2N	1 1 E
Fresco →	127	7 15 S	51 30W
Freshfield, C.	5	68 25 S	151 10 E
Fresnay	18	48 17N	0 1 E
Fresnillo	120	23 10N	103 0W
Fresno	119	36 47N	119 50W
Fresno Alhandiga	30	40 42N	5 37W
Fresno Res.	118	48 40N	110 0W
Freudenstadt	25	48 27N	8 25 E
Frévent	19	50 15N	2 17 E
Freycinet Pen.	97	42 10 S	148 25 E
Freyung	25	48 48N	13 33 E
Fria	84	10 27N	13 38W
Fria, C.	92	18 0 S	12 0 E
Frias	124	28 40 S	65 5W
Fribourg	25	46 49N	7 9 E
Fribourg □	25	46 40N	7 0 E
Fridafors	49	56 25N	14 39 E
Friedberg, Bayern, Ger.	25	48 21N	10 59 E
Friedberg, Hessen, Ger.	25	50 21N	8 46 E
Friedland	24	53 40N	13 33 E
Friedrichshafen	25	47 39N	9 29 E
Friedrichskoog	24	54 1N	8 52 E
Friedrichsort	24	54 24N	10 11 E
Friedrichstadt	24	54 23N	9 6 E
Friendly (Tonga) Is.	101	22 0 S	173 0W
Friesach	26	46 57N	14 24 E
Friesack	24	52 43N	12 35 E
Friesland □	16	53 5N	5 50 E
Friesoythe	24	53 1N	7 51 E
Frijoles	120	9 11N	79 48W
Frillesås	49	57 20N	12 12 E
Frinnaryd	49	57 55N	14 50 E
Frio →	117	28 30N	98 10W
Friona	117	34 40N	102 42W
Frisian Is.	24	53 30N	6 0 E
Fristad	49	57 50N	13 0 E
Fritch	117	35 40N	101 35W
Fritsla	49	57 33N	12 47 E
Fritzlar	24	51 8N	9 19 E
Friuli-Venezia Giulia □	39	46 0N	13 0 E
Friville-Escarbotin	19	50 5N	1 33 E
Frobisher B.	105	62 30N	66 0W
Frobisher Bay	105	63 44N	68 31W
Frobisher L.	109	56 20N	108 15W
Frohavet	50	63 50N	9 35 E
Froid	116	48 20N	104 29W
Frolovo	57	49 45N	43 40 E
Fromberg	118	45 25N	108 58W
Frombork	28	54 21N	19 41 E
Frome	13	51 16N	2 17W
Frome, L.	97	30 45 S	139 45 E
Fromentine	18	46 53N	2 9W
Frómista	30	42 16N	4 25W
Front Range	118	40 0N	105 40W
Front Royal	114	38 55N	78 10W
Fronteira	31	39 3N	7 39W
Frontera	120	18 30N	92 40W
Frontignan	20	43 27N	3 45 E
Frosinone	40	41 38N	13 20 E
Frosolone	41	41 34N	14 27 E
Frostburg	114	39 43N	78 57W
Frostisen	50	68 14N	17 10 E
Frouard	19	48 47N	6 8 E
Frövi	48	59 28N	15 24 E
Frøya	47	63 43N	8 40 E
Fruges	19	50 30N	2 8 E
Frumoasa	46	46 28N	25 48 E
Frunze	58	42 54N	74 46 E
Fruška Gora	42	45 7N	19 30 E
Frutal	127	20 0 S	49 0W
Frutigen	25	46 35N	7 38 E
Frýdek-Místek	27	49 40N	18 20 E
Frýdlant, Severočeský, Czech.	26	50 56N	15 9 E
Frýdlant, Severomoravsky, Czech.	27	49 35N	18 20 E
Fryvaldov = Jesenik	27	50 0N	17 8 E
Fthiótis □	45	38 50N	22 25 E
Fu Xian, Liaoning, China	76	39 38N	121 58 E
Fu Xian, Shaanxi, China	76	36 0N	109 20 E
Fucécchio	38	43 44N	10 51 E
Fucheng	76	37 50N	116 10 E
Fuchou = Fuzhou	75	26 5N	119 16 E
Fuchuan	77	24 50N	111 5 E
Fuchun Jiang →	77	30 5N	120 5 E
Fúcino, Conca del	39	42 1N	13 31 E
Fuding	77	27 20N	120 12 E
Fuencaliente	31	38 25N	4 18W
Fuengirola	31	36 32N	4 41W
Fuente Alamo	33	38 44N	1 24W
Fuente Álamo	33	37 42N	1 6W
Fuente de Cantos	31	38 15N	6 18W
Fuente de San Esteban, La	30	40 49N	6 15W
Fuente del Maestre	31	38 31N	6 28W
Fuente el Fresno	31	39 14N	3 46W
Fuente Ovejuna	31	38 15N	5 25W
Fuentes de Andalucía	31	37 28N	5 20W
Fuentes de Ebro	32	41 31N	0 38W
Fuentes de León	31	38 5N	6 32W
Fuentes de Oñoro	30	40 33N	6 52W
Fuentesaúco	30	41 15N	5 30W
Fuerte →	120	25 50N	109 25W
Fuerte Olimpo	124	21 0 S	57 51W
Fuerteventura	80	28 30N	14 0W
Füget, Munţii	46	45 50N	22 9 E
Fugløysund	50	70 15N	20 20 E
Fugou	77	34 3N	114 25 E
Fuhai	75	47 2N	87 25 E
Fuji-no-miya	74	35 10N	138 40 E
Fuji-San	74	35 22N	138 44 E
Fujian □	75	26 0N	118 0 E
Fujin	76	47 16N	132 1 E
Fujisawa	74	35 22N	139 29 E
Fukien = Fujian □	75	26 0N	118 0 E
Fukuchiyama	74	35 19N	135 9 E
Fukui	74	36 0N	136 10 E
Fukui □	74	36 0N	136 12 E
Fukuoka	74	33 39N	130 21 E
Fukuoka □	74	33 30N	131 0 E
Fukushima	74	37 44N	140 28 E
Fukushima □	74	37 30N	140 15 E
Fukuyama	74	34 35N	133 20 E
Fulda	24	50 32N	9 41 E
Fulda →	24	51 27N	9 40 E
Fuling	77	29 40N	107 20 E
Fullerton, Calif., U.S.A.	119	33 52N	117 58W
Fullerton, Nebr., U.S.A.	116	41 25N	98 0W
Fulton, Mo., U.S.A.	116	38 50N	91 55W
Fulton, N.Y., U.S.A.	114	43 20N	76 22W
Fulton, Tenn., U.S.A.	115	36 30N	88 53W
Fuluälven	48	61 18N	13 4 E
Fulufjället	48	61 32N	12 41 E
Fumay	19	50 0N	4 40 E
Fumel	20	44 30N	0 58 E
Funabashi	74	35 45N	140 0 E
Funafuti	94	8 30 S	179 0 E
Funchal	80	32 38N	16 54W
Fundación	126	10 31N	74 11W
Fundão	30	40 8N	7 30W
Fundy, B. of	107	45 0N	66 0W
Funing, Jiangsu, China	77	33 45N	119 50 E
Funing, Yunnan, China	77	23 35N	105 45 E
Funiu Shan	77	33 30N	112 20 E
Funsi	84	10 21N	1 54W
Funtua	85	11 30N	7 18 E
Fuping	76	38 48N	114 12 E
Fuqing	77	25 41N	119 21 E
Fur	49	56 50N	9 0 E
Furāt, Nahr al →	64	31 0N	47 25 E
Furmanov	55	57 10N	41 9 E
Furmanovo	57	49 42N	49 25 E
Furnas, Reprêsa de	125	20 50 S	45 0W
Furneaux Group	97	40 10 S	147 50 E
Furness, Pen.	12	54 12N	3 10W
Fürstenau	24	52 32N	7 40 E
Fürstenberg	24	53 11N	13 9 E
Fürstenfeld	26	47 3N	16 3 E
Fürstenfeldbruck	25	48 10N	11 15 E
Fürstenwalde	24	52 20N	14 3 E
Fürth	25	49 29N	11 0 E
Furth im Wald	25	49 19N	12 51 E
Furtwangen	25	48 3N	8 14 E
Furudal	48	61 10N	15 11 E
Furusund	48	59 40N	18 55 E
Fury and Hecla Str.	105	69 56N	84 0W
Fusa	47	60 12N	5 37 E
Fusagasuga	126	4 21N	74 22W
Fuscaldo	41	39 25N	16 1 E
Fushan	76	37 30N	121 15 E
Fushë Arrëzi	44	42 4N	20 2 E
Fushun	76	41 50N	123 56 E
Fusong	76	42 20N	127 15 E
Füssen	25	47 35N	10 43 E
Fusui	77	22 40N	107 56 E
Futuna	94	14 25 S	178 20 E
Fuwa	86	31 12N	30 33 E
Fuxin	76	42 5N	121 48 E
Fuyang, Anhui, China	77	33 0N	115 48 E
Fuyang, Zhejiang, China	77	30 5N	119 57 E
Fuyu	76	45 12N	124 43 E
Fuyuan	75	48 20N	134 5 E
Füzesgyarmat	27	47 6N	21 14 E
Fuzhou, Fujian, China	75	26 5N	119 16 E
Fuzhou, Jiangxi, China	75	28 0N	116 25 E
Fylde	12	53 50N	2 58W
Fyn	49	55 20N	10 30 E
Fyne, L.	14	56 0N	5 20W
Fyns Amtskommune □	49	55 15N	10 30 E
Fyresvatn	47	59 6N	8 10 E

G

Gaanda	85	10 10N	12 27 E
Gabarin	85	11 8N	10 27 E
Gabas →	20	43 46N	0 42W
Gabela	88	11 0 S	14 24 E
Gabès	83	33 53N	10 2 E
Gabès, Golfe de	83	34 0N	10 30 E
Gabgaba, W.	86	22 10N	33 5 E
Gabin	28	52 23N	19 41 E
Gabon ■	88	0 10 S	10 0 E
Gaborone	92	24 45 S	25 57 E
Gabriels	113	44 26N	74 12W
Gabrovo	43	42 52N	25 19 E
Gacé	18	48 49N	0 20 E
Gach Sārān	65	30 15N	50 45 E
Gacko	42	43 10N	18 33 E
Gadag-Batgeri	70	15 30N	75 45 E
Gadamai	87	17 11N	36 10 E
Gadap	68	25 5N	67 28 E
Gadarwara	68	22 50N	78 50 E
Gadebusch	24	53 41N	11 6 E
Gadein	87	8 10N	28 45 E
Gadhada	68	22 0N	71 35 E
Gádor, Sierra de	33	36 57N	2 45W
Gadsden, Ala., U.S.A.	115	34 1N	86 0W
Gadsden, Ariz., U.S.A.	119	32 35N	114 47W
Gadwal	70	16 10N	77 50 E
Gadyach	54	50 21N	34 0 E
Găeşti	46	44 48N	25 19 E
Gaeta	40	41 12N	13 35 E
Gaeta, G. di	40	41 0N	13 25 E
Gaffney	115	35 3N	81 40W
Gafsa	83	32 24N	8 43 E
Gagarin (Gzhatsk)	54	55 38N	35 0 E
Gagetown	107	45 46N	66 10W
Gagino	55	55 15N	45 1 E
Gagliano del Capo	41	39 50N	18 23 E
Gagnef	48	60 36N	15 5 E
Gagnoa	84	6 56N	5 16W
Gagnon	107	51 50N	68 5W
Gagnon, L.	109	62 3N	110 27W
Gagra	57	43 20N	40 10 E
Gahini	90	1 50 S	30 30 E
Gahmar	69	25 27N	83 49 E
Gai Xian	76	40 22N	122 20 E
Gaibanda	69	25 20N	89 36 E
Gaïdhouronisi	45	34 53N	25 41 E
Gail	117	32 48N	101 25W
Gail →	26	46 36N	13 53 E
Gaillac	20	43 54N	1 54 E
Gaillon	18	49 10N	1 20 E
Gaines	112	41 46N	77 35W
Gainesville, Fla., U.S.A.	115	29 38N	82 20W
Gainesville, Ga., U.S.A.	115	34 17N	83 47W
Gainesville, Mo., U.S.A.	117	36 35N	92 26W
Gainesville, Tex., U.S.A.	117	33 40N	97 10W
Gainsborough	12	53 23N	0 46W
Gairdner L.	96	31 30 S	136 0 E
Gairloch, L.	14	57 43N	5 45W
Gaj	42	45 28N	17 3 E
Gal Oya Res.	70	7 5N	81 30 E
Galachipa	69	22 8N	90 26 E
Galán, Cerro	124	25 55 S	66 52W
Galana →	90	3 9 S	40 8 E
Galangue	89	13 42 S	16 9 E
Galanta	27	48 11N	17 45 E
Galápagos	95	0 0	89 0W
Galas →	71	4 55N	101 57 E
Galashiels	14	55 37N	2 50W
Galatás	45	37 30N	23 26 E
Galaţi	46	45 27N	28 2 E
Galaţi □	46	45 45N	27 30 E
Galatina	41	40 10N	18 10 E
Galátone	41	40 8N	18 3 E
Galax	115	36 42N	80 57W
Galaxidhion	45	38 22N	22 23 E
Galbraith	98	16 25 S	141 30 E
Galcaio	63	6 30N	47 30 E
Galdhøpiggen	47	61 38N	8 18 E
Galela	73	1 50N	127 49 E
Galera	33	37 45N	2 33W
Galesburg	116	40 57N	90 23W
Galeton	112	41 43N	77 40W
Gali	57	42 37N	41 46 E
Galicea Mare	46	44 4N	23 19 E
Galich	55	58 23N	42 12 E
Galiche	43	43 34N	23 50 E
Galicia	30	42 43N	7 45W
Galilee = Hagalil	62	32 53N	35 18 E
Galilee, L.	98	22 20 S	145 50 E
Galion	112	40 43N	82 48W
Galite, Is. de la	83	37 30N	8 59 E
Galiuro Mts.	119	32 40N	110 30W
Galiabat	81	12 58N	36 11 E
Gallarate	38	45 40N	8 48 E
Gallardon	19	48 32N	1 47 E
Gallatin	115	36 24N	86 27W
Galle	70	6 5N	80 10 E
Gállego →	32	41 39N	0 51W
Gallegos →	128	51 35 S	69 0W
Galley Hd.	15	51 32N	8 56W

Galliate	**38**	45 27N	8 44 E
Gallinas, Pta.	**126**	12 28N	71 40W
Gallipoli	**41**	40 8N	18 0 E
Gallipoli = Gelibolu	**44**	40 28N	26 43 E
Gallipolis	**114**	38 50N	82 10W
Gällivare	**50**	67 9N	20 40 E
Gallo, C.	**40**	38 13N	13 19 E
Gallocanta, Laguna de	**32**	40 58N	1 30W
Galloway	**14**	55 0N	4 25W
Galloway, Mull of	**14**	54 38N	4 50W
Gallup	**119**	35 30N	108 45W
Gallur	**32**	41 52N	1 19W
Gal'on	**62**	31 38N	34 51 E
Galong	**99**	34 37 S	148 34 E
Galtström	**48**	62 10N	17 30 E
Galtür	**26**	46 58N	10 11 E
Galty Mts.	**15**	52 22N	8 10W
Galtymore	**15**	52 22N	8 12W
Galva	**116**	41 10N	90 0W
Galve de Sorbe	**32**	41 13N	3 10W
Galveston	**117**	29 15N	94 48W
Galveston B.	**117**	29 30N	94 50W
Gálvez, Argent.	**124**	32 0 S	61 14W
Gálvez, Spain	**31**	39 42N	4 16W
Galway	**15**	53 16N	9 4W
Galway □	**15**	53 16N	9 3W
Galway B.	**15**	53 10N	9 20W
Gamari, L.	**87**	11 32N	41 40 E
Gamawa	**85**	12 10N	10 31 E
Gambaga	**85**	10 30N	0 28W
Gambat	**68**	27 17N	68 26 E
Gambela	**87**	8 14N	34 38 E
Gambia ■	**84**	13 25N	16 0W
Gambia →	**84**	13 28N	16 34W
Gamboa	**120**	9 8N	79 42W
Gamboli	**68**	29 53N	68 24 E
Gambos	**89**	14 37 S	14 40 E
Gamerco	**119**	35 33N	108 56W
Gammon →	**109**	51 24N	95 44W
Gammouda	**83**	35 3N	9 39 E
Gan	**20**	43 12N	0 27W
Gan Goriama, Mts.	**85**	7 44N	12 45 E
Gan Jiang →	**75**	29 15N	116 0 E
Gan Shemu'el	**62**	32 28N	34 56 E
Gan Yavne	**62**	31 48N	34 42 E
Ganado, Ariz., U.S.A.	**119**	35 46N	109 41W
Ganado, Tex., U.S.A.	**117**	29 4N	96 31W
Gananoque	**106**	44 20N	76 10W
Ganaveh	**65**	29 35N	50 35 E
Gancheng	**77**	18 51N	108 37 E
Gand = Gent	**16**	51 2N	3 42 E
Ganda	**89**	13 3 S	14 35 E
Gandak →	**69**	25 39N	85 13 E
Gandava	**68**	28 32N	67 32 E
Gander	**107**	48 58N	54 35W
Gander L.	**107**	48 58N	54 35W
Ganderowe Falls	**91**	17 20 S	29 10 E
Gandesa	**32**	41 3N	0 26 E
Gandhi Sagar	**68**	24 40N	75 40 E
Gandi	**85**	12 55N	5 49 E
Gandia	**33**	38 58N	0 9W
Gandino	**38**	45 50N	9 52 E
Gandole	**85**	8 28N	11 35 E
Ganedidalem = Gani	**73**	0 48 S	128 14 E
Ganetti	**86**	18 0N	31 10 E
Ganga →	**69**	23 20N	90 30 E
Ganga, Mouths of the	**69**	21 30N	90 0 E
Ganganagar	**68**	29 56N	73 56 E
Gangapur	**68**	26 32N	76 49 E
Gangara	**85**	14 35N	8 29 E
Gangavati	**70**	15 30N	76 36 E
Gangaw	**67**	22 5N	94 5 E
Gangdisê Shan	**67**	31 20N	81 0 E
Ganges	**20**	43 56N	3 42 E
Ganges = Ganga →	**69**	23 20N	90 30 E
Gangoh	**68**	29 46N	77 18 E
Gangtok	**69**	27 20N	88 37 E
Gani	**73**	0 48 S	128 14 E
Ganj	**68**	27 45N	78 57 E
Gannat	**20**	46 7N	3 11 E
Gannett Pk.	**118**	43 15N	109 38W
Gannvalley	**116**	44 3N	98 57W
Ganquan	**76**	36 20N	109 20 E
Gänserdorf	**27**	48 20N	16 43 E
Gansu □	**75**	36 0N	104 0 E
Ganta (Gompa)	**84**	7 15N	8 59W
Gantheaume B.	**96**	27 40 S	114 10 E
Gantheaume, C.	**99**	36 4 S	137 32 E
Gantsevichi	**54**	52 49N	26 30 E
Ganyu	**77**	34 50N	119 8 E
Ganyushkino	**57**	46 35N	49 20 E
Ganzhou	**75**	25 51N	114 56 E
Gao □	**85**	18 0N	1 0 E
Gao Bang	**71**	22 37N	106 18 E
Gao'an	**77**	28 26N	115 17 E
Gaomi	**76**	36 20N	119 42 E
Gaoping	**76**	35 45N	112 55 E
Gaoua	**84**	10 20N	3 8W
Gaoual	**84**	11 45N	13 25W
Gaoxiong	**75**	22 38N	120 18 E
Gaoyou	**77**	32 47N	119 26 E
Gaoyou Hu	**77**	32 45N	119 20 E
Gaoyuan	**76**	37 8N	117 58 E
Gap	**21**	44 33N	6 5 E
Gar	**75**	32 10N	79 58 E
Garachiné	**121**	8 0N	78 12W
Garanhuns	**127**	8 50 S	36 30W
Garawe	**84**	4 35N	8 0W
Garba Tula	**90**	0 30N	38 32 E
Garber	**117**	36 30N	97 36W
Garberville	**118**	40 11N	123 50W
Gard	**63**	9 30N	49 6 E
Gard □	**21**	44 2N	4 10 E
Gard →	**21**	43 51N	4 37 E
Garda, L. di	**38**	45 40N	10 40 E
Gardala	**81**	5 40N	37 25 E
Gardanne	**21**	43 27N	5 27 E
Garde L.	**109**	62 50N	106 13W
Gardelegen	**24**	52 32N	11 21 E
Garden City, Kans., U.S.A.	**117**	38 0N	100 45W
Garden City, Tex., U.S.A.	**117**	31 52N	101 28W
Gardez	**66**	33 37N	69 9 E
Gardhíki	**45**	38 50N	21 55 E
Gardiner	**118**	45 3N	110 42W
Gardiners I.	**113**	41 4N	72 5W
Gardner	**114**	42 35N	72 0W
Gardner Canal	**108**	53 27N	128 8W
Gardnerville	**118**	38 59N	119 47W
Gardno, Jezioro	**28**	54 40N	17 7 E
Garešnica	**42**	45 36N	16 56 E
Garéssio	**38**	44 12N	8 1 E
Garfield	**118**	47 3N	117 8W
Gargaliánoi	**45**	37 4N	21 38 E
Gargano, Mte.	**41**	41 43N	15 43 E
Gargans, Mt.	**20**	45 37N	1 39 E
Gargouna	**85**	15 56N	0 13 E
Garhshankar	**68**	31 13N	76 11 E
Garibaldi Prov. Park	**108**	49 50N	122 40W
Garies	**92**	30 32 S	17 59 E
Garigliano →	**40**	41 13N	13 44 E
Garissa	**90**	0 25 S	39 40 E
Garissa □	**90**	0 20 S	40 0 E
Garkida	**85**	10 27N	12 36 E
Garko	**85**	11 45N	8 53 E
Garland	**118**	41 47N	112 10W
Garlasco	**38**	45 11N	8 55 E
Garm	**58**	39 0N	70 20 E
Garmisch-Partenkirchen	**25**	47 30N	11 5 E
Garmsār	**65**	35 20N	52 25 E
Garner	**116**	43 4N	93 37W
Garnett	**116**	38 18N	95 12W
Garo Hills	**69**	25 30N	90 30 E
Garob	**92**	26 37 S	16 0 E
Garoe	**63**	8 25N	48 33 E
Garonne →	**20**	45 2N	0 36W
Garoua (Garwa)	**85**	9 19N	13 21 E
Garrel	**24**	52 58N	7 59 E
Garrigues	**20**	43 40N	3 30 E
Garrison, Mont., U.S.A.	**118**	46 30N	112 56W
Garrison, N.D., U.S.A.	**116**	47 39N	101 27W
Garrison, Tex., U.S.A.	**117**	31 50N	94 28W
Garrison Res.	**116**	47 30N	102 0W
Garrovillas	**31**	39 40N	6 33W
Garrucha	**33**	37 11N	1 49W
Garry →	**14**	56 47N	3 47W
Garry L.	**104**	65 58N	100 18W
Garsen	**90**	2 20 S	40 5 E
Garson →	**109**	56 20N	110 1W
Garson L.	**109**	56 19N	110 2W
Gartempe →	**20**	46 47N	0 49 E
Gartz	**24**	53 12N	14 23 E
Garu	**85**	10 55N	0 11W
Garut	**73**	7 14 S	107 53 E
Garvão	**31**	37 42N	8 21W
Garvie Mts.	**101**	45 30 S	168 50 E
Garwa	**69**	24 11N	83 47 E
Garwolin	**28**	51 55N	21 38 E
Gary	**114**	41 35N	87 20W
Garz	**24**	54 17N	13 21 E
Garzê	**75**	31 39N	99 58 E
Garzón	**126**	2 10N	75 40W
Gasan Kuli	**58**	37 40N	54 20 E
Gascogne	**20**	43 45N	0 20 E
Gascogne, G. de	**32**	44 0N	2 0W
Gascony = Gascogne	**20**	43 45N	0 20 E
Gascoyne →	**96**	24 52 S	113 37 E
Gascueña	**32**	40 18N	2 31W
Gash, Wadi →	**87**	16 48N	35 51 E
Gashaka	**85**	7 20N	11 29 E
Gashua	**85**	12 54N	11 0 E
Gaspé	**107**	48 52N	64 30W
Gaspé, C.	**107**	48 48N	64 7W
Gaspé, Pén. de	**107**	48 45N	65 40W
Gaspésie, Parc Prov. de la	**107**	48 55N	65 50W
Gassaway	**114**	38 42N	80 43W
Gássino Torinese	**38**	45 8N	7 50 E
Gassol	**85**	8 34N	10 25 E
Gastonia	**115**	35 17N	81 10W
Gastoúni	**45**	37 51N	21 15 E
Gastoúri	**44**	39 34N	19 54 E
Gastre	**128**	42 20 S	69 15W
Gata, C. de	**33**	36 41N	2 13W
Gata, Sierra de	**30**	40 20N	6 45W
Gataga →	**108**	58 35N	126 59W
Gătaia	**42**	45 26N	21 30 E
Gatchina	**54**	59 35N	30 9 E
Gateshead	**12**	54 57N	1 37W
Gatesville	**117**	31 29N	97 45W
Gaths	**91**	20 2 S	30 32 E
Gatico	**124**	22 29 S	70 20W
Gâtinais	**19**	48 5N	2 40 E
Gâtine, Hauteurs de	**20**	46 35N	0 45W
Gatineau	**113**	45 29N	75 39W
Gatineau →	**106**	45 27N	75 42W
Gatineau, Parc de la	**106**	45 40N	76 0W
Gatooma	**91**	18 20 S	29 52 E
Gattinara	**38**	45 37N	8 22 E
Gatun	**120**	9 16N	79 55W
Gatun Dam	**120**	9 16N	79 55W
Gatun, L.	**120**	9 7N	79 56W
Gatun Locks	**120**	9 16N	79 55W
Gaucín	**31**	36 31N	5 19W
Gauer L.	**109**	57 0N	97 50W
Gauhati	**67**	26 10N	91 45 E
Gauja →	**54**	57 10N	24 16 E
Gaula →	**47**	63 21N	10 14 E
Gaussberg	**5**	66 45 S	89 0 E
Gausta	**47**	59 50N	8 37 E
Gavá	**32**	41 18N	2 0 E
Gavarnie	**20**	42 44N	0 3W
Gaväter	**65**	25 10N	61 31 E
Gavdhopoúla	**45**	34 56N	24 0 E
Gávdhos	**45**	34 50N	24 5 E
Gavião	**31**	39 28N	7 56W
Gävle	**48**	60 40N	17 9 E
Gävleborgs län □	**48**	61 30N	16 15 E
Gavorrano	**38**	42 55N	10 49 E
Gavray	**18**	48 55N	1 20W
Gavrilov Yam	**55**	57 18N	39 49 E
Gávrion	**45**	37 54N	24 44 E
Gawachab	**92**	27 4 S	17 55 E
Gawilgarh Hills	**68**	21 15N	76 45 E
Gawler	**97**	34 30 S	138 42 E
Gawler Ranges	**96**	32 30 S	135 45 E
Gaxun Nur	**75**	42 22N	100 30 E
Gay	**52**	51 27N	58 27 E
Gaya, India	**69**	24 47N	85 4 E
Gaya, Niger	**85**	11 52N	3 28 E
Gaya, Nigeria	**85**	11 57N	9 0 E
Gaylord	**114**	45 1N	84 41W
Gayndah	**97**	25 35 S	151 32 E
Gaysin	**56**	48 57N	28 25 E
Gayvoron	**56**	48 22N	29 52 E
Gaza	**62**	31 30N	34 28 E
Gaza □	**93**	23 10 S	32 45 E
Gaza Strip	**62**	31 29N	34 25 E
Gazaoua	**85**	13 32N	7 55 E
Gazelle Pen.	**98**	4 40 S	152 0 E
Gazi	**90**	1 3N	24 30 E
Gaziantep	**64**	37 6N	37 23 E
Gazli	**58**	40 14N	63 24 E
Gbarnga	**84**	7 19N	9 13W
Gbekebo	**85**	6 20N	4 56 E
Gboko	**85**	7 17N	9 4 E
Gbongan	**85**	7 28N	4 20 E
Gcuwa	**93**	32 20 S	28 11 E
Gdańsk	**28**	54 22N	18 40 E
Gdańsk □	**28**	54 10N	18 30 E
Gdańska, Zatoka	**28**	54 30N	19 20 E
Gdov	**54**	58 48N	27 55 E
Gdynia	**28**	54 35N	18 33 E
Ge'a	**62**	31 38N	34 37 E
Gebe	**73**	0 5N	129 25 E
Gebeit Mine	**86**	21 3N	36 29 E
Gebel Mûsa	**86**	28 32N	33 59 E
Gecha	**87**	7 30N	35 18 E
Gedaref	**87**	14 2N	35 28 E
Gede, Tanjung	**72**	6 46 S	105 12 E
Gedera	**62**	31 49N	34 46 E
Gedo	**87**	9 2N	37 25 E
Gèdre	**20**	42 47N	0 2 E
Gedser	**49**	54 35N	11 55 E
Gedser Odde	**49**	54 30N	11 58 E
Geelong	**97**	38 10 S	144 22 E
Geestenseth	**24**	53 31N	8 51 E
Geesthacht	**24**	53 25N	10 20 E
Geidam	**85**	12 57N	11 57 E
Geikie →	**109**	57 45N	103 52W
Geili	**87**	16 1N	32 37 E
Geilo	**47**	60 32N	8 14 E
Geinica	**27**	48 51N	20 55 E
Geisingen	**25**	47 55N	8 37 E
Geislingen	**25**	48 37N	9 51 E
Geita	**90**	2 48 S	32 12 E
Geita □	**90**	2 50 S	32 10 E
Gejiu	**75**	23 20N	103 10 E
Gel →	**87**	7 5N	29 10 E
Gel River	**87**	7 5N	29 10 E
Gela	**41**	37 6N	14 18 E
Gela, Golfo di	**41**	37 0N	14 8 E
Geladi	**63**	6 59N	46 30 E
Gelderland □	**16**	52 5N	6 10 E
Geldermalsen	**16**	51 53N	5 17 E
Geldern	**24**	51 32N	6 18 E
Geldrop	**16**	51 25N	5 32 E
Geleen	**16**	50 57N	5 49 E
Gelehun	**84**	8 20N	11 40W
Gelendzhik	**56**	44 33N	38 10 E
Gelibolu	**44**	40 28N	26 43 E
Gelnhausen	**25**	50 12N	9 12 E
Gelsenkirchen	**24**	51 30N	7 5 E
Gelting	**24**	54 43N	9 53 E
Gemas	**71**	2 37N	102 36 E
Gembloux	**16**	50 34N	4 43 E
Gemena	**88**	3 13N	19 48 E
Gemerek	**64**	39 15N	36 10 E
Gemona del Friuli	**39**	46 16N	13 7 E
Gemsa	**86**	27 39N	33 35 E
Gemu-Gofa □	**87**	5 40N	36 40 E
Gemünden	**25**	50 3N	9 43 E
Gen He →	**76**	50 16N	119 32 E
Genale	**87**	6 0N	39 30 E
Gençay	**20**	46 23N	0 23 E
Gendringen	**16**	51 52N	6 21 E
Geneina, Gebel	**86**	29 2N	33 55 E
General Acha	**124**	37 20 S	64 38W
General Alvear, Buenos Aires, Argent.	**124**	36 0 S	60 0W
General Alvear, Mendoza, Argent.	**124**	35 0 S	67 40W
General Artigas	**124**	26 52 S	56 16W
General Belgrano	**124**	36 35 S	58 47W
General Cabrera	**124**	32 53 S	63 52W
General Guido	**124**	36 40 S	57 50W
General Juan Madariaga	**124**	37 0 S	57 0W
General La Madrid	**124**	37 17 S	61 20W
General MacArthur	**73**	11 18N	125 28 E
General Martin Miguel de Güemes	**124**	24 35 S	65 0W
General Paz	**124**	27 45 S	57 36W
General Pico	**124**	35 45 S	63 50W
General Pinedo	**124**	27 15 S	61 20W
General Pinto	**124**	34 45 S	61 50W
General Santos	**73**	6 5N	125 14 E
General Toshevo	**43**	43 42N	28 6 E
General Trías	**120**	28 21N	106 22W
General Viamonte	**124**	35 1 S	61 3W
General Villegas	**124**	35 0 S	63 0W
Genesee, Idaho, U.S.A.	**118**	46 31N	116 59W
Genesee, Pa., U.S.A.	**112**	42 0N	77 54W
Genesee →	**114**	42 35N	78 0W
Geneseo, Ill., U.S.A.	**116**	41 25N	90 10W
Geneseo, Kans., U.S.A.	**116**	38 32N	98 8W
Geneseo, N.Y., U.S.A.	**112**	42 49N	77 49W
Geneva, Ala., U.S.A.	**115**	31 2N	85 52W
Geneva, N.Y., U.S.A.	**114**	42 53N	77 0W
Geneva, Nebr., U.S.A.	**116**	40 35N	97 35W
Geneva, Ohio, U.S.A.	**114**	41 49N	80 58W
Geneva = Genève	**25**	46 12N	6 9 E
Geneva, L.	**114**	42 38N	88 30W
Geneva, L. = Léman, Lac	**25**	46 26N	6 30 E
Genève	**25**	46 12N	6 9 E
Genève □	**25**	46 10N	6 10 E
Gengenbach	**25**	48 25N	8 0 E
Genichesk	**56**	46 12N	34 50 E
Genil →	**31**	37 42N	5 19W
Génissiat, Barrage de	**21**	46 1N	5 48 E
Genjem	**73**	2 46 S	140 12 E
Genk	**16**	50 58N	5 32 E
Genlis	**19**	47 15N	5 12 E
Gennargentu, Mti. del	**40**	40 0N	9 10 E
Gennep	**16**	51 41N	5 59 E
Gennes	**18**	47 20N	0 17W
Genoa, Austral.	**99**	37 29 S	149 35 E
Genoa, N.Y., U.S.A.	**113**	42 40N	76 32W
Genoa, Nebr., U.S.A.	**116**	41 31N	97 44W
Genoa = Génova	**38**	44 24N	8 57 E
Génova	**38**	44 24N	8 56 E
Génova, Golfo di	**38**	44 0N	9 0 E
Gent	**16**	51 2N	3 42 E
Genthin	**24**	52 24N	12 10 E
Geographe B.	**96**	33 30 S	115 15 E
Geographe Chan.	**96**	24 30 S	113 0 E
Geokchay	**57**	40 42N	47 43 E
Georga, Zemlya	**58**	80 30N	49 0 E
George	**92**	33 58 S	22 29 E
George →	**107**	58 49N	66 10W
George, L., N.S.W., Austral.	**99**	35 10 S	149 25 E
George, L., S. Austral., Austral.	**99**	37 25 S	140 0 E
George, L., Uganda	**90**	0 5N	30 10 E
George, L., Fla., U.S.A.	**115**	29 15N	81 35W
George, L., N.Y., U.S.A.	**113**	43 30N	73 30W
George River = Port Nouveau	**105**	58 30N	65 50W
George Sound	**101**	44 52 S	167 25 E
George Town, Austral.	**99**	41 5 S	146 49 E
George Town, Bahamas	**121**	23 33N	75 47W
George Town, Malay.	**71**	5 25N	100 15 E
George V Coast	**5**	69 0 S	148 0 E
George VI Sound	**5**	71 0 S	68 0W
George West	**117**	28 18N	98 5W
Georgetown, Austral.	**97**	18 17 S	143 33 E
Georgetown, Ont., Can.	**106**	43 40N	79 56W
Georgetown, P.E.I., Can.	**107**	46 13N	62 24W
Georgetown, Gambia	**84**	13 30N	14 47W
Georgetown, Guyana	**126**	6 50N	58 12W
Georgetown, Colo., U.S.A.	**118**	39 46N	105 49W
Georgetown, Ky., U.S.A.	**114**	38 13N	84 33W
Georgetown, Ohio, U.S.A.	**114**	38 50N	83 50W
Georgetown, S.C., U.S.A.	**115**	33 22N	79 15W
Georgetown, Tex., U.S.A.	**117**	30 40N	97 45W
Georgi Dimitrov	**43**	42 15N	23 54 E
Georgi Dimitrov, Yazovir	**43**	42 37N	25 18 E
Georgia □	**115**	32 0N	82 0W
Georgia, Str. of	**108**	49 25N	124 0W
Georgian B.	**106**	45 15N	81 0W
Georgian S.S.R. □	**57**	42 0N	43 0 E
Georgievsk	**57**	44 12N	43 28 E
Georgina →	**97**	23 30 S	139 47 E
Georgiu-Dezh	**55**	51 3N	39 30 E
Gera	**24**	50 53N	12 11 E
Gera □	**24**	50 45N	11 45 E
Geraardsbergen	**16**	50 45N	3 53 E
Geral de Goiás, Serra	**127**	12 0 S	46 0W
Geral, Serra	**125**	26 25 S	50 0W
Geraldine	**118**	47 36N	110 18W
Geraldton, Austral.	**96**	28 48 S	114 32 E
Geraldton, Can.	**106**	49 44N	86 59W
Gérardmer	**19**	48 3N	6 50 E
Gerede	**56**	40 45N	32 10 E
Gereshk	**65**	31 47N	64 35 E
Gérgal	**33**	37 7N	2 31W
Gerik	**71**	5 25N	101 0 E
Gering	**116**	41 51N	103 30W
Gerizim	**62**	32 13N	35 15 E
Gerlach	**118**	40 43N	119 27W
Gerlachovka	**27**	49 11N	20 7 E
Gerlogubi	**63**	6 53N	45 3 E
German Planina	**42**	42 20N	22 0 E
Germansen Landing	**108**	55 43N	124 40W
Germany, East ■	**24**	52 0N	12 0 E
Germany, West ■	**24**	52 0N	9 0 E
Germersheim	**25**	49 13N	8 20 E
Germiston	**93**	26 15 S	28 10 E
Gernsheim	**25**	49 44N	8 29 E
Gerolstein	**25**	50 12N	6 40 E
Gerolzhofen	**25**	49 54N	10 21 E
Gerona	**32**	41 58N	2 46 E
Gerona □	**32**	42 11N	2 30 E
Gerrard	**108**	50 30N	117 17W
Gers □	**20**	43 35N	0 38 E
Gers →	**20**	44 9N	0 39 E
Gersfeld	**24**	50 27N	9 57 E
Gersoppa Falls	**70**	14 12N	74 46 E
Gerufa	**92**	19 17 S	26 0 E
Geseke	**24**	51 38N	8 29 E
Geser	**73**	3 50 S	130 54 E
Gesso →	**38**	44 24N	7 33 E
Gestro, Wabi →	**87**	4 12N	42 2 E
Getafe	**30**	40 18N	3 44W
Gethsémani	**107**	50 13N	60 40W
Gettysburg, Pa., U.S.A.	**114**	39 47N	77 18W
Gettysburg, S.D., U.S.A.	**116**	45 3N	99 56W
Getz Ice Shelf	**5**	75 0 S	130 0W
Gévaudan	**20**	44 40N	3 40 E
Gevgelija	**42**	41 9N	22 30 E
Gévora →	**31**	38 53N	6 57W
Gex	**21**	46 21N	6 3 E
Geyikh	**44**	39 50N	26 12 E
Geyser	**118**	47 17N	110 30W
Geysir	**50**	64 19N	20 18W
Ghaghara →	**69**	25 45N	84 40 E
Ghalla, Wadi el →	**87**	10 25N	27 32 E
Ghana ■	**85**	6 0N	1 0W
Ghansor	**69**	22 39N	80 1 E
Ghanzi	**92**	21 50 S	21 34 E
Ghanzi □	**92**	21 50 S	21 45 E
Gharbîya, Es Sahrâ el	**86**	27 40N	26 30 E
Ghard Abû Muharik	**86**	26 50N	30 0 E
Ghardaïa	**82**	32 20N	3 37 E
Ghârib, G.	**86**	28 6N	32 54 E
Ghârib, Râs	**86**	28 6N	33 18 E
Gharyān	**83**	32 10N	13 0 E
Gharyān □	**83**	30 35N	12 0 E
Ghat	**83**	24 59N	10 11 E
Ghatal	**69**	22 40N	87 46 E
Ghatampur	**69**	26 8N	80 13 E
Ghatprabha →	**70**	16 15N	75 20 E
Ghayl	**64**	21 40N	46 20 E

Ghazal, Bahr el → 81 15 0N 17 0 E
Ghazāl, Bahr el → 87 9 31N 30 25 E
Ghazaouet 82 35 8N 1 50W
Ghaziabad 68 28 42N 77 26 E
Ghazipur 69 25 38N 83 35 E
Ghazni 66 33 30N 68 28 E
Ghaznī □ 65 33 0N 68 0 E
Ghedi 38 45 24N 10 16 E
Chelari 46 45 38N 22 45 E
Ghèlinsor 63 6 28N 46 39 E
Ghent = Gand 16 51 2N 3 42 E
Gheorghe Gheorghiu-Dej 46 46 17N 26 47 E
Gheorgheni 46 46 43N 25 41 E
Ghergani 46 44 37N 25 37 E
Gherla 46 47 0N 23 57 E
Ghilarza 40 40 8N 8 50 E
Ghisonaccia 21 42 1N 9 26 E
Ghod → 70 18 30N 74 35 E
Ghot Ogrein 86 31 10N 25 20 E
Ghotaru 68 27 20N 70 1 E
Ghotki 68 28 5N 69 21 E
Ghowr □ 65 34 0N 64 20 E
Ghudāmis 83 30 11N 9 29 E
Ghugri 69 22 39N 80 41 E
Ghugus 70 19 58N 79 12 E
Ghulam Mohammad Barrage 68 25 30N 68 20 E
Ghūriān 65 34 17N 61 25 E
Gia Nghia 71 12 0N 107 42 E
Gian 73 5 45N 125 20 E
Giannutri 38 42 16N 11 5 E
Giant Mts. = Krkonoše 26 50 50N 16 10 E
Giant's Causeway 15 55 15N 6 30W
Giarre 41 37 44N 15 10 E
Giaveno 38 45 3N 7 20 E
Gibara 121 21 9N 76 11W
Gibbon 116 40 49N 98 45W
Gibe → 87 7 20N 37 36 E
Gibellina 40 37 48N 13 0 E
Gibeon 92 25 7 S 17 45 E
Gibraléon 31 37 23N 6 58W
Gibraltar 31 36 7N 5 22W
Gibraltar, Str. of 31 35 55N 5 40W
Gibson Des. 96 24 0 S 126 0 E
Gibsons 108 49 24N 123 32W
Giddalur 70 15 20N 78 57 E
Giddings 117 30 11N 96 58W
Gidole 87 5 40N 37 25 E
Gien 19 47 40N 2 36 E
Giessen 24 50 34N 8 40 E
Gifatin, Geziret 86 27 10N 33 50 E
Gifhorn 24 52 29N 10 32 E
Gifu 74 35 30N 136 45 E
Gifu □ 74 35 40N 137 0 E
Gigant 57 46 28N 41 20 E
Giganta, Sa. de la 120 25 30N 111 30W
Gigen 43 43 40N 24 28 E
Gigha 14 55 42N 5 45W
Giglio 38 42 20N 10 52 E
Gignac 20 43 39N 3 32 E
Gigüela → 33 39 8N 3 44W
Gijón 30 43 32N 5 42W
Gil I. 108 53 12N 129 15W
Gila → 119 32 43N 114 33W
Gila Bend 119 33 0N 112 46W
Gila Bend Mts. 119 33 15N 113 0W
Gilan □ 64 37 0N 48 0 E
Gilău 46 46 45N 23 23 E
Gilbert → 97 16 35 S 141 15 E
Gilbert Is. = Kiribati ■ 94 1 0N 176 0 E
Gilbert Plains 109 51 9N 100 28W
Gilbert River 98 18 9 S 142 52 E
Gilberton 98 19 16 S 143 35 E
Gilf el Kebîr, Hadabat el 86 23 50N 25 50 E
Gilford I. 108 50 40N 126 30W
Gilgandra 97 31 43 S 148 39 E
Gilgil 90 0 30 S 36 20 E
Gilgit 69 35 50N 74 15 E
Giljeva Planina 42 43 9N 20 0 E
Gillam 109 56 20N 94 40W
Gilleleje 49 56 8N 12 19 E
Gillette 116 44 20N 105 30W
Gilliat 98 20 40 S 141 28 E
Gillingham 13 51 23N 0 34 E
Gilmer 117 32 44N 94 55W
Gilmore 99 35 20 S 148 12 E
Gilmour 106 44 48N 77 37W
Gilo → 87 8 10N 33 15 E
Gilort → 46 44 38N 23 32 E
Gilroy 119 37 1N 121 37W
Gimbi 87 9 3N 35 42 E
Gimigliano 41 38 58N 16 32 E
Gimli 109 50 40N 97 0W
Gimo 48 60 11N 18 12 E
Gimone → 20 44 0N 1 6 E
Gimont 20 43 38N 0 52 E
Gimzo 62 31 56N 34 56 E
Gin → 70 6 5N 80 7 E
Gin Gin 99 25 0 S 151 58 E
Ginâh 86 25 21N 30 30 E
Gindie 98 23 44 S 148 8 E
Gineta, La 33 39 8N 2 1W
Gîngiova 46 43 54N 23 50 E
Ginir 87 7 6N 40 40 E
Ginosa 41 40 35N 16 45 E
Ginzo de Limia 30 42 3N 7 47W
Giohar 63 2 48N 45 30 E
Gióia del Colle 41 40 49N 16 55 E
Gióia, G. di 41 38 30N 15 50 E
Gióia Táuro 41 38 26N 15 53 E
Gioiosa Iónica 41 38 20N 16 19 E
Gióna, Óros 45 38 38N 22 14 E
Giong, Teluk 73 4 50N 118 20 E
Giovi, Passo dei 38 44 33N 8 57 E
Giovinazzo 41 41 10N 16 40 E
Gippsland 97 37 45 S 147 15 E
Gir Hills 68 21 0N 71 0 E
Girab 68 26 2N 70 38 E
Giraltovce 27 49 7N 21 32 E
Girard, Kans., U.S.A. 117 37 30N 94 50W
Girard, Ohio, U.S.A. 112 41 10N 80 42W
Girard, Pa., U.S.A. 112 42 1N 80 21W
Girardot 126 4 18N 74 48W
Girdle Ness 14 57 9N 2 2W
Giresun 64 40 55N 38 30 E
Girga 86 26 17N 31 55 E
Giridih 69 24 10N 86 21 E
Girifalco 41 38 49N 16 25 E
Girilambone 99 31 16 S 146 57 E
Giro 85 11 7N 4 42 E
Giromagny 19 47 44N 6 50 E
Gironde □ 20 44 45N 0 30W
Gironde → 20 45 32N 1 7W
Gironella 32 42 2N 1 53 E
Giru 98 19 30 S 147 5 E
Girvan 14 55 15N 4 50W
Gisborne 101 38 39 S 178 5 E
Gisenyi 90 1 41 S 29 15 E
Giske 47 62 30N 6 3 E
Gislaved 49 57 19N 13 32 E
Gisors 19 49 15N 1 47 E
Gitega (Kitega) 90 3 26 S 29 56 E
Giuba → 63 1 30N 42 35 E
Giugliano in Campania 41 40 55N 14 12 E
Giulianova 39 42 45N 13 58 E
Giurgeni 46 44 45N 27 48 E
Giurgiu 46 43 52N 25 57 E
Giv'at Brenner 62 31 52N 34 47 E
Giv'atayim 62 32 4N 34 49 E
Give 49 55 51N 9 13 E
Givet 19 50 8N 4 49 E
Givors 21 45 35N 4 45 E
Givry 19 46 41N 4 46 E
Giyon 87 8 33N 38 1 E
Giza = El Gîza 86 30 1N 31 11 E
Gizhiga 59 62 3N 160 30 E
Gizhiginskaya, Guba 59 61 0N 158 0 E
Giżycko 28 54 2N 21 48 E
Gizzeria 41 38 57N 16 10 E
Gjegjan 44 41 58N 20 3 E
Gjerstad 47 58 54N 9 0 E
Gjirokastra 44 40 7N 20 10 E
Gjoa Haven 104 68 20N 96 8W
Gjøl 49 57 4N 9 42 E
Gjøvik 47 60 47N 10 43 E
Glace Bay 107 46 11N 59 58W
Glacier B. 108 58 30N 136 10W
Glacier Nat. Park, Can. 108 51 15N 117 30W
Glacier Nat. Park, U.S.A. 118 48 35N 113 40W
Glacier Park 118 48 30N 113 18W
Glacier Peak Mt. 118 48 7N 121 7W
Gladewater 117 32 30N 94 58W
Gladstone, Austral. 99 33 15 S 138 22 E
Gladstone, Can. 109 50 13N 98 57W
Gladstone, U.S.A. 114 45 52N 87 1W
Gladwin 114 43 59N 84 29W
Gladys L. 108 59 50N 133 0W
Glafsfjorden 48 59 30N 12 37 E
Głagów Małapolski 27 50 10N 21 56 E
Gláma 50 65 48N 23 0W
Glåma → 47 59 12N 10 57 E
Glamoč 39 44 3N 16 51 E
Glan 49 58 37N 16 0 E
Glarus 25 47 3N 9 4 E
Glasco, Kans., U.S.A. 116 39 25N 97 50W
Glasco, N.Y., U.S.A. 113 42 3N 73 57W
Glasgow, U.K. 14 55 52N 4 14W
Glasgow, Ky., U.S.A. 114 37 2N 85 55W
Glasgow, Mont., U.S.A. 118 48 12N 106 35W
Glastonbury, U.K. 13 51 9N 2 42W
Glastonbury, U.S.A. 113 41 42N 72 27W
Glauchau 24 50 50N 12 33 E
Glazov 55 58 9N 52 40 E
Gleisdorf 26 47 6N 15 44 E
Gleiwitz = Gliwice 28 50 22N 18 41 E
Glen 113 44 7N 71 10W
Glen Affric 14 57 15N 5 0W
Glen Canyon Dam 119 37 0N 111 25W
Glen Canyon Nat. Recreation Area 119 37 30N 111 0W
Glen Coe 12 56 40N 5 0W
Glen Cove 113 40 51N 73 37W
Glen Garry 14 57 3N 5 7W
Glen Innes 97 29 44 S 151 44 E
Glen Lyon 113 41 10N 76 7W
Glen Mor 14 57 12N 4 37 E
Glen Moriston 14 57 10N 4 58W
Glen Orchy 14 56 27N 4 52W
Glen Spean 14 56 53N 4 40W
Glen Ullin 116 46 48N 101 46W
Glénans, Îles. de 18 47 42N 4 0W
Glenburnie 100 37 51 S 140 50 E
Glencoe, Can. 112 42 45N 81 43W
Glencoe, S. Afr. 93 28 11 S 30 11 E
Glencoe, U.S.A. 116 44 45N 94 10W
Glendale, Ariz., U.S.A. 119 33 40N 112 8W
Glendale, Calif., U.S.A. 119 34 7N 118 18W
Glendale, Oreg., U.S.A. 118 42 44N 123 29W
Glendale, Zimb. 91 17 22 S 31 5 E
Glendive 116 47 7N 104 40W
Glendo 116 42 30N 105 0W
Glenelg 99 34 58 S 138 31 E
Glenelg → 99 38 4 S 140 59 E
Glengarriff 15 51 45N 9 33W
Glengyle 98 24 48 S 139 37 E
Glenmora 117 31 1N 92 34W
Glenmorgan 99 27 14 S 149 42 E
Glenns Ferry 118 43 0N 115 15W
Glenorchy 99 42 49 S 147 18 E
Glenore 98 17 50 S 141 12 E
Glenormiston 98 22 55 S 138 50 E
Glenreagh 99 30 2 S 153 1 E
Glenrock 118 42 53N 105 55W
Glenrothes 14 56 12N 3 11W
Glens Falls 114 43 20N 73 40W
Glenties 15 54 48N 8 18W
Glenville 114 38 56N 80 50W
Glenwood, Alta., Can. 108 49 21N 113 31W
Glenwood, Newf., Can. 107 49 0N 54 58W
Glenwood, Ark., U.S.A. 117 34 20N 93 30W
Glenwood, Hawaii, U.S.A. 110 19 29N 155 10W
Glenwood, Iowa, U.S.A. 116 41 7N 95 41W
Glenwood, Minn., U.S.A. 116 45 38N 95 21W
Glenwood Sprs. 118 39 39N 107 21W
Glina 39 45 20N 16 6 E
Glinojeck 28 52 49N 20 21 E
Glittertind 47 61 40N 8 32 E
Gliwice 28 50 22N 18 41 E
Globe 119 33 25N 110 53W
Glodeanu Siliştea 46 44 50N 26 48 E
Glödnitz 26 46 53N 14 7 E
Glodyany 46 47 45N 27 31 E
Gloggnitz 26 47 41N 15 56 E
Głogów 28 51 37N 16 5 E
Głogowek 28 50 21N 17 53 E
Glorieuses, Îles 93 11 30 S 47 20 E
Glossop 12 53 27N 1 56W
Gloucester, Austral. 99 32 0 S 151 59 E
Gloucester, U.K. 13 51 52N 2 15W
Gloucester, U.S.A. 113 42 38N 70 39W
Gloucester, C. 98 5 26 S 148 21 E
Gloucester I. 98 20 0 S 148 30 E
Gloucestershire □ 13 51 44N 2 10W
Gloversville 114 43 5N 74 18W
Glovertown 107 48 40N 54 03W
Główno 28 51 59N 19 42 E
Głubczyce 27 50 13N 17 52 E
Glubokiy 57 48 35N 40 25 E
Glubokoye 54 55 10N 27 45 E
Glűbovo 43 42 8N 25 55 E
Głuchołazy 28 50 19N 17 24 E
Glücksburg 24 54 48N 9 34 E
Glückstadt 24 53 46N 9 28 E
Glukhov 54 51 40N 33 58 E
Glussk 54 52 53N 28 41 E
Glyngøre 49 56 46N 8 52 E
Gmünd, Kärnten, Austria 26 46 54N 13 31 E
Gmünd, Niederösterreich, Austria 26 48 45N 15 0 E
Gmunden 26 47 55N 13 48 E
Gnarp 48 62 3N 17 16 E
Gnesta 48 59 3N 17 17 E
Gniew 28 53 50N 18 50 E
Gniewkowo 28 52 54N 18 25 E
Gniezno 28 52 30N 17 35 E
Gnjilane 42 42 28N 21 29 E
Gnoien 24 53 58N 12 41 E
Gnosjö 49 57 22N 13 43 E
Gnowangerup 96 33 58 S 117 59 E
Go Cong 71 10 22N 106 40 E
Goa 70 15 33N 73 59 E
Goa □ 70 15 33N 73 59 E
Goageb 92 26 49 S 17 15 E
Goalen Hd. 99 36 33 S 150 4 E
Goalpara 69 26 10N 90 40 E
Goalundo Ghat 69 23 50N 89 47 E
Goaso 84 6 48N 2 30W
Goat Fell 14 55 37N 5 11W
Goba 87 7 1N 39 59 E
Gobabis 92 22 30 S 19 0 E
Gobi 75 44 0N 111 0 E
Gobichettipalayam 70 11 31N 77 21 E
Gobo 87 5 40N 31 10 E
Goch 24 51 40N 6 9 E
Gochas 92 24 59 S 18 55 E
Godavari → 70 16 25N 82 18 E
Godavari Point 70 17 0N 82 20 E
Godbout 107 49 20N 67 38W
Godda 69 24 50N 87 13 E
Goddua 83 26 26N 14 19 E
Godech 42 43 1N 23 4 E
Godegård 49 58 43N 15 8 E
Goderich 106 43 45N 81 41W
Goderville 18 49 38N 0 22 E
Godhavn 4 69 15N 53 38W
Godhra 68 22 49N 73 40 E
Gödöllö 27 47 38N 19 25 E
Godoy Cruz 124 32 56 S 68 52W
Gods → 109 56 22N 92 51W
Gods L. 109 54 40N 94 15W
Godthåb 4 64 10N 51 35W
Godwin Austen (K2) 69 36 0N 77 0 E
Goeie Hoop, Kaap die 92 34 24 S 18 30 E
Goéland, L. au 106 49 50N 76 48W
Goeree 16 51 50N 4 0 E
Goes 16 51 30N 3 55 E
Gogama 106 47 35N 81 43W
Gogango 98 23 40 S 150 2 E
Gogebic, L. 116 46 20N 89 34W
Gogha 68 21 40N 72 20 E
Gogolin 28 50 30N 18 0 E
Gogra = Ghaghara → 67 26 0N 84 20 E
Gogriâl 87 8 30N 28 8 E
Goiânia 127 16 43 S 49 20W
Goiás 127 15 55 S 50 10W
Goiás □ 127 12 10 S 48 0W
Góis 30 40 10N 8 6W
Goisern 26 47 38N 13 38 E
Gojam □ 87 10 55N 36 30 E
Gojeb, Wabi → 87 7 12N 36 40 E
Gojra 68 31 10N 72 40 E
Gokak 70 16 11N 74 52 E
Gokarannath 69 27 57N 80 39 E
Gokarn 70 14 33N 74 17 E
Gökçeada 44 40 10N 25 50 E
Gokteik 67 22 26N 97 0 E
Gokurt 68 29 40N 67 26 E
Gola 69 28 3N 80 32 E
Golakganj 69 26 8N 89 52 E
Golaya Pristen 56 46 29N 32 32 E
Golchikha 4 71 45N 83 30 E
Golconda 118 40 58N 117 32W
Gold Beach 118 42 25N 124 25W
Gold Coast, Austral. 99 28 0 S 153 25 E
Gold Coast, W. Afr. 85 4 0N 1 40W
Gold Hill 118 42 28N 123 2W
Gold River 108 49 46N 126 3 E
Gołdap 28 54 19N 22 18 E
Goldberg 24 53 34N 12 6 E
Golden, Can. 108 51 20N 117 59W
Golden, U.S.A. 116 39 42N 105 15W
Golden Bay 101 40 40 S 172 50 E
Golden Gate 118 37 54N 122 30W
Golden Hinde 108 49 40N 125 44W
Golden Lake 112 45 34N 77 21W
Golden Prairie 109 50 13N 109 37W
Golden Rock 70 10 45N 78 48 E
Golden Vale 15 52 33N 8 17W
Goldendale 118 45 53N 120 48W
Goldfield 119 37 45N 117 13W
Goldfields 109 59 28N 108 29W
Goldsand L. 109 57 2N 101 8W
Goldsboro 115 35 24N 77 59W
Goldsmith 117 32 0N 102 40W
Goldthwaite 117 31 25N 98 32W
Golegã 31 39 24N 8 29W
Golęniów 28 53 35N 14 50 E
Golfito 121 8 41N 83 5W
Golfo Aranci 40 41 0N 9 35 E
Goliad 117 28 40N 97 22W
Golija, Crna Gora, Yugo. 42 43 5N 18 45 E
Golija, Srbija, Yugo. 42 43 22N 20 15 E
Golina 28 52 15N 18 4 E
Göllersdorf 27 48 29N 16 7 E
Golo → 21 42 31N 9 32 E
Golovanevsk 56 48 25N 30 30 E
Golspie 14 57 58N 3 58W
Golub Dobrzyń 28 53 7N 19 2 E
Golubac 42 44 38N 21 38 E
Golyam Perelik 43 41 36N 24 33 E
Golyama Kamchiya → 43 43 10N 27 55 E
Goma, Rwanda 90 2 11 S 29 18 E
Goma, Zaïre 90 1 37 S 29 10 E
Gomare 92 19 25 S 22 8 E
Gomati → 69 25 32N 83 11 E
Gombari 90 2 45N 29 3 E
Gombe 85 10 19N 11 2 E
Gombe → 90 4 38 S 31 40 E
Gombi 85 10 12N 12 30 E
Gomel 54 52 28N 31 0 E
Gomera 80 28 7N 17 14W
Gómez Palacio 120 25 40N 104 0W
Gommern 24 52 5N 11 47 E
Gomogomo 73 6 39 S 134 43 E
Gomotartsi 42 44 6N 22 57 E
Gomphoi 44 39 31N 21 27 E
Gonābād 65 34 15N 58 45 E
Gonaïves 121 19 20N 72 42W
Gonâve, G. de la 121 19 29N 72 42W
Gonbab-e Kāvūs 65 37 20N 55 25 E
Gönc 27 48 28N 21 14 E
Gonda 69 27 9N 81 58 E
Gondal 68 21 58N 70 52 E
Gonder 87 12 39N 37 30 E
Gondia 69 21 23N 80 10 E
Gondola 91 19 10 S 33 37 E
Gondomar, Port. 30 41 10N 8 35W
Gondomar, Spain 30 42 7N 8 45W
Gondrecourt-le-Château 19 48 26N 5 30 E
Gonghe 75 36 18N 100 32 E
Gongola □ 85 8 0N 12 0 E
Gongola → 85 9 30N 12 4 E
Goniadz 28 53 30N 22 44 E
Goniri 85 11 30N 12 15 E
Gonnesa 40 39 17N 8 27 E
Gónnos 44 39 52N 22 29 E
Gonnosfanadiga 40 39 30N 8 39 E
Gonzales, Calif., U.S.A. 119 36 35N 121 30W
Gonzales, Tex., U.S.A. 117 29 30N 97 30W
González Chaves 124 38 02 S 60 05W
Good Hope, C. of = Goeie Hoop, K. die 92 34 24 S 18 30 E
Goodenough I. 98 9 20 S 150 15 E
Gooderham 106 44 54N 78 21W
Goodeve 109 51 4N 103 10W
Gooding 118 43 0N 114 44W
Goodland 116 39 22N 101 44W
Goodnight 117 35 4N 101 13W
Goodooga 99 29 3 S 147 28 E
Goodsoil 109 54 24N 109 13W
Goodsprings 119 35 51N 115 30W
Goole 12 53 42N 0 52W
Goolgowi 99 33 58 S 145 41 E
Goombalie 99 29 59 S 145 26 E
Goonda 91 19 48 S 33 57 E
Goondiwindi 97 28 30 S 150 21 E
Goor 16 52 13N 6 33 E
Gooray 99 28 25 S 150 2 E
Goose → 107 53 20N 60 35W
Goose Bay 107 53 15N 60 20W
Goose L. 118 42 0N 120 30W
Gooty 70 15 7N 77 41 E
Gopalganj, Bangla. 69 23 1N 89 50 E
Gopalganj, India 69 26 28N 84 30 E
Göppingen 25 48 42N 9 40 E
Gor 33 37 23N 2 58W
Góra, Leszno, Poland 28 51 40N 16 31 E
Góra, Płock, Poland 28 52 39N 20 6 E
Góra Kalwaria 28 51 59N 21 14 E
Gorakhpur 69 26 47N 83 23 E
Goražde 42 43 38N 18 58 E
Gorbatov 55 56 12N 43 2 E
Gorbea, Peña 32 43 1N 2 50W
Gorda, Punta 121 14 20N 83 10W
Gordon, Austral. 99 32 7 S 138 20 E
Gordon, U.S.A. 116 42 49N 102 12W
Gordon → 99 42 27 S 145 30 E
Gordon Downs 96 18 48 S 128 33 E
Gordon L., Alta., Can. 109 56 30N 110 25W
Gordon L., N.W.T., Can. 108 63 5N 113 11W
Gordonia 92 28 13 S 21 10 E
Gordonvale 98 17 5 S 145 50 E
Gore 99 28 17 S 151 30 E
Goré 81 7 59N 16 31 E
Gore, Ethiopia 87 8 12N 35 32 E
Gore, N.Z. 101 46 5 S 168 58 E
Gore Bay 106 45 57N 82 28W
Gorey 15 52 41N 6 18W
Gorgān 65 36 55N 54 30 E
Gorgona 38 43 27N 9 52 E
Gorgona, I. 126 3 0N 78 10W
Gorgora 87 12 15N 37 17 E
Gorham 113 44 23N 71 10W
Gori 57 42 0N 44 7 E
Gorinchem 16 51 50N 4 59 E
Goritsy 55 57 4N 36 43 E
Gorízia 39 45 56N 13 37 E
Górka 28 51 39N 16 58 E
Gorki 54 54 17N 30 59 E

Gorki = Gorkiy 55 56 20N 44 0 E
Gorkiy 55 56 20N 44 0 E
Gorkovskoye Vdkhr. 55 57 2N 43 4 E
Gørlev 49 55 30N 11 15 E
Gorlice 27 49 35N 21 11 E
Görlitz 24 51 10N 14 59 E
Gorlovka 56 48 19N 38 5 E
Gorman 117 32 15N 98 43W
Gorna Oryakhovitsa 43 43 7N 25 40 E
Gornja Radgona 39 46 40N 16 2 E
Gornja Tuzla 42 44 35N 18 46 E
Gornji Grad 39 46 20N 14 52 E
Gornji Milanovac 42 44 00N 20 29 E
Gornji Vakuf 42 43 57N 17 34 E
Gorno Ablanovo 43 43 37N 25 43 E
Gorno-Altaysk 58 51 50N 86 5 E
Gorno Slinkino 58 60 5N 70 0 E
Gornyatski 52 67 32N 64 3 E
Gornyy 55 51 50N 48 30 E
Gorodenka 56 48 41N 25 29 E
Gorodets 55 56 38N 43 28 E
Gorodische 55 53 13N 45 40 E
Gorodishche 56 49 17N 31 27 E
Gorodnitsa 54 50 46N 27 19 E
Gorodnya 54 51 55N 31 33 E
Gorodok, Byelorussia, U.S.S.R. 54 55 30N 30 3 E
Gorodok, Ukraine, U.S.S.R. 54 49 46N 23 32 E
Goroka 98 6 7S 145 25 E
Gorokhov 54 50 30N 24 45 E
Gorokhovets 55 56 13N 42 39 E
Gorom Gorom 85 14 26N 0 14W
Goromonzi 91 17 52S 31 22 E
Gorong, Kepulauan 73 4 5S 131 25 E
Gorongosa, Sa. da 91 18 27S 34 2 E
Gorongose → 93 20 30S 34 40 E
Gorontalo 73 0 35N 123 5 E
Goronyo 85 13 29N 5 39 E
Górowo Iławeckie 28 54 17N 20 30 E
Gorron 18 48 25N 0 50W
Gort 15 53 4N 8 50W
Gorumahisani 69 22 20N 86 24 E
Gorzkowice 28 51 13N 19 36 E
Gorzno 28 53 12N 19 38 E
Gorzów Śląski 28 51 3N 18 22 E
Gorzów Wielkopolski 28 52 43N 15 15 E
Gorzów Wielkopolski □ 28 52 45N 15 30 E
Gosford 99 33 23S 151 18 E
Goshen, S. Afr. 92 25 50S 25 0 E
Goshen, Ind., U.S.A. 114 41 36N 85 46W
Goshen, N.Y., U.S.A. 113 41 23N 74 21W
Goslar 24 51 55N 10 23 E
Gospič 39 44 35N 15 23 E
Gosport 13 50 48N 1 8W
Gostivar 42 41 48N 20 57 E
Gostyń 28 51 50N 17 3 E
Gostynin 28 52 26N 19 29 E
Göta älv → 49 57 42N 11 54 E
Göteborg 49 57 43N 11 59 E
Götene 49 58 32N 13 30 E
Gotha 24 50 56N 10 42 E
Gothenburg 116 40 58N 100 8W
Gotland 49 57 30N 18 33 E
Gotō-Rettō 74 32 55N 129 5 E
Gotse Delchev (Nevrokop) 43 41 43N 23 46 E
Göttingen 24 51 31N 9 55 E
Gottwaldov (Zlin) 27 49 14N 17 40 E
Goubangzi 76 41 20N 121 52 E
Gouda 16 52 1N 4 42 E
Goudiry 84 14 15N 12 45W
Gough I. 7 40 10S 9 45W
Gouin Rés. 106 48 35N 74 40W
Gouitafla 84 7 30N 5 53W
Goula Touila 82 21 50N 1 57W
Goulburn 97 34 44S 149 44 E
Goulburn → 100 36 6S 144 55 E
Goulburn Is. 96 11 40S 133 20 E
Goulia 84 10 1N 7 11W
Goulimine 82 28 56N 10 0W
Goulmina 82 31 41N 4 57W
Gouménissa 44 40 56N 22 37 E
Gounou-Gaya 81 9 38N 15 31 E
Goúra 45 37 56N 22 20 E
Gourara 82 29 0N 0 30 E
Gouraya 82 36 31N 1 56 E
Gourdon 20 44 44N 1 23 E
Gouré 85 14 0N 10 10 E
Gouri 81 19 36N 19 36 E
Gourits → 92 34 21S 21 52 E
Gourma Rharous 85 16 55N 1 50W
Gournay-en-Bray 19 49 29N 1 44 E
Gourock Ra. 99 36 0S 149 25 E
Goursi 84 12 42N 2 37W
Gouverneur 113 44 18N 75 30W
Gouzon 20 46 12N 2 14 E
Govan 109 51 20N 105 0W
Gove 97 12 25S 136 55 E
Governador Valadares 127 18 15S 41 57W
Gowan Ra. 98 25 0S 145 0 E
Gowanda 114 42 29N 78 58W
Gowd-e Zirreh 65 29 45N 62 0 E
Gower, The 13 51 35N 4 10W
Gowna, L. 15 53 52N 7 35W
Gowrie, Carse of 14 56 30N 3 10W
Goya 124 29 10S 59 10W
Goyllarisquisga 126 10 31S 76 24W
Goz Beïda 81 12 10N 21 20 E
Goz Regeb 87 16 3N 35 33 E
Gozdnica 28 51 28N 15 4 E
Gozo (Ghawdex) 36 36 0N 14 13 E
Graaff-Reinet 92 32 13S 24 32 E
Grabow 24 53 17N 11 31 E
Grabów 28 51 31N 18 7 E
Gračac 39 44 18N 15 57 E
Gračanica 42 44 43N 18 18 E
Graçay 19 47 10N 1 50 E
Grace 118 42 38N 111 46W
Graceville 116 45 36N 96 23W
Gracias a Dios, C. 121 15 0N 83 10W
Gradačac 42 44 52N 18 26 E
Gradeśka Planina 42 41 30N 22 15 E
Gradets 43 42 46N 26 30 E
Grado, Italy 39 45 40N 13 20 E
Grado, Spain 30 43 23N 6 4W
Gradule 99 28 32S 149 15 E
Grady 117 34 52N 103 15W
Graeca, Lacul 46 44 5N 26 10 E
Graénalon, L. 50 64 10N 17 20W
Grafenau 25 48 51N 13 24 E
Gräfenberg 25 49 39N 11 15 E
Grafton, Austral. 97 29 38S 152 58 E
Grafton, U.S.A. 116 48 30N 97 25W
Grafton, C. 97 16 51S 146 0 E
Gragnano 41 40 42N 14 30 E
Graham, Can. 106 49 20N 90 30W
Graham, N.C., U.S.A. 115 36 5N 79 22W
Graham, Tex., U.S.A. 117 33 7N 98 38W
Graham → 108 56 31N 122 17W
Graham Bell, Os. 58 80 5N 70 0 E
Graham I. 108 53 40N 132 30W
Graham Land 5 65 0S 64 0W
Graham Mt. 119 32 46N 109 58W
Grahamdale 109 51 23N 98 30W
Grahamstown 92 33 19S 26 31 E
Grahovo 42 42 40N 18 40 E
Graïba 83 34 30N 10 13 E
Graie, Alpi 38 45 30N 7 10 E
Grain Coast 84 4 20N 10 0W
Grajaú 127 5 50S 46 4W
Grajaú → 127 3 41S 44 48W
Grajewo 28 53 39N 22 30 E
Gral. Martin Miguel de Gäemes 124 24 50S 65 0W
Gramada 42 43 49N 22 39 E
Gramat 20 44 48N 1 43 E
Grammichele 41 37 12N 14 37 E
Grámmos, Óros 44 40 18N 20 47 E
Grampian □ 14 57 0N 3 0W
Grampian Mts. 14 56 50N 4 0W
Grampians, Mts. 99 37 0S 142 20 E
Gran Canaria 80 27 55N 15 35W
Gran Chaco 124 25 0S 61 0W
Gran Paradiso 38 45 33N 7 17 E
Gran Sasso d'Italia 39 42 25N 13 30 E
Granada, Nic. 121 11 58N 86 0W
Granada, Spain 33 37 10N 3 35W
Granada, U.S.A. 117 38 5N 102 20W
Granada □ 31 37 18N 3 0W
Granard 15 53 47N 7 30W
Granbury 117 32 28N 97 48W
Granby 106 45 25N 72 45W
Grand →, Mo., U.S.A. 116 39 23N 93 6W
Grand →, Mo., U.S.A. 116 39 23N 93 6W
Grand →, S.D., U.S.A. 116 45 40N 100 32W
Grand Bahama 121 26 40N 78 30W
Grand Bank 107 47 6N 55 48W
Grand Bassam 84 5 10N 3 49W
Grand Bérèby 84 4 38N 6 55W
Grand-Bourge 121 15 53N 61 19W
Grand Canyon 119 36 3N 112 9W
Grand Canyon National Park 119 36 15N 112 20W
Grand Cayman 121 19 20N 81 20W
Grand Cess 84 4 40N 8 12W
Grand-Combe, La 21 44 13N 4 2 E
Grand Coulee 118 47 48N 119 1W
Grand Coulee Dam 118 48 0N 118 50W
Grand Erg Occidental 82 30 20N 1 0 E
Grand Erg Oriental 83 30 0N 6 30 E
Grand Falls 107 48 56N 55 40W
Grand Forks, Can. 108 49 0N 118 30W
Grand Forks, U.S.A. 116 48 0N 97 3W
Grand-Fougeray 18 47 44N 1 43W
Grand Haven 114 43 3N 86 13W
Grand I. 106 46 30N 86 40W
Grand Island 116 40 59N 98 25W
Grand Isle 117 29 15N 89 58W
Grand Junction 119 39 0N 108 30W
Grand L., N.B., Can. 107 45 57N 66 7W
Grand L., Newf., Can. 107 53 40N 60 30W
Grand L., Newf., Can. 107 49 0N 57 30W
Grand L., U.S.A. 117 29 55N 92 45W
Grand Lac Victoria 106 47 35N 77 35W
Grand Lahou 84 5 10N 5 0W
Grand Lake 118 40 20N 105 54W
Grand-Lieu, Lac de 18 47 6N 1 40W
Grand-Luce, Le 18 47 52N 0 28 E
Grand Manan I. 107 44 45N 66 52W
Grand Marais, Can. 116 47 45N 90 25W
Grand Marais, U.S.A. 114 46 39N 85 59W
Grand Mère 106 46 36N 72 40W
Grand Popo 85 6 15N 1 57 E
Grand Portage 106 47 58N 89 41W
Grand-Pressigny, Le 18 46 55N 0 48 E
Grand Rapids, Can. 109 53 12N 99 19W
Grand Rapids, Mich., U.S.A. 114 42 57N 86 40W
Grand Rapids, Minn., U.S.A. 116 47 15N 93 29W
Grand St.-Bernard, Col. du 25 45 53N 7 11 E
Grand Teton 118 43 54N 111 50W
Grand Valley 118 39 30N 108 2W
Grand View 109 51 10N 100 42W
Grandas de Salime 30 43 13N 6 53W
Grande →, Jujuy, Argent. 124 24 20S 65 2W
Grande →, Mendoza, Argent. 124 36 52S 69 45W
Grande →, Boliv. 126 15 51S 64 39W
Grande →, Bahia, Brazil 127 11 30S 44 30W
Grande →, Minas Gerais, Brazil 127 20 6S 51 4W
Grande →, Spain 33 39 6N 0 48W
Grande →, U.S.A. 117 25 57N 97 9W
Grande, B. 128 50 30S 68 20W
Grande Baie 107 48 19N 70 52W
Grande Baleine → 106 55 20N 77 50W
Grande Cache 108 53 53N 119 8W
Grande, Coxilha 125 28 18S 51 30W
Grande de Santiago → 120 21 20N 105 50W
Grande-Entrée 107 47 30N 61 40W
Grande, La 118 45 15N 118 0W
Grande-Motte, La 21 43 23N 4 3 E
Grande Prairie 108 55 10N 118 50W
Grande-Rivière 107 48 26N 64 30W
Grande-Saulde → 19 47 22N 1 55 E
Grande-Vallée 107 49 14N 65 8W
Grandes-Bergeronnes 107 48 16N 69 35W
Grandfalls 117 31 21N 102 51W
Grandoe Mines 108 56 29N 129 54W
Grândola 31 38 12N 8 35W
Grandpré 19 49 20N 4 50 E
Grandview 118 46 13N 119 58W
Grandvilliers 19 49 40N 1 57 E
Graneros 124 34 5S 70 45W
Grange, La, Ga., U.S.A. 115 33 4N 85 0W
Grange, La, Ky., U.S.A. 114 38 20N 85 20W
Grange, La, Tex., U.S.A. 117 29 54N 96 52W
Grangemouth 14 56 1N 3 43W
Granger, U.S.A. 118 46 25N 120 5W
Granger, Wyo., U.S.A. 118 41 35N 109 58W
Grängesberg 48 60 6N 15 1 E
Grangeville 118 45 57N 116 4W
Granite City 116 38 45N 90 3W
Granite Falls 116 44 45N 95 35W
Granite Pk. 118 45 8N 109 52W
Granity 101 41 39S 171 51 E
Granja 127 3 7S 40 50W
Granja de Moreruela 30 41 48N 5 44W
Granja de Torrehermosa 31 38 19N 5 35W
Gränna 49 58 1N 14 28 E
Granollers 32 41 39N 2 18 E
Gransee 24 53 0N 13 10 E
Grant 116 40 53N 101 42W
Grant City 116 40 30N 94 25W
Grant, Mt. 118 38 34N 118 48W
Grant, Pt. 100 38 32S 145 6 E
Grant Range Mts. 119 38 30N 115 30W
Grantham 12 52 55N 0 39W
Grantown-on-Spey 14 57 19N 3 36W
Grants 119 35 14N 107 51W
Grants Pass 118 42 30N 123 22W
Grantsburg 116 45 46N 92 44W
Grantsville 118 40 35N 112 32W
Granville, France 18 48 50N 1 35W
Granville, N.D., U.S.A. 116 48 18N 100 48W
Granville, N.Y., U.S.A. 114 43 24N 73 16W
Granville L. 109 56 18N 100 30W
Grao de Gandía 33 39 0N 0 7W
Grapeland 117 31 30N 95 31W
Gras, L. de 104 64 30N 110 30W
Graskop 93 24 56S 30 49 E
Gräsö 48 60 28N 18 35 E
Grass → 109 56 3N 96 33W
Grass Range 118 47 0N 109 0W
Grass River Prov. Park 109 54 40N 100 50W
Grass Valley, Calif., U.S.A. 118 39 18N 121 0W
Grass Valley, Oreg., U.S.A. 118 45 22N 120 48W
Grassano 41 40 38N 16 17 E
Grasse 21 43 38N 6 56 E
Graubünden (Grisons) □ 25 46 45N 9 30 E
Graulhet 20 43 45N 1 58 E
Graus 32 42 11N 0 20 E
Grave, Pte. de 20 45 34N 1 4W
Gravelbourg 109 49 50N 106 35W
Gravelines 19 51 0N 2 10 E
's-Gravenhage 16 52 7N 4 17 E
Gravenhurst 112 44 52N 79 20W
Gravesend, Austral. 99 29 35S 150 20 E
Gravesend, U.K. 13 51 25N 0 22 E
Gravina di Púglia 41 40 48N 16 25 E
Gravois, Pointe-à- 121 16 15N 73 56W
Gravone → 21 41 58N 8 45 E
Gray 19 47 27N 5 35 E
Grayling 114 44 40N 84 42W
Grayling → 108 59 21N 125 0W
Grays Harbor 118 46 55N 124 8W
Grays L. 118 43 8N 111 30W
Grayson 109 50 45N 102 40W
Graz 26 47 4N 15 27 E
Grazalema 31 36 46N 5 23W
Grdelica 42 42 55N 22 3 E
Greasy L. 108 62 55N 122 12W
Great Abaco I. 121 26 25N 77 10W
Great Australia Basin 97 26 0S 140 0 E
Great Australian Bight 96 33 30S 130 0 E
Great Bahama Bank 121 23 15N 78 0W
Great Barrier I. 101 36 11S 175 25 E
Great Barrier Reef 97 18 0S 146 50 E
Great Barrington 113 42 11N 73 22W
Great Basin 118 40 0N 116 30W
Great Bear → 104 65 0N 124 0W
Great Bear L. 104 65 30N 120 0W
Great Bena 113 41 57N 75 45W
Great Bend 116 38 25N 98 55W
Great Blasket I. 15 52 5N 10 30W
Great Britain 8 54 0N 2 15W
Great Bushman Land 92 29 20S 19 20 E
Great Central 108 49 20N 125 10W
Great Divide, The 100 35 0S 149 17 E
Great Dividing Ra. 97 23 0S 146 0 E
Great Exuma I. 121 23 30N 75 50W
Great Falls, Can. 109 50 27N 96 1W
Great Falls, U.S.A. 118 47 27N 111 12W
Great Fish →, C. Prov., S. Afr. 92 31 30S 20 16 E
Great Fish →, C. Prov., S. Afr. 92 33 28S 27 5 E
Great Guana Cay 121 24 0N 76 20W
Great Harbour Deep 107 50 25N 56 32W
Great I. 109 58 53N 96 35W
Great Inagua I. 121 21 0N 73 20W
Great Indian Desert = Thar Desert 68 28 0N 72 0 E
Great Lake 97 41 50S 146 40 E
Great Orme's Head 12 53 20N 3 52W
Great Ouse → 12 52 47N 0 22 E
Great Palm I. 98 18 45S 146 40 E
Great Plains 102 47 0N 105 0W
Great Ruaha → 90 7 56S 37 52 E
Great Salt Lake 102 41 0N 112 30W
Great Salt Lake Desert 118 40 20N 113 50W
Great Salt Plains Res. 117 36 40N 98 15W
Great Sandy Desert 96 21 0S 124 0 E
Great Scarcies → 84 9 0N 13 0W
Great Slave L. 108 61 23N 115 38W
Great Smoky Mt. Nat. Park 115 35 39N 83 30W
Great Stour → 13 51 15N 1 20 E
Great Victoria Des. 96 29 30S 126 30 E
Great Wall 76 38 30N 109 30 E
Great Whernside 12 54 9N 1 59W
Great Winterhoek 92 33 07S 19 10 E
Great Yarmouth 12 52 40N 1 45 E
Greater Antilles 121 17 40N 74 0W
Greater London □ 13 51 30N 0 5W
Greater Manchester □ 12 53 30N 2 15W
Greater Sunda Is. 72 7 0S 112 0 E
Grebbestad 49 58 42N 11 15 E
Grebenka 54 50 9N 32 22 E
Greco, Mte. 40 41 48N 14 0 E
Gredos, Sierra de 30 40 20N 5 0W
Greece ■ 44 40 0N 23 0 E
Greeley, Colo., U.S.A. 116 40 30N 104 40W
Greeley, Nebr., U.S.A. 116 41 36N 98 32W
Green →, Ky., U.S.A. 114 37 54N 87 30W
Green →, Utah, U.S.A. 119 38 11N 109 53W
Green B. 114 45 0N 87 30W
Green Bay 114 44 30N 88 0W
Green C. 99 37 13S 150 1 E
Green Cove Springs 115 29 59N 81 40W
Green Is. 98 4 35S 154 10 E
Green Island 101 45 55S 170 26 E
Green River 119 38 59N 110 10W
Greenbush, Mich., U.S.A. 112 44 35N 83 19W
Greenbush, Minn., U.S.A. 116 48 46N 96 10W
Greencastle 114 39 40N 86 48W
Greene 113 42 20N 75 45W
Greenfield, Ind., U.S.A. 114 39 47N 85 51W
Greenfield, Iowa, U.S.A. 116 41 18N 94 28W
Greenfield, Mass., U.S.A. 114 42 38N 72 38W
Greenfield, Miss., U.S.A. 117 37 28N 93 50W
Greenfield Park 113 45 29N 73 29W
Greenland □ 4 66 0N 45 0W
Greenland Sea 4 73 0N 10 0W
Greenock 14 55 57N 4 46W
Greenore 15 54 2N 6 8W
Greenore Pt. 15 52 15N 6 20W
Greenport 113 41 5N 72 23W
Greensboro, Ga., U.S.A. 115 33 34N 83 12W
Greensboro, N.C., U.S.A. 115 36 7N 79 46W
Greensburg, Ind., U.S.A. 114 39 20N 85 30W
Greensburg, Kans., U.S.A. 117 37 38N 99 20W
Greensburg, Pa., U.S.A. 114 40 18N 79 31W
Greenville, Liberia 84 5 1N 9 6W
Greenville, Ala., U.S.A. 115 31 50N 86 37W
Greenville, Calif., U.S.A. 118 40 8N 121 0W
Greenville, Ill., U.S.A. 116 38 53N 89 22W
Greenville, Me., U.S.A. 107 45 30N 69 32W
Greenville, Mich., U.S.A. 114 43 12N 85 14W
Greenville, Miss., U.S.A. 117 33 25N 91 0W
Greenville, N.C., U.S.A. 115 35 37N 77 26W
Greenville, Ohio, U.S.A. 114 40 5N 84 38W
Greenville, Pa., U.S.A. 114 41 23N 80 22W
Greenville, S.C., U.S.A. 115 34 54N 82 24W
Greenville, Tenn., U.S.A. 115 36 13N 82 51W
Greenville, Tex., U.S.A. 117 33 5N 96 5W
Greenwater Lake Prov. Park 109 52 32N 103 30W
Greenwich, U.K. 13 51 28N 0 0
Greenwich, Conn., U.S.A. 113 41 1N 73 38W
Greenwich, N.Y., U.S.A. 113 43 2N 73 36W
Greenwich, Ohio, U.S.A. 112 41 1N 82 32W
Greenwood, Can. 108 49 10N 118 40W
Greenwood, Miss., U.S.A. 117 33 30N 90 4W
Greenwood, S.C., U.S.A. 115 34 13N 82 13W
Gregory 116 43 14N 99 20W
Gregory → 98 17 53S 139 17 E
Gregory Downs 98 18 35S 138 45 E
Gregory, L. 97 28 55S 139 0 E
Gregory Lake 96 20 10S 127 30 E
Gregory Ra. 97 19 30S 143 40 E
Greiffenberg 24 53 6N 13 57 E
Greifswald 24 54 6N 13 23 E
Greifswalder Bodden 24 54 12N 13 35 E
Greifswalder Oie 24 54 15N 13 55 E
Grein 26 48 14N 14 51 E
Greiner Wald 26 48 30N 15 0 E
Greiz 24 50 39N 12 12 E
Gremikha 52 67 50N 39 40 E
Grenå 49 56 25N 10 53 E
Grenada 117 33 45N 89 50W
Grenada ■ 121 12 10N 61 40W
Grenade 20 43 47N 1 17 E
Grenadines 121 12 40N 61 20W
Grenen 49 57 44N 10 40 E
Grenfell, Austral. 99 33 52S 148 8 E
Grenfell, Can. 109 50 30N 102 56W
Grenoble 21 45 12N 5 42 E
Grenora 116 48 38N 103 54W
Grenville, C. 97 12 0S 143 13 E
Grenville Chan. 108 53 40N 129 46W
Gréoux-les-Bains 21 43 45N 5 52 E
Gresham 118 45 30N 122 25W
Gresik 73 7 13S 112 38 E
Grëssoney St. Jean 38 45 49N 7 47 E
Gretna Green 14 55 0N 3 3W
Greven 24 52 7N 7 36 E
Grevená 44 40 4N 21 25 E
Grevená □ 44 40 2N 21 25 E
Grevenbroich 24 51 6N 6 32 E
Grevenmacher 16 49 41N 6 26 E
Grevesmühlen 24 53 51N 11 10 E
Grevie 49 56 22N 12 46 E
Grey → 101 42 27S 171 12 E
Grey, C. 97 13 0S 136 35 E
Grey Range 97 27 0S 143 30 E
Grey Res. 107 48 20N 56 30W
Greybull 118 44 30N 108 3W
Greytown, N.Z. 101 41 5S 175 29 E
Greytown, S. Afr. 93 29 1S 30 36 E
Gribanovskiy 55 51 28N 41 50 E
Gribbell I. 108 53 23N 129 0W
Gridley 118 39 27N 121 47W
Griekwastad 92 28 49S 23 15 E
Griffin 115 33 17N 84 14W
Griffith 97 34 18S 146 2 E
Grillby 48 59 38N 17 15 E
Grim, C. 97 40 45S 144 45 E
Grimari 88 5 43N 20 6 E
Grimaylov 54 49 20N 26 5 E
Grimma 24 51 14N 12 44 E
Grimmen 24 54 6N 13 2 E
Grimsby, Can. 112 43 12N 79 34W
Grimsby, U.K. 12 53 35N 0 5W
Grimsey 50 66 33N 18 0W
Grimshaw 108 56 10N 117 40W
Grimstad 47 58 22N 8 35 E
Grindelwald 25 46 38N 8 2 E
Grindsted 49 55 46N 8 55 E

Grindu 46 44 44N 26 50 E
Grinnell 116 41 45N 92 43W
Griñón 30 40 13N 3 51W
Grintavec 39 46 22N 14 32 E
Grip 47 63 16N 7 37 E
Griqualand East 93 30 30 S 29 0 E
Griqualand West 92 28 40 S 23 30 E
Grisolles 20 43 49N 1 19 E
Grisslehamn 48 60 5N 18 49 E
Griz Nez, C. 19 50 50N 1 35 E
Grmeč Planina 39 44 43N 16 16 E
Groais I. 107 50 55N 55 35W
Groblersdal 93 25 15 S 29 25 E
Grobming 26 47 27N 13 54 E
Grocka 42 44 40N 20 42 E
Gródek 28 53 6N 23 40 E
Grodkow 28 50 43N 17 21 E
Grodno 54 53 42N 23 52 E
Grodzisk Mázowiecki 28 52 7N 20 37 E
Grodzisk Wielkopolski 28 52 15N 16 22 E
Grodzyanka 54 53 31N 28 42 E
Groesbeck 117 31 32N 96 34W
Groix 18 47 38N 3 29W
Groix, I. de 18 47 38N 3 28W
Grójec 28 51 50N 20 58 E
Gronau, Niedersachsen, Ger. 24 52 5N 9 47 E
Gronau, Nordrhein-Westfalen, Ger. 24 52 13N 7 2 E
Grong 50 64 25N 12 8 E
Groningen 16 53 15N 6 35 E
Groningen □ 16 53 16N 6 40 E
Grönskåra 49 57 5N 15 43 E
Groom 117 35 12N 100 59W
Groot → 92 33 45 S 24 36 E
Groot Berg → 92 32 47 S 18 8 E
Groot-Brakrivier 92 34 2 S 22 18 E
Groot Karoo 92 32 35 S 23 0 E
Groote Eylandt 97 14 0 S 136 40 E
Grootfontein 92 19 31 S 18 6 E
Grootlaagte → 92 20 55 S 21 27 E
Gros C. 108 61 59N 113 32W
Grosa, P. 33 39 6N 1 36 E
Grósio 38 46 18N 10 17 E
Grosne → 21 46 42N 4 56 E
Gross Glockner 26 47 5N 12 40 E
Gross Ottersleben 24 52 5N 11 33 E
Grossenbrode 24 54 21N 11 4 E
Grossenhain 24 51 17N 13 32 E
Grosseto 38 42 45N 11 7 E
Grossgerungs 26 48 34N 14 57 E
Groswater B. 107 54 20N 57 40W
Groton, Conn., U.S.A. 113 41 22N 72 12W
Groton, S.D., U.S.A. 116 45 27N 98 6W
Grottáglie 41 40 32N 17 25 E
Grottaminarda 41 41 5N 15 4 E
Grottammare 39 42 59N 13 52 E
Grouard Mission 108 55 33N 116 9W
Grouin, Pointe du 18 48 43N 1 51W
Groundhog → 106 48 45N 82 58W
Grouse Creek 118 41 44N 113 57W
Grove City 112 41 10N 80 5W
Groveton, N.H., U.S.A. 114 44 34N 71 30W
Groveton, Tex., U.S.A. 117 31 5N 95 4W
Grožnjan 39 45 22N 13 43 E
Groznyy 57 43 20N 45 45 E
Grubišno Polje 42 45 44N 17 12 E
Grudovo 43 42 21N 27 10 E
Grudusk 28 53 3N 20 38 E
Grudziądz 28 53 30N 18 47 E
Gruissan 20 43 8N 3 7 E
Grumo Appula 41 41 2N 16 43 E
Grums 48 59 22N 13 5 E
Grünberg 24 50 37N 8 55 E
Grundy Center 116 42 22N 92 45W
Grungedal 47 59 44N 7 43 E
Gruver 117 36 19N 101 20W
Gruyères 25 46 35N 7 4 E
Gruža 42 43 54N 20 46 E
Gryazi 55 52 30N 39 58 E
Gryazovets 55 58 50N 40 10 E
Grybów 27 49 36N 20 55 E
Grycksbo 48 60 40N 15 29 E
Gryfice 28 53 55N 15 13 E
Gryfino 28 53 16N 14 29 E
Gryfow Sl. 28 51 2N 15 24 E
Grythyttan 48 59 41N 14 32 E
Grytviken 5 53 50 S 37 10W
Gstaad 25 46 28N 7 18 E
Guacanayabo, G. de 121 20 40N 77 20W
Guachípas → 124 25 40 S 65 30W
Guadajoz → 31 37 50N 4 51W
Guadalajara, Mexico 120 20 40N 103 20W
Guadalajara, Spain 32 40 37N 3 12W
Guadalajara □ 32 40 47N 3 0W
Guadalcanal, Solomon Is. 94 9 32 S 160 12 E
Guadalcanal, Spain 31 38 5N 5 52W
Guadalén → 31 38 5N 3 32W
Guadales 124 34 30 S 67 55W
Guadalete → 31 36 35N 6 13W
Guadalhorce → 31 36 41N 4 27W
Guadalimar → 33 38 5N 3 28W
Guadalmena → 33 38 19N 2 56W
Guadalmez → 31 38 46N 5 4W
Guadalope → 32 41 15N 0 3W
Guadalquivir → 31 36 47N 6 22W
Guadalupe, Spain 31 39 27N 5 17W
Guadalupe, U.S.A. 119 34 59N 120 33W
Guadalupe → 117 28 30N 96 53W
Guadalupe Bravos 120 31 20N 106 10W
Guadalupe I. 95 21 20N 118 50W
Guadalupe Pk. 119 31 50N 105 30W
Guadalupe, Sierra de 31 39 28N 5 30W
Guadarrama, Sierra de 30 41 0N 4 0W
Guadeloupe 121 16 20N 61 40W
Guadeloupe Passage 121 16 50N 62 15W
Guadiamar → 31 36 55N 6 24W
Guadiana → 31 37 14N 7 22W
Guadiana Menor → 33 37 56N 3 15W
Guadiaro → 31 36 17N 5 17W
Guadiato → 31 37 48N 5 5W
Guadiela → 32 40 22N 2 49W
Guadix 33 37 18N 3 11W
Guafo, Boca del 128 43 35 S 74 0W
Guaíra 125 24 5 S 54 10W
Guaira, La 126 10 36N 66 56W
Guaitecas, Islas 128 44 0 S 74 30W
Guajará-Mirim 126 10 50 S 65 20W
Guajira, Pen. de la 126 12 0N 72 0W
Gualdo Tadino 39 43 14N 12 46 E
Gualeguay 124 33 10 S 59 14W
Gualeguaychú 124 33 3 S 59 31W
Guam 94 13 27N 144 45 E
Guaminí 124 37 1 S 62 28W
Guamúchil 120 25 25N 108 3W
Guan Xian 75 31 2N 103 38 E
Guanabacoa 121 23 8N 82 18W
Guanacaste, Cordillera del 121 10 40N 85 4W
Guanaceví 120 25 40N 106 0W
Guanahani = San Salvador, I. 121 24 0N 74 40W
Guanajay 121 22 56N 82 42W
Guanajuato 120 21 0N 101 20W
Guanajuato □ 120 20 40N 101 20W
Guanare 126 8 42N 69 12W
Guandacol 124 29 30 S 68 40W
Guane 121 22 10N 84 7W
Guang'an 77 30 28N 106 35 E
Guangde 77 30 54N 119 25 E
Guangdong □ 75 23 0N 113 0 E
Guanghua 75 32 22N 111 38 E
Guangshun 77 26 8N 106 21 E
Guangxi Zhuangzu Zizhiqu □ 75 24 0N 109 0 E
Guangyuan 77 32 26N 105 51 E
Guangze 77 27 30N 117 12 E
Guangzhou 75 23 5N 113 10 E
Guanipa → 126 9 56N 62 26W
Guantánamo 121 20 10N 75 14W
Guantao 76 36 42N 115 25 E
Guanyun 77 34 20N 119 18 E
Guápiles 121 10 10N 83 46W
Guaporé → 126 11 55 S 65 4W
Guaqui 126 16 41 S 68 54W
Guara, Sierra de 32 42 19N 0 15W
Guarapari 125 20 40 S 40 30W
Guarapuava 125 25 20 S 51 30W
Guaratinguetá 125 22 49 S 45 9W
Guaratuba 125 25 53 S 48 38W
Guarda 30 40 32N 7 20W
Guarda □ 30 40 40N 7 20W
Guardafui, C. = Asir, Ras 63 11 55N 51 16 E
Guardamar del Segura 33 38 5N 0 39W
Guardavalle 41 38 31N 16 30 E
Guardia, La 30 41 56N 8 52W
Guardiagrele 39 42 11N 14 11 E
Guardo 30 42 47N 4 50W
Guareña 31 38 51N 6 6W
Guareña → 30 41 29N 5 23W
Guaria □ 124 25 45 S 56 30W
Guarujá 125 24 2 S 46 25W
Guarus 125 21 44 S 41 20W
Guasdualito 126 7 15N 70 44W
Guasipati 126 7 28N 61 54W
Guastalla 38 44 55N 10 40 E
Guatemala 120 14 40N 90 22W
Guatemala ■ 120 15 40N 90 30W
Guatire 126 10 28N 66 32W
Guaviare → 126 4 3N 67 44W
Guaxupé 125 21 10 S 47 5W
Guayama 121 17 59N 66 7W
Guayaquil 126 2 15 S 79 52W
Guayaquil, G. de 126 3 10 S 81 0W
Guaymas 120 27 59N 110 54W
Guazhou 77 32 17N 119 21 E
Guba 91 10 38 S 26 27 E
Gûbâl 86 27 30N 34 0 E
Gúbbio 39 43 20N 12 34 E
Gubin 28 51 57N 14 43 E
Gubio 85 12 30N 12 42 E
Gubkin 55 51 17N 37 32 E
Guča 42 43 46N 20 15 E
Guchil 71 5 35N 102 10 E
Gudalur 70 11 30N 76 29 E
Gudata 57 43 7N 40 10 E
Gudenå 49 56 27N 9 40 E
Gudermes 57 43 24N 46 5 E
Gudhjem 49 55 12N 14 58 E
Gudiña, La 30 42 4N 7 8W
Gudivada 70 16 30N 81 3 E
Gudiyatam 70 12 57N 78 55 E
Gudur 70 14 12N 79 55 E
Guebwiller 19 47 55N 7 12 E
Guecho 32 43 21N 2 59W
Guékédou 84 8 40N 10 5W
Guelma 83 36 25N 7 29 E
Guelph 106 43 35N 80 20W
Guelt es Stel 82 35 12N 3 1 E
Guelttara 82 29 23N 2 10W
Guemar 83 33 30N 6 49 E
Guéméné-Penfao 18 47 38N 1 50W
Guéméné-sur-Scorff 18 48 4N 3 13W
Guéné 85 11 44N 3 16 E
Guer 18 47 54N 2 8W
Güera, La 80 20 51N 17 0W
Guérande 18 47 20N 2 26W
Guerche, La 18 47 57N 1 16W
Guerche-sur-l'Aubois, La 19 46 58N 2 56 E
Guercif 82 34 14N 3 21W
Guéréda 81 14 31N 22 5 E
Guéret 20 46 11N 1 51 E
Guérigny 19 47 6N 3 10 E
Guernica 32 43 19N 2 40W
Guernsey, Chan. Is. 18 49 30N 2 35W
Guernsey, U.S.A. 116 42 19N 104 45W
Guerrara, Oasis, Alg. 83 32 51N 4 22 E
Guerrara, Saoura, Alg. 82 28 5N 0 8W
Guerrero □ 120 17 30N 100 0W
Guerzim 82 29 39N 1 40W
Guest I. 5 76 18 S 148 0W
Gueugnon 21 46 36N 4 4 E
Gueydan 117 30 3N 92 30W
Guglionesi 41 41 55N 14 54 E
Gui Jiang → 77 23 30N 111 15 E
Gui Xian 77 23 8N 109 35 E
Guia Lopes da Laguna 125 21 26 S 56 7W
Guichi 77 30 39N 117 27 E
Guider 85 9 56N 13 57 E
Guidimouni 85 13 42N 9 31 E
Guidong 77 26 7N 113 57 E
Guiglo 84 6 45N 7 30W
Guijo de Coria 30 40 6N 6 28W
Guildford 13 51 14N 0 34W
Guilford 107 45 12N 69 25W
Guilin 75 25 18N 110 15 E
Guillaumes 21 44 5N 6 52 E
Guillestre 21 44 39N 6 40 E
Guilvinec 18 47 48N 4 17W
Guimarães 127 2 9 S 44 42W
Guimarãis 30 41 28N 8 24W
Guimaras 73 10 35N 122 37 E
Guinea ■ 84 10 20N 10 0W
Guinea-Bissau ■ 84 12 0N 15 0W
Guinea, Gulf of 85 3 0N 2 30 E
Güines 121 22 50N 82 0W
Guingamp 18 48 34N 3 10W
Guipavas 18 48 26N 4 29W
Guiping 75 23 21N 110 2 E
Guipúzcoa □ 32 43 12N 2 15W
Guir, O. → 82 31 29N 2 17W
Güiria 126 10 32N 62 18W
Guiscard 19 49 40N 3 0 E
Guise 19 49 52N 3 35 E
Guitiriz 30 43 11N 7 50W
Guiuan 73 11 5N 125 55 E
Guixi 77 28 16N 117 15 E
Guiyang, Guizhou, China 75 26 32N 106 40 E
Guiyang, Hunan, China 77 25 46N 112 42 E
Guizhou □ 75 27 0N 107 0 E
Gujan-Mestras 20 44 38N 1 4W
Gujarat □ 68 23 20N 71 0 E
Gujranwala 68 32 10N 74 12 E
Gujrat 68 32 40N 74 2 E
Gukovo 57 48 1N 39 58 E
Gulargambone 100 31 20 S 148 30 E
Gulbarga 70 17 20N 76 50 E
Gulbene 54 57 8N 26 52 E
Guledgud 70 16 3N 75 48 E
Gulf Basin 96 15 20 S 129 0 E
Gulfport 117 30 21N 89 3W
Gulgong 99 32 20 S 149 49 E
Gulistan 68 30 30N 66 35 E
Gull Lake 109 50 10N 108 29W
Gullringen 49 57 48N 15 44 E
Gulma 85 12 40N 4 23 E
Gülpinar 44 39 32N 26 10 E
Gulshad 58 46 45N 74 25 E
Gulsvik 47 60 24N 9 38 E
Gulu 90 2 48N 32 17 E
Gulwe 90 6 30 S 36 25 E
Gulyaypole 56 47 45N 36 21 E
Gum Lake 99 32 42 S 143 9 E
Gumal → 68 31 40N 71 50 E
Gumbaz 68 30 2N 69 0 E
Gumel 85 12 39N 9 22 E
Gumiel de Hizán 32 41 46N 3 41W
Gumlu 98 19 53 S 147 41 E
Gumma □ 74 36 30N 138 20 E
Gummersbach 24 51 2N 7 32 E
Gummi 85 12 4N 5 9 E
Gümüsane 64 40 30N 39 30 E
Gümüşhaciköy 56 40 50N 35 18 E
Gumzai 73 5 28 S 134 42 E
Guna 68 24 40N 77 19 E
Guna Mt. 87 11 50N 37 40 E
Gundagai 99 35 3 S 148 6 E
Gundelfingen 25 48 33N 10 22 E
Gundih 73 7 10 S 110 56 E
Gundlakamma → 70 15 30N 80 15 E
Gungu 88 5 43 S 19 20 E
Gunisao → 109 53 56N 97 53W
Gunisao L. 109 53 33N 96 15W
Gunnedah 97 30 59 S 150 15 E
Gunning 100 34 47 S 149 14 E
Gunnison, Colo., U.S.A. 119 38 32N 106 56W
Gunnison, Utah, U.S.A. 118 39 11N 111 48W
Gunnison → 119 39 3N 108 30W
Guntakal 70 15 11N 77 27 E
Guntersville 115 34 18N 86 16W
Guntur 70 16 23N 80 30 E
Gunung-Sitoli 72 1 15N 97 30 E
Gunungapi 73 6 45 S 126 30 E
Gunupur 70 19 5N 83 50 E
Günz → 25 48 27N 10 16 E
Gunza 88 10 50 S 13 50 E
Günzburg 25 48 27N 10 16 E
Gunzenhausen 25 49 6N 10 45 E
Guo He → 77 32 59N 117 10 E
Guoyang 77 33 32N 116 12 E
Gupis 69 36 15N 73 20 E
Gura 68 25 12N 71 39 E
Gura Humorului 46 47 35N 25 53 E
Gura-Teghii 46 45 30N 26 25 E
Gurag 87 8 20N 38 20 E
Gürchañ 64 34 55N 49 25 E
Gurdaspur 68 32 5N 75 31 E
Gurdon 117 33 55N 93 10W
Gurdzhaani 57 41 43N 45 52 E
Gurgaon 68 28 27N 77 1 E
Gurghiu, Munţii 46 46 41N 25 15 E
Gurk → 26 46 35N 14 31 E
Gurkha 69 28 5N 84 40 E
Gurley 99 29 45 S 149 48 E
Gurun 71 5 49N 100 27 E
Gurupá 127 1 25 S 51 35W
Gurupá, I. Grande de 127 1 25 S 51 45W
Gurupi → 127 1 13 S 46 6W
Guryev 57 47 5N 52 0 E
Gus-Khrustalnyy 55 55 42N 40 44 E
Gusau 85 12 12N 6 40 E
Gusev 54 54 35N 22 10 E
Gushan 76 39 50N 123 35 E
Gushi 77 32 11N 115 41 E
Gushiago 85 9 55N 0 15W
Gusinje 42 42 35N 19 50 E
Gúspini 40 39 32N 8 38 E
Gusselby 48 59 38N 15 14 E
Güssing 27 47 3N 16 20 E
Gustanj 39 46 36N 14 49 E
Gustine 119 37 14N 121 0 E
Güstrow 24 53 47N 12 12 E
Gusum 49 58 16N 16 30 E
Guta = Kalárovo 27 47 54N 18 0 E
Gütersloh 24 51 54N 8 25 E
Guthalongra 98 19 52 S 147 50 E
Guthega Dam 100 36 20 S 148 27 E
Guthrie 117 35 55N 97 30W
Guttenberg 116 42 46N 91 10W
Guyana ■ 126 5 0N 59 0W
Guyang 76 41 0N 110 5 E
Guyenne 20 44 30N 0 40 E
Guymon 117 36 45N 101 30W
Guyra 99 30 15 S 151 40 E
Guyuan 76 36 0N 106 20 E
Guzhen 77 33 22N 117 18 E
Guzmán, Laguna de 120 31 25N 107 25W
Gwa 67 17 36N 94 34 E
Gwaai 91 19 15 S 27 45 E
Gwabegar 99 30 31 S 149 0 E
Gwadabawa 85 13 28N 5 15 E
Gwādar 66 25 10N 62 18 E
Gwagwada 85 10 15N 7 15 E
Gwalior 68 26 12N 78 10 E
Gwanda 91 20 55 S 29 0 E
Gwandu 85 12 30N 4 41 E
Gwane 90 4 45N 25 48 E
Gwaram 85 10 15N 10 25 E
Gwarzo 85 12 20N 8 55 E
Gwda → 28 53 3N 16 44 E
Gweebarra B. 15 54 52N 8 21W
Gweedore 15 55 4N 8 15W
Gwelo 91 19 28 S 29 45 E
Gwent □ 13 51 45N 2 55W
Gwi 85 9 0N 7 10 E
Gwinn 114 46 15N 87 29W
Gwio Kura 85 12 40N 11 2 E
Gwol 84 10 58N 1 59W
Gwoza 85 11 5N 13 40 E
Gwydir → 97 29 27 S 149 48 E
Gwynedd □ 12 53 0N 4 0W
Gyaring Hu 75 34 50N 97 40 E
Gydanskiy P-ov. 58 70 0N 78 0 E
Gyland 47 58 24N 6 45 E
Gympie 97 26 11 S 152 38 E
Gyoda 74 36 10N 139 30 E
Gyoma 27 46 56N 20 50 E
Gyöngyös 27 47 48N 20 0 E
Györ 27 47 41N 17 40 E
Györ-Sopron □ 27 47 40N 17 20 E
Gypsum Pt. 108 61 53N 114 35W
Gypsumville 109 51 45N 98 40W
Gyttorp 48 59 31N 14 58 E
Gyula 27 46 38N 21 17 E
Gzhatsk = Gagarin 54 55 30N 35 0 E

H

Ha 'Arava 62 30 50N 35 20 E
Haag 25 48 11N 12 12 E
Haapamäki 50 62 18N 24 28 E
Haapsalu 54 58 56N 23 30 E
Haarlem 16 52 23N 4 39 E
Haast → 101 43 50 S 169 2 E
Hab Nadi Chauki 66 25 0N 66 50 E
Habana, La 121 23 8N 82 22W
Habaswein 90 1 2N 39 30 E
Habay 108 58 50N 118 44W
Habiganj 69 24 24N 91 30 E
Hablingbo 49 57 12N 18 16 E
Habo 49 57 55N 14 6 E
Hachenburg 24 50 40N 7 49 E
Hachijō-Jima 74 33 5N 139 45 E
Hachinohe 74 40 30N 141 29 E
Hachiōji 74 35 40N 139 20 E
Hadali 68 32 16N 72 11 E
Hadarba, Ras 86 22 4N 36 51 E
Hadd, Ras al 65 22 35N 59 50 E
Haddington 14 55 57N 2 48W
Hadejia 85 12 30N 10 5 E
Hadejia → 85 12 50N 10 51 E
Haden 99 27 13 S 151 54 E
Ḥadera 62 32 27N 34 55 E
Ḥadera, N. → 62 32 28N 34 52 E
Haderslev 49 55 15N 9 30 E
Hadhra 86 20 10N 41 5 E
Hadhramaut = Ḥaḍramawt 63 15 30N 49 30 E
Hadibu 63 12 35N 54 2 E
Hadjeb El Aïoun 83 35 21N 9 32 E
Ḥaḍramawt 63 15 30N 49 30 E
Hadrians Wall 12 55 0N 2 30W
Hadsten 49 56 19N 10 3 E
Hadsund 49 56 44N 10 8 E
Haeju 76 38 3N 125 45 E
Haerhpin = Harbin 76 45 48N 126 40 E
Ḥafar al Bāṭin 64 28 25N 46 0 E
Hafizabad 68 32 5N 73 40 E
Haflong 67 25 10N 93 5 E
Hafnarfjörður 50 64 4N 21 57W
Haft-Gel 64 31 30N 49 32 E
Hafun, Ras 63 10 29N 51 30 E
Hagalil 62 32 53N 35 18 E
Hagari → 70 15 40N 77 0 E
Hagen 24 51 21N 7 29 E
Hagenow 24 53 25N 11 10 E
Hagerman 117 33 5N 104 22W
Hagerstown 114 39 39N 77 46W
Hagetmau 20 43 39N 0 37W
Hagfors 48 60 3N 13 45 E
Häggenås 48 63 24N 14 55 E
Hagi, Iceland 50 65 28N 23 25W
Hagi, Japan 74 34 30N 131 22 E
Hagolan 62 33 0N 35 45 E
Hags Hd. 15 52 57N 9 30W
Hague, C. de la 18 49 44N 1 56W
Hague, The = 's-Gravenhage 16 52 7N 4 17 E
Haguenau 19 48 49N 7 47 E
Hai □ 90 3 10 S 37 10 E
Haicheng 76 40 50N 122 45 E
Haifeng 77 22 58N 115 10 E

Haiger 24 50 44N 8 12 E
Haikang 77 20 52N 110 8 E
Haikou 75 20 1N 110 16 E
Ḩā'il 64 27 28N 41 45 E
Hailar 75 49 10N 119 38 E
Hailar He → 76 49 30N 117 50 E
Hailey 118 43 30N 114 15W
Haileybury 106 47 30N 79 38W
Hailin 76 44 37N 129 30 E
Hailing Dao 77 21 35N 111 47 E
Hailong 76 42 32N 125 40 E
Hailun 75 47 28N 126 50 E
Hailuoto 50 65 3N 24 45 E
Haimen 77 31 52N 121 10 E
Hainan 77 19 0N 110 0 E
Hainan Dao 75 19 0N 109 30 E
Hainaut □ 16 50 30N 4 0 E
Hainburg 27 48 9N 16 56 E
Haines 118 44 51N 117 59W
Haines City 115 28 6N 81 35W
Haines Junction 108 60 45N 137 30W
Hainfeld 26 48 3N 15 48 E
Haining 77 30 28N 120 40 E
Haiphong 71 20 47N 106 41 E
Haiti ■ 121 19 0N 72 30W
Haiya Junction 86 18 20N 36 21 E
Haiyan 77 30 28N 120 58 E
Haiyang 76 36 47N 121 9 E
Haiyuan 76 36 35N 105 52 E
Haja 73 3 19 S 129 37 E
Hajar Bangar 81 10 40N 22 45 E
Hajar, Jabal 64 26 5N 39 10 E
Hajdú-Bihar □ 27 47 30N 21 30 E
Hajdúböszörmény 27 47 40N 21 30 E
Hajdúdurog 27 47 48N 21 30 E
Hajdúhadház 27 47 40N 21 40 E
Hajdúnánás 27 47 50N 21 26 E
Hajdúsámson 27 47 37N 21 42 E
Hajdúszobaszló 27 47 27N 21 22 E
Hajipur 69 25 45N 85 13 E
Hajówka 28 52 47N 23 35 E
Hajr 65 24 0N 56 34 E
Hakansson, Mts. 91 8 40 S 25 45 E
Håkantorp 49 58 18N 12 55 E
Hakken-Zan 74 34 10N 135 54 E
Hakodate 74 41 45N 140 44 E
Ḩalab = Aleppo 64 36 10N 37 15 E
Ḩalabjah 64 35 10N 45 58 E
Halaib 86 22 12N 36 30 E
Halbe 86 19 40N 42 15 E
Halberstadt 24 51 53N 11 2 E
Halcombe 101 40 8 S 175 30 E
Halcyon, Mt. 73 13 0N 121 30 E
Halden 47 59 9N 11 23 E
Haldensleben 24 52 17N 11 30 E
Haldia 67 22 5N 88 3 E
Haldwani-cum-Kathgodam 69 29 31N 79 30 E
Haleakala Crater 110 20 43N 156 12W
Haleyville 115 34 15N 87 40W
Half Assini 84 5 1N 2 50W
Halfway 118 44 56N 117 8W
Halfway → 108 56 12N 121 32W
Ḩalḩul 62 31 35N 35 7 E
Hali, Si. Arab. 86 18 40N 41 15 E
Hali, Yemen 63 18 30N 41 30 E
Haliburton 106 45 3N 78 30W
Halicarnassus 45 37 3N 27 30 E
Halifax, Austral. 98 18 32 S 146 22 E
Halifax, Can. 107 44 38N 63 35W
Halifax, U.K. 12 53 43N 1 51W
Halifax B. 97 18 50 S 147 0 E
Halifax I. 92 26 38 S 15 4 E
Halīl Rūd → 65 27 40N 58 30 E
Hall 26 47 17N 11 30 E
Hall Beach 105 68 46N 81 12W
Hallabro 49 56 22N 15 5 E
Hallands län □ 49 56 50N 12 50 E
Hallands Väderö 49 56 27N 12 34 E
Hallandsås 49 56 22N 13 0 E
Halle, Belg. 16 50 44N 4 13 E
Halle, Halle, Ger. 24 51 29N 12 0 E
Halle, Nordrhein-Westfalen, Ger. 24 52 4N 8 20 E
Halle □ 24 51 28N 11 58 E
Hällefors 48 59 47N 14 31 E
Hallefors 49 59 46N 14 30 E
Hallein 26 47 40N 13 5 E
Hällekis 49 58 38N 13 27 E
Hallett 99 33 25 S 138 55 E
Hallettsville 117 29 28N 96 57W
Hällevadsholm 49 58 35N 11 33 E
Halley Bay 5 75 31 S 26 36W
Hallia → 70 16 55N 79 20 E
Halliday 116 47 20N 102 25W
Halliday L. 109 61 21N 108 56W
Hallingskeid 47 60 40N 7 17 E
Hällnäs 50 64 19N 19 36 E
Hallock 109 48 47N 97 0W
Halls Creek 96 18 16 S 127 38 E
Hallsberg 48 59 5N 15 7 E
Hallstahammar 48 59 38N 16 15 E
Hallstatt 26 47 33N 13 38 E
Hallstavik 48 60 5N 18 37 E
Hallstead 113 41 56N 75 45W
Halmahera 73 0 40N 128 0 E
Halmeu 46 47 57N 23 2 E
Halmstad 49 56 41N 12 52 E
Halq el Oued 83 36 53N 10 18 E
Hals 49 56 59N 10 18 E
Halsa 47 63 3N 8 14 E
Halsafjorden 47 63 5N 8 10 E
Hälsingborg = Helsingborg 49 56 3N 12 42 E
Halstad 116 47 21N 96 50W
Haltdalen 47 62 56N 11 8 E
Haltern 24 51 44N 7 10 E
Halul 65 25 40N 52 40 E
Ham 19 49 45N 3 4 E
Hamab 92 28 7 S 19 16 E
Hamad 87 15 20N 33 32 E
Hamada 74 34 56N 132 4 E
Hamadān 64 34 52N 48 32 E
Hamadān □ 64 35 0N 49 0 E
Hamadia 82 35 28N 1 57 E
Hamāh 64 35 5N 36 40 E
Hamamatsu 74 34 45N 137 45 E
Hamar 47 60 48N 11 7 E
Hamarøy 50 68 5N 15 38 E
Hamâta, Gebel 86 24 17N 35 0 E
Hamber Prov. Park 108 52 20N 118 0W
Hamburg, Ger. 24 53 32N 9 59 E
Hamburg, Ark., U.S.A. 117 33 15N 91 47W
Hamburg, Iowa, U.S.A. 116 40 37N 95 38W
Hamburg, N.Y., U.S.A. 112 42 44N 78 50W
Hamburg, Pa., U.S.A. 113 40 33N 76 0W
Hamburg □ 24 53 30N 10 0 E
Hamden 113 41 21N 72 56W
Hamdh, W. → 86 24 55N 36 20 E
Hämeen lääni □ 51 61 24N 24 10 E
Hämeenlinna 50 61 0N 24 28 E
Hamélé 84 10 56N 2 45W
Hameln 24 52 7N 9 24 E
Hamer Koke 87 5 15N 36 45 E
Hamersley Ra. 96 22 0 S 117 45 E
Hamhung 76 39 54N 127 30 E
Hami 75 42 55N 93 25 E
Hamilton, Austral. 97 37 45 S 142 2 E
Hamilton, Berm. 121 32 15N 64 45W
Hamilton, Can. 106 43 15N 79 50W
Hamilton, N.Z. 101 37 47 S 175 19 E
Hamilton, U.K. 14 55 47N 4 2W
Hamilton, Mo., U.S.A. 116 39 45N 93 59W
Hamilton, Mont., U.S.A. 118 46 20N 114 6W
Hamilton, N.Y., U.S.A. 114 42 49N 75 31W
Hamilton, Ohio, U.S.A. 114 39 20N 84 35W
Hamilton, Tex., U.S.A. 117 31 40N 98 5W
Hamilton → 98 23 30 S 139 47 E
Hamilton Hotel 98 22 45 S 140 40 E
Hamilton Inlet 107 54 0N 57 30W
Hamiota 109 50 11N 100 38W
Hamlet 115 34 56N 79 40W
Hamley Bridge 99 34 17 S 138 35 E
Hamlin, N.Y., U.S.A. 112 43 17N 77 55W
Hamlin, Tex., U.S.A. 117 32 58N 100 8W
Hamm 24 51 40N 7 49 E
Hammam Bouhadjar 82 35 23N 0 58W
Hammamet 83 36 24N 10 38 E
Hammamet, G. de 83 36 10N 10 48 E
Hammarstrand 48 63 7N 16 20 E
Hammel 49 56 16N 9 52 E
Hammelburg 25 50 7N 9 54 E
Hammeren 49 55 18N 14 47 E
Hammerfest 50 70 39N 23 41 E
Hammond, Ind., U.S.A. 114 41 40N 87 30W
Hammond, La., U.S.A. 117 30 32N 90 30W
Hammonton 114 39 40N 74 47W
Hamneda 49 56 41N 13 51 E
Hamoyet, Jebel 86 17 33N 38 2 E
Hampden 101 45 18 S 170 50 E
Hampshire □ 13 51 3N 1 20W
Hampshire Downs 13 51 10N 1 10W
Hampton, Ark., U.S.A. 117 33 35N 92 29W
Hampton, Iowa, U.S.A. 116 42 42N 93 12W
Hampton, N.H., U.S.A. 113 42 56N 70 48W
Hampton, S.C., U.S.A. 115 32 52N 81 2W
Hampton, Va., U.S.A. 114 37 4N 76 18W
Hampton Harbour 96 20 30 S 116 30 E
Hampton Tableland 96 32 0 S 127 0 E
Hamrat esh Sheykh 87 14 38N 27 55 E
Han Jiang → 77 23 25N 116 40 E
Han Shui → 77 30 35N 114 18 E
Hana 110 20 45N 155 59W
Hanak 86 25 32N 37 0 E
Hanang 90 4 30 S 35 25 E
Hanau 25 50 8N 8 56 E
Hancheng 76 35 31N 110 25 E
Hancock, Mich., U.S.A. 116 47 10N 88 40W
Hancock, Minn., U.S.A. 116 45 26N 95 46W
Hancock, Pa., U.S.A. 113 41 57N 75 19W
Handa, Japan 74 34 53N 137 0 E
Handa, Somalia 63 10 37N 51 2 E
Handan 76 36 35N 114 28 E
Handen 48 59 12N 18 12 E
Handeni 90 5 25 S 38 2 E
Handeni □ 90 5 30 S 38 0 E
Handlová 27 48 45N 18 35 E
Handub 86 19 15N 37 16 E
Hanegev 62 30 50N 35 0 E
Haney 108 49 12N 122 40W
Hanford 119 36 23N 119 39W
Hangang → 76 37 50N 126 30 E
Hangayn Nuruu 75 47 30N 100 0 E
Hangchou = Hangzhou 75 30 18N 120 11 E
Hanggin Houqi 76 40 58N 107 4 E
Hangklip, K. 92 34 26 S 18 48 E
Hangö 51 59 50N 22 57 E
Hangu 76 39 18N 117 53 E
Hangzhou 75 30 18N 120 11 E
Hangzhou Wan 75 30 15N 120 45 E
Ḩanīsh J. 63 13 45N 42 46 E
Haniska 27 48 37N 21 15 E
Hanita 62 33 5N 35 10 E
Hankinson 116 46 9N 96 58W
Hanko 51 59 59N 22 57 E
Hankou 77 30 35N 114 30 E
Hanksville 119 38 19N 110 45W
Hanmer 101 42 32 S 172 50 E
Hann, Mt. 96 16 0 S 126 0 E
Hanna 108 51 40N 111 54W
Hannaford 116 47 23N 98 11W
Hannah 116 48 58N 98 42W
Hannah B. 106 51 40N 80 0W
Hannibal 116 39 42N 91 22W
Hannik 86 18 12N 32 20 E
Hannover 24 52 23N 9 43 E
Hanö 49 56 2N 14 50 E
Hanöbukten 49 55 35N 14 30 E
Hanoi 71 21 5N 105 55 E
Hanover, Can. 112 44 9N 81 2W
Hanover, S. Afr. 92 31 4 S 24 29 E
Hanover, N.H., U.S.A. 113 43 43N 72 17W
Hanover, Ohio, U.S.A. 112 40 5N 82 17W
Hanover, Pa., U.S.A. 114 39 46N 76 59W
Hanover = Hannover 24 52 23N 9 43 E
Hanover, I. 128 51 0 S 74 50W
Hansi 68 29 10N 75 57 E
Hansjö 48 61 10N 14 40 E
Hanson Range 96 27 0 S 136 30 E
Hanwood 100 34 22 S 146 2 E
Hanyang 77 30 35N 114 2 E
Hanyin 77 32 54N 108 28 E
Hanzhong 75 33 10N 107 1 E
Hanzhuang 77 34 33N 117 23 E
Haparanda 50 65 52N 24 8 E
Happy 117 34 47N 101 50W
Happy Camp 118 41 52N 123 22W
Happy Valley 107 53 15N 60 20W
Hapur 68 28 45N 77 45 E
Ḩaql 86 29 10N 35 0 E
Har 73 5 16 S 133 14 E
Har Hu 75 38 20N 97 38 E
Har Us Nuur 75 48 0N 92 0 E
Har Yehuda 62 31 35N 34 57 E
Ḩaraḑ 64 24 22N 49 0 E
Haraisan Plateau 64 23 0N 47 40 E
Haramsøya 47 62 39N 6 12 E
Harardera 63 4 33N 47 38 E
Harat 87 16 5N 39 26 E
Harazé, Chad 81 14 20N 19 12 E
Harazé, Chad 81 9 57N 20 48 E
Harbin 76 45 48N 126 40 E
Harboør 49 56 38N 8 10 E
Harbor Beach 114 43 50N 82 38W
Harbor Springs 114 45 28N 85 0W
Harbour Breton 107 47 29N 55 50W
Harbour Grace 107 47 40N 53 22W
Harburg 24 53 27N 9 58 E
Hårby 49 55 13N 10 7 E
Harcourt 98 24 17 S 149 55 E
Harda 68 22 27N 77 5 E
Hardangerfjorden 47 60 15N 6 0 E
Hardangerjøkulen 47 60 30N 7 0 E
Hardangervidda 47 60 20N 7 20 E
Hardap Dam 92 24 32 S 17 50 E
Hardenberg 16 52 34N 6 37 E
Harderwijk 16 52 21N 5 38 E
Hardin 118 45 44N 107 35W
Harding 93 30 35 S 29 55 E
Hardisty 108 52 40N 111 18W
Hardman 118 45 12N 119 40W
Hardoi 69 27 26N 80 6 E
Hardwar 68 29 58N 78 9 E
Hardwick 113 44 30N 72 20W
Hardy 117 36 20N 91 30W
Hardy, Pen. 128 55 30 S 68 20W
Hare B. 107 51 15N 55 45W
Hare Gilboa 62 32 31N 35 25 E
Hare Meron 62 32 59N 35 24 E
Haren 24 52 47N 7 18 E
Harer 87 9 20N 42 8 E
Harer □ 87 7 12N 42 0 E
Hareto 87 9 23N 37 6 E
Harfleur 18 49 30N 0 10 E
Hargeisa 63 9 30N 44 2 E
Harghita □ 46 46 30N 25 30 E
Harghita, Mţii 46 46 25N 25 35 E
Hargshamn 48 60 12N 18 30 E
Hari → 72 1 16 S 104 5 E
Haricha, Hamada el 82 22 40N 3 15W
Harihar 70 14 32N 75 44 E
Haringhata → 69 22 0N 89 58 E
Haripad 70 9 14N 76 28 E
Harīrūd 65 35 0N 61 0 E
Harīrūd → 65 34 20N 62 30 E
Harkat 86 20 25N 39 40 E
Harlan, Iowa, U.S.A. 116 41 37N 95 20W
Harlan, Tenn., U.S.A. 115 36 50N 83 20W
Harlech 12 52 52N 4 7W
Harlem 118 48 29N 108 47W
Harlingen, Neth. 16 53 11N 5 25 E
Harlingen, U.S.A. 117 26 20N 97 50W
Harlowton 118 46 30N 109 54W
Harmånger 48 61 55N 17 20 E
Harmil 87 16 30N 40 10 E
Harney Basin 118 43 30N 119 0W
Harney L. 118 43 0N 119 0W
Harney Pk. 116 43 52N 103 33W
Härnön 48 62 36N 18 0 E
Härnösand 48 62 38N 18 0 E
Haro 32 42 35N 2 55W
Haro, C. 120 27 50N 110 55W
Harp L. 107 55 5N 61 50W
Harpanahalli 70 14 47N 76 2 E
Harpe, La 116 40 30N 91 0W
Harper 84 4 25N 7 43W
Harplinge 49 56 45N 12 45 E
Harrand 68 29 28N 70 3 E
Ḩarrat al Kishb 64 22 30N 40 15 E
Harrat al 'Uwairidh 64 26 50N 38 0 E
Harrat Khaibar 86 25 45N 40 0 E
Harrat Nawāṣīf 86 21 30N 42 0 E
Harriman 115 36 0N 84 35W
Harrington Harbour 107 50 31N 59 30W
Harris 14 57 50N 6 55W
Harris L. 96 31 10 S 135 10 E
Harris, Sd. of 14 57 44N 7 6W
Harrisburg, Ill., U.S.A. 117 37 42N 88 30W
Harrisburg, Nebr., U.S.A. 116 41 36N 103 46W
Harrisburg, Oreg., U.S.A. 118 44 16N 123 10W
Harrisburg, Pa., U.S.A. 114 40 18N 76 52W
Harrismith 93 28 15 S 29 8 E
Harrison, Ark., U.S.A. 117 36 10N 93 4W
Harrison, Idaho, U.S.A. 118 47 30N 116 51W
Harrison, Nebr., U.S.A. 116 42 42N 103 52W
Harrison B. 104 70 25N 151 30W
Harrison, C. 107 54 55N 57 55W
Harrison L. 108 49 33N 121 50W
Harrisonburg 114 38 28N 78 52W
Harrisonville 116 38 39N 94 21W
Harriston 106 43 57N 80 53W
Harrisville 106 44 40N 83 19W
Harrogate 12 53 59N 1 32W
Harrow, Can. 112 42 2N 82 55W
Harrow, U.K. 13 51 35N 0 15W
Harsefeld 24 53 26N 9 31 E
Harstad 50 68 48N 16 30 E
Hart 114 43 42N 86 21W
Hartbees → 92 28 45 S 20 32 E
Hartberg 26 47 17N 15 58 E
Hartford, Conn., U.S.A. 114 41 47N 72 41W
Hartford, Ky., U.S.A. 114 37 26N 86 50W
Hartford, S.D., U.S.A. 116 43 40N 96 58W
Hartford, Wis., U.S.A. 116 43 18N 88 25W
Hartford City 114 40 22N 85 20W
Hartland 107 46 20N 67 32W
Hartland Pt. 13 51 2N 4 32W
Hartlepool 12 54 42N 1 11W
Hartley 91 18 10 S 30 14 E
Hartley Bay 108 53 25N 129 15W
Hartmannberge 92 17 0 S 13 0 E
Hartney 109 49 30N 100 35W
Hartselle 115 34 25N 86 55W
Hartshorne 117 34 51N 95 30W
Hartsville 115 34 23N 80 2W
Hartwell 115 34 21N 82 52W
Harunabad 68 29 35N 73 8 E
Harur 70 12 3N 78 29 E
Harvey, Ill., U.S.A. 114 41 40N 87 40W
Harvey, N.D., U.S.A. 116 47 50N 99 58W
Harwich 13 51 56N 1 18 E
Haryana □ 68 29 0N 76 10 E
Harz 24 51 40N 10 40 E
Harzgerode 24 51 38N 11 8 E
Hasa 64 26 0N 49 0 E
Hasaheisa 87 14 44N 33 20 E
Hasani 86 25 0N 37 8 E
Hasanpur 68 28 43N 78 17 E
Haselünne 24 52 40N 7 30 E
Hasharon 62 32 12N 34 49 E
Hashefela 62 31 30N 34 43 E
Håsjö 48 63 1N 16 5 E
Haskell, Okla., U.S.A. 117 35 51N 95 40W
Haskell, Tex., U.S.A. 117 33 10N 99 45W
Haslach 25 48 16N 8 7 E
Hasle 49 55 11N 14 44 E
Haslev 49 55 18N 11 57 E
Hasparren 20 43 24N 1 18W
Hasselt 16 50 56N 5 21 E
Hassene, Ad. 82 21 0N 4 0 E
Hassfurt 25 50 2N 10 30 E
Hassi Berrekrem 83 33 45N 5 16 E
Hassi bou Khelala 82 30 17N 0 18W
Hassi Daoula 83 33 4N 5 38 E
Hassi Djafou 82 30 55N 3 35 E
Hassi el Abiod 82 31 47N 3 37 E
Hassi el Biod 83 28 30N 6 0 E
Hassi el Gassi 83 30 52N 6 5 E
Hassi el Hadjar 83 31 28N 4 45 E
Hassi er Rmel 82 32 56N 3 17 E
Hassi Imoulaye 83 29 54N 9 10 E
Hassi Inifel 82 29 50N 3 41 E
Hassi Marroket 82 30 10N 3 0 E
Hassi Messaoud 83 31 43N 6 8 E
Hassi Rhénami 83 31 50N 5 58 E
Hassi Tartrat 83 30 5N 6 28 E
Hassi Zerzour 82 30 51N 3 56W
Hastings, Can. 112 44 18N 77 57W
Hastings, N.Z. 101 39 39 S 176 52 E
Hastings, U.K. 13 50 51N 0 36 E
Hastings, Mich., U.S.A. 114 42 40N 85 20W
Hastings, Minn., U.S.A. 116 44 41N 92 51W
Hastings, Nebr., U.S.A. 116 40 34N 98 22W
Hastings Ra. 99 31 15 S 152 14 E
Hästveda 49 56 17N 13 55 E
Hat Nhao 71 14 46N 106 32 E
Hatch 119 32 45N 107 8W
Hatches Creek 96 20 56 S 135 12 E
Hatchet L. 109 58 36N 103 40W
Haţeg 46 45 36N 22 55 E
Haţeg, Mţii. 46 45 25N 23 0 E
Hatfield P.O. 99 33 54 S 143 49 E
Hatgal 75 50 26N 100 9 E
Hathras 68 27 36N 78 6 E
Hattah 99 34 48 S 142 17 E
Hatteras, C. 115 35 10N 75 30W
Hattiesburg 117 31 20N 89 20W
Hatvan 27 47 40N 19 45 E
Hau Bon 71 13 25N 108 28 E
Haug 47 60 23N 10 26 E
Haugastøl 47 60 30N 7 50 E
Haugesund 47 59 23N 5 13 E
Haultain → 109 55 51N 106 46W
Hauraki Gulf 101 36 35 S 175 5 E
Hauran 62 32 50N 36 15 E
Hausruck 26 48 6N 13 30 E
Haut Atlas 82 32 30N 5 0W
Haut-Rhin □ 19 48 0N 7 15 E
Haut Zaïre □ 90 2 20N 26 0 E
Hautah, Wahāt al 64 23 40N 47 0 E
Haute-Corse □ 21 42 30N 9 30 E
Haute-Garonne □ 20 43 28N 1 30 E
Haute-Loire □ 20 45 5N 3 50 E
Haute-Marne □ 19 48 10N 5 20 E
Haute-Saône □ 19 47 45N 6 10 E
Haute-Savoie □ 21 46 0N 6 20 E
Haute-Vienne □ 20 45 50N 1 10 E
Hauterive 107 49 10N 68 16W
Hautes-Alpes □ 21 44 42N 6 20 E
Hautes-Pyrénées □ 20 43 0N 0 10 E
Hauteville 21 45 58N 5 36 E
Hautmont 19 50 15N 3 55 E
Hauts-de-Seine □ 19 48 52N 2 15 E
Hauts Plateaux 82 34 14N 1 0 E
Hauzenberg 25 48 39N 13 38 E
Havana 116 40 19N 90 3W
Havana = La Habana 121 23 8N 82 22W
Havasu, L. 119 34 18N 114 28W
Havdhem 49 57 10N 18 20 E
Havelange 16 50 23N 5 15 E
Havelock, N.B., Can. 107 46 2N 65 24W
Havelock, Ont., Can. 106 44 26N 77 53W
Havelock, N.Z. 101 41 17 S 173 48 E
Havelock I. 71 11 55N 93 2 E
Haverfordwest 13 51 48N 4 59W
Haverhill 114 42 50N 71 2W
Haveri 70 14 53N 75 24 E
Havering 13 51 33N 0 20 E
Haverstraw 113 41 12N 73 58W
Håverud 49 58 50N 12 28 E

Havîrna 46 48 4N 26 43 E
Havlíčkův Brod 26 49 36N 15 33 E
Havneby 49 55 5N 8 34 E
Havre 118 48 34N 109 40W
Havre-St.-Pierre 107 50 18N 63 33W
Havre-Aubert 107 47 12N 61 56W
Havre, Le 18 49 30N 0 5 E
Havza 64 41 0N 35 35 E
Haw → 115 35 36N 79 3W
Hawaii □ 110 20 30N 157 0W
Hawaii 110 20 0N 155 0W
Hawaiian Is. 110 20 30N 156 0W
Hawaiian Ridge 95 24 0N 165 0W
Hawarden, Can. 109 51 25N 106 36W
Hawarden, U.S.A. 116 43 2N 96 28W
Hawea Lake 101 44 28 S 169 19 E
Hawera 101 39 35 S 174 19 E
Hawick 14 55 25N 2 48W
Hawk Junction 106 48 5N 84 38W
Hawke B. 101 39 25 S 177 20 E
Hawke, C. 100 32 13 S 152 34 E
Hawker 97 31 59 S 138 22 E
Hawke's Bay □ 101 39 45 S 176 35 E
Hawkesbury 106 45 37N 74 37W
Hawkesbury → 97 33 30 S 151 10 E
Hawkesbury I. 108 53 37N 129 3W
Hawkinsville 115 32 17N 83 30W
Hawkwood 99 25 45 S 150 50 E
Hawley 116 46 58N 96 20W
Hawrân 62 32 45N 36 15 E
Hawthorne 118 38 31N 118 37W
Hawzen 87 13 58N 39 28 E
Haxtun 116 40 40N 102 39W
Hay, Austral. 97 34 30 S 144 51 E
Hay, U.K. 13 52 4N 3 9W
Hay →, Austral. 97 25 14 S 138 0 E
Hay →, Can. 108 60 50N 116 26W
Hay L. 108 58 50N 118 50W
Hay Lakes 108 53 12N 113 2W
Hay River 108 60 51N 115 44W
Hay Springs 116 42 40N 102 38W
Hayange 19 49 20N 6 2 E
Hayden, Ariz., U.S.A. 119 33 2N 110 48W
Hayden, Colo., U.S.A. 118 40 30N 107 22W
Haydon 98 18 0 S 141 30 E
Haye-Descartes, La 18 46 58N 0 42 E
Haye-du-Puits, La 18 49 17N 1 33W
Hayes 116 44 22N 101 1W
Hayes → 109 57 3N 92 12W
Haynesville 117 33 0N 93 7W
Hays, Can. 108 50 6N 111 48W
Hays, U.S.A. 116 38 55N 99 25W
Hayward 116 46 2N 91 30W
Hayward's Heath 13 51 0N 0 5W
Hazard 114 37 18N 83 10W
Hazaribagh 69 23 58N 85 26 E
Hazaribagh Road 69 24 12N 85 57 E
Hazebrouck 19 50 42N 2 31 E
Hazelton, Can. 108 55 20N 127 42W
Hazelton, U.S.A. 116 46 30N 100 15W
Hazen, N.D., U.S.A. 116 47 18N 101 38W
Hazen, Nev., U.S.A. 118 39 37N 119 2W
Hazlehurst, Ga., U.S.A. 115 31 50N 82 35W
Hazlehurst, Miss., U.S.A. 117 31 52N 90 24W
Hazleton 114 40 58N 76 0W
Hazor 62 33 2N 35 32 E
He Xian 77 24 27N 111 30 E
Head of Bight 96 31 30 S 131 25 E
Headlands 91 18 15 S 32 2 E
Healdsburg 118 38 33N 122 51W
Healdton 117 34 16N 97 31W
Healesville 99 37 35 S 145 30 E
Heanor 12 53 1N 1 20W
Heard I. 3 53 0 S 74 0 E
Hearne 117 30 54N 96 35W
Hearne B. 109 60 10N 99 10W
Hearne L. 108 62 20N 113 10W
Hearst 106 49 40N 83 41W
Heart → 116 46 40N 100 51W
Heart's Content 107 47 54N 53 27W
Heath Pt. 107 49 8N 61 40W
Heath Steele 107 47 17N 66 5W
Heavener 117 34 54N 94 36W
Hebbronville 117 27 20N 98 40W
Hebei □ 76 39 0N 116 0 E
Hebel 99 28 58 S 147 47 E
Heber Springs 117 35 29N 91 59W
Hebert 109 50 30N 107 10W
Hebgen, L. 118 44 50N 111 15W
Hebi 76 35 57N 114 7 E
Hebrides 14 57 30N 7 0W
Hebrides, Inner Is. 14 57 20N 6 40W
Hebrides, Outer Is. 14 57 30N 7 40W
Hebron, Can. 105 58 5N 62 30W
Hebron, N.D., U.S.A. 116 46 56N 102 2W
Hebron, Nebr., U.S.A. 116 40 15N 97 33W
Hebron = Al Khalil 62 31 32N 35 6 E
Heby 48 59 56N 16 53 E
Hecate Str. 108 53 10N 130 30W
Hechi 75 24 40N 108 2 E
Hechingen 25 48 20N 8 58 E
Hechuan 75 30 2N 106 12 E
Hecla 116 45 56N 98 8W
Hecla I. 109 51 10N 96 43W
Heddal 47 59 36N 9 9 E
Hédé 18 48 18N 1 49W
Hede 48 62 23N 13 30 E
Hedemora 48 60 18N 15 58 E
Hedley 117 34 53N 100 39W
Hedmark fylke □ 47 61 17N 11 40 E
Hedrum 47 59 7N 10 5 E
Heemstede 16 52 22N 4 37 E
Heerde 16 52 24N 6 2 E
Heerenveen 16 52 57N 5 55 E
Heerlen 16 50 55N 6 0 E
Hefa 62 32 46N 35 0 E
Hefei 75 31 52N 117 18 E
Hegang 75 47 20N 130 19 E
Hegyalja 27 48 25N 21 25 E
Heide 24 54 10N 9 7 E
Heidelberg, Ger. 25 49 23N 8 41 E
Heidelberg, C. Prov., S. Afr. 92 34 6 S 20 59 E
Heidelberg, Trans., S. Afr. 93 26 30 S 28 23 E
Heidenheim 25 48 40N 10 10 E
Heilbron 93 27 16 S 27 59 E
Heilbronn 25 49 8N 9 13 E
Heiligenblut 26 47 2N 12 51 E
Heiligenhafen 24 54 21N 10 58 E
Heiligenstadt 24 51 22N 10 9 E
Heilongjiang □ 75 48 0N 126 0 E
Heilunkiang = Heilongjiang □ 75 48 0N 126 0 E
Heim 47 63 26N 9 5 E
Heinola 51 61 13N 26 2 E
Heinze Is. 71 14 25N 97 45 E
Hejaz = Ḥijāz 64 26 0N 37 30 E
Hejian 76 38 25N 116 5 E
Hejiang 77 28 43N 105 46 E
Hekimhan 64 38 50N 38 0 E
Hekla 50 63 56N 19 35W
Hekou 75 22 30N 103 59 E
Hel 28 54 37N 18 47 E
Helagsfjället 48 62 54N 12 25 E
Helan Shan 76 39 0N 105 55 E
Helechosa 31 39 22N 4 53W
Helena, Ark., U.S.A. 117 34 30N 90 35W
Helena, Mont., U.S.A. 118 46 40N 112 0W
Helensburgh, Austral. 100 34 11 S 151 1 E
Helensburgh, U.K. 14 56 0N 4 44W
Helensville 101 36 41 S 174 29 E
Helez 62 31 36N 34 39 E
Helgasjön 49 57 0N 14 50 E
Helgeroa 47 59 0N 9 45 E
Helgoland 24 54 10N 7 51 E
Heligoland = Helgoland 24 54 10N 7 51 E
Heliopolis 86 30 6N 31 17 E
Hell-Ville 93 13 25 S 48 16 E
Hellebæk 49 56 4N 12 32 E
Helleland 47 58 33N 6 7 E
Hellendoorn 16 52 24N 6 27 E
Hellevoetsluis 16 51 50N 4 8 E
Hellin 33 38 31N 1 40W
Helmand □ 65 31 20N 64 0 E
Helmand → 66 31 12N 61 34 E
Helmand, Hamun 65 31 15N 61 15 E
Helme → 24 51 40N 11 20 E
Helmond 16 51 29N 5 41 E
Helmsdale 14 58 7N 3 40W
Helmstedt 24 52 16N 11 0 E
Helnæs 49 55 9N 10 0 E
Helper 118 39 44N 110 56W
Helsingborg 49 56 3N 12 42 E
Helsinge 49 56 2N 12 12 E
Helsingfors 51 60 15N 25 3 E
Helsingør 49 56 2N 12 35 E
Helsinki 51 60 15N 25 3 E
Helska, Mierzeja 28 54 45N 18 40 E
Helston 13 50 7N 5 17W
Helvellyn 12 54 31N 3 1W
Helwân 86 29 50N 31 20 E
Hemavati → 70 12 30N 76 20 E
Hemet 119 33 45N 116 59W
Hemingford 116 42 21N 103 4W
Hemphill 117 31 21N 93 49W
Hempstead 117 30 5N 96 5W
Hemse 49 57 15N 18 22 E
Hemsö 48 62 43N 18 5 E
Henan □ 75 34 0N 114 0 E
Henares → 32 40 24N 3 30W
Hendaye 20 43 23N 1 47W
Henderson, Argent. 124 36 18 S 61 43W
Henderson, Ky., U.S.A. 114 37 50N 87 38W
Henderson, N.C., U.S.A. 115 36 20N 78 25W
Henderson, Nev., U.S.A. 119 36 2N 115 0W
Henderson, Pa., U.S.A. 115 35 25N 88 40W
Henderson, Tex., U.S.A. 117 32 5N 94 49W
Hendersonville 115 35 21N 82 28W
Hendon 99 28 5 S 151 50 E
Hendorf 46 46 4N 24 55 E
Heng Xian 77 22 40N 109 17 E
Hengdaohezi 76 44 52N 129 0 E
Hengelo 16 52 3N 6 19 E
Hengshan, Hunan, China 77 27 16N 112 45 E
Hengshan, Shaanxi, China 76 37 58N 109 5 E
Hengshui 76 37 41N 115 40 E
Hengyang 75 26 52N 112 33 E
Hénin-Beaumont 19 50 25N 2 58 E
Henlopen, C. 114 38 48N 75 5W
Hennan, L. 48 62 3N 55 46 E
Hennebont 18 47 49N 3 19W
Hennenman 92 27 59 S 27 1 E
Hennessy 117 36 8N 97 53W
Hennigsdorf 24 52 38N 13 13 E
Henrichemont 19 47 20N 2 30 E
Henrietta 117 33 50N 98 15W
Henrietta Maria C. 106 55 9N 82 20W
Henrietta, Ostrov 59 77 6N 156 30 E
Henry 116 41 5N 89 20W
Henryetta 117 35 30N 96 0W
Hensall 112 43 26N 81 30W
Hentiyn Nuruu 75 48 30N 108 30 E
Henty 99 35 30 S 147 0 E
Henzada 67 17 38N 95 26 E
Hephaestia 44 39 55N 25 14 E
Heping 77 24 29N 115 0 E
Heppner 118 45 21N 119 34W
Hepu 77 21 40N 109 12 E
Hepworth 112 44 37N 81 9W
Herad 47 58 8N 6 47 E
Héraðsflói 50 65 42N 14 12W
Héraðsvötn → 50 65 45N 19 25W
Herāt 65 34 20N 62 7 E
Herāt □ 65 35 0N 62 0 E
Hérault □ 20 43 34N 3 15 E
Hérault → 20 43 17N 3 26 E
Herbault 18 47 36N 1 8 E
Herbert → 98 18 31 S 146 17 E
Herbert Downs 98 23 7 S 139 9 E
Herberton 98 17 20 S 145 25 E
Herbiers, Les 18 46 52N 1 0W
Herbignac 18 47 27N 2 18W
Herborn 24 50 40N 8 19 E
Herby 28 50 45N 18 50 E
Hercegnovi 42 42 30N 18 33 E
Herðubreið 50 65 11N 16 21W
Hereford, U.K. 13 52 4N 2 42W
Hereford, U.S.A. 117 34 50N 102 28W
Hereford and Worcester □ 13 52 10N 2 30W
Herefoss 47 58 32N 8 23 E
Herentals 16 51 12N 4 51 E
Herfølge 49 55 26N 12 9 E
Herford 24 52 7N 8 40 E
Héricourt 19 47 32N 6 45 E
Herington 116 38 43N 97 0W
Herisau 25 47 22N 9 17 E
Hérisson 20 46 32N 2 42 E
Herkimer 114 43 0N 74 59W
Herm 18 49 30N 2 28W
Hermagor-Pressegger See 26 46 38N 13 23 E
Herman 116 45 51N 96 8W
Hermann 116 38 40N 91 25W
Hermannsburg 24 52 49N 10 6 E
Hermanus 92 34 27 S 19 12 E
Herment 20 45 45N 2 24 E
Hermidale 99 31 30 S 146 42 E
Hermiston 118 45 50N 119 16W
Hermitage 101 43 44 S 170 5 E
Hermite, I. 128 55 50 S 68 0W
Hermon, Mt. = Ash Shaykh, J. 64 33 20N 35 51 E
Hermosillo 120 29 10N 111 0W
Hernad → 27 47 56N 21 8 E
Hernandarias 125 25 20 S 54 40W
Hernando, Argent. 124 32 28 S 63 40W
Hernando, U.S.A. 117 34 50N 89 59W
Herne 24 51 33N 7 12 E
Herne Bay 13 51 22N 1 8 E
Herning 49 56 8N 8 58 E
Heroica Nogales = Nogales 120 31 20N 110 56W
Heron Bay 106 48 40N 86 25W
Herowābād 64 38 37N 48 32 E
Herreid 116 45 53N 100 5W
Herrera 31 37 26N 4 55W
Herrera de Alcántar 31 39 39N 7 25W
Herrera de Pisuerga 30 42 35N 4 20W
Herrera del Duque 31 39 10N 5 3W
Herrick 99 41 5 S 147 55 E
Herrin 117 37 50N 89 0W
Herrljunga 49 58 5N 13 1 E
Hersbruck 25 49 30N 11 25 E
Herstal 16 50 40N 5 38 E
Hersvik 47 61 10N 4 53 E
Hertford 13 51 47N 0 4W
Hertford □ 13 51 51N 0 5W
's-Hertogenbosch 16 51 42N 5 17 E
Hertzogville 92 28 9 S 25 30 E
Hervás 30 40 16N 5 52W
Hervey B. 97 25 0 S 152 52 E
Hervey Is. 95 19 30 S 159 0W
Herzberg, Cottbus, Ger. 24 51 40N 13 13 E
Herzberg, Niedersachsen, Ger. 24 51 38N 10 20 E
Herzliyya 62 32 10N 34 50 E
Herzogenburg 26 48 17N 15 41 E
Hesdin 19 50 21N 2 0 E
Hesel 24 53 18N 7 36 E
Heskestad 47 58 28N 6 22 E
Hespeler 112 43 26N 80 19W
Hesse = Hessen 24 50 40N 9 20 E
Hessen □ 24 50 40N 9 20 E
Hettinger 116 46 0N 102 38W
Hettstedt 24 51 39N 11 30 E
Hève, C. de la 18 49 30N 0 5 E
Heves □ 27 47 50N 20 0 E
Hevron → 62 31 12N 34 42 E
Hewett, C. 105 70 16N 67 45W
Hex River 92 33 30 S 19 35 E
Hexham 12 54 58N 2 7W
Hexigten Qi 76 43 18N 117 30 E
Heyfield 100 37 59 S 146 47 E
Heysham 12 54 5N 2 53W
Heywood 99 38 8 S 141 37 E
Hi-no-Misaki 74 35 26N 132 38 E
Hialeah 115 25 49N 80 17W
Hiawatha, Kans., U.S.A. 116 39 55N 95 33W
Hiawatha, Utah, U.S.A. 118 39 29N 111 1W
Hibbing 116 47 30N 93 0W
Hickman 117 36 35N 89 8W
Hickory 115 35 46N 81 17W
Hicks Pt. 97 37 49 S 149 17 E
Hicksville 113 40 46N 73 30W
Hida 46 47 10N 23 19 E
Hida-Sammyaku 74 36 30N 137 40 E
Hidalgo 120 24 15N 99 26W
Hidalgo del Parral 120 26 58N 105 40W
Hidalgo, Presa M. 120 26 30N 108 35W
Hiddensee 24 54 30N 13 6 E
Hieflau 26 47 36N 14 46 E
Hiendelaencina 32 41 5N 3 0W
Hierro 80 27 44N 18 0 E
Higashiōsaka 74 34 40N 135 37 E
Higgins 117 36 9N 100 1W
High Atlas = Haut Atlas 82 32 30N 5 0W
High I. 107 56 40N 61 10W
High Island 117 29 32N 94 22W
High Level 108 58 31N 117 8W
High Point 115 35 57N 79 58W
High Prairie 108 55 30N 116 30W
High River 108 50 30N 113 50W
High Springs 115 29 50N 82 40W
High Tatra 27 49 30N 20 00 E
High Wycombe 13 51 37N 0 45W
Highbury 98 16 25 S 143 9 E
Highland □ 14 57 30N 5 0W
Highland Park 114 42 10N 87 50W
Highmore 116 44 35N 99 26W
Highrock L. 109 57 5N 105 32W
Higley 119 33 27N 111 46W
Hihya 86 30 40N 31 36 E
Hiiumaa 54 58 50N 22 45 E
Hijar 32 41 10N 0 27W
Ḥijārah, Şaḥrā' al 64 30 25N 44 30 E
Hiko 119 37 30N 115 13W
Hikone 74 35 15N 136 10 E
Hildburghhausen 25 50 24N 10 43 E
Hildesheim 24 52 9N 9 55 E
Hill City, Idaho, U.S.A. 118 43 20N 115 2W
Hill City, Kans., U.S.A. 116 39 25N 99 51W
Hill City, Minn., U.S.A. 116 46 57N 93 35W
Hill City, S.D., U.S.A. 116 43 58N 103 35W
Hill Island L. 109 60 30N 109 50W
Hillared 49 57 37N 13 10 E
Hillegom 16 52 18N 4 35 E
Hillerød 49 55 56N 12 19 E
Hillerstorp 49 57 20N 13 52 E
Hillingdon 13 51 33N 0 29W
Hillman 114 45 5N 83 52W
Hillmond 109 53 26N 109 41W
Hillsboro, Kans., U.S.A. 116 38 22N 97 10W
Hillsboro, N. Mex., U.S.A. 119 33 0N 107 35W
Hillsboro, N.D., U.S.A. 116 47 23N 97 9W
Hillsboro, N.H., U.S.A. 114 43 8N 71 56W
Hillsboro, Oreg., U.S.A. 118 45 31N 123 0W
Hillsboro, Tex., U.S.A. 117 32 0N 97 10W
Hillsdale, Mich., U.S.A. 114 41 55N 84 40W
Hillsdale, N.Y., U.S.A. 113 42 11N 73 30W
Hillsport 106 49 27N 85 34W
Hillston 97 33 30 S 145 31 E
Hilo 110 19 44N 155 5W
Hilonghilong 73 9 10N 125 45 E
Hilton 112 43 16N 77 48W
Hilversum 16 52 14N 5 10 E
Himachal Pradesh □ 68 31 30N 77 0 E
Himalaya 67 29 0N 84 0 E
Himara 44 40 8N 19 43 E
Himeji 74 34 50N 134 40 E
Himi 74 36 50N 137 0 E
Himmerland 49 56 45N 9 30 E
Ḥimş 64 34 40N 36 45 E
Hinako, Kepulauan 72 0 50N 97 20 E
Hinchinbrook I. 97 18 20 S 146 15 E
Hinckley, U.K. 13 52 33N 1 21W
Hinckley, U.S.A. 118 39 18N 112 41W
Hindås 49 57 42N 12 27 E
Hindaun 68 26 44N 77 5 E
Hindmarsh L. 99 36 5 S 141 55 E
Hindol 69 20 40N 85 10 E
Hindsholm 49 55 30N 10 40 E
Hindu Bagh 68 30 56N 67 50 E
Hindu Kush 65 36 0N 71 0 E
Hindupur 70 13 49N 77 32 E
Hines Creek 108 56 20N 118 40W
Hinganghat 68 20 30N 78 52 E
Hingham 118 48 34N 110 29W
Hingoli 70 19 41N 77 15 E
Hinlopenstretet 4 79 35N 18 40 E
Hinna 85 10 25N 11 35 E
Hinojosa del Duque 31 38 30N 5 9W
Hinsdale 118 48 26N 107 2W
Hinterrhein → 25 46 40N 9 25 E
Hinton, Can. 108 53 26N 117 34W
Hinton, U.S.A. 114 37 40N 80 51W
Hippolytushoef 16 52 54N 4 58 E
Hirakud 69 21 32N 83 51 E
Hirakud Dam 69 21 32N 83 45 E
Hiratsuka 74 35 19N 139 21 E
Hirhafok 83 23 49N 5 45 E
Hîrlău 46 47 23N 27 0 E
Hirosaki 74 40 34N 140 28 E
Hiroshima 74 34 24N 132 30 E
Hiroshima □ 74 34 50N 133 0 E
Hirsoholmene 49 57 30N 10 36 E
Hirson 19 49 55N 4 4 E
Hîrşova 46 44 40N 27 59 E
Hirtshals 49 57 36N 9 57 E
Ḥişn Dibā 65 25 45N 56 16 E
Hispaniola 121 19 0N 71 0W
Hissar 68 29 12N 75 45 E
Hita 74 33 20N 130 58 E
Hitachi 74 36 36N 140 39 E
Hitchin 13 51 57N 0 16W
Hitoyoshi 74 32 13N 130 45 E
Hitra 47 63 30N 8 45 E
Hitzacker 24 53 9N 11 1 E
Hiyyon, N. → 62 30 25N 35 10 E
Hjalmar L. 109 61 33N 109 25W
Hjälmare kanal 48 59 20N 15 59 E
Hjälmaren 48 59 18N 15 40 E
Hjartdal 47 59 37N 8 41 E
Hjerkinn 47 62 13N 9 33 E
Hjørring 49 57 29N 9 59 E
Hjorted 49 57 37N 16 19 E
Hjortkvarn 49 58 54N 15 26 E
Hlinsko 26 49 45N 15 54 E
Hlohovec 27 48 26N 17 49 E
Hňak 4 70 40N 52 10W
Ho 85 6 37N 0 27 E
Ho Chi Minh, Phanh Bho 71 10 58N 106 40 E
Hoa Binh 71 20 50N 105 20 E
Hoai Nhon (Bon Son) 71 14 28N 109 1 E
Hoare B. 105 65 17N 62 30W
Hobart, Austral. 97 42 50 S 147 21 E
Hobart, U.S.A. 117 35 0N 99 5W
Hobbs 117 32 40N 103 3W
Hobbs Coast 5 74 50 S 131 0W
Hoboken, Belg. 16 51 11N 4 21 E
Hoboken, U.S.A. 113 40 45N 74 4W
Hobro 49 56 39N 9 46 E
Hoburgen 49 56 55N 18 7 E
Hochatown 117 34 11N 94 39W
Hochschwab 26 47 35N 15 0 E
Höchst 25 50 6N 8 33 E
Höchstadt 25 49 42N 10 48 E
Hockenheim 25 49 18N 8 33 E
Hodgson 109 51 13N 97 36W
Hódmezővásárhely 27 46 28N 20 22 E
Hodna, Chott el 83 35 30N 5 0 E
Hodna, Monts du 83 35 52N 4 42 E
Hodonín 27 48 50N 17 10 E
Hoëdic 18 47 21N 2 52W
Hoek van Holland 16 52 0N 4 7 E
Hoëveld 93 26 30 S 30 0 E
Hof, Ger. 25 50 18N 11 55 E
Hof, Iceland 50 64 33N 14 40W
Höfðakaupstaður 50 65 50N 20 19W
Hofgeismar 24 51 29N 9 23 E
Hofors 48 60 31N 16 15 E
Hofsjökull 50 64 49N 18 48W
Hofsós 50 65 53N 19 26W
Hōfu 74 34 3N 131 34 E
Hogansville 115 33 14N 84 50W

Hogeland 118 48 51N 108 40W
Hogenakai Falls 70 12 6N 77 50 E
Högfors 48 59 58N 15 3 E
Högsäter 49 58 38N 12 5 E
Högsby 49 57 10N 16 1 E
Högsjö 48 59 4N 15 44 E
Hoh Xil Shan 75 35 0N 89 0 E
Hohe Rhön 25 50 24N 9 58 E
Hohe Tauern 26 47 11N 12 40 E
Hohe Venn 16 50 30N 6 5 E
Hohenau 27 48 36N 16 55 E
Hohenems 26 47 22N 9 42 E
Hohenstein Ernstthal 24 50 48N 12 43 E
Hohenwald 115 35 35N 87 30W
Hohenwestedt 24 54 6N 9 30 E
Hohhot 76 40 52N 111 40 E
Hohoe 85 7 8N 0 32 E
Hoi An 71 15 30N 108 19 E
Hoi Xuan 71 20 25N 105 9 E
Hoisington 116 38 33N 98 50W
Højer 49 54 58N 8 42 E
Hok 49 57 31N 14 16 E
Hökensås 49 58 0N 14 5 E
Hökerum 49 57 51N 13 16 E
Hokianga Harbour 101 35 31 S 173 22 E
Hokitika 101 42 42 S 171 0 E
Hokkaidō □ 74 43 30N 143 0 E
Hokksund 47 59 44N 9 59 E
Hol-Hol 87 11 20N 42 50 E
Holbæk 49 55 43N 11 43 E
Holbrook, Austral. 99 35 42 S 147 18 E
Holbrook, U.S.A. 119 35 54N 110 10W
Holden, Can. 108 53 13N 112 11W
Holden, U.S.A. 118 39 0N 112 26W
Holdenville 117 35 5N 96 25W
Holderness 12 53 45N 0 5W
Holdfast 109 50 58N 105 25W
Holdrege 116 40 26N 99 22W
Hole 47 60 6N 10 12 E
Hole-Narsipur 70 12 48N 76 16 E
Holešov 27 49 20N 17 35 E
Holguín 121 20 50N 76 20W
Holíč 27 48 49N 17 10 E
Hollabrunn 26 48 34N 16 5 E
Hollams Bird I. 92 24 40 S 14 30 E
Holland 114 42 47N 86 7W
Hollandia = Jayapura 73 2 28 S 140 38 E
Höllen 47 58 6N 7 49 E
Hollfeld 25 49 56N 11 18 E
Hollick Kenyon Plateau 5 82 0 S 110 0W
Hollidaysburg 114 40 26N 78 25W
Hollis 117 34 45N 99 55W
Hollister, Calif., U.S.A. 119 36 51N 121 24W
Hollister, Idaho, U.S.A. 118 42 21N 114 40W
Holly 116 38 7N 102 7W
Holly Hill 115 29 15N 81 3W
Holly Springs 117 34 45N 89 25W
Hollywood, Calif., U.S.A. 110 34 7N 118 25W
Hollywood, Fla., U.S.A. 115 26 0N 80 9W
Holm 48 62 40N 16 40 E
Holman Island 104 70 42N 117 41W
Hólmavík 50 65 42N 21 40W
Holmedal 47 61 22N 5 11 E
Holmegil 48 59 10N 11 44 E
Holmestrand 47 59 31N 10 14 E
Holmsbu 47 59 32N 10 27 E
Holmsjön 48 62 26N 15 20 E
Holmsland Klit 49 56 0N 8 5 E
Holmsund 50 63 41N 20 20 E
Holod 46 46 49N 22 8 E
Holon 62 32 2N 34 47 E
Holroyd → 97 14 10 S 141 36 E
Holstebro 49 56 22N 8 37 E
Holsworthy 13 50 48N 4 21W
Holt 50 63 33N 19 48W
Holte 49 55 50N 12 29 E
Holton, Can. 107 54 31N 57 12W
Holton, U.S.A. 116 39 28N 95 44W
Holtville 119 32 50N 115 27W
Holum 47 58 6N 7 32 E
Holwerd 16 53 22N 5 54 E
Holy Cross 104 62 10N 159 52W
Holy I., England, U.K. 12 55 42N 1 48W
Holy I., Wales, U.K. 12 53 17N 4 37W
Holyhead 12 53 18N 4 38W
Holyoke, Colo., U.S.A. 116 40 39N 102 18W
Holyoke, Mass., U.S.A. 114 42 14N 72 37W
Holyrood 107 47 27N 53 8W
Holzkirchen 25 47 53N 11 42 E
Holzminden 24 51 49N 9 31 E
Homa Bay 90 0 36 S 34 30 E
Homa Bay □ 90 0 50 S 34 30 E
Homalin 67 24 55N 95 0 E
Homberg 24 51 2N 9 20 E
Hombori 85 15 20N 1 38W
Homburg 25 49 19N 7 21 E
Home B. 105 68 40N 67 10W
Home Hill 97 19 43 S 147 25 E
Homedale 118 43 42N 116 59W
Homer, Alaska, U.S.A. 104 59 40N 151 35W
Homer, La., U.S.A. 117 32 50N 93 4W
Homestead, Austral. 98 20 20 S 145 40 E
Homestead, Fla., U.S.A. 115 25 29N 80 27W
Homestead, Oreg., U.S.A. 118 45 5N 116 57W
Hominy 117 36 26N 96 24W
Homnabad 70 17 45N 77 11 E
Homoine 93 23 55 S 35 8 E
Homoljske Planina 42 44 10N 21 45 E
Homorod 46 46 5N 25 15 E
Homs = Ḥimş 64 34 40N 36 45 E
Hon Chong 71 10 25N 104 30 E
Honan = Henan □ 75 34 0N 114 0 E
Honda 126 5 12N 74 45W
Hondeklipbaai 92 30 19 S 17 17 E
Hondo 117 29 22N 99 6W
Hondo → 120 18 25N 88 21W
Honduras ■ 121 14 40N 86 30W
Honduras, Golfo de 120 16 50N 87 0W
Honesdale 113 41 34N 75 17W
Honey L. 118 40 13N 120 14W
Honfleur 18 49 25N 0 13 E
Hong Kong ■ 75 22 11N 114 14 E
Hong'an 77 31 20N 114 40 E
Hongha → 71 22 0N 104 0 E
Honghai Wan 77 22 40N 115 0 E
Honghu 77 29 50N 113 30 E
Hongjiang 75 27 7N 109 59 E
Hongshui He → 75 23 48N 109 30 E
Hongtong 76 36 16N 111 40 E
Honguedo, Détroit d' 107 49 15N 64 0W
Hongze Hu 75 33 15N 118 35 E
Honiara 94 9 27 S 159 57 E
Honiton 13 50 48N 3 11W
Honkorâb, Ras 86 24 35N 35 10 E
Honolulu 110 21 19N 157 52W
Honshū 74 36 0N 138 0 E
Hontoria del Pinar 32 41 50N 3 10W
Hood Mt. 118 45 24N 121 41W
Hood, Pt. 96 34 23 S 119 34 E
Hood River 118 45 45N 121 31W
Hoodsport 118 47 24N 123 7W
Hooge 24 54 31N 8 36 E
Hoogeveen 16 52 44N 6 30 E
Hoogezand 16 53 11N 6 45 E
Hooghly → 69 21 56N 88 4 E
Hooghly-Chinsura 69 22 53N 88 27 E
Hook Hd. 15 52 8N 6 57W
Hook I. 98 20 4 S 149 0 E
Hook of Holland = Hoek van Holland 16 52 0N 4 7 E
Hooker 117 36 55N 101 10W
Hoopeston 114 40 30N 87 40W
Hoopstad 92 27 50 S 25 55 E
Hoorn 16 52 38N 5 4 E
Hoover Dam 119 36 0N 114 45W
Hooversville 112 40 8N 78 57W
Hop Bottom 113 41 41N 75 47W
Hopà 57 41 28N 41 30 E
Hope, Can. 108 49 25N 121 25 E
Hope, Ark., U.S.A. 117 33 40N 93 36W
Hope, N.D., U.S.A. 116 47 21N 97 42W
Hope Bay 5 65 0 S 55 0W
Hope, L. 99 28 24 S 139 18 E
Hope Pt. 104 68 20N 166 50W
Hope Town 121 26 35N 76 57W
Hopedale 107 55 28N 60 13W
Hopefield 92 33 3 S 18 22 E
Hopei = Hebei □ 76 39 0N 116 0 E
Hopelchén 120 19 46N 89 50W
Hopen 47 63 27N 8 2 E
Hopetoun, Vic., Austral. 99 35 42 S 142 22 E
Hopetoun, W. Australia, Austral. 100 33 57 S 120 7 E
Hopetown 92 29 34 S 24 3 E
Hopkins 116 40 31N 94 45W
Hopkins → 100 38 25 S 142 30 E
Hopkinsville 115 36 52N 87 26W
Hopland 118 39 0N 123 7W
Hoptrup 49 55 11N 9 28 E
Hoquiam 118 46 50N 123 55W
Horazdovice 26 49 19N 13 42 E
Horcajo de Santiago 32 39 50N 3 1W
Hordaland fylke □ 47 60 25N 6 15 E
Horden Hills 96 20 40 S 130 20 E
Horezu 46 45 6N 24 0 E
Horgen 25 47 15N 8 35 E
Horgoš 42 46 10N 20 0 E
Horice 26 50 21N 15 39 E
Horlick Mts. 5 84 0 S 102 0W
Hormoz 65 27 35N 55 0 E
Hormoz, Jaz. ye 65 27 8N 56 28 E
Hormuz Str. 65 26 30N 56 30 E
Horn, Austria 26 48 39N 15 40 E
Horn, Ísafjarðarsýsla, Iceland 50 66 28N 22 28W
Horn, Suður-Múlasýsla, Iceland 50 65 10N 13 31W
Horn → 108 61 30N 118 1W
Horn, Cape = Hornos, Cabo de 128 55 50 S 67 30W
Horn Head 15 55 13N 8 0W
Horn, I. 115 30 17N 88 40W
Horn Mts. 108 62 15N 119 15W
Hornachuelos 31 37 50N 5 14W
Hornavan 50 66 15N 17 30 E
Hornbæk 49 56 5N 12 26 E
Hornbeck 117 31 22N 93 20W
Hornbrook 118 41 58N 122 37W
Hornburg 24 52 2N 10 36 E
Horncastle 12 53 13N 0 8W
Horndal 48 60 18N 16 23 E
Hornell 114 42 23N 77 41W
Hornell L. 108 62 20N 119 25W
Hornepayne 106 49 14N 84 48W
Hornindal 47 61 58N 6 30 E
Hornnes 47 58 34N 7 45 E
Hornos, Cabo de 128 55 50 S 67 30W
Hornoy 19 49 50N 1 54 E
Hornsby 99 33 42 S 151 2 E
Hornsea 12 53 55N 0 10W
Hornslandet 48 61 35N 17 37 E
Hornslet 49 56 18N 10 19 E
Hörnum 24 54 44N 8 18 E
Horovice 26 49 48N 13 53 E
Horqin Youyi Qianqi 75 46 5N 122 3 E
Horqueta 124 23 15 S 56 55W
Horra, La 30 41 44N 3 53W
Horred 49 57 22N 12 28 E
Horse Cr. → 116 41 57N 103 58W
Horse Is. 107 50 15N 55 50W
Horsefly L. 108 52 25N 121 0W
Horsens 49 55 52N 9 51 E
Horsens Fjord 49 55 50N 10 0 E
Horseshoe Dam 119 33 45N 111 35W
Horsham, Austral. 97 36 44 S 142 13 E
Horsham, U.K. 13 51 4N 0 20W
Horšovský Týn 26 49 31N 12 58 E
Horten 47 59 25N 10 32 E
Hortobágy → 27 47 30N 21 6 E
Horton 116 39 42N 95 30W
Horton → 104 69 56N 126 52W
Hörvik 49 56 2N 14 45 E
Horwood, L. 106 48 5N 82 20W
Hosaina 87 7 30N 37 47 E
Hosdurga 70 13 49N 76 17 E
Hose, Pegunungan 72 2 5N 114 6 E
Hoshangabad 68 22 45N 77 45 E
Hoshiarpur 68 31 30N 75 58 E
Hosmer 116 45 36N 99 29W
Hospet 70 15 15N 76 20 E
Hospitalet de Llobregat 32 41 21N 2 6 E
Hospitalet, L' 20 42 36N 1 47 E
Hoste, I. 128 55 0 S 69 0W
Hostens 20 44 30N 0 40W
Hot 71 18 8N 98 29 E
Hot Creek Ra. 118 39 0N 116 0W
Hot Springs, Ari., U.S.A. 117 34 30N 93 0W
Hot Springs, S.D., U.S.A. 116 43 25N 103 30W
Hotagen 50 63 50N 14 30 E
Hotan 75 37 25N 79 55 E
Hotazel 92 27 17 S 23 00 E
Hotchkiss 119 38 47N 107 47W
Hoting 50 64 8N 16 15 E
Hotolishti 44 41 10N 20 25 E
Hottentotsbaai 92 26 8 S 14 59 E
Houat 18 47 24N 2 58W
Houck 119 35 15N 109 15W
Houdan 19 48 48N 1 35 E
Houffalize 16 50 8N 5 48 E
Houghton 116 47 9N 88 39W
Houghton L. 114 44 20N 84 40W
Houghton-le-Spring 12 54 51N 1 28W
Houhora 101 34 49 S 173 9 E
Houlton 107 46 5N 67 50W
Houma 117 29 35N 90 44W
Houndé 84 11 34N 3 31W
Hourtin 20 45 11N 1 4W
Hourtin, Étang d' 20 45 10N 1 6W
Houston, Can. 108 54 25N 126 39W
Houston, Mo., U.S.A. 117 37 20N 92 0W
Houston, Tex., U.S.A. 117 29 50N 95 20W
Houtman Abrolhos 96 28 43 S 113 48 E
Hov 49 55 55N 10 15 E
Hova 49 58 53N 14 14 E
Høvåg 47 58 10N 8 16 E
Hovd (Jargalant) 75 48 2N 91 37 E
Hovden 47 59 33N 7 22 E
Hove 13 50 50N 0 10W
Hovmantorp 49 56 47N 15 7 E
Hövsgöl Nuur 75 51 0N 100 30 E
Hovsta 48 59 22N 15 15 E
Howakil 87 15 10N 40 16 E
Howar, Wadi → 87 17 30N 27 8 E
Howard, Austral. 99 25 16 S 152 32 E
Howard, Kans., U.S.A. 117 37 30N 96 16W
Howard, Pa., U.S.A. 112 41 0N 77 40W
Howard, S.D., U.S.A. 116 44 2N 97 30W
Howard L. 109 62 15N 105 57W
Howe 118 43 48N 113 0W
Howe, C. 97 37 30 S 150 0 E
Howell 114 42 38N 83 56W
Howick, Can. 113 45 11N 73 51W
Howick, S. Afr. 93 29 28 S 30 14 E
Howick Group 98 14 20 S 145 30 E
Howitt, L. 99 27 40 S 138 40 E
Howley 107 49 12N 57 2W
Howrah 69 22 37N 88 20 E
Howth Hd. 15 53 21N 6 0W
Höxter 24 51 45N 9 26 E
Hoy I. 14 58 50N 3 15W
Hoya 24 52 47N 9 10 E
Hoyerswerda 24 51 26N 14 14 E
Hoyos 30 40 9N 6 45W
Hpungan Pass 67 27 30N 96 55 E
Hrádec Králové 26 50 15N 15 50 E
Hrádek 27 48 46N 16 16 E
Hranice 27 49 34N 17 45 E
Hron → 27 47 49N 18 45 E
Hrubieszów 28 50 49N 23 51 E
Hrubý Nízký Jeseník 27 50 7N 17 10 E
Hrvatska 39 45 20N 16 0 E
Hrvatska □ 42 45 20N 18 0 E
Hsenwi 67 23 22N 97 55 E
Hsiamen = Xiamen 75 24 25N 118 4 E
Hsian = Xi'an 77 34 15N 109 0 E
Hsinhailien = Lianyungang 77 34 40N 119 11 E
Hsüchou = Xuzhou 77 34 18N 117 18 E
Hua Hin 71 12 34N 99 58 E
Hua Xian, Henan, China 77 35 30N 114 30 E
Hua Xian, Shaanxi, China 77 34 30N 109 48 E
Huacheng 77 24 4N 115 37 E
Huacho 126 11 10 S 77 35W
Huachón 126 10 35 S 76 0W
Huachuan 76 46 50N 130 21 E
Huade 76 41 55N 113 59 E
Huadian 76 43 0N 126 40 E
Huai He → 75 33 0N 118 30 E
Huai'an 77 33 30N 119 10 E
Huaide 76 43 30N 124 40 E
Huainan 75 32 38N 116 58 E
Huaiyang 77 33 40N 114 52 E
Huaiyuan 77 24 31N 108 22 E
Huajianzi 76 41 23N 125 20 E
Huajuapan de Leon 120 17 50N 97 48W
Hualian 77 23 59N 121 37 E
Huallaga → 126 5 0 S 75 30W
Hualpai Pk. 119 35 8N 113 58W
Huambo 89 12 42 S 15 54 E
Huan Jiang → 76 34 28N 109 0 E
Huan Xian 76 36 33N 107 7 E
Huancabamba 126 5 10 S 79 15W
Huancane 126 15 10 S 69 44W
Huancapi 126 13 40 S 74 0W
Huancavelica 126 12 50 S 75 5W
Huancayo 126 12 5 S 75 12W
Huang He 75 37 55N 118 50 E
Huangchuan 77 32 15N 115 10 E
Huangliu 75 18 20N 108 50 E
Huanglong 76 35 30N 109 59 E
Huangshi 75 30 10N 115 3 E
Huangyan 77 28 38N 121 19 E
Huánuco 126 9 55 S 76 15W
Huaraz 126 9 30 S 77 32W
Huarmey 126 10 5 S 78 5W
Huascarán 126 9 8 S 77 36W
Huasco 124 28 30 S 71 15W
Huasco → 124 28 27 S 71 13W
Huatabampo 120 26 50N 109 50W
Huay Namota 120 21 56N 104 30W
Huayllay 126 11 03 S 76 21W
Hubbard 117 31 50N 96 50W
Hubbart Pt. 109 59 21N 94 41W
Hubei □ 75 31 0N 112 0 E
Hubli 70 15 22N 75 15 E
Hückelhoven-Ratheim 24 51 6N 6 13 E
Huczwa → 28 50 49N 23 58 E
Huddersfield 12 53 38N 1 49W
Hudi 86 17 43N 34 18 E
Hudiksvall 48 61 43N 17 10 E
Hudson, Can. 109 50 6N 92 09W
Hudson, Mass., U.S.A. 113 42 23N 71 35W
Hudson, Mich., U.S.A. 114 41 50N 84 20W
Hudson, N.Y., U.S.A. 114 42 15N 73 46W
Hudson, Wis., U.S.A. 116 44 57N 92 45W
Hudson, Wyo., U.S.A. 118 42 54N 108 37W
Hudson → 114 40 42N 74 2W
Hudson Bay, Can. 105 60 0N 86 0W
Hudson Bay, Sask., Can. 109 52 51N 102 23W
Hudson Falls 114 43 18N 73 34W
Hudson Hope 108 56 0N 121 54W
Hudson Mts. 5 74 32 S 99 20W
Hudson Str. 105 62 0N 70 0W
Hue 71 16 30N 107 35 E
Huebra → 30 41 2N 6 48W
Huedin 46 46 52N 23 2 E
Huelgoat 18 48 22N 3 46W
Huelma 33 37 39N 3 28W
Huelva 31 37 18N 6 57W
Huelva □ 31 37 40N 7 0W
Huelva → 31 37 27N 6 0W
Huentelauquén 124 31 38 S 71 33W
Huércal Overa 33 37 23N 1 57W
Huerta, Sa. de la 124 31 10 S 67 30W
Huertas, C. de las 33 38 21N 0 24W
Huerva → 32 41 39N 0 52W
Huesca 32 42 8N 0 25W
Huesca □ 32 42 20N 0 1 E
Huéscar 33 37 44N 2 35W
Huetamo 120 18 36N 100 54W
Huete 32 40 10N 2 43W
Hugh → 96 25 1 S 134 1 E
Hughenden 97 20 52 S 144 10 E
Hughes 104 66 0N 154 20W
Hugo 116 39 12N 103 27W
Hugoton 117 37 11N 101 22W
Hui Xian 76 35 27N 113 12 E
Hui'an 77 25 1N 118 43 E
Huichang 77 25 32N 115 45 E
Huichapán 120 20 24N 99 40W
Huihe 76 48 12N 119 17 E
Huila, Nevado del 126 3 0N 76 0W
Huilai 77 23 0N 116 18 E
Huimin 76 37 27N 117 28 E
Huinan 76 42 40N 126 2 E
Huinca Renancó 124 34 51 S 64 22W
Huining 76 35 38N 105 0 E
Huinong 76 39 5N 106 35 E
Huisne → 18 47 59N 0 11 E
Huize 75 26 24N 103 15 E
Huizhou 77 23 0N 114 23 E
Hukawng Valley 67 26 30N 96 30 E
Hukou 77 29 45N 116 21 E
Hukuntsi 92 23 58 S 21 45 E
Hula 87 6 33N 38 30 E
Hulan 75 46 1N 126 37 E
Ḥulayfā' 64 25 58N 40 45 E
Huld 75 45 5N 105 30 E
Hulda 62 31 50N 34 51 E
Hulin 76 45 48N 132 59 E
Hull, Can. 106 45 25N 75 44W
Hull, U.K. 12 53 45N 0 20W
Hull → 12 53 43N 0 25W
Hulst 16 51 17N 4 2 E
Hultsfred 49 57 30N 15 52 E
Hulun Nur 75 49 0N 117 30 E
Huma 76 51 43N 126 38 E
Huma He → 76 51 42N 126 42 E
Humahuaca 124 23 10 S 65 25W
Humaitá, Brazil 126 7 35 S 63 1W
Humaitá, Parag. 124 27 2 S 58 31W
Humansdorp 92 34 2 S 24 46 E
Humbe 92 16 40 S 14 55 E
Humber → 12 53 40N 0 10W
Humberside □ 12 53 50N 0 30W
Humble 117 29 59N 93 18W
Humboldt, Can. 109 52 15N 105 9W
Humboldt, Iowa, U.S.A. 116 42 42N 94 15W
Humboldt, Tenn., U.S.A. 117 35 50N 88 55W
Humboldt → 118 40 2N 118 31W
Humboldt Gletscher 4 79 30N 62 0W
Hume, L. 97 36 0 S 147 0 E
Humenné 27 48 55N 21 50 E
Humphreys Pk. 119 35 24N 111 38W
Humpolec 26 49 31N 15 20 E
Hūn 83 29 2N 16 0 E
Húnaflói 50 65 50N 20 50W
Hunan □ 75 27 30N 112 0 E
Hunchun 76 42 52N 130 28 E
Hundested 49 55 58N 11 52 E
Hundred Mile House 108 51 38N 121 18W
Hunedoara 46 45 40N 22 50 E
Hunedoara □ 46 45 50N 22 54 E
Hünfeld 24 50 40N 9 47 E
Hungary ■ 27 47 20N 19 20 E
Hungary, Plain of 9 47 0N 20 0 E
Hungerford 99 28 58 S 144 24 E
Hüngnam 76 39 49N 127 45 E
Huni Valley 84 5 33N 1 56W
Hunsberge 92 27 45 S 17 12 E
Hunsrück 25 49 30N 7 0 E
Hunstanton 12 52 57N 0 30 E
Hunsur 70 12 16N 76 16 E
Hunte → 24 52 30N 8 19 E
Hunter, N.D., U.S.A. 116 47 12N 97 17W
Hunter, N.Y., U.S.A. 113 42 13N 74 13W
Hunter → 100 32 52 S 151 46 E
Hunter I., Austral. 97 40 30 S 144 45 E
Hunter I., Can. 108 51 55N 128 0W
Hunter Ra. 99 32 45 S 150 15 E
Hunters Road 91 19 9 S 29 49 E
Hunterton 99 26 12 S 148 30 E
Hunterville 101 39 56 S 175 35 E

Huntingburg 114 38 20N 86 58W
Huntingdon, Can. 106 45 6N 74 10W
Huntingdon, U.K. 13 52 20N 0 11W
Huntingdon, U.S.A. 114 40 28N 78 1W
Huntington, Ind., U.S.A. 114 40 52N 85 30W
Huntington, N.Y., U.S.A. 113 40 52N 73 25W
Huntington, Oreg., U.S.A. 118 44 22N 117 21W
Huntington, Ut., U.S.A. 118 39 24N 111 1W
Huntington, W. Va., U.S.A. 114 38 20N 82 30W
Huntington Beach 119 33 40N 118 0W
Huntington Park 119 33 58N 118 15W
Huntly, N.Z. 101 37 34 S 175 11 E
Huntly, U.K. 14 57 27N 2 48W
Huntsville, Can. 106 45 20N 79 14W
Huntsville, Ala., U.S.A. 115 34 45N 86 35W
Huntsville, Tex., U.S.A. 117 30 45N 95 35W
Hunyani → 91 15 57 S 30 39 E
Huo Xian 76 36 36N 111 42 E
Huon, G. 98 7 0 S 147 30 E
Huonville 97 43 0 S 147 5 E
Huoqiu 77 32 20N 116 12 E
Huoshao Dao 77 22 40N 121 30 E
Hupeh □ = Hubei □ 75 31 0N 112 0 E
Hurbanovo 27 47 51N 18 11 E
Hure Qi 76 42 45N 121 45 E
Hurezani 46 44 49N 23 40 E
Hurghada 86 27 15N 33 50 E
Hurley, N. Mex., U.S.A. 119 32 45N 108 7W
Hurley, Wis., U.S.A. 116 46 26N 90 10W
Huron, Ohio, U.S.A. 112 41 22N 82 34W
Huron, S.D., U.S.A. 116 44 22N 98 12W
Huron, L. 112 45 0N 83 0W
Hurricane 119 37 10N 113 12W
Hurso 87 9 35N 41 33 E
Hurum, Buskerud, Norway 47 59 36N 10 23 E
Hurum, Oppland, Norway 47 61 9N 8 46 E
Hurunui → 101 42 54 S 173 18 E
Hurup 49 56 46N 8 25 E
Húsavík 50 66 3N 17 21W
Huşi 46 46 41N 28 7 E
Huskvarna 49 57 47N 14 15 E
Husøy 47 61 3N 4 44 E
Hussar 108 51 3N 112 41W
Hustopéce 27 48 57N 16 43 E
Husum, Ger. 24 54 27N 9 3 E
Husum, Sweden 48 63 21N 19 12 E
Hutchinson, Kans., U.S.A. 117 38 3N 97 59W
Hutchinson, Minn., U.S.A. 116 44 50N 94 22W
Hutou 76 45 58N 133 38 E
Huttenberg 26 46 56N 14 33 E
Hüttental 24 50 52N 8 1 E
Huttig 117 33 5N 92 10W
Hutton, Mt. 99 25 51 S 148 20 E
Huwun 87 4 23N 40 6 E
Ḩuwwārah 62 32 9N 35 15 E
Huy 16 50 31N 5 15 E
Hvaler 47 59 4N 11 1 E
Hvammur 50 65 13N 21 49W
Hvar 39 43 11N 16 28 E
Hvarski Kanal 39 43 15N 16 35 E
Hvítá 50 64 40N 21 5W
Hvítá → 50 64 0N 20 58W
Hvítárvatn 50 64 37N 19 50W
Hvitsten 47 59 35N 10 42 E
Hwang Ho = Huang He → 76 37 50N 118 50 E
Hyannis 116 42 0N 101 45W
Hyargas Nuur 75 49 0N 93 0 E
Hyatts 114 38 59N 76 55W
Hybo 48 61 49N 16 15 E
Hyderabad, India 70 17 22N 78 29 E
Hyderabad, Pak. 68 25 23N 68 24 E
Hyderabad □ 68 25 3N 68 24 E
Hyères 21 43 8N 6 9 E
Hyères, Îles d' 21 43 0N 6 28 E
Hyesan 76 41 20N 128 10 E
Hyland → 108 59 52N 128 12W
Hylestad 47 59 6N 7 29 E
Hyltebruk 49 56 59N 13 15 E
Hyndman Pk. 118 43 50N 114 10W
Hyōgo □ 74 35 15N 135 0 E
Hyrum 118 41 35N 111 56W
Hysham 118 46 21N 107 11W
Hythe 13 51 4N 1 5 E
Hyvinkää 51 60 38N 24 50 E

I

I-n-Azaoua 83 20 45N 7 31 E
I-n-Échaï 82 20 10N 2 5W
I-n-Gall 85 16 51N 7 1 E
I-n-Tabedog 82 19 48N 1 11 E
Iabès, Erg 82 27 30N 2 2W
Iaco → 126 9 3 S 68 34W
Iacobeni 46 47 25N 25 20 E
Iakora 93 23 6 S 46 40 E
Ialomiţa □ 46 44 30N 27 30 E
Ialomiţa → 46 44 42N 27 51 E
Ianca 46 45 6N 27 29 E
Iara 46 46 31N 23 35 E
Iaşi 46 47 20N 27 0 E
Iba 73 15 22N 120 0 E
Ibadan 85 7 22N 3 58 E
Ibagué 126 4 20N 75 20W
Iballja 44 42 12N 20 0 E
Ibăneşti 46 46 45N 24 50 E
Ibar → 42 43 43N 20 45 E
Ibaraki □ 74 36 10N 140 10 E
Ibarra 126 0 21N 78 7W
Ibba 87 4 49N 29 2 E
Ibba, Bahr el 87 5 30N 28 55 E
Ibbenbüren 24 52 16N 7 41 E
Ibembo 90 2 35N 23 35 E
Ibera, Laguna 124 28 30 S 57 9W
Iberian Peninsula 8 40 0N 5 0W
Iberville 106 45 19N 73 17W
Iberville, Lac d' 106 55 55N 73 15W
Ibi 85 8 15N 9 44 E
Ibiá 127 19 30 S 46 30W
Ibicuy 124 33 55 S 59 10W
Ibioapaba, Sa. da 127 4 0 S 41 30W
Ibiza 33 38 54N 1 26 E
Íblei, Monti 41 37 15N 14 45 E
Ibo 91 12 22 S 40 40 E
Ibonma 73 3 29 S 133 31 E
Ibotirama 127 12 13 S 43 12W
Ibriktepe 44 41 2N 26 33 E
Ibshawâi 86 29 21N 30 40 E
Ibu 73 1 35N 127 33 E
Iburg 24 52 10N 8 3 E
Icá 126 14 0 S 75 48W
Içá → 126 2 55 S 67 58W
Içana 126 0 21N 67 19W
Iceland ■ 50 65 0N 19 0W
Icha 59 55 30N 156 0 E
Ich'ang = Yichang 75 30 40N 111 20 E
Ichchapuram 70 19 10N 84 40 E
Ichihara 74 35 28N 140 5 E
Ichihawa 74 35 44N 139 55 E
Ichilo → 126 15 57 S 64 50W
Ichinomiya 74 35 18N 136 48 E
Ichnya 54 50 52N 32 24 E
Icht 82 29 6N 8 54W
Icy Str. 108 58 20N 135 30W
Ida Grove 116 42 20N 95 25W
Idabel 117 33 53N 94 50W
Idaga Hamus 87 14 13N 39 48 E
Idah 85 7 5N 6 40 E
Idaho □ 118 44 10N 114 0W
Idaho City 118 43 50N 115 52W
Idaho Falls 118 43 30N 112 1W
Idaho Springs 118 39 49N 105 30W
Idanha-a-Nova 30 39 50N 7 15W
Idar-Oberstein 25 49 43N 7 19 E
Idd el Ghanam 81 11 30N 24 19 E
Iddan 63 6 10N 48 55 E
Idehan 83 27 10N 11 30 E
Idehan Marzūq 83 24 50N 13 51 E
Idelès 83 23 50N 5 53 E
Idfû 86 25 0N 32 49 E
Ídhi Óros 45 35 15N 24 45 E
Ídhra 45 37 20N 23 28 E
Idi 72 5 2N 97 37 E
Idi Amin Dada, L. 90 0 25 S 29 40 E
Idiofa 88 4 55 S 19 42 E
Idkerberget 48 60 22N 15 15 E
Idku, Bahra el 86 31 18N 30 18 E
Idlip 64 35 55N 36 38 E
Idna 62 31 34N 34 58 E
Idrija 39 46 0N 14 5 E
Idritsa 54 56 25N 28 30 E
Idstein 25 50 13N 8 17 E
Idutywa 93 32 8 S 28 18 E
Ieper 16 50 51N 2 53 E
Ierápetra 45 35 0N 25 44 E
Ierissós 44 40 22N 23 52 E
Ierissóu Kólpos 44 40 27N 23 57 E
Ierzu 40 39 48N 9 32 E
Iesi 39 43 32N 13 12 E
Ifach, Punta 33 38 38N 0 5 E
Ifanadiana 93 21 19 S 47 39 E
Ife 85 7 30N 4 31 E
Iférouâne 85 19 5N 8 24 E
Iffley 98 18 53 S 141 12 E
Ifni 82 29 29N 10 12W
Ifon 85 6 58N 5 40 E
Iforas, Adrar des 85 19 40N 1 40 E
Ifrane 82 33 33N 5 7W
Iganga 90 0 37N 33 28 E
Igarapava 127 20 3 S 47 47W
Igarapé Açu 127 1 4 S 47 33W
Igarka 59 67 30N 86 33 E
Igatimi 125 24 5 S 55 40W
Igatpuri 70 19 40N 73 35 E
Igbetti 85 8 44N 4 8 E
Igbo-Ora 85 7 29N 3 15 E
Igboho 85 8 53N 3 50 E
Iggesund 48 61 39N 17 10 E
Ighil Izane 82 35 44N 0 31 E
Iglene 82 22 57N 4 58 E
Iglésias 40 39 19N 8 27 E
Igli 82 30 25N 2 19W
Igloolik 105 69 20N 81 49W
Igma 82 29 9N 6 24W
Igma, Gebel el 86 28 55N 34 0 E
Ignace 106 49 30N 91 40W
Igoshevo 55 59 25N 42 35 E
Igoumenítsa 44 39 32N 20 18 E
Iguaçu → 125 25 36 S 54 36W
Iguaçu, Cat. del 125 25 41 S 54 26W
Iguala 120 18 20N 99 40W
Igualada 32 41 37N 1 37 E
Iguassu = Iguaçu 125 25 41N 54 26W
Iguatu 127 6 20 S 39 18W
Iguéla 88 2 0 S 9 16 E
Igunga □ 90 4 20 S 33 45 E
Ihiala 85 5 51N 6 55 E
Ihosy 93 22 24 S 46 8 E
Ihotry, L. 93 21 56 S 43 41 E
Ii 50 65 19N 25 22 E
Iida 74 35 35N 137 50 E
Iijoki → 50 65 20N 25 20 E
Iisalmi 50 63 32N 27 10 E
Iizuka 74 33 38N 130 42 E
Ijebu-Igbo 85 6 56N 4 1 E
Ijebu-Ode 85 6 47N 3 58 E
IJmuiden 16 52 28N 4 35 E
IJssel → 16 52 35N 5 50 E
IJsselmeer 16 52 45N 5 20 E
Ijuí → 125 27 58 S 55 20W
Ikale 85 7 40N 5 37 E
Ikare 85 7 32N 5 40 E
Ikaría 45 37 35N 26 10 E
Ikast 49 56 8N 9 10 E
Ikeja 85 6 36N 3 23 E
Ikela 88 1 6 S 23 6 E
Ikerre-Ekiti 85 7 25N 5 19 E
Ikhtiman 43 42 27N 23 48 E
Iki 74 33 45N 129 42 E
Ikimba L. 90 1 30 S 31 20 E
Ikire 85 7 23N 4 15 E
Ikom 85 6 0N 8 42 E
Ikopa → 93 16 45 S 46 40 E
Ikot Ekpene 85 5 12N 7 40 E
Ikungu 90 1 33 S 33 42 E
Ikurun 85 7 54N 4 40 E
Ila 85 8 0N 4 39 E
Ilagan 73 17 7N 121 53 E
Ilam 69 26 58N 87 58 E
Ilanskiy 59 56 14N 96 3 E
Ilaro 85 6 53N 3 3 E
Iława 28 53 36N 19 34 E
Ilayangudi 70 9 34N 78 37 E
Ilbilbie 98 21 45 S 149 20 E
Île-à-la Crosse 109 55 27N 107 53W
Île-à-la-Crosse, Lac 109 55 40N 107 45W
Île-Bouchard, L' 18 47 7N 0 26 E
Île-de-France 19 49 0N 2 20 E
Île-sur-le-Doubs, L' 19 47 26N 6 34 E
Ilebo 88 4 17 S 20 55 E
Ileje □ 91 9 30 S 33 25 E
Ilek 58 51 32N 53 21 E
Ilek → 52 51 30N 53 22 E
Ilero 85 8 0N 3 20 E
Ilesha, Oyo, Nigeria 85 7 37N 4 40 E
Ilesha, Oyo, Nigeria 85 8 57N 3 28 E
Ilford 109 56 4N 95 35W
Ilfov □ 46 44 20N 26 0 E
Ilfracombe, Austral. 97 23 30 S 144 30 E
Ilfracombe, U.K. 13 51 13N 4 8W
Ílhavo 30 40 33N 8 43W
Ilhéus 127 14 49 S 39 2W
Ilia 46 45 57N 22 40 E
Ilia □ 45 37 45N 21 35 E
Ilich 58 40 50N 68 27 E
Iliff 116 40 50N 103 3W
Iligan 73 8 12N 124 13 E
Ilikí, L. 45 38 24N 23 15 E
Iliodhrómia 44 39 12N 23 50 E
Ilion 114 43 0N 75 3W
Ilirska-Bistrica 39 45 34N 14 14 E
Ilkal 70 15 57N 76 8 E
Ilkeston 12 52 59N 1 19W
Illana B. 73 7 35N 123 45 E
Illapel 124 32 0 S 71 10W
'Illār 62 32 23N 35 7 E
Ille 20 42 40N 2 37 E
Ille-et-Vilaine □ 18 48 10N 1 30W
Iller → 25 48 23N 9 58 E
Illescas 30 40 8N 3 51W
Illiers 18 48 18N 1 15 E
Illimani 126 16 30 S 67 50W
Illinois □ 111 40 15N 89 30W
Illinois → 111 38 55N 90 28W
Illium = Troy 44 39 57N 26 12 E
Illizi 83 26 31N 8 32 E
Illora 31 37 17N 3 53W
Ilm → 24 51 7N 11 45 E
Ilmen, Oz. 54 58 15N 31 10 E
Ilmenau 24 50 41N 10 55 E
Ilo 126 17 40 S 71 20W
Ilobu 85 7 45N 4 25 E
Iloilo 73 10 45N 122 33 E
Ilok 42 45 15N 19 20 E
Ilora 85 7 45N 3 50 E
Ilorin 85 8 30N 4 35 E
Iloulya 57 49 15N 44 2 E
Ilovatka 55 50 30N 45 50 E
Ilovlya → 57 49 14N 43 54 E
Iłowa 28 51 30N 15 10 E
Ilubabor □ 87 7 25N 35 0 E
Ilukste 54 55 55N 26 20 E
Ilva Mică 46 47 17N 24 40 E
Ilwaki 73 7 55 S 126 30 E
Ilyichevsk 56 46 10N 30 35 E
Iłża 28 51 10N 21 15 E
Iłzanka → 28 51 14N 21 48 E
Imabari 74 34 4N 133 0 E
Imaloto → 93 23 27 S 45 13 E
Imandra, Oz. 52 67 30N 33 0 E
Imari 74 33 15N 129 52 E
Imasa 86 18 0N 36 12 E
Imathía □ 44 40 30N 22 15 E
Imbâbah 86 30 5N 31 12 E
Imbler 118 45 31N 118 0W
Imdahane 82 32 8N 7 0W
imeni 26 Bakinskikh Komissarov (Neft-chala) 53 39 19N 49 12 E
imeni 26 Bakinskikh Komissarov (Vyshzha) 53 39 22N 54 10 E
Imeni Poliny Osipenko 59 52 30N 136 29 E
Imeri, Serra 126 0 50N 65 25W
Imerimandroso 93 17 26 S 48 35 E
Imi (Hinna) 87 6 28N 42 10 E
Imishly 57 39 49N 48 4 E
Imitek 82 29 43N 8 10W
Imlay 118 40 45N 118 9W
Imlay City 112 43 0N 83 2W
Immenstadt 25 47 34N 10 13 E
Immingham 12 53 37N 0 12W
Immokalee 115 26 25N 81 26W
Imo □ 85 5 15N 7 20 E
Imola 39 44 20N 11 42 E
Imotski 42 43 27N 17 12 E
Imperatriz 127 5 30 S 47 29W
Impéria 38 43 52N 8 0 E
Imperial, Can. 109 51 21N 105 28W
Imperial, Calif., U.S.A. 119 32 52N 115 34W
Imperial, Nebr., U.S.A. 116 40 38N 101 39W
Imperial Dam 119 32 50N 114 30W
Impfondo 88 1 40N 18 0 E
Imphal 67 24 48N 93 56 E
Imphy 19 46 56N 3 15 E
İmroz = Gökçeada 44 40 10N 25 50 E
Imst 26 47 15N 10 44 E
Imuruan B. 73 10 40N 119 10 E
In Belbel 82 27 55N 1 12 E
In Delimane 85 15 52N 1 31 E
In Rhar 82 27 10N 1 59 E
In Salah 82 27 10N 2 32 E
In Tallak 85 16 19N 3 15 E
Ina 74 35 50N 138 0 E
Ina-Bonchi 74 35 45N 137 58 E
Inangahua Junc. 101 41 52 S 171 59 E
Inanwatan 73 2 10 S 132 14 E
Iñapari 126 11 0 S 69 40W
Inari 50 68 54N 27 5 E
Inarijärvi 50 69 0N 28 0 E
Inawashiro-Ko 74 37 29N 140 6 E
Inca 32 39 43N 2 54 E
Incaguasi 124 29 12 S 71 5W
İnce-Burnu 56 42 7N 34 56 E
Inchon 76 37 27N 126 40 E
Incio 30 42 39N 7 21W
Incomáti → 93 25 46 S 32 43 E
Incudine, L' 21 41 50N 9 12 E
Inda Silase 87 14 10N 38 15 E
Indalsälven → 48 62 36N 17 30 E
Indaw 67 24 15N 96 5 E
Indbir 87 8 7N 37 52 E
Independence, Calif., U.S.A. 119 36 51N 118 14W
Independence, Iowa, U.S.A. 116 42 27N 91 52W
Independence, Kans., U.S.A. 117 37 10N 95 43W
Independence, Mo., U.S.A. 116 39 3N 94 25W
Independence, Oreg., U.S.A. 118 44 53N 123 12W
Independence Fjord 4 82 10N 29 0W
Independence Mts. 118 41 30N 116 2W
Independenţa 46 45 25N 27 42 E
Inderborskiy 57 48 30N 51 42 E
India ■ 3 20 0N 78 0 E
Indian → 115 27 59N 80 34W
Indian-Antarctic Ridge 94 49 0 S 120 0 E
Indian Cabins 108 59 52N 117 40W
Indian Harbour 107 54 27N 57 13W
Indian Head 109 50 30N 103 41W
Indian Ocean 3 5 0 S 75 0 E
Indiana 114 40 38N 79 9W
Indiana □ 114 40 0N 86 0W
Indianapolis 114 39 42N 86 10W
Indianola, Iowa, U.S.A. 116 41 20N 93 32W
Indianola, Miss., U.S.A. 117 33 27N 90 40W
Indiga 52 67 50N 48 50 E
Indigirka → 59 70 48N 148 54 E
Inđija 42 45 6N 20 7 E
Indio 119 33 46N 116 15W
Indonesia ■ 72 5 0 S 115 0 E
Indore 68 22 42N 75 53 E
Indramayu 73 6 21 S 108 20 E
Indramayu, Tg. 73 6 20 S 108 20 E
Indravati → 70 19 20N 80 20 E
Indre □ 19 46 50N 1 39 E
Indre → 18 47 16N 0 19 E
Indre-et-Loire □ 18 47 12N 0 40 E
Indus → 68 24 20N 67 47 E
Indus, Mouth of the 68 24 00N 68 00 E
İnebolu 64 41 55N 33 40 E
İnegöl 64 40 5N 29 31 E
Ineu 42 46 26N 21 51 E
Inezgane 82 30 25N 9 29W
Infante, Kaap 92 34 27 S 20 51 E
Infantes 33 38 43N 3 1W
Infiernillo, Presa del 120 18 9N 102 0W
Infiesto 30 43 21N 5 21W
Ingende 88 0 12 S 18 57 E
Ingenio Santa Ana 124 27 25 S 65 40W
Ingersoll 112 43 4N 80 55W
Ingham 97 18 43 S 146 10 E
Ingleborough 12 54 11N 2 23W
Inglewood, Queensland, Austral. 99 28 25 S 151 2 E
Inglewood, Vic., Austral. 99 36 29 S 143 53 E
Inglewood, N.Z. 101 39 9 S 174 14 E
Inglewood, U.S.A. 119 33 58N 118 21W
Ingólfshöfði 50 63 48N 16 39W
Ingolstadt 25 48 45N 11 26 E
Ingomar 118 46 35N 107 21W
Ingonish 107 46 42N 60 18W
Ingore 84 12 24N 15 48W
Ingrid Christensen Coast 5 69 30 S 76 00 E
Ingul → 56 46 50N 32 15 E
Ingulec 56 47 42N 33 14 E
Ingulets → 56 46 41N 32 48 E
Inguri →, U.S.S.R. 57 42 38N 41 35 E
Inguri →, U.S.S.R. 57 42 15N 41 48 E
Inhaca, I. 93 26 1 S 32 57 E
Inhafenga 93 20 36 S 33 53 E
Inhambane 93 23 54 S 35 30 E
Inhambane □ 93 22 30 S 34 20 E
Inhaminga 91 18 26 S 35 0 E
Inharrime 93 24 30 S 35 0 E
Inharrime → 93 24 30 S 35 0 E
Iniesta 33 39 27N 1 45W
Ining = Yining 75 43 58N 81 10 E
Inírida → 126 3 55N 67 52W
Inishbofin 15 53 35N 10 12W
Inishmore 15 53 8N 9 45W
Inishowen 15 55 14N 7 15W
Injune 97 25 53 S 148 32 E
Inklin 108 58 56N 133 5W
Inklin → 108 58 50N 133 10W
Inkom 118 42 51N 112 15W
Inle L. 67 20 30N 96 58 E
Inn → 25 48 35N 13 28 E
Innamincka 99 27 44 S 140 46 E
Inner Hebrides 14 57 0N 6 30W
Inner Mongolia = Nei Monggol Zizhiqu □ 76 42 0N 112 0 E
Inner Sound 14 57 30N 5 55W
Innerkip 112 43 13N 80 42W
Innerste → 24 52 45N 9 40 E
Innetalling I. 106 56 0N 79 0W
Innisfail, Austral. 97 17 33 S 146 5 E
Innisfail, Can. 108 52 0N 113 57W
Innsbruck 26 47 16N 11 23 E
Inny → 15 53 30N 7 50W
Inongo 88 1 55 S 18 30 E
Inoucdjouac (Port Harrison) 105 58 25N 78 15W
Inowrocław 28 52 50N 18 12 E
Inquisivi 126 16 50 S 67 10W
Insein 67 16 50N 96 5 E
Însurăţei 46 44 50N 27 40 E
Inta 52 66 5N 60 8 E
Intendente Alvear 125 35 12 S 63 32W
Interior 116 43 46N 101 59W
Interlaken 25 46 41N 7 50 E
International Falls 116 48 36N 93 25W
Interview I. 71 12 55N 92 42 E
Inthanon, Doi 71 18 35N 98 29 E

Intiyaco 124 28 43 S 60 5W
Inútil, B. 128 53 30 S 70 15W
Inuvik 104 68 16N 133 40W
Inveraray 14 56 13N 5 5W
Inverbervie 14 56 50N 2 17W
Invercargill 101 46 24 S 168 24 E
Inverell 97 29 45 S 151 8 E
Invergordon 14 57 41N 4 10W
Invermere 108 50 30N 116 2W
Inverness, Can. 107 46 15N 61 19W
Inverness, U.K. 14 57 29N 4 12W
Inverness, U.S.A. 115 28 50N 82 20W
Inverurie 14 57 15N 2 21W
Investigator Group 96 34 45 S 134 20 E
Investigator Str. 97 35 30 S 137 0 E
Invona 112 40 46N 78 35W
Inya 58 50 28N 86 37 E
Inyanga 91 18 12 S 32 40 E
Inyangani 91 18 5 S 32 50 E
Inyantue 91 18 30 S 26 40 E
Inyazura 91 18 40 S 32 16 E
Inyo Range 119 37 0N 118 0W
Inyokern 119 35 38N 117 48W
Inza 55 53 55N 46 25 E
Inzhavino 55 52 22N 42 30 E
Ioánnina 44 39 42N 20 47 E
Ioánnina (Janinà) □ 44 39 39N 20 57 E
Iola 117 38 0N 95 20W
Ion Corvin 46 44 7N 27 50 E
Iona 14 56 20N 6 25W
Ione, Calif., U.S.A. 118 38 20N 120 56W
Ione, Wash., U.S.A. 118 48 44N 117 29W
Ionia 114 42 59N 85 7W
Ionian Is. = Iónioi Nísoi 45 38 40N 20 0 E
Ionian Sea 35 37 30N 17 30 E
Iónioi Nísoi 45 38 40N 20 0 E
Iori → 57 41 3N 46 17 E
Íos 45 36 41N 25 20 E
Iowa □ 116 42 18N 93 30W
Iowa City 116 41 40N 91 35W
Iowa Falls 116 42 30N 93 15W
Ipala 90 4 30 S 32 52 E
Ipameri 127 17 44 S 48 9W
Ipáti 45 38 52N 22 14 E
Ipatovo 57 45 45N 42 50 E
Ipel → 27 48 10N 19 35 E
Ipiales 126 0 50N 77 37W
Ipin = Yibin 75 28 45N 104 32 E
Ípiros □ 44 39 30N 20 30 E
Ipixuna 126 7 0 S 71 40W
Ipoh 71 4 35N 101 5 E
Ippy 88 6 5N 21 7 E
Ipsala 44 40 55N 26 23 E
Ipsárion Óros 44 40 40N 24 40 E
Ipswich, Austral. 97 27 35 S 152 40 E
Ipswich, U.K. 13 52 4N 1 9 E
Ipswich, Mass., U.S.A. 113 42 40N 70 50W
Ipswich, S.D., U.S.A. 116 45 28N 99 1W
Ipu 127 4 23 S 40 44W
Iput → 54 52 26N 31 2 E
Iquique 126 20 19 S 70 5W
Iquitos 126 3 45 S 73 10W
Iracoubo 127 5 30N 53 10W
Iráklia 45 36 50N 25 28 E
Iráklion 45 35 20N 25 12 E
Iráklion □ 45 35 10N 25 10 E
Iralá 125 25 55 S 54 35W
Iramba □ 90 4 30 S 34 30 E
Iran ■ 65 33 0N 53 0 E
Iran, Pegunungan 72 2 20N 114 50 E
Iranamadu Tank 70 9 23N 80 29 E
Īrānshahr 65 27 15N 60 40 E
Irapuato 120 20 40N 101 30W
Iraq ■ 64 33 0N 44 0 E
Irarrar, O. → 82 20 0N 1 30 E
Irati 125 25 25 S 50 38W
Irbid 62 32 35N 35 48 E
Irebu 88 0 40 S 17 46 E
Iregua → 32 42 27N 2 24 E
Ireland ■ 15 53 0N 8 0W
Ireland I. 121 32 16N 64 50W
Ireland's Eye 15 53 25N 6 4W
Irele 85 7 40N 5 40 E
Iret 59 60 3N 154 20 E
Irgiz, Bol. 55 52 10N 49 10 E
Irhârharene 83 27 37N 7 30 E
Irharrhar, O. → 83 28 3N 6 15 E
Irherm 82 30 7N 8 18W
Irhil Mgoun 82 31 30N 6 28W
Irian Jaya □ 73 4 0 S 137 0 E
Irié 84 8 15N 9 10W
Iringa 90 7 48 S 35 43 E
Iringa □ 90 7 48 S 35 43 E
Irinjalakuda 70 10 21N 76 14 E
Iriri → 127 3 52 S 52 37W
Irish Sea 12 54 0N 5 0W
Irkineyeva 59 58 30N 96 49 E
Irkutsk 59 52 18N 104 20 E
Irma 109 52 55N 111 14W
Iroise, Mer d' 18 48 15N 4 45W
Iron Baron 99 32 58 S 137 11 E
Iron Gate = Portile de Fier 46 44 42N 22 30 E
Iron Knob 97 32 46 S 137 8 E
Iron Mountain 114 45 49N 88 4W
Iron River 116 46 6N 88 40W
Ironbridge 13 52 38N 2 29W
Ironstone Kopje 92 25 17 S 24 5 E
Ironton, Mo., U.S.A. 117 37 40N 90 40W
Ironton, Ohio, U.S.A. 114 38 35N 82 40W
Ironwood 116 46 30N 90 10W
Iroquois Falls 106 48 46N 80 41W
Irpen 54 50 30N 30 15 E
Irrara Cr. → 99 29 35 S 145 31 E
Irrawaddy □ 67 17 0N 95 0 E
Irrawaddy → 67 15 50N 95 6 E
Irsina 41 40 45N 16 15 E
Irtysh → 58 61 4N 68 52 E
Irumu 90 1 32N 29 53 E
Irún 32 43 20N 1 52W
Irurzun 32 42 55N 1 50W
Irvine, Can. 109 49 57N 110 16W
Irvine, U.K. 14 55 37N 4 40W
Irvine, U.S.A. 114 37 42N 83 58W
Irvinestown 15 54 28N 7 38W
Irymple 99 34 14 S 142 8 E
Is-sur-Tille 19 47 30N 5 10 E
Isa 85 13 14N 6 24 E
Isaac → 97 22 55 S 149 20 E
Isabel 116 45 27N 101 22W
Isabela, I. 120 21 51N 105 55W
Isabella, Cord. 121 13 30N 85 25W
Ísafjarðardjúp 50 66 10N 23 0W
Ísafjörður 50 66 5N 23 9W
Isagarh 68 24 48N 77 51 E
Isaka 90 3 56 S 32 59 E
Isangi 88 0 52N 24 10 E
Isar → 25 48 49N 12 58 E
Isarco → 39 46 57N 11 18 E
Ísari 45 37 22N 22 0 E
Isbergues 19 50 36N 2 24 E
Isbiceni 46 43 45N 24 40 E
Íschia 40 40 45N 13 51 E
Ise 74 34 25N 136 45 E
Ise-Wan 74 34 43N 136 43 E
Isefjord 49 55 53N 11 50 E
Iseo 38 45 40N 10 3 E
Iseo, L. d' 38 45 45N 10 3 E
Iseramagazi 90 4 37 S 32 10 E
Isère □ 21 45 15N 5 40 E
Isère → 21 44 59N 4 51 E
Iserlohn 24 51 22N 7 40 E
Isérnia 41 41 35N 14 12 E
Iseyin 85 8 0N 3 36 E
Ishikari-Wan (Otaru-Wan) 74 43 25N 141 1 E
Ishikawa □ 74 36 30N 136 30 E
Ishim 58 56 10N 69 30 E
Ishim → 58 57 45N 71 10 E
Ishinomaki 74 38 32N 141 20 E
Ishmi 44 41 33N 19 34 E
Ishpeming 114 46 30N 87 40W
Isigny-sur-Mer 18 49 19N 1 6W
Isil Kul 58 54 55N 71 16 E
Isiolo 90 0 24N 37 33 E
Isiolo □ 90 2 30N 37 30 E
Isipingo Beach 93 30 00 S 30 57 E
Isiro 90 2 53N 27 40 E
Isisford 98 24 15 S 144 21 E
İskenderun 64 36 32N 36 10 E
İskilip 56 40 50N 34 20 E
Iskŭr → 43 43 45N 24 25 E
Iskŭr, Yazovir 43 42 23N 23 30 E
Iskut → 108 56 45N 131 49W
Isla → 14 56 32N 3 20W
Isla Cristina 31 37 13N 7 17W
Islamabad 66 33 40N 73 10 E
Islamkot 68 24 42N 70 13 E
Islampur 70 17 2N 74 20 E
Island → 108 60 25N 121 12W
Island Falls, Can. 106 49 35N 81 20W
Island Falls, U.S.A. 107 46 0N 68 16W
Island L. 109 53 47N 94 25W
Island Pond 114 44 50N 71 50W
Islands, B. of, Can. 107 49 11N 58 15W
Islands, B. of, N.Z. 101 35 20 S 174 20 E
Islay 14 55 46N 6 10W
Isle → 20 44 55N 0 15W
Isle-Adam, L' 19 49 6N 2 14 E
Isle aux Morts 107 47 35N 59 0W
Isle-Jourdain, L', Gers, France 20 43 36N 1 5 E
Isle-Jourdain, L', Vienne, France 20 46 13N 0 31 E
Isle of Wight □ 13 50 40N 1 20W
Isle Royale 116 48 0N 88 50W
Isleta 119 34 58N 106 46W
Ismail 56 45 22N 28 46 E
Ismâ'ilîya 86 30 37N 32 18 E
Ismaning 25 48 14N 11 41 E
Ismay 116 46 33N 104 44W
Isna 86 25 17N 32 30 E
Isola del Gran Sasso d'Italia 39 42 30N 13 40 E
Ísola del Liri 40 41 39N 13 32 E
Ísola della Scala 38 45 16N 11 0 E
Ísola di Capo Rizzuto 41 38 56N 17 5 E
Isparta 64 37 47N 30 30 E
Isperikh 43 43 43N 26 50 E
Íspica 41 36 47N 14 53 E
İspir 57 40 40N 40 50 E
Israel ■ 62 32 0N 34 50 E
Issia 84 6 33N 6 33W
Issoire 20 45 32N 3 15 E
Issoudun 19 46 57N 2 0 E
Issyk-Kul, Ozero 58 42 25N 77 15 E
Ist 39 44 17N 14 47 E
İstanbul 64 41 0N 29 0 E
Istiaía 45 38 57N 23 9 E
Istok 42 42 45N 20 24 E
Istokpoga, L. 115 27 22N 81 14W
Istra, U.S.S.R. 55 55 55N 36 50 E
Istra, Yugo. 39 45 10N 14 0 E
Istranca Dağları 43 41 48N 27 30 E
Istres 21 43 31N 4 59 E
Istria = Istra 39 45 10N 14 0 E
Itá 124 25 29 S 57 21W
Itabaiana 127 7 18 S 35 19W
Itaberaba 127 12 32 S 40 18W
Itabira 127 19 37 S 43 13W
Itabirito 125 20 15 S 43 48W
Itabuna 127 14 48 S 39 16W
Itaituba 127 4 10 S 55 50W
Itajaí 125 27 50 S 48 39W
Itajubá 125 22 24 S 45 30W
Itaka 91 8 50 S 32 49 E
Italy ■ 36 42 0N 13 0 E
Itampolo 93 24 41 S 43 57 E
Itapecuru-Mirim 127 3 24 S 44 20W
Itaperuna 127 21 10 S 41 54W
Itapetininga 125 23 36 S 48 7W
Itapeva 125 23 59 S 48 59W
Itapicuru →, Bahia, Brazil 127 11 47 S 37 32W
Itapicuru →, Maranhão, Brazil 127 2 52 S 44 12W
Itapuá □ 125 26 40 S 55 40W
Itaquari 125 20 20 S 40 25W
Itaquatiara 126 2 58 S 58 30W
Itaquí 124 29 8 S 56 30W
Itararé 125 24 6 S 49 23W
Itarsi 68 22 36N 77 51 E
Itatí 124 27 16 S 58 15W
Itatuba 126 5 46 S 63 20W
Itchen → 13 50 57N 1 20W
Itéa 45 38 25N 22 25 E
Ithaca 114 42 25N 76 30W
Ithaca = Itháki 45 38 25N 20 43 E
Itháki 45 38 25N 20 40 E
Ito 74 34 58N 139 5 E
Itoman 77 26 7N 127 40 E
Iton → 18 49 9N 1 12 E
Itonamas → 126 12 28 S 64 24W
Itsa 86 29 15N 30 47 E
Ittiri 40 40 38N 8 32 E
Itu, Brazil 125 23 17 S 47 15W
Itu, Nigeria 85 5 10N 7 58 E
Ituaçu 127 13 50 S 41 18W
Ituiutaba 127 19 0 S 49 25W
Itumbiara 127 18 20 S 49 10W
Ituna 109 51 10N 103 24W
Itunge Port 91 9 40 S 33 55 E
Iturbe 124 23 0 S 65 25W
Ituri → 90 1 40N 27 1 E
Iturup, Ostrov 59 45 0N 148 0 E
Ituyuro → 124 22 40 S 63 50W
Itzehoe 24 53 56N 9 31 E
Ivaí → 125 23 18 S 53 42W
Ivalo 50 68 38N 27 35 E
Ivalojoki → 50 68 40N 27 40 E
Ivangorod 54 59 37N 28 40 E
Ivangrad 42 42 51N 19 52 E
Ivanhoe 97 32 56 S 144 20 E
Ivanhoe L. 109 60 25N 106 30W
Ivanić Grad 39 45 41N 16 25 E
Ivanjica 42 43 35N 20 12 E
Ivanjšcice 39 46 12N 16 13 E
Ivankoyskoye Vdkhr. 55 56 37N 36 32 E
Ivano-Frankovsk 56 48 56N 24 43 E
Ivano-Frankovsk (Stanislav) 54 48 40N 24 40 E
Ivanovo, Byelorussia, U.S.S.R. 54 52 7N 25 29 E
Ivanovo, R.S.F.S.R., U.S.S.R. 55 57 5N 41 0 E
Ivato 93 20 37 S 47 10 E
Ivaylovgrad 43 41 32N 26 8 E
Ivdel 52 60 42N 60 24 E
Ivinheima → 125 23 14 S 53 42W
Iviza = Ibiza 33 39 0N 1 30 E
Ivohibe 93 22 31 S 46 57 E
Ivory Coast ■ 84 7 30N 5 0W
Ivösjön 49 56 8N 14 25 E
Ivrea 38 45 30N 7 52 E
Ivugivik, (N.D. d'Ivugivic) 105 62 24N 77 55W
Iwahig 72 8 35N 117 32 E
Iwaki 74 37 3N 140 55 E
Iwakuni 74 34 15N 132 8 E
Iwata 74 34 42N 137 51 E
Iwate □ 74 39 30N 141 30 E
Iwate-San 74 39 51N 141 0 E
Iwo 85 7 39N 4 9 E
IwoniczZdrój 27 49 37N 21 47 E
Ixiamas 126 13 50 S 68 5W
Ixopo 93 30 11 S 30 5 E
Ixtepec 120 16 32N 95 10W
Ixtlán de Juárez 120 17 23N 96 28W
Ixtlán del Río 120 21 5N 104 21W
Izabel, L. de 120 15 30N 89 10W
Izamal 120 20 56N 89 1W
Izberbash 57 42 35N 47 52 E
Izbica 28 50 53N 23 10 E
Izbica Kujawska 28 52 25N 18 30 E
Izegem 16 50 55N 3 12 E
Izgrev 43 43 36N 26 58 E
Izhevsk 52 56 51N 53 14 E
İzmir (Smyrna) 53 38 25N 27 8 E
İzmit 64 40 45N 29 50 E
Iznajar 31 37 15N 4 19W
Iznalloz 33 37 24N 3 30W
Izobil'nyy 57 45 25N 41 44 E
Izola 39 45 32N 13 39 E
Izra 62 32 51N 36 15 E
Izra' 62 32 52N 36 5 E
Iztochni Rodopi 43 41 45N 25 30 E
Izumi-sano 74 34 23N 135 18 E
Izumo 74 35 20N 132 46 E
Izyaslav 54 50 5N 26 50 E
Izyum 56 49 12N 37 19 E

J

Jaba 87 6 20N 35 7 E
Jaba' 62 32 20N 35 13 E
Jabal el Awlîya 87 15 10N 32 31 E
Jabalón → 31 38 53N 4 5W
Jabalpur 69 23 9N 79 58 E
Jabālyah 62 31 32N 34 27 E
Jablah 64 35 20N 36 0 E
Jablanac 39 44 42N 14 56 E
Jablonec 26 50 43N 15 10 E
Jablonica 27 48 37N 17 26 E
Jabłonowo 28 53 23N 19 10 E
Jaboticabal 125 21 15 S 48 17W
Jabukovac 42 44 22N 22 21 E
Jaburu 126 5 30 S 64 0W
Jaca 32 42 35N 0 33W
Jacareí 125 23 20 S 46 0W
Jacarèzinho 125 23 5 S 50 0W
Jáchymov 26 50 22N 12 55 E
Jackman 107 45 35N 70 17W
Jacksboro 117 33 14N 98 15W
Jackson, Austral. 99 26 39 S 149 39 E
Jackson, Ala., U.S.A. 115 31 32N 87 53W
Jackson, Calif., U.S.A. 118 38 19N 120 47W
Jackson, Ky., U.S.A. 114 37 35N 83 22W
Jackson, Mich., U.S.A. 114 42 18N 84 25W
Jackson, Minn., U.S.A. 116 43 35N 95 0W
Jackson, Miss., U.S.A. 117 32 20N 90 10W
Jackson, Mo., U.S.A. 117 37 25N 89 42W
Jackson, Ohio, U.S.A. 114 39 0N 82 40W
Jackson, Tenn., U.S.A. 115 35 40N 88 50W
Jackson, Wyo., U.S.A. 118 43 30N 110 49W
Jackson Bay 101 43 58 S 168 42 E
Jackson, L. 118 43 55N 110 40W
Jacksons 101 42 46 S 171 32 E
Jacksonville, Ala., U.S.A. 115 33 49N 85 45W
Jacksonville, Fla., U.S.A. 115 30 15N 81 38W
Jacksonville, Ill., U.S.A. 116 39 42N 90 15W
Jacksonville, N.C., U.S.A. 115 34 50N 77 29W
Jacksonville, Oreg., U.S.A. 118 42 19N 122 56W
Jacksonville, Tex., U.S.A. 117 31 58N 95 19W
Jacksonville Beach 115 30 19N 81 26W
Jacmel 121 18 14N 72 32W
Jacob Lake 119 36 45N 112 12W
Jacobabad 68 28 20N 68 29 E
Jacobina 127 11 11 S 40 30W
Jacob's Well 62 32 13N 35 13 E
Jacques-Cartier, Mt. 107 48 57N 66 0W
Jacqueville 84 5 12N 4 25W
Jacuí → 125 30 2 S 51 15W
Jacundá → 127 1 57 S 50 26W
Jade 24 53 22N 8 14 E
Jadebusen 24 53 30N 8 15 E
Jadotville = Likasi 91 10 55 S 26 48 E
Jadovnik 42 43 20N 19 45 E
Jadów 28 52 28N 21 38 E
Jadraque 32 40 55N 2 55W
Jādū 83 32 0N 12 0 E
Jaén, Peru 126 5 25 S 78 40W
Jaén, Spain 31 37 44N 3 43W
Jaén □ 31 37 50N 3 30W
Jaerens Rev 47 58 45N 5 45 E
Jafène 82 20 35N 5 30W
Jaffa = Tel Aviv-Yafo 62 32 4N 34 48 E
Jaffa, C. 99 36 58 S 139 40 E
Jaffna 70 9 45N 80 2 E
Jagadhri 68 30 10N 77 20 E
Jagadishpur 69 25 30N 84 21 E
Jagdalpur 70 19 3N 82 0 E
Jagersfontein 92 29 44 S 25 27 E
Jagst → 25 49 14N 9 11 E
Jagtial 70 18 50N 79 0 E
Jaguariaíva 125 24 10 S 49 50W
Jaguaribe → 127 4 25 S 37 45W
Jagüey Grande 121 22 35N 81 7W
Jahangirabad 68 28 19N 78 4 E
Jahrom 65 28 30N 53 31 E
Jailolo 73 1 5N 127 30 E
Jailolo, Selat 73 0 5N 129 5 E
Jainti 69 26 45N 89 40 E
Jaipur 68 27 0N 75 50 E
Jajce 42 44 19N 17 17 E
Jajpur 69 20 53N 86 22 E
Jakarta 73 6 9 S 106 49 E
Jakobstad (Pietarsaari) 50 63 40N 22 43 E
Jakupica 42 41 45N 21 22 E
Jal 117 32 8N 103 8W
Jalai Nur 76 49 27N 117 42 E
Jalalabad, Afghan. 66 34 30N 70 29 E
Jalalabad, India 69 27 41N 79 42 E
Jalalpur Jattan 68 32 38N 74 11 E
Jalapa, Guat. 120 14 39N 89 59W
Jalapa, Mexico 120 19 30N 96 56W
Jalas, Jabal al 64 27 30N 36 30 E
Jalaun 69 26 8N 79 25 E
Jaleswar 69 26 38N 85 48 E
Jalgaon, Maharashtra, India 68 21 0N 75 42 E
Jalgaon, Maharashtra, India 68 21 2N 76 31 E
Jalingo 85 8 55N 11 25 E
Jalisco □ 120 20 0N 104 0W
Jallas → 30 42 54N 9 8W
Jalna 70 19 48N 75 38 E
Jalón → 32 41 47N 1 4W
Jalpa 120 21 38N 102 58W
Jalpaiguri 69 26 32N 88 46 E
Jalq 65 27 35N 62 46 E
Jaluit I. 94 6 0N 169 30 E
Jamaari 85 11 44N 9 53 E
Jamaica ■ 121 18 10N 77 30W
Jamalpur, Bangla. 69 24 52N 89 56 E
Jamalpur, India 69 25 18N 86 28 E
Jamalpurganj 69 23 2N 88 1 E
Jamanxim → 127 4 43 S 56 18W
Jambe 73 1 15 S 132 10 E
Jambi 72 1 38 S 103 30 E
Jambi □ 72 1 30 S 102 30 E
Jambusar 68 22 3N 72 51 E
James → 116 42 52N 97 18W
James B. 106 51 30N 80 0W
James Range 96 24 10 S 132 30 E
James Ross I. 5 63 58 S 57 50W
Jamestown, Austral. 97 33 10 S 138 32 E
Jamestown, S. Afr. 92 31 6 S 26 45 E
Jamestown, Ky., U.S.A. 114 37 0N 85 5W
Jamestown, N.D., U.S.A. 116 46 54N 98 42W
Jamestown, N.Y., U.S.A. 114 42 5N 79 18W
Jamestown, Pa., U.S.A. 112 41 32N 80 27W
Jamestown, Tenn., U.S.A. 115 36 25N 85 0W
Jamkhaudi 70 16 30N 75 15 E
Jammā'în 62 32 8N 35 12 E
Jammalamadugu 70 14 51N 78 25 E
Jammerbugt 49 57 15N 9 20 E
Jammu 68 32 43N 74 54 E
Jammu & Kashmir □ 66 34 25N 77 0 E
Jamnagar 68 22 30N 70 6 E
Jamner 68 20 45N 75 52 E
Jampur 68 29 39N 70 40 E
Jamrud Fort 66 33 59N 71 24 E
Jamshedpur 69 22 44N 86 12 E
Jamtara 69 23 59N 86 49 E
Jämtlands län □ 48 62 40N 13 50 E
Jan Kemp 92 27 55 S 24 51 E
Jan L. 109 54 56N 102 55W
Jan Mayen Is. 4 71 0N 9 0W
Jand 66 33 30N 72 6 E
Janda, Laguna de la 31 36 15N 5 45W
Jandaq 65 34 3N 54 22 E
Jandola 68 32 20N 70 9 E
Jandowae 99 26 45 S 151 7 E
Jándula → 31 38 3N 4 6W
Janesville 116 42 39N 89 1W
Janga 85 10 5N 1 0W
Jangaon 70 17 44N 79 5 E
Jangeru 72 2 20 S 116 29 E
Janikowo 28 52 45N 18 7 E

Janīn 62 32 28N 35 18 E
Janja 42 44 40N 19 17 E
Janjevo 42 42 35N 21 19 E
Janjina 42 42 58N 17 25 E
Jánoshalma 27 46 18N 19 21 E
Jánosháza 27 47 8N 17 12 E
Jánossomorja 27 47 47N 17 11 E
Janów 28 50 44N 19 27 E
Janów Lubelski 28 50 48N 22 23 E
Janów Podlaski 28 52 11N 23 11 E
Janowiec Wielkopolski 28 52 45N 17 30 E
Januária 127 15 25 S 44 25W
Janub Dârfûr □ 87 11 0N 25 0 E
Janub Kordofân □ 87 12 0N 30 0 E
Janville 19 48 10N 1 50 E
Janzé 18 47 55N 1 28W
Jaora 68 23 40N 75 10 E
Japan ■ 74 36 0N 136 0 E
Japan, Sea of 74 40 0N 135 0 E
Japan Trench 94 32 0N 142 0 E
Japara 73 6 30 S 110 40 E
Japen = Yapen 73 1 50 S 136 0 E
Japurá → 126 3 8 S 64 46W
Jaque 126 7 27N 78 8W
Jara, La 119 37 16N 106 0W
Jaraicejo 31 39 40N 5 49W
Jaraiz 30 40 4N 5 45W
Jarales 119 34 39N 106 51W
Jarama → 32 40 2N 3 39W
Jarandilla 30 40 8N 5 39W
Jaranwala 68 31 15N 73 26 E
Jarash 62 32 17N 35 54 E
Jarbidge 118 41 56N 115 27W
Jardim 124 21 28 S 56 2W
Jardín → 33 38 50N 2 10W
Jardines de la Reina, Is. 121 20 50N 78 50W
Jargalant (Kobdo) 75 48 2N 91 37 E
Jargeau 19 47 50N 2 1 E
Jarmen 24 53 56N 13 20 E
Jarnac 20 45 40N 0 11W
Jarny 19 49 9N 5 53 E
Jarocin 28 51 59N 17 29 E
Jaroměř 26 50 22N 15 52 E
Jarosław 27 50 2N 22 42 E
Järpås 49 58 23N 12 57 E
Järpen 48 63 21N 13 26 E
Jarso 87 5 15N 37 30 E
Jarvis 112 42 53N 80 6W
Jarvis I. 95 0 15 S 159 55W
Jarvornik 27 50 23N 17 2 E
Jarwa 69 27 38N 82 30 E
Jaša Tomić 42 45 26N 20 50 E
Jasien 28 51 46N 15 0 E
Jasin 71 2 20N 102 26 E
Jāsk 65 25 38N 57 45 E
Jasło 27 49 45N 21 30 E
Jasper, Alta., Can. 108 52 55N 118 5W
Jasper, Ont., Can. 113 44 52N 75 57W
Jasper, Ala., U.S.A. 115 33 48N 87 16W
Jasper, Fla., U.S.A. 115 30 31N 82 58W
Jasper, Minn., U.S.A. 116 43 52N 96 22W
Jasper, Tex., U.S.A. 117 30 59N 93 58W
Jasper Nat. Park 108 52 50N 118 8W
Jassy = Iaşi 46 47 10N 27 40 E
Jastrebarsko 39 45 41N 15 39 E
Jastrowie 28 53 26N 16 49 E
Jastrzębie Zdrój 27 49 57N 18 35 E
Jászapáti 27 47 32N 20 10 E
Jászárokszállás 27 47 39N 20 1 E
Jászberény 27 47 30N 19 55 E
Jászkiser 27 47 27N 20 20 E
Jászladány 27 47 23N 20 10 E
Jataí 127 17 58 S 51 48W
Jati 68 24 20N 68 19 E
Jatibarang 73 6 28 S 108 18 E
Jatinegara 73 6 13 S 106 52 E
Játiva 33 39 0N 0 32W
Jatobal 127 4 35 S 49 33W
Jatt 62 32 24N 35 2 E
Jaú 125 22 10 S 48 30W
Jauja 126 11 45 S 75 15W
Jaunjelgava 54 56 35N 25 0 E
Jaunpur 69 25 46N 82 44 E
Java = Jawa 73 7 0 S 110 0 E
Java Sea 72 4 35 S 107 15 E
Java Trench 94 10 0 S 110 0W
Javadi Hills 70 12 40N 78 40 E
Jávea 33 38 48N 0 10 E
Javhlant = Ulyasutay 75 47 56N 97 28 E
Javla 70 17 18N 75 9 E
Javron 18 48 25N 0 25W
Jawa 73 7 0 S 110 0 E
Jawor 28 51 4N 16 11 E
Jaworzno 27 50 13N 19 11 E
Jay 117 36 25N 94 46W
Jaya, Puncak 73 3 57 S 137 17 E
Jayapura 73 2 28 S 140 38 E
Jayawijaya, Pegunungan 73 5 0 S 139 0 E
Jayton 117 33 17N 100 35W
Jean 119 35 47N 115 20W
Jean Marie River 104 61 32N 120 38W
Jean Rabel 121 19 50N 73 5W
Jeanerette 117 29 52N 91 38W
Jeanette, Ostrov 59 76 43N 158 0 E
Jeannette 112 40 20N 79 36W
Jebba, Moroc. 82 35 11N 4 43W
Jebba, Nigeria 85 9 9N 4 48 E
Jebel, Bahr el → 81 15 38N 32 31 E
Jebel Qerri 87 16 16N 32 50 E
Jedburgh 14 55 28N 2 33W
Jedlicze 27 49 43N 21 40 E
Jedlnia-Letnisko 28 51 25N 21 19 E
Jędrzejów 28 50 35N 20 15 E
Jedwabne 28 53 17N 22 18 E
Jedway 108 52 17N 131 14W
Jeetze → 24 53 9N 11 6 E
Jefferson, Iowa, U.S.A. 116 42 3N 94 25W
Jefferson, Ohio, U.S.A. 112 41 40N 80 46W
Jefferson, Tex., U.S.A. 117 32 45N 94 23W
Jefferson, Wis., U.S.A. 116 43 0N 88 49W
Jefferson City, Mo., U.S.A. 116 38 34N 92 10W
Jefferson City, Tenn., U.S.A. 115 36 8N 83 30W
Jefferson, Mt., Nev., U.S.A. 118 38 51N 117 0W
Jefferson, Mt., Oreg., U.S.A. 118 44 45N 121 50W
Jeffersonville 114 38 20N 85 42W
Jega 85 12 15N 4 23 E
Jekabpils 54 56 29N 25 57 E
Jelenia Góra 28 50 50N 15 45 E
Jelenia Góra □ 28 51 0N 15 30 E
Jelgava 54 56 41N 23 49 E
Jelica 42 43 50N 20 17 E
Jelli 87 5 25N 31 45 E
Jellicoe 106 49 40N 87 30W
Jelšava 27 48 37N 20 15 E
Jemaja 72 3 5N 105 45 E
Jember 73 8 11 S 113 41 E
Jembongan 72 6 45N 117 20 E
Jemeppe 16 50 37N 5 30 E
Jemnice 26 49 1N 15 34 E
Jena, Ger. 24 50 56N 11 33 E
Jena, U.S.A. 117 31 41N 92 7W
Jenbach 26 47 24N 11 47 E
Jendouba 83 36 29N 8 47 E
Jenkins 114 37 13N 82 41W
Jennings 117 30 10N 92 45W
Jennings → 108 59 38N 132 5W
Jenny 49 57 47N 16 35 E
Jeparit 99 36 8 S 142 1 E
Jequié 127 13 51 S 40 5W
Jequitinhonha 127 16 30 S 41 0W
Jequitinhonha → 127 15 51 S 38 53W
Jerada 82 34 17N 2 10W
Jerantut 71 3 56N 102 22 E
Jérémie 121 18 40N 74 10W
Jerez de García Salinas 120 22 39N 103 0W
Jerez de la Frontera 31 36 41N 6 7W
Jerez de los Caballeros 31 38 20N 6 45W
Jerez, Punta 120 22 58N 97 40W
Jericho 98 23 38 S 146 6 E
Jericho = El Arīhā 62 31 52N 35 27 E
Jerichow 24 52 30N 12 2 E
Jerilderie 99 35 20 S 145 41 E
Jermyn 113 41 31N 75 31W
Jerome 119 34 50N 112 0W
Jerrobert 109 51 56N 109 8W
Jersey City 114 40 41N 74 8W
Jersey, I. 18 49 13N 2 7W
Jersey Shore 114 41 17N 77 18W
Jerseyville 116 39 5N 90 20W
Jerusalem 62 31 47N 35 10 E
Jervis B. 97 35 8 S 150 46 E
Jesenice 39 46 28N 14 3 E
Jesenik 27 50 0N 17 8 E
Jesenké 27 48 20N 20 10 E
Jesselton = Kota Kinabalu 72 6 0N 116 4 E
Jessnitz 24 51 42N 12 19 E
Jessore 69 23 10N 89 10 E
Jesup 115 31 36N 81 54W
Jesús María 124 30 59 S 64 5W
Jetmore 117 38 10N 99 57W
Jetpur 68 21 45N 70 10 E
Jevnaker 47 60 15N 10 26 E
Jewett, Ohio, U.S.A. 112 40 22N 81 2W
Jewett, Tex., U.S.A. 117 31 20N 96 8W
Jewett City 113 41 36N 72 0W
Jeypore 70 18 50N 82 38 E
Jeziorak, Jezioro 28 53 40N 19 35 E
Jeziorany 28 53 58N 20 46 E
Jeziorka → 28 51 59N 20 57 E
Jhajjar 68 28 37N 76 42 E
Jhal Jhao 66 26 20N 65 35 E
Jhalawar 68 24 40N 76 10 E
Jhang Maghiana 68 31 15N 72 22 E
Jhansi 68 25 30N 78 36 E
Jharia 69 23 45N 86 26 E
Jharsuguda 69 21 56N 84 5 E
Jhelum 68 33 0N 73 45 E
Jhelum → 68 31 20N 72 10 E
Jhunjhunu 68 28 10N 75 30 E
Ji Xian 76 36 7N 110 40 E
Jia Xian 76 38 12N 110 28 E
Jiamusi 75 46 40N 130 26 E
Ji'an 75 27 6N 114 59 E
Jianchuan 75 26 38N 99 55 E
Jiande 77 29 23N 119 15 E
Jiangbei 77 29 40N 106 34 E
Jiange 77 32 4N 105 32 E
Jiangjin 77 29 14N 106 14 E
Jiangling 75 30 25N 112 12 E
Jiangmen 75 22 32N 113 0 E
Jiangshan 77 28 40N 118 37 E
Jiangsu □ 75 33 0N 120 0 E
Jiangxi □ 75 27 30N 116 0 E
Jiangyin 77 31 54N 120 17 E
Jiangyong 77 25 20N 111 22 E
Jiangyou 77 31 44N 104 43 E
Jianning 77 26 50N 116 50 E
Jian'ou 75 27 3N 118 17 E
Jianshi 77 30 37N 109 38 E
Jianshui 75 23 36N 102 43 E
Jianyang 77 27 20N 118 5 E
Jiao Xian 76 36 18N 120 1 E
Jiaohe 76 38 2N 116 20 E
Jiaozhou Wan 76 36 5N 120 10 E
Jiaozuo 77 35 16N 113 12 E
Jiawang 77 34 28N 117 26 E
Jiaxing 75 30 49N 120 45 E
Jiayi 75 23 30N 120 24 E
Jibāl 63 22 10N 56 8 E
Jibiya 85 13 5N 7 12 E
Jibou 46 47 15N 23 17 E
Jibuti = Djibouti ■ 63 12 0N 43 0 E
Jičín 26 50 25N 15 28 E
Jiddah 64 21 29N 39 10 E
Jido 67 29 2N 94 58 E
Jifnā 62 31 58N 35 13 E
Jihlava 26 49 28N 15 35 E
Jihlava → 26 48 55N 16 36 E
Jihočeský □ 26 49 8N 14 35 E
Jihomoravský □ 27 49 5N 16 30 E
Jijel 83 36 52N 5 50 E
Jijiga 63 9 20N 42 50 E
Jijona 33 38 34N 0 30W
Jikamshi 85 12 12N 7 45 E
Jilin 76 43 44N 126 30 E
Jilin □ 76 44 0N 124 0 E
Jiloca → 32 41 21N 1 39W
Jilong 75 25 8N 121 42 E
Jílové 26 49 52N 14 29 E
Jima 87 7 40N 36 47 E
Jimbolia 42 45 47N 20 43 E
Jimena de la Frontera 31 36 27N 5 24W
Jiménez 120 27 10N 104 54W
Jimo 76 36 23N 120 30 E
Jin Xian 76 38 55N 121 42 E
Jinan 76 36 38N 117 1 E
Jincheng 76 35 29N 112 50 E
Jind 68 29 19N 76 22 E
Jindabyne 99 36 25 S 148 35 E
Jindabyne L. 100 36 20 S 148 38 E
Jindrichuv Hradeç 26 49 10N 15 2 E
Jing He → 77 34 27N 109 4 E
Jing Xian 77 26 33N 109 40 E
Jingchuan 76 35 20N 107 20 E
Jingdezhen 75 29 20N 117 11 E
Jinggu 75 23 35N 100 41 E
Jinghai 76 38 55N 116 55 E
Jingle 76 38 20N 111 55 E
Jingmen 77 31 0N 112 10 E
Jingning 76 35 30N 105 43 E
Jingshan 77 31 1N 113 7 E
Jingtai 76 37 10N 104 6 E
Jingxi 75 23 8N 106 27 E
Jingyu 76 42 25N 126 45 E
Jingyuan 76 36 30N 104 40 E
Jingziguan 77 33 15N 111 0 E
Jinhe 76 51 18N 121 32 E
Jinhua 75 29 8N 119 38 E
Jining, Nei Mongol Zizhiqu, China 76 41 5N 113 0 E
Jining, Shandong, China 77 35 22N 116 34 E
Jinja 90 0 25N 33 12 E
Jinjini 84 7 26N 3 42W
Jinmen Dao 77 24 25N 118 25 E
Jinnah Barrage 65 32 58N 71 33 E
Jinotega 121 13 6N 85 59W
Jinotepe 121 11 50N 86 10W
Jinshi 75 29 40N 111 50 E
Jinxiang 77 35 5N 116 22 E
Jinzhou 76 41 5N 121 3 E
Jiparaná (Machado) → 126 8 3 S 62 52W
Jipijapa 126 1 0 S 80 40W
Jiquilpan 120 19 57N 102 42W
Jishou 77 28 21N 109 43 E
Jisr al Ḥusayn (Allenby) Br. 62 31 53N 35 33 E
Jisr ash Shughūr 64 35 49N 36 18 E
Jitra 71 6 16N 100 25 E
Jiu → 46 44 40N 23 25 E
Jiudengkou 76 39 56N 106 40 E
Jiujiang 75 29 42N 115 58 E
Jiuling Shan 77 28 40N 114 40 E
Jiuquan 75 39 50N 98 20 E
Jixi 76 45 20N 130 50 E
Jizera → 26 50 10N 14 43 E
Jizl Wadi 86 25 30N 38 30 E
Joaçaba 125 27 5 S 51 31W
João Pessoa 127 7 10 S 34 52W
Joaquín V. González 124 25 10 S 64 0W
Jobourg, Nez de 18 49 41N 1 57W
Jódar 33 37 50N 3 21W
Jodhpur 68 26 23N 73 8 E
Joensuu 52 62 37N 29 49 E
Jœuf 19 49 12N 6 1 E
Joggins 107 45 42N 64 27W
Jogjakarta = Yogyakarta 73 7 49 S 110 22 E
Johannesburg 93 26 10 S 28 2 E
Johansfors 49 56 42N 15 32 E
John Day 118 44 25N 118 57W
John Day → 118 45 44N 120 39W
John H. Kerr Res. 115 36 20N 78 30W
John o' Groats 14 58 39N 3 3W
Johnson 117 37 35N 101 48W
Johnson City, N.Y., U.S.A. 114 42 7N 75 57W
Johnson City, Tenn., U.S.A. 115 36 18N 82 21W
Johnson City, Tex., U.S.A. 117 30 15N 98 24W
Johnsonburg 112 41 30N 78 40W
Johnson's Crossing 108 60 29N 133 18W
Johnston Falls = Mambilima Falls 91 10 31 S 28 45 E
Johnston I. 95 17 10N 169 8W
Johnstone Str. 108 50 28N 126 0W
Johnstown, N.Y., U.S.A. 114 43 1N 74 20W
Johnstown, Pa., U.S.A. 114 40 19N 78 53W
Johor □ 71 2 5N 103 20 E
Joigny 19 48 0N 3 20 E
Joinvile 125 26 15 S 48 55 E
Joinville 19 48 27N 5 10 E
Joinville I. 5 65 0 S 55 30W
Jokkmokk 50 66 35N 19 50 E
Jökulsá á Brú → 50 65 40N 14 16W
Jökulsá Fjöllum → 50 66 10N 16 30W
Joliet 114 41 30N 88 0W
Joliette 106 46 3N 73 24W
Jolo 73 6 0N 121 0 E
Jombang 73 7 33 S 112 14 E
Jome 73 1 16 S 127 30 E
Jomfruland 49 58 52N 9 36 E
Jönåker 49 58 44N 16 40 E
Jonava 54 55 8N 24 12 E
Jones Sound 4 76 0N 85 0W
Jonesboro, Ark., U.S.A. 117 35 50N 90 45W
Jonesboro, Ill., U.S.A. 117 37 26N 89 18W
Jonesboro, La., U.S.A. 117 32 15N 92 41W
Jonesport 107 44 32N 67 38W
Jonglei 87 6 25N 30 50 E
Joniskis 54 56 13N 23 35 E
Jönköping 49 57 45N 14 10 E
Jönköpings län □ 49 57 30N 14 30 E
Jonquière 107 48 27N 71 14W
Jonsberg 49 58 30N 16 48 E
Jonsered 49 57 45N 12 10 E
Jonzac 20 45 27N 0 28W
Joplin 117 37 0N 94 31W
Jordan, Phil. 73 10 41N 122 38 E
Jordan, U.S.A. 118 47 25N 106 58W
Jordan ■ 64 31 0N 36 0 E
Jordan → 62 31 48N 35 32 E
Jordan Valley 118 43 0N 117 2W
Jordanów 27 49 41N 19 49 E
Jorhat 67 26 45N 94 12 E
Jorm 65 36 50N 70 52 E
Jörn 50 65 4N 20 1 E
Jørpeland 47 59 3N 6 1 E
Jorquera → 124 28 3 S 69 58W
Jos 85 9 53N 8 51 E
Jošanička Banja 42 43 24N 20 47 E
José Batlle y Ordóñez 125 33 20 S 55 10W
Joseni 46 46 42N 25 29 E
Joseph 118 45 27N 117 13W
Joseph Bonaparte G. 96 14 35 S 128 50 E
Joseph City 119 35 0N 110 16W
Joseph, L., Newf., Can. 107 52 45N 65 18W
Joseph, L., Ont., Can. 112 45 10N 79 44W
Josselin 18 47 57N 2 33W
Jostedal 47 61 35N 7 15 E
Jotunheimen 47 61 35N 8 25 E
Jourdanton 117 28 54N 98 32W
Joussard 108 55 22N 115 50W
Jovellanos 121 22 40N 81 10W
Jowzjān □ 65 36 10N 66 0 E
Joyeuse 21 44 29N 4 16 E
Józefów 28 52 10N 21 11 E
Ju Xian 77 36 35N 118 20 E
Juan Aldama 120 24 20N 103 23W
Juan Bautista 119 36 55N 121 33W
Juan Bautista Alberdi 124 34 26 S 61 48W
Juan de Fuca Str. 118 48 15N 124 0W
Juan de Nova 93 17 3 S 43 45 E
Juan Fernández, Arch. de 95 33 50 S 80 0W
Juan José Castelli 124 25 27 S 60 57W
Juan L. Lacaze 124 34 26 S 57 25W
Juárez 124 37 40 S 59 43W
Juárez, Sierra de 120 32 0N 116 0W
Juàzeiro 127 9 30 S 40 30W
Juàzeiro do Norte 127 7 10 S 39 18W
Jubbulpore = Jabalpur 69 23 9N 79 58 E
Jübek 24 54 31N 9 24 E
Jubga 57 44 19N 38 48 E
Juby, C. 80 28 0N 12 59W
Júcar → 33 39 5N 0 10W
Juchitán 120 16 27N 95 5W
Judaea = Yehuda 62 31 35N 34 57 E
Judenburg 26 47 12N 14 38 E
Judith → 118 47 44N 109 38W
Judith Gap 118 46 40N 109 46W
Judith Pt. 113 41 20N 71 30W
Jugoslavia = Yugoslavia ■ 37 44 0N 20 0 E
Juigalpa 121 12 6N 85 26W
Juillac 20 45 20N 1 19 E
Juist 24 53 40N 7 0 E
Juiz de Fora 127 21 43 S 43 19W
Jujuy □ 124 23 20 S 65 40W
Julesberg 116 41 0N 102 20W
Juli 126 16 10 S 69 25W
Julia Cr. → 98 20 0 S 141 11 E
Julia Creek 97 20 39 S 141 44 E
Juliaca 126 15 25 S 70 10W
Julian 119 33 4N 116 38W
Julian Alps = Julijske Alpe 39 46 15N 14 1 E
Julianehåb 4 60 43N 46 0W
Jülich 24 50 55N 6 20 E
Julijske Alpe 39 46 15N 14 1 E
Jullundur 68 31 20N 75 40 E
Julu 76 37 15N 115 2 E
Jumbo 91 17 30 S 30 58 E
Jumentos Cays 121 23 0N 75 40 E
Jumet 16 50 27N 4 25 E
Jumilla 33 38 28N 1 19W
Jumla 69 29 15N 82 13 E
Jumna = Yamuna → 68 25 30N 81 53 E
Junagadh 68 21 30N 70 30 E
Junction, Tex., U.S.A. 117 30 29N 99 48W
Junction, Utah, U.S.A. 119 38 10N 112 15W
Junction B. 96 11 52 S 133 55 E
Junction City, Kans., U.S.A. 116 39 4N 96 55W
Junction City, Oreg., U.S.A. 118 44 14N 123 12W
Jundah 97 24 46 S 143 2 E
Jundiaí 125 24 30 S 47 0W
Juneau 104 58 20N 134 20W
Junee 97 34 53 S 147 35 E
Jungfrau 25 46 32N 7 58 E
Junggar Pendi 75 44 30N 86 0 E
Jungshahi 68 24 52N 67 44 E
Juniata → 112 40 30N 77 40W
Junín 124 34 33 S 60 57W
Junín de los Andes 128 39 45 S 71 0W
Jūniyah 64 33 59N 35 38 E
Junnar 70 19 12N 73 58 E
Junquera, La 32 42 25N 2 53 E
Junta, La 117 38 0N 103 30W
Juntura 118 43 44N 118 4W
Jupiter → 107 49 29N 63 37W
Jur, Nahr el → 87 8 45N 29 15 E
Jura, France 19 46 35N 6 5 E
Jura, U.K. 14 56 0N 5 50W
Jura □ 19 46 47N 5 45 E
Jura, Sd. of 14 55 57N 5 45W
Jura Suisse 25 47 10N 7 0 E
Jurado 126 7 7N 77 46W
Jurien B. 96 30 17 S 115 0 E
Jurilovca 46 44 46N 28 52 E
Juruá → 126 2 37 S 65 44W
Juruena → 126 7 20 S 58 3W
Juruti 127 2 9 S 56 4W
Jussey 19 47 50N 5 55 E
Justo Daract 124 33 52 S 65 12W
Jüterbog 24 52 0N 13 6 E
Juticalpa 121 14 40N 86 12W
Jutland = Jylland 8 56 25N 9 30 E
Juvigny-sous-Andaine 18 48 32N 0 30W
Juvisy 19 48 43N 2 23 E
Juwain 65 31 45N 61 30 E
Juzennecourt 19 48 10N 4 48 E
Jylland 8 56 25N 9 30 E
Jyväskylä 72 62 14N 25 50 E

K

K2 66 35 58N 76 32 E
Kaalasin 71 16 26N 103 30 E
Kaap die Goeie Hoop 92 34 24S 18 30 E
Kaap Plato 92 28 30S 24 0 E
Kaapkruis 92 21 43S 14 0 E
Kaapstad = Cape Town 92 33 55S 18 22 E
Kabaena 73 5 15S 122 0 E
Kabala 84 9 38N 11 37W
Kabale 90 1 15S 30 0 E
Kabalo 90 6 0S 27 0 E
Kabambare 90 4 41S 27 39 E
Kabango 91 8 35S 28 30 E
Kabanjahe 72 3 6N 98 30 E
Kabara 84 16 40N 2 50W
Kabardinka 56 44 40N 37 57 E
Kabardino-Balkar-A.S.S.R. □ 57 43 30N 43 30 E
Kabare 73 0 4S 130 58 E
Kabarega Falls 90 2 15N 31 30 E
Kabasalan 73 7 47N 122 44 E
Kabba 85 7 50N 6 3 E
Kabi 85 13 30N 12 35 E
Kabinakagami L. 106 48 54N 84 25W
Kabīr Kūh 64 33 0N 47 30 E
Kabīr, Zab al 64 36 0N 43 0 E
Kabkabīyah 81 13 50N 24 0 E
Kabna 86 19 6N 32 40 E
Kabompo 91 13 36S 24 14 E
Kabompo → 89 14 10S 23 11 E
Kabondo 91 8 58S 25 40 E
Kabongo 90 7 22S 25 33 E
Kabou 85 9 28N 0 55 E
Kaboudia, Rass 83 35 13N 11 10 E
Kabra 98 23 25S 150 25 E
Kabūd Gonbad 65 37 5N 59 45 E
Kabul 66 34 28N 69 11 E
Kabúl □ 65 34 30N 69 0 E
Kabul → 66 33 55N 72 14 E
Kabunga 90 1 38S 28 3 E
Kaburuang 73 3 50N 126 30 E
Kabushiya 87 16 54N 33 41 E
Kabwe 91 14 30S 28 29 E
Kačanik 42 42 13N 21 12 E
Kachanovo 54 57 25N 27 38 E
Kachebera 91 13 50S 32 50 E
Kachin □ 67 26 0N 97 30 E
Kachira, L. 90 0 40S 31 7 E
Kachiry 58 53 10N 75 50 E
Kachisi 87 9 40N 37 50 E
Kackar 57 40 45N 41 10 E
Kadan Kyun 72 12 30N 98 20 E
Kadarkút 27 46 13N 17 39 E
Kadayanallur 70 9 3N 77 22 E
Kade 85 6 7N 0 56W
Kadi 68 23 18N 72 23 E
Kadina 97 34 0S 137 43 E
Kadiri 70 14 12N 78 13 E
Kadirli 64 37 23N 36 5 E
Kadiyevka 57 48 35N 38 40 E
Kadoka 116 43 50N 101 31W
Kadom 55 54 37N 42 30 E
Kâdugli 81 11 0N 29 45 E
Kaduna 85 10 30N 7 21 E
Kaduna □ 85 11 0N 7 30 E
Kaédi 84 16 9N 13 28W
Kaelé 85 10 7N 14 27 E
Kaesŏng 76 37 58N 126 35 E
Kâf 64 31 25N 37 29 E
Kafakumba 88 9 38S 23 46 E
Kafan 53 39 18N 46 15 E
Kafanchan 85 9 40N 8 20 E
Kafareti 85 10 25N 11 12 E
Kaffrine 84 14 8N 15 36W
Kafia Kingi 81 9 20N 24 25 E
Kafinda 91 12 32S 30 20 E
Kafirévs, Ákra 45 38 9N 24 38 E
Kafr 'Ayn 62 32 3N 35 7 E
Kafr el Dauwâr 86 31 8N 30 8 E
Kafr el Sheikh 86 31 15N 30 50 E
Kafr Kammā 62 32 44N 35 26 E
Kafr Kannā 62 32 45N 35 20 E
Kafr Mālik 62 32 0N 35 18 E
Kafr Mandā 62 32 49N 35 15 E
Kafr Quaddūm 62 32 14N 35 7 E
Kafr Rā'ī 62 32 23N 35 9 E
Kafr Şīr 62 33 19N 35 23 E
Kafr Yāsīf 62 32 58N 35 10 E
Kafue 91 15 46S 28 9 E
Kafue Flats 91 15 40S 27 25 E
Kafulwe 91 9 0S 29 1 E
Kaga Bandoro 88 7 0N 19 10 E
Kagan 58 39 43N 64 33 E
Kagawa □ 74 34 15N 134 0 E
Kagera → 90 0 57S 31 47 E
Kağizman 64 40 5N 43 10 E
Kagoshima 74 31 35N 130 33 E
Kagoshima □ 74 31 30N 130 30 E
Kagoshima-Wan 74 31 25N 130 40 E
Kagul 56 45 50N 28 15 E
Kahajan → 72 3 40S 114 0 E
Kahama 90 4 8S 32 30 E
Kahama □ 90 3 50S 32 0 E
Kahe 90 3 30S 37 25 E
Kahemba 88 7 18S 18 55 E
Kahil, Djebel bou 83 34 26N 4 0 E
Kahniah → 108 58 15N 120 55W
Kahnūj 65 27 55N 57 40 E
Kahoka 116 40 25N 91 42W
Kahoolawe 110 20 33N 156 35W
Kai Besar 73 5 35S 133 0 E
Kai Kai 92 19 52S 21 15 E
Kai, Kepulauan 73 5 55S 132 45W
Kai-Ketjil 73 5 45S 132 40 E
Kaiama 85 9 36N 4 1 E
Kaiapoi 101 42 24S 172 40 E
Kaieteur Falls 126 5 1N 59 10W
Kaifeng 77 34 48N 114 21 E
Kaihua 77 29 12N 118 20 E
Kaiingveld 92 30 0S 22 0 E
Kaikohe 101 35 25S 173 49 E
Kaikoura 101 42 25S 173 43 E
Kaikoura Pen. 101 42 25S 173 43 E
Kaikoura Ra. 101 41 59S 173 41 E
Kailahun 84 8 18N 10 39W
Kaili 77 26 33N 107 59 E
Kailu 76 43 38N 121 18 E
Kailua 110 19 39N 156 0W
Kaimana 73 3 39S 133 45 E
Kaimanawa Mts. 101 39 15S 175 56 E
Kaimganj 69 27 33N 79 24 E
Kaimur Hill 69 24 30N 82 0 E
Kainantu 98 6 18S 145 52 E
Kaingaroa Forest 101 38 24S 176 30 E
Kainji Res. 85 10 1N 4 40 E
Kaipara Harbour 101 36 25S 174 14 E
Kaiping 77 22 23N 112 42 E
Kaipokok B. 107 54 54N 59 47W
Kairana 68 29 24N 77 15 E
Kaironi 73 0 47S 133 40 E
Kairouan 83 35 45N 10 5 E
Kairuku 98 8 51S 146 35 E
Kaiserslautern 25 49 30N 7 43 E
Kaitaia 101 35 8S 173 17 E
Kaitangata 101 46 17S 169 51 E
Kaithal 68 29 48N 76 26 E
Kaiwi Channel 110 21 13N 157 30W
Kaiyuan 76 42 28N 124 1 E
Kajaani 50 64 17N 27 46 E
Kajabbi 97 20 0S 140 1 E
Kajan → 72 2 55N 117 35 E
Kajang 71 2 59N 101 48 E
Kajiado 90 1 53S 36 48 E
Kajiado □ 90 2 0S 36 30 E
Kajo Kaji 87 3 58N 31 40 E
Kajoa 73 0 1N 127 28 E
Kaka 81 10 38N 32 10 E
Kakabeka Falls 106 48 24N 89 37W
Kakamega 90 0 20N 34 46 E
Kakamega □ 90 0 20N 34 46 E
Kakanj 42 44 9N 18 7 E
Kakanui Mts. 101 45 10S 170 30 E
Kakegawa 74 34 45N 138 1 E
Kakhib 57 42 28N 46 34 E
Kakhovka 56 46 40N 33 15 E
Kakhovskoye Vdkhr. 56 47 5N 34 16 E
Kakinada (Cocanada) 70 16 57N 82 11 E
Kakisa → 108 61 3N 118 10W
Kakisa L. 108 60 56N 117 43W
Kakwa → 108 54 37N 118 28W
Kala 85 12 2N 14 40 E
Kala Oya → 70 8 20N 79 45 E
Kalaa-Kebira 83 35 59N 10 32 E
Kalabagh 68 33 0N 71 28 E
Kalabahi 73 8 13S 124 31 E
Kalabáka 44 39 42N 21 39 E
Kalabo 89 14 58S 22 40 E
Kalach 55 50 22N 41 0 E
Kalach na Donu 57 48 43N 43 32 E
Kaladan → 67 20 20N 93 5 E
Kaladar 112 44 37N 77 5W
Kalahari 92 24 0S 21 30 E
Kalahari Gemsbok Nat. Park 92 25 30S 20 30 E
Kalahasti 70 13 45N 79 44 E
Kalakamati 93 20 40S 27 25 E
Kalakan 59 55 15N 116 45 E
Kalama, U.S.A. 118 46 0N 122 55W
Kalama, Zaïre 90 2 52S 28 35 E
Kalamariá 44 40 33N 22 55 E
Kalamata 45 37 3N 22 10 E
Kalamazoo 114 42 20N 85 35W
Kalamazoo → 114 42 40N 86 12W
Kalamb 70 18 3N 74 48 E
Kalambo Falls 91 8 37S 31 35 E
Kálamos, Greece 45 38 37N 20 55 E
Kálamos, Greece 45 38 17N 23 52 E
Kalamoti 45 38 15N 26 4 E
Kalan 64 39 7N 39 32 E
Kalao 73 7 21S 121 0 E
Kalaotoa 73 7 20S 121 50 E
Kälarne 48 62 59N 16 8 E
Kalárovo 27 47 54N 18 0 E
Kalasin 71 16 26N 103 30 E
Kalat 66 29 8N 66 31 E
Kalat □ 68 27 30N 66 0 E
Kálathos (Calato) 45 36 9N 28 8 E
Kalaus → 57 45 40N 44 7 E
Kalávrita 45 38 3N 22 8 E
Kalecik 56 40 4N 33 26 E
Kalegauk Kyun 67 15 33N 97 35 E
Kalehe 90 2 6S 28 50 E
Kalema 90 1 12S 31 55 E
Kalemie 90 5 55S 29 9 E
Kalety 28 50 35N 18 52 E
Kalewa 67 23 10N 94 15 E
Kálfafellsstaður 50 64 11N 15 53W
Kalgan = Zhangjiakou 76 40 48N 114 55 E
Kalgoorlie 96 30 40S 121 22 E
Kaliakra, Nos 43 43 21N 28 30 E
Kalianda 72 5 50S 105 45 E
Kalibo 73 11 43N 122 22 E
Kaliganj Town 69 22 25N 89 8 E
Kalima 90 2 33S 26 32 E
Kalimantan Barat □ 72 0 0 110 30 E
Kalimantan Selatan □ 72 2 30S 115 30 E
Kalimantan Tengah □ 72 2 0S 113 30 E
Kalimantan Timur □ 72 1 30N 116 30 E
Kálimnos 45 37 0N 27 0 E
Kalimpong 69 27 4N 88 35 E
Kalinadi → 70 14 50N 74 7 E
Kalinin 55 56 55N 35 55 E
Kaliningrad 54 54 42N 20 32 E
Kalinkovichi 54 52 12N 29 20 E
Kalinovik 42 43 31N 18 29 E
Kalipetrovo (Stančevo) 43 44 5N 27 14 E
Kaliro 90 0 56N 33 30 E
Kalirrákhi 44 40 40N 24 35 E
Kalispell 118 48 10N 114 22W
Kalisz 28 51 45N 18 8 E
Kalisz □ 28 51 30N 18 0 E
Kalisz Pomorski 28 53 17N 15 55 E
Kaliua 90 5 5S 31 48 E
Kaliveli Tank 70 12 5N 79 50 E
Kalix, → 50 65 50N 23 11 E
Kalka 68 30 46N 76 57 E
Kalkaska 106 44 44N 85 11W
Kalkfeld 92 20 57S 16 14 E
Kalkfontein 92 22 4S 20 57 E
Kalkrand 92 24 1S 17 35 E
Kallakurichi 70 11 44N 79 1 E
Kållandsö 49 58 40N 13 5 E
Kallia 62 31 46N 35 30 E
Kallidaikurichi 70 8 38N 77 31 E
Kallinge 49 56 15N 15 18 E
Kallithéa 45 37 55N 23 41 E
Kallmeti 44 41 51N 19 41 E
Kallonis, Kólpos 45 39 10N 26 10 E
Kallsjön 50 63 38N 13 0 E
Kalmalo 85 13 40N 5 20 E
Kalmar 49 56 40N 16 20 E
Kalmar län □ 49 57 25N 16 0 E
Kalmar sund 49 56 40N 16 25 E
Kalmyk A.S.S.R. □ 57 46 5N 46 1 E
Kalmykovo 57 49 0N 51 47 E
Kalna 69 23 13N 88 25 E
Kalo 98 10 1S 147 48 E
Kalocsa 27 46 32N 19 0 E
Kalofer 43 42 37N 24 59 E
Kaloko 90 6 47S 25 48 E
Kalol, Gujarat, India 68 23 15N 72 33 E
Kalol, Gujarat, India 68 22 37N 73 31 E
Kalolimnos 45 37 4N 27 8 E
Kalomo 91 17 0S 26 30 E
Kaloneròn 45 37 20N 21 38 E
Kalpi 69 26 8N 79 47 E
Kalrayan Hills 70 11 45N 78 40 E
Kalsubai 70 19 35N 73 45 E
Kaltungo 85 9 48N 11 19 E
Kalu 68 25 5N 67 39 E
Kaluga 55 54 35N 36 10 E
Kalulushi 91 12 50S 28 3 E
Kalundborg 49 55 41N 11 5 E
Kalush 54 49 3N 24 23 E
Kałuszyn 28 52 13N 21 52 E
Kalutara 70 6 35N 80 0 E
Kalwaria 27 49 53N 19 41 E
Kalya 52 60 15N 59 59 E
Kalyan 68 20 30N 74 3 E
Kalyazin 55 57 15N 37 55 E
Kam Keut 71 18 20N 104 48 E
Kama 90 3 30S 27 5 E
Kama → 52 55 45N 52 0 E
Kamachumu 90 1 37S 31 37 E
Kamaishi 74 39 20N 142 0 E
Kamalia 68 30 44N 72 42 E
Kamandorskiye Ostrava 59 55 0N 167 0 E
Kamapanda 91 12 5S 24 0 E
Kamaran 63 15 21N 42 35 E
Kamativi 91 18 15S 27 27 E
Kamba 85 11 50N 3 45 E
Kambam 70 9 45N 77 16 E
Kambar 68 27 37N 68 1 E
Kambarka 52 56 15N 54 11 E
Kambia 84 9 3N 12 53W
Kambolé 91 8 47S 30 48 E
Kambove 91 10 51S 26 33 E
Kamchatka, P-ov. 59 57 0N 160 0 E
Kamen 58 53 50N 81 30 E
Kamen Kashirskiy 54 51 39N 24 56 E
Kamenica, Srbija, Yugo. 42 44 25N 19 40 E
Kamenica, Srbija, Yugo. 42 43 27N 22 27 E
Kamenice 26 49 18N 15 2 E
Kamenjak, Rt 39 44 47N 13 55 E
Kamenka, R.S.F.S.R., U.S.S.R. 52 65 58N 44 0 E
Kamenka, R.S.F.S.R., U.S.S.R. 55 50 47N 39 20 E
Kamenka, R.S.F.S.R., U.S.S.R. 55 53 10N 44 5 E
Kamenka, Ukraine S.S.R., U.S.S.R. 56 49 3N 32 6 E
Kamenka Bugskaya 54 50 8N 24 16 E
Kamenka Dneprovskaya 56 47 29N 34 14 E
Kameno 43 42 34N 27 18 E
Kamenolomini 57 47 40N 40 14 E
Kamensk-Shakhtinskiy 57 48 23N 40 20 E
Kamensk Uralskiy 58 56 25N 62 2 E
Kamenskiy, R.S.F.S.R., U.S.S.R. 55 50 48N 45 25 E
Kamenskiy, R.S.F.S.R., U.S.S.R. 57 49 20N 41 15 E
Kamenskoye 59 62 45N 165 30 E
Kamenyak 43 43 24N 26 57 E
Kamenz 24 51 17N 14 7 E
Kami 44 42 17N 20 18 E
Kamiah 118 46 12N 116 2W
Kamień Krajeński 28 53 32N 17 32 E
Kamień Pomorski 28 53 57N 14 50 E
Kamienna → 28 51 6N 21 47 E
Kamienna Góra 28 50 47N 16 2 E
Kamieńsk 28 51 12N 19 29 E
Kamilukuak, L. 109 62 22N 101 40W
Kamina 91 8 45S 25 0 E
Kaminak L. 109 62 10N 95 0W
Kamituga 90 3 2S 28 10 E
Kamloops 108 50 40N 120 20W
Kamloops L. 108 50 45N 120 40W
Kamnik 39 46 14N 14 37 E
Kamo 57 40 21N 45 7 E
Kamoke 68 32 4N 74 4 E
Kamp → 26 48 23N 15 42 E
Kampala 90 0 20N 32 30 E
Kampar 71 4 18N 101 9 E
Kampar → 72 0 30N 103 8 E
Kampen 16 52 33N 5 53 E
Kampolombo, L. 91 11 37S 29 42 E
Kampot 71 10 36N 104 10 E
Kamptee 68 21 9N 79 19 E
Kampti 84 10 7N 3 25W
Kampuchea = Cambodia ■ 71 13 0N 105 0 E
Kampung → 73 5 44S 138 24 E
Kampungbaru = Tolitoli 73 1 5N 120 50 E
Kamrau, Teluk 73 3 30S 133 36 E
Kamsack 109 51 34N 101 54W
Kamskoye Ustye 55 55 10N 49 20 E
Kamskoye Vdkhr. 52 58 0N 56 0 E
Kamuchawie L. 109 56 18N 101 59W
Kamyshin 55 50 10N 45 24 E
Kamyzyak 57 46 4N 48 10 E
Kanaaupscow 106 54 2N 76 30W
Kanab 119 37 3N 112 29W
Kanab Creek 119 37 0N 112 40W
Kanagawa □ 74 35 20N 139 20 E
Kanairiktok → 107 55 2N 60 18W
Kanakapura 70 12 33N 77 28 E
Kanália 44 39 30N 22 53 E
Kananga 88 5 55S 22 18 E
Kanarraville 119 37 34N 113 12W
Kanash 55 55 30N 47 32 E
Kanastraíon, Ákra 44 39 57N 23 45 E
Kanawha → 114 38 50N 82 8W
Kanazawa 74 36 30N 136 38 E
Kanchanaburi 71 14 2N 99 31 E
Kanchenjunga 69 27 50N 88 10 E
Kanchipuram (Conjeeveram) 70 12 52N 79 45 E
Kańczuga 27 49 59N 22 25 E
Kanda Kanda 88 6 52S 23 48 E
Kandahar 65 31 32N 65 30 E
Kandalaksha 52 67 9N 32 30 E
Kandalakshkiy Zaliv 52 66 0N 35 0 E
Kandangan 72 2 50S 115 20 E
Kandanos 45 35 19N 23 44 E
Kandhíla 45 37 46N 22 22 E
Kandhkot 68 28 16N 69 8 E
Kandhla 68 29 18N 77 19 E
Kandi, Benin 85 11 7N 2 55 E
Kandi, India 69 23 58N 88 5 E
Kandla 68 23 0N 70 10 E
Kandos 99 32 45S 149 58 E
Kandukur 70 15 12N 79 57 E
Kandy 70 7 18N 80 43 E
Kane 114 41 39N 78 53W
Kane Bassin 4 79 30N 68 0W
Kanevskaya 57 46 3N 39 3 E
Kanfanar 39 45 7N 13 50 E
Kangaba 84 11 56N 8 25W
Kangar 71 6 27N 100 12 E
Kangaroo I. 97 35 45S 137 0 E
Kangaroo Mts. 98 23 25S 142 0 E
Kangavar 64 34 40N 48 0 E
Kangean, Kepulauan 72 6 55S 115 23 E
Kangerdlugsuak 4 68 10N 32 20W
Kanggyee 76 41 0N 126 35 E
Kangnŭng 76 37 45N 128 54 E
Kango 88 0 11N 10 5 E
Kangto 67 27 50N 92 35 E
Kanhangad 70 12 21N 74 58 E
Kanheri 70 19 13N 72 50 E
Kani 84 8 29N 6 36W
Kaniama 90 7 30S 24 12 E
Kaniapiskau → 107 56 40N 69 30W
Kaniapiskau L. 107 54 10N 69 55W
Kanin Nos, Mys 52 68 45N 43 20 E
Kanin, P-ov. 52 68 0N 45 0 E
Kanina 44 40 23N 19 30 E
Kaniva 99 36 22S 141 18 E
Kanjiža 42 46 3N 20 4 E
Kankakee 114 41 6N 87 50W
Kankakee → 114 41 23N 88 16W
Kankan 84 10 23N 9 15W
Kanker 70 20 10N 81 40 E
Kankunskiy 59 57 37N 126 8 E
Kannapolis 115 35 32N 80 37W
Kannauj 69 27 3N 79 56 E
Kano 85 12 2N 8 30 E
Kano □ 85 11 45N 9 0 E
Kanoroba 84 9 7N 6 8W
Kanowit 72 2 14N 112 20 E
Kanowna 96 30 32S 121 31 E
Kanoya 74 31 25N 130 50 E
Kanpetlet 67 21 10N 93 59 E
Kanpur 69 26 28N 80 20 E
Kansas □ 116 38 40N 98 0W
Kansas → 116 39 7N 94 36W
Kansas City, Kans., U.S.A. 116 39 0N 94 40W
Kansas City, Mo., U.S.A. 116 39 3N 94 30W
Kansenia 91 10 20S 26 0 E
Kansk 59 56 20N 95 37 E
Kansu = Gansu □ 75 37 0N 103 0 E
Kantang 71 7 25N 99 31 E
Kantché 85 13 31N 8 30 E
Kanté 85 9 57N 1 3 E
Kantemirovka 57 49 43N 39 55 E
Kanturk 15 52 10N 8 55W
Kanuma 74 36 34N 139 42 E
Kanus 92 27 50S 18 39 E
Kanye 92 25 0S 25 28 E
Kanyu 92 20 7S 24 37 E
Kanzenze 91 10 30S 25 12 E
Kanzi, Ras 90 7 1S 39 33 E
Kaohsiung = Gaoxiong 75 22 38N 120 18 E
Kaokoveld 92 18 20S 13 37 E
Kaolack 84 14 5N 16 8W
Kapadvanj 68 23 5N 73 0 E
Kapanga 88 8 30S 22 40 E
Kapchagai 58 43 50N 77 10 E
Kapéllo, Ákra 45 36 9N 23 3 E
Kapema 91 10 45S 28 22 E
Kapfenberg 26 47 26N 15 18 E
Kapiri Mposhi 91 13 59S 28 43 E
Kapisa □ 65 35 0N 69 20 E
Kapiskau → 106 52 47N 81 55W
Kapit 72 2 0N 112 55 E
Kapiti I. 101 40 50S 174 56 E
Kaplice 26 48 42N 14 30 E
Kapoeta 87 4 50N 33 35 E
Kápolnásnyék 27 47 16N 18 41 E
Kapos → 27 46 44N 18 30 E
Kaposvár 27 46 25N 17 47 E
Kappeln 24 54 37N 9 56 E
Kapps 92 22 32S 17 18 E
Kaprije 39 43 42N 15 43 E
Kapsukas 54 54 33N 23 19 E
Kapuas → 72 0 25S 109 20 E
Kapuas Hulu, Pegunungan 72 1 30N 113 30 E
Kapulo 91 8 18S 29 15 E
Kapunda 99 34 20S 138 56 E
Kapurthala 68 31 23N 75 25 E
Kapuskasing 106 49 25N 82 30W
Kapuskasing → 106 49 49N 82 0W
Kapustin Yar 57 48 37N 45 40 E
Kaputir 90 2 5N 35 28 E

Kapuvár 27 47 36N 17 1 E
Kara, Turkey 45 36 58N 27 30 E
Kara, U.S.S.R. 58 69 10N 65 0 E
Kara Bogaz Gol, Zaliv 53 41 0N 53 30 E
Kara Burun 45 38 41N 26 28 E
Kara Kalpak A.S.S.R. □ 58 43 0N 60 0 E
Kara Sea 58 75 0N 70 0 E
Kara, Wadi 86 20 0N 41 25 E
Karabük 64 41 12N 32 37 E
Karaburuni 44 40 25N 19 20 E
Karabutak 58 49 59N 60 14 E
Karachala 57 39 45N 48 53 E
Karachayevsk 57 43 50N 42 0 E
Karachev 54 53 10N 35 5 E
Karachi 68 24 53N 67 0 E
Karachi □ 68 25 30N 67 0 E
Karád 27 46 41N 17 51 E
Karad 70 17 15N 74 10 E
Karadeniz Boğazı 64 41 10N 29 10 E
Karaga 85 9 58N 0 28W
Karaganda 58 49 50N 73 10 E
Karagayly 58 49 26N 76 0 E
Karaginskiy, Ostrov 59 58 45N 164 0 E
Karagiye Depression 53 43 27N 51 45 E
Karagwe □ 90 2 0S 31 0 E
Karaikkudi 70 10 0N 78 45 E
Karaitivu I. 70 9 45N 79 52 E
Karaitivu, I. 70 8 22N 79 47 E
Karaj 65 35 48N 51 0 E
Karakas 58 48 20N 83 30 E
Karakitang 73 3 14N 125 28 E
Karakoram Pass 66 35 33N 77 50 E
Karakoram Ra. 66 35 30N 77 0 E
Karakum, Peski 58 39 30N 60 0 E
Karalon 59 57 5N 115 50 E
Karaman 64 37 14N 33 13 E
Karamay 75 45 30N 84 58 E
Karambu 72 3 53S 116 6 E
Karamea Bight 101 41 22S 171 40 E
Karamoja □ 90 3 0N 34 15 E
Karamsad 68 22 35N 72 50 E
Karanganjar 73 7 38S 109 37 E
Karanja 68 20 29N 77 31 E
Karasburg 92 28 0S 18 44 E
Karasino 58 66 50N 86 50 E
Karasjok 50 69 27N 25 30 E
Karasuk 58 53 44N 78 2 E
Karatau 58 43 10N 70 28 E
Karatau, Khrebet 58 43 30N 69 30 E
Karauli 68 26 30N 77 4 E
Karávi 45 36 49N 23 37 E
Karawanken 26 46 30N 14 40 E
Karazhal 58 48 2N 70 49 E
Karbalā 64 32 36N 44 3 E
Kårböle 48 61 59N 15 22 E
Karcag 27 47 19N 20 57 E
Karda 59 55 0N 103 16 E
Kardhámila 45 38 35N 26 5 E
Kardhítsa 44 39 23N 21 54 E
Kardhítsa □ 44 39 15N 21 50 E
Kärdla 54 58 50N 22 40 E
Kareeberge 92 30 50S 22 0 E
Kareima 86 18 30N 31 49 E
Karelian A.S.S.R. □ 52 65 30N 32 30 E
Karen 71 12 49N 92 53 E
Kargānrūd 64 37 55N 49 0 E
Kargasok 58 59 3N 80 53 E
Kargat 58 55 10N 80 15 E
Kargı 56 41 11N 34 30 E
Kargil 69 34 32N 76 12 E
Kargopol 52 61 30N 38 58 E
Kargowa 28 52 5N 15 51 E
Karguéri 85 13 27N 10 30 E
Karia ba Mohammed 82 34 22N 5 12W
Kariaí 44 40 14N 24 19 E
Kariba 91 16 28S 28 50 E
Kariba Gorge 91 16 30S 28 50 E
Kariba Lake 91 16 40S 28 25 E
Karibib 92 21 0S 15 56 E
Karikal 70 10 59N 79 50 E
Karimata, Kepulauan 72 1 25S 109 0 E
Karimata, Selat 72 2 0S 108 40 E
Karimnagar 70 18 26N 79 10 E
Karimunjawa, Kepulauan 72 5 50S 110 30 E
Karin 63 10 50N 45 52 E
Káristos 45 38 1N 24 29 E
Kariya 74 34 58N 137 1 E
Karkal 70 13 15N 74 56 E
Karkar I. 98 4 40S 146 0 E
Karkaralinsk 58 49 26N 75 30 E
Karkinitskiy Zaliv 56 45 56N 33 0 E
Karkur 62 32 29N 34 57 E
Karkur Tohl 86 22 5N 25 5 E
Karl Libknekht 54 51 40N 35 35 E
Karl-Marx-Stadt 24 50 50N 12 55 E
Karl-Marx-Stadt □ 24 50 45N 13 0 E
Karla, L. = Voiviïs, L. 44 39 30N 22 45 E
Karlino 28 54 3N 15 53 E
Karlobag 39 44 32N 15 5 E
Karlovac 39 45 31N 15 36 E
Karlovka 56 49 29N 35 8 E
Karlovy Vary 26 50 13N 12 51 E
Karlsborg 49 58 33N 14 33 E
Karlshamn 49 56 10N 14 51 E
Karlskoga 48 59 22N 14 33 E
Karlskrona 49 56 10N 15 35 E
Karlsruhe 25 49 3N 8 23 E
Karlstad, Sweden 48 59 23N 13 30 E
Karlstad, U.S.A. 116 48 38N 96 30W
Karlstadt 25 49 57N 9 46 E
Karmøy 47 59 15N 5 15 E
Karnal 68 29 42N 77 2 E
Karnali → 69 29 0N 83 20 E
Karnaphuli Res. 67 22 40N 92 20 E
Karnataka □ 70 14 15N 76 0 E
Karnes City 117 28 53N 97 53W
Karnische Alpen 26 46 36N 13 0 E
Kärnten □ 26 46 52N 13 30 E
Karo 84 12 16N 3 18W
Karoi 91 16 48S 29 45 E
Karonga 91 9 57S 33 55 E
Karoonda 99 35 1S 139 59 E
Káros 45 36 54N 25 40 E
Karousádhes 44 39 47N 19 45 E
Kárpathos 45 35 37N 27 10 E
Karpáthos, Stenón 45 36 0N 27 30 E
Karpinsk 52 59 45N 60 1 E
Karpogory 52 63 59N 44 27 E
Karrebæk 49 55 12N 11 39 E
Kars, Turkey 64 40 40N 43 5 E
Kars, U.S.S.R. 56 40 36N 43 5 E
Karsakpay 58 47 55N 66 40 E
Karsha 57 49 45N 51 35 E
Karshi 58 38 53N 65 48 E
Karst 39 45 35N 14 0 E
Karsun 55 54 14N 46 57 E
Kartál Óros 44 41 15N 25 13 E
Kartaly 58 53 3N 60 40 E
Kartapur 68 31 27N 75 32 E
Karthaus 112 41 8N 78 9W
Kartuzy 28 54 22N 18 10 E
Karufa 73 3 50S 133 20 E
Karumba 98 17 31S 140 50 E
Karumo 90 2 25S 32 50 E
Karumwa 90 3 12S 32 38 E
Karungu 90 0 50S 34 10 E
Karup 49 56 19N 9 10 E
Karur 70 10 59N 78 2 E
Karviná 27 49 53N 18 25 E
Karwi 69 25 12N 80 57 E
Kas Kong 71 11 27N 102 12 E
Kasache 91 13 25S 34 20 E
Kasai → 88 3 30S 16 10 E
Kasai Oriental □ 90 5 0S 24 30 E
Kasaji 91 10 25S 23 27 E
Kasama 91 10 16S 31 9 E
Kasane 92 17 34S 24 50 E
Kasanga 91 8 30S 31 10 E
Kasangulu 88 4 33S 15 15 E
Kasaragod 70 12 30N 74 58 E
Kasba L. 109 60 20N 102 10W
Kasba Tadla 82 32 36N 6 17W
Kasempa 91 13 30S 25 44 E
Kasenga 91 10 20S 28 45 E
Kasese 90 0 13N 30 3 E
Kasewa 91 14 28S 28 53 E
Kasganj 68 27 48N 78 42 E
Kashabowie 106 48 40N 90 26W
Kāshān 65 34 5N 51 30 E
Kashi 75 39 30N 76 2 E
Kashimbo 91 11 12S 26 19 E
Kashin 55 57 20N 37 36 E
Kashipur, Orissa, India 70 19 16N 83 3 E
Kashipur, Ut. P., India 68 29 15N 79 0 E
Kashira 55 54 45N 38 10 E
Kāshmar 65 35 16N 58 26 E
Kashmir 69 34 0N 76 0 E
Kashmor 68 28 28N 69 32 E
Kashpirovka 55 53 0N 48 30 E
Kashun Noerh = Gaxun Nur 75 42 22N 100 30 E
Kasimov 55 54 55N 41 20 E
Kasinge 90 6 15S 26 58 E
Kasiruta 73 0 25S 127 12 E
Kaskaskia → 116 37 58N 89 57W
Kaskattama → 109 57 3N 90 4W
Kaskinen 50 62 22N 21 15 E
Kaskö 50 62 22N 21 15 E
Kaslo 108 49 55N 116 55W
Kasmere L. 109 59 34N 101 10W
Kasongo 90 4 30S 26 33 E
Kasongo Lunda 88 6 35S 16 49 E
Kásos 45 35 20N 26 55 E
Kasos, Stenón 45 35 30N 26 30 E
Kaspi 57 41 54N 44 17 E
Kaspichan 43 43 18N 27 11 E
Kaspiysk 57 42 52N 47 40 E
Kaspiyskiy 57 45 22N 47 23 E
Kassab ed Doleib 87 13 30N 33 35 E
Kassaba 86 22 40N 29 55 E
Kassala 87 16 0N 36 0 E
Kassalâ □ 87 15 20N 36 26 E
Kassándra 44 40 0N 23 30 E
Kassel 24 51 19N 9 32 E
Kassinga 89 15 5S 16 4 E
Kassinger 86 18 46N 31 51 E
Kassue 73 6 58S 139 21 E
Kastamonu 64 41 25N 33 43 E
Kastav 39 45 22N 14 20 E
Kastélli 45 35 29N 23 38 E
Kastéllion 45 35 12N 25 20 E
Kastellorizon = Megiste 35 36 8N 29 34 E
Kastellou, Ákra 45 35 30N 27 15 E
Kastlösa 49 56 26N 16 25 E
Kastóri 45 37 10N 22 17 E
Kastoría 44 40 30N 21 19 E
Kastoría □ 44 40 30N 21 15 E
Kastorías, L. 44 40 30N 21 20 E
Kastornoye 55 51 55N 38 2 E
Kastós 45 38 35N 20 55 E
Kástron 44 39 50N 25 2 E
Kastrosikiá 44 39 6N 20 36 E
Kasulu 90 4 37S 30 5 E
Kasulu □ 90 4 37S 30 5 E
Kasumkent 57 41 47N 48 15 E
Kasungu 91 13 0S 33 29 E
Kasur 68 31 5N 74 25 E
Kata 59 58 46N 102 40 E
Kataba 91 16 5S 25 10 E
Katako Kombe 90 3 25S 24 20 E
Katákolon 45 37 38N 21 19 E
Katale 90 4 52S 31 7 E
Katamatite 99 36 6S 145 41 E
Katanda, Zaïre 90 0 55S 29 21 E
Katanda, Zaïre 90 7 52S 24 13 E
Katangi 69 21 56N 79 50 E
Katangli 59 51 42N 143 14 E
Katanning 96 33 40S 117 33 E
Katastári 45 37 50N 20 45 E
Katavi Swamp 90 6 50S 31 10 E
Kateríni 44 40 18N 22 37 E
Katha 67 24 10N 96 30 E
Katherîna, Gebel 86 28 30N 33 57 E
Katherine 96 14 27S 132 20 E
Kathiawar 68 22 20N 71 0 E
Kati 84 12 41N 8 4W
Katiet 72 2 21S 99 54 E
Katihar 69 25 34N 87 36 E
Katima Mulilo 92 17 28S 24 13 E
Katimbira 91 12 40S 34 0 E
Katiola 84 8 10N 5 10W
Katkopberg 92 30 0S 20 0 E
Katlanovo 42 41 52N 21 40 E
Katmandu 69 27 45N 85 20 E
Kato Akhaïa 45 38 8N 21 33 E
Káto Stavros 44 40 39N 23 43 E
Katol 68 21 17N 78 38 E
Katompe 90 6 2S 26 23 E
Katonga → 90 0 34N 31 50 E
Katoomba 97 33 41S 150 19 E
Katowice 28 50 17N 19 5 E
Katowice □ 28 50 10N 19 0 E
Katrine, L. 14 56 15N 4 30W
Katrineholm 48 59 9N 16 12 E
Katsepe 93 15 45S 46 15 E
Katsina Ala → 85 7 10N 9 20 E
Katsuura 74 35 10N 140 20 E
Kattawaz-Urgun □ 65 32 10N 68 20 E
Kattegatt 49 57 0N 11 20 E
Katumba 90 7 40S 25 17 E
Katungu 90 2 55S 40 3 E
Katwa 69 23 30N 88 5 E
Katwijk-aan-Zee 16 52 12N 4 24 E
Katy 28 51 2N 16 45 E
Kauai 110 22 0N 159 30W
Kauai Chan. 110 21 45N 158 50W
Kaub 25 50 5N 7 46 E
Kaufbeuren 25 47 50N 10 37 E
Kaufman 117 32 35N 96 20W
Kaukauna 114 44 20N 88 13W
Kaukauveld 92 20 0S 20 15 E
Kaukonen 50 67 31N 24 53 E
Kauliranta 50 66 27N 23 41 E
Kaunas 54 54 54N 23 54 E
Kaura Namoda 85 12 37N 6 33 E
Kautokeino 50 69 0N 23 4 E
Kavacha 59 60 16N 169 51 E
Kavadarci 42 41 26N 22 3 E
Kavaja 44 41 11N 19 33 E
Kavali 70 14 55N 80 1 E
Kaválla 44 40 57N 24 28 E
Kaválla □ 44 41 5N 24 30 E
Kaválla Kólpos 44 40 50N 24 25 E
Kavarna 43 43 26N 28 22 E
Kavieng 98 2 36S 150 51 E
Kavkaz, Bolshoi 57 42 50N 44 0 E
Kavoúsi 45 35 7N 25 51 E
Kaw = Caux 127 4 30N 52 15W
Kawa 87 13 42N 32 34 E
Kawagama L. 112 45 18N 78 45W
Kawagoe 74 35 55N 139 29 E
Kawaguchi 74 35 52N 139 45 E
Kawaihae 110 20 3N 155 50W
Kawambwa 91 9 48S 29 3 E
Kawardha 69 22 0N 81 17 E
Kawasaki 74 35 35N 139 42 E
Kawene 106 48 45N 91 15W
Kawerau 101 38 7S 176 42 E
Kawhia Harbour 101 38 5S 174 51 E
Kawio, Kepulauan 73 4 30N 125 30 E
Kawnro 67 22 48N 99 8 E
Kawthaung 71 10 5N 98 36 E
Kawthoolei □ = Kawthule 67 18 0N 97 30 E
Kawthule □ 67 18 0N 97 30 E
Kaya 85 13 4N 1 10W
Kayah □ 67 19 15N 97 15 E
Kayangulam 70 9 10N 76 33 E
Kaycee 118 43 45N 106 46W
Kayeli 73 3 20S 127 10 E
Kayenta 119 36 46N 110 15W
Kayes 84 14 25N 11 30W
Kayima 84 8 54N 11 15W
Kayomba 91 13 11S 24 2 E
Kayoro 85 11 0N 1 28W
Kayrunnera 99 30 40S 142 30 E
Kaysatskoye 57 49 47N 46 49 E
Kayseri 64 38 45N 35 30 E
Kaysville 118 41 2N 111 58W
Kayuagung 72 3 24S 104 50 E
Kazachinskoye 59 56 16N 107 36 E
Kazachye 59 70 52N 135 58 E
Kazakh S.S.R. □ 58 50 0N 70 0 E
Kazan 55 55 48N 49 3 E
Kazanlúk 43 42 38N 25 20 E
Kazanskaya 57 49 50N 41 10 E
Kazatin 56 49 45N 28 50 E
Kazbek 57 42 42N 44 30 E
Kāzerūn 65 29 38N 51 40 E
Kazi Magomed 57 40 3N 49 0 E
Kazimierz Dolny 28 51 19N 21 57 E
Kazimierza Wielka 28 50 15N 20 30 E
Kazincbarcika 27 48 17N 20 36 E
Kaztalovka 57 49 47N 48 43 E
Kazumba 88 6 25S 22 5 E
Kazym → 58 63 54N 65 50 E
Kcynia 28 53 0N 17 30 E
Ké-Macina 84 13 58N 5 22W
Kéa 45 37 35N 24 22 E
Kea 45 37 30N 24 22 E
Keams Canyon 119 35 53N 110 9W
Kearney 116 40 45N 99 3W
Keban 64 38 50N 38 50 E
Kébi 84 9 18N 6 37W
Kebili 83 33 47N 9 0 E
Kebnekaise 50 67 53N 18 33 E
Kebri Dehar 63 6 45N 44 17 E
Kebumen 73 7 42S 109 40 E
Kecel 27 46 31N 19 16 E
Kechika → 108 59 41N 127 12W
Kecskemét 27 46 57N 19 42 E
Kedada 87 5 25N 35 58 E
Kedah □ 71 5 50N 100 40 E
Kedainiai 54 55 15N 24 2 E
Kedgwick 107 47 40N 67 20W
Kedia Hill 92 21 28S 24 37 E
Kediri 73 7 51S 112 1 E
Kédougou 84 12 35N 12 10W
Kedzierzyn 28 50 20N 18 12 E
Keefers 108 50 0N 121 40W
Keeley L. 109 54 54N 108 8W
Keeling Is. = Cocos Is. 94 12 12S 96 55 E
Keene 114 42 57N 72 17W
Keeper Hill 15 52 46N 8 17W
Keer-Weer, C. 97 14 0S 141 32 E
Keeseville 113 44 29N 73 30W
Keetmanshoop 92 26 35S 18 8 E
Keewatin 116 47 23N 93 0W
Keewatin □ 109 63 20N 95 0W
Keewatin → 109 56 29N 100 46W
Kefa □ 87 6 55N 36 30 E
Kefallinía 45 38 20N 20 30 E
Kefamenanu 73 9 28S 124 29 E
Kefar 'Eqron 62 31 52N 34 49 E
Kefar Ḥasīdim 62 32 47N 35 5 E
Kefar Naḥum 62 32 54N 35 34 E
Kefar Sava 62 32 11N 34 54 E
Kefar Szold 62 33 11N 35 39 E
Kefar Vitkin 62 32 22N 34 53 E
Kefar Yehezqel 62 32 34N 35 22 E
Kefar Yona 62 32 20N 34 54 E
Kefar Zekharya 62 31 43N 34 57 E
Kefar Zetim 62 32 48N 35 27 E
Keffi 85 8 55N 7 43 E
Keflavík 50 64 2N 22 35W
Keg River 108 57 54N 117 55W
Kegahka 107 50 9N 61 18W
Kegalla 70 7 15N 80 21 E
Kehl 25 48 34N 7 50 E
Keighley 12 53 52N 1 54W
Keimoes 92 28 41S 21 0 E
Keita 85 14 46N 5 56 E
Keith, Austral. 99 36 6S 140 20 E
Keith, U.K. 14 57 33N 2 58W
Keith Arm 104 64 20N 122 15W
Kekri 68 26 0N 75 10 E
Kël 59 69 30N 124 10 E
Kelamet 87 16 0N 38 30 E
Kelan 76 38 43N 111 31 E
Kelang 71 3 2N 101 26 E
Kelani Ganga → 70 6 58N 79 50 E
Kelantan □ 71 5 10N 102 0 E
Kelantan → 71 6 13N 102 14 E
Këlcyra 44 40 22N 20 12 E
Kelheim 25 48 58N 11 57 E
Kelibia 83 36 50N 11 3 E
Kellé 88 0 8S 14 38 E
Keller 118 48 2N 118 44W
Kellerberrin 96 31 36S 117 38 E
Kellett C. 4 72 0N 126 0W
Kelleys I. 112 41 35N 82 42W
Kellogg 118 47 30N 116 5W
Kelloselkä 50 66 56N 28 53 E
Kells = Ceanannus Mor 15 53 42N 6 53W
Kélo 81 9 10N 15 45 E
Kelowna 108 49 50N 119 25W
Kelsey Bay 108 50 25N 126 0W
Kelso, N.Z. 101 45 54S 169 15 E
Kelso, U.K. 14 55 36N 2 27W
Kelso, U.S.A. 118 46 10N 122 57W
Keluang 71 2 3N 103 18 E
Kelvington 109 52 10N 103 30W
Kem 52 65 0N 34 38 E
Kem → 52 64 57N 34 41 E
Kem-Kem 82 30 40N 4 30W
Kema 73 1 22N 125 8 E
Kemah <4 39 32N 39 5 E
Kemano 108 53 35N 128 0W
Kembolcha 87 11 2N 39 42 E
Kemenets-Podolskiy 56 48 40N 26 40 E
Kemerovo 58 55 20N 86 5 E
Kemi 50 65 44N 24 34 E
Kemi älv = Kemijoki → 50 65 47N 24 32 E
Kemijärvi 50 66 43N 27 22 E
Kemijoki → 50 65 47N 24 32 E
Kemmerer 118 41 52N 110 30W
Kemp Coast 5 69 0S 55 0 E
Kemp L. 117 33 45N 99 15W
Kempsey 97 31 1S 152 50 E
Kempt, L. 106 47 25N 74 22W
Kempten 25 47 42N 10 18 E
Kemptville 106 45 0N 75 38W
Kenadsa 82 31 48N 2 26W
Kendal, Indon. 72 6 56S 110 14 E
Kendal, U.K. 12 54 19N 2 44W
Kendall 99 31 35S 152 44 E
Kendall → 98 14 4S 141 35 E
Kendallville 114 41 25N 85 15W
Kendari 73 3 50S 122 30 E
Kendawangan 72 2 32S 110 17 E
Kende 85 11 30N 4 12 E
Kendervicës, m. e. 44 40 15N 19 52 E
Kendrapara 69 20 35N 86 30 E
Kendrick 118 46 43N 116 41W
Kenedy 117 28 49N 97 51W
Kenema 84 7 50N 11 14W
Keng Tung 67 21 0N 99 30 E
Kenge 88 4 50S 17 4 E
Kengeja 90 5 26S 39 45 E
Kenhardt 92 29 19S 21 12 E
Kénitra (Port Lyautey) 82 34 15N 6 40W
Kenmare, Ireland 15 51 52N 9 35W
Kenmare, U.S.A. 116 48 40N 102 4W
Kenmare → 15 51 40N 10 0W
Kenmore 100 34 44S 149 45 E
Kenn Reef 97 21 12S 155 46 E
Kennebec 116 43 56N 99 54W
Kennedy 91 18 52S 27 10 E
Kennedy Taungdeik 67 23 15N 93 45 E
Kennet → 13 51 24N 0 58W
Kennett 117 36 7N 90 0W
Kennewick 118 46 11N 119 2W
Kénogami 107 48 25N 71 15W
Kenogami → 106 51 6N 84 28W
Kenora 109 49 47N 94 29W
Kenosha 114 42 33N 87 48W
Kensington, Can. 107 46 28N 63 34W
Kensington, U.S.A. 116 39 48N 99 2W
Kensington Downs 98 22 31S 144 19 E
Kent, Ohio, U.S.A. 114 41 8N 81 20W

Kent, Oreg., U.S.A. 118 45 11N 120 45W
Kent, Tex., U.S.A. 117 31 5N 104 12W
Kent □ 13 51 12N 0 40 E
Kent Group 99 39 30 S 147 20 E
Kent Pen. 104 68 30N 107 0W
Kentau 58 43 32N 68 36 E
Kentland 114 40 45N 87 25W
Kenton 114 40 40N 83 35W
Kentucky □ 114 37 20N 85 0W
Kentucky → 114 38 41N 85 11W
Kentucky Dam 114 37 2N 88 15W
Kentucky L. 115 36 25N 88 0W
Kentville 107 45 6N 64 29W
Kentwood 117 31 0N 90 30W
Kenya ■ 90 1 0N 38 0 E
Kenya, Mt. 90 0 10 S 37 18 E
Keokuk 116 40 25N 91 24W
Kep-i-Gjuhës 44 40 28N 19 15 E
Kepi 73 6 32 S 139 19 E
Kepice 28 54 16N 16 51 E
Kępno 28 51 18N 17 58 E
Keppel B. 97 23 21 S 150 55 E
Kepsut 64 39 40N 28 9 E
Kerala □ 70 11 0N 76 15 E
Kerang 97 35 40 S 143 55 E
Keratéa 45 37 48N 23 58 E
Keraudren, C. 99 19 58 S 119 45 E
Keray 65 26 15N 57 30 E
Kerch 56 45 20N 36 20 E
Kerchenskiy Proliv 56 45 10N 36 30 E
Kerchoual 85 17 12N 0 20 E
Kerem Maharal 62 32 39N 34 59 E
Keremma 98 7 58 S 145 50 E
Keren 87 15 45N 38 28 E
Kerewan 84 13 29N 16 10W
Kerguelen 3 48 15 S 69 10 E
Keri 45 37 40N 20 49 E
Keri Kera 87 12 21N 32 42 E
Kericho 90 0 22 S 35 15 E
Kericho □ 90 0 30 S 35 15 E
Kerinci 72 1 40 S 101 15 E
Kerkenna, Iles 83 34 48N 11 11 E
Kerki 58 37 50N 65 12 E
Kerkinitis, Límni 44 41 12N 23 10 E
Kérkira 44 39 38N 19 50 E
Kerkrade 16 50 53N 6 4 E
Kerma 86 19 33N 30 32 E
Kermadec Is. 94 30 0 S 178 15W
Kermadec Trench 94 30 30 S 176 0W
Kermān 65 30 15N 57 1 E
Kermān □ 65 30 0N 57 0 E
Kermānshāh 64 34 23N 47 0 E
Kermānshāhān □ 64 34 0N 46 30 E
Kerme Körfezi 45 36 55N 27 50 E
Kermen 43 42 30N 26 16 E
Kermit 117 31 56N 103 3W
Kern → 119 35 16N 119 18W
Kerrobert 109 52 0N 109 11W
Kerrville 117 30 1N 99 8W
Kerry □ 15 52 7N 9 35W
Kerry Hd. 15 52 26N 9 56W
Kersa 87 9 28N 41 48 E
Kerteminde 49 55 28N 10 39 E
Kertosono 73 7 38 S 112 9 E
Kerulen → 75 48 48N 117 0 E
Kerzaz 82 29 29N 1 37W
Kesagami → 106 51 40N 79 45W
Kesagami L. 106 50 23N 80 15W
Keşan 44 40 49N 26 38 E
Keski-Suomen lääni □ 50 62 0N 25 30 E
Kestell 93 28 17 S 28 42 E
Kestenga 52 66 0N 31 50 E
Keswick 12 54 35N 3 9W
Keszthely 27 46 50N 17 15 E
Ket → 58 58 55N 81 32 E
Keta 85 5 49N 1 0 E
Ketapang 72 1 55 S 110 0 E
Ketchikan 104 55 25N 131 40W
Ketchum 118 43 41N 114 27W
Kete Krachi 85 7 46N 0 1W
Ketef, Khalîg Umm el 86 23 40N 35 35 E
Keti Bandar 68 24 8N 67 27 E
Ketri 68 28 1N 75 50 E
Kętrzyn 28 54 7N 21 22 E
Kettering 13 52 24N 0 44W
Kettle → 109 56 40N 89 34W
Kettle Falls 118 48 41N 118 2W
Kety 27 49 51N 19 16 E
Kevin 118 48 45N 111 58W
Kewanee 116 41 18N 89 55W
Kewaunee 114 44 27N 87 30W
Keweenaw B. 114 46 56N 88 23W
Keweenaw Pen. 114 47 30N 88 0W
Keweenaw Pt. 114 47 26N 87 40W
Key Harbour 106 45 50N 80 45W
Key West 121 24 33N 82 0W
Keyport 113 40 26N 74 12W
Keyser 114 39 26N 79 0W
Keystone, S.D., U.S.A. 116 43 54N 103 27W
Keystone, W. Va., U.S.A. 114 37 30N 81 30W
Kezhma 59 58 59N 101 9 E
Kežmarok 27 49 10N 20 28 E
Khabarovo 58 69 30N 60 30 E
Khabarovsk 59 48 30N 135 5 E
Khābūr → 64 35 0N 40 30 E
Khachmas 57 41 31N 48 42 E
Khachraud 68 23 25N 75 20 E
Khadari, W. el → 87 10 29N 27 15 E
Khadro 68 26 11N 68 50 E
Khadyzhensk 57 44 26N 39 32 E
Khagaria 69 25 30N 86 32 E
Khaibar 86 25 49N 39 16 E
Khaipur, Bahawalpur, Pak. 68 29 34N 72 17 E
Khaipur, Hyderabad, Pak. 68 27 32N 68 49 E
Khair 68 27 57N 77 46 E
Khairabad 69 27 33N 80 47 E
Khairagarh Raj 69 21 27N 81 2 E
Khairpur □ 68 27 20N 69 8 E
Khakhea 92 24 48 S 23 22 E
Khalfallah 82 34 20N 0 16 E
Khalij-e-Fars □ 65 28 20N 51 45 E
Khalilabad 69 26 48N 83 5 E
Khálki 44 39 36N 22 30 E
Khalkidhikí □ 44 40 25N 23 20 E
Khalkís 45 38 27N 23 42 E
Khalmer-Sede = Tazovskiy 58 67 30N 78 30 E
Khalmer Yu 58 67 58N 65 1 E
Khalturin 55 58 40N 48 50 E
Khamaria 69 23 10N 80 52 E
Khamas Country 92 21 45 S 26 30 E
Khambhalia 68 22 14N 69 41 E
Khamgaon 68 20 42N 76 37 E
Khamilonísion 45 35 50N 26 15 E
Khamir 63 16 0N 44 0 E
Khammam 70 17 11N 80 6 E
Khān Yūnis 62 31 21N 34 18 E
Khānābād 65 36 45N 69 5 E
Khānaqīn 64 34 23N 45 25 E
Khandrá 45 35 3N 26 8 E
Khandwa 68 21 49N 76 22 E
Khandyga 59 62 42N 135 35 E
Khanewal 68 30 20N 71 55 E
Khanh Hung 71 9 37N 105 50 E
Khaniá 45 35 30N 24 4 E
Khaniá □ 45 35 30N 24 0 E
Khanion Kólpos 45 35 33N 23 55 E
Khanka, Oz. 59 45 0N 132 30 E
Khanna 68 30 42N 76 16 E
Khanpur 68 28 42N 70 35 E
Khanty-Mansiysk 58 61 0N 69 0 E
Khapcheranga 59 49 42N 112 24 E
Kharagpur 69 22 20N 87 25 E
Kharaij 86 21 25N 41 0 E
Kharan Kalat 66 28 34N 65 21 E
Kharānaq 65 32 20N 54 45 E
Kharda 70 18 40N 75 34 E
Khârga, El Wâhât el 86 25 10N 30 35 E
Khargon 68 21 45N 75 40 E
Kharit, Wadi el → 86 24 26N 33 3 E
Khārk, Jazireh 64 29 15N 50 28 E
Kharkov 56 49 58N 36 20 E
Kharmanli 43 41 55N 25 55 E
Kharovsk 55 59 56N 40 13 E
Kharsānīya 64 27 10N 49 10 E
Khartoum = El Khartûm 87 15 31N 32 35 E
Khasab 65 26 14N 56 15 E
Khasavyurt 57 43 16N 46 40 E
Khasebake 92 20 42 S 24 29 E
Khāsh 65 28 15N 61 15 E
Khashm el Girba 87 14 59N 35 58 E
Khashuri 57 41 58N 43 35 E
Khasi Hills 69 25 30N 91 30 E
Khaskovo 43 41 56N 25 30 E
Khatanga 59 72 0N 102 20 E
Khatanga → 59 72 55N 106 0 E
Khatangskiy, Saliv 4 66 0N 112 0 E
Khatauli 68 29 17N 77 43 E
Khatyrka 59 62 3N 175 15 E
Khavār □ 64 37 20N 47 0 E
Khaybar, Harrat 64 25 45N 40 0 E
Khazzân Jabal el Awliyâ 87 15 24N 32 20 E
Khed, Maharashtra, India 70 17 43N 73 27 E
Khed, Maharashtra, India 70 18 51N 73 56 E
Khekra 68 28 52N 77 20 E
Khemelnik 56 49 33N 27 58 E
Khemis Miliana 82 36 11N 2 14 E
Khemissèt 82 33 50N 6 1W
Khemmarat 71 16 10N 105 15 E
Khenchela 83 35 28N 7 11 E
Khenifra 82 32 58N 5 46W
Kherrata 83 36 27N 5 13 E
Khérson 44 41 5N 22 47 E
Kherson 56 46 35N 32 35 E
Khersónisos Akrotiri 45 35 30N 24 10 E
Kheta → 59 71 54N 102 6 E
Khiliomódhion 45 37 48N 22 51 E
Khilok 59 51 30N 110 45 E
Khimki 55 55 50N 37 20 E
Khíos 45 38 27N 26 9 E
Khisar-Momina Banya 43 42 30N 24 44 E
Khiuma = Hiiumaa 54 58 50N 22 45 E
Khiva 58 41 30N 60 18 E
Khiyāv 64 38 30N 47 45 E
Khlebarovo 43 43 37N 26 15 E
Khlong → 71 15 30N 98 50 E
Khmelnitskiy 56 49 23N 27 0 E
Khmer Rep. = Cambodia ■ 71 12 15N 105 0 E
Khojak P. 65 30 55N 66 30 E
Khokholskiy 55 51 35N 38 40 E
Kholm, Afghan. 65 36 45N 67 40 E
Kholm, U.S.S.R. 54 57 10N 31 15 E
Kholmsk 59 47 40N 142 5 E
Khomas Hochland 92 22 40 S 16 0 E
Khomayn 64 33 40N 50 7 E
Khomo 92 21 7 S 24 35 E
Khon Kaen 71 16 30N 102 47 E
Khong 71 14 5N 105 56 E
Khong → 71 15 0N 106 50 E
Khonu 59 66 30N 143 12 E
Khoper → 55 49 30N 42 20 E
Khor el 'Atash 87 13 20N 34 15 E
Khóra 45 37 3N 21 42 E
Khóra Sfakion 45 35 15N 24 9 E
Khorāsān □ 65 34 0N 58 0 E
Khorat = Nakhon Ratchasima 71 14 59N 102 12 E
Khorat, Cao Nguyen 71 15 30N 102 50 E
Khorb el Ethel 82 28 30N 6 17W
Khorixas 92 20 16 S 14 59 E
Khorog 58 37 30N 71 36 E
Khorol 56 49 48N 33 15 E
Khorramābād 64 33 30N 48 25 E
Khorramshahr 64 30 29N 48 15 E
Khotin 56 48 31N 26 27 E
Khouribga 82 32 58N 6 57W
Khowai 67 24 5N 91 40 E
Khoyniki 54 51 54N 29 55 E
Khrami → 57 41 30N 45 0 E
Khrenovoye 55 51 4N 40 16 E
Khristianá 45 36 14N 25 13 E
Khtapodhiá 45 37 24N 25 34 E
Khu Khan 71 14 42N 104 12 E
Khulna 69 22 45N 89 34 E
Khulo 57 41 33N 42 19 E
Khumago 92 20 26 S 24 32 E
Khunzakh 57 42 35N 46 42 E
Khūr 65 32 55N 58 18 E
Khurai 68 24 3N 78 23 E
Khurayş 64 24 55N 48 5 E
Khurja 68 28 15N 77 58 E
Khūryān Mūryān, Jazā 'ir 63 17 30N 55 58 E
Khushab 68 32 20N 72 20 E
Khuzdar 66 27 52N 66 30 E
Khūzetān □ 64 31 0N 50 0 E
Khvalynsk 55 52 30N 48 2 E
Khvatovka 55 52 24N 46 32 E
Khvor 65 33 45N 55 0 E
Khvormūj 65 28 40N 51 30 E
Khvoy 64 38 35N 45 0 E
Khvoynaya 54 58 58N 34 28 E
Khyber Pass 66 34 10N 71 8 E
Kiabukwa 91 8 40 S 24 48 E
Kiadho → 70 19 37N 77 40 E
Kiama 99 34 40 S 150 50 E
Kiamba 73 6 2N 124 46 E
Kiambi 90 7 15 S 28 0 E
Kiambu 90 1 8 S 36 50 E
Kiangsi = Jiangxi □ 75 27 30N 116 0 E
Kiangsu = Jiangsu □ 75 33 0N 120 0 E
Kiáton 45 38 2N 22 43 E
Kibæk 49 56 2N 8 51 E
Kibanga Port 90 0 10N 32 58 E
Kibangou 88 3 26 S 12 22 E
Kibara 90 2 8 S 33 30 E
Kibare, Mts. 90 8 25 S 27 10 E
Kibombo 90 3 57 S 25 53 E
Kibondo 90 3 35 S 30 45 E
Kibondo □ 90 4 0 S 30 55 E
Kibumbu 90 3 32 S 29 45 E
Kibungu 90 2 10 S 30 32 E
Kibuye, Burundi 90 3 39 S 29 59 E
Kibuye, Rwanda 90 2 3 S 29 21 E
Kibwesa 90 6 30 S 29 58 E
Kibwezi 90 2 27 S 37 57 E
Kičevo 42 41 34N 20 59 E
Kichiga 59 59 50N 163 5 E
Kicking Horse Pass 108 51 28N 116 16W
Kidal 85 18 26N 1 22 E
Kidderminster 13 52 24N 2 13W
Kidete 90 6 25 S 37 17 E
Kidira 84 14 28N 12 13W
Kidnappers, C. 101 39 38 S 177 5 E
Kidston 98 18 52 S 144 8 E
Kidugallo 90 6 49 S 38 15 E
Kiel 24 54 16N 10 8 E
Kiel Kanal = Nord-Ostee-Kanal 24 54 15N 9 40 E
Kielce 28 50 52N 20 42 E
Kielce □ 28 50 40N 20 40 E
Kieler Bucht 24 54 30N 10 30 E
Kienge 91 10 30 S 27 30 E
Kiessé 85 13 29N 4 1 E
Kiev = Kiyev 54 50 30N 30 28 E
Kifār 'Aşyūn 62 31 39N 35 7 E
Kiffa 84 16 37N 11 24W
Kifisiá 45 38 4N 23 49 E
Kifissós → 45 38 35N 23 20 E
Kifrī 64 34 45N 45 0 E
Kigali 90 1 59 S 30 4 E
Kigarama 90 1 1 S 31 50 E
Kigoma □ 90 5 0 S 30 0 E
Kigoma-Ujiji 90 4 55 S 29 36 E
Kigomasha, Ras 90 4 58 S 38 58 E
Kihee 99 27 23 S 142 37 E
Kii-Suidō 74 33 40N 135 0 E
Kikinda 42 45 50N 20 30 E
Kikládhes 45 37 20N 24 30 E
Kikládhes □ 45 37 0N 25 0 E
Kikori 98 7 25 S 144 15 E
Kikori → 98 7 38 S 144 20 E
Kikwit 88 5 5 S 18 45 E
Kilafors 48 61 14N 16 36 E
Kilakarai 70 9 12N 78 47 E
Kilalki 45 36 15N 27 35 E
Kilauea Crater 110 19 24N 155 17W
Kilcoy 99 26 59 S 152 30 E
Kildare 15 53 10N 6 50W
Kildare □ 15 53 10N 6 50W
Kilgore 117 32 22N 94 55W
Kilifi 90 3 40 S 39 48 E
Kilifi □ 90 3 30 S 39 40 E
Kilimanjaro 90 3 7 S 37 20 E
Kilimanjaro □ 90 4 0 S 38 0 E
Kilindini 90 4 4 S 39 40 E
Kilis 64 36 50N 37 10 E
Kiliya 56 45 28N 29 16 E
Kilju 76 40 57N 129 25 E
Kilkee 15 52 41N 9 40W
Kilkenny 15 52 40N 7 17W
Kilkenny □ 15 52 35N 7 15W
Kilkieran B. 15 53 18N 9 45W
Kilkis 44 40 58N 22 57 E
Kilkis □ 44 41 5N 22 50 E
Killala 15 54 13N 9 12W
Killala B. 15 54 20N 9 12W
Killaloe 15 52 48N 8 28W
Killaloe Sta. 112 45 33N 77 25W
Killam 108 52 47N 111 51W
Killarney, Can. 106 45 55N 81 30W
Killarney, Ireland 15 52 2N 9 30W
Killarney, Lakes of 15 52 0N 9 30W
Killary Harbour 15 53 38N 9 52W
Killdeer, Can. 109 49 6N 106 22W
Killdeer, U.S.A. 116 47 26N 102 48W
Killeen 117 31 7N 97 45W
Killiecrankie, Pass of 14 56 44N 3 46W
Killin 14 56 28N 4 20W
Killíni, Ilía, Greece 45 37 55N 21 8 E
Killíni, Korinthía, Greece 45 37 54N 22 25 E
Killybegs 15 54 38N 8 26W
Kilmarnock 14 55 36N 4 30W
Kilmez 55 56 58N 50 55 E
Kilmez → 55 56 58N 50 28 E
Kilmore 99 37 25 S 144 53 E
Kilondo 91 9 45 S 34 20 E
Kilosa 90 6 48 S 37 0 E
Kilosa □ 90 6 48 S 37 0 E
Kilrush 15 52 39N 9 30W
Kilsmo 48 59 6N 15 35 E
Kilwa □ 91 9 0 S 39 0 E
Kilwa Kisiwani 91 8 58 S 39 32 E
Kilwa Kivinje 91 8 45 S 39 25 E
Kilwa Masoko 91 8 55 S 39 30 E
Kim 117 37 18N 103 20W
Kimaam 73 7 58 S 138 53 E
Kimamba 90 6 45 S 37 10 E
Kimba 97 33 8 S 136 23 E
Kimball, Nebr., U.S.A. 116 41 17N 103 40W
Kimball, S.D., U.S.A. 116 43 47N 98 57W
Kimbe 98 5 33 S 150 11 E
Kimbe B. 98 5 15 S 150 30 E
Kimberley, Austral. 96 16 20 S 127 0 E
Kimberley, Can. 108 49 40N 115 59W
Kimberley, S. Afr. 92 28 43 S 24 46 E
Kimberly 118 42 33N 114 25W
Kimchaek 76 40 40N 129 10 E
Kimchŏn 76 36 11N 128 4 E
Kími 45 38 38N 24 6 E
Kímolos 45 36 48N 24 37 E
Kimovsk 55 54 0N 38 29 E
Kimparana 84 12 48N 5 0W
Kimry 55 56 55N 37 15 E
Kimsquit 108 52 45N 126 57W
Kimstad 49 58 35N 15 58 E
Kinabalu 72 6 0N 116 0 E
Kínaros 45 36 59N 26 15 E
Kinaskan L. 108 57 38N 130 8W
Kincaid 109 49 40N 107 0W
Kincardine 106 44 10N 81 40W
Kinda 91 9 18 S 25 4 E
Kindersley 109 51 30N 109 10W
Kindia 84 10 0N 12 52W
Kindu 90 2 55 S 25 50 E
Kinel 55 53 15N 50 40 E
Kineshma 55 57 30N 42 5 E
Kinesi 90 1 25 S 33 50 E
King City 119 36 11N 121 8W
King Cr. → 98 24 35 S 139 30 E
King Frederick VI Land = Kong Frederik VI.s. Kyst 4 63 0N 43 0W
King George B. 128 51 30 S 60 30W
King George I. 5 60 0 S 60 0W
King George Is. 105 57 20N 80 30W
King George Sd. 96 35 5 S 118 0 E
King I., Austral. 97 39 50 S 144 0 E
King I., Can. 108 52 10N 127 40W
King I. = Kadah Kyun 71 12 30N 98 20 E
King Leopold Ranges 96 17 30 S 125 45 E
King, Mt. 99 25 10 S 147 30 E
King Sd. 96 16 50 S 123 20 E
King William I. 104 69 10N 97 25W
King William's Town 92 32 51 S 27 22 E
Kingaroy 97 26 32 S 151 51 E
Kingfisher 117 35 50N 97 55W
Kingisepp 54 59 25N 28 40 E
Kingisepp (Kuressaare) 54 58 15N 22 30 E
Kingman, Ariz., U.S.A. 119 35 12N 114 2W
Kingman, Kans., U.S.A. 117 37 41N 98 9W
Kings → 119 36 10N 119 50W
Kings Canyon National Park 119 37 0N 118 35W
King's Lynn 12 52 45N 0 25 E
Kings Mountain 115 35 13N 81 20W
King's Peak 118 40 46N 110 27W
Kingsbridge 13 50 17N 3 46W
Kingsburg 119 36 35N 119 36W
Kingscote 99 35 40 S 137 38 E
Kingscourt 15 53 55N 6 48W
Kingsley 116 42 37N 95 58W
Kingsley Dam 116 41 20N 101 40W
Kingsport 115 36 33N 82 36W
Kingston, Can. 106 44 14N 76 30W
Kingston, Jamaica 121 18 0N 76 50W
Kingston, N.Z. 101 45 20 S 168 43 E
Kingston, N.Y., U.S.A. 114 41 55N 74 0W
Kingston, Pa., U.S.A. 114 41 19N 75 58W
Kingston, R.I., U.S.A. 113 41 29N 71 30W
Kingston South East 97 36 51 S 139 55 E
Kingston-upon-Thames 13 51 23N 0 20W
Kingstown 121 13 10N 61 10W
Kingstree 115 33 40N 79 48W
Kingsville, Can. 106 42 2N 82 45W
Kingsville, U.S.A. 117 27 30N 97 53W
Kingussie 14 57 5N 4 2W
Kinistino 109 52 57N 105 2W
Kinkala 88 4 18 S 14 49 E
Kinleith 101 38 20 S 175 56 E
Kinmount 112 44 48N 78 45W
Kinn 47 61 34N 4 45 E
Kinna 49 57 32N 12 42 E
Kinnaird 108 49 17N 117 39W
Kinnairds Hd. 14 57 40N 2 0W
Kinnared 49 57 2N 13 7 E
Kinneret 62 32 44N 35 34 E
Kinneret, Yam 62 32 45N 35 35 E
Kinoje → 106 52 8N 81 25W
Kinoni 90 0 41 S 30 28 E
Kinross 14 56 13N 3 25W
Kinsale 15 51 42N 8 31W
Kinsale, Old Hd. of 15 51 37N 8 32W
Kinsarvik 47 60 22N 6 43 E
Kinshasa 88 4 20 S 15 15 E
Kinsley 117 37 57N 99 30W
Kinston 115 35 18N 77 35W
Kintampo 85 8 5N 1 41W
Kintap 72 3 51 S 115 13 E
Kintyre 14 55 30N 5 35W
Kintyre, Mull of 14 55 17N 5 55W
Kinushseo → 106 55 15N 83 45W
Kinuso 108 55 20N 115 25W
Kinyangiri 90 4 25 S 34 37 E
Kinzig → 25 48 37N 7 49 E
Kinzua 112 41 52N 78 58W
Kinzua Dam 112 41 53N 79 0W
Kíoni 45 38 27N 20 41 E
Kiosk 106 46 6N 78 53W
Kiowa, Kans., U.S.A. 117 37 3N 98 30W
Kiowa, Okla., U.S.A. 117 34 45N 95 50W
Kipahigan L. 109 55 20N 101 55W
Kipanga 90 6 15 S 35 20 E
Kiparissía 45 37 15N 21 40 E

Kiparissiakós Kólpos 45 37 25N 21 25 E
Kipembawe 90 7 38 S 33 27 E
Kipengere Ra. 91 9 12 S 34 15 E
Kipili 90 7 28 S 30 32 E
Kipini 90 2 30 S 40 32 E
Kipling 109 50 6N 102 38W
Kippure 15 53 11N 6 23W
Kipushi 91 11 48 S 27 12 E
Kirandul 70 18 33N 81 10 E
Kiratpur 68 29 32N 78 12 E
Kirchhain 24 50 49N 8 54 E
Kirchheim 25 48 38N 9 20 E
Kirchheim-Bolanden 25 49 40N 8 0 E
Kirchschlag 27 47 30N 16 19 E
Kirensk 59 57 50N 107 55 E
Kirgiz S.S.R. □ 58 42 0N 75 0 E
Kirgiziya Steppe 53 50 0N 55 0 E
Kiri 88 1 29 S 19 0 E
Kiribati ■ 94 1 0N 176 0 E
Kiriburu 69 22 0N 85 0 E
Kırıkkale 64 39 51N 33 32 E
Kirillov 55 59 51N 38 14 E
Kirin = Jilin 76 43 55N 126 30 E
Kirin = Jilin □ 76 44 0N 126 0 E
Kirindi ~→ 70 6 15N 81 20 E
Kirishi 54 59 28N 31 59 E
Kirkcaldy 14 56 7N 3 10W
Kirkcudbright 14 54 50N 4 3W
Kirkee 70 18 34N 73 56 E
Kirkenær 47 60 27N 12 3 E
Kirkenes 50 69 40N 30 5 E
Kirkintilloch 14 55 57N 4 10W
Kirkjubæjarklaustur 50 63 47N 18 4W
Kirkland 119 34 29N 112 46W
Kirkland Lake 106 48 9N 80 2W
Kırklareli 43 41 44N 27 15 E
Kirksville 116 40 8N 92 35W
Kirkük 64 35 30N 44 21 E
Kirkwall 14 58 59N 2 59W
Kirkwood 92 33 22 S 25 15 E
Kirlampudi 70 17 12N 82 12 E
Kirn 25 49 46N 7 29 E
Kirov, R.S.F.S.R., U.S.S.R. 54 54 3N 34 20 E
Kirov, R.S.F.S.R., U.S.S.R. 58 58 35N 49 40 E
Kirovabad 57 40 45N 46 20 E
Kirovakan 57 40 48N 44 30 E
Kirovo-Chepetsk 55 58 28N 50 0 E
Kirovograd 56 48 35N 32 20 E
Kirovsk, R.S.F.S.R., U.S.S.R. 52 67 48N 33 50 E
Kirovsk, Turkmen S.S.R., U.S.S.R. 58 37 42N 60 23 E
Kirovsk, Ukraine S.S.R., U.S.S.R. 57 48 35N 38 30 E
Kirovski 57 45 51N 48 11 E
Kirovskiy 59 54 27N 155 42 E
Kirriemuir, Can. 109 51 56N 110 20W
Kirriemuir, U.K. 14 56 41N 3 0W
Kirsanov 55 52 35N 42 40 E
Kırşehir 64 39 14N 34 5 E
Kirstonia 92 25 30 S 23 45 E
Kirtachi 85 12 52N 2 30 E
Kirteh 65 32 15N 63 0 E
Kirthar Range 68 27 0N 67 0 E
Kiruna 50 67 52N 20 15 E
Kirundu 90 0 50 S 25 35 E
Kirya 55 55 5N 46 45 E
Kiryū 74 36 24N 139 20 E
Kisa 49 58 0N 15 39 E
Kisaga 90 4 30 S 34 23 E
Kisámou, Kólpos 45 35 30N 23 38 E
Kisanga 90 2 30N 26 35 E
Kisangani 90 0 35N 25 15 E
Kisar 73 8 5 S 127 10 E
Kisaran 72 3 0N 99 37 E
Kisarawe 90 6 53 S 39 0 E
Kisarawe □ 90 7 3 S 39 0 E
Kisarazu 74 35 23N 139 55 E
Kisbér 27 47 30N 18 0 E
Kiselevsk 58 54 5N 86 39 E
Kishanganj 69 26 3N 88 14 E
Kishangarh 68 27 50N 70 30 E
Kishi 85 9 1N 3 52 E
Kishinev 56 47 0N 28 50 E
Kishiwada 74 34 28N 135 22 E
Kishon 62 32 49N 35 2 E
Kishorganj 69 24 26N 90 40 E
Kishtwar 69 33 20N 75 48 E
Kisii 90 0 40 S 34 45 E
Kisii □ 90 0 40 S 34 45 E
Kisiju 90 7 23 S 39 19 E
Kısır, Dağ 57 41 0N 43 5 E
Kisizi 90 1 0 S 29 58 E
Kiska I. 104 52 0N 177 30 E
Kiskatinaw ~→ 108 56 8N 120 10W
Kiskittogisu L. 109 54 13N 98 20W
Kiskomárom = Zalakomár 27 46 33N 17 10 E
Kiskőrös 27 46 37N 19 20 E
Kiskundorozsma 27 46 16N 20 5 E
Kiskunfélegyháza 27 46 42N 19 53 E
Kiskunhalas 27 46 28N 19 37 E
Kiskunmajsa 27 46 30N 19 48 E
Kislovodsk 57 43 50N 42 45 E
Kiso-Sammyaku 74 35 45N 137 45 E
Kisoro 90 1 17 S 29 48 E
Kispest 27 47 27N 19 9 E
Kissidougou 84 9 5N 10 0W
Kissimmee 115 28 18N 81 22W
Kissimmee ~→ 115 27 20N 80 55W
Kississing L. 109 55 10N 101 20W
Kistanje 39 43 58N 15 55 E
Kisterenye 27 48 3N 19 50 E
Kisújszállás 27 47 12N 20 50 E
Kisumu 90 0 3 S 34 45 E
Kisvárda 27 48 14N 22 4 E
Kiswani 90 4 5 S 37 57 E
Kiswere 91 9 27 S 39 30 E
Kit Carson 116 38 48N 102 45W
Kita 84 13 5N 9 25W
Kitab 58 39 7N 66 52 E
Kitaibaraki 74 36 50N 140 45 E
Kitakami-Gawa ~→ 74 38 25N 141 19 E
Kitakyūshū 74 33 50N 130 50 E
Kitale 90 1 0N 35 0 E
Kitangiri, L. 90 4 5 S 34 20 E
Kitaya 91 10 38 S 40 8 E
Kitchener 106 43 27N 80 29W
Kitega = Citega 90 3 30 S 29 58 E
Kitengo 90 7 26 S 24 8 E
Kiteto □ 90 5 0 S 37 0 E
Kitgum 90 3 17N 32 52 E
Kíthira 45 36 9N 23 0 E
Kíthnos 45 37 26N 24 27 E
Kitimat 108 54 3N 128 38W
Kitinen ~→ 50 67 34N 26 40 E
Kitiyab 87 17 13N 33 35 E
Kítros 44 40 22N 22 34 E
Kittakittaooloo, L. 99 28 3 S 138 14 E
Kittanning 114 40 49N 79 30W
Kittatinny Mts. 113 41 0N 75 0W
Kittery 114 43 7N 70 42W
Kitui 90 1 17 S 38 0 E
Kitui □ 90 1 30 S 38 25 E
Kitwe 91 12 54 S 28 13 E
Kitzbühel 26 47 27N 12 24 E
Kitzingen 25 49 44N 10 9 E
Kivalo 50 66 18N 26 0 E
Kivarli 68 24 33N 72 46 E
Kivotós 44 40 13N 21 26 E
Kivu □ 90 3 10 S 27 0 E
Kivu, L. 90 1 48 S 29 0 E
Kiyev 54 50 30N 30 28 E
Kiyevskoye Vdkhr. 54 51 0N 30 0 E
Kizel 52 59 3N 57 40 E
Kiziguru 90 1 46 S 30 23 E
Kızıl Irmak ~→ 56 39 15N 36 0 E
Kizil Yurt 57 43 13N 46 54 E
Kızılcahamam 56 40 30N 32 30 E
Kizimkazi 90 6 28 S 39 30 E
Kizlyar 57 43 51N 46 40 E
Kizyl-Arvat 58 38 58N 56 15 E
Kjellerup 49 56 17N 9 25 E
Kladanj 42 44 14N 18 42 E
Kladnica 42 43 23N 20 2 E
Kladno 26 50 10N 14 7 E
Kladovo 42 44 36N 22 33 E
Klagenfurt 26 46 38N 14 20 E
Klagshamn 49 55 32N 12 53 E
Klagstorp 49 55 22N 13 23 E
Klaipeda 54 55 43N 21 10 E
Klamath ~→ 118 41 40N 124 4W
Klamath Falls 118 42 20N 121 50W
Klamath Mts. 118 41 20N 123 0W
Klanjec 39 46 3N 15 45 E
Klappan ~→ 108 58 0N 129 43W
Klaten 73 7 43 S 110 36 E
Klatovy 26 49 23N 13 18 E
Klawak 108 55 35N 133 0W
Klawer 92 31 44 S 18 36 E
Klecko 28 52 38N 17 25 E
Kleczew 28 52 22N 18 9 E
Kleena Kleene 108 52 0N 124 59W
Klein 118 46 26N 108 31W
Klein-Karas 92 27 33 S 18 7 E
Klein Karoo 92 33 45 S 21 30 E
Klekovača 39 44 25N 16 32 E
Klemtu 108 52 35N 128 55W
Klenovec, Czech. 27 48 36N 19 54 E
Klenovec, Yugo. 42 41 32N 20 49 E
Klerksdorp 92 26 51 S 26 38 E
Kleszczele 28 52 35N 23 19 E
Kletnya 54 53 23N 33 12 E
Kletsk 54 53 5N 26 45 E
Kletskiy 57 49 20N 43 0 E
Kleve 24 51 46N 6 10 E
Klickitat 118 45 50N 121 10W
Klimovichi 54 53 36N 32 0 E
Klin 55 56 20N 36 48 E
Klinaklini ~→ 108 51 21N 125 40W
Klintsey 54 52 50N 32 10 E
Klipplaat 92 33 0 S 24 22 E
Klisura 43 42 40N 24 28 E
Klitmøller 49 57 3N 8 30 E
Kljajićevo 42 45 45N 19 17 E
Ključ 39 44 32N 16 48 E
Kłobuck 28 50 55N 18 55 E
Kłodawa 28 52 15N 18 55 E
Kłodzko 28 50 28N 16 38 E
Klondike 104 64 0N 139 26W
Klosi 44 41 28N 20 10 E
Klosterneuburg 27 48 18N 16 19 E
Klosters 25 46 52N 9 52 E
Klötze 24 52 38N 11 9 E
Klouto 85 6 57N 0 44 E
Kluane L. 104 61 15N 138 40W
Kluczbork 28 50 58N 18 12 E
Klyuchevskaya, Guba 59 55 50N 160 30 E
Knaresborough 12 54 1N 1 29W
Knee L., Man., Can. 109 55 3N 94 45W
Knee L., Sask., Can. 109 55 51N 107 0W
Kneïss, I. 83 34 22N 10 18 E
Knezha 43 43 30N 24 5 E
Knić 42 43 53N 20 45 E
Knight Inlet 108 50 45N 125 40W
Knighton 13 52 21N 3 2W
Knight's Landing 118 38 50N 121 43W
Knin 39 44 1N 16 17 E
Knittelfeld 26 47 13N 14 51 E
Knjaževac 42 43 35N 22 18 E
Knob, C. 96 34 32 S 119 16 E
Knockmealdown Mts. 15 52 16N 8 0W
Knokke 16 51 20N 3 17 E
Knossos 45 35 16N 25 10 E
Knox 114 41 18N 86 36W
Knox, C. 108 54 11N 133 5W
Knox City 117 33 26N 99 49W
Knox Coast 5 66 30 S 108 0 E
Knoxville, Iowa, U.S.A. 116 41 20N 93 5W
Knoxville, Tenn., U.S.A. 115 35 58N 83 57W
Knurów 27 50 13N 18 38 E
Knutshø 47 62 18N 9 41 E
Knysna 92 34 2 S 23 2 E
Knyszyn 28 53 20N 22 56 E
Ko Chang 71 12 0N 102 20 E
Ko Kut 71 11 40N 102 32 E
Ko Phra Thong 71 9 6N 98 15 E
Ko Tao 71 10 6N 99 48 E
Koartac (Notre Dame de Koartac) 105 60 55N 69 40W
Koba, Aru, Indon. 73 6 37 S 134 37 E
Koba, Bangka, Indon. 72 2 26 S 106 14 E
Kobarid 39 46 15N 13 30 E
Kobayashi 74 31 56N 130 59 E
Kobdo = Hovd 75 48 2N 91 37 E
Kōbe 74 34 45N 135 10 E
Kobelyaki 56 49 11N 34 9 E
København 49 55 41N 12 34 E
Koblenz 25 50 21N 7 36 E
Kobo 87 12 2N 39 56 E
Kobrin 54 52 15N 24 22 E
Kobroor, Kepulauan 73 6 10 S 134 30 E
Kobuleti 57 41 55N 41 45 E
Kobylin 28 51 43N 17 12 E
Kobyłka 28 52 21N 21 10 E
Kobylkino 55 54 8N 43 56 E
Kobylnik 54 54 58N 26 39 E
Kočane 42 43 12N 21 52 E
Kočani 42 41 55N 22 25 E
Koçarlı 45 37 45N 27 43 E
Koceljevo 42 44 28N 19 50 E
Kočevje 39 45 39N 14 50 E
Kochas 69 25 15N 83 56 E
Kocher ~→ 25 49 14N 9 12 E
Kocheya 59 52 32N 120 42 E
Kōchi 74 33 30N 133 35 E
Kōchi □ 74 33 40N 133 30 E
Kochiu = Gejiu 75 23 20N 103 10 E
Kock 28 51 38N 22 27 E
Koddiyar Bay 70 8 33N 81 15 E
Kodiak 104 57 30N 152 45W
Kodiak I. 104 57 30N 152 45W
Kodiang 71 6 21N 100 18 E
Kodinar 68 20 46N 70 46 E
Kodori ~→ 57 42 47N 41 10 E
Koes 92 26 0 S 19 15 E
Kofiau 73 1 11 S 129 50 E
Köflach 26 47 4N 15 5 E
Koforidua 85 6 3N 0 17W
Kōfu 74 35 40N 138 30 E
Kogaluk ~→ 107 56 12N 61 44W
Kogin Baba 85 7 55N 11 35 E
Koh-i-Bābā 65 34 30N 67 0 E
Kohat 66 33 40N 71 29 E
Kohima 67 25 35N 94 10 E
Kohler Ra. 5 77 0 S 110 0W
Kohtla Järve 54 59 20N 27 20 E
Kojetín 27 49 21N 17 20 E
Koka 86 20 5N 30 35 E
Kokand 58 40 30N 70 57 E
Kokanee Glacier Prov. Park 108 49 47N 117 10W
Kokas 73 2 42 S 132 26 E
Kokava 27 48 35N 19 50 E
Kokchetav 58 53 20N 69 25 E
Kokemäenjoki ~→ 51 61 32N 21 44 E
Kokhma 55 56 55N 41 18 E
Kokkola (Gamlakarleby) 50 63 50N 23 8 E
Koko 85 11 28N 4 29 E
Koko Kyunzu 71 14 10N 93 25 E
Kokoda 98 8 54 S 147 47 E
Kokolopozo 84 5 8N 6 5W
Kokomo 114 40 30N 86 6W
Kokonau 73 4 43 S 136 26 E
Kokopo 98 4 22 S 152 19 E
Kokoro 85 14 12N 0 55 E
Koksoak ~→ 105 58 30N 68 10W
Kokstad 93 30 32 S 29 29 E
Kokuora 59 71 35N 144 50 E
Kola, Indon. 73 5 35 S 134 30 E
Kola, U.S.S.R. 52 68 45N 33 8 E
Kola Pen. = Kolskiy P-ov. 52 67 30N 38 0 E
Kolahun 84 8 15N 10 4W
Kolaka 73 4 3 S 121 46 E
Kolar 70 13 12N 78 15 E
Kolar Gold Fields 70 12 58N 78 16 E
Kolari 50 67 20N 23 48 E
Kolarovgrad 43 43 18N 26 55 E
Kolašin 42 42 50N 19 31 E
Kolby Kås 49 55 48N 10 32 E
Kolchugino 55 56 17N 39 22 E
Kolda 84 12 55N 14 57W
Kolding 49 55 30N 9 29 E
Kole 88 3 16 S 22 42 E
Koléa 82 36 38N 2 46 E
Kolepom, Pulau 73 8 0 S 138 30 E
Kolguyev, Ostrov 52 69 20N 48 30 E
Kolhapur 70 16 43N 74 15 E
Kolia 84 9 46N 6 28W
Kolín 26 50 2N 15 9 E
Kolind 49 56 21N 10 34 E
Kölleda 24 51 11N 11 14 E
Kollegal 70 12 9N 77 9 E
Kolleru L. 70 16 40N 81 10 E
Kolmanskop 92 26 45 S 15 14 E
Köln 24 50 56N 6 58 E
Kolno 28 53 25N 21 56 E
Koło 28 52 14N 18 40 E
Kołobrzeg 28 54 10N 15 35 E
Kologriv 55 58 48N 44 25 E
Kolokani 84 13 35N 7 45W
Kolomna 55 55 8N 38 45 E
Kolomyya 56 48 31N 25 2 E
Kolondiéba 84 11 5N 6 54W
Kolonodale 73 2 3 S 121 25 E
Kolosib 67 24 15N 92 45 E
Kolpashevo 58 58 20N 83 5 E
Kolpino 54 59 44N 30 39 E
Kolpny 55 52 12N 37 10 E
Kolskiy Poluostrov 52 67 30N 38 0 E
Kolskiy Zaliv 52 69 23N 34 0 E
Kolubara ~→ 42 44 35N 20 15 E
Kolumna 28 51 36N 19 14 E
Koluszki 28 51 45N 19 46 E
Kolwezi 91 10 40 S 25 25 E
Kolyberovo 55 55 15N 38 40 E
Kolyma ~→ 59 69 30N 161 0 E
Kolymskoye, Okhotsko 59 63 0N 157 0 E
Kôm Ombo 86 24 25N 32 52 E
Komárno 27 47 49N 18 5 E
Komárom 27 47 43N 18 7 E
Komárom □ 27 47 35N 18 20 E
Komarovo 54 58 38N 33 40 E
Komatipoort 93 25 25 S 31 55 E
Kombissiri 85 12 4N 1 20W
Kombori 84 13 26N 3 56W
Kombóti 45 39 6N 21 5 E
Komen 39 45 49N 13 45 E
Komenda 85 5 4N 1 28W
Komi A.S.S.R. □ 52 64 0N 55 0 E
Komiža 39 43 3N 16 11 E
Komló 27 46 15N 18 16 E
Kommamur Canal 70 16 0N 80 25 E
Kommunarsk 57 48 30N 38 45 E
Kommunizma, Pik 58 39 0N 72 2 E
Komnes 47 59 30N 9 55 E
Komodo 73 8 37 S 119 20 E
Komoé 84 5 12N 3 44W
Komono 88 3 10 S 13 20 E
Komoran, Pulau 73 8 18 S 138 45 E
Komotini 44 41 9N 25 26 E
Komovi 42 42 41N 19 39 E
Kompong Cham 71 12 0N 105 30 E
Kompong Chhnang 71 12 20N 104 35 E
Kompong Speu 71 11 26N 104 32 E
Kompong Thom 71 12 35N 104 51 E
Komrat 56 46 18N 28 40 E
Komsberge 92 32 40 S 20 45 E
Komsomolets, Ostrov 59 80 30N 95 0 E
Komsomolsk, R.S.F.S.R., U.S.S.R. 55 57 2N 40 20 E
Komsomolsk, R.S.F.S.R., U.S.S.R. 59 50 30N 137 0 E
Komsomolskaya 5 66 33 S 93 1 E
Komsomolskiy 55 53 30N 49 30 E
Konakovo 55 56 52N 36 45 E
Konarhá □ 65 35 30N 71 3 E
Konawa 117 34 59N 96 46W
Kondagaon 70 19 35N 81 35 E
Kondakovo 59 69 36N 152 0 E
Konde 90 4 57 S 39 45 E
Kondiá 44 39 49N 25 10 E
Kondoa 90 4 55 S 35 50 E
Kondoa □ 90 5 0 S 36 0 E
Kondopaga 52 62 12N 34 17 E
Kondratyevo 59 57 22N 98 15 E
Konduga 85 11 35N 13 26 E
Konevo 52 62 8N 39 20 E
Kong 84 8 54N 4 36W
Kong Christian IX.s Land 4 68 0N 36 0W
Kong Christian X.s Land 4 74 0N 29 0W
Kong Franz Joseph Fd. 4 73 20N 24 30W
Kong Frederik IX.s Land 4 67 0N 52 0W
Kong Frederik VI.s Kyst 4 63 0N 43 0W
Kong Frederik VIII.s Land 4 78 30N 26 0W
Kong, Koh 71 11 20N 103 0 E
Kong Oscar Fjord 4 72 20N 24 0W
Konga 49 56 30N 15 6 E
Kongeå 49 55 24N 9 39 E
Kongju 76 36 30N 127 0 E
Konglu 67 27 13N 97 57 E
Kongolo, Kasai Or., Zaïre 90 5 26 S 24 49 E
Kongolo, Shaba, Zaïre 90 5 22 S 27 0 E
Kongor 81 7 1N 31 27 E
Kongoussi 85 13 19N 1 32W
Kongsberg 47 59 39N 9 39 E
Kongsvinger 47 60 12N 12 2 E
Kongwa 90 6 11 S 36 26 E
Koni 91 10 40 S 27 11 E
Koni, Mts. 91 10 36 S 27 10 E
Koniecpol 28 50 46N 19 40 E
Königsberg = Kaliningrad 54 54 42N 20 32 E
Königshofen 25 50 18N 10 29 E
Königslutter 24 52 14N 10 50 E
Königswusterhausen 24 52 19N 13 38 E
Konin 28 52 12N 18 15 E
Konin □ 28 52 15N 18 30 E
Konispoli 44 39 42N 20 10 E
Kónitsa 44 40 5N 20 48 E
Konjic 42 43 42N 17 58 E
Konjice 39 46 20N 15 28 E
Konkouré ~→ 84 9 50N 13 42W
Könnern 24 51 40N 11 45 E
Konnur 70 16 14N 74 49 E
Kono 84 8 30N 11 5W
Konongo 85 6 40N 1 15W
Konosha 52 61 0N 40 5 E
Konotop 54 51 12N 33 7 E
Konqi He ~→ 75 40 45N 90 10 E
Końskie 28 51 15N 20 23 E
Konsmo 47 58 16N 7 23 E
Konstantinovka 56 48 32N 37 39 E
Konstantinovski 57 47 33N 41 10 E
Konstantynów Łódźki 28 51 45N 19 20 E
Konstanz 25 47 39N 9 10 E
Kontagora 85 10 23N 5 27 E
Kontum 71 14 24N 108 0 E
Konya 64 37 52N 32 35 E
Konya Ovasi 64 38 30N 33 0 E
Konz 25 49 41N 6 36 E
Konza 90 1 45 S 37 7 E
Koo-wee-rup 100 38 13 S 145 28 E
Koolan I. 96 16 0 S 123 45 E
Kooloonong 99 34 48 S 143 10 E
Koondrook 99 35 33 S 144 8 E
Koorawatha 99 34 2 S 148 33 E
Kooskia 118 46 9N 115 59W
Koostatak 109 51 26N 97 26W
Kootenai ~→ 118 49 15N 117 39W
Kootenay L. 108 49 45N 116 50W
Kootenay Nat. Park 108 51 0N 116 0W
Kopanovka 57 47 28N 46 50 E
Kopaonik Planina 42 43 10N 21 50 E
Kopargaon 70 19 51N 74 28 E
Kópavogur 50 64 6N 21 55W
Koper 39 45 31N 13 44 E
Kopervik 47 59 17N 5 17 E
Kopeysk 58 55 7N 61 37 E
Köping 48 59 31N 16 3 E
Kopiste 39 42 48N 16 42 E
Kopliku 44 42 15N 19 25 E

Köpmanholmen 48 63 10N 18 35 E
Koppal 70 15 23N 76 5 E
Koppang 47 61 34N 11 3 E
Kopparbergs län □ 48 61 20N 14 15 E
Koppeh Dāgh 65 38 0N 58 0 E
Kopperå 47 63 24N 11 50 E
Koppom 48 59 43N 12 10 E
Koprivlen 43 41 36N 23 53 E
Koprivnica 39 46 12N 16 45 E
Koprivshtitsa 43 42 40N 24 19 E
Kopychintsy 54 49 7N 25 58 E
Kopys 54 54 20N 30 17 E
Korab 42 41 44N 20 40 E
Korakiána 44 39 42N 19 45 E
Koraput 70 18 50N 82 40 E
Korba 69 22 20N 82 45 E
Korbach 24 51 17N 8 50 E
Korça 44 40 37N 20 50 E
Korça □ 44 40 40N 20 50 E
Korčula 39 42 57N 17 8 E
Korčulanski Kanal 39 43 3N 16 40 E
Kordestan 64 35 30N 42 0 E
Kordestān □ 64 36 0N 47 0 E
Korea Bay 76 39 0N 124 0 E
Koregaon 70 17 40N 74 10 E
Korenevo 54 51 27N 34 55 E
Korenovsk 57 45 30N 39 22 E
Korets 54 50 40N 27 5 E
Korgus 86 19 16N 33 29 E
Korhogo 84 9 29N 5 28W
Koribundu 84 7 41N 11 46W
Korim 73 0 58 S 136 10 E
Korinthía □ 45 37 50N 22 35 E
Korinthiakós Kólpos 45 38 16N 22 30 E
Kórinthos 45 37 56N 22 55 E
Korioumé 84 16 35N 3 0W
Kōriyama 74 37 24N 140 23 E
Körmend 27 47 5N 16 35 E
Kornat 39 43 50N 15 20 E
Korneshty 56 47 21N 28 1 E
Korneuburg 27 48 20N 16 20 E
Kornsjø 47 58 57N 11 39 E
Kornstad 47 62 59N 7 27 E
Koro, Fiji 101 17 19 S 179 23 E
Koro, Ivory C. 84 8 32N 7 30W
Koro, Mali 84 14 1N 2 58W
Koro Sea 101 17 30 S 179 45W
Korocha 55 50 55N 37 30 E
Korogwe 90 5 5 S 38 25 E
Korogwe □ 90 5 0 S 38 20 E
Koroit 99 38 18 S 142 24 E
Koróni 45 36 48N 21 57 E
Korónia, Limni 44 40 47N 23 37 E
Koronis 45 37 12N 25 35 E
Koronowo 28 53 19N 17 55 E
Koror 73 7 20N 134 28 E
Körös → 27 46 43N 20 12 E
Köröstarcsa 27 46 53N 21 3 E
Korosten 54 50 57N 28 25 E
Korotoyak 55 51 1N 39 2 E
Korraraika, Helodranon' i 93 17 45 S 43 57 E
Korsakov 59 46 36N 142 42 E
Korshunovo 59 58 37N 110 10 E
Korsun Shevchenkovskiy 56 49 26N 31 16 E
Korsze 28 54 11N 21 9 E
Korti 86 18 6N 31 33 E
Kortrijk 16 50 50N 3 17 E
Korwai 68 24 7N 78 5 E
Koryakskiy Khrebet 59 61 0N 171 0 E
Kos 45 36 50N 27 15 E
Kosa 87 7 50N 36 50 E
Kosaya Gora 55 54 10N 37 30 E
Koschagyl 53 46 40N 54 0 E
Kościan 28 52 5N 16 40 E
Kościerzyna 28 54 8N 17 59 E
Kosciusko 117 33 3N 89 34W
Kosciusko I. 108 56 0N 133 40W
Kosciusko, Mt. 97 36 27 S 148 16 E
Kösély → 27 47 25N 21 5 E
Kosgi 70 16 58N 77 43 E
Kosha 86 20 50N 30 30 E
K'oshih = Kashi 75 39 30N 76 2 E
Koshk-e Kohneh 65 34 55N 62 30 E
Kosi 68 27 48N 77 29 E
Kosi-meer 93 27 0 S 32 50 E
Košice 27 48 42N 21 15 E
Kosjerić 42 44 0N 19 55 E
Koslan 52 63 28N 48 52 E
Kosŏng 76 38 40N 128 22 E
Kosovo, Pokrajina 42 42 40N 21 5 E
Kosovo, Soc. Aut. Pokrajina □ 42 42 30N 21 0 E
Kosovska-Mitrovica 42 42 54N 20 52 E
Kostajnica 39 45 17N 16 30 E
Kostamuksa 52 62 34N 32 44 E
Kostanjevica 39 45 51N 15 27 E
Kostelec 27 50 14N 16 35 E
Kostenets 43 42 15N 23 52 E
Koster 92 25 52 S 26 54 E
Kôstī 87 13 8N 32 43 E
Kostolac 42 44 37N 21 15 E
Kostopol 54 50 51N 26 22 E
Kostroma 55 57 50N 40 58 E
Kostromskoye Vdkhr. 55 57 52N 40 49 E
Kostrzyn, Poland 28 52 24N 17 14 E
Kostrzyn, Poland 28 52 35N 14 39 E
Kostyukovichi 54 53 20N 32 4 E
Koszalin 28 53 50N 16 8 E
Koszalin □ 28 53 40N 16 10 E
Kőszeg 27 47 23N 16 33 E
Kot Adu 68 30 30N 71 0 E
Kot Moman 68 32 13N 73 0 E
Kota 68 25 14N 75 49 E
Kota Baharu 71 6 7N 102 14 E
Kota Belud 72 6 21N 116 26 E
Kota Kinabalu 72 6 0N 116 4 E
Kota Tinggi 71 1 44N 103 53 E
Kotaagung 72 5 38 S 104 29 E
Kotabaru 72 3 20 S 116 20 E
Kotabumi 72 4 49 S 104 54 E
Kotagede 73 7 54 S 110 26 E
Kotamobagu 73 0 57N 124 31 E
Kotaneelee → 108 60 11N 123 42W
Kotawaringin 72 2 28 S 111 27 E
Kotcho L. 108 59 7N 121 12W
Kotel 43 42 52N 26 26 E
Kotelnich 55 58 20N 48 10 E
Kotelnikovo 57 47 38N 43 8 E
Kotelnyy, Ostrov 59 75 10N 139 0 E
Kothagudam 70 17 30N 80 40 E
Kothapet 70 19 21N 79 28 E
Köthen 24 51 44N 11 59 E
Kothi 69 24 45N 80 40 E
Kotiro 68 26 17N 67 13 E
Kotka 51 60 28N 26 58 E
Kotlas 52 61 15N 47 0 E
Kotlenska Planina 43 42 56N 26 30 E
Kotli 66 33 30N 73 55 E
Kotonkoro 85 11 3N 5 58 E
Kotor 42 42 25N 18 47 E
Kotor Varoš 42 44 38N 17 22 E
Kotoriba 39 46 23N 16 48 E
Kotovo 55 50 22N 44 45 E
Kotovsk 56 47 45N 29 35 E
Kotputli 68 27 43N 76 12 E
Kotri 68 25 22N 68 22 E
Kotri → 70 19 15N 80 35 E
Kótronas 45 36 38N 22 29 E
Kötschach-Mauthern 26 46 41N 13 1 E
Kottayam 70 9 35N 76 33 E
Kottur 70 10 34N 76 56 E
Kotuy → 59 71 54N 102 6 E
Kotzebue 104 66 50N 162 40W
Kouango 88 5 0N 20 10 E
Koudougou 84 12 10N 2 20W
Koufonísi 45 34 56N 26 8 E
Koufonísia 45 36 57N 25 35 E
Kougaberge 92 33 48 S 23 50 E
Kouibli 84 7 15N 7 14W
Kouilou → 88 4 10 S 12 5 E
Kouki 88 7 22N 17 3 E
Koula Moutou 88 1 15 S 12 25 E
Koulen 71 13 50N 104 40 E
Koulikoro 84 12 40N 7 50W
Koumala 98 21 38 S 149 15 E
Koumankou 84 11 58N 6 6W
Koumbia, Guin. 84 11 48N 13 29W
Koumbia, Upp. Vol. 84 11 10N 3 50W
Koumboum 84 10 25N 13 0W
Koumpenntoum 84 13 59N 14 34W
Koumra 81 8 50N 17 35 E
Koundara 84 12 29N 13 18W
Kounradskiy 58 46 59N 75 0 E
Kountze 117 30 20N 94 22W
Koupéla 85 12 11N 0 21W
Kourizo, Passe de 83 22 28N 15 27 E
Kouroussa 84 10 45N 9 45W
Koussané 84 14 53N 11 14W
Kousseri 81 12 0N 14 55 E
Koutiala 84 12 25N 5 23W
Kouto 84 9 53N 6 25W
Kouvé 85 6 25N 1 25 E
Kovačica 42 45 5N 20 38 E
Kovdor 52 67 34N 30 24 E
Kovel 54 51 10N 24 20 E
Kovilpatti 70 9 10N 77 50 E
Kovin 42 44 44N 20 59 E
Kovrov 55 56 25N 41 25 E
Kovur, Andhra Pradesh, India 70 17 3N 81 39 E
Kovur, Andhra Pradesh, India 70 14 30N 80 1 E
Kowal 28 52 32N 19 7 E
Kowalewo Pomorskie 28 53 10N 18 52 E
Kowkash 106 50 20N 87 12W
Kowloon 75 22 20N 114 15 E
Koyabuti 73 2 36 S 140 37 E
Koyan, Pegunungan 72 3 15N 114 30 E
Koyuk 104 64 55N 161 20W
Koyukuk → 104 64 56N 157 30W
Koyulhisar 56 40 20N 37 52 E
Koza 77 26 19N 127 46 E
Kozan 64 37 35N 35 50 E
Kozáni 44 40 19N 21 47 E
Kozáni □ 44 40 18N 21 45 E
Kozara 39 45 0N 17 0 E
Kozarac 39 44 58N 16 48 E
Kozelsk 54 54 2N 35 48 E
Kozhikode = Calicut 70 11 15N 75 43 E
Kozhva 52 65 10N 57 0 E
Koziegłowy 28 50 37N 19 8 E
Kozienice 28 51 35N 21 34 E
Kozje 39 46 5N 15 35 E
Kozle 28 50 20N 18 8 E
Kozloduy 43 43 45N 23 42 E
Kozlovets 43 43 30N 25 20 E
Koźmin 28 51 48N 17 27 E
Kozmodemyansk 55 56 20N 46 36 E
Kozuchów 28 51 45N 15 31 E
Kpabia 85 9 10N 0 20W
Kpalimé 85 6 57N 0 44 E
Kpandae 85 8 30N 0 2W
Kpessi 85 8 4N 1 16 E
Kra Buri 71 10 22N 98 46 E
Kra, Isthmus of = Kra, Kho Khot 71 10 15N 99 30 E
Kra, Kho Khot 71 10 15N 99 30 E
Kragan 73 6 43 S 111 38 E
Kragerø 47 58 52N 9 25 E
Kragujevac 42 44 2N 20 56 E
Krajenka 28 53 18N 16 59 E
Krakatau = Rakata, Pulau 72 6 10 S 105 20 E
Kraków 27 50 4N 19 57 E
Kraków □ 27 50 0N 20 0 E
Kraksaan 73 7 43 S 113 23 E
Kråkstad 47 59 39N 10 55 E
Králiky 27 50 6N 16 45 E
Kraljevo 42 43 44N 20 41 E
Kralovice 26 49 59N 13 29 E
Královský Chlmec 27 48 27N 22 0 E
Kralupy 26 50 13N 14 20 E
Kramatorsk 56 48 50N 37 30 E
Kramer 119 35 0N 117 38W
Kramfors 48 62 55N 17 48 E
Kramis, C. 82 36 26N 0 45 E
Krångede 48 63 9N 16 10 E
Kraniá 44 39 53N 21 18 E
Kranídhion 45 37 20N 23 10 E
Kranj 39 46 16N 14 22 E
Kranjska Gora 39 46 29N 13 48 E
Krapina 39 46 10N 15 52 E
Krapina → 39 45 50N 15 50 E
Krapivna 55 53 58N 37 10 E
Krapkowice 28 50 29N 17 56 E
Krasavino 52 60 58N 46 29 E
Kraskino 59 42 44N 130 48 E
Kraslice 26 50 19N 12 31 E
Krasnaya Gorbatka 55 55 52N 41 45 E
Krasnaya Polyana 57 43 40N 40 13 E
Kraśnik 28 50 55N 22 5 E
Kraśnik Fabryczny 28 50 58N 22 11 E
Krasnoarmeisk 56 48 18N 37 11 E
Krasnoarmeysk, R.S.F.S.R., U.S.S.R. 55 51 0N 45 42 E
Krasnoarmeysk, R.S.F.S.R., U.S.S.R. 57 48 30N 44 25 E
Krasnodar 57 45 5N 39 0 E
Krasnodon 57 48 17N 39 44 E
Krasnodonetskaya 57 48 5N 40 50 E
Krasnogorskiy 55 56 10N 48 28 E
Krasnograd 56 49 27N 35 27 E
Krasnogvardeyskoye 57 45 52N 41 33 E
Krasnogvardyesk 56 45 32N 34 16 E
Krasnokamsk 52 58 4N 55 48 E
Krasnokutsk 54 50 10N 34 50 E
Krasnoperekopsk 56 46 0N 33 54 E
Krasnoselkupsk 58 65 20N 82 10 E
Krasnoslobodsk, R.S.F.S.R., U.S.S.R. 55 54 25N 43 45 E
Krasnoslobodsk, R.S.F.S.R., U.S.S.R. 57 48 42N 44 33 E
Krasnoturinsk 58 59 46N 60 12 E
Krasnoufimsk 52 56 57N 57 46 E
Krasnouralsk 52 58 21N 60 3 E
Krasnovishersk 52 60 23N 57 3 E
Krasnovodsk 53 40 0N 52 52 E
Krasnoyarsk 59 56 8N 93 0 E
Krasnoye, Kalmyk A.S.S.R., U.S.S.R. 57 46 16N 45 0 E
Krasnoye, R.S.F.S.R., U.S.S.R. 55 59 15N 47 40 E
Krasnoye = Krasnyy 54 54 25N 31 30 E
Krasnozavodsk 55 56 27N 38 25 E
Krasny Liman 56 48 58N 37 50 E
Krasny Sulin 57 47 52N 40 8 E
Krasnystaw 28 50 57N 23 5 E
Krasnyy 54 54 25N 31 30 E
Krasnyy Kholm 55 58 10N 37 10 E
Krasnyy Kut 55 50 50N 47 0 E
Krasnyy Luch 57 48 13N 39 0 E
Krasnyy Profintern 55 57 45N 40 27 E
Krasnyy Yar, Kalmyk A.S.S.R., U.S.S.R. 57 46 43N 48 23 E
Krasnyy Yar, R.S.F.S.R., U.S.S.R. 55 53 30N 50 22 E
Krasnyy Yar, R.S.F.S.R., U.S.S.R. 55 50 42N 44 45 E
Krasnyye Baki 55 57 8N 45 10 E
Krasnyyoskolskoye Vdkhr. 56 49 30N 37 30 E
Kraszna → 27 48 0N 22 20 E
Kratie 71 12 32N 106 10 E
Kratovo 42 42 6N 22 10 E
Krau 73 3 19 S 140 5 E
Kravanh, Chuor Phnum 71 12 0N 103 32 E
Krawang 73 6 19N 107 18 E
Krefeld 24 51 20N 6 32 E
Krémaston, Límni 45 38 52N 21 30 E
Kremenchug 56 49 5N 33 25 E
Kremenchugskoye Vdkhr. 56 49 20N 32 30 E
Kremenets 56 50 8N 25 43 E
Kremenica 42 40 55N 21 25 E
Kremennaya 56 49 1N 38 10 E
Kremges = Svetlovodsk 56 49 5N 33 15 E
Kremikovtsi 43 42 46N 23 28 E
Kremmen 24 52 45N 13 1 E
Kremmling 118 40 10N 106 30W
Kremnica 27 48 45N 18 50 E
Krems 26 48 25N 15 36 E
Kremsmünster 26 48 3N 14 8 E
Kretinga 54 55 53N 21 15 E
Krettamia 82 28 47N 3 27W
Krettsy 54 58 15N 32 30 E
Kreuzberg 25 50 22N 9 58 E
Kribi 88 2 57N 9 56 E
Krichem 43 42 8N 24 28 E
Krichev 54 53 45N 31 50 E
Krim 39 45 53N 14 30 E
Krionéri 45 38 20N 21 35 E
Krishna → 70 15 57N 80 59 E
Krishnagiri 70 12 32N 78 16 E
Krishnanagar 69 23 24N 88 33 E
Krishnaraja Sagara 70 12 20N 76 30 E
Kristiansand 47 58 9N 8 1 E
Kristianstad 49 56 2N 14 9 E
Kristiansund 47 63 7N 7 45 E
Kristiinankaupunki 50 62 16N 21 21 E
Kristinehamn 48 59 18N 14 13 E
Kristinestad 50 62 16N 21 21 E
Kriti 45 35 15N 25 0 E
Kritsá 45 35 10N 25 41 E
Kriva → 42 42 5N 21 47 E
Kriva Palanka 42 42 11N 22 19 E
Krivaja → 42 44 27N 18 9 E
Krivelj 42 44 8N 22 5 E
Krivoy Rog 56 47 51N 33 20 E
Križevci 39 46 3N 16 32 E
Krk 39 45 8N 14 40 E
Krka → 39 45 50N 15 30 E
Krkonoše 26 50 50N 15 35 E
Krnov 27 50 5N 17 40 E
Krobia 28 51 47N 16 59 E
Kročehlavy 26 50 8N 14 9 E
Krøderen 47 60 9N 9 49 E
Krokawo 28 54 47N 18 9 E
Krokeaí 45 36 53N 22 32 E
Krokom 48 63 20N 14 30 E
Krolevets 54 51 35N 33 20 E
Kroměříz 27 49 18N 17 21 E
Krompachy 27 48 54N 20 52 E
Kromy 54 52 40N 35 48 E
Kronach 25 50 14N 11 19 E
Kronobergs län □ 49 56 45N 14 30 E
Kronprins Olav Kyst 5 69 0 S 42 0 E
Kronprinsesse Märtha Kyst 5 73 30 S 10 0 E
Kronshtadt 54 60 5N 29 45 E
Kroonstad 92 27 43 S 27 19 E
Kröpelin 24 54 4N 11 48 E
Kropotkin, R.S.F.S.R., U.S.S.R. 57 45 28N 40 28 E
Kropotkin, R.S.F.S.R., U.S.S.R. 59 59 0N 115 30 E
Kropp 24 54 24N 9 32 E
Krościenko 27 49 29N 20 25 E
Krośniewice 28 52 15N 19 11 E
Krosno 27 49 42N 21 46 E
Krosno □ 27 49 35N 22 0 E
Krosno Odrzańskie 28 52 3N 15 7 E
Krotoszyn 28 51 42N 17 23 E
Krraba 44 41 13N 20 0 E
Krško 39 45 57N 15 30 E
Krstača 42 42 57N 20 8 E
Kruger Nat. Park 93 24 0 S 31 40 E
Krugersdorp 93 26 5 S 27 46 E
Kruis, Kaap 92 21 55 S 13 57 E
Kruja 44 41 32N 19 46 E
Krulevshchina 54 55 5N 27 45 E
Kruma 44 42 14N 20 28 E
Krumbach 25 48 15N 10 22 E
Krumovgrad 43 41 29N 25 38 E
Krung Thep 71 13 45N 100 35 E
Krupanj 42 44 25N 19 22 E
Krupina 27 48 22N 19 5 E
Krupinica → 27 48 15N 18 52 E
Kruševac 42 43 35N 21 28 E
Kruševo 42 41 23N 21 19 E
Kruszwica 28 52 40N 18 20 E
Kruzof I. 108 57 10N 135 40W
Krylbo 48 60 7N 16 15 E
Krymsk Abinsk 56 44 50N 38 0 E
Krymskiy P-ov. 56 45 0N 34 0 E
Krynica 27 49 25N 20 57 E
Krynica Morska 28 54 23N 19 28 E
Krynki 28 53 17N 23 43 E
Krzepice 28 50 58N 18 50 E
Krzeszów 28 50 24N 22 21 E
Krzeszowice 27 50 8N 19 37 E
Krzna → 28 51 59N 22 47 E
Krzywiń 28 51 58N 16 50 E
Krzyz 28 52 52N 16 0 E
Ksabi 82 32 51N 4 13W
Ksar Chellala 82 35 13N 2 19 E
Ksar el Boukhari 82 35 51N 2 52 E
Ksar el Kebir 82 35 0N 6 0W
Ksar es Souk = Ar Rachidiya 82 31 58N 4 20W
Ksar Rhilane 83 33 0N 9 39 E
Ksiba, El 82 32 46N 6 0W
Ksour, Mts. des 82 32 45N 0 30W
Kstovo 55 56 12N 44 13 E
Kuala 72 2 55N 105 47 E
Kuala Kangsar 71 4 46N 100 56 E
Kuala Kerai 71 5 30N 102 12 E
Kuala Kubu Baharu 71 3 34N 101 39 E
Kuala Lipis 71 4 10N 102 3 E
Kuala Lumpur 71 3 9N 101 41 E
Kuala Sedili Besar 71 1 55N 104 5 E
Kuala Terengganu 71 5 20N 103 8 E
Kualakapuas 72 2 55 S 114 20 E
Kualakurun 72 1 10 S 113 50 E
Kualapembuang 72 3 14 S 112 38 E
Kualasimpang 72 4 17N 98 3 E
Kuandang 73 0 56N 123 1 E
Kuandian 76 40 45N 124 45 E
Kuangchou = Guangzhou 75 23 5N 113 10 E
Kuantan 71 3 49N 103 20 E
Kuba 57 41 21N 48 32 E
Kubak 66 27 10N 63 10 E
Kuban → 56 45 20N 37 30 E
Kubenskoye, Oz. 55 59 40N 39 25 E
Kuberle 57 47 0N 42 20 E
Kubrat 43 43 49N 26 31 E
Kučevo 42 44 30N 21 40 E
Kuchaman 68 27 13N 74 47 E
Kuchenspitze 26 47 7N 10 12 E
Kuching 72 1 33N 110 25 E
Kuçove = Qytet Stalin 44 40 47N 19 57 E
Kücük Kuyu 44 39 35N 26 27 E
Kudalier → 70 18 35N 79 48 E
Kudat 72 6 55N 116 55 E
Kudremukh, Mt. 70 13 15N 75 20 E
Kudus 73 6 48 S 110 51 E
Kudymkar 58 59 1N 54 39 E
Kueiyang = Guiyang 75 26 32N 106 40 E
Kufrinjah 62 32 20N 35 41 E
Kufstein 26 47 35N 12 11 E
Kugong I. 106 56 18N 79 50W
Kūh-e 'Alījūq 65 31 30N 51 41 E
Kūh-e Dīnār 65 30 40N 51 0 E
Kūh-e-Hazārān 65 29 35N 57 20 E
Kūh-e-Jebāl Bārez 65 29 0N 58 0 E
Kūh-e Sorkh 65 35 30N 58 45 E
Kūh-e Taftān 65 28 40N 61 0 E
Kūhak 65 27 12N 63 10 E
Kūhhā-ye-Bashākerd 65 26 45N 59 0 E
Kūhhā-ye Sabalān 64 38 15N 47 45 E
Kuhnsdorf 26 46 37N 14 38 E
Kūhpāyeh 65 32 44N 52 20 E
Kuile He → 76 49 32N 124 42 E
Kuito 89 12 22 S 16 55 E
Kukavica 42 42 48N 21 57 E
Kukawa 85 12 58N 13 27 E
Kukësi 44 42 5N 20 20 E
Kukësi □ 44 42 25N 20 15 E
Kukmor 55 56 11N 50 54 E
Kukvidze 55 50 40N 43 15 E
Kula, Bulg. 42 43 52N 22 36 E
Kula, Yugo. 42 45 37N 19 32 E
Kulai 71 1 44N 103 35 E
Kulal, Mt. 90 2 42N 36 57 E
Kulaly, O. 57 45 0N 50 0 E
Kulasekharapattanam 70 8 20N 78 0 E
Kuldiga 54 56 58N 21 59 E
Kuldja = Yining 75 43 58N 81 10 E
Kuldu 87 12 50N 28 30 E
Kulebaki 55 55 22N 42 25 E
Kulen Vakuf 39 44 35N 16 2 E

Kuli 57 42 2N 47 12 E
Küllük 45 37 12N 27 36 E
Kulm 116 46 22N 98 58W
Kulmbach 25 50 6N 11 27 E
Kulsary 58 46 59N 54 1 E
Kultay 57 45 5N 51 40 E
Kulti 69 23 43N 86 50 E
Kulunda 58 52 35N 78 57 E
Kulwin 99 35 0 S 142 42 E
Kulyab 58 37 55N 69 50 E
Kum Tekei 58 43 10N 79 30 E
Kuma → 57 44 55N 47 0 E
Kumaganum 85 13 8N 10 38 E
Kumagaya 74 36 9N 139 22 E
Kumai 72 2 44 S 111 43 E
Kumamba, Kepulauan 73 1 36 S 138 45 E
Kumamoto 74 32 45N 130 45 E
Kumamoto □ 74 32 55N 130 55 E
Kumanovo 42 42 9N 21 42 E
Kumara 101 42 37 S 171 12 E
Kumasi 84 6 41N 1 38W
Kumba 88 4 36N 9 24 E
Kumbakonam 70 10 58N 79 25 E
Kumbarilla 99 27 15 S 150 55 E
Kumbo 85 6 15N 10 36 E
Kumbukkan Oya → 70 6 35N 81 40 E
Kumeny 55 58 10N 49 47 E
Kumertau 52 52 46N 55 47 E
Kumi 90 1 30N 33 58 E
Kumkale 44 40 0N 26 13 E
Kumla 48 59 8N 15 10 E
Kummerower See 24 53 47N 12 52 E
Kumo 85 10 1N 11 12 E
Kumon Bum 67 26 30N 97 15 E
Kumta 70 14 29N 74 25 E
Kumtorkala 57 43 2N 46 50 E
Kumylzhenskaya 57 49 51N 42 38 E
Kunágota 27 46 26N 21 3 E
Kunama 99 35 35 S 148 4 E
Kunashir, Ostrov 59 44 0N 146 0 E
Kunch 68 26 0N 79 10 E
Kunda 54 59 30N 26 34 E
Kundiawa 98 6 2 S 145 1 E
Kundla 68 21 21N 71 25 E
Kungala 99 29 58 S 153 7 E
Kungälv 49 57 53N 11 59 E
Kunghit I. 108 52 6N 131 3W
Kungrad 58 43 6N 58 54 E
Kungsbacka 49 57 30N 12 5 E
Kungur 52 57 25N 56 57 E
Kungurri 98 21 3 S 148 46 E
Kunhegyes 27 47 22N 20 36 E
Kuningan 73 6 59 S 108 29 E
Kunlong 67 23 20N 98 50 E
Kunlun Shan 75 36 0N 85 0 E
Kunmadaras 27 47 28N 20 45 E
Kunming 75 25 1N 102 41 E
Kunnamkulam 70 10 38N 76 7 E
Kunsan 76 35 59N 126 45 E
Kunshan 77 31 22N 120 58 E
Kunszentmárton 27 46 50N 20 20 E
Kununurra 96 15 40 S 128 50 E
Kunwarara 98 22 55 S 150 9 E
Kunya-Urgenoh 58 42 19N 59 10 E
Künzelsau 25 49 17N 9 41 E
Kuopio 50 62 53N 27 35 E
Kuopion lääni □ 50 63 25N 27 10 E
Kupa → 39 45 28N 16 24 E
Kupang 73 10 19 S 123 39 E
Kupres 42 44 1N 17 15 E
Kupyansk 56 49 52N 37 35 E
Kupyansk-Uzlovoi 56 49 45N 37 34 E
Kuqa 75 41 35N 82 30 E
Kura → 57 39 50N 49 20 E
Kuranda 98 16 48 S 145 35 E
Kurashiki 74 34 40N 133 50 E
Kurayoshi 74 35 26N 133 50 E
Kurduvadi 70 18 8N 75 29 E
Kürdzhali 43 41 38N 25 21 E
Kure 74 34 14N 132 32 E
Kuressaare = Kingisepp 54 58 15N 22 15 E
Kurgaldzhino 58 50 35N 70 20 E
Kurgan 58 55 26N 65 18 E
Kurganinsk 57 44 54N 40 34 E
Kurgannaya = Kurganinsk 57 44 54N 40 34 E
Kuria Maria I. = Khūryān Mūryān, Jazā 'ir 63 17 30N 55 58 E
Kurichchi 70 11 36N 77 35 E
Kuridala P.O 98 21 16 S 140 29 E
Kuril Is. = Kurilskiye Os. 59 45 0N 150 0 E
Kuril Trench 94 44 0N 153 0 E
Kurilsk 59 45 14N 147 53 E
Kurilskiye Ostrova 59 45 0N 150 0 E
Kuring Kuru 92 17 42 S 18 32 E
Kurkur 86 23 50N 32 0 E
Kurkūrah 83 31 30N 20 1 E
Kurla 70 19 5N 72 52 E
Kurlovskiy 55 55 25N 40 40 E
Kurmuk 87 10 33N 34 21 E
Kurnool 70 15 45N 78 0 E
Kurovskoye 55 55 35N 38 55 E
Kurow 101 44 44 S 170 29 E
Kurów 28 51 23N 22 12 E
Kurrajong 99 33 33 S 150 42 E
Kurri Kurri 99 32 50 S 151 28 E
Kursavka 57 44 29N 42 32 E
Kuršenai 54 56 1N 23 3 E
Kurseong 69 26 56N 88 18 E
Kursk 55 51 42N 36 11 E
Kuršumlija 42 43 9N 21 19 E
Kuršumlijska Banja 42 43 3N 21 11 E
Kuru (Chel), Bahr el 87 8 10N 26 50 E
Kuruktag 75 41 0N 89 0 E
Kuruman 92 27 28 S 23 28 E
Kurume 74 33 15N 130 30 E
Kurunegala 70 7 30N 80 23 E
Kurya 59 61 15N 108 10 E
Kuşada Körfezı 45 37 56N 27 0 E
Kuşadası 45 37 52N 27 15 E
Kusawa L. 108 60 20N 136 13W
Kusel 25 49 31N 7 25 E
Kushchevskaya 57 46 33N 39 35 E
Kushiro 74 43 0N 144 25 E
Kushiro → 74 42 59N 144 23 E
Kushka 58 35 20N 62 18 E
Kushtia 69 23 55N 89 5 E
Kushum → 57 49 0N 50 20 E
Kushva 52 58 18N 59 45 E
Kuskokwim → 104 60 17N 162 27W
Kuskokwim Bay 104 59 50N 162 56W
Kussharo-Ko 74 43 38N 144 21 E
Kustanay 58 53 10N 63 35 E
Kütahya 64 39 30N 30 2 E
Kutaisi 57 42 19N 42 40 E
Kutaraja = Banda Aceh 72 5 35N 95 20 E
Kutch, G. of 68 22 50N 69 15 E
Kutch, Rann of 68 24 0N 70 0 E
Kutina 39 45 29N 16 48 E
Kutiyana 68 21 36N 70 2 E
Kutjevo 42 45 23N 17 55 E
Kutkashen 57 40 58N 47 47 E
Kutná Hora 26 49 57N 15 16 E
Kutno 28 52 15N 19 23 E
Kuttabul 98 21 5 S 148 48 E
Kutu 88 2 40 S 18 11 E
Kutum 87 14 10N 24 40 E
Kúty 27 48 40N 17 3 E
Kuvshinovo 54 57 2N 34 11 E
Kuwait = Al Kuwayt 64 29 30N 47 30 E
Kuwait ■ 64 29 30N 47 30 E
Kuwana 74 35 0N 136 43 E
Kuybyshev 58 55 27N 78 19 E
Kuybyshev 58 53 8N 50 6 E
Kuybyshevskoye Vdkhr. 55 55 2N 49 30 E
Küysanjaq 64 36 5N 44 38 E
Kuyto, Oz. 52 64 40N 31 0 E
Kuyumba 59 60 58N 96 59 E
Kuzey Anadolu Dağlari 64 41 30N 35 0 E
Kuzhithura 70 8 18N 77 11 E
Kuzmin 42 45 2N 19 25 E
Kuznetsk 55 53 12N 46 40 E
Kuzomen 52 66 22N 36 50 E
Kvænangen 50 70 5N 21 15 E
Kvam 47 61 40N 9 42 E
Kvamsøy 47 61 7N 6 28 E
Kvareli 57 41 27N 45 47 E
Kvarner 39 44 50N 14 10 E
Kvarnerič 39 44 43N 14 37 E
Kvernes 47 63 1N 7 44 E
Kvillsfors 49 57 24N 15 29 E
Kvine → 47 58 17N 6 56 E
Kvinesdal 47 58 19N 6 57 E
Kviteseid 47 59 24N 8 29 E
Kwabhaga 93 30 51 S 29 0 E
Kwadacha → 108 57 28N 125 38W
Kwakhanai 92 21 39 S 21 16 E
Kwakoegron 127 5 12N 55 25W
Kwale, Kenya 90 4 15 S 39 31 E
Kwale, Nigeria 85 5 46N 6 26 E
Kwale □ 90 4 15 S 39 10 E
Kwamouth 88 3 9 S 16 12 E
Kwando → 92 18 27 S 23 32 E
Kwangsi-Chuang = Guangxi Zhuangzu □ 75 24 0N 109 0 E
Kwangtung = Guangdong □ 75 23 0N 113 0 E
Kwara □ 85 8 0N 5 0 E
Kwataboahegan → 106 51 9N 80 50W
Kwatisore 73 3 18 S 134 50 E
Kweichow = Guizhou □ 75 27 0N 107 0 E
Kwidzyn 28 53 44N 18 55 E
Kwiguk 104 63 45N 164 35W
Kwimba □ 90 3 0S 33 0 E
Kwinana 96 32 15 S 115 47 E
Kwisa → 28 51 34N 15 24 E
Kwoka 73 0 31 S 132 27 E
Kyabé 81 9 30N 19 0 E
Kyabra Cr. → 99 25 36 S 142 55 E
Kyabram 99 36 19 S 145 4 E
Kyaikto 71 17 20N 97 3 E
Kyakhta 59 50 30N 106 25 E
Kyangin 67 18 20N 95 20 E
Kyaukpadaung 67 20 52N 95 8 E
Kyaukpyu 67 19 28N 93 30 E
Kyaukse 67 21 36N 96 10 E
Kyenjojo 90 0 40N 30 37 E
Kyle Dam 91 20 15 S 31 0 E
Kyle of Lochalsh 14 57 17N 5 43W
Kyll → 25 49 48N 6 42 E
Kyllburg 25 50 2N 6 35 E
Kyneton 99 37 10 S 144 29 E
Kynuna 98 21 37 S 141 55 E
Kyō-ga-Saki 74 35 45N 135 15 E
Kyoga, L. 90 1 35N 33 0 E
Kyogle 99 28 40 S 153 0 E
Kyongju 76 35 51N 129 14 E
Kyongpyaw 67 17 12N 95 10 E
Kyōto 74 35 0N 135 45 E
Kyōto □ 74 35 15N 135 45 E
Kyren 59 51 45N 101 45 E
Kyrenia 64 35 20N 33 20 E
Kyritz 24 52 57N 12 25 E
Kystatyam 59 67 20N 123 10 E
Kytal Ktakh 59 65 30N 123 40 E
Kyulyunken 59 64 10N 137 5 E
Kyunhla 67 23 25N 95 15 E
Kyuquot 108 50 3N 127 25W
Kyurdamir 57 40 25N 48 3 E
Kyūshū 74 33 0N 131 0 E
Kyūshū-Sanchi 74 32 35N 131 17 E
Kyustendil 42 42 16N 22 41 E
Kyusyur 59 70 39N 127 15 E
Kywong 99 34 58 S 146 44 E
Kyzyl 59 51 50N 94 30 E
Kyzyl-Kiya 58 40 16N 72 8 E
Kyzylkum, Peski 58 42 30N 65 0 E
Kzyl-Orda 58 44 48N 65 28 E

L

Laa 27 48 43N 16 23 E
Laaber → 25 49 0N 12 3 E
Laage 24 53 55N 12 21 E
Laasphe 24 50 56N 8 23 E
Laba → 57 45 11N 39 42 E
Labastide 20 43 28N 2 39 E
Labastide-Murat 20 44 39N 1 33 E
Labbézenga 85 15 2N 0 48 E
Labdah = Leptis Magna 83 32 40N 14 12 E
Labé 84 11 24N 12 16W
Labe = Elbe → 26 50 50N 14 12 E
Laberec → 27 48 37N 21 58 E
Laberge, L. 108 61 11N 135 12W
Labin 39 45 5N 14 8 E
Labinsk 57 44 40N 40 48 E
Labis 71 2 22N 103 2 E
Labiszyn 28 52 57N 17 54 E
Laboe 24 54 25N 10 13 E
Labouheyre 20 44 13N 0 55W
Laboulaye 124 34 10 S 63 30W
Labra, Peña 30 43 3N 4 26W
Labrador City 107 52 57N 66 55W
Labrador, Coast of □ 105 53 20N 61 0W
Lábrea 126 7 15 S 64 51W
Labrède 20 44 41N 0 32W
Labuan 72 5 21N 115 13 E
Labuha 73 0 30 S 127 30 E
Labuhan 73 6 26 S 105 50 E
Labuhanbajo 73 8 28 S 120 1 E
Labuk, Telok 72 6 10N 117 50 E
Labytnangi 58 66 39N 66 21 E
Łabżenica 28 53 18N 17 15 E
Lac Allard 107 50 33N 63 24W
Lac Bouchette 107 48 16N 72 11W
Lac du Flambeau 116 46 1N 89 51W
Lac Édouard 106 47 40N 72 16W
Lac la Biche 108 54 45N 111 58W
Lac la Martre 104 63 8N 117 16W
Lac-Mégantic 107 45 35N 70 53W
Lac Seul 109 50 28N 92 0W
Lacanau, Étang de 20 44 58N 1 7W
Lacanau-Médoc 20 44 59N 1 5W
Lacantúm → 120 16 36N 90 40W
Lacara → 31 38 55N 6 25W
Lacaune 20 43 43N 2 40 E
Lacaune, Mts. de 20 43 43N 2 50 E
Laccadive Is. = Lakshadweep Is. 60 10 0N 72 30 E
Lacepede B. 99 36 40 S 139 40 E
Lacepede Is. 96 16 55 S 122 0 E
Lacerdónia 91 18 3 S 35 35 E
Lachine 106 45 30N 73 40W
Lachlan → 99 34 22 S 143 55 E
Lachmangarh 68 27 50N 75 4 E
Lachute 106 45 39N 74 21W
Lackawanna 114 42 49N 78 50W
Lacolle 113 45 5N 73 22W
Lacombe 108 52 30N 113 44W
Lacona 113 43 37N 76 5W
Láconi 40 39 54N 9 4 E
Laconia 114 43 32N 71 30W
Lacq 20 43 25N 0 35W
Lacrosse 118 46 51N 117 58W
Ladakh Ra. 69 34 0N 78 0 E
Lądekzdrój 28 50 21N 16 53 E
Ládhon → 45 37 40N 21 50 E
Ladik 56 40 57N 35 58 E
Ladismith 92 33 28 S 21 15 E
Lādīz 65 28 55N 61 15 E
Ladnun 68 27 38N 74 25 E
Ladoga, L. = Ladozhskoye Oz. 52 61 15N 30 30 E
Ladon 19 48 0N 2 30 E
Ladozhskoye Ozero 52 61 15N 30 30 E
Lady Grey 92 30 43 S 27 13 E
Ladybrand 92 29 9 S 27 29 E
Ladysmith, Can. 108 49 0N 123 49W
Ladysmith, S. Afr. 93 28 32 S 29 46 E
Ladysmith, U.S.A. 116 45 27N 91 4W
Lae 94 6 40 S 147 2 E
Læsø 49 57 15N 10 53 E
Læsø Rende 49 57 20N 10 45 E
Lafayette, Colo., U.S.A. 116 40 0N 105 2W
Lafayette, Ga., U.S.A. 115 34 44N 85 15W
Lafayette, La., U.S.A. 117 30 18N 92 0W
Lafayette, Tenn., U.S.A. 115 36 35N 86 0W
Laferte → 108 61 53N 117 44W
Lafia 85 8 30N 8 34 E
Lafiagi 85 8 52N 5 20 E
Lafleche 109 49 45N 106 40W
Lafon 87 5 5N 32 29 E
Laforsen 48 61 56N 15 3 E
Lagan →, Sweden 49 56 56N 13 58 E
Lagan →, U.K. 15 54 35N 5 55W
Lagarfljót → 50 65 40N 14 18W
Lage, Ger. 24 52 0N 8 47 E
Lage, Spain 30 43 13N 9 0W
Lågen →, Oppland, Norway 47 61 8N 10 25 E
Lågen →, Vestfold, Norway 47 59 3N 10 5 E
Lägerdorf 24 53 53N 9 35 E
Laggers Pt. 99 30 52 S 153 4 E
Laghán □ 65 34 20N 70 0 E
Laghouat 82 33 50N 2 59 E
Lagnieu 21 45 55N 5 20 E
Lagny 19 48 52N 2 40 E
Lago 41 39 9N 16 8 E
Lagôa 31 37 8N 8 27W
Lagoaça 30 41 11N 6 44W
Lagodekhi 57 41 50N 46 22 E
Lagónegro 41 40 8N 15 45 E
Lagonoy Gulf 73 13 50N 123 50 E
Lagos, Nigeria 85 6 25N 3 27 E
Lagos, Port. 31 37 5N 8 41W
Lagos de Moreno 120 21 21N 101 55W
Lagrange 96 18 45 S 121 43 E
Laguardia 32 42 33N 2 35W
Laguépie 20 44 8N 1 57 E
Laguna, Brazil 125 28 30 S 48 50W
Laguna, U.S.A. 119 35 3N 107 28W
Laguna Beach 119 33 31N 117 52W
Laguna Dam 119 32 55N 114 30W
Laguna de la Janda 31 36 15N 5 45W
Laguna Limpia 124 26 32 S 59 45W
Laguna Madre 120 27 0N 97 20W
Lagunas, Chile 124 21 0 S 69 45W
Lagunas, Peru 126 5 10 S 75 35W
Laha 76 48 12N 124 35 E
Lahad Datu 73 5 0N 118 20 E
Laharpur 69 27 43N 80 56 E
Lahat 72 3 45 S 103 30 E
Lahewa 72 1 22N 97 12 E
Lahijan 64 37 10N 50 6 E
Lahn → 25 50 52N 8 35 E
Laholm 49 56 30N 13 2 E
Laholmsbukten 49 56 30N 12 45 E
Lahontan Res. 118 39 28N 118 58W
Lahore 68 31 32N 74 22 E
Lahore □ 68 31 55N 74 5 E
Lahr 25 48 20N 7 52 E
Lahti 51 60 58N 25 40 E
Laï 81 9 25N 16 18 E
Lai Chau 71 22 5N 103 3 E
Laibin 75 23 42N 109 14 E
Laidley 99 27 39 S 152 20 E
Laifeng 77 29 27N 109 20 E
Laignes 19 47 50N 4 20 E
Laikipia □ 90 0 30N 36 30 E
Laingsburg 92 33 9 S 20 52 E
Lairg 14 58 1N 4 24W
Lais 72 3 35 S 102 0 E
Laiyang 76 36 59N 120 45 E
Laizhou Wan 76 37 30N 119 30 E
Laja → 120 20 55N 100 46W
Lajere 85 11 58N 11 25 E
Lajes 125 27 48 S 50 20W
Lajkovac 42 44 27N 20 14 E
Lajosmizse 27 47 3N 19 32 E
Lakaband 68 31 2N 69 15 E
Lakar 73 8 15 S 128 17 E
Lake Andes 116 43 10N 98 32W
Lake Anse 114 46 42N 88 25W
Lake Arthur 117 30 8N 92 40W
Lake Cargelligo 97 33 15 S 146 22 E
Lake Charles 117 30 15N 93 10W
Lake City, Colo, U.S.A. 119 38 3N 107 27W
Lake City, Fla., U.S.A. 115 30 10N 82 40W
Lake City, Iowa, U.S.A. 116 42 12N 94 42W
Lake City, Mich., U.S.A. 114 44 20N 85 10W
Lake City, Minn., U.S.A. 116 44 28N 92 21W
Lake City, Pa., U.S.A. 112 42 2N 80 20W
Lake City, S.C., U.S.A. 115 33 51N 79 44W
Lake George 113 43 25N 73 43W
Lake Harbour 105 62 50N 69 50W
Lake Havasu City 119 34 25N 114 29W
Lake Lenore 109 52 24N 104 59W
Lake Louise 108 51 30N 116 10W
Lake Mead Nat. Rec. Area 119 36 0N 114 30W
Lake Mills 116 43 23N 93 33W
Lake Nash 98 20 57 S 138 0 E
Lake Providence 117 32 49N 91 12W
Lake River 106 54 30N 82 31W
Lake Superior Prov. Park 106 47 45N 84 45W
Lake Village 117 33 20N 91 19W
Lake Wales 115 27 55N 81 32W
Lake Worth 115 26 36N 80 3W
Lakefield 106 44 25N 78 16W
Lakeland 115 28 0N 82 0W
Lakemba 101 18 13 S 178 47W
Lakes Entrance 99 37 50 S 148 0 E
Lakeside, Ariz., U.S.A. 119 34 12N 109 59W
Lakeside, Nebr., U.S.A. 116 42 5N 102 24W
Lakeview 118 42 15N 120 22W
Lakewood, N.J., U.S.A. 114 40 5N 74 13W
Lakewood, Ohio, U.S.A. 114 41 28N 81 50W
Lakhaniá 45 35 58N 27 54 E
Lákhi 45 35 24N 23 57 E
Lakhpat 68 23 48N 68 47 E
Laki 50 64 4N 18 14W
Lakin 117 37 58N 101 18W
Lakitusaki → 106 54 21N 82 25W
Lakonía □ 45 36 55N 22 30 E
Lakonikós Kólpos 45 36 40N 22 40 E
Lakota, Ivory C. 84 5 50N 5 30W
Lakota, U.S.A. 116 48 0N 98 22W
Laksefjorden 50 70 45N 26 50 E
Lakselv 50 70 2N 24 56 E
Lakshmi Kantapur 69 22 5N 88 20 E
Lala Ghat 67 24 30N 92 40 E
Lala Musa 68 32 40N 73 57 E
Lalago 90 3 28 S 33 58 E
Lalapanzi 91 19 20 S 30 15 E
Lalganj 69 25 52N 85 13 E
Lalibela 87 12 2N 39 2 E
Lalin 76 45 12N 127 0 E
Lalín 30 42 40N 8 5W
Lalinde 20 44 50N 0 44 E
Lalitpur 68 24 42N 78 28 E
Lama Kara 85 9 30N 1 15 E
Lamaing 67 15 25N 97 53 E
Lamar, Colo., U.S.A. 116 38 9N 102 35W
Lamar, Mo., U.S.A. 117 37 30N 94 20W
Lamas 126 6 28 S 76 31W
Lamastre 21 44 59N 4 35 E
Lambach 26 48 6N 13 51 E
Lamballe 18 48 29N 2 31W
Lambaréné 88 0 41 S 10 12 E
Lambasa 101 16 30 S 179 10 E
Lambay I. 15 53 30N 6 0W
Lambert 116 47 44N 104 39W
Lambert Glacier 5 71 0 S 70 0 E
Lambesc 21 43 39N 5 16 E
Lambi Kyun (Sullivan I.) 71 10 50N 98 20 E
Lámbia 45 37 52N 21 53 E
Lambro → 38 45 8N 9 32 E
Lame 85 45 35N 106 40W
Lame Deer 118 45 45N 106 40W
Lamego 30 41 5N 7 52W
Lamèque 107 47 45N 64 38W
Lameroo 99 35 19 S 140 33 E
Lamesa 117 32 45N 101 57W
Lamía 45 38 55N 22 26 E
Lamitan 73 6 40N 122 10 E
Lammermuir Hills 14 55 50N 2 40W
Lamoille 118 40 47N 115 31W
Lamon Bay 73 14 30N 122 20 E
Lamont 108 53 46N 112 50W
Lampa 126 15 22 S 70 22W
Lampang, Thai. 71 18 18N 99 31 E
Lampang, Thai. 71 18 16N 99 32 E

Lampasas **117** 31 5N 98 10W
Lampaul **18** 48 28N 5 7W
Lampazos de Naranjo **120** 27 2N 100 32W
Lampedusa **36** 35 36N 12 40 E
Lampeter **13** 52 6N 4 6W
Lampione **83** 35 33N 12 20 E
Lampman **109** 49 25N 102 50W
Lamprechtshausen **26** 48 0N 12 58 E
Lamprey **109** 58 33N 94 8W
Lampung □ **72** 5 30 S 104 30 E
Lamu **90** 2 16 S 40 55 E
Lamu □ **90** 2 0 S 40 45 E
Lamut, Tg. **72** 3 50 S 105 58 E
Lamy **119** 35 30N 105 58W
Lan Xian **76** 38 15N 111 35 E
Lan Yu **77** 22 5N 121 35 E
Lanai I. **110** 20 50N 156 55W
Lanak La **69** 34 27N 79 32 E
Lanak'o Shank'ou = Lanak La **69** 34 27N 79 32 E
Lanao, L. **73** 7 52N 124 15 E
Lanark, Can. **113** 45 1N 76 22W
Lanark, U.K. **14** 55 40N 3 48W
Lancashire □ **12** 53 40N 2 30W
Lancaster, Can. **113** 45 10N 74 30W
Lancaster, U.K. **12** 54 3N 2 48W
Lancaster, Calif., U.S.A. **119** 34 47N 118 8W
Lancaster, Ky., U.S.A. **114** 37 40N 84 40W
Lancaster, N.H., U.S.A. **114** 44 27N 71 33W
Lancaster, N.Y., U.S.A. **112** 42 53N 78 43W
Lancaster, Pa., U.S.A. **114** 40 4N 76 19W
Lancaster, S.C., U.S.A. **115** 34 45N 80 47W
Lancaster, Wis., U.S.A. **116** 42 48N 90 43W
Lancaster Sd. **4** 74 13N 84 0W
Lancer **109** 50 48N 108 53W
Lanchow = Lanzhou **76** 36 1N 103 52 E
Lanciano **39** 42 15N 14 22 E
Łancut **27** 50 10N 22 13 E
Lándana **88** 5 11 S 12 5 E
Landau, Bayern, Ger. **25** 48 41N 12 41 E
Landau, Rhld-Pfz., Ger. **25** 49 12N 8 7 E
Landeck **26** 47 9N 10 34 E
Landen **16** 50 45N 5 5 E
Lander **118** 42 50N 108 49W
Landerneau **18** 48 28N 4 17W
Landeryd **49** 57 7N 13 15 E
Landes □ **20** 43 57N 0 48W
Landes, Les **20** 44 20N 1 0W
Landete **32** 39 56N 1 25W
Landi Kotal **66** 34 7N 71 6 E
Landivisiau **18** 48 31N 4 6W
Landquart **25** 46 58N 9 32 E
Landrecies **19** 50 7N 3 40 E
Land's End **13** 50 4N 5 43W
Landsberg **25** 48 3N 10 52 E
Landsborough Cr. → **98** 22 28 S 144 35 E
Landsbro **49** 57 24N 14 56 E
Landshut **25** 48 31N 12 10 E
Landskrona **49** 55 53N 12 50 E
Landstuhl **25** 49 25N 7 34 E
Landvetter **49** 57 41N 12 17 E
Lanesboro **113** 41 57N 75 34W
Lanett **115** 33 0N 85 15W
Lang Bay **108** 49 45N 124 21W
Lang Shan **76** 41 0N 106 30 E
Lang Son **71** 21 52N 106 42 E
La'nga Co **67** 30 45N 81 15 E
Lángadhás **44** 40 46N 23 2 E
Langádhia **45** 37 43N 22 1 E
Långan → **48** 63 19N 14 44 E
Langara I. **108** 54 14N 133 1W
Langdon **116** 48 47N 98 24W
Langeac **20** 45 7N 3 29 E
Langeais **18** 47 20N 0 24 E
Langeb Baraka → **86** 17 28N 36 50 E
Langeberge, C. Prov., S. Afr. **92** 33 55 S 21 40 E
Langeberge, C. Prov., S. Afr. **92** 28 15 S 22 33 E
Langeland **49** 54 56N 10 48 E
Langen **25** 49 59N 8 40 E
Langenburg **109** 50 51N 101 43W
Langeness **24** 54 34N 8 35 E
Langenlois **26** 48 29N 15 40 E
Langeoog **24** 53 44N 7 33 E
Langeskov **49** 55 22N 10 35 E
Langesund **47** 59 0N 9 45 E
Länghem **49** 57 36N 13 14 E
Langhirano **38** 44 39N 10 16 E
Langholm **14** 55 9N 2 59W
Langjökull **50** 64 39N 20 12W
Langkawi, P. **71** 6 25N 99 45 E
Langkon **72** 6 30N 116 40 E
Langlade **107** 46 50N 56 20W
Langlois **118** 42 54N 124 26W
Langnau **25** 46 56N 7 47 E
Langogne **20** 44 43N 3 50 E
Langon **20** 44 33N 0 16W
Langøya **50** 68 45N 14 50 E
Langpran, Gunong **72** 1 0N 114 23 E
Langres **19** 47 52N 5 20 E
Langres, Plateau de **19** 47 45N 5 3 E
Langsa **72** 4 30N 97 57 E
Långsele **48** 63 12N 17 4 E
Långshyttan **48** 60 27N 16 2 E
Langtry **117** 29 50N 101 33W
Languedoc **20** 43 58N 4 0 E
Langxiangzhen **76** 39 43N 116 8 E
Langzhong **75** 31 38N 105 58 E
Lanigan **109** 51 51N 105 2W
Lankao **77** 34 48N 114 50 E
Lannemezan **20** 43 8N 0 23 E
Lannilis **18** 48 35N 4 32W
Lannion **18** 48 46N 3 29W
Lanouaille **20** 45 24N 1 9 E
Lansdale **113** 40 14N 75 18W
Lansdowne, Austral. **99** 31 48 S 152 30 E
Lansdowne, Can. **113** 44 24N 76 1W
Lansdowne House **106** 52 14N 87 53W
Lansford **113** 40 48N 75 55W
Lansing **114** 42 47N 84 40W
Lanslebourg **21** 45 17N 6 52 E
Lant, Pulau **72** 4 10 S 116 0 E
Lanus **124** 34 44 S 58 27W
Lanusei **40** 39 53N 9 31 E
Lanxi **77** 29 13N 119 28 E
Lanzarote **80** 29 0N 13 40W
Lanzhou **76** 36 1N 103 52 E
Lanzo Torinese **38** 45 16N 7 29 E
Lao → **41** 39 45N 15 45 E
Lao Cai **71** 22 30N 103 57 E
Laoag **73** 18 7N 120 34 E
Laoang **73** 12 32N 125 8 E
Laoha He → **76** 43 25N 120 35 E
Laois □ **15** 53 0N 7 20W
Laon **19** 49 33N 3 35 E
Laona **114** 45 32N 88 41W
Laos ■ **71** 17 45N 105 0 E
Lapa **125** 25 46 S 49 44W
Lapalisse **20** 46 15N 3 38 E
Laparan Cap **73** 6 0N 120 0 E
Lapeer **114** 43 3N 83 20W
Lapi □ **50** 67 0N 27 0 E
Lapland = Lappland **50** 68 7N 24 0 E
Laporte **113** 41 27N 76 30W
Lapovo **42** 44 10N 21 2 E
Lappland **50** 68 7N 24 0 E
Laprairie **113** 45 20N 73 30W
Laprida **124** 37 34 S 60 45W
Laptev Sea **59** 76 0N 125 0 E
Lapuş, Munţii **46** 47 20N 23 50 E
Lapush **118** 47 56N 124 33W
Lăpusul → **46** 47 25N 23 40 E
Łapy **28** 52 59N 22 52 E
Lār **65** 27 40N 54 14 E
Larabanga **84** 9 16N 1 56W
Laracha **30** 43 15N 8 35W
Larache **82** 35 10N 6 5W
Laragne-Monteglin **21** 44 18N 5 49 E
Laramie **116** 41 20N 105 38W
Laramie Mts. **116** 42 0N 105 30W
Laranjeiras do Sul **125** 25 23 S 52 23W
Larantuka **73** 8 21 S 122 55 E
Larap **73** 14 18N 122 39 E
Larat **73** 7 0 S 132 0 E
Lårdal **47** 59 25N 8 10 E
Larde **91** 16 28 S 39 43 E
Larder Lake **106** 48 5N 79 40W
Lárdhos, Ákra **45** 36 4N 28 10 E
Laredo, Spain **32** 43 26N 3 28W
Laredo, U.S.A. **117** 27 34N 99 29W
Laredo Sd. **108** 52 30N 128 53W
Largentière **21** 44 34N 4 18 E
Largs **14** 55 48N 4 51W
Lari **38** 43 34N 10 35 E
Lariang **73** 1 26 S 119 17 E
Larimore **116** 47 55N 97 35W
Larino **41** 41 48N 14 54 E
Lárisa **44** 39 49N 22 28 E
Lárisa □ **44** 39 39N 22 24 E
Larkana **68** 27 32N 68 18 E
Larkollen **47** 59 20N 10 41 E
Larnaca **64** 35 0N 33 35 E
Larne **15** 54 52N 5 50W
Larned **116** 38 15N 99 10W
Larrimah **96** 15 35 S 133 12 E
Larsen Ice Shelf **5** 67 0 S 62 0W
Larvik **47** 59 4N 10 0 E
Laryak **58** 61 15N 80 0 E
Larzac, Causse du **20** 44 0N 3 17 E
Las Animas **117** 38 8N 103 18W
Las Anod **63** 8 26N 47 19 E
Las Blancos **33** 37 38N 0 49W
Las Brenãs **124** 27 5 S 61 7W
Las Cabezas de San Juan **31** 37 0N 5 58W
Las Cascadas **120** 9 5N 79 41W
Las Cruces **119** 32 18N 106 50W
Las Flores **124** 36 10 S 59 7W
Las Heras **124** 32 51 S 68 49W
Las Khoreh **63** 11 10N 48 20 E
Las Lajas **128** 38 30 S 70 25W
Las Lomitas **124** 24 43 S 60 35W
Las Marismas **31** 37 5N 6 20W
Las Navas de la Concepción **31** 37 56N 5 30W
Las Navas de Tolosa **31** 38 18N 3 38W
Las Palmas, Argent. **124** 27 8 S 58 45W
Las Palmas, Canary Is. **80** 28 7N 15 26W
Las Palmas □ **80** 28 10N 15 28W
Las Piedras **125** 34 44 S 56 14W
Las Pipinas **124** 35 30 S 57 19W
Las Plumas **128** 43 40 S 67 15W
Las Rosas **124** 32 30 S 61 35W
Las Tablas **121** 7 49N 80 14W
Las Termas **124** 27 29 S 64 52W
Las Varillas **124** 31 50 S 62 50W
Las Vegas, N. Mex., U.S.A. **119** 35 35N 105 10W
Las Vegas, Nev., U.S.A. **119** 36 10N 115 5W
Lascano **125** 33 35 S 54 12W
Lascaux **20** 45 5N 1 10 E
Lashburn **109** 53 10N 109 40W
Lashio **67** 22 56N 97 45 E
Lashkar **68** 26 10N 78 10 E
Łasin **28** 53 30N 19 2 E
Lasíthi □ **45** 35 5N 25 50 E
Lask **28** 51 34N 19 8 E
Łaskarzew **28** 51 48N 21 36 E
Laško **39** 46 10N 15 16 E
Lassay **18** 48 27N 0 30W
Lassen Pk. **118** 40 29N 121 31W
Last Mountain L. **109** 51 5N 105 14W
Lastoursville **88** 0 55 S 12 38 E
Lastovo **39** 42 46N 16 55 E
Lastovski Kanal **39** 42 50N 17 0 E
Latacunga **126** 0 50 S 78 35W
Latakia = Al Lādhiqīyah **64** 35 30N 35 45 E
Latchford **106** 47 20N 79 50W
Laterza **41** 40 38N 16 47 E
Lathen **24** 52 51N 7 21 E
Latiano **41** 40 33N 17 43 E
Latina **40** 41 26N 12 53 E
Latisana **39** 45 47N 13 1 E
Latium = Lazio **39** 42 10N 12 30 E
Latorica → **27** 48 28N 21 50 E
Latouche Treville, C. **96** 18 27 S 121 49 E
Latrobe **112** 40 19N 79 21W
Latrónico **41** 40 5N 16 0 E
Latrun **62** 31 50N 34 58 E
Latur **70** 18 25N 76 40 E
Latvian S.S.R. □ **54** 56 50N 24 0 E
Lau (Eastern) Group **101** 17 0 S 178 30W
Lauchhammer **24** 51 35N 13 48 E
Laudal **47** 58 15N 7 30 E
Lauenburg **24** 53 23N 10 33 E
Lauffen **25** 49 4N 9 9 E
Laugarbakki **50** 65 20N 20 55W
Laujar **33** 37 0N 2 54W
Launceston, Austral. **97** 41 24 S 147 8 E
Launceston, U.K. **13** 50 38N 4 21W
Laune → **15** 52 5N 9 40W
Launglon Bok **71** 13 50N 97 54 E
Laupheim **25** 48 13N 9 53 E
Laura **97** 15 32 S 144 32 E
Laureana di Borrello **41** 38 28N 16 5 E
Laurel, Miss., U.S.A. **117** 31 41N 89 9W
Laurel, Mont., U.S.A. **118** 45 46N 108 49W
Laurencekirk **14** 56 50N 2 30W
Laurens **115** 34 32N 82 2W
Laurentian Plat. **107** 52 0N 70 0W
Laurentides, Parc Prov. des **107** 47 45N 71 15W
Lauria **41** 40 3N 15 50 E
Laurie I. **5** 60 44 S 44 37W
Laurie L. **109** 56 35N 101 57W
Laurinburg **115** 34 50N 79 25W
Laurium **114** 47 14N 88 26W
Lausanne **25** 46 32N 6 38 E
Laut, Kepulauan **72** 4 45N 108 0 E
Laut Ketil, Kepulauan **72** 4 45 S 115 40 E
Lauterbach **24** 50 39N 9 23 E
Lauterecken **25** 49 38N 7 35 E
Lautoka **101** 17 37 S 177 27 E
Lauzon **107** 46 48N 71 10W
Lava Hot Springs **118** 42 38N 112 1W
Lavadores **30** 42 14N 8 41W
Lavagna **38** 44 18N 9 22 E
Laval **18** 48 4N 0 48W
Lavalle **124** 28 15 S 65 15W
Lavandou, Le **21** 43 8N 6 22 E
Lávara **44** 41 19N 26 22 E
Lavardac **20** 44 12N 0 20 E
Lavaur **20** 43 30N 1 49 E
Lavaveix **20** 46 5N 2 8 E
Lavelanet **20** 42 57N 1 51 E
Lavello **41** 41 4N 15 47 E
Laverendrye Prov. Park **106** 46 15N 17 15W
Laverne **117** 36 43N 99 58W
Laverton **96** 28 44 S 122 29 E
Lavi **62** 32 47N 35 25 E
Lavik **47** 61 6N 5 25 E
Lávkos **45** 39 9N 23 14 E
Lavos **30** 40 6N 8 49W
Lavras **125** 21 20 S 45 0W
Lavre **31** 38 46N 8 22W
Lavrentiya **59** 65 35N 171 0W
Lávrion **45** 37 40N 24 4 E
Lavumisa **93** 27 20 S 31 55 E
Lawas **72** 4 55N 115 25 E
Lawele **73** 5 16 S 123 3 E
Lawn Hill **98** 18 36 S 138 33 E
Lawng Pit **67** 25 30N 97 25 E
Lawra **84** 10 39N 2 51W
Lawrence, Kans., U.S.A. **116** 39 0N 95 10W
Lawrence, Mass., U.S.A. **114** 42 40N 71 9W
Lawrenceburg, Ind., U.S.A. **114** 39 5N 84 50W
Lawrenceburg, Tenn., U.S.A. **115** 35 12N 87 19W
Lawrenceville **115** 33 55N 83 59W
Lawton **117** 34 33N 98 25W
Lawu **73** 7 40 S 111 13 E
Laxford, L. **14** 58 25N 5 10W
Laxmeshwar **70** 15 9N 75 28 E
Laylá **64** 22 10N 46 40 E
Layon → **18** 47 20N 0 45W
Laysan I. **95** 25 30N 167 0W
Laytonville **118** 39 44N 123 29W
Lazarevac **42** 44 23N 20 17 E
Lazio □ **39** 42 10N 12 30 E
Łazy **28** 50 27N 19 24 E
Lea → **13** 51 30N 0 10W
Lead **116** 44 20N 103 40W
Leader **109** 50 50N 109 30W
Leadhills **14** 55 25N 3 47W
Leadville **119** 39 17N 106 23W
Leaf → **117** 31 0N 88 45W
Leakey **117** 29 45N 99 45W
Leamington, Can. **106** 42 3N 82 36W
Leamington, U.K. **13** 52 18N 1 32W
Leamington, U.S.A. **118** 39 37N 112 17W
Leandro Norte Alem **125** 27 34 S 55 15W
Learmonth **96** 22 13 S 114 10 E
Leask **109** 53 5N 106 45W
Leavenworth, Mo., U.S.A. **116** 39 25N 95 0W
Leavenworth, Wash., U.S.A. **118** 47 44N 120 37W
Łeba **28** 54 45N 17 32 E
Łeba → **28** 54 46N 17 33 E
Lebak **73** 6 32N 124 5 E
Lebane **42** 42 56N 21 44 E
Lebanon, Ind., U.S.A. **114** 40 3N 86 28W
Lebanon, Kans., U.S.A. **116** 39 50N 98 35W
Lebanon, Ky., U.S.A. **114** 37 35N 85 15W
Lebanon, Mo., U.S.A. **117** 37 40N 92 40W
Lebanon, Oreg., U.S.A. **118** 44 31N 122 57W
Lebanon, Pa., U.S.A. **114** 40 20N 76 28W
Lebanon, Tenn., U.S.A. **115** 36 15N 86 20W
Lebanon ■ **64** 34 0N 36 0 E
Lebec **119** 34 50N 118 59W
Lebedin **54** 50 35N 34 30 E
Lebedyan **55** 53 0N 39 10 E
Lebombo-berge **93** 24 30 S 32 0 E
Lębork **28** 54 33N 17 46 E
Lebrija **31** 36 53N 6 5W
Łebsko, Jezioro **28** 54 40N 17 25 E
Lebu **124** 37 40 S 73 47W
Lecce **41** 40 20N 18 10 E
Lecco **38** 45 50N 9 27 E
Lecco, L. di. **38** 45 51N 9 22 E
Lécera **32** 41 13N 0 43W
Lech **26** 47 13N 10 9 E
Lech → **25** 48 44N 10 56 E
Lechang **77** 25 10N 113 20 E
Lechtaler Alpen **26** 47 15N 10 30 E
Lectoure **20** 43 56N 0 38 E
Łeczna **28** 51 18N 22 53 E
Łeczyca **28** 52 5N 19 15 E
Ledbury **13** 52 3N 2 25W
Ledeč **26** 49 41N 15 18 E
Ledesma **30** 41 6N 5 59W
Ledong **77** 18 41N 109 5 E
Leduc **108** 53 15N 113 30W
Ledyczek **28** 53 33N 16 59 E
Lee, Mass., U.S.A. **113** 42 17N 73 18W
Lee, Nev., U.S.A. **118** 40 35N 115 36W
Lee → **15** 51 50N 8 30W
Leech L. **116** 47 9N 94 23W
Leedey **117** 35 53N 99 24W
Leeds, U.K. **12** 53 48N 1 34W
Leeds, U.S.A. **115** 33 32N 86 30W
Leek **12** 53 7N 2 2W
Leer **24** 53 13N 7 29 E
Leesburg **115** 28 47N 81 52W
Leesville **117** 31 12N 93 15W
Leeton **97** 34 33 S 146 23 E
Leetonia **112** 40 53N 80 45W
Leeuwarden **16** 53 15N 5 48 E
Leeuwin, C. **96** 34 20 S 115 9 E
Leeward Is., Atl. Oc. **121** 16 30N 63 30W
Leeward Is., Pac. Oc. **95** 16 0 S 147 0W
Lefors **117** 35 30N 100 50W
Lefroy, L. **96** 31 21 S 121 40 E
Łeg → **28** 50 42N 21 50 E
Legal **108** 53 55N 113 35W
Legazpi **73** 13 10N 123 45 E
Leghorn = Livorno **38** 43 32N 10 18 E
Legion **91** 21 25 S 28 30 E
Legionowo **28** 52 25N 20 50 E
Legnago **39** 45 10N 11 19 E
Legnano **38** 45 35N 8 55 E
Legnica **28** 51 12N 16 10 E
Legnica □ **28** 51 30N 16 0 E
Legrad **39** 46 17N 16 51 E
Legume **99** 28 20 S 152 19 E
Leh **69** 34 9N 77 35 E
Lehi **118** 40 20N 111 51W
Lehighton **113** 40 50N 75 44W
Lehliu **46** 44 29N 26 20 E
Lehrte **24** 52 22N 9 58 E
Lehututu **92** 23 54 S 21 55 E
Leiah **68** 30 58N 70 58 E
Leibnitz **26** 46 47N 15 34 E
Leicester **13** 52 39N 1 9W
Leicester □ **13** 52 40N 1 10W
Leichhardt → **97** 17 35 S 139 48 E
Leichhardt Ra. **98** 20 46 S 147 40 E
Leiden **16** 52 9N 4 30 E
Leie → **16** 51 2N 3 45 E
Leigh Creek **97** 30 28 S 138 24 E
Leikanger **47** 61 10N 6 52 E
Leine → **24** 52 20N 9 50 E
Leinster □ **15** 53 0N 7 10W
Leinster, Mt. **15** 52 38N 6 47W
Leipzig **24** 51 20N 12 23 E
Leipzig □ **24** 51 20N 12 30 E
Leiria **31** 39 46N 8 53W
Leiria □ **31** 39 46N 8 53W
Leith **14** 55 59N 3 10W
Leith Hill **13** 51 10N 0 23W
Leitha → **27** 48 0N 16 35 E
Leitrim **15** 54 0N 8 5W
Leitrim □ **15** 54 8N 8 0W
Leiyang **77** 26 27N 112 45 E
Leiza **32** 43 5N 1 55W
Leizhou Bandao **77** 21 0N 110 0 E
Leizhou Wan **77** 20 50N 110 20 E
Lek → **16** 52 0N 6 0 E
Lekáni **44** 41 10N 24 35 E
Lekhainá **45** 37 57N 21 16 E
Leksula **73** 3 46 S 126 31 E
Leland **117** 33 25N 90 52W
Leland Lakes **109** 60 0N 110 59W
Leleque **128** 42 28 S 71 0W
Lelystad **16** 52 30N 5 25 E
Lema **85** 12 58N 4 13 E
Léman, Lac **25** 46 26N 6 30 E
Lemera **90** 3 0 S 28 55 E
Lemery **73** 13 51N 120 56 E
Lemgo **24** 52 2N 8 52 E
Lemhi Ra. **118** 44 30N 113 30W
Lemmer **16** 52 51N 5 43 E
Lemmon **116** 45 59N 102 10W
Lemoore **119** 36 23N 119 46W
Lempdes **20** 45 22N 3 17 E
Lemvig **49** 56 33N 8 20 E
Lena → **59** 72 52N 126 40 E
Lenartovce **27** 48 18N 20 19 E
Lencloître **18** 46 50N 0 20 E
Lendinara **39** 45 4N 11 37 E
Lengau de Vaca, Pta. **124** 30 14 S 71 38W
Lengerich **24** 52 12N 7 50 E
Lenggong **71** 5 6N 100 58 E
Lenggries **25** 47 41N 11 34 E
Lengyeltóti **27** 46 40N 17 40 E
Lenhovda **49** 57 0N 15 16 E
Lenin **57** 48 20N 40 56 E
Leninabad **58** 40 17N 69 37 E
Leninakan **57** 40 47N 43 50 E
Leningrad **54** 59 55N 30 20 E
Lenino **56** 45 17N 35 46 E
Leninogorsk **58** 50 20N 83 30 E
Leninsk, R.S.F.S.R., U.S.S.R. **57** 48 40N 45 15 E
Leninsk, R.S.F.S.R., U.S.S.R. **57** 46 10N 43 46 E
Leninsk-Kuznetskiy **58** 54 44N 86 10 E
Leninskaya Sloboda **55** 56 7N 44 29 E
Leninskoye, R.S.F.S.R., U.S.S.R. **55** 58 23N 47 3 E
Leninskoye, R.S.F.S.R., U.S.S.R. **59** 47 56N 132 38 E
Lenk **25** 46 27N 7 28 E
Lenkoran **53** 39 45N 48 50 E
Lenmalu **73** 1 45 S 130 15 E
Lenne → **24** 51 25N 7 30 E
Lennoxville **113** 45 22N 71 51W
Leno **38** 45 24N 10 14 E
Lenoir **115** 35 55N 81 36W
Lenoir City **115** 35 40N 84 20W
Lenora **116** 39 39N 100 1W

Lenore L. 109 52 30N 104 59W
Lenox 113 42 20N 73 18W
Lens 19 50 26N 2 50 E
Lensk (Mukhtuya) 59 60 48N 114 55 E
Lenskoye 56 45 3N 34 1 E
Lenti 27 46 37N 16 33 E
Lentini 41 37 18N 15 0 E
Lentvaric 54 54 39N 25 3 E
Lenzen 24 53 6N 11 26 E
Léo 84 11 3N 2 2W
Leoben 26 47 22N 15 5 E
Leola 116 45 47N 98 58W
Leominster, U.K. 13 52 15N 2 43W
Leominster, U.S.A. 114 42 32N 71 45W
Léon 20 43 53N 1 18W
León, Mexico 120 21 7N 101 30W
León, Nic. 121 12 20N 86 51W
León, Spain 30 42 38N 5 34W
Leon 116 40 40N 93 40W
León □ 30 42 40N 5 55W
León, Montañas de 30 42 30N 6 18W
Leonardtown 114 38 19N 76 39W
Leonforte 41 37 39N 14 22 E
Leongatha 99 38 30S 145 58 E
Leonídhion 45 37 9N 22 52 E
Leonora 96 28 49S 121 19 E
Léopold II, Lac = Mai-Ndombe 88 2 0S 18 20 E
Leopoldina 125 21 28S 42 40W
Leopoldsburg 16 51 7N 5 13 E
Léopoldville = Kinshasa 88 4 20S 15 15 E
Leoti 116 38 31N 101 19W
Leoville 109 53 39N 107 33W
Lépa, L. do 92 17 0S 19 0 E
Lepe 31 37 15N 7 12W
Lepel 54 54 50N 28 40 E
Lepikha 59 64 45N 125 55 E
Leping 77 28 47N 117 7 E
Lepontino, Alpi 38 46 22N 8 27 E
Lepsény 27 47 0N 18 15 E
Leptis Magna 83 32 40N 14 12 E
Lequeitio 32 43 20N 2 32W
Lercara Friddi 40 37 42N 13 36 E
Léré 81 9 39N 14 13 E
Lere 85 9 43N 9 18 E
Leribe 93 28 51S 28 3 E
Lérici 38 44 4N 9 58 E
Lérida 32 41 37N 0 39 E
Lérida □ 32 42 6N 1 0 E
Lérins, Is. de 21 43 31N 7 3 E
Lerma 30 42 0N 3 47W
Léros 45 37 10N 26 50 E
Lérouville 19 48 50N 5 30 E
Lerwick 14 60 10N 1 10W
Les 46 46 58N 21 50 E
Lesbos, I. = Lésvos 45 39 10N 26 20 E
Leshukonskoye 52 64 54N 45 46 E
Lésina, L. di 39 41 53N 15 25 E
Lesja 47 62 7N 8 51 E
Lesjaverk 47 62 12N 8 34 E
Lesko 27 49 30N 22 23 E
Leskov I. 5 56 0S 28 0W
Leskovac 42 43 0N 21 58 E
Leskoviku 44 40 10N 20 34 E
Leslie 117 35 50N 92 35W
Lesna 28 51 0N 15 15 E
Lesneven 18 48 35N 4 20W
Lešnica 42 44 39N 19 20 E
Lesnoye 54 58 15N 35 18 E
Lesotho ■ 93 29 40S 28 0 E
Lesozavodsk 59 45 30N 133 29 E
Lesparre-Médoc 20 45 18N 0 57W
Lessay 18 49 14N 1 30W
Lesse → 16 50 15N 4 54 E
Lesser Antilles 121 15 0N 61 0W
Lesser Slave L. 108 55 30N 115 25W
Lessines 16 50 42N 3 50 E
Lestock 109 51 19N 103 59W
Lésvos 45 39 10N 26 20 E
Leszno 28 51 50N 16 30 E
Leszno □ 28 51 45N 16 30 E
Letchworth 13 51 58N 0 13W
Letea, Ostrov 46 45 18N 29 20 E
Lethbridge 108 49 45N 112 45W
Leti 73 8 10S 127 40 E
Leti, Kepulauan 73 8 10S 128 0 E
Letiahau → 92 21 16S 24 0 E
Leticia 126 4 9S 70 0W
Leting 76 39 23N 118 55 E
Letlhakeng 92 24 0S 24 59 E
Letpadan 67 17 45N 95 45 E
Letpan 67 19 28N 94 10 E
Letsôk-aw Kyun (Domel I.) 71 11 30N 98 25 E
Letterkenny 15 54 57N 7 42W
Leu 46 44 10N 24 0 E
Leucate 20 42 56N 3 3 E
Leucate, Étang de 20 42 50N 3 0 E
Leuk 25 46 19N 7 37 E
Leuser, G. 72 3 46N 97 12 E
Leutkirch 25 47 49N 10 1 E
Leuven (Louvain) 16 50 52N 4 42 E
Leuze, Hainaut, Belg. 16 50 36N 3 37 E
Leuze, Namur, Belg. 16 50 33N 4 54 E
Lev Tolstoy 55 53 13N 39 29 E
Levádhia 45 38 27N 22 54 E
Levan 118 39 37N 111 52W
Levanger 47 63 45N 11 19 E
Levani 44 40 40N 19 28 E
Levant, I. du 21 43 3N 6 28 E
Lévanto 38 44 10N 9 37 E
Levanzo 40 38 0N 12 19 E
Levelland 117 33 38N 102 23W
Leven 14 56 12N 3 0W
Leven, L. 14 56 12N 3 22W
Leven, Toraka 93 12 30S 47 45 E
Levens 21 43 50N 7 12 E
Leveque C. 96 16 20S 123 0 E
Leverano 41 40 16N 18 0 E
Leverkusen 24 51 2N 6 59 E
Levet 19 46 56N 2 22 E
Levice 27 48 13N 18 35 E
Levick, Mt. 5 75 0S 164 0 E
Levico 39 46 0N 11 18 E
Levie 21 41 40N 9 7 E
Levier 19 46 58N 6 8 E
Levin 101 40 37S 175 18 E
Lévis 107 46 48N 71 9W
Levis, L. 108 62 37N 117 58W
Levítha 45 37 0N 26 28 E
Levittown, N.Y., U.S.A. 113 40 41N 73 31W
Levittown, Pa., U.S.A. 113 40 10N 74 51W
Levka 43 41 52N 26 15 E
Lévka 45 35 18N 24 3 E
Levkás 45 38 40N 20 43 E
Levkimmi 44 39 25N 20 3 E
Levkôsia = Nicosia 64 35 10N 33 25 E
Levoča 27 49 2N 20 35 E
Levroux 19 47 0N 1 38 E
Levski 43 43 21N 25 10 E
Levskigrad 43 42 38N 24 47 E
Lewellen 116 41 22N 102 5W
Lewes, U.K. 13 50 53N 0 2 E
Lewes, U.S.A. 114 38 45N 75 8W
Lewin Brzeski 28 50 45N 17 37 E
Lewis 14 58 10N 6 40W
Lewis, Butt of 14 58 30N 6 12W
Lewis Ra. 118 48 0N 113 15W
Lewisburg, Pa., U.S.A. 112 40 57N 76 57W
Lewisburg, Tenn., U.S.A. 115 35 29N 86 46W
Lewisporte 107 49 15N 55 3W
Lewiston, Idaho, U.S.A. 118 46 25N 117 0W
Lewiston, Utah, U.S.A. 118 41 58N 111 56W
Lewistown, Mont., U.S.A. 118 47 0N 109 25W
Lewistown, Pa., U.S.A. 114 40 37N 77 33W
Lexington, Ill., U.S.A. 116 40 37N 88 47W
Lexington, Ky., U.S.A. 114 38 6N 84 30W
Lexington, Miss., U.S.A. 117 33 8N 90 2W
Lexington, Mo., U.S.A. 116 39 7N 93 55W
Lexington, N.C., U.S.A. 115 35 50N 80 13W
Lexington, Nebr., U.S.A. 116 40 48N 99 45W
Lexington, Ohio, U.S.A. 112 40 39N 82 35W
Lexington, Oreg., U.S.A. 118 45 29N 119 46W
Lexington, Tenn., U.S.A. 115 35 38N 88 25W
Lexington Park 114 38 16N 76 27W
Leyre → 20 44 39N 1 1W
Leyte 73 11 0N 125 0 E
Lezajsk 28 50 16N 22 25 E
Lezay 20 46 17N 0 0 E
Lezha 44 41 47N 19 42 E
Lézignan-Corbières 20 43 13N 2 43 E
Lezoux 20 45 49N 3 21 E
Lgov 54 51 42N 35 16 E
Lhasa 75 29 25N 90 58 E
Lhazê 75 29 5N 87 38 E
Lhokseumawe 72 5 10N 97 10 E
Lhuntsi Dzong 67 27 39N 91 10 E
Li Shui → 77 29 24N 112 1 E
Li Xian, Gansu, China 77 34 10N 105 5 E
Li Xian, Hunan, China 77 29 36N 111 42 E
Liádhoi 45 36 50N 26 11 E
Lianga 73 8 38N 126 6 E
Liangdang 77 33 56N 106 18 E
Lianhua 77 27 3N 113 54 E
Lianjiang 77 26 12N 119 27 E
Lianping 77 24 26N 114 30 E
Lianshanguan 76 40 53N 123 43 E
Lianyungang 77 34 40N 119 11 E
Liao He → 76 41 0N 121 50 E
Liaocheng 76 36 28N 115 58 E
Liaodong Bandao 76 40 0N 122 30 E
Liaodong Wan 76 40 20N 121 10 E
Liaoning □ 76 42 0N 122 0 E
Liaoyang 76 41 15N 122 58 E
Liaoyuan 76 42 58N 125 2 E
Liaozhong 76 41 23N 122 50 E
Liapádhes 44 39 42N 19 40 E
Liard → 108 61 51N 121 18W
Libau = Liepaja 54 56 30N 21 0 E
Libby 118 48 20N 115 33W
Libenge 88 3 40N 18 55 E
Liberal, Kans., U.S.A. 117 37 4N 101 0W
Liberal, Mo., U.S.A. 117 37 35N 94 30W
Liberec 26 50 47N 15 7 E
Liberia 121 10 40N 85 30W
Liberia ■ 84 6 30N 9 30W
Liberty, Mo., U.S.A. 116 39 15N 94 24W
Liberty, Tex., U.S.A. 117 30 5N 94 50W
Libiaz 27 50 7N 19 21 E
Libo 77 25 22N 107 53 E
Libobo, Tanjung 73 0 54S 128 28 E
Libohava 44 40 3N 20 10 E
Libonda 89 14 28S 23 12 E
Libourne 20 44 55N 0 14W
Libramont 16 49 55N 5 23 E
Librazhdi 44 41 12N 20 22 E
Libreville 88 0 25N 9 26 E
Libya ■ 81 27 0N 17 0 E
Libyan Plateau = Ed-Déffa 86 30 40N 26 30 E
Licantén 124 35 55S 72 0W
Licata 40 37 6N 13 55 E
Lichfield 12 52 40N 1 50W
Lichinga 91 13 13S 35 11 E
Lichtenburg 92 26 8S 26 8 E
Lichtenfels 25 50 7N 11 4 E
Lichuan 77 30 18N 108 57 E
Licosa, Punta 41 40 15N 14 53 E
Lida, U.S.A. 119 37 30N 117 30W
Lida, U.S.S.R. 54 53 53N 25 15 E
Lidhult 49 56 50N 13 27 E
Lidingö 48 59 22N 18 8 E
Lidköping 49 58 31N 13 14 E
Lido, Italy 39 45 25N 12 23 E
Lido, Niger 85 12 54N 3 44 E
Lido di Ostia 40 41 44N 12 14 E
Lidzbark 28 53 15N 19 49 E
Lidzbark Warminski 28 54 7N 20 34 E
Liebenwalde 24 52 51N 13 23 E
Lieberose 24 51 59N 14 18 E
Liebling 42 45 36N 21 20 E
Liechtenstein ■ 25 47 8N 9 35 E
Liège 16 50 38N 5 35 E
Liège □ 16 50 32N 5 35 E
Liegnitz = Legnica 28 51 12N 16 10 E
Lienart 90 3 3N 25 31 E
Lienyünchiangshih = Lianyungang 77 34 40N 119 11 E
Lienz 26 46 50N 12 46 E
Liepaja 54 56 30N 21 0 E
Lier 16 51 7N 4 34 E
Lieşta 46 45 38N 27 34 E
Liévin 19 50 24N 2 47 E
Lièvre → 106 45 31N 75 26W
Liezen 26 47 34N 14 15 E
Liffey → 15 53 21N 6 20W
Lifford 15 54 50N 7 30W
Liffré 18 48 12N 1 30W
Lifjell 47 59 27N 8 45 E
Lightning Ridge 99 29 22S 148 0 E
Lignano 39 45 42N 13 8 E
Ligny-en-Barrois 19 48 36N 5 20 E
Ligny-le-Châtel 19 47 54N 3 45 E
Ligoúrion 45 37 37N 23 2 E
Ligua, La 124 32 30S 71 16W
Ligueil 18 47 2N 0 49 E
Liguria □ 38 44 30N 9 0 E
Ligurian Sea 38 43 20N 9 0 E
Lihir Group 98 3 0S 152 35 E
Lihou Reefs and Cays 97 17 25S 151 40 E
Lihue 110 21 59N 159 24W
Lijiang 75 26 55N 100 20 E
Likasi 91 10 55S 26 48 E
Likati 88 3 20N 24 0 E
Likhoslavl 54 57 12N 35 30 E
Likhovski 57 48 10N 40 10 E
Likoma I. 91 12 3S 34 45 E
Likumburu 91 9 43S 35 8 E
Liling 77 27 42N 113 29 E
Lille 19 50 38N 3 3 E
Lille Bælt 49 55 20N 9 45 E
Lillebonne 18 49 30N 0 32 E
Lillehammer 47 61 8N 10 30 E
Lillers 19 50 35N 2 28 E
Lillesand 47 58 15N 8 23 E
Lilleshall 13 52 45N 2 22W
Lillestrøm 47 59 58N 11 5 E
Lillo 32 39 45N 3 20W
Lillooet → 108 49 15N 121 57W
Lilongwe 91 14 0S 33 48 E
Liloy 73 8 4N 122 39 E
Lim → 42 43 0N 19 40 E
Lima, Indon. 73 3 37S 128 4 E
Lima, Peru 126 12 0S 77 0W
Lima, Sweden 48 60 55N 13 20 E
Lima, Mont., U.S.A. 118 44 41N 112 38W
Lima, Ohio, U.S.A. 114 40 42N 84 5W
Lima → 30 41 41N 8 50W
Limages 113 45 20N 75 16W
Liman 57 45 45N 47 12 E
Limanowa 27 49 42N 20 22 E
Limassol 64 34 42N 33 1 E
Limavady 15 55 3N 6 58W
Limavady □ 15 55 0N 6 55W
Limay → 128 39 0S 68 0W
Limay Mahuida 124 37 10S 66 45W
Limbang 72 4 42N 115 6 E
Limbara, Monti 40 40 50N 9 10 E
Limbdi 68 22 34N 71 51 E
Limbri 99 31 3S 151 5 E
Limburg 25 50 22N 8 4 E
Limburg □, Belg. 16 51 2N 5 25 E
Limburg □, Neth. 16 51 20N 5 55 E
Limedsforsen 48 60 52N 13 25 E
Limeira 125 22 35S 47 28W
Limenária 44 40 38N 24 32 E
Limerick 15 52 40N 8 38W
Limerick □ 15 52 30N 8 50W
Limestone 112 42 2N 78 39W
Limestone → 109 56 31N 94 7W
Limfjorden 49 56 55N 9 0 E
Limia → 30 41 41N 8 50W
Limmared 49 57 34N 13 20 E
Limmen Bight 96 14 40S 135 35 E
Límni 45 38 43N 23 18 E
Límnos 44 39 50N 25 5 E
Limoeiro do Norte 127 5 5S 38 0W
Limoges 20 45 50N 1 15 E
Limón 121 10 0N 83 2W
Limon, Panama 120 9 17N 79 45W
Limon, U.S.A. 116 39 18N 103 38W
Limon B. 120 9 22N 79 56W
Limone Piemonte 38 44 12N 7 32 E
Limousin 20 46 0N 1 0 E
Limousin, Plateaux du 20 46 0N 1 0 E
Limoux 20 43 4N 2 12 E
Limpopo → 93 25 15S 33 30 E
Limuru 90 1 2S 36 35 E
Linares, Chile 124 35 50S 71 40W
Linares, Mexico 120 24 50N 99 40W
Linares, Spain 33 38 10N 3 40W
Linares □ 124 36 0S 71 0W
Linas Mte. 40 39 25N 8 38 E
Lincheng 76 37 25N 114 30 E
Linchuan 75 27 57N 116 15 E
Lincoln, Argent. 124 34 55S 61 30W
Lincoln, N.Z. 101 43 38S 172 30 E
Lincoln, U.K. 12 53 14N 0 32W
Lincoln, Ill., U.S.A. 116 40 10N 89 20W
Lincoln, Kans., U.S.A. 116 39 6N 98 9W
Lincoln, Maine, U.S.A. 107 45 27N 68 29W
Lincoln, N. Mex., U.S.A. 119 33 30N 105 26W
Lincoln, N.H., U.S.A. 113 44 3N 71 40W
Lincoln, Nebr., U.S.A. 116 40 50N 96 42W
Lincoln □ 12 53 14N 0 32W
Lincoln Sea 4 84 0N 55 0W
Lincoln Wolds 12 53 20N 0 5W
Lincolnton 115 35 30N 81 15W
Lind 118 47 0N 118 33W
Lindås, Norway 47 60 44N 5 9 E
Lindås, Sweden 49 56 38N 15 35 E
Lindau 25 47 33N 9 41 E
Linden, Guyana 126 6 0N 58 10W
Linden, U.S.A. 117 33 0N 94 20W
Linderöd 49 55 56N 13 47 E
Linderödsåsen 49 55 53N 13 53 E
Lindesberg 48 59 36N 15 15 E
Lindesnes 47 57 58N 7 3 E
Lindi 91 9 58S 39 38 E
Lindi □ 91 9 40S 38 30 E
Lindi → 90 0 33N 25 5 E
Lindian 76 47 11N 124 52 E
Lindoso 30 41 52N 8 11W
Lindow 24 52 58N 12 58 E
Lindsay, Can. 106 44 22N 78 43W
Lindsay, Calif., U.S.A. 119 36 14N 119 6W
Lindsay, Okla., U.S.A. 117 34 51N 97 37W
Lindsborg 116 38 35N 97 40W
Línea de la Concepción, La 31 36 15N 5 23W
Linfen 76 36 3N 111 30 E
Ling Xian 76 37 22N 116 30 E
Lingao 77 19 56N 109 42 E
Lingayen 73 16 1N 120 14 E
Lingayen G. 73 16 10N 120 15 E
Lingchuan 77 25 26N 110 21 E
Lingen 24 52 32N 7 21 E
Lingga 72 0 12S 104 37 E
Lingga, Kepulauan 72 0 10S 104 30 E
Linghed 48 60 48N 15 55 E
Lingle 116 42 10N 104 18W
Lingling 77 26 17N 111 37 E
Lingshan 77 22 25N 109 18 E
Lingshi 76 36 48N 111 48 E
Lingshui 77 18 27N 110 0 E
Lingtai 77 35 0N 107 40 E
Linguéré 84 15 25N 15 5W
Lingyuan 76 41 10N 119 15 E
Lingyun 75 25 2N 106 35 E
Linh Cam 71 18 31N 105 31 E
Linhai 75 28 50N 121 8 E
Linhe 76 40 48N 107 20 E
Linjiang 76 41 50N 127 0 E
Linköping 49 58 28N 15 36 E
Linkou 76 45 15N 130 18 E
Linlithgow 14 55 58N 3 38W
Linn, Mt. 118 40 0N 123 0W
Linnhe, L. 14 56 36N 5 25W
Linosa, I. 83 35 51N 12 50 E
Linqing 76 36 50N 115 42 E
Lins 125 21 40S 49 44W
Lintao 76 35 18N 103 52 E
Linth → 25 47 7N 9 7W
Linthal 25 46 54N 9 0 E
Lintlaw 109 52 4N 103 14W
Linton, Can. 107 47 15N 72 16W
Linton, Ind., U.S.A. 114 39 0N 87 10W
Linton, N. Dak., U.S.A. 116 46 21N 100 12W
Linville 99 26 50S 152 11 E
Linwood 112 43 35N 80 43W
Linwu 77 25 19N 112 31 E
Linxe 20 43 56N 1 13W
Linxi 76 43 36N 118 2 E
Linxia 75 35 36N 103 10 E
Linyanti → 92 17 50S 25 5 E
Linyi 77 35 5N 118 21 E
Linz, Austria 26 48 18N 14 18 E
Linz, Ger. 24 50 33N 7 18 E
Lion-d'Angers, Le 18 47 37N 0 43W
Lion, G. du 20 43 0N 4 0 E
Lioni 41 40 52N 15 10 E
Lion's Den 91 17 15S 30 5 E
Lion's Head 106 44 58N 81 15W
Liozno 54 55 0N 30 50 E
Lipali 91 15 50S 35 50 E
Lipari 41 38 26N 14 58 E
Lipari, Is. 41 38 30N 14 50 E
Lipetsk 55 52 37N 39 35 E
Lipiany 28 53 2N 14 58 E
Liping 77 26 15N 109 7 E
Lipkany 56 48 14N 26 48 E
Lipljan 42 42 31N 21 7 E
Lipnik 27 49 32N 17 36 E
Lipno 28 52 49N 19 15 E
Lipova 42 46 8N 21 42 E
Lipovets 56 49 12N 29 1 E
Lippe → 24 51 39N 6 38 E
Lippstadt 24 51 40N 8 19 E
Lipscomb 117 36 16N 100 16W
Lipsko 28 51 9N 21 40 E
Lipsói 45 37 19N 26 50 E
Liptovsky Svaty Milkulaš 27 49 6N 19 35 E
Liptrap C. 99 38 50S 145 55 E
Lira 90 2 17N 32 57 E
Liri → 40 41 25N 13 52 E
Liria 32 39 37N 0 35W
Lisala 88 2 12N 21 38 E
Lisboa 31 38 42N 9 10W
Lisboa □ 31 39 0N 9 12W
Lisbon, N. Dak., U.S.A. 116 46 30N 97 46W
Lisbon, N.H., U.S.A. 113 44 13N 71 52W
Lisbon, Ohio, U.S.A. 112 40 45N 80 42W
Lisbon = Lisboa 31 38 42N 9 10W
Lisburn 15 54 30N 6 9W
Lisburne, C. 104 68 50N 166 0W
Liscannor, B. 15 52 57N 9 24W
Liscia → 40 41 11N 9 9 E
Lishi 76 37 31N 111 8 E
Lishui 75 28 28N 119 54 E
Lisianski I. 94 26 2N 174 0W
Lisichansk 56 48 55N 38 30 E
Lisieux 18 49 10N 0 12 E
Lisle-sur-Tarn 20 43 52N 1 49 E
Lismore, Austral. 97 28 44S 153 21 E
Lismore, Ireland 15 52 8N 7 58W
Lisse 16 52 16N 4 33 E
List 24 55 1N 8 26 E
Lista 47 58 7N 6 39 E
Lister, Mt. 5 78 0S 162 0 E
Liston 99 28 39S 152 6 E
Listowel, Can. 106 43 44N 80 58W
Listowel, Ireland 15 52 27N 9 30W
Lit-et-Mixe 20 44 2N 1 15W
Litang, China 77 23 12N 109 8 E
Litang, Malay. 73 5 27N 118 31 E
Litani →, Leb. 62 33 20N 35 14 E
Litani →, Surinam 62 3 40N 54 0W
Litchfield, Conn., U.S.A. 113 41 44N 73 12W
Litchfield, Ill., U.S.A. 116 39 10N 89 40W
Litchfield, Minn., U.S.A. 116 45 5N 94 31W
Liteni 46 47 32N 26 32 E

Lithgow 97 33 25S 150 8 E
Líthinon, Ákra 45 34 55N 24 44 E
Lithuanian S.S.R. □ 54 55 30N 24 0 E
Litija 39 46 3N 14 50 E
Litókhoron 44 40 8N 22 34 E
Litoměřice 26 50 33N 14 10 E
Litomysl 27 49 52N 16 20 E
Litschau 26 48 58N 15 4 E
Little Abaco I. 121 26 50N 77 30W
Little America 5 79 0S 160 0W
Little Andaman I. 71 10 40N 92 15 E
Little Barrier I. 101 36 12S 175 8 E
Little Belt Mts. 118 46 50N 111 0W
Little Blue → 116 39 41N 96 40W
Little Bushman Land 92 29 10S 18 10 E
Little Cadotte → 108 56 41N 117 6W
Little Churchill → 109 57 30N 95 22W
Little Colorado → 119 36 11N 111 48W
Little Current 106 45 55N 82 0W
Little Current → 106 50 57N 84 36W
Little Falls, Minn., U.S.A. 116 45 58N 94 19W
Little Falls, N.Y., U.S.A. 114 43 3N 74 50W
Little Fork → 116 48 31N 93 35W
Little Grand Rapids 109 52 0N 95 29W
Little Humboldt → 118 41 0N 117 43W
Little Inagua I. 121 21 40N 73 50W
Little Lake 119 35 58N 117 58W
Little Marais 116 47 24N 91 8W
Little Minch 14 57 35N 6 45W
Little Missouri → 116 47 30N 102 25W
Little Namaqualand 92 29 0S 17 9 E
Little Ouse → 13 52 25N 0 50 E
Little Rann of Kutch 68 23 25N 71 25 E
Little Red → 117 35 11N 91 27W
Little River 101 43 45S 172 49 E
Little Rock 117 34 41N 92 10W
Little Ruaha → 90 7 57S 37 53 E
Little Sable Pt. 114 43 40N 86 32W
Little Sioux → 116 41 49N 96 4W
Little Smoky → 108 54 44N 117 11W
Little Snake → 118 40 27N 108 26W
Little Valley 112 42 15N 78 48W
Little Wabash → 114 37 54N 88 5W
Littlefield 117 33 57N 102 17W
Littlefork 116 48 24N 93 35W
Littlehampton 13 50 48N 0 32W
Littleton 114 44 19N 71 47W
Liuba 77 33 38N 106 55 E
Liucheng 77 24 38N 109 14 E
Liukang Tenggaja 73 6 45S 118 50 E
Liuli 91 11 3S 34 38 E
Liuwa Plain 89 14 20S 22 30 E
Liuyang 77 28 10N 113 37 E
Liuzhou 75 24 22N 109 22 E
Livada 46 47 52N 23 5 E
Livadherón 44 40 2N 21 57 E
Livarot 18 49 0N 0 9 E
Live Oak 115 30 17N 83 0W
Livermore, Mt. 117 30 45N 104 8W
Liverpool, Austral. 97 33 54S 150 58 E
Liverpool, Can. 107 44 5N 64 41W
Liverpool, U.K. 12 53 25N 3 0W
Liverpool Plains 97 31 15S 150 15 E
Liverpool Ra. 97 31 50S 150 30 E
Livingston, Guat. 120 15 50N 88 50W
Livingston, U.S.A. 118 45 40N 110 40W
Livingstone, U.S.A. 117 30 44N 94 54W
Livingstone, Zambia 91 17 46S 25 52 E
Livingstone I. 5 63 0S 60 15W
Livingstone Memorial 91 12 20S 30 18 E
Livingstone Mts. 91 9 40S 34 20 E
Livingstonia 91 10 38S 34 5 E
Livno 42 43 50N 17 0 E
Livny 55 52 30N 37 30 E
Livorno 38 43 32N 10 18 E
Livramento 125 30 55S 55 30W
Livron-sur-Drôme 21 44 46N 4 51 E
Liwale 91 9 48S 37 58 E
Liwale □ 91 9 0S 38 0 E
Liwiec → 28 52 36N 21 34 E
Lixoúrion 45 38 14N 20 24 E
Lizard I. 98 14 42S 145 30 E
Lizard Pt. 13 49 57N 5 11W
Lizzano 41 40 23N 17 25 E
Ljig 42 44 13N 20 18 E
Ljubija 39 44 55N 16 35 E
Ljubinje 42 42 58N 18 5 E
Ljubljana 39 46 4N 14 33 E
Ljubno 39 46 25N 14 46 E
Ljubovija 42 44 11N 19 22 E
Ljubuški 42 43 12N 17 34 E
Ljung 49 58 1N 13 3 E
Ljungan → 48 62 18N 17 23 E
Ljungaverk 48 62 30N 16 5 E
Ljungby 49 56 49N 13 55 E
Ljusdal 48 61 46N 16 3 E
Ljusnan → 48 61 12N 17 8 E
Ljusne 48 61 13N 17 7 E
Ljutomer 39 46 31N 16 11 E
Llagostera 32 41 50N 2 54 E
Llancanelo, Salina 124 35 40S 69 8W
Llandeilo 13 51 53N 4 0W
Llandovery 13 51 59N 3 49W
Llandrindod Wells 13 52 15N 3 23W
Llandudno 12 53 19N 3 51W
Llanelli 13 51 41N 4 11W
Llanes 30 43 25N 4 50W
Llangollen 12 52 58N 3 10W
Llanidloes 13 52 28N 3 31W
Llano 117 30 45N 98 41W
Llano → 117 30 50N 98 25W
Llano Estacado 117 34 0N 103 0W
Llanos 126 5 0N 71 35W
Llera 120 23 19N 99 1W
Llerena 31 38 17N 6 0W
Llico 124 34 46S 72 5W
Llobregat → 32 41 19N 2 9 E
Lloret de Mar 32 41 41N 2 53 E
Lloyd B. 98 12 45S 143 27 E
Lloyd L. 109 57 22N 108 57W
Lloydminster 109 53 17N 110 0W
Lluchmayor 33 39 29N 2 53 E
Llullaillaco, volcán 124 24 43S 68 30W
Loa 119 38 18N 111 40W
Loa → 124 21 26S 70 41W
Loano 38 44 8N 8 14 E
Lobatse 92 25 12S 25 40 E
Löbau 24 51 5N 14 42 E
Lobenstein 24 50 25N 11 39 E
Lobería 124 38 10S 58 40W
Łobez 28 53 38N 15 39 E
Lobito 89 12 18S 13 35 E
Lobón, Canal de 31 38 50N 6 55W
Lobos 124 35 10S 59 0W
Lobos, I. 120 27 15N 110 30W
Lobos, Is. 122 6 57S 80 45W
Lobstick L. 107 54 0N 65 0W
Loc Binh 71 21 46N 106 54 E
Loc Ninh 71 11 50N 106 34 E
Locarno 25 46 10N 8 47 E
Lochaber 14 56 55N 5 0W
Lochcarron 14 57 25N 5 30W
Loche, La 109 56 29N 109 26W
Lochem 16 52 9N 6 26 E
Loches 18 47 7N 1 0 E
Lochgelly 14 56 7N 3 18W
Lochgilphead 14 56 2N 5 37W
Lochinver 14 58 9N 5 15W
Lochnagar, Austral. 98 23 33S 145 38 E
Lochnagar, U.K. 14 56 57N 3 14W
Łochów 28 52 33N 21 42 E
Lochy → 14 56 52N 5 3W
Lock 99 33 34S 135 46 E
Lock Haven 114 41 7N 77 31W
Lockeport 107 43 47N 65 4W
Lockerbie 14 55 7N 3 21W
Lockhart, Austral. 99 35 14S 146 40 E
Lockhart, U.S.A. 117 29 55N 97 40W
Lockney 117 34 7N 101 27W
Lockport 114 43 12N 78 42W
Locle, Le 25 47 3N 6 44 E
Locminé 18 47 54N 2 51W
Locri 41 38 14N 16 14 E
Locronan 18 48 7N 4 15W
Loctudy 18 47 50N 4 12W
Lod 62 31 57N 34 54 E
Lodalskåpa 47 61 47N 7 13 E
Loddon → 100 35 31S 143 51 E
Lodeinoye Pole 52 60 44N 33 33 E
Lodève 20 43 44N 3 19 E
Lodge Grass 118 45 21N 107 20W
Lodgepole 116 41 12N 102 40W
Lodgepole Cr. → 116 41 20N 104 30W
Lodhran 68 29 32N 71 30 E
Lodi, Italy 38 45 19N 9 30 E
Lodi, U.S.A. 118 38 12N 121 16W
Lodja 90 3 30S 23 23 E
Lodosa 32 42 25N 2 4W
Lödöse 49 58 2N 12 9 E
Lodwar 90 3 10N 35 40 E
Łódź 28 51 45N 19 27 E
Łódź □ 28 51 45N 19 27 E
Loengo 90 4 48S 26 30 E
Lofer 26 47 35N 12 41 E
Lofoten 50 68 30N 15 0 E
Lofsdalen 48 62 10N 13 20 E
Lofsen → 48 62 7N 13 57 E
Loftahammar 49 57 54N 16 41 E
Logan, Kans., U.S.A. 116 39 40N 99 35W
Logan, Ohio, U.S.A. 114 39 25N 82 22W
Logan, Utah, U.S.A. 118 41 45N 111 50W
Logan, W. Va., U.S.A. 114 37 51N 81 59W
Logan, Mt. 104 60 31N 140 22W
Logan Pass 108 48 41N 113 44W
Logansport, Ind., U.S.A. 114 40 45N 86 21W
Logansport, La., U.S.A. 117 31 58N 93 58W
Logar □ 65 34 0N 69 0 E
Logo 87 5 20N 30 18 E
Logroño 32 42 28N 2 27W
Logroño □ 32 42 28N 2 27W
Logrosán 31 39 20N 5 32W
Løgstør 49 56 58N 9 14 E
Lohardaga 69 23 27N 84 45 E
Lohja 51 60 12N 24 5 E
Lohr 25 50 0N 9 35 E
Loi-kaw 67 19 40N 97 17 E
Loimaa 51 60 50N 23 5 E
Loir → 18 47 33N 0 32W
Loir-et-Cher □ 18 47 40N 1 20 E
Loire □ 21 45 40N 4 5 E
Loire → 18 47 16N 2 10W
Loire-Atlantique □ 18 47 25N 1 40W
Loiret □ 19 47 58N 2 10 E
Loitz 24 53 58N 13 8 E
Loja, Ecuador 126 3 59S 79 16W
Loja, Spain 31 37 10N 4 10W
Loji 73 1 38S 127 28 E
Loka 87 4 13N 31 0 E
Lokandu 90 2 30S 25 45 E
Løken 47 59 48N 11 29 E
Lokeren 16 51 6N 3 59 E
Lokhvitsa 54 50 25N 33 18 E
Lokichokio 90 4 19N 34 13 E
Lokitaung 90 4 12N 35 48 E
Lokka 50 67 49N 27 45 E
Løkken 49 57 22N 9 41 E
Løkkenverk 47 63 8N 9 45 E
Loknya 54 56 49N 30 4 E
Lokoja 85 7 47N 6 45 E
Lokolama 88 2 35S 19 50 E
Lokwei 77 19 5N 110 31 E
Lol → 87 9 13N 26 30 E
Lola 84 7 52N 8 29W
Lolibai, Gebel 87 3 50N 33 0 E
Lolimi 87 4 35N 34 0 E
Loliondo 90 2 2S 35 39 E
Lolland 49 54 45N 11 30 E
Lollar 24 50 39N 8 43 E
Lolo 118 46 50N 114 8W
Lolodorf 85 3 16N 10 49 E
Lom 43 43 48N 23 12 E
Lom → 42 43 45N 23 15 E
Loma 118 47 59N 110 29W
Lomami → 90 0 46N 24 16 E
Lomas de Zamóra 124 34 45S 58 25W
Lombard 118 46 7N 111 28W
Lombardia □ 38 45 35N 9 45 E
Lombardy = Lombardia 38 45 35N 9 45 E
Lombez 20 43 29N 0 55 E
Lomblen 73 8 30S 123 32 E
Lombok 72 8 45S 116 30 E
Lomé 85 6 9N 1 20 E
Lomela 88 2 19S 23 15 E
Lomela → 88 1 30S 22 50 E
Lomello 38 45 5N 8 46 E
Lometa 117 31 15N 98 25W
Lomié 88 3 13N 13 38 E
Lomma 49 55 43N 13 6 E
Lomond 108 50 24N 112 36W
Lomond, L. 14 56 8N 4 38W
Lomonosov 54 59 57N 29 53 E
Lompobatang 73 5 24S 119 56 E
Lompoc 119 34 41N 120 32W
Lomsegga 47 61 49N 8 21 E
Łomza 28 53 10N 22 2 E
Łomza □ 28 53 0N 22 30 E
Lonavla 70 18 46N 73 29 E
Loncoche 128 39 20S 72 50W
Londa 70 15 30N 74 30 E
Londe, La 21 43 8N 6 14 E
Londiani 90 0 10S 35 33 E
Londinières 18 49 50N 1 25 E
London, Can. 106 42 59N 81 15W
London, U.K. 13 51 30N 0 5W
London, Ky., U.S.A. 114 37 11N 84 5W
London, Ohio, U.S.A. 114 39 54N 83 28W
London, Greater □ 13 51 30N 0 5W
Londonderry 15 55 0N 7 20W
Londonderry □ 15 55 0N 7 20W
Londonderry, C. 96 13 45S 126 55 E
Londonderry, I. 128 55 0S 71 0W
Londrina 125 23 18S 51 10W
Lone Pine 119 36 35N 118 2W
Long Beach, Calif., U.S.A. 119 33 46N 118 12W
Long Beach, N.Y., U.S.A. 113 40 35N 73 40W
Long Beach, Wash., U.S.A. 118 46 20N 124 1W
Long Branch 114 40 19N 74 0W
Long Creek 118 44 43N 119 6W
Long Eaton 12 52 54N 1 16W
Long I., Austral. 98 22 8S 149 53 E
Long I., Bahamas 121 23 20N 75 10W
Long I., P.N.G. 98 5 20S 147 5 E
Long I., U.S.A. 114 40 50N 73 20W
Long I. Sd. 113 41 10N 73 0W
Long L. 106 49 30N 86 50W
Long Lake 113 43 57N 74 25W
Long Pine 116 42 33N 99 41W
Long Pt., Newf., Can. 107 48 47N 58 46W
Long Pt., Ont., Can. 112 42 35N 80 2W
Long Point B. 112 42 40N 80 10W
Long Range Mts. 107 49 30N 57 30W
Long Str. 4 70 0N 175 0 E
Long Xian 77 34 55N 106 55 E
Long Xuyen 71 10 19N 105 28 E
Longá 45 36 53N 21 55 E
Long'an 77 23 10N 107 40 E
Longarone 39 46 15N 12 18 E
Longchuan 77 24 5N 115 17 E
Longde 76 35 30N 106 20 E
Longeau 19 47 47N 5 20 E
Longford, Austral. 99 41 32S 147 3 E
Longford, Ireland 15 53 43N 7 50W
Longford □ 15 53 42N 7 45W
Longhua 76 41 18N 117 45 E
Longido 90 2 43S 36 42 E
Longiram 72 0 5S 115 45 E
Longjiang 76 47 20N 123 12 E
Longkou 76 37 40N 120 18 E
Longlac 106 49 45N 86 25W
Longlin 77 24 47N 105 20 E
Longmen 77 23 40N 114 18 E
Longmont 116 40 10N 105 4W
Longnan 77 24 55N 114 47 E
Longnawan 72 1 51N 114 55 E
Longobucco 41 39 27N 16 37 E
Longone → 81 10 0N 15 40 E
Longquan 77 28 7N 119 10 E
Longreach 97 23 28S 144 14 E
Longs Peak 118 40 20N 105 37W
Longshan 77 29 29N 109 25 E
Longsheng 77 25 48N 110 0 E
Longton 98 20 58S 145 55 E
Longtown 13 51 58N 2 59W
Longué 18 47 22N 0 8W
Longueau 19 49 52N 2 21 E
Longueuil 113 45 32N 73 28W
Longuyon 19 49 27N 5 35 E
Longview, Can. 108 50 32N 114 10W
Longview, Tex., U.S.A. 117 32 30N 94 45W
Longview, Wash., U.S.A. 118 46 9N 122 58W
Longwy 19 49 30N 5 45 E
Longxi 76 34 53N 104 40 E
Longzhou 77 22 22N 106 50 E
Lonigo 39 45 23N 11 22 E
Löningen 24 52 43N 7 44 E
Lonja → 39 45 30N 16 40 E
Lonoke 117 34 48N 91 57W
Lons-le-Saunier 19 46 40N 5 31 E
Lønstrup 49 57 29N 9 47 E
Looc 73 12 20N 112 5 E
Lookout, C., Can. 106 55 18N 83 56W
Lookout, C., U.S.A. 115 34 30N 76 30W
Loolmalasin 90 3 0S 35 53 E
Loon →, Alta., Can. 108 57 8N 115 3W
Loon →, Man., Can. 109 55 53N 101 59W
Loon Lake 109 54 2N 109 10W
Loop Hd. 15 52 34N 9 55W
Lop Nor = Lop Nur 75 40 20N 90 10 E
Lop Nur 75 40 20N 90 10 E
Lopare 42 44 39N 18 46 E
Lopatin 57 43 50N 47 35 E
Lopatina, G. 59 50 47N 143 10 E
Lopaye 87 6 37N 33 40 E
Lopera 31 37 56N 4 14W
Lopez, C. 88 0 47S 8 40 E
Lopphavet 50 70 27N 21 15 E
Lora →, Afghan. 65 32 0N 67 15 E
Lora →, Norway 47 62 8N 8 42 E
Lora del Río 31 37 39N 5 33W
Lora, Hamun-i- 66 29 38N 64 58 E
Lora, La 30 42 45N 4 0W
Lorain 114 41 28N 82 55W
Loralai 68 30 20N 68 41 E
Lorca 33 37 41N 1 42W
Lord Howe I. 94 31 33S 159 6 E
Lord Howe Ridge 94 30 0S 162 30 E
Lordsburg 119 32 22N 108 45W
Lorengau 98 2 1S 147 15 E
Loreto, Brazil 127 7 5S 45 10W
Loreto, Italy 39 43 26N 13 36 E
Loreto Aprutina 39 42 24N 13 59 E
Lorgues 21 43 28N 6 22 E
Lorient 18 47 45N 3 23W
Loristān □ 64 33 20N 47 0 E
Lorn 14 56 26N 5 10W
Lorn, Firth of 14 56 20N 5 40W
Lorne 99 38 33S 143 59 E
Lörrach 25 47 36N 7 38 E
Lorraine 19 49 0N 6 0 E
Lorrainville 106 47 21N 79 23W
Los Alamos 119 35 57N 106 17W
Los Andes 124 32 50S 70 40W
Los Angeles, Chile 124 37 28S 72 23W
Los Angeles, U.S.A. 119 34 0N 118 10W
Los Angeles Aqueduct 119 35 25N 118 0W
Los Banos 119 37 8N 120 56W
Los Barrios 31 36 11N 5 30W
Los Blancos 124 23 40S 62 30W
Los Gatos 119 37 15N 121 59W
Los Hermanos 126 11 45N 84 25W
Los, Îles de 84 9 30N 13 50W
Los Lamentos 120 30 36N 105 50W
Los Lunas 119 34 48N 106 47W
Los Mochis 120 25 45N 109 5W
Los Monegros 32 41 29N 0 13W
Los Olivos 119 34 40N 120 7W
Los Palacios y Villafranca 31 37 10N 5 55W
Los Roques 126 11 50N 66 45W
Los Santos de Maimona 31 38 27N 6 22W
Los Testigos 126 11 23N 63 6W
Los Vilos 124 32 10S 71 30W
Los Yébenes 31 39 36N 3 55W
Loshkalakh 59 62 45N 147 20 E
Łosice 28 52 13N 22 43 E
Lošinj 39 44 30N 14 30 E
Lossiemouth 14 57 43N 3 17W
Losuia 98 8 30S 151 4 E
Lot □ 20 44 39N 1 40 E
Lot → 20 44 18N 0 20 E
Lot-et-Garonne □ 20 44 22N 0 30 E
Lota 124 37 5S 73 10W
Løten 47 60 51N 11 21 E
Lothian □ 14 55 50N 3 0W
Lothiers 19 46 42N 1 33 E
Lotschbergtunnel 25 46 26N 7 43 E
Lottefors 48 61 25N 16 24 E
Loubomo 88 4 9S 12 47 E
Loudéac 18 48 11N 2 47W
Loudon 115 35 35N 84 22W
Loudonville 112 40 40N 82 15W
Loudun 18 47 0N 0 5 E
Loué 18 47 59N 0 9W
Loue → 19 47 1N 5 27 E
Louga 84 15 45N 16 5W
Loughborough 12 52 46N 1 11W
Loughrea 15 53 11N 8 33W
Loughros More B. 15 54 48N 8 30W
Louhans 21 46 38N 5 12 E
Louis Trichardt 93 23 0S 29 43 E
Louis XIV, Pte. 106 54 37N 79 45W
Louisa 114 38 5N 82 40W
Louisbourg 107 45 55N 60 0W
Louise I. 108 52 55N 131 50W
Louiseville 106 46 20N 72 56W
Louisiade Arch. 94 11 10S 153 0 E
Louisiana 116 39 25N 91 0W
Louisiana □ 117 30 50N 92 0W
Louisville, Ky., U.S.A. 114 38 15N 85 45W
Louisville, Miss., U.S.A. 117 33 7N 89 3W
Loulay 20 46 3N 0 30W
Loulé 31 37 9N 8 0W
Lount L. 109 50 10N 94 20W
Louny 26 50 20N 13 48 E
Loup City 116 41 19N 98 57W
Loupe, La 18 48 29N 1 1 E
Lourdes 20 43 6N 0 3W
Lourdes-du-Blanc-Sablon 107 51 24N 57 12W
Lourenço-Marques = Maputo 93 25 58S 32 32 E
Loures 31 38 50N 9 9W
Lourinhã 31 39 14N 9 17W
Louroux-Béconnais, Le 18 47 30N 0 55W
Lousã 30 40 7N 8 14W
Louth, Austral. 99 30 30S 145 8 E
Louth, Ireland 15 53 47N 6 33W
Louth, U.K. 12 53 23N 0 0W
Louth □ 15 53 55N 6 30W
Loutrá Aidhipsoú 45 38 54N 23 2 E
Loutráki 45 38 0N 22 57 E
Louvière, La 16 50 27N 4 10 E
Louviers 18 49 12N 1 10 E
Lovat → 54 58 14N 30 28 E
Lovćen 42 42 23N 18 51 E
Love 109 53 29N 104 10W
Lovech 43 43 8N 24 42 E
Loveland 116 40 27N 105 4W
Lovell 118 44 51N 108 20W
Lovelock 118 40 17N 118 25W
Lóvere 38 45 50N 10 4 E
Loviisa 51 60 28N 26 12 E
Loving 117 32 17N 104 4W
Lovington 117 33 0N 103 20W
Lovios 30 41 55N 8 4W
Lovisa 51 60 28N 26 12 E
Lovosice 26 50 30N 14 2 E
Lovran 39 45 18N 14 15 E
Lovrin 42 45 58N 20 48 E
Lövstabukten 48 60 35N 17 45 E
Low Rocky Pt. 97 42 59S 145 29 E

Lowa **90** 1 25S 25 47 E
Lowa → **90** 1 24S 25 51 E
Lowell **114** 42 38N 71 19W
Lower Arrow L. **108** 49 40N 118 5W
Lower Austria = Niederösterreich □ **26** 48 25N 15 40 E
Lower Hutt **101** 41 10S 174 55 E
Lower L. **118** 41 17N 120 3W
Lower Lake **118** 38 56N 122 36W
Lower Neguac **107** 47 20N 65 10W
Lower Post **108** 59 58N 128 30W
Lower Red L. **116** 47 58N 95 0W
Lower Saxony = Niedersachsen □ **24** 52 45N 9 0 E
Lowestoft **13** 52 29N 1 44 E
Łowicz **28** 52 6N 19 55 E
Lowville **114** 43 48N 75 30W
Loxton **97** 34 28S 140 31 E
Loyalty Is. = Loyauté, Is. **94** 21 0S 167 30 E
Loyang = Luoyang **77** 34 40N 112 26 E
Loyev, U.S.S.R. **54** 51 55N 30 40 E
Loyev, U.S.S.R. **54** 51 56N 30 46 E
Loyoro **90** 3 22N 34 14 E
Lož **39** 45 43N 30 14 E
Lozère □ **20** 44 35N 3 30 E
Loznica **42** 44 32N 19 14 E
Lozovaya **56** 49 0N 36 20 E
Luachimo **88** 7 23S 20 48 E
Luacono **88** 11 15S 21 37 E
Lualaba → **90** 0 26N 25 20 E
Luampa **91** 15 4S 24 20 E
Lu'an **77** 31 45N 116 29 E
Luan Chau **71** 21 38N 103 24 E
Luan Xian **76** 39 40N 118 40 E
Luanda **88** 8 50S 13 15 E
Luang Prabang **71** 19 52N 102 10 E
Luangwa Valley **91** 13 30S 31 30 E
Luanping **76** 40 53N 117 23 E
Luanshya **91** 13 3S 28 28 E
Luapula □ **91** 11 0S 29 0 E
Luapula → **91** 9 26S 28 33 E
Luarca **30** 43 32N 6 32W
Luashi **91** 10 50S 23 36 E
Luau **88** 10 40S 22 10 E
Lubaczów **28** 50 10N 23 8 E
Lubalo **88** 9 10S 19 15 E
Lubań **28** 51 5N 15 15 E
Lubana, Ozero **54** 56 45N 27 0 E
Lubang Is. **73** 13 50N 120 12 E
Lubartów **28** 51 28N 22 42 E
Lubawa **28** 53 30N 19 48 E
Lübben **24** 51 56N 13 54 E
Lübbenau **24** 51 49N 13 59 E
Lubbock **117** 33 40N 101 53W
Lübeck **24** 53 52N 10 41 E
Lübecker Bucht **24** 54 3N 11 0 E
Lubefu **90** 4 47S 24 27 E
Lubefu → **90** 4 10S 23 0 E
Lubero = Luofu **90** 0 1S 29 15 E
Lubicon L. **108** 56 23N 115 56W
Lubień Kujawski **28** 52 23N 19 9 E
Lubin **28** 51 24N 16 11 E
Lublin **28** 51 12N 22 38 E
Lublin □ **28** 51 5N 22 30 E
Lubliniec **28** 50 43N 18 45 E
Lubny **54** 50 3N 32 58 E
Lubok Antu **72** 1 3N 111 50 E
Lubon **28** 52 21N 16 51 E
Lubongola **90** 2 35S 27 50 E
Lubotin **27** 49 17N 20 53 E
Lubran **64** 34 0N 36 0 E
Lubraniec **28** 52 33N 18 50 E
Lubsko **28** 51 45N 14 57 E
Lübtheen **24** 53 18N 11 4 E
Lubuagan **73** 17 21N 121 10 E
Lubudi → **91** 9 0S 25 35 E
Lubuklinggau **72** 3 15S 102 55 E
Lubuksikaping **72** 0 10N 100 15 E
Lubumbashi **91** 11 40S 27 28 E
Lubunda **90** 5 12S 26 41 E
Lubungu **91** 14 35S 26 24 E
Lubutu **90** 0 45S 26 30 E
Luc-en-Diois **21** 44 36N 5 28 E
Luc, Le **21** 43 23N 6 21 E
Lucan **112** 43 11N 81 24W
Lucca **38** 43 50N 10 30 E
Luce Bay **14** 54 45N 4 48W
Lucea **121** 18 25N 78 10W
Lucedale **115** 30 55N 88 34W
Lucena, Phil. **73** 13 56N 121 37 E
Lucena, Spain **31** 37 27N 4 31W
Lucena del Cid **32** 40 9N 0 17W
Lučenec **27** 48 18N 19 42 E
Lucera **41** 41 30N 15 20 E
Lucerne = Luzern **25** 47 3N 8 18 E
Luchena → **33** 37 44N 1 50W
Lucheringo → **91** 11 43S 36 17 E
Lüchow **24** 52 58N 11 8 E
Lucira **89** 14 0S 12 35 E
Luckau **24** 51 50N 13 43 E
Luckenwalde **24** 52 5N 13 11 E
Lucknow **69** 26 50N 81 0 E
Luçon **20** 46 28N 1 10W
Lüda **76** 38 50N 121 40 E
Luda Kamchiya → **43** 43 3N 27 29 E
Ludbreg **39** 46 15N 16 38 E
Lüdenscheid **24** 51 13N 7 37 E
Lüderitz **92** 26 41S 15 8 E
Ludewe □ **91** 10 0S 34 50 E
Ludhiana **68** 30 57N 75 56 E
Lüdinghausen **24** 51 46N 7 28 E
Ludington **114** 43 58N 86 27W
Ludlow, U.K. **13** 52 23N 2 42W
Ludlow, Calif., U.S.A. **119** 34 43N 116 10W
Ludlow, Vt., U.S.A. **113** 43 25N 72 40W
Ludus **46** 46 29N 24 5 E
Ludvika **48** 60 8N 15 14 E
Ludwigsburg **25** 48 53N 9 11 E
Ludwigshafen **25** 49 27N 8 27 E
Ludwigslust **24** 53 19N 11 28 E
Ludza **54** 56 32N 27 43 E
Luebo **88** 5 21S 21 23 E
Lueki **90** 3 20S 25 48 E
Luena, Zaïre **91** 9 28S 25 43 E
Luena, Zambia **91** 10 40S 30 25 E
Lüeyang **77** 33 22N 106 10 E
Lufeng **77** 22 57N 115 38 E
Lufkin **117** 31 25N 94 40W
Lufupa **91** 10 37S 24 56 E
Luga **54** 58 40N 29 55 E
Luga → **54** 59 40N 28 18 E
Lugang **77** 24 4N 120 23 E
Lugano **25** 46 0N 8 57 E
Lugano, L. di **25** 46 0N 9 0 E
Lugansk = Voroshilovgrad **57** 48 35N 39 20 E
Lugard's Falls **90** 3 6S 38 41 E
Lugela **91** 16 25S 36 43 E
Lugenda → **91** 11 25S 38 33 E
Lugh Ganana **63** 3 48N 42 34 E
Lugnaquilla **15** 52 58N 6 28W
Lugnvik **48** 62 56N 17 55 E
Lugo, Italy **39** 44 25N 11 53 E
Lugo, Spain **30** 43 2N 7 35W
Lugo □ **30** 43 0N 7 30W
Lugoj **42** 45 42N 21 57 E
Lugones **30** 43 26N 5 50W
Lugovoy **58** 42 54N 72 45 E
Luhe → **24** 53 18N 10 11 E
Luiana **92** 17 25S 22 59 E
Luino **38** 46 0N 8 42 E
Luís Correia **127** 3 0S 41 35W
Luitpold Coast **5** 78 30S 32 0W
Luize **88** 7 40S 22 30 E
Luizi **90** 6 0S 27 25 E
Luján **124** 34 45S 59 5W
Lukanga Swamps **91** 14 30S 27 40 E
Lukenie → **88** 3 0S 18 50 E
Lukhisaral **69** 25 11N 86 5 E
Lŭki **43** 41 50N 24 43 E
Lukolela, Equateur, Zaïre **88** 1 10S 17 12 E
Lukolela, Kasai Or., Zaïre **90** 5 23S 24 32 E
Lukosi **91** 18 30S 26 30 E
Lukovit **43** 43 13N 24 11 E
Łuków **28** 51 55N 22 23 E
Lukoyanov **55** 55 2N 44 29 E
Lule älv → **50** 65 35N 22 10 E
Luleå **50** 65 35N 22 10 E
Lüleburgaz **43** 41 23N 27 22 E
Luling **117** 29 45N 97 40W
Lulong **76** 39 53N 118 51 E
Lulonga → **88** 1 0N 19 0 E
Lulua → **88** 6 30S 22 50 E
Luluabourg = Kananga **88** 5 55S 22 26 E
Lumai **89** 13 13S 21 25 E
Lumajang **73** 8 8S 113 16 E
Lumbala **89** 14 18S 21 18 E
Lumberton, Miss., U.S.A. **117** 31 4N 89 28W
Lumberton, N. Mex., U.S.A. **119** 36 58N 106 57W
Lumberton, N.C., U.S.A. **115** 34 37N 78 59W
Lumbres **19** 50 40N 2 5 E
Lumbwa **90** 0 12S 35 28 E
Lumby **108** 50 10N 118 50W
Lumsden **101** 45 44S 168 27 E
Lumut **71** 4 13N 100 37 E
Lunavada **68** 23 8N 73 37 E
Lunca **46** 47 22N 25 1 E
Lund, Sweden **49** 55 44N 13 12 E
Lund, U.S.A. **118** 38 53N 115 0W
Lundazi **91** 12 20S 33 7 E
Lunde **47** 59 17N 9 5 E
Lunderskov **49** 55 29N 9 19 E
Lundi → **91** 21 43S 32 34 E
Lundu **72** 1 40N 109 50 E
Lundy **13** 51 10N 4 41W
Lune → **12** 54 0N 2 51W
Lüneburg **24** 53 15N 10 23 E
Lüneburg Heath = Lüneburger Heide **24** 53 0N 10 0 E
Lüneburger Heide **24** 53 0N 10 0 E
Lunel **21** 43 39N 4 9 E
Lünen **24** 51 36N 7 31 E
Lunenburg **107** 44 22N 64 18W
Lunéville **19** 48 36N 6 30 E
Lunga → **91** 14 34S 26 25 E
Lungi Airport **84** 8 40N 13 17W
Lungleh **67** 22 55N 92 45 E
Luni **68** 26 0N 73 6 E
Lūni → **68** 24 41N 71 14 E
Luninets **54** 52 15N 26 50 E
Luning **118** 38 30N 118 10W
Lunino **55** 53 35N 45 6 E
Lunner **47** 60 19N 10 35 E
Lunsemfwa → **91** 14 54S 30 12 E
Lunsemfwa Falls **91** 14 30S 29 6 E
Luo He → **77** 34 35N 110 20 E
Luobei **76** 47 35N 130 50 E
Luocheng **77** 24 48N 108 53 E
Luochuan **76** 35 45N 109 26 E
Luoding **77** 22 45N 111 40 E
Luodong **77** 24 41N 121 46 E
Luofu **90** 0 10S 29 15 E
Luoning **77** 34 35N 111 40 E
Luoyang **77** 34 40N 112 26 E
Luoyuan **77** 26 28N 119 30 E
Luozi **88** 4 54S 14 0 E
Lupeni **46** 45 21N 23 13 E
Łupków **27** 49 15N 22 4 E
Luque, Parag. **124** 25 19S 57 25W
Luque, Spain **31** 37 35N 4 16W
Luray **114** 38 39N 78 26W
Lure **19** 47 40N 6 30 E
Luremo **88** 8 30S 17 50 E
Lurgan **15** 54 28N 6 20W
Lusaka **91** 15 28S 28 16 E
Lusambo **90** 4 58S 23 28 E
Lusangaye **90** 4 54S 26 0 E
Luseland **109** 52 5N 109 24W
Lushan **77** 33 45N 112 55 E
Lushih **77** 34 3N 111 3 E
Lushnja **44** 40 55N 19 41 E
Lushoto **90** 4 47S 38 20 E
Lushoto □ **90** 4 45S 38 20 E
Lüshun **76** 38 45N 121 15 E
Lusignan **20** 46 26N 0 8 E
Lusigny-sur-Barse **19** 48 16N 4 15 E
Lusk **116** 42 47N 104 27W
Lussac-les-Châteaux **20** 46 24N 0 43 E
Luta = Lüda **76** 38 50N 121 40 E
Luton **13** 51 53N 0 24W
Lutong **72** 4 30N 114 0 E
Lutsk **54** 50 50N 25 15 E
Lützow Holmbukta **5** 69 10S 37 30 E
Luverne **116** 43 35N 96 12W
Luvua **91** 8 48S 25 17 E
Luwegu → **91** 8 31S 37 23 E
Luwuk **73** 0 56S 122 47 E
Luxembourg **16** 49 37N 6 9 E
Luxembourg ■ **16** 50 0N 6 0 E
Luxembourg □ **16** 49 58N 5 30 E
Luxeuil-les-Bains **19** 47 49N 6 24 E
Luxi **77** 28 20N 110 7 E
Luxor = El Uqsur **86** 25 41N 32 38 E
Luy → **20** 43 39N 1 9W
Luy-de-Béarn → **20** 43 39N 0 48W
Luy-de-France → **20** 43 39N 0 48W
Luz-St-Sauveur **20** 42 53N 0 1 E
Luza **52** 60 39N 47 10 E
Luzern **25** 47 3N 8 18 E
Luzern □ **25** 47 2N 7 55 E
Luzhai **77** 24 29N 109 42 E
Luzhou **75** 28 52N 105 20 E
Luziânia **127** 16 20S 48 0W
Luzon **73** 16 0N 121 0 E
Luzy **19** 46 47N 3 58 E
Luzzi **41** 39 28N 16 17 E
Lvov **54** 49 50N 24 0 E
Lwówek **28** 52 28N 16 10 E
Lwówek Śląski **28** 51 7N 15 38 E
Lyakhovichi **24** 53 2N 26 32 E
Lyakhovskiye, Ostrova **59** 73 40N 141 0 E
Lyaki **57** 40 34N 47 22 E
Lyallpur = Shah Faisalabad **68** 31 30N 73 5 E
Lyaskovets **43** 43 6N 25 44 E
Lychen **24** 53 13N 13 20 E
Lyckeby **49** 56 12N 15 37 E
Lycksele **50** 64 38N 18 40 E
Lycosura **45** 37 20N 22 3 E
Lydda = Lod **62** 31 57N 34 54 E
Lydenburg **93** 25 10S 30 29 E
Lyell **101** 41 48S 172 4 E
Lyell I. **108** 52 40N 131 35W
Lyell Range **101** 41 38S 172 20 E
Lygnern **49** 57 30N 12 15 E
Lykling **47** 59 42N 5 12 E
Lyman **118** 41 24N 110 15W
Lyme Regis **13** 50 44N 2 57W
Lymington **13** 50 46N 1 32W
Łyńa → **28** 54 37N 21 14 E
Lynchburg **114** 37 23N 79 10W
Lynd → **98** 16 28S 143 18 E
Lynd Ra. **99** 25 30S 149 20 E
Lynden, Can. **112** 43 14N 80 9W
Lynden, U.S.A. **118** 48 56N 122 32W
Lyndhurst **99** 30 15S 138 18 E
Lyndonville, N.Y., U.S.A. **112** 43 19N 78 25W
Lyndonville, Vt., U.S.A. **113** 44 32N 72 1W
Lyngdal, Aust-Agder, Norway **47** 58 8N 7 7 E
Lyngdal, Buskerud, Norway **47** 59 54N 9 32 E
Lynn **114** 42 28N 70 57W
Lynn Canal **108** 58 50N 135 20W
Lynn Lake **109** 56 51N 101 3W
Lynton **13** 51 14N 3 50W
Lyntupy **54** 55 4N 26 23 E
Lynx L. **109** 62 25N 106 15W
Lyø **49** 55 3N 10 9 E
Lyon **21** 45 46N 4 50 E
Lyonnais **21** 45 45N 4 15 E
Lyons, Colo., U.S.A. **116** 40 17N 105 15W
Lyons, Ga., U.S.A. **115** 32 10N 82 15W
Lyons, Kans., U.S.A. **116** 38 24N 98 13W
Lyons, N.Y., U.S.A. **114** 43 3N 77 0W
Lyons = Lyon **21** 45 46N 4 50 E
Lyrestad **49** 58 48N 14 4 E
Lys → **19** 50 39N 2 24 E
Lysá **26** 50 11N 14 51 E
Lysekil **49** 58 17N 11 26 E
Lyskovo **55** 56 0N 45 3 E
Lysva **52** 58 07N 57 49 E
Lysvik **48** 60 1N 13 9 E
Lytle **117** 29 14N 98 46W
Lyttelton **101** 43 35S 172 44 E
Lytton **108** 50 13N 121 31W
Lyuban **54** 59 16N 31 18 E
Lyubcha **54** 53 46N 26 1 E
Lyubertsy **55** 55 39N 37 50 E
Lyubim **55** 58 20N 40 39 E
Lyubimets **43** 41 50N 26 5 E
Lyuboml, U.S.S.R. **54** 51 10N 24 2 E
Lyuboml, U.S.S.R. **54** 51 11N 24 4 E
Lyubotin **56** 50 0N 36 0 E
Lyubytino **54** 58 50N 33 16 E
Lyudinovo **54** 53 52N 34 28 E

M

Mā'ad **62** 32 37N 35 36 E
Ma'alah **64** 26 31N 47 20 E
Maamba **92** 17 17S 26 28 E
Ma'ānn **64** 30 12N 35 44 E
Ma'anshan **77** 31 44N 118 29 E
Ma'arrat un Nu'man **64** 35 38N 36 40 E
Maas → **16** 51 45N 4 32 E
Maaseik **16** 51 6N 5 45 E
Maassluis **16** 51 56N 4 16 E
Maastricht **16** 50 50N 5 40 E
Maave **93** 21 4S 34 47 E
Mabel L. **108** 50 35N 118 43W
Mabenge **90** 4 15N 24 12 E
Mablethorpe **12** 53 21N 0 14 E
Maboma **90** 2 30N 28 10 E
Mabrouk **85** 19 29N 1 15W
Mabton **118** 46 15N 120 12W
Mac Nutt **109** 51 5N 101 36W
Mac Tier **112** 45 9N 79 46W
Macachín **124** 37 10S 63 43W
Macaé **125** 22 20S 41 43W
McAlester **117** 34 57N 95 46W
McAllen **117** 26 12N 98 15W
Macallister → **100** 38 2S 146 59 E
Macamic **106** 48 45N 79 0W
Macão **31** 39 35N 7 59W
Macao = Macau ■ **75** 22 16N 113 35 E
Macapá **127** 0 5N 51 4W
McArthur → **97** 15 54S 136 40 E
McArthur River **97** 16 27S 136 7 E
Macau **127** 5 0S 36 40W
Macau ■ **75** 22 16N 113 35 E
McBride **108** 53 20N 120 19W
McCall **118** 44 55N 116 6W
McCamey **117** 31 8N 102 15W
McCammon **118** 42 41N 112 11W
McCauley I. **108** 53 40N 130 15W
Macclesfield **12** 53 16N 2 9W
McClintock **109** 57 50N 94 10W
McCloud **118** 41 14N 122 5W
McClure **112** 40 42N 77 20W
McClure Str. **4** 75 0N 119 0W
McClusky **116** 47 30N 100 31W
McComb **117** 31 13N 90 30W
McCook **116** 40 15N 100 35W
McCusker → **109** 55 32N 108 39W
McDame **108** 59 44N 128 59W
McDermitt **118** 42 0N 117 45W
Macdonald → **100** 33 22S 151 0 E
McDonald Is. **3** 54 0S 73 0 E
Macdonald L. **96** 23 30S 129 0 E
Macdonnell Ranges **96** 23 40S 133 0 E
Macdougall L. **104** 66 0N 98 27W
MacDowell L. **106** 52 15N 92 45W
Macduff **14** 57 40N 2 30W
Maceda **30** 42 16N 7 39W
Macedo de Cavaleiros **88** 11 25S 16 45 E
Macedonia = Makedhonia **44** 40 39N 22 0 E
Macedonia = Makedonija **42** 41 53N 21 40 E
Maceió **127** 9 40S 35 41W
Maceira **31** 39 41N 8 55W
Macenta **84** 8 35N 9 32W
Macerata **39** 43 19N 13 28 E
McFarlane → **109** 59 12N 107 58W
Macfarlane, L. **97** 32 0S 136 40 E
McGehee **117** 33 40N 91 25W
McGill **118** 39 27N 114 50W
Macgillycuddy's Reeks **15** 52 2N 9 45W
MacGregor **109** 49 57N 98 48W
McGregor, Iowa, U.S.A. **116** 42 58N 91 15W
McGregor, Minn., U.S.A. **116** 46 37N 93 17W
McGregor → **108** 55 10N 122 0W
McGregor Ra. **99** 27 0S 142 45 E
Mach **66** 29 50N 67 20 E
Machado = Jiparana → **126** 8 3S 62 52W
Machagai **124** 26 56S 60 2W
Machakos **90** 1 30S 37 15 E
Machakos □ **90** 1 30S 37 15 E
Machala **126** 3 20S 79 57W
Machanga **93** 20 59S 35 0 E
Machattie, L. **97** 24 50S 139 48 E
Machava **93** 25 54S 32 28 E
Machece **91** 19 15S 35 32 E
Machecoul **18** 47 0N 1 49W
Macheng **77** 31 12N 115 2 E
Machevna **59** 61 20N 172 20 E
Machezo **31** 39 21N 4 20W
Machias **107** 44 40N 67 28W
Machichaco, Cabo **32** 43 28N 2 47W
Machichi → **109** 57 3N 92 6W
Machilipatnam **70** 16 12N 81 8 E
Machine, La **19** 46 54N 3 27 E
Machiques **126** 10 4N 72 34W
Machupicchu **126** 13 8S 72 30W
Machynlleth **13** 52 36N 3 51W
Macias Nguema Biyoga **85** 3 30N 8 40 E
Maciejowice **28** 51 36N 21 26 E
McIlwraith Ra. **97** 13 50S 143 20 E
Măcin **46** 45 16N 28 8 E
Macina **84** 14 50N 5 0W
McIntosh **116** 45 57N 101 20W
McIntosh L. **109** 55 45N 105 0W
Macintyre → **97** 28 37S 150 47 E
Macizo Galaico **30** 42 30N 7 30W
Mackay, Austral. **97** 21 8S 149 11 E
Mackay, U.S.A. **118** 43 58N 113 37W
Mackay → **108** 57 10N 111 38W
Mackay, L. **96** 22 30S 129 0 E
McKees Rock **112** 40 27N 80 3W
McKeesport **114** 40 21N 79 50W
Mackenzie **108** 55 20N 123 05W
McKenzie **115** 36 10N 88 31W
Mackenzie □ **104** 61 30N 115 0W
Mackenzie →, Austral. **97** 23 38S 149 46 E
Mackenzie →, Can. **104** 69 10N 134 20W
McKenzie → **118** 44 2N 123 6W
Mackenzie City = Linden **126** 6 0N 58 10W
Mackenzie Highway **108** 58 0N 117 15W
Mackenzie Mts. **104** 64 0N 130 0W
Mackinaw City **114** 45 47N 84 44W
McKinlay **98** 21 16S 141 18 E
McKinlay → **98** 20 50S 141 28 E
McKinley, Mt. **104** 63 2N 151 0W
McKinley Sea **4** 84 0N 10 0W
McKinney **117** 33 10N 96 40W
Mackinnon Road **90** 3 40S 39 1 E
McKittrick **119** 35 18N 119 39W
Macksville **99** 30 40S 152 56 E
McLaughlin **116** 45 50N 100 50W
Maclean **97** 29 26S 153 16 E
McLean **117** 35 15N 100 35W
McLeansboro **116** 38 5N 88 30W
Maclear **93** 31 2S 28 23 E
Macleay → **97** 30 56S 153 0 E
McLennan **108** 55 42N 116 50W
MacLeod, B. **109** 62 53N 110 0W
McLeod L. **96** 24 9S 113 47 E
MacLeod Lake **108** 54 58N 123 0W
M'Clintock Chan. **104** 72 0N 102 0W
McLoughlin, Mt. **118** 42 10N 122 19W
McLure **108** 51 2N 120 13W

McMechen 112 39 57N 80 44W
McMillan L. 117 32 40N 104 20W
McMinnville, Oreg., U.S.A. 118 45 16N 123 11W
McMinnville, Tenn., U.S.A. 115 35 43N 85 45W
McMorran 109 51 19N 108 42W
McMurdo Sd. 5 77 0S 170 0E
McMurray = Fort McMurray 108 56 45N 111 27W
McNary 119 34 4N 109 53W
McNaughton L. 108 52 0N 118 10W
Macodoene 93 23 32S 35 5E
Macomb 116 40 25N 90 40W
Macomer 40 40 16N 8 48E
Mâcon 21 46 19N 4 50E
Macon, Ga., U.S.A. 115 32 50N 83 37W
Macon, Miss., U.S.A. 115 33 7N 88 31W
Macon, Mo., U.S.A. 116 39 40N 92 26W
Macondo 89 12 37S 23 46E
Macossa 91 17 55S 33 56E
Macoun L. 109 56 32N 103 40W
Macovane 93 21 30S 35 0E
McPherson 116 38 25N 97 40W
Macpherson Ra. 99 28 15S 153 15E
Macquarie → 97 30 5S 147 30E
Macquarie Harbour 97 42 15S 145 23E
Macquarie Is. 94 54 36S 158 55E
Macquarie, L. 100 33 4S 151 36E
MacRobertson Coast 5 68 30S 63 0E
Macroom 15 51 54N 8 57W
Macubela 91 16 53S 37 49E
Macugnaga 38 45 57N 7 58E
Macuiza 91 18 7S 34 29E
Macuse 91 17 45S 37 10E
Macuspana 120 17 46N 92 36W
Macusse 92 17 48S 20 23E
Mácuzari, Presa 120 27 10N 109 10W
McVille 116 47 46N 98 11W
Madā 'in Salih 86 26 51N 37 58E
Madagali 85 10 56N 13 33E
Madagascar ■ 93 20 0S 47 0E
Madā'in Sālih 64 26 46N 37 57E
Madama 83 22 0N 13 40E
Madame I. 107 45 30N 60 58W
Madan 43 41 30N 24 57E
Madanapalle 70 13 33N 78 28E
Madang 94 5 12S 145 49E
Madaoua 85 14 5N 6 27E
Madara 85 11 45N 10 35E
Madaripur 69 23 19N 90 15E
Madauk 67 17 56N 96 52E
Madawaska 112 45 30N 77 55W
Madawaska → 106 45 27N 76 21W
Madaya 67 22 12N 96 10E
Madbar 87 6 17N 30 45E
Maddalena 40 41 15N 9 23E
Maddalena, La 40 41 13N 9 25E
Maddaloni 41 41 4N 14 23E
Madden Dam 120 9 13N 79 37W
Madden Lake 120 9 20N 79 37W
Madeira 80 32 50N 17 0W
Madeira → 126 3 22S 58 45W
Madeleine, Îs. de la 107 47 30N 61 40W
Madera 119 37 0N 120 1W
Madha 70 18 0N 75 30E
Madhubani 69 26 21N 86 7E
Madhya Pradesh □ 68 21 50N 81 0E
Madill 117 34 5N 96 49W
Madimba 88 5 0S 15 0E
Madīnat ash Sha'b 63 12 50N 45 0E
Madingou 88 4 10S 13 33E
Madirovalo 93 16 26S 46 32E
Madison, Fla., U.S.A. 115 30 29N 83 39W
Madison, Ind., U.S.A. 114 38 42N 85 20W
Madison, Nebr., U.S.A. 116 41 53N 97 25W
Madison, Ohio, U.S.A. 112 41 45N 81 4W
Madison, S.D., U.S.A. 116 44 0N 97 8W
Madison, Wis., U.S.A. 116 43 5N 89 25W
Madison → 118 45 56N 111 30W
Madison Junc. 118 44 42N 110 56W
Madisonville, Ky., U.S.A. 114 37 20N 87 30W
Madisonville, Tex., U.S.A. 117 30 57N 95 55W
Madista 92 21 15S 25 6E
Madiun 73 7 38S 111 32E
Madley 13 52 3N 2 51W
Madol 87 9 3N 27 45E
Madon → 19 48 36N 6 6E
Madona 54 56 53N 26 5E
Madonie, Le 40 37 50N 13 50E
Madras, India 70 13 8N 80 19E
Madras, U.S.A. 118 44 40N 121 10W
Madras = Tamil Nadu □ 70 11 0N 77 0E
Madre de Dios → 126 10 59S 66 8W
Madre de Dios, I. 128 50 20S 75 10W
Madre del Sur, Sierra 120 17 30N 100 0W
Madre, Laguna, Mexico 120 25 0N 97 30W
Madre, Laguna, U.S.A. 117 25 0N 97 40W
Madre Occidental, Sierra 120 27 0N 107 0W
Madre Oriental, Sierra 120 25 0N 100 0W
Madre, Sierra, Mexico 120 16 0N 93 0W
Madre, Sierra, Phil. 73 17 0N 122 0E
Madri 68 24 16N 73 32E
Madrid 30 40 25N 3 45W
Madrid □ 30 40 30N 3 45W
Madridejos 31 39 28N 3 33W
Madrigal de las Altas Torres 30 41 5N 5 0W
Madrona, Sierra 31 38 27N 4 16W
Madroñera 31 39 26N 5 42W
Madu 87 14 37N 26 4E
Madura, Selat 73 7 30S 113 20E
Madurai 70 9 55N 78 10E
Madurantakam 70 12 30N 79 50E
Madzhalis 57 42 9N 47 47E
Mae Hong Son 71 19 16N 98 1E
Mae Sot 71 16 43N 98 34E
Maebashi 74 36 24N 139 4E
Maella 32 41 8N 0 7E
Măeruş 46 45 53N 25 31E
Maesteg 13 51 36N 3 40W
Maestra, Sierra 121 20 15N 77 0W
Maestrazgo, Mts. del 32 40 30N 0 25W
Maevatanana 93 16 56N 46 49E
Ma'fan 83 25 56N 14 29E
Mafeking, Can. 109 52 40N 101 10W
Mafeking, S. Afr. 92 25 50S 25 38E
Maféré 84 5 30N 3 2W
Mafeteng 92 29 51S 27 15E
Maffra 99 37 53S 146 58E
Mafia 90 7 45S 39 50E
Mafra, Brazil 125 26 10S 50 0W
Mafra, Port. 31 38 55N 9 20W
Mafungabusi Plateau 91 18 30S 29 8E
Magadan 59 59 38N 150 50E
Magadi 90 1 54S 36 19E
Magadi, L. 90 1 54S 36 19E
Magaliesburg 93 26 1S 27 32E
Magallanes, Estrecho de 128 52 30S 75 0W
Magangué 126 9 14N 74 45W
Magaria 85 13 4N 9 5E
Magburaka 84 8 47N 12 0W
Magdalena, Argent. 124 35 5S 57 30W
Magdalena, Boliv. 126 13 13S 63 57W
Magdalena, Malay. 72 4 25N 117 55E
Magdalena, Mexico 120 30 50N 112 0W
Magdalena, U.S.A. 119 34 10N 107 20W
Magdalena →, Colomb. 126 11 6N 74 51W
Magdalena →, Mexico 120 30 40N 112 25W
Magdalena, B. 120 24 30N 112 10W
Magdalena, I. 120 24 40N 112 15W
Magdalena, Llano de la 120 25 0N 111 30W
Magdeburg 24 52 8N 11 36E
Magdeburg □ 24 52 20N 11 30E
Magdi'el 62 32 10N 34 54E
Magdub 87 13 42N 25 5E
Magee 117 31 53N 89 45W
Magee, I. 15 54 48N 5 44W
Magelang 73 7 29S 110 13E
Magellan's Str. = Magallanes, Est. de 128 52 30S 75 0W
Magenta 38 45 28N 8 53E
Maggia → 25 46 18N 8 36E
Maggiorasca, Mte. 38 44 33N 9 29E
Maggiore, L. 38 46 0N 8 35E
Maghama 84 15 32N 12 57W
Maghār 62 32 54N 35 24E
Magherafelt 15 54 44N 6 37W
Maghnia 82 34 50N 1 43W
Magione 39 43 10N 12 12E
Maglaj 42 44 33N 18 7E
Magliano in Toscana 39 42 36N 11 18E
Máglie 41 40 8N 18 17E
Magnac-Laval 20 46 13N 1 11E
Magnetic Pole, 1976 (North) 4 76 12N 100 12W
Magnetic Pole, 1976 (South) 5 68 48S 139 30E
Magnisia □ 44 39 15N 22 45E
Magnitogorsk 52 53 27N 59 4E
Magnolia, Ark., U.S.A. 117 33 18N 93 12W
Magnolia, Miss., U.S.A. 117 31 8N 90 28W
Magnor 47 59 56N 12 15E
Magny-en-Vexin 19 49 9N 1 47E
Magog 107 45 18N 72 9W
Magoro 90 1 45N 34 12E
Magosa = Famagusta 64 35 8N 33 55E
Magoye 91 16 1S 27 30E
Magpie L. 107 51 0N 64 41W
Magrath 108 49 25N 112 50W
Magro → 33 39 11N 0 25W
Magrur, Wadi → 87 16 5N 26 30E
Magu □ 90 2 31S 33 28E
Maguarinho, C. 127 0 15S 48 30W
Maguse L. 109 61 40N 95 10W
Maguse Pt. 109 61 20N 93 50W
Magwe 67 20 10N 95 0E
Mahābād 64 36 50N 45 45E
Mahabaleshwar 70 17 58N 73 43E
Mahabharat Lekh 69 28 30N 82 0E
Mahabo 93 20 23S 44 40E
Mahad 70 18 6N 73 29E
Mahadeo Hills 68 22 20N 78 30E
Mahadeopur 70 18 48N 80 0E
Mahagi 90 2 20N 31 0E
Mahajamba → 93 15 33S 47 8E
Mahajamba, Helodranon' i 93 15 24S 47 5E
Mahajan 68 28 48N 73 56E
Mahajanga □ 93 17 0S 47 0E
Mahajilo → 93 19 42S 45 22E
Mahakam → 72 0 35S 117 17E
Mahalapye 92 23 1S 26 51E
Maḥallāt 65 33 55N 50 30E
Mahanadi → 69 20 20N 86 25E
Mahanoro 93 19 54S 48 48E
Mahanoy City 113 40 48N 76 10W
Maharashtra □ 70 20 30N 75 30E
Maharès 83 34 32N 10 29E
Mahari Mts. 90 6 20S 30 0E
Mahasolo 93 19 7S 46 22E
Mahaweli → Ganga 70 8 30N 81 15E
Mahboobabad 70 17 42N 80 2E
Mahbubnagar 70 16 45N 77 59E
Mahdia 83 35 28N 11 0E
Mahé 70 11 42N 75 34E
Mahendra Giri 70 8 20N 77 30E
Mahenge 91 8 45S 36 41E
Maheno 101 45 10S 170 50E
Mahia Pen. 101 39 9S 177 55E
Mahirija 82 34 0N 3 16W
Mahmiya 87 17 12N 33 43E
Mahmud Kot 68 30 16N 71 0E
Mahmudia 46 45 5N 29 5E
Mahnomen 116 47 22N 95 57W
Mahoba 69 25 15N 79 55E
Mahón 32 39 53N 4 16E
Mahone Bay 107 44 30N 64 20W
Mahuta 85 11 32N 4 58E
Mai-Ndombe, L. 88 2 0S 18 20E
Maîche 19 47 16N 6 48E
Maicurú → 127 2 14S 54 17W
Máida 41 38 51N 16 21E
Maidenhead 13 51 31N 0 42W
Maidi 87 16 20N 42 45E
Maidstone, Can. 109 53 5N 109 20W
Maidstone, U.K. 13 51 16N 0 31E
Maiduguri 85 12 0N 13 20E
Maignelay 19 49 32N 2 30E
Maigudo 87 7 30N 37 8E
Maijdi 69 22 48N 91 10E
Maikala Ra. 69 22 0N 81 0E
Mailly-le-Camp 19 48 41N 4 12E
Mailsi 68 29 48N 72 15E
Main →, Ger. 25 50 0N 8 18E
Main →, U.K. 15 54 49N 6 20W
Main Centre 109 50 35N 107 21W
Mainburg 25 48 37N 11 49E
Maine 18 48 0N 0 0E
Maine □ 107 45 20N 69 0W
Maine → 15 52 10N 9 40W
Maine-et-Loire □ 18 47 31N 0 30W
Maïne-Soroa 85 13 13N 12 2E
Maingkwan 67 26 15N 96 37E
Mainit, L. 73 9 31N 125 30E
Mainland, Orkney, U.K. 14 59 0N 3 10W
Mainland, Shetland, U.K. 14 60 15N 1 22W
Mainpuri 68 27 18N 79 4E
Maintenon 19 48 35N 1 35E
Maintirano 93 18 3S 44 1E
Mainz 25 50 0N 8 17E
Maipú 124 36 52S 57 50W
Maiquetía 126 10 36N 66 57W
Maira → 38 44 49N 7 38E
Mairabari 67 26 30N 92 22E
Maisi, Pta. de 121 20 10N 74 10W
Maisse 19 48 24N 2 21E
Maitland, N.S.W., Austral. 97 32 33S 151 36E
Maitland, S. Australia, Austral. 99 34 23S 137 40E
Maitland → 112 43 45N 81 33W
Maiyema 85 12 5N 4 25E
Maizuru 74 35 25N 135 22E
Majalengka 73 6 55S 108 14E
Majd el Kurūm 62 32 56N 35 15E
Majene 73 3 38S 118 57E
Majevica Planina 42 44 45N 18 50E
Maji 87 6 12N 35 30E
Major 109 51 52N 109 37W
Majorca, I. = Mallorca 32 39 30N 3 0E
Maka 84 13 40N 14 10W
Makak 85 3 36N 11 0E
Makale 73 3 6S 119 51E
Makamba 90 4 8S 29 49E
Makari 88 12 35N 14 28E
Makarikari = Makgadikgadi Salt Pans 92 20 40S 25 45E
Makarovo 59 57 40N 107 45E
Makarska 42 43 20N 17 2E
Makaryev 55 57 52N 43 50E
Makasar = Ujung Pandang 73 5 10S 119 20E
Makasar, Selat 73 1 0S 118 20E
Makat 58 47 39N 53 19E
Makedhonia □ 44 40 39N 22 0E
Makedonija □ 42 41 53N 21 40E
Makena 110 20 39N 156 27W
Makeni 84 8 55N 12 5W
Makeyevka 56 48 0N 38 0E
Makgadikgadi Salt Pans 92 20 40S 25 45E
Makhachkala 57 43 0N 47 30E
Makhambet, U.S.S.R. 57 47 43N 51 40E
Makhambet, U.S.S.R. 57 47 40N 51 35E
Makharadze 57 41 55N 42 2E
Makian 73 0 20N 127 20E
Makin 94 3 30N 174 0E
Makindu 90 2 18S 37 50E
Makinsk 58 52 37N 70 26E
Makkah 86 21 30N 39 54E
Makkovik 107 55 10N 59 10W
Maklakovo 59 58 16N 92 29E
Makó 27 46 14N 20 33E
Makokou 88 0 40N 12 50E
Makongo 90 3 25N 26 17E
Makoro 90 3 10N 29 59E
Makoua 88 0 5S 15 50E
Maków Mazowiecki 28 52 52N 21 6E
Maków Podhal 27 49 43N 19 45E
Makrá 45 36 15N 25 54E
Makran 65 26 13N 61 30E
Makran Coast Range 66 25 40N 64 0E
Makrana 68 27 2N 74 46E
Mákri 44 40 52N 25 40E
Maksimkin Yar 58 58 42N 86 50E
Maktar 83 35 48N 9 12E
Mākū 64 39 15N 44 31E
Makumbi 88 5 50S 20 43E
Makunda 92 22 30S 20 7E
Makurazaki 74 31 15N 130 20E
Makurdi 85 7 43N 8 35E
Makwassie 92 27 17S 26 0E
Mal B. 15 52 50N 9 30W
Mal i Gjalicës së Lumës 44 42 2N 20 25E
Mal i Gribës 44 40 17N 19 45E
Mal i Nemërçkës 44 40 15N 20 15E
Mal i Tomorit 44 40 42N 20 11E
Mala Kapela 39 44 45N 15 30E
Mala, Pta. 121 7 28N 80 2W
Malabang 73 7 36N 124 3E
Malabar Coast 70 11 0N 75 0E
Malacca, Str. of 71 3 0N 101 0E
Malacky 27 48 27N 17 0E
Malad City 118 42 10N 112 20E
Málaga 31 36 43N 4 23W
Malaga 117 32 12N 104 2W
Málaga □ 31 36 38N 4 58W
Malagarasi 90 5 5S 30 50E
Malagarasi → 90 5 12S 29 47E
Malagón 31 39 11N 3 52W
Malagón → 31 37 35N 7 29W
Malaimbandy 93 20 20S 45 36E
Malakâl 87 9 33N 31 40E
Malakand 66 34 40N 71 55E
Malakoff 117 32 10N 95 55W
Malamyzh 59 50 0N 136 50E
Malang 73 7 59S 112 45E
Malange 88 9 36S 16 17E
Mälaren 48 59 30N 17 10E
Malargüe 124 35 32S 69 30W
Malartic 106 48 9N 78 9W
Malatya 64 38 25N 38 20E
Malawi ■ 91 13 0S 34 0E
Malawi, L. 91 12 30S 34 30E
Malay Pen. 71 7 25N 100 0E
Malaya □ 71 4 0N 102 0E
Malaya Belozërka 56 47 12N 34 56E
Malaya Vishera 54 58 55N 32 25E
Malaya Viska 56 48 39N 31 36E
Malaybalay 73 8 5N 125 7E
Malāyer 64 34 19N 48 51E
Malaysia ■ 72 5 0N 110 0E
Malazgirt 64 39 10N 42 33E
Malbaie, La 107 47 40N 70 10W
Malbon 98 21 5S 140 17E
Malbork 28 54 3N 19 1E
Malcésine 38 45 46N 10 48E
Malchin 24 53 43N 12 44E
Malchow 24 53 29N 12 25E
Malcolm 96 28 51S 121 25E
Malczyce 28 51 14N 16 29E
Maldegem 16 51 14N 3 26E
Malden, Mass., U.S.A. 113 42 26N 71 5W
Malden, Mo., U.S.A. 117 36 35N 90 0W
Malden I. 95 4 3S 155 1W
Maldives ■ 60 7 0N 73 0E
Maldonado 125 35 0S 55 0W
Maldonado, Punta 120 16 19N 98 35W
Malé 38 46 20N 10 55E
Malé Karpaty 27 48 30N 17 20E
Maléa, Ákra 45 36 28N 23 7E
Malegaon 68 20 30N 74 38E
Malei 91 17 12S 36 58E
Malela 90 4 22S 26 8E
Målerås 49 56 54N 15 34E
Malerkotla 68 30 32N 75 58E
Máles 45 35 6N 25 35E
Malesherbes 19 48 15N 2 24E
Maleshevska Planina 42 41 38N 23 7E
Malestroit 18 47 49N 2 25W
Malfa 41 38 35N 14 50E
Malgobek 57 43 30N 44 34E
Malgomaj 50 64 40N 16 30E
Malgrat 32 41 39N 2 46E
Malha 81 15 8N 25 10E
Malheur → 118 44 3N 116 59W
Malheur L. 118 43 19N 118 42W
Mali 84 12 10N 12 20W
Mali ■ 85 15 0N 2 0W
Mali → 67 25 40N 97 40E
Mali Kanal 42 45 36N 19 24E
Mali Kyun 71 13 0N 98 20E
Malih → 62 32 20N 35 34E
Malik 73 0 39S 123 16E
Malili 73 2 42S 121 6E
Malimba, Mts. 90 7 30S 29 30E
Malin 54 50 46N 29 3E
Malin Hd. 15 55 18N 7 24W
Malinau 72 3 35N 116 40E
Malindi 90 3 12S 40 5E
Maling 73 1 0N 121 0E
Malingping 73 6 45S 106 2E
Malinyi 91 8 56S 36 0E
Maliqi 44 40 45N 20 48E
Malita 73 6 19N 125 39E
Maljenik 42 43 59N 21 55E
Malkapur, Maharashtra, India 68 20 53N 73 58E
Malkapur, Maharashtra, India 70 16 57N 73 58E
Małkinia Górna 28 52 42N 22 5E
Malko Tŭrnovo 43 41 59N 27 31E
Mallacoota 100 37 40S 149 40E
Mallacoota Inlet 97 37 34S 149 40E
Mallaig 14 57 0N 5 50W
Mallawan 69 27 4N 80 12E
Mallawi 86 27 44N 30 44E
Mallemort 21 43 44N 5 11E
Málles Venosta 38 46 42N 10 32E
Mállia 45 35 17N 25 27E
Mallorca 32 39 30N 3 0E
Mallorytown 113 44 29N 75 53W
Mallow 15 52 8N 8 40W
Malmbäck 49 57 34N 14 28E
Malmberget 50 67 11N 20 40E
Malmédy 16 50 25N 6 2E
Malmesbury 92 33 28S 18 41E
Malmö 49 55 36N 12 59E
Malmöhus län □ 49 55 45N 13 30E
Malmslätt 49 58 27N 15 33E
Malmyzh 55 56 35N 50 41E
Malnaş 46 46 2N 25 49E
Malo Konare 43 42 12N 24 24E
Maloarkhangelsk 55 52 28N 36 30E
Malolos 73 14 50N 120 49E
Malombe L. 91 14 40S 35 15E
Malomir 43 42 16N 26 30E
Malone 114 44 50N 74 19W
Malorad 43 43 28N 23 4! E
Malorita 54 51 50N 24 3E
Maloyaroslovets 55 55 2N 36 20E
Malozemelskaya Tundra 52 67 0N 50 0E
Malpartida 31 39 26N 6 30W
Malpelo 126 4 3N 81 35W
Malpica 30 43 19N 8 50W
Malprabha → 70 16 20N 76 5E
Malta, Idaho, U.S.A. 118 42 15N 113 30W
Malta, Mont., U.S.A. 118 48 20N 107 55W
Malta ■ 36 35 50N 14 30E
Malta Channel 40 36 40N 14 0E
Malton, Can. 112 43 42N 79 38W
Malton, U.K. 12 54 9N 0 48W
Maluku 73 1 0S 127 0E
Maluku □ 73 3 0S 128 0E
Maluku, Kepulauan 73 3 0S 128 0E
Malumfashi 85 11 48N 7 39E
Malung 48 60 42N 13 44E
Malvalli 70 12 28N 77 8E
Malvan 70 16 2N 73 30E
Malvern, U.K. 13 52 7N 2 19W
Malvern, U.S.A. 117 34 22N 92 50W
Malvern Hills 13 52 0N 2 19W
Malvérnia 93 22 6S 31 42E
Malvik 47 63 25N 10 40E
Malvinas, Is. = Falkland Is. 128 51 30S 59 0W
Malya 90 3 5S 33 38E
Malyy Lyakhovskiy, Ostrov 59 74 7N 140 36E
Mama 59 58 18N 112 54E
Mamadysh 55 55 44N 51 23E
Mamahatun 64 39 50N 40 23E

Mamaia **46** 44 18N 28 37 E
Mamanguape **127** 6 50 S 35 4W
Mamasa **73** 2 55 S 119 20 E
Mambasa **90** 1 22N 29 3 E
Mamberamo → **73** 2 0 S 137 50 E
Mambilima **91** 10 31 S 28 45 E
Mambirima **91** 11 25 S 27 33 E
Mambo **90** 4 52 S 38 22 E
Mambrui **90** 3 5 S 40 5 E
Mamburao **73** 13 13N 120 39 E
Mameigwess L. **106** 52 35N 87 50W
Mamers **18** 48 21N 0 22 E
Mamfe **85** 5 50N 9 15 E
Mámmola **41** 38 23N 16 13 E
Mammoth **119** 32 46N 110 43W
Mamoré → **126** 10 23 S 65 53W
Mamou **84** 10 15N 12 0W
Mampatá **84** 11 54N 14 53W
Mampawah **72** 0 30N 109 5 E
Mampong **85** 7 6N 1 26W
Mamry, Jezioro **28** 54 5N 21 50 E
Mamuju **73** 2 41 S 118 50 E
Man **84** 7 30N 7 40W
Man → **70** 17 31N 75 32 E
Man, I. of **12** 54 15N 4 30W
Man Na **67** 23 27N 97 19 E
Mana **127** 5 45N 53 55W
Måna → **47** 59 55N 8 50 E
Manaar, Gulf of **70** 8 30N 79 0 E
Manacapuru **126** 3 16 S 60 37W
Manacor **32** 39 34N 3 13 E
Manado **73** 1 29N 124 51 E
Managua **121** 12 6N 86 20W
Managua, L. **121** 12 20N 86 30W
Manakara **93** 22 8 S 48 1 E
Manam I. **98** 4 5 S 145 0 E
Manamāh, Al **65** 26 11N 50 35 E
Manambao → **93** 17 35 S 44 0 E
Manambato **93** 13 43 S 49 7 E
Manambolo → **93** 19 18 S 44 22 E
Manambolosy **93** 16 2 S 49 40 E
Mananara **93** 16 10 S 49 46 E
Mananara → **93** 23 21 S 47 42 E
Mananjary **93** 21 13 S 48 20 E
Manantenina **93** 24 17 S 47 19 E
Manaos = Manaus **126** 3 0 S 60 0W
Manapouri **101** 45 34 S 167 39 E
Manapouri, L. **101** 45 32 S 167 32 E
Manar → **70** 18 50N 77 20 E
Manas **75** 44 17N 85 56 E
Manasir **65** 24 30N 51 10 E
Manaslu, Mt. **69** 28 33N 84 33 E
Manasquan **113** 40 7N 74 3W
Manassa **119** 37 12N 105 58W
Manaung **67** 18 45N 93 40 E
Manaus **126** 3 0 S 60 0W
Manawan L. **109** 55 24N 103 14W
Manay **73** 7 17N 126 33 E
Mancelona **114** 44 54N 85 5W
Mancha, La **33** 39 10N 2 54W
Mancha Real **31** 37 48N 3 39W
Manche □ **18** 49 10N 1 20W
Manchegorsk **52** 67 40N 32 40 E
Manchester, U.K. **12** 53 30N 2 15W
Manchester, Conn., U.S.A. **114** 41 47N 72 30W
Manchester, Ga., U.S.A. **115** 32 53N 84 32W
Manchester, Iowa, U.S.A. **116** 42 28N 91 27W
Manchester, Ky., U.S.A. **114** 37 9N 83 45W
Manchester, N.H., U.S.A. **114** 42 58N 71 29W
Manchester, N.Y., U.S.A. **112** 42 56N 77 16W
Manchester, Vt., U.S.A. **113** 43 10N 73 5W
Manchester L. **109** 61 28N 107 29W
Manciano **39** 42 35N 11 30 E
Mancifa **87** 6 53N 41 50 E
Mand → **65** 28 20N 52 30 E
Manda, Chunya, Tanz. **90** 6 51 S 32 29 E
Manda, Ludewe, Tanz. **91** 10 30 S 34 40 E
Mandaguari **125** 23 32 S 51 42W
Mandal **47** 58 2N 7 25 E
Mandalay **67** 22 0N 96 4 E
Mandale = Mandalay **67** 22 0N 96 4 E
Mandalī **64** 33 43N 45 28 E
Mandalya Körfezi **45** 37 15N 27 20 E
Mandan **116** 46 50N 101 0W
Mandapeta **70** 16 47N 81 56 E
Mandar, Teluk **73** 3 35 S 119 15 E
Mandas **40** 39 40N 9 8 E
Mandasaur **68** 24 3N 75 8 E
Mandasor = Mandasaur **68** 24 3N 75 8 E
Mandawai (Katingan) → **72** 3 30 S 113 0 E
Mandelieu-la-Napoule **21** 43 34N 6 57 E
Mandera **90** 3 55N 41 53 E
Mandera □ **90** 3 30N 41 0 E
Mandi **68** 31 39N 76 58 E
Mandioli **73** 0 40 S 127 20 E
Mandla **69** 22 39N 80 30 E
Mandø **49** 55 18N 8 33 E
Mandoto **93** 19 34 S 46 17 E
Mandoúdhion **45** 38 48N 23 29 E
Mandráki **45** 36 36N 27 11 E
Mandrare → **93** 25 10 S 46 30 E
Mandritsara **93** 15 50 S 48 49 E
Mandúria **41** 40 25N 17 38 E
Mandvi **68** 22 51N 69 22 E
Mandya **70** 12 30N 77 0 E
Mandzai **68** 30 55N 67 6 E
Mané **85** 12 59N 1 21W
Manengouba, Mts. **85** 5 0N 9 50 E
Maner → **70** 18 30N 79 40 E
Maneroo **98** 23 22 S 143 53 E
Maneroo Cr. → **98** 23 21 S 143 53 E
Manfalût **86** 27 20N 30 52 E
Manfred **99** 33 19 S 143 45 E
Manfredónia **41** 41 40N 15 55 E
Manfredónia, G. di **41** 41 30N 16 10 E
Manga, Niger **85** 15 0N 14 0 E
Manga, Upp. Vol. **85** 11 40N 1 4W
Mangaia **101** 21 55 S 157 55W
Mangalagiri **70** 16 26N 80 36 E
Mangalia **46** 43 50N 28 35 E
Mangalore **70** 12 55N 74 47 E
Manganeses **30** 41 45N 5 43W
Mangaon **70** 18 15N 73 20 E
Manger **47** 60 38N 5 3 E
Manggar **72** 2 50 S 108 10 E
Manggawitu **73** 4 8 S 133 32 E
Mangkalihat, Tanjung **73** 1 2N 118 59 E
Manglaur **68** 29 44N 77 49 E
Mangnai **75** 37 52N 91 43 E
Mango **85** 10 20N 0 30 E
Mangoky → **93** 21 29 S 43 41 E
Mangole **73** 1 50 S 125 55 E
Mangombe **90** 1 20 S 26 48 E
Mangonui **101** 35 1 S 173 32 E
Mangualde **30** 40 38N 7 48W
Mangueigne **81** 10 30N 21 15 E
Mangueira, Lagoa da **125** 33 0 S 52 50W
Manguéni, Hamada **83** 22 35N 12 40 E
Mangum **117** 34 50N 99 30W
Mangyshlak P-ov. **57** 44 30N 52 30 E
Mangyshlakskiy Zaliv **57** 44 40N 50 50 E
Manhattan, Kans., U.S.A. **116** 39 10N 96 40W
Manhattan, Nev., U.S.A. **119** 38 31N 117 3W
Manhiça **93** 25 23 S 32 49 E
Manhuaçu **127** 20 15 S 42 2W
Mania → **93** 19 42 S 45 22 E
Maniago **39** 46 11N 12 40 E
Manica e Sofala □ **93** 19 10 S 33 45 E
Manicaland □ **91** 19 0 S 32 30 E
Manicoré **126** 5 48 S 61 16W
Manicouagan → **107** 49 30N 68 30W
Manicouagan L. **107** 51 25N 68 15W
Manīfah **64** 27 44N 49 0 E
Manigotagan **109** 51 6N 96 18W
Manigotagan L. **109** 50 52N 95 37W
Manihiki **95** 10 24 S 161 1W
Manika, Plat. de la **91** 10 0 S 25 5 E
Manila, Phil. **73** 14 40N 121 3 E
Manila, U.S.A. **118** 41 0N 109 44W
Manila B. **73** 14 0N 120 0 E
Manilla **99** 30 45 S 150 43 E
Manimpé **84** 14 11N 5 28W
Manipur □ **67** 25 0N 94 0 E
Manipur → **67** 23 45N 94 20 E
Manisa **64** 38 38N 27 30 E
Manistee **114** 44 15N 86 20W
Manistee → **114** 44 15N 86 21W
Manistique **114** 45 59N 86 18W
Manito L. **109** 52 43N 109 43W
Manitoba □ **109** 55 30N 97 0W
Manitoba, L. **109** 51 0N 98 45W
Manitou **109** 49 15N 98 32W
Manitou I. **106** 47 22N 87 30W
Manitou Is. **114** 45 8N 86 0W
Manitou L., Ont., Can. **109** 49 15N 93 0W
Manitou L., Qué., Can. **107** 50 55N 65 17W
Manitou Springs **116** 38 52N 104 55W
Manitoulin I. **106** 45 40N 82 30W
Manitowaning **106** 45 46N 81 49W
Manitowoc **114** 44 8N 87 40W
Manizales **126** 5 5N 75 32W
Manja **93** 21 26 S 44 20 E
Manjakandriana **93** 18 55 S 47 47 E
Manjeri **70** 11 7N 76 11 E
Manjhand **68** 25 50N 68 10 E
Manjil **64** 36 46N 49 30 E
Manjimup **96** 34 15 S 116 6 E
Manjra → **70** 18 49N 77 52 E
Mankato, Kans., U.S.A. **116** 39 49N 98 11W
Mankato, Minn., U.S.A. **116** 44 8N 93 59W
Mankayana **93** 26 38 S 31 6 E
Mankono **84** 8 1N 6 10W
Mankota **109** 49 25N 107 5W
Manlleu **32** 42 2N 2 17 E
Manly **99** 33 48 S 151 17 E
Manmad **70** 20 18N 74 28 E
Manna **72** 4 25 S 102 55 E
Mannahill **99** 32 25 S 140 0 E
Mannar **70** 9 1N 79 54 E
Mannar, G. of **70** 8 30N 79 0 E
Mannar I. **70** 9 5N 79 45 E
Mannargudi **70** 10 45N 79 51 E
Mannheim **25** 49 28N 8 29 E
Manning, Can. **108** 56 53N 117 39W
Manning, U.S.A. **115** 33 40N 80 9W
Manning → **100** 31 52 S 152 43 E
Manning Prov. Park **108** 49 5N 120 45W
Mannington **114** 39 35N 80 25W
Mannu → **40** 39 15N 9 32 E
Mannu, C. **40** 40 2N 8 24 E
Mannum **99** 34 50 S 139 20 E
Mano **84** 8 3N 12 2W
Manokwari **73** 0 54 S 134 0 E
Manolás **45** 38 4N 21 21 E
Manombo **93** 22 57 S 43 28 E
Manono **90** 7 15 S 27 25 E
Manosque **21** 43 49N 5 47 E
Manouane L. **107** 50 45N 70 45W
Manresa **32** 41 48N 1 50 E
Mans, Le **18** 48 0N 0 10 E
Mansa, Gujarat, India **68** 23 27N 72 45 E
Mansa, Punjab, India **68** 30 0N 75 27 E
Mansa, Zambia **91** 11 13 S 28 55 E
Mansel I. **105** 62 0N 80 0W
Mansfield, Austral. **100** 37 4 S 146 6 E
Mansfield, U.K. **12** 53 8N 1 12W
Mansfield, La., U.S.A. **117** 32 2N 93 40W
Mansfield, Mass., U.S.A. **113** 42 2N 71 12W
Mansfield, Ohio, U.S.A. **114** 40 45N 82 30W
Mansfield, Pa., U.S.A. **112** 41 48N 77 4W
Mansfield, Wash., U.S.A. **118** 47 51N 119 44W
Mansilla de las Mulas **30** 42 30N 5 25W
Mansle **20** 45 52N 0 9 E
Mansoa **84** 12 0N 15 20W
Manson Creek **108** 55 37N 124 32W
Mansoura **83** 36 1N 4 31 E
Manta **126** 1 0 S 80 40W
Mantalingajan, Mt. **72** 8 55N 117 45 E
Mantare **90** 2 42 S 33 13 E
Manteca **119** 37 50N 121 12W
Manteo **115** 35 55N 75 41W
Mantes-la-Jolie **19** 49 0N 1 41 E
Manthani **70** 18 40N 79 35 E
Manthelan **18** 47 9N 0 47 E
Manti **118** 39 23N 111 32W
Mantiqueira, Serra da **125** 22 0 S 44 0W
Manton **114** 44 23N 85 25W
Mantorp **49** 58 21N 15 20 E
Mántova **38** 45 20N 10 42 E
Mänttä **50** 62 0N 24 40 E
Mantua = Mántova **38** 45 20N 10 42 E
Manturovo **55** 58 30N 44 30 E
Manu **126** 12 10 S 70 51W
Manua Is. **101** 14 13 S 169 35W
Manuel Alves → **127** 11 19 S 48 28W
Manui **73** 3 35 S 123 5 E
Manukan **73** 8 14N 123 3 E
Manus I. **98** 2 0 S 147 0 E
Manvi **70** 15 57N 76 59 E
Manville **116** 42 48N 104 36W
Manwath **70** 19 19N 76 32 E
Many **117** 31 36N 93 28W
Manyane **92** 23 21 S 21 42 E
Manyara, L. **90** 3 40 S 35 50 E
Manych → **57** 47 15N 40 0 E
Manych-Gudilo, Oz. **57** 46 24N 42 38 E
Manyonga → **90** 4 10 S 34 15 E
Manyoni **90** 5 45 S 34 55 E
Manyoni □ **90** 6 30 S 34 30 E
Manzai **68** 32 12N 70 15 E
Manzala, Bahra el **86** 31 10N 31 56 E
Manzanares **33** 39 0N 3 22W
Manzaneda, Cabeza de **30** 42 12N 7 15W
Manzanillo, Cuba **121** 20 20N 77 31W
Manzanillo, Mexico **120** 19 0N 104 20W
Manzanillo, Pta. **121** 9 30N 79 40W
Manzano Mts. **119** 34 30N 106 45W
Manzhouli **75** 49 35N 117 25 E
Manzini **93** 26 30 S 31 25 E
Mao **81** 14 4N 15 19 E
Maoke, Pegunungan **73** 3 40 S 137 30 E
Maoming **75** 21 50N 110 54 E
Mapam Yumco **75** 30 45N 81 28 E
Mapia, Kepulauan **73** 0 50N 134 20 E
Mapimí **120** 25 50N 103 50W
Mapimí, Bolsón de **120** 27 30N 104 15W
Mapinga **90** 6 40 S 39 12 E
Mapinhane **93** 22 20 S 35 0 E
Maple Creek **109** 49 55N 109 29W
Mapleton **118** 44 4N 123 58W
Maplewood **116** 38 33N 90 18W
Maprik **98** 3 44 S 143 3 E
Mapuca **70** 15 36N 73 46 E
Mapuera → **126** 1 5 S 57 2W
Maputo **93** 25 58 S 32 32 E
Maputo, B. de **93** 25 50 S 32 45 E
Maqnā **64** 28 25N 34 50 E
Maquela do Zombo **88** 6 0 S 15 15 E
Maquinchao **128** 41 15 S 68 50W
Maquoketa **116** 42 4N 90 40W
Mår → **47** 59 59N 8 46 E
Mar Chiquita, L. **124** 30 40 S 62 50W
Mar del Plata **124** 38 0 S 57 30W
Mar Menor, L. **33** 37 40N 0 45W
Mar, Serra do **125** 25 30 S 49 0W
Mara **90** 1 30 S 34 32 E
Mara □ **90** 1 45 S 34 20 E
Maraã **126** 1 52 S 65 25W
Marabá **127** 5 20 S 49 5W
Maracá, I. de **127** 2 10N 50 30W
Maracaibo **126** 10 40N 71 37W
Maracaibo, Lago de **126** 9 40N 71 30W
Maracaju **125** 21 38 S 55 9W
Maracay **126** 10 15N 67 28W
Marādah **83** 29 15N 19 15 E
Maradi **85** 13 29N 8 10 E
Maradun **85** 12 35N 6 18 E
Marāgheh **64** 37 30N 46 12 E
Marāh **64** 25 0N 45 35 E
Marajó, Ilha de **127** 1 0 S 49 30W
Maralal **90** 1 0N 36 38 E
Maralinga **96** 30 13 S 131 32 E
Marama **99** 35 10 S 140 10 E
Marampa **84** 8 45N 12 28W
Maramureş □ **46** 47 45N 24 0 E
Marana **119** 32 30N 111 9W
Maranchón **32** 41 6N 2 15W
Marand **64** 38 30N 45 45 E
Marandellas **91** 18 5 S 31 42 E
Maranguape **127** 3 55 S 38 50W
Maranhão = São Luis **127** 2 39 S 44 15W
Maranhão □ **127** 5 0 S 46 0W
Marano, L. di **39** 45 42N 13 13 E
Maranoa → **97** 27 50 S 148 37 E
Marañón → **126** 4 30 S 73 35W
Maraş **64** 37 37N 36 53 E
Mărăşeşti **46** 45 52N 27 14 E
Maratea **41** 39 59N 15 43 E
Marateca **31** 38 34N 8 40W
Marathókambos **45** 37 43N 26 42 E
Marathon, Austral. **98** 20 51 S 143 32 E
Marathon, Can. **106** 48 44N 86 23W
Marathón **45** 38 11N 23 58 E
Marathon, N.Y., U.S.A. **113** 42 25N 76 3W
Marathon, Tex., U.S.A. **117** 30 15N 103 15W
Maratua **73** 2 10N 118 35 E
Marbella **31** 36 30N 4 57W
Marble Bar **96** 21 9 S 119 44 E
Marble Falls **117** 30 30N 98 15W
Marblehead **113** 42 29N 70 51W
Marburg **24** 50 49N 8 36 E
Marby **48** 63 7N 14 18 E
Marcal → **27** 47 41N 17 32 E
Marcali **27** 46 35N 17 25 E
Marcaria **38** 45 7N 10 34 E
March **13** 52 33N 0 5 E
Marchand = Rommani **82** 33 20N 6 40W
Marché **20** 46 0N 1 20 E
Marche □ **39** 43 22N 13 10 E
Marche-en-Famenne **16** 50 14N 5 19 E
Marchena **31** 37 18N 5 23W
Marches = Marche **39** 43 22N 13 10 E
Marciana Marina **38** 42 44N 10 12 E
Marcianise **41** 41 3N 14 16 E
Marcigny **21** 46 17N 4 2 E
Marcillac-Vallon **20** 44 29N 2 27 E
Marcillat **20** 46 12N 2 38 E
Marck **19** 50 57N 1 57 E
Marckolsheim **19** 48 10N 7 30 E
Marcos Juárez **124** 32 42 S 62 5W
Marcus **94** 24 0N 153 45 E
Marcus Necker Ridge **94** 20 0N 175 0 E
Marcy Mt. **113** 44 7N 73 55W
Mardin **64** 37 20N 40 43 E
Maree L. **14** 57 40N 5 30W
Mareeba **97** 16 59 S 145 28 E
Marek **73** 4 41 S 120 24 E
Marek = Stanke Dimitrov **42** 42 17N 23 9 E
Maremma **38** 42 45N 11 15 E
Maréna **84** 14 0N 7 20W
Marenberg **39** 46 38N 15 13 E
Marengo **116** 41 42N 92 5W
Marennes **20** 45 49N 1 7W
Marenyi **90** 4 22 S 39 8 E
Marerano **93** 21 23 S 44 52 E
Maréttimo **40** 37 58N 12 5 E
Mareuil-sur-Lay **20** 46 32N 1 14W
Marfa **117** 30 15N 104 0W
Marganets **56** 47 40N 34 40 E
Margao **70** 15 12N 73 58 E
Margaret Bay **108** 51 20N 126 35W
Margaret L. **108** 58 56N 115 25W
Margarita **120** 9 20N 79 55W
Margarita, Isla de **126** 11 0N 64 0W
Margarítion **44** 39 22N 20 26 E
Margate, S. Afr. **93** 30 50 S 30 20 E
Margate, U.K. **13** 51 23N 1 24 E
Margeride, Mts. de la **20** 44 43N 3 38 E
Margherita di Savola **41** 41 25N 16 5 E
Marghita **46** 47 22N 22 22 E
Margonin **28** 52 58N 17 5 E
Marguerite **108** 52 30N 122 25W
Marhoum **82** 34 27N 0 11W
Mari, A.S.S.R. □ **55** 56 30N 48 0 E
María Elena **124** 22 18 S 69 40W
María Grande **124** 31 45 S 59 55W
Maria I. **96** 14 52 S 135 45 E
Maria van Diemen, C. **101** 34 29 S 172 40 E
Mariager **49** 56 40N 10 0 E
Mariager Fjord **49** 56 42N 10 19 E
Mariakani **90** 3 50 S 39 27 E
Marian L. **108** 63 0N 116 15W
Mariana Is. **94** 17 0N 145 0 E
Mariana Trench **94** 13 0N 145 0 E
Marianao **121** 23 8N 82 24W
Marianna, Ark., U.S.A. **117** 34 48N 90 48W
Marianna, Fla., U.S.A. **115** 30 45N 85 15W
Mariannelund **49** 57 37N 15 35 E
Mariánské Lázně **26** 49 48N 12 41 E
Marias → **118** 47 56N 110 30W
Mariato, Punta **121** 7 12N 80 52W
Mariazell **26** 47 47N 15 19 E
Ma'rib **63** 15 25N 45 30 E
Maribo **49** 54 48N 11 30 E
Maribor **39** 46 36N 15 40 E
Marico → **92** 23 35 S 26 57 E
Maricopa, Ariz., U.S.A. **119** 33 5N 112 2W
Maricopa, Calif., U.S.A. **119** 35 7N 119 27W
Marîdî **87** 4 55N 29 25 E
Maridi, Wadi → **87** 6 15N 29 21 E
Marie-Galante **121** 15 56N 61 16W
Mariecourt **105** 61 30N 72 0W
Mariefred **48** 59 15N 17 12 E
Mariehamn **51** 60 5N 19 55 E
Marienberg, Ger. **24** 50 40N 13 10 E
Marienberg, Neth. **16** 52 30N 6 35 E
Marienbourg **16** 50 6N 4 31 E
Mariental **92** 24 36 S 18 0 E
Marienville **112** 41 27N 79 8W
Mariestad **49** 58 43N 13 50 E
Marietta, Ga., U.S.A. **115** 34 0N 84 30W
Marietta, Ohio, U.S.A. **114** 39 27N 81 27W
Marieville **113** 45 26N 73 10W
Marignane **21** 43 25N 5 13 E
Mariinsk **58** 56 10N 87 20 E
Mariinskiy Posad **55** 56 10N 47 45 E
Marília **125** 22 13 S 50 0W
Marín **30** 42 23N 8 42W
Marina di Cirò **41** 39 22N 17 8 E
Mariña, La **30** 43 30N 7 40W
Marina Plains **98** 14 37 S 143 57 E
Marinduque **73** 13 25N 122 0 E
Marine City **114** 42 45N 82 29W
Marinel, Le **91** 10 25 S 25 17 E
Marineo **40** 37 57N 13 23 E
Marinette, Ariz., U.S.A. **119** 33 41N 112 16W
Marinette, Wis., U.S.A. **114** 45 4N 87 40W
Maringá **125** 23 26 S 52 2W
Marinha Grande **31** 39 45N 8 56W
Marion, Ala., U.S.A. **115** 32 33N 87 20W
Marion, Ill., U.S.A. **117** 37 45N 88 55W
Marion, Ind., U.S.A. **114** 40 35N 85 40W
Marion, Iowa, U.S.A. **116** 42 2N 91 36W
Marion, Kans., U.S.A. **116** 38 25N 97 2W
Marion, Mich., U.S.A. **114** 44 7N 85 8W
Marion, N.C., U.S.A. **115** 35 42N 82 0W
Marion, Ohio, U.S.A. **114** 40 38N 83 8W
Marion, S.C., U.S.A. **115** 34 11N 79 22W
Marion, Va., U.S.A. **115** 36 51N 81 29W
Marion, L. **115** 33 30N 80 15W
Marion Reef **97** 19 10 S 152 17 E
Mariposa **119** 37 31N 119 59W
Mariscal Estigarribia **124** 22 3 S 60 40W
Maritime Alps = Alpes Maritimes **38** 44 10N 7 10 E
Maritsa **43** 42 1N 25 50 E
Maritsá **45** 36 22N 28 10 E
Maritsa → **43** 42 15N 24 0 E
Mariyampole = Kapsukas **54** 54 33N 23 19 E
Marka **86** 18 14N 41 19 E
Markapur **70** 15 44N 79 19 E
Markaryd **49** 56 28N 13 35 E
Markdale **112** 44 19N 80 39W
Marked Tree **117** 35 35N 90 24W
Markelsdorfer Huk **24** 54 33N 11 0 E
Marken **16** 52 26N 5 12 E
Market Drayton **12** 52 55N 2 30W
Market Harborough **13** 52 29N 0 55W

Markham	**112**	43 52N	79 16W
Markham →	**98**	6 41 S	147 2 E
Markham I.	**4**	84 0N	0 45W
Markham L.	**109**	62 30N	102 35W
Markham Mt.	**5**	83 0 S	164 0 E
Marki	**28**	52 20N	21 2 E
Markoupoulon	**45**	37 53N	23 57 E
Markovac	**42**	44 14N	21 7 E
Markovo	**59**	64 40N	169 40 E
Markoye	**85**	14 39N	0 2 E
Marks	**55**	51 45N	46 50 E
Marksville	**117**	31 10N	92 2W
Markt Schwaben	**25**	48 14N	11 49 E
Marktredwitz	**25**	50 1N	12 2 E
Marlboro	**113**	42 19N	71 33W
Marlborough	**98**	22 46 S	149 52 E
Marlborough □	**101**	41 45 S	173 33 E
Marlborough Downs	**13**	51 25N	1 55W
Marle	**19**	49 43N	3 47 E
Marlin	**117**	31 25N	96 50W
Marlow, Ger.	**24**	54 8N	12 34 E
Marlow, U.S.A.	**117**	34 40N	97 58W
Marmagao	**70**	15 25N	73 56 E
Marmande	**20**	44 30N	0 10 E
Marmara	**56**	40 35N	27 38 E
Marmara Denizi	**64**	40 45N	28 15 E
Marmara, Sea of = Marmara Denizi	**64**	40 45N	28 15 E
Marmaris	**64**	36 50N	28 14 E
Marmarth	**116**	46 21N	103 52W
Marmion L.	**106**	48 55N	91 20W
Marmolada, Mte.	**39**	46 25N	11 55 E
Marmolejo	**31**	38 3N	4 13W
Marmora	**106**	44 28N	77 41W
Marnay	**19**	47 20N	5 48 E
Marne	**24**	53 57N	9 1 E
Marne □	**19**	49 0N	4 10 E
Marne →	**19**	8 23N	18 36 E
Marnoo	**100**	36 40 S	142 54 E
Marnueli	**57**	41 30N	44 48 E
Maroala	**93**	15 23 S	47 59 E
Maroantsetra	**93**	15 26 S	49 44 E
Maromandia	**93**	14 13 S	48 5 E
Maroni →	**127**	4 0N	52 0W
Marónia	**44**	40 53N	25 24 E
Maroochydore	**99**	26 29 S	153 5 E
Maroona	**99**	37 27 S	142 54 E
Maros →	**27**	46 15N	20 13 E
Marosakoa	**93**	15 26 S	46 38 E
Marostica	**39**	45 44N	11 40 E
Maroua	**85**	10 40N	14 20 E
Marovoay	**93**	16 6 S	46 39 E
Marquard	**92**	28 40 S	27 28 E
Marqueira	**31**	38 41N	9 9W
Marquesas Is.	**95**	9 30 S	140 0W
Marquette	**114**	46 30N	87 21W
Marquise	**19**	50 50N	1 40 E
Marra, Gebel	**87**	7 20N	27 35 E
Marradi	**39**	44 5N	11 37 E
Marrakech	**82**	31 9N	8 0W
Marrawah	**99**	40 55 S	144 42 E
Marree	**97**	29 39 S	138 1 E
Marrimane	**93**	22 58 S	33 34 E
Marronne →	**20**	45 4N	1 56 E
Marroquí, Punta	**31**	36 0N	5 37W
Marrowie Creek	**99**	33 23 S	145 40 E
Marrubane	**91**	18 0 S	37 0 E
Marrupa	**91**	13 8 S	37 30 E
Mars, Le	**116**	43 0N	96 0W
Marsa Brega	**83**	30 24N	19 37 E
Marsá Susah	**81**	32 52N	21 59 E
Marsabit	**90**	2 18N	38 0 E
Marsabit □	**90**	2 45N	37 45 E
Marsala	**40**	37 48N	12 25 E
Marsaxlokk (Medport)	**36**	35 47N	14 32 E
Marsciano	**39**	42 54N	12 20 E
Marsden	**99**	33 47 S	147 32 E
Marseillan	**20**	43 23N	3 31 E
Marseille	**21**	43 18N	5 23 E
Marseilles = Marseille	**21**	43 18N	5 23 E
Marsh I.	**117**	29 35N	91 50W
Marsh L.	**116**	45 5N	96 0W
Marshall, Liberia	**84**	6 8N	10 22W
Marshall, Ark., U.S.A.	**117**	35 58N	92 40W
Marshall, Mich., U.S.A.	**114**	42 17N	84 59W
Marshall, Minn., U.S.A.	**116**	44 25N	95 45W
Marshall, Mo., U.S.A.	**116**	39 8N	93 15W
Marshall, Tex., U.S.A.	**117**	32 29N	94 20W
Marshall Is.	**94**	9 0N	171 0 E
Marshalltown	**116**	42 5N	92 56W
Marshfield, Mo., U.S.A.	**117**	37 20N	92 58W
Marshfield, Wis., U.S.A.	**116**	44 42N	90 10W
Mársico Nuovo	**41**	40 26N	15 43 E
Märsta	**48**	59 37N	17 52 E
Marstal	**49**	54 51N	10 30 E
Marstrand	**49**	57 53N	11 35 E
Mart	**117**	31 34N	96 51W
Marta →	**39**	42 14N	11 42 E
Martaban	**67**	16 30N	97 35 E
Martaban, G. of	**67**	16 5N	96 30 E
Martagne	**18**	46 59N	0 57W
Martano	**41**	40 14N	18 18 E
Martapura, Kalimantan, Indon.	**72**	3 22 S	114 47 E
Martapura, Sumatera, Indon.	**72**	4 19 S	104 22 E
Marte	**85**	12 23N	13 46 E
Martel	**20**	44 57N	1 37 E
Martelange	**16**	49 49N	5 43 E
Martés, Sierra	**33**	39 20N	1 0W
Marthaguy Creek →	**99**	30 16 S	147 35 E
Martha's Vineyard	**114**	41 25N	70 35W
Martigné-Ferchaud	**18**	47 50N	1 20W
Martigny	**25**	46 6N	7 3 E
Martigues	**21**	43 24N	5 4 E
Martil	**82**	35 36N	5 15W
Martin, Czech.	**27**	49 6N	18 48 E
Martin, S.D., U.S.A.	**116**	43 11N	101 45W
Martin, Tenn., U.S.A.	**117**	36 23N	88 51W
Martín →	**32**	41 18N	0 19W
Martin, L.	**115**	32 45N	85 50W
Martina Franca	**41**	40 42N	17 20 E
Martinborough	**101**	41 14 S	175 29 E
Martinique	**121**	14 40N	61 0W
Martinique Passage	**121**	15 15N	61 0W
Martínon	**45**	38 35N	23 15 E
Martinópolis	**125**	22 11 S	51 12W
Martins Ferry	**113**	40 5N	80 46W
Martinsberg	**26**	48 22N	15 9 E
Martinsburg, Pa., U.S.A.	**112**	40 18N	78 21W
Martinsburg, W. Va., U.S.A.	**114**	39 30N	77 57W
Martinsville, Ind., U.S.A.	**114**	39 29N	86 23W
Martinsville, Va., U.S.A.	**115**	36 41N	79 52W
Marton	**101**	40 4 S	175 23 E
Martorell	**32**	41 28N	1 56 E
Martos	**31**	37 44N	3 58W
Martuni	**57**	40 9N	45 10 E
Maru	**85**	12 22N	6 22 E
Marudi	**72**	4 10N	114 19 E
Ma'ruf	**65**	31 30N	67 6 E
Marugame	**74**	34 15N	133 40 E
Marúggio	**41**	40 20N	17 33 E
Marulan	**99**	34 43 S	150 3 E
Marunga	**92**	17 28 S	20 2 E
Marungu, Mts.	**90**	7 30 S	30 0 E
Mårvatn	**47**	60 8N	8 14 E
Marvejols	**20**	44 33N	3 19 E
Marwar	**68**	25 43N	73 45 E
Mary	**58**	37 40N	61 50 E
Mary Frances L.	**109**	63 19N	106 13W
Mary Kathleen	**97**	20 44 S	139 48 E
Maryborough, Queens., Austral.	**97**	25 31 S	152 37 E
Maryborough, Vic., Austral.	**97**	37 0 S	143 44 E
Maryfield	**109**	49 50N	101 35W
Maryland □	**114**	39 10N	76 40W
Maryland Jc.	**91**	17 45 S	30 31 E
Maryport	**12**	54 43N	3 30W
Mary's Harbour	**107**	52 18N	55 51W
Marystown	**107**	47 10N	55 10W
Marysvale	**119**	38 25N	112 17W
Marysville, Can.	**108**	49 35N	116 0W
Marysville, Calif., U.S.A.	**118**	39 14N	121 40W
Marysville, Kans., U.S.A.	**116**	39 50N	96 49W
Marysville, Mich., U.S.A.	**112**	42 55N	82 29W
Marysville, Ohio, U.S.A.	**114**	40 15N	83 20W
Maryvale	**99**	28 4 S	152 12 E
Maryville	**115**	35 50N	84 0W
Marzūq	**83**	25 53N	13 57 E
Masada = Mesada	**62**	31 20N	35 19 E
Masahunga	**90**	2 6 S	33 18 E
Masai Steppe	**90**	4 30 S	36 30 E
Masaka	**90**	0 21 S	31 45 E
Masalembo, Kepulauan	**72**	5 35 S	114 30 E
Masalima, Kepulauan	**72**	5 4 S	117 5 E
Masamba	**73**	2 30 S	120 15 E
Masan	**76**	35 11N	128 32 E
Masanasa	**33**	39 25N	0 25W
Masandam, Ras	**65**	26 30N	56 30 E
Masasi	**91**	10 45 S	38 52 E
Masasi □	**91**	10 45 S	38 50 E
Masaya	**121**	12 0N	86 7W
Masba	**85**	10 35N	13 1 E
Masbate	**73**	12 21N	123 36 E
Mascara	**82**	35 26N	0 6 E
Mascota	**120**	20 30N	104 50W
Masela	**73**	8 9 S	129 51 E
Maseru	**92**	29 18 S	27 30 E
Mashaba	**91**	20 2 S	30 29 E
Mashābih	**64**	25 35N	36 30 E
Mashan	**77**	23 40N	108 11 E
Mashhad	**65**	36 20N	59 35 E
Mashi	**85**	13 0N	7 54 E
Mashike	**74**	43 31N	141 30 E
Mashkel, Hamun-i-	**66**	28 30N	63 0 E
Mashki Chah	**66**	29 5N	62 30 E
Mashtaga	**57**	40 35N	50 0 E
Masi	**50**	69 26N	23 40 E
Masi Manimba	**88**	4 40 S	17 54 E
Masindi	**90**	1 40N	31 43 E
Masindi Port	**90**	1 43N	32 2 E
Masisea	**126**	8 35 S	74 22W
Masisi	**90**	1 23 S	28 49 E
Masjed Soleyman	**64**	31 55N	49 18 E
Mask, L.	**15**	53 36N	9 24W
Maski	**70**	15 56N	76 46 E
Maslen Nos	**43**	42 18N	27 48 E
Maslinica	**39**	43 24N	16 13 E
Masnou	**32**	41 28N	2 20 E
Masoala, Tanjon' i	**93**	15 59 S	50 13 E
Masoarivo	**93**	19 3 S	44 19 E
Masohi	**73**	3 2 S	128 15 E
Masomeloka	**93**	20 17 S	48 37 E
Mason, S.D., U.S.A.	**116**	45 12N	103 27W
Mason, Tex., U.S.A.	**117**	30 45N	99 15W
Mason City, Iowa, U.S.A.	**116**	43 9N	93 12W
Mason City, Wash., U.S.A.	**118**	48 0N	119 0W
Masqat	**65**	23 37N	58 36 E
Massa	**38**	44 2N	10 7 E
Massa Maríttima	**38**	43 3N	10 52 E
Massa, O. →	**82**	30 2N	9 40W
Massachusetts □	**114**	42 25N	72 0W
Massachusetts B.	**113**	42 30N	70 0W
Massada	**62**	33 41N	35 36 E
Massafra	**41**	40 35N	17 8 E
Massaguet	**81**	12 28N	15 26 E
Massakory	**81**	13 0N	15 49 E
Massangena	**93**	21 34 S	33 0 E
Massarosa	**38**	43 53N	10 17 E
Massat	**20**	42 53N	1 21 E
Massawa = Mitsiwa	**87**	15 35N	39 25 E
Massena	**114**	44 52N	74 55W
Massénya	**81**	11 21N	16 9 E
Masset	**108**	54 2N	132 10W
Massiac	**20**	45 15N	3 11 E
Massif Central	**20**	45 30N	2 21 E
Massillon	**114**	40 47N	81 30W
Massinga	**93**	23 46 S	32 4 E
Masson	**113**	45 32N	75 25W
Masson I.	**5**	66 10 S	93 20 E
Mastaba	**86**	20 52N	39 30 E
Mastanli = Momchilgrad	**43**	41 33N	25 23 E
Masterton	**101**	40 56 S	175 39 E
Mástikho, Ákra	**45**	38 10N	26 2 E
Mastuj	**69**	36 20N	72 36 E
Mastung	**66**	29 50N	66 56 E
Mastura	**86**	23 7N	38 52 E
Masuda	**74**	34 40N	131 51 E
Maswa □	**90**	3 30 S	34 0 E
Matabeleland North □	**91**	19 0 S	28 0 E
Matabeleland South □	**91**	21 0 S	29 0 E
Mataboor	**73**	1 41 S	138 3 E
Matachel →	**31**	38 50N	6 17W
Matachewan	**106**	47 56N	80 39W
Matad	**75**	47 11N	115 27 E
Matadi	**88**	5 52 S	13 31 E
Matagalpa	**121**	13 0N	85 58W
Matagami	**106**	49 45N	77 34W
Matagami, L.	**106**	49 50N	77 40W
Matagorda	**117**	28 43N	96 0W
Matagorda B.	**117**	28 30N	96 15W
Matagorda I.	**117**	28 10N	96 40W
Matak, P.	**72**	3 18N	106 16 E
Matakana	**99**	32 59 S	145 54 E
Matale	**70**	7 30N	80 37 E
Matam	**84**	15 34N	13 17W
Matameye	**85**	13 26N	8 28 E
Matamoros, Coahuila, Mexico	**120**	25 33N	103 15W
Matamoros, Puebla, Mexico	**120**	18 2N	98 17W
Matamoros, Tamaulipas, Mexico	**120**	25 50N	97 30W
Ma'ṭan as Sarra	**81**	21 45N	22 0 E
Matandu →	**91**	8 45 S	34 19 E
Matane	**107**	48 50N	67 33W
Matankari	**85**	13 46N	4 1 E
Matanuska	**104**	61 39N	149 19W
Matanzas	**121**	23 0N	81 40W
Matapan, C. = Taínaron, Akra	**45**	36 22N	22 27 E
Matapédia	**107**	48 0N	66 59W
Matara	**70**	5 58N	80 30 E
Mataram	**72**	8 41 S	116 10 E
Matarani	**126**	77 0 S	72 10W
Mataranka	**96**	14 55 S	133 4 E
Mataró	**32**	41 32N	2 29 E
Matarraña →	**32**	41 14N	0 22 E
Mataruška Banja	**42**	43 40N	20 45 E
Matatiele	**93**	30 20 S	28 49 E
Mataura	**101**	46 11 S	168 51 E
Matehuala	**120**	23 40N	100 40W
Mateke Hills	**91**	21 48 S	31 0 E
Matélica	**39**	43 15N	13 0 E
Matera	**41**	40 40N	16 37 E
Mátészalka	**27**	47 58N	22 20 E
Matetsi	**91**	18 12 S	26 0 E
Mateur	**83**	37 0N	9 40 E
Matfors	**48**	62 21N	17 2 E
Matha	**20**	45 52N	0 20W
Matheson Island	**109**	51 45N	96 56W
Mathis	**117**	28 4N	97 48W
Mathura	**68**	27 30N	77 40 E
Mati	**73**	6 55N	126 15 E
Mati →	**44**	41 40N	20 0 E
Matías Romero	**120**	16 53N	95 2W
Matibane	**91**	14 49 S	40 45 E
Matima	**92**	20 15 S	24 26 E
Matlock	**12**	53 8N	1 32W
Matmata	**83**	33 37N	9 59 E
Matna	**87**	13 49N	35 10 E
Mato Grosso □	**127**	14 0 S	55 0W
Mato Grosso, Planalto do	**127**	15 0 S	59 57W
Matochkin Shar	**58**	73 10N	56 40 E
Matopo Hills	**91**	20 36 S	28 20 E
Matopos	**91**	20 20 S	28 29 E
Matosinhos	**30**	41 11N	8 42W
Matour	**21**	46 19N	4 29 E
Matrah	**65**	23 37N	58 30 E
Matrûh	**86**	31 19N	27 9 E
Matsena	**85**	13 5N	10 5 E
Matsesta	**57**	43 34N	39 51 E
Matsue	**74**	35 25N	133 10 E
Matsumoto	**74**	36 15N	138 0 E
Matsuyama	**74**	33 45N	132 45 E
Mattagami →	**106**	50 43N	81 29W
Mattancheri	**70**	9 50N	76 15 E
Mattawa	**106**	46 20N	78 45W
Mattawamkeag	**107**	45 30N	68 21W
Matterhorn	**25**	45 58N	7 39 E
Mattersburg	**27**	47 44N	16 24 E
Matthew Town	**121**	20 57N	73 40W
Matthew's Ridge	**126**	7 37N	60 10W
Mattice	**106**	49 40N	83 20W
Mattituck	**113**	40 58N	72 32W
Mattmar	**48**	63 18N	13 45 E
Matua	**72**	2 58 S	110 46 E
Matuba	**93**	24 28 S	32 49 E
Matucana	**126**	11 55 S	76 25W
Matun	**66**	33 22N	69 58 E
Maturín	**126**	9 45N	63 11W
Matveyev Kurgan	**57**	47 35N	38 47 E
Mau-é-ele	**93**	24 18 S	34 2 E
Mau Escarpment	**90**	0 40 S	36 0 E
Mau Ranipur	**68**	25 16N	79 8 E
Maubeuge	**19**	50 17N	3 57 E
Maubourguet	**20**	43 29N	0 1 E
Maude	**99**	34 29 S	144 18 E
Maudheim	**5**	71 5 S	11 0W
Maudin Sun	**67**	16 0N	94 30 E
Maués	**126**	3 20 S	57 45W
Maui	**110**	20 45N	156 20 E
Mauke	**101**	20 09 S	157 20W
Maule □	**124**	36 5 S	72 30W
Mauléon-Licharre	**20**	43 14N	0 54W
Maumee	**114**	41 35N	83 40W
Maumee →	**114**	41 42N	83 28W
Maumere	**73**	8 38 S	122 13 E
Maun	**92**	20 0 S	23 26 E
Mauna Kea	**110**	19 50N	155 28W
Mauna Loa	**110**	21 8N	157 10W
Maunath Bhanjan	**69**	25 56N	83 33 E
Maungmagan Kyunzu	**71**	14 0N	97 48 E
Maupin	**118**	45 12N	121 9W
Maure-de-Bretagne	**18**	47 53N	2 0W
Maurepas L.	**117**	30 18N	90 35W
Maures	**21**	43 15N	6 15 E
Mauriac	**20**	45 13N	2 19 E
Maurice L.	**96**	29 30 S	131 0 E
Mauritania ■	**80**	20 50N	10 0W
Mauritius ■	**3**	20 0 S	57 0 E
Mauron	**18**	48 9N	2 18W
Maurs	**20**	44 43N	2 12 E
Mauston	**116**	43 48N	90 5W
Mauterndorf	**26**	47 9N	13 40 E
Mauvezin	**20**	43 44N	0 53 E
Mauzé-sur-le-Mignon	**20**	46 12N	0 41W
Mavelikara	**70**	9 14N	76 32 E
Mavinga	**89**	15 50 S	20 21 E
Mavli	**68**	24 45N	73 55 E
Mavqi'im	**62**	31 38N	34 32 E
Mavrova	**44**	40 26N	19 32 E
Mavuradonha Mts.	**91**	16 30 S	31 30 E
Mawa	**90**	2 45N	26 40 E
Mawana	**68**	29 6N	77 58 E
Mawand	**68**	29 33N	68 38 E
Mawk Mai	**67**	20 14N	97 37 E
Mawson Base	**5**	67 30 S	62 53 E
Max	**116**	47 50N	101 20W
Maxcanú	**120**	20 40N	92 0W
Maxhamish L.	**108**	59 50N	123 17W
Maxixe	**93**	23 54 S	35 17 E
Maxville	**113**	45 17N	74 51W
Maxwelton	**98**	20 43 S	142 41 E
May Downs	**98**	22 38 S	148 55 E
May Glacier Tongue	**5**	66 08 S	130 35 E
May Pen	**121**	17 58N	77 15W
Maya	**32**	43 12N	1 29W
Maya →	**59**	54 31N	134 41 E
Maya Mts.	**120**	16 30N	89 0W
Mayaguana	**121**	22 30N	72 44W
Mayagüez	**121**	18 12N	67 9W
Mayahi	**85**	13 58N	7 40 E
Mayals	**32**	41 22N	0 30 E
Mayarí	**121**	20 40N	75 41W
Mayavaram = Mayuram	**70**	11 3N	79 42 E
Maybell	**118**	40 30N	108 4W
Maychew	**87**	12 50N	39 31 E
Maydena	**99**	42 45 S	146 30 E
Maydos	**44**	40 13N	26 20 E
Mayen	**25**	50 18N	7 10 E
Mayenne	**18**	48 20N	0 38W
Mayenne □	**18**	48 10N	0 40W
Mayenne →	**18**	47 30N	0 32W
Mayer	**119**	34 28N	112 17W
Mayerthorpe	**108**	53 57N	115 8W
Mayfield	**115**	36 45N	88 40W
Mayhill	**119**	32 58N	105 30W
Maykop	**57**	44 35N	40 25 E
Maymyo	**71**	22 2N	96 28 E
Maynooth	**15**	53 22N	6 38W
Mayo	**104**	63 38N	135 57W
Mayo □	**15**	53 47N	9 7W
Mayo →	**120**	26 45N	109 47W
Mayo L.	**104**	63 45N	135 0W
Mayon, Mt.	**73**	13 15N	123 42 E
Mayor I.	**101**	37 16 S	176 17 E
Mayorga	**30**	42 10N	5 16W
Mayskiy	**57**	43 47N	44 2 E
Mayson L.	**109**	57 55N	107 10W
Maysville	**114**	38 39N	83 46W
Maythalūn	**62**	32 21N	35 16 E
Mayu	**73**	1 30N	126 30 E
Mayuram	**70**	11 3N	79 42 E
Mayville, N.D., U.S.A.	**116**	47 30N	97 23W
Mayville, N.Y., U.S.A.	**112**	42 14N	79 31W
Mayya	**59**	61 44N	130 18 E
Mazabuka	**91**	15 52 S	27 44 E
Mazagán = El Jadida	**82**	33 11N	8 17W
Mazagão	**127**	0 7 S	51 16W
Mazamet	**20**	43 30N	2 20 E
Mazán	**126**	3 30 S	73 0W
Mazan Deran □	**65**	36 30N	52 0 E
Mazar-e Sharīf	**65**	36 41N	67 0 E
Mazar, O. →	**82**	31 50N	1 36 E
Mazara del Vallo	**40**	37 40N	12 34 E
Mazarredo	**128**	47 10 S	66 50W
Mazarrón	**33**	37 38N	1 19W
Mazarrón, Golfo de	**33**	37 27N	1 19W
Mazaruni →	**126**	6 25N	58 35W
Mazatenango	**120**	14 35N	91 30W
Mazatlán	**120**	23 10N	106 30W
Mažeikiai	**54**	56 20N	22 20 E
Māzhān	**65**	32 30N	59 0 E
Mazīnān	**65**	36 19N	56 56 E
Mazoe, Mozam.	**91**	16 42 S	33 7 E
Mazoe, Zimb.	**91**	17 28 S	30 58 E
Mazrûb	**87**	14 0N	29 20 E
Mazu Dao	**77**	26 10N	119 55 E
Mazurian Lakes = Mazurski, Pojezierze	**28**	53 50N	21 0 E
Mazurski, Pojezierze	**28**	53 50N	21 0 E
Mazzarino	**41**	37 19N	14 12 E
Mbaba	**84**	14 59N	16 44W
Mbabane	**93**	26 18 S	31 6 E
Mbagne	**84**	16 6N	14 47W
M'bahiakro	**84**	7 33N	4 19W
Mbaïki	**88**	3 53N	18 1 E
Mbala	**91**	8 46 S	31 24 E
Mbale	**90**	1 8N	34 12 E
Mbalmayo	**88**	3 33N	11 33 E
Mbamba Bay	**91**	11 13 S	34 49 E
Mbandaka	**88**	0 1N	18 18 E
Mbanga	**85**	4 30N	9 33 E
Mbanza Congo	**88**	6 18 S	14 16 E
Mbanza Ngungu	**88**	5 12 S	14 53 E
Mbarara	**90**	0 35 S	30 40 E
Mbatto	**84**	6 28N	4 22W
Mbenkuru →	**91**	9 25 S	39 50 E
Mberubu	**85**	6 10N	7 38 E
Mbesuma	**91**	10 0 S	32 2 E
Mbeya	**91**	8 54 S	33 29 E
Mbeya □	**90**	8 15 S	33 30 E
Mbinga	**91**	10 50 S	35 0 E
Mbinga □	**91**	10 50 S	35 0 E
Mbini □	**88**	1 30N	10 0 E
Mboki	**87**	5 19N	25 58 E
Mboro	**84**	15 9N	16 54W
Mboune	**84**	14 42N	13 34W
Mbour	**84**	14 22N	16 54W
Mbout	**84**	16 1N	12 38W
Mbozi □	**91**	9 0 S	32 50 E
Mbuji-Mayi	**90**	6 9 S	23 40 E
Mbulu	**90**	3 45 S	35 30 E
Mbulu □	**90**	3 52 S	35 33 E

Mburucuyá 124 28 1S 58 14W
Mcherrah 82 27 0N 4 30W
Mchinja 91 9 44S 39 45E
Mchinji 91 13 47S 32 58E
Mdennah 82 24 37N 6 0W
Mdina 36 35 51N 14 25E
Mead, L. 119 36 1N 114 44W
Meade 117 37 18N 100 25W
Meadow Lake 109 54 10N 108 26W
Meadow Lake Prov. Park 109 54 27N 109 0W
Meadow Valley Wash → 119 36 39N 114 35W
Meadville 114 41 39N 80 9W
Meaford 106 44 36N 80 35W
Mealhada 30 40 22N 8 27W
Mealy Mts. 107 53 10N 58 0W
Meander River 108 59 2N 117 42W
Meares, C. 118 45 37N 124 0W
Mearim → 127 3 4S 44 35W
Meath □ 15 53 32N 6 40W
Meath Park 109 53 27N 105 22W
Meaulne 20 46 36N 2 36E
Meaux 19 48 58N 2 50E
Mecanhelas 91 15 12S 35 54E
Mecca 119 33 37N 116 3W
Mecca = Makkah 86 21 30N 39 54E
Mechanicsburg 112 40 12N 77 0W
Mechanicville 113 42 54N 73 41W
Mechara 87 8 36N 40 20E
Mechelen 16 51 2N 4 29E
Mecheria 82 33 35N 0 18W
Mechernich 24 50 35N 6 39E
Mechetinskaya 57 46 45N 40 32E
Mechra Benâbbou 82 32 39N 7 48W
Mecidiye 44 40 38N 26 32E
Mecitözü 56 40 32N 35 17E
Meconta 91 14 59S 39 50E
Meda 30 40 57N 7 18W
Meda → 96 17 20S 123 50E
Medak 70 18 1N 78 15E
Medan 72 3 40N 98 38E
Medanosa, Pta. 128 48 8S 66 0W
Medawachchiya 70 8 30N 80 30E
Medéa 82 36 12N 2 50E
Mededa 42 43 44N 19 15E
Medellín 126 6 15N 75 35W
Medemblik 16 52 46N 5 8E
Médenine 83 33 21N 10 30E
Mederdra 84 17 0N 15 38W
Medford, Oreg., U.S.A. 118 42 20N 122 52W
Medford, Wis., U.S.A. 116 45 9N 90 21W
Medgidia 46 44 15N 28 19E
Medi 87 5 4N 30 42E
Media Agua 124 31 58S 68 25W
Media Luna 124 34 45S 66 44W
Mediaş 46 46 9N 24 22E
Medical Lake 118 47 35N 117 42W
Medicina 39 44 29N 11 38E
Medicine Bow 118 41 56N 106 11W
Medicine Bow Pk. 118 41 21N 106 19W
Medicine Bow Ra. 118 41 10N 106 25W
Medicine Hat 109 50 0N 110 45W
Medicine Lake 116 48 30N 104 30W
Medicine Lodge 117 37 20N 98 37W
Medina, N.D., U.S.A. 116 46 57N 99 20W
Medina, N.Y., U.S.A. 114 43 15N 78 27W
Medina, Ohio, U.S.A. 114 41 9N 81 50W
Medina = Al Madīnah 64 24 35N 39 35E
Medina → 117 29 10N 98 20W
Medina de Ríoseco 30 41 53N 5 3W
Medina del Campo 30 41 18N 4 55W
Medina L. 117 29 35N 98 58W
Medina-Sidonia 31 36 28N 5 57W
Medinaceli 32 41 12N 2 30W
Mediterranean Sea 34 35 0N 15 0E
Medjerda, O. → 83 37 7N 10 13E
Medley 109 54 25N 110 16W
Médoc 20 45 10N 0 56W
Medstead 109 53 19N 108 5W
Medulin 39 44 49N 13 55E
Medveda 42 42 50N 21 32E
Medveditsa →, R.S.F.S.R., U.S.S.R. 55 49 35N 42 41E
Medveditsa →, R.S.F.S.R., U.S.S.R. 55 57 5N 37 30E
Medvedok 55 57 20N 50 1E
Medvezhi, Ostrava 59 71 0N 161 0E
Medvezhyegorsk 52 63 0N 34 25E
Medway → 13 51 28N 0 45E
Medyn 55 54 58N 35 52E
Medzev 27 48 43N 20 55E
Medzilaborce 27 49 17N 21 52E
Meekatharra 96 26 32S 118 29E
Meeker 118 40 1N 107 58W
Meerane 24 50 51N 12 30E
Meersburg 25 47 42N 9 16E
Meerut 68 29 1N 77 42E
Meeteetse 118 44 10N 108 56W
Mega 87 3 57N 38 19E
Megálo Khorío 45 36 27N 27 24E
Megálo Petalí 45 38 0N 24 15E
Megalópolis 45 37 25N 22 7E
Meganísi 45 38 39N 20 48E
Mégara 45 37 58N 23 22E
Megarine 83 33 14N 6 2E
Megdhova → 45 39 10N 21 45E
Mégève 21 45 51N 6 37E
Meghezez, Mt. 87 9 18N 39 26E
Meghna → 69 22 50N 90 50E
Megiddo 62 32 36N 35 11E
Mégiscane, L. 106 48 35N 75 55W
Megiste 35 36 8N 29 34E
Mehadia 46 44 56N 22 23E
Mehaïguene, O. → 82 32 15N 2 59E
Meharry, Mt. 96 22 59S 118 35E
Mehedinţi □ 46 44 40N 22 45E
Meheisa 86 19 38N 32 57E
Mehndawal 69 26 58N 83 5E
Mehsana 68 23 39N 72 26E
Mehun-sur-Yèvre 19 47 10N 2 13E
Mei Jiang → 77 24 25N 116 35E
Mei Xian 75 24 16N 116 6E
Meiganga 88 6 30N 14 25E
Meiktila 67 20 53N 95 54E
Meiningen 24 50 32N 10 25E
Me'ir Shefeya 62 32 35N 34 58E
Meira, Sierra de 30 43 15N 7 15W
Meiringen 25 46 43N 8 12E
Meissen 24 51 10N 13 29E
Meissner 24 51 13N 9 51E
Meitan 77 27 45N 107 29E
Méjean, Causse 20 44 15N 3 30E
Mejillones 124 23 10S 70 30W
Mékambo 88 1 2N 13 50E
Mekdela 87 11 24N 39 10E
Mekele 87 13 33N 39 30E
Meklong = Samut Songkhram 71 13 24N 100 1E
Meknès 82 33 57N 5 33W
Meko 85 7 27N 2 52E
Mekong → 71 9 30N 106 15E
Mekongga 73 3 39S 121 15E
Melagiri Hills 70 12 20N 77 30E
Melah, Sebkhet el 82 29 20N 1 30W
Melaka 71 2 15N 102 15E
Melaka □ 71 2 20N 102 15E
Melalap 72 5 10N 116 5E
Mélambes 45 35 8N 24 40E
Melanesia 94 4 0S 155 0E
Melapalaiyam 70 8 39N 77 44E
Melbourne, Austral. 97 37 50S 145 0E
Melbourne, U.S.A. 115 28 4N 80 35W
Melchor Múzquiz 120 27 50N 101 30W
Melchor Ocampo (San Pedro Ocampo) 120 24 52N 101 40W
Méldola 39 44 7N 12 3E
Meldorf 24 54 5N 9 5E
Mêle-sur-Sarthe, Le 18 48 31N 0 22E
Melegnano 38 45 21N 9 20E
Melenci 42 45 32N 20 20E
Melenki 55 55 20N 41 37E
Mélèzes → 105 57 30N 71 0W
Melfi, Chad 81 11 0N 17 59E
Melfi, Italy 41 41 0N 15 33E
Melfort, Can. 109 52 50N 104 37W
Melfort, Zimb. 91 18 0S 31 25E
Melgaço 30 42 7N 8 15W
Melgar de Fernamental 30 42 27N 4 17W
Melhus 47 63 17N 10 18E
Meligalá 45 37 15N 21 59E
Melilla 82 35 21N 2 57W
Melilot 62 31 22N 34 37E
Melipilla 124 33 42S 71 15W
Mélissa Óros 45 37 32N 26 4E
Melita 109 49 15N 101 0W
Mélito di Porto Salvo 41 37 55N 15 47E
Melitopol 56 46 50N 35 22E
Melk 26 48 13N 15 20E
Mellan-Fryken 48 59 45N 13 10E
Mellansel 50 63 25N 18 17E
Melle, France 20 46 14N 0 10W
Melle, Ger. 24 52 12N 8 20E
Mellégue, O. → 83 36 32N 8 51E
Mellen 116 46 19N 90 36W
Mellerud 49 58 41N 12 28E
Mellette 116 45 11N 98 29W
Mellid 30 42 55N 8 1W
Mellish Reef 97 17 25S 155 50E
Mellit 87 14 7N 25 34E
Mellrichstadt 25 50 26N 10 19E
Melnik 43 41 30N 23 25E
Mělník 26 50 22N 14 23E
Melo 125 32 20S 54 10W
Melolo 73 9 53S 120 40E
Melovoye 57 49 25N 40 5E
Melrhir, Chott 83 34 25N 6 24E
Melrose, Austral. 99 32 42S 146 57E
Melrose, U.K. 14 53 35N 2 44W
Melrose, U.S.A. 117 34 27N 103 33W
Melstone 118 46 36N 107 50W
Melsungen 24 51 8N 9 34E
Melton Mowbray 12 52 46N 0 52W
Melun 19 48 32N 2 39E
Melur 70 10 2N 78 23E
Melut 87 10 30N 32 13E
Melville 109 50 55N 102 50W
Melville B. 97 12 0S 136 45E
Melville, C. 97 14 11S 144 30E
Melville I., Austral. 96 11 30S 131 0E
Melville I., Can. 4 75 30N 112 0W
Melville, L. 107 53 30N 60 0W
Melville Pen. 105 68 0N 84 0W
Melvin → 108 59 11N 117 31W
Mélykút 27 46 11N 19 25E
Memaliaj 44 40 25N 19 58E
Memba 91 14 11S 40 30E
Memboro 73 9 30S 119 30E
Membrilla 33 38 59N 3 21W
Memel 93 27 38S 29 36E
Memel = Klaipeda 54 55 43N 21 10E
Memmingen 25 47 59N 10 12E
Memphis, Tenn., U.S.A. 117 35 7N 90 0W
Memphis, Tex., U.S.A. 117 34 45N 100 30W
Mena 117 34 40N 94 15W
Mena → 87 5 40N 40 50E
Menai Strait 12 53 14N 4 10W
Ménaka 85 15 59N 2 18E
Menan = Chao Phraya → 71 13 32N 100 36E
Menarandra → 93 25 17S 44 30E
Menard 117 30 57N 99 48W
Menasha 114 44 13N 88 27W
Menate 72 0 12S 113 3E
Mendawai → 72 3 17S 113 21E
Mende 20 44 31N 3 30E
Mendebo Mts. 87 7 0N 39 22E
Menderes → 64 37 25N 28 45E
Mendi, Ethiopia 87 9 47N 35 4E
Mendi, P.N.G. 98 6 11S 143 39E
Mendip Hills 13 51 17N 2 40W
Mendocino 118 39 26N 123 50W
Mendocino Seascarp 95 41 0N 140 0W
Mendota, Calif., U.S.A. 119 36 46N 120 24W
Mendota, Ill., U.S.A. 116 41 35N 89 5W
Mendoza 124 32 50S 68 52W
Mendoza □ 124 33 0S 69 0W
Mene Grande 126 9 49N 70 56W
Menemen 64 38 34N 27 3E
Menen 16 50 47N 3 7E
Menfi 40 37 36N 12 57E
Mengcheng 77 33 18N 116 31E
Mengeš 39 46 24N 14 35E
Menggala 72 4 30S 105 15E
Mengíbar 31 37 58N 3 48W
Mengoub 82 29 49N 5 26W
Mengshan 77 24 14N 110 55E
Mengzi 75 23 20N 103 22E
Menihek L. 107 54 0N 67 0W
Menin = Menen 16 50 47N 3 7E
Menindee 97 32 20S 142 25E
Menindee, L. 99 32 20S 142 25E
Meningie 99 35 35S 139 0E
Menominee 114 45 9N 87 39W
Menominee → 114 45 5N 87 36W
Menomonie 116 44 50N 91 54W
Menongue 89 14 48S 17 52E
Menorca 32 40 0N 4 0E
Mentawai, Kepulauan 72 2 0S 99 0E
Menton 21 43 50N 7 29E
Mentor 112 41 40N 81 21W
Menzel-Bourguiba 83 39 9N 9 49E
Menzel Chaker 83 35 0N 10 26E
Menzel-Temime 83 36 46N 11 0E
Menzelinsk 52 55 53N 53 1E
Menzies 96 29 40S 120 58E
Me'ona (Tarshiha) 62 33 1N 35 15E
Mepaco 91 15 57S 30 48E
Meppel 16 52 42N 6 12E
Meppen 24 52 41N 7 20E
Mequinenza 32 41 22N 0 17E
Mer Rouge 117 32 47N 91 48W
Merabéllou, Kólpos 45 35 10N 25 50E
Merak 73 5 56S 106 0E
Meran = Merano 39 46 40N 11 10E
Merano 39 46 40N 11 10E
Merate 38 45 42N 9 23E
Merauke 73 8 29S 140 24E
Merbabu 73 7 30S 110 40E
Merbein 99 34 10S 142 2E
Merca 63 1 48N 44 50E
Mercadal 32 39 59N 4 5E
Mercara 70 12 30N 75 45E
Mercato Saraceno 39 43 57N 12 11E
Merced 119 37 18N 120 30W
Mercedes, Buenos Aires, Argent. 124 34 40S 59 30W
Mercedes, Corrientes, Argent. 124 29 10S 58 5W
Mercedes, San Luis, Argent. 124 33 40S 65 21W
Mercedes, Uruguay 124 33 12S 58 0W
Merceditas 124 28 20S 70 35W
Mercer, N.Z. 101 37 16S 175 5E
Mercer, U.S.A. 112 41 14N 80 13W
Mercy C. 105 65 0N 63 30W
Merdrignac 18 48 11N 2 27W
Meredith C. 128 52 15S 60 40W
Meredith, L. 117 35 30N 101 35W
Merei 46 45 7N 26 43E
Méréville 19 48 20N 2 5E
Mergenevsky 57 49 59N 51 15E
Mergui Arch. = Myeik Kyunzu 71 11 30N 97 30E
Mérida, Mexico 120 20 9N 89 40W
Mérida, Spain 31 38 55N 6 25W
Mérida, Venez. 126 8 24N 71 8W
Meriden 114 41 33N 72 47W
Meridian, Idaho, U.S.A. 118 43 41N 116 25W
Meridian, Miss., U.S.A. 115 32 20N 88 42W
Meridian, Tex., U.S.A. 117 31 55N 97 37W
Mering 25 48 15N 11 0E
Meringur 100 34 20S 141 19E
Meriruma 127 1 15N 54 50W
Merkel 117 32 30N 100 0W
Merksem 16 51 16N 4 25E
Merlebach 19 49 5N 6 52E
Merlerault, Le 18 48 41N 0 16E
Mern 49 55 3N 12 3E
Merowe 86 18 29N 31 46E
Merredin 96 31 28S 118 18E
Merrick 14 55 8N 4 30W
Merrickville 113 44 55N 75 50W
Merrill, Oregon, U.S.A. 118 42 2N 121 37W
Merrill, Wis., U.S.A. 116 45 11N 89 41W
Merriman 116 42 55N 101 42W
Merritt 108 50 10N 120 45W
Merriwa 99 32 6S 150 22E
Merriwagga 99 33 47S 145 43E
Merry I. 106 55 29N 77 31W
Merrygoen 99 31 51S 149 12E
Merryville 117 30 47N 93 31W
Mersa Fatma 87 14 57N 40 17E
Mersch 16 49 44N 6 7E
Merseburg 24 51 20N 12 0E
Mersey → 12 53 20N 2 56W
Merseyside □ 12 53 25N 2 55W
Mersin 64 36 51N 34 36E
Mersing 71 2 25N 103 50E
Merta 68 26 39N 74 4E
Merthyr Tydfil 13 51 45N 3 23W
Mértola 31 37 40N 7 40E
Mertzon 117 31 17N 100 48W
Méru 19 49 13N 2 8E
Meru, Kenya 90 0 3N 37 40E
Meru, Tanz. 90 3 15S 36 46E
Meru □ 90 0 3N 37 46E
Merville 19 50 38N 2 38E
Méry-sur-Seine 19 48 31N 3 54E
Merzifon 56 40 53N 35 32E
Merzig 25 49 26N 6 37E
Merzouga, Erg Tin 83 24 0N 11 4E
Mesa 119 33 20N 111 56W
Mesa, La, Calif., U.S.A. 119 32 48N 117 5W
Mesa, La, N. Mex., U.S.A. 119 32 6N 106 48W
Mesach Mellet 83 24 30N 11 30E
Mesada 62 31 20N 35 19E
Mesagne 41 40 34N 17 48E
Mesaras, Kólpos 45 35 6N 24 47E
Meschede 24 51 20N 8 17E
Mesfinto 87 13 20N 37 22E
Mesgouez, L. 106 51 20N 75 0W
Meshchovsk 54 54 22N 35 17E
Meshed = Mashhad 65 36 20N 59 35E
Meshoppen 113 41 36N 76 3W
Meshra er Req 81 8 25N 29 18E
Mesick 114 44 24N 85 42W
Mesilinka → 108 56 6N 124 30W
Mesilla 119 32 20N 106 50W
Meslay-du-Maine 18 47 58N 0 33W
Mesocco 25 46 23N 9 12E
Mesolóngion 45 38 21N 21 28E
Mesopotamia = Al Jazirah 64 33 30N 44 0E
Mesoraca 41 39 5N 16 47E
Mésou Volímais 45 37 53N 20 35E
Mess Cr. → 108 57 55N 131 14W
Messac 18 47 49N 1 50W
Messad 82 34 8N 3 30E
Messalo → 91 12 25S 39 15E
Méssaména 85 3 48N 12 49E
Messeix 20 45 37N 2 33E
Messeue 45 37 12N 21 58E
Messina, Italy 41 38 10N 15 32E
Messina, S. Afr. 93 22 20S 30 0E
Messina, Str. di 41 38 5N 15 35E
Messíni 45 37 4N 22 1E
Messínia □ 45 37 10N 22 0E
Messiniakós, Kólpos 45 36 45N 22 5E
Messkirch 25 47 59N 9 7E
Mesta → 43 41 30N 24 0E
Mestá, Ákra 45 38 16N 25 53E
Mestanza 31 38 35N 4 4W
Město Teplá 26 49 59N 12 52E
Mestre 39 45 30N 12 13E
Městys Zelezná Ruda 26 49 8N 13 15E
Meta → 126 6 12N 67 28W
Metairie 117 29 59N 90 9W
Metalici, Munţii 46 46 15N 22 50E
Metaline Falls 118 48 52N 117 22W
Metán 124 25 30S 65 0W
Metauro → 39 43 50N 13 3E
Metema 87 12 56N 36 13E
Metengobalame 91 14 49S 34 30E
Méthana 45 37 35N 23 23E
Methóni 45 36 49N 21 42E
Methven 101 43 38S 171 40E
Methy L. 109 56 28N 109 30W
Metkovets 43 43 37N 23 10E
Metković 42 43 6N 17 39E
Metlakatla 108 55 10N 131 33W
Metlaoui 83 34 24N 8 24E
Metlika 39 45 40N 15 20E
Metropolis 117 37 10N 88 47W
Métsovon 44 39 48N 21 12E
Mettuppalaiyam 70 11 18N 76 59E
Mettur 70 11 48N 77 47E
Mettur Dam 70 11 45N 77 45E
Metulla 62 33 17N 35 34E
Metz 19 49 8N 6 10E
Meulaboh 72 4 11N 96 3E
Meulan 19 49 0N 1 52E
Meung-sur-Loire 19 47 50N 1 40E
Meureudu 72 5 19N 96 10E
Meurthe → 19 48 47N 6 9E
Meurthe-et-Moselle □ 19 48 52N 6 0E
Meuse □ 19 49 8N 5 25E
Meuse → 16 50 45N 5 41E
Meuselwitz 24 51 3N 12 18E
Mexborough 12 53 29N 1 18W
Mexia 117 31 38N 96 32W
Mexiana, I. 127 0 0 49 30W
Mexicali 120 32 40N 115 30W
México 120 19 20N 99 10W
Mexico, Me., U.S.A. 113 44 35N 70 30W
Mexico, Mo., U.S.A. 116 39 10N 91 55W
Mexico ■ 120 20 0N 100 0W
México □ 120 19 20N 99 10W
Mexico, G. of 120 25 0N 90 0W
Meyenburg 24 53 19N 12 15E
Meymac 20 45 32N 2 10E
Meymaneh 65 35 53N 64 38E
Meyrargues 21 43 38N 5 32E
Meyrueis 20 44 12N 3 27E
Meyssac 20 45 3N 1 40E
Mezdra 43 43 12N 23 42E
Mèze 20 43 27N 3 36E
Mezen 52 65 50N 44 20E
Mézenc 21 44 55N 4 11E
Mezeş, Munţii 46 47 5N 23 5E
Mezha → 54 55 50N 31 45E
Mézidon 18 49 5N 0 1W
Mézilhac 21 44 49N 4 21E
Mézin 20 44 4N 0 16E
Mezöberény 27 46 49N 21 3E
Mezöfalva 27 46 55N 18 49E
Mezöhegyes 27 46 19N 20 49E
Mezökovácsháza 27 46 25N 20 57E
Mezökövesd 27 47 49N 20 35E
Mézos 20 44 5N 1 10W
Mezötúr 27 47 0N 20 41E
Mezquital 120 23 29N 104 23W
Mezzolombardo 38 46 13N 11 5E
Mgeta 91 8 22S 36 6E
Mglin 54 53 2N 32 50E
Mhlaba Hills 91 18 30S 30 30E
Mhow 68 22 33N 75 50E
Miahuatlán 120 16 21N 96 36W
Miajadas 31 39 9N 5 54W
Mialar 68 26 15N 70 20E
Miallo 98 16 28S 145 22E
Miami, Ariz., U.S.A. 119 33 25N 110 54W
Miami, Fla., U.S.A. 115 25 45N 80 15W
Miami, Tex., U.S.A. 117 35 44N 100 38W
Miami → 114 39 20N 84 40W
Miami Beach 115 25 49N 80 6W
Miamisburg 114 39 40N 84 11W
Mian Xian 77 33 10N 106 32E
Mianchi 77 34 48N 111 48E
Mīāndow āb 64 37 0N 46 5E
Miandrivazo 93 19 31S 45 29E
Mīāneh 64 37 30N 47 40E
Mianwali 68 32 38N 71 28E
Mianyang, Hubei, China 77 30 25N 113 25E
Mianyang, Sichuan, China 77 31 22N 104 47E
Miaoli 75 24 37N 120 49E
Miarinarivo 93 18 57S 46 55E

Miass **52** 54 59N 60 6 E
Miasteczko Kraj **28** 53 7N 17 1 E
Miastko **28** 54 0N 16 58 E
Micăsasa **46** 46 7N 24 7 E
Michalovce **27** 48 47N 21 58 E
Michelstadt **25** 49 40N 9 0 E
Michigan □ **111** 44 40N 85 40W
Michigan City **114** 41 42N 86 56W
Michigan, L. **114** 44 0N 87 0W
Michipicoten **106** 47 55N 84 55W
Michipicoten I. **106** 47 40N 85 40W
Michoacan □ **120** 19 0N 102 0W
Michurin **43** 42 9N 27 51 E
Michurinsk **55** 52 58N 40 27 E
Miclere **98** 22 34 S 147 32 E
Mico, Pta. **121** 12 0N 83 30W
Micronesia **94** 11 0N 160 0 E
Mid Glamorgan □ **13** 51 40N 3 25W
Mid-Indian Ridge **94** 40 0 S 75 0 E
Mid-Oceanic Ridge **94** 42 0 S 90 0 E
Midai, P. **72** 3 0N 107 47 E
Midale **109** 49 25N 103 20W
Midas **118** 41 14N 116 48W
Middagsfjället **48** 63 27N 12 19 E
Middelburg, Neth. **16** 51 30N 3 36 E
Middelburg, C. Prov., S. Afr. **92** 31 30 S 25 0 E
Middelburg, Trans., S. Afr. **93** 25 49 S 29 28 E
Middelfart **49** 55 30N 9 43 E
Middle Alkali L. **118** 41 30N 120 3W
Middle Andaman I. **71** 12 30N 92 30 E
Middle Loup → **116** 41 17N 98 23W
Middleboro **113** 41 56N 70 52W
Middleburg, N.Y., U.S.A. **113** 42 36N 74 19W
Middleburg, Pa., U.S.A. **112** 40 46N 77 5W
Middlebury **113** 44 0N 73 9W
Middleport **114** 39 0N 82 5W
Middlesboro **115** 36 36N 83 43W
Middlesbrough **12** 54 35N 1 14W
Middlesex **113** 40 36N 74 30W
Middleton **107** 44 57N 65 4W
Middleton Cr. → **98** 22 35 S 141 51 E
Middleton P.O. **98** 22 22 S 141 32 E
Middletown, Conn., U.S.A. **114** 41 37N 72 40W
Middletown, N.Y., U.S.A. **114** 41 28N 74 28W
Middletown, Ohio, U.S.A. **114** 39 29N 84 25W
Middletown, Pa., U.S.A. **113** 40 12N 76 44W
Midelt **82** 32 46N 4 44W
Midi, Canal du **20** 43 45N 1 21 E
Midi d'Ossau **32** 42 50N 0 25W
Midland, Austral. **96** 31 54 S 115 59 E
Midland, Can. **106** 44 45N 79 50W
Midland, Mich., U.S.A. **114** 43 37N 84 17W
Midland, Pa., U.S.A. **112** 40 39N 80 27W
Midland, Tex., U.S.A. **117** 32 0N 102 3W
Midlands □ **91** 19 40 S 29 0 E
Midleton **15** 51 52N 8 12W
Midlothian **117** 32 30N 97 0W
Midnapore **69** 22 25N 87 21 E
Midongy Atsimo **93** 23 35 S 47 1 E
Midongy, Tangorombohitr' i **93** 23 30 S 47 0 E
Midour → **20** 43 54N 0 30W
Midouze → **20** 43 48N 0 51W
Midvale **118** 40 39N 111 58W
Midway Is. **94** 28 13N 177 22W
Midwest **118** 43 27N 106 19W
Midyat **64** 37 25N 41 23 E
Midzur **42** 43 24N 22 40 E
Mie □ **74** 34 30N 136 10 E
Miechów **28** 50 21N 20 5 E
Miedwie, Jezioro **28** 53 17N 14 54 E
Międzybód **28** 51 25N 17 34 E
Międzychód **28** 52 35N 15 53 E
Międzylesie **28** 50 8N 16 40 E
Międzyrzec Podlaski **28** 51 58N 22 45 E
Międzyrzecz **28** 52 26N 15 35 E
Międzyzdroje **28** 53 56N 14 26 E
Miejska **28** 51 39N 16 58 E
Miélan **20** 43 27N 0 19 E
Mielec **28** 50 15N 21 25 E
Mienga **92** 17 12 S 19 48 E
Miercurea Ciuc **46** 46 21N 25 48 E
Mieres **30** 43 18N 5 48W
Mieroszów **28** 50 40N 16 11 E
Mieso **87** 9 15N 40 43 E
Mieszkowice **28** 52 47N 14 30 E
Migdāl **62** 32 51N 35 30 E
Migdal Afeq **62** 32 5N 34 58 E
Migennes **19** 47 58N 3 31 E
Migliarino **39** 44 45N 11 56 E
Miguel Alemán, Presa **120** 18 15N 96 40W
Miguel Alves **127** 4 11 S 42 55W
Mihara **74** 34 24N 133 5 E
Mijares → **32** 39 55N 0 1W
Mijas **31** 36 36N 4 40W
Mikese **90** 6 48 S 37 55 E
Mikha-Tskhakaya **57** 42 15N 42 7 E
Mikhailovka **56** 47 36N 35 16 E
Mikhaylov **55** 54 14N 39 0 E
Mikhaylovgrad **43** 43 27N 23 16 E
Mikhaylovka, Azerbaijan, U.S.S.R. **57** 41 31N 48 52 E
Mikhaylovka, R.S.F.S.R., U.S.S.R. **55** 50 3N 43 5 E
Mikhnevo **55** 55 4N 37 59 E
Mikínai **45** 37 43N 22 46 E
Mikindani **91** 10 15 S 40 2 E
Mikkeli **51** 61 43N 27 15 E
Mikkeli □ **50** 62 0N 28 0 E
Mikkwa → **108** 58 25N 114 46W
Mikniya **87** 17 0N 33 45 E
Mikołajki **28** 53 49N 21 37 E
Mikołów **27** 50 10N 18 50 E
Mikonos **45** 37 30N 25 25 E
Mikrí Préspa, Límni **44** 40 47N 21 3 E
Mikrón Dhérion **44** 41 19N 26 6 E
Mikstat **28** 51 32N 17 59 E
Mikulov **27** 48 48N 16 39 E
Mikumi **90** 7 26 S 37 0 E
Mikun **52** 62 20N 50 0 E
Mikura-Jima **74** 33 52N 139 36 E
Milaca **116** 45 45N 93 40W
Milagro **126** 2 11 S 79 36W
Milan, Mo., U.S.A. **116** 40 10N 93 5W
Milan, Tenn., U.S.A. **115** 35 55N 88 45W
Milan = Milano **38** 45 28N 9 10 E
Milange **91** 16 3 S 35 45 E
Milano **38** 45 28N 9 10 E
Milâs **64** 37 20N 27 50 E
Milazzo **41** 38 13N 15 13 E
Milbank **116** 45 17N 96 38W
Milden **109** 51 29N 107 32W
Mildmay **112** 44 3N 81 7W
Mildura **97** 34 13 S 142 9 E
Miléai **44** 39 20N 23 9 E
Miles, Austral. **97** 26 40 S 150 9 E
Miles, U.S.A. **117** 31 39N 100 11W
Miles City **116** 46 24N 105 50W
Milestone **109** 49 59N 104 31W
Mileto **41** 38 37N 16 3 E
Miletto, Mte. **41** 41 26N 14 23 E
Miletus **45** 37 20N 27 33 E
Milevsko **26** 49 27N 14 21 E
Milford, Conn., U.S.A. **113** 41 13N 73 4W
Milford, Del., U.S.A. **114** 38 52N 75 27W
Milford, Mass., U.S.A. **113** 42 8N 71 30W
Milford, Pa., U.S.A. **113** 41 20N 74 47W
Milford, Utah, U.S.A. **119** 38 20N 113 0W
Milford Haven **13** 51 43N 5 2W
Milford Haven, B. **13** 51 40N 5 10W
Milford Sd. **101** 44 41 S 167 47 E
Milḥ, Baḥr al **64** 32 40N 43 35 E
Milḥ, Ras al **81** 31 54N 25 6 E
Miliana, Aïn Salah, Alg. **82** 27 20N 2 32 E
Miliana, Médéa, Alg. **82** 36 20N 2 15 E
Milicz **28** 51 31N 17 19 E
Militello in Val di Catánia **41** 37 16N 14 46 E
Milk → **118** 48 5N 106 15W
Milk River **108** 49 10N 112 5W
Milk, Wadi el → **86** 17 55N 30 20 E
Mill City **118** 44 45N 122 28W
Mill I. **5** 66 0 S 101 30 E
Millau **20** 44 8N 3 4 E
Millbridge **112** 44 41N 77 36W
Millbrook **112** 44 10N 78 29W
Mille **115** 33 7N 83 15W
Mille Lacs, L. **116** 46 10N 93 30W
Mille Lacs, L. des **106** 48 45N 90 35W
Millen **115** 32 50N 81 57W
Miller **116** 44 35N 98 59W
Millerovo **57** 48 57N 40 28 E
Millersburg, Ohio, U.S.A. **112** 40 32N 81 52W
Millersburg, Pa., U.S.A. **112** 40 32N 76 58W
Millerton **113** 41 57N 73 32W
Millevaches, Plateau de **20** 45 45N 2 0 E
Millicent **97** 37 34 S 140 21 E
Millinocket **107** 45 45N 68 45W
Millmerran **99** 27 53 S 151 16 E
Mills L. **108** 61 30N 118 20W
Millsboro **112** 40 0N 80 0W
Milltown Malbay **15** 52 51N 9 25W
Millville **114** 39 22N 75 0W
Millwood Res. **117** 33 45N 94 0W
Milly **19** 48 24N 2 28 E
Milna **39** 43 20N 16 28 E
Milne Inlet **105** 72 30N 80 0W
Milnor **116** 46 19N 97 29W
Milo **108** 50 34N 112 53W
Mílos **45** 36 44N 24 25 E
Miloševo **42** 45 42N 20 20 E
Miłosław **28** 52 12N 17 32 E
Milparinka P.O. **99** 29 46 S 141 57 E
Miltenberg **25** 49 41N 9 13 E
Milton, Can. **112** 43 33N 79 53W
Milton, N.Z. **101** 46 7 S 169 59 E
Milton, U.K. **14** 57 18N 4 32W
Milton, Fla., U.S.A. **115** 30 38N 87 0W
Milton, Pa., U.S.A. **114** 41 0N 76 53W
Milton-Freewater **118** 45 57N 118 24W
Milton Keynes **13** 52 3N 0 42W
Miltou **81** 10 14N 17 26 E
Milverton **112** 43 34N 80 55W
Milwaukee **114** 43 9N 87 58W
Milwaukie **118** 45 27N 122 39W
Mim **84** 6 57N 2 33W
Mimizan **20** 44 12N 1 13W
Mimon **26** 50 38N 14 43 E
Min Jiang →, Fujian, China **75** 26 0N 119 35 E
Min Jiang →, Sichuan, China **75** 28 45N 104 40 E
Min Xian **77** 34 25N 104 0 E
Mina **119** 38 21N 118 9W
Mina Pirquitas **124** 22 40 S 66 30W
Mīnā Su'ud **64** 28 45N 48 28 E
Mīnā'al Aḥmadī **64** 29 5N 48 10 E
Mīnāb **65** 27 10N 57 1 E
Minago → **109** 54 33N 98 59W
Minaki **109** 49 59N 94 40W
Minamata **74** 32 10N 130 30 E
Minas **125** 34 20 S 55 10W
Minas Basin **107** 45 20N 64 12W
Minas de Rio Tinto **31** 37 42N 6 35W
Minas de San Quintín **31** 38 49N 4 23W
Minas Gerais □ **127** 18 50 S 46 0W
Minas, Sierra de las **120** 15 9N 89 31W
Minatitlán **120** 17 58N 94 35W
Minbu **67** 20 10N 94 52 E
Mincio → **38** 45 4N 10 59 E
Mindanao **73** 8 0N 125 0 E
Mindanao Sea **73** 9 0N 124 0 E
Mindanao Trench **73** 8 0N 128 0 E
Mindel → **25** 48 31N 10 23 E
Mindelheim **25** 48 4N 10 30 E
Minden, Can. **112** 44 55N 78 43W
Minden, Ger. **24** 52 18N 8 45 E
Minden, U.S.A. **117** 32 40N 93 20W
Mindiptana **73** 5 55 S 140 22 E
Mindona, L. **100** 33 6 S 142 6 E
Mindoro **73** 13 0N 121 0 E
Mindoro Strait **73** 12 30N 120 30 E
Mindouli **88** 4 12 S 14 28 E
Minehead **13** 51 12N 3 29W
Mineoia **117** 32 40N 95 30W
Mineral Wells **117** 32 50N 98 5W
Mineralnyye Vody **57** 44 2N 43 8 E
Minersville, Pa., U.S.A. **113** 40 11N 76 17W
Minersville, Utah, U.S.A. **119** 38 14N 112 58W
Minerva **112** 40 43N 81 8W
Minervino Murge **41** 41 6N 16 4 E
Minetto **113** 43 24N 76 28W
Mingan **107** 50 20N 64 0W
Mingechaur **57** 40 45N 47 0 E
Mingechaurskoye Vdkhr. **57** 40 56N 47 20 E
Mingela **98** 19 52 S 146 38 E
Mingera Cr. → **98** 20 38 S 138 10 E
Minggang **77** 32 24N 114 3 E
Mingin **67** 22 50N 94 30 E
Minglanilla **32** 39 34N 1 38W
Mingorria **30** 40 45N 4 40W
Mingxi **77** 26 18N 117 12 E
Minićevo **42** 43 42N 22 18 E
Minidoka **118** 42 47N 113 34W
Minigwal L. **96** 29 31 S 123 14 E
Minipi, L. **107** 52 25N 60 45W
Mink L. **108** 61 54N 117 40W
Minna **85** 9 37N 6 30 E
Minneapolis, Kans., U.S.A. **116** 39 11N 97 40W
Minneapolis, Minn., U.S.A. **116** 44 58N 93 20W
Minnedosa **109** 50 14N 99 50W
Minnesota □ **116** 46 40N 94 0W
Minnesund **47** 60 23N 11 14 E
Minnitaki L. **106** 49 57N 92 10W
Miño → **30** 41 52N 8 40W
Minoa **45** 35 6N 25 45 E
Minorca = Menorca **32** 40 0N 4 0 E
Minore **99** 32 14 S 148 27 E
Minot **116** 48 10N 101 15W
Minqing **77** 26 15N 118 50 E
Minquiers, Les **18** 48 58N 2 8W
Minsen **24** 53 43N 7 58 E
Minsk **54** 53 52N 27 30 E
Mińsk Mazowiecki **28** 52 10N 21 33 E
Mintaka Pass **69** 37 0N 74 58 E
Minto **104** 64 55N 149 20W
Minton **109** 49 10N 104 35W
Minturn **118** 39 35N 106 25W
Minturno **40** 41 15N 13 43 E
Minûf **86** 30 26N 30 52 E
Minusinsk **59** 53 50N 91 20 E
Minutang **67** 28 15N 96 30 E
Minvoul **88** 2 9N 12 8 E
Minya el Qamh **86** 30 31N 31 21 E
Mionica **42** 44 14N 20 6 E
Mir **85** 14 5N 11 59 E
Mir-Bashir **57** 40 20N 46 58 E
Mira, Italy **39** 45 26N 12 9 E
Mira, Port. **30** 40 26N 8 44W
Mira → **31** 37 43N 8 47W
Mirabella Eclano **41** 41 3N 14 59 E
Miraflores Locks **120** 8 59N 79 36W
Miraj **70** 16 50N 74 45 E
Miram **98** 21 15 S 148 55 E
Miramar, Argent. **124** 38 15 S 57 50W
Miramar, Mozam. **93** 23 50 S 35 35 E
Miramas **21** 43 33N 4 59 E
Mirambeau **20** 45 23N 0 35W
Miramichi B. **107** 47 15N 65 0W
Miramont-de-Guyenne **20** 44 37N 0 21 E
Miranda **127** 20 10 S 56 15W
Miranda de Ebro **32** 42 41N 2 57W
Miranda do Corvo **30** 40 6N 8 20W
Miranda do Douro **30** 41 30N 6 16W
Mirande **20** 43 31N 0 25 E
Mirandela **30** 41 32N 7 10W
Mirando City **117** 27 28N 98 59W
Mirandola **38** 44 53N 11 2 E
Mirandópolis **125** 21 9 S 51 6W
Mirango **91** 13 32 S 34 58 E
Mirano **39** 45 29N 12 6 E
Mirassol **125** 20 46 S 49 28W
Mirbāṭ **63** 17 0N 54 45 E
Mirear **86** 23 15N 35 41 E
Mirebeau, Côte-d'or, France **19** 47 25N 5 20 E
Mirebeau, Vienne, France **18** 46 49N 0 10 E
Mirecourt **19** 48 20N 6 10 E
Mirgorod **54** 49 58N 33 37 E
Miri **72** 4 18N 114 0 E
Miriam Vale **98** 24 20 S 151 33 E
Mirim, Lagoa **125** 32 45 S 52 50W
Mirnyy, Antarct. **5** 66 33 S 93 1 E
Mirnyy, U.S.S.R. **59** 62 33N 113 53 E
Miroč **42** 44 32N 22 16 E
Mirond L. **109** 55 6N 102 47W
Mirosławiec **28** 53 20N 16 5 E
Mirpur Bibiwari **68** 28 33N 67 44 E
Mirpur Khas **68** 25 30N 69 0 E
Mirpur Sakro **68** 24 33N 67 41 E
Mirria **85** 13 43N 9 7 E
Mirror **108** 52 30N 113 7W
Mirşani **46** 44 1N 23 59 E
Mirsk **28** 50 58N 15 23 E
Miryang **76** 35 31N 128 44 E
Mirzaani **57** 41 24N 46 5 E
Mirzapur-cum-Vindhyachal **69** 25 10N 82 34 E
Miscou I. **107** 47 57N 64 31W
Mish'āb, Ra'as al **64** 28 15N 48 43 E
Mishan **75** 45 37N 131 48 E
Mishawaka **114** 41 40N 86 8W
Mishbih, Gebel **86** 22 38N 34 44 E
Mishima **74** 35 10N 138 52 E
Mishmar Ayyalon **62** 31 52N 34 57 E
Mishmar Ha' Emeq **62** 32 37N 35 7 E
Mishmar Ha Negev **62** 31 22N 34 48 E
Mishmar Ha Yarden **62** 33 0N 35 36 E
Misilmeri **40** 38 2N 13 25 E
Misima I. **98** 10 40 S 152 45 E
Misiones □, Argent. **125** 27 0 S 55 0W
Misiones □, Parag. **124** 27 0 S 56 0W
Miskīn **65** 23 44N 56 52 E
Miskitos, Cayos **121** 14 26N 82 50W
Miskolc **27** 48 7N 20 50 E
Misoke **90** 0 42 S 28 2 E
Misool **73** 1 52 S 130 10 E
Misrātah **83** 32 24N 15 3 E
Misrātah □ **83** 29 0N 16 0 E
Misriç **64** 37 55N 41 40 E
Missanabie **106** 48 20N 84 6W
Missinaibi → **106** 50 43N 81 29W
Missinaibi L. **106** 48 23N 83 40W
Mission, S.D., U.S.A. **116** 43 21N 100 36W
Mission, Tex., U.S.A. **117** 26 15N 98 20W
Mission City **108** 49 10N 122 15W
Missisa L. **106** 52 20N 85 7W
Mississagi → **106** 46 15N 83 9W
Mississippi → **117** 29 0N 89 15W
Mississippi, Delta of the **117** 29 15N 90 30W
Mississippi L. **113** 45 5N 76 10W
Mississippi Sd. **117** 30 25N 89 0W
Missoula **118** 46 52N 114 0W
Missouri □ **116** 38 25N 92 30W
Missouri → **116** 38 50N 90 8W
Missouri Valley **116** 41 33N 95 53W
Mistake B. **109** 62 8N 93 0W
Mistassini → **107** 48 42N 72 20W
Mistassini L. **106** 51 0N 73 30W
Mistastin L. **107** 55 57N 63 20W
Mistatim **109** 52 52N 103 22W
Mistelbach **27** 48 34N 16 34 E
Misterbianco **41** 37 32N 15 0 E
Mistretta **41** 37 56N 14 20 E
Misty L. **109** 58 53N 101 40W
Mît Ghamr **86** 30 42N 31 12 E
Mitatib **87** 15 59N 36 12 E
Mitchell, Austral. **97** 26 29 S 147 58 E
Mitchell, Can. **112** 43 28N 81 12W
Mitchell, Ind., U.S.A. **114** 38 42N 86 25W
Mitchell, Nebr., U.S.A. **116** 41 58N 103 45W
Mitchell, Oreg., U.S.A. **118** 44 31N 120 8W
Mitchell, S.D., U.S.A. **116** 43 40N 98 0W
Mitchell → **97** 15 12 S 141 35 E
Mitchell, Mt. **115** 35 40N 82 20W
Mitchelstown **15** 52 16N 8 18W
Mitha Tiwana **68** 32 13N 72 6 E
Mithimna **44** 39 20N 26 12 E
Mitiaro, I. **101** 19 49 S 157 43W
Mitilini **45** 39 6N 26 35 E
Mitilinoí **45** 37 42N 26 56 E
Mitla **120** 16 55N 96 24W
Mito **74** 36 20N 140 30 E
Mitsinjo **93** 16 1 S 45 52 E
Mitsiwa **87** 15 35N 39 25 E
Mitsiwa Channel **87** 15 30N 40 0 E
Mitta Mitta → **100** 36 14 S 147 10 E
Mittagong **99** 34 28 S 150 29 E
Mittelland Kanal **24** 52 23N 7 45 E
Mittenwalde **24** 52 16N 13 33 E
Mitterteich **25** 49 57N 12 15 E
Mittweida **24** 50 59N 13 0 E
Mitú **126** 1 8N 70 3W
Mitumba **90** 7 8 S 31 2 E
Mitumba, Chaîne des **90** 6 0 S 29 0 E
Mitwaba **91** 8 2 S 27 17 E
Mityana **90** 0 23N 32 2 E
Mitzic **88** 0 45N 11 40 E
Mixteco → **120** 18 11N 98 30W
Miyagi □ **74** 38 15N 140 45 E
Miyâh, W. el → **86** 25 0N 33 23 E
Miyake-Jima **74** 34 0N 139 30 E
Miyako **74** 39 40N 141 59 E
Miyakonojō **74** 31 40N 131 5 E
Miyazaki **74** 31 56N 131 30 E
Miyazaki □ **74** 32 30N 131 30 E
Miyazu **74** 35 35N 135 10 E
Miyet, Bahr el **64** 31 30N 35 30 E
Miyun **76** 40 28N 116 50 E
Mizal **64** 23 59N 45 11 E
Mizamis = Ozamiz **73** 8 15N 123 50 E
Mizdah **83** 31 30N 13 0 E
Mizen Hd., Cork, Ireland **15** 51 27N 9 50W
Mizen Hd., Wicklow, Ireland **15** 52 52N 6 4W
Mizhi **76** 37 47N 110 12 E
Mizil **46** 44 59N 26 29 E
Mizoram □ **67** 23 30N 92 40 E
Mizpe Ramon **62** 30 34N 34 49 E
Mjöbäck **49** 57 28N 12 53 E
Mjölby **49** 58 20N 15 10 E
Mjømna **47** 60 55N 4 55 E
Mjörn **49** 57 55N 12 25 E
Mjøsa **47** 60 48N 11 0 E
Mkata **90** 5 45 S 38 20 E
Mkokotoni **90** 5 55 S 39 15 E
Mkomazi **90** 4 40 S 38 7 E
Mkulwe **91** 8 37 S 32 20 E
Mkumbi, Ras **90** 7 38 S 39 55 E
Mkushi **91** 14 25 S 29 15 E
Mkushi River **91** 13 32 S 29 45 E
Mkuze → **93** 27 45 S 32 30 E
Mladá Boleslav **26** 50 27N 14 53 E
Mladenovac **42** 44 28N 20 44 E
Mlala Hills **90** 6 50 S 31 40 E
Mlange **91** 16 2 S 35 33 E
Mlava → **42** 44 45N 21 13 E
Mława **28** 53 9N 20 25 E
Mlinište **39** 44 15N 16 50 E
Mljet **42** 42 43N 17 30 E
Mljetski Kanal **42** 42 48N 17 35 E
Młynąry **28** 54 12N 19 46 E
Mlynary **28** 54 12N 19 43 E
Mme **85** 6 18N 10 14 E
Mo **47** 59 28N 7 50 E
Mo i Rana **50** 66 15N 14 7 E
Moa **73** 8 0 S 128 0 E
Moa → **84** 6 59N 11 36 E
Moab **119** 38 40N 109 35W
Moabi **88** 2 24 S 10 59 E
Moala **101** 18 36 S 179 53 E
Moalie Park **99** 29 42 S 143 3 E
Moaña **30** 42 18N 8 43W
Moapa **119** 36 45N 114 37W
Moba **90** 7 0 S 29 48 E
Mobaye **88** 4 25N 21 5 E
Mobayi **88** 4 15N 21 8 E
Moberley **116** 39 25N 92 25W
Moberly → **108** 56 12N 120 55W
Mobile **115** 30 41N 88 3W
Mobile B. **115** 30 30N 88 0W
Mobile, Pt. **115** 30 15N 88 0W
Mobridge **116** 45 31N 100 28W
Mobutu Sese Seko, L. **90** 1 30N 31 0 E

Mocabe Kasari 91 9 58 S 26 12 E
Moçambique 91 15 3 S 40 42 E
Moçambique □ 91 14 45 S 38 30 E
Moçâmedes 89 15 7 S 12 11 E
Moçâmedes □ 92 16 35 S 12 30 E
Mochudi 92 24 27 S 26 7 E
Mocimboa da Praia 91 11 25 S 40 20 E
Mociu 46 46 46N 24 3 E
Möckeln 49 56 40N 14 15 E
Moclips 118 47 14N 124 10W
Mocoa 126 1 7N 76 35W
Mococa 125 21 28 S 47 0W
Mocorito 120 25 30N 107 53W
Moctezuma 120 29 50N 109 0W
Moctezuma → 120 21 59N 98 34W
Mocuba 91 16 54 S 36 57 E
Modalen 47 60 49N 5 48 E
Modane 21 45 12N 6 40 E
Modasa 68 23 30N 73 21 E
Modder → 92 29 2 S 24 37 E
Modderrivier 92 29 2 S 24 38 E
Módena 38 44 39N 10 55 E
Modena 119 37 55N 113 56W
Modesto 119 37 43N 121 0W
Módica 41 36 52N 14 45 E
Modigliana 39 44 9N 11 48 E
Modlin 28 52 24N 20 41 E
Mödling 27 48 5N 16 17 E
Modo 87 5 31N 30 33 E
Modra 27 48 19N 17 20 E
Modriča 42 44 57N 18 17 E
Moe 97 38 12 S 146 19 E
Moebase 91 17 3 S 38 41 E
Moei → 71 17 25N 98 10 E
Moëlan-sur-Mer 18 47 49N 3 38W
Moengo 127 5 45N 54 20W
Moffat 14 55 20N 3 27W
Moga 68 30 48N 75 8 E
Mogadishu = Muqdisho 63 2 2N 45 25 E
Mogador = Essaouira 82 31 32N 9 48W
Mogadouro 30 41 22N 6 47W
Mogami → 74 38 45N 140 0 E
Mogaung 67 25 20N 97 0 E
Møgeltønder 49 54 57N 8 48 E
Mogente 33 38 52N 0 45W
Mogho 87 4 54N 40 16 E
Mogi das Cruzes 125 23 31 S 46 11W
Mogi-Guaçu → 125 20 53 S 48 10W
Mogi-Mirim 125 22 29 S 47 0W
Mogielnica 28 51 42N 20 41 E
Mogilev 54 53 55N 30 18 E
Mogilev-Podolskiy 56 48 20N 27 40 E
Mogilno 28 52 39N 17 55 E
Mogincual 91 15 35 S 40 25 E
Mogliano Véneto 39 45 33N 12 15 E
Mogocha 59 53 40N 119 50 E
Mogoi 73 1 55 S 133 10 E
Mogok 67 23 0N 96 40 E
Mogollon 119 33 25N 108 48W
Mogollon Mesa 119 35 0N 111 0W
Moguer 31 37 15N 6 52W
Mohács 27 45 58N 18 41 E
Mohall 116 48 46N 101 30W
Moḩammadābād 65 37 52N 59 5 E
Mohammadia 82 35 33N 0 3 E
Mohammedia 82 33 44N 7 21W
Mohawk 119 32 45N 113 50W
Mohawk → 113 42 47N 73 42W
Mohe 76 53 28N 122 17 E
Moheda 49 57 1N 14 35 E
Möhne → 24 51 29N 7 57 E
Moholm 49 58 37N 14 5 E
Mohon 19 49 45N 4 44 E
Mohoro 90 8 6 S 39 8 E
Moia 87 5 3N 28 2 E
Moidart, L. 14 56 47N 5 40W
Moinabad 70 17 44N 77 16 E
Moineşti 46 46 28N 26 31 E
Mointy 58 47 10N 73 18 E
Moirans 21 45 20N 5 33 E
Moirans-en-Montagne 21 46 26N 5 43 E
Moíres 45 35 4N 24 56 E
Moisakula 54 58 3N 25 12 E
Moisie 107 50 12N 66 1W
Moisie → 107 50 14N 66 5W
Moissac 20 44 7N 1 5 E
Moïssala 81 8 21N 17 46 E
Moita 31 38 38N 8 58W
Mojácar 33 37 6N 1 55W
Mojados 30 41 26N 4 40W
Mojave 119 35 8N 118 8W
Mojave Desert 119 35 0N 116 30W
Mojo, Boliv. 124 21 48 S 65 33W
Mojo, Ethiopia 87 8 35N 39 5 E
Mojo, Indon. 72 8 10 S 117 40 E
Mojokerto 73 7 29 S 112 25 E
Mokai 101 38 32 S 175 56 E
Mokambo 91 12 25 S 28 20 E
Mokameh 69 25 24N 85 55 E
Mokhós 45 35 16N 25 27 E
Mokhotlong 93 29 22 S 29 2 E
Moknine 83 35 35N 10 58 E
Mokokchung 67 26 15N 94 30 E
Mokra Gora 42 42 50N 20 30 E
Mokronog 39 45 57N 15 9 E
Moksha → 55 54 45N 41 53 E
Mokshan 55 53 25N 44 35 E
Mol 16 51 11N 5 5 E
Mola, C. de la 32 39 40N 4 20 E
Mola di Bari 41 41 3N 17 5 E
Moláoi 45 36 49N 22 56 E
Molat 39 44 15N 14 50 E
Molchanovo 58 57 40N 83 50 E
Mold 12 53 10N 3 10W
Moldava nad Bodvou 27 48 38N 21 0 E
Moldavia = Moldova 46 46 30N 27 0 E
Moldavian S.S.R. □ 56 47 0N 28 0 E
Molde 47 62 45N 7 9 E
Moldova 46 46 30N 27 0 E
Moldova Nouă 42 44 45N 21 41 E
Moldoveanu 43 45 36N 24 45 E
Molepolole 92 24 28 S 25 28 E
Molfetta 41 41 12N 16 35 E
Molina de Aragón 32 40 46N 1 52W
Moline 116 41 30N 90 30W
Molinella 39 44 38N 11 40 E
Molinos 124 25 28 S 66 15W
Moliro 90 8 12 S 30 30 E
Molise □ 39 41 45N 14 30 E
Moliterno 41 40 14N 15 50 E
Mollahat 69 22 56N 89 48 E
Mölle 49 56 17N 12 31 E
Molledo 30 43 8N 4 6W
Mollendo 126 17 0 S 72 0W
Mollerusa 32 41 37N 0 54 E
Mollina 31 37 8N 4 38W
Mölln 24 53 37N 10 41 E
Mölltorp 49 58 30N 14 26 E
Mölndal 49 57 40N 12 3 E
Molochansk 56 47 15N 35 35 E
Molochnaya → 56 47 0N 35 30 E
Molodechno 54 54 20N 26 50 E
Molokai 110 21 8N 157 0W
Moloma → 55 58 20N 48 15 E
Molong 99 33 5 S 148 54 E
Molopo → 92 28 30 S 20 13 E
Mólos 45 38 47N 22 37 E
Moloundou 88 2 8N 15 15 E
Molsheim 19 48 33N 7 29 E
Molson L. 109 54 22N 96 40W
Molteno 92 31 22 S 26 22 E
Molu 73 6 45 S 131 40 E
Molucca Sea 73 4 0 S 124 0 E
Moluccas = Maluku 73 1 0 S 127 0 E
Molusi 92 20 21 S 24 29 E
Moma, Mozam. 91 16 47 S 39 4 E
Moma, Zaïre 90 1 35 S 23 52 E
Momanga 92 18 7 S 21 41 E
Mombasa 90 4 2 S 39 43 E
Mombuey 30 42 3N 6 20W
Momchilgrad 43 41 33N 25 23 E
Momi 90 1 42 S 27 0 E
Mompós 126 9 14N 74 26W
Møn 49 54 57N 12 15 E
Mon → 67 20 25N 94 30 E
Mona, Canal de la 121 18 30N 67 45W
Mona, I. 121 18 5N 67 54W
Mona, Pta. 121 9 37N 82 36W
Mona, Punta 31 36 43N 3 45W
Monach Is. 14 57 32N 7 40W
Monaco ■ 21 43 46N 7 23 E
Monadhliath Mts. 14 57 10N 4 4W
Monaghan 15 54 15N 6 58W
Monaghan □ 15 54 10N 7 0W
Monahans 117 31 35N 102 50W
Monapo 91 14 56 S 40 19 E
Monarch Mt. 108 51 55N 125 57W
Monastier-sur-Gazeille, Le 20 44 57N 3 59 E
Monastir 83 35 50N 10 49 E
Monastyriska 54 49 8N 25 14 E
Moncada 32 39 30N 0 24W
Moncalieri 38 45 0N 7 40 E
Moncalvo 38 45 3N 8 15 E
Moncão 30 42 4N 8 27W
Moncarapacho 31 37 5N 7 46W
Moncayo, Sierra del 32 41 48N 1 50W
Mönchengladbach 24 51 12N 6 23 E
Monchique 31 37 19N 8 38W
Monclova 120 26 50N 101 30W
Moncontour 18 48 22N 2 38W
Moncoutant 18 46 43N 0 35W
Moncton 107 46 7N 64 51W
Mondego → 30 40 9N 8 52W
Mondego, Cabo 30 40 11N 8 54W
Mondeodo 73 3 34 S 122 9 E
Mondolfo 39 43 45N 13 8 E
Mondoñedo 30 43 25N 7 23W
Mondovi 38 44 23N 7 49 E
Mondovi 116 44 37N 91 40W
Mondragon 21 44 13N 4 44 E
Mondragone 40 41 8N 13 52 E
Monduli □ 90 3 0 S 36 0 E
Monemvasía 45 36 41N 23 3 E
Monessen 114 40 9N 79 50W
Monesterio 31 38 6N 6 15W
Monestier-de-Clermont 21 44 55N 5 38 E
Monêtier-les-Bains, Le 21 44 58N 6 30 E
Monett 117 36 55N 93 56W
Monfalcone 39 45 49N 13 32 E
Monflanquin 20 44 32N 0 47 E
Monforte 31 39 6N 7 25W
Monforte de Lemos 30 42 31N 7 33W
Mong Cai 71 21 27N 107 54 E
Mong Hsu 67 21 54N 98 30 E
Mong Kung 67 21 35N 97 35 E
Mong Lang 71 21 29N 97 52 E
Mong Nai 67 20 32N 97 46 E
Mong Pawk 67 22 4N 99 16 E
Mong Ton 67 20 17N 98 45 E
Mong Wa 67 21 26N 100 27 E
Mong Yai 67 22 21N 98 3 E
Mongalla 87 5 8N 31 42 E
Mongers, L. 96 29 25 S 117 5 E
Monghyr 69 25 23N 86 30 E
Mongla 69 22 8N 89 35 E
Mongo 81 12 14N 18 43 E
Mongolia ■ 75 47 0N 103 0 E
Mongonu 85 12 40N 13 32 E
Mongororo 81 12 3N 22 26 E
Mongu 89 15 16 S 23 12 E
Môngua 92 16 43 S 15 20 E
Monistrol 20 45 57N 3 38 E
Monistrol-St-Loire 21 45 17N 4 11 E
Monkey Bay 91 14 7 S 35 1 E
Mońki 28 53 23N 22 48 E
Monkira 98 24 46 S 140 30 E
Monkoto 88 1 38 S 20 35 E
Monmouth, U.K. 13 51 48N 2 43W
Monmouth, U.S.A. 116 40 50N 90 40W
Mono, L. 119 38 0N 119 9W
Monongahela 112 40 12N 79 56W
Monópoli 41 40 57N 17 18 E
Monor 27 47 21N 19 27 E
Monóvar 33 38 28N 0 53W
Monqoumba 88 3 33N 18 40 E
Monreal del Campo 32 40 47N 1 20W
Monreale 40 38 6N 13 16 E
Monroe, Ga., U.S.A. 115 33 47N 83 43W
Monroe, La., U.S.A. 117 32 32N 92 4W
Monroe, Mich., U.S.A. 114 41 55N 83 26W
Monroe, N.C., U.S.A. 115 35 2N 80 37W
Monroe, N.Y., U.S.A. 113 41 19N 74 11W
Monroe, Utah, U.S.A. 119 38 45N 112 5W
Monroe, Wis., U.S.A. 116 42 38N 89 40W
Monroe City 116 39 40N 91 40W
Monroeville 115 31 33N 87 15W
Monrovia, Liberia 84 6 18N 10 47W
Monrovia, U.S.A. 119 34 7N 118 1W
Mons 16 50 27N 3 58 E
Monsaraz 31 38 28N 7 22W
Monse 73 4 0 S 123 10 E
Monségur 20 44 38N 0 4 E
Monsélice 39 45 16N 11 46 E
Mont-de-Marsan 20 43 54N 0 31W
Mont d'Or, Tunnel 19 46 45N 6 18 E
Mont-Dore, Le 20 45 35N 2 50 E
Mont-Joli 107 48 37N 68 10W
Mont Laurier 106 46 35N 75 30W
Mont-sous-Vaudrey 19 46 58N 5 36 E
Mont-St-Michel, Le 18 48 40N 1 30W
Mont Tremblant Prov. Park 106 46 30N 74 30W
Montabaur 24 50 26N 7 49 E
Montagnac 20 43 29N 3 28 E
Montagnana 39 45 13N 11 29 E
Montagu 92 33 45 S 20 8 E
Montagu I. 5 58 25 S 26 20W
Montague, Can. 107 46 10N 62 39W
Montague, Calif., U.S.A. 118 41 47N 122 30W
Montague, Mass., U.S.A. 113 42 31N 72 33W
Montague, I. 120 31 40N 114 56W
Montague I. 104 60 0N 147 0W
Montague Sd. 96 14 28 S 125 20 E
Montaigu 18 46 59N 1 18W
Montalbán 32 40 50N 0 45W
Montalbano di Elicona 41 38 1N 15 0 E
Montalbano Iónico 41 40 17N 16 33 E
Montalbo 32 39 53N 2 42W
Montalcino 39 43 4N 11 30 E
Montalegre 30 41 49N 7 47W
Montalto di Castro 39 42 20N 11 36 E
Montalto Uffugo 41 39 25N 16 9 E
Montamarta 30 41 39N 5 49W
Montaña 126 6 0 S 73 0W
Montana □ 110 47 0N 110 0W
Montánchez 31 39 15N 6 8W
Montargis 19 48 0N 2 43 E
Montauban 20 44 0N 1 21 E
Montauk 114 41 3N 71 57W
Montauk Pt. 113 41 4N 71 52W
Montbard 19 47 38N 4 20 E
Montbéliard 19 47 31N 6 48 E
Montblanch 32 41 23N 1 4 E
Montbrison 21 45 36N 4 3 E
Montcalm, Pic de 20 42 40N 1 25 E
Montceau-les-Mines 19 46 40N 4 23 E
Montchanin 38 46 47N 4 30 E
Montclair 113 40 53N 74 13W
Montcornet 19 49 40N 4 0 E
Montcuq 20 44 21N 1 13 E
Montdidier 19 49 38N 2 35 E
Monte Alegre 127 2 0 S 54 0W
Monte Azul 127 15 9 S 42 53W
Monte Bello Is. 96 20 30 S 115 45 E
Monte-Carlo 21 43 46N 7 23 E
Monte Caseros 124 30 10 S 57 50W
Monte Comán 124 34 40 S 67 53W
Monte Lindo → 124 23 56 S 57 12W
Monte Quemado 124 25 53 S 62 41W
Monte Redondo 30 39 53N 8 50W
Monte San Giovanni 40 41 39N 13 33 E
Monte San Savino 39 43 20N 11 42 E
Monte Sant' Ángelo 41 41 42N 15 59 E
Monte Santu, C. di 40 40 5N 9 42 E
Monte Vista 119 37 40N 106 8W
Monteagudo 125 27 14 S 54 8W
Montealegre 33 38 48N 1 17W
Montebello 106 45 40N 74 55W
Montebelluna 39 45 47N 12 3 E
Montebourg 18 49 30N 1 20W
Montecastrilli 39 42 40N 12 30 E
Montecatini Terme 38 43 55N 10 48 E
Montecristi 126 1 0 S 80 40W
Montecristo 38 42 20N 10 20 E
Montefalco 39 42 53N 12 38 E
Montefiascone 39 42 31N 12 2 E
Montefrío 31 37 20N 4 0W
Montego Bay 121 18 30N 78 0W
Montegranaro 39 43 13N 13 38 E
Montehanin 19 46 46N 4 44 E
Montejicar 33 37 33N 3 30W
Montélimar 21 44 33N 4 45 E
Montella 41 40 50N 15 0 E
Montellano 31 36 59N 5 36W
Montello 116 43 49N 89 21W
Montelupo Fiorentino 38 43 44N 11 2 E
Montemor-o-Novo 31 38 40N 8 12W
Montemor-o-Velho 30 40 11N 8 40W
Montemorelos 120 25 11N 99 42W
Montendre 20 45 16N 0 26W
Montenegro 125 29 39 S 51 29W
Montenegro = Crna Gora □ 42 42 40N 19 20 E
Montenero di Bisaccia 39 42 0N 14 47 E
Montepuez 91 13 8 S 38 59 E
Montepuez → 91 12 32 S 40 27 E
Montepulciano 39 43 5N 11 46 E
Montereale 39 42 31N 13 13 E
Montereau 19 48 22N 2 57 E
Monterey 119 36 35N 121 57W
Montería 126 8 46N 75 53W
Monteros 124 27 11 S 65 30W
Monterotondo 39 42 3N 12 36 E
Monterrey 120 25 40N 100 30W
Montes Claros 127 16 30 S 43 50W
Montesano 118 47 0N 123 39W
Montesárchio 41 41 5N 14 37 E
Montescaglioso 41 40 34N 16 40 E
Montesilvano 39 42 30N 14 8 E
Montevarchi 39 43 30N 11 32 E
Montevideo 125 34 50 S 56 11W
Montezuma 116 41 32N 92 35W
Montfaucon, Haute-Loire, France 21 45 11N 4 20 E
Montfaucon, Meuse, France 19 49 16N 5 8 E
Montfort-l'Amaury 19 48 47N 1 49 E
Montfort-sur-Meu 18 48 8N 1 58W
Montgenèvre 21 44 56N 6 42 E
Montgomery, U.K. 13 52 34N 3 9W
Montgomery, Ala., U.S.A. 115 32 20N 86 20W
Montgomery, W. Va., U.S.A. 114 38 9N 81 21W
Montgomery = Sahiwal 68 30 45N 73 8 E
Montguyon 20 45 12N 0 12W
Monthey 25 46 15N 6 56 E
Monticelli d'Ongina 38 45 3N 9 56 E
Monticello, Ark., U.S.A. 117 33 40N 91 48W
Monticello, Fla., U.S.A. 115 30 35N 83 50W
Monticello, Ind., U.S.A. 114 40 40N 86 45W
Monticello, Iowa, U.S.A. 116 42 18N 91 12W
Monticello, Ky., U.S.A. 115 36 52N 84 50W
Monticello, Minn., U.S.A. 116 45 17N 93 52W
Monticello, Miss., U.S.A. 117 31 35N 90 8W
Monticello, N.Y., U.S.A. 113 41 37N 74 42W
Monticello, Utah, U.S.A. 119 37 55N 109 27W
Montichiari 38 45 28N 10 29 E
Montier 19 48 30N 4 45 E
Montignac 20 45 4N 1 10 E
Montigny-les-Metz 19 49 7N 6 10 E
Montigny-sur-Aube 19 47 57N 4 45 E
Montijo 31 38 52N 6 39W
Montijo, Presa de 31 38 55N 6 26W
Montilla 31 37 36N 4 40W
Montivideo 116 44 55N 95 40W
Montlhéry 19 48 39N 2 15 E
Montluçon 20 46 22N 2 36 E
Montmagny 107 46 58N 70 34W
Montmarault 20 46 19N 2 57 E
Montmartre 109 50 14N 103 27W
Montmédy 19 49 30N 5 20 E
Montmélian 21 45 30N 6 4 E
Montmirail 19 48 51N 3 30 E
Montmoreau-St-Cybard 20 45 23N 0 8 E
Montmorency 107 46 53N 71 11W
Montmorillon 20 46 26N 0 50 E
Montmort 19 48 55N 3 49 E
Monto 97 24 52 S 151 6 E
Montoire 18 47 45N 0 52 E
Montório al Vomano 39 42 35N 13 38 E
Montoro 31 38 1N 4 27W
Montour Falls 112 42 20N 76 51W
Montpelier, Idaho, U.S.A. 118 42 15N 111 20W
Montpelier, Ohio, U.S.A. 114 41 34N 84 40W
Montpelier, Vt., U.S.A. 114 44 15N 72 38W
Montpellier 20 43 37N 3 52 E
Montpezat-de-Quercy 20 44 15N 1 30 E
Montpon 20 45 2N 0 11 E
Montréal, Can. 106 45 31N 73 34W
Montréal, France 20 43 13N 2 8 E
Montreal L. 109 54 20N 105 45W
Montreal Lake 109 54 3N 105 46W
Montredon-Labessonniè 20 43 45N 2 18 E
Montréjeau 20 43 6N 0 35 E
Montrésor 18 47 10N 1 10 E
Montreuil 19 50 27N 1 45 E
Montreuil-Bellay 18 47 8N 0 9W
Montreux 25 46 26N 6 55 E
Montrevault 18 47 17N 1 2W
Montrevel-en-Bresse 21 46 21N 5 8 E
Montrichard 18 47 20N 1 10 E
Montrose, U.K. 14 56 43N 2 28W
Montrose, Col., U.S.A. 119 38 30N 107 52W
Montrose, Pa., U.S.A. 113 41 50N 75 55W
Monts, Pte des 107 49 20N 67 12W
Monts-sur-Guesnes 18 46 55N 0 13 E
Montsalvy 20 44 41N 2 30 E
Montsant, Sierra de 32 41 17N 1 0 E
Montsauche 19 47 13N 4 0 E
Montsech, Sierra del 32 42 0N 0 45 E
Montseny 32 41 55N 2 25W
Montserrat, Spain 32 41 36N 1 49 E
Montserrat, W. Indies 121 16 40N 62 10W
Montuenga 30 41 3N 4 38W
Montuiri 32 39 34N 2 59 E
Monveda 88 2 52N 21 30 E
Monywa 67 22 7N 95 11 E
Monza 38 45 35N 9 15 E
Monze 91 16 17 S 27 29 E
Monze, C. 66 24 47N 66 37 E
Monzón 32 41 52N 0 10 E
Moolawatana 99 29 55 S 139 45 E
Moonah → 98 22 3 S 138 33 E
Moonbeam 106 49 20N 82 10W
Moonie 99 27 46 S 150 20 E
Moonie → 97 29 19 S 148 43 E
Moonta 99 34 6 S 137 32 E
Mooraberree 99 25 13 S 140 54 E
Moorcroft 116 44 17N 104 58W
Moore, L. 96 29 50 S 117 35 E
Moorefield 114 39 5N 78 59W
Moores Res. 113 44 45N 71 50W
Mooresville 115 35 36N 80 45W
Moorfoot Hills 14 55 44N 3 8W
Moorhead 116 46 51N 96 44W
Mooroopna 99 36 25 S 145 22 E
Moorreesburg 92 33 6 S 18 38 E
Moosburg 25 48 28N 11 57 E
Moose → 106 51 20N 80 25W
Moose Factory 106 51 16N 80 32W
Moose I. 109 51 42N 97 10W
Moose Jaw 109 50 24N 105 30W
Moose Jaw Cr. → 109 50 34N 105 18W
Moose Lake, Can. 109 53 43N 100 20W
Moose Lake, U.S.A. 116 46 27N 92 48W
Moose Mountain Cr. → 109 49 13N 102 12W
Moose Mountain Prov. Park 109 49 48N 102 25W
Moose River 106 50 48N 81 17W
Moosehead L. 107 45 34N 69 40W
Moosomin 109 50 9N 101 40W
Moosonee 106 51 17N 80 39W
Moosup 113 41 44N 71 52W

Mopipi	**92**	21 6S	24 55 E
Mopoi	**90**	5 6N	26 54 E
Mopti	**84**	14 30N	4 0W
Moqatta	**87**	14 38N	35 50 E
Moquegua	**126**	17 15S	70 46W
Mór	**27**	47 25N	18 12 E
Móra	**31**	38 55N	8 10W
Mora, Sweden	**48**	61 2N	14 38 E
Mora, Minn., U.S.A.	**116**	45 52N	93 19W
Mora, N. Mex., U.S.A.	**119**	35 58N	105 21W
Mora de Ebro	**32**	41 6N	0 38 E
Mora de Rubielos	**32**	40 15N	0 45W
Mora la Nueva	**32**	41 7N	0 39 E
Morača →	**42**	42 20N	19 9 E
Moradabad	**68**	28 50N	78 50 E
Morafenobe	**93**	17 50S	44 53 E
Morąg	**28**	53 55N	19 56 E
Moral de Calatrava	**33**	38 51N	3 33W
Moraleja	**30**	40 6N	6 43W
Moran, Kans., U.S.A.	**117**	37 53N	94 35W
Moran, Wyo., U.S.A.	**118**	43 53N	110 37W
Morano Cálabro	**41**	39 51N	16 8 E
Morant Cays	**121**	17 22N	76 0W
Morant Pt.	**121**	17 55N	76 12W
Morar L.	**14**	56 57N	5 40W
Moratalla	**33**	38 14N	1 49W
Moratuwa	**70**	6 45N	79 55 E
Morava →	**27**	48 10N	16 59 E
Moravia	**116**	40 50N	92 50W
Moravian Hts. = Ceskemoravská V.	**26**	49 30N	15 40 E
Moravica →	**42**	43 52N	20 8 E
Moravice →	**27**	49 50N	17 43 E
Moraviţa	**42**	45 17N	21 14 E
Moravská Třebová	**27**	49 45N	16 40 E
Moravské Budějovice	**26**	49 4N	15 49 E
Morawhanna	**126**	8 30N	59 40W
Moray Firth	**14**	57 50N	3 30W
Morbach	**25**	49 48N	7 7 E
Morbegno	**38**	46 8N	9 34 E
Morbihan □	**18**	47 55N	2 50W
Morcenx	**20**	44 0N	0 55W
Mordelles	**18**	48 5N	1 52W
Morden	**109**	49 15N	98 10W
Mordialloc	**100**	38 1S	145 6 E
Mordovian A.S.S.R. □	**55**	54 20N	44 30 E
Mordovo	**55**	52 6N	40 50 E
Mordy	**28**	52 13N	22 31 E
Møre og Romsdal fylke □	**47**	62 30N	8 0 E
Morea	**9**	37 45N	22 10 E
Moreau →	**116**	45 15N	100 43W
Morecambe	**12**	54 5N	2 52W
Morecambe B.	**12**	54 7N	3 0W
Moree	**97**	29 28S	149 54 E
Morehead	**114**	38 12N	83 22W
Morehead City	**115**	34 46N	76 44W
Morelia	**120**	19 40N	101 11W
Morella, Austral.	**98**	23 0S	143 52 E
Morella, Spain	**32**	40 35N	0 5W
Morelos □	**120**	18 40N	99 10W
Morena, Sierra	**31**	38 20N	4 0W
Morenci	**119**	33 7N	109 20W
Moreni	**46**	44 59N	25 36 E
Moresby I.	**108**	52 30N	131 40W
Morestel	**21**	45 40N	5 28 E
Moret	**19**	48 22N	2 58 E
Moreton	**98**	12 22S	142 30 E
Moreton B.	**97**	27 10S	153 10 E
Moreton I.	**97**	27 10S	153 25 E
Moreuil	**19**	49 46N	2 30 E
Morez	**21**	46 31N	6 2 E
Morgan, Austral.	**99**	34 0S	139 35 E
Morgan, U.S.A.	**118**	41 3N	111 44W
Morgan City	**117**	29 40N	91 15W
Morganfield	**114**	37 40N	87 55W
Morganton	**115**	35 46N	81 48W
Morgantown	**114**	39 39N	79 58W
Morganville	**99**	25 10S	151 50 E
Morgat	**18**	48 15N	4 32W
Morgenzon	**93**	26 45S	29 36 E
Morges	**25**	46 31N	6 29 E
Morhange	**19**	48 55N	6 38 E
Mori	**38**	45 51N	10 59 E
Moriarty	**119**	35 3N	106 2W
Morice L.	**108**	53 50N	127 40W
Moriki	**85**	12 52N	6 30 E
Morinville	**108**	53 49N	113 41W
Morioka	**74**	39 45N	141 8 E
Morkalla	**99**	34 23S	141 10 E
Morlaàs	**20**	43 21N	0 18W
Morlaix	**18**	48 36N	3 52W
Mormanno	**41**	39 53N	15 59 E
Mormant	**19**	48 37N	2 52 E
Mornington	**99**	38 15S	145 5 E
Mornington I.	**97**	16 30S	139 30 E
Mornington, I.	**128**	49 50S	75 30W
Mórnos →	**45**	38 30N	22 0 E
Moro	**87**	10 50N	30 9 E
Moro G.	**73**	6 30N	123 0 E
Morobe	**98**	7 49S	147 38 E
Morocco ■	**82**	32 0N	5 50W
Morococha	**126**	11 40S	76 5W
Morogoro	**90**	6 50S	37 40 E
Morogoro □	**90**	8 0S	37 0 E
Moroleón	**120**	20 8N	101 32W
Morombe	**93**	21 45S	43 22 E
Moron	**124**	34 39S	58 37W
Morón	**121**	22 8N	78 39W
Mörön →	**75**	47 14N	110 37 E
Morón de Almazán	**32**	41 29N	2 27W
Morón de la Frontera	**31**	37 6N	5 28W
Morondava	**93**	20 17S	44 17 E
Morondo	**84**	8 57N	6 47W
Moronou	**84**	6 16N	4 59W
Morotai	**73**	2 10N	128 30 E
Moroto	**90**	2 28N	34 42 E
Moroto Summit	**90**	2 30N	34 43 E
Morozov (Bratan)	**43**	42 30N	25 10 E
Morozovsk	**57**	48 25N	41 50 E
Morpeth	**12**	55 11N	1 41W
Morphou	**64**	35 12N	32 59 E
Morrilton	**117**	35 10N	92 45W
Morrinhos	**127**	17 45S	49 10W
Morrinsville	**101**	37 40S	175 32 E
Morris, Can.	**109**	49 25N	97 22W
Morris, Ill., U.S.A.	**114**	41 20N	88 20W
Morris, Minn., U.S.A.	**116**	45 33N	95 56W
Morrisburg	**106**	44 55N	75 7W
Morrison	**116**	41 47N	90 0W
Morristown, Ariz., U.S.A.	**119**	33 54N	112 35W
Morristown, N.J., U.S.A.	**113**	40 48N	74 30W
Morristown, S.D., U.S.A.	**116**	45 57N	101 44W
Morristown, Tenn., U.S.A.	**115**	36 18N	83 20W
Morro Bay	**119**	35 27N	120 54W
Morro, Pta.	**124**	27 6S	71 0W
Morrosquillo, Golfo de	**121**	9 35N	75 40W
Mörrum	**49**	56 12N	14 45 E
Mors	**49**	56 50N	8 45 E
Morshansk	**55**	53 28N	41 50 E
Mörsil	**48**	63 19N	13 40 E
Mortagne	**20**	45 28N	0 49W
Mortagne →	**19**	48 33N	6 27 E
Mortagne-au-Perche	**18**	48 31N	0 33 E
Mortain	**18**	48 40N	0 57W
Mortara	**38**	45 15N	8 43 E
Morteau	**19**	47 3N	6 35 E
Morteros	**124**	30 50S	62 0W
Mortes, R. das →	**127**	11 45S	50 44W
Mortlake	**99**	38 5S	142 50 E
Morton, Tex., U.S.A.	**117**	33 39N	102 49W
Morton, Wash., U.S.A.	**118**	46 33N	122 17W
Morundah	**99**	34 57S	146 19 E
Moruya	**99**	35 58S	150 3 E
Morvan, Mts. du	**19**	47 5N	4 0 E
Morven	**99**	26 22S	147 5 E
Morvern	**14**	56 38N	5 44W
Morvi	**68**	22 50N	70 42 E
Morwell	**97**	38 10S	146 22 E
Moryn	**28**	52 51N	14 22 E
Morzhovets, Ostrov	**52**	66 44N	42 35 E
Mosalsk	**54**	54 30N	34 55 E
Mosbach	**25**	49 21N	9 9 E
Mošćenice	**39**	45 17N	14 16 E
Mosciano Sant' Ángelo	**39**	42 42N	13 52 E
Moscos Is.	**72**	14 0N	97 30 E
Moscow	**118**	46 45N	116 59W
Moscow = Moskva	**55**	55 45N	37 35 E
Mosel →	**16**	50 22N	7 36 E
Moselle = Mosel →	**16**	50 22N	7 36 E
Moselle □	**19**	48 59N	6 33 E
Moses Lake	**118**	47 9N	119 17W
Mosgiel	**101**	45 53S	170 21 E
Moshi	**90**	3 22S	37 18 E
Moshi □	**90**	3 22S	37 18 E
Moshupa	**92**	24 46S	25 29 E
Mośina	**28**	52 15N	16 50 E
Mosjøen	**50**	65 51N	13 12 E
Moskenesøya	**50**	67 58N	13 0 E
Moskenstraumen	**50**	67 47N	12 45 E
Moskva	**55**	55 45N	37 35 E
Moskva →	**55**	55 5N	38 51 E
Moslavačka Gora	**39**	45 40N	16 37 E
Mosomane (Artesia)	**92**	24 2S	26 19 E
Mosonmagyaróvár	**27**	47 52N	17 18 E
Mošorin	**42**	45 19N	20 4 E
Mospino	**56**	47 52N	38 0 E
Mosquera	**126**	2 35N	78 24W
Mosquero	**117**	35 48N	103 57W
Mosqueruela	**32**	40 21N	0 27W
Mosquitos, Golfo de los	**121**	9 15N	81 10W
Moss	**47**	59 27N	10 40 E
Moss Vale	**99**	34 32S	150 25 E
Mossaka	**88**	1 15S	16 45 E
Mossbank	**109**	49 56N	105 56W
Mossburn	**101**	45 41S	168 15 E
Mosselbaai	**92**	34 11S	22 8 E
Mossendjo	**88**	2 55S	12 42 E
Mossgiel	**99**	33 15S	144 5 E
Mossman	**97**	16 21S	145 15 E
Mossoró	**127**	5 10S	37 15W
Møsstrand	**47**	59 51N	8 4 E
Mossuril	**91**	14 58S	40 42 E
Mossy →	**109**	54 5N	102 58W
Most	**26**	50 31N	13 38 E
Mostaganem	**82**	35 54N	0 5 E
Mostar	**42**	43 22N	17 50 E
Mostardas	**125**	31 2S	50 51W
Mostefa, Rass	**83**	36 55N	11 3 E
Mosterøy	**47**	59 5N	5 37 E
Mostiska	**54**	49 48N	23 4 E
Mosty	**54**	53 27N	24 38 E
Mosul = Al Mawşil	**64**	36 20N	43 5 E
Mosvatn	**47**	59 52N	8 5 E
Mota del Cuervo	**32**	39 30N	2 52W
Mota del Marqués	**30**	41 38N	5 11W
Motagua →	**120**	15 44N	88 14W
Motala	**49**	58 32N	15 1 E
Mothe-Achard, La	**18**	46 37N	1 40W
Motherwell	**14**	55 48N	4 0W
Motihari	**69**	26 30N	84 55 E
Motilla del Palancar	**32**	39 34N	1 55W
Motnik	**39**	46 14N	14 54 E
Motovun	**39**	45 20N	13 50 E
Motozintla de Mendoza	**120**	15 21N	92 14W
Motril	**33**	36 31N	3 37W
Motru →	**46**	44 44N	22 59 E
Mott	**116**	46 25N	102 29W
Motte-Chalançon, La	**21**	44 30N	5 21 E
Motte, La	**21**	44 20N	6 3 E
Móttola	**41**	40 38N	17 0 E
Motueka	**101**	41 7S	173 1 E
Motul	**120**	21 0N	89 20W
Mouanda	**88**	1 28S	13 7 E
Mouchalagane →	**107**	50 56N	68 41W
Moucontant	**18**	46 43N	0 36W
Moúdhros	**44**	39 50N	25 18 E
Moudjeria	**84**	17 50N	12 28W
Moudon	**25**	46 40N	6 49 E
Mouila	**88**	1 50S	11 0 E
Moulamein	**99**	35 3S	144 1 E
Moule	**121**	16 20N	61 22W
Moulins	**20**	46 35N	3 19 E
Moulmein	**67**	16 30N	97 40 E
Moulouya, O. →	**82**	35 5N	2 25W
Moulton	**117**	29 35N	97 8W
Moultrie	**115**	31 11N	83 47W
Moultrie, L.	**115**	33 25N	80 10W
Mound City, Mo., U.S.A.	**116**	40 2N	95 25W
Mound City, S.D., U.S.A.	**116**	45 46N	100 3W
Moúnda, Ákra	**45**	38 5N	20 45 E
Moundou	**81**	8 40N	16 10 E
Moundsville	**114**	39 53N	80 43W
Mount Airy	**115**	36 31N	80 37W
Mount Albert	**112**	44 8N	79 19W
Mount Angel	**118**	45 4N	122 46W
Mount Barker, S.A., Austral.	**99**	35 5S	138 52 E
Mount Barker, W.A., Austral.	**96**	34 38S	117 40 E
Mount Carmel, Ill., U.S.A.	**114**	38 20N	87 48W
Mount Carmel, Pa., U.S.A.	**114**	40 46N	76 25W
Mount Clemens	**106**	42 35N	82 50W
Mount Coolon	**98**	21 25S	147 25 E
Mount Darwin	**91**	16 45S	31 33 E
Mount Desert I.	**107**	44 15N	68 25W
Mount Dora	**115**	28 49N	81 32W
Mount Douglas	**98**	21 35S	146 50 E
Mount Edgecumbe	**108**	57 8N	135 22W
Mount Enid	**96**	21 42S	116 26 E
Mount Forest	**106**	43 59N	80 43W
Mount Gambier	**97**	37 50S	140 46 E
Mount Garnet	**98**	17 37S	145 6 E
Mount Hope	**114**	37 52N	81 9W
Mount Horeb	**116**	43 0N	89 42W
Mount Howitt	**99**	26 31S	142 16 E
Mount Isa	**97**	20 42S	139 26 E
Mount Larcom	**98**	23 48S	150 59 E
Mount Lofty Ra.	**97**	34 35S	139 5 E
Mount McKinley Nat. Park	**104**	64 0N	150 0W
Mount Magnet	**96**	28 2S	117 47 E
Mount Margaret	**99**	26 54S	143 21 E
Mount Maunganui	**101**	37 40S	176 14 E
Mount Morgan	**97**	23 40S	150 25 E
Mount Morris	**114**	42 43N	77 50W
Mount Mulligan	**98**	16 45S	144 47 E
Mount Nicholas	**96**	22 54S	120 27 E
Mount Oxide Mine	**98**	19 30S	139 29 E
Mount Pearl	**107**	47 31N	52 47W
Mount Perry	**99**	25 13S	151 42 E
Mount Pleasant, Iowa, U.S.A.	**116**	41 0N	91 35W
Mount Pleasant, Mich., U.S.A.	**114**	43 35N	84 47W
Mount Pleasant, Pa., U.S.A.	**112**	40 9N	79 31W
Mount Pleasant, S.C., U.S.A.	**115**	32 45N	79 48W
Mount Pleasant, Tenn., U.S.A.	**115**	35 31N	87 11W
Mount Pleasant, Tex., U.S.A.	**117**	33 5N	95 0W
Mount Pleasant, Ut., U.S.A.	**118**	39 40N	111 29W
Mount Pocono	**113**	41 8N	75 21W
Mount Rainier Nat. Park.	**118**	46 50N	121 43W
Mount Revelstoke Nat. Park	**108**	51 5N	118 30W
Mount Robson	**108**	52 56N	119 15W
Mount Robson Prov. Park	**108**	53 0N	119 0W
Mount Shasta	**118**	41 20N	122 18W
Mount Sterling, Ill., U.S.A.	**116**	40 0N	90 40W
Mount Sterling, Ky., U.S.A.	**114**	38 0N	84 0W
Mount Surprise	**98**	18 10S	144 17 E
Mount Union	**112**	40 22N	77 51W
Mount Vernon, Ind., U.S.A.	**116**	38 17N	88 57W
Mount Vernon, N.Y., U.S.A.	**114**	40 57N	73 49W
Mount Vernon, Ohio, U.S.A.	**114**	40 20N	82 30W
Mount Vernon, Wash., U.S.A.	**108**	48 25N	122 20W
Mount Whaleback	**96**	23 18S	119 44 E
Mountain City, Nev., U.S.A.	**118**	41 54N	116 0W
Mountain City, Tenn., U.S.A.	**115**	36 30N	81 50W
Mountain Grove	**117**	37 5N	92 20W
Mountain Home, Ark., U.S.A.	**117**	36 20N	92 25W
Mountain Home, Idaho, U.S.A.	**118**	43 11N	115 45W
Mountain Iron	**116**	47 30N	92 37W
Mountain Park.	**108**	52 50N	117 15W
Mountain View, Ark., U.S.A.	**117**	35 52N	92 10W
Mountain View, Calif., U.S.A.	**119**	37 26N	122 5W
Mountainair	**119**	34 35N	106 15W
Mountmellick	**15**	53 7N	7 20W
Moura, Austral.	**98**	24 35S	149 58 E
Moura, Brazil	**126**	1 32S	61 38W
Moura, Port.	**31**	38 7N	7 30W
Mourão	**31**	38 22N	7 22W
Mourdi Depression	**81**	18 10N	23 0 E
Mourdiah	**84**	14 35N	7 25W
Moure, La	**116**	46 27N	98 17W
Mourenx	**20**	43 23N	0 36W
Mouri	**85**	5 6N	1 14W
Mourilyan	**98**	17 35S	146 3 E
Mourmelon-le-Grand	**19**	49 8N	4 22 E
Mourne →	**15**	54 45N	7 39W
Mourne Mts.	**15**	54 10N	6 0W
Mouscron	**16**	50 45N	3 12 E
Moussoro	**81**	13 41N	16 35 E
Mouthe	**19**	46 44N	6 12 E
Moutier	**25**	47 16N	7 21 E
Moûtiers	**21**	45 29N	6 31 E
Moutong	**73**	0 28N	121 13 E
Mouy	**19**	49 18N	2 20 E
Mouzáki	**44**	39 25N	21 37 E
Moville	**15**	55 11N	7 3W
Moy →	**15**	54 5N	8 50W
Moyale, Ethiopia	**87**	3 34N	39 4 E
Moyale, Kenya	**90**	3 30N	39 0 E
Moyamba	**84**	8 4N	12 30W
Moyen Atlas	**80**	32 0N	5 0W
Moyle □	**15**	55 10N	6 15W
Moyobamba	**126**	6 0S	77 0W
Moyyero →	**59**	68 44N	103 42 E
Mozambique = Moçambique	**91**	15 3S	40 42 E
Mozambique ■	**91**	19 0S	35 0 E
Mozambique Chan.	**93**	20 0S	39 0 E
Mozdok	**57**	43 45N	44 48 E
Mozhaysk	**55**	55 30N	36 2 E
Mozhga	**55**	56 26N	52 15 E
Mozirje	**39**	46 22N	14 58 E
Mozyr	**54**	52 0N	29 15 E
Mpanda	**90**	6 23S	31 1 E
Mpanda □	**90**	6 23S	31 40 E
Mpésoba	**84**	12 31N	5 39W
Mpika	**91**	11 51S	31 25 E
Mpulungu	**91**	8 51S	31 5 E
Mpwapwa	**90**	6 23S	36 30 E
Mpwapwa □	**90**	6 30S	36 20 E
Mrągowo	**28**	53 52N	21 18 E
Mramor	**42**	43 20N	21 45 E
Mrimina	**82**	29 50N	7 9W
Mrkonjić Grad	**42**	44 26N	17 4 E
Mrkopalj	**39**	45 21N	14 52 E
Mrocza	**28**	53 16N	17 35 E
Msab, Oued en →	**83**	32 25N	5 20 E
Msaken	**83**	35 49N	10 33 E
Msambansovu	**91**	15 50S	30 3 E
M'sila	**83**	35 46N	4 30 E
Msta →	**54**	58 25N	31 20 E
Mstislavl	**54**	54 0N	31 50 E
Mszana Dolna	**27**	49 41N	20 5 E
Mszczonów	**28**	51 58N	20 33 E
Mtama	**91**	10 17S	39 21 E
Mtilikwe →	**91**	21 9S	31 30 E
Mtsensk	**55**	53 25N	36 30 E
Mtskheta	**57**	41 52N	44 45 E
Mtwara-Mikindani	**91**	10 20S	40 20 E
Mu Us Shamo	**76**	39 0N	109 0 E
Muaná	**127**	1 25S	49 15W
Muang Chiang Rai	**71**	19 52N	99 50 E
Muang Lamphun	**71**	18 40N	99 2 E
Muang Phichit	**71**	16 29N	100 21 E
Muar	**71**	2 3N	102 34 E
Muar →	**71**	2 15N	102 48 E
Muarabungo	**72**	1 28S	102 52 E
Muaradjuloi	**72**	0 12S	114 3 E
Muaraenim	**72**	3 40S	103 50 E
Muarakaman	**72**	0 2S	116 45 E
Muaratebo	**72**	1 30S	102 26 E
Muaratembesi	**72**	1 42S	103 8 E
Muaratewe	**72**	0 58S	114 52 E
Mubarakpur	**69**	26 6N	83 18 E
Mubende	**90**	0 33N	31 22 E
Mubi	**85**	10 18N	13 16 E
Mücheln	**24**	51 18N	11 49 E
Muchinga Mts.	**91**	11 30S	31 30 E
Muchkapskiy	**55**	51 52N	42 28 E
Muck	**14**	56 50N	6 15W
Muckadilla	**99**	26 35S	148 23 E
Mucuri	**127**	18 0S	39 36W
Mucusso	**92**	18 1S	21 25 E
Mudanjiang	**76**	44 38N	129 30 E
Mudanya	**56**	40 25N	28 50 E
Muddy →	**119**	38 0N	110 22W
Mudgee	**97**	32 32S	149 31 E
Mudjatik →	**109**	56 1N	107 36W
Muecate	**91**	14 55S	39 40 E
Muêda	**91**	11 36S	39 28 E
Muela, La	**32**	41 36N	1 7W
Muerto, Mar	**120**	16 10N	94 10W
Muertos, Punta de los	**33**	36 57N	1 54W
Mufindi □	**91**	8 30S	35 20 E
Mufulira	**91**	12 32S	28 15 E
Mufumbiro Range	**90**	1 25S	29 30 E
Mugardos	**30**	43 27N	8 15W
Muge	**31**	39 3N	8 40W
Muge →	**31**	39 8N	8 44W
Múggia	**39**	45 36N	13 47 E
Mugia	**30**	43 3N	9 10W
Mugila, Mts.	**90**	7 0S	28 50 E
Muğla	**64**	37 15N	28 22 E
Mŭglizh	**43**	42 37N	25 32 E
Mugshin	**63**	19 35N	54 40 E
Mugu	**69**	29 45N	82 30 E
Muhammad Qol	**86**	20 53N	37 9 E
Muhammad Râs	**86**	27 42N	34 13 E
Muhammadabad	**69**	26 4N	83 25 E
Muharraqa = Sa'ad	**62**	31 28N	34 33 E
Muhesi →	**90**	7 0S	35 20 E
Muheza □	**90**	5 0S	39 0 E
Mühldorf	**25**	48 14N	12 33 E
Mühlhausen	**24**	51 12N	10 29 E
Mühlig Hofmann fjella	**5**	72 30S	5 0 E
Muhutwe	**90**	1 35S	31 45 E
Mui Bai Bung	**71**	8 35N	104 42 E
Mui Ron	**71**	18 7N	106 27 E
Muikamachi	**74**	37 15N	138 50 E
Muine Bheag	**15**	52 42N	6 57W
Muiños	**30**	41 58N	7 59W
Mukachevo	**54**	48 27N	22 45 E
Mukah	**72**	2 55N	112 5 E
Mukawwa, Geziret	**86**	23 55N	35 53 E
Mukden = Shenyang	**76**	41 48N	123 27 E
Mukhtolovo	**55**	55 29N	43 15 E
Mukishi	**91**	8 30S	24 44 E
Mukomuko	**72**	2 30S	101 10 E
Mukomwenze	**90**	6 49S	27 15 E
Muktsar	**68**	30 30N	74 30 E
Mukur	**66**	32 50N	67 42 E
Mukutawa →	**109**	53 10N	97 24W
Mukwela	**91**	17 0S	26 40 E
Mula	**33**	38 3N	1 33W
Mula →	**70**	18 34N	74 21 E
Mulange	**90**	3 40S	27 10 E
Mulatas, Arch. de las	**121**	9 50N	78 31W
Mulchén	**124**	37 45S	72 20W
Mulde →	**24**	51 10N	12 48 E
Mule Creek	**116**	43 19N	104 8W
Muleba	**90**	1 50S	31 37 E
Muleba □	**90**	2 0S	31 30 E
Muleshoe	**117**	34 17N	102 42W
Mulgrave	**107**	45 38N	61 31W
Mulgrave I.	**98**	10 5S	142 10 E
Mulhacén	**33**	37 4N	3 20W
Mülheim	**24**	51 26N	6 53 E
Mulhouse	**19**	47 40N	7 20 E
Muling He →	**76**	45 53N	133 30 E
Mull	**14**	56 27N	6 0W
Mullaittvu	**70**	9 15N	80 49 E
Mullen	**116**	42 5N	101 0W
Mullengudgery	**99**	31 43S	147 23 E
Mullens	**114**	37 34N	81 22W
Muller, Pegunungan	**72**	0 30N	113 30 E
Mullet Pen.	**15**	54 10N	10 2W
Mullewa	**96**	28 29S	115 30 E
Müllheim	**25**	47 48N	7 37 E
Mulligan →	**98**	26 40S	139 0 E
Mullin	**117**	31 33N	98 38W
Mullingar	**15**	53 31N	7 20W
Mullins	**115**	34 12N	79 15W
Mullsjö	**49**	57 56N	13 55 E

Mullumbimby 99 28 30S 153 30E
Mulobezi 91 16 45S 25 7E
Mulshi L. 70 18 30N 73 48E
Multai 68 21 50N 78 21E
Multan 68 30 15N 71 36E
Multan □ 68 30 29N 72 29E
Multrå 48 63 10N 17 24E
Mulumbe, Mts. 91 8 40S 27 30E
Mulungushi Dam 91 14 48S 28 48E
Mulvane 117 37 30N 97 15W
Mulwad 86 18 45N 30 39E
Mulwala 100 35 59S 146 0E
Mumra 57 45 45N 47 41E
Mun → 71 15 17N 103 0E
Muna 73 5 0S 122 30E
Munamagi 54 57 43N 27 4E
Münchberg 25 50 11N 11 48E
Muncheberg 24 52 30N 14 9E
München 25 48 8N 11 33E
Munchen-Gladbach = Mönchengladbach 24 51 12N 6 23E
Muncho Lake 108 59 0N 125 50W
Muncie 114 40 10N 85 20W
Mundakayam 70 9 30N 76 50E
Mundala, Puncak 73 4 30S 141 0E
Mundare 108 53 35N 112 20W
Munday 117 33 26N 99 39W
Münden 24 51 25N 9 42E
Mundo → 33 38 30N 2 15W
Mundo Novo 127 11 50S 40 29W
Mundra 68 22 54N 69 48E
Munera 33 39 2N 2 29W
Muneru → 70 16 45N 80 3E
Mungallala 99 26 28S 147 34E
Mungallala Cr. → 99 28 53S 147 5E
Mungana 98 17 8S 144 27E
Mungaoli 68 24 24N 78 7E
Mungari 91 17 12S 33 30E
Mungbere 90 2 36N 28 28E
Mungindi 97 28 58S 149 1E
Munhango 89 12 10S 18 38E
Munich = München 25 48 8N 11 33E
Munising 114 46 25N 86 39W
Munjiye 86 18 47N 41 20E
Munka-Ljungby 49 56 16N 12 58E
Munkedal 49 58 28N 11 40E
Munkfors 48 59 50N 13 30E
Munku-Sardyk 59 51 45N 100 20E
Münnerstadt 25 50 15N 10 11E
Muñoz Gamero, Pen. 128 52 30S 73 5E
Munroe L. 109 59 13N 98 35W
Munster, France 19 48 2N 7 8E
Munster, Ger. 24 52 59N 10 5E
Münster 24 51 58N 7 37E
Munster □ 15 52 20N 8 40W
Muntele Mare 46 46 30N 23 12E
Muntok 72 2 5S 105 10E
Munyak 58 43 30N 59 15E
Munyama 91 16 5S 28 31E
Muon Pak Beng 71 19 51N 101 4E
Muonio 50 67 57N 23 40E
Mupa 89 16 5S 15 50E
Muping 76 37 22N 121 36E
Muqaddam, Wadi → 86 18 4N 31 30E
Muqdisho 63 2 2N 45 25E
Mur → 26 46 18N 16 53E
Mur-de-Bretagne 18 48 12N 3 0W
Mura → 39 46 18N 16 53E
Murallón, Cuerro 128 49 48S 73 30W
Muranda 90 1 52S 29 20E
Murang'a 90 0 45S 37 9E
Murashi 55 59 30N 49 0E
Murat 20 45 7N 2 53E
Murau 26 47 6N 14 10E
Muravera 40 39 25N 9 35E
Murça 30 41 24N 7 28W
Murchison → 96 27 45S 114 0E
Murchison Falls = Kabarega Falls 90 2 15N 31 38E
Murchison Ra. 96 20 0S 134 10E
Murchison Rapids 91 15 55S 34 35E
Murcia 33 38 20N 1 10W
Murcia □ 33 37 50N 1 30W
Murdo 116 43 56N 100 43W
Murdoch Pt. 98 14 37S 144 55E
Mure, La 21 44 55N 5 48E
Mureş □ 46 46 45N 24 40E
Mureş (Mureşul) → 46 46 15N 20 13E
Muret 20 43 30N 1 20E
Murfatlar 46 44 10N 28 26E
Murfreesboro 115 35 50N 86 21W
Murg → 25 48 55N 8 10E
Murgab 58 38 10N 74 2E
Murgeni 46 46 12N 28 1E
Murgon 97 26 15S 151 54E
Muriaé 125 21 8S 42 23W
Murias de Paredes 30 42 52N 6 11W
Muriel Mine 91 17 14S 30 40E
Müritz see 24 53 25N 12 40E
Murka 90 3 27S 38 0E
Murmansk 52 68 57N 33 10E
Murnau 25 47 40N 11 11E
Muro, France 21 42 34N 8 54E
Muro, Spain 32 39 44N 3 3E
Muro, C. de 21 41 44N 8 37E
Muro Lucano 41 40 45N 15 30E
Murom 55 55 35N 42 3E
Muroran 74 42 25N 141 0E
Muros 30 42 45N 9 5W
Muros y de Noya, Ría de 30 42 45N 9 0W
Muroto-Misaki 74 33 15N 134 10E
Murowana Goślina 28 52 35N 17 0E
Murphy 118 43 11N 116 33W
Murphysboro 117 37 50N 89 20W
Murrat 86 18 51N 29 33E
Murray, Ky., U.S.A. 115 36 40N 88 20W
Murray, Utah, U.S.A. 118 40 41N 111 58W
Murray →, Austral. 97 35 20S 139 22E
Murray →, Can. 108 56 11N 120 45W
Murray Bridge 97 35 6S 139 14E
Murray Harbour 107 46 0N 62 28W
Murray, L., P.N.G. 98 7 0S 141 35E
Murray, L., U.S.A. 115 34 8N 81 30W
Murray Seascarp 95 30 0N 135 0W
Murraysburg 92 31 58S 23 47E
Murrayville 100 35 16S 141 11E
Murree 66 33 56N 73 28E
Murrumbidgee → 97 34 43S 143 12E
Murrumburrah 99 34 32S 148 22E
Murrurundi 99 31 42S 150 51E
Mursala 72 1 41N 98 28E
Murshid 86 21 40N 31 10E
Murshidabad 69 24 11N 88 19E
Murska Sobota 39 46 39N 16 12E
Murtazapur 68 20 40N 77 25E
Murtle L. 108 52 8N 119 38W
Murtoa 99 36 35S 142 28E
Murtosa 30 40 44N 8 40W
Murungu 90 4 12S 31 10E
Murwara 69 23 46N 80 28E
Murwillumbah 97 28 18S 153 27E
Muryo 73 6 36S 110 53E
Mürz → 26 47 30N 15 25E
Mürzzuschlag 26 47 36N 15 41E
Muş 64 38 45N 41 30E
Musa Khel Bazar 68 30 59N 69 52E
Mūsá Qal'eh 65 32 20N 64 50E
Musairik, Wadi → 86 19 30N 43 10E
Musala 43 42 13N 23 37E
Musan, Kor., N. 76 42 12N 129 12E
Musan, Kor., N. 76 42 12N 129 12E
Musangu 91 10 28S 23 55E
Musasa 90 3 25S 31 30E
Musay'id 65 25 0N 51 33E
Muscat = Masqat 65 23 37N 58 36E
Muscat & Oman = Oman ■ 63 23 0N 58 0E
Muscatine 116 41 25N 91 5W
Musel 30 43 34N 5 42W
Musgrave Ras. 96 26 0S 132 0E
Mushie 88 2 56S 16 55E
Mushin 85 6 32N 3 21E
Musi →, India 70 16 41N 79 40E
Musi →, Indon. 72 2 20S 104 56E
Muskeg → 108 60 20N 123 20W
Muskegon 114 43 15N 86 17W
Muskegon → 114 43 25N 86 0W
Muskegon Hts. 114 43 12N 86 17W
Muskogee 117 35 50N 95 25W
Muskwa → 108 58 47N 122 48W
Musmar 86 18 13N 35 40E
Musofu 91 13 30S 29 0E
Musoma 90 1 30S 33 48E
Musoma □ 90 1 50S 34 30E
Musquaro, L. 107 50 38N 61 5W
Musquodoboit Harbour 107 44 50N 63 9W
Musselburgh 14 55 57N 3 3W
Musselshell → 118 47 21N 107 58W
Mussidan 20 45 2N 0 22E
Mussomeli 40 37 35N 13 43E
Mussooree 68 30 27N 78 6E
Mussuco 92 17 2S 19 3E
Mustang 69 29 10N 83 55E
Musters, L. 128 45 20S 69 25W
Muswellbrook 97 32 16S 150 56E
Muszyna 27 49 22N 20 55E
Mût 86 25 28N 28 58E
Mut 64 36 40N 33 28E
Mutanda, Mozam. 93 21 0S 33 34E
Mutanda, Zambia 91 12 24S 26 13E
Mutaray 59 60 56N 101 0E
Muting 73 7 23S 140 20E
Mutshatsha 91 10 35S 24 20E
Muttaburra 97 22 38S 144 29E
Mutuáli 91 14 55S 37 0E
Muvatupusha 70 9 53N 76 35E
Muxima 88 9 33S 13 58E
Muy, Le 21 43 28N 6 34E
Muya 59 56 27N 115 50E
Muyinga 90 3 14S 30 33E
Muzaffarabad 69 34 25N 73 30E
Muzaffargarh 68 30 5N 71 14E
Muzaffarnagar 68 29 26N 77 40E
Muzaffarpur 69 26 7N 85 23E
Muzhi 58 65 25N 64 40E
Muzillac 18 47 35N 2 30W
Muzon C. 108 54 40N 132 40W
Muztag 75 36 20N 87 28E
Mvôlô 87 6 2N 29 53E
Mwadui 90 3 26S 33 32E
Mwambo 91 10 30S 40 22E
Mwandi 91 17 30S 24 51E
Mwanza, Tanz. 90 2 30S 32 58E
Mwanza, Zaïre 90 7 55S 26 43E
Mwanza, Zambia 91 16 58S 24 28E
Mwanza □ 90 2 0S 33 0E
Mwaya 91 9 32S 33 55E
Mweelrea 15 53 37N 9 48W
Mweka 88 4 50S 21 34E
Mwenga 90 3 1S 28 28E
Mweru, L. 91 9 0S 28 40E
Mweza Range 91 21 0S 30 0E
Mwilambwe 90 8 7S 25 0E
Mwimbi 91 8 38S 31 39E
Mwinilunga 91 11 43S 24 25E
My Tho 71 10 29N 106 23E
Mya, O. → 83 30 46N 4 54E
Myall → 100 32 30S 152 15E
Myanaung 67 18 18N 95 22E
Myaungmya 67 16 30N 94 40E
Mycenae = Mikinai 45 37 43N 22 46E
Myeik Kyunzu 71 11 30N 97 30E
Myerstown 113 40 22N 76 18W
Myitkyina 67 25 24N 97 26E
Myjava 27 48 41N 17 37E
Mymensingh 69 24 45N 90 24E
Myndus 45 37 3N 27 14E
Mynydd ddu 13 51 45N 3 45W
Myrdal 47 60 43N 7 10E
Mýrdalsjökull 50 63 40N 19 6W
Myrtle Beach 115 33 43N 78 50W
Myrtle Creek 118 43 0N 123 9W
Myrtle Point 118 43 0N 124 4W
Myrtleford 100 36 34S 146 44E
Mysen 47 59 33N 11 20E
Myslenice 27 49 51N 19 57E
Myślibórz 28 52 55N 14 50E
Mysłowice 27 50 15N 19 12E
Mysore 70 12 17N 76 41E
Mysore □ = Karnataka 70 13 15N 77 0E
Mystic 113 41 21N 71 58W
Mystishchi 55 55 50N 37 50E
Myszków 28 50 45N 19 22E
Myszyniec 28 53 23N 21 21E
Myton 118 40 10N 110 2W
Mývatn 50 65 36N 17 0W
Mze → 26 49 46N 13 24E
Mzimba 91 11 55S 33 39E
Mzimvubu → 93 31 38S 29 33E
Mzuzu 91 11 30S 33 55E

N

N' Dioum 84 16 31N 14 39W
Naab → 25 49 1N 12 2E
Na'am 87 9 42N 28 27E
Na'an 62 31 53N 34 52E
Naantali 51 60 29N 22 2E
Naas 15 53 12N 6 40W
Nababiep 92 29 36S 17 46E
Nabadwip 69 23 34N 88 20E
Nabas 73 11 47N 122 6E
Nabburg 25 49 27N 12 11E
Naberezhnyje Celny 58 55 42N 52 19E
Nabeul 83 36 30N 10 44E
Nabha 68 30 26N 76 14E
Nabire 73 3 15S 135 26E
Nabisar 68 25 8N 69 40E
Nabisipi → 107 50 14N 62 13W
Nabiswera 90 1 27N 32 15E
Nablus = Nābulus 62 32 14N 35 15E
Naboomspruit 93 24 32S 28 40E
Nābulus 62 32 14N 35 15E
Nacala-Velha 91 14 32S 40 34E
Nacaroa 91 14 22S 39 56E
Naches 118 46 48N 120 42W
Nachingwea 91 10 23S 38 49E
Nachingwea □ 91 10 30S 38 30E
Nachna 68 27 34N 71 41E
Náchod 27 50 25N 16 8E
Nacka 48 59 17N 18 12E
Nackara 99 32 48S 139 12E
Naco 119 31 24N 109 58W
Nacogdoches 117 31 33N 94 39W
Nacozari 120 30 24N 109 39W
Nadi 86 18 40N 33 41E
Nadiad 68 22 41N 72 56E
Nădlac 42 46 10N 20 50E
Nador 82 35 14N 2 58W
Nadūshan 65 32 2N 53 35E
Nadvoitsy 52 63 52N 34 14E
Nadvornaya 56 48 37N 24 30E
Nadym 58 65 35N 72 42E
Nadym → 58 66 12N 72 0E
Nærbø 47 58 40N 5 39E
Næstved 49 55 13N 11 44E
Nafada 85 11 8N 11 20E
Naft-e Shāh 64 34 0N 45 30E
Nafūd ad Dahy 64 22 0N 45 0E
Nafūsah, Jabal 83 32 12N 12 30E
Nag Hammâdi 86 26 2N 32 18E
Naga 73 13 38N 123 15E
Naga, Kreb en 82 24 12N 6 0W
Nagagami → 106 49 40N 84 40W
Nagaland □ 67 26 0N 94 30E
Nagano 74 36 40N 138 10E
Nagano □ 74 36 15N 138 0E
Nagaoka 74 37 27N 138 50E
Nagappattinam 70 10 46N 79 51E
Nagar Parkar 68 24 28N 70 46E
Nagari Hills 70 13 3N 79 45E
Nagarjuna Sagar 70 16 35N 79 17E
Nagasaki 74 32 47N 129 50E
Nagasaki □ 74 32 50N 129 40E
Nagaur 68 27 15N 73 45E
Nagbhil 70 20 34N 79 55E
Nagercoil 70 8 12N 77 26E
Nagina 68 29 30N 78 30E
Nagineh 65 34 20N 57 15E
Nago 77 26 36N 128 0E
Nagold 25 34 14N 57 2E
Nagold → 25 48 52N 8 42E
Nagoorin 98 24 17S 151 15E
Nagornyy 59 55 58N 124 57E
Nagorsk 55 59 18N 50 48E
Nagoya 74 35 10N 136 50E
Nagpur 68 21 8N 79 10E
Nagyatád 27 46 14N 17 22E
Nagyecsed 27 47 53N 22 24E
Nagykanizsa 27 46 28N 17 0E
Nagykörös 27 47 5N 19 48E
Nagyléta 27 47 23N 21 55E
Naha 77 26 13N 127 42E
Nahalal 62 32 41N 35 12E
Nahanni Butte 108 61 2N 123 31W
Nahanni Nat. Park 108 61 15N 125 0W
Nahariyya 62 33 1N 35 5E
Nahāvand 64 34 10N 48 22E
Nahe → 25 49 58N 7 57E
Nahf 62 32 56N 35 18E
Nahīya, Wadi → 86 28 55N 31 0E
Nahlin 108 58 55N 131 38W
Nahud 86 18 12N 41 40E
Naicam 109 52 30N 104 30W
Nā'ifah 63 19 59N 50 46E
Naila 25 50 19N 11 43E
Nain 107 56 34N 61 40W
Nā'īn 65 32 54N 53 0E
Naini Tal 69 29 30N 79 30E
Naintré 18 46 46N 0 29E
Naipu 46 44 12N 25 47E
Naira 73 4 28S 130 0E
Nairn 14 57 35N 3 54W
Nairobi 90 1 17S 36 48E
Naivasha 90 0 40S 36 30E
Naivasha L. 90 0 48S 36 20E
Najac 20 44 14N 1 58E
Najafābād 65 32 40N 51 15E
Najd 64 26 30N 42 0E
Nájera 32 42 26N 2 48W
Najerilla → 32 42 32N 2 48W
Najibabad 68 29 40N 78 20E
Najin 76 42 12N 130 15E
Nakalagba 90 2 50N 27 58E
Nakamura 74 33 0N 133 0E
Nakfa 87 16 40N 38 32E
Nakhichevan A.S.S.R. □ 53 39 14N 45 30E
Nakhl 86 29 55N 33 43E
Nakhodka 59 42 53N 132 54E
Nakhon Phanom 71 17 23N 104 43E
Nakhon Ratchasima (Khorat) 71 14 59N 102 12E
Nakhon Sawan 71 15 35N 100 10E
Nakhon Si Thammarat 71 8 29N 100 0E
Nakina, B.C., Can. 108 59 12N 132 52W
Nakina, Ont., Can. 106 50 10N 86 40W
Nakło nad Notecią 28 53 9N 17 38E
Nakodar 68 31 8N 75 31E
Nakskov 49 54 50N 11 8E
Näkten 48 62 48N 14 38E
Naktong → 76 35 7N 128 57E
Nakuru 90 0 15S 36 4E
Nakuru □ 90 0 15S 35 5E
Nakuru, L. 90 0 23S 36 5E
Nakusp 108 50 20N 117 45W
Nal → 66 25 20N 65 30E
Nalchik 57 43 30N 43 33E
Nälden 48 63 21N 14 14E
Näldsjön 48 63 25N 14 15E
Nalerigu 85 10 35N 0 25W
Nalgonda 70 17 6N 79 15E
Nalhati 69 24 17N 87 52E
Nallamalai Hills 70 15 30N 78 50E
Nalón → 30 43 32N 6 4W
Nālūt 83 31 54N 11 0E
Nam Co 75 30 30N 90 45E
Nam Dinh 71 20 25N 106 5E
Nam-Phan 72 10 30N 106 0E
Nam Phong 71 16 42N 102 52E
Nam Tha 71 20 58N 101 30E
Nama unde 92 17 18S 15 50E
Namak, Daryācheh-ye 65 34 30N 52 0E
Namak, Kavir-e 65 34 30N 57 30E
Namakkal 70 11 13N 78 13E
Namaland 92 24 30S 17 0E
Namangan 58 41 0N 71 40E
Namapa 91 13 43S 39 50E
Namaqualand 92 30 0S 18 0E
Namasagali 90 1 2N 33 0E
Namatanai 98 3 40S 152 29E
Namber 73 1 2S 134 49E
Nambour 97 26 32S 152 58E
Nambucca Heads 99 30 37S 153 0E
Namche Bazar 69 27 51N 86 47E
Namecunda 91 14 54S 37 37E
Nameh 72 2 34N 116 21E
Nameponda 91 15 50S 39 50E
Náměšť nad Oslavou 27 49 12N 16 10E
Námestovo 27 49 24N 19 25E
Nametil 91 15 40S 39 21E
Namew L. 109 54 14N 101 56W
Namib Desert = Namib Woestyn 92 22 30S 15 0E
Namib-Woestyn 92 22 30S 15 0E
Namibia ■ 92 22 0S 18 9E
Namlea 73 3 18S 127 5E
Namoi → 99 30 12S 149 30E
Namous, O. en → 82 31 0N 0 15W
Nampa 118 43 34N 116 34W
Nampula 91 15 6N 39 15E
Namrole 73 3 46S 126 46E
Namse Shankou 67 30 0N 82 25E
Namsen → 50 64 27N 11 42E
Namsos 50 64 29N 11 30E
Namtay 59 62 43N 129 37E
Namtu 67 23 5N 97 28E
Namtumbo 91 10 30S 36 4E
Namu 108 51 52N 127 50W
Namucha Shank'ou 69 30 0N 82 28E
Namur 16 50 27N 4 52E
Namur □ 16 50 17N 5 0E
Namutoni 92 18 49S 16 55E
Namwala 91 15 44S 26 30E
Namysłów 28 51 6N 17 42E
Nan 71 18 52N 100 42E
Nana 46 44 17N 26 34E
Nanaimo 108 49 10N 124 0W
Nanam 76 41 44N 129 40E
Nanan 77 24 59N 118 21E
Nanango 97 26 40S 152 0E
Nan'ao 77 23 28N 117 5E
Nanao 74 37 0N 137 0E
Nanbu 77 31 18N 106 3E
Nanchang 75 28 42N 115 55E
Nancheng 77 27 33N 116 35E
Nanching = Nanjing 75 32 2N 118 47E
Nanchong 75 30 43N 106 2E
Nanchuan 77 29 9N 107 6E
Nancy 19 48 42N 6 12E
Nanda Devi 69 30 23N 79 59E
Nandan 77 24 58N 107 29E
Nander 70 19 10N 77 20E
Nandewar Ra. 99 30 15S 150 35E
Nandi 101 17 42S 177 20E
Nandi □ 90 0 15N 35 0E
Nandikotkur 70 15 52N 78 18E
Nandura 68 20 52N 76 25E
Nandurbar 68 21 20N 74 15E
Nandyal 70 15 30N 78 30E
Nanga-Eboko 88 4 41N 12 22E
Nanga Parbat 69 35 10N 74 35E
Nangade 91 11 5S 39 36E
Nangapinoh 72 0 20S 111 44E
Nangarhár □ 65 34 20N 70 0E
Nangatayap 72 1 32S 110 34E
Nangeya Mts. 90 3 30N 33 30E
Nangis 19 48 33N 3 0E
Nanjangud 70 12 6N 76 43E
Nanjeko 91 15 31S 23 30E

Nanjiang 77 32 28N 106 51 E
Nanjing 75 32 2N 118 47 E
Nanjirinji 91 9 41 S 39 5 E
Nankana Sahib 68 31 27N 73 38 E
Nankang 77 25 40N 114 45 E
Nanking = Nanjing 75 32 2N 118 47 E
Nannine 96 26 51 S 118 18 E
Nanning 75 22 48N 108 20 E
Nanpara 69 27 52N 81 33 E
Nanpi 76 38 2N 116 45 E
Nanping 75 26 38N 118 10 E
Nanripe 91 13 52 S 38 52 E
Nansei-Shotō 74 26 0N 128 0 E
Nansen Sd. 4 81 0N 91 0W
Nansio 90 2 3 S 33 4 E
Nant 20 44 1N 3 18 E
Nantes 18 47 12N 1 33W
Nanteuil-le-Haudouin 19 49 9N 2 48 E
Nantiat 20 46 1N 1 11 E
Nanticoke 114 41 12N 76 1W
Nanton 108 50 21N 113 46W
Nantong 77 32 1N 120 52 E
Nantua 21 46 10N 5 35 E
Nantucket I. 102 41 16N 70 3W
Nanuque 127 17 50 S 40 21W
Nanxiong 77 25 6N 114 15 E
Nanyang 75 33 11N 112 30 E
Nanyuan 76 39 44N 116 22 E
Nanyuki 90 0 2N 37 4 E
Nanzhang 77 31 45N 111 50 E
Náo, C. de la 33 38 44N 0 14 E
Naococane L. 107 52 50N 70 45W
Naoetsu 74 37 12N 138 10 E
Naogaon 69 24 52N 88 52 E
Naoli He → 76 47 18N 134 9 E
Náousa 44 40 42N 22 9 E
Napa 118 38 18N 122 17W
Napanee 106 44 15N 77 0W
Napanoch 113 41 44N 74 22W
Napier 101 39 30 S 176 56 E
Naples 115 26 10N 81 45W
Naples = Nápoli 41 40 50N 14 17 E
Napo → 126 3 20 S 72 40W
Napoleon, N. Dak., U.S.A. 116 46 32N 99 49W
Napoleon, Ohio, U.S.A. 114 41 24N 84 7W
Nápoli 41 40 50N 14 17 E
Nápoli, G. di 41 40 40N 14 10 E
Napopo 90 4 15N 28 0 E
Nappa Merrie 99 27 36 S 141 7 E
Naqâda 86 25 53N 32 42 E
Nara, Japan 74 34 40N 135 49 E
Nara, Mali 84 15 10N 7 20W
Nara □ 74 34 30N 136 0 E
Nara, Canal 68 24 30N 69 20 E
Nara Visa 117 35 39N 103 10W
Naracoorte 97 36 58 S 140 45 E
Naradhan 99 33 34 S 146 17 E
Narasapur 70 16 26N 81 40 E
Narasaropet 70 16 14N 80 4 E
Narathiwat 71 6 30N 101 48 E
Narayanganj 69 23 40N 90 33 E
Narayanpet 70 16 45N 77 30 E
Narbonne 20 43 11N 3 0 E
Narcea → 30 43 33N 6 44W
Nardò 41 40 10N 18 0 E
Narew 28 52 55N 23 31 E
Narew → 28 52 26N 20 41 E
Nari → 68 29 40N 68 0 E
Narindra, Helodranon' i 93 14 55 S 47 30 E
Narmada → 68 21 38N 72 36 E
Narnaul 68 28 5N 76 11 E
Narni 39 42 30N 12 30 E
Naro, Ghana 84 10 22N 2 27W
Naro, Italy 40 37 18N 13 48 E
Naro Fominsk 55 55 23N 36 43 E
Narodnaya, G. 52 65 5N 60 0 E
Narok 90 1 55 S 33 52 E
Narok □ 90 1 20 S 36 30 E
Narón 30 43 32N 8 9W
Narooma 99 36 14 S 150 4 E
Narowal 68 32 6N 74 52 E
Narrabri 97 30 19 S 149 46 E
Narran → 99 28 37 S 148 12 E
Narrandera 97 34 42 S 146 31 E
Narraway → 108 55 44N 119 55W
Narrogin 96 32 58 S 117 14 E
Narromine 97 32 12 S 148 12 E
Narsampet 70 17 57N 79 58 E
Narsimhapur 68 22 54N 79 14 E
Nartkala 57 43 33N 43 51 E
Narva 54 59 23N 28 12 E
Narva → 54 59 27N 28 2 E
Narvik 50 68 28N 17 26 E
Narvskoye Vdkhr. 54 59 18N 28 14 E
Narwana 68 29 39N 76 6 E
Naryan-Mar 52 68 0N 53 0 E
Naryilco 99 28 37 S 141 53 E
Narym 58 59 0N 81 30 E
Narymskoye 58 49 10N 84 15 E
Naryn 58 41 26N 75 58 E
Nasa 50 66 29N 15 23 E
Nasarawa 85 8 32N 7 41 E
Năsăud 46 47 19N 24 29 E
Naseby 101 45 1 S 170 10 E
Naser, Buheirat en 86 23 0N 32 30 E
Nashua, Iowa, U.S.A. 116 42 55N 92 34W
Nashua, Mont., U.S.A. 118 48 10N 106 25W
Nashua, N.H., U.S.A. 114 42 50N 71 25W
Nashville, Ark., U.S.A. 117 33 56N 93 50W
Nashville, Ga., U.S.A. 115 31 3N 83 15W
Nashville, Tenn., U.S.A. 115 36 12N 86 46W
Našice 42 45 32N 18 4 E
Nasielsk 28 52 35N 20 50 E
Nasik 70 19 58N 73 50 E
Nasirabad 68 26 15N 74 45 E
Naskaupi → 107 53 47N 60 51W
Naso 41 38 8N 14 46 E
Nass → 108 55 0N 129 40W
Nassau, Bahamas 121 25 0N 77 20W
Nassau, U.S.A. 113 42 30N 73 34W
Nassau, Bahia 128 55 20 S 68 0W
Nasser City = Kôm Ombo 86 24 25N 32 52 E
Nasser, L. = Naser, Buheiret en 86 23 0N 32 30 E
Nassian 84 8 28N 3 28W
Nässjö 49 57 39N 14 42 E
Nastopoka Is. 106 57 0N 77 0W
Näsum 49 56 10N 14 29 E
Näsviken 48 61 46N 16 52 E
Nat Kyizin 71 14 57N 97 59 E
Nata 92 20 12 S 26 12 E
Natagaima 126 3 37N 75 6W
Natal, Brazil 127 5 47 S 35 13W
Natal, Can. 108 49 43N 114 51W
Natal, Indon. 72 0 35N 99 7 E
Natal □ 93 28 30 S 30 30 E
Natalinci 42 44 15N 20 49 E
Naṭanz 65 33 30N 51 55 E
Natashquan 107 50 14N 61 46W
Natashquan → 107 50 7N 61 50W
Natchez 117 31 35N 91 25W
Natchitoches 117 31 47N 93 4W
Nathalia 99 36 1 S 145 13 E
Nathdwara 68 24 55N 73 50 E
Natick 113 42 16N 71 19W
Natih 65 22 25N 56 30 E
Natimuk 99 36 42 S 142 0 E
Nation → 108 55 30N 123 32W
National City 119 32 39N 117 7W
Natitingou 85 10 20N 1 26 E
Natividad, I. 120 27 50N 115 10W
Natoma 116 39 14N 99 0W
Natron, L. 90 2 20 S 36 0 E
Natrona 112 40 39N 79 43W
Natrûn, W. el. → 86 30 25N 30 13 E
Natuna Besar, Kepulauan 72 4 0N 108 15 E
Natuna Selatan, Kepulauan 72 2 45N 109 0 E
Natural Bridge 113 44 5N 75 30W
Naturaliste, C. 96 33 32 S 115 0 E
Naturaliste C. 99 40 50 S 148 15 E
Naturaliste Channel 96 25 20 S 113 0 E
Naubinway 106 46 7N 85 27W
Naucelle 20 44 13N 2 20 E
Nauders 26 46 54N 10 30 E
Nauen 24 52 36N 12 52 E
Naugatuck 113 41 28N 73 4W
Naujoji Vilnia 54 54 48N 25 27 E
Naumburg 24 51 10N 11 48 E
Nauru 94 1 0 S 166 0 E
Nauru Is. 94 0 32 S 166 55 E
Nauta 126 4 31 S 73 35W
Nautla 120 20 20N 96 50W
Nava del Rey 30 41 22N 5 6W
Navacerrada, Puerto de 30 40 47N 4 0W
Navahermosa 31 39 41N 4 28W
Navajo Res. 119 36 55N 107 30W
Navalcarnero 30 40 17N 4 5W
Navalmoral de la Mata 30 39 52N 5 33W
Navalvillar de Pela 31 39 9N 5 24W
Navan = An Uaimh 15 53 39N 6 40W
Navare 20 43 20N 1 20W
Navarino, I. 128 55 0 S 67 40W
Navarra □ 32 42 40N 1 40W
Navarre, France 20 43 15N 1 20W
Navarre, U.S.A. 112 40 43N 81 31W
Navarrenx 20 43 20N 0 45W
Navas del Marqués, Las 30 40 36N 4 20W
Navasota 117 30 20N 96 5W
Navassa 121 18 30N 75 0W
Nave 38 45 35N 10 17 E
Naver → 14 58 34N 4 15W
Navia 30 43 35N 6 42W
Navia → 30 43 15N 6 50W
Navia de Suarna 30 42 58N 6 59W
Navidad 124 33 57 S 71 50W
Navlya 54 52 53N 34 30 E
Navoi 58 40 9N 65 22 E
Navojoa 120 27 0N 109 30W
Navolok 52 62 33N 39 57 E
Návpaktos 45 38 23N 21 50 E
Návplion 45 37 33N 22 50 E
Navrongo 85 10 51N 1 3W
Navsari 68 20 57N 72 59 E
Nawa Kot 68 28 21N 71 24 E
Nawabganj, Bangla. 69 24 35N 88 14 E
Nawabganj, India 69 26 56N 81 14 E
Nawabganj, Bareilly 69 28 32N 79 40 E
Nawabshah 68 26 15N 68 25 E
Nawada 69 24 50N 85 33 E
Nawakot 69 27 55N 85 10 E
Nawalgarh 68 27 50N 75 15 E
Nawapara 69 20 46N 82 33 E
Nawāsīf, Harrat 64 21 20N 42 10 E
Nawi 86 18 32N 30 50 E
Náxos 45 37 8N 25 25 E
Nay 20 43 10N 0 18W
Nāy Band 65 27 20N 52 40 E
Nayakhan 59 61 56N 159 0 E
Nayarit □ 120 22 0N 105 0W
Nayé 84 14 28N 12 12W
Nazaré 31 39 36N 9 4W
Nazas 120 25 10N 104 6W
Nazas → 120 25 35N 103 25W
Naze, The 13 51 53N 1 19 E
Nazerat 62 32 42N 35 17 E
Nazir Hat 67 22 35N 91 49 E
Nazko 108 53 1N 123 37W
Nazko → 108 53 7N 123 34W
Nazret 87 8 32N 39 22 E
Nchanga 91 12 30 S 27 49 E
Ncheu 91 14 50 S 34 47 E
Ndala 90 4 45 S 33 15 E
Ndalatando 88 9 12 S 14 48 E
Ndali 85 9 50N 2 46 E
Ndareda 90 4 12 S 35 30 E
Ndélé 81 8 25N 20 36 E
Ndendé 88 2 22 S 11 23 E
Ndjamena 81 12 10N 14 59 E
Ndjolé 88 0 10 S 10 45 E
Ndola 91 13 0 S 28 34 E
Ndoto Mts. 90 2 0N 37 0 E
Nduguti 90 4 18 S 34 41 E
Nea → 47 63 15N 11 0 E
Néa Epídhavros 45 37 40N 23 7 E
Néa Flippiás 44 39 12N 20 53 E
Néa Kallikrátia 44 40 21N 23 1 E
Néa Víssi 44 41 34N 26 33 E
Neagh, Lough 15 54 35N 6 25W
Neah Bay 118 48 25N 124 40W
Neamţ □ 46 47 0N 26 20 E
Neápolis, Kozan, Greece 44 40 20N 21 24 E
Neápolis, Lakonia, Greece 45 36 27N 23 8 E
Near Is. 104 53 0N 172 0 E
Neath 13 51 39N 3 49W
Nebbou 85 11 9N 1 51W
Nebine Cr. → 99 29 27 S 146 56 E
Nebit Dag 58 39 30N 54 22 E
Nebolchy, U.S.S.R. 54 59 12N 32 58 E
Nebolchy, U.S.S.R. 54 59 8N 33 18 E
Nebraska □ 116 41 30N 100 0W
Nebraska City 116 40 40N 95 52W
Nébrodi, Monti 40 37 55N 14 50 E
Necedah 116 44 2N 90 7W
Nechako → 108 53 30N 122 44W
Neches → 117 29 55N 93 52W
Neckar → 25 49 31N 8 26 E
Necochea 124 38 30 S 58 50W
Nedelišće 39 46 23N 16 22 E
Nédha → 45 37 25N 21 45 E
Nedroma 82 35 1N 1 45W
Nedstrand 47 59 21N 5 49 E
Needles 119 34 50N 114 35W
Needles, The 13 50 39N 1 35W
Ñeembucú □ 124 27 0 S 58 0W
Neemuch (Nimach) 68 24 30N 74 56 E
Neenah 114 44 10N 88 30W
Neepawa 109 50 15N 99 30W
Nefta 83 33 53N 7 50 E
Neftah Sidi Boubekeur 82 35 1N 0 4 E
Neftegorsk 57 44 25N 39 45 E
Neftyannyye Kamni 53 40 20N 50 55 E
Negapatam = Nagappattinam 70 10 46N 79 50 E
Negaunee 114 46 30N 87 36W
Negba 62 31 40N 34 41 E
Negele 87 5 20N 39 36 E
Negeri Sembilan □ 71 2 50N 102 10 E
Negev = Hanegev 62 30 50N 35 0 E
Negoiu 46 45 35N 24 32 E
Negombo 70 7 12N 79 50 E
Negotin 42 44 16N 22 37 E
Negotino 42 41 29N 22 9 E
Negra, La 124 23 46 S 70 18W
Negra, Peña 30 42 11N 6 30W
Negra Pt. 73 18 40N 120 50 E
Negreira 30 42 54N 8 45W
Negreşti 46 46 50N 27 30 E
Négrine 83 34 30N 7 30 E
Negro →, Argent. 128 41 2 S 62 47W
Negro →, Brazil 126 3 0 S 60 0W
Negro →, Uruguay 125 33 24 S 58 22W
Negros 73 10 0N 123 0 E
Negru Vodă 46 43 47N 28 21 E
Nehbandān 65 31 35N 60 5 E
Neheim-Hüsten 24 51 27N 7 58 E
Nehoiaşu 46 45 24N 26 20 E
Nei Monggol Zizhiqu □ 76 42 0N 112 0 E
Neidpath 109 50 12N 107 20W
Neihart 118 47 0N 110 44W
Neijiang 75 29 35N 104 55 E
Neilton 118 17 24N 123 52W
Neira de Jusá 30 42 53N 7 14W
Neisse → 24 52 4N 14 46 E
Neiva 126 2 56N 75 18W
Neixiang 77 33 10N 111 52 E
Nejanilini L. 109 59 33N 97 48W
Nejo 87 9 30N 35 28 E
Nekemte 87 9 4N 36 30 E
Někheb 86 25 10N 32 48 E
Neksø 49 55 4N 15 8 E
Nelas 30 40 32N 7 52W
Nelaug 47 58 39N 8 40 E
Nelia 98 20 39 S 142 12 E
Nelidovo 54 56 13N 32 49 E
Neligh 116 42 11N 98 2W
Nelkan 59 57 40N 136 4 E
Nellikuppam 70 11 46N 79 43 E
Nellore 70 14 27N 79 59 E
Nelma 59 47 39N 139 0 E
Nelson, Austral. 100 38 3 S 141 2 E
Nelson, Can. 108 49 30N 117 20W
Nelson, N.Z. 101 41 18 S 173 16 E
Nelson, U.K. 12 53 50N 2 14W
Nelson, Ariz., U.S.A. 119 35 35N 113 16W
Nelson, Nev., U.S.A. 119 35 46N 114 48W
Nelson □ 101 42 11 S 172 15 E
Nelson → 109 54 33N 98 2W
Nelson, C., Austral. 99 38 26 S 141 32 E
Nelson, C., P.N.G. 98 9 0 S 149 20 E
Nelson, Estrecho 128 51 30 S 75 0W
Nelson Forks 108 59 30N 124 0W
Nelson House 109 55 47N 98 51W
Nelson L. 109 55 48N 100 7W
Nelspruit 93 25 29 S 30 59 E
Néma 84 16 40N 7 15W
Neman (Nemunas) → 54 55 25N 21 10 E
Neméa 45 37 49N 22 40 E
Nemeiben L. 109 55 20N 105 20W
Nemira 46 46 17N 26 19 E
Nemours 19 48 16N 2 40 E
Nemunas = Neman → 54 55 25N 21 10 E
Nemuro 74 43 20N 145 35 E
Nemuro-Kaikyō 74 43 30N 145 30 E
Nemuy 59 55 40N 136 9 E
Nen Jiang → 76 45 28N 124 30 E
Nenagh 15 52 52N 8 11W
Nenana 104 64 30N 149 20W
Nene → 12 52 38N 0 13 E
Nenjiang 75 49 10N 125 10 E
Neno 91 15 25 S 34 40 E
Nenusa, Kepulauan 73 4 45N 127 1 E
Neodesha 117 37 30N 95 37W
Néon Petrítsi 44 41 16N 23 15 E
Neosho 117 36 56N 94 28W
Neosho → 117 35 59N 95 10W
Nepal ■ 69 28 0N 84 30 E
Nepalganj 69 28 5N 81 40 E
Nephi 118 39 43N 111 52W
Nephin 15 54 1N 9 21W
Nepomuk 26 49 29N 13 35 E
Neptune City 113 40 13N 74 4W
Néra → 42 44 48N 21 25 E
Nérac 20 44 8N 0 21 E
Nerchinsk 59 52 0N 116 39 E
Nerchinskiy Zavod 59 51 20N 119 40 E
Nereju 46 45 43N 26 43 E
Nerekhta 55 57 26N 40 38 E
Néret L. 107 54 45N 70 44W
Neretva → 42 43 1N 17 27 E
Neretvanski Kanal 42 43 7N 17 10 E
Neringa 54 55 30N 21 5 E
Nerja 31 36 43N 3 55W
Nerl → 55 56 11N 40 34 E
Nerokoúrou 45 35 29N 24 3 E
Nerpio 33 38 11N 2 16W
Nerva 31 37 42N 6 30W
Nes 50 65 53N 17 24W
Nes Ziyyona 62 31 56N 34 48W
Nesbyen 47 60 34N 9 35 E
Nesebûr 43 42 41N 27 46 E
Nesflaten 47 59 38N 6 48 E
Neskaupstaður 50 65 9N 13 42W
Nesland 47 59 31N 7 59 E
Neslandsvatn 47 58 57N 9 10 E
Nesle 19 49 45N 2 53 E
Nesodden 47 59 48N 10 40 E
Nesque → 21 43 59N 4 59 E
Ness, Loch 14 57 15N 4 30W
Nestórion Óros 44 40 24N 21 5 E
Néstos → 44 41 20N 24 35 E
Nesttun 47 60 19N 5 21 E
Nesvizh 54 53 14N 26 38 E
Netanya 62 32 20N 34 51 E
Nète → 16 51 7N 4 14 E
Nether Stowey 13 51 0N 3 10W
Netherbury 13 50 46N 2 45W
Netherdale 97 21 10 S 148 33 E
Netherlands ■ 16 52 0N 5 30 E
Netherlands Guiana = Surinam ■ 127 4 0N 56 0W
Neto → 41 39 13N 17 8 E
Netrakona 69 24 53N 90 47 E
Nettancourt 19 48 51N 4 57 E
Nettilling L. 105 66 30N 71 0W
Nettuno 40 41 29N 12 40 E
Netzahualcoyotl, Presa 120 17 10N 93 30W
Neu-Isenburg 25 50 3N 8 42 E
Neu-Ulm 25 48 23N 10 2 E
Neubrandenburg 24 53 33N 13 17 E
Neubrandenburg □ 24 53 30N 13 20 E
Neubukow 24 54 1N 11 40 E
Neuburg 25 48 43N 11 11 E
Neuchâtel 25 47 0N 6 55 E
Neuchâtel □ 25 47 0N 6 55 E
Neuchâtel, Lac de 25 46 53N 6 50 E
Neudau 26 47 11N 16 6 E
Neuenhaus 24 52 30N 6 55 E
Neuf-Brisach 19 48 0N 7 30 E
Neufahrn 25 48 44N 12 11 E
Neufchâteau, Belg. 16 49 50N 5 25 E
Neufchâteau, France 19 48 21N 5 40 E
Neufchâtel 19 49 43N 1 30 E
Neufchâtel-sur-Aisne 19 49 26N 4 0 E
Neuhaus 24 53 16N 10 54 E
Neuillé-Pont-Pierre 18 47 33N 0 33 E
Neuilly-St-Front 19 49 10N 3 15 E
Neukalen 24 53 49N 12 48 E
Neumarkt 25 49 16N 11 28 E
Neumarkt-Sankt Veit 25 48 22N 12 30 E
Neumünster 24 54 4N 9 58 E
Neung-sur-Beuvron 19 47 30N 1 50 E
Neunkirchen, Austria 26 47 43N 16 4 E
Neunkirchen, Ger. 25 49 23N 7 12 E
Neuquén 128 38 55 S 68 0 E
Neuquén □ 124 38 0 S 69 50W
Neuruppin 24 52 56N 12 48 E
Neuse → 115 35 5N 76 30W
Neusiedl 27 47 57N 16 50 E
Neusiedler See 27 47 50N 16 47 E
Neuss 24 51 12N 6 39 E
Neussargues-Moissac 20 45 9N 3 1 E
Neustadt, Baden-W., Ger. 25 47 54N 8 13 E
Neustadt, Bayern, Ger. 25 50 23N 11 0 E
Neustadt, Bayern, Ger. 25 49 42N 12 10 E
Neustadt, Bayern, Ger. 25 48 48N 11 47 E
Neustadt, Bayern, Ger. 25 49 34N 10 37 E
Neustadt, Gera, Ger. 24 50 45N 11 43 E
Neustadt, Hessen, Ger. 24 50 51N 9 9 E
Neustadt, Niedersachsen, Ger. 24 52 30N 9 30 E
Neustadt, Potsdam, Ger. 24 52 50N 12 27 E
Neustadt, Rhld-Pfz., Ger. 25 49 21N 8 10 E
Neustadt, Schleswig-Holstein, Ger. 24 54 6N 10 49 E
Neustrelitz 24 53 22N 13 4 E
Neuvic 20 45 23N 2 16 E
Neuville, Rhône, France 21 45 52N 4 51 E
Neuville, Vienne, France 18 46 41N 0 15 E
Neuville-aux-Bois 19 48 4N 2 3 E
Neuvy-le-Roi 18 47 36N 0 36 E
Neuvy-St-Sépulchure 20 46 35N 1 48 E
Neuvy-sur-Barangeon 19 47 20N 2 15 E
Neuwerk 24 53 55N 8 30 E
Neuwied 24 50 26N 7 29 E
Neva → 52 59 50N 30 30 E
Nevada 117 37 51N 94 22W
Nevada □ 118 39 20N 117 0W
Nevada City 118 39 20N 121 0W
Nevada de Sta. Marta, Sa. 126 10 55N 73 50W
Nevada, Sierra, Spain 33 37 3N 3 15W
Nevada, Sierra, U.S.A. 118 39 0N 120 30W
Nevado, Cerro 124 35 30 S 68 32W
Nevanka 59 56 31N 98 55 E
Nevasa 70 19 34N 75 0 E
Nevel 54 56 0N 29 55 E
Nevers 19 47 0N 3 9 E
Nevertire 99 31 50 S 147 44 E
Nevesinje 42 43 14N 18 6 E
Neville 109 49 58N 107 39W
Nevinnomyssk 57 44 40N 42 0 E
Nevis 121 17 0N 62 30W

Nevlunghavn 47 55 58N 9 52 E
Nevrokop = Gotse Delchev 43 41 33N 23 46 E
Nevşehir 64 38 33N 34 40 E
Nevyansk 52 57 30N 60 13 E
New Albany, Ind., U.S.A. 114 38 20N 85 50W
New Albany, Miss., U.S.A. 117 34 30N 89 0W
New Albany, Pa., U.S.A. 113 41 35N 76 28W
New Amsterdam 126 6 15N 57 36W
New Bedford 114 41 40N 70 52W
New Bern 115 35 8N 77 3W
New Bethlehem 112 41 0N 79 22W
New Bloomfield 112 40 24N 77 12W
New Boston 117 33 27N 94 21W
New Braunfels 117 29 43N 98 9W
New Brighton, N.Z. 101 43 29 S 172 43 E
New Brighton, U.S.A. 112 40 42N 80 19W
New Britain, P.N.G. 94 5 50 S 150 20 E
New Britain, U.S.A. 114 41 41N 72 47W
New Brunswick 114 40 30N 74 28W
New Brunswick □ 107 46 50N 66 30W
New Bussa 85 9 53N 4 31 E
New Byrd 5 80 0 S 120 0W
New Caledonia = Nouvelle-Calédonie 94 21 0 S 165 0 E
New Castile = Castilla La Neuva 31 39 45N 3 20W
New Castle, Ind., U.S.A. 114 39 55N 85 23W
New Castle, Pa., U.S.A. 114 41 0N 80 20W
New City 113 41 8N 74 0W
New Cristóbal 120 9 22N 79 40W
New Cumberland 112 40 30N 80 36W
New Delhi 68 28 37N 77 13 E
New Denver 108 50 0N 117 25W
New England 116 46 36N 102 47W
New England Ra. 97 30 20 S 151 45 E
New Forest 13 50 53N 1 40W
New Glasgow 107 45 35N 62 36W
New Guinea 94 4 0 S 136 0 E
New Hamburg 112 43 23N 80 42W
New Hampshire □ 114 43 40N 71 40W
New Hampton 116 43 2N 92 20W
New Hanover, P.N.G. 98 2 30 S 150 10 E
New Hanover, S. Afr. 93 29 22 S 30 31 E
New Haven, Conn., U.S.A. 114 41 20N 72 54W
New Haven, Mich., U.S.A. 112 42 44N 82 46W
New Hazelton 108 55 20N 127 30W
New Hebrides 94 15 0 S 168 0 E
New Iberia 117 30 2N 91 54W
New Ireland 94 3 20 S 151 50 E
New Jersey □ 114 40 30N 74 10W
New Kensington 114 40 36N 79 43W
New Lexington 114 39 40N 82 15W
New Liskeard 106 47 31N 79 41W
New London, Conn., U.S.A. 114 41 23N 72 8W
New London, Minn., U.S.A. 116 45 17N 94 55W
New London, Ohio, U.S.A. 112 41 4N 82 25W
New London, Wis., U.S.A. 116 44 23N 88 43W
New Madrid 117 36 40N 89 30W
New Meadows 118 45 0N 116 32W
New Mexico □ 110 34 30N 106 0W
New Milford, Conn., U.S.A. 113 41 35N 73 25W
New Milford, Pa., U.S.A. 113 41 50N 75 45W
New Norfolk 97 42 46 S 147 2 E
New Orleans 117 30 0N 90 5W
New Philadelphia 114 40 29N 81 25W
New Plymouth, N.Z. 101 39 4 S 174 5 E
New Plymouth, U.S.A. 118 43 58N 116 49W
New Providence 121 25 25N 78 35W
New Radnor 13 52 15N 3 10W
New Richmond 116 45 6N 92 34W
New Roads 117 30 43N 91 30W
New Rochelle 113 40 55N 73 46W
New Rockford 116 47 44N 99 7W
New Ross 15 52 24N 6 58W
New Salem 116 46 51N 101 25W
New Siberian Is. = Novosibirskiye Os. 59 75 0N 142 0 E
New Smyrna Beach 115 29 0N 80 50W
New South Wales □ 97 33 0 S 146 0 E
New Town 116 47 59N 102 30W
New Ulm 116 44 15N 94 30W
New Waterford 107 46 13N 60 4W
New Westminster 108 49 13N 122 55W
New York □ 114 42 40N 76 0W
New York City 114 40 45N 74 0W
New Zealand ■ 94 40 0 S 176 0 E
Newala 91 10 58 S 39 18 E
Newala □ 91 10 46 S 39 20 E
Newark, Del., U.S.A. 114 39 42N 75 45W
Newark, N.J., U.S.A. 114 40 41N 74 12W
Newark, N.Y., U.S.A. 114 43 2N 77 10W
Newark, Ohio, U.S.A. 114 40 5N 82 24W
Newark-on-Trent 12 53 6N 0 48W
Newaygo 114 43 25N 85 48W
Newberg 118 45 22N 123 0W
Newberry, Mich., U.S.A. 114 46 20N 85 32W
Newberry, S.C., U.S.A. 115 34 17N 81 37W
Newbrook 108 54 24N 112 57W
Newburgh 114 41 30N 74 1W
Newbury, U.K. 13 51 24N 1 19W
Newbury, U.S.A. 113 44 7N 72 6W
Newburyport 114 42 48N 70 50W
Newcastle, Austral. 97 33 0 S 151 46 E
Newcastle, Can. 107 47 1N 65 38W
Newcastle, S. Afr. 93 27 45 S 29 58 E
Newcastle, U.K. 15 54 13N 5 54W
Newcastle, U.S.A. 116 43 50N 104 12W
Newcastle Emlyn 13 52 2N 4 29W
Newcastle Ra. 97 15 45 S 130 15 E
Newcastle-under-Lyme 12 53 2N 2 15W
Newcastle-upon-Tyne 12 54 59N 1 37W
Newcastle Waters 96 17 30 S 133 28 E
Newdegate 96 33 6 S 119 0 E
Newe Etan 62 32 30N 35 32 E
Newe Sha'anan 62 32 47N 34 59 E
Newe Zohar 62 31 9N 35 21 E
Newell 116 44 48N 103 25W
Newenham, C. 104 58 40N 162 15W
Newfoundland 107 48 30N 56 0W
Newfoundland □ 107 53 0N 58 0W
Newhalem 108 48 41N 121 16W
Newham 13 51 31N 0 2 E
Newhaven 13 50 47N 0 4 E
Newkirk 117 36 52N 97 3W
Newman, Mt. 96 23 20 S 119 34 E
Newmarket, Can. 112 44 3N 79 28W
Newmarket, Ireland 15 52 13N 9 0W
Newmarket, U.K. 13 52 15N 0 23 E
Newmarket, U.S.A. 113 43 4N 70 57W
Newnan 115 33 22N 84 48W
Newnes 99 33 9 S 150 16 E
Newport, Gwent, U.K. 13 51 35N 3 0W
Newport, I. of W., U.K. 13 50 42N 1 18W
Newport, Salop, U.K. 13 52 47N 2 22W
Newport, Ark., U.S.A. 117 35 38N 91 15W
Newport, Ky., U.S.A. 114 39 5N 84 23W
Newport, N.H., U.S.A. 114 43 23N 72 8W
Newport, Oreg., U.S.A. 118 44 41N 124 2W
Newport, Pa., U.S.A. 112 40 28N 77 8W
Newport, R.I., U.S.A. 114 41 13N 71 19W
Newport, Tenn., U.S.A. 115 35 59N 83 12W
Newport, Vt., U.S.A. 114 44 57N 72 17W
Newport, Wash., U.S.A. 118 48 11N 117 2W
Newport Beach 119 33 40N 117 58W
Newport News 114 37 2N 76 30W
Newquay 13 50 24N 5 6W
Newry 15 54 10N 6 20W
Newry & Mourne □ 15 54 10N 6 15W
Newton, Iowa, U.S.A. 116 41 40N 93 3W
Newton, Mass., U.S.A. 114 42 21N 71 10W
Newton, Miss., U.S.A. 117 32 19N 89 10W
Newton, N.C., U.S.A. 115 35 42N 81 10W
Newton, N.J., U.S.A. 114 41 3N 74 46W
Newton, Texas, U.S.A. 117 30 54N 93 42W
Newton Abbot 13 50 32N 3 37W
Newton Boyd 99 29 45 S 152 16 E
Newton Stewart 14 54 57N 4 30W
Newtonmore 14 57 4N 4 7W
Newtown 13 52 31N 3 19W
Newtownabbey 15 54 40N 5 55W
Newtownabbey □ 15 54 45N 6 0W
Newtownards 15 54 37N 5 40W
Newville 112 40 10N 77 24W
Nexon 20 45 41N 1 11 E
Neya 55 58 21N 43 49 E
Neyrīz 65 29 15N 54 19 E
Neyshābūr 65 36 10N 58 50 E
Neyyattinkara 70 8 26N 77 5 E
Nezhin 54 51 5N 31 55 E
Nezperce 118 46 13N 116 15W
Ngabang 72 0 23N 109 55 E
Ngabordamlu, Tanjung 73 6 56 S 134 11 E
Ngambé 85 5 48N 11 29 E
Ngami Depression 92 20 30 S 22 46 E
Ngamo 91 19 3 S 27 32 E
Nganglong Kangri 67 33 0N 81 0 E
Nganjuk 73 7 32 S 111 55 E
Ngaoundéré 88 7 15N 13 35 E
Ngapara 101 44 57 S 170 46 E
Ngara 90 2 29 S 30 40 E
Ngara □ 90 2 29 S 30 40 E
Ngau 101 18 2 S 179 18 E
Ngawi 73 7 24 S 111 26 E
Ngha Lo 71 21 33N 104 28 E
Ngiva 92 16 48 S 15 50 E
Ngoma 91 13 8 S 33 45 E
Ngomahura 91 20 26 S 30 43 E
Ngomba 91 8 20 S 32 53 E
Ngop 87 6 17N 30 9 E
Ngoring Hu 75 34 55N 97 5 E
Ngorkou 84 15 40N 3 41W
Ngorongoro 90 3 11 S 35 32 E
Ngozi 90 2 54 S 29 50 E
Ngudu 90 2 58 S 33 25 E
Nguigmi 81 14 20N 13 20 E
Ngunga 90 3 37 S 33 37 E
Ngunza 88 11 10 S 13 48 E
Nguru 85 12 56N 10 29 E
Nguru Mts. 90 6 0 S 37 30 E
Nha Trang 71 12 16N 109 10 E
Nhacoongo 93 24 18 S 35 14 E
Nhangutazi, L. 93 24 0 S 34 30 E
Nhill 99 36 18 S 141 40 E
Nia-nia 90 1 30N 27 40 E
Niafounké 84 16 0N 4 5W
Niagara 114 45 45N 88 0W
Niagara Falls, Can. 106 43 7N 79 5W
Niagara Falls, U.S.A. 114 43 5N 79 0W
Niagara-on-the-Lake 112 43 15N 79 4W
Niah 72 3 58N 113 46 E
Nialia, L. 100 33 20 S 141 42 E
Niamey 85 13 27N 2 6 E
Nianforando 84 9 37N 10 36W
Nianfors 48 61 36N 16 46 E
Niangara 90 3 42N 27 50 E
Nianzishan 76 47 31N 122 53 E
Nias 72 1 0N 97 30 E
Niassa □ 91 13 30 S 36 0 E
Nibbiano 38 44 54N 9 20 E
Nibe 49 56 59N 9 38 E
Nibong Tebal 71 5 10N 100 29 E
Nicaragua ■ 121 11 40N 85 30W
Nicaragua, Lago de 121 12 0N 85 30W
Nicastro 41 39 0N 16 18 E
Nice 21 43 42N 7 14 E
Niceville 115 30 30N 86 30W
Nichinan 74 31 38N 131 23 E
Nicholás, Canal 121 23 30N 80 5W
Nicholasville 114 37 54N 84 31W
Nichols 113 42 1N 76 22W
Nicholson 113 41 37N 75 47W
Nicobar Is. 60 9 0N 93 0 E
Nicola 108 50 12N 120 40W
Nicolet 106 46 17N 72 35W
Nicolls Town 121 25 8N 78 0W
Nicopolis 45 39 2N 20 37 E
Nicosia, Cyprus 64 35 10N 33 25 E
Nicosia, Italy 41 37 45N 14 22 E
Nicótera 41 38 33N 15 57 E
Nicoya, G. de 121 10 0N 85 0W
Nicoya, Pen. de 121 9 45N 85 40W
Nidd → 12 54 1N 1 32W
Nidda 24 50 24N 9 2 E
Nidda → 25 50 6N 8 34 E
Nidzica 28 53 25N 20 28 E
Niebüll 24 54 47N 8 49 E
Nied → 19 49 23N 6 40 E
Niederaula 24 50 48N 9 37 E
Niederbronn 19 48 57N 7 39 E
Niedere Tauern 26 47 20N 14 0 E
Niedermarsberg 24 51 28N 8 52 E
Niederösterreich □ 26 48 25N 15 40 E
Niedersachsen □ 24 52 45N 9 0 E
Niellé 84 10 5N 5 38W
Niemba 90 5 58 S 28 24 E
Niemcza 28 50 42N 16 47 E
Niemodlin 28 50 38N 17 38 E
Niemur 100 35 17 S 144 9 E
Nienburg 24 52 38N 9 15 E
Niepołomice 27 50 3N 20 13 E
Niers → 24 51 45N 5 58 E
Niesky 24 51 18N 14 48 E
Nieszawa 28 52 52N 18 50 E
Nieuw Amsterdam 127 5 53N 55 5W
Nieuw Nickerie 127 6 0N 56 59W
Nieuwpoort 16 51 8N 2 45 E
Nieves 30 42 7N 8 26W
Nièvre □ 19 47 10N 3 40 E
Niğde 64 38 0N 34 40 E
Nigel 93 26 27 S 28 25 E
Niger ■ 85 13 30N 10 0 E
Niger □ 85 10 0N 5 0 E
Niger → 85 5 33N 6 33 E
Nigeria ■ 85 8 30N 8 0 E
Nightcaps 101 45 57 S 168 2 E
Nigríta 44 40 56N 23 29 E
Nihtaur 69 29 20N 78 23 E
Nii-Jima 74 34 20N 139 15 E
Niigata 74 37 58N 139 0 E
Niigata □ 74 37 15N 138 45 E
Niihama 74 33 55N 133 16 E
Niihau 110 21 55N 160 10W
Nijar 33 36 53N 2 15W
Nijkerk 16 52 13N 5 30 E
Nijmegen 16 51 50N 5 52 E
Nijverdal 16 52 22N 6 28 E
Nike 85 6 26N 7 29 E
Nikel 50 69 24N 30 12 E
Nikiniki 73 9 49 S 124 30 E
Nikítas 44 40 13N 23 34 E
Nikki 85 9 58N 3 12 E
Nikkō 74 36 45N 139 35 E
Nikolayev 56 46 58N 32 0 E
Nikolayevsk 55 50 0N 45 35 E
Nikolayevsk-na-Amur 59 53 8N 140 44 E
Nikolsk 55 59 30N 45 28 E
Nikolskoye 59 55 12N 166 0 E
Nikopol, Bulg. 43 43 43N 24 54 E
Nikopol, U.S.S.R. 56 47 35N 34 25 E
Niksar 56 40 31N 37 2 E
Nikshahr 65 26 15N 60 10 E
Nikšić 42 42 50N 18 57 E
Nîl el Abyad → 87 15 38N 32 31 E
Nîl el Azraq → 87 15 38N 32 31 E
Nîl, Nahr en → 86 30 10N 31 6 E
Niland 119 33 16N 115 30W
Nile = Nîl, Nahr en → 86 30 10N 31 6 E
Nile □ 90 2 0N 31 30 E
Nile Delta 86 31 40N 31 0 E
Niles 114 41 8N 80 40W
Nilgiri Hills 70 11 30N 76 30 E
Nimach = Neemuch 68 24 30N 74 56 E
Nimbahera 68 24 37N 74 45 E
Nîmes 21 43 50N 4 23 E
Nimfaíon, Ákra- 44 40 5N 24 20 E
Nimingarra 96 20 31 S 119 55 E
Nimmitabel 99 36 29 S 149 15 E
Nimneryskiy 59 57 50N 125 10 E
Nimrod Glacier 5 82 27 S 161 0 E
Nimule 87 3 32N 32 3 E
Nin 39 44 16N 15 12 E
Nindigully 99 28 21 S 148 50 E
Ninemile 108 56 0N 130 7W
Ninety Mile Beach, The 97 38 15 S 147 24 E
Nineveh = Nīnawá 64 36 25N 43 10 E
Ning'an 76 44 22N 129 20 E
Ningbo 75 29 51N 121 28 E
Ningde 75 26 38N 119 23 E
Ningdu 77 26 25N 115 59 E
Ningjin 76 37 35N 114 57 E
Ningming 77 22 8N 107 4 E
Ningpo = Ningbo 75 29 51N 121 28 E
Ningqiang 77 32 47N 106 15 E
Ningshan 77 33 21N 108 21 E
Ningsia Hui A.R. = Ningxia Huizu Zizhiqu □ 76 38 0N 106 0 E
Ningwu 76 39 0N 112 18 E
Ningxia Huizu Zizhiqu □ 76 38 0N 106 0 E
Ningxiang 77 28 15N 112 30 E
Ningyuan 77 25 37N 111 57 E
Ninh Binh 71 20 15N 105 55 E
Ninove 16 50 51N 4 2 E
Nioaque 125 21 5 S 55 50W
Niobrara 116 42 48N 97 59W
Niobrara → 116 42 45N 98 0W
Niono 84 14 15N 6 0W
Nioro du Rip 84 13 40N 15 50W
Nioro du Sahel 84 15 15N 9 30W
Niort 20 46 19N 0 29W
Nipani 70 16 20N 74 25 E
Nipawin 109 53 20N 104 0W
Nipawin Prov. Park 109 54 0N 104 37W
Nipigon 106 49 0N 88 17W
Nipigon, L. 106 49 50N 88 30W
Nipin → 109 55 46N 108 35W
Nipishish L. 107 54 12N 60 45W
Nipissing L. 106 46 20N 80 0W
Nipomo 119 35 4N 120 29W
Niquelândia 127 14 33 S 48 23W
Nira → 70 17 58N 75 8 E
Nirmal 70 19 3N 78 20 E
Nirmali 69 26 20N 86 35 E
Niš 42 43 19N 21 58 E
Nisa 31 39 30N 7 41W
Nişāb 63 14 25N 46 29 E
Nišava → 42 43 20N 21 46 E
Niscemi 41 37 8N 14 21 E
Nishinomiya 74 34 45N 135 20 E
Nísiros 45 36 35N 27 12 E
Niskibi → 106 56 29N 88 9W
Nisko 28 50 35N 22 7 E
Nisporeny 46 47 4N 28 10 E
Nissafors 49 57 25N 13 37 E
Nissan → 49 56 40N 12 51 E
Nissedal 47 59 10N 8 30 E
Nisser 47 59 7N 8 28 E
Nissum Fjord 49 56 20N 8 11 E
Nisutlin → 108 60 14N 132 34W
Nitā' 64 27 15N 48 35 E
Nitchequon 107 53 10N 70 58W
Niterói 125 22 52 S 43 0W
Nith → 14 55 20N 3 5W
Nitra 27 48 19N 18 4 E
Nitra → 27 47 46N 18 10 E
Nittedal 47 60 1N 10 57 E
Nittendau 25 49 12N 12 16 E
Niuafo'ou 101 15 30 S 175 58W
Niue I. (Savage I.) 95 19 2 S 169 54W
Niut 72 0 55N 110 6 E
Nivelles 16 50 35N 4 20 E
Nivernais 19 47 0N 3 40 E
Nixon, Nev., U.S.A. 118 39 54N 119 22W
Nixon, Tex., U.S.A. 117 29 17N 97 45W
Nizam Sagar 70 18 10N 77 58 E
Nizamabad 70 18 45N 78 7 E
Nizamghat 67 28 20N 95 45 E
Nizhne Kolymsk 59 68 34N 160 55 E
Nizhne-Vartovskoye 58 60 56N 76 38 E
Nizhneangarsk 59 55 47N 109 30 E
Nizhnegorskiy 56 45 27N 34 38 E
Nizhneudinsk 59 54 54N 99 3 E
Nizhneyansk 59 71 26N 136 4 E
Nizhniy Lomov 55 53 34N 43 38 E
Nizhniy Novgorod = Gorkiy 55 56 20N 44 0 E
Nizhniy Tagil 52 57 55N 59 57 E
Nizhnyaya Tunguska → 59 64 20N 93 0 E
Nizip 64 37 5N 37 50 E
Nizké Tatry 27 48 55N 20 0 E
Nizza Monferrato 38 44 46N 8 22 E
Njakwa 91 11 1 S 33 56 E
Njanji 91 14 25 S 31 46 E
Njinjo 91 8 48 S 38 54 E
Njombe 91 9 20 S 34 50 E
Njombe □ 91 9 20 S 34 49 E
Njombe → 90 6 56 S 35 6 E
Nkambe 85 6 35N 10 40 E
Nkana 91 12 50 S 28 8 E
Nkawkaw 85 6 36N 0 49W
Nkhota Kota 91 12 56 S 34 15 E
Nkongsamba 88 4 55N 9 55 E
Nkwanta 84 6 10N 2 10W
Noatak 104 67 32N 162 59W
Nobel 112 45 25N 80 6W
Nobeoka 74 32 36N 131 41 E
Noblejas 32 39 58N 3 26W
Noblesville 114 40 1N 85 59W
Noce → 38 46 9N 11 4 E
Nocera Inferiore 41 40 45N 14 37 E
Nocera Terinese 41 39 2N 16 9 E
Nocera Umbra 39 43 8N 12 47 E
Noci 41 40 47N 17 7 E
Nockatunga 99 27 42 S 142 42 E
Nocona 117 33 48N 97 45W
Nocrich 46 45 55N 24 26 E
Noel 117 36 36N 94 29W
Nogales, Mexico 120 31 20N 110 56W
Nogales, U.S.A. 119 31 33N 110 56W
Nogat → 28 54 17N 19 17 E
Nōgata 74 33 48N 130 44 E
Nogent-en-Bassigny 19 48 0N 5 20 E
Nogent-le-Rotrou 18 48 20N 0 50 E
Nogent-sur-Seine 19 48 30N 3 30 E
Noginsk, Moskva, U.S.S.R. 55 55 50N 38 25 E
Noginsk, Sib., U.S.S.R. 59 64 30N 90 50 E
Nogoa → 97 23 40 S 147 55 E
Nogoyá 124 32 24 S 59 48W
Nógrád □ 27 48 0N 19 30 E
Nogueira de Ramuin 30 42 21N 7 43W
Noguera Pallaresa → 32 42 15N 1 0 E
Noguera Ribagorzana → 32 41 40N 0 43 E
Nohar 68 29 11N 74 49 E
Noi → 71 14 50N 100 15 E
Noire, Mt. 18 48 11N 3 40W
Noirétable 20 45 48N 3 46 E
Noirmoutier 18 47 0N 2 15W
Noirmoutier, Î. de 18 46 58N 2 10W
Nojane 92 23 15 S 20 14 E
Nok Kundi 66 28 50N 62 45 E
Nokaneng 92 19 40 S 22 17 E
Nokhtuysk 59 60 0N 117 45 E
Nokomis 109 51 35N 105 0W
Nokomis L. 109 57 0N 103 0W
Nol 49 57 56N 12 5 E
Nola, C. Afr. Rep. 88 3 35N 16 4 E
Nola, Italy 41 40 54N 14 29 E
Nolay 19 46 58N 4 35 E
Noli, C. di 38 44 12N 8 26 E
Nolinsk 55 57 28N 49 57 E
Noma Omuramba → 92 18 52 S 20 53 E
Noman L. 109 62 15N 108 55W
Nome 104 64 30N 165 24W
Nonacho L. 109 61 42N 109 40W
Nonancourt 18 48 47N 1 11 E
Nonant-le-Pin 18 48 42N 0 12 E
Nonda 98 20 40 S 142 28 E
Nong Khae 71 14 29N 100 53 E
Nong Khai 71 17 50N 102 46 E
Nong'an 76 44 25N 125 5 E
Nonoava 120 27 28N 106 44W
Nontron 20 45 31N 0 40 E
Noonan 116 48 51N 102 59W
Noondoo 99 28 35 S 148 30 E
Noord Brabant □ 16 51 40N 5 0 E
Noord Holland □ 16 52 30N 4 45 E
Noordbeveland 16 51 35N 3 50 E
Noordoostpolder 16 52 45N 5 45 E
Noordwijk aan Zee 16 52 14N 4 26 E
Nootka 108 49 38N 126 38W
Nootka I. 108 49 32N 126 42W

Nóqui 88 5 55 S 13 30 E
Nora, Ethiopia 87 16 6N 40 4 E
Nora, Sweden 48 59 32N 15 2 E
Noranda 106 48 20N 79 0W
Norberg 48 60 4N 15 56 E
Nórcia 39 42 50N 13 5 E
Nord □ 19 50 15N 3 30 E
Nord-Ostee Kanal 24 54 15N 9 40 E
Nord-Süd Kanal 24 53 0N 10 32 E
Nord-Trøndelag fylke □ 50 64 20N 12 0 E
Nordagutu 47 59 25N 9 20 E
Nordaustlandet 4 79 14N 23 0 E
Nordborg 49 55 5N 9 50 E
Nordby, Arhus, Denmark 49 55 58N 10 32 E
Nordby, Ribe, Denmark 49 55 27N 8 24 E
Norddal 47 62 15N 7 14 E
Norddalsfjord 47 61 39N 5 23 E
Norddeich 24 53 37N 7 10 E
Nordegg 108 52 29N 116 5W
Norden 24 53 35N 7 12 E
Nordenham 24 53 29N 8 28 E
Norderhov 47 60 7N 10 17 E
Norderney 24 53 42N 7 15 E
Nordfjord 47 61 55N 5 30 E
Nordfriesische Inseln 24 54 40N 8 20 E
Nordhausen 24 51 29N 10 47 E
Nordhorn 24 52 27N 7 4 E
Nordjyllands Amtskommune □ 49 57 0N 10 0 E
Nordkapp, Norway 50 71 10N 25 44 E
Nordkapp, Svalb. 4 80 31N 20 0 E
Nordkinn 9 71 8N 27 40 E
Nordland fylke □ 50 65 40N 13 0 E
Nördlingen 25 48 50N 10 30 E
Nordrhein-Westfalen □ 24 51 45N 7 30 E
Nordstrand 24 54 27N 8 50 E
Nordvik 59 74 2N 111 32 E
Nore 47 60 10N 9 0 E
Nore → 15 52 40N 7 20W
Norefjell 47 60 16N 9 29 E
Norembega 106 48 59N 80 43W
Noresund 47 60 11N 9 37 E
Norfolk, Nebr., U.S.A. 116 42 3N 97 25W
Norfolk, Va., U.S.A. 114 36 40N 76 15W
Norfolk □ 12 52 39N 1 0 E
Norfolk Broads 12 52 30N 1 15 E
Norfolk I. 94 28 58 S 168 3 E
Norfork Res. 117 36 13N 92 15W
Norilsk 59 69 20N 88 6 E
Norley 99 27 45 S 143 48 E
Norma, Mt. 98 20 55 S 140 42 E
Normal 116 40 30N 89 0W
Norman 117 35 12N 97 30W
Norman → 97 17 28 S 140 49 E
Norman Wells 104 65 17N 126 51W
Normanby → 97 14 23 S 144 10 E
Normanby I. 98 10 55 S 151 5 E
Normandie 18 48 45N 0 10 E
Normandie, Collines de Normandie 18 48 55N 0 45W
Normandin 106 48 49N 72 31W
Normandy = Normandie 18 48 45N 0 10 E
Normanton 97 17 40 S 141 10 E
Norquay 109 51 53N 102 5W
Norquinco 128 41 51 S 70 55W
Norrahammar 49 57 43N 14 7 E
Norrbotten □ 50 66 30N 22 30 E
Norrby 50 64 55N 18 15 E
Nørre Åby 49 55 27N 9 52 E
Nørre Nebel 49 55 47N 8 17 E
Nørresundby 49 57 5N 9 52 E
Norris 118 45 40N 111 40W
Norristown 114 40 9N 75 21W
Norrköping 49 58 37N 16 11 E
Norrland □ 50 66 50N 18 0 E
Norrtälje 48 59 46N 18 42 E
Norsholm 49 58 31N 15 59 E
Norsk 59 52 30N 130 0 E
North Adams 114 42 42N 73 6W
North America 102 40 0N 100 0W
North Andaman I. 71 13 15N 92 40 E
North Atlantic Ocean 6 30 0N 50 0W
North Battleford 109 52 50N 108 17W
North Bay 106 46 20N 79 30W
North Belcher Is. 106 56 50N 79 50W
North Bend, Can. 108 49 50N 121 27W
North Bend, Oreg., U.S.A. 118 43 28N 124 14W
North Bend, Pa., U.S.A. 112 41 20N 77 42W
North Berwick, U.K. 14 56 4N 2 44W
North Berwick, U.S.A. 113 43 18N 70 43W
North Buganda □ 90 1 0N 32 0 E
North Canadian → 117 35 17N 95 31W
North C., Antarct. 5 71 0 S 166 0 E
North C., Can. 107 47 2N 60 20W
North C., N.Z. 101 34 23 S 173 4 E
North Caribou L. 106 52 50N 90 40W
North Carolina □ 115 35 30N 80 0W
North Channel, Br. Is. 14 55 0N 5 30W
North Channel, Can. 106 46 0N 83 0W
North Chicago 114 42 19N 87 50W
North Dakota □ 116 47 30N 100 0W
North Down □ 15 54 40N 5 45W
North Downs 13 51 17N 0 30 E
North East 112 42 17N 79 50W
North East Frontier Agency = Arunachal Pradesh □ 67 28 0N 95 0 E
North East Providence Chan. 121 26 0N 76 0W
North Eastern □ 90 1 30N 40 0 E
North Esk → 14 56 44N 2 25W
North European Plain 9 55 0N 20 0 E
North Foreland 13 51 22N 1 28 E
North Frisian Is. = Nordfr'sche Inseln 24 54 50N 8 20 E
North Henik L. 109 61 45N 97 40W
North Horr 90 3 20N 37 8 E
North I., Kenya 90 4 5N 36 5 E
North I., N.Z. 101 38 0 S 175 0 E
North Kingsville 112 41 53N 80 42W
North Knife → 109 58 53N 94 45W
North Koel → 69 24 45N 83 50 E
North Korea ■ 76 40 0N 127 0 E
North Lakhimpur 67 27 14N 94 7 E
North Las Vegas 119 36 15N 115 6W
North Loup → 116 41 17N 98 23W
North Mashonaland □ 91 16 30 S 30 0 E
North Minch 14 58 5N 5 55W
North Nahanni → 108 62 15N 123 20W
North Ossetian A.S.S.R. □ 57 43 30N 44 30 E
North Palisade 119 37 6N 118 32W
North Platte 116 41 10N 100 50W
North Platte → 116 41 15N 100 45W
North Pt. 107 47 5N 64 0W
North Pole 4 90 0N 0 0 E
North Portal 109 49 0N 102 33W
North Powder 118 45 2N 117 59W
North Ronaldsay 14 59 20N 2 30W
North Sea 8 56 0N 4 0 E
North Sentinel I. 71 11 35N 92 15 E
North Sporades = Voríai Sporádhes 45 39 15N 23 30 E
North Stradbroke I. 97 27 35 S 153 28 E
North Sydney 107 46 12N 60 15W
North Thompson → 108 50 40N 120 20W
North Tonawanda 114 43 5N 78 50W
North Troy 113 44 59N 72 24W
North Truchas Pk. 119 36 0N 105 30W
North Twin I. 106 53 20N 80 0W
North Tyne → 12 54 59N 2 7W
North Uist 14 57 40N 7 15W
North Vancouver 108 49 25N 123 3W
North Vernon 114 39 0N 85 35W
North Village 121 32 15N 64 45W
North Wabiskaw L. 108 56 0N 113 55W
North Walsham 12 52 49N 1 22 E
North West Basin 96 25 45 S 115 0 E
North West C. 96 21 45 S 114 9 E
North West Christmas I. Ridge 95 6 30N 165 0W
North West Highlands 14 57 35N 5 2W
North West Providence Channel 121 26 0N 78 0W
North West River 107 53 30N 60 10W
North Western □ 91 13 30 S 25 30 E
North York Moors 12 54 25N 0 50W
North Yorkshire □ 12 54 15N 1 25W
Northallerton 12 54 20N 1 26W
Northam 96 31 35 S 116 42 E
Northampton, Austral. 96 28 27 S 114 33 E
Northampton, U.K. 13 52 14N 0 54W
Northampton, Mass., U.S.A. 114 42 22N 72 31W
Northampton, Pa., U.S.A. 113 40 38N 75 24W
Northampton □ 13 52 16N 0 55W
Northampton Downs 98 24 35 S 145 48 E
Northbridge 113 42 12N 71 40W
Northeim 24 51 42N 10 0 E
Northern □, Malawi 91 11 0 S 34 0 E
Northern □, Uganda 90 3 5N 32 30 E
Northern □, Zambia 91 10 30 S 31 0 E
Northern Circars 70 17 30N 82 30 E
Northern Group 101 10 00 S 160 00W
Northern Indian L. 109 57 20N 97 20W
Northern Ireland □ 15 54 45N 7 0W
Northern Light, L. 106 48 15N 90 39W
Northern Province □ 84 9 15N 11 30W
Northern Territory □ 96 16 0 S 133 0 E
Northfield 116 44 30N 93 10W
Northome 116 47 53N 94 15W
Northport, Ala., U.S.A. 115 33 15N 87 35W
Northport, Mich., U.S.A. 114 45 8N 85 39W
Northport, Wash., U.S.A. 118 48 55N 117 48W
Northumberland □ 12 55 12N 2 0W
Northumberland, C. 97 38 5 S 140 40 E
Northumberland Is. 98 21 30 S 149 50 E
Northumberland Str. 107 46 20N 64 0W
Northwest Territories □ 104 65 0N 100 0W
Northwich 12 53 16N 2 30W
Northwood, Iowa, U.S.A. 116 43 27N 93 0W
Northwood, N.D., U.S.A. 116 47 44N 97 30W
Norton, U.S.A. 116 39 50N 99 53W
Norton, Zimb. 91 17 52 S 30 40 E
Norton Sd. 104 64 0N 164 0W
Nortorf 24 54 14N 9 47 E
Norwalk, Conn., U.S.A. 114 41 9N 73 25W
Norwalk, Ohio, U.S.A. 114 41 13N 82 38W
Norway 114 45 46N 87 57W
Norway House 109 53 59N 97 50W
Norwegian Dependency 5 66 0 S 15 0 E
Norwegian Sea 6 66 0N 1 0 E
Norwich, Can. 112 42 59N 80 36W
Norwich, U.K. 12 52 38N 1 17 E
Norwich, Conn., U.S.A. 113 41 33N 72 5W
Norwich, N.Y., U.S.A. 114 42 32N 75 30W
Norwood, Can. 112 44 23N 77 59W
Norwood, U.S.A. 113 42 10N 71 10W
Nosok 58 70 10N 82 20 E
Nosovka 54 50 50N 31 37 E
Noşratābād 65 29 55N 60 0 E
Noss Hd. 14 58 29N 3 4W
Nossebro 49 58 12N 12 43 E
Nossob → 92 26 55 S 20 37 E
Nosy Boraha 93 16 50 S 49 55 E
Nosy Varika 93 20 35 S 48 32 E
Noteć → 28 52 44N 15 26 E
Notigi Dam 109 56 40N 99 10W
Notikewin → 108 57 2N 117 38W
Notios Evvoïkos Kólpos 45 38 20N 24 0 E
Noto 41 36 52N 15 4 E
Noto, G. di 41 36 50N 15 10 E
Noto-Hanto 74 37 0N 137 0 E
Notodden 47 59 35N 9 17 E
Notre-Dame 107 46 18N 64 46W
Notre Dame B. 107 49 45N 55 30W
Notre Dame de Koartac 105 60 55N 69 40W
Notsé 85 7 0N 1 17 E
Nottaway → 106 51 22N 78 55W
Nøtterøy 47 59 14N 10 24 E
Nottingham 12 52 57N 1 10W
Nottingham □ 12 53 10N 1 0W
Nottoway → 114 36 33N 76 55W
Notwani → 92 23 35 S 26 58 E
Nouâdhibou 80 20 54N 17 0W
Nouâdhibou, Ras 80 20 50N 17 0W
Nouakchott 84 18 9N 15 58W
Noumea 94 22 17 S 166 30 E
Noupoort 92 31 10 S 24 57 E
Nouveau Comptoir (Paint Hills) 106 53 0N 78 49W
Nouvelle Calédonie 94 21 0 S 165 0 E
Nouzonville 19 49 48N 4 44 E
Nová Baña 27 48 28N 18 39 E
Nová Bystřice 26 49 2N 15 8 E
Nova Chaves 88 10 31 S 21 15 E
Nova Cruz 127 6 28 S 35 25W
Nova Esperança 125 23 8 S 52 24W
Nova Friburgo 125 22 16 S 42 30W
Nova Gaia 88 10 10 S 17 35 E
Nova Gradiška 42 45 17N 17 28 E
Nova Iguaçu 125 22 45 S 43 28W
Nova Iorque 127 7 0 S 44 5W
Nova Lamego 84 12 19N 14 11W
Nova Lima 125 19 59 S 43 51W
Nova Lisboa = Huambo 89 12 42 S 15 44 E
Nova Lusitânia 91 19 50 S 34 34 E
Nova Mambone 93 21 0 S 35 3 E
Nova Mesto 39 45 47N 15 12 E
Nova Paka 26 50 29N 15 30 E
Nova Scotia □ 107 45 10N 63 0W
Nova Sofala 93 20 7 S 34 42 E
Nova Varoš 42 43 29N 19 48 E
Nova Venécia 127 18 45 S 40 24W
Nova Zagora 43 42 32N 25 59 E
Novaci, Romania 46 45 10N 23 42 E
Novaci, Yugo. 42 41 5N 21 29 E
Noval Iorque 127 6 48 S 44 0W
Novaleksandrovskaya 57 45 29N 41 17 E
Novannenskiy 55 50 32N 42 39 E
Novara 38 45 27N 8 36 E
Novaya Kakhovka 56 46 42N 33 27 E
Novaya Ladoga 52 60 7N 32 16 E
Novaya Lyalya 58 59 10N 60 35 E
Novaya Sibir, O. 59 75 10N 150 0 E
Novaya Zemlya 58 75 0N 56 0 E
Nové Město 27 48 45N 17 50 E
Nové Zámky 27 48 0N 18 8 E
Novelda 33 38 24N 0 45W
Novellara 38 44 50N 10 43 E
Noventa Vicentina 39 45 18N 11 30 E
Novgorod 54 58 30N 31 25 E
Novgorod-Severskiy 54 52 2N 33 10 E
Novi Bečej 42 45 36N 20 10 E
Novi Grad 39 45 19N 13 33 E
Novi Kneževa 42 46 4N 20 8 E
Novi Krichim 43 42 8N 24 31 E
Novi Lígure 38 44 45N 8 47 E
Novi Pazar, Bulg. 43 43 25N 27 15 E
Novi Pazar, Yugo. 42 43 12N 20 28 E
Novi Sad 42 45 18N 19 52 E
Novi Vinodolski 39 45 10N 14 48 E
Novigrad 39 44 10N 15 32 E
Nôvo Hamburgo 125 29 37 S 51 7W
Novo-Zavidovskiy 55 56 32N 36 29 E
Novoakrainka 56 48 25N 31 30 E
Novoaltaysk 58 53 30N 84 0 E
Novoazovsk 56 47 15N 38 4 E
Novobelitsa 54 52 27N 31 2 E
Novobogatinskoye 57 47 20N 51 26 E
Novocherkassk 57 47 27N 40 5 E
Novodevichye 55 53 37N 48 50 E
Novograd-Volynskiy 54 50 34N 27 35 E
Novogrudok 54 53 40N 25 50 E
Novokayakent 57 42 30N 47 52 E
Novokazalinsk 58 45 48N 62 6 E
Novokhopersk 55 51 5N 41 39 E
Novokuybyshevsk 55 53 7N 49 58 E
Novokuznetsk 58 53 45N 87 10 E
Novomirgorod 56 48 45N 31 33 E
Novomoskovsk, R.S.F.S.R., U.S.S.R. 55 54 5N 38 15 E
Novomoskovsk, Ukraine, U.S.S.R. 56 48 33N 35 17 E
Novopolotsk 54 55 32N 28 37 E
Novorossiysk 56 44 43N 37 46 E
Novorybnoye 59 72 50N 105 50 E
Novorzhev 54 57 3N 29 25 E
Novoselitsa 56 48 14N 26 15 E
Novoshakhtinsk 57 47 46N 39 58 E
Novosibirsk 58 55 0N 83 5 E
Novosibirskiye Ostrava 59 75 0N 142 0 E
Novosil 55 52 58N 36 58 E
Novosokolniki 54 56 33N 30 5 E
Novotroitsk 52 51 10N 58 15 E
Novotulskiy 55 54 10N 37 43 E
Novouzensk 55 50 32N 48 17 E
Novovolynsk 54 50 45N 24 4 E
Novovyatsk 55 58 29N 49 44 E
Novozybkov 54 52 30N 32 0 E
Novska 42 45 19N 17 0 E
Novvy Port 58 67 40N 72 30 E
Novy Bug 56 47 34N 32 29 E
Nový Bydzov 26 50 14N 15 29 E
Novy Dwór Mazowiecki 28 52 26N 20 44 E
Nový Jičín 27 49 30N 18 0 E
Novyy Afon 57 43 7N 40 50 E
Novyy Oskol 55 50 44N 37 55 E
Now Shahr 65 36 40N 51 30 E
Nowa Deba 28 50 26N 21 41 E
Nowa Huta 27 50 5N 20 30 E
Nowa Ruda 28 50 35N 16 30 E
Nowa Skalmierzyce 28 51 43N 18 0 E
Nowa Sól 28 51 48N 15 44 E
Nowe 28 53 41N 18 44 E
Nowe Miasteczko 28 51 42N 15 42 E
Nowe Miasto 28 51 38N 20 34 E
Nowe Miasto Lubawskie 28 53 27N 19 33 E
Nowe Warpno 28 53 42N 14 18 E
Nowgong 67 26 20N 92 50 E
Nowingi 100 34 33 S 142 15 E
Nowogard 28 53 41N 15 10 E
Nowogród 28 53 14N 21 53 E
Nowra 97 34 53 S 150 35 E
Nowy Dwór, Białystok, Poland 28 53 40N 23 30 E
Nowy Dwór, Gdansk, Poland 28 54 13N 19 7 E
Nowy Korczyn 28 50 19N 20 48 E
Nowy Sącz 27 49 40N 20 41 E
Nowy Sącz □ 27 49 30N 20 30 E
Nowy Staw 28 54 13N 19 2 E
Nowy Tomyśl 28 52 19N 16 10 E
Noxen 113 41 25N 76 4W
Noxon 118 48 0N 115 43W
Noya 30 42 48N 8 53W
Noyant 18 47 30N 0 6 E
Noyers 19 47 40N 4 0 E
Noyes I. 108 55 30N 133 40W
Noyon 19 49 34N 3 0 E
Nozay 18 47 34N 1 38W
Nsa, O. en → 83 32 28N 5 24 E
Nsanje 91 16 55 S 35 12 E
Nsawam 85 5 50N 0 24W
Nsomba 91 10 45 S 29 51 E
Nsukka 85 6 51N 7 29 E
Nuanetsi → 91 22 40 S 31 50 E
Nuba Mts. = Nubah, Jibalan 87 12 0N 31 0 E
Nubah, Jibalan 87 12 0N 31 0 E
Nûbîya, Es Sahrâ En 86 21 30N 33 30 E
Ñuble □ 124 37 0 S 72 0W
Nuboai 73 2 10 S 136 30 E
Nueces → 117 27 50N 97 30W
Nueima → 62 31 54N 35 25 E
Nueltin L. 109 60 30N 99 30W
Nueva Gerona 121 21 53N 82 49W
Nueva Imperial 128 38 45 S 72 58W
Nueva Palmira 124 33 52 S 58 20W
Nueva Rosita 120 28 0N 101 11W
Nueva San Salvador 120 13 40N 89 18W
Nuéve de Julio 124 35 30 S 61 0W
Nuevitas 121 21 30N 77 20W
Nuevo, Golfo 128 43 0 S 64 30W
Nuevo Laredo 120 27 30N 99 30W
Nuevo León □ 120 25 0N 100 0W
Nugget Pt. 101 46 27 S 169 50 E
Nugrus, Gebel 86 24 47N 34 35 E
Nuhaka 101 39 3 S 177 45 E
Nuits 19 47 44N 4 12 E
Nuits-St-Georges 19 47 10N 4 56 E
Nukheila (Merga) 86 19 1N 26 21 E
Nuku'alofa 101 21 10 S 174 0W
Nukus 58 42 20N 59 7 E
Nulato 104 64 40N 158 10W
Nules 32 39 51N 0 9W
Nullagine 96 21 53 S 120 6 E
Nullarbor Plain 96 30 45 S 129 0 E
Numalla, L. 99 28 43 S 144 20 E
Numan 85 9 29N 12 3 E
Numata 74 36 45N 139 4 E
Numatinna → 87 7 38N 27 20 E
Numazu 74 35 7N 138 51 E
Numfoor 73 1 0 S 134 50 E
Numurkah 99 36 5 S 145 26 E
Nunaksaluk I. 107 55 49N 60 20W
Nuneaton 13 52 32N 1 29W
Nungo 91 13 23 S 37 43 E
Nungwe 90 2 48 S 32 2 E
Nunivak 104 60 0N 166 0W
Nunkun 69 33 57N 76 2 E
Nunspeet 16 52 21N 5 45 E
Nuomin He → 76 46 45N 126 55 E
Nuoro 40 40 20N 9 20 E
Nuqayy, Jabal 83 23 11N 19 30 E
Nure → 38 45 3N 9 49 E
Nuremburg = Nürnberg 25 49 26N 11 5 E
Suriootpa 99 34 27 S 139 0 E
Nurlat 55 54 29N 50 45 E
Nürnberg 25 49 26N 11 5 E
Nurran, L. = Terewah, L. 99 29 52 S 147 35 E
Nurri 40 39 43N 9 13 E
Nurzec → 28 52 37N 22 25 E
Nusa Barung 73 8 22 S 113 20 E
Nusa Kambangan 73 7 47 S 109 0 E
Nusa Tenggara Barat □ 72 8 50 S 117 30 E
Nusa Tenggara Timur □ 73 9 30 S 122 0 E
Nushki 66 29 35N 66 0 E
Nutak 105 57 28N 61 59W
Nuwakot 69 28 10N 83 55 E
Nuwara Eliya 70 6 58N 80 48 E
Nuweiba' 86 28 58N 34 40 E
Nuweveldberge 92 32 10 S 21 45 E
Nuyts Arch. 96 32 35 S 133 20 E
Nuyts, Pt. 96 35 4 S 116 38 E
Nuzvid 70 16 47N 80 53 E
Nxau-Nxau 92 18 57 S 21 4 E
Nyaake (Webo) 84 4 52N 7 37W
Nyabing 96 33 30 S 118 7 E
Nyack 113 41 5N 73 57W
Nyadal 48 62 48N 17 59 E
Nyah West 100 35 16 S 143 21 E
Nyahanga 90 2 20 S 33 37 E
Nyahua 90 5 25 S 33 23 E
Nyahururu 90 0 2N 36 27 E
Nyainqentanglha Shan 75 30 0N 90 0 E
Nyakanazi 90 3 2 S 31 10 E
Nyakrom 85 5 40N 0 50W
Nyâlâ 87 12 2N 24 58 E
Nyamandhlovu 91 19 55 S 28 16 E
Nyambiti 90 2 48 S 33 27 E
Nyamwaga 90 1 27 S 34 33 E
Nyandekwa 90 3 57 S 32 32 E
Nyanding → 87 8 40N 32 41 E
Nyandoma 52 61 40N 40 12 E
Nyangana 92 18 0 S 20 40 E
Nyanguge 90 2 30 S 33 12 E
Nyankpala 85 9 21N 0 58W
Nyanza, Burundi 90 4 21 S 29 36 E
Nyanza, Rwanda 90 2 20 S 29 42 E
Nyanza □ 90 0 10 S 34 15 E
Nyarling → 108 60 41N 113 23W
Nyasa, L. = Malawi, L. 91 12 0 S 34 30 E
Nyazepetrovsk 52 56 3N 59 36 E
Nyazwidzi → 91 20 0 S 31 17 E
Nyborg 49 55 18N 10 47 E
Nybro 49 56 44N 15 55 E
Nyda 58 66 40N 72 58 E
Nyeri 90 0 23 S 36 56 E
Nyerol 87 8 41N 32 1 E
Nyhem 48 62 54N 15 37 E
Nyiel 87 6 9N 31 13 E
Nyinahin 84 6 43N 2 3W
Nyirbátor 27 47 49N 22 9 E
Nyíregyháza 27 47 58N 21 47 E
Nykarleby 50 63 22N 22 31 E
Nykøbing, Sjælland, Denmark 49 55 55N 11 40 E
Nykøbing, Storstrøm, Denmark 49 54 56N 11 52 E
Nykøbing, Viborg, Denmark 49 56 48N 8 51 E
Nyköping 49 58 45N 17 0 E

Nykroppa 48 59 37N 14 18 E
Nykvarn 48 59 11N 17 25 E
Nyland 48 63 1N 17 45 E
Nylstroom 93 24 42 S 28 22 E
Nymagee 99 32 7 S 146 20 E
Nymburk 26 50 10N 15 1 E
Nynäshamn 48 58 54N 17 57 E
Nyngan 99 31 30 S 147 8 E
Nyon 25 46 23N 6 14 E
Nyong → 85 3 17N 9 54 E
Nyons 21 44 22N 5 10 E
Nyord 49 55 4N 12 13 E
Nyou 85 12 42N 2 1W
Nysa 28 50 30N 17 22 E
Nysa →, Poland 28 52 4N 14 46 E
Nysa →, Poland 28 50 49N 17 40 E
Nyssa 118 43 56N 117 2W
Nysted 49 54 40N 11 44 E
Nyunzu 90 5 57 S 27 58 E
Nyurba 59 63 17N 118 28 E
Nzega 90 4 10 S 33 12 E
Nzega □ 90 4 10 S 33 10 E
N'Zérékoré 84 7 49N 8 48W
Nzeto 88 7 10 S 12 52 E
Nzilo, Chutes de 91 10 18 S 25 27 E
Nzubuka 90 4 45 S 32 50 E

O

Oacoma 116 43 50N 99 26W
Oahe 116 44 33N 100 29W
Oahe Dam 116 44 28N 100 25W
Oahe Res. 116 45 30N 100 25W
Oahu 110 21 30N 158 0W
Oak Creek 118 40 15N 106 59W
Oak Harb. 118 48 20N 122 38W
Oak Hill 114 38 0N 81 7W
Oak Park 114 41 55N 87 45W
Oak Ridge 115 36 1N 84 12W
Oakbank 99 33 4 S 140 33 E
Oakdale, Calif., U.S.A. 119 46 14N 98 4W
Oakdale, La., U.S.A. 117 30 50N 92 38W
Oakengates 12 52 42N 2 29W
Oakes 116 46 14N 98 4W
Oakesdale 118 47 11N 117 15W
Oakey 99 27 25 S 151 43 E
Oakham 12 52 40N 0 43W
Oakland, Calif., U.S.A. 119 37 50N 122 18W
Oakland, Oreg., U.S.A. 118 43 23N 123 18W
Oakland City 114 38 20N 87 20W
Oakleigh 100 37 54 S 145 6 E
Oakley, Id., U.S.A. 118 42 14N 113 55W
Oakley, Kans., U.S.A. 116 39 8N 100 51W
Oakridge 118 43 47N 122 31W
Oakwood 117 31 35N 94 45W
Oamaru 101 45 5 S 170 59 E
Oates Coast 5 69 0 S 160 0 E
Oatman 119 35 1N 114 19W
Oaxaca 120 17 2N 96 40W
Oaxaca □ 120 17 0N 97 0W
Ob → 58 66 45N 69 30 E
Oba 106 49 4N 84 7W
Obala 85 4 9N 11 32 E
Oban, N.Z. 101 46 55 S 168 10 E
Oban, U.K. 14 56 25N 5 30W
Obbia 63 5 25N 48 30 E
Obed 108 53 30N 117 10W
Obera 125 27 21 S 55 2W
Oberammergau 25 47 35N 11 3 E
Oberdrauburg 26 46 44N 12 58 E
Oberengadin 25 46 35N 9 55 E
Oberhausen 24 51 28N 6 50 E
Oberkirch 25 48 31N 8 5 E
Oberlin, Kans., U.S.A. 116 39 52N 100 31W
Oberlin, La., U.S.A. 117 30 42N 92 42W
Oberlin, Ohio, U.S.A. 112 41 15N 82 10W
Obernai 19 48 28N 7 30 E
Oberndorf 25 48 17N 8 35 E
Oberon 99 33 45 S 149 52 E
Oberösterreich □ 26 48 10N 14 0 E
Oberpfälzer Wald 25 49 30N 12 25 E
Oberstdorf 25 47 25N 10 16 E
Obi, Kepulauan 73 1 23 S 127 45 E
Obiaruku 85 5 51N 6 9 E
Óbidos, Brazil 127 1 50 S 55 30W
Óbidos, Port. 31 39 19N 9 10W
Obihiro 74 42 56N 143 12 E
Obilatu 73 1 25 S 127 20 E
Obilnoye 57 47 32N 44 30 E
Obing 25 48 0N 12 25 E
Obisfelde 24 52 27N 10 57 E
Objat 20 45 16N 1 24 E
Obluchye 59 49 1N 131 4 E
Obninsk 55 55 8N 36 37 E
Obo, C. Afr. Rep. 90 5 20N 26 32 E
Obo, Ethiopia 87 3 46N 38 52 E
Oboa, Mt. 90 1 45N 34 45 E
Obock 87 12 0N 43 20 E
Oborniki 28 52 39N 16 50 E
Oborniki Śląskie 28 51 17N 16 53 E
Oboyan 55 51 13N 36 37 E
Obrenovac 42 44 40N 20 11 E
Obrovac 39 44 11N 15 41 E
Observatory Inlet 108 55 10N 129 54W
Obshchi Syrt 9 52 0N 53 0 E
Obskaya Guba 58 69 0N 73 0 E
Obuasi 85 6 17N 1 40W
Obubra 85 6 8N 8 20 E
Obzor 43 42 50N 27 52 E
Ocala 115 29 11N 82 5W
Ocampo 120 28 9N 108 24W
Ocaña 32 39 55N 3 30W
Oconomowoc 116 43 7N 88 30W
Ocate 117 36 12N 104 59W
Occidental, Cordillera 126 5 0N 76 0W
Ocean City 114 39 18N 74 34W
Ocean, I. = Banaba 94 0 52 S 169 35 E
Ocean Park 118 46 30N 124 2W
Oceanlake 118 45 0N 124 0W
Oceanport 113 40 20N 74 3W
Oceanside 119 33 13N 117 26W
Ochagavia 32 42 55N 1 5W
Ochamchire 57 42 46N 41 32 E
Ochil Hills 14 56 14N 3 40W
Ochre River 109 51 4N 99 47W
Ochsenfurt 25 49 38N 10 3 E
Ochsenhausen 25 48 4N 9 57 E
Ocilla 115 31 35N 83 12W
Ockelbo 48 60 54N 16 45 E
Ocmulgee → 115 31 58N 82 32W
Ocna Mureş 46 46 23N 23 55 E
Ocna Sibiului 46 45 52N 24 2 E
Ocnele Mari 46 45 8N 24 18 E
Oconee → 115 31 58N 82 32W
Oconto 114 44 52N 87 53W
Oconto Falls 114 44 52N 88 10W
Ocotal 121 13 41N 86 31W
Ocotlán 120 20 21N 102 42W
Ocreza → 31 39 32N 7 50W
Öcsa 27 47 17N 19 15 E
Octave 119 34 10N 112 43W
Octeville 18 49 38N 1 40W
Ocumare del Tuy 126 10 7N 66 46W
Ocussi 73 9 20 S 124 23 E
Oda 85 5 50N 0 51W
Oda, Jebel 86 20 21N 36 39 E
Ódáðahraun 50 65 5N 17 0W
Ödåkra 49 56 7N 12 45 E
Odawara 74 35 20N 139 6 E
Odda 47 60 3N 6 35 E
Odder 49 55 58N 10 10 E
Oddur 63 4 11N 43 52 E
Ödeborg 49 58 32N 11 58 E
Odei → 109 56 6N 96 54W
Odemira 31 37 35N 8 40W
Ödemiş 64 38 15N 28 0 E
Odendaalsrus 92 27 48 S 26 45 E
Odense 49 55 22N 10 23 E
Odenwald 25 49 40N 9 0 E
Oder → 24 53 33N 14 38 E
Oderzo 39 45 47N 12 29 E
Odessa, Can. 113 44 17N 76 43W
Odessa, Tex., U.S.A. 117 31 51N 102 23W
Odessa, Wash., U.S.A. 118 47 19N 118 35W
Odessa, U.S.S.R. 56 46 30N 30 45 E
Odiakwe 92 20 12 S 25 17 E
Odiel → 31 37 10N 6 55W
Odienné 84 9 30N 7 34W
Odobeşti 46 45 43N 27 4 E
Odolanów 28 51 34N 17 40 E
O'Donnell 117 33 0N 101 48W
Odorheiul Secuiesc 46 46 21N 25 21 E
Odoyevo 55 53 56N 36 42 E
Odra →, Poland 28 53 33N 14 38 E
Odra →, Spain 30 42 14N 4 17W
Odžaci 42 45 30N 19 17 E
Odžak 42 45 3N 18 18 E
Oeiras, Brazil 127 7 0 S 42 8W
Oeiras, Port. 31 38 41N 9 18W
Oelrichs 116 43 11N 103 14W
Oelsnitz 24 50 24N 12 11 E
Oelwein 116 42 41N 91 55W
Ofanto → 41 41 22N 16 13 E
Offa 85 8 13N 4 42 E
Offaly □ 15 53 15N 7 30W
Offenbach 25 50 6N 8 46 E
Offenburg 25 48 29N 7 56 E
Offerdal 48 63 28N 14 0 E
Offida 39 42 56N 13 40 E
Offranville 18 49 52N 1 0 E
Ofidhousa 45 36 33N 26 8 E
Ofotfjorden 50 68 27N 16 40 E
Oga-Hantō 74 39 58N 139 47 E
Ogahalla 106 50 6N 85 51W
Ōgaki 74 35 21N 136 37 E
Ogallala 116 41 12N 101 40W
Ogbomosho 85 8 1N 4 11 E
Ogden, Iowa, U.S.A. 116 42 3N 94 0W
Ogden, Utah, U.S.A. 118 41 13N 112 1W
Ogdensburg 114 44 40N 75 27W
Ogeechee → 115 31 51N 81 6W
Oglio → 38 45 2N 10 39 E
Ogmore 98 22 37 S 149 35 E
Ogna 47 58 31N 5 48 E
Ognon → 19 47 16N 5 28 E
Ogoja 85 6 38N 8 39 E
Ogoki → 106 51 38N 85 57W
Ogoki L. 106 50 50N 87 10W
Ogoki Res. 106 50 45N 88 15W
Ogooué → 88 1 0 S 10 0 E
Ogosta → 43 43 48N 23 55 E
Ogowe = Ogooué → 88 1 0 S 10 0 E
Ograźden 42 41 30N 22 50 E
Ogrein 86 17 55N 34 50 E
Ogulin 39 45 16N 15 16 E
Ogun □ 85 7 0N 3 0 E
Oguta 85 5 44N 6 44 E
Ogwashi-Uku 85 6 15N 6 30 E
Ogwe 85 5 0N 7 14 E
Ohai 101 44 55 S 168 0 E
Ohakune 101 39 24 S 175 24 E
Ohau, L. 101 44 15 S 169 53 E
Ohey 16 50 26N 5 8 E
O'Higgins □ 124 34 15 S 70 45W
Ohio □ 114 40 20N 14 10 E
Ohio → 114 38 0N 86 0W
Ohre →, Czech. 26 50 30N 14 10 E
Ohre →, Ger. 24 52 18N 11 47 E
Ohrid 42 41 8N 20 52 E
Ohridsko, Jezero 42 41 8N 20 52 E
Ohrigstad 93 24 19 S 30 36 E
Öhringen 25 49 11N 9 31 E
Oil City 114 41 26N 79 40W
Oinousa 45 38 33N 26 14 E
Oise □ 19 49 28N 2 30 E
Oise → 19 49 0N 2 4 E
Ōita 74 33 14N 131 36 E
Ōita □ 74 33 15N 131 30 E
Oiticica 127 5 3 S 41 5W
Ojai 119 34 28N 119 16W
Ojinaga 120 29 34N 104 25W
Ojos del Salado, Cerro 124 27 0 S 68 40W
Oka → 55 56 20N 43 59 E
Okaba 73 8 6 S 139 42 E
Okahandja 92 22 0 S 16 59 E
Okahukura 94 38 48 S 175 14 E
Okanagan L. 108 50 0N 119 30W
Okandja 88 0 35 S 13 45 E
Okanogan 118 48 6N 119 43W
Okanogan → 118 48 6N 119 43W
Okány 27 46 52N 21 21 E
Okaputa 92 20 5 S 17 0 E
Okara 68 30 50N 73 31 E
Okarito 101 43 15 S 170 9 E
Okavango Swamps 92 18 45 S 22 45 E
Okaya 74 36 0N 138 10 E
Okayama 74 34 40N 133 54 E
Okayama □ 74 35 0N 133 50 E
Okazaki 74 34 57N 137 10 E
Oke-Iho 85 8 1N 3 18 E
Okeechobee 115 27 16N 80 46W
Okeechobee L. 115 27 0N 80 50W
Okefenokee Swamp 115 30 50N 82 15W
Okehampton 13 50 44N 4 1W
Okene 85 7 32N 6 11 E
Oker → 24 52 30N 10 22 E
Okha 59 53 40N 143 0 E
Ókhi Óros 45 38 5N 24 25 E
Okhotsk 59 59 20N 143 10 E
Okhotsk, Sea of 59 55 0N 145 0 E
Okhotskiy Perevoz 59 61 52N 135 35 E
Okhotsko Kolymskoye 59 63 0N 157 0 E
Oki-Shotō 74 36 5N 133 15 E
Okiep 92 29 39 S 17 53 E
Okigwi 85 5 52N 7 20 E
Okija 85 5 54N 6 55 E
Okinawa □ 77 26 40N 128 0 E
Okitipupa 85 6 31N 4 50 E
Oklahoma □ 117 35 20N 97 30W
Oklahoma City 117 35 25N 97 30W
Okmulgee 117 35 38N 96 0W
Oknitsa 56 48 25N 27 30 E
Okolo 90 2 37N 31 8 E
Okolona 117 34 0N 88 45W
Okondeka 92 21 38 S 15 37 E
Okonek 28 53 32N 16 51 E
Okrika 85 4 40N 7 10 E
Oktabrsk 58 49 28N 57 25 E
Oktyabrsk 55 53 11N 48 40 E
Oktyabrskiy, Byelorussia, U.S.S.R. 54 52 38N 28 53 E
Oktyabrskiy, R.S.F.S.R., U.S.S.R. 52 54 28N 53 28 E
Oktyabrskoy Revolyutsii, Os. 59 79 30N 97 0 E
Oktyabrskoye 58 62 28N 66 3 E
Oktyabrskoye = Zhovtnevoye 56 47 54N 32 2 E
Okulovka 54 58 25N 33 19 E
Okuru 101 43 55 S 168 55 E
Okushiri-Tō 74 42 15N 139 30 E
Okuta 85 9 14N 3 12 E
Okwa → 92 22 30 S 23 0 E
Ola 117 35 2N 93 10W
Ólafsfjörður 50 66 4N 18 39W
Ólafsvík 50 64 53N 23 43W
Olancha 119 36 15N 118 1W
Olanchito 121 15 30N 86 30W
Öland 49 56 45N 16 38 E
Olargues 20 43 34N 2 53 E
Olary 99 32 18 S 140 19 E
Olascoaga 124 35 15 S 60 39W
Olathe 116 38 50N 94 50W
Olavarría 124 36 55 S 60 20W
Oława 28 50 57N 17 20 E
Ólbia 40 40 55N 9 30 E
Ólbia, G. di 40 40 55N 9 35 E
Old Bahama Chan. = Bahama, Canal Viejo de 121 22 10N 77 30W
Old Castile = Castilla la Vieja □ 30 41 55N 4 0W
Old Castle 15 53 46N 7 10W
Old Cork 98 22 57 S 141 52 E
Old Crow 104 67 30N 140 5 E
Old Dongola 86 18 11N 30 44 E
Old Forge, N.Y., U.S.A. 113 43 43N 74 58W
Old Forge, Pa., U.S.A. 113 41 20N 75 46W
Old Fort → 109 58 36N 110 24W
Old Shinyanga 90 3 33 S 33 27 E
Old Speckle, Mt. 113 44 35N 70 57W
Old Town 107 45 0N 68 41W
Old Wives L. 109 50 5N 106 0W
Oldbury 13 51 38N 2 30W
Oldeani 90 3 22 S 35 35 E
Oldenburg, Niedersachsen, Ger. 24 53 10N 8 10 E
Oldenburg, Schleswig-Holstein, Ger. 24 54 16N 10 53 E
Oldenzaal 16 52 19N 6 53 E
Oldham 12 53 33N 2 8W
Oldman → 108 49 57N 111 42W
Olds 108 51 50N 114 10W
Olean 114 42 8N 78 25W
Olecko 28 54 2N 22 31 E
Oléggio 38 45 36N 8 38 E
Oleiros 30 39 56N 7 56W
Olekma → 59 60 22N 120 42 E
Olekminsk 59 60 25N 120 30 E
Olenegorsk 52 68 9N 33 18 E
Olenek 59 68 28N 112 18 E
Olenek → 59 73 0N 120 10 E
Olenino 54 56 15N 33 30 E
Oléron, Île d' 20 45 55N 1 15W
Oleśnica 28 51 13N 17 22 E
Olesno 28 50 51N 18 26 E
Olevsk 54 51 12N 27 39 E
Olga 59 43 50N 135 14 E
Olga, L. 106 49 47N 77 15W
Olga, Mt. 96 25 20 S 130 50 E
Olgastretet 4 78 35N 25 0 E
Ølgod 49 55 49N 8 36 E
Olhão 31 37 3N 7 48W
Olib 39 44 23N 14 44 E
Olib, I. 39 44 23N 14 44 E
Oliena 40 40 18N 9 22 E
Oliete 32 41 1N 0 41W
Olifants → 93 24 5 S 31 20 E
Olifantshoek 92 27 57 S 22 42 E
Ólimbos 45 35 44N 27 11 E
Ólimbos, Óros 44 40 6N 22 23 E
Olímpia 125 20 44 S 48 54W
Olimpo □ 124 20 30 S 58 45W
Olite 32 42 29N 1 40W
Oliva, Argent. 124 32 0 S 63 38W
Oliva, Spain 33 38 58N 0 9W
Oliva de la Frontera 31 38 17N 6 54W
Oliva, Punta del 30 43 37N 5 28W
Olivares 32 39 46N 2 20W
Oliveira 127 20 39 S 44 50W
Oliveira de Azemeis 30 40 49N 8 29W
Olivença 91 11 47 S 35 13 E
Olivenza 31 38 41N 7 9W
Oliver 108 49 13N 119 37W
Oliver L. 109 56 56N 103 22W
Olkhovka 57 49 48N 44 32 E
Olkusz 28 50 18N 19 33 E
Ollagüe 124 21 15 S 68 10W
Olmedo 30 41 20N 4 43W
Olney, Ill., U.S.A. 114 38 40N 88 0W
Olney, Tex., U.S.A. 117 33 25N 98 45W
Olofström 49 56 17N 14 32 E
Oloma 85 3 29N 11 19 E
Olomane → 107 50 14N 60 37W
Olomouc 27 49 38N 17 12 E
Olonets 52 61 10N 33 0 E
Olongapo 73 14 50N 120 18 E
Oloron, Gave d' 20 43 33N 1 5W
Oloron-Ste-Marie 20 43 11N 0 38W
Olot 32 42 11N 2 30 E
Olovo 42 44 8N 18 35 E
Olovyannaya 59 50 58N 115 35 E
Oloy → 59 66 29N 159 29 E
Olpe 24 51 2N 7 50 E
Olshanka 56 48 16N 30 58 E
Olshany 56 50 3N 35 53 E
Olsztyn 28 53 48N 20 29 E
Olsztyn □ 28 54 0N 21 0 E
Olsztynek 28 53 34N 20 19 E
Olt □ 46 44 20N 24 30 E
Olt → 46 43 50N 24 40 E
Olten 25 47 21N 7 53 E
Olteniţa 46 44 7N 26 42 E
Olton 117 34 16N 102 7W
Oltu 64 40 35N 41 58 E
Olvega 32 41 47N 2 0W
Olvera 31 36 55N 5 18W
Olympia, Greece 45 37 39N 21 39 E
Olympia, U.S.A. 118 47 0N 122 58W
Olympic Mts. 118 47 50N 123 45W
Olympic Nat. Park 118 47 48N 123 30W
Olympus, Mt. 118 47 52N 123 40W
Olympus, Mt. = Ólimbos, Óros 44 40 6N 22 23 E
Olyphant 113 41 27N 75 36W
Om → 58 54 59N 73 22 E
Om Hajer 87 14 20N 36 41 E
Ōmachi 74 36 30N 137 50 E
Omagh 15 54 36N 7 20W
Omagh □ 15 54 35N 7 15W
Omaha 116 41 15N 96 0W
Omak 118 48 24N 119 31W
Oman ■ 63 23 0N 58 0 E
Oman, G. of 65 24 30N 58 30 E
Omaruru 92 21 26 S 16 0 E
Omaruru → 92 22 7 S 14 15 E
Omate 126 16 45 S 71 0W
Ombai, Selat 73 8 30 S 124 50 E
Ombo 47 59 18N 6 0 E
Omboué 88 1 35 S 9 15 E
Ombrone → 38 42 39N 11 0 E
Omchi 83 21 22N 17 53 E
Omdurmân 87 15 40N 32 28 E
Omegna 38 45 52N 8 23 E
Omeonga 90 3 40 S 24 22 E
Ometepe, Isla de 121 11 32N 85 35W
Ometepec 120 16 39N 98 23W
Omez 62 32 22N 35 0 E
Omineca → 108 56 3N 124 16W
Omiš 39 43 28N 16 40 E
Omisalj 39 45 13N 14 32 E
Omitara 92 22 16 S 18 2 E
Ōmiya 74 35 54N 139 38 E
Omme Å → 49 55 56N 8 32 E
Ommen 16 52 31N 6 26 E
Omo → 81 6 25N 36 10 E
Omolon → 59 68 42N 158 36 E
Omsk 58 55 0N 73 12 E
Omsukchan 59 62 32N 155 48 E
Omul, Vf. 46 45 27N 25 29 E
Omulew → 28 53 5N 21 33 E
Ōmura 74 32 56N 130 0 E
Omurtag 43 43 8N 26 26 E
Ōmuta 74 33 0N 130 26 E
Omutninsk 55 58 45N 52 4 E
Oña 32 42 43N 3 25W
Onaga 116 39 32N 96 12W
Onalaska 116 43 53N 91 14W
Onamia 116 46 4N 93 38W
Onancock 114 37 42N 75 49W
Onang 73 3 2 S 118 49 E
Onaping L. 106 47 3N 81 30W
Onarheim 47 59 57N 5 35 E
Oñate 32 43 3N 2 25W
Onavas 120 28 28N 109 30W
Onawa 116 42 2N 96 2W
Onaway 114 45 21N 84 11W
Oncesti 46 43 56N 25 52 E
Oncócua 92 16 30 S 13 25 E
Onda 32 39 55N 0 17W
Ondangua 92 17 57 S 16 4 E
Ondárroa 32 43 19N 2 25W
Ondava → 27 48 27N 21 48 E
Ondo 85 7 4N 4 47 E
Ondo □ 85 7 0N 5 0 E
Öndörhaan 75 47 19N 110 39 E
Öndverðarnes 50 64 52N 24 0W
Onega 52 64 0N 38 10 E
Onega → 52 63 58N 37 55 E
Onega, G. of = Onezhskaya G. 52 64 30N 37 0 E
Onega, L. = Onezhskoye Oz. 52 62 0N 35 30 E
Onehunga 101 36 55 S 174 48 E

Oneida 114 43 5N 75 40W
Oneida L. 114 43 12N 76 0W
O'Neill 116 42 30N 98 38W
Onekotan, Ostrov 59 49 25N 154 45 E
Onema 90 4 35 S 24 30 E
Oneonta, Ala., U.S.A. 115 33 58N 86 29W
Oneonta, N.Y., U.S.A. 114 42 26N 75 5W
Onezhskaya Guba 52 64 30N 37 0 E
Onezhskoye Ozero 52 62 0N 35 30 E
Ongarue 101 38 42 S 175 19 E
Ongniud Qi 76 43 0N 118 38 E
Ongoka 90 1 20 S 26 0 E
Ongole 70 15 33N 80 2 E
Onguren 59 53 38N 107 36 E
Oni 57 42 33N 43 26 E
Onida 116 44 42N 100 5W
Onilahy → 93 23 34 S 43 45 E
Onitsha 85 6 6N 6 42 E
Onoda 74 34 2N 131 25 E
Ons, Islas d' 30 42 23N 8 55W
Onsala 49 57 26N 12 0 E
Onslow 96 21 40 S 115 12 E
Onslow B. 115 34 20N 77 20W
Onstwedde 16 53 2N 7 4 E
Ontake-San 74 35 53N 137 29 E
Ontaneda 30 43 12N 3 57W
Ontario, Calif., U.S.A. 119 34 2N 117 40W
Ontario, Oreg., U.S.A. 118 44 1N 117 1W
Ontario □ 106 52 0N 88 10W
Ontario, L. 106 43 40N 78 0W
Onteniente 33 38 50N 0 35W
Ontonagon 116 46 52N 89 19W
Ontur 33 38 38N 1 29W
Oodnadatta 96 27 33 S 135 30 E
Ooldea 96 30 27 S 131 50 E
Oona River 108 53 57N 130 16W
Oorindi 98 20 40 S 141 1 E
Oost-Vlaanderen □ 16 51 5N 3 50 E
Oostende 16 51 15N 2 50 E
Oosterhout 16 51 39N 4 47 E
Oosterschelde 16 51 33N 4 0 E
Ootacamund 70 11 30N 76 44 E
Ootsa L. 108 53 50N 126 2W
Ootsi 92 25 2 S 25 45 E
Opaka 43 43 28N 26 10 E
Opala, U.S.S.R. 59 51 58N 156 30 E
Opala, Zaïre 88 0 40 S 24 20 E
Opalenica 28 52 18N 16 24 E
Opan 43 42 13N 25 41 E
Opanake 70 6 35N 80 40 E
Opasatika 106 49 30N 82 50W
Opasquia 109 53 16N 93 34W
Opatija 39 45 21N 14 17 E
Opatów 28 50 50N 21 27 E
Opava 27 49 57N 17 58 E
Opelousas 117 30 35N 92 7W
Opémisca L. 106 50 0N 75 0W
Opheim 118 48 52N 106 30W
Ophir 104 63 10N 156 40W
Ophthalmia Ra. 96 23 15 S 119 30 E
Opi 85 6 36N 7 28 E
Opinaca → 106 52 15N 78 2W
Opinaca L. 106 52 39N 76 20W
Opiskotish, L. 107 53 10N 67 50W
Opobo 85 4 35N 7 34 E
Opochka 54 56 42N 28 45 E
Opoczno 28 51 22N 20 18 E
Opole 28 50 42N 17 58 E
Opole □ 28 50 40N 17 56 E
Oporto = Porto 30 41 8N 8 40W
Opotiki 101 38 1 S 177 19 E
Opp 115 31 19N 86 13W
Oppegård 47 59 48N 10 48 E
Oppenheim 25 49 50N 8 22 E
Óppido Mamertina 41 38 16N 15 59 E
Oppland fylke □ 47 61 15N 9 40 E
Oppstad 47 60 17N 11 40 E
Oprtalj 39 45 23N 13 50 E
Opua 101 35 19 S 174 9 E
Opunake 101 39 26 S 173 52 E
Opuzen 42 43 1N 17 34 E
Or Yehuda 62 32 2N 34 50 E
Ora, Israel 62 30 55N 35 1 E
Ora, Italy 39 46 20N 11 19 E
Oracle 119 32 36N 110 46W
Oradea 46 47 2N 21 58 E
Öræfajökull 50 64 2N 16 39W
Orahovac 42 42 24N 20 40 E
Orahovica 42 45 35N 17 52 E
Orai 69 25 58N 79 30 E
Oraison 21 43 55N 5 55 E
Oran, Alg. 82 35 45N 0 39W
Oran, Argent. 124 23 10 S 64 20W
Orange, Austral. 97 33 15 S 149 7 E
Orange, France 21 44 8N 4 47 E
Orange, Mass., U.S.A. 113 42 35N 72 15W
Orange, Tex., U.S.A. 117 30 10N 93 50W
Orange, Va., U.S.A. 114 38 17N 78 5W
Orange, C. 127 4 20N 51 30W
Orange Free State = Oranje Vrystaat □ 92 28 30 S 27 0 E
Orange Grove 117 27 57N 97 57W
Orange Walk 120 18 6N 88 33W
Orangeburg 115 33 35N 80 53W
Orangeville 106 43 55N 80 5W
Oranienburg 24 52 45N 13 15 E
Oranje → 92 28 41 S 16 28 E
Oranje Vrystaat □ 92 28 30 S 27 0 E
Oranjemund 92 28 38 S 16 29 E
Or'Aquiva 62 32 30N 34 54 E
Oras 73 12 9N 125 28 E
Orašje 42 45 1N 18 42 E
Orăştie 46 45 50N 23 10 E
Oraşul Stalin = Braşov 46 45 38N 25 35 E
Orava → 27 49 24N 19 20 E
Oravita 42 45 2N 21 43 E
Orb → 20 43 17N 3 17 E
Orba → 38 44 53N 8 37 E
Ørbæk 49 55 17N 10 39 E
Orbe 25 46 43N 6 32 E
Orbec 18 49 1N 0 23 E
Orbetello 39 42 26N 11 11 E
Órbigo → 30 42 5N 5 42W
Orbost 97 37 40 S 148 29 E
Örbyhus 48 60 15N 17 43 E
Orce 33 37 44N 2 28W
Orce → 33 37 44N 2 28W
Orchies 19 50 28N 3 14 E
Orchila, Isla 126 11 48N 66 10W
Orco → 38 45 10N 7 52 E
Ord → 96 15 33 S 138 15 E
Ord, Mt. 96 17 20 S 125 34 E
Ordenes 30 43 5N 8 29W
Orderville 119 37 18N 112 43W
Ordos = Mu Us Shamo 76 39 0N 109 0 E
Ordu 64 40 55N 37 53 E
Orduña, Álava, Spain 32 42 58N 2 58 E
Orduña, Granada, Spain 33 37 20N 3 30W
Ordway 116 38 15N 103 42W
Ordzhonikidze, R.S.F.S.R., U.S.S.R. 57 43 0N 44 43 E
Ordzhonikidze, Ukraine S.S.R., U.S.S.R. 56 47 39N 34 3 E
Ore, Sweden 48 61 8N 15 10 E
Ore, Zaïre 90 3 17N 29 30 E
Ore Mts. = Erzgebirge 24 50 25N 13 0 E
Orebić 42 43 0N 17 11 E
Örebro 48 59 20N 15 18 E
Örebro län □ 48 59 27N 15 0 E
Oregon 116 42 1N 89 20W
Oregon □ 118 44 0N 121 0W
Oregon City 118 45 21N 122 35W
Öregrund 48 60 21N 18 30 E
Öregrundsgrepen 48 60 25N 18 15 E
Orekhov 56 47 30N 35 48 E
Orekhovo-Zuyevo 55 55 50N 38 55 E
Orel 55 52 57N 36 3 E
Orel → 56 48 30N 34 54 E
Orellana, Canal de 31 39 2N 6 0W
Orellana la Vieja 31 39 1N 5 32W
Orellana, Pantano de 31 39 5N 5 10W
Orem 118 40 20N 111 45W
Oren 45 37 3N 27 57 E
Orenburg 52 51 45N 55 6 E
Orense 30 42 19N 7 55W
Orense □ 30 42 15N 7 51W
Orepuki 101 46 19 S 167 46 E
Orestiás 44 41 30N 26 33 E
Øresund 49 55 45N 12 45 E
Orford Ness 13 52 6N 1 31 E
Orgañà 32 42 13N 1 20 E
Orgaz 31 39 39N 3 53W
Orgeyev 56 47 24N 28 50 E
Orgon 21 43 47N 5 3 E
Orgūn 65 32 55N 69 12 E
Orhon Gol → 75 49 30N 106 0 E
Ória 41 40 30N 17 38 E
Orient 99 28 7 S 142 50 E
Oriental, Cordillera 126 6 0N 73 0W
Oriente 124 38 44 S 60 37W
Origny-Ste-Benoîte 19 49 50N 3 30 E
Orihuela 33 38 7N 0 55W
Orihuela del Tremedal 32 40 33N 1 39W
Oriku 44 40 20N 19 30 E
Orinoco → 126 9 15N 61 30W
Orissa □ 69 20 0N 84 0 E
Oristano 40 39 54N 8 35 E
Oristano, Golfo di 40 39 50N 8 22 E
Orizaba 120 18 50N 97 10W
Orizare 43 42 44N 27 39 E
Ørje 47 59 29N 11 39 E
Orjen 42 42 35N 18 34 E
Orjiva 33 36 53N 3 24W
Orkanger 47 63 18N 9 52 E
Orkelljunga 49 56 17N 13 17 E
Örkény 27 47 9N 19 26 E
Orkla → 47 63 18N 9 51 E
Orkney 92 26 58 S 26 40 E
Orkney □ 14 59 0N 3 0W
Orkney Is. 14 59 0N 3 0W
Orla 28 52 42N 23 20 E
Orland 118 39 46N 122 12W
Orlando 115 28 30N 81 25W
Orlando, C. d' 41 38 10N 14 43 E
Orléanais 19 48 0N 2 0 E
Orléans 19 47 54N 1 52 E
Orleans 113 44 49N 72 10W
Orléans, Î. d' 107 46 54N 70 58W
Orlice → 26 50 5N 16 10 E
Orlické Hory 27 50 15N 16 30 E
Orlik 59 52 30N 99 55 E
Orlov 27 49 17N 20 51 E
Orlov Gay 55 50 56N 48 19 E
Orlovat 42 45 14N 20 33 E
Ormara 66 25 16N 64 33 E
Ormea 38 44 9N 7 54 E
Ormília 44 40 16N 23 39 E
Ormoc 73 11 0N 124 37 E
Ormond, N.Z. 101 38 33 S 177 56 E
Ormond, U.S.A. 115 29 13N 81 5W
Ormož 39 46 25N 16 10 E
Ormstown 113 45 8N 74 0W
Ornans 19 47 7N 6 10 E
Orne □ 18 48 40N 0 5 E
Orne → 18 49 18N 0 15W
Orneta 28 54 8N 20 9 E
Ørnhøj 49 56 13N 8 34 E
Ornö 48 59 4N 18 24 E
Örnsköldsvik 48 63 17N 18 40 E
Oro → 120 25 35N 105 2W
Orocué 126 4 48N 71 20W
Orodo 85 5 34N 7 4 E
Orogrande 119 32 20N 106 4W
Orol 30 43 34N 7 39W
Oromocto 107 45 54N 66 29W
Oron 85 4 48N 8 14 E
Orono 112 43 59N 78 37W
Oropesa 30 39 57N 5 10W
Oroqen Zizhiqi 76 50 34N 123 43 E
Oroquieta 73 8 32N 123 44 E
Orós 127 6 15 S 38 55W
Orosei, G. di 40 40 15N 9 40 E
Orosháza 27 46 32N 20 42 E
Orotukan 59 62 16N 151 42 E
Oroville, Calif., U.S.A. 118 39 31N 121 30W
Oroville, Wash., U.S.A. 118 48 58N 119 30W
Orrefors 49 56 50N 15 45 E
Orroroo 99 32 43 S 138 38 E
Orrville 112 40 50N 81 46W
Orsa 48 61 7N 14 37 E
Orsara di Púglia 41 41 17N 15 16 E
Orsasjön 48 61 7N 14 37 E
Orsha 54 54 30N 30 25 E
Orsk 52 51 12N 58 34 E
Ørslev 49 55 3N 11 56 E
Orsogna 39 42 13N 14 17 E
Orşova 46 44 41N 22 25 E
Ørsted 49 56 30N 10 20 E
Orta, L. d' 38 45 48N 8 21 E
Orta Nova 41 41 20N 15 40 E
Orte 39 42 28N 12 23 E
Ortegal, C. 30 43 43N 7 52W
Orthez 20 43 29N 0 48W
Ortigueira 30 43 40N 7 50W
Ortles 38 46 31N 10 33 E
Ortón → 126 10 50 S 67 0W
Ortona 39 42 21N 14 24 E
Orune 40 40 25N 9 20 E
Oruro 126 18 0 S 67 9W
Orust 49 58 10N 11 40 E
Orūzgān □ 65 33 30N 66 0 E
Orvault 18 47 17N 1 38W
Orvieto 39 42 43N 12 8 E
Orwell 112 41 32N 80 52W
Orwell → 13 52 2N 1 12 E
Oryakhovo 43 43 40N 23 57 E
Orzinuovi 38 45 24N 9 55 E
Orzyc → 28 52 46N 21 14 E
Orzysz 28 53 50N 21 58 E
Os 47 60 9N 5 30 E
Osa 52 57 17N 55 26 E
Osa → 28 53 33N 18 46 E
Osa, Pen. de 121 8 0N 84 0W
Osage, Iowa, U.S.A. 116 43 15N 92 50W
Osage, Wyo., U.S.A. 116 43 59N 104 25W
Osage → 116 38 35N 91 57W
Osage City 116 38 43N 95 51W
Ōsaka 74 34 40N 135 30 E
Ōsaka □ 74 34 30N 135 30 E
Osawatomie 116 38 30N 94 55W
Osborne 116 39 30N 98 45W
Osby 49 56 23N 13 59 E
Osceola, Ark., U.S.A. 117 35 40N 90 0W
Osceola, Iowa, U.S.A. 116 41 0N 93 20W
Oschatz 24 51 17N 13 8 E
Oschersleben 24 52 2N 11 13 E
Óschiri 40 40 43N 9 7 E
Oscoda 114 44 26N 83 20W
Oscoda-Au-Sable 112 44 26N 83 20W
Osečina 42 44 23N 19 34 E
Ösel = Saaremaa 54 58 30N 22 30W
Osëry 55 54 52N 38 28 E
Osh 58 40 37N 72 49 E
Oshawa 106 43 50N 78 50W
ŌShima 74 34 44N 139 24 E
Oshkosh, Nebr., U.S.A. 116 41 27N 102 20W
Oshkosh, Wis., U.S.A. 116 44 3N 88 35W
Oshmyany 54 54 26N 25 52 E
Oshogbo 85 7 48N 4 37 E
Oshwe 88 3 25 S 19 28 E
Osica de Jos 46 44 14N 24 20 E
Osieczna 28 51 55N 16 40 E
Osijek 42 45 34N 18 41 E
Ósilo 40 40 45N 8 41 E
Osimo 39 43 28N 13 30 E
Osintorf 54 54 40N 30 39 E
Osipenko = Berdyansk 56 46 45N 36 50 E
Osipovichi 54 53 19N 28 33 E
Oskaloosa 116 41 18N 92 40W
Oskarshamn 49 57 15N 16 27 E
Oskélanéo 106 48 5N 75 15W
Oskol → 55 49 6N 37 25 E
Oslo 47 59 55N 10 45 E
Oslob 73 9 31N 123 26 E
Oslofjorden 47 59 20N 10 35 E
Osmanabad 70 18 5N 76 10 E
Osmancık 56 40 45N 34 47 E
Osmaniye 64 37 5N 36 10 E
Ösmo 48 58 58N 17 55 E
Osnabrück 24 52 16N 8 2 E
Ošno Lubuskie 28 52 28N 14 51 E
Osobláha 27 50 17N 17 44 E
Osogovska Planina 42 42 10N 22 30 E
Osor 38 44 42N 14 24 E
Osorio 125 29 53 S 50 17W
Osorno, Chile 128 40 25 S 73 0W
Osorno, Spain 30 42 24N 4 22W
Osoyoos 108 49 0N 119 30W
Ospika → 108 56 20N 124 0W
Osprey Reef 97 13 52 S 146 36 E
Oss 16 51 46N 5 32 E
Ossa de Montiel 33 38 58N 2 45W
Ossa, Mt. 97 41 52 S 146 3 E
Óssa, Oros 44 39 47N 22 42 E
Ossabaw I. 115 31 45N 81 8W
Osse → 20 44 7N 0 17 E
Ossining 114 41 9N 73 50W
Ossipee 113 43 41N 71 9W
Ossokmanuan L. 107 53 25N 65 0W
Ossora 59 59 20N 163 13 E
Ostashkov 54 57 4N 33 2 E
Oste → 24 53 30N 9 12 E
Ostend = Oostende 16 51 15N 2 50 E
Oster 54 50 57N 30 53 E
Osterburg 24 52 47N 11 44 E
Osterburken 25 49 26N 9 25 E
Österbybruk 48 60 13N 17 55 E
Österbymo 49 57 49N 15 15 E
Östergötlands län □ 49 58 35N 15 45 E
Osterholz-Scharmbeck 24 53 14N 8 48 E
Østerild 49 57 2N 8 51 E
Österkorsberga 49 57 18N 15 6 E
Osterøya 47 60 32N 5 30 E
Östersund 48 63 10N 14 38 E
Østfold fylke □ 47 59 25N 11 25 E
Ostfreisland 24 53 20N 7 30 E
Ostfriesische Inseln 24 53 45N 7 15 E
Ostia, Lido di (Lido di Roma) 40 41 43N 12 17 E
Ostiglía 39 45 4N 11 9 E
Ostra 39 43 40N 13 5 E
Ostrava 27 49 51N 18 18 E
Ostróda 28 53 42N 19 58 E
Ostrog 54 50 20N 26 30 E
Ostrogozhsk 55 50 55N 39 7 E
Ostrogróg Szamotuły 28 52 37N 16 33 E
Ostrołeka 28 53 4N 21 32 E
Ostrołeka □ 28 53 0N 21 30 E
Ostrov, Bulg. 43 43 40N 24 9 E
Ostrov, Romania 46 44 6N 27 24 E
Ostrov, U.S.S.R. 54 57 25N 28 20 E
Ostrów Lubelski 28 51 29N 22 51 E
Ostrów Mazowiecka 28 52 50N 21 51 E
Ostrów Wielkopolski 28 51 36N 17 44 E
Ostrowiec-Świętokrzyski 28 50 55N 21 22 E
Ostrozac 42 43 43N 17 49 E
Ostrzeszów 28 51 25N 17 52 E
Ostseebad-Külungsborn 24 54 10N 11 40 E
Ostuni 41 40 44N 17 34 E
Osum → 43 43 40N 24 50 E
Osumi → 44 40 40N 20 10 E
Ōsumi-Kaikyō 74 30 55N 131 0 E
Osuna 31 37 14N 5 8W
Oswego 114 43 29N 76 30W
Oswestry 12 52 52N 3 3W
Oświecim 27 50 2N 19 11 E
Otago □ 101 44 44 S 169 10 E
Otago Harb. 101 45 47 S 170 42 E
Ōtake 74 34 12N 132 13 E
Otaki 101 40 45 S 175 10 E
Otaru 74 43 10N 141 0 E
Otava → 26 49 26N 14 12 E
Otavalo 126 0 13N 78 20W
Otavi 92 19 40 S 17 24 E
Otchinjau 92 16 30 S 13 56 E
Otelec 42 45 36N 20 50 E
Otero de Rey 30 43 6N 7 36W
Othello 118 46 53N 119 8W
Othonoí 44 39 52N 19 22 E
Óthris, Óros 45 39 4N 22 42 E
Otira Gorge 101 42 53 S 171 33 E
Otis 116 40 12N 102 58W
Otjiwarongo 92 20 30 S 16 33 E
Otmuchów 28 50 28N 17 10 E
Otočac 39 44 53N 15 12 E
Otorohanga 101 38 12 S 175 14 E
Otoskwin → 106 52 13N 88 6W
Otosquen 109 53 17N 102 1W
Otra → 47 58 8N 8 1 E
Otranto 41 40 9N 18 28 E
Otranto, C. d' 41 40 7N 18 30 E
Otranto, Str. of 41 40 15N 18 40 E
Ōtsu 74 35 0N 135 50 E
Otta 47 61 46N 9 32 E
Otta → 47 61 46N 9 32 E
Ottapalam 70 10 46N 76 23 E
Ottawa, Can. 106 45 27N 75 42W
Ottawa, Ill., U.S.A. 116 41 20N 88 55W
Ottawa, Kans., U.S.A. 116 38 40N 95 6W
Ottawa = Outaouais → 106 45 27N 74 8W
Ottawa Is. 105 59 35N 80 10W
Ottélé 85 3 38N 11 19 E
Ottenby 49 56 15N 16 24 E
Otter L. 109 55 35N 104 39W
Otter Rapids, Ont., Can. 106 50 11N 81 39W
Otter Rapids, Sask., Can. 109 55 38N 104 44W
Otterberg 25 49 30N 7 46 E
Otterndorf 24 53 47N 8 52 E
Ottersheim 26 48 21N 14 12 E
Otterup 49 55 30N 10 22 E
Otterville 112 42 55N 80 36W
Otto Beit Bridge 91 15 59 S 28 56 E
Ottosdal 92 26 46 S 25 59 E
Ottoshoop 92 25 45 S 25 58 E
Ottsjö 48 63 13N 13 2 E
Ottumwa 116 41 0N 92 25W
Otu 85 8 14N 3 22 E
Otukpa (Al Owuho) 85 7 9N 7 41 E
Oturkpo 85 7 16N 8 8 E
Otway, Bahía 128 53 30 S 74 0W
Otway, C. 97 38 52 S 143 30 E
Otwock 28 52 5N 21 20 E
Ötz 26 47 13N 10 53 E
Ötz → 26 47 14N 10 50 E
Ötztaler Alpen 26 46 45N 11 0 E
Ou → 71 20 4N 102 13 E
Ou-Sammyaku 74 39 20N 140 35 E
Ouachita → 117 31 38N 91 49W
Ouachita, L. 117 34 40N 93 25W
Ouachita Mts. 117 34 50N 94 30W
Ouadâne 80 20 50N 11 40W
Ouadda 81 8 15N 22 20 E
Ouagadougou 85 12 25N 1 30W
Ouahigouya 84 13 31N 2 25W
Ouahila 82 27 50N 5 0W
Ouahran = Oran 82 35 49N 0 39W
Oualâta 84 17 20N 6 55W
Ouallene 82 24 41N 1 11 E
Ouanda Djallé 81 8 55N 22 53 E
Ouango 88 4 19N 22 30 E
Ouargla 83 31 59N 5 16 E
Ouarkziz, Djebel 82 28 50N 8 0W
Ouarzazate 82 30 55N 6 50W
Ouatagouna 85 15 11N 0 43 E
Oubangi → 88 1 0N 17 50 E
Oubarakai, O. → 83 27 20N 9 0 E
Ouche → 19 47 6N 5 16 E
Ouddorp 16 51 50N 3 57 E
Oude Rijn → 16 52 12N 4 24 E
Oudenaarde 16 50 50N 3 37 E
Oudon 18 47 22N 1 19W
Oudon → 18 47 38N 1 18 E
Oudtshoorn 92 33 35 S 22 14 E
Oued Zem 82 32 52N 6 34W
Ouellé 84 7 26N 4 1W
Ouenza 83 35 57N 8 4 E
Ouessa 84 11 4N 2 47W
Ouessant, Île d' 18 48 28N 5 6W
Ouesso 88 1 37N 16 5 E

Ouest, Pte. **107** 49 52N 64 40W
Ouezzane **82** 34 51N 5 35W
Ouidah **85** 6 25N 2 0 E
Ouistreham **18** 49 17N 0 18W
Oujda **82** 34 41N 1 55W
Oujeft **80** 20 2N 13 0W
Ould Yenjé **84** 15 38N 12 16W
Ouled Djellal **83** 34 28N 5 2 E
Ouled Naïl, Mts. des **82** 34 30N 3 30 E
Oulmès **82** 33 17N 6 0W
Oulu **50** 65 1N 25 29 E
Oulu □ **50** 65 10N 27 20 E
Oulujärvi **50** 64 25N 27 15 E
Oulujoki → **50** 65 1N 25 30 E
Oulx **38** 45 2N 6 49 E
Oum Chalouba **81** 15 48N 20 46 E
Oum-el-Bouaghi **83** 35 55N 7 6 E
Oum el Ksi **82** 29 4N 6 59W
Oum-er-Rbia, O. → **82** 33 19N 8 21W
Oumè **84** 6 21N 5 27W
Ounane, Dj. **83** 25 4N 7 19 E
Ounguati **92** 21 54S 15 46 E
Ounianga-Kébir **81** 19 4N 20 29 E
Ounianga Sérir **81** 18 54N 19 51 E
Our → **16** 49 55N 6 5 E
Ouray **119** 38 3N 107 40W
Ourcq → **19** 49 1N 3 1 E
Oureg, Oued el → **82** 32 34N 2 10 E
Ouricuri **127** 7 53S 40 5W
Ourinhos **125** 23 0S 49 54W
Ourique **31** 37 38N 8 16W
Ouro Fino **125** 22 16S 46 25W
Ouro Prêto **125** 20 20S 43 30W
Ouro Sogui **84** 15 36N 13 19W
Oursi **85** 14 41N 0 27W
Ourthe → **16** 50 29N 5 35 E
Ouse **99** 42 38S 146 42 E
Ouse →, Sussex, U.K. **13** 50 43N 0 3 E
Ouse →, Yorks., U.K. **12** 54 3N 0 7 E
Oust **20** 42 52N 1 13 E
Oust → **18** 47 35N 2 6W
Outaouais → **106** 45 27N 74 8W
Outardes → **107** 49 24N 69 30W
Outat Oulad el Haj **82** 33 22N 3 42W
Outer Hebrides **14** 57 30N 7 40W
Outer I. **107** 51 10N 58 35W
Outes **30** 42 52N 8 55W
Outjo **92** 20 5S 16 7 E
Outlook, Can. **109** 51 30N 107 0W
Outlook, U.S.A. **116** 48 53N 104 46W
Outreau **19** 50 40N 1 36 E
Ouvèze → **21** 43 59N 4 51 E
Ouyen **97** 35 1S 142 22 E
Ouzouer-le-Marché **18** 47 54N 1 32 E
Ovada **38** 44 39N 8 40 E
Ovalau **101** 17 40S 178 48 E
Ovalle **124** 30 33S 71 18W
Ovar **30** 40 51N 8 40W
Ovens → **100** 36 2S 146 12 E
Over Flakkee **16** 51 45N 4 5 E
Overijssel □ **16** 52 25N 6 35 E
Overpelt **16** 51 12N 5 20 E
Overton **119** 36 32N 114 31W
Övertorneå **50** 66 23N 23 38 E
Överum **49** 58 0N 16 20 E
Ovid **116** 41 0N 102 17W
Ovidiopol **56** 46 15N 30 30 E
Oviedo **30** 43 25N 5 50W
Oviedo □ **30** 43 20N 6 0W
Oviken **48** 63 0N 14 23 E
Oviksfjällen **48** 63 0N 13 49 E
Ovoro **85** 5 26N 7 16 E
Övre Sirdal **47** 58 48N 6 43 E
Ovruch **54** 51 25N 28 45 E
Owaka **101** 46 27S 169 40 E
Owambo **92** 17 20S 16 30 E
Owase **74** 34 7N 136 12 E
Owatonna **116** 44 3N 93 10W
Owbeh **65** 34 28N 63 10 E
Owego **114** 42 6N 76 17W
Owen Falls **90** 0 30N 33 5 E
Owen Sound **106** 44 35N 80 55W
Owen Stanley Range **98** 8 30S 147 0 E
Owendo **88** 0 17N 9 30 E
Owens L. **119** 36 20N 118 0W
Owensboro **114** 37 40N 87 5W
Owensville **116** 38 20N 91 30W
Owerri **85** 5 29N 7 0 E
Owl → **109** 57 51N 92 44W
Owo **85** 7 10N 5 39 E
Owosso **114** 43 0N 84 10W
Owyhee **118** 42 0N 116 3W
Owyhee → **118** 43 46N 117 2W
Owyhee Res. **118** 43 40N 117 16W
Ox Mts. **15** 54 6N 9 0W
Oxberg **48** 61 7N 14 11 E
Oxelösund **49** 58 43N 17 15 E
Oxford, N.Z. **101** 43 18S 172 11 E
Oxford, U.K. **13** 51 45N 1 15W
Oxford, Miss., U.S.A. **117** 34 22N 89 30W
Oxford, N.C., U.S.A. **115** 36 19N 78 36W
Oxford, Ohio, U.S.A. **114** 39 30N 84 40W
Oxford □ **13** 51 45N 1 15W
Oxford L. **109** 54 51N 95 37W
Oxia **45** 38 16N 21 5 E
Oxílithos **45** 38 35N 24 7 E
Oxley **99** 34 11S 144 6 E
Oxnard **119** 34 10N 119 14W
Oya **72** 2 55N 111 55 E
Oyem **88** 1 34N 11 31 E
Oyen **109** 51 22N 110 28W
Öyeren **47** 59 50N 11 15 E
Oykel → **14** 57 55N 4 26W
Oymyakon **59** 63 25N 142 44 E
Oyo **85** 7 46N 3 56 E
Oyo □ **85** 8 0N 3 30 E
Oyonnax **21** 46 16N 5 40 E
Oyster B. **113** 40 52N 73 32W
Øystese **47** 60 22N 6 9 E
Ozamis (Mizamis) **73** 8 15N 123 50 E
Ozark, Ala., U.S.A. **115** 31 29N 85 39W
Ozark, Ark., U.S.A. **117** 35 30N 93 50W
Ozark, Mo., U.S.A. **117** 37 0N 93 15W
Ozark Plateau **117** 37 20N 91 40W
Ozarks, L. of **116** 38 10N 92 40W
Ózd **27** 48 14N 20 15 E
Ozieri **40** 40 35N 9 0 E
Ozimek **28** 50 41N 18 11 E
Ozona **117** 30 43N 101 11W
Ozorków **28** 51 57N 19 16 E
Ozren **42** 43 55N 18 29 E
Ozuluama **120** 21 40N 97 50W
Ozun **46** 45 47N 25 50 E

P

Pa **84** 11 33N 3 19W
Pa-an **67** 16 51N 97 40 E
Pa Sak → **71** 15 30N 101 0 E
Paar → **25** 48 13N 10 59 E
Paarl **92** 33 45S 18 56 E
Paatsi → **50** 68 55N 29 0 E
Paauilo **110** 20 3N 155 22W
Pab Hills **66** 26 30N 66 45 E
Pabianice **28** 51 40N 19 20 E
Pabna **69** 24 1N 89 18 E
Pabo **90** 3 1N 32 10 E
Pacaja → **127** 1 56S 50 50W
Pacaraima, Sierra **126** 4 0N 62 30W
Pacasmayo **126** 7 20S 79 35W
Pacaudière, La **20** 46 11N 3 52 E
Paceco **40** 37 59N 12 32 E
Pachhar **68** 24 40N 77 42 E
Pachino **41** 36 43N 15 4 E
Pachora **68** 20 38N 75 29 E
Pachuca **120** 20 10N 98 40W
Pacific **108** 54 48N 128 28W
Pacific-Antarctic Basin **95** 46 0S 95 0W
Pacific-Antarctic Ridge **95** 43 0S 115 0W
Pacific Grove **119** 36 38N 121 58W
Pacific Ocean **94** 10 0N 140 0W
Pacitan **73** 8 12S 111 7 E
Pacofi **108** 53 0N 132 30W
Pacov **26** 49 27N 15 0 E
Pacsa **27** 46 44N 17 2 E
Paczków **28** 50 28N 17 0 E
Padaido, Kepulauan **73** 1 5S 138 0 E
Padalarang **73** 7 50S 107 30 E
Padang **72** 1 0S 100 20 E
Padangpanjang **72** 0 40S 100 20 E
Padangsidempuan **72** 1 30N 99 15 E
Padborg **49** 54 49N 9 21 E
Paddockwood **109** 53 30N 105 30W
Paderborn **24** 51 42N 8 44 E
Padeşul **46** 45 40N 22 22 E
Padina **46** 44 50N 27 8 E
Padloping Island **105** 67 0N 62 50W
Padmanabhapuram **70** 8 16N 77 17 E
Pádova **39** 45 24N 11 52 E
Padra **68** 22 15N 73 7 E
Padrauna **69** 26 54N 83 59 E
Padre I. **117** 27 0N 97 20W
Padrón **30** 42 41N 8 39W
Padstow **12** 50 33N 4 57W
Padua = Pádova **39** 45 24N 11 52 E
Paducah, Ky., U.S.A. **114** 37 0N 88 40W
Paducah, Tex., U.S.A. **117** 34 3N 100 16W
Padul **31** 37 1N 3 38W
Padula **41** 40 20N 15 40 E
Padwa **70** 18 27N 82 47 E
Paeroa **101** 37 23S 175 41 E
Paesana **38** 44 40N 7 18 E
Pag **39** 44 30N 14 50 E
Paga **85** 11 1N 1 8W
Pagadian **73** 7 55N 123 30 E
Pagai Selatan **72** 3 0S 100 15W
Pagai Utara **72** 2 35S 100 0 E
Pagalu **79** 1 25S 5 36 E
Pagastikós Kólpos **44** 39 15N 23 0 E
Pagatan **72** 3 33S 115 59 E
Page, Ariz., U.S.A. **119** 36 57N 111 27W
Page, N.D., U.S.A. **116** 47 11N 97 37W
Paglieta **39** 42 10N 14 30 E
Pagny-sur-Moselle **19** 48 59N 6 2 E
Pago Pago **101** 14 16S 170 43W
Pagosa Springs **119** 37 16N 107 4W
Pagwa River **106** 50 2N 85 14W
Pahala **110** 19 12N 155 25W
Pahang □ **71** 3 40N 102 20 E
Pahang → **71** 3 30N 103 9 E
Pahiatua **101** 40 27S 175 50 E
Pahokee **115** 26 50N 80 40W
Pahrump **119** 36 15N 116 0W
Paia **110** 20 54N 156 22W
Paide **54** 58 57N 25 31 E
Paignton **13** 50 26N 3 33W
Päijänne, L. **51** 61 30N 25 30 E
Pailin **71** 12 46N 102 36 E
Paimbœuf **18** 47 17N 2 0W
Paimpol **18** 48 48N 3 4W
Painan **72** 1 21S 100 34 E
Painesville **114** 41 42N 81 18W
Paint I. **109** 55 28N 97 57W
Paint Rock **117** 31 30N 99 56W
Painted Desert **119** 36 0N 111 30W
Paintsville **114** 37 50N 82 50W
Paisley, Can. **112** 44 18N 81 16W
Paisley, U.K. **14** 55 51N 4 27W
Paisley, U.S.A. **118** 42 43N 120 40W
Paita **126** 5 11S 81 9W
Paiva → **30** 41 4N 8 16W
Pajares **30** 43 1N 5 46W
Pajares, Puerto de **30** 43 0N 5 46W
Pajeczno **28** 51 10N 19 0 E
Pak Lay **71** 18 15N 101 27 E
Pakala **70** 13 29N 79 8 E
Pakanbaru **72** 0 30N 101 15 E
Pakaraima Mts. **126** 6 0N 60 0W
Pakistan ■ **66** 30 0N 70 0 E
Pakistan, East = Bangladesh ■ **67** 24 0N 90 0 E
Pakokku **67** 21 20N 95 0 E
Pakosc **28** 52 48N 18 6 E
Pakpattan **68** 30 25N 73 27 E
Pakrac **42** 45 27N 17 12 E
Paks **27** 46 38N 18 55 E
Pakse **71** 15 5N 105 52 E
Paktīā □ **65** 33 0N 69 15 E
Pakwach **90** 2 28N 31 27 E
Pala, Chad **81** 9 25N 15 5 E
Pala, Zaïre **90** 6 45S 29 30 E
Palabek **90** 3 22N 32 33 E
Palacios **117** 28 44N 96 12W
Palafrugell **32** 41 55N 3 10 E
Palagiano **41** 40 35N 17 0 E
Palagonía **41** 37 20N 14 43 E
Palagruža **39** 42 24N 16 15 E
Palaiokastron **45** 35 12N 26 18 E
Palaiokhóra **45** 35 16N 23 39 E
Pálairos **45** 38 45N 20 51 E
Palais, Le **18** 47 20N 3 10W
Palakol **70** 16 31N 81 46 E
Palam **70** 19 0N 77 0 E
Palamás **44** 39 26N 22 4 E
Palamós **32** 41 50N 3 10 E
Palampur **68** 32 10N 76 30 E
Palana, Austral. **99** 39 45S 147 55 E
Palana, U.S.S.R. **59** 59 10N 159 59 E
Palanan **73** 17 8N 122 29 E
Palanan Pt. **73** 17 17N 122 30 E
Palangkaraya **72** 2 16S 113 56 E
Palanpur **68** 24 10N 72 25 E
Palapye **92** 22 30S 27 7 E
Palar → **70** 12 27N 80 13 E
Palatka, U.S.A. **115** 29 40N 81 40W
Palatka, U.S.S.R. **59** 60 6N 150 54 E
Palau Is. **94** 7 30N 134 30 E
Palauig **73** 15 26N 119 54 E
Palauk **71** 13 10N 98 40 E
Palavas **20** 43 32N 3 56 E
Palawan **72** 9 30N 118 30 E
Palayancottai **70** 8 45N 77 45 E
Palazzo San Gervásio **41** 40 53N 15 58 E
Palazzolo Acreide **41** 37 4N 14 54 E
Paldiski **54** 59 23N 24 9 E
Pale **42** 43 50N 18 38 E
Paleleh **73** 1 10N 121 50 E
Palembang **72** 3 0S 104 50 E
Palencia **30** 42 1N 4 34W
Palencia □ **30** 42 31N 4 33W
Palermo, Italy **40** 38 8N 13 20 E
Palermo, U.S.A. **118** 39 30N 121 37W
Palestine, Asia **62** 32 0N 35 0 E
Palestine, U.S.A. **117** 31 42N 95 35W
Palestrina **40** 41 50N 12 52 E
Paletwa **67** 21 10N 92 50 E
Palghat **70** 10 46N 76 42 E
Pali **68** 25 50N 73 20 E
Palinuro, C. **41** 40 1N 15 14 E
Palisade **116** 40 21N 101 10W
Palitana **68** 21 32N 71 49 E
Palizada **120** 18 18N 92 8W
Palizzi **41** 37 58N 15 59 E
Palk Bay **70** 9 30N 79 15 E
Palk Strait **70** 10 0N 79 45 E
Palkonda **70** 18 36N 83 48 E
Palkonda Ra. **70** 13 50N 79 20 E
Pallanza = Verbánia **38** 45 50N 8 55 E
Pallasovka **55** 50 4N 47 0 E
Palleru → **70** 16 45N 80 2 E
Pallisa **90** 1 12N 33 43 E
Pallu **68** 28 59N 74 14 E
Palm Beach **115** 26 46N 80 0W
Palm Is. **97** 18 40S 146 35 E
Palm Springs **119** 33 51N 116 35W
Palma, Canary Is. **8** 28 40N 17 50W
Palma, Mozam. **91** 10 46S 40 29 E
Palma → **127** 12 33S 47 52W
Palma, B. de **33** 39 30N 2 39 E
Palma de Mallorca **32** 39 35N 2 39 E
Palma del Río **31** 37 43N 5 17W
Palma di Montechiaro **40** 37 12N 13 46 E
Palma, La, Canary Is. **80** 28 40N 17 50W
Palma, La, Panama **121** 8 15N 78 0W
Palma, La, Spain **31** 37 21N 6 38W
Palma Soriano **121** 20 15N 76 0W
Palmahim **62** 31 56N 34 44 E
Palmanova **39** 45 54N 13 18 E
Palmares **127** 8 41S 35 28W
Palmarola **40** 40 57N 12 50 E
Palmas **125** 26 29S 52 0W
Palmas, C. **84** 4 27N 7 46W
Pálmas, G. di **40** 39 0N 8 30 E
Palmdale **119** 34 36N 118 7W
Palmeira dos Índios **127** 9 25S 36 37W
Palmeirinhas, Pta. das **88** 9 2S 12 57 E
Palmela **31** 38 32N 8 57W
Palmer, Alaska, U.S.A. **104** 61 35N 149 10W
Palmer, Mass., U.S.A. **113** 42 9N 72 21W
Palmer →, N. Terr., Austral. **96** 24 46S 133 25 E
Palmer →, Queens., Austral. **98** 15 34S 142 26 E
Palmer Arch **5** 64 15S 65 0W
Palmer Lake **116** 39 10N 104 52W
Palmer Land **5** 73 0S 60 0W
Palmerston **112** 43 50N 80 51W
Palmerston, C. **97** 21 32S 149 29 E
Palmerston North **101** 40 21S 175 39 E
Palmerton **113** 40 47N 75 36W
Palmetto **115** 27 33N 82 33W
Palmi **41** 38 21N 15 51 E
Palmira, Argent. **124** 32 59S 68 34W
Palmira, Colomb. **126** 3 32N 76 16W
Palms **112** 43 37N 82 47W
Palmyra, Mo., U.S.A. **116** 39 45N 91 30W
Palmyra, N.Y., U.S.A. **112** 42 5N 77 18W
Palmyra = Tudmur **64** 34 30N 37 17 E
Palmyra Is. **95** 5 52N 162 6W
Palni **70** 10 30N 77 30 E
Palni Hills **70** 10 14N 77 33 E
Palo Alto **119** 37 25N 122 8W
Palo del Colle **41** 41 4N 16 43 E
Paloma, La **124** 30 35S 71 0W
Palombara Sabina **39** 42 4N 12 45 E
Palopo **73** 3 0S 120 16 E
Palos, Cabo de **33** 37 38N 0 40W
Palouse **118** 46 59N 117 5W
Palparara **98** 24 47S 141 28 E
Pålsboda **49** 59 3N 15 22 E
Palu, Indon. **73** 1 0S 119 52 E
Palu, Turkey **64** 38 45N 40 0 E
Paluan **73** 13 26N 120 29 E
Palwal **68** 28 8N 77 19 E
Pama **85** 11 19N 0 44 E
Pamamaroo, L. **100** 32 17S 142 28 E
Pamanukan **73** 6 16S 107 49 E
Pamban I. **70** 9 15N 79 20 E
Pamekasan **73** 7 10S 113 29 E
Pameungpeuk **73** 7 38S 107 44 E
Pamiers **20** 43 7N 1 39 E
Pamirs **58** 37 40N 73 0 E
Pamlico → **115** 35 25N 76 30W
Pamlico Sd. **115** 35 20N 76 0W
Pampa **117** 35 35N 100 58W
Pampa de las Salinas **124** 32 1S 66 58W
Pampa, La □ **124** 36 50S 66 0W
Pampanua **73** 4 16S 120 8 E
Pamparato **38** 44 16N 7 54 E
Pampas, Argent. **124** 35 0S 63 0W
Pampas, Peru **126** 12 20S 74 50W
Pamplona, Colomb. **126** 7 23N 72 39W
Pamplona, Spain **32** 42 48N 1 38W
Pampoenpoort **92** 31 3S 22 40 E
Pana **116** 39 25N 89 10W
Panaca **119** 37 51N 114 23W
Panagyurishte **43** 42 30N 24 15 E
Panaitan **73** 6 35S 105 10 E
Panaji (Panjim) **70** 15 25N 73 50 E
Panamá **121** 9 0N 79 25W
Panama ■ **121** 8 48N 79 55W
Panama Canal **121** 9 10N 79 37W
Panama City **115** 30 10N 85 41W
Panamá, Golfo de **121** 8 4N 79 20W
Panamint Mts. **119** 36 30N 117 20W
Panão **126** 9 55S 75 55W
Panarea **41** 38 38N 15 3 E
Panaro → **38** 44 55N 11 25 E
Panarukan **73** 7 40S 113 52 E
Panay **73** 11 10N 122 30 E
Panay, G. **73** 11 0N 122 30 E
Pancake Ra. **119** 38 30N 116 0W
Pančevo **42** 44 52N 20 41 E
Panciu **46** 45 54N 27 8 E
Panco **73** 8 42S 118 40 E
Pancorbo, Paso **32** 42 32N 3 5W
Pandan **73** 11 45N 122 10 E
Pandeglang **73** 6 25S 106 0 E
Pandharpur **70** 17 41N 75 20 E
Pandhurna **68** 21 36N 78 35 E
Pandilla **32** 41 32N 3 43W
Pando **125** 34 44S 56 0W
Pando, L. = Hope L. **99** 28 24S 139 18 E
Panevezys **54** 55 42N 24 25 E
Panfilov **58** 44 10N 80 0 E
Panfilovo **55** 50 25N 42 46 E
Pang-Long **67** 23 11N 98 45 E
Pang-Yang **67** 22 7N 98 48 E
Panga **90** 1 52N 26 18 E
Pangaion Óros **44** 40 50N 24 0 E
Pangalanes, Canal des **93** 22 48S 47 50 E
Pangani **90** 5 25S 38 58 E
Pangani □ **90** 5 25S 39 0 E
Pangani → **90** 5 26S 38 58 E
Pangfou = Bengbu **77** 32 56N 117 20 E
Pangil **90** 3 10S 26 35 E
Pangkah, Tanjung **73** 6 51S 112 33 E
Pangkalanberandan **72** 4 1N 98 20 E
Pangkalanbuun **72** 2 41S 111 37 E
Pangkalansusu **72** 4 2N 98 13 E
Pangkoh **72** 3 5S 114 8 E
Pangnirtung **105** 66 8N 65 54W
Pangrango **73** 6 46S 107 1 E
Panguitch **119** 37 52N 112 30W
Pangutaran Group **73** 6 18N 120 34 E
Panhandle **117** 35 23N 101 23W
Pani Mines **68** 22 29N 73 50 E
Pania-Mutombo **90** 5 11S 23 51 E
Panipat **68** 29 25N 77 2 E
Panjal Range **68** 32 30N 76 50 E
Panjgur **66** 27 0N 64 5 E
Panjim = Panaji **70** 15 25N 73 50 E
Panjinad Barrage **65** 29 22N 71 15 E
Pankajene **73** 4 46S 119 34 E
Pankalpinang **72** 2 0S 106 0 E
Pankshin **85** 9 16N 9 25 E
Panna **69** 24 40N 80 15 E
Panna Hills **69** 24 40N 81 15 E
Pannuru **70** 16 5N 80 34 E
Panorama **125** 21 21S 51 51W
Panruti **70** 11 46N 79 35 E
Panshan **76** 41 3N 122 2 E
Panshi **76** 42 58N 126 5 E
Pantano **119** 32 0N 110 32W
Pantar **73** 8 28S 124 10 E
Pantelleria **40** 36 52N 12 0 E
Pantón **30** 42 31N 7 37W
Pánuco **120** 22 0N 98 15W
Panyam **85** 9 27N 9 8 E
Panyu **77** 22 51N 113 20 E
Páola **41** 39 21N 16 2 E
Paola **116** 38 36N 94 50W
Paonia **119** 38 56N 107 37W
Paoting = Baoding **76** 38 50N 115 28 E
Paot'ou = Baotou **76** 40 32N 110 2 E
Paoua **88** 7 9N 16 20 E
Papá **27** 47 22N 17 30 E
Papagayo → **120** 16 36N 99 43W
Papagayo, Golfo de **121** 10 30N 85 50W
Papagni → **70** 15 35N 77 45 E
Papakura **101** 37 4S 174 59 E
Papantla **120** 20 30N 97 30W
Papar **72** 5 45N 116 0 E
Pápas, Ákra **45** 38 13N 21 20 E
Papenburg **24** 53 7N 7 25 E
Papigochic → **120** 29 9N 109 40W
Paposo **124** 25 0S 70 30W
Papua, Gulf of **98** 9 0S 144 50 E
Papua New Guinea ■ **94** 8 0S 145 0 E

Papuča 39 44 22N 15 30 E
Papudo 124 32 29 S 71 27W
Papuk 42 45 30N 17 30 E
Papun 67 18 0N 97 30 E
Pará = Belém 127 1 20 S 48 30W
Pará □ 127 3 20 S 52 0W
Parábita 41 40 3N 18 8 E
Paraburdoo 96 23 14 S 117 32 E
Paracatu 127 17 10 S 46 50W
Parachilna 99 31 10 S 138 21 E
Parachinar 66 33 55N 70 5 E
Paraćin 42 43 54N 21 27 E
Paradas 31 37 18N 5 29W
Paradela 30 42 44N 7 37W
Paradip 69 20 15N 86 35 E
Paradise 118 47 27N 114 17W
Paradise → 107 53 27N 57 19W
Paradise Valley 118 41 30N 117 28W
Parado 73 8 42 S 118 30 E
Paradyz 28 51 19N 20 2 E
Paragould 117 36 5N 90 30W
Paragua → 126 6 55N 62 55W
Paragua, La 126 6 50N 63 20W
Paraguaçu → 127 12 45 S 38 54W
Paraguaçu Paulista 125 22 22 S 50 35W
Paraguaná, Pen. de 126 12 0N 70 0W
Paraguarí 124 25 36 S 57 0W
Paraguarí □ 124 26 0 S 57 10W
Paraguay ■ 124 23 0 S 57 0W
Paraguay → 124 27 18 S 58 38W
Paraíba = João Pessoa 127 7 10 S 35 0W
Paraíba □ 127 7 0 S 36 0W
Paraíba do Sul → 125 21 37 S 41 3W
Parainen 51 60 18N 22 18 E
Parakhino Paddubye 54 58 26N 33 10 E
Parakou 85 9 25N 2 40 E
Parálion-Astrous 45 37 25N 22 45 E
Paramagudi 70 9 31N 78 39 E
Paramaribo 127 5 50N 55 10W
Paramithiá 44 39 30N 20 35 E
Paramushir, Ostrov 59 50 24N 156 0 E
Paran → 62 30 20N 35 10 E
Paraná 124 31 45 S 60 30W
Paranã 127 12 30 S 47 48W
Paraná □ 125 24 30 S 51 0W
Paraná → 124 33 43 S 59 15W
Paranaguá 125 25 30 S 48 30W
Paranaíba → 127 20 6 S 51 4W
Paranapanema → 125 22 40 S 53 9W
Paranapiacaba, Serra do 125 24 31 S 48 35W
Paranavaí 125 23 4 S 52 56W
Parang, Jolo, Phil. 73 5 55N 120 54 E
Parang, Mindanao, Phil. 73 7 23N 124 16 E
Parapóla 45 36 55N 23 27 E
Paraspóri, Ákra 45 35 55N 27 15 E
Paratinga 127 12 40 S 43 10W
Paratoo 99 32 42 S 139 40 E
Parattah 99 42 22 S 147 23 E
Paray-le-Monial 21 46 27N 4 7 E
Parbati → 68 25 50N 76 30 E
Parbhani 68 19 8N 76 52 E
Parchim 24 53 25N 11 50 E
Parczew 28 51 40N 22 52 E
Pardes Hanna 62 32 28N 34 57 E
Pardilla 30 41 33N 3 43W
Pardo →, Bahia, Brazil 127 15 40 S 39 0W
Pardo →, Mato Grosso, Brazil 125 21 46 S 52 9W
Pardo →, São Paulo, Brazil 127 20 10 S 48 38W
Pardubice 26 50 3N 15 45 E
Pare 73 7 43 S 112 12 E
Pare □ 90 4 10 S 38 0 E
Pare Mts. 90 4 0 S 37 45 E
Parecis, Serra dos 126 13 0 S 60 0W
Paredes de Nava 30 42 9N 4 42W
Paren 59 62 30N 163 15 E
Parent 106 47 55N 74 35W
Parent, Lac. 106 48 31N 77 1W
Parentis-en-Born 20 44 21N 1 4W
Parepare 73 4 0 S 119 40 E
Parfino 54 57 59N 31 34 E
Parfuri 93 22 28 S 31 17 E
Parguba 52 62 20N 34 27 E
Parham 113 44 39N 76 43W
Pariaguán 126 8 51N 64 34W
Pariaman 72 0 47 S 100 11 E
Paricutín, Cerro 120 19 28N 102 15W
Parigi, Java, Indon. 73 7 42 S 108 29 E
Parigi, Sulawesi, Indon. 73 0 50 S 120 5 E
Parika 126 6 50N 58 20W
Parima, Serra 126 2 30N 64 0W
Parinari 126 4 35 S 74 25W
Parincea 46 46 27N 27 9 E
Parîng 46 45 20N 23 37 E
Parintins 127 2 40 S 56 50W
Pariparit Kyun 67 14 55 S 93 45 E
Paris, Can. 106 43 12N 80 25W
Paris, France 19 48 50N 2 20 E
Paris, Idaho, U.S.A. 118 42 13N 111 30W
Paris, Ky., U.S.A. 114 38 12N 84 12W
Paris, Tenn., U.S.A. 115 36 20N 88 20W
Paris, Tex., U.S.A. 117 33 40N 95 30W
Paris, Ville de □ 19 48 50N 2 20 E
Parish 113 43 24N 76 9W
Pariti 73 10 15 S 123 45 E
Park City 118 40 42N 111 35W
Park Falls 116 45 58N 90 27W
Park Range 118 40 0N 106 30W
Park Rapids 116 46 56N 95 0W
Park River 116 48 25N 97 43W
Park Rynie 93 30 25 S 30 45 E
Park View 119 36 45N 106 37W
Parker, Ariz., U.S.A. 119 34 8N 114 16W
Parker, S.D., U.S.A. 116 43 25N 97 7W
Parker Dam 119 34 13N 114 5W
Parkersburg 114 39 18N 81 31W
Parkerview 109 51 21N 103 18W
Parkes, A.C.T., Austral. 97 35 18 S 149 8 E
Parkes, N.S.W., Austral. 97 33 9 S 148 11 E
Parkside 109 53 10N 106 33W
Parkston 116 43 25N 98 0W
Parksville 108 49 20N 124 21W
Parlakimedi 70 18 45N 84 5 E
Parma, Italy 38 44 50N 10 20 E
Parma, Idaho, U.S.A. 118 43 49N 116 59W
Parma, Ohio, U.S.A. 112 41 25N 81 42W
Parma → 38 44 56N 10 26 E
Parnaguá 127 10 10 S 44 38W
Parnaíba, Piauí, Brazil 127 2 54 S 41 47W
Parnaíba, São Paulo, Brazil 127 19 34 S 51 14W
Parnaíba → 127 3 0 S 41 50W
Parnassós 45 38 35N 22 30 E
Párnis 45 38 14N 23 45 E
Párnon Óros 45 37 15N 22 45 E
Pärnu 54 58 28N 24 33 E
Parola 68 20 47N 75 7 E
Paroo → 97 31 28 S 143 32 E
Paroo Chan. 97 30 50 S 143 35 E
Páros, Greece 45 37 5N 25 9 E
Páros, Greece 45 37 5N 25 12 E
Parowan 119 37 54N 112 56W
Parpaillon 21 44 30N 6 40 E
Parral 124 36 10 S 71 52W
Parramatta 99 33 48 S 151 1 E
Parras 120 25 30N 102 20W
Parrett → 13 51 7N 2 58W
Parris I. 115 32 20N 80 30W
Parrsboro 107 45 30N 64 25W
Parry Is. 4 77 0N 110 0W
Parry Sound 106 45 20N 80 0W
Parsberg 25 49 10N 11 43 E
Parseta → 28 54 11N 15 34 E
Parshall 116 47 56N 102 11W
Parsnip → 108 55 10N 123 2W
Parsons 117 37 20N 95 17W
Partabpur 70 20 0N 80 42 E
Partanna 40 37 43N 12 51 E
Partapgarh 68 24 2N 74 40 E
Parthenay 18 46 38N 0 16W
Partinico 40 38 3N 13 6 E
Partur 70 19 40N 76 14 E
Paru → 127 1 33 S 52 38W
Parur 70 10 13N 76 14 E
Paruro 126 13 45 S 71 50W
Parván □ 65 35 0N 69 0 E
Parvatipuram 70 18 50N 83 25 E
Parys 92 26 52 S 27 29 E
Pas-de-Calais □ 19 50 30N 2 30 E
Pasadena, Calif., U.S.A. 119 34 5N 118 9W
Pasadena, Tex., U.S.A. 117 29 45N 95 14W
Pasaje 126 3 23 S 79 50W
Pasaje → 124 25 39 S 63 56W
Pascagoula 117 30 21N 88 30W
Pascagoula → 117 30 21N 88 35W
Paşcani 46 47 14N 26 45 E
Pasco 118 46 10N 119 0W
Pasco, Cerro de 126 10 45 S 76 10W
Pasewalk 24 53 30N 14 0 E
Pasfield L. 109 58 24N 105 20W
Pasha → 54 60 29N 32 55 E
Pashmakli = Smolyan 43 41 36N 24 38 E
Pasing 25 48 9N 11 27 E
Pasir Mas 71 6 2N 102 8 E
Pasir Puteh 71 5 50N 102 24 E
Pasirian 73 8 13 S 113 8 E
Pasłeka → 28 54 26N 19 46 E
Pasley, C. 96 33 52 S 123 35 E
Pašman 39 43 58N 15 20 E
Pasni 66 25 15N 63 27 E
Paso de Indios 128 43 55 S 69 0W
Paso de los Libres 124 29 44 S 57 10W
Paso de los Toros 124 32 45 S 56 30W
Paso Robles 119 35 40N 120 45W
Paspébiac 107 48 3N 65 17W
Pasrur 68 32 16N 74 43 E
Passage West 15 51 52N 8 20W
Passaic 113 40 50N 74 8W
Passau 25 48 34N 13 27 E
Passero, C. 41 36 42N 15 8 E
Passo Fundo 125 28 10 S 52 20W
Passos 127 20 45 S 46 37W
Passow 24 53 13N 14 10 E
Passy 21 45 55N 6 41 E
Pastaza → 126 4 50 S 76 52W
Pastęk 28 54 3N 19 41 E
Pasto 126 1 13N 77 17W
Pastrana 32 40 27N 2 53W
Pasuruan 73 7 40 S 112 44 E
Pasym 28 53 48N 20 49 E
Pásztó 27 47 52N 19 43 E
Patagonia, Argent. 128 45 0 S 69 0W
Patagonia, U.S.A. 119 31 35N 110 45W
Patan, Gujarat, India 70 17 22N 73 57 E
Patan, Maharashtra, India 68 23 54N 72 14 E
Patani 73 0 20N 128 50 E
Pataudi 68 28 18N 76 48 E
Patay 19 48 2N 1 40 E
Patchewollock 99 35 22 S 142 12 E
Patchogue 114 40 46N 73 1W
Patea 101 39 45 S 174 30 E
Pategi 85 8 50N 5 45 E
Patensie 92 33 46 S 24 49 E
Paternò 41 37 34N 14 53 E
Paternoster, Kepulauan 72 7 5 S 118 15 E
Pateros 118 48 4N 119 58W
Paterson, Austral. 100 32 37 S 151 39 E
Paterson, U.S.A. 114 40 55N 74 10W
Pathankot 68 32 18N 75 45 E
Pathfinder Res. 118 42 30N 107 0W
Pati 73 6 45 S 111 3 E
Patiala 68 30 23N 76 26 E
Patine Kouka 84 12 45N 13 45W
Patkai Bum 67 27 0N 95 30 E
Pátmos 45 37 21N 26 36 E
Patna 69 25 35N 85 12 E
Patonga 90 2 45N 33 15 E
Patos de Minas 127 18 35 S 46 32W
Patos, Lag. dos 125 31 20 S 51 0 E
Patosi 44 40 42N 19 38 E
Patquia 124 25 30N 102 11W
Pátrai 45 38 14N 21 47 E
Pátraikós, Kólpos 45 38 17N 21 30 E
Patrocínio 127 18 57 S 47 0W
Patta 90 2 10 S 41 0 E
Pattada 40 40 35N 9 7 E
Pattanapuram 70 9 6N 76 50 E
Pattani 71 6 48N 101 15 E
Patten 107 45 59N 68 28W
Patterson, Calif., U.S.A. 119 37 30N 121 9W
Patterson, La., U.S.A. 117 29 44N 91 20W
Patti, India 68 31 17N 74 54 E
Patti, Italy 41 38 8N 14 57 E
Pattoki 68 31 5N 73 52 E
Patton 112 40 38N 78 40W
Pattukkottai 70 10 25N 79 20 E
Patuakhali 69 22 20N 90 25 E
Patuca → 121 15 50N 84 18W
Patuca, Punta 121 15 49N 84 14W
Pátzcuaro 120 19 30N 101 40W
Pau 20 43 19N 0 25W
Pau, Gave de 20 43 33N 1 12W
Pauillac 20 45 11N 0 46W
Pauini → 126 1 42 S 62 50W
Pauk 67 21 27N 94 30 E
Paul I. 107 56 30N 61 20W
Paulhan 20 43 33N 3 28 E
Paulis = Isiro 90 2 47N 27 37 E
Paulistana 127 8 9 S 41 9W
Paullina 116 42 55N 95 40W
Paulo Afonso 127 9 21 S 38 15W
Paulpietersburg 93 27 23 S 30 50 E
Pauls Valley 117 34 40N 97 17W
Pauni 69 20 48N 79 40 E
Pavelets 55 53 49N 39 14 E
Pavia 38 45 10N 9 10 E
Pavlikeni 43 43 14N 25 20 E
Pavlodar 58 52 33N 77 0 E
Pavlograd 56 48 30N 35 52 E
Pavlovo, Gorkiy, U.S.S.R. 55 55 58N 43 5 E
Pavlovo, Yakut A.S.S.R., U.S.S.R. 59 63 5N 115 25 E
Pavlovsk 55 50 26N 40 5 E
Pavlovskaya 57 46 17N 39 47 E
Pavlovskiy-Posad 55 55 47N 38 42 E
Pavullo nel Frignano 38 44 20N 10 50 E
Pawhuska 117 36 40N 96 25W
Pawling 113 41 35N 73 37W
Pawnee 117 36 24N 96 50W
Pawnee City 116 40 8N 96 10W
Pawtucket 114 41 51N 71 22W
Paximádhia 45 35 0N 24 35 E
Paxoí 44 39 14N 20 12 E
Paxton, Ill., U.S.A. 114 40 25N 88 7W
Paxton, Nebr., U.S.A. 116 41 12N 101 27W
Paya Bakri 71 2 3N 102 44 E
Payakumbah 72 0 20 S 100 35 E
Payerne 25 46 49N 6 56 E
Payette 118 44 0N 117 0W
Paymogo 31 37 44N 7 21W
Payne L. 105 59 30N 74 30W
Paynesville, Liberia 84 6 20N 10 45W
Paynesville, U.S.A. 116 45 21N 94 44W
Pays Basque 20 43 15N 1 0W
Paysandú 124 32 19 S 58 8W
Payson, Ariz., U.S.A. 119 34 17N 111 15W
Payson, Utah, U.S.A. 118 40 8N 111 41W
Paz → 120 13 44N 90 10W
Paz, Bahía de la 120 24 15N 110 25W
Paz, La, Entre Ríos, Argent. 124 30 50 S 59 45W
Paz, La, San Luis, Argent. 124 33 30 S 67 20W
Paz, La, Boliv. 126 16 20 S 68 10W
Paz, La, Hond. 120 14 20N 87 47W
Paz, La, Mexico 120 24 10N 110 20W
Pazar 64 41 10N 40 50 E
Pazardzhik 43 42 12N 24 20 E
Pazin 39 45 14N 13 56 E
Pčinja → 42 41 50N 21 45 E
Pe Ell 118 46 30N 123 18W
Peabody 113 42 31N 70 56W
Peace → 108 59 0N 111 25W
Peace Point 108 59 7N 112 27W
Peace River 108 56 15N 117 18W
Peach Springs 119 35 36N 113 30W
Peak Downs 98 22 14 S 148 0 E
Peak Hill 99 32 47 S 148 11 E
Peak Range 97 22 50 S 148 20 E
Peak, The 12 53 24N 1 53W
Peake 99 35 25 S 140 0 E
Peale Mt. 119 38 25N 109 12W
Pearce 119 31 57N 109 56W
Pearl → 117 30 23N 89 45W
Pearl Banks 70 8 45N 79 45 E
Pearl City 110 21 24N 158 0W
Pearsall 117 28 55N 99 8W
Pearse I. 108 54 52N 130 14W
Peary Land 4 82 40N 33 0W
Pease → 117 34 12N 99 7W
Pebane 91 17 10 S 38 8 E
Pebas 126 3 10 S 71 46W
Peč 42 42 40N 20 17 E
Péccioli 38 43 32N 10 43 E
Pechea 46 45 36N 27 49 E
Pechenezhin 56 48 30N 24 48 E
Pechenga 52 69 30N 31 25 E
Pechnezhskoye Vdkhr. 55 50 0N 37 10 E
Pechora → 52 68 13N 54 15 E
Pechorskaya Guba 52 68 40N 54 0 E
Pechory 54 57 48N 27 40 E
Pecica 42 46 10N 21 3 E
Pečka 42 44 18N 19 33 E
Pécora, C. 40 39 28N 8 23 E
Pecos 117 31 25N 103 35W
Pecos → 117 29 42N 102 30W
Pécs 27 46 5N 18 15 E
Peddapalli 70 18 40N 79 24 E
Peddapuram 70 17 6N 8 13 E
Pedra Azul 127 16 2 S 41 17W
Pedreiras 127 4 32 S 44 40W
Pedrera, La 126 1 18 S 69 43W
Pedro Afonso 127 9 0 S 48 10W
Pedro Cays 121 17 5N 77 48W
Pedro de Valdivia 124 22 55 S 69 38W
Pedro Juan Caballero 125 22 30 S 55 40W
Pedro Miguel Locks 120 9 1N 79 36W
Pedro Muñoz 33 39 25N 2 56W
Pedrógão Grande 30 39 55N 8 9W
Peduyim 62 31 20N 34 37 E
Peebinga 99 34 52 S 140 57 E
Peebles 14 55 40N 3 12W
Peekskill 114 41 18N 73 57W
Peel 12 54 14N 4 40W
Peel →, Austral. 99 30 50 S 150 29 E
Peel →, Can. 104 67 0N 135 0W
Peene → 24 54 9N 13 46 E
Peera Peera Poolanna L. 99 26 30 S 138 0 E
Peers 108 53 40N 116 0W
Pegasus Bay 101 43 20 S 173 10 E
Peggau 26 47 12N 15 21 E
Pegnitz 25 49 45N 11 33 E
Pegnitz → 25 49 29N 10 59 E
Pego 33 38 51N 0 8W
Pegu Yoma 67 19 0N 96 0 E
Pehčevo 42 41 41N 22 55 E
Pehuajó 124 35 45 S 62 0W
Peine, Chile 124 23 45 S 68 8W
Peine, Ger. 24 52 19N 10 12 E
Peip'ing = Beijing 76 39 55N 116 20 E
Peiss 25 47 58N 11 47 E
Peissenberg 25 47 48N 11 4 E
Peitz 24 51 50N 14 23 E
Peixe 127 12 0 S 48 40W
Pek → 42 44 45N 21 29 E
Pekalongan 73 6 53 S 109 40 E
Pekan 71 3 30N 103 25 E
Pekin 116 40 35N 89 40W
Peking = Beijing 76 39 55N 116 20 E
Pelabuhan Ratu, Teluk 73 7 5 S 106 30 E
Pelabuhanratu 73 7 0 S 106 32 E
Pélagos 44 39 17N 24 4 E
Pelaihari 72 3 55 S 114 45 E
Pelat, Mont 21 44 16N 6 42 E
Pelczyce 28 53 3N 15 16 E
Peleaga 46 45 22N 22 55 E
Pelee I. 106 41 47N 82 40W
Pelée, Mt. 121 14 48N 61 0W
Pelee, Pt. 106 41 54N 82 31W
Pelekech, mt. 90 3 52N 35 8 E
Peleng 73 1 20 S 123 30 E
Pelham 115 31 5N 84 6W
Pelhřimov 26 49 24N 15 12 E
Pelican L. 109 52 28N 100 20W
Pelican Narrows 109 55 10N 102 56W
Pelican Portage 108 55 51N 112 35W
Pelican Rapids 109 52 45N 100 42W
Peljesac 42 42 55N 17 25 E
Pelkosenniemi 50 67 6N 27 28 E
Pella, Greece 44 40 46N 22 23 E
Pella, U.S.A. 116 41 30N 93 0W
Pélla □ 44 40 52N 22 0 E
Péllaro 41 38 1N 15 40 E
Pellworm 24 54 30N 8 40 E
Pelly → 104 62 47N 137 19W
Pelly Bay 105 68 38N 89 50W
Pelly L. 104 66 0N 102 0W
Peloponnes = Pelóponnisos □ 45 37 10N 22 0 E
Pelóponnisos □ 45 37 10N 22 0 E
Peloritani, Monti 41 38 2N 15 25 E
Peloro, C. 41 38 15N 15 40 E
Pelorus Sound 101 40 59 S 173 59 E
Pelotas 125 31 42 S 52 23W
Pelòvo 43 43 26N 24 17 E
Pelvoux, Massif de 21 44 52N 6 20 E
Pemalang 73 6 53 S 109 23 E
Pematang 72 0 12 S 102 4 E
Pematangsiantar 72 2 57N 99 5 E
Pemba, Mozam. 91 12 58 S 40 30 E
Pemba, Tanz. 90 5 0 S 39 45 E
Pemba, Zambia 91 16 30 S 27 28 E
Pemba Channel 90 5 0 S 39 37 E
Pemberton, Austral. 96 34 30 S 116 0 E
Pemberton, Can. 108 50 25N 122 50W
Pembina 109 48 58N 97 15W
Pembina → 109 49 0N 98 12W
Pembine 114 45 38N 87 59W
Pembino 116 48 58N 97 15W
Pembroke, Can. 106 45 50N 77 7W
Pembroke, U.K. 13 51 41N 4 57W
Pembroke, U.S.A. 115 32 5N 81 32W
Pen-y-Ghent 12 54 10N 2 15W
Peña de Francia, Sierra de 30 40 32N 6 10W
Peña, Sierra de la 32 42 32N 0 45W
Penafiel 30 41 12N 8 17W
Peñafiel 30 41 35N 4 7W
Peñaflor 31 37 43N 5 21W
Peñalara, Pico 30 40 51N 3 57W
Penamacôr 30 40 10N 7 10W
Penang = Pinang 71 5 25N 100 15 E
Penápolis 125 21 30 S 50 0W
Peñaranda de Bracamonte 30 40 53N 5 13W
Peñarroya-Pueblonuevo 31 38 19N 5 16W
Peñas, C. de 30 43 42N 5 52W
Peñas de San Pedro 33 38 44N 2 0W
Penas, G. de 128 47 0 S 75 0W
Peñausende 30 41 17N 5 52W
Pench'i = Benxi 76 41 20N 123 48 E
Pend Oreille → 118 49 4N 117 37W
Pend Oreille, L. 118 48 0N 116 30W
Pendálofon 44 40 14N 21 12 E
Pendelikón 45 38 10N 23 53 E
Pendembu 84 9 7N 12 14W
Pendleton 118 45 35N 118 50W
Penedo 127 10 15 S 36 36W
Penetanguishene 106 44 50N 79 55W
Pengalengan 73 7 9 S 107 30 E
Penge, Kasai Oriental, Congo 90 5 30 S 24 33 E
Penge, Kivu, Congo 90 4 27 S 28 25 E
Penglai 76 37 48N 120 42 E
Pengshui 77 29 17N 108 12 E
Penguin 99 41 8 S 146 6 E
Penhalonga 91 18 52 S 32 40 E
Peniche 31 39 19N 9 22W
Penicuik 14 55 50N 3 14W
Penida 72 8 45 S 115 30 E
Peñíscola 32 40 22N 0 24 E
Penmarch 18 47 49N 4 21W
Penmarch, Pte. de 18 47 48N 4 22W
Pennabilli 39 43 50N 12 17 E
Pennant 109 50 32N 108 14W
Penne 39 42 28N 13 56 E

Pennel Glacier **5** 69 20S 157 27 E
Penner → **70** 14 35N 80 10 E
Pennine, Alpi **38** 46 4N 7 30 E
Pennines **12** 54 50N 2 20W
Pennino, Mte. **39** 43 6N 12 54 E
Pennsylvania □ **114** 40 50N 78 0W
Penny **108** 53 51N 121 20W
Pennyan **114** 42 39N 77 7W
Peno **54** 57 2N 32 49 E
Penola **97** 37 25S 140 21 E
Penong **96** 31 59S 133 5 E
Penonomé **121** 8 31N 80 21W
Penrhyn Is. **95** 9 0S 158 30W
Penrith, Austral. **97** 33 43S 150 38 E
Penrith, U.K. **12** 54 40N 2 45W
Pensacola **115** 30 30N 87 10W
Pensacola Mts. **5** 84 0S 40 0W
Pense **109** 50 25N 104 59W
Penshurst **99** 37 49S 142 20 E
Penticton **108** 49 30N 119 38W
Pentland **97** 20 32S 145 25 E
Pentland Firth **14** 58 43N 3 10W
Pentland Hills **14** 55 48N 3 25W
Penukonda **70** 14 5N 77 38 E
Penylan L. **109** 61 50N 106 20W
Penza **55** 53 15N 45 5 E
Penzance **13** 50 7N 5 32W
Penzberg **25** 47 46N 11 23 E
Penzhino **59** 63 30N 167 55 E
Penzhinskaya Guba **59** 61 30N 163 0 E
Penzlin **24** 53 32N 13 6 E
Peoria, Ariz., U.S.A. **119** 33 40N 112 15W
Peoria, Ill., U.S.A. **116** 40 40N 89 40W
Pepperwood **118** 40 23N 124 0W
Peqini **44** 41 4N 19 44 E
Pera Hd. **98** 12 55S 141 37 E
Perabumilih **72** 3 27S 104 15 E
Perak → **71** 5 10N 101 4 E
Perakhóra **45** 38 2N 22 56 E
Perales de Alfambra **32** 40 38N 1 0W
Perales del Puerto **30** 40 10N 6 40W
Peralta **32** 42 21N 1 49W
Pérama **45** 35 20N 24 40 E
Perast **42** 42 31N 18 47 E
Percé **107** 48 31N 64 13W
Perche **18** 48 31N 1 1 E
Perche, Collines du **18** 48 30N 0 40 E
Percy **18** 48 55N 1 11W
Percy Is. **98** 21 39S 150 16 E
Pereira **126** 4 49N 75 43W
Perekerten **99** 34 55S 143 40 E
Perekop **56** 46 10N 33 42 E
Pereslavi-Zalesskiy **55** 56 45N 38 50 E
Pereyaslav Khmelnitskiy **54** 50 3N 31 28 E
Pérez, I. **120** 22 24N 89 42W
Perg **26** 48 15N 14 38 E
Pergamino **124** 33 52S 60 30W
Pérgine Valsugano **39** 46 4N 11 15 E
Pérgola **39** 43 35N 12 50 E
Perham **116** 46 36N 95 36W
Perhentian, Kepulauan **71** 5 54N 102 42 E
Periam **42** 46 2N 20 59 E
Péribonca → **107** 48 45N 72 5W
Péribonca, L. **107** 50 1N 71 10W
Perico **124** 24 20S 65 5W
Pericos **120** 25 3N 107 42W
Périers **18** 49 11N 1 25W
Périgord **20** 45 0N 0 40 E
Périgueux **20** 45 10N 0 42 E
Perijá, Sierra de **126** 9 30N 73 3W
Peristéra **45** 39 15N 23 58 E
Periyakulam **70** 10 5N 77 30 E
Periyar → **70** 10 15N 76 10 E
Periyar, L. **70** 9 25N 77 10 E
Perkam, Tg. **73** 1 35S 137 50 E
Perković **39** 43 41N 16 10 E
Perlas, Arch. de las **121** 8 41N 79 7W
Perlas, Punta de **121** 12 30N 83 30W
Perleberg **24** 53 5N 11 50 E
Perlevka **55** 51 48N 38 57 E
Perlez **42** 45 11N 20 22 E
Perlis □ **71** 6 30N 100 15 E
Perm (Molotov) **52** 58 0N 57 10 E
Përmeti **44** 40 15N 20 21 E
Pernambuco = Recife **127** 8 0S 35 0W
Pernambuco □ **127** 8 0S 37 0W
Pernik **42** 42 35N 23 2 E
Péronne **19** 49 55N 2 57 E
Perosa Argentina **38** 44 57N 7 11 E
Perow **108** 54 35N 126 10W
Perpendicular Pt. **99** 31 37S 152 52 E
Perpignan **20** 42 42N 2 53 E
Perros-Guirec **18** 48 49N 3 28W
Perry, Fla., U.S.A. **115** 30 9N 83 40W
Perry, Ga., U.S.A. **115** 32 25N 83 41W
Perry, Iowa, U.S.A. **116** 41 48N 94 5W
Perry, Maine, U.S.A. **115** 44 59N 67 20W
Perry, Okla., U.S.A. **117** 36 20N 97 20W
Perryton **117** 36 28N 100 48W
Perryville **117** 37 42N 89 50W
Persberg **48** 59 47N 14 15 E
Persepolis **65** 29 55N 52 50 E
Persia = Iran ■ **65** 35 0N 50 0 E
Persian Gulf **65** 27 0N 50 0 E
Perstorp **49** 56 10N 13 25 E
Perth, Austral. **96** 31 57S 115 52 E
Perth, Can. **106** 44 55N 76 15W
Perth, U.K. **14** 56 24N 3 27W
Perth Amboy **114** 40 31N 74 16W
Perthus, Le **20** 42 30N 2 53 E
Pertuis **21** 43 42N 5 30 E
Peru, Ill., U.S.A. **116** 41 18N 89 12W
Peru, Ind., U.S.A. **114** 40 42N 86 0W
Peru ■ **126** 8 0S 75 0W
Peru-Chile Trench **95** 20 0S 72 0W
Perúgia **39** 43 6N 12 24 E
Perušić **39** 44 40N 15 22 E
Pervomaysk, R.S.F.S.R., U.S.S.R. **55** 54 56N 43 58 E
Pervomaysk, Ukraine S.S.R., U.S.S.R. **56** 48 10N 30 46 E
Pervouralsk **52** 56 55N 60 0 E
Pésaro **39** 43 55N 12 53 E
Pescara **39** 42 28N 14 13 E
Pescara → **39** 42 28N 14 13 E
Peschanokopskoye **57** 46 14N 41 4 E
Pèscia **38** 43 54N 10 40 E
Pescina **39** 42 0N 13 39 E
Peshawar **66** 34 2N 71 37 E
Peshawar □ **66** 33 30N 71 20 E
Peshkopia **44** 41 41N 20 25 E
Peshtera **43** 42 2N 24 18 E
Peshtigo **114** 45 4N 87 46W
Peski **55** 51 14N 42 29 E
Peskovka **55** 59 23N 52 20 E
Pêso da Régua **30** 41 10N 7 47W
Pesqueira **127** 8 20S 36 42W
Pesqueria → **120** 25 54N 99 11W
Pessac **20** 44 48N 0 37W
Pest □ **27** 47 29N 19 5 E
Pestovo **54** 58 33N 35 42 E
Pestravka **55** 52 28N 49 57 E
Péta **45** 39 10N 21 2 E
Petah Tiqwa **62** 32 6N 34 53 E
Petalídhion **45** 36 57N 21 55 E
Petaling Jaya **71** 3 4N 101 42 E
Petaluma **118** 38 13N 122 39W
Petange **16** 49 33N 5 55 E
Petatlán **120** 17 31N 101 16W
Petauke **91** 14 14S 31 20 E
Petawawa **106** 45 54N 77 17W
Petén Itzá, Lago **120** 16 58N 89 50W
Peter 1st, I. **5** 69 0S 91 0W
Peter Pond L. **109** 55 55N 108 44W
Peterbell **106** 48 36N 83 21W
Peterborough, Austral. **97** 32 58S 138 51 E
Peterborough, Can. **112** 44 20N 78 20W
Peterborough, U.K. **13** 52 35N 0 14W
Peterborough, U.S.A. **113** 42 55N 71 59W
Peterhead **14** 57 30N 1 49W
Petersburg, Alas., U.S.A. **108** 56 50N 133 0W
Petersburg, Ind., U.S.A. **114** 38 30N 87 15W
Petersburg, Va., U.S.A. **114** 37 17N 77 26W
Petersburg, W. Va., U.S.A. **114** 38 59N 79 10W
Petford **98** 17 20S 144 58 E
Petília Policastro **41** 39 7N 16 48 E
Petit Bois I. **115** 30 16N 88 25W
Petit-Cap **107** 48 3N 64 30W
Petit Goâve **121** 18 27N 72 51W
Petit-Quevilly, Le **18** 49 26N 1 0 E
Petit Saint Bernard, Col du **38** 45 40N 6 52 E
Petitcodiac **107** 45 57N 65 11W
Petite Baleine → **106** 55 50N 77 0W
Petite Saguenay **107** 48 15N 70 4W
Petitsikapau, L. **107** 54 37N 66 25W
Petlad **68** 22 30N 72 45 E
Peto **120** 20 10N 88 53W
Petone **101** 41 13S 174 53 E
Petoskey **106** 45 22N 84 57W
Petra, Jordan **62** 30 20N 35 22 E
Petra, Spain **32** 39 37N 3 6 E
Petra, Ostrova **4** 76 15N 118 30 E
Petralia **41** 37 49N 14 4 E
Petrel **33** 38 30N 0 46W
Petrich **43** 41 24N 23 13 E
Petrijanec **39** 46 23N 16 17 E
Petrikov **54** 52 11N 28 29 E
Petrila **46** 45 29N 23 29 E
Petrinja **39** 45 28N 16 18 E
Petrolândia **127** 9 5S 38 20W
Petrolia **106** 42 54N 82 9W
Petrolina **127** 9 24S 40 30W
Petromagoúla **45** 38 31N 23 0 E
Petropavlovsk **58** 54 53N 69 13 E
Petropavlovsk-Kamchatskiy **59** 53 3N 158 43 E
Petrópolis **125** 22 33S 43 9W
Petroşeni **46** 45 28N 23 20 E
Petroskey **114** 45 22N 84 57W
Petrova Gora **39** 45 15N 15 45 E
Petrovac, Crna Gora, Yugo. **42** 42 13N 18 57 E
Petrovac, Srbija, Yugo. **42** 44 22N 21 26 E
Petrovaradin **42** 45 16N 19 55 E
Petrovsk **55** 52 22N 45 19 E
Petrovsk-Zabaykalskiy **59** 51 20N 108 55 E
Petrovskoye = Svetlograd **57** 45 25N 42 58 E
Petrozavodsk **52** 61 41N 34 20 E
Petrus Steyn **93** 27 38S 28 8 E
Petrusburg **92** 29 4S 25 26 E
Petukhovka **54** 53 42N 30 54 E
Peumo **124** 34 21S 71 12W
Peureulak **72** 4 48N 97 45 E
Pevek **59** 69 41N 171 19 E
Peveragno **38** 44 20N 7 37 E
Peyrehorade **20** 43 34N 1 7W
Peyruis **21** 44 1N 5 56 E
Pézenas **20** 43 28N 3 24 E
Pezinok **27** 48 17N 17 17 E
Pfaffenhofen **25** 48 31N 11 31 E
Pfarrkirchen **25** 48 25N 12 57 E
Pfeffenhausen **25** 48 40N 11 58 E
Pforzheim **25** 48 53N 8 43 E
Pfullendorf **25** 47 55N 9 15 E
Pfungstadt **25** 49 47N 8 36 E
Phala **92** 23 45S 26 50 E
Phalodi **68** 27 12N 72 24 E
Phalsbourg **19** 48 46N 7 15 E
Phan Rang **71** 11 34N 109 0 E
Phan Thiet **71** 11 1N 108 9 E
Phanae **45** 38 8N 25 87 E
Phangan, Ko **71** 9 45N 100 0 E
Phangnga **71** 8 28N 98 30 E
Phanh Bho Ho Chi Minh **71** 10 58N 106 40 E
Pharenda **69** 27 5N 83 17 E
Phatthalung **71** 7 39N 100 6 E
Phelps, N.Y., U.S.A. **112** 42 57N 77 5W
Phelps, Wis., U.S.A. **116** 46 2N 89 2W
Phelps L. **109** 59 15N 103 15W
Phenix City **115** 32 30N 85 0W
Phetchabun **71** 16 25N 101 8 E
Phetchabun, Thiu Khao **71** 16 0N 101 20 E
Phetchaburi **71** 13 1N 99 55 E
Phichai **71** 17 22N 100 10 E
Philadelphia, Miss., U.S.A. **117** 32 47N 89 5W
Philadelphia, N.Y., U.S.A. **113** 44 9N 75 40W
Philadelphia, Pa., U.S.A. **114** 40 0N 75 10W
Philip **116** 44 4N 101 42W
Philippeville **16** 50 12N 4 33 E
Philippi **44** 41 1N 24 16 E
Philippi L. **98** 24 20S 138 55 E
Philippines ■ **73** 12 0N 123 0 E
Philippolis **92** 30 15S 25 16 E
Philippopolis = Plovdiv **43** 42 8N 24 44 E
Philipsburg, Mont., U.S.A. **118** 46 20N 113 21W
Philipsburg, Pa., U.S.A. **112** 40 53N 78 10W
Philipstown **92** 30 28S 24 30 E
Phillip **97** 38 30S 145 12 E
Phillips, Texas, U.S.A. **117** 35 48N 101 17W
Phillips, Wis., U.S.A. **116** 45 41N 90 22W
Phillipsburg, Kans., U.S.A. **116** 39 48N 99 20W
Phillipsburg, Pa., U.S.A. **113** 40 43N 75 12W
Phillott **99** 27 53S 145 50 E
Philmont **113** 42 14N 73 37W
Philomath **118** 44 28N 123 21W
Phitsanulok **71** 16 50N 100 12 E
Phnom Dangrek **71** 14 20N 104 0 E
Phnom Penh **71** 11 33N 104 55 E
Phnom Thbeng **71** 13 50N 104 56 E
Phoenix, Ariz., U.S.A. **119** 33 30N 112 10W
Phoenix, N.Y., U.S.A. **113** 43 13N 76 18W
Phoenix Is. **94** 3 30S 172 0W
Phoenixville **113** 40 12N 75 29W
Phong Saly **71** 21 42N 102 9 E
Phra Chedi Sam Ong **71** 15 16N 98 23 E
Phra Nakhon Si Ayutthaya **71** 14 25N 100 30 E
Phrae **71** 18 7N 100 9 E
Phrao **71** 19 23N 99 15 E
Phu Doan **71** 21 40N 105 10 E
Phu Loi **71** 20 14N 103 14 E
Phu Ly **71** 20 35N 105 50 E
Phu Qui **71** 19 20N 105 20 E
Phuket **71** 7 52N 98 22 E
Phulera (Phalera) **68** 26 52N 75 16 E
Phuoc Le (Baria) **71** 10 30N 107 10 E
Piacenza **38** 45 2N 9 42 E
Piádena **38** 45 8N 10 22 E
Pialba **97** 25 20S 152 45 E
Pian Cr. → **99** 30 2S 148 12 E
Piana **21** 42 15N 8 34 E
Pianella **39** 42 24N 14 5 E
Pianoro **39** 44 20N 11 20 E
Pianosa, Puglia, Italy **39** 42 12N 15 44 E
Pianosa, Toscana, Italy **38** 42 36N 10 4 E
Piapot **109** 49 59N 109 8W
Piare → **39** 45 32N 12 44 E
Pias **31** 38 1N 7 29W
Piaseczno **28** 52 5N 21 2 E
Piaski **28** 51 8N 22 52 E
Piastów **28** 52 12N 20 48 E
Piatra **46** 43 51N 25 9 E
Piatra Neamţ **46** 46 56N 26 21 E
Piatra Olt **46** 44 22N 24 16 E
Piauí □ **127** 7 0S 43 0W
Piave → **39** 45 32N 12 44 E
Piazza Ármerina **41** 37 21N 14 20 E
Pibor → **87** 7 35N 33 0 E
Pibor Post **87** 6 47N 33 3 E
Pica **126** 20 35S 69 25W
Picardie **19** 50 0N 2 15 E
Picardie, Plaine de **19** 50 0N 2 0 E
Picardy = Picardie **19** 50 0N 2 15 E
Picayune **117** 30 31N 89 40W
Picerno **41** 40 40N 15 37 E
Pichilemu **124** 34 22S 72 0W
Pickerel L. **106** 48 40N 91 25W
Pickle Lake **106** 51 30N 90 12W
Pico **8** 38 28N 28 18W
Pico Truncado **128** 46 40S 68 0W
Picos Ancares, Sierra de **30** 42 51N 6 52W
Picquigny **19** 49 56N 2 10 E
Picton, Austral. **99** 34 12S 150 34 E
Picton, Can. **106** 44 1N 77 9W
Picton, N.Z. **101** 41 18S 174 3 E
Pictou **107** 45 41N 62 42W
Picture Butte **108** 49 55N 112 45W
Picún Leufú **128** 39 30S 69 5W
Pidurutalagala **70** 7 10N 80 50 E
Piedad, La **120** 20 20N 102 1W
Piedicavallo **38** 45 41N 7 57 E
Piedmont **115** 33 55N 85 39W
Piedmont = Piemonte **38** 45 0N 7 30 E
Piedmont Plat. **115** 34 0N 81 30W
Piedmonte d'Alife **41** 41 22N 14 22 E
Piedra → **32** 41 18N 1 47W
Piedrabuena **31** 39 0N 4 10W
Piedrahita **30** 40 28N 5 23W
Piedras Blancas Pt. **119** 35 45N 121 18W
Piedras Negras **120** 28 35N 100 35W
Piedras, R. de las → **126** 12 30S 69 15W
Piemonte □ **38** 45 0N 7 30 E
Piensk **28** 51 16N 15 2 E
Pierce **118** 46 29N 115 53W
Piercefield **113** 44 13N 74 35W
Piería □ **44** 40 13N 22 25 E
Pierre, France **19** 46 54N 5 13 E
Pierre, U.S.A. **116** 44 23N 100 20W
Pierre Benite, Barrage **21** 45 42N 4 49 E
Pierrefeu **21** 43 8N 6 9 E
Pierrefonds **19** 49 20N 3 0 E
Pierrefontaine **19** 47 14N 6 32 E
Pierrefort **20** 44 55N 2 50 E
Pierrelatte **21** 44 23N 4 43 E
Piešťany **27** 48 38N 17 55 E
Piesting → **27** 48 6N 16 40 E
Pieszyce **28** 50 43N 16 33 E
Piet Retief **93** 27 1S 30 50 E
Pietarsaari **50** 63 40N 22 43 E
Pietermaritzburg **93** 29 35S 30 25 E
Pietersburg **93** 23 54S 29 25 E
Pietraperzia **41** 37 26N 14 8 E
Pietrasanta **38** 43 57N 10 12 E
Pietrosu **46** 47 12N 25 8 E
Pietrosul **46** 47 35N 24 43 E
Pieve di Cadore **39** 46 25N 12 22 E
Pieve di Teco **38** 44 3N 7 54 E
Pievepélago **38** 44 12N 10 35 E
Pigádhia **45** 35 30N 27 12 E
Pigadhítsa **44** 39 59N 21 23 E
Pigeon **114** 43 50N 83 17W
Pigeon I. **70** 14 2N 74 20 E
Piggott **117** 36 20N 90 10W
Pigna **38** 43 57N 7 40 E
Pigüe **124** 37 36S 62 25W
Pihani **69** 27 36N 80 15 E
Pikalevo **54** 59 37N 34 0 E
Pikes Peak **116** 38 50N 105 10W
Piketberg **92** 32 55S 18 40 E
Pikeville **114** 37 30N 82 30W
Pikwitonei **109** 55 35N 97 9W
Piła **28** 53 10N 16 48 E
Pila **33** 38 16N 1 11W
Piła □ **28** 53 0N 17 0 E
Pilaía **44** 40 32N 22 59 E
Pilani **68** 28 22N 75 33 E
Pilar, Brazil **127** 9 36S 35 56W
Pilar, Parag. **124** 26 50S 58 20W
Pilas **73** 6 39N 121 37 E
Pilawa **28** 51 57N 21 32 E
Pilbara **96** 21 15S 118 16 E
Pilcomayo → **124** 25 21S 57 42W
Pili **45** 36 50N 27 15 E
Pilibhit **69** 28 40N 79 50 E
Pilica → **28** 51 52N 21 17 E
Pilion **44** 39 27N 23 7 E
Pilis **27** 47 17N 19 35 E
Pilisvörösvár **27** 47 38N 18 56 E
Pilkhawa **68** 28 43N 77 42 E
Pílos **45** 36 55N 21 42 E
Pilot Mound **109** 49 15N 98 54W
Pilot Point **117** 33 26N 97 0W
Pilot Rock **118** 45 30N 118 50W
Pilsen = Plzen **26** 49 45N 13 22 E
Pilštanj **39** 46 8N 15 39 E
Pilzno **27** 50 0N 21 16 E
Pima **119** 32 54N 109 50W
Pimba **97** 31 18S 136 46 E
Pimenta Bueno **126** 11 35S 61 10W
Pimentel **126** 6 45S 79 55W
Pina **32** 41 29N 0 33W
Pinang **71** 5 25N 100 15 E
Pinar del Río **121** 22 26N 83 40W
Pinaroo **97** 35 17S 140 53 E
Pincehely **27** 46 41N 18 27 E
Pincher Creek **108** 49 30N 113 57W
Pinchi L. **108** 54 38N 124 30W
Pinckneyville **116** 38 5N 89 20W
Pîncota **42** 46 20N 21 45 E
Pińczów **28** 50 32N 20 32 E
Pind Dadan Khan **68** 32 36N 73 7 E
Pindiga **85** 9 58N 10 53 E
Pindos Óros **44** 40 0N 21 0 E
Pindus Mts. = Pindos Óros **44** 40 0N 21 0 E
Pine **119** 34 27N 111 30W
Pine → **109** 58 50N 105 38W
Pine Bluff **117** 34 10N 92 0W
Pine, C. **107** 46 37N 53 32W
Pine City **116** 45 46N 93 0W
Pine Creek **96** 13 50S 132 10 E
Pine Falls **109** 50 34N 96 11W
Pine, La **118** 43 40N 121 30W
Pine Pass **108** 55 25N 122 42W
Pine Point **108** 60 50N 114 28W
Pine Ridge **116** 43 0N 102 35W
Pine River, Can. **109** 51 45N 100 30W
Pine River, U.S.A. **116** 46 43N 94 24W
Pinedale **119** 34 23N 110 16W
Pinega → **52** 64 8N 46 54 E
Pinehill **98** 23 38S 146 57 E
Pinerolo **38** 44 47N 7 21 E
Pineto **39** 42 36N 14 4 E
Pinetop **119** 34 10N 109 57W
Pinetown **93** 29 48S 30 54 E
Pinetree **118** 43 42N 105 52W
Pineville, Ky., U.S.A. **115** 36 42N 83 42W
Pineville, La., U.S.A. **117** 31 22N 92 30W
Piney **19** 48 22N 4 21 E
Ping → **71** 15 42N 100 9 E
Pingding **76** 37 47N 113 38 E
Pingdingshan **77** 33 43N 113 27 E
Pingdong **75** 22 39N 120 30 E
Pingdu **76** 36 42N 119 59 E
Pingguo **77** 23 19N 107 36 E
Pinghe **77** 24 17N 117 21 E
Pingjiang **77** 28 45N 113 36 E
Pingle **77** 24 40N 110 40 E
Pingliang **76** 35 35N 106 31 E
Pingluo **76** 38 52N 106 30 E
Pingnan **77** 23 33N 110 22 E
Pingtan Dao **77** 25 29N 119 47 E
Pingwu **75** 32 25N 104 30 E
Pingxiang, Guangxi Zhuangzu, China **75** 22 6N 106 46 E
Pingxiang, Jiangxi, China **77** 27 43N 113 48 E
Pingyao **76** 37 12N 112 10 E
Pinhal **125** 22 10S 46 46W
Pinhel **30** 40 50N 7 1W
Pini **72** 0 10N 98 40 E
Piniós →, Ilia, Greece **45** 37 48N 21 20 E
Piniós →, Trikkala, Greece **44** 39 55N 22 10 E
Pinjarra **96** 32 37S 115 52 E
Pink → **109** 56 50N 103 50W
Pinkafeld **27** 47 22N 16 9 E
Pinneberg **24** 53 39N 9 48 E
Pinos **120** 22 20N 101 40W
Pinos, I. de **121** 21 40N 82 40W
Pinos Pt. **119** 36 38N 121 57W
Pinos Puente **31** 37 15N 3 45W
Pinrang **73** 3 46S 119 41 E
Pinsk **54** 52 10N 26 1 E
Pintados **126** 20 35S 69 40W
Pinyang **77** 27 42N 120 31 E
Pinyug **52** 60 5N 48 0 E
Pinzolo **38** 46 9N 10 45 E
Pioche **119** 38 0N 114 35W
Piombino **38** 42 54N 10 30 E
Piombino, Canale di **38** 42 50N 10 25 E
Pioner, Os. **59** 79 50N 92 0 E
Pionki **28** 51 29N 21 28 E
Piorini, L. **126** 3 15S 62 35W

Piotrków Trybunalski 28 51 23N 19 43 E
Piotrków Trybunalski □ 28 51 30N 19 45 E
Piove di Sacco 39 45 18N 12 1 E
Pip 65 26 45N 60 10 E
Pipar 68 26 25N 73 31 E
Pipariya 68 22 45N 78 23 E
Pipéri 44 39 20N 24 19 E
Pipestone 116 44 0N 96 20W
Pipestone → 106 52 53N 89 23W
Pipestone Cr. → 109 49 42N 100 45W
Pipmuacan, Rés. 107 49 45N 70 30W
Pipriac 18 47 49N 1 58W
Piqua 114 40 10N 84 10W
Piquiri → 125 24 3 S 54 14W
Piracicaba 125 22 45 S 47 40W
Piracuruca 127 3 50 S 41 50W
Piræus = Piraiévs 45 37 57N 23 42 E
Piraiévs 45 37 57N 23 42 E
Piraiévs □ 45 37 0N 23 30 E
Piráino 41 38 10N 14 52 E
Pirajuí 125 21 59 S 49 29W
Piran (Pirano) 39 45 31N 13 33 E
Pirané 124 25 42 S 59 6W
Pirapora 127 17 20 S 44 56W
Pirdop 43 42 40N 24 10 E
Pirganj 69 25 51N 88 24 E
Pirgos, Ilía, Greece 45 37 40N 21 27 E
Pírgos, Messinia, Greece 45 36 50N 22 16 E
Pirgovo 43 43 44N 25 43 E
Piriac-sur-Mer 18 47 22N 2 33W
Piribebuy 124 25 26 S 57 2W
Pirin Planina 43 41 40N 23 30 E
Pirineos 32 42 40N 1 0 E
Piripiri 127 4 15 S 41 46W
Pirmasens 25 49 12N 7 30 E
Pirna 24 50 57N 13 57 E
Pirojpur 69 22 35N 90 1 E
Pirot 42 43 9N 22 39 E
Pirtleville 119 31 25N 109 35W
Piru 73 3 4 S 128 12 E
Piryatin 54 50 15N 32 25 E
Piryí 45 38 13N 25 59 E
Pisa 38 43 43N 10 23 E
Pisa → 28 53 14N 21 52 E
Pisagua 126 19 40 S 70 15W
Pisarovina 39 45 35N 15 50 E
Pisciotta 41 40 7N 15 12 E
Pisco 126 13 50 S 76 12W
Piscu 46 45 30N 27 43 E
Písek 26 49 19N 14 10 E
Pishan 75 37 30N 78 33 E
Pising 73 5 8 S 121 53 E
Pissos 20 44 19N 0 49W
Pisticci 41 40 24N 16 33 E
Pistóia 38 43 57N 10 53 E
Pistol B. 109 62 25N 92 37W
Pisuerga → 30 41 33N 4 52W
Pisz 28 53 38N 21 49 E
Pitarpunga, L. 99 34 24 S 143 30 E
Pitcairn I. 95 25 5 S 130 5W
Pite älv → 50 65 20N 21 25 E
Piteå 50 65 20N 21 25 E
Piterka 55 50 41N 47 29 E
Piteşti 46 44 52N 24 54 E
Pithapuram 70 17 10N 82 15 E
Píthion 44 41 24N 26 40 E
Pithiviers 19 48 10N 2 13 E
Pitigliano 39 42 38N 11 40 E
Pitlochry 14 56 43N 3 43W
Pitt I. 108 53 30N 129 50W
Pittsburg, Calif., U.S.A. 118 38 1N 121 50W
Pittsburg, Kans., U.S.A. 117 37 21N 94 43W
Pittsburg, Tex., U.S.A. 117 32 59N 94 58W
Pittsburgh 114 40 25N 79 55W
Pittsfield, Ill., U.S.A. 116 39 35N 90 46W
Pittsfield, Mass., U.S.A. 114 42 28N 73 17W
Pittsfield, N.H., U.S.A. 113 43 17N 71 18W
Pittston 114 41 19N 75 50W
Pittsworth 99 27 41 S 151 37 E
Pituri → 98 22 35 S 138 30 E
Piura 126 5 15 S 80 38W
Piva → 42 43 20N 18 50 E
Piwniczna 27 49 27N 20 42 E
Piyai 44 39 17N 21 25 E
Pizzo 41 38 44N 16 10 E
Placentia 107 47 20N 54 0W
Placentia B. 107 47 0N 54 40W
Placerville 118 38 47N 120 51W
Placetas 121 22 15N 79 44W
Plačkovica 42 41 45N 22 30 E
Plain Dealing 117 32 56N 93 41W
Plainfield 114 40 37N 74 28W
Plains, Kans., U.S.A. 117 37 20N 100 35W
Plains, Mont., U.S.A. 118 47 27N 114 57W
Plains, Tex., U.S.A. 117 33 11N 102 50W
Plainview, Nebr., U.S.A. 116 42 25N 97 48W
Plainview, Tex., U.S.A. 117 34 10N 101 40W
Plainville 116 39 18N 99 19W
Plainwell 114 42 28N 85 40W
Plaisance 20 43 36N 0 3 E
Pláka 44 40 0N 25 24 E
Plakenska Planina 42 41 14N 21 2 E
Plakhino 58 67 45N 86 5 E
Planá 26 49 50N 12 44 E
Plancoët 18 48 32N 2 13W
Plandište 42 45 16N 21 10 E
Planina, Slovenija, Yugo. 39 46 10N 15 20 E
Planina, Slovenija, Yugo. 39 45 47N 14 19 E
Plankinton 116 43 45N 98 27W
Plano 117 33 0N 96 45W
Plant City 115 28 0N 82 8W
Plant, La 116 45 11N 100 40W
Plaquemine 117 30 20N 91 15W
Plasencia 30 40 3N 6 8W
Plaški 39 45 4N 15 22 E
Plassen 48 61 9N 12 30 E
Plaster Rock 107 46 53N 67 22W
Plata, La 124 35 0 S 57 55W
Plata, Río de la 124 34 45 S 57 30W
Platani → 40 37 23N 13 16 E
Plateau 5 79 55 S 40 0 E
Plateau □ 85 8 0N 8 30 E
Plateau du Coteau du Missouri 116 47 9N 101 5W
Platí, Ákra- 44 40 27N 24 0 E
Plato 126 9 47N 74 47W
Platte 116 43 28N 98 50W
Platte → 116 39 16N 94 50W
Platteville 116 40 18N 104 47W
Plattling 25 48 46N 12 53 E
Plattsburg 114 44 41N 73 30W
Plattsmouth 116 41 0N 95 50W
Plau 24 53 27N 12 16 E
Plauen 24 50 29N 12 9 E
Plav 42 42 38N 19 57 E
Plavinas 54 56 35N 25 46 E
Plavnica 42 42 20N 19 13 E
Plavsk 55 53 40N 37 18 E
Playgreen L. 109 54 0N 98 15W
Pleasant Bay 107 46 51N 60 48W
Pleasant Hill 116 38 48N 94 14W
Pleasanton 117 29 0N 98 30W
Pleasantville 114 39 25N 74 30W
Pléaux 20 45 8N 2 13 E
Pleiku (Gia Lai) 71 13 57N 108 0 E
Plélan-le-Grand 18 48 0N 2 7W
Plémet 18 48 11N 2 36W
Pléneuf-Val-André 18 48 35N 2 32W
Pleniţa 46 44 14N 23 10 E
Plenty, Bay of 101 37 45 S 177 0 E
Plentywood 116 48 45N 104 35W
Plesetsk 52 62 40N 40 10 E
Plessisville 107 46 14N 71 47W
Plestin-les-Grèves 18 48 40N 3 39W
Pleszew 28 51 53N 17 47 E
Pleternica 42 45 17N 17 48 E
Pletipi L. 107 51 44N 70 6W
Pleven 43 43 26N 24 37 E
Plevlja 42 43 21N 19 21 E
Ploče 42 43 4N 17 26 E
Płock 28 52 32N 19 40 E
Płock □ 28 52 30N 19 45 E
Plöcken Passo 39 46 37N 12 57 E
Ploëmeur 18 47 44N 3 26W
Ploërmel 18 47 55N 2 26W
Ploieşti 46 44 57N 26 5 E
Plomárion 45 38 58N 26 24 E
Plomb du Cantal 20 45 2N 2 48 E
Plombières 19 47 59N 6 27 E
Plomin 39 45 8N 14 10 E
Plön 24 54 8N 10 22 E
Plöner See 24 45 10N 10 22 E
Plonge, Lac La 109 55 8N 107 20W
Płońsk 28 52 37N 20 21 E
Płoty 28 53 48N 15 18 E
Plouaret 18 48 37N 3 28W
Plouay 18 47 55N 3 21W
Ploučnice → 26 50 46N 14 13 E
Ploudalmézeau 18 48 34N 4 41W
Plougasnou 18 48 42N 3 49W
Plouha 18 48 41N 2 57W
Plouhinec 18 48 0N 4 29W
Plovdiv 43 42 8N 24 44 E
Plum I. 113 41 10N 72 12W
Plummer 118 47 21N 116 59W
Plumtree 91 20 27 S 27 55 E
Plunge 54 55 53N 21 59 E
Pluvigner 18 47 46N 3 1W
Plymouth, U.K. 13 50 23N 4 9W
Plymouth, Ind., U.S.A. 114 41 20N 86 19W
Plymouth, Mass., U.S.A. 113 41 58N 70 40W
Plymouth, N.C., U.S.A. 115 35 54N 76 46W
Plymouth, N.H., U.S.A. 113 43 44N 71 41W
Plymouth, Pa., U.S.A. 113 41 17N 76 0W
Plymouth, Wis., U.S.A. 114 43 42N 87 58W
Plymouth Sd. 13 50 20N 4 10W
Plynlimon = Pumlumon Fawr 13 52 29N 3 47W
Plyussa 54 58 40N 29 20 E
Plyussa → 54 58 40N 29 0 E
Plzen 26 49 45N 13 22 E
Pniewy 28 52 31N 16 16 E
Pô 85 11 14N 1 5W
Po → 38 44 57N 12 4 E
Po, Foci del 39 44 55N 12 30 E
Po Hai = Bo Hai 76 39 0N 120 0 E
Pobé 85 7 0N 2 56 E
Pobeda 59 65 12N 146 12 E
Pobedino 59 49 51N 142 49 E
Pobedy Pik 58 40 45N 79 58 E
Pobiedziska 28 52 29N 17 11 E
Pobla de Lillet, La 32 42 16N 1 59 E
Pobla de Segur 32 42 15N 0 58 E
Pobladura de Valle 30 42 6N 5 44W
Pocahontas, Arkansas, U.S.A. 117 36 18N 91 0W
Pocahontas, Iowa, U.S.A. 116 42 41N 94 42W
Pocatello 118 42 50N 112 25W
Počátky 26 49 15N 15 14 E
Pochep 54 52 58N 33 29 E
Pochinki 55 54 41N 44 59 E
Pochinok 54 54 28N 32 29 E
Pöchlarn 26 48 12N 15 12 E
Pochontas 108 53 10N 117 51W
Pochutla 120 15 50N 96 31W
Pocomoke City 114 38 4N 75 32W
Poços de Caldas 125 21 50 S 46 33W
Poddebice 28 51 54N 18 58 E
Poděbrady 26 50 9N 15 8 E
Podensac 20 44 40N 0 22W
Podgorač 42 45 27N 18 13 E
Podgorica = Titograd 42 42 30N 19 19 E
Podkamennaya Tunguska → 59 61 50N 90 13 E
Podlapac 39 44 37N 15 47 E
Podmokly 26 50 48N 14 10 E
Podoleni 46 46 46N 26 39 E
Podolínec 27 49 16N 20 31 E
Podolsk 55 55 25N 37 30 E
Podor 84 16 40N 15 2W
Podporozhy 52 60 55N 34 2 E
Podravska Slatina 42 45 42N 17 45 E
Podu Turcului 46 46 11N 27 25 E
Podujevo 42 42 54N 21 10 E
Poel 24 54 0N 11 25 E
Pofadder 92 29 10 S 19 22 E
Pogamasing 106 46 55N 81 50W
Poggiardo 41 40 3N 18 21 E
Poggibonsi 39 43 27N 11 8 E
Pogoanele 46 44 55N 27 0 E
Pogorzela 28 51 50N 17 12 E
Pogradeci 44 40 57N 20 37 E
Poh 73 0 46 S 122 51 E
Pohang 76 36 1N 129 23 E
Pohorelá 27 48 50N 20 2 E
Pohořelice 27 48 59N 16 31 E
Pohorje 39 46 30N 15 20 E
Poiana Mare 46 43 57N 23 5 E
Poiana Ruscăi, Munţii 46 45 45N 22 25 E
Poinsett, C. 5 65 42 S 113 18 E
Point Edward 106 43 0N 82 30W
Point Pedro 70 9 50N 80 15 E
Point Pleasant, U.S.A. 113 40 5N 74 4W
Point Pleasant, W. Va., U.S.A. 114 38 50N 82 7W
Pointe-à-la Hache 117 29 35N 89 55W
Pointe-à-Pitre 121 16 10N 61 30W
Pointe Noire 88 4 48 S 11 53 E
Poirino 38 44 55N 7 50 E
Poissy 19 48 55N 2 0 E
Poitiers 18 46 35N 0 20 E
Poitou, Plaines et Seuil du 20 46 30N 0 1W
Poix 19 49 47N 2 0 E
Poix-Terron 19 49 38N 4 38 E
Pojoaque 119 35 55N 106 0W
Pokataroo 99 29 30 S 148 36 E
Poko, Sudan 87 5 41N 31 55 E
Poko, Zaïre 90 3 7N 26 52 E
Pokrov 55 55 55N 39 7 E
Pokrovsk 59 61 29N 126 12 E
Pol 30 43 9N 7 20W
Pola de Allande 30 43 16N 6 37W
Pola de Gordón, La 30 42 51N 5 41W
Pola de Lena 30 43 10N 5 49W
Pola de Siero 30 43 24N 5 39W
Pola de Somiedo 30 43 5N 6 15W
Polacca 119 35 52N 110 25W
Polan 65 25 30N 61 10 E
Poland ■ 28 52 0N 20 0 E
Polanów 28 54 7N 16 41 E
Polar Sub-Glacial Basin 5 85 0 S 110 0 E
Polcura 124 37 17 S 71 43W
Połczyn Zdrój 28 53 47N 16 5 E
Polden Hills 13 51 7N 2 50W
Polessk 54 54 50N 21 8 E
Polevskoy 52 56 26N 60 11 E
Polewali, Sulawesi, Indon. 73 4 8 S 119 43 E
Polewali, Sulawesi, Indon. 73 3 21 S 119 23 E
Polgar 27 47 54N 21 6 E
Poli 88 8 34N 13 15 E
Políaigos 45 36 45N 24 38 E
Policastro, Golfo di 41 39 55N 15 35 E
Police 28 53 33N 14 33 E
Polička 27 49 43N 16 15 E
Polignano a Mare 41 41 0N 17 12 E
Poligny 19 46 50N 5 42 E
Políkhnitas 45 39 4N 26 10 E
Polillo Is. 73 14 56N 122 0 E
Polístena 41 38 25N 16 4 E
Políyiros 44 40 23N 23 25 E
Polk 112 41 22N 79 57W
Polkowice 28 51 29N 16 3 E
Polla 41 40 31N 15 27 E
Pollachi 70 10 35N 77 0 E
Pollensa 32 39 54N 3 1 E
Pollensa, B. de 32 39 53N 3 8 E
Pòllica 41 40 13N 15 3 E
Pollino, Mte. 41 39 54N 16 13 E
Pollock 116 45 58N 100 18W
Polna 54 58 31N 28 0 E
Polnovat 58 63 50N 65 54 E
Polo 116 42 0N 89 38W
Pologi 56 47 29N 36 15 E
Polonnoye 54 50 6N 27 30 E
Polotsk 54 55 30N 28 50 E
Polski Trŭmbesh 43 43 20N 25 38 E
Polsko Kosovo 43 43 23N 25 38 E
Polson 118 47 45N 114 12W
Poltava 56 49 35N 34 35 E
Polunochnoye 52 60 52N 60 25 E
Polur 70 12 32N 79 11 E
Polyanovgrad 43 42 39N 26 59 E
Polyarny 52 69 8N 33 20 E
Polynesia 95 10 0 S 162 0W
Pomarance 38 43 18N 10 51 E
Pomarico 41 40 31N 16 33 E
Pombal, Brazil 127 6 45 S 37 50W
Pombal, Port. 30 39 55N 8 40W
Pómbia 45 35 0N 24 51 E
Pomeroy, Ohio, U.S.A. 114 39 0N 82 0W
Pomeroy, Wash., U.S.A. 118 46 30N 117 33W
Pomona 119 34 2N 117 49W
Pomorie 43 42 32N 27 41 E
Pomoshnaya 56 48 13N 31 36 E
Pompano Beach 115 26 12N 80 6W
Pompei 41 40 45N 14 30 E
Pompey 19 48 50N 6 2 E
Pompeys Pillar 118 46 0N 108 0W
Ponape 94 6 55N 158 10 E
Ponask, L. 106 54 0N 92 41W
Ponass L. 109 52 16N 103 58W
Ponca 116 42 38N 96 41W
Ponca City 117 36 40N 97 5W
Ponce 121 18 1N 66 37W
Ponchatoula 117 30 27N 90 25W
Poncheville, L. 106 50 10N 76 55W
Poncin 21 46 6N 5 25 E
Pond Inlet 105 72 40N 77 0W
Pondicherry 70 11 59N 79 50 E
Pondoland 93 31 10 S 29 30 E
Ponds, I. of 107 53 27N 55 52W
Ponferrada 30 42 32N 6 35W
Pongo, Wadi → 87 8 42N 27 40 E
Poniatowa 28 51 11N 22 3 E
Poniec 28 51 48N 16 50 E
Ponikva 39 46 16N 15 26 E
Ponnaiyar → 70 11 50N 79 45 E
Ponnani 70 10 45N 75 59 E
Ponneri 70 13 20N 80 15 E
Ponnyadaung 67 22 0N 94 10 E
Ponoi 52 67 0N 41 0 E
Ponoi → 52 66 59N 41 17 E
Ponoka 108 52 42N 113 40W
Ponorogo 73 7 52 S 111 29 E
Pons, France 20 45 35N 0 34W
Pons, Spain 32 41 55N 1 12 E
Ponsul → 31 39 40N 7 31W
Pont-à-Mousson 19 48 54N 6 1 E
Pont-Audemer 18 49 21N 0 30 E
Pont-Aven 18 47 51N 3 47W
Pont Canavese 38 45 24N 7 33 E
Pont-de-Roide 19 47 23N 6 45 E
Pont-de-Salars 20 44 18N 2 44 E
Pont-de-Vaux 19 46 26N 4 56 E
Pont-de-Veyle 21 46 17N 4 53 E
Pont-l'Abbé 18 47 52N 4 15W
Pont-l'Évêque 18 49 18N 0 11 E
Pont-St-Esprit 21 44 16N 4 40 E
Pont-sur-Yonne 19 48 18N 3 10 E
Ponta Grossa 125 25 7 S 50 10W
Ponta Pora 125 22 20 S 55 35W
Pontacq 20 43 11N 0 8W
Pontailler 19 47 18N 5 24 E
Pontarlier 19 46 54N 6 20 E
Pontassieve 39 43 47N 11 25 E
Pontaubault 18 48 40N 1 20W
Pontaumur 20 45 52N 2 40 E
Pontcharra 21 45 26N 6 1 E
Pontchartrain, L. 117 30 12N 90 0W
Pontchâteau 18 47 25N 2 5W
Ponte da Barca 30 41 48N 8 25W
Ponte de Sor 31 39 17N 7 57W
Ponte dell 'Olio 38 44 52N 9 39 E
Ponte di Legno 38 46 15N 10 30 E
Ponte do Lima 30 41 46N 8 35W
Ponte do Pungué 91 19 30 S 34 33 E
Ponte Leccia 21 42 28N 9 13 E
Ponte Macassar 73 9 30 S 123 58 E
Ponte nell' Alpi 39 46 10N 12 18 E
Ponte Nova 125 20 25 S 42 54W
Ponte San Martino 38 45 36N 7 47 E
Ponte San Pietro 38 45 42N 9 35 E
Pontebba 39 46 30N 13 17 E
Pontecorvo 40 41 28N 13 40 E
Pontedera 38 43 40N 10 37 E
Pontefract 12 53 42N 1 19W
Ponteix 109 49 46N 107 29W
Pontelandolfo 41 41 17N 14 41 E
Pontevedra 30 42 26N 8 40W
Pontevedra □ 30 42 25N 8 39W
Pontevedra, R. de → 30 42 22N 8 45W
Pontevico 38 45 16N 10 6 E
Pontiac, Ill., U.S.A. 116 40 50N 88 40W
Pontiac, Mich., U.S.A. 114 42 40N 83 20W
Pontian Kechil 71 1 29N 103 23 E
Pontianak 72 0 3 S 109 15 E
Pontine Is. = Ponziane, Isole 40 40 55N 13 0 E
Pontine Mts. = Karadeniz D. 64 41 30N 35 0 E
Pontinia 40 41 25N 13 2 E
Pontivy 18 48 5N 3 0W
Pontoise 19 49 3N 2 5 E
Ponton → 108 58 27N 116 11W
Pontorson 18 48 34N 1 30W
Pontrémoli 38 44 22N 9 52 E
Pontrieux 18 48 42N 3 10W
Ponts-de-Cé, Les 18 47 25N 0 30W
Pontypool, Can. 112 44 6N 78 38W
Pontypool, U.K. 13 51 42N 3 1W
Pontypridd 13 51 36N 3 21W
Ponza 40 40 55N 12 57 E
Ponziane, Isole 40 40 55N 13 0 E
Poole 13 50 42N 1 58W
Pooley I. 108 52 45N 128 15W
Poona = Pune 70 18 29N 73 57 E
Poonamallee 70 13 3N 80 10 E
Pooncarie 99 33 22 S 142 31 E
Poopelloe, L. 99 31 40 S 144 0 E
Poopó, Lago de 126 18 30 S 67 35W
Popayán 126 2 27N 76 36W
Poperinge 16 50 51N 2 42 E
Popigay 59 72 1N 110 39 E
Popilta, L. 99 33 10 S 141 42 E
Popina 43 44 7N 26 57 E
Popio, L. 99 33 10 S 141 52 E
Poplar 116 48 3N 105 9W
Poplar →, Man., Can. 109 53 0N 97 19W
Poplar →, N.W.T., Can. 108 61 22N 121 52W
Poplar Bluff 117 36 45N 90 22W
Poplarville 117 30 55N 89 30W
Popocatepetl 120 19 10N 98 40W
Popokabaka 88 5 41 S 16 40 E
Pópoli 39 42 12N 13 50 E
Popondetta 98 8 48 S 148 17 E
Popovača 39 45 30N 16 41 E
Popovo 43 43 21N 26 18 E
Poprád 27 49 3N 20 18 E
Poprád → 27 49 38N 20 42 E
Porbandar 68 21 44N 69 43 E
Porcher I. 108 53 50N 130 30W
Porcuna 31 37 52N 4 11W
Porcupine →, Can. 109 59 11N 104 46W
Porcupine →, U.S.A. 104 66 35N 145 15W
Pordenone 39 45 58N 12 40 E
Pordim 43 43 23N 24 51 E
Poreč 39 45 14N 13 36 E
Poretskoye 55 55 9N 46 21 E
Pori 51 61 29N 21 48 E
Porí 45 35 58N 23 13 E
Porjus 50 66 57N 19 50 E
Porkhov 54 57 45N 29 38 E
Porkkala 51 59 59N 24 26 E
Porlamar 126 10 57N 63 51W
Porlezza 38 46 2N 9 8 E
Porma → 30 42 49N 5 28W
Pornic 18 47 7N 2 5W
Poronaysk 59 49 13N 143 0 E
Póros 45 37 30N 23 30 E
Poroshiri-Dake 74 42 41N 142 52 E
Poroszló 27 47 39N 20 40 E
Poroto Mts. 91 9 0 S 33 30 E
Porquerolles, Îles de 21 43 0N 6 13 E
Porrentruy 25 47 25N 7 6 E
Porreras 32 39 31N 3 2 E

Porretta, Passo di	38	44 2N	10 56 E
Porsangen	50	70 40N	25 40 E
Porsgrunn	47	59 10N	9 40 E
Port	19	47 43N	6 4 E
Port Adelaide	99	34 46 S	138 30 E
Port Alberni	108	49 40N	124 50W
Port Albert	100	38 42 S	146 42 E
Port Albert Victor	68	21 0N	71 30 E
Port Alfred, Can.	107	48 18N	70 53W
Port Alfred, S. Afr.	92	33 36 S	26 55 E
Port Alice	108	50 20N	127 25W
Port Allegany	114	41 49N	78 17W
Port Allen	117	30 30N	91 15W
Port Alma	98	23 38 S	150 53 E
Port Angeles	118	48 7N	123 30W
Port Antonio	121	18 10N	76 30W
Port Aransas	117	27 49N	97 4W
Port Arthur, Austral.	97	43 7 S	147 50 E
Port Arthur, U.S.A.	117	30 0N	94 0W
Port au Port B.	107	48 40N	58 50W
Port-au-Prince	121	18 40N	72 20W
Port Augusta	97	32 30 S	137 50 E
Port Augusta West	97	32 29 S	137 29 E
Port Austin	106	44 3N	82 59W
Port Bell	90	0 18N	32 35 E
Port Bergé Vaovao	93	15 33 S	47 40 E
Port Blair	71	11 40N	92 30 E
Port Blandford	107	48 20N	54 10W
Port Bolivar	117	29 20N	94 40W
Port Bou	32	42 25N	3 9 E
Port Bouët	84	5 16N	3 57W
Port Bradshaw	97	12 30 S	137 20 E
Port Broughton	99	33 37 S	137 56 E
Port Burwell	106	42 40N	80 48W
Port-Cartier	107	50 2N	66 50W
Port Chalmers	101	45 49 S	170 30 E
Port Chester	114	41 0N	73 41W
Port Clements	108	53 40N	132 10W
Port Clinton	114	41 30N	82 58W
Port Colborne	106	42 50N	79 10W
Port Coquitlam	108	49 15N	122 45W
Port Credit	112	43 33N	79 35W
Port Dalhousie	112	43 13N	79 16W
Port Darwin, Austral.	96	12 24 S	130 45 E
Port Darwin, Falk. Is.	128	51 50 S	59 0W
Port Davey	97	43 16 S	145 55 E
Port-de-Bouc	21	43 24N	4 59 E
Port-de-Paix	121	19 50N	72 50W
Port Dickson	71	2 30N	101 49 E
Port Douglas	98	16 30 S	145 30 E
Port Dover	112	42 47N	80 12W
Port Edward	108	54 12N	130 10W
Port Elgin	106	44 25N	81 25W
Port Elizabeth	92	33 58 S	25 40 E
Port Ellen	14	55 38N	6 10W
Port-en-Bessin	18	49 21N	0 45W
Port Erin	12	54 5N	4 45W
Port Etienne = Nouâdhibou	80	20 54N	17 0W
Port Fairy	97	38 22 S	142 12 E
Port Fouâd = Bûr Fuad	86	31 15N	32 20 E
Port-Gentil	88	0 40 S	8 50 E
Port Gibson	117	31 57N	91 0W
Port Glasgow	14	55 57N	4 40W
Port Harcourt	85	4 40N	7 10 E
Port Hardy	108	50 41N	127 30W
Port Harrison	105	58 25N	78 15W
Port Hawkesbury	107	45 36N	61 22W
Port Hedland	96	20 25 S	118 35 E
Port Henry	114	44 0N	73 30W
Port Hood	107	46 0N	61 32W
Port Hope	106	43 56N	78 20W
Port Huron	114	43 0N	82 28W
Port Isabel	117	26 4N	97 9W
Port Jackson	97	33 50 S	151 18 E
Port Jefferson	114	40 58N	73 5W
Port Jervis	113	41 22N	74 42W
Port-Joinville	18	46 45N	2 23W
Port Katon	57	46 52N	38 46 E
Port Kelang	71	3 0N	101 23 E
Port Kembla	99	34 52 S	150 49 E
Port-la-Nouvelle	20	43 1N	3 3 E
Port Laoise	15	53 2N	7 20W
Port Lavaca	117	28 38N	96 38W
Port-Leucate-Barcarès	20	42 53N	3 3 E
Port Lincoln	96	34 42 S	135 52 E
Port Loko	84	8 48N	12 46W
Port Louis	18	47 42N	3 22W
Port Lyautey = Kenitra	82	34 15N	6 40W
Port Macdonnell	99	38 0 S	140 48 E
Port Macquarie	97	31 25 S	152 25 E
Port Maria	121	18 25N	77 5W
Port Mellon	108	49 32N	123 31W
Port-Menier	107	49 51N	64 15W
Port Moresby	94	9 24 S	147 8 E
Port Mouton	107	43 58N	64 50W
Port Musgrave	97	11 55 S	141 50 E
Port-Navalo	18	47 34N	2 54W
Port Nelson	109	57 3N	92 36W
Port Nolloth	92	29 17 S	16 52 E
Port Nouveau-Québec (George River)	105	58 30N	65 59W
Port O'Connor	117	28 26N	96 24W
Port of Spain	121	10 40N	61 31W
Port Orchard	118	47 31N	122 38W
Port Oxford	118	42 45N	124 28W
Port Pegasus	101	47 12 S	167 41 E
Port Perry	106	44 6N	78 56W
Port Phillip B.	97	38 10 S	144 50 E
Port Pirie	97	33 10 S	138 1 E
Port Pólnocny	28	54 25N	18 42 E
Port Radium = Echo Bay	104	66 10N	117 40W
Port Renfrew	108	48 30N	124 20W
Port Rowan	106	42 40N	80 30W
Port Safaga = Bûr Safâga	86	26 43N	33 57 E
Port Said = Bûr Sa'îd	86	31 16N	32 18 E
Port St. Joe	115	29 49N	85 20W
Port St. Louis	93	13 7 S	48 48 E
Port-St-Louis-du-Rhône	21	43 23N	4 49 E
Port Sanilac	106	43 26N	82 33W
Port Saunders	107	50 40N	57 18W
Port Severn	112	44 48N	79 43W
Port Shepstone	93	30 44 S	30 28 E
Port Simpson	108	54 30N	130 20W
Port Stanley	106	42 40N	81 10W
Port Stephens	97	32 38 S	152 12 E
Port Sudan = Bûr Sûdân	86	19 32N	37 9 E
Port Talbot	13	51 35N	3 48W
Port Taufiq = Bûr Taufiq	86	29 54N	32 32 E
Port Townsend	118	48 7N	122 50W
Port-Vendres	20	42 32N	3 8 E
Port Vladimir	52	69 25N	33 6 E
Port Washington	114	43 25N	87 52W
Port Weld	71	4 50N	100 38 E
Portachuelo	126	17 10 S	63 20W
Portadown	15	54 27N	6 26W
Portage	116	43 31N	89 25W
Portage La Prairie	109	49 58N	98 18W
Portageville	117	36 25N	89 40W
Portalegre	31	39 19N	7 25W
Portalegre □	31	39 20N	7 40W
Portales	117	34 12N	103 25W
Portarlington	15	53 10N	7 10W
Porte, La	114	41 36N	86 43W
Portel	31	38 19N	7 41W
Porter L., N.W.T., Can.	109	61 41N	108 5W
Porter L., Sask., Can.	109	56 20N	107 20W
Porterville, S. Afr.	92	33 0 S	18 57 E
Porterville, U.S.A.	119	36 5N	119 0W
Porthcawl	13	51 28N	3 42W
Porthill	118	49 0N	116 30W
Portile de Fier	46	44 42N	22 30 E
Portimão	31	37 8N	8 32W
Portland, N.S.W., Austral.	99	33 20 S	150 0 E
Portland, Victoria, Austral.	97	38 20 S	141 35 E
Portland, Can.	113	44 42N	76 12W
Portland, Conn., U.S.A.	113	41 34N	72 39W
Portland, Me., U.S.A.	107	43 40N	70 15W
Portland, Mich., U.S.A.	114	42 52N	84 58W
Portland, Oreg., U.S.A.	118	45 35N	122 40W
Portland B.	99	38 15 S	141 45 E
Portland, Bill of	13	50 31N	2 27W
Portland, C.	97	40 46 S	148 0 E
Portland, I. of	13	50 32N	2 25W
Portland Prom.	105	58 40N	78 33W
Portneuf	107	46 43N	71 55W
Porto	30	41 8N	8 40W
Porto □	30	41 8N	8 20W
Pôrto Alegre	125	30 5 S	51 10W
Porto Alexandre	92	15 55 S	11 55 E
Porto Amboim = Gunza	88	10 50 S	13 50 E
Porto Argentera	38	44 15N	7 27 E
Porto Azzurro	38	42 46N	10 24 E
Porto Botte	40	39 3N	8 33 E
Porto Civitanova	39	43 19N	13 44 E
Pôrto de Móz	127	1 41 S	52 13W
Porto Empédocle	40	37 18N	13 30 E
Pôrto Esperança	126	19 37 S	57 29W
Pôrto Franco	127	6 20 S	47 24W
Porto Garibaldi	39	44 41N	12 14 E
Porto, G. de	21	42 17N	8 34 E
Pórto Lágo	44	40 58N	25 6 E
Porto Mendes	125	24 30 S	54 15W
Pôrto Murtinho	126	21 45 S	57 55W
Pôrto Nacional	127	10 40 S	48 30W
Porto Novo, Benin	85	6 23N	2 42 E
Porto Novo, India	70	11 30N	79 38 E
Porto Recanati	39	43 26N	13 40 E
Porto San Giórgio	39	43 11N	13 49 E
Porto Santo	80	33 45N	16 25W
Porto Santo Stefano	38	42 26N	11 7 E
Pôrto São José	125	22 43 S	53 10W
Pôrto Seguro	127	16 26 S	39 5W
Porto Tolle	39	44 57N	12 20 E
Porto Tórres	40	40 50N	8 23 E
Pôrto União	125	26 10 S	51 10W
Pôrto Válter	126	8 15 S	72 40W
Porto-Vecchio	21	41 35N	9 16 E
Pôrto Velho	126	8 46 S	63 54W
Portoferráio	38	42 50N	10 20 E
Portogruaro	39	45 47N	12 50 E
Portola	118	39 49N	120 28W
Portomaggiore	39	44 41N	11 47 E
Portoscuso	40	39 12N	8 22 E
Portovénere	38	44 2N	9 50 E
Portoviejo	126	1 7 S	80 28W
Portpatrick	14	54 50N	5 7W
Portree	14	57 25N	6 11W
Portrush	15	55 13N	6 40W
Portsall	18	48 37N	4 45W
Portsmouth, Domin.	121	15 34N	61 27W
Portsmouth, U.K.	13	50 48N	1 6W
Portsmouth, N.H., U.S.A.	114	43 5N	70 45W
Portsmouth, Ohio, U.S.A.	114	38 45N	83 0W
Portsmouth, R.I., U.S.A.	113	41 35N	71 15W
Portsmouth, Va., U.S.A.	114	36 50N	76 20W
Portsoy	14	57 41N	2 41W
Porttipahta	50	68 5N	26 40 E
Portugal ■	30	40 0N	7 0W
Portugalete	32	43 19N	3 4W
Portuguese-Guinea = Guinea-Bissau ■	84	12 0N	15 0W
Portuguese Timor □ = Timor	73	8 0 S	126 30 E
Portumna	15	53 5N	8 12W
Portville	112	42 3N	78 21W
Porvenir	128	53 10 S	70 16W
Porvoo	51	60 24N	25 40 E
Porzuna	31	39 9N	4 9W
Posada →	40	40 40N	9 45 E
Posadas, Argent.	125	27 30 S	55 50W
Posadas, Spain	31	37 47N	5 11W
Poschiavo	25	46 19N	10 4 E
Posets	32	42 39N	0 25 E
Poshan = Boshan	76	36 28N	117 49 E
Posidhion, Ákra	44	39 57N	23 30 E
Posidium	45	35 30N	27 10 E
Poso	73	1 20 S	120 55 E
Posse	127	14 4 S	46 18W
Possel	88	5 5N	19 10 E
Possession I.	5	72 4 S	172 0 E
Pössneck	24	50 42N	11 34 E
Post	117	33 13N	101 21W
Post Falls	118	47 46N	116 59W
Postavy	54	55 4N	26 50 E
Poste Maurice Cortier (Bidon 5)	82	22 14N	1 2 E
Postmasburg	92	28 18 S	23 5 E
Postojna	39	45 46N	14 12 E
Potamós, Andikíthira, Greece	45	36 18N	22 58 E
Potamós, Kíthira, Greece	45	36 15N	22 58 E
Potchefstroom	92	26 41 S	27 7 E
Potcoava	46	44 30N	24 39 E
Poteau	117	35 5N	94 37W
Poteet	117	29 4N	98 35W
Potelu, Lacul	46	43 44N	24 20 E
Potenza	41	40 40N	15 50 E
Potenza →	39	43 27N	13 38 E
Potenza Picena	39	43 22N	13 37 E
Poteriteri, L.	101	46 5 S	167 10 E
Potes	30	43 15N	4 42W
Potgietersrus	93	24 10 S	28 55 E
Poti	57	42 10N	41 38 E
Potiskum	85	11 39N	11 2 E
Potlogi	46	44 34N	25 34 E
Potomac →	114	38 0N	76 23W
Potosí	126	19 38 S	65 50W
Pototan	73	10 54N	122 38 E
Potrerillos	124	26 30 S	69 30W
Potsdam, Ger.	24	52 23N	13 4 E
Potsdam, U.S.A.	114	44 40N	74 59W
Potsdam □	24	52 40N	12 50 E
Pottenstein	25	49 46N	11 25 E
Potter	116	41 15N	103 20W
Pottery Hill = Abu Ballas	86	24 26N	27 36 E
Pottstown	114	40 17N	75 40W
Pottsville	114	40 39N	76 12W
Pouancé	18	47 44N	1 10W
Pouce Coupé	108	55 40N	120 10W
Poughkeepsie	114	41 40N	73 57W
Pouilly	19	47 18N	2 57 E
Poulaphouca Res.	15	53 8N	6 30W
Pouldu, Le	18	47 41N	3 36W
Poulsbo	118	47 45N	122 39W
Pourri, Mont	21	45 32N	6 52 E
Pouso Alegre, Mato Grosso, Brazil	127	11 46 S	57 16W
Pouso Alegre, Minas Gerais, Brazil	125	22 14 S	45 57W
Pouzages	20	46 40N	0 50W
Pouzauges	18	46 47N	0 50W
Povenets	52	62 50N	34 50 E
Poverty Bay	101	38 43 S	178 2 E
Povlen	42	44 9N	19 44 E
Póvoa de Lanhosa	30	41 33N	8 15W
Póvoa de Varzim	30	41 25N	8 46W
Povorino	55	51 12N	42 5 E
Powassan	106	46 5N	79 25W
Powder →	116	46 47N	105 12W
Powder River	118	43 5N	107 0W
Powell	118	44 45N	108 45W
Powell Creek	96	18 6 S	133 46 E
Powell, L.	119	37 25N	110 45W
Powell River	108	49 50N	124 35W
Powers, Mich., U.S.A.	114	45 40N	87 32W
Powers, Oreg., U.S.A.	118	42 53N	124 2W
Powers Lake	116	48 37N	102 38W
Powys □	13	52 20N	3 20W
Poyang Hu	75	29 5N	116 20 E
Poyarkovo	59	49 36N	128 41 E
Poysdorf	27	48 40N	16 37 E
Poza de la Sal	32	42 35N	3 31W
Poza Rica	120	20 33N	97 27W
Požarevac	42	44 35N	21 18 E
Požega	42	43 53N	20 2 E
Poznań	28	52 25N	16 55 E
Poznań □	28	52 50N	17 0 E
Pozo Alcón	33	37 42N	2 56W
Pozo Almonte	126	20 10 S	69 50W
Pozo Colorado	124	23 30 S	58 45W
Pozoblanco	31	38 23N	4 51W
Pozzallo	41	36 44N	14 52 E
Pozzuoli	41	40 46N	14 6 E
Pra →	85	5 1N	1 37W
Prabuty	28	53 47N	19 15 E
Prača	42	43 47N	18 43 E
Prachatice	26	49 1N	14 0 E
Prachin Buri	71	14 0N	101 25 E
Prachuap Khiri Khan	71	11 49N	99 48 E
Pradelles	20	44 46N	3 52 E
Prades	20	42 38N	2 23 E
Prado	127	17 20 S	39 13W
Prado del Rey	31	36 48N	5 33W
Præstø	49	55 8N	12 2 E
Pragersko	39	46 27N	15 42 E
Prague = Praha	26	50 5N	14 22 E
Praha	26	50 5N	14 22 E
Prahecq	20	46 19N	0 26W
Prahita →	70	19 0N	79 55 E
Prahova □	46	45 10N	26 0 E
Prahova →	46	44 50N	25 50 E
Prahovo	42	44 18N	22 39 E
Praid	46	46 32N	25 10 E
Prainha, Amazonas, Brazil	126	7 10 S	60 30W
Prainha, Pará, Brazil	127	1 45 S	53 30W
Prairie	98	20 50 S	144 35 E
Prairie →	117	34 30N	99 23W
Prairie City	118	44 27N	118 44W
Prairie du Chien	116	43 1N	91 9W
Praja	72	8 39 S	116 17 E
Pramánda	44	39 32N	21 8 E
Prang	85	8 1N	0 56W
Prapat	72	2 41N	98 58 E
Praszka	28	51 5N	18 31 E
Prata	127	19 25 S	48 54W
Prática di Mare	40	41 40N	12 26 E
Prato	38	43 53N	11 5 E
Prátola Peligna	39	42 7N	13 51 E
Pratovécchio	39	43 44N	11 43 E
Prats-de-Mollo	20	42 25N	2 27 E
Pratt	117	37 40N	98 45W
Prattville	115	32 30N	86 28W
Pravara →	70	19 35N	74 45 E
Pravdinsk	55	56 29N	43 28 E
Pravia	30	43 30N	6 12W
Pré-en-Pail	18	48 28N	0 12W
Pré St. Didier	38	45 45N	7 0 E
Precordillera	124	30 0 S	69 1W
Predáppio	39	44 7N	11 58 E
Predazzo	39	46 19N	11 37 E
Predejane	42	42 51N	22 9 E
Preeceville	109	51 57N	102 40W
Préfailles	18	47 9N	2 11W
Pregrada	39	46 11N	15 45 E
Preko	39	44 7N	15 14 E
Prelate	109	50 51N	109 24W
Prelog	39	46 18N	16 32 E
Premier	108	56 4N	129 56W
Premier Downs	96	30 30 S	126 30 E
Premont	117	27 19N	98 8W
Premuda	39	44 20N	14 36 E
Prenj	42	43 33N	17 53 E
Prenjasi	44	41 6N	20 32 E
Prentice	116	45 31N	90 19W
Prenzlau	24	53 19N	13 51 E
Prepansko Jezero	44	40 55N	21 0 E
Preparis North Channel	71	15 12N	93 40 E
Preparis South Channel	71	14 36N	93 40 E
Přerov	27	49 28N	17 27 E
Presanella	38	46 13N	10 40 E
Prescott, Can.	106	44 45N	75 30W
Prescott, Ariz., U.S.A.	119	34 35N	112 30W
Prescott, Ark., U.S.A.	117	33 49N	93 22W
Preservation Inlet	101	46 8 S	166 35 E
Preševo	42	42 19N	21 39 E
Presho	116	43 56N	100 4W
Presicce	41	39 53N	18 13 E
Presidencia de la Plaza	124	27 0 S	29 50W
Presidencia Roque Saenz Peña	124	26 45 S	60 30W
Presidente Epitácio	127	21 56 S	52 6W
Presidente Hayes □	124	24 0 S	59 0W
Presidente Hermes	126	11 17 S	61 55W
Presidente Prudente	125	22 5 S	51 25W
Presidio	117	29 30N	104 20W
Preslav	43	43 10N	26 52 E
Preslavska Planina	43	43 10N	26 45 E
Prešov	27	49 0N	21 15 E
Prespa	43	41 44N	24 55 E
Prespa, L. = Prepansko Jezero	44	40 55N	21 0 E
Presque Isle	107	46 40N	68 0W
Presseger See	26	46 37N	13 26 E
Prestbury	13	51 54N	2 2W
Prestea	84	5 22N	2 7W
Presteigne	13	52 17N	3 0W
Přeštice	26	49 34N	13 20 E
Preston, Can.	112	43 23N	80 21W
Preston, U.K.	12	53 46N	2 42W
Preston, Idaho, U.S.A.	118	42 10N	111 55W
Preston, Minn., U.S.A.	116	43 39N	92 3W
Preston, Nev., U.S.A.	118	38 59N	115 2W
Preston, C.	96	20 51 S	116 12 E
Prestonpans	14	55 58N	3 0W
Prestwick	14	55 30N	4 38W
Pretoria	93	25 44 S	28 12 E
Preuilly-sur-Claise	18	46 51N	0 56 E
Préveza	45	38 57N	20 47 E
Préveza □	44	39 20N	20 40 E
Prey-Veng	71	11 35N	105 29 E
Priazovskoye	56	46 44N	35 40 E
Pribilof Is.	4	56 0N	170 0W
Priboj	42	43 35N	19 32 E
Pribram	26	49 41N	14 2 E
Price	118	39 40N	110 48W
Price I.	108	52 23N	128 41W
Prichalnaya	57	48 57N	44 33 E
Priego	32	40 26N	2 21W
Priego de Córdoba	31	37 27N	4 12W
Priekule	54	57 27N	21 45 E
Prien	25	47 52N	12 20 E
Prieska	92	29 40 S	22 42 E
Priest L.	118	48 30N	116 55W
Priest River	118	48 11N	116 55W
Priestly	108	54 8N	125 20W
Prievidza	27	48 46N	18 36 E
Prijedor	39	44 58N	16 41 E
Prijepolje	42	43 27N	19 40 E
Prikaspiyskaya Nizmennost	57	47 0N	48 0 E
Prikumsk	56	44 50N	44 10 E
Prilep	42	41 21N	21 37 E
Priluki	54	50 30N	32 24 E
Primorsko	43	42 15N	27 44 E
Primorsko-Akhtarsk	56	46 2N	38 10 E
Primorskoye	56	47 10N	37 38 E
Primrose L.	109	54 55N	109 45W
Prince Albert	109	53 15N	105 50W
Prince Albert Mts.	5	76 0 S	161 30 E
Prince Albert Nat. Park	109	54 0N	106 25W
Prince Albert Pen.	104	72 30N	116 0W
Prince Albert Sd.	104	70 25N	115 0W
Prince Alfred C.	4	74 20N	124 40W
Prince Charles I.	105	67 47N	76 12W
Prince Charles Mts.	5	72 0 S	67 0 E
Prince Edward I. □	107	46 20N	63 20W
Prince Edward Is.	3	45 15 S	39 0 E
Prince George	108	53 55N	122 50W
Prince of Wales I.	104	55 30N	133 0W
Prince of Wales Is.	97	10 40 S	142 10 E
Prince Patrick I.	4	77 0N	120 0W
Prince Regent Inlet	4	73 0N	90 0W
Prince Rupert	108	54 20N	130 20W
Princess Charlotte B.	97	14 25 S	144 0 E
Princess Royal I.	108	53 0N	128 40W
Princeton, Can.	108	49 27N	120 30W
Princeton, Ill., U.S.A.	116	41 25N	89 25W
Princeton, Ind., U.S.A.	114	38 20N	87 35W
Princeton, Ky., U.S.A.	114	37 6N	87 55W
Princeton, Mo., U.S.A.	116	40 23N	93 35W
Princeton, N.J., U.S.A.	114	40 18N	74 40W
Princeton, W. Va., U.S.A.	114	37 21N	81 8W
Principe Chan.	108	53 28N	130 0W
Principe da Beira	126	12 20 S	64 30W
Príncipe, I. de	79	1 37N	7 27 E
Prineville	118	44 17N	120 50W
Prins Albert	92	33 12 S	22 2 E
Prins Harald Kyst	5	70 0 S	35 1 E
Prinsesse Astrid Kyst	5	70 45 S	12 30 E
Prinsesse Ragnhild Kyst	5	70 15 S	27 30 E
Prior, C.	30	43 34N	8 17W
Priozersk	52	61 2N	30 7 E
Pripet = Pripyat →	54	51 20N	30 9 E
Pripet Marshes = Polesye	54	52 0N	28 10 E

Pripyat → 54 51 20N 30 9 E
Prislop, Pasul 46 47 37N 25 15 E
Pristen 55 51 15N 36 44 E
Priština 42 42 40N 21 13 E
Pritchard 115 30 47N 88 5W
Pritzwalk 24 53 10N 12 11 E
Privas 21 44 45N 4 37 E
Priverno 40 41 29N 13 10 E
Privolzhsk 55 57 23N 41 16 E
Privolzhskaya Vozvyshennost 55 51 0N 46 0 E
Privolzhskiy 55 51 25N 46 3 E
Privolzhye 55 52 52N 48 33 E
Priyutnoye 57 46 12N 43 40 E
Prizren 42 42 13N 20 45 E
Prizzi 40 37 44N 13 24 E
Prnjavor 42 44 52N 17 43 E
Probolinggo 73 7 46S 113 13 E
Prochowice 28 51 17N 16 20 E
Procida 40 40 46N 14 0 E
Proddatur 70 14 45N 78 30 E
Proença-a-Nova 31 39 45N 7 54W
Progreso 120 21 20N 89 40W
Prokhladnyy 57 43 50N 44 2 E
Prokletije 44 42 30N 19 45 E
Prokopyevsk 58 54 0N 86 45 E
Prokuplje 42 43 16N 21 36 E
Proletarskaya 57 46 42N 41 50 E
Prome = Pyè 67 18 45N 95 30 E
Prophet → 108 58 48N 122 40W
Propriá 127 10 13S 36 51W
Propriano 21 41 41N 8 52 E
Proserpine 97 20 21S 148 36 E
Prosna 28 51 1N 18 30 E
Prosser 118 46 11N 119 52W
Prostějov 27 49 30N 17 9 E
Prostki 28 53 42N 22 25 E
Proston 99 26 8S 151 32 E
Proszowice 27 50 13N 20 16 E
Protection 117 37 16N 99 30W
Próti 45 37 5N 21 32 E
Provadiya 43 43 12N 27 30 E
Provence 21 43 40N 5 46 E
Providence, Ky., U.S.A. 114 37 25N 87 46W
Providence, R.I., U.S.A. 114 41 50N 71 28W
Providence Bay 106 45 41N 82 15W
Providence Mts. 119 35 0N 115 30W
Providencia, I. de 121 13 25N 81 26W
Provideniya 59 64 23N 173 18W
Provins 19 48 33N 3 15 E
Provo 118 40 16N 111 37W
Provost 109 52 25N 110 20W
Prozor 42 43 50N 17 34 E
Prud'homme 109 52 20N 105 54W
Prudnik 28 50 20N 17 38 E
Prüm 25 50 14N 6 22 E
Pruszcz Gd. 28 54 17N 18 40 E
Pruszków 28 52 9N 20 49 E
Prut → 46 46 3N 28 10 E
Pruzhany 54 52 33N 24 28 E
Prvič 39 44 55N 14 47 E
Prydz B. 5 69 0S 74 0 E
Pryor 117 36 17N 95 20W
Przasnysz 28 53 2N 20 45 E
Przedbórz 28 51 6N 19 53 E
Przedecz 28 52 20N 18 53 E
Przemyśl 27 49 50N 22 45 E
Przeworsk 27 50 6N 22 32 E
Przewóz 28 51 28N 14 57 E
Przhevalsk 58 42 30N 78 20 E
Przysucha 28 51 22N 20 38 E
Psakhná 45 38 34N 23 35 E
Psará 45 38 37N 25 38 E
Psathoúra 44 39 30N 24 12 E
Psel → 56 49 5N 33 20 E
Pserimos 45 36 56N 27 12 E
Pskov 54 57 50N 28 25 E
Psunj 42 45 25N 17 19 E
Pszczyna 27 49 59N 18 58 E
Pteleón 45 39 3N 22 57 E
Ptich → 54 52 9N 28 52 E
Ptolemaís 44 40 30N 21 43 E
Ptuj 39 46 28N 15 50 E
Ptujska Gora 39 46 23N 15 47 E
Puán 124 37 30S 62 45W
Pucallpa 126 8 25S 74 30W
Pucheng 77 27 59N 118 31 E
Pucheni 46 45 12N 25 17 E
Pučišće 39 43 22N 16 43 E
Puck 28 54 45N 18 23 E
Pucka, Zatoka 28 54 30N 18 40 E
Pudozh 52 61 48N 36 32 E
Pudukkottai 70 10 28N 78 47 E
Puebla 120 19 0N 98 10W
Puebla □ 120 18 30N 98 0W
Puebla de Alcocer 31 38 59N 5 14W
Puebla de Cazalla, La 31 37 10N 5 20W
Puebla de Don Fadrique 33 37 58N 2 25W
Puebla de Don Rodrigo 31 39 5N 4 37W
Puebla de Guzmán 31 37 37N 7 15W
Puebla de los Infantes, La 31 37 47N 5 24W
Puebla de Montalbán, La 30 39 52N 4 22W
Puebla de Sanabria 30 42 4N 6 38W
Puebla de Trives 30 42 20N 7 10W
Puebla del Caramiñal 30 42 37N 8 56W
Puebla, La 32 39 46N 3 1 E
Pueblo 116 38 20N 104 40W
Pueblo Bonito 119 36 4N 107 57W
Pueblo Hundido 124 26 20S 70 5W
Puelches 124 38 5S 65 51W
Puelén 124 37 32S 67 38W
Puente Alto 124 33 32S 70 35W
Puente del Arzobispo 30 39 48N 5 10W
Puente-Genil 31 37 22N 4 47W
Puente la Reina 32 42 40N 1 49W
Puenteareas 30 42 10N 8 28W
Puentedeume 30 43 24N 8 10W
Puentes de Garcia Rodriguez 30 43 27N 7 50W
Puerco → 119 34 22N 107 50W
Puerta, La 33 38 22N 2 45W
Puerto Aisén 128 45 27S 73 0W
Puerto Armuelles 121 8 20N 82 51W
Puerto Ayacucho 126 5 40N 67 35W
Puerto Barrios 120 15 40N 88 32W
Puerto Bermejo 124 26 55S 58 34W
Puerto Bermúdez 126 10 20S 75 0W
Puerto Bolívar 126 3 19S 79 55W
Puerto Cabello 126 10 28N 68 1W
Puerto Cabezas 121 14 0N 83 30W
Puerto Capaz = Jebba 82 35 11N 4 43W
Puerto Carreño 126 6 12N 67 22W
Puerto Castilla 121 16 0N 86 0W
Puerto Chicama 126 7 45S 79 20W
Puerto Coig 128 50 54S 69 15W
Puerto Cortes 121 8 55N 84 0W
Puerto Cortés 120 15 51N 88 0W
Puerto Cumarebo 126 11 29N 69 30W
Puerto de Santa María 31 36 36N 6 13W
Puerto del Rosario 80 28 30N 13 52W
Puerto Deseado 128 47 55S 66 0W
Puerto Heath 126 12 34S 68 39W
Puerto Juárez 120 21 11N 86 49W
Puerto La Cruz 126 10 13N 64 38W
Puerto Leguízamo 126 0 12S 74 46W
Puerto Libertad 120 29 55N 112 41W
Puerto Lobos 128 42 0S 65 3W
Puerto Lumbreras 33 37 34N 1 48W
Puerto Madryn 128 42 48S 65 4W
Puerto Maldonado 126 12 30S 69 10W
Puerto Mazarrón 33 37 34N 1 15W
Puerto Montt 128 41 28S 73 0W
Puerto Morelos 120 20 49N 86 52W
Puerto Natales 128 51 45S 72 15W
Puerto Padre 121 21 13N 76 35W
Puerto Páez 126 6 13N 67 28W
Puerto Peñasco 120 31 20N 113 33W
Puerto Pinasco 124 22 36S 57 50W
Puerto Pirámides 128 42 35S 64 20W
Puerto Plata 121 19 48N 70 45W
Puerto Princesa 73 9 46N 118 45 E
Puerto Quellón 128 43 7S 73 37W
Puerto Quepos 121 9 29N 84 6W
Puerto Real 31 36 33N 6 12W
Puerto Rico ■ 121 18 15N 66 45W
Puerto Sastre 124 22 2S 57 55W
Puerto Suárez 126 18 58S 57 52W
Puerto Vallarta 120 20 36N 105 15W
Puerto Wilches 126 7 21N 73 54W
Puertollano 31 38 43N 4 7W
Puertomarin 30 42 48N 7 36W
Pueyrredón, L. 128 47 20S 72 0W
Pugachev 55 52 0N 48 49 E
Puge 90 4 45S 33 11 E
Puget Sd. 118 47 15N 122 30W
Puget-Théniers 21 43 58N 6 53 E
Púglia □ 41 41 0N 16 30 E
Pugu 90 6 55S 39 4 E
Pui 46 45 30N 23 4 E
Puieşti 46 46 25N 27 33 E
Puig Mayor, Mte. 32 39 48N 2 47 E
Puigcerdá 32 42 24N 1 50 E
Puigmal 32 42 23N 2 7 E
Puisaye, Collines de 19 47 34N 3 18 E
Puiseaux 19 48 11N 2 30 E
Puka 44 42 2N 19 53 E
Pukaki L. 101 44 4S 170 1 E
Pukatawagan 109 55 45N 101 20W
Pukekohe 101 37 12S 174 55 E
Pukou 77 32 7N 118 38 E
Pula 40 39 0N 9 0 E
Pula (Pola) 39 44 54N 13 57 E
Pulaski, N.Y., U.S.A. 114 43 32N 76 9W
Pulaski, Tenn., U.S.A. 115 35 10N 87 0W
Pulaski, Va., U.S.A. 114 37 4N 80 49W
Pulawy 28 51 23N 21 59 E
Pulgaon 68 20 44N 78 21 E
Pulicat, L. 70 13 40N 80 15 E
Puliyangudi 70 9 11N 77 24 E
Pullman 118 46 49N 117 10W
Pulog, Mt. 73 16 40N 120 50 E
Puloraja 72 4 55N 95 24 E
Pultusk 28 52 43N 21 6 E
Pumlumon Fawr 13 52 29N 3 47W
Puna 126 19 45S 65 28W
Puná, I. 126 2 55S 80 5W
Punakha 69 27 42N 89 52 E
Punalur 70 9 0N 76 56 E
Punasar 68 27 6N 73 6 E
Punata 126 17 32S 65 50W
Punch 69 33 48N 74 4 E
Pune 70 18 29N 73 57 E
Pungue, Ponte de 91 19 0S 34 0 E
Puning 77 23 20N 116 12 E
Punjab □ 68 31 0N 76 0 E
Puno 126 15 55S 70 3W
Punta Alta 128 38 53S 62 4W
Punta Arenas 128 53 10S 71 0W
Punta de Díaz 124 28 0S 70 45W
Punta Gorda, Belize 120 16 10N 88 45W
Punta Gorda, U.S.A. 115 26 55N 82 0W
Puntarenas 121 10 0N 84 50W
Punto Fijo 126 11 50N 70 13W
Punxsutawney 114 40 56N 79 0W
Puqi 77 29 40N 113 50 E
Puquio 126 14 45S 74 10W
Pur → 58 67 31N 77 55 E
Purace, Vol. 126 2 21N 76 23W
Puračić 42 44 33N 18 28 E
Purari → 98 7 49S 145 0 E
Purbeck, Isle of 13 50 40N 2 5W
Purcell 117 35 0N 97 25W
Purchena Tetica 33 37 21N 2 21W
Puri 69 19 50N 85 58 E
Purli 68 18 50N 76 35 E
Purmerend 16 52 30N 4 58 E
Purna → 70 19 6N 77 2 E
Purnea 69 25 45N 87 31 E
Pursat 71 12 34N 103 50 E
Purukcahu 72 0 35S 114 35 E
Purulia 69 23 17N 86 24 E
Purus → 126 3 42S 61 28W
Pŭrvomay 43 42 8N 25 17 E
Purwakarta 73 6 35S 107 29 E
Purwodadi, Jawa, Indon. 73 7 51S 110 0 E
Purwodadi, Jawa, Indon. 73 7 7S 110 55 E
Purwokerto 73 7 25S 109 14 E
Purworedjo 73 7 43S 110 2 E
Pus → 70 19 55N 77 55 E
Pusad 70 19 56N 77 36 E
Pusan 76 35 5N 129 0 E
Pushchino 59 54 10N 158 0 E
Pushkin 54 59 45N 30 25 E
Pushkino, R.S.F.S.R., U.S.S.R. 55 51 16N 47 0 E
Pushkino, R.S.F.S.R., U.S.S.R. 55 56 2N 37 49 E
Püspökladány 27 47 19N 21 6 E
Pustoshka 54 56 20N 29 30 E
Puszczykowo 28 52 18N 16 49 E
Putahow L. 109 59 54N 100 40W
Putao 67 27 28N 97 30 E
Putaruru 101 38 2S 175 50 E
Putbus 24 54 19N 13 29 E
Puţeni 46 45 49N 27 42 E
Puthein Myit → 67 15 56N 94 18 E
Putian 77 25 23N 119 0 E
Putignano 41 40 50N 17 5 E
Puting, Tanjung 72 3 31S 111 46 E
Putlitz 24 53 15N 12 3 E
Putna 46 47 50N 25 33 E
Putna → 46 45 42N 27 26 E
Putnam 113 41 55N 71 55W
Putnok 27 48 18N 20 26 E
Putorana, Gory 59 69 0N 95 0 E
Puttalam Lagoon 70 8 15N 79 45 E
Putten 16 52 16N 5 36 E
Puttgarden 24 54 28N 11 15 E
Puttur 70 12 46N 75 12 E
Putumayo → 126 3 7S 67 58W
Putussibau 72 0 50N 112 56 E
Puy-de-Dôme 20 45 46N 2 57 E
Puy-de-Dôme □ 20 45 47N 3 0 E
Puy-de-Sancy 20 45 32N 2 48 E
Puy-Guillaume 20 45 57N 3 29 E
Puy, Le 20 45 3N 3 52 E
Puy l'Évêque 20 44 31N 1 9 E
Puyallup 118 47 10N 122 22W
Puyang 76 35 40N 115 1 E
Puylaurens 20 43 35N 2 0 E
Puyôo 20 43 33N 0 56W
Pwani □ 90 7 0S 39 0 E
Pweto 91 8 25S 28 51 E
Pwllheli 12 52 54N 4 26W
Pya-ozero 52 66 5N 30 58 E
Pyana → 55 55 30N 46 0 E
Pyapon 67 16 20N 95 40 E
Pyasina → 59 73 30N 87 0 E
Pyatigorsk 57 44 2N 43 6 E
Pyatikhatki 56 48 28N 33 38 E
Pydna 44 40 20N 22 34 E
Pyinmana 67 19 45N 96 12 E
Pyŏngyang 76 39 0N 125 30 E
Pyote 117 31 34N 103 5W
Pyramid L. 118 40 0N 119 30W
Pyramids 86 29 58N 31 9 E
Pyrénées 20 42 45N 0 18 E
Pyrenees = Pyrénées 20 42 45N 0 18 E
Pyrénées-Atlantiques □ 20 43 15N 1 0W
Pyrénées-Orientales □ 20 42 35N 2 26 E
Pyrzyce 28 53 10N 14 55 E
Pyshchug 55 58 57N 45 47 E
Pytalovo 54 57 5N 27 55 E
Pyttegga 47 62 13N 7 42 E
Pyu 67 18 30N 96 28 E
Pyzdry 28 52 11N 17 42 E

Q

Qabalān 62 32 8N 35 17 E
Qabātiyah 62 32 25N 35 16 E
Qaidam Pendi 75 37 0N 95 0 E
Qa'iya 64 24 33N 43 15 E
Qal' at Shajwa 86 25 2N 38 57 E
Qala-i-Jadid (Spin Baldak) 68 31 1N 66 25 E
Qalāt 65 32 15N 66 58 E
Qal'at al Akhḍar 64 28 0N 37 10 E
Qal'at al Mu'azzam 64 27 45N 37 31 E
Qal'at Saura 86 26 10N 38 40 E
Qal'eh-ye Now 65 35 0N 63 5 E
Qalqīlya 62 32 12N 34 58 E
Qalyûb 86 30 12N 31 11 E
Qam 62 32 36N 35 43 E
Qamar, Ghubbat al 63 16 20N 52 30 E
Qamruddin Karez 68 31 45N 68 20 E
Qāna 62 33 12N 35 17 E
Qâra 86 29 38N 26 30 E
Qarachuk 64 37 0N 42 2 E
Qārah 64 29 55N 40 3 E
Qardud 87 10 20N 29 56 E
Qarqan 75 38 5N 85 20 E
Qarqan He → 75 39 30N 88 30 E
Qarrasa 87 14 38N 32 5 E
Qasim 64 26 0N 43 0 E
Qāsim 62 32 59N 36 2 E
Qaşr Bū Hadi 83 31 1N 16 45 E
Qaşr-e Qand 65 26 15N 60 45 E
Qasr Farâfra 86 27 0N 28 1 E
Qatar ■ 65 25 30N 51 15 E
Qattâra 86 30 12N 27 3 E
Qattâra Depression = Qattâra, Munkhafed el 86 29 30N 27 30 E
Qattâra, Munkhafed el 86 29 30N 27 30 E
Qāyen 65 33 40N 59 10 E
Qazvin 64 36 15N 50 0 E
Qena 86 26 10N 32 43 E
Qena, Wadi → 86 26 12N 32 44 E
Qeshm 65 26 55N 56 10 E
Qezi'ot 62 30 52N 34 26 E
Qian Xian 77 34 31N 108 15 E
Qianshan 77 30 37N 116 35 E
Qianxi 77 27 3N 106 3 E
Qianyang 77 27 18N 110 10 E
Qijiang 77 28 57N 106 35 E
Qila Safed 66 29 0N 61 30 E
Qila Saifulla 68 30 45N 68 17 E
Qilian Shan 75 38 30N 96 0 E
Qin Ling = Qinling Shandi 77 33 50N 108 10 E
Qin'an 77 34 48N 105 40 E
Qingdao 76 36 5N 120 20 E
Qinghai □ 75 36 0N 98 0 E
Qinghai Hu 75 36 40N 100 10 E
Qingjiang, Jiangsu, China 77 33 30N 119 2 E
Qingjiang, Jiangxi, China 77 28 4N 115 29 E
Qingliu 77 26 11N 116 48 E
Qingshuihe 76 39 55N 111 35 E
Qingyang 76 36 2N 107 55 E
Qingyuan 77 23 40N 112 59 E
Qinhuangdao 76 39 56N 119 30 E
Qinling Shandi 77 33 50N 108 10 E
Qinyang 77 35 7N 112 57 E
Qinyuan 76 36 29N 112 20 E
Qinzhou 75 21 58N 108 38 E
Qiongshan 77 19 51N 110 26 E
Qiongzhou Haixia 77 20 10N 110 15 E
Qiqihar 75 47 26N 124 0 E
Qiryat 'Anavim 62 31 49N 35 7 E
Qiryat Ata 62 32 47N 35 6 E
Qiryat Bialik 62 32 50N 35 5 E
Qiryat Gat 62 31 32N 34 46 E
Qiryat Hayyim 62 32 49N 35 4 E
Qiryat Mal'akhi 62 31 44N 34 44 E
Qiryat Shemona 62 33 13N 35 35 E
Qiryat Yam 62 32 51N 35 4 E
Qishan 77 22 52N 120 25 E
Qishon → 62 32 49N 35 2 E
Qishrān 86 20 14N 40 2 E
Qitai 75 44 2N 89 35 E
Qiyahe 76 53 0N 120 35 E
Qiyang 77 26 35N 111 50 E
Qizan 87 16 57N 42 34 E
Qizān 63 17 0N 42 20 E
Qom 65 34 40N 51 0 E
Qomolangma Feng (Mt. Everest) 75 28 0N 86 45 E
Qondūz 65 36 50N 68 50 E
Qondūz □ 65 36 50N 68 50 E
Qu Jiang → 77 30 1N 106 24 E
Qu Xian, Sichuan, China 77 30 48N 106 58 E
Qu Xian, Zhejiang, China 75 28 57N 118 54 E
Quackenbrück 24 52 40N 7 59 E
Quakertown 113 40 27N 75 20W
Quambatook 99 35 49S 143 34 E
Quambone 99 30 57S 147 53 E
Quan Long 71 9 7N 105 8 E
Quanan 117 34 20N 99 45W
Quandialla 99 34 1S 147 47 E
Quang Ngai 71 15 13N 108 58 E
Quang Yen 71 20 56N 106 52 E
Quantock Hills 13 51 8N 3 10W
Quanzhou, Fujian, China 75 24 55N 118 34 E
Quanzhou, Guangxi Zhuangzu, China 77 25 57N 111 5 E
Quaraí 124 30 15S 56 20W
Quarré-les-Tombes 19 47 21N 4 0 E
Quartu Sant' Elena 40 39 15N 9 10 E
Quartzsite 119 33 44N 114 16W
Quatsino 108 50 30N 127 40W
Quatsino Sd. 108 50 25N 127 58W
Qubab = Mishmar Ayyalon 62 31 52N 34 57 E
Qūchān 65 37 10N 58 27 E
Que Que 91 18 58S 29 48 E
Queanbeyan 97 35 17S 149 14 E
Québec 107 46 52N 71 13W
Québec □ 107 50 0N 70 0W
Quedlinburg 24 51 47N 11 9 E
Queen Alexandra Ra. 5 85 0S 170 0 E
Queen Charlotte 108 53 15N 132 2W
Queen Charlotte Is. 108 53 20N 132 10W
Queen Charlotte Str. 108 51 0N 128 0W
Queen Elizabeth Is. 102 76 0N 95 0W
Queen Elizabeth Nat. Park 90 0 0S 30 0 E
Queen Mary Coast 5 70 0S 95 0 E
Queen Maud G. 104 68 15N 102 30W
Queen Maud Ra. 5 86 0S 160 0W
Queens Chan. 96 15 0S 129 30 E
Queenscliff 97 38 16S 144 39 E
Queensland □ 97 22 0S 142 0 E
Queenstown, Austral. 97 42 4S 145 35 E
Queenstown, N.Z. 101 45 1S 168 40 E
Queenstown, S. Afr. 92 31 52S 26 52 E
Queguay Grande → 124 32 9S 58 9W
Queimadas 127 11 0S 39 38W
Quela 88 9 10S 16 56 E
Quelimane 91 17 53S 36 58 E
Quelpart = Cheju Do 77 33 29N 126 34 E
Quemado, N. Mex., U.S.A. 119 34 17N 108 28W
Quemado, Tex., U.S.A. 117 28 58N 100 35W
Quemú-Quemú 124 36 3S 63 36W
Quequén 124 38 30S 58 30W
Querétaro 120 20 40N 100 23W
Querétaro □ 120 20 30N 100 0W
Querfurt 24 51 22N 11 33 E
Querqueville 18 49 40N 1 42W
Quesada 33 37 51N 3 4W
Queshan 77 32 55N 114 2 E
Quesnel 108 53 0N 122 30W
Quesnel → 108 52 58N 122 29W
Quesnel L. 108 52 30N 121 20W
Quesnoy, Le 19 50 15N 3 38 E
Questa 119 36 45N 105 35W
Questembert 18 47 40N 2 28W
Quetico Prov. Park 106 48 30N 91 45W
Quetta 66 30 15N 66 55 E
Quetta □ 66 30 15N 66 55 E
Quezaltenango 120 14 50N 91 30W
Quezon City 73 14 38N 121 0 E
Qui Nhon 71 13 40N 109 13 E
Quiaca, La 124 22 5S 65 35W
Quibaxe 88 8 24S 14 27 E
Quibdo 126 5 42N 76 40W
Quiberon 18 47 29N 3 9W
Quick 108 54 36N 126 54W
Quickborn 24 53 42N 9 52 E
Quiet L. 108 61 5N 133 5W
Quiindy 124 25 58S 57 14W
Quilán, C. 128 43 15S 74 30W
Quilengues 89 14 12S 14 12 E
Quilimarí 124 32 5S 71 30W
Quilino 124 30 14S 64 29W
Quillabamba 126 12 50S 72 50W

Quillagua 124 21 40S 69 40W
Quillaicillo 124 31 17S 71 40W
Quillan 20 42 53N 2 10 E
Quillebeuf 18 49 28N 0 30 E
Quillota 124 32 54S 71 16W
Quilmes 124 34 43S 58 15W
Quilon 70 8 50N 76 38 E
Quilpie 97 26 35S 144 11 E
Quilpué 124 33 5S 71 33W
Quilua 91 16 17S 39 54 E
Quimilí 124 27 40S 62 30W
Quimper 18 48 0N 4 9W
Quimperlé 18 47 53N 3 33W
Quincy, Calif., U.S.A. 118 39 56N 121 0W
Quincy, Fla., U.S.A. 115 30 34N 84 34W
Quincy, Ill., U.S.A. 116 39 55N 91 20W
Quincy, Mass., U.S.A. 114 42 14N 71 0W
Quincy, Wash., U.S.A. 118 47 22N 119 56W
Quines 124 32 13S 65 48W
Quinga 91 15 49S 40 15 E
Quingey 19 47 7N 5 52 E
Quintana de la Serena 31 38 45N 5 40W
Quintana Roo □ 120 19 0N 88 0W
Quintanar de la Orden 32 39 36N 3 5W
Quintanar de la Sierra 32 41 57N 2 55W
Quintanar del Rey 33 39 21N 1 56W
Quintero 124 32 45S 71 30W
Quintin 18 48 26N 2 56W
Quinto 32 41 25N 0 32W
Quinyambie 99 30 15S 141 0 E
Quipar → 33 38 15N 1 40W
Quirihue 124 36 15S 72 35W
Quirindi 99 31 28S 150 40 E
Quiroga 30 42 28N 7 18W
Quissac 21 43 55N 4 0 E
Quissanga 91 12 24S 40 28 E
Quitilipi 124 26 50S 60 13W
Quitman, Ga., U.S.A. 115 30 49N 83 35W
Quitman, Miss., U.S.A. 115 32 2N 88 42W
Quitman, Tex., U.S.A. 117 32 48N 95 25W
Quito 126 0 15S 78 35W
Quixadá 127 4 55S 39 0W
Quixaxe 91 15 17S 40 4 E
Qul'ân, Jazâ'ir 86 24 22N 35 31 E
Qumrân 62 31 43N 35 27 E
Quneitra 62 33 7N 35 48 E
Quoin Pt. 92 34 46S 19 37 E
Quondong 99 33 6S 140 18 E
Quorn 97 32 25S 138 0 E
Qurein 87 13 30N 34 50 E
Qûs 86 25 55N 32 50 E
Quseir 86 26 7N 34 16 E
Qusrah 62 32 5N 35 20 E
Quthing 93 30 25S 27 36 E
Qytet Stalin (Kuçove) 44 40 47N 19 57 E

R

Råå 49 56 0N 12 45 E
Raab 26 48 21N 13 39 E
Raahe 50 64 40N 24 28 E
Ra'ananna 62 32 12N 34 52 E
Raasay 14 57 25N 6 4W
Raasay, Sd. of 14 57 30N 6 8W
Rab 39 44 45N 14 45 E
Raba 73 8 36S 118 55 E
Rába → 27 47 38N 17 38 E
Raba → 27 50 8N 20 30 E
Rabaçal → 30 41 30N 7 12W
Rabah 85 13 5N 5 30 E
Rabai 90 3 50S 39 31 E
Rabastens, Hautes-Pyrénées, France 20 43 25N 0 10 E
Rabastens, Tarn, France 20 43 50N 1 43 E
Rabat, Malta 36 35 53N 14 25 E
Rabat, Moroc. 82 34 2N 6 48W
Rabaul 94 4 24S 152 18 E
Rabbit → 108 59 41N 127 12W
Rabbit Lake 109 53 8N 107 46W
Rabbitskin → 108 61 47N 120 42W
Râbigh 64 22 50N 39 5 E
Rabka 27 49 37N 19 59 E
Rača 42 44 14N 21 0 E
Răcale 41 39 57N 18 6 E
Racalmuto 40 37 25N 13 41 E
Răcăşdia 42 44 59N 21 36 E
Racconigi 38 44 47N 7 41 E
Race, C. 107 46 40N 53 5W
Rach Gia 71 10 5N 105 5 E
Raciąż 28 52 46N 20 10 E
Racibórz 27 50 7N 18 18 E
Racine 114 42 41N 87 51W
Radama, Nosy 93 14 0S 47 47 E
Radama, Saikanosy 93 14 16S 47 53 E
Radan 42 42 59N 21 29 E
Rădăuţi 46 47 50N 25 59 E
Radbuza → 26 49 35N 13 5 E
Råde 47 59 21N 10 53 E
Radeburg 24 51 6N 13 55 E
Radeče 39 46 5N 15 14 E
Radekhov 54 50 25N 24 32 E
Radew → 28 54 2N 15 52 E
Radford 114 37 8N 80 32W
Radhanpur 68 23 50N 71 38 E
Radhwa, Jabal 64 24 34N 38 18 E
Radiska → 42 41 38N 20 37 E
Radisson 109 52 30N 107 20W
Radium Hill 97 32 30S 140 42 E
Radium Hot Springs 108 50 35N 116 2W
Radja, Kepulauan 73 0 30S 130 00 E
Radków 28 50 30N 16 24 E
Radlin 27 50 3N 18 29 E
Radna 42 46 7N 21 41 E
Radnevo 43 42 17N 25 58 E
Radnice 26 49 51N 13 35 E
Radnor Forest 13 52 17N 3 10W
Radolfzell 25 47 44N 8 58 E
Radom 28 51 23N 21 12 E
Radom □ 28 51 30N 21 0 E
Radomir 42 42 37N 23 4 E
Radomka → 28 51 31N 21 11 E
Radomsko 28 51 5N 19 28 E
Radomyshl 54 50 30N 29 12 E
Radomysl Wielki 27 50 14N 21 15 E
Radoszyce 28 51 4N 20 15 E
Radoviš 42 41 38N 22 28 E
Radovljica 39 46 22N 14 12 E
Radstadt 26 47 24N 13 28 E
Radstock 13 51 17N 2 25W
Răducăneni 46 46 58N 27 54 E
Raduša 42 42 7N 21 15 E
Radviliškis 54 55 49N 23 33 E
Radville 109 49 30N 104 15W
Radymno 27 49 59N 22 52 E
Radzanów 28 52 56N 20 8 E
Radziejów 28 52 40N 18 30 E
Radzymin 28 52 25N 21 11 E
Radzyń Chełmiński 28 53 23N 18 55 E
Radzyń Podlaski 28 51 47N 22 37 E
Rae 108 62 50N 116 3W
Rae Bareli 69 26 18N 81 20 E
Rae Isthmus 105 66 40N 87 30W
Raeren 16 50 41N 6 7 E
Raeside, L. 96 29 20S 122 0 E
Raetihi 101 39 25S 175 17 E
Rafaela 124 31 10S 61 30W
Rafah 86 31 18N 34 14 E
Rafai 90 4 59N 23 58 E
Raffadali 40 37 23N 13 29 E
Rafḩā 64 29 35N 43 35 E
Rafsanjān 65 30 30N 56 5 E
Ragag 87 10 59N 24 40 E
Raglan, Austral. 98 23 42S 150 49 E
Raglan, N.Z. 101 37 55S 174 55 E
Ragunda 48 63 6N 16 23 E
Ragusa 41 36 56N 14 42 E
Raha 73 4 55S 123 0 E
Rahad al Bardī 81 11 20N 23 40 E
Rahad, Nahr ed → 87 14 28N 33 31 E
Rahden 24 52 26N 8 36 E
Raheita 87 12 46N 43 4 E
Rahimyar Khan 68 28 30N 70 25 E
Raichur 70 16 10N 77 20 E
Raiganj 69 25 37N 88 10 E
Raigarh, Madhya Pradesh, India 69 21 56N 83 25 E
Raigarh, Orissa, India 70 19 51N 82 6 E
Raiis 64 23 33N 38 43 E
Raijua 73 10 37S 121 36 E
Railton 99 41 25S 146 28 E
Rainbow Lake 108 58 30N 119 23W
Rainier 118 46 4N 123 0W
Rainier, Mt. 118 46 50N 121 50W
Rainy L. 109 48 42N 93 10W
Rainy River 109 48 43N 94 29W
Raipur 69 21 17N 81 45 E
Raja, Kepulauan 73 0 30S 129 40 E
Raja, Ujung 72 3 40N 96 25 E
Rajahmundry 70 17 1N 81 48 E
Rajang → 72 2 30N 112 0 E
Rajapalaiyam 70 9 25N 77 35 E
Rajasthan □ 68 26 45N 73 30 E
Rajasthan Canal 68 28 0N 72 0 E
Rajbari 69 23 47N 89 41 E
Rajgarh, Mad. P., India 68 24 2N 76 45 E
Rajgarh, Raj., India 68 28 40N 75 25 E
Rajgród 28 53 42N 22 42 E
Rajhenburg 39 46 1N 15 29 E
Rajkot 68 22 15N 70 56 E
Rajmahal Hills 69 24 30N 87 30 E
Rajnandgaon 69 21 5N 81 5 E
Rajojooseppi 50 68 25N 28 30 E
Rajpipla 68 21 50N 73 30 E
Rajpura 68 30 25N 76 32 E
Rajshahi 69 24 22N 88 39 E
Rajshahi □ 69 25 0N 89 0 E
Rakaia 101 43 45S 172 1 E
Rakaia → 101 43 36S 172 15 E
Rakan, Ra's 65 26 10N 51 20 E
Rakaposhi 69 36 10N 74 25 E
Rakha 86 18 25N 41 30 E
Rakhni 68 30 4N 69 56 E
Rakitovo 43 41 59N 24 5 E
Rakkestad 47 59 25N 11 21 E
Rakoniewice 28 52 10N 16 16 E
Rakops 92 21 1S 24 28 E
Rákospalota 27 47 30N 19 5 E
Rakov 54 53 58N 26 59 E
Rakovica 39 44 59N 15 38 E
Rakovník 26 50 6N 13 42 E
Rakovski 43 42 21N 24 57 E
Rakvere 54 59 30N 26 25 E
Raleigh 115 35 47N 78 39W
Raleigh B. 115 34 50N 76 15W
Ralja 42 44 33N 20 34 E
Ralls 117 33 40N 101 20W
Ram → 108 62 1N 123 41W
Rām Allāh 62 31 55N 35 10 E
Rama 62 32 56N 35 21 E
Ramacca 41 37 24N 14 40 E
Ramachandrapuram 70 16 50N 82 4 E
Ramales de la Victoria 32 43 15N 3 28W
Ramanathapuram 70 9 25N 78 55 E
Ramanetaka, B. de 93 14 13S 47 52 E
Ramas C. 70 15 5N 73 55 E
Ramat Gan 62 32 4N 34 48 E
Ramat HaSharon 62 32 7N 34 50 E
Ramatlhabama 92 25 37S 25 33 E
Rambervillers 19 48 20N 6 38 E
Rambipuji 73 8 12S 113 37 E
Rambla, La 31 37 37N 4 45W
Rambouillet 19 48 40N 1 48 E
Ramdurg 70 15 58N 75 22 E
Rame Hd. 99 37 47S 149 30 E
Ramea 107 47 28N 57 4W
Ramechhap 69 27 25N 86 10 E
Ramelau 73 8 55S 126 22 E
Ramenskoye 55 55 32N 38 15 E
Ramgarh, Bihar, India 69 23 40N 85 35 E
Ramgarh, Rajasthan, India 68 27 16N 75 14 E
Ramgarh, Rajasthan, India 68 27 30N 70 36 E
Rāmhormoz 64 31 15N 49 35 E
Ramla 62 31 55N 34 52 E
Ramlat Zalṭan 83 28 30N 19 30 E
Ramlu 87 13 32N 41 40 E
Ramme 49 56 30N 8 11 E
Rammūn 62 31 55N 35 17 E
Ramnad = Ramanathapuram 70 9 25N 78 55 E
Ramnäs 48 59 46N 16 12 E
Ramon 55 51 55N 39 21 E
Ramon, Har 62 30 30N 34 38 E
Ramona 119 33 1N 116 56W
Ramore 106 48 30N 80 25W
Ramos → 120 25 35N 105 3W
Ramoutsa 92 24 50S 25 52 E
Rampart 104 65 0N 150 15W
Rampur, H.P., India 68 31 26N 77 43 E
Rampur, Mad. P., India 68 23 25N 73 53 E
Rampur, Orissa, India 69 21 48N 83 58 E
Rampur, U.P., India 68 28 50N 79 5 E
Rampura 68 24 30N 75 27 E
Rampurhat 69 24 10N 87 50 E
Ramree Kyun 67 19 0N 94 0 E
Ramsey, Can. 106 47 25N 82 20W
Ramsey, U.K. 12 54 20N 4 21W
Ramsgate 13 51 20N 1 25 E
Ramsjö 48 62 11N 15 37 E
Ramtek 69 21 20N 79 15 E
Ramu → 98 4 0S 144 41 E
Ramvik 48 62 49N 17 51 E
Ranaghat 69 23 15N 88 35 E
Ranahu 68 25 55N 69 45 E
Ranau 72 6 2N 116 40 E
Rancagua 124 34 10S 70 50W
Rance → 18 48 34N 1 59W
Rance, Barrage de la 18 48 30N 2 3W
Rancheria → 108 60 13N 129 7W
Ranchester 118 44 57N 107 12W
Ranchi 69 23 19N 85 27 E
Rancu 46 44 32N 24 15 E
Rand 100 35 33S 146 32 E
Randan 20 46 2N 3 21 E
Randazzo 41 37 53N 14 56 E
Randers 49 56 29N 10 1 E
Randers Fjord 49 56 37N 10 20 E
Randfontein 93 26 8S 27 45 E
Randolph, Mass., U.S.A. 113 42 10N 71 3W
Randolph, N.Y., U.S.A. 112 42 10N 78 59W
Randolph, Utah, U.S.A. 118 41 43N 111 10W
Randolph, Vt., U.S.A. 113 43 55N 72 39W
Randsburg 119 35 22N 117 44W
Randsfjorden 47 60 15N 10 25 E
Råne älv → 50 65 50N 22 20 E
Rangaunu B. 101 34 51S 173 15 E
Rångedala 49 57 47N 13 9 E
Rangeley 114 44 58N 70 33W
Rangely 118 40 3N 108 53W
Ranger 117 32 30N 98 42W
Rangia 67 26 28N 91 38 E
Rangiora 101 43 19S 172 36 E
Rangitaiki → 101 37 54S 176 49 E
Rangitata → 101 43 45S 171 15 E
Rangkasbitung 73 6 22S 106 16 E
Rangon → 67 16 28N 96 40 E
Rangoon 67 16 45N 96 20 E
Ranibennur 70 14 35N 75 30 E
Raniganj 69 23 40N 87 5 E
Ranipet 70 12 56N 79 23 E
Rankin 117 31 16N 101 56W
Rankin Inlet 104 62 30N 93 0W
Rankins Springs 99 33 49S 146 14 E
Rannoch, L. 14 56 41N 4 20W
Rannoch Moor 14 56 38N 4 48W
Ranobe, Helodranon' i 93 23 3S 43 33 E
Ranohira 93 22 29S 45 24 E
Ranomafana, Tamatave, Madag. 93 18 57S 48 50 E
Ranomafana, Tuléar, Madag. 93 24 34S 47 0 E
Ranong 71 9 56N 98 40 E
Ransiki 73 1 30S 134 10 E
Rantau 72 2 56S 115 9 E
Rantauprapat 72 2 15N 99 50 E
Rantemario 73 3 15S 119 57 E
Rantīs 62 32 4N 35 3 E
Rantoul 114 40 18N 88 10W
Ranum 49 56 54N 9 14 E
Ranwanlenau 92 19 37S 22 49 E
Raohe 76 46 47N 134 0 E
Raon l'Étape 19 48 24N 6 50 E
Raoui, Erg er 82 29 0N 2 0W
Rapa Iti 95 27 35S 144 20W
Rapallo 38 44 21N 9 12 E
Rapang 73 3 45S 119 55 E
Rāpch 65 25 40N 59 15 E
Rapid → 108 59 15N 129 5W
Rapid City 116 44 0N 103 0W
Rapid River 114 45 55N 87 0W
Rapides des Joachims 106 46 13N 77 43W
Rapla 54 59 1N 24 52 E
Rarotonga 95 21 30S 160 0W
Ra's al Khaymah 65 25 50N 56 5 E
Ra's al-Unuf 83 30 25N 18 15 E
Ras Bânâs 81 23 57N 35 59 E
Ras Dashen 87 13 8N 38 26 E
Ras el Ma 82 34 26N 0 50W
Ras Mallap 86 29 18N 32 50 E
Ra's Tannūrah 64 26 40N 50 10 E
Râs Timirist 84 19 21N 16 30W
Rasa, Punta 128 40 50S 62 15W
Raseiniai 54 55 25N 23 5 E
Rashad 87 11 55N 31 0 E
Rashîd 86 31 21N 30 22 E
Rashîd, Masabb 86 31 22N 30 17 E
Rasht 64 37 20N 49 40 E
Rasipuram 70 11 30N 78 15 E
Raška 42 43 19N 20 39 E
Rason, L. 96 28 45S 124 25 E
Raşova 46 44 15N 27 55 E
Rasovo 43 43 42N 23 17 E
Rasra 69 25 50N 83 50 E
Rass el Oued 83 35 57N 5 2 E
Rasskazovo 55 52 35N 41 50 E
Rastatt 25 48 50N 8 12 E
Rastu 46 43 53N 23 16 E
Raszków 28 51 43N 17 40 E
Rat Buri 71 13 30N 99 54 E
Rat Is. 104 51 50N 178 15 E
Rat River 108 61 7N 112 36W
Ratangarh 68 28 5N 74 35 E
Rath 69 25 36N 79 37 E
Rath Luirc (Charleville) 15 52 21N 8 40W
Rathdrum, Ireland 15 52 57N 6 13W
Rathdrum, U.S.A. 118 47 50N 116 58W
Rathenow 24 52 38N 12 23 E
Rathkeale 15 52 32N 8 57W
Rathlin I. 15 55 18N 6 14W
Rathlin O'Birne I. 15 54 40N 8 50W
Ratibor = Racibórz 27 50 7N 18 18 E
Rätikon 26 47 0N 9 55 E
Ratlam 68 23 20N 75 0 E
Ratnagiri 70 16 57N 73 18 E
Ratnapura 70 6 40N 80 20 E
Raton 117 37 0N 104 30W
Ratten 26 47 28N 15 44 E
Rattray Hd. 14 57 38N 1 50W
Rättvik 48 60 52N 15 7 E
Ratz, Mt. 108 57 23N 132 12W
Ratzeburg 24 53 41N 10 46 E
Raub 71 3 47N 101 52 E
Rauch 124 36 45S 59 5W
Raufarhöfn 50 66 27N 15 57W
Raufoss 47 60 44N 10 37 E
Raukumara Ra. 101 38 5S 177 55 E
Rauland 47 59 43N 8 0 E
Rauma 51 61 10N 21 30 E
Rauma → 47 62 34N 7 43 E
Raundal 47 60 40N 6 37 E
Raung 73 8 8S 114 4 E
Raurkela 69 22 14N 84 50 E
Rava Russkaya 54 50 15N 23 42 E
Ravanusa 40 37 16N 13 58 E
Rāvar 65 31 20N 56 51 E
Ravena 113 42 28N 73 49W
Ravenna, Italy 39 44 28N 12 15 E
Ravenna, Nebr., U.S.A. 116 41 3N 98 58W
Ravenna, Ohio, U.S.A. 112 41 11N 81 15W
Ravensburg 25 47 48N 9 38 E
Ravenshoe 97 17 37S 145 29 E
Ravensthorpe 96 33 35S 120 2 E
Ravenswood, Austral. 98 20 6S 146 54 E
Ravenswood, U.S.A. 114 38 58N 81 47W
Ravi → 68 30 35N 71 49 E
Ravna Gora 39 45 24N 14 50 E
Ravna Reka 42 43 59N 21 35 E
Rawa Mazowiecka 28 51 46N 20 12 E
Rawalpindi 66 33 38N 73 8 E
Rawāndūz 64 36 40N 44 30 E
Rawang 71 3 20N 101 35 E
Rawdon 106 46 3N 73 40W
Rawene 101 35 25S 173 32 E
Rawicz 28 51 36N 16 52 E
Rawka → 28 52 9N 20 8 E
Rawlinna 96 30 58S 125 28 E
Rawlins 118 41 50N 107 20W
Rawlinson Range 96 24 40S 128 30 E
Rawson 128 43 15S 65 0W
Ray 116 48 21N 103 6W
Ray, C. 107 47 33N 59 15W
Rayachoti 70 14 4N 78 50 E
Rayadrug 70 14 40N 76 50 E
Rayagada 70 19 15N 83 20 E
Raychikhinsk 59 49 46N 129 25 E
Raymond, Can. 108 49 30N 112 35W
Raymond, U.S.A. 118 46 45N 123 48W
Raymondville 117 26 30N 97 50W
Raymore 109 51 25N 104 31W
Rayne 117 30 16N 92 16W
Rayong 71 12 40N 101 20 E
Rayville 117 32 30N 91 45W
Raz, Pte. du 18 48 2N 4 47W
Ražana 42 44 6N 19 55 E
Ražanj 42 43 40N 21 31 E
Razdelna 43 43 13N 27 41 E
Razdel'naya 56 46 50N 30 2 E
Razdolnoye 56 45 46N 33 29 E
Razelm, Lacul 46 44 50N 29 0 E
Razgrad 43 43 33N 26 34 E
Razlog 43 41 53N 23 28 E
Razmak 68 32 45N 69 50 E
Razole 70 16 36N 81 48 E
Ré, Île de 20 46 12N 1 30W
Reading, U.K. 13 51 27N 0 57W
Reading, U.S.A. 114 40 20N 75 53W
Realicó 124 35 0S 64 15W
Réalmont 20 43 48N 2 10 E
Ream 71 10 34N 103 39 E
Rebais 19 48 50N 3 10 E
Rebi 73 6 23S 134 7 E
Rebiana 81 24 12N 22 10 E
Rebun-Tō 74 45 23N 141 2 E
Recanati 39 43 24N 13 32 E
Recaş 42 45 46N 21 30 E
Recherche, Arch. of the 96 34 15S 122 50 E
Rechitsa 54 52 13N 30 15 E
Recife 127 8 0S 35 0W
Recklinghausen 24 51 36N 7 10 E
Reconquista 124 29 10S 59 45W
Recreo 124 29 25S 65 10W
Recz 28 53 16N 15 31 E
Red →, Can. 109 50 24N 96 48W
Red →, Minn., U.S.A. 116 48 10N 97 0W
Red →, Tex., U.S.A. 117 31 0N 91 40W
Red Bank 113 40 21N 74 4W
Red Bay 107 51 44N 56 25W
Red Bluff 118 40 11N 122 11W
Red Bluff L. 117 31 59N 103 58W
Red Cloud 116 40 8N 98 33W
Red Deer 108 52 20N 113 50W
Red Deer →, Alta., Can. 109 50 58N 110 0W
Red Deer →, Man., Can. 109 52 53N 101 1W
Red Deer L. 109 52 55N 101 20W
Red Indian L. 107 48 35N 57 0W
Red Lake 109 51 3N 93 49W
Red Lake Falls 116 47 54N 96 15W
Red Lodge 118 45 10N 109 10W
Red Oak 116 41 0N 95 10W
Red Rock 106 48 55N 88 15W
Red Rock, L. 116 41 30N 93 15W

Red Sea 63 25 0N 36 0 E
Red Sucker L 109 54 9N 93 40W
Red Tower Pass = Turnu Rosu P. 46 45 33N 24 17 E
Red Wing 116 44 32N 92 35W
Reda 28 54 40N 18 19 E
Redbridge 13 51 35N 0 7 E
Redcar 12 54 37N 1 4W
Redcliff 109 50 10N 110 50W
Redcliffe 99 27 12 S 153 0 E
Reddersburg 92 29 41 S 26 10 E
Redding 118 40 30N 122 25W
Redditch 13 52 18N 1 57W
Redfield 116 45 0N 98 30W
Redknife → 108 61 14N 119 22W
Redlands 119 34 0N 117 11W
Redmond 118 44 19N 121 11W
Redon 18 47 40N 2 6W
Redonda 121 16 58N 62 19W
Redondela 30 42 15N 8 38W
Redondo 31 38 39N 7 37W
Redondo Beach 119 33 52N 118 26W
Redrock Pt. 108 62 11N 115 2W
Redruth 13 50 14N 5 14W
Redvers 109 49 35N 101 40W
Redwater 108 53 55N 113 6W
Redwood 113 44 18N 75 48W
Redwood City 119 37 30N 122 15W
Redwood Falls 116 44 30N 95 2W
Ree, L. 15 53 35N 8 0W
Reed City 114 43 52N 85 30W
Reed, L 109 54 38N 100 30W
Reeder 116 46 7N 102 52W
Reedley 119 36 36N 119 27W
Reedsburg 116 43 34N 90 5W
Reedsport 118 43 45N 124 4W
Reefton 101 42 6 S 171 51 E
Reftele 49 57 11N 13 35 E
Refugio 117 28 18N 97 17W
Rega → 28 54 10N 15 18 E
Regalbuto 41 37 40N 14 38 E
Regavim 62 32 32N 35 2 E
Regen 25 48 58N 13 9 E
Regen → 25 49 2N 12 6 E
Regensburg 25 49 1N 12 7 E
Réggio di Calábria 41 38 7N 15 38 E
Réggio nell' Emilia 38 44 42N 10 38 E
Regina 109 50 27N 104 35W
Registro 125 24 29 S 47 49W
Reguengos de Monsaraz 31 38 25N 7 32W
Rehar → 69 23 55N 82 40 E
Rehoboth 92 23 15 S 17 4 E
Rehovot 62 31 54N 34 48 E
Rei-Bouba 81 8 40N 14 15 E
Reichenbach 24 50 36N 12 19 E
Reid River 98 19 40 S 146 48 E
Reidsville 115 36 21N 79 40W
Reigate 13 51 14N 0 11W
Reillo 32 39 54N 1 53W
Reims 19 49 15N 4 0 E
Reina 62 32 43N 35 18 E
Reina Adelaida, Arch. 128 52 20 S 74 0W
Reinbeck 116 42 18N 92 0W
Reindeer → 109 55 36N 103 11W
Reindeer I. 109 52 30N 98 0W
Reindeer L. 109 57 15N 102 15W
Reine, La 32 48 50N 79 30W
Reinga, C. 101 34 25 S 172 43 E
Reinosa 30 43 2N 4 15W
Reinosa, Paso 30 42 56N 4 10W
Reitz 93 27 48 S 28 29 E
Reivilo 92 27 36 S 24 8 E
Rejmyra 49 58 50N 15 55 E
Rejowiec Fabryczny 28 51 5N 23 17 E
Reka → 39 45 40N 14 0 E
Rekinniki 59 60 51N 163 40 E
Rekovac 42 43 51N 21 3 E
Reliance 109 63 0N 109 20W
Remad, Oued → 82 33 28N 1 20W
Rémalard 18 48 26N 0 47 E
Remanso 127 9 41 S 42 4W
Remarkable, Mt. 99 32 48 S 138 10 E
Rembang 73 6 42 S 111 21 E
Remchi 82 35 2N 1 26W
Remeshk 65 26 55N 58 50 E
Remetea 46 46 45N 25 29 E
Remich 16 49 32N 6 22 E
Remiremont 19 48 0N 6 36 E
Remo 87 6 48N 41 20 E
Remontnoye 57 46 34N 43 37 E
Remoulins 21 43 55N 4 35 E
Remscheid 24 51 11N 7 12 E
Rena 47 61 8N 11 20 E
Rena → 47 61 8N 11 23 E
Rende 41 39 19N 16 11 E
Rendína 45 39 4N 21 58 E
Rendsburg 24 54 18N 9 41 E
Rene 59 66 2N 179 25W
Renfrew, Can. 106 45 30N 76 40W
Renfrew, U.K. 14 55 52N 4 24W
Rengat 72 0 30 S 102 45 E
Rengo 124 34 24 S 70 50W
Renhuai 77 27 48N 106 24 E
Reni 56 45 28N 28 15 E
Renigunta 70 13 38N 79 30 E
Renk 81 11 50N 32 50 E
Renkum 16 51 58N 5 43 E
Renmark 97 34 11 S 140 43 E
Rennell Sd. 108 53 23N 132 35W
Renner Springs T.O. 96 18 20 S 133 47 E
Rennes 18 48 7N 1 41W
Rennes, Bassin de 18 48 12N 1 33W
Rennesøy 47 59 6N 5 43 E
Reno 118 39 30N 119 50W
Reno → 39 44 37N 12 17 E
Renovo 114 41 20N 77 47W
Rensselaer, Ind., U.S.A. 114 40 57N 87 10W
Rensselaer, N.Y., U.S.A. 113 42 38N 73 41W
Rentería 32 43 19N 1 54W
Renton 118 47 30N 122 9W
Réo 84 12 28N 2 35W
Réole, La 20 44 35N 0 1W
Reotipur 69 25 33N 83 45 E
Repalle 70 16 2N 80 45 E
Répcelak 27 47 24N 17 1 E
Republic, Mich., U.S.A. 114 46 25N 87 59W
Republic, Wash., U.S.A. 118 48 38N 118 42W
Republican → 116 39 3N 96 48W
Republican City 116 40 9N 99 20W
Repulse B., Antarct. 5 64 30 S 99 30 E
Repulse B., Austral. 97 20 31 S 148 45 E
Repulse Bay 105 66 30N 86 30W
Requena, Peru 126 5 5 S 73 52W
Requena, Spain 33 39 30N 1 4W
Resele 48 63 20N 17 5 E
Resen 42 41 5N 21 0 E
Reserve, Can. 109 52 28N 102 39W
Reserve, U.S.A. 119 33 50N 108 54W
Resht = Rasht 64 37 20N 49 40 E
Resistencia 124 27 30 S 59 0W
Reşiţa 42 45 18N 21 53 E
Resko 28 53 47N 15 25 E
Resolution I., Can. 105 61 30N 65 0W
Resolution I., N.Z. 101 45 40 S 166 40 E
Ressano Garcia 93 25 25 S 32 0 E
Reston 109 49 33N 101 6W
Reszel 28 54 4N 21 10 E
Retalhuleu 120 14 33N 91 46W
Reteag 46 47 10N 24 0 E
Retenue, Lac de 91 11 0 S 27 0 E
Rethel 19 49 30N 4 20 E
Rethem 24 52 47N 9 25 E
Réthímnon 45 35 18N 24 30 E
Réthímnon □ 45 35 23N 24 28 E
Rétiers 18 47 55N 1 25W
Retortillo 30 40 48N 6 21W
Rétság 27 47 58N 19 10 E
Réunion 3 22 0 S 56 0 E
Reus 32 41 10N 1 5 E
Reuss → 25 47 16N 8 24 E
Reuterstadt Stavenhagen 24 53 41N 12 54 E
Reutlingen 25 48 28N 9 13 E
Reutte 26 47 29N 10 42 E
Reval = Tallinn 54 59 29N 24 58 E
Revda 52 56 48N 59 57 E
Revel 20 43 28N 2 0 E
Revelganj 69 25 50N 84 40 E
Revelstoke 108 51 0N 118 10W
Reventazón 126 6 10 S 81 0W
Revigny 19 48 50N 5 0 E
Revilla Gigedo, Is. 95 18 40N 112 0W
Revillagigedo I. 108 55 50N 131 20W
Revin 19 49 55N 4 39 E
Revuè → 91 19 50 S 34 0 E
Rewa 69 24 33N 81 25 E
Rewari 68 28 15N 76 40 E
Rexburg 118 43 55N 111 50W
Rey Malabo 88 3 45N 8 50 E
Rey, Rio del → 85 4 30N 8 48 E
Reykjahlið 50 65 40N 16 55W
Reykjanes 50 63 48N 22 40W
Reykjavík 50 64 10N 21 57 E
Reynolds 109 49 40N 95 55W
Reynolds Ra. 96 22 30 S 133 0 E
Reynoldsville 112 41 5N 78 58W
Reynosa 120 26 5N 98 18W
Rezā'īyeh 64 37 40N 45 0 E
Rezā'īyeh, Daryācheh-ye 64 37 50N 45 30 E
Rezekne 54 56 30N 27 17 E
Rezovo 43 42 0N 28 0 E
Rgotina 42 44 1N 22 17 E
Rhamnus 45 38 12N 24 3 E
Rharis, O. → 83 26 0N 5 4 E
Rhayader 13 52 19N 3 30W
Rheden 16 52 0N 6 3 E
Rhein 109 51 25N 102 15W
Rhein → 24 51 52N 6 20 E
Rhein-Main-Donau-Kanal 25 49 1N 11 27 E
Rheinbach 24 50 38N 6 54 E
Rheine 24 52 17N 7 25 E
Rheinland-Pfalz □ 25 50 0N 7 0 E
Rheinsberg 24 53 6N 12 52 E
Rheriss ,Oued → 82 30 50N 4 34W
Rheydt 24 51 10N 6 24 E
Rhin = Rhein → 24 51 52N 6 20 E
Rhinau 19 48 19N 7 43 E
Rhine = Rhein → 24 51 52N 6 20 E
Rhinelander 116 45 38N 89 29W
Rhino Camp 90 3 0N 31 22 E
Rhir, Cap 82 30 38N 9 54W
Rho 38 45 31N 9 2 E
Rhode Island □ 114 41 38N 71 37W
Rhodes = Ródhos 45 36 15N 28 10 E
Rhodes' Tomb 91 20 30 S 28 30 E
Rhodesia = Zimbabwe ■ 91 20 0 S 30 0 E
Rhodope Mts. = Rhodopi Planina 43 41 40N 24 20 E
Rhodopi Planina 43 41 40N 24 20 E
Rhondda 13 51 39N 3 30W
Rhône □ 21 45 54N 4 35 E
Rhône → 21 43 28N 4 42 E
Rhum 14 57 0N 6 20W
Rhumney 13 51 32N 3 7W
Rhyl 12 53 19N 3 29W
Ri-Aba 85 3 28N 8 40 E
Riachão 127 7 20 S 46 37W
Riaño 30 42 59N 5 0W
Rians 21 43 37N 5 44 E
Riansares → 32 39 32N 3 18W
Riasi 69 33 10N 74 50 E
Riau □ 72 0 0 102 35 E
Riau, Kepulauan 72 0 30N 104 20 E
Riaza 32 41 18N 3 30W
Riaza → 32 41 42N 3 55W
Riba de Saelices 32 40 55N 2 17W
Ribadavia 30 42 17N 8 8W
Ribadeo 30 43 35N 7 5W
Ribadesella 30 43 30N 5 7W
Ribas 32 42 19N 2 15 E
Ribble → 12 54 13N 2 20W
Ribe 49 55 19N 8 44 E
Ribeauvillé 19 48 10N 7 20 E
Ribécourt 19 49 30N 2 55 E
Ribeira 30 42 36N 8 58W
Ribeirão Prêto 125 21 10 S 47 50W
Ribemont 19 49 47N 3 27 E
Ribera 40 37 30N 13 13 E
Ribérac 20 45 15N 0 20 E
Riberalta 126 11 0 S 66 0W
Ribnica 39 45 45N 14 45 E
Ribnitz-Damgarten 24 54 14N 12 24 E
Ričany 26 50 0N 14 40 E
Riccarton 101 43 32 S 172 37 E
Riccia 41 41 30N 14 50 E
Riccione 39 44 0N 12 39 E
Rice L. 112 44 12N 78 10W
Rice Lake 116 45 30N 91 42W
Riceys, Les 19 47 59N 4 22 E
Rich 82 32 16N 4 30W
Rich Hill 117 38 5N 94 22W
Richards Bay 93 28 48 S 32 6 E
Richards L. 109 59 10N 107 10W
Richardson → 109 58 25N 111 14W
Richardton 116 46 56N 102 22W
Richelieu 18 47 0N 0 20 E
Richey 116 47 42N 105 5W
Richfield, Idaho, U.S.A. 118 43 2N 114 5W
Richfield, Utah, U.S.A. 119 38 50N 112 0W
Richford 113 45 0N 72 40W
Richibucto 107 46 42N 64 54W
Richland, Ga., U.S.A. 115 32 7N 84 40W
Richland, Oreg., U.S.A. 118 44 49N 117 9W
Richland, Wash., U.S.A. 118 46 15N 119 15W
Richland Center 116 43 21N 90 22W
Richlands 114 37 7N 81 49W
Richmond, N.S.W., Austral. 100 33 35 S 150 42 E
Richmond, Queens., Austral. 97 20 43 S 143 8 E
Richmond, N.Z. 101 41 20 S 173 12 E
Richmond, S. Afr. 93 29 51 S 30 18 E
Richmond, N. Yorks., U.K. 12 54 24N 1 43W
Richmond, Surrey, U.K. 13 51 28N 0 18W
Richmond, Calif., U.S.A. 118 37 58N 122 21W
Richmond, Ind., U.S.A. 114 39 50N 84 50W
Richmond, Ky., U.S.A. 114 37 40N 84 20W
Richmond, Mich., U.S.A. 112 42 47N 82 45W
Richmond, Mo., U.S.A. 116 39 15N 93 58W
Richmond, Tex., U.S.A. 117 29 32N 95 42W
Richmond, Utah, U.S.A. 118 41 55N 111 48W
Richmond, Va., U.S.A. 114 37 33N 77 27W
Richmond, Ra. 99 29 0 S 152 45 E
Richton 115 31 23N 88 58W
Richwood 114 38 17N 80 32W
Ricla 32 41 31N 1 24W
Riddarhyttan 48 59 49N 15 33 E
Ridgedale 109 53 0N 104 10W
Ridgeland 115 32 30N 80 58W
Ridgelands 98 23 16 S 150 17 E
Ridgetown 106 42 26N 81 52W
Ridgewood 113 40 59N 74 7W
Ridgway 114 41 25N 78 43W
Riding Mt. Nat. Park 109 50 50N 100 0W
Ried 26 48 14N 13 30 E
Riedlingen 25 48 9N 9 28 E
Rienza → 39 46 49N 11 47 E
Riesa 24 51 19N 13 19 E
Riesi 41 37 16N 14 4 E
Rieti 39 42 23N 12 50 E
Rieupeyroux 20 44 19N 2 12 E
Riez 21 43 49N 6 6 E
Rifle 118 39 40N 107 50W
Rifstangi 50 66 32N 16 12W
Rift Valley □ 90 0 20N 36 0 E
Rig Rig 81 14 13N 14 25 E
Riga 54 56 53N 24 8 E
Riga, G. of = Rīgas Jūras Līcis 54 57 40N 23 45 E
Rīgas Jūras Līcis 54 57 40N 23 45 E
Rigaud 113 45 29N 74 18W
Rigby 118 43 41N 111 58W
Rīgestān □ 65 30 15N 65 0 E
Riggins 118 45 29N 116 26W
Rignac 20 44 25N 2 16 E
Rigolet 107 54 10N 58 23W
Riihimäki 51 60 45N 24 48 E
Riiser-Larsen-halvøya 5 68 0 S 35 0 E
Rijau 85 11 8N 5 17 E
Rijeka 39 45 20N 14 21 E
Rijeka Crnojevica 42 42 24N 19 1 E
Rijn → 16 52 12N 4 21 E
Rijssen 16 52 19N 6 30 E
Rijswijk 16 52 4N 4 22 E
Rike 87 10 50N 39 53 E
Rila 43 42 7N 23 7 E
Rila Planina 42 42 10N 23 0 E
Riley 118 43 35N 119 33W
Rilly 19 49 11N 4 3 E
Rima → 85 13 4N 5 10 E
Rimah, Wadi ar → 64 26 5N 41 30 E
Rimavská Sobota 27 48 22N 20 2 E
Rimbey 108 52 35N 114 15W
Rimbo 48 59 44N 18 21 E
Rimforsa 49 58 6N 15 43 E
Rimi 85 12 58N 7 43 E
Rímini 39 44 3N 12 33 E
Rîmna → 46 45 36N 27 3 E
Rîmnicu Sărat 46 45 26N 27 3 E
Rîmnicu Vîlcea 46 45 9N 24 21 E
Rimouski 107 48 27N 68 30W
Rinca 73 8 45 S 119 35 E
Rinconada 124 22 26 S 66 10W
Rineanna 15 52 42N 85 7W
Ringarum 49 58 21N 16 26 E
Ringe 49 55 13N 10 28 E
Ringim 85 12 13N 9 10 E
Ringkøbing 49 56 5N 8 15 E
Ringling 118 46 16N 110 56W
Ringsaker 47 60 54N 10 45 E
Ringsjön 49 55 55N 13 30 E
Ringsted 49 55 25N 11 46 E
Ringvassøy 50 69 56N 19 15 E
Rinía 45 37 23N 25 13 E
Rinjani 72 8 24 S 116 28 E
Rinteln 24 52 11N 9 3 E
Rio Branco 126 9 58 S 67 49W
Río Branco 125 32 40 S 53 40W
Rio Brilhante 125 21 48 S 54 33W
Rio Claro, Brazil 125 22 19 S 47 35W
Rio Claro, Trin. 121 10 20N 61 25W
Río Colorado 128 39 0 S 64 0W
Río Cuarto 124 33 10 S 64 25W
Rio das Pedras 93 23 8 S 35 28 E
Rio de Janeiro 125 23 0 S 43 12W
Rio de Janeiro □ 125 22 50 S 43 0W
Rio do Sul 125 27 13 S 49 37W
Río Gallegos 128 51 35 S 69 15W
Río Grande 128 53 50 S 67 45W
Rio Grande 125 32 0 S 52 20W
Rio Grande → 117 25 57N 97 9W
Rio Grande City 117 26 23N 98 49W
Río Grande del Norte → 110 26 0N 97 0W
Rio Grande do Norte □ 127 5 40 S 36 0W
Rio Grande do Sul □ 125 30 0 S 53 0W
Rio Largo 127 9 28 S 35 50W
Rio Maior 31 39 19N 8 57W
Rio Marina 38 42 48N 10 25 E
Río Mulatos 126 19 40 S 66 50W
Río Muni = Mbini □ 88 1 30N 10 0 E
Rio Negro 125 26 0 S 50 0W
Rio Pardo 125 30 0 S 52 30W
Río, Punta del 33 36 49N 2 24W
Río Segundo 124 31 40 S 63 59W
Río Tercero 124 32 15 S 64 8W
Rio Tinto 30 41 11N 8 34W
Rio Verde 127 17 50 S 51 0W
Río Verde 120 21 56N 99 59W
Rio Vista 118 38 11N 121 44W
Ríobamba 126 1 50 S 78 45W
Ríohacha 126 11 33N 72 55W
Rioja, La, Argent. 124 29 20 S 67 0W
Rioja, La, Spain 32 42 20N 2 20W
Rioja, La □ 124 29 30 S 67 0W
Riom 20 45 54N 3 7 E
Riom-ès-Montagnes 20 45 17N 2 39 E
Rion-des-Landes 20 43 55N 0 56W
Rionero in Vúlture 41 40 55N 15 40 E
Rioni → 57 42 5N 41 50 E
Rios 30 41 58N 7 16W
Riosucio 126 5 30N 75 40W
Ríosucio 126 7 27N 77 7W
Riou L. 109 59 7N 106 25W
Rioz 19 47 25N 6 04 E
Riparia, Dora → 38 45 7N 7 24 E
Ripatransone 39 43 0N 13 45 E
Ripley, Can. 112 44 4N 81 35W
Ripley, N.Y., U.S.A. 112 42 16N 79 44W
Ripley, Tenn., U.S.A. 117 35 43N 89 34W
Ripoll 32 42 15N 2 13 E
Ripon, U.K. 12 54 8N 1 31W
Ripon, U.S.A. 114 43 51N 88 50W
Riposto 41 37 44N 15 12 E
Risan 42 42 32N 18 42 E
Riscle 20 43 39N 0 5W
Rishiri-Tō, Japan 74 45 11N 141 15 E
Rishiri-Tō, Japan 74 45 11N 141 15 E
Rishon le Ziyyon 62 31 58N 34 48 E
Rishpon 62 32 12N 34 49 E
Risle → 18 49 26N 0 23 E
Rîsnov 46 45 35N 25 27 E
Rison 117 33 57N 92 11W
Risør 47 58 43N 9 13 E
Ritchies Archipelago 71 12 5N 94 0 E
Riti 85 7 57N 9 41 E
Rittman 112 40 57N 81 48W
Ritzville 118 47 10N 118 21W
Riva Bella 18 49 17N 0 18W
Riva del Garda 38 45 53N 10 50 E
Rivadavia, Buenos Aires, Argent. 124 35 29 S 62 59W
Rivadavia, Mendoza, Argent. 124 33 13 S 68 30W
Rivadavia, Salta, Argent. 124 24 5 S 62 54W
Rivadavia, Chile 124 29 57 S 70 35W
Rivarolo Canavese 38 45 20N 7 42 E
Rivas 121 11 30N 85 50W
Rive-de-Gier 21 45 32N 4 37 E
River Cess 84 5 30N 9 32W
Rivera 125 31 0 S 55 50W
Riverdsale 92 34 7 S 21 15 E
Riverhead 114 40 53N 72 40W
Riverhurst 109 50 55N 106 50W
Riverina 97 35 30 S 145 20 E
Rivers 109 50 2N 100 14W
Rivers □ 85 5 0N 6 30 E
Rivers Inl. 108 51 40N 127 20W
Rivers, L. of the 109 49 49N 105 44W
Riverside, Calif., U.S.A. 119 34 0N 117 22W
Riverside, Wyo., U.S.A. 118 41 12N 106 57W
Riversleigh 98 19 5 S 138 40 E
Riverton, Austral. 99 34 10 S 138 46 E
Riverton, Can. 109 51 1N 97 0W
Riverton, N.Z. 101 46 21 S 168 0 E
Riverton, U.S.A. 118 43 1N 108 27W
Rives 21 45 21N 5 31 E
Rivesaltes 20 42 47N 2 50 E
Riviera 38 44 0N 8 30 E
Riviera di Levante 36 44 23N 9 15 E
Riviera di Ponente 36 43 50N 7 58 E
Rivière-à-Pierre 107 46 59N 72 11W
Rivière-au-Renard 107 48 59N 64 23W
Rivière-du-Loup 107 47 50N 69 30W
Rivière-Pentecôte 107 49 57N 67 1W
Rívoli 38 45 3N 7 31 E
Rivoli B. 99 37 32 S 140 3 E
Riyadh = Ar Riyāḍ 64 24 41N 46 42 E
Rize 64 41 0N 40 30 E
Rizhao 77 35 25N 119 30 E
Rizzuto, C. 41 38 54N 17 5 E
Rjukan 47 59 54N 8 33 E
Rjuven 47 59 9N 7 8 E
Roa, Norway 47 60 17N 10 37 E
Roa, Spain 30 41 41N 3 56W
Roag, L. 14 58 10N 6 55W
Roanne 21 46 3N 4 4 E
Roanoke, Ala., U.S.A. 115 33 9N 85 23W
Roanoke, Va., U.S.A. 114 37 19N 79 55W
Roanoke → 115 35 56N 76 43W
Roanoke I. 115 35 55N 75 40W
Roanoke Rapids 115 36 28N 77 42W
Roatán 121 16 18N 86 35W
Robbins I. 99 40 42 S 145 0 E
Robe → 15 53 38N 9 10W
Robe, Mt. 100 31 40 S 141 20 E
Röbel 24 53 24N 12 37 E

Robert Lee **117** 31 55N 100 26W
Roberts **118** 43 44N 112 8W
Robertsganj **69** 24 44N 83 4 E
Robertson **92** 33 46 S 19 50 E
Robertson I. **5** 65 15 S 59 30W
Robertsport **84** 6 45N 11 26W
Robertstown **99** 33 58 S 139 5 E
Roberval **107** 48 32N 72 15W
Robeson Ch. **4** 82 0N 61 30W
Robinson Crusoe I. **95** 33 38 S 78 52W
Robinson Ranges **96** 25 40 S 119 0 E
Robinvale **99** 34 40 S 142 45 E
Robla, La **30** 42 50N 5 41W
Roblin **109** 51 14N 101 21W
Roboré **126** 18 10 S 59 45W
Robson, Mt. **108** 53 10N 119 10W
Robstown **117** 27 47N 97 40W
Roc, Pointe du **18** 48 50N 1 37W
Roca, C. da **31** 38 40N 9 31W
Rocas, I. **127** 4 0 S 34 1W
Rocca d'Aspidé **41** 40 27N 15 10 E
Rocca San Casciano **39** 44 3N 11 45 E
Roccalbegna **39** 42 47N 11 30 E
Roccastrada **39** 43 0N 11 10 E
Roccella Iónica **41** 38 20N 16 24 E
Rocha **125** 34 30 S 54 25W
Rochdale **12** 53 36N 2 10W
Roche-Bernard, La **18** 47 31N 2 19W
Roche-Canillac, La **20** 45 12N 1 57 E
Roche, La **21** 46 4N 6 19 E
Roche-sur-Yon, La **18** 46 40N 1 25W
Rochechouart **20** 45 50N 0 49 E
Rochefort, Belg. **16** 50 9N 5 12 E
Rochefort, France **20** 45 56N 0 57W
Rochefort-en-Terre **18** 47 42N 2 22W
Rochefoucauld, La **20** 45 44N 0 24 E
Rochelle **116** 41 55N 89 5W
Rochelle, La **20** 46 10N 1 9W
Rocher River **108** 61 23N 112 44W
Rocheservière **18** 46 57N 1 30W
Rochester, Austral. **100** 36 22 S 144 41 E
Rochester, Can. **108** 54 22N 113 27W
Rochester, U.K. **13** 51 22N 0 30 E
Rochester, Ind., U.S.A. **114** 41 5N 86 15W
Rochester, Minn., U.S.A. **116** 44 1N 92 28W
Rochester, N.H., U.S.A. **114** 43 19N 70 57W
Rochester, N.Y., U.S.A. **114** 43 10N 77 40W
Rochester, Pa., U.S.A. **112** 40 41N 80 17W
Rociana **31** 37 19N 6 35W
Rociu **46** 44 43N 25 2 E
Rock → **108** 60 7N 127 7W
Rock Hill **115** 34 55N 81 2W
Rock Island **116** 41 30N 90 35W
Rock Port **116** 40 26N 95 30W
Rock Rapids **116** 43 25N 96 10W
Rock River **118** 41 49N 106 0W
Rock Sound **121** 24 54N 76 12W
Rock Sprs., Ariz., U.S.A. **119** 34 2N 112 11W
Rock Sprs., Mont., U.S.A. **118** 46 55N 106 11W
Rock Sprs., Tex., U.S.A. **117** 30 2N 100 11W
Rock Sprs., Wyo., U.S.A. **118** 41 40N 109 10W
Rock Valley **116** 43 10N 96 17W
Rockall **8** 57 37N 13 42W
Rockdale **117** 30 40N 97 0W
Rockefeller Plat. **5** 80 0 S 140 0W
Rockford **116** 42 20N 89 0W
Rockglen **109** 49 11N 105 57W
Rockhampton **97** 23 22 S 150 32 E
Rockingham B. **98** 18 5 S 146 10 E
Rockingham Forest **13** 52 28N 0 42W
Rocklake **116** 48 50N 99 13W
Rockland, Can. **113** 45 33N 75 17W
Rockland, Idaho, U.S.A. **118** 42 37N 112 57W
Rockland, Me., U.S.A. **107** 44 6N 69 6W
Rockland, Mich., U.S.A. **116** 46 40N 89 10W
Rocklands Reservoir **100** 37 15 S 142 5 E
Rockmart **115** 34 1N 85 2W
Rockport **117** 28 2N 97 3W
Rockville, Conn., U.S.A. **113** 41 51N 72 27W
Rockville, Md., U.S.A. **114** 39 7N 77 10W
Rockwall **117** 32 55N 96 30W
Rockwell City **116** 42 20N 94 35W
Rockwood **115** 35 52N 84 40W
Rocky Ford **116** 38 7N 103 45W
Rocky Lane **108** 58 31N 116 22W
Rocky Mount **115** 35 55N 77 48W
Rocky Mountain House **108** 52 22N 114 55W
Rocky Mts. **108** 55 0N 121 0W
Rocky Pt. **96** 33 30 S 123 57 E
Rocky River **112** 41 30N 81 40W
Rockyford **108** 51 14N 113 10W
Rocroi **19** 49 55N 4 30 E
Rod **66** 28 10N 63 5 E
Roda, La, Albacete, Spain **33** 39 13N 2 15W
Roda, La, Sevilla, Spain **31** 37 12N 4 46W
Rødberg **47** 60 17N 8 56 E
Rødby **49** 54 41N 11 23 E
Rødbyhavn **49** 54 39N 11 22 E
Roddickton **107** 50 51N 56 8W
Rødding **49** 55 23N 9 3 E
Rødekro **49** 55 4N 9 20 E
Rødenes **47** 59 35N 11 34 E
Rodenkirchen **24** 53 24N 8 26 E
Roderick I. **108** 52 38N 128 22W
Rodez **20** 44 21N 2 33 E
Rodholivas **44** 40 55N 24 0 E
Rodhópi □ **44** 41 5N 25 30 E
Ródhos **45** 36 15N 28 10 E
Rodi Garganico **41** 41 55N 15 53 E
Rodna **46** 47 25N 24 50 E
Rodnei, Munţii **46** 47 35N 24 35 E
Rodney **112** 42 34N 81 41W
Rodney, C. **101** 36 17 S 174 50 E
Rodniki **55** 57 7N 41 47 E
Rodriguez **3** 19 45 S 63 20 E
Rodstock, C. **96** 33 12 S 134 20 E
Roe → **15** 55 10N 6 59W
Roebling **113** 40 7N 74 45W
Roebourne **96** 20 44 S 117 9 E
Roebuck B. **96** 18 5 S 122 20 E
Roermond **16** 51 12N 6 0 E
Roes Welcome Sd. **105** 65 0N 87 0W
Roeselare **16** 50 57N 3 7 E
Rogachev **54** 53 8N 30 5 E
Rogaçica **42** 44 4N 19 40 E
Rogagua, L. **126** 13 43 S 66 50W
Rogaland fylke □ **47** 59 12N 6 20 E
Rogaška Slatina **39** 46 15N 15 42 E
Rogatec **39** 46 15N 15 46 E
Rogatica **42** 43 47N 19 0 E
Rogatin **54** 49 24N 24 36 E
Rogers **117** 36 20N 94 5W
Rogers City **114** 45 25N 83 49W
Rogerson **118** 42 10N 114 40W
Rogersville **115** 36 27N 83 1W
Roggan **106** 54 25N 79 32W
Roggeveldberge **92** 32 10 S 20 10 E
Roggiano Gravina **41** 39 37N 16 9 E
Rogliano, France **21** 42 57N 9 30 E
Rogliano, Italy **41** 39 11N 16 20 E
Rogoaguado, L. **126** 13 0 S 65 30W
Rogowo **28** 52 43N 17 38 E
Rogozno **28** 52 45N 16 59 E
Rogue → **118** 42 30N 124 0W
Rohan **18** 48 4N 2 45W
Rohrbach **19** 49 3N 7 15 E
Rohri **68** 27 45N 68 51 E
Rohri Canal **68** 26 15N 68 27 E
Rohtak **68** 28 55N 76 43 E
Roi Et **71** 16 4N 103 40 E
Roisel **19** 49 58N 3 6 E
Rojas **124** 34 10 S 60 45W
Rojo, C. **120** 21 33N 97 20W
Rokan → **72** 2 0N 100 50 E
Rokeby **98** 13 39 S 142 40 E
Rokiskis **54** 55 55N 25 35 E
Rokitno **54** 50 57N 35 56 E
Rokycany **26** 49 43N 13 35 E
Rolândia **125** 23 18 S 51 23W
Røldal **47** 59 47N 6 50 E
Rolette **116** 48 42N 99 50W
Rolla, Kansas, U.S.A. **117** 37 10N 101 40W
Rolla, Mo., U.S.A. **117** 37 56N 91 42W
Rolla, N. Dak., U.S.A. **116** 48 50N 99 36W
Rollag **47** 60 2N 9 18 E
Rolleston **98** 24 28 S 148 35 E
Rollingstone **98** 19 2 S 146 24 E
Rom **87** 9 54N 32 16 E
Roma, Austral. **97** 26 32 S 148 49 E
Roma, Italy **40** 41 54N 12 30 E
Roman, Bulg. **43** 43 8N 23 54 E
Roman, Romania **46** 46 57N 26 55 E
Roman, U.S.S.R. **59** 66 4N 112 14 E
Roman-Kosh, Gora **56** 44 37N 34 15 E
Romana, La **121** 18 27N 68 57W
Romanche → **21** 45 5N 5 43 E
Romang **73** 7 30 S 127 20 E
Români **86** 30 59N 32 38 E
Romania ■ **46** 46 0N 25 0 E
Romanija Planina **42** 43 50N 18 45 E
Romano, Cayo **121** 22 0N 77 30W
Romano di Lombardia **38** 45 32N 9 45 E
Romanovka = Bessarabka **56** 46 21N 28 58 E
Romans **21** 45 3N 5 3 E
Romanshorn **25** 47 33N 9 22 E
Romblon **73** 12 33N 122 17 E
Rombo □ **90** 3 10 S 37 30 E
Rome, Ga., U.S.A. **115** 34 20N 85 0W
Rome, N.Y., U.S.A. **114** 43 14N 75 29W
Rome = Roma **40** 41 54N 12 30 E
Romeleåsen **49** 55 34N 13 33 E
Romenay **21** 46 30N 5 1 E
Romerike **47** 60 7N 11 10 E
Romilly **19** 48 31N 3 44 E
Romîni **46** 44 59N 24 11 E
Rommani **82** 33 31N 6 40W
Romney **114** 39 21N 78 45W
Romney Marsh **13** 51 0N 1 0 E
Romny **54** 50 48N 33 28 E
Rømø **49** 55 10N 8 30 E
Romodan **54** 50 0N 33 15 E
Romodanovo **55** 54 26N 45 23 E
Romont **25** 46 42N 6 54 E
Romorantin-Lanthenay **19** 47 21N 1 45 E
Romsdalen **47** 62 25N 8 0 E
Rona **14** 57 33N 6 0W
Ronan **118** 47 30N 114 6W
Roncador, Cayos **121** 13 32N 80 4W
Roncador, Serra do **127** 12 30 S 52 30W
Roncesvalles, Paso **32** 43 1N 1 19W
Ronceverte **114** 37 45N 80 28W
Ronciglione **39** 42 18N 12 12 E
Ronco → **39** 44 24N 12 12 E
Ronda **31** 36 46N 5 12W
Ronda, Serranía de **31** 36 44N 5 3W
Rondane **47** 61 57N 9 50 E
Rondônia □ **126** 11 0 S 63 0W
Rondonópolis **127** 16 28 S 54 38W
Rong, Koh **71** 10 45N 103 15 E
Rong Xian **77** 29 23N 104 22 E
Rong'an **77** 25 14N 109 22 E
Ronge, L. la **109** 55 6N 105 17W
Ronge, La **109** 55 5N 105 20W
Rongshui **77** 25 5N 109 12 E
Ronne Land **5** 83 0 S 70 0W
Ronneby **49** 56 12N 15 17 E
Ronse **16** 50 45N 3 35 E
Roof Butte **119** 36 29N 109 5W
Roorkee **68** 29 52N 77 59 E
Roosendaal **16** 51 32N 4 29 E
Roosevelt, Minn., U.S.A. **116** 48 51N 95 2W
Roosevelt, Utah, U.S.A. **118** 40 19N 110 1W
Roosevelt I. **5** 79 30 S 162 0W
Roosevelt, Mt. **108** 58 26N 125 20W
Roosevelt Res. **119** 33 46N 111 0W
Ropczyce **27** 50 4N 21 38 E
Roper → **96** 14 43 S 135 27 E
Ropesville **117** 33 25N 102 10W
Roque Pérez **124** 35 25 S 59 24W
Roquebrou, La **20** 44 58N 2 12 E
Roquefort **20** 44 2N 0 20W
Roquefort-sur-Soulzon **20** 43 58N 2 59 E
Roquemaure **21** 44 3N 4 48 E
Roquetas **32** 40 50N 0 30 E
Roquevaire **21** 43 20N 5 36 E
Roraima □ **126** 2 0N 61 30W
Roraima, Mt. **126** 5 10N 60 40W
Rorketon **109** 51 24N 99 35W
Røros **47** 62 35N 11 23 E
Rorschach **25** 47 28N 9 30 E
Rosa **91** 9 33 S 31 15 E
Rosa, C. **83** 37 0N 8 16 E
Rosa, Monte **25** 45 57N 7 53 E
Rosal **30** 41 57N 8 51W
Rosal de la Frontera **31** 37 59N 7 13W
Rosalia **118** 47 14N 117 25W
Rosans **21** 44 24N 5 29 E
Rosario **124** 33 0 S 60 40W
Rosário **127** 3 0 S 44 15W
Rosario, Baja Calif. N., Mexico **120** 30 0N 115 50W
Rosario, Durango, Mexico **120** 26 30N 105 35W
Rosario, Sinaloa, Mexico **120** 23 0N 105 52W
Rosario, Parag. **124** 24 30 S 57 35W
Rosario de la Frontera **124** 25 50 S 65 0W
Rosario de Lerma **124** 24 59 S 65 35W
Rosario del Tala **124** 32 20 S 59 10W
Rosário do Sul **125** 30 15 S 54 55W
Rosarno **41** 38 29N 15 59 E
Rosas **32** 42 19N 3 10 E
Roscoe **116** 45 27N 99 20W
Roscoff **18** 48 44N 4 0W
Roscommon, Ireland **15** 53 38N 8 11W
Roscommon, U.S.A. **114** 44 27N 84 35W
Roscommon □ **15** 53 40N 8 15W
Roscrea **15** 52 58N 7 50W
Rose Blanche **107** 47 38N 58 45W
Rose Harbour **108** 52 15N 131 10W
Rose Pt. **108** 54 11N 131 39W
Rose Valley **109** 52 19N 103 49W
Roseau, Domin. **121** 15 20N 61 24W
Roseau, U.S.A. **116** 48 51N 95 46W
Rosebery **99** 41 46 S 145 33 E
Rosebud, Austral. **100** 38 21 S 144 54 E
Rosebud, U.S.A. **117** 31 5N 97 0W
Roseburg **118** 43 10N 123 20W
Rosedale, Austral. **98** 24 38 S 151 53 E
Rosedale, U.S.A. **117** 33 51N 91 0W
Rosemary **108** 50 46N 112 5W
Rosenberg **117** 29 30N 95 48W
Rosendaël **19** 51 3N 2 24 E
Rosenheim **25** 47 51N 12 9 E
Roseto degli Abruzzi **39** 42 40N 14 2 E
Rosetown **109** 51 35N 107 59W
Rosetta = Rashîd **86** 31 21N 30 22 E
Roseville **118** 38 46N 121 17W
Rosewood **99** 27 38 S 152 36 E
Rosh Haniqra, Kefar **62** 33 5N 35 5 E
Rosh Pinna **62** 32 58N 35 32 E
Rosières **19** 49 49N 2 43 E
Rosignano Marittimo **38** 43 23N 10 28 E
Rosignol **126** 6 15N 57 30W
Roşiori de Vede **46** 44 9N 25 0 E
Rositsa **43** 43 57N 27 57 E
Rositsa → **43** 43 10N 25 30 E
Roskilde **49** 55 38N 12 3 E
Roskilde Amtskommune □ **49** 55 35N 12 5 E
Roskilde Fjord **49** 55 50N 12 2 E
Roslavl **54** 53 57N 32 55 E
Roslyn **99** 34 29 S 149 37 E
Rosmaninhal **31** 39 44N 7 5W
Røsnæs **49** 55 44N 10 55 E
Rosolini **41** 36 49N 14 58 E
Rosporden **18** 47 57N 3 50W
Ross, Austral. **99** 42 2 S 147 30 E
Ross, N.Z. **101** 42 53 S 170 49 E
Ross Dependency □ **5** 70 0 S 170 5W
Ross I. **5** 77 30 S 168 0 E
Ross Ice Shelf **5** 80 0 S 180 0W
Ross L. **118** 48 50N 121 5W
Ross on Wye **13** 51 55N 2 34W
Ross Sea **5** 74 0 S 178 0 E
Rossan Pt. **15** 54 42N 8 47W
Rossano Cálabro **41** 39 36N 16 39 E
Rossburn **109** 50 40N 100 49W
Rosseau **112** 45 16N 79 39W
Rossignol, L., N.S., Can. **107** 44 12N 65 10W
Rossignol, L., Qué., Can. **106** 52 43N 73 40W
Rossland **108** 49 6N 117 50W
Rosslare **15** 52 17N 6 23W
Rosslau **24** 51 52N 12 15 E
Rosso **84** 16 40N 15 45W
Rossosh **57** 50 15N 39 28 E
Rossport **106** 48 50N 87 30W
Røssvatnet **50** 65 45N 14 5 E
Rossville **98** 15 48 S 145 15 E
Rosthern **109** 52 40N 106 20W
Rostock **24** 54 4N 12 9 E
Rostock □ **24** 54 10N 12 30 E
Rostov, Don, U.S.S.R. **57** 47 15N 39 45 E
Rostov, Moskva, U.S.S.R. **55** 57 14N 39 25 E
Rostrenen **18** 48 14N 3 21W
Roswell **117** 33 26N 104 32W
Rosyth **14** 56 2N 3 26W
Rota **31** 36 37N 6 20W
Rotälven → **48** 61 15N 14 3 E
Rotan **117** 32 52N 100 30W
Rotenburg **24** 53 6N 9 24 E
Roth **25** 49 15N 11 6 E
Rothaargebirge **22** 51 0N 8 20 E
Rothenburg ob der Tauber **25** 49 21N 10 11 E
Rother → **13** 50 59N 0 40 E
Rotherham **12** 53 26N 1 21W
Rothes **14** 57 31N 3 12W
Rothesay, Can. **107** 45 23N 66 0W
Rothesay, U.K. **14** 55 50N 5 3W
Roti **73** 10 50 S 123 0 E
Roto **97** 33 0 S 145 30 E
Rotondella **41** 40 10N 16 30 E
Rotoroa, L. **101** 41 55 S 172 39 E
Rotorua **101** 38 9 S 176 16 E
Rotorua, L. **101** 38 5 S 176 18 E
Rott → **25** 48 26N 13 26 E
Rottenburg **25** 48 28N 8 56 E
Rottenmann **26** 47 31N 14 22 E
Rotterdam **16** 51 55N 4 30 E
Rottumeroog **16** 53 33N 6 34 E
Rottweil **25** 48 9N 8 38 E
Rotuma **94** 12 25 S 177 5 E
Roubaix **19** 50 40N 3 10 E
Roudnice **26** 50 25N 14 15 E
Rouen **18** 49 27N 1 4 E
Rouillac **20** 45 47N 0 4W
Rouleau **109** 50 10N 104 56W
Round Mt. **97** 30 26 S 152 16 E
Round Mountain **118** 38 46N 117 3W
Roundup **118** 46 25N 108 35W
Rousay **14** 59 10N 3 2W
Rouses Point **113** 44 58N 73 22W
Rousse, L'Île **21** 42 37N 8 57 E
Roussillon, Isère, France **21** 45 24N 4 49 E
Roussillon, Pyrénées-Or., France **20** 42 30N 2 35 E
Rouxville **92** 30 25 S 26 50 E
Rouyn **106** 48 20N 79 0W
Rovaniemi **50** 66 29N 25 41 E
Rovato **38** 45 34N 10 0 E
Rovenki **57** 48 5N 39 21 E
Rovereto **38** 45 53N 11 3 E
Rovigo **39** 45 4N 11 48 E
Rovinari **46** 44 56N 23 10 E
Rovinj **39** 45 5N 13 40 E
Rovno **54** 50 40N 26 10 E
Rovnoye **55** 50 52N 46 3 E
Rovuma → **91** 10 29 S 40 28 E
Rowena **99** 29 48 S 148 55 E
Rowley Shoals **96** 17 30 S 119 0 E
Roxa **84** 11 15N 15 45W
Roxas **73** 11 36N 122 49 E
Roxboro **115** 36 24N 78 59W
Roxborough Downs **98** 22 30 S 138 45 E
Roxburgh **101** 45 33 S 169 19 E
Roxen **49** 58 30N 15 40 E
Roy, Mont., U.S.A. **118** 47 17N 109 0W
Roy, N. Mex., U.S.A. **117** 35 57N 104 8W
Roy, Le **117** 38 8N 95 35W
Roya, Peña **32** 40 25N 0 40W
Royal Oak **114** 42 30N 83 5W
Royan **20** 45 37N 1 2W
Roye **19** 49 42N 2 48 E
Røyken **47** 59 45N 10 23 E
Rožaj **42** 42 50N 20 15 E
Różan **28** 52 52N 21 25 E
Rozay **19** 48 40N 2 56 E
Rozhishche **54** 50 54N 25 15 E
Rozier, Le **20** 44 13N 3 12 E
Rožnava **27** 48 37N 20 35 E
Rozogi **28** 53 48N 21 9 E
Rozoy-sur-Serre **19** 49 40N 4 8 E
Rozwadów **28** 50 37N 22 2 E
Rrësheni **44** 41 47N 19 49 E
Rrogozhino **44** 41 2N 19 50 E
Rtanj **42** 43 45N 21 50 E
Rtishchevo **55** 55 16N 43 50 E
Rúa **30** 42 24N 7 6W
Ruacaná **92** 17 20 S 14 12 E
Ruahine Ra. **101** 39 55 S 176 2 E
Ruapehu **101** 39 17 S 175 35 E
Ruapuke I. **101** 46 46 S 168 31 E
Ruaus, Wadi → **83** 30 26N 15 24 E
Rubeho Mts. **90** 6 50 S 36 25 E
Rubezhnoye **56** 49 6N 38 25 E
Rubh a' Mhail **14** 55 55N 6 10W
Rubha Hunish **14** 57 42N 6 20W
Rubicone → **39** 44 8N 12 28 E
Rubino **84** 6 4N 4 18W
Rubio **126** 7 43N 72 22W
Rubtsovsk **58** 51 30N 81 10 E
Ruby **104** 64 40N 155 35W
Ruby L. **118** 40 10N 115 28W
Ruby Mts. **118** 40 30N 115 30W
Rubyvale **98** 23 25 S 147 45 E
Rucava **54** 56 9N 21 12 E
Ruciane-Nida **28** 53 40N 21 32 E
Rud **47** 60 1N 10 1 E
Ruda **49** 57 6N 16 7 E
Ruda Śląska **28** 50 16N 18 50 E
Ruden **24** 54 13N 13 47 E
Rüdersdorf **24** 52 28N 13 48 E
Rudewa **91** 10 7 S 34 40 E
Rudkøbing **49** 54 56N 10 41 E
Rudna **28** 51 30N 16 17 E
Rudnichnyy **52** 59 38N 52 26 E
Rudnik, Bulg. **43** 42 36N 27 30 E
Rudnik, Poland **28** 50 26N 22 15 E
Rudnik, Yugo. **42** 44 8N 20 30 E
Rudnik, Yugo. **43** 44 7N 20 35 E
Rudnogorsk **59** 57 15N 103 42 E
Rudnya **54** 54 55N 31 7 E
Rudnyy **58** 52 57N 63 7 E
Rudo **42** 43 41N 19 23 E
Rudolf, Ostrov **58** 81 45N 58 30 E
Rudolstadt **24** 50 44N 11 20 E
Rudozem **43** 41 29N 24 51 E
Rudyard **114** 46 14N 84 35W
Rue **19** 50 15N 1 40 E
Ruelle **20** 45 41N 0 14 E
Rufa'a **87** 14 44N 33 22 E
Ruffec-Charente **20** 46 2N 0 12 E
Rufiji □ **90** 8 0 S 38 30 E
Rufiji → **90** 7 50 S 39 15 E
Rufino **124** 34 20 S 62 50W
Rufisque **84** 14 40N 17 15W
Rufunsa **91** 15 4 S 29 34 E
Rugao **77** 32 23N 120 31 E
Rugby, U.K. **13** 52 23N 1 16W
Rugby, U.S.A. **116** 48 21N 100 0W
Rügen **24** 54 22N 13 25 E
Rugles **18** 48 50N 0 40 E
Ruhama **62** 31 31N 34 43 E
Ruhengeri **90** 1 30 S 29 36 E
Ruhla **24** 50 53N 10 21 E
Ruhland **24** 51 27N 13 52 E
Ruhr → **24** 51 25N 6 44 E
Ruhuhu → **91** 10 31 S 34 34 E
Rui'an **77** 27 47N 120 40 E
Ruidosa **117** 29 59N 104 39W
Ruidoso **119** 33 19N 105 39W
Ruj **42** 42 52N 22 42 E
Rujen **42** 42 9N 22 30 E

Place	Map	Lat.	Long.
Ruk	68	27 50N	68 42 E
Rukwa □	90	7 0S	31 30 E
Rukwa L.	90	8 0S	32 20 E
Rum Cay	121	23 40N	74 58W
Rum Jungle	96	13 0S	130 59 E
Ruma	42	45 0N	19 50 E
Rumāḩ	64	25 29N	47 10 E
Rumania = Romania ■	46	46 0N	25 0 E
Rumbêk	87	6 54N	29 37 E
Rumburk	26	50 57N	14 32 E
Rumford	114	44 30N	70 30W
Rumia	28	54 37N	18 25 E
Rumilly	21	45 53N	5 56 E
Rumoi	74	43 56N	141 39W
Rumonge	90	3 59S	29 26 E
Rumsey	108	51 51N	112 48W
Rumula	98	16 35S	145 20 E
Rumuruti	90	0 17N	36 32 E
Runan	77	33 0N	114 30 E
Runanga	101	42 25S	171 15 E
Runaway, C.	101	37 32S	178 2 E
Runcorn	12	53 20N	2 44W
Rungwa	90	6 55S	33 32 E
Rungwa →	90	7 36S	31 50 E
Rungwe	91	9 11S	33 32 E
Rungwe □	91	9 25S	33 32 E
Runka	85	12 28N	7 20 E
Runn	48	60 30N	15 40 E
Ruoqiang	75	38 55N	88 10 E
Rupa	67	27 15N	92 21 E
Rupar	68	31 2N	76 38 E
Rupat	72	1 45N	101 40 E
Rupea	46	46 2N	25 13 E
Rupert →	106	51 29N	78 45W
Rupert House = Fort Rupert	106	51 30N	78 40W
Rupsa	69	21 44N	89 30 E
Rur →	24	51 20N	6 0 E
Rurrenabaque	126	14 30S	67 32W
Rus →	33	39 30N	2 30W
Rusambo	91	16 30S	32 4 E
Rusape	91	18 35S	32 8 E
Ruschuk = Ruse	43	43 48N	25 59 E
Ruse	43	43 48N	25 59 E
Ruşeţu	46	44 57N	27 14 E
Rushden	13	52 17N	0 37W
Rushford	116	43 48N	91 46W
Rushville, Ill., U.S.A.	116	40 6N	90 35W
Rushville, Ind., U.S.A.	114	39 38N	85 22W
Rushville, Nebr., U.S.A.	116	42 43N	102 28W
Rushworth	100	36 32S	145 1 E
Rusken	49	57 15N	14 20 E
Russas	127	4 55S	37 50W
Russell, Can.	109	50 50N	101 20W
Russell, N.Z.	101	35 16S	174 10 E
Russell, U.S.A.	116	38 56N	98 55W
Russell L., Man., Can.	109	56 15N	101 30W
Russell L., N.W.T., Can.	108	63 5N	115 44W
Russellkonda	69	19 57N	84 42 E
Russellville, Ala., U.S.A.	115	34 30N	87 44W
Russellville, Ark., U.S.A.	117	35 15N	93 8W
Russellville, Ky., U.S.A.	115	36 50N	86 50W
Russi	39	44 21N	12 1 E
Russian S.F.S.R. □	59	62 0N	105 0 E
Russkaya Polyana	58	53 47N	73 53 E
Russkoye Ustie	4	71 0N	149 0 E
Rust	27	47 49N	16 42 E
Rustavi	57	41 30N	45 0 E
Rustenburg	92	25 41S	27 14 E
Ruston	117	32 30N	92 58W
Rutana	90	3 55S	30 0 E
Rute	31	37 19N	4 23W
Ruteng	73	8 35S	120 30 E
Ruth, Mich., U.S.A.	112	43 42N	82 45W
Ruth, Nev., U.S.A.	118	39 15N	115 1W
Rutherglen, Austral.	100	36 5S	146 29 E
Rutherglen, U.K.	14	55 50N	4 11W
Rutigliano	41	41 1N	17 0 E
Rutland I.	71	11 25N	92 40 E
Rutland Plains	98	15 38S	141 43 E
Rutledge →	109	61 4N	112 0W
Rutledge L.	109	61 33N	110 47W
Rutshuru	90	1 13S	29 25 E
Ruurlo	16	52 5N	6 24 E
Ruvo di Púglia	41	41 7N	16 27 E
Ruvu	90	6 49S	38 43 E
Ruvu →	90	6 23S	38 52 E
Ruvuma □	91	10 20S	36 0 E
Ruwenzori	90	0 30N	29 55 E
Ruyigi	90	3 29S	30 15 E
Ruzayevka	55	54 4N	45 0 E
Růžhevo Konare	43	42 23N	24 46 E
Ružomberok	27	49 3N	19 17 E
Rwanda ■	90	2 0S	30 0 E
Ry	49	56 5N	9 45 E
Ryakhovo	43	44 0N	26 18 E
Ryan, L.	14	55 0N	5 2W
Ryazan	55	54 40N	39 40 E
Ryazhsk	55	53 45N	40 3 E
Rybache	58	46 40N	81 20 E
Rybachiy Poluostrov	52	69 43N	32 0 E
Rybinsk	55	58 5N	38 50 E
Rybinskoye Vdkhr.	55	58 30N	38 25 E
Rybnik	27	50 6N	18 32 E
Rybnitsa	56	47 45N	29 0 E
Rybnoye	55	54 45N	39 30 E
Rychwał	28	52 4N	18 10 E
Ryd	49	56 27N	14 42 E
Ryde	13	50 44N	1 9W
Rydöbruk	49	56 58N	13 7 E
Rydsnäs	49	57 47N	15 9 E
Rydultowy	27	50 4N	18 23 E
Rydzyna	28	51 47N	16 39 E
Rye	13	50 57N	0 46 E
Rye →	12	54 12N	0 53W
Rye Patch Res.	118	40 38N	118 20W
Ryegate	118	46 21N	109 15W
Ryki	28	51 38N	21 56 E
Rylsk	54	51 36N	34 43 E
Rylstone	99	32 46S	149 58 E
Rymanów	27	49 35N	21 51 E
Ryn	28	53 57N	21 34 E
Rypin	28	53 3N	19 25 E
Ryūkyū Is. = Nansei-Shotō	74	26 0N	128 0 E
Rzepin	28	52 20N	14 49 E
Rzeszów	27	50 5N	21 58 E
Rzeszów □	27	50 0N	22 0 E
Rzhev	54	56 20N	34 20 E

S

Place	Map	Lat.	Long.
Sa Dec	71	10 20N	105 46 E
Sa'ad (Muharraqa)	62	31 28N	34 33 E
Sa'ādatābād	65	30 10N	53 5 E
Saale →	24	51 57N	11 56 E
Saaler Bodden	24	54 20N	12 25 E
Saalfeld	24	50 39N	11 21 E
Saalfelden	26	47 25N	12 51 E
Saane →	25	46 23N	7 18 E
Saar (Sarre) →	19	49 42N	6 34 E
Saarbrücken	25	49 15N	6 58 E
Saarburg	25	49 36N	6 32 E
Saaremaa	54	58 30N	22 30 E
Saariselkä	50	68 16N	28 15 E
Saarland □	25	49 15N	7 0 E
Saarlouis	25	49 19N	6 45 E
Saba	121	17 42N	63 26W
Šabac	42	44 48N	19 42 E
Sabadell	32	41 28N	2 7 E
Sabagalet	72	1 36S	98 40 E
Sabah □	72	6 0N	117 0 E
Sábana de la Mar	121	19 7N	69 24W
Sábanalarga	126	10 38N	74 55W
Sabang	72	5 50N	95 15 E
Sabará	127	19 55S	43 46W
Sabarania	73	2 5S	138 18 E
Sabari →	70	17 35N	81 16 E
Sabasṭiyah	62	32 17N	35 12 E
Sabattis	113	44 6N	74 40W
Sabáudia	40	41 17N	13 2 E
Sabhah	83	27 9N	14 29 E
Sabhah □	83	26 0N	14 0 E
Sabie	93	25 10S	30 48 E
Sabinal, Mexico	120	30 58N	107 25W
Sabinal, U.S.A.	117	29 20N	99 27W
Sabinal, Punta del	33	36 43N	2 44W
Sabinas	120	27 50N	101 10W
Sabinas Hidalgo	120	26 33N	100 10W
Sabine	117	29 42N	93 54W
Sabine →	117	30 0N	93 35W
Sabine L.	117	29 50N	93 50W
Sabinov	27	49 6N	21 5 E
Sabirabad	57	40 5N	48 30 E
Sabkhat Tāwurghā'	83	31 48N	15 30 E
Sablayan	73	12 50N	120 50 E
Sable, C., Can.	107	43 29N	65 38W
Sable, C., U.S.A.	121	25 13N	81 0W
Sable I.	107	44 0N	60 0W
Sablé-sur-Sarthe	18	47 50N	0 20W
Sables-d'Olonne, Les	20	46 30N	1 45W
Sabolev	59	54 20N	155 30 E
Sabor →	30	41 10N	7 7W
Sabou	84	12 1N	2 15W
Sabrātah	83	32 47N	12 29 E
Sabria	83	33 22N	8 45 E
Sabrina Coast	5	68 0S	120 0 E
Sabugal	30	40 20N	7 5W
Sabzevār	65	36 15N	57 40 E
Sabzvārān	65	28 45N	57 50 E
Sac City	116	42 26N	95 0W
Sacedón	32	40 29N	2 41W
Sachigo →	106	55 6N	88 58W
Sachigo, L.	106	53 50N	92 12W
Sachkhere	57	42 25N	43 28 E
Sacile	39	45 58N	12 30 E
Sackets Harbor	113	43 56N	76 7W
Säckingen	25	47 34N	7 56 E
Saco, Me., U.S.A.	115	43 30N	70 27W
Saco, Mont., U.S.A.	118	48 28N	107 19W
Sacramento	118	38 33N	121 30 E
Sacramento →	118	38 3N	121 56W
Sacramento Mts.	119	32 30N	105 30W
Sacratif, Cabo	33	36 42N	3 28W
Săcueni	46	47 20N	22 5 E
Sada	30	43 22N	8 15W
Sádaba	32	42 19N	1 12W
Sadani	90	5 58S	38 35 E
Sadao	71	6 38N	100 26 E
Sadasivpet	70	17 38N	77 59 E
Sadd el Aali	86	23 54N	32 54 E
Sade	85	11 22N	10 45 E
Sadimi	91	9 25S	23 32 E
Sado	74	38 0N	138 25 E
Sado →	31	38 29N	8 55W
Sado, Shima	74	38 15N	138 30 E
Sadon, Burma	67	25 28N	98 0 E
Sadon, U.S.S.R.	57	42 52N	43 58 E
Sæby	49	57 21N	10 30 E
Saegerstown	112	41 42N	80 10W
Saelices	32	39 55N	2 49W
Safaga	86	26 42N	34 0 E
Safaha	86	26 25N	39 0 E
Šafárikovo	27	48 25N	20 20 E
Säffle	48	59 8N	12 55 E
Safford	119	32 50N	109 43W
Saffron Walden	13	52 2N	0 15 E
Safi	82	32 18N	9 20W
Safīd Kūh	65	34 45N	63 0 E
Safonovo	54	55 4N	33 16 E
Safranbolu	56	41 15N	32 41 E
Sag Harbor	113	40 59N	72 17W
Saga	73	2 40S	132 55 E
Saga □	74	33 15N	130 20 E
Sagala	84	14 9N	6 38W
Sagara	70	14 14N	75 6 E
Sagara, L.	90	5 20S	31 0 E
Saghīr, Zab al	64	35 10N	43 20 E
Sagil	75	50 15N	91 15 E
Saginaw	114	43 26N	83 55W
Saginaw B.	106	43 50N	83 40W
Sagleipie	84	7 0N	8 52W
Saglouc (Sugluk)	105	62 10N	74 40W
Sagone	21	42 7N	8 42 E
Sagone, G. de	21	42 4N	8 40 E
Sagra, La >	33	37 57N	2 35W
Sagres	31	37 0N	8 58W
Sagua la Grande	121	22 50N	80 10W
Saguache	119	38 10N	106 10W
Saguenay →	107	48 22N	71 0W
Sagunto	32	39 42N	0 18W
Sahaba	86	18 57N	30 25 E
Sahagún	30	42 18N	5 2W
Saham	62	32 42N	35 46 E
Saḩam al Jawlān	62	32 45N	35 55 E
Sahand, Kūh-e	64	37 44N	46 27 E
Sahara	82	23 0N	5 0 E
Saharanpur	68	29 58N	77 33 E
Saharien Atlas	82	33 30N	1 0 E
Sahasinaka	93	21 49S	47 49 E
Sahaswan	68	28 5N	78 45 E
Sahel, Canal du	84	14 20N	6 0W
Sahibganj	69	25 12N	87 40 E
Sahiwal	68	30 45N	73 8 E
Sahtaneh →	108	59 2N	122 28W
Sahuaripa	120	29 0N	109 13W
Sahuarita	119	31 58N	110 59W
Sahuayo	120	20 4N	102 43W
Sahy	27	48 4N	18 55 E
Saibai I.	98	9 25S	142 40 E
Sa'id Bundas	81	8 24N	24 48 E
Saïda	82	34 50N	0 11 E
Saïdābād	65	29 30N	55 45 E
Saïdia	82	35 5N	2 14W
Saidu	69	34 43N	72 24 E
Saignes	20	45 20N	2 31 E
Saigon = Phanh Bho Ho Chi Minh	71	10 46N	106 40 E
Saih-al-Malih	65	23 37N	58 31 E
Saijō	74	33 55N	133 11 E
Saikhoa Ghat	67	27 50N	95 40 E
Saiki	74	32 58N	131 51 E
Saillans	21	44 42N	5 12 E
Sailolof	73	1 7S	130 46 E
St. Abb's Head	14	55 55N	2 10W
St. Aegyd	26	47 52N	15 33 E
St-Affrique	20	43 57N	2 53 E
St-Agrève	21	45 0N	4 23 E
St-Aignan	18	47 16N	1 22 E
St. Alban's	107	47 51N	55 50W
St. Albans, U.K.	13	51 44N	0 19W
St. Albans, Vt., U.S.A.	114	44 49N	73 7W
St. Albans, W. Va., U.S.A.	114	38 21N	81 50W
St. Alban's Head	13	50 34N	2 3W
St. Albert	108	53 37N	113 32W
St-Amand	19	50 25N	3 26 E
St-Amand-en-Puisaye	19	47 32N	3 5 E
St-Amand-Mont-Rond	20	46 43N	2 30 E
St-Amarin	19	47 54N	7 0 E
St-Amour	21	46 26N	5 21 E
St-André-de-Cubzac	20	44 59N	0 26W
St-André-de-l'Eure	18	48 54N	1 16 E
St-André-les-Alpes	21	43 58N	6 30 E
St. André, Tanjona	93	16 11S	44 27 E
St. Andrew's	107	47 45N	59 15W
St. Andrews	14	56 20N	2 48W
St-Anicet	113	45 8N	74 22W
St. Ann B.	107	46 22N	60 25W
St. Anne	18	49 43N	2 11W
St. Anthony, Can.	107	51 22N	55 35W
St. Anthony, U.S.A.	118	44 0N	111 40W
St-Antonin-Noble-Val	20	44 10N	1 45 E
St. Arnaud	99	36 40S	143 16 E
St. Arthur	107	47 33N	67 46W
St. Asaph	12	53 15N	3 27W
St-Astier	20	45 8N	0 31 E
St-Aubin-du-Cormier	18	48 15N	1 26W
St. Augustin	93	23 33S	43 46 E
St-Augustin-Saguenay	107	51 13N	58 38W
St. Augustine	115	29 52N	81 20W
St. Austell	13	50 20N	4 48W
St-Avold	19	49 6N	6 43 E
St.-Barthélemy, I.	121	17 50N	62 50W
St. Bee's Hd.	12	54 30N	3 38 E
St-Benoît-du-Sault	20	46 26N	1 24 E
St. Bernard, Col du Grand	25	45 53N	7 11 E
St. Boniface	109	49 53N	97 5W
St-Bonnet	21	44 40N	6 5 E
St-Brévin-les-Pins	18	47 14N	2 10W
St-Brice-en-Coglès	18	48 25N	1 22W
St. Bride's	107	46 56N	54 10W
St. Bride's B.	13	51 48N	5 15W
St-Brieuc	18	48 30N	2 46W
St-Calais	18	47 55N	0 45 E
St-Cast	18	48 37N	2 18W
St. Catharines	106	43 10N	79 15W
St. Catherines I.	115	31 35N	81 10W
St. Catherine's Pt.	13	50 34N	1 18W
St-Céré	20	44 51N	1 54 E
St.-Cergue	25	46 27N	6 10 E
St-Cernin	20	45 5N	2 25 E
St-Chamond	21	45 28N	4 31 E
St. Charles, Ill., U.S.A	114	41 55N	88 21W
St. Charles, Mo., U.S.A.	116	38 46N	90 30W
St-Chély-d'Apcher	20	44 48N	3 17 E
St-Chinian	20	43 25N	2 56 E
St. Christopher (St. Kitts)	121	17 20N	62 40W
St-Ciers-sur-Gironde	20	45 17N	0 37W
St. Clair, Mich, U.S.A.	112	42 47N	82 27W
St. Clair, Pa., U.S.A.	113	40 42N	76 12W
St. Clair, L.	106	42 30N	82 45W
St. Clairsville	112	40 5N	80 53W
St-Claud	20	45 54N	0 28 E
St. Claude	109	49 40N	98 20W
St-Claude	21	46 22N	5 52 E
St-Cloud	18	48 51N	2 12 E
St. Cloud, Fla., U.S.A.	115	28 15N	81 15W
St. Cloud, Minn., U.S.A.	116	45 30N	94 11W
St-Coeur de Marie	107	48 39N	71 43W
St. Croix	121	17 45N	64 45W
St. Croix →	116	44 45N	92 50W
St. Croix Falls	116	45 18N	92 22W
St-Cyprien	20	42 37N	3 0 E
St-Cyr	21	43 11N	5 43 E
St. David's, Can.	107	48 12N	58 52W
St. David's, U.K.	13	51 54N	5 16W
St. David's Head	13	51 55N	5 16W
St-Denis	19	48 56N	2 22 E
St-Denis-d'Orques	18	48 2N	0 17W
St-Dié	19	48 17N	6 56 E
St-Dizier	19	48 40N	5 0 E
St-Egrève	21	45 14N	5 41 E
St. Elias, Mt.	104	60 14N	140 50W
St Elias Mts.	108	60 33N	139 28W
St-Éloy-les-Mines	20	46 10N	2 51 E
St-Émilion	20	44 53N	0 9W
St-Étienne	21	45 27N	4 22 E
St-Étienne-de-Tinée	21	44 16N	6 56 E
St. Eugène	113	45 30N	74 28W
St. Eustatius	121	17 20N	63 0W
St-Félicien	106	48 40N	72 25W
St-Florent	21	42 41N	9 18 E
St-Florent-sur-Cher	19	46 59N	2 15 E
St-Florentin	19	48 0N	3 45 E
St-Flour	20	45 2N	3 6 E
St-Fons	21	45 42N	4 52 E
St. Francis	116	39 48N	101 47W
St. Francis →	117	34 38N	90 36W
St. Francis, C.	92	34 14S	24 49 E
St-Francis, L.	113	45 10N	74 22W
St. Francisville	117	30 48N	91 22W
St-Fulgent	18	46 50N	1 10W
St-Gabriel-de-Brandon	106	46 17N	73 24W
St-Gaudens	20	43 6N	0 44 E
St-Gengoux-le-National	21	46 37N	4 40 E
St-Geniez-d'Olt	20	44 27N	2 58 E
St. George, Austral.	97	28 1S	148 30 E
St. George, Berm.	121	32 24N	64 42W
St. George, Can.	107	45 11N	66 50W
St. George, S.C., U.S.A.	115	33 13N	80 37W
St. George, Utah, U.S.A.	119	37 10N	113 35W
St. George, C., Can.	107	48 30N	59 16W
St. George, C., U.S.A.	115	29 36N	85 2W
St-Georges	16	50 37N	5 20 E
St. George's	107	48 26N	58 31W
St. Georges	106	46 42N	72 35W
St-Georges	107	46 8N	70 40W
St. Georges	127	4 0N	52 0W
St. George's	121	12 5N	61 43W
St. George's B.	107	48 24N	58 53W
Saint George's Channel	98	4 10S	152 20 E
St. George's Channel	11	52 0N	6 0W
St-Georges-de-Didonne	20	45 36N	1 0W
St. Georges Head	100	35 12S	150 42 E
St-Germain	19	48 53N	2 5 E
St-Germain-Lembron	20	45 27N	3 14 E
St-Germain-de-Calberte	20	44 13N	3 48 E
St-Germain-des-Fossés	20	46 12N	3 26 E
St-Germain-du-Plain	19	46 42N	4 58 E
St-Germain-Laval	21	45 50N	4 1 E
St-Gers	20	45 18N	0 37W
St-Gervais, Haute Savoie, France	21	45 53N	6 42 E
St-Gervais, Puy de Dôme, France	20	46 4N	2 50 E
St-Gildas, Pte. de	18	47 8N	2 14W
St-Gilles-Croix-de-Vie	18	46 41N	1 55W
St-Gilles-du-Gard	21	43 40N	4 26 E
St-Girons	20	42 59N	1 8 E
St. Goar	25	50 12N	7 43 E
St-Gualtier	18	46 39N	1 26 E
St-Guénolé	18	47 49N	4 23W
St. Helena, Atl. Oc.	7	15 55S	5 44W
St. Helena, U.S.A.	118	38 29N	122 30W
St. Helenabaai	92	32 40S	18 10 E
St. Helens, U.K.	12	53 28N	2 44W
St. Helens, U.S.A.	118	45 55N	122 50W
St. Helier	18	49 11N	2 6W
St-Hilaire	18	48 35N	1 7W
St-Hippolyte	19	47 20N	6 50 E
St-Hippolyte-du-Fort	20	43 58N	3 52 E
St-Honoré	19	46 54N	3 50 E
St-Hubert	16	50 2N	5 23 E
St-Hyacinthe	106	45 40N	72 58W
St. Ignace	114	45 53N	84 43W
St. Ignace I.	106	48 45N	88 0W
St. Ignatius	118	47 19N	114 8W
St-Imier	25	47 9N	6 58 E
St. Ives, Cambs., U.K.	13	52 20N	0 5W
St. Ives, Cornwall, U.K.	13	50 13N	5 29W
St-James	18	48 31N	1 20W
St. James	116	43 57N	94 40W
St. Jean	106	45 20N	73 20W
St-Jean	21	45 30N	5 10 E
St-Jean →	107	50 17N	64 20W
St. Jean Baptiste	109	49 15N	97 20W
St-Jean-d'Angély	20	45 57N	0 31W
St-Jean-de-Maurienne	21	45 16N	6 21 E
St-Jean-de-Luz	20	43 23N	1 39W
St-Jean-de-Monts	18	46 47N	2 4W
St-Jean-du-Gard	20	44 7N	3 52 E
St-Jean-en-Royans	21	45 1N	5 18 E
St-Jean, L.	107	48 40N	72 0W
St-Jean-Port-Joli	107	47 15N	70 13W
St-Jérôme, Qué., Can.	106	45 47N	74 0W
St-Jérôme, Qué., Can.	107	48 26N	71 53W
St. John, Can.	107	45 20N	66 8W
St. John, Kans., U.S.A.	117	37 59N	98 45W
St. John, N.D., U.S.A.	116	48 58N	99 40W
St. John →	107	45 15N	66 4W
St. John, C.	107	50 0N	55 32W
St. John's, Antigua	121	17 6N	61 51W
St. John's, Can.	107	47 35N	52 40W
St. Johns, Ariz., U.S.A.	119	34 31N	109 26W
St. Johns, Mich., U.S.A.	114	43 0N	84 31W
St. John's →	115	30 20N	81 30W
St. Johnsbury	114	44 25N	72 1W
St. Johnsville	113	43 0N	74 43W
St. Joseph, La., U.S.A.	117	31 55N	91 15W
St. Joseph, Mich., U.S.A.	114	42 5N	86 30W
St. Joseph, Mo., U.S.A.	116	39 46N	94 50W
St. Joseph →	114	42 7N	86 30W
St. Joseph, I.	106	46 12N	83 58W
St. Joseph, L.	106	51 10N	90 35W
St-Jovite	106	46 8N	74 38W
St-Juéry	20	43 55N	2 12 E
St-Julien	21	46 8N	6 5 E
St-Julien-Chapteuil	21	45 2N	4 4 E
St-Julien-du-Sault	19	48 1N	3 17 E
St-Junien	20	45 53N	0 55 E

St-Just-en-Chaussée 19 49 30N 2 25 E
St-Just-en-Chevalet 20 45 55N 3 50 E
St-Justin 20 43 59N 0 14W
St. Kilda, N.Z. 101 45 53 S 170 31 E
St. Kilda, U.K. 8 57 9N 8 34W
St. Kitts 121 17 20N 62 40W
St. Laurent 109 50 25N 97 58W
St-Laurent 127 5 29N 54 3W
St-Laurent-du-Pont 21 45 23N 5 45 E
St-Laurent-en-Grandvaux 21 46 35N 5 58 E
St. Lawrence 107 46 54N 55 23W
St. Lawrence → 107 49 30N 66 0W
St. Lawrence, Gulf of 107 48 25N 62 0W
St. Lawrence I. 104 63 0N 170 0W
St. Leonard 107 47 12N 67 58W
St-Léonard-de-Noblat 20 45 49N 1 29 E
St. Lewis → 107 52 26N 56 11W
St-Lô 18 49 7N 1 5W
St-Louis 84 16 8N 16 27W
St. Louis, Mich., U.S.A. 114 43 27N 84 38W
St. Louis, Mo., U.S.A. 116 38 40N 90 12W
St. Louis → 116 47 15N 92 45W
St-Loup-sur-Semouse 19 47 53N 6 16 E
St. Lucia ■ 121 14 0N 60 50W
St. Lucia, C. 93 28 32 S 32 29 E
St. Lucia Channel 121 14 15N 61 0W
St. Lucia, Lake 93 28 5 S 32 30 E
St. Lunaire-Griquet 107 51 31N 55 28W
St. Maarten 121 18 0N 63 5W
St-Maixent-l'École 20 46 24N 0 12W
St-Malo 18 48 39N 2 1W
St-Malo, G. de 18 48 50N 2 30W
St-Mandrier 21 43 4N 5 56 E
St-Marc 121 19 10N 72 41W
St-Marcellin 21 45 9N 5 20 E
St-Marcouf, Îs. 18 49 30N 1 10W
St. Maries 118 47 17N 116 34W
St-Martin, Charente-M., France 20 46 12N 1 22W
St-Martin, Pas-de-Calais, France 19 50 42N 1 38 E
St-Martin, I. 121 18 0N 63 0W
St. Martin L. 109 51 40N 98 30W
St-Martin-Vésubie 21 44 4N 7 15 E
St. Martins 107 45 22N 65 34W
St. Martinsville 117 30 10N 91 50W
St-Martory 20 43 9N 0 56 E
St. Mary B. 107 46 50N 53 50W
St. Mary Is. 70 13 20N 74 35 E
St. Mary Pk. 97 31 32 S 138 34 E
St. Marys, Austral. 97 41 35 S 148 11 E
St. Marys, Can. 112 43 20N 81 10W
St. Mary's, U.K. 13 49 55N 6 17W
St. Mary's, U.S.A. 114 40 33N 84 20W
St. Marys 114 41 27N 78 33W
St. Marys Bay 107 44 25N 66 10W
St. Mary's, C. 107 46 50N 54 12W
St. Mathews I. = Zadetkyi Kyun 71 10 0N 98 25 E
St-Mathieu, Pte. de 18 48 20N 4 45W
St-Maur-des-Fossés 19 48 48N 2 30 E
St-Maurice → 106 46 21N 72 31W
St-Médard-de-Guizières 20 45 1N 0 4W
St-Méen-le-Grand 18 48 11N 2 12W
St. Michaels 119 35 38N 109 5W
St. Michael's Mt. 13 50 7N 5 30W
St-Michel 21 45 15N 6 29 E
St-Mihiel 19 48 54N 5 30 E
St-Nazaire 18 47 17N 2 12W
St. Neots 13 52 14N 0 16W
St-Nicolas-de-Port 19 48 38N 6 18 E
St-Omer 19 50 45N 2 15 E
St. Ouen 19 48 50N 2 20 E
St-Ouen 19 50 2N 2 7 E
St-Pacome 107 47 24N 69 58W
St-Palais 20 45 40N 1 8W
St-Pamphile 107 46 58N 69 48W
St-Pardoux-la-Rivière 20 45 29N 0 45 E
St. Pascal 107 47 32N 69 48W
St. Paul, Can. 108 54 0N 111 17W
St. Paul, Ind. Oc. 3 30 40 S 77 34 E
St. Paul, Minn., U.S.A. 116 44 54N 93 5W
St. Paul, Nebr., U.S.A. 116 41 15N 98 30W
St-Paul-de-Fenouillet 20 42 50N 2 28 E
St. Paul, I. 107 47 12N 60 9W
St-Péray 21 44 57N 4 50 E
St-Père-en-Retz 18 47 11N 2 2W
St. Peter 116 44 21N 93 57W
St. Peter Port 18 49 27N 2 31W
St. Peters, N.S., Can. 107 45 40N 60 53W
St. Peters, P.E.I., Can. 107 46 25N 62 35W
St. Petersburg 115 27 45N 82 40W
St-Philbert-de-Grand-Lieu 18 47 2N 1 39W
St Pierre 107 46 46N 56 12W
St-Pierre-d'Oléron 20 45 57N 1 19W
St-Pierre-Église 18 49 40N 1 24W
St-Pierre-en-Port 18 49 48N 0 30 E
St-Pierre et Miquelon □ 107 46 55N 56 10W
St-Pierre, L. 106 46 12N 72 52W
St-Pierre-le-Moûtier 19 46 47N 3 7 E
St.-Pierre-sur-Dives 18 49 2N 0 1W
St.-Pol 19 50 21N 2 20 E
St-Pol-de-Léon 18 48 41N 4 0W
St-Pol-sur-Mer 19 51 1N 2 20 E
St-Pons 20 43 30N 2 45 E
St-Pourçain-sur-Sioule 20 46 18N 3 18 E
St-Quay-Portrieux 18 48 39N 2 51W
St-Quentin 19 49 50N 3 16 E
St-Rambert-d'Albon 21 45 17N 4 49 E
St-Raphaël 21 43 25N 6 46 E
St. Regis, Mont., U.S.A. 118 47 20N 115 3W
St. Regis, N.Y., U.S.A. 113 44 39N 74 34W
St-Rémy-de-Provence 21 43 48N 4 50 E
St-Renan 18 48 26N 4 37W
St-Saëns 18 49 41N 1 16 E
St-Sauveur-en-Puisaye 19 47 37N 3 12 E
St-Sauveur-le-Vicomte 18 49 23N 1 32W
St-Savin 20 46 34N 0 50 E
St-Savinien 20 45 53N 0 42W
St. Sebastien, Tanjon' i 93 12 26 S 48 44 E
St-Seine-l'Abbaye 19 47 26N 4 47 E
St-Sernin 20 43 54N 2 35 E
St-Servan-sur-Mer 18 48 38N 2 0W
St-Sever 20 43 46N 0 34W
St-Sever-Calvados 18 48 50N 1 3W
St-Siméon 107 47 51N 69 54W
St. Stephen 107 45 16N 67 17W
St-Sulpice-Laurière 20 46 3N 1 29 E
St-Sulpice-la-Pointe 20 43 46N 1 41 E
St-Thégonnec 18 48 31N 3 57W
St. Thomas, Can. 106 42 45N 81 10W
St. Thomas, W. Indies 121 18 21N 64 55W
St-Tite 106 46 45N 72 34W
St-Tropez 21 43 17N 6 38 E
St. Troud = Sint Truiden 16 50 48N 5 10 E
St-Vaast-la-Hougue 18 49 35N 1 17W
St-Valéry 19 50 10N 1 38 E
St-Valéry-en-Caux 18 49 52N 0 43 E
St-Vallier 21 45 11N 4 50 E
St-Vallier-de-Thiey 21 43 42N 6 51 E
St-Varent 18 46 53N 0 13W
St. Vincent 6 18 0N 26 1W
St. Vincent ■ 121 13 10N 61 10W
St-Vincent-de-Tyrosse 20 43 39N 1 18W
St. Vincent, G. 97 35 0 S 138 0 E
St. Vincent Passage 121 13 30N 61 0W
St. Vincent, Tanjona 93 21 58 S 43 20 E
St-Vith 16 50 17N 6 9 E
St-Yrieux-la-Perche 20 45 31N 1 12 E
Ste-Adresse 18 49 31N 0 5 E
Ste-Agathe-des-Monts 106 46 3N 74 17W
Ste Anne de Beaupré 107 47 2N 70 58W
Ste-Anne-des-Monts 107 49 8N 66 30W
Ste-Énimie 20 44 22N 3 26 E
Ste-Foy-la-Grande 20 44 50N 0 13 E
Ste. Genevieve 116 37 59N 90 2W
Ste-Hermine 20 46 32N 1 4W
Ste-Livrade-sur-Lot 20 44 24N 0 36 E
Ste-Marguerite → 107 50 9N 66 36W
Ste Marie 121 14 48N 61 1W
Ste-Marie-aux-Mines 19 48 10N 7 12 E
Ste-Marie de la Madeleine 107 46 26N 71 0W
Ste-Maure-de-Touraine 18 47 7N 0 37 E
Ste-Maxime 21 43 19N 6 39 E
Ste-Menehould 19 49 5N 4 54 E
Ste-Mère-Église 18 49 24N 1 19W
Ste-Rose 121 16 20N 61 45W
Ste.-Rose du lac 109 51 4N 99 30W
Saintes 20 45 45N 0 37W
Saintes, Île des 121 15 50N 61 35W
Saintes-Maries-de-la-Mer 21 43 26N 4 26 E
Saintonge 20 45 40N 0 50W
Sairang 67 23 50N 92 45 E
Sairecábur, Cerro 124 22 43 S 67 54W
Saitama □ 74 36 25N 139 30 E
Sajama 126 18 7 S 69 0W
Sajan 42 45 50N 20 20 E
Sajószentpéter 27 48 12N 20 44 E
Sakai 74 34 30N 135 30 E
Sakākah 64 30 0N 40 8 E
Sakami, L. 106 53 15N 77 0W
Sâkâne, 'Erg i-n 82 20 30N 1 30W
Sakania 91 12 43 S 28 30 E
Sakarya → 56 41 7N 30 39 E
Sakata 74 38 55N 139 50 E
Sakeny → 93 20 0 S 45 25 E
Sakété 85 6 40N 2 45 E
Sakhalin, Ostrov 59 51 0N 143 0 E
Sakhi Gopal 69 19 58N 85 50 E
Sakhnīn 62 32 52N 35 12 E
Saki 56 45 9N 33 34 E
Sakiai 54 54 59N 23 0 E
Sakołow Małopolski 28 50 10N 22 9 E
Sakon Nakhon 71 17 10N 104 9 E
Sakrand 68 26 10N 68 15 E
Sakri 68 21 2N 74 20 E
Sakskøbing 49 54 49N 11 39 E
Sal → 57 47 31N 40 45 E
Šal'a 27 48 10N 17 50 E
Sala 48 59 58N 16 35 E
Sala Consilina 41 40 23N 15 35 E
Sala-y-Gómez 95 26 28 S 105 28W
Salaberry-de-Valleyfield 106 45 15N 74 8W
Saladas 124 28 15 S 58 40W
Saladillo 124 35 40 S 59 55W
Salado →, Buenos Aires, Argent. 124 35 44 S 57 22W
Salado →, La Pampa, Argent. 128 37 30 S 67 0W
Salado →, Santa Fe, Argent. 124 31 40 S 60 41W
Salado →, Mexico 120 26 52N 99 19W
Salaga 85 8 31N 0 31W
Sălaj □ 46 47 15N 23 0 E
Salala, Liberia 84 6 42N 10 7W
Salala, Sudan 86 21 17N 36 16 E
Salālah 63 16 56N 53 59 E
Salamanca, Chile 124 31 46 S 70 59W
Salamanca, Spain 30 40 58N 5 39W
Salamanca, U.S.A. 114 42 10N 78 42W
Salamanca □ 30 40 57N 5 40W
Salamis 45 37 56N 23 30 E
Salar de Atacama 124 23 30 S 68 25W
Salar de Uyuni 126 20 30 S 67 45W
Sălard 46 47 12N 22 3 E
Salas 30 43 25N 6 15W
Salas de los Infantes 32 42 2N 3 17W
Salatiga 73 7 19 S 110 30 E
Salavat 52 53 21N 55 55 E
Salaverry 126 8 15 S 79 0W
Salawati 73 1 7 S 130 52 E
Salayar 73 6 7 S 120 30 E
Salazar → 32 42 40N 1 20W
Salbris 19 47 25N 2 3 E
Salcia 46 43 56N 24 55 E
Salcombe 13 50 14N 3 47W
Saldaña 30 42 32N 4 48W
Saldanha 92 33 0 S 17 58 E
Saldanhabaai 92 33 6 S 18 0 E
Saldus 54 56 38N 22 30 E
Sale 97 38 6 S 147 6 E
Salé 82 34 3N 6 48W
Sale 12 53 26N 2 19W
Salebabu 73 3 55N 126 40 E
Salekhard 58 66 30N 66 35 E
Salem, India 70 11 40N 78 11 E
Salem, Ind., U.S.A. 114 38 38N 86 6W
Salem, Mass., U.S.A. 114 42 29N 70 53W
Salem, Mo., U.S.A. 117 37 40N 91 30W
Salem, N.J., U.S.A. 114 39 34N 75 29W
Salem, Ohio, U.S.A. 114 40 52N 80 50W
Salem, Oreg., U.S.A. 118 45 0N 123 0W
Salem, S.D., U.S.A. 116 43 44N 97 23W
Salem, Va., U.S.A. 114 37 19N 80 8W
Salemi 40 37 49N 12 47 E
Salernes 21 43 34N 6 15 E
Salerno 41 40 40N 14 44 E
Salerno, G. di 41 40 35N 14 45 E
Salfit 62 32 5N 35 11 E
Salford 12 53 30N 2 17W
Salgir → 56 45 38N 35 1 E
Salgótarján 27 48 5N 19 47 E
Salies-de-Béarn 20 43 28N 0 56W
Salina, Italy 41 38 35N 14 50 E
Salina, U.S.A. 116 38 50N 97 40W
Salina Cruz 120 16 10N 95 10W
Salinas, Brazil 127 16 10 S 42 10W
Salinas, Chile 124 23 31 S 69 29W
Salinas, Ecuador 126 2 10 S 80 58W
Salinas, U.S.A. 119 36 40N 121 41W
Salinas →, Mexico 120 16 28N 90 31W
Salinas →, U.S.A. 119 36 45N 121 48W
Salinas Ambargasta 124 29 0 S 65 0W
Salinas, B. de 121 11 4N 85 45W
Salinas, C. de 33 39 16N 3 4 E
Salinas (de Hidalgo) 120 22 30N 101 40W
Salinas Grandes 124 30 0 S 65 0W
Salinas, Pampa de las 124 31 58 S 66 42W
Saline →, Ark., U.S.A. 117 33 10N 92 8W
Saline →, Kans., U.S.A. 116 38 51N 97 30W
Salinópolis 127 0 40 S 47 20W
Salins 19 46 57N 5 53 E
Salins-les-Bains 19 46 58N 5 52 E
Salir 31 37 14N 8 2W
Salisbury, Austral. 99 34 46 S 138 40 E
Salisbury, U.K. 13 51 4N 1 48W
Salisbury, Md., U.S.A. 114 38 20N 75 38W
Salisbury, N.C., U.S.A. 115 35 20N 80 29W
Salisbury, Zimb. 91 17 43 S 31 2 E
Salisbury Plain 13 51 13N 1 50W
Săliște 46 45 45N 23 56 E
Salka 85 10 20N 4 58 E
Salle, La 116 41 20N 89 6W
Sallent 32 41 49N 1 54 E
Salles-Curan 20 44 11N 2 48 E
Salling 49 56 40N 8 55 E
Sallisaw 117 35 26N 94 45W
Sallom Junction 86 19 17N 37 6 E
Salmerón 32 40 33N 2 29W
Salmo 108 49 10N 117 20W
Salmon 118 45 12N 113 56W
Salmon →, Can. 108 54 3N 122 40W
Salmon →, U.S.A. 118 45 51N 116 46W
Salmon Arm 108 50 40N 119 15W
Salmon Falls 118 42 48N 114 59W
Salmon Res. 107 48 05N 56 00W
Salmon River Mts. 118 45 0N 114 30W
Salo 51 60 22N 23 10 E
Salò 38 45 37N 10 32 E
Salobreña 31 36 44N 3 35W
Salome 119 33 51N 113 37W
Salon-de-Provence 21 43 39N 5 6 E
Salonica = Thessaloníki 44 40 38N 22 58 E
Salonta 46 46 49N 21 42 E
Salop = Shropshire □ 13 52 36N 2 45W
Salor → 31 39 39N 7 3W
Salou, Cabo 32 41 3N 1 10 E
Salsacate 124 31 20 S 65 5W
Salses 20 42 50N 2 55 E
Salsette I. 70 19 5N 72 50 E
Salsk 57 46 28N 41 30 E
Salso → 41 37 6N 13 55 E
Salsomaggiore 38 44 48N 9 59 E
Salt →, Can. 108 60 0N 112 25W
Salt →, U.S.A. 119 33 23N 112 18W
Salt Creek 99 36 8 S 139 38 E
Salt Fork → 117 36 37N 97 7W
Salt Lake City 118 40 45N 111 58W
Salt Range 68 32 30N 72 25 E
Salta 124 24 57 S 65 25W
Salta □ 124 24 48 S 65 30W
Saltcoats 14 55 38N 4 47W
Saltee Is. 15 52 7N 6 37W
Saltfjorden 50 67 15N 14 10 E
Saltholm 49 55 38N 12 43 E
Salthólmavík 50 65 24N 21 57W
Saltillo 120 25 30N 100 57W
Salto, Argent. 124 34 20 S 60 15W
Salto, Uruguay 124 31 27 S 57 50W
Salton Sea 119 33 20N 115 50W
Saltpond 85 5 15N 1 3W
Saltsjöbaden 49 59 15N 18 20 E
Saltspring 108 48 54N 123 37W
Saltville 114 36 53N 81 46W
Saluda → 115 34 0N 81 4W
Salûm 86 31 31N 25 7 E
Salûm, Khâlig el 86 31 30N 25 9 E
Salur 70 18 27N 83 18 E
Saluzzo 38 44 39N 7 29 E
Salvador, Brazil 127 13 0 S 38 30W
Salvador, Can. 109 52 10N 109 32W
Salvador, L. 117 29 46N 90 16W
Salvaterra de Magos 31 39 1N 8 47W
Sálvora, Isla 30 42 30N 8 58W
Salwa 65 24 45N 50 55 E
Salween → 67 16 31N 97 37 E
Salyany 53 39 10N 48 50 E
Salyersville 114 37 45N 83 4W
Salza → 26 47 40N 14 43 E
Salzach → 26 48 12N 12 56 E
Salzburg 26 47 48N 13 2 E
Salzburg □ 26 47 15N 13 0 E
Salzgitter 24 52 13N 10 22 E
Salzwedel 24 52 50N 11 11 E
Sam Neua 71 20 29N 104 0 E
Sam Ngao 71 17 18N 99 0 E
Sam Rayburn Res. 117 31 15N 94 20W
Sama 58 60 12N 60 22 E
Sama de Langreo 30 43 18N 5 40W
Samagaltai 59 50 36N 95 3 E
Samales Group 73 6 0N 122 0 E
Samalkot 70 17 3N 82 13 E
Samâlût 86 28 20N 30 42 E
Samana 68 30 10N 76 13 E
Samanga 91 8 20 S 39 13 E
Samangán □ 65 36 15N 68 3 E
Samangwa 90 4 23 S 24 10 E
Samar 73 12 0N 125 0 E
Samarai 98 10 39 S 150 41 E
Samaria = Shōmrōn 62 32 15N 35 13 E
Samarinda 72 0 30 S 117 9 E
Samarkand 58 39 40N 66 55 E
Sāmarrā" 64 34 16N 43 55 E
Samastipur 69 25 50N 85 50 E
Samatan 20 43 29N 0 55 E
Samba 90 4 38 S 26 22 E
Sambalpur 69 21 28N 84 4 E
Sambar, Tanjung 72 2 59 S 110 19 E
Sambas 72 1 20N 109 20 E
Sambava 93 14 16 S 50 10 E
Sambawizi 91 18 24 S 26 13 E
Sambhal 68 28 35N 78 37 E
Sambhar 68 26 52N 75 6 E
Sambiase 41 38 58N 16 16 E
Sambonifacio 38 45 24N 11 16 E
Sambor, Camb. 71 12 46N 106 0 E
Sambor, U.S.S.R. 54 49 30N 23 10 E
Sambre → 16 50 27N 4 52 E
Sambuca di Sicilia 40 37 39N 13 6 E
Samburu □ 90 1 10N 37 0 E
Samchŏk 76 37 30N 129 10 E
Same 90 4 2 S 37 38 E
Samer 19 50 38N 1 44 E
Samfya 91 11 22 S 29 31 E
Sámi 45 38 15N 20 39 E
Samna 86 25 12N 37 17 E
Samnū 83 27 15N 14 55 E
Samo Alto 124 30 22 S 71 0W
Samobor 39 45 47N 15 44 E
Samoëns 21 46 5N 6 45 E
Samokov 43 42 18N 23 35 E
Samoorombón, Bahía 124 36 5 S 57 20W
Samorogouan 84 11 21N 4 57W
Sámos 45 37 45N 26 50 E
Samos 30 42 44N 7 20W
Samoš 42 45 13N 20 49 E
Samotharáki 44 39 48N 19 31 E
Samothráki 44 40 28N 25 28 E
Samoylovka 55 51 12N 43 43 E
Sampa 84 8 0N 2 36W
Sampacho 124 33 20 S 64 50W
Sampang 73 7 11 S 113 13 E
Samper de Calanda 32 41 11N 0 28W
Sampit 72 2 34 S 113 0 E
Sampit, Teluk 72 3 5 S 113 3 E
Samra 64 25 35N 41 0 E
Samsø 49 55 50N 10 35 E
Samsø Bælt 49 55 45N 10 45 E
Samsun 64 41 15N 36 22 E
Samsun Daği 45 37 45N 27 10 E
Samtredia 57 42 7N 42 24 E
Samui, Ko 71 9 30N 100 0 E
Samur → 57 41 53N 48 32 E
Samusole 91 10 2 S 24 0 E
Samut Prakan 71 13 32N 100 40 E
Samut Sakhon 71 13 31N 100 13 E
Samut Songkhram (Mekong) 71 13 24N 100 1 E
Samwari 68 28 30N 66 46 E
San 84 13 15N 4 57W
San → 27 50 45N 21 51 E
San Adrián, C. de 30 43 21N 8 50W
San Agustin, C. 73 6 20N 126 13 E
San Agustín de Valle Fértil 124 30 35 S 67 30W
San Ambrosio 95 26 28 S 79 53W
San Andreas 118 38 0N 120 39W
San Andrés, I. de 121 12 42N 81 46W
San Andres Mts. 119 33 0N 106 45W
San Andrés Tuxtla 120 18 30N 95 20W
San Angelo 117 31 30N 100 30W
San Antonio, Chile 124 33 40 S 71 40W
San Antonio, N. Mex., U.S.A. 119 33 58N 106 57W
San Antonio, Tex., U.S.A. 117 29 30N 98 30W
San Antonio → 117 28 30N 96 50W
San Antonio Abad 33 38 59N 1 19 E
San Antonio, C., Argent. 124 36 15 S 56 40W
San Antonio, C., Cuba 121 21 50N 84 57W
San Antonio, C. de 33 38 48N 0 12 E
San Antonio de los Baños 121 22 54N 82 31W
San Antonio de los Cobres 124 24 10 S 66 17W
San Antonio Oeste 128 40 40 S 65 0W
San Augustine 117 31 30N 94 7W
San Bartolomeo in Galdo 41 41 23N 15 2 E
San Benedetto 38 45 2N 10 57 E
San Benedetto del Tronto 39 42 57N 13 52 E
San Benito 117 26 5N 97 39W
San Bernardino 119 34 7N 117 18W
San Bernardino Str. 73 13 0N 125 0 E
San Bernardo 124 33 40 S 70 50W
San Bernardo, I. de 126 9 45N 75 50W
San Blas 120 26 4N 108 46W
San Blas, C. 115 29 40N 85 12W
San Borja 126 14 50 S 66 52W
San Buenaventura 120 27 5N 101 32W
San Carlos, Argent. 124 33 50 S 69 0W
San Carlos, Chile 124 36 10 S 72 0W
San Carlos, Mexico 120 29 0N 100 54W
San Carlos, Nic. 121 11 12N 84 50W
San Carlos, Phil. 73 10 29N 123 25 E
San Carlos, Uruguay 125 34 46 S 54 58W
San Carlos, U.S.A. 119 33 24N 110 27W
San Carlos, Amazonas, Venez. 126 1 55N 67 4W
San Carlos, Cojedes, Venez. 126 9 40N 68 36W
San Carlos = Butuku-Luba 85 3 29N 8 33 E
San Carlos de Bariloche 128 41 10 S 71 25W
San Carlos de la Rápita 32 40 37N 0 35 E
San Carlos del Zulia 126 9 1N 71 55W
San Carlos L. 119 33 15N 110 25W
San Cataldo 40 37 30N 13 58 E
San Celoni 32 41 42N 2 30 E
San Clemente, Chile 124 35 30 S 71 29W
San Clemente, Spain 33 39 24N 2 25W
San Clemente, U.S.A. 119 33 29N 117 36W
San Clemente I. 119 32 53N 118 30W
San Constanzo 39 43 46N 13 5 E

San Cristóbal, Argent. 124 30 20S 61 10W
San Cristóbal, Dom. Rep. 121 18 25N 70 6W
San Cristóbal, Venez. 126 16 50N 92 40W
San Cristóbal de las Casas 120 16 50N 92 33W
San Damiano d'Asti 38 44 51N 8 4 E
San Daniele del Friuli 39 46 10N 13 0 E
San Demétrio Corone 41 39 34N 16 22 E
San Diego, Calif., U.S.A. 119 32 43N 117 10W
San Diego, Tex., U.S.A. 117 27 47N 98 15W
San Diego, C. 128 54 40S 65 10W
San Donà di Piave 39 45 38N 12 34 E
San Elpídio a Mare 39 43 16N 13 41 E
San Estanislao 124 24 39S 56 26W
San Esteban de Gormaz 32 41 34N 3 13W
San Felice sul Panaro 38 44 51N 11 9 E
San Felipe, Chile 124 32 43S 70 42W
San Felipe, Mexico 120 31 0N 114 52W
San Felipe, Venez. 126 10 20N 68 44W
San Feliu de Guíxols 32 41 45N 3 1 E
San Feliu de Llobregat 32 41 23N 2 2 E
San Félix 95 26 23S 80 0W
San Fernando, Chile 124 34 30S 71 0W
San Fernando, Mexico 120 30 0N 115 10W
San Fernando, Luzon, Phil. 73 16 40N 120 23 E
San Fernando, Luzon, Phil. 73 15 5N 120 37 E
San Fernando, Spain 31 36 28N 6 17W
San Fernando, Trin. 121 10 20N 61 30W
San Fernando, U.S.A. 119 34 15N 118 29W
San Fernando → 120 24 55N 98 10W
San Fernando de Apure 126 7 54N 67 15W
San Fernando de Atabapo 126 4 3N 67 42W
San Fernando di Púglia 41 41 18N 16 5 E
San Francisco, Argent. 124 31 30S 62 5W
San Francisco, U.S.A. 119 37 47N 122 30W
San Francisco → 119 32 59N 109 22W
San Francisco de Macorîs 121 19 19N 70 15W
San Francisco del Monte de Oro 124 32 36S 66 8W
San Francisco del Oro 120 26 52N 105 50W
San Francisco Javier 33 38 42N 1 26 E
San Francisco, Paso de 124 27 0S 68 0W
San Fratello 41 38 1N 14 33 E
San Gavino Monreale 40 39 33N 8 47 E
San Gil 126 6 33N 73 8W
San Gimignano 38 43 28N 11 3 E
San Giórgio di Nogaro 39 45 50N 13 13 E
San Giórgio Iónico 41 40 27N 17 23 E
San Giovanni Bianco 38 45 52N 9 40 E
San Giovanni in Fiore 41 39 16N 16 42 E
San Giovanni in Persieceto 39 44 39N 11 12 E
San Giovanni Rotondo 41 41 41N 15 42 E
San Giovanni Valdarno 39 43 32N 11 30 E
San Giuliano Terme 38 43 45N 10 26 E
San Gottardo, Paso del 25 46 33N 8 33 E
San Grcángelo 40 40 14N 16 14 E
San Gregorio 125 32 37S 55 40W
San Guiseppe Iato 40 37 57N 13 11 E
San Ignacio, Boliv. 126 16 20S 60 55W
San Ignacio, Parag. 124 26 52S 57 3W
San Ignacio, Laguna 120 26 50N 113 11W
San Ildefonso, C. 73 16 0N 122 1 E
San Isidro 124 34 29S 58 31W
San Javier, Misiones, Argent. 125 27 55S 55 5W
San Javier, Santa Fe, Argent. 124 30 40S 59 55W
San Javier, Boliv. 126 16 18S 62 30W
San Javier, Chile 124 35 40S 71 45W
San Javier, Spain 33 37 49N 0 50W
San Joaquin → 119 37 4N 121 51W
San Jorge 124 31 54S 61 50W
San Jorge, Bahía de 120 31 20N 113 20W
San Jorge, Golfo 128 46 0S 66 0W
San Jorge, G. de 32 40 50N 0 55W
San José, Boliv. 126 17 53S 60 50W
San José, C. Rica 121 10 0N 84 2W
San José, Guat. 120 14 0N 90 50W
San José, Mexico 120 25 0N 110 50W
San Jose, Luzon, Phil. 73 15 45N 120 55 E
San Jose, Mindoro, Phil. 73 12 27N 121 4 E
San Jose, Panay, Phil. 73 10 50N 122 5 E
San José 33 38 55N 1 18 E
San Jose, Calif., U.S.A. 119 37 20N 121 53W
San Jose, N. Mex., U.S.A. 119 35 26N 105 30W
San Jose → 119 34 58N 106 7W
San José de Feliciano 124 30 26S 58 46W
San José de Jáchal 124 30 15S 68 46W
San José de Mayo 124 34 27S 56 40W
San José de Ocune 126 4 15N 70 20W
San José del Cabo 120 23 0N 109 40W
San José del Guaviare 126 2 35N 72 38W
San Juan, Argent. 124 31 30S 68 30W
San Juan, Dom. Rep. 121 18 45N 72 45W
San Juan, Mexico 120 21 20N 102 50W
San Juan, Phil. 73 8 25N 126 20 E
San Juan, Pto. Rico 121 18 28N 66 8W
San Juan □ 124 31 9S 69 0W
San Juan →, Argent. 124 32 20S 67 25W
San Juan →, Nic. 121 10 56N 83 42W
San Juan →, U.S.A. 119 37 20N 110 20W
San Juan Bautista, Parag. 124 26 37S 57 6W
San Juan Bautista, Spain 33 39 5N 1 31 E
San Juan, C. 88 1 5N 9 20 E
San Juan Capistrano 119 33 29N 117 40W
San Juan de los Morros 126 9 55N 67 21W
San Juan del Norte, B. de 121 11 0N 83 40W
San Juan del Puerto 31 37 20N 6 50W
San Juan del Río 120 20 25N 100 0W
San Juan del Sur 121 11 20N 85 51W
San Juan Mts. 119 38 30N 108 30W
San Julián 128 49 15S 67 45W
San Just, Sierra de 32 40 45N 0 49W
San Justo 124 30 47S 60 30W
San Lázaro, C. 120 24 50N 112 18W
San Lázaro, Sa. de 120 23 25N 110 0W
San Leandro 119 37 40N 122 6W
San Leonardo 32 41 51N 3 5W
San Lorenzo, Argent. 124 32 45S 60 45W
San Lorenzo, Ecuador 126 1 15N 78 50W
San Lorenzo, Parag. 124 25 20S 57 32W
San Lorenzo → 120 24 15N 107 24W
San Lorenzo de la Parrilla 32 39 51N 2 22W
San Lorenzo de Morunys 32 42 8N 1 35 E
San Lorenzo, I., Mexico 120 28 35N 112 50W
San Lorenzo, I., Peru 126 12 7S 77 15W
San Lorenzo, Mt. 128 47 40S 72 20W
San Lucas, Boliv. 126 20 5S 65 7W
San Lucas, Mexico 120 27 10N 112 14W
San Lucas, C. de 120 22 50N 110 0W
San Lúcido 41 39 18N 16 3 E
San Luis, Argent. 124 33 20S 66 20W
San Luis, U.S.A. 119 37 3N 105 26W
San Luis □ 124 34 0S 66 0W
San Luis de la Paz 120 21 19N 100 32W
San Luis, I. 120 29 58N 114 26W
San Luis Obispo 119 35 21N 120 38W
San Luis Potosí 120 22 9N 100 59W
San Luis Potosí □ 120 22 10N 101 0W
San Luis Río Colorado 120 32 29N 114 58W
San Luis, Sierra de 124 32 30S 66 10W
San Marco Argentano 41 39 34N 16 8 E
San Marco dei Cavoti 41 41 20N 14 50 E
San Marco in Lámis 41 41 43N 15 38 E
San Marcos, Guat. 120 14 59N 91 52W
San Marcos, Mexico 120 27 13N 112 6W
San Marcos, U.S.A. 117 29 53N 98 0W
San Marino 39 43 56N 12 25 E
San Marino ■ 39 43 56N 12 25 E
San Martín 124 33 5S 68 28W
San Martín de Valdeiglesias 30 40 21N 4 24W
San Martín, L. 128 48 50S 72 50W
San Martino de Calvi 38 45 57N 9 41 E
San Mateo, Spain 32 40 28N 0 10 E
San Mateo, U.S.A. 119 37 32N 122 19W
San Matías 126 16 25S 58 20W
San Matías, Golfo 128 41 30S 64 0W
San Matias, G. of 122 41 30S 64 0W
San Miguel, El Sal. 120 13 30N 88 12W
San Miguel, Spain 33 39 3N 1 26 E
San Miguel, U.S.A. 119 35 45N 120 42W
San Miguel → 126 13 52S 63 56W
San Miguel de Salinas 33 37 59N 0 47W
San Miguel de Tucumán 124 26 50S 65 20W
San Miguel del Monte 124 35 23S 58 50W
San Miniato 38 43 40N 10 50 E
San Narciso 73 15 2N 120 3 E
San Nicolás de los Arroyas 124 33 25S 60 10W
San Nicolas I. 119 33 16N 119 30W
San Pablo 124 21 43S 66 38W
San Paolo di Civitate 41 41 44N 15 16 E
San Pedro, Buenos Aires, Argent. 125 26 30S 54 10W
San Pedro, Jujuy, Argent. 124 24 12S 64 55W
San-Pédro 84 4 50N 6 33W
San Pedro □ 124 24 0S 57 0W
San Pedro →, Chihuahua, Mexico 120 28 20N 106 10W
San Pedro →, Nayarit, Mexico 120 21 45N 105 30W
San Pedro →, U.S.A. 119 33 0N 110 50W
San Pedro de Atacama 124 22 55S 68 15W
San Pedro de Jujuy 124 24 12S 64 55W
San Pedro de las Colonias 120 25 50N 102 59W
San Pedro de Lloc 126 7 15S 79 28W
San Pedro de Macorís 121 18 30N 69 18W
San Pedro del Paraná 124 26 43S 56 13W
San Pedro del Pinatar 33 37 50N 0 50W
San Pedro Mártir, Sierra 120 31 0N 115 30W
San Pedro Mixtepec 120 16 2N 97 7W
San Pedro Ocampo = Melchor Ocampo 120 24 52N 101 40W
San Pedro, Pta. 124 25 30S 70 38W
San Pedro, Sierra de 31 39 18N 6 40W
San Pedro Sula 120 15 30N 88 0W
San Pedro,Pta. 124 25 30S 70 38W
San Pietro, I. 40 39 9N 8 17 E
San Pietro Vernótico 41 40 28N 18 0 E
San Quintin 73 16 1N 120 56 E
San Rafael, Argent. 124 34 40S 68 21W
San Rafael, Calif., U.S.A. 118 37 59N 122 32W
San Rafael, N. Mex., U.S.A. 119 35 6N 107 58W
San Ramón de la Nueva Orán 124 23 10S 64 20W
San Remo 38 43 48N 7 47 E
San Roque, Argent. 124 28 25S 58 45W
San Roque, Spain 31 36 17N 5 21W
San Rosendo 124 37 16S 72 43W
San Saba 117 31 12N 98 45W
San Salvador 120 13 40N 89 10W
San Salvador de Jujuy 124 24 10S 64 48W
San Salvador I. 121 24 0N 74 32W
San Sebastián, Argent. 128 53 10S 68 30W
San Sebastián, Spain 32 43 17N 1 58W
San Serverino Marche 39 43 13N 13 10 E
San Simon 119 32 14N 109 16W
San Stéfano di Cadore 39 46 34N 12 33 E
San Valentin, Mte. 128 46 30S 73 30W
San Vicente de Alcántara 31 39 22N 7 8W
San Vicente de la Barquera 30 43 23N 4 29W
San Vincenzo 38 43 6N 10 29 E
San Vito 40 39 26N 9 32 E
San Vito al Tagliamento 39 45 55N 12 50 E
San Vito, C. 40 38 11N 12 41 E
San Vito Chietino 39 42 19N 14 27 E
San Vito dei Normanni 41 40 40N 17 40 E
San Ygnacio 117 27 6N 99 24W
Sana' 63 15 27N 44 12 E
Sana → 39 45 3N 16 23 E
Sanaba 84 12 25N 3 47W
Sanabria, La 30 42 0N 6 30W
Sanâfir 86 27 55N 34 37 E
Sanaga → 88 3 35N 9 38 E
Sanak I. 104 53 30N 162 30W
Sanana 73 2 5S 125 59 E
Sanand 68 22 59N 72 25 E
Sanandaj 64 35 18N 47 1 E
Sanandita 124 21 40S 63 45W
Sanary 21 43 7N 5 48 E
Sanawad 68 22 11N 76 5 E
Sancergues 19 47 10N 2 54 E
Sancerre 19 47 20N 2 50 E
Sancerrois, Coll. du 19 47 20N 2 40 E
Sancha He → 77 26 48N 106 7 E
Sanchor 68 24 45N 71 55 E
Sanco, Pt. 73 8 15N 126 24 E
Sancoins 19 46 47N 2 55 E
Sancti-Spíritus 121 21 52N 79 33W
Sand → 93 22 25S 30 5 E
Sand Springs 117 36 12N 96 5W
Sandah 86 20 35N 39 32 E
Sandakan 72 5 53N 118 4 E
Sandan 71 12 46N 106 0 E
Sandanski 43 41 35N 23 16 E
Sandaré 84 14 40N 10 15W
Sanday 14 59 15N 2 30W
Sande, Möre og Romsdal, Norway 47 62 15N 5 27 E
Sande, Sogn og Fjordane, Norway 47 61 20N 5 47 E
Sandefjord 47 59 10N 10 15 E
Sandeid 47 59 33N 5 52 E
Sanders 119 35 12N 109 25W
Sanderson 117 30 5N 102 30W
Sandfly L. 109 55 43N 106 6W
Sandgate 99 27 18S 153 3 E
Sandia 126 14 10S 69 30W
Sandıklı 64 38 30N 30 20 E
Sandnes 47 58 50N 5 45 E
Sandness 14 60 18N 1 38W
Sandoa 88 9 41S 23 0 E
Sandomierz 28 50 40N 21 43 E
Sandover → 97 21 43S 136 32 E
Sandoway 67 18 20N 94 30 E
Sandpoint 118 48 20N 116 34W
Sandringham 12 52 50N 0 30 E
Sandslån 48 63 2N 17 49 E
Sandspit 108 53 14N 131 49W
Sandstone 96 27 59S 119 16 E
Sandusky, Mich., U.S.A. 106 43 26N 82 50W
Sandusky, Ohio, U.S.A. 114 41 25N 82 40W
Sandvig 49 55 18N 14 48 E
Sandviken 48 60 38N 16 46 E
Sandwich B., Can. 107 53 40N 57 15W
Sandwich B., S. Afr. 92 23 25S 14 20 E
Sandwich, C. 98 18 14S 146 18 E
Sandwich Group 5 57 0S 27 0W
Sandwip Chan. 67 22 35N 91 35 E
Sandy C., Queens., Austral. 97 24 42S 153 15 E
Sandy C., Tas., Austral. 97 41 25S 144 45 E
Sandy Cr. → 118 41 15N 109 47W
Sandy L. 106 53 2N 93 0W
Sandy Lake 106 53 0N 93 15W
Sandy Narrows 109 55 5N 103 4W
Sanford, Fla., U.S.A. 115 28 45N 81 20W
Sanford, Me., U.S.A. 113 43 28N 70 47W
Sanford, N.C., U.S.A. 115 35 30N 79 10W
Sanford → 96 27 22S 115 53 E
Sanford Mt. 104 62 30N 143 0W
Sanga 91 12 22S 35 21 E
Sanga → 88 1 5S 17 0 E
Sanga-Tolon 59 61 50N 149 40 E
Sangamner 70 19 37N 74 15 E
Sangar 59 64 2N 127 31 E
Sangasanga 72 0 36S 117 13 E
Sange 90 6 58S 28 21 E
Sangeang 73 8 12S 119 6 E
Sanger 119 36 41N 119 35W
Sangerhausen 24 51 28N 11 18 E
Sanggan He → 76 38 12N 117 15 E
Sanggau 72 0 5N 110 30 E
Sangihe, Kepulauan 73 3 0N 126 0 E
Sangihe, P. 73 3 45N 125 30 E
Sangkapura 72 5 52S 112 40 E
Sangli 70 16 55N 74 33 E
Sangmélina 88 2 57N 12 1 E
Sangonera → 33 37 59N 1 4W
Sangre de Cristo Mts. 117 37 0N 105 0W
Sangro → 39 42 14N 14 32 E
Sangudo 108 53 50N 114 54W
Sangüesa 32 42 37N 1 17W
Sanguinaires, Îs. 21 41 51N 8 36 E
Sangzhi 77 29 25N 110 12 E
Sanhala 84 10 3N 6 51W
Sanish 116 48 0N 102 30W
Sanje 90 0 49S 31 30 E
Sanjiang 77 25 48N 109 37 E
Sankaranayinarkovil 70 9 10N 77 35 E
Sankeshwar 70 16 23N 74 32 E
Sankt Andra 26 46 46N 14 50 E
Sankt Blasien 25 47 47N 8 7 E
Sankt Gallen 25 47 26N 9 22 E
Sankt Gallen □ 25 47 25N 9 22 E
Sankt Gotthard P. = San Gottardo, Paso del 25 46 33N 8 33 E
Sankt Ingbert 25 49 16N 7 6 E
Sankt Johann, Salzburg, Austria 26 47 22N 13 12 E
Sankt Johann, Tirol, Austria 26 47 30N 12 25 E
Sankt Moritz 25 46 30N 9 50 E
Sankt Olof 49 55 37N 14 8 E
Sankt Pölten 26 48 12N 15 38 E
Sankt Valentin 26 48 11N 14 33 E
Sankt Veit 26 46 54N 14 22 E
Sankt Wendel 25 49 27N 7 9 E
Sankt Wolfgang 26 47 43N 13 27 E
Sankuru → 88 4 17S 20 25 E
Sanlúcar de Barrameda 31 36 46N 6 21W
Sanlúcar la Mayor 31 37 26N 6 18W
Sanluri 40 39 35N 8 55 E
Sanmenxia 77 34 47N 111 12 E
Sannaspos 92 29 6S 26 34 E
Sannicandro Gargánico 41 41 50N 15 34 E
Sannidal 47 58 55N 9 15 E
Sannieshof 92 26 30S 25 47 E
Sanok 27 49 35N 22 10 E
Sanquhar 14 55 21N 3 56W
Sansanding Dam 84 13 48N 6 0W
Sansepolcro 39 43 34N 12 8 E
Sanshui 75 23 10N 112 56 E
Sanski Most 39 44 46N 16 40 E
Sant' Ágata de Goti 41 41 6N 14 30 E
Sant' Ágata di Militello 41 38 2N 14 8 E
Santa Ana, Boliv. 126 13 50S 65 40W
Santa Ana, Ecuador 126 1 16S 80 20W
Santa Ana, El Sal. 120 14 0N 89 31W
Santa Ana, Mexico 120 30 31N 111 8W
Santa Ana, U.S.A. 119 33 48N 117 55W
Sant' Ángelo Lodigiano 38 45 14N 9 25 E
Sant' Antíoco 40 39 2N 8 30 E
Sant' Arcángelo di Romagna 39 44 4N 12 26 E
Santa Bárbara, Mexico 120 26 48N 105 50W
Santa Bárbara, Spain 32 40 42N 0 29 E
Santa Barbara 119 34 25N 119 40W
Santa Bárbara, Mt. 33 37 23N 2 50W
Santa Catalina 120 25 40N 110 50W
Santa Catalina, G. of 119 33 0N 118 0W
Santa Catalina I. 119 33 20N 118 30W
Santa Catarina □ 125 27 25S 48 30W
Santa Catarina, I. de 125 27 30S 48 40W
Santa Caterina Villarmosa 41 37 37N 14 1 E
Santa Cecília 125 26 56S 50 18W
Santa Clara, Cuba 121 22 20N 80 0W
Santa Clara, Calif., U.S.A. 119 37 21N 122 0W
Santa Clara, Utah, U.S.A. 119 37 10N 113 38W
Santa Clara de Olimar 125 32 50S 54 54W
Santa Clara Pk. 119 35 58N 106 45W
Santa Clotilde 126 2 33S 73 45W
Santa Coloma de Farnés 32 41 50N 2 39 E
Santa Coloma de Gramanet 32 41 27N 2 13 E
Santa Comba 30 43 2N 8 49W
Santa Croce Camerina 41 36 50N 14 30 E
Santa Croce di Magliano 41 41 43N 14 59 E
Santa Cruz, Argent. 128 50 0S 68 32W
Santa Cruz, Boliv. 126 17 43S 63 10W
Santa Cruz, Chile 124 34 38S 71 27W
Santa Cruz, C. Rica 121 10 15N 85 35W
Santa Cruz, Phil. 73 14 20N 121 24 E
Santa Cruz, Calif., U.S.A. 119 36 55N 122 1W
Santa Cruz, N. Mexico, U.S.A. 119 35 59N 106 1W
Santa Cruz □ 126 17 43S 63 10W
Santa Cruz → 128 50 10S 68 20W
Santa Cruz de Mudela 33 38 39N 3 28W
Sta. Cruz de Tenerife 80 28 28N 16 15W
Santa Cruz del Retamar 30 40 8N 4 14W
Santa Cruz del Sur 121 20 44N 78 0W
Santa Cruz do Rio Pardo 125 22 54S 49 37W
Santa Cruz do Sul 125 29 42S 52 25W
Santa Cruz I. 119 34 0N 119 45W
Santa Cruz, Is. 94 10 30S 166 0 E
Santa Domingo, Cay 121 21 25N 75 15W
Santa Elena, Argent. 124 30 58S 59 47W
Santa Elena, Ecuador 126 2 16S 80 52W
Santa Elena, C. 121 10 54N 85 56W
Sant' Eufémia, Golfo di 41 38 50N 16 10 E
Santa Eulalia 33 38 59N 1 32 E
Santa Fe, Argent. 124 31 35S 60 41W
Santa Fe, Spain 31 37 11N 3 43W
Santa Fe, U.S.A. 119 35 40N 106 0W
Santa Fé □ 124 31 50S 60 55W
Santa Filomena 127 9 6S 45 50W
Santa Genoveva 120 23 18N 109 52W
Santa Inés 31 38 32N 5 37W
Santa Inés, I. 128 54 0S 73 0W
Santa Isabel, Argent. 124 36 10S 66 54W
Santa Isabel, Brazil 127 11 45S 51 30W
Santa Isabel = Rey Malabo 85 3 45N 8 50 E
Santa Isabel, Pico 85 3 36N 8 49 E
Santa Lucía, Corrientes, Argent. 124 28 58S 59 5W
Santa Lucía, San Juan, Argent. 124 31 30S 68 30W
Santa Lucía, Spain 33 37 35N 0 58W
Santa Lucia 124 34 27S 56 24W
Santa Lucia Range 119 36 0N 121 20W
Santa Margarita, Argent. 124 38 28S 61 35W
Santa Margarita, Mexico 120 24 30N 111 50W
Santa Margherita 38 44 20N 9 11 E
Santa María 124 26 40S 66 0W
Santa Maria, Brazil 125 29 40S 53 48W
Santa Maria, Spain 32 39 38N 2 47 E
Santa Maria, U.S.A. 119 34 58N 120 29W
Santa Maria, Zambia 91 11 5S 29 58 E
Santa María → 120 31 0N 107 14W
Santa María, Bahía de 120 25 10N 108 40W
Santa Maria, Cabo de 31 36 58N 7 53W
Santa Maria Capua Vetere 41 41 3N 14 15 E
Santa Maria da Vitória 127 13 24S 44 12W
Santa María del Oro 120 25 58N 105 20W
Santa Maria di Leuca, C. 41 39 48N 18 20 E
Santa María la Real de Nieva 30 41 4N 4 24W
Santa Marta, Colomb. 126 11 15N 74 13W
Santa Marta, Spain 31 38 37N 6 39W
Santa Marta Grande, C. 125 28 43S 48 50W
Santa Marta, Ría de 30 43 44N 7 45W
Santa Marta, Sierra Nevada de 126 10 55N 73 50W
Santa Maura = Levkás 45 38 40N 20 43 E
Santa Monica 119 34 0N 118 30W
Santa Olalla, Huelva, Spain 31 37 54N 6 14W
Santa Olalla, Toledo, Spain 30 40 2N 4 25W
Sant' Onofrio 41 38 42N 16 10 E
Santa Paula 119 34 20N 119 2W
Santa Pola 33 38 13N 0 35W
Santa Rita 119 32 50N 108 0W
Santa Rosa, La Pampa, Argent. 124 36 40S 64 17W
Santa Rosa, San Luis, Argent. 124 32 21S 65 10W
Santa Rosa, Boliv. 126 10 36S 67 20W
Santa Rosa, Brazil 125 27 52S 54 29W
Santa Rosa, Calif., U.S.A. 118 38 26N 122 43W
Santa Rosa, N. Mexico, U.S.A. 117 34 58N 104 40W
Santa Rosa de Copán 120 14 47N 88 46W
Santa Rosa de Río Primero 124 31 8S 63 20W
Santa Rosa I., Calif., U.S.A. 119 34 0N 120 6W
Santa Rosa I., Fla., U.S.A. 115 30 23N 87 0W
Santa Rosa Mts. 118 41 45N 117 30W
Santa Rosalía 120 27 20N 112 20W
Santa Sofia 39 43 57N 11 55 E
Santa Sylvina 124 27 50S 61 10W
Santa Tecla = Nueva San Salvador 120 13 40N 89 25W
Santa Teresa 124 33 25S 60 47W
Santa Teresa di Riva 41 37 58N 15 21 E
Santa Teresa Gallura 40 41 14N 9 12 E
Santa Vitória do Palmar 125 33 32S 53 25W
Santadi 40 39 5N 8 42 E
Santai 75 31 5N 104 58 E
Santana, Coxilha de 125 30 50S 55 35W
Santana do Livramento 125 30 55S 55 30W
Santanayi 33 39 20N 3 5 E
Santander 30 43 27N 3 51W
Santander □ 30 43 25N 4 0W
Santander Jiménez 120 24 11N 98 29W
Santaquin 118 40 0N 111 51W
Santarém, Brazil 127 2 25S 54 42W
Santarém, Port. 31 39 12N 8 42W
Santarém □ 31 39 10N 8 40W
Santaren Channel 121 24 0N 79 30W
Santéramo in Colle 41 40 48N 16 45 E

Santerno → 39 44 10N 11 38 E
Santhia 38 45 20N 8 10 E
Santiago, Brazil 125 29 11 S 54 52W
Santiago, Chile 124 33 24 S 70 40W
Santiago, Panama 121 8 0N 81 0W
Santiago □ 124 33 30 S 70 50W
Santiago de Compostela 30 42 52N 8 37W
Santiago de Cuba 121 20 0N 75 49W
Santiago de los Cabelleros 121 19 30N 70 40W
Santiago del Estero 124 27 50 S 64 15W
Santiago del Estero □ 124 27 40 S 63 15W
Santiago do Cacém 31 38 1N 8 42W
Santiago Ixcuintla 120 21 50N 105 11W
Santiago Papasquiaro 120 25 0N 105 20W
Santiago, Punta de 85 3 12N 8 40 E
Santiaguillo, L. de 120 24 50N 104 50W
Santillana del Mar 30 43 24N 4 6W
Santipur 69 23 17N 88 25 E
Santisteban del Puerto 33 38 17N 3 15W
Santo Amaro 127 12 30 S 38 43W
Santo Anastácio 125 21 58 S 51 39W
Santo André 125 23 39 S 46 29W
Santo Ângelo 125 28 15 S 54 15W
Santo Antonio 127 15 50 S 56 0W
Santo Corazón 126 18 0 S 58 45W
Santo Domingo, Dom. Rep. 121 18 30N 64 54W
Santo Domingo, Baja Calif. N., Mexico 120 30 43N 116 2W
Santo Domingo, Baja Calif. S., Mexico 120 25 32N 112 2W
Santo Domingo, Nic. 121 12 14N 84 59W
Santo Domingo de la Calzada 32 42 26N 2 57W
Santo Stéfano di Camastro 41 38 1N 14 22 E
Santo Stino di Livenza 39 45 45N 12 40 E
Santo Tirso 30 41 21N 8 28W
Santo Tomás 126 14 26 S 72 8W
Santo Tomé 125 28 40 S 56 5W
Santo Tomé de Guayana 126 8 22N 62 40W
Santoña 30 43 29N 3 27W
Santos 125 24 0 S 46 20W
Santos Dumont 125 22 55 S 43 10W
Santos, Sierra de los 31 38 7N 5 12W
Şanūr 62 32 22N 35 15 E
Sanvignes-les-Mines 19 46 40N 4 18 E
Sanyuan 77 34 35N 108 58 E
Sanza Pombo 88 7 18 S 15 56 E
São Anastácio 125 22 0 S 51 40W
São Bartolomeu de Messines 31 37 15N 8 17W
São Borja 125 28 39 S 56 0W
São Bras d'Alportel 31 37 8N 7 37W
São Carlos 125 22 0 S 47 50W
São Cristóvão 127 11 1 S 37 15W
São Domingos 127 13 25 S 46 19W
São Francisco 127 16 0 S 44 50W
São Francisco → 127 10 30 S 36 24W
São Francisco do Sul 125 26 15 S 48 36W
São Gabriel 125 30 20 S 54 20W
São Gonçalo 125 22 48 S 43 5W
Sao Hill 91 8 20 S 35 12 E
São João da Boa Vista 125 22 0 S 46 52W
São João da Pesqueira 30 41 8N 7 24W
São João del Rei 125 21 8 S 44 15W
São João do Araguaia 127 5 23 S 48 46W
São João do Piauí 127 8 21 S 42 15W
São José do Rio Prêto 125 20 50 S 49 20W
São José dos Campos 125 23 7 S 45 52W
São Leopoldo 125 29 50 S 51 10W
São Lourenço 125 22 7 S 45 3W
São Lourenço → 127 17 53 S 57 27W
São Luís Gonzaga 125 28 25 S 55 0W
São Luís (Maranhão) 127 2 39 S 44 15W
São Marcos → 127 18 15 S 47 37W
São Marcos, B. de 127 2 0 S 44 0W
São Martinho 30 40 18N 8 8W
São Mateus 127 18 44 S 39 50W
São Miguel 8 37 33N 25 27W
São Paulo 125 23 32 S 46 37W
São Paulo □ 125 22 0 S 49 0W
Sao Paulo, I. 6 0 50N 31 40W
São Pedro do Sul 30 40 46N 8 4W
São Roque, C. de 127 5 30 S 35 16W
São Sebastião do Paraíso 125 20 54 S 46 59W
São Sebastião, I. de 125 23 50 S 45 18W
São Teotónio 31 37 30N 8 42W
São Tomé 79 0 10N 6 39 E
São Tomé, C. de 125 22 0 S 40 59W
São Vicente 125 23 57 S 46 23W
São Vicente, Cabo de 31 37 0N 9 0W
Saona, I. 121 18 10N 68 40W
Saône → 19 45 44N 4 50 E
Saône-et-Loire □ 19 46 25N 4 50 E
Saonek 73 0 22 S 130 55 E
Saoura, O. → 82 29 0N 0 55W
Sápai 44 41 2N 25 43 E
Saparua 73 3 33 S 128 40 E
Sapele 85 5 50N 5 40 E
Sapelo I. 115 31 28N 81 15W
Sapiéntza 45 36 45N 21 43 E
Sapone 85 12 3N 1 35W
Saposoa 126 6 55 S 76 45W
Sapozhok 55 53 59N 40 41 E
Sapphire Mts. 118 46 20N 113 45W
Sapporo 74 43 0N 141 21 E
Sapri 41 40 5N 15 37 E
Sapudi 73 7 2 S 114 17 E
Sapulpa 117 36 0N 96 0W
Saqqez 64 36 15N 46 20 E
Sar-e Pol 65 36 10N 66 0 E
Sar Planina 42 42 10N 21 0 E
Sara 84 11 40N 3 53W
Sarāb 64 38 0N 47 30 E
Saragossa = Zaragoza 32 41 39N 0 53W
Saraguro 126 3 35 S 79 16W
Saraipalli 69 21 20N 82 59 E
Sarajevo 42 43 52N 18 26 E
Saralu 46 44 43N 28 10 E
Saran 86 19 35N 40 30 E
Saran, G. 72 0 30 S 111 25 E
Saranac Lake 114 44 20N 74 10W
Saranda, Alb. 44 39 52N 19 55 E
Saranda, Tanz. 90 5 45 S 34 59 E
Sarandí del Yi 125 33 18 S 55 38W
Sarandí Grande 124 33 44 S 56 20W
Sarangani B. 73 6 0N 125 13 E
Sarangani Is. 73 5 25N 125 25 E
Sarangarh 69 21 30N 83 5 E
Saransk 55 54 10N 45 10 E
Sarapul 52 56 28N 53 48 E
Sarasota 115 27 20N 82 30W
Saratoga 118 41 30N 106 48W
Saratoga Springs 114 43 5N 73 47W
Saratov 55 51 30N 46 2 E
Saravane 71 15 43N 106 25 E
Sarawak □ 72 2 0N 113 0 E
Saraya 84 12 50N 11 45W
Sarbāz 65 26 38N 61 19 E
Sarbīsheh 65 32 30N 59 40 E
Sårbogård 27 46 50N 18 40 E
Sarca → 38 45 52N 10 52 E
Sardalas 83 25 50N 10 34 E
Sardarshahr 68 28 30N 74 29 E
Sardegna 40 39 57N 9 0 E
Sardhana 68 29 9N 77 39 E
Sardinia = Sardegna 40 39 57N 9 0 E
Sarengrad 42 45 14N 19 16 E
Saréyamou 84 16 7N 3 10W
Sargasso Sea 6 27 0N 72 0W
Sargent 116 41 42N 99 24W
Sargodha 68 32 10N 72 40 E
Sargodha □ 68 31 50N 72 0 E
Sarh 81 9 5N 18 23 E
Sarhro, Djebel 82 31 6N 5 0W
Sārī 65 36 30N 53 4 E
Sária 45 35 54N 27 17 E
Sarida → 62 32 4N 34 45 E
Sarikamiş 64 40 22N 42 35 E
Sarikei 72 2 8N 111 30 E
Sarina 97 21 22 S 149 13 E
Sariñena 32 41 47N 0 10W
Sarīr Tibasti 83 22 50N 18 30 E
Sarita 117 27 14N 97 49W
Sariyer 43 41 10N 29 3 E
Sark 18 49 25N 2 20W
Sarkad 27 46 47N 21 23 E
Sarlat-la-Canéda 20 44 54N 1 13 E
Sarles 116 48 58N 99 0W
Sărmaşu 46 46 45N 24 13 E
Sarmi 73 1 49 S 138 44 E
Sarmiento 128 45 35 S 69 5W
Särna 48 61 41N 13 8 E
Sarnano 39 43 2N 13 17 E
Sarnen 25 46 53N 8 13 E
Sarnia 106 42 58N 82 23W
Sarno 41 40 48N 14 35 E
Sarnowa 28 51 39N 16 53 E
Sarny 54 51 17N 26 40 E
Särö 49 57 31N 11 57 E
Sarolangun 72 2 19 S 102 42 E
Saronikós Kólpos 45 37 45N 23 45 E
Saronno 38 45 38N 9 2 E
Saros Körfezi 44 40 30N 26 15 E
Sárospatak 27 48 18N 21 33 E
Sarosul Romănesc 42 45 34N 21 43 E
Sarova 55 54 55N 43 19 E
Sarpsborg 47 59 16N 11 12 E
Sarracín 32 42 15N 3 45W
Sarralbe 19 48 55N 7 1 E
Sarre = Saar → 19 49 7N 7 4 E
Sarre, La 106 48 45N 79 15W
Sarre-Union 19 48 55N 7 4 E
Sarrebourg 19 48 43N 7 3 E
Sarreguemines 19 49 1N 7 4 E
Sarriá 30 42 49N 7 29W
Sarrión 32 40 9N 0 49W
Sarro 84 13 40N 5 15W
Sarstedt 24 52 13N 9 50 E
Sartène 21 41 38N 8 58 E
Sarthe □ 18 47 58N 0 10 E
Sarthe → 18 47 33N 0 31W
Sartilly 18 48 45N 1 28W
Sartynya 58 63 22N 63 11 E
Sarum 86 21 11N 39 10 E
Sarūr 65 23 17N 58 4 E
Sárvár 27 47 15N 16 56 E
Sarvestān 65 29 20N 53 10 E
Särvfjället 48 62 42N 13 30 E
Sárviz → 27 46 24N 18 41 E
Sary-Tash 58 39 44N 73 15 E
Sarych, Mys. 56 44 25N 33 45 E
Saryshagan 58 46 12N 73 38 E
Sarzana 38 44 5N 9 59 E
Sarzeau 18 47 31N 2 48W
Sasa 62 33 2N 35 23 E
Sasabeneh 63 7 59N 44 43 E
Sasaram 69 24 57N 84 5 E
Sasca Montană 42 44 50N 21 45 E
Sasebo 74 33 10N 129 43 E
Saser Mt. 69 34 50N 77 50 E
Saskatchewan □ 109 54 40N 106 0W
Saskatchewan → 109 53 37N 100 40W
Saskatoon 109 52 10N 106 38W
Saskylakh 59 71 55N 114 1 E
Sasnovka 55 56 20N 51 4 E
Sasolburg 93 26 46 S 27 49 E
Sasovo 55 54 25N 41 55 E
Sassandra 84 5 0N 6 8W
Sassandra → 84 4 58N 6 5W
Sássari 40 40 44N 8 33 E
Sassnitz 24 54 29N 13 39 E
Sasso Marconi 39 44 22N 11 12 E
Sassocorvaro 39 43 47N 12 30 E
Sassoferrato 39 43 26N 12 51 E
Sassuolo 38 44 31N 10 47 E
Sástago 32 41 19N 0 21W
Sastown 84 4 45N 8 27W
Sasumua Dam 90 0 45 S 36 40 E
Sasyk, Ozero 46 45 45N 30 0 E
Sata-Misaki 74 30 59N 130 40 E
Satadougou 84 12 25N 11 25W
Satanta 117 37 30N 101 0W
Satara 70 17 44N 73 58 E
Satilla → 115 30 59N 81 28W
Satka 52 55 3N 59 1 E
Satkhira 69 22 43N 89 8 E
Satmala Hills 70 20 15N 74 40 E
Satna 69 24 35N 80 50 E
Sator 39 44 11N 16 37 E
Sátoraljaújhely 27 48 25N 21 41 E
Satpura Ra. 68 21 25N 76 10 E
Satrup 24 54 39N 9 38 E
Sattenapalle 70 16 25N 80 6 E
Satu Mare 46 47 46N 22 55 E
Satui 72 3 50 S 115 27 E
Satumare □ 46 47 45N 23 0 E
Satun 71 6 43N 100 2 E
Saturnina → 126 12 15 S 58 10W
Sauce 124 30 5 S 58 46W
Saucillo 120 28 1N 105 17W
Sauda 47 59 40N 6 20 E
Sauðarkrókur 50 65 45N 19 40W
Saudi Arabia ■ 64 26 0N 44 0 E
Sauerland 24 51 0N 8 0 E
Saugeen → 112 44 30N 81 22W
Saugerties 114 42 4N 73 58W
Saugues 20 44 58N 3 32 E
Sauherad 47 59 25N 9 15 E
Saujon 20 45 41N 0 55W
Sauk Center 116 45 42N 94 56W
Sauk Rapids 116 45 35N 94 10W
Saulgau 25 48 4N 9 32 E
Saulieu 19 47 17N 4 14 E
Sault 21 44 6N 5 24 E
Sault Ste. Marie, Can. 106 46 30N 84 20W
Sault Ste. Marie, U.S.A. 114 46 27N 84 22W
Saumlaki 73 7 55 S 131 20 E
Saumur 18 47 15N 0 5W
Saunders C. 101 45 53 S 170 45 E
Saunders I. 5 57 48 S 26 28W
Saurbær, Borgarfjarðarsýsla, Iceland 50 64 24N 21 35W
Saurbær, Eyjafjarðarsýsla, Iceland 50 65 27N 18 13W
Sauri 85 11 42N 6 44 E
Saurimo 88 9 40 S 20 12 E
Sauveterre 20 43 25N 0 57W
Sauzé-Vaussais 20 46 8N 0 8 E
Sava 39 40 28N 17 32 E
Sava → 39 44 50N 20 26 E
Savage 116 47 27N 104 20W
Savai'i 101 13 28 S 172 24W
Savalou 85 7 57N 1 58 E
Savane 91 19 37 S 35 8 E
Savanna 116 42 5N 90 10W
Savanna la Mar 121 18 10N 78 10W
Savannah, Ga., U.S.A. 115 32 4N 81 4W
Savannah, Mo., U.S.A. 116 39 55N 94 46W
Savannah, Tenn., U.S.A. 115 35 12N 88 18W
Savannah → 115 32 2N 80 53W
Savannakhet 71 16 30N 104 49 E
Savant L. 106 50 16N 90 44W
Savant Lake 106 50 14N 90 40W
Savantvadi 70 15 55N 73 54 E
Savanur 70 14 59N 75 21 E
Savda 68 21 9N 75 56 E
Savé 85 8 2N 2 29 E
Save → 20 43 47N 1 17 E
Säveh 64 35 2N 50 20 E
Savelugu 85 9 38N 0 54W
Savenay 18 47 20N 1 55W
Saverdun 20 43 14N 1 34 E
Saverne 19 48 39N 7 20 E
Savigliano 38 44 39N 7 40 E
Savigny-sur-Braye 18 47 53N 0 49 E
Saviñao 30 42 35N 7 38W
Savio → 39 44 19N 12 20 E
Šavnik 42 42 59N 19 10 E
Savoie □ 21 45 26N 6 35 E
Savona 38 44 19N 8 29 E
Savonlinna 52 61 52N 28 53 E
Sävsjö 49 57 20N 14 40 E
Sävsjøström 49 57 1N 15 25 E
Sawahlunto 72 0 40 S 100 52 E
Sawai 73 3 0 S 129 5 E
Sawai Madhopur 68 26 0N 76 25 E
Sawara 74 35 55N 140 30 E
Sawatch Mts. 119 38 30N 106 30W
Sawdā, Jabal as 83 28 51N 15 12 E
Sawel, Mt. 15 54 48N 7 5W
Sawfajjin, W. 83 31 46N 14 30 E
Sawknah 81 29 4N 15 47 E
Sawmills 91 19 30 S 28 2 E
Sawu 73 10 35 S 121 50 E
Sawu Sea 73 9 30 S 121 50 E
Sawyerville 113 45 20N 71 34W
Saxby → 98 18 25 S 140 53 E
Saxony, Lower = Niedersachsen □ 24 52 45N 9 0 E
Saxton 112 40 12N 78 18W
Say 85 13 8N 2 22 E
Saya 85 9 30N 3 18 E
Sayabec 107 48 35N 67 41W
Sayán 126 11 8 S 77 12W
Sayan, Vostochnyy 59 54 0N 96 0 E
Sayan, Zapadnyy 59 52 30N 94 0 E
Sayasan 57 42 56N 46 15 E
Saydā 64 33 35N 35 25 E
Şayghān 65 35 10N 67 55 E
Sayhut 63 15 12N 51 10 E
Saynshand 75 44 55N 110 11 E
Sayre, Okla., U.S.A. 117 35 20N 99 40W
Sayre, Pa., U.S.A. 114 42 0N 76 30W
Sayula 120 19 50N 103 40W
Sayville 113 40 45N 73 7W
Sazan 44 40 30N 19 20 E
Sázava → 26 49 53N 14 24 E
Sazin 69 35 35N 73 30 E
Sazlika → 43 41 59N 25 50 E
Sbeïtla 83 35 12N 9 7 E
Scaër 18 48 2N 3 42W
Scafell Pikes 12 54 26N 3 14W
Scalea 41 39 49N 15 47 E
Scalpay 14 57 51N 6 40W
Scandia 108 50 20N 112 0W
Scandiano 38 44 36N 10 40 E
Scandinavia 9 64 0N 12 0 E
Scansano 39 42 40N 11 20 E
Scapa Flow 14 58 52N 3 6W
Scarborough, Trin. 121 11 11N 60 42W
Scarborough, U.K. 12 54 17N 0 24W
Scarpe → 19 50 31N 3 27 E
Scedro 39 43 6N 16 43 E
Scenic 116 43 49N 102 32W
Schaal See 24 53 40N 10 57 E
Schaffhausen □ 25 47 42N 8 36 E
Schagen 16 52 49N 4 48 E
Schärding 26 48 27N 13 27 E
Scharhörn 24 53 58N 8 24 E
Scharnitz 26 47 23N 11 15 E
Scheessel 24 53 10N 9 33 E
Schefferville 107 54 48N 66 50W
Scheibbs 26 48 1N 15 9 E
Schelde → 16 51 15N 4 16 E
Schenectady 114 42 50N 73 58W
Scherfede 24 51 32N 9 2 E
Schesslitz 25 49 59N 11 2 E
Scheveningen 16 52 6N 4 16 E
Schiedam 16 51 55N 4 25 E
Schiermonnikoog 16 53 30N 6 15 E
Schifferstadt 25 49 22N 8 23 E
Schiltigheim 19 48 35N 7 45 E
Schio 39 45 42N 11 21 E
Schirmeck 19 48 29N 7 12 E
Schladming 26 47 23N 13 41 E
Schlei → 24 54 45N 9 52 E
Schleiden 24 50 32N 6 26 E
Schleiz 24 50 35N 11 49 E
Schleswig 24 54 32N 9 34 E
Schleswig-Holstein □ 24 54 10N 9 40 E
Schlüchtern 25 50 20N 9 32 E
Schmalkalden 24 50 43N 10 28 E
Schmölin 24 50 54N 12 22 E
Schmölln 24 53 15N 14 6 E
Schneeberg, Austria 26 47 47N 15 48 E
Schneeberg, Ger. 24 50 35N 12 39 E
Schofield 116 44 54N 89 39W
Schönberg, Rostock, Ger. 24 53 50N 10 55 E
Schönberg, Schleswig-Holstein, Ger. 24 54 23N 10 20 E
Schönebeck 24 52 2N 11 42 E
Schongau 25 47 49N 10 54 E
Schöningen 24 52 8N 10 57 E
Schortens 24 53 37N 7 51 E
Schouten I. 99 42 20 S 148 20 E
Schouten, Kepulauan 73 1 0 S 136 0 E
Schouwen 16 51 43N 3 45 E
Schramberg 25 48 12N 8 24 E
Schrankogl 26 47 3N 11 7 E
Schreiber 106 48 45N 87 20W
Schrobenhausen 25 48 33N 11 16 E
Schruns 26 47 5N 9 56 E
Schuler 109 50 20N 110 6W
Schumacher 106 48 30N 81 16W
Schurz 118 38 57N 118 48W
Schuyler 116 41 30N 97 3W
Schuylkill Haven 113 40 37N 76 11W
Schwabach 25 49 19N 11 3 E
Schwäbisch Gmünd 25 48 49N 9 48 E
Schwäbisch Hall 25 49 7N 9 45 E
Schwäbische Alb 25 48 30N 9 30 E
Schwabmünchen 25 48 11N 10 45 E
Schwandorf 25 49 20N 12 7 E
Schwarmstedt 24 52 41N 9 37 E
Schwarzach → 26 46 56N 12 35 E
Schwärze 24 52 50N 13 49 E
Schwarzenberg 24 50 31N 12 49 E
Schwarzwald 25 48 0N 8 0 E
Schwaz 26 47 20N 11 44 E
Schwedt 24 53 4N 14 18 E
Schweinfurt 25 50 3N 10 12 E
Schweizer Reneke 92 27 11 S 25 18 E
Schwerin 24 53 37N 11 22 E
Schwerin □ 24 53 35N 11 20 E
Schweriner See 24 53 45N 11 26 E
Schwetzingen 25 49 22N 8 35 E
Schwyz 25 47 2N 8 39 E
Schwyz □ 25 47 2N 8 39 E
Sciacca 40 37 30N 13 3 E
Scicli 41 36 48N 14 41 E
Scie, La 107 49 57N 55 36W
Scilla 41 38 18N 15 44 E
Scilly, Isles of 13 49 55N 6 15W
Ścinawa 28 51 25N 16 26 E
Scione 44 39 57N 23 36 E
Scioto → 114 38 44N 83 0W
Scobey 116 48 47N 105 30W
Scone, Austral. 99 32 5 S 150 52 E
Scone, U.K. 14 56 25N 3 26W
Scordia 41 37 19N 14 50 E
Scoresbysund 4 70 20N 23 0W
Scorno, Punta dello 40 41 7N 8 23 E
Scotia, Calif., U.S.A. 118 40 36N 124 4W
Scotia, N.Y., U.S.A. 113 42 50N 73 58W
Scotia Sea 5 56 5 S 56 0W
Scotland 116 43 10N 97 45W
Scotland □ 13 57 0N 4 0W
Scotland Neck 115 36 6N 77 32W
Scott 5 77 0 S 165 0 E
Scott, C. 5 71 30 S 168 0 E
Scott City 116 38 30N 100 52W
Scott Glacier 5 66 15 S 100 5 E
Scott I. 5 67 0 S 179 0 E
Scott Inlet 105 71 0N 71 0W
Scott Is. 108 50 48N 128 40W
Scott L. 109 59 55N 106 18W
Scott Reef 96 14 0 S 121 50 E
Scottburgh 93 30 15 S 30 47 E
Scottdale 112 40 8N 79 35W
Scottsbluff 116 41 55N 103 35W
Scottsboro 115 34 40N 86 0W
Scottsburg 114 38 40N 85 46W
Scottsdale 97 41 9 S 147 31 E
Scottsville, Ky., U.S.A. 115 36 48N 86 10W
Scottsville, N.Y., U.S.A. 112 43 2N 77 47W
Scottville, Austral. 98 20 33 S 147 49 E
Scottville, U.S.A. 114 43 57N 86 18W
Scranton 114 41 22N 75 41W
Scugog, L. 112 44 10N 78 55W
Scunthorpe 12 53 35N 0 38W

Scusciuban 63 10 18N 50 12 E
Sea Breeze 112 43 12N 77 32W
Seaford, Austral. 100 38 10S 145 11 E
Seaford, U.S.A. 114 38 37N 75 36W
Seaforth 106 43 35N 81 25W
Seagraves 117 32 56N 102 30W
Seal → 109 58 50N 97 30W
Seal Cove 107 49 57N 56 22W
Seal L. 107 54 20N 61 30W
Sealy 117 29 46N 96 9W
Searchlight 119 35 31N 114 55W
Searcy 117 35 15N 91 45W
Searles L. 119 35 47N 117 17W
Seaside 118 45 59N 123 55W
Seaspray 99 38 25S 147 15 E
Seattle 118 47 41N 122 15W
Seaview Ra. 97 18 40S 145 45 E
Sebastián Vizcaíno, Bahía 120 28 0N 114 30W
Sebastopol 118 38 24N 122 49W
Sebastopol = Sevastopol 56 44 35N 33 30 E
Sebderat 87 15 26N 36 42 E
Sebdou 82 34 38N 1 19W
Sebeş 46 45 58N 23 34 E
Sebeşului, Munţii 46 45 36N 23 40 E
Sebewaing 114 43 45N 83 27W
Sebezh 54 56 14N 28 22 E
Sébi 84 15 50N 4 12W
Şebinkarahisar 56 40 22N 38 28 E
Sebiş 46 46 23N 22 13 E
Sebkhet Te-n-Dghâmcha 84 18 30N 15 55W
Sebkra Azzel Mati 82 26 10N 0 43 E
Sebkra Mekerghene 82 26 21N 1 30 E
Sebnitz 24 50 58N 14 17 E
Sebou, Oued → 82 34 16N 6 40W
Sebring, Fla., U.S.A. 115 27 30N 81 26W
Sebring, Ohio, U.S.A. 112 40 55N 81 2W
Sebringville 112 43 24N 81 4W
Sebta = Ceuta 82 35 52N 5 19W
Sebuku 72 3 30S 116 25 E
Sebuku, Teluk 72 4 0N 118 10 E
Sečanj 42 45 25N 20 47 E
Secchia → 38 44 4N 11 0 E
Sechelt 108 49 25N 123 42W
Sechura, Desierto de 126 6 0S 80 30W
Seclin 19 50 33N 3 2 E
Secondigny 18 46 37N 0 26W
Sečovce 27 48 42N 21 40 E
Secretary I. 101 45 15S 166 56 E
Secunderabad 70 17 28N 78 30 E
Sedalia 116 38 40N 93 18W
Sedan, Austral. 99 34 34S 139 19 E
Sedan, France 19 49 43N 4 57 E
Sedan, U.S.A. 117 37 10N 96 11W
Sedano 32 42 43N 3 49W
Seddon 101 41 40S 174 7 E
Seddonville 101 41 33S 172 1 E
Sede Ya'aqov 62 32 43N 35 7 E
Sedgewick 108 52 48N 111 41W
Sedhiou 84 12 44N 15 30W
Sedičany 26 49 40N 14 25 E
Sedico 39 46 8N 12 6 E
Sedienie 43 42 16N 24 33 E
Sedley 109 50 10N 104 0W
Sedom 62 31 5N 35 20 E
Sedova, Pik 58 73 29N 54 58 E
Sedrata 83 36 7N 7 31 E
Sedro Woolley 118 48 30N 122 15W
Seduva 54 55 45N 23 45 E
Sedziszów Małapolski 27 50 5N 21 45 E
Seebad Ahlbeck 24 53 56N 14 10 E
Seefeld 26 47 19N 11 13 E
Seehausen 24 52 52N 11 43 E
Seeheim 92 26 50S 17 45 E
Seekoe → 92 30 18S 25 1 E
Seelaw 24 52 32N 14 22 E
Se'elim, Nahal 62 31 21N 35 24 E
Sées 18 48 38N 0 10 E
Seesen 24 51 53N 10 10 E
Sefadu 84 8 35N 10 58W
Séfeto 84 14 8N 9 49W
Sefrou 82 33 52N 4 52W
Sefwi Bekwai 84 6 10N 2 25W
Seg-ozero 54 63 0N 33 10 E
Segamat 71 2 30N 102 50 E
Segarcea 46 44 6N 23 43 E
Segbwema 84 8 0N 11 0W
Seget 73 1 24S 130 58 E
Segezha 52 63 44N 34 19 E
Segueur, O. → 82 32 4N 2 4 E
Segid 87 16 55N 42 0 E
Segonzac 20 45 36N 0 14W
Segorbe 32 39 50N 0 30W
Ségou 84 13 30N 6 16W
Segovia 30 40 57N 4 10W
Segovia = Coco → 121 15 0N 83 8W
Segovia □ 30 40 55N 4 10W
Segré 18 47 40N 0 52W
Segre → 32 41 40N 0 43 E
Séguéla 84 7 55N 6 40W
Seguin 117 29 34N 97 58W
Segundo 117 37 12N 104 50W
Segundo → 124 30 53S 62 44W
Segura → 33 38 6N 0 54W
Segura, Sierra de 33 38 5N 2 45W
Sehore 68 23 10N 77 5 E
Sehwan 68 26 28N 67 53 E
Şeica Mare 46 46 1N 24 7 E
Seiland 50 70 25N 23 15 E
Seiling 117 36 10N 98 56W
Seille →, Moselle, France 19 49 7N 6 11 E
Seille →, Saône-et-Loire, France 21 46 31N 4 57 E
Sein, Î. de 18 48 2N 4 52W
Seinäjoki → 50 62 40N 22 45 E
Seine → 18 49 26N 0 26 E
Seine, B. de la 18 49 40N 0 40W
Seine-et-Marne □ 19 48 45N 3 0 E
Seine-Maritime □ 18 49 40N 1 0 E
Seine-Saint-Denis □ 19 48 58N 2 24 E
Seini 46 47 44N 23 21 E
Seistan 65 30 50N 61 0 E
Seistan-Balūchestān □ 65 27 0N 62 0 E
Sejerø 49 55 54N 11 9 E
Sejerø Bugt 49 55 53N 11 15 E
Sejny 28 54 6N 23 21 E
Seka 87 8 10N 36 52 E
Sekayu 72 2 51S 103 51 E
Seke 90 3 20S 33 31 E
Sekenke 90 4 18S 34 11 E
Sekiu 118 48 16N 124 18W
Sekken Veøy 47 62 45N 7 30 E
Sekondi-Takoradi 84 4 58N 1 45W
Sekuma 92 24 36S 23 50 E
Selah 118 46 44N 120 30W
Selama 71 5 12N 100 42 E
Selangor □ 71 3 20N 101 30 E
Selárgius 40 39 14N 9 14 E
Selaru 73 8 9S 131 0 E
Selb 25 50 9N 12 9 E
Selby, U.K. 12 53 47N 1 5W
Selby, U.S.A. 116 45 34N 100 2W
Selca 39 43 20N 16 50 E
Selden 116 39 33N 100 39W
Seldovia 104 59 30N 151 45W
Sele → 41 40 27N 14 58 E
Selemdzha → 59 51 42N 128 53 E
Selenge → 75 49 25N 103 59 E
Selenica 44 40 33N 19 39 E
Selenter See 24 54 19N 10 26 E
Sélestat 19 48 16N 7 26 E
Seletan, Tg. 72 4 10S 114 40 E
Seletin 46 47 50N 25 12 E
Selevac 42 44 28N 20 52 E
Selfridge 116 46 3N 100 57W
Sélibabi 84 15 10N 12 15W
Seliger, Oz. 54 57 15N 33 0 E
Seligman 119 35 17N 112 56W
Şelim 57 40 30N 42 46 E
Selîma, El Wâhât el 86 21 22N 29 19 E
Selinda Spillway 92 18 35S 23 10 E
Selinoús 45 37 35N 21 37 E
Selizharovo 54 56 51N 33 27 E
Selje 47 62 3N 5 22 E
Seljord 47 59 30N 8 40 E
Selkirk, Can. 109 50 10N 96 55W
Selkirk, U.K. 14 55 33N 2 50W
Selkirk I. 109 53 20N 99 6W
Selkirk Mts. 108 51 15N 117 40W
Selles-sur-Cher 19 47 16N 1 33 E
Sellières 19 46 50N 5 32 E
Sells 119 31 57N 111 57W
Sellye 27 45 52N 17 51 E
Selma, Ala., U.S.A. 115 32 30N 87 0W
Selma, Calif., U.S.A. 119 36 39N 119 39W
Selma, N.C., U.S.A. 115 35 32N 78 15W
Selmer 115 35 9N 88 36W
Selo 44 41 10N 25 53 E
Selongey 19 47 36N 5 10 E
Selowandoma Falls 91 21 15S 31 50 E
Selpele 73 0 1S 130 5 E
Selsey Bill 13 50 44N 0 47W
Seltz 19 48 48N 8 4 E
Selu 73 7 32S 130 55 E
Selukwe 91 19 40S 30 0 E
Sélune → 18 48 38N 1 22W
Selva, Argent. 124 29 50S 62 0W
Selva, Italy 39 46 33N 11 46 E
Selva, Spain 32 41 13N 1 8 E
Selva, La 32 42 0N 2 45 E
Selvas 126 6 30S 67 0W
Selwyn L. 109 60 0N 104 30W
Selwyn P.O. 97 21 32S 140 30 E
Selwyn Ra. 97 21 10S 140 0 E
Seman → 44 40 45N 19 50 E
Semara 82 26 48N 11 41W
Semarang 73 7 0S 110 26 E
Semau 73 10 13S 123 22 E
Sembabule 90 0 4S 31 25 E
Sémé 84 15 4N 13 41W
Semeih 87 12 43N 30 53 E
Semenov 55 56 43N 44 30 E
Semenovka, Ukraine S.S.R., U.S.S.R. 54 52 8N 32 36 E
Semenovka, Ukraine S.S.R., U.S.S.R. 56 49 37N 33 10 E
Semeru 73 8 4S 112 55 E
Semiluki 55 51 41N 39 2 E
Seminoe Res. 118 42 0N 107 0W
Seminole, Okla., U.S.A. 117 35 15N 96 45W
Seminole, Tex., U.S.A. 117 32 41N 102 38W
Semiozernoye 58 52 22N 64 8 E
Semipalatinsk 58 50 30N 80 10 E
Semirara Is. 73 12 0N 121 20 E
Semisopochnoi 104 52 0N 179 40W
Semitau 72 0 29N 111 57 E
Semiyarskoye 58 50 55N 78 23 E
Semmering Pass 26 47 41N 15 45 E
Semnān 65 35 55N 53 25 E
Semnān □ 65 36 0N 54 0 E
Semois → 16 49 53N 4 44 E
Semporna 73 4 30N 118 33 E
Semuda 72 2 51S 112 58 E
Semur-en-Auxois 19 47 30N 4 20 E
Sen → 71 13 45N 105 12 E
Sena 91 17 25S 35 0 E
Sena Madureira 126 9 5S 68 45W
Senador Pompeu 127 5 40S 39 20W
Senai 71 1 38N 103 38 E
Senaja 72 6 45N 117 3 E
Senanga 92 16 2S 23 14 E
Senatobia 117 34 38N 89 57W
Sendafa 87 9 11N 39 3 E
Sendai, Kagoshima, Japan 74 31 50N 130 20 E
Sendai, Miyagi, Japan 74 38 15N 140 53 E
Sendamangalam 70 11 17N 78 17 E
Sendeling's Drift 92 28 12S 16 52 E
Sendenhorst 24 51 50N 7 49 E
Sendurjana 68 21 32N 78 17 E
Senec 27 48 12N 17 23 E
Seneca, Oreg., U.S.A. 118 44 10N 119 2W
Seneca, S.C., U.S.A. 115 34 43N 82 59W
Seneca Falls 114 42 55N 76 50W
Seneca L. 114 42 40N 76 58W
Senegal ■ 84 14 30N 14 30W
Senegal → 84 15 48N 16 32W
Senekal 93 28 30S 27 36 E
Senftenberg 24 51 30N 14 1 E
Senga Hill 91 9 19S 31 11 E
Senge Khambab (Indus) → 68 28 40N 70 10 E
Sengerema □ 90 2 10S 32 20 E
Sengiley 55 53 58N 48 46 E
Sengkang 73 4 8S 120 1 E
Sengua → 91 17 7S 28 5 E
Senhor-do-Bonfim 127 10 30S 40 10W
Senica 27 48 41N 17 25 E
Senigállia 39 43 42N 13 12 E
Senio → 39 44 35N 12 15 E
Senise 40 40 6N 16 15 E
Senj 39 45 0N 14 58 E
Senja 50 69 25N 17 30 E
Senlis 19 49 13N 2 35 E
Senmonorom 71 12 27N 107 12 E
Sennâr 87 13 30N 33 35 E
Senneterre 106 48 25N 77 15W
Senniquelle 84 7 19N 8 38W
Senno 54 54 45N 29 43 E
Sennori 40 40 49N 8 36 E
Senonches 18 48 34N 1 2 E
Senorbì 40 39 33N 9 8 E
Senožeče 39 45 43N 14 3 E
Sens 19 48 11N 3 15 E
Senta 42 45 55N 20 3 E
Sentein 20 42 53N 0 58 E
Sentery 90 5 17S 25 42 E
Sentinel 119 32 45N 113 13W
Sentolo 73 7 55S 110 13 E
Senya Beraku 85 5 28N 0 31W
Seo de Urgel 32 42 22N 1 23 E
Seohara 68 29 15N 78 33 E
Seoni 69 22 5N 79 30 E
Seoriuarayan 69 21 45N 82 34 E
Seoul = Sŏul 76 37 31N 127 6 E
Separation Point 107 53 37N 57 25W
Sepik → 98 3 49S 144 30 E
Sępólno Krajeńskie 28 53 26N 17 30 E
Sepone 71 16 45N 106 13 E
Sepopa 92 18 49S 22 12 E
Sepopol 28 54 16N 21 2 E
Sept-Îles 107 50 13N 66 22W
Septemvri 43 42 13N 24 6 E
Septimus 98 21 13S 148 47 E
Sepúlveda 30 41 18N 3 45W
Sequeros 30 40 31N 6 2W
Sequim 118 48 3N 123 9W
Sequoia Nat. Park 119 36 30N 118 30W
Serafimovich 57 49 36N 42 43 E
Seraing 16 50 35N 5 32 E
Seram 73 3 10S 129 0 E
Seram Sea 73 2 30S 128 30 E
Serampore 69 22 44N 88 21 E
Serang 73 6 8S 106 10 E
Serasan 72 2 29N 109 4 E
Seravezza 38 43 59N 10 13 E
Serbia = Srbija 42 43 30N 21 0 E
Sercaia 46 45 49N 25 9 E
Serdo 87 11 56N 41 14 E
Serdobsk 55 52 28N 44 10 E
Seredka 54 58 12N 28 10 E
Seregno 38 45 40N 9 12 E
Seremban 71 2 43N 101 53 E
Serena, La, Chile 124 29 55S 71 10W
Serena, La, Spain 31 38 45N 5 40W
Serengeti □ 90 2 0S 34 30 E
Serengeti Plain 90 2 40S 35 0 E
Sereth = Siret → 46 47 58N 26 5 E
Sergach 55 55 30N 45 30 E
Serge → 32 41 54N 0 50 E
Sergino 58 62 30N 65 38 E
Sergipe □ 127 10 30S 37 30W
Seria 72 4 37N 114 23 E
Serian 72 1 10N 110 31 E
Seriate 38 45 42N 9 43 E
Seribu, Kepulauan 72 5 36S 106 33 E
Sérifontaine 19 49 20N 1 45 E
Sérifos 45 37 9N 24 30 E
Sérignan 20 43 17N 3 17 E
Sermaize-les-Bains 19 48 47N 4 54 E
Sermata 73 8 15S 128 50 E
Sérmide 39 45 0N 11 17 E
Sernovodsk 55 53 54N 51 16 E
Serny Zavod 58 39 59N 58 50 E
Serock 28 52 31N 21 4 E
Serón 33 37 20N 2 29W
Serós 32 41 27N 0 24 E
Serov 58 59 29N 60 35 E
Serowe 92 22 25S 26 43 E
Serpa 31 37 57N 7 38 E
Serpeddi, Punta 40 39 19N 9 18 E
Serpentara 40 39 8N 9 38 E
Serpis → 33 38 59N 0 9W
Serpukhov 55 54 55N 37 28 E
Serra San Bruno 41 38 31N 16 23 E
Serracapriola 41 41 47N 15 12 E
Serradilla 30 39 50N 6 9W
Sérrai 44 41 5N 23 31 E
Sérrai □ 44 41 5N 23 37 E
Serramanna 40 39 26N 8 56 E
Serrat, C. 83 37 14N 9 10 E
Serre-Poncon, Barrage de 21 44 22N 6 20 E
Serres 21 44 26N 5 43 E
Serrezuela 124 30 40S 65 20W
Serrinha 127 11 39S 39 0W
Sersale 41 39 1N 16 44 E
Sertã 30 39 48N 8 6W
Sertânia 127 8 5S 37 20W
Sertanópolis 125 23 4S 51 2W
Serua 73 6 18S 130 1 E
Serui 73 1 53S 136 10 E
Serule 92 21 57S 27 20 E
Sérvia 44 40 9N 21 58 E
Sese Is. 90 0 20S 32 20 E
Sesepe 73 1 30S 127 59 E
Sesfontein 92 19 7S 13 39 E
Sesheke 92 17 29S 24 13 E
Sesia → 38 45 5N 8 37 E
Sesimbra 31 38 28N 9 6W
Sessa Aurunca 40 41 14N 13 55 E
Sestao 32 43 18N 3 0W
Sesto S. Giovanni 38 45 32N 9 14 E
Sestos 44 40 16N 26 23 E
Sestri Levante 38 44 17N 9 22 E
Sestrières 38 44 58N 6 56 E
Sestrunj 39 44 10N 15 0 E
Sestu 40 39 18N 9 6 E
Sète 20 43 25N 3 42 E
Sete Lagôas 127 19 27S 44 16W
Sétif 83 36 9N 5 26 E
Setonaikai 74 34 20N 133 30 E
Settat 82 33 0N 7 40W
Setté-Cama 88 2 32S 9 45 E
Séttimo Tor 38 45 9N 7 46 E
Setting L. 109 55 0N 98 38W
Settle 12 54 5N 2 18W
Settlement Pt. 115 26 40N 79 0W
Setto Calende 38 45 44N 8 37 E
Setúbal 31 38 30N 8 58W
Setúbal □ 31 38 25N 8 35W
Setúbal, B. de 31 38 40N 8 56W
Seugne → 20 45 42N 0 32W
Seul, Lac-Rés. 106 50 25N 92 30W
Seulimeum 72 5 27N 95 15 E
Sevan 57 40 33N 44 56 E
Sevan, Ozero 57 40 30N 45 20 E
Sevastopol 56 44 35N 33 30 E
Seven Sisters 108 54 56N 128 10W
Sever → 31 39 40N 7 32W
Sévérac-le-Château 20 44 20N 3 5 E
Severn →, Can. 106 56 2N 87 36W
Severn →, U.K. 13 51 35N 2 38W
Severn L. 106 53 54N 90 48W
Severnaya Zemlya 59 79 0N 100 0 E
Severnyye Uvaly 52 58 0N 48 0 E
Severo-Kurilsk 59 50 40N 156 8 E
Severo-Yeniseyskiy 59 60 22N 93 1 E
Severočeský □ 26 50 30N 14 0 E
Severodinsk 52 64 27N 39 58 E
Severodonetsk 57 48 58N 38 30 E
Severomoravský □ 27 49 38N 17 40 E
Severomorsk 52 69 5N 33 27 E
Severouralsk 52 60 9N 59 57 E
Sevier 119 38 39N 112 11W
Sevier → 119 39 10N 113 6W
Sevier L. 118 39 0N 113 20W
Sevilla 31 37 23N 6 0W
Sevilla □ 31 37 25N 5 30W
Seville = Sevilla 31 37 23N 6 0W
Sevlievo 43 43 2N 25 3 E
Sevnica 39 46 2N 15 19 E
Sèvre-Nantaise → 18 47 12N 1 33W
Sèvre Niortaise → 20 46 18N 1 8W
Sevsk 54 52 10N 34 30 E
Seward, Alaska, U.S.A. 104 60 6N 149 26W
Seward, Nebr., U.S.A. 116 40 55N 97 6W
Seward Pen. 104 65 0N 164 0W
Sewell 124 34 10S 70 23W
Sewer 73 5 53S 134 40 E
Sewickley 112 40 33N 80 12W
Sexsmith 108 55 21N 118 47W
Seychelles ■ 3 5 0S 56 0 E
Seyðisfjörður 50 65 16N 14 0W
Seym → 54 51 27N 32 34 E
Seymchan 59 62 54N 152 30 E
Seymour, Austral. 99 37 0S 145 10 E
Seymour, Conn., U.S.A. 113 41 23N 73 5W
Seymour, Ind., U.S.A. 114 39 0N 85 50W
Seymour, Tex., U.S.A. 117 33 35N 99 18W
Seymour, Wis., U.S.A. 114 44 30N 88 20W
Seyne 21 44 21N 6 22 E
Seyne-sur-Mer, La 21 43 7N 5 52 E
Seyssel 21 45 57N 5 50 E
Sežana 39 45 43N 13 41 E
Sézanne 19 48 40N 3 40 E
Sezze 40 41 30N 13 3 E
Sfax 83 34 49N 10 48 E
Sfîntu Gheorghe 46 45 52N 25 48 E
Sha Xian 77 26 23N 117 45 E
Shaanxi □ 77 35 0N 109 0 E
Shaba 90 8 0S 25 0 E
Shabani 91 20 17S 30 2 E
Shabla 43 43 31N 28 32 E
Shabunda 90 2 40S 27 16 E
Shache 75 38 20N 77 10 E
Shackleton 5 78 30S 36 1W
Shackleton Ice Shelf 5 66 0S 100 0 E
Shackleton Inlet 5 83 0S 160 0 E
Shaddad 86 21 25N 40 2 E
Shadrinsk 58 56 5N 63 32 E
Shaffa 85 10 30N 12 6 E
Shafter, Calif., U.S.A. 119 35 32N 119 14W
Shafter, Tex., U.S.A. 117 29 49N 104 18W
Shaftesbury 13 51 0N 2 12W
Shagamu 85 6 51N 3 39 E
Shah Bunder 68 24 13N 67 56 E
Shah Faisalabad 68 31 30N 73 5 E
Shahabad, Andhra Pradesh, India 70 17 10N 76 54 E
Shahabad, Punjab, India 68 30 10N 76 55 E
Shahabad, Raj., India 68 25 15N 77 11 E
Shahabad, Ut. P., India 69 27 36N 79 56 E
Shāhābād, Kermanshāhān, Iran 64 34 10N 46 30 E
Shāhābād, Khorāsān, Iran 65 37 40N 56 50 E
Shahada 68 21 33N 74 30 E
Shahadpur 68 25 55N 68 35 E
Shahapur 70 15 50N 74 34 E
Shahdād 65 30 30N 57 40 E
Shahdadkot 68 27 50N 67 55 E
Shahganj 69 26 3N 82 44 E
Shahḥāt 81 32 48N 21 54 E
Shāhī 65 36 30N 52 55 E
Shahjahanpur 69 27 54N 79 57 E
Shahpur, Mad. P., India 68 22 12N 77 58 E
Shahpur, Mysore, India 70 16 40N 76 48 E
Shāhpūr 64 38 12N 44 45 E
Shahpur 68 28 46N 68 27 E
Shahpura 69 23 10N 80 45 E
Shahr Kord 65 32 15N 50 55 E
Shahrezā 65 32 0N 51 55 E
Shahrig 68 30 15N 67 40 E
Shāhrūd 65 36 30N 55 0 E

Shahsād, Namakzār-e **65** 30 20N 58 20 E
Shahsavār **65** 36 45N 51 12 E
Shaibara **86** 25 26N 36 47 E
Shaikhabad **66** 34 2N 68 45 E
Shajapur **68** 23 27N 76 21 E
Shakargarh **68** 32 17N 75 10 E
Shakawe **92** 18 28 S 21 49 E
Shaker Heights **112** 41 29N 81 36W
Shakhty **57** 47 40N 40 16 E
Shakhunya **55** 57 40N 46 46 E
Shaki **85** 8 41N 3 21 E
Shakopee **116** 44 45N 93 30W
Shala, L. **87** 7 30N 38 30 E
Shallow Lake **112** 44 36N 81 5W
Sham, J. ash **65** 23 10N 57 5 E
Shamâl Dârfûr □ **87** 15 0N 25 0 E
Shamâl Kordofân □ **87** 15 0N 30 0 E
Shamattawa **109** 55 51N 92 5W
Shamattawa → **106** 55 1N 85 23W
Shambe **87** 7 8N 30 46 E
Shambu **87** 9 32N 37 3 E
Shamgong Dzong **69** 27 13N 90 35 E
Shamīl **65** 27 30N 56 55 E
Shamkhor **57** 40 50N 46 0 E
Shamli **68** 29 32N 77 18 E
Shammar, Jabal **64** 27 40N 41 0 E
Shamo, L. **87** 5 45N 37 30 E
Shamokin **114** 40 47N 76 33W
Shamrock **117** 35 15N 100 15W
Shan □ **67** 21 30N 98 30 E
Shanan → **87** 8 0N 40 20 E
Shanchengzhen **76** 42 20N 125 20 E
Shandong □ **76** 36 0N 118 0 E
Shang Xian **77** 33 50N 109 58 E
Shangalowe **91** 10 50 S 26 30 E
Shangani **91** 19 41 S 29 20 E
Shangani → **91** 18 41 S 27 10 E
Shangbancheng **76** 40 50N 118 1 E
Shangcheng **77** 31 47N 115 26 E
Shangchuan Dao **77** 21 40N 112 50 E
Shangdu **76** 41 30N 113 30 E
Shanggao **77** 28 17N 114 55 E
Shanghai **75** 31 15N 121 26 E
Shangqiu **77** 34 26N 115 36 E
Shangrao **75** 28 25N 117 59 E
Shangshui **77** 33 42N 114 35 E
Shangsi **77** 22 8N 107 58 E
Shangyou **77** 25 48N 114 32 E
Shangzhi **76** 45 22N 127 56 E
Shani **85** 10 14N 12 2 E
Shaniko **118** 45 0N 120 50W
Shannon, Greenl. **4** 75 10N 18 30W
Shannon, N.Z. **101** 40 33 S 175 25 E
Shannon → **15** 52 35N 9 30W
Shansi = Shanxi □ **76** 37 0N 112 0 E
Shantar, Ostrov Bolshoy **59** 55 9N 137 40 E
Shantou **75** 23 18N 116 40 E
Shantung = Shandong □ **76** 36 0N 118 0 E
Shanxi □ **76** 37 0N 112 0 E
Shanyang **77** 33 31N 109 55 E
Shaoguan **75** 24 48N 113 35 E
Shaowu **75** 27 22N 117 28 E
Shaoxing **75** 30 0N 120 35 E
Shaoyang **75** 27 14N 111 25 E
Shapinsay **14** 59 2N 2 50W
Shaqrā', Si. Arab. **64** 25 15N 45 16 E
Shaqrā', Yemen, S. **63** 13 22N 45 44 E
Sharafa (Ogr) **87** 11 59N 27 7 E
Sharavati → **70** 14 20N 74 25 E
Sharbot Lake **113** 44 46N 76 41W
Shark B. **96** 25 55 S 113 32 E
Sharm el Sheikh **86** 27 53N 34 15 E
Sharon, Mass., U.S.A. **113** 42 5N 71 11W
Sharon, Pa., U.S.A. **114** 41 18N 80 30W
Sharon, Plain of = Hasharon **62** 32 12N 34 49 E
Sharon Springs **116** 38 54N 101 45W
Sharp Pt. **98** 10 58 S 142 43 E
Sharpe L. **109** 54 5N 93 40W
Sharpsville **112** 41 16N 80 28W
Shary **64** 27 14N 43 29 E
Sharya **55** 58 22N 45 20 E
Shasha **87** 6 29N 35 59 E
Shashemene **87** 7 13N 38 33 E
Shashi **75** 30 25N 112 14 E
Shashi → **91** 21 14 S 29 20 E
Shasta, Mt. **118** 41 30N 122 12W
Shasta Res. **118** 40 50N 122 15W
Shatsk **55** 54 0N 41 45 E
Shattuck **117** 36 17N 99 55W
Shatura **55** 55 34N 39 31 E
Shaumyani **57** 41 22N 41 45 E
Shaunavon **109** 49 35N 108 25W
Shaw → **96** 20 21 S 119 17 E
Shaw I. **98** 20 30 S 149 2 E
Shawan **75** 44 34N 85 50 E
Shawanaga **112** 45 31N 80 17W
Shawano **114** 44 45N 88 38W
Shawinigan **106** 46 35N 72 50W
Shawnee **117** 35 15N 97 0W
Shayib el Banat, Bebel **86** 26 59N 33 29 E
Shchekino **55** 54 1N 37 34 E
Shcherbakov = Rybinsk **55** 58 5N 38 50 E
Shchigri **55** 51 55N 36 58 E
Shchors **54** 51 48N 31 56 E
Shchuchiosk **58** 52 56N 70 12 E
She Xian **77** 29 50N 118 25 E
Shebekino **55** 50 28N 36 54 E
Shebele, Wabi → **87** 2 0N 44 0 E
Sheboygan **114** 43 46N 87 45W
Shechem **62** 32 13N 35 21 E
Shediac **107** 46 14N 64 32W
Sheelin, Lough **15** 53 48N 7 20W
Sheep Haven **15** 55 12N 7 55W
Sheerness **13** 51 26N 0 47 E
Sheet Harbour **107** 44 56N 62 31W
Shefar'am **62** 32 48N 35 10 E
Sheffield, U.K. **12** 53 23N 1 28W
Sheffield, Ala., U.S.A. **115** 34 45N 87 42W
Sheffield, Mass., U.S.A. **113** 42 6N 73 23W
Sheffield, Pa., U.S.A. **112** 41 42N 79 3W
Sheffield, Tex., U.S.A. **117** 30 42N 101 49W
Shegaon **68** 20 48N 76 47 E
Sheho **109** 51 35N 103 13W
Shehojele **87** 10 40N 35 9 E
Sheikhpura **69** 25 9N 85 53 E
Shek Hasan **87** 12 5N 35 58 E
Shekhupura **68** 31 42N 73 58 E
Sheki **57** 41 10N 47 5 E
Sheksna → **55** 59 0N 38 30 E
Shelburne, N.S., Can. **107** 43 47N 65 20W
Shelburne, Ont., Can. **106** 44 4N 80 15W
Shelburne, U.S.A. **113** 44 23N 73 15W
Shelburne B. **97** 11 50 S 142 50 E
Shelburne Falls **113** 42 36N 72 45W
Shelby, Mich., U.S.A. **114** 43 34N 86 27W
Shelby, Mont., U.S.A. **118** 48 30N 111 52W
Shelby, N.C., U.S.A. **115** 35 18N 81 34W
Shelby, Ohio, U.S.A. **112** 40 52N 82 40W
Shelbyville, Ill., U.S.A. **116** 39 25N 88 45W
Shelbyville, Ind., U.S.A. **114** 39 30N 85 42W
Shelbyville, Tenn., U.S.A. **115** 35 30N 86 25W
Sheldon **116** 43 6N 95 40W
Sheldrake **107** 50 20N 64 51W
Shelikhova, Zaliv **59** 59 30N 157 0 E
Shell Creek Ra. **118** 39 15N 114 30W
Shell Lake **109** 53 19N 107 2W
Shellbrook **109** 53 13N 106 24W
Shellharbour **97** 34 31 S 150 51 E
Shelling Rocks **15** 51 45N 10 35W
Shelon → **54** 58 10N 30 30 E
Shelton, Conn., U.S.A. **113** 41 18N 73 7W
Shelton, Wash., U.S.A. **118** 47 15N 123 6W
Shemakha **57** 40 38N 48 37 E
Shenandoah, Iowa, U.S.A. **116** 40 50N 95 25W
Shenandoah, Pa., U.S.A. **114** 40 49N 76 13W
Shenandoah, Va., U.S.A. **114** 38 30N 78 38W
Shenandoah → **114** 39 19N 77 44W
Shenchi **76** 39 8N 112 10 E
Shencottah **70** 8 59N 77 18 E
Shendam **85** 8 49N 9 30 E
Shendî **87** 16 46N 33 22 E
Shendurni **70** 20 39N 75 36 E
Sheng Xian **77** 29 35N 120 50 E
Shëngjergji **44** 41 17N 20 10 E
Shëngjini **44** 41 50N 19 35 E
Shenmëria **44** 42 7N 20 13 E
Shenmu **76** 38 50N 110 29 E
Shenqiucheng **77** 33 24N 115 2 E
Shensi = Shaanxi □ **77** 35 0N 109 0 E
Shenyang **76** 41 48N 123 27 E
Shepetovka **54** 50 10N 27 10 E
Shephelah = Hashefela **62** 31 30N 34 43 E
Shepparton **97** 36 23 S 145 26 E
Sheqi **77** 33 12N 112 57 E
Sherada **87** 7 18N 36 30 E
Sherborne **13** 50 56N 2 31W
Sherbro I. **84** 7 30N 12 40W
Sherbrooke **107** 45 28N 71 57W
Sherda **83** 20 7N 16 46 E
Shereik **86** 18 44N 33 47 E
Sheridan, Ark., U.S.A. **117** 34 20N 92 25W
Sheridan, Col., U.S.A. **116** 39 44N 105 3W
Sheridan, Wyo., U.S.A. **118** 44 50N 107 0W
Sherkot **68** 29 22N 78 35 E
Sherman **117** 33 40N 96 35W
Sherpur **69** 25 0N 90 0 E
Sherridon **109** 55 8N 101 5W
Sherwood, N.D., U.S.A. **116** 48 59N 101 36W
Sherwood, Tex., U.S.A. **117** 31 18N 100 45W
Sherwood Forest **12** 53 5N 1 5W
Sheslay **108** 58 17N 131 52W
Sheslay → **108** 58 48N 132 5W
Shethanei L. **109** 58 48N 97 50W
Shetland □ **14** 60 30N 1 30W
Shetland Is. **14** 60 30N 1 30W
Shevaroy Hills **70** 11 58N 78 12 E
Shewa □ **87** 9 33N 38 10 E
Shewa Gimira **87** 7 4N 35 51 E
Sheyenne **116** 47 52N 99 8W
Sheyenne → **116** 47 5N 96 50W
Shibām **63** 16 0N 48 36 E
Shibîn El Kôm **86** 30 31N 30 55 E
Shibîn el Qanâtir **86** 30 19N 31 19 E
Shibogama L. **106** 53 35N 88 15W
Shibushi **74** 31 25N 131 8 E
Shidao **76** 36 50N 122 25 E
Shiel, L. **14** 56 48N 5 32W
Shiga □ **74** 35 20N 136 0 E
Shigaib **81** 15 5N 23 35 E
Shiguaigou **76** 40 52N 110 15 E
Shihchiachuangi = Shijiazhuang **76** 38 2N 114 28 E
Shijaku **44** 41 21N 19 33 E
Shijiazhuang **76** 38 2N 114 28 E
Shikarpur, India **68** 28 17N 78 7 E
Shikarpur, Pak. **68** 27 57N 68 39 E
Shikoku **74** 33 30N 133 30 E
Shikoku □ **74** 33 30N 133 30 E
Shikoku-Sanchi **74** 33 30N 133 30 E
Shilabo **63** 6 22N 44 32 E
Shilka **59** 52 0N 115 55 E
Shilka → **59** 53 20N 121 26 E
Shillelagh **15** 52 46N 6 32W
Shillong **67** 25 35N 91 53 E
Shilo **62** 32 4N 35 18 E
Shilong **75** 23 5N 113 52 E
Shilovo **55** 54 25N 40 57 E
Shimabara **74** 32 48N 130 20 E
Shimada **74** 34 49N 138 10 E
Shimane □ **74** 35 0N 132 30 E
Shimanovsk **59** 52 15N 127 30 E
Shimizu **74** 35 0N 138 30 E
Shimodate **74** 36 20N 139 55 E
Shimoga **70** 13 57N 75 32 E
Shimoni **90** 4 38 S 39 20 E
Shimonoseki **74** 33 58N 131 0 E
Shimpuru Rapids **92** 17 45 S 19 55 E
Shimsha → **70** 13 15N 77 10 E
Shimsk **54** 58 15N 30 50 E
Shin, L. **14** 58 7N 4 30W
Shin-Tone → **74** 35 44N 140 51 E
Shinano → **74** 36 50N 138 30 E
Shīndand **65** 33 12N 62 8 E
Shingleton **106** 46 25N 86 33W
Shingū **74** 33 40N 135 55 E
Shinkafe **85** 13 8N 6 29 E
Shinyanga **90** 3 45 S 33 27 E
Shinyanga □ **90** 3 50 S 34 0 E
Shio-no-Misaki **74** 33 25N 135 45 E
Ship I. **117** 30 16N 88 55W
Shipehenski Prokhod **43** 42 45N 25 15 E
Shippegan **107** 47 45N 64 45W
Shippensburg **114** 40 4N 77 32W
Shiprock **119** 36 51N 108 45W
Shiqian **77** 27 32N 108 13 E
Shiqma, N. → **62** 31 37N 34 30 E
Shiquan **77** 33 5N 108 15 E
Shīr Kūh **65** 31 39N 54 3 E
Shīrāz **65** 29 42N 52 30 E
Shirbin **86** 31 11N 31 32 E
Shire → **91** 17 42 S 35 19 E
Shiretoko-Misaki **74** 44 21N 145 20 E
Shiringushi **55** 53 51N 42 46 E
Shiriya-Zaki **74** 41 25N 141 30 E
Shirol **70** 16 47N 74 41 E
Shirpur **68** 21 21N 74 57 E
Shīrvān **65** 37 30N 57 50 E
Shishmanova **43** 42 58N 23 12 E
Shisur **63** 17 30N 54 0 E
Shitai **77** 30 12N 117 25 E
Shivali (Sirkali) **70** 11 15N 79 41 E
Shivpuri **68** 25 26N 77 42 E
Shivta **62** 30 53N 34 40 E
Shiwei **76** 51 19N 119 55 E
Shixing **77** 24 46N 114 5 E
Shiyata **86** 29 25N 25 7 E
Shizuishan **76** 39 15N 106 50 E
Shizuoka **74** 35 0N 138 24 E
Shizuoka □ **74** 35 15N 138 40 E
Shklov **54** 54 16N 30 15 E
Shkoder = Shkodra **44** 42 6N 19 1 E
Shkodra **44** 42 6N 19 20 E
Shkodra □ **44** 42 25N 19 20 E
Shkumbini → **44** 41 5N 19 50 E
Shmidt, O. **59** 81 0N 91 0 E
Shoal Lake **109** 50 30N 100 35W
Shoalhaven → **100** 34 54 S 150 42 E
Shoeburyness **13** 51 31N 0 49 E
Sholapur **70** 17 43N 75 56 E
Shologontsy **59** 66 13N 114 0 E
Shomera **62** 33 4N 35 17 E
Shōmrōn **62** 32 15N 35 13 E
Shongopovi **119** 35 49N 110 37W
Shoranur **70** 10 46N 76 19 E
Shorapur **70** 16 31N 76 48 E
Shoshone **118** 43 0N 114 27W
Shoshone L. **118** 44 30N 110 40W
Shoshone Mts. **118** 39 30N 117 30W
Shoshong **92** 22 56 S 26 31 E
Shoshoni **118** 43 13N 108 5W
Shostka **54** 51 57N 33 32 E
Shouyang **76** 37 54N 113 8 E
Show Low **119** 34 16N 110 0W
Shpola **56** 49 1N 31 30 E
Shreveport **117** 32 30N 93 50W
Shrewsbury **12** 52 42N 2 45W
Shrivardhan **70** 18 4N 73 3 E
Shropshire □ **13** 52 36N 2 45W
Shuangcheng **76** 45 20N 126 15 E
Shuangliao **76** 43 29N 123 30 E
Shuangyashan **75** 46 28N 131 5 E
Shucheng **77** 31 28N 116 57 E
Shu'eib, Wadi **62** 31 54N 35 38 E
Shuguri Falls **91** 8 33 S 37 22 E
Shujalpur **68** 23 18N 76 46 E
Shulan **76** 44 28N 127 0 E
Shule **75** 39 25N 76 3 E
Shumagin Is. **104** 55 0N 159 0W
Shumerlya **55** 55 30N 46 25 E
Shumikha **58** 55 10N 63 15 E
Shunchang **77** 26 54N 117 48 E
Shunde **77** 22 42N 113 14 E
Shungay **57** 48 30N 46 45 E
Shungnak **104** 66 55N 157 10W
Shuo Xian **76** 39 20N 112 33 E
Shūr → **65** 28 30N 55 0 E
Shurma **55** 56 58N 50 21 E
Shūsf **65** 31 50N 60 5 E
Shūshtar **64** 32 0N 48 50 E
Shuswap L. **108** 50 55N 119 3W
Shuwaykah **62** 32 20N 35 1 E
Shuya **55** 56 50N 41 28 E
Shwebo **67** 22 30N 95 45 E
Shwegu **67** 24 15N 96 26 E
Shweli → **67** 23 45N 96 45 E
Shyok **69** 34 15N 78 12 E
Shyok → **69** 35 13N 75 53 E
Si Kiang = Xi Jiang → **75** 22 5N 113 20 E
Si Racha **71** 13 10N 100 48 E
Siah **64** 22 0N 47 0 E
Siahan Range **66** 27 30N 64 40 E
Siaksrinderapura **72** 0 51N 102 0 E
Sialkot **68** 32 32N 74 30 E
Siam = Thailand ■ **71** 16 0N 102 0 E
Siam, G. of **71** 11 30N 101 0 E
Sian = Xi'an **77** 34 15N 109 0 E
Siantan, P. **72** 3 10N 106 15 E
Sīāreh **65** 28 5N 60 14 E
Siargao **73** 9 52N 126 3 E
Siasi **73** 5 34N 120 50 E
Siátista **44** 40 15N 21 33 E
Siau **73** 2 50N 125 25 E
Siauliai **54** 55 56N 23 15 E
Siaya □ **90** 0 0N 34 20 E
Siazan **57** 41 3N 49 10 E
Sibâi, Gebel el **86** 25 45N 34 10 E
Sibari **41** 39 47N 16 27 E
Sibay **52** 52 42N 58 39 E
Sibaya, L. **93** 27 20 S 32 45 E
Šibenik **39** 43 48N 15 54 E
Siberia **60** 60 0N 100 0 E
Siberut **72** 1 30 S 99 0 E
Sibi **68** 29 30N 67 54 E
Sibil **73** 4 59 S 140 35 E
Sibiti **88** 3 38 S 13 19 E
Sibiu **46** 45 45N 24 9 E
Sibiu □ **46** 45 50N 24 15 E
Sibley, Iowa, U.S.A. **116** 43 21N 95 43W
Sibley, La., U.S.A. **117** 32 34N 93 16W
Sibolga **72** 1 42N 98 45 E
Sibsagar **67** 27 0N 94 36 E
Sibu **72** 2 18N 111 49 E
Sibuco **73** 7 20N 122 10 E
Sibuguey B. **73** 7 50N 122 45 E
Sibutu **73** 4 45N 119 30 E
Sibutu Passage **73** 4 50N 120 0 E
Sibuyan **73** 12 25N 122 40 E
Sibuyan Sea **73** 12 30N 122 20 E
Sicamous **108** 50 49N 119 0W
Siccus → **99** 31 42 S 139 25 E
Sichuan □ **75** 31 0N 104 0 E
Sicilia **41** 37 30N 14 30 E
Sicilia, Canale di **40** 37 25N 12 30 E
Sicilian Channel = Sicilia, Canale di **40** 37 25N 12 30 E
Sicily = Sicilia **41** 37 30N 14 30 E
Sicuani **126** 14 21 S 71 10W
Siculiana **40** 37 20N 13 23 E
Šid **42** 45 8N 19 14 E
Sidamo □ **87** 5 0N 37 50 E
Sidaouet **85** 18 34N 8 3 E
Siddipet **70** 18 0N 78 51 E
Sidéradougou **84** 10 42N 4 12W
Siderno Marina **41** 38 16N 16 17 E
Sidheros, Ákra **45** 35 19N 26 19 E
Sidhirókastron **44** 41 13N 23 24 E
Sidhpur **68** 23 56N 72 25 E
Sîdi Abd el Rahmân **86** 30 55N 29 44 E
Sîdi Barrâni **86** 31 38N 25 58 E
Sidi-bel-Abbès **82** 35 13N 0 39W
Sidi Bennour **82** 32 40N 8 25W
Sidi Haneish **86** 31 10N 27 35 E
Sidi Kacem **82** 34 11N 5 49W
Sidi Moussa, O. → **82** 26 58N 3 54 E
Sidi Omar **86** 31 24N 24 57 E
Sidi Slimane **82** 34 16N 5 56W
Sidi Smaïl **82** 32 50N 8 31W
Sidlaw Hills **14** 56 32N 3 10W
Sidley, Mt. **5** 77 2 S 126 2W
Sidmouth **13** 50 40N 3 13W
Sidmouth, C. **98** 13 25 S 143 36 E
Sidney, Can. **108** 48 39N 123 24W
Sidney, Mont., U.S.A. **116** 47 42N 104 7W
Sidney, N.Y., U.S.A. **114** 42 18N 75 20W
Sidney, Ohio, U.S.A. **114** 40 18N 84 6W
Sidoarjo **73** 7 30 S 112 46 E
Sidra, G. of = Khalīj Surt **35** 31 40N 18 30 E
Siedlce **28** 52 10N 22 20 E
Siedlce □ **28** 52 0N 22 0 E
Sieg → **24** 50 46N 7 7 E
Siegburg **24** 50 48N 7 12 E
Siegen **24** 50 52N 8 2 E
Siem Reap **71** 13 20N 103 52 E
Siena **39** 43 20N 11 20 E
Sieniawa **27** 50 11N 22 38 E
Sieradź **28** 51 37N 18 41 E
Sieraków **28** 52 39N 16 2 E
Sierck-les-Bains **19** 49 26N 6 20 E
Sierpc **28** 52 55N 19 43 E
Sierra Blanca, N. Mex., U.S.A. **119** 33 20N 105 54W
Sierra Blanca, Tex., U.S.A. **119** 31 11N 105 17W
Sierra City **118** 39 34N 120 42W
Sierra Colorada **128** 40 35 S 67 50W
Sierra de Yeguas **31** 37 7N 4 52W
Sierra Gorda **124** 22 50 S 69 15W
Sierra Leone ■ **84** 9 0N 12 0W
Sierra Mojada **120** 27 19N 103 42W
Sierre **25** 46 17N 7 31 E
Sif Fatima **83** 31 6N 8 41 E
Sífnos **45** 37 0N 24 45 E
Sifton **109** 51 21N 100 8W
Sifton Pass **108** 57 52N 126 15W
Sig **82** 35 32N 0 12W
Sigdal **47** 60 4N 9 38 E
Sigean **20** 43 2N 2 58 E
Sighetul Marmatiei **46** 47 57N 23 52 E
Sighişoara **46** 46 12N 24 50 E
Sigli **72** 5 25N 96 0 E
Siglufjörður **50** 66 12N 18 55W
Sigma **73** 11 29N 122 40 E
Sigmaringen **25** 48 5N 9 13 E
Signakhi **57** 41 40N 45 57 E
Signy I. **5** 60 45 S 45 56W
Signy-l'Abbaye **19** 49 40N 4 25 E
Sigsig **126** 3 0 S 78 50W
Sigtuna **48** 59 36N 17 44 E
Sigüenza **32** 41 3N 2 40W
Siguiri **84** 11 31N 9 10W
Sigulda **54** 57 10N 24 55 E
Sigurd **119** 38 49N 112 0W
Sihanoukville = Kompong Som **71** 10 40N 103 30 E
Sihui **77** 23 20N 112 40 E
Si'īr **62** 31 35N 35 9 E
Siirt **64** 37 57N 41 55 E
Sijarira Ra. **91** 17 36 S 27 45 E
Sikar **68** 27 33N 75 10 E
Sikasso **84** 11 18N 5 35W
Sikeston **117** 36 52N 89 35W
Sikhote Alin, Khrebet **59** 46 0N 136 0 E
Sikiá. **44** 40 2N 23 56 E
Síkinos **45** 36 40N 25 8 E
Sikkani Chief → **108** 57 47N 122 15W
Sikkim □ **69** 27 50N 88 30 E
Siklós **27** 45 50N 18 19 E
Sil → **30** 42 27N 7 43W
Sila, La **41** 39 15N 16 35 E
Silandro **38** 46 38N 10 48 E
Sīlat az Zahr **62** 32 19N 35 11 E
Silba **39** 44 24N 14 41 E
Silchar **67** 24 49N 92 48 E
Silcox **109** 57 12N 94 10W
Siler City **115** 35 44N 79 30W
Sileru → **70** 17 49N 81 24 E
Silesia = Slask **22** 51 0N 16 30 E
Silet **82** 22 44N 4 37 E
Silgarhi Doti **69** 29 15N 81 0 E
Silghat **67** 26 35N 93 0 E
Silifke **64** 36 22N 33 58 E
Siliguri **69** 26 45N 88 25 E

Siling Co 75 31 50N 89 20 E
Siliqua 40 39 20N 8 49 E
Silistra 43 44 6N 27 19 E
Siljan, L. 48 60 55N 14 45 E
Silkeborg 49 56 10N 9 32 E
Sillajhuay, Cordillera 126 19 46 S 68 40W
Sillé-le-Guillaume 18 48 10N 0 8W
Siloam Springs 117 36 15N 94 31W
Silogui 72 1 10 S 9 0 E
Silsbee 117 30 20N 94 8W
Silute 54 55 21N 21 33 E
Silva Porto = Bié 89 12 22 S 16 55 E
Silver City, Panama 120 9 19N 79 53W
Silver City, N. Mex., U.S.A. 119 32 50N 108 18W
Silver City, Nev., U.S.A. 118 39 15N 119 48W
Silver Cr. ~→ 118 43 16N 119 13W
Silver Creek 114 42 33N 79 9W
Silver Lake 118 43 9N 121 4W
Silverton, Austral. 100 31 52 S 141 10 E
Silverton, Colo., U.S.A. 119 37 51N 107 45W
Silverton, Tex., U.S.A. 117 34 30N 101 16W
Silves 31 37 11N 8 26W
Silvi 39 42 32N 14 5 E
Silvies ~→ 118 43 22N 118 48W
Silvretta Gruppe 25 46 50N 10 6 E
Silwa Bahari 86 24 45N 32 55 E
Silwād 62 31 59N 35 15 E
Silz 26 47 16N 10 56 E
Sim, C. 82 31 26N 9 51W
Simanggang 72 1 15N 111 32 E
Simard, L. 106 47 40N 78 40W
Sîmărtin 46 46 19N 25 58 E
Simba 90 2 10 S 37 36 E
Simbach 25 48 16N 13 3 E
Simbo 90 4 51 S 29 41 E
Simcoe 106 42 50N 80 20W
Simcoe, L. 106 44 25N 79 20W
Simenga 59 62 42N 108 25 E
Simeto ~→ 41 37 25N 15 10 E
Simeulue 72 2 45N 95 45 E
Simferopol 56 44 55N 34 3 E
Sími 45 36 35N 27 50 E
Simikot 69 30 0N 81 50 E
Simitli 42 41 52N 23 7 E
Simla 68 31 2N 77 9 E
Şimleu-Silvaniei 46 47 17N 22 50 E
Simmern 25 49 59N 7 32 E
Simmie 109 49 56N 108 6W
Simojärvi 50 66 5N 27 3 E
Simojoki ~→ 50 65 35N 25 1 E
Simonette ~→ 108 55 9N 118 15W
Simonstown 92 34 14 S 18 26 E
Simontornya 27 46 45N 18 33 E
Simpang, Indon. 72 1 16 S 104 5 E
Simpang, Malay. 71 4 50N 100 40 E
Simplon Pass 25 46 15N 8 0 E
Simplon Tunnel 25 46 15N 8 7 E
Simpson Des. 97 25 0 S 137 0 E
Simrishamn 49 55 33N 14 22 E
Simunjan 72 1 25N 110 45 E
Simushir, Ostrov 59 46 50N 152 30 E
Sina ~→ 70 17 30N 75 55 E
Sinabang 72 2 30N 96 24 E
Sinadogo 63 5 50N 47 0 E
Sinai = Es Sînâ' 86 29 0N 34 0 E
Sinai, Mt. = Mûsa, G. 86 28 32N 33 59 E
Sinaia 46 45 21N 25 38 E
Sinaloa 120 25 50N 108 20W
Sinaloa □ 120 25 0N 107 30W
Sinalunga 39 43 12N 11 43 E
Sinan 77 27 56N 108 13 E
Sînandrei 46 45 52N 21 13 E
Sīnāwan 83 31 0N 10 37 E
Sincelejo 126 9 18N 75 24W
Sinclair 118 41 47N 107 10W
Sinclair Mills 108 54 5N 121 40W
Sincorá, Serra do 127 13 30 S 41 0W
Sind 68 26 0N 68 30 E
Sind Sagar Doab 68 32 0N 71 30 E
Sindal 49 57 28N 10 10 E
Sindangan 73 8 10N 123 5 E
Sindangbarang 73 7 27 S 107 1 E
Sinde 91 17 28 S 25 51 E
Sinegorski 57 48 0N 40 52 E
Sinelnikovo 56 48 25N 35 30 E
Sines 31 37 56N 8 51W
Sines, Cabo de 31 37 58N 8 53W
Sineu 32 39 38N 3 1 E
Sinfra 84 6 35N 5 56W
Singa 87 13 10N 33 57 E
Singanallur 70 11 2N 77 1 E
Singaparna 73 7 23 S 108 4 E
Singapore ■ 71 1 17N 103 51 E
Singapore, Straits of 71 1 15N 104 0 E
Singaraja 72 8 6 S 115 10 E
Singen 25 47 45N 8 50 E
Singida 90 4 49 S 34 48 E
Singida □ 90 6 0 S 34 30 E
Singitikós Kólpos 44 40 6N 24 0 E
Singkaling Hkamti 67 26 0N 95 39 E
Singkawang 72 1 0N 108 57 E
Singkep 72 0 30 S 104 20 E
Singleton 97 32 33 S 151 0 E
Singleton, Mt. 96 29 27 S 117 15 E
Singö 48 60 12N 18 45 E
Singoli 68 25 0N 75 22 E
Siniátsikon, Óros 44 40 25N 21 35 E
Siniscóla 40 40 35N 9 40 E
Sinj 39 43 42N 16 39 E
Sinjai 73 5 7 S 120 20 E
Sinjajevina, Planina 42 42 57N 19 22 E
Sinjār 64 36 19N 41 52 E
Sinjil 62 32 3N 35 15 E
Sinkat 86 18 55N 36 49 E
Sinkiang Uighur = Xinjiang Uygur □ 75 42 0N 86 0 E
Sinnai 40 39 18N 9 13 E
Sinnar 70 19 48N 74 0 E
Sinni ~→ 41 40 9N 16 42 E
Sînnicolau Maré 42 46 5N 20 39 E
Sinnuris 86 29 26N 30 31 E
Sinoe, L. 46 44 35N 28 50 E
Sinoia 91 17 20 S 30 8 E
Sinop 64 42 1N 35 11 E
Sinskoye 59 61 8N 126 48 E
Sint Maarten 121 18 0N 63 5W
Sint Niklaas 16 51 10N 4 9 E
Sint Truiden 16 50 48N 5 10 E
Sîntana 46 46 20N 21 30 E
Sintang 72 0 5N 111 35 E
Sinton 117 28 1N 97 30W
Sintra 31 38 47N 9 25W
Sinŭiju 76 40 5N 124 24 E
Sinyukha ~→ 56 48 3N 30 51 E
Siocon 73 7 40N 122 10 E
Siófok 27 16 39 S 23 36 E
Sioma 92 16 25 S 23 28 E
Sion 25 46 14N 7 20 E
Sioux City 116 42 32N 96 25W
Sioux Falls 116 43 35N 96 40W
Sioux Lookout 106 50 10N 91 50W
Šipan 42 42 45N 17 52 E
Siping 76 43 8N 124 21 E
Sipiwesk L. 109 55 5N 97 35W
Sipora 72 2 18 S 99 40 E
Siquia ~→ 121 12 10N 84 20W
Siquijor 73 9 12N 123 35 E
Sir Edward Pellew Group 97 15 40 S 137 10 E
Sira 70 13 41N 76 49 E
Siracusa 41 37 4N 15 17 E
Sirajganj 69 24 25N 89 47 E
Sirakoro 84 12 41N 9 14W
Sirasso 84 9 16N 6 6W
Siret 46 47 55N 26 5 E
Siret ~→ 46 47 58N 26 5 E
Şiria 42 46 16N 21 38 E
Sirino, Monte 41 40 7N 15 50 E
Sirkali (Shivali) 70 11 15N 79 41 E
Sírna. 45 36 22N 26 42 E
Sirohi 68 24 52N 72 53 E
Široki Brijeg 42 43 21N 17 36 E
Sironj 68 24 5N 77 39 E
Síros 45 37 28N 24 57 E
Sirsa 68 29 33N 75 4 E
Sirsi 70 14 40N 74 49 E
Siruela 31 38 58N 5 3W
Sisak 39 45 30N 16 21 E
Sisaket 71 15 8N 104 23 E
Sisante 33 39 25N 2 12W
Sisargas, Islas 30 43 21N 8 50W
Sishen 92 27 47 S 22 59 E
Sishui 77 34 48N 113 15 E
Sisipuk L. 109 55 45N 101 50W
Sisophon 71 13 38N 102 59 E
Sisseton 116 45 43N 97 3W
Sissonne 19 49 34N 3 51 E
Sistema Central 30 40 40N 5 55W
Sistema Iberico 32 41 0N 2 10W
Sisteron 21 44 12N 5 57 E
Sisters 118 44 21N 121 32W
Sitamarhi 69 26 37N 85 30 E
Sitapur 69 27 38N 80 45 E
Siteki 93 26 32 S 31 58 E
Sitges 32 41 17N 1 47 E
Sithoniá 44 40 0N 23 45 E
Sitía 45 35 13N 26 6 E
Sitka 104 57 9N 135 20W
Sitoti 92 23 15 S 23 40 E
Sitra 86 28 40N 26 53 E
Sittang ~→ 67 17 10N 96 58 E
Sittang Myit ~→ 67 17 20N 96 45 E
Sittard 16 51 0N 5 52 E
Sittensen 24 53 17N 9 32 E
Sittona 87 14 25N 37 23 E
Situbondo 73 7 45 S 114 0 E
Sivaganga 70 9 50N 78 28 E
Sivagiri 70 9 16N 77 26 E
Sivakasi 70 9 24N 77 47 E
Sivana 68 28 37N 78 6 E
Sīvand 65 30 5N 52 55 E
Sivas 64 39 43N 36 58 E
Siverek 64 37 50N 39 19 E
Sivomaskinskiy 52 66 40N 62 35 E
Sivrihisar 64 39 30N 31 35 E
Sîwa 86 29 11N 25 31 E
Sîwa, El Wâhât es 86 29 10N 25 30 E
Siwalik Range 69 28 0N 83 0 E
Siwan 69 26 13N 84 21 E
Siyâl, Jazâ'ir 86 22 49N 3C 12 E
Sizewell 13 52 13N 1 38 E
Sjælland 49 55 30N 11 30 E
Sjællands Odde 49 56 0N 11 15 E
Själevad 48 63 18N 18 36 E
Sjarinska Banja 42 42 45N 21 38 E
Sjenica 42 43 16N 20 0 E
Sjoa 47 61 41N 9 33 E
Sjöbo 49 55 37N 13 45 E
Sjösa 49 58 47N 17 4 E
Skadarsko Jezero 42 42 10N 19 20 E
Skadovsk 56 46 17N 32 52 E
Skagafjörður 50 65 54N 19 35W
Skagastølstindane 47 61 28N 7 52 E
Skagen 49 57 43N 10 35 E
Skagern 48 59 0N 14 20 E
Skagerrak 49 57 30N 9 0 E
Skagway 104 59 23N 135 20W
Skaidi 50 70 26N 24 30 E
Skala Podolskaya 56 48 50N 26 15 E
Skalat 54 49 23N 25 55 E
Skalbmierz 28 50 20N 20 25 E
Skalica 27 48 50N 17 15 E
Skalni Dol = Kamenyak 43 43 24N 26 57 E
Skals 49 56 34N 9 24 E
Skanderborg 49 56 2N 9 55 E
Skånevik 47 59 43N 5 53 E
Skänninge 49 58 24N 15 5 E
Skanör 49 55 24N 12 50 E
Skantzoúra 45 39 5N 24 6 E
Skara 49 58 25N 13 30 E
Skaraborgs län □ 49 58 20N 13 30 E
Skardu 69 35 20N 75 44 E
Skarrild 49 55 58N 8 53 E
Skarszewy 28 54 4N 18 25 E
Skaryszew 28 51 19N 21 15 E
Skarzysko Kamienna 28 51 7N 20 52 E
Skattungbyn 48 61 10N 14 56 E
Skebokvarn 48 59 7N 16 45 E
Skeena ~→ 108 54 9N 130 5W
Skeena Mts. 108 56 40N 128 30W
Skegness 12 53 9N 0 20 E
Skeldon 126 5 55N 57 20W
Skellefte älv ~→ 50 64 45N 21 10 E
Skellefteå 50 64 45N 20 58 E
Skelleftehamn 50 64 47N 20 59 E
Skender Vakuf 42 44 29N 17 22 E
Skene 49 57 30N 12 37 E
Skerries, The 12 53 27N 4 40W
Skhíza 45 36 41N 21 40 E
Skhoinoúsa 45 36 53N 25 31 E
Skhwaner, Pegunungan 72 1 0 S 112 30 E
Ski 47 59 43N 10 52 E
Skíathos 45 39 12N 23 30 E
Skibbereen 15 51 33N 9 16W
Skiddaw 12 54 39N 3 9W
Skien 47 59 12N 9 35 E
Skierniewice 28 51 58N 20 10 E
Skierniewice □ 28 52 0N 20 10 E
Skikda 83 36 50N 6 58 E
Skillingaryd 49 57 27N 14 5 E
Skillinge 49 55 30N 14 16 E
Skillingmark 48 59 48N 12 1 E
Skinári, Ákra 45 37 56N 20 40 E
Skipton, Austral. 99 37 39 S 143 40 E
Skipton, U.K. 12 53 57N 2 1W
Skiropoúla 45 38 50N 24 21 E
Skíros 45 38 55N 24 34 E
Skivarp 49 55 26N 13 34 E
Skive 49 56 33N 9 2 E
Skjåk 47 61 52N 8 22 E
Skjálfandafljót ~→ 50 65 59N 17 25W
Skjálfandi 50 66 5N 17 30W
Skjeberg 47 59 12N 11 12 E
Skjern 49 55 57N 8 30 E
Skoczów 27 49 49N 18 45 E
Skodje 47 62 30N 6 43 E
Škofja Loka 39 46 9N 14 19 E
Skoghall 48 59 20N 13 30 E
Skoki 28 52 40N 17 11 E
Skole 54 49 3N 23 30 E
Skópelos 45 39 9N 23 47 E
Skopin 55 53 55N 39 32 E
Skopje 42 42 1N 21 32 E
Skórcz 28 53 47N 18 30 E
Skottfoss 47 59 12N 9 30 E
Skovorodino 59 54 0N 125 0 E
Skowhegan 107 44 49N 69 40W
Skownan 109 51 58N 99 35W
Skradin 39 43 52N 15 53 E
Skreanäs 49 56 52N 12 35 E
Skrwa ~→ 28 52 35N 19 32 E
Skull 15 51 32N 9 40W
Skultorp 49 58 24N 13 51 E
Skunk ~→ 116 40 42N 91 7W
Skuodas 54 56 21N 21 45 E
Skurup 49 55 28N 13 30 E
Skutskär 49 60 37N 17 25 E
Skvira 56 49 44N 29 40 E
Skwierzyna 28 52 33N 15 30 E
Skye 14 57 15N 6 10W
Skykomish 118 47 43N 121 16W
Skyros = Skíros 45 38 52N 24 37 E
Slagelse 49 55 23N 11 19 E
Slamet, G. 72 7 16 S 109 8 E
Slaney ~→ 15 52 52N 6 45W
Slangerup 49 55 50N 12 11 E
Slănic 46 45 14N 25 58 E
Slankamen 42 45 8N 20 15 E
Slano 42 42 48N 17 53 E
Slantsy 54 59 7N 28 5 E
Slany 26 50 13N 14 6 E
Slask 22 51 0N 16 30 E
Slate Is. 106 48 40N 87 0W
Slatina 46 44 28N 24 22 E
Slaton 117 33 27N 101 38W
Slave ~→ 108 61 18N 113 39W
Slave Coast 85 6 0N 2 30 E
Slave Lake 108 55 17N 114 43W
Slave Pt. 108 61 11N 115 56W
Slavgorod 58 53 1N 78 37 E
Slavinja 42 43 9N 22 50 E
Slavkov (Austerlitz) 27 49 10N 16 52 E
Slavnoye 54 54 24N 29 15 E
Slavonska Požega 42 45 20N 17 40 E
Slavonski Brod 42 45 11N 18 0 E
Slavuta 54 50 15N 27 2 E
Slavyansk 56 48 55N 37 36 E
Slavyansk-na-Kubani 56 45 15N 38 11 E
Sława 28 51 52N 16 2 E
Sławno 28 54 20N 16 41 E
Sławoborze 28 53 55N 15 42 E
Sleaford 12 53 0N 0 22W
Sleat, Sd. of 14 57 5N 5 47W
Sleeper Is. 105 58 30N 81 0W
Sleepy Eye 116 44 15N 94 45W
Sleman 73 7 40 S 110 20 E
Slemon L. 108 63 13N 116 4W
Ślesin 28 52 22N 18 14 E
Slidell 117 30 20N 89 48W
Sliedrecht 16 51 50N 4 45 E
Slieve Aughty 15 53 4N 8 30W
Slieve Bloom 15 53 4N 7 40W
Slieve Donard 15 54 10N 5 57W
Slieve Gullion 15 54 8N 6 26W
Slieve Mish 15 52 12N 9 50W
Slievenamon 15 52 25N 7 37W
Sligo 15 54 17N 8 28W
Sligo □ 15 54 10N 8 35W
Sligo B. 15 54 20N 8 40W
Slite 51 57 42N 18 48 E
Sliven 43 42 42N 26 19 E
Slivnitsa 42 42 50N 23 0 E
Sljeme 39 45 57N 15 58 E
Sloansville 113 42 45N 74 22W
Slobodskoy 52 58 40N 50 6 E
Slobozia, Ialomiţa, Romania 46 44 34N 27 23 E
Slobozia, Valahia, Romania 46 44 30N 25 14 E
Slocan 108 49 48N 117 28W
Slochteren 16 53 12N 6 48 E
Slöinge 49 56 51N 12 42 E
Słomniki 28 50 16N 20 4 E
Slonim 54 53 4N 25 19 E
Slough 13 51 30N 0 35W
Slovakia = Slovensko 27 48 30N 19 0 E
Slovakian Ore Mts. = Slovenské Rudohorie 27 48 45N 20 0 E
Slovenia = Slovenija 39 45 58N 14 30 E
Slovenija □ 39 45 58N 14 30 E
Slovenj Gradec 39 46 31N 15 5 E
Slovenska Bistrica 39 46 24N 15 35 E
Slovenská Socialisticka Republika □ 27 48 30N 10 0 E
Slovenské Rudohorie 27 48 45N 20 0 E
Slovensko □ 27 48 30N 19 0 E
Słubice 28 52 22N 14 35 E
Sluch ~→ 54 51 37N 26 38 E
Sluis 16 51 18N 3 23 E
Slunchev Bryag 43 42 40N 27 41 E
Slunj 39 45 6N 15 33 E
Słupca 28 52 15N 17 52 E
Słupia ~→ 28 54 35N 16 51 E
Słupsk 28 54 30N 17 3 E
Słupsk □ 28 54 15N 17 30 E
Slurry 92 25 49 S 25 42 E
Slutsk 54 53 2N 27 31 E
Slyne Hd. 15 53 25N 10 10W
Slyudyanka 59 51 40N 103 40 E
Smålandsfarvandet 49 55 10N 11 20 E
Smalandsstenar 49 57 9N 13 24 E
Smalltree L. 109 61 0N 105 0W
Smallwood Reservoir 107 54 20N 63 10W
Smarje 39 46 15N 15 34 E
Smart Syndicate Dam 92 30 45 S 23 10 E
Smeaton 109 53 30N 104 49W
Smederevo 42 44 40N 20 57 E
Smederevska Palanka 42 44 22N 20 58 E
Smela 56 49 15N 31 58 E
Smethport 112 41 50N 78 28W
Smidovich 59 48 36N 133 49 E
Smigiel 28 52 1N 16 32 E
Smiley 109 51 38N 109 29W
Smilyan 43 41 29N 24 46 E
Smith 108 55 10N 114 0W
Smith ~→ 108 59 34N 126 30W
Smith Arm 104 66 15N 123 0W
Smith Center 116 39 50N 98 50W
Smith Sund 4 78 30N 74 0W
Smithburne ~→ 98 17 3 S 140 57 E
Smithers 108 54 45N 127 10W
Smithfield, Madag. 93 30 9 S 26 30 E
Smithfield, N.C., U.S.A. 115 35 31N 78 16W
Smithfield, Utah, U.S.A. 118 41 50N 111 50W
Smiths Falls 106 44 55N 76 0W
Smithton 99 40 53 S 145 6 E
Smithtown 99 30 58 S 152 48 E
Smithville, Can. 112 43 6N 79 33W
Smithville, U.S.A. 117 30 2N 97 12W
Smoky ~→ 108 56 10N 117 21W
Smoky Falls 106 50 4N 82 10W
Smoky Hill ~→ 116 39 3N 96 48W
Smoky Lake 108 54 10N 112 30W
Smøla 47 63 23N 8 3 E
Smolensk 54 54 45N 32 0 E
Smolikas, Óros 44 40 9N 20 58 E
Smolník 27 48 43N 20 44 E
Smolyan 43 41 36N 24 38 E
Smooth Rock Falls 106 49 17N 81 37W
Smoothstone L. 109 54 40N 106 50W
Smorgon 54 54 20N 26 24 E
Smulţi 46 45 57N 27 44 E
Smyadovo 43 43 2N 27 1 E
Smyrna = İzmir 64 38 25N 27 8 E
Snaefell 12 54 18N 4 26W
Snaefellsjökull 50 64 45N 23 46W
Snake ~→ 118 46 12N 119 2W
Snake I. 99 38 47 S 146 33 E
Snake L. 109 55 32N 106 35W
Snake Ra. 118 39 0N 114 30W
Snake River 118 44 10N 110 42W
Snake River Plain 118 43 13N 113 0W
Snarum 47 60 1N 9 54 E
Snedsted 49 56 55N 8 32 E
Sneek 16 53 2N 5 40 E
Snejbjerg 49 56 8N 8 54 E
Snezhnoye 57 48 0N 38 58 E
Sněžka 26 50 41N 15 50 E
Snežnik 39 45 36N 14 35 E
Sniadowo 28 53 2N 22 0 E
Sniardwy, Jezioro 28 53 48N 21 50 E
Snigirevka 56 47 2N 32 49 E
Snina 27 49 0N 22 9 E
Snizort, L. 14 57 33N 6 28W
Snøhetta 47 62 19N 9 16 E
Snohomish 118 47 53N 122 6W
Snonuten 47 59 31N 6 50 E
Snow Hill 114 38 10N 75 21W
Snow Lake 109 54 52N 100 3W
Snowbird L. 109 60 45N 103 0W
Snowdon 12 53 4N 4 8W
Snowdrift 109 62 24N 110 44W
Snowdrift ~→ 109 62 24N 110 44W
Snowflake 119 34 30N 110 4W
Snowshoe Pk. 118 48 13N 115 41W
Snowtown 99 33 46 S 138 14 E
Snowville 118 41 59N 112 47W
Snowy ~→ 97 37 46 S 148 30 E
Snowy Mts. 99 36 30 S 148 20 E
Snyatyn 56 48 30N 25 50 E
Snyder, Okla., U.S.A. 117 34 40N 99 0W
Snyder, Tex., U.S.A. 117 32 45N 100 57W
Soahanina 93 18 42 S 44 13 E
Soalala 93 16 6 S 45 20 E
Soanierana-Ivongo 93 16 55 S 49 35 E
Soap Lake 118 47 23N 119 31W
Sobat, Nahr ~→ 87 9 22N 31 33 E
Soběslav 26 49 16N 14 45 E
Sobhapur 68 22 47N 78 17 E
Sobinka 55 56 0N 40 0 E
Sobótka 28 50 54N 16 44 E

Sobrado **30** 43 2N 8 2W
Sobral **127** 3 50 S 40 20W
Sobreira Formosa **31** 39 46N 7 51W
Soča → **39** 46 20N 13 40 E
Sochaczew **28** 52 15N 20 13 E
Soch'e = Shache **75** 38 20N 77 10 E
Sochi **57** 43 35N 39 40 E
Société, Is. de la **95** 17 0 S 151 0W
Society Is. = Société, Is. de la **95** 17 0 S 151 0W
Socompa, Portezuelo de **124** 24 27 S 68 18W
Socorro, Colomb. **126** 6 29N 73 16W
Socorro, U.S.A. **119** 34 4N 106 54W
Socotra **63** 12 30N 54 0 E
Socúellmos **33** 39 16N 2 47W
Soda L. **119** 35 7N 116 2W
Soda Plains **69** 35 30N 79 0 E
Soda Springs **118** 42 40N 111 40W
Söderfors **48** 60 23N 17 25 E
Söderhamn **48** 61 18N 17 10 E
Söderköping **48** 58 31N 16 20 E
Södermanlands län □ **48** 59 10N 16 30 E
Södertälje **48** 59 12N 17 39 E
Sodiri **81** 14 27N 29 0 E
Sodo **87** 7 0N 37 41 E
Södra Vi **49** 57 45N 15 45 E
Sodražica **39** 45 45N 14 39 E
Sodus **112** 43 13N 77 5W
Soekmekaar **93** 23 30 S 29 55 E
Soest, Ger. **24** 51 34N 8 7 E
Soest, Neth. **16** 52 9N 5 19 E
Sofádhes **44** 39 20N 22 4 E
Sofara **84** 13 59N 4 9W
Sofia = Sofiya **43** 42 45N 23 20 E
Sofia → **93** 15 27 S 47 23 E
Sofievka **56** 48 6N 33 55 E
Sofiiski **59** 52 15N 133 59 E
Sofikón **45** 37 47N 23 3 E
Sofiya **43** 42 45N 23 20 E
Sogad **73** 10 30N 125 0 E
Sogakofe **85** 6 2N 0 39 E
Sogamoso **126** 5 43N 72 56W
Sögel **24** 52 50N 7 32 E
Sogn og Fjordane fylke □ **47** 61 40N 6 0 E
Sognefjorden **47** 61 10N 5 50 E
Sohâg **86** 26 33N 31 43 E
Soignies **16** 50 35N 4 5 E
Soira, Mt. **87** 14 45N 39 30 E
Soissons **19** 49 25N 3 19 E
Sōja **74** 34 40N 133 45 E
Sojat **68** 25 55N 73 45 E
Sok → **55** 53 24N 50 8 E
Sokal **54** 50 31N 24 15 E
Söke **45** 37 48N 27 28 E
Sokelo **91** 9 55 S 24 36 E
Sokhós **44** 40 48N 23 22 E
Sokki, Oued In → **82** 29 30N 3 42 E
Sokna **47** 60 16N 9 50 E
Soknedal **47** 62 57N 10 13 E
Soko Banja **42** 43 40N 21 51 E
Sokodé **85** 9 0N 1 11 E
Sokol **55** 59 30N 40 5 E
Sokolac **42** 43 56N 18 48 E
Sokółka **28** 53 25N 23 30 E
Sokolo **84** 14 53N 6 8W
Sokolov **26** 50 12N 12 40 E
Sokołów Małpolski **27** 50 12N 22 7 E
Sokołów Podlaski **28** 52 25N 22 15 E
Sokoły **28** 52 59N 22 42 E
Sokoto **85** 13 2N 5 16 E
Sokoto □ **85** 12 30N 5 0 E
Sokoto → **85** 11 20N 4 10 E
Sol Iletsk **52** 51 10N 55 0 E
Sola **47** 58 53N 5 36 E
Sola → **27** 50 4N 19 15 E
Solai **90** 0 2N 36 12 E
Solana, La **33** 38 59N 3 14W
Solano **73** 16 31N 121 15 E
Solares **30** 43 23N 3 43W
Solberga **49** 57 45N 14 43 E
Solca **46** 47 40N 25 50 E
Solec Kujawski **28** 53 5N 18 14 E
Soledad, U.S.A. **119** 36 27N 121 16W
Soledad, Venez. **126** 8 10N 63 34W
Solent, The **13** 50 45N 1 25W
Solenzara **21** 41 53N 9 23 E
Solesmes **19** 50 10N 3 30 E
Solfonn **47** 60 2N 6 57 E
Soligalich **55** 59 5N 42 10 E
Soligorsk **54** 52 51N 27 27 E
Solikamsk **58** 59 38N 56 50 E
Solila **93** 21 25 S 46 37 E
Solimões → = Amazonas → **126** 2 15 S 66 30W
Solingen **24** 51 10N 7 4 E
Sollebrunn **49** 58 8N 12 32 E
Sollefteå **48** 63 12N 17 20 E
Sollentuna **48** 59 26N 17 56 E
Sóller **32** 39 46N 2 43 E
Solling **24** 51 44N 9 36 E
Solna **48** 59 22N 18 1 E
Solnechnogorsk **55** 56 10N 36 57 E
Sologne **19** 47 40N 2 0 E
Solok **72** 0 45 S 100 40 E
Sololá **120** 14 49N 91 10 E
Solomon Is. ■ **94** 6 0 S 155 0 E
Solomon, N. Fork → **116** 39 29N 98 26W
Solomon Sea **98** 7 0 S 150 0 E
Solomon, S. Fork → **116** 39 25N 99 12W
Solomon's Pools = Birak Sulaymān **62** 31 42N 35 7 E
Solon **75** 46 32N 121 10 E
Solon Springs **116** 46 19N 91 47W
Solor **73** 8 27 S 123 0 E
Solotcha **55** 54 48N 39 53 E
Solothurn **25** 47 13N 7 32 E
Solothurn □ **25** 47 18N 7 40 E
Solsona **32** 42 0N 1 31 E
Solt **27** 46 45N 19 1 E
Solta **39** 43 24N 16 15 E
Solţānābād **65** 36 29N 58 5 E
Solţāniyeh **64** 36 20N 48 55 E
Soltau **24** 52 59N 9 50 E
Soltsy **54** 58 10N 30 30 E
Solund **47** 61 5N 4 50 E
Solunska Glava **42** 41 44N 21 31 E
Solvay **114** 43 5N 76 17W
Sölvesborg **49** 56 5N 14 35 E
Solvychegodsk **52** 61 21N 46 56 E
Solway Firth **12** 54 45N 3 38W
Solwezi **91** 12 11 S 26 21 E
Somali Rep. ■ **63** 7 0N 47 0 E
Sombe Dzong **69** 27 13N 89 8 E
Sombernon **19** 47 20N 4 40 E
Sombor **42** 45 46N 19 9 E
Sombra **112** 42 43N 82 29W
Sombrerete **120** 23 40N 103 40W
Sombrero **121** 18 37N 63 30W
Somers **118** 48 4N 114 18W
Somerset, Berm. **121** 32 16N 64 55W
Somerset, Can. **109** 49 25N 98 39W
Somerset, Colo., U.S.A. **119** 38 55N 107 30W
Somerset, Ky., U.S.A. **114** 37 5N 84 40W
Somerset, Mass., U.S.A. **113** 41 45N 71 10W
Somerset, Pa., U.S.A. **112** 40 1N 79 4W
Somerset □ **13** 51 9N 3 0W
Somerset East **92** 32 42 S 25 35 E
Somerset I. **104** 73 30N 93 0W
Somerset West **92** 34 8 S 18 50 E
Somersworth **113** 43 15N 70 51W
Somerton **119** 32 35N 114 47W
Somerville **113** 40 34N 74 36W
Someş → **46** 47 15N 23 45 E
Someşul Mare → **46** 47 18N 24 30 E
Somma Lombardo **38** 45 41N 8 42 E
Somma Vesuviana **41** 40 52N 14 23 E
Sommariva **99** 26 24 S 146 36 E
Sommatino **40** 37 20N 14 0 E
Somme □ **19** 50 0N 2 20 E
Somme, B. de la **18** 50 14N 1 33 E
Sommen **49** 58 12N 15 0 E
Sommen, L. **49** 58 0N 15 15 E
Sommepy-Tahure **19** 49 15N 4 31 E
Sömmerda **24** 51 10N 11 8 E
Sommesous **19** 48 44N 4 12 E
Sommières **21** 43 47N 4 6 E
Somogy □ **27** 46 19N 17 30 E
Somogyszob **27** 46 18N 17 20 E
Sompolno **28** 52 26N 18 30 E
Somport, Paso **32** 42 48N 0 31W
Somport, Puerto de **32** 42 48N 0 31W
Son, Norway **47** 59 32N 10 42 E
Son, Spain **30** 42 43N 8 58W
Son La **71** 21 20N 103 50 E
Sonamukhi **69** 23 18N 87 27 E
Soncino **38** 45 24N 9 52 E
Sondags → **92** 33 44 S 25 51 E
Sóndalo **38** 46 20N 10 20 E
Sønder Omme **49** 55 50N 8 54 E
Sønder Ternby **49** 57 31N 9 58 E
Sønderborg **49** 54 55N 9 49 E
Sonderjyllands Amtskommune □ **49** 55 10N 9 10 E
Sondershausen **24** 51 22N 10 50 E
Sóndrio **38** 46 10N 9 53 E
Sone **91** 17 23 S 34 55 E
Sonepat **68** 29 0N 77 5 E
Sonepur **69** 20 55N 83 50 E
Song Cau **71** 13 27N 109 18 E
Song Xian **77** 34 12N 112 8 E
Songea **91** 10 40 S 35 40 E
Songea □ **91** 10 30 S 36 0 E
Songeons **19** 49 32N 1 50 E
Songhua Hu **76** 43 35N 126 50 E
Songhua Jiang → **75** 47 45N 132 30 E
Songjiang **77** 31 1N 121 12 E
Songkhla **71** 7 13N 100 37 E
Songling **76** 48 2N 121 9 E
Songpan **75** 32 40N 103 30 E
Songtao **77** 28 11N 109 10 E
Songwe **90** 3 20 S 26 16 E
Songwe → **91** 9 44 S 33 58 E
Songzi **77** 30 12N 111 45 E
Sonkovo **55** 57 50N 37 5 E
Sonmiani **66** 25 25N 66 40 E
Sonnino **40** 41 25N 13 13 E
Sono → **127** 9 58 S 48 11W
Sonora, Calif., U.S.A. **119** 37 59N 120 27W
Sonora, Texas, U.S.A. **117** 30 33N 100 37W
Sonora □ **120** 29 0N 111 0W
Sonora → **120** 28 50N 111 33W
Sonora P. **118** 38 17N 119 35W
Sonsomate **120** 13 43N 89 44W
Sonthofen **25** 47 31N 10 16 E
Soo Junction **114** 46 20N 85 14W
Soochow = Suzhou **75** 31 19N 120 38 E
Sopi **73** 2 34N 128 28 E
Sopo, Nahr → **87** 8 40N 26 30 E
Sopot, Poland **28** 54 27N 18 31 E
Sopot, Yugo. **42** 44 29N 20 30 E
Sopotnica **42** 41 23N 21 13 E
Sopron **27** 47 45N 16 32 E
Sop's Arm **107** 49 46N 56 56W
Sør-Rondane **5** 72 0 S 25 0 E
Sør-Trøndelag fylke □ **47** 63 0N 10 0 E
Sora **40** 41 45N 13 36 E
Sorada **70** 19 45N 84 26 E
Sorah **68** 27 13N 68 56 E
Söråker **48** 62 30N 17 32 E
Sorano **39** 42 40N 11 42 E
Sorata **126** 15 50 S 68 40W
Sorbas **33** 37 6N 2 7W
Sorel **106** 46 0N 73 10W
Sorento **99** 38 22 S 144 47 E
Soreq, N. → **62** 31 57N 34 43 E
Soresina **38** 45 17N 9 51 E
Sorgono **40** 40 01N 9 06 E
Sorgues **21** 44 1N 4 53 E
Soria **32** 41 43N 2 32W
Soria □ **32** 41 46N 2 28W
Soriano **124** 33 24 S 58 19W
Soriano nel Cimino **39** 42 25N 12 14 E
Sorkh, Kuh-e **65** 35 40N 58 30 E
Sorø **49** 55 26N 11 32 E
Soro **84** 10 9N 9 48W
Sorocaba **125** 23 31 S 47 27W
Sorochinsk **52** 52 26N 53 10 E
Soroki **56** 48 8N 28 12 E
Soroksár **27** 47 24N 19 9 E
Soron **68** 27 55N 78 45 E
Sorong **73** 0 55 S 131 15 E
Soroti **90** 1 43N 33 35 E
Sørøya **50** 70 40N 22 30 E
Sørøyane **47** 62 25N 5 32 E
Sørøysundet **50** 70 25N 23 0 E
Sorraia → **31** 38 55N 8 53W
Sorrento **41** 40 38N 14 23 E
Sorris Sorris **92** 21 0 S 14 46 E
Sorsele **50** 65 31N 17 30 E
Sorso **40** 40 50N 8 34 E
Sorsogon **73** 13 0N 124 0 E
Sortavala **52** 61 42N 30 41 E
Sortino **41** 37 9N 15 1 E
Sorvizhi **55** 57 52N 48 32 E
Sos **32** 42 30N 1 13W
Soscumica, L. **106** 50 15N 77 27W
Sosna → **55** 52 42N 38 55 E
Sosnogorsk **52** 63 37N 53 51 E
Sosnovka, R.S.F.S.R., U.S.S.R. **55** 53 13N 41 24 E
Sosnovka, R.S.F.S.R., U.S.S.R. **59** 54 9N 109 35 E
Sosnowiec **28** 50 20N 19 10 E
Sospel **21** 43 52N 7 27 E
Sostanj **39** 46 23N 15 4 E
Sosva **52** 59 10N 61 50 E
Soto la Marina → **120** 23 40N 97 40W
Soto y Amío **30** 42 46N 5 53W
Sotteville-lès-Rouen **18** 49 24N 1 5 E
Sotuta **120** 20 29N 89 43W
Souanké **88** 2 10N 14 3 E
Soúdhas, Kólpos **45** 35 25N 24 10 E
Souflíon **44** 41 12N 26 18 E
Souillac **20** 44 53N 1 29 E
Souk-Ahras **83** 36 23N 7 57 E
Souk el Arba du Rharb **82** 34 43N 5 59W
Sŏul **76** 37 31N 126 58 E
Soulac-sur-Mer **20** 45 30N 1 7W
Soultz **19** 48 57N 7 52 E
Soúnion, Ákra **45** 37 37N 24 1 E
Sour el Ghozlane **83** 36 10N 3 45 E
Sources, Mt. aux **93** 28 45 S 28 50 E
Sourdeval **18** 48 43N 0 55W
Soure, Brazil **127** 0 35 S 48 30W
Soure, Port. **30** 40 4N 8 38W
Souris, Man., Can. **109** 49 40N 100 20W
Souris, P.E.I., Can. **107** 46 21N 62 15W
Souris → **109** 49 40N 99 34W
Soúrpi **45** 39 6N 22 54 E
Sousa **127** 6 45 S 38 10W
Sousel, Brazil **127** 2 38 S 52 29W
Sousel, Port. **31** 38 57N 7 40W
Souss, O. → **82** 30 27N 9 31W
Sousse **83** 35 50N 10 38 E
Soustons **20** 43 45N 1 19W
Souterraine, La **20** 46 15N 1 30 E
South Africa, Rep. of, ■ **89** 32 0 S 17 0 E
South America **122** 10 0 S 60 0W
South Atlantic Ocean **7** 20 0 S 10 0W
South Aulatsivik I. **107** 56 45N 61 30W
South Australia □ **96** 32 0 S 139 0 E
South Baldy, Mt. **119** 34 6N 107 27W
South Bend, Ind., U.S.A. **114** 41 38N 86 20W
South Bend, Wash., U.S.A. **118** 46 44N 123 52W
South Boston **115** 36 42N 78 58W
South Branch **107** 47 55N 59 2W
South Brook **107** 49 26N 56 5W
South Buganda □ **90** 0 15 S 31 30 E
South Carolina □ **115** 33 45N 81 0W
South Charleston **114** 38 20N 81 40W
South China Sea **71** 10 0N 113 0 E
South Dakota □ **116** 45 0N 100 0W
South Downs **13** 50 53N 0 10W
South East C. **97** 43 40 S 146 50 E
South-East Indian Rise **94** 43 0 S 80 0 E
South Esk → **14** 56 44N 3 3W
South Foreland **13** 51 7N 1 23 E
South Fork → **118** 47 54N 113 15W
South Gamboa **120** 9 4N 79 40W
South Georgia **5** 54 30 S 37 0W
South Glamorgan □ **13** 51 30N 3 20W
South Grafton **99** 29 41 S 152 57 E
South Haven **114** 42 22N 86 20W
South Henik, L. **109** 61 30N 97 30W
South Honshu Ridge **94** 23 0N 143 0 E
South Horr **90** 2 12N 36 56 E
South I., Kenya **90** 2 35N 36 35 E
South I., N.Z. **101** 44 0 S 170 0 E
South Invercargill **101** 46 26 S 168 23 E
South Knife → **109** 58 55N 94 37W
South Korea ■ **76** 36 0N 128 0 E
South Loup → **116** 41 4N 98 40W
South Mashonaland □ **91** 18 0 S 31 30 E
South Milwaukee **114** 42 50N 87 52W
South Molton **13** 51 1N 3 50W
South Nahanni → **108** 61 3N 123 21W
South Negril Pt. **121** 18 14N 78 30W
South Orkney Is. **5** 63 0 S 45 0W
South Pass **118** 42 20N 108 58W
South Passage **96** 26 07 S 113 09 E
South Pines **115** 35 10N 79 25W
South Pittsburg **115** 35 1N 85 42W
South Platte → **116** 41 7N 100 42W
South Pole **5** 90 0 S 0 0 E
South Porcupine **106** 48 30N 81 12W
South River, Can. **106** 45 52N 79 23W
South River, U.S.A. **113** 40 27N 74 23W
South Ronaldsay **14** 58 46N 2 58W
South Sandwich Is. **7** 57 0 S 27 0W
South Saskatchewan → **109** 53 15N 105 5W
South Seal → **109** 58 48N 98 8W
South Sentinel I. **71** 11 1N 92 16 E
South Shetland Is. **5** 62 0 S 59 0W
South Shields **12** 54 59N 1 26W
South Sioux City **116** 42 30N 96 24W
South Taranaki Bight **101** 39 40 S 174 5 E
South Thompson → **108** 50 40N 120 20W
South Twin I. **106** 53 7N 79 52W
South Tyne → **12** 54 46N 2 25W
South Uist **14** 57 20N 7 15W
South West Africa = Namibia ■ **92** 22 0 S 18 9 E
South West C. **99** 43 34 S 146 3 E
South Yemen ■ **63** 15 0N 48 0 E
South Yorkshire □ **12** 53 30N 1 20W
Southampton, Can. **106** 44 30N 81 25W
Southampton, U.K. **13** 50 54N 1 23W
Southampton, U.S.A. **114** 40 54N 72 22W
Southampton I. **105** 64 30N 84 0W
Southbridge, N.Z. **101** 43 48 S 172 16 E
Southbridge, U.S.A. **113** 42 4N 72 2W
Southeast Pacific Basin **95** 16 30 S 92 0W
Southend **109** 56 19N 103 22W
Southend-on-Sea **13** 51 32N 0 42 E
Southern □, Malawi **91** 15 0 S 35 0 E
Southern □, S. Leone **84** 8 0N 12 30W
Southern □, Zambia **91** 16 20 S 26 20 E
Southern Alps **101** 43 41 S 170 11 E
Southern Cross **96** 31 12 S 119 15 E
Southern Indian L. **109** 57 10N 98 30W
Southern Ocean **5** 62 0 S 60 0 E
Southern Uplands **14** 55 30N 3 3W
Southington **113** 41 37N 72 53W
Southold **113** 41 4N 72 26W
Southport, Austral. **97** 27 58 S 153 25 E
Southport, U.K. **12** 53 38N 3 1W
Southport, U.S.A. **115** 33 55N 78 0W
Southwestern Pacific Basin **94** 42 0 S 170 0W
Southwold **13** 52 19N 1 41 E
Soutpansberge **93** 23 0 S 29 30 E
Souvigny **20** 46 33N 3 10 E
Sovata **46** 46 35N 25 3 E
Sovetsk, Lithuania, U.S.S.R. **54** 55 6N 21 50 E
Sovetsk, R.S.F.S.R., U.S.S.R. **55** 57 38N 48 53 E
Sovetskaya **57** 49 1N 42 7 E
Sovetskaya Gavan **59** 48 50N 140 0 E
Sovicille **39** 43 16N 11 12 E
Sovra **42** 42 44N 17 34 E
Sōya-Misaki **74** 45 30N 142 0 E
Soyo **88** 6 13 S 12 20 E
Sozh → **54** 51 57N 30 48 E
Sozopol **43** 42 23N 27 42 E
Spa **16** 50 29N 5 53 E
Spain ■ **29** 40 0N 5 0W
Spalding, Austral. **99** 33 30 S 138 37 E
Spalding, U.K. **12** 52 47N 0 9W
Spalding, U.S.A. **116** 41 45N 98 27W
Spangereid **47** 58 3N 7 9 E
Spangler **112** 40 39N 78 48W
Spaniard's Bay **107** 47 38N 53 20W
Spanish **106** 46 12N 82 20W
Spanish Fork **118** 40 10N 111 37W
Spanish Town **121** 18 0N 76 57W
Sparks **118** 39 30N 119 45W
Sparta, Ga., U.S.A. **115** 33 18N 82 59W
Sparta, Wis., U.S.A. **116** 43 55N 90 47W
Sparta = Spárti **45** 37 5N 22 25 E
Spartanburg **115** 35 0N 82 0W
Spartansburg **112** 41 48N 79 43W
Spartel, C. **82** 35 47N 5 56W
Spárti **45** 37 5N 22 25 E
Spartivento, C., Calabria, Italy **41** 37 56N 16 4 E
Spartivento, C., Sard., Italy **40** 38 52N 8 50 E
Spas-Demensk **54** 54 20N 34 0 E
Spas-Klepiki **55** 55 10N 40 10 E
Spassk-Dalniy **59** 44 40N 132 48 E
Spassk-Ryazanskiy **55** 54 24N 40 25 E
Spátha, Akra **45** 35 42N 23 43 E
Spatsizi → **108** 57 42N 128 7W
Spearfish **116** 44 32N 103 52W
Spearman **117** 36 15N 101 10W
Speers **109** 52 43N 107 34W
Speightstown **121** 13 15N 59 39W
Speke Gulf **90** 2 20 S 32 50 E
Spenard **104** 61 11N 149 50W
Spence Bay **104** 69 32N 93 32W
Spencer, Idaho, U.S.A. **118** 44 18N 112 8W
Spencer, Iowa, U.S.A. **116** 43 5N 95 19W
Spencer, N.Y., U.S.A. **113** 42 14N 76 30W
Spencer, Nebr., U.S.A. **116** 42 52N 98 43W
Spencer, W. Va., U.S.A. **114** 38 47N 81 24W
Spencer B. **92** 25 30 S 14 47 E
Spencer, C. **97** 35 20 S 136 53 E
Spencer G. **97** 34 0 S 137 20 E
Spencerville **113** 44 51N 75 33W
Spences Bridge **108** 50 25N 121 20W
Spenser Mts. **101** 42 15 S 172 45 E
Sperkhiós → **45** 38 57N 22 3 E
Sperrin Mts. **15** 54 50N 7 0W
Spessart **25** 50 10N 9 20 E
Spétsai **45** 37 15N 23 10 E
Spey → **14** 57 26N 3 25W
Speyer **25** 49 19N 8 26 E
Speyer → **25** 49 19N 8 27 E
Spézia, La **38** 44 8N 9 50 E
Spezzano Albanese **41** 39 41N 16 19 E
Spiekeroog **24** 53 45N 7 42 E
Spielfeld **39** 46 43N 15 38 E
Spiez **25** 46 40N 7 40 E
Spíli **45** 35 13N 24 31 E
Spilimbergo **39** 46 7N 12 53 E
Spinazzola **41** 40 58N 16 5 E
Spind **47** 58 6N 6 53 E
Spineni **46** 44 43N 24 37 E
Spirit Lake **118** 47 56N 116 56W
Spirit River **108** 55 45N 118 50W
Spiritwood **109** 53 24N 107 33W
Spišská Nová Ves **27** 48 58N 20 34 E
Spišské Podhradie **27** 49 0N 20 48 E
Spital **26** 47 42N 14 18 E
Spithead **13** 50 43N 1 5W
Spittal **26** 46 48N 13 31 E
Spitzbergen = Svalbard **4** 78 0N 17 0 E
Split **39** 43 31N 16 26 E
Split L. **109** 56 8N 96 15W
Splitski Kanal **39** 43 31N 16 20 E
Splügenpass **25** 46 30N 9 20 E
Spoffard **117** 29 10N 100 27W
Spokane **118** 47 45N 117 25W
Spoleto **39** 42 46N 12 47 E
Spooner **116** 45 49N 91 51W
Sporádhes **45** 39 0N 24 30 E
Sporyy Navolok, Mys **58** 75 50N 68 40 E
Spragge **106** 46 15N 82 40W

Sprague 118 47 18N 117 59W
Sprague River 118 42 28N 121 31W
Spratly, I. 72 8 20N 112 0 E
Spray 118 44 50N 119 46W
Spree → 24 52 32N 13 13 E
Spring City 118 39 31N 111 28W
Spring Mts. 119 36 20N 115 43W
Spring Valley, Minn., U.S.A. 116 43 40N 92 23W
Spring Valley, N.Y., U.S.A. 113 41 7N 74 4W
Springbok 92 29 42S 17 54 E
Springburn 101 43 40S 171 32 E
Springdale, Can. 107 49 30N 56 6W
Springdale, Ark., U.S.A. 117 36 10N 94 5W
Springdale, Wash., U.S.A. 118 48 1N 117 50W
Springe 24 52 12N 9 35 E
Springer 117 36 22N 104 36W
Springerville 119 34 10N 109 16W
Springfield, Can. 112 42 50N 80 56W
Springfield, N.Z. 101 43 19S 171 56 E
Springfield, Colo., U.S.A. 117 37 26N 102 40W
Springfield, Ill., U.S.A. 116 39 48N 89 40W
Springfield, Mass., U.S.A. 114 42 8N 72 37W
Springfield, Mo., U.S.A. 117 37 15N 93 20W
Springfield, Ohio, U.S.A. 114 39 58N 83 48W
Springfield, Oreg., U.S.A. 118 44 2N 123 0W
Springfield, Tenn., U.S.A. 115 36 35N 86 55W
Springfield, Vt., U.S.A. 113 43 20N 72 30W
Springfontein 92 30 15S 25 40 E
Springhill 107 45 40N 64 4W
Springhouse 108 51 56N 122 7W
Springhurst 99 36 10S 146 31 E
Springs 93 26 13S 28 25 E
Springsure 97 24 8S 148 6 E
Springvale, Austral. 98 23 33S 140 42 E
Springvale, U.S.A. 113 43 28N 70 48W
Springville, N.Y., U.S.A. 114 42 31N 78 41W
Springville, Utah, U.S.A. 118 40 14N 111 35W
Springwater 109 51 58N 108 23W
Spruce-Creek 112 40 36N 78 9W
Spur 117 33 28N 100 50W
Spurn Hd. 12 53 34N 0 8 E
Spuž 42 42 32N 19 10 E
Spuzzum 108 49 37N 121 23W
Squam L. 113 43 45N 71 32W
Squamish 108 49 45N 123 10W
Square Islands 107 52 47N 55 47W
Squillace, Golfo di 41 38 43N 16 35 E
Squinzano 41 40 27N 18 1 E
Sragen 73 7 28S 110 59 E
Srbac 42 45 7N 17 30 E
Srbija □ 42 43 30N 21 0 E
Srbobran 42 45 32N 19 48 E
Sre Umbell 71 11 8N 103 46 E
Srebrnica 42 44 10N 19 18 E
Sredinnyy Khrebet 59 57 0N 160 0 E
Središče 39 46 24N 16 17 E
Sredna Gora 43 42 40N 24 20 E
Sredne Tambovskoye 59 50 55N 137 45 E
Srednekolymsk 59 67 27N 153 40 E
Srednevilyuysk 59 63 50N 123 5 E
Sredni Rodopi 43 41 40N 24 45 E
Šrem 28 52 6N 17 2 E
Sremska Mitrovica 42 44 59N 19 33 E
Sremski Karlovci 42 45 12N 19 56 E
Sretensk 59 52 10N 117 40 E
Sri Lanka ■ 70 7 30N 80 50 E
Sriharikota, I. 70 13 40N 80 20 E
Srikakulam 70 18 14N 83 58 E
Srinagar 66 34 5N 74 50 E
Sripur 69 24 14N 90 30 E
Srirangam 70 10 54N 78 42 E
Srirangapatnam 70 12 26N 76 43 E
Srivilliputtur 70 9 31N 77 40 E
Šroda Šląska 28 51 10N 16 36 E
Šroda Wielkopolski 28 52 15N 17 19 E
Srokowo 28 54 13N 21 31 E
Srpska Crnja 42 45 38N 20 44 E
Srpska Itabej 42 45 35N 20 44 E
Staaten → 98 16 24S 141 17 E
Staberhuk 24 54 23N 11 18 E
Stade 24 53 35N 9 31 E
Staðarhólskirkja 50 65 23N 21 58W
Städjan 48 61 56N 12 52 E
Stadlandet 47 62 10N 5 10 E
Stadskanaal 16 53 4N 6 55 E
Stadthagen 24 52 20N 9 14 E
Stadtlohn 24 52 0N 6 52 E
Stadtroda 24 50 51N 11 44 E
Stafafell 50 64 25N 14 52W
Staffa 14 56 26N 6 21W
Stafford, U.K. 12 52 49N 2 9W
Stafford, U.S.A. 117 38 0N 98 35W
Stafford □ 12 52 53N 2 10W
Stafford Springs 113 41 58N 72 20W
Stagnone 40 37 50N 12 28 E
Staines 13 51 26N 0 30W
Stainz 26 46 53N 15 17 E
Stalač 42 43 43N 21 28 E
Stalingrad = Volgograd 57 48 40N 44 25 E
Staliniri = Tskhinvali 57 42 14N 44 1 E
Stalino = Donetsk 56 48 0N 37 45 E
Stalinogorsk = Novomoskovsk 55 54 5N 38 15 E
Stalowa Wola 28 50 34N 22 3 E
Stalybridge 12 53 29N 2 4W
Stamford, Austral. 98 21 15S 143 46 E
Stamford, U.K. 13 52 39N 0 29W
Stamford, Conn., U.S.A. 114 41 5N 73 30W
Stamford, Tex., U.S.A. 117 32 58N 99 50W
Stamps 117 33 22N 93 30W
Stanberry 116 40 12N 94 32W
Standerton 93 26 55S 29 7 E
Standish 114 43 58N 83 57W
Stanford 118 47 11N 110 10W
Stange 47 60 43N 11 5 E
Stanger 93 29 27S 31 14 E
Stanišić 42 45 56N 19 10 E
Stanislav = Ivano-Frankovsk 54 49 0N 24 40 E
Stanisławów 28 52 18N 21 33 E
Stanke Dimitrov 42 42 17N 23 9 E
Stanley, Austral. 99 40 46S 145 19 E
Stanley, N.B., Can. 107 46 20N 66 44W
Stanley, Sask., Can. 109 55 24N 104 22W
Stanley, Falk. Is. 128 51 40S 59 51W
Stanley, Idaho, U.S.A. 118 44 10N 114 59W
Stanley, N.D., U.S.A. 116 48 20N 102 23W
Stanley, N.Y., U.S.A. 112 42 48N 77 6W
Stanley, Wis., U.S.A. 116 44 57N 91 0W
Stanley Res. 70 11 50N 77 40 E
Stann Creek 120 17 0N 88 13W
Stanovoy Khrebet 59 55 0N 130 0 E
Stanthorpe 97 28 36S 151 59 E
Stanton 117 32 8N 101 45W
Staples 116 46 21N 94 48W
Stapleton 116 41 30N 100 31W
Staporków 28 51 9N 20 31 E
Star City 109 52 50N 104 20W
Stara-minskaya 57 46 33N 39 0 E
Stara Moravica 42 45 50N 19 30 E
Stara Pazova 42 45 0N 20 10 E
Stara Planina 43 43 15N 23 0 E
Stara Zagora 43 42 26N 25 39 E
Starachowice 28 51 3N 21 2 E
Starashcherbinovskaya 57 46 40N 38 53 E
Staraya Russa 54 57 58N 31 23 E
Starbuck I. 95 5 37S 155 55W
Stargard 24 53 29N 13 19 E
Stargard Szczeciński 28 53 20N 15 0 E
Stari Bar 42 42 7N 19 13 E
Stari Trg 39 45 29N 15 7 E
Staritsa 54 56 33N 35 0 E
Starke 115 30 0N 82 10W
Starkville, Colo., U.S.A. 117 37 10N 104 31W
Starkville, Miss., U.S.A. 115 33 26N 88 48W
Starnberg 25 48 0N 11 20 E
Starnberger See 25 47 55N 11 20 E
Starobelsk 57 49 16N 39 0 E
Starodub 54 52 30N 32 50 E
Starogard 28 53 59N 18 30 E
Starokonstantinov 56 49 48N 27 10 E
Starosielce 28 53 8N 23 5 E
Start Pt. 13 50 13N 3 38W
Stary Sącz 27 49 33N 20 35 E
Staryy Biryuzyak 57 44 46N 46 50 E
Staryy Chartoriysk 54 51 15N 25 54 E
Staryy Kheydzhan 59 60 0N 144 50 E
Staryy Krym 56 45 3N 35 8 E
Staryy Oskol 55 51 19N 37 55 E
Stassfurt 24 51 51N 11 34 E
Staszów 28 50 33N 21 10 E
State College 114 40 47N 77 49W
Staten I. 113 40 35N 74 10W
Staten, I. = Los Estados, I. de 128 54 40S 64 30W
Statesboro 115 32 26N 81 46W
Statesville 115 35 48N 80 51W
Staunton, Ill., U.S.A. 116 39 0N 89 49W
Staunton, Va., U.S.A. 114 38 7N 79 4W
Stavanger 47 58 57N 5 40 E
Stavelot 16 50 23N 5 55 E
Staveren 16 52 53N 5 22 E
Stavern 47 59 0N 10 1 E
Stavre 48 62 51N 15 19 E
Stavropol 57 45 5N 42 0 E
Stavroúpolis 44 41 12N 24 45 E
Stawell 97 37 5S 142 47 E
Stawell → 96 20 20S 142 55 E
Stawiski 28 53 22N 22 9 E
Stawiszyn 28 51 56N 18 4 E
Stayner 112 44 25N 80 5W
Steamboat Springs 118 40 30N 106 50W
Stębark 28 53 30N 20 10 E
Stebleva 44 41 18N 20 33 E
Steele 116 46 56N 99 52W
Steelton 114 40 17N 76 50W
Steelville 117 37 57N 91 21W
Steen River 108 59 40N 117 12W
Steenvoorde 19 50 48N 2 33 E
Steenwijk 16 52 47N 6 7 E
Steep Pt. 96 26 08S 113 8 E
Steep Rock 109 51 30N 98 48W
Ştefăneşti 46 47 44N 27 15 E
Stefanie L. = Chew Bahir 87 4 40N 36 50 E
Stefansson Bay 5 67 20S 59 8 E
Stege 49 55 0N 12 18 E
Steiermark □ 26 47 26N 15 0 E
Steigerwald 25 49 45N 10 30 E
Steinbach 109 49 32N 96 40W
Steinfort 16 49 39N 5 55 E
Steinheim 24 51 50N 9 6 E
Steinhuder Meer 24 52 48N 9 20 E
Steinkjer 50 63 59N 11 31 E
Stellaland 92 26 45S 24 50 E
Stellarton 107 45 32N 62 30W
Stellenbosch 92 33 58S 18 50 E
Stemshaug 47 63 19N 8 44 E
Stendal 24 52 36N 11 50 E
Stensele 50 65 3N 17 8 E
Stenstorp 49 58 17N 13 45 E
Stepanakert 53 39 40N 46 25 E
Stephan 116 48 30N 96 53W
Stephens Creek 99 31 50S 141 30 E
Stephens I. 108 54 10N 130 45W
Stephenville, Can. 107 48 31N 58 35W
Stephenville, U.S.A. 117 32 12N 98 12W
Stepnica 28 53 38N 14 36 E
Stepnoi = Elista 57 46 16N 44 14 E
Stepnyak 58 52 50N 70 50 E
Steppe 60 50 0N 50 0 E
Stereá Ellas □ 45 38 50N 22 0 E
Sterkstroom 92 31 32S 26 32 E
Sterling, Colo., U.S.A. 116 40 40N 103 15W
Sterling, Ill., U.S.A. 116 41 45N 89 45W
Sterling, Kans., U.S.A. 116 38 17N 98 13W
Sterling City 117 31 50N 100 59W
Sterling Run 112 41 25N 78 12W
Sterlitamak 52 53 40N 56 0 E
Šternberg 24 53 42N 11 48 E
Šternberk 27 49 45N 17 15 E
Stettin = Szczecin 28 53 27N 14 27 E
Stettiner Haff 24 53 50N 14 25 E
Stettler 108 52 19N 112 40W
Steubenville 114 40 21N 80 39W
Stevens Port 116 44 32N 89 34W
Stevenson L. 109 53 55N 96 0W
Stevns Klint 49 55 17N 12 28 E
Stewart, B.C., Can. 108 55 56N 129 57W
Stewart, N.W.T., Can. 104 63 19N 139 26W
Stewart, I. 128 54 50S 71 15W
Stewart I. 101 46 58S 167 54 E
Stewiacke 107 45 9N 63 22W
Steynsburg 92 31 15S 25 49 E
Steyr 26 48 3N 14 25 E
Steyr → 26 48 17N 14 15 E
Steytlerville 92 33 17S 24 19 E
Stia 39 43 48N 11 41 E
Stigler 117 35 19N 95 6W
Stigliano 41 40 24N 16 13 E
Stigsnæs 49 55 13N 11 18 E
Stigtomta 49 58 47N 16 48 E
Stikine → 104 56 40N 132 30W
Stilfontein 92 26 50S 26 50 E
Stilís 45 38 55N 22 47 E
Stillwater, Minn., U.S.A. 116 45 3N 92 47W
Stillwater, N.Y., U.S.A. 113 42 55N 73 41W
Stillwater, Okla., U.S.A. 117 36 5N 97 3W
Stillwater Mts 118 39 45N 118 6W
Stilwell 117 35 52N 94 36W
Stimfalías, L. 45 37 51N 22 27 E
Štip 42 41 42N 22 10 E
Stira 45 38 9N 24 14 E
Stiring-Wendel 19 49 12N 6 57 E
Stirling, Austral. 98 17 12S 141 35 E
Stirling, Can. 108 49 30N 112 30W
Stirling, U.K. 14 56 7N 3 57W
Stirling Ra. 96 34 23S 118 0 E
Stittsville 113 45 15N 75 55W
Stockach 25 47 51N 9 01 E
Stockaryd 49 57 19N 14 36 E
Stockerau 27 48 24N 16 12 E
Stockett 118 47 23N 111 7W
Stockholm 48 59 20N 18 3 E
Stockholms län □ 48 59 30N 18 20 E
Stockinbingal 100 34 30S 147 53 E
Stockport 12 53 25N 2 11W
Stockton, Austral. 100 32 50S 151 47 E
Stockton, Calif., U.S.A. 119 38 0N 121 20W
Stockton, Kans., U.S.A. 116 39 30N 99 20W
Stockton, Mo., U.S.A. 117 37 40N 93 48W
Stockton-on-Tees 12 54 34N 1 20W
Stockvik 48 62 17N 17 23 E
Stoczek Łukowski 28 51 58N 22 0 E
Stöde 48 62 28N 16 35 E
Stogovo 42 41 31N 20 38 E
Stoke-on-Trent 12 53 1N 2 11W
Stokes Bay 106 45 0N 81 28W
Stokes Pt. 99 40 10S 143 56 E
Stokkseyri 50 63 50N 21 2W
Stokksnes 50 64 14N 14 58W
Stolac 42 43 8N 17 59 E
Stolberg 24 50 48N 6 13 E
Stolbovaya, R.S.F.S.R., U.S.S.R. 55 55 10N 37 32 E
Stolbovaya, R.S.F.S.R., U.S.S.R. 59 64 50N 153 50 E
Stolbovoy, Ostrov 59 56 44N 163 14 E
Stolbtsy 54 53 30N 26 43 E
Stolin 54 51 53N 26 50 E
Stolnici 46 44 31N 24 48 E
Ston 42 42 51N 17 43 E
Stonehaven 14 56 58N 2 11W
Stonehenge 98 24 22S 143 17 E
Stonewall 109 50 10N 97 19W
Stonington I. 5 68 11S 67 0W
Stony L., Man., Can. 109 58 51N 98 40W
Stony L., Ont., Can. 112 44 30N 78 0W
Stony Rapids 109 59 16N 105 50W
Stony Tunguska = Tunguska, Nizhnyaya → 59 65 48N 88 4 E
Stopnica 28 50 27N 20 57 E
Stora Gla 48 59 30N 12 30 E
Stora Karlsö 49 57 17N 17 59 E
Stora Lulevatten 50 67 10N 19 30 E
Stora Sjöfallet 50 67 29N 18 40 E
Storavan 50 65 45N 18 10 E
Stordal 47 63 28N 10 56 E
Store Bælt 49 55 20N 11 0 E
Store Creek 99 32 54S 149 6 E
Store Heddinge 49 55 18N 12 23 E
Støren 47 63 3N 10 18 E
Storfjorden 47 62 25N 6 30 E
Storm B. 97 43 10S 147 30 E
Storm Lake 116 42 35N 95 11W
Stormberg 92 31 16S 26 17 E
Stormsrivier 92 33 59S 23 52 E
Stornoway 14 58 12N 6 23W
Storozhinets 56 48 14N 25 45 E
Storsjö 48 62 49N 13 5 E
Storsjöen, Hedmark, Norway 47 60 20N 11 40 E
Storsjöen, Hedmark, Norway 47 61 30N 11 14 E
Storsjön, Gävleborg, Sweden 48 60 35N 16 45 E
Storsjön, Jämtland, Sweden 48 62 50N 13 8 E
Storstrøms Amt. □ 49 54 50N 11 45 E
Storuman 50 65 5N 17 10 E
Storuman,sjö 50 65 13N 16 50 E
Storvik 48 60 35N 16 33 E
Stoughton 109 49 40N 103 0W
Stour →, Dorset, U.K. 13 50 48N 2 7W
Stour →, Here. & Worcs., U.K. 13 52 25N 2 13W
Stour →, Suffolk, U.K. 13 51 55N 1 5 E
Stour (Gt. Stour) → 13 51 15N 1 20 E
Stourbridge 13 52 28N 2 8W
Stout, L. 109 52 0N 94 40W
Stowmarket 13 52 11N 1 0 E
Strabane 15 54 50N 7 28W
Strabane □ 15 54 45N 7 25W
Stracin 42 42 13N 22 2 E
Stradella 38 45 4N 9 20 E
Strahan 97 42 9S 145 20 E
Strakonice 26 49 15N 13 53 E
Straldzha 43 42 35N 26 40 E
Stralsund 24 54 17N 13 5 E
Strand, Norway 47 61 17N 11 17 E
Strand, S. Afr. 92 34 9S 18 48 E
Stranda 47 62 19N 6 58 E
Strandebarm 47 60 17N 6 0 E
Strandvik 47 60 9N 5 41 E
Strangford, L. 15 54 30N 5 37W
Strängnäs 48 59 23N 17 2 E
Stranraer 14 54 54N 5 0W
Strasbourg, Can. 109 51 4N 104 55W
Strasbourg, France 19 48 35N 7 42 E
Strasburg, Ger. 24 53 30N 13 44 E
Strasburg, U.S.A. 116 46 12N 100 9W
Stratford, Austral. 100 37 59S 147 7 E
Stratford, Can. 106 43 23N 81 0W
Stratford, N.Z. 101 39 20S 174 19 E
Stratford, Calif., U.S.A. 119 36 10N 119 49W
Stratford, Conn., U.S.A. 113 41 13N 73 8W
Stratford, Tex., U.S.A. 117 36 20N 102 3W
Stratford-on-Avon 13 52 12N 1 42W
Strath Spey 14 57 15N 3 40W
Strathalbyn 99 35 13S 138 53 E
Strathclyde □ 14 56 0N 4 50W
Strathcona Prov. Park 108 49 38N 125 40W
Strathmore, Austral. 98 17 50S 142 35 E
Strathmore, Can. 108 51 5N 113 18W
Strathmore, U.K. 14 56 40N 3 4W
Strathnaver 108 53 20N 122 33W
Strathpeffer 14 57 35N 4 32W
Strathroy 106 42 58N 81 38W
Strathy Pt. 14 58 35N 4 0W
Stratton, U.K. 12 51 41N 1 45W
Stratton, U.S.A. 116 39 20N 102 36W
Straubing 25 48 53N 12 35 E
Straumnes 50 66 26N 23 8W
Strausberg 24 52 40N 13 52 E
Strawberry Res. 118 40 10N 111 7W
Strawn 117 32 36N 98 30W
Strážnice 27 48 54N 17 19 E
Streaky Bay 96 32 48S 134 13 E
Streator 116 41 9N 88 52W
Středočeský □ 26 49 55N 14 30 E
Středoslovenský □ 27 48 30N 19 15 E
Streeter 116 46 39N 99 21W
Streetsville 112 43 35N 79 42W
Strehaia 46 44 37N 23 10 E
Strelcha 43 42 25N 24 19 E
Strelka 59 58 5N 93 3 E
Strésa 38 45 52N 8 28 E
Strezhevoy 58 60 42N 77 34 E
Střibro 26 49 44N 13 0 E
Strickland → 98 7 35S 141 36 E
Strimón → 44 40 46N 23 51 E
Strimonikós Kólpos 44 40 33N 24 0 E
Strofádhes 45 37 15N 21 0 E
Strombacka 48 61 58N 16 44 E
Strómboli 41 38 48N 15 12 E
Stromeferry 14 57 20N 5 33W
Stromness 14 58 58N 3 18W
Ströms vattudal 50 64 15N 14 55 E
Strömsnäsbruk 49 56 35N 13 45 E
Strömstad 48 58 55N 11 15 E
Strömsund 50 63 51N 15 33 E
Strongoli 41 39 16N 17 2 E
Stronsay 14 59 8N 2 38W
Stronsburg 116 41 7N 97 36W
Stropkov 27 49 13N 21 39 E
Stroud 13 51 44N 2 12W
Stroud Road 99 32 18S 151 57 E
Stroudsberg 113 40 59N 75 15W
Struer 49 56 30N 8 35 E
Struga 42 41 13N 20 44 E
Strugi Krasnyye 54 58 21N 29 1 E
Strumica 42 41 28N 22 41 E
Strumica → 42 41 20N 22 22 E
Struthers, Can. 106 48 41N 85 51W
Struthers, U.S.A. 114 41 6N 80 38W
Stryama 43 42 16N 24 54 E
Stryi 54 49 16N 23 48 E
Stryker 108 48 40N 114 44W
Stryków 28 51 55N 19 33 E
Strzegom 28 50 58N 16 20 E
Strzelce Krajeńskie 28 52 52N 15 33 E
Strzelce Opolskie 28 50 31N 18 18 E
Strzelecki Cr. → 97 29 37S 139 59 E
Strzelin 28 50 46N 17 2 E
Strzelno 28 52 35N 18 9 E
Strzybnica 28 50 28N 18 48 E
Strzyżów 27 49 52N 21 47 E
Stuart, Fla., U.S.A. 115 27 11N 80 12W
Stuart, Nebr., U.S.A. 116 42 39N 99 8W
Stuart → 108 54 0N 123 35W
Stuart L. 108 54 30N 124 30W
Stuart Range 96 29 10S 134 56 E
Stuart Town 100 32 44S 149 4 E
Stubbekøbing 49 54 53N 12 9 E
Stuben 26 47 10N 10 8 E
Studen Kladenets, Yazovir 43 41 37N 25 30 E
Stugun 48 63 10N 15 40 E
Stühlingen 25 47 44N 8 26 E
Stull, L. 109 54 24N 92 34W
Stung Treng 71 13 31N 105 58 E
Stupart → 109 56 0N 93 25W
Stupino 55 54 57N 38 2 E
Sturgeon B. 109 52 0N 97 50W
Sturgeon Bay 114 44 52N 87 20W
Sturgeon Falls 106 46 25N 79 57W
Sturgeon L., Alta., Can. 108 55 6N 117 32W
Sturgeon L., Ont., Can. 106 50 0N 90 45W
Sturgeon L., Ont., Can. 112 44 28N 78 43W
Sturgis, Mich., U.S.A. 114 41 50N 85 25W
Sturgis, S.D., U.S.A. 116 44 25N 103 30W
Sturkö 49 56 5N 15 42 E
Štúrovo 27 47 48N 18 41 E
Sturt Cr. → 96 20 8S 127 24 E
Stutterheim 92 32 33S 27 28 E
Stuttgart, Ger. 25 48 46N 9 10 E
Stuttgart, U.S.A. 117 34 30N 91 33W
Stuyvesant 113 42 23N 73 45W
Stykkishólmur 50 65 2N 22 40W
Styr → 54 52 7N 26 35 E
Styria = Steiermark □ 26 47 26N 15 0 E
Su Xian 77 33 41N 116 59 E
Suakin 86 19 8N 37 20 E
Suaqui 120 29 12N 109 41W
Subang 73 6 34S 107 45 E
Subi 72 2 58N 108 50 E
Subiaco 39 41 56N 13 5 E
Subotica 42 46 6N 19 49 E
Success 109 50 28N 108 6W
Suceava 46 47 38N 26 16 E

EIL

Suceava □ 46 47 37N 25 40 E
Suceava → 46 47 38N 26 16 E
Sucha-Beskidzka 27 49 44N 19 35 E
Suchan 28 53 18N 15 18 E
Suchedniów 28 51 3N 20 49 E
Suchitoto 120 13 56N 89 0W
Suchou = Suzhou 75 31 18N 120 36 E
Süchow = Xuzhou 77 34 18N 117 10 E
Suchowola 28 53 33N 23 3 E
Suck → 15 53 17N 8 18W
Suckling, Mt. 98 9 49 S 148 53 E
Sucre 126 19 0 S 65 15W
Sućuraj 39 43 10N 17 8 E
Sud-Ouest, Pte. du 107 49 23N 63 36W
Sud, Pte. 107 49 3N 62 14W
Suda → 55 59 0N 37 40 E
Sudair 64 26 0N 45 0 E
Sudak 56 44 51N 34 57 E
Sudan 117 34 4N 102 32W
Sudan ■ 81 15 0N 30 0 E
Suday 55 59 0N 43 0 E
Sudbury 106 46 30N 81 0W
Sûdd 87 8 20N 30 0 E
Süderbrarup 24 54 38N 9 47 E
Süderlügum 24 54 50N 8 55 E
Süderoog-Sand 24 54 27N 8 30 E
Sudetan Mts. = Sudety 27 50 20N 16 45 E
Sudety 27 50 20N 16 45 E
Sudi 91 10 11 S 39 57 E
Sudirman, Pegunungan 73 4 30 S 137 0 E
Sudiţi 46 44 35N 27 38 E
Sudogda 55 55 55N 40 50 E
Sudr 86 29 40N 32 42 E
Sudzha 54 51 14N 35 17 E
Sueca 33 39 12N 0 21W
Suedala 49 55 30N 13 15 E
Sueur, Le 116 44 25N 93 52W
Suez = El Suweis 86 28 40N 33 0 E
Suez Canal = Suweis, Qanâl es 86 31 0N 33 20 E
Sûf 62 32 19N 35 49 E
Şufaynah 64 23 6N 40 33 E
Suffield 109 50 12N 111 10W
Suffolk 114 36 47N 76 33W
Suffolk □ 13 52 16N 1 0 E
Sufuk 65 23 50N 51 50 E
Şugag 46 45 47N 23 37 E
Sugar City 116 38 18N 103 38W
Sugluk = Sagloue 105 62 30N 74 15W
Suhaia, L. 46 43 45N 25 15 E
Suhār 65 24 20N 56 40 E
Suhbaatar 75 50 17N 106 10 E
Suhl 24 50 35N 10 40 E
Suhl □ 24 50 37N 10 43 E
Sui Xian, Henan, China 77 34 25N 115 2 E
Sui Xian, Henan, China 77 31 42N 113 24 E
Suichang 77 28 29N 119 15 E
Suichuan 77 26 20N 114 32 E
Suide 76 37 30N 110 12 E
Suifenhe 76 44 25N 131 10 E
Suihua 75 46 32N 126 55 E
Suining, Hunan, China 77 26 35N 110 10 E
Suining, Sichuan, China 77 30 26N 105 35 E
Suiping 77 33 10N 113 59 E
Suippes 19 49 8N 4 30 E
Suir → 15 52 15N 7 10W
Suixi 77 21 19N 110 18 E
Suizhong 76 40 21N 120 20 E
Sujangarh 68 27 42N 74 31 E
Sujica 42 43 52N 17 11 E
Sukabumi 73 6 56 S 106 50 E
Sukadana, Kalimantan, Indon. 72 1 10 S 110 0 E
Sukadana, Sumatera, Indon. 72 5 5 S 105 33 E
Sukaradja 72 2 28 S 110 25 E
Sukarnapura = Jayapura 73 2 37 S 140 38 E
Sukhindol 43 43 11N 25 10 E
Sukhinichi 54 54 8N 35 10 E
Sukhona → 52 60 30N 45 0 E
Sukhumi 57 43 0N 41 0 E
Sukkur 68 27 42N 68 54 E
Sukkur Barrage 68 27 40N 68 50 E
Sukma 70 18 24N 81 45 E
Sukovo 42 43 4N 22 37 E
Sukunka → 108 55 45N 121 15W
Sula → 54 49 40N 32 41 E
Sula, Kepulauan 73 1 45 S 125 0 E
Sulaiman Range 68 30 30N 69 50 E
Sulak → 57 43 20N 47 34 E
Sulam Tsor 62 33 4N 35 6 E
Sulawesi □ 73 2 0 S 120 0 E
Sulechów 28 52 5N 15 40 E
Sulęcin 28 52 26N 15 10 E
Sulejów 28 51 26N 19 53 E
Sulejówek 28 52 13N 21 17 E
Sulima 84 6 58N 11 32W
Sulina 46 45 10N 29 40 E
Sulingen 24 52 41N 8 47 E
Suliţa 46 47 39N 26 59 E
Sulitälma 50 67 17N 17 28 E
Sulitjelma 50 67 9N 16 3 E
Sułkowice 27 49 50N 19 49 E
Sullana 126 4 52 S 80 39W
Sullivan, Ill., U.S.A. 116 39 40N 88 40W
Sullivan, Ind., U.S.A. 114 39 5N 87 26W
Sullivan, Mo., U.S.A. 116 38 10N 91 10W
Sullivan Bay 108 50 55N 126 50W
Sully-sur-Loire 19 47 45N 2 20 E
Sulmierzyce 28 51 37N 17 32 E
Sulmona 39 42 3N 13 55 E
Sulphur, La., U.S.A. 117 30 13N 93 22W
Sulphur, Okla., U.S.A. 117 34 35N 97 0W
Sulphur Pt. 108 60 56N 114 48W
Sulphur Springs 117 33 5N 95 36W
Sulphur Springs, Cr. → 117 32 12N 101 36W
Sultan 106 47 36N 82 47W
Sultanpur 69 26 18N 82 4 E
Sultsa 52 63 27N 46 2 E
Sulu Arch. 73 6 0N 121 0 E
Sulu Sea 73 8 0N 120 0 E
Sululta 87 9 10N 38 43 E
Suluq 83 31 44N 20 14 E
Sulzbach 25 49 18N 7 4 E
Sulzbach-Rosenberg 25 49 30N 11 46 E
Sumalata 73 1 0N 122 31 E
Sumampa 124 29 25 S 63 29W
Sumatera □ 72 0 40N 100 20 E
Sumatera Barat □ 72 1 0 S 100 0 E
Sumatera Selatan □ 72 3 30 S 104 0 E
Sumatera Utara □ 72 2 0N 99 0 E
Sumatra 118 46 38N 107 31W
Sumatra = Sumatera □ 72 0 40N 100 20 E
Sumba 73 9 45 S 119 35 E
Sumba, Selat 73 9 0 S 118 40 E
Sumbawa 72 8 26 S 117 30 E
Sumbawa Besar 72 8 30 S 117 26 E
Sumbawanga □ 90 8 0 S 31 30 E
Sumbing 73 7 19 S 110 3 E
Sumburgh Hd. 14 59 52N 1 17W
Sumedang 73 6 49 S 107 56 E
Sümeg 27 46 59N 17 20 E
Sumenep 73 7 3 S 113 51 E
Sumgait 57 40 34N 49 38 E
Summer L. 118 42 50N 120 50W
Summerland 108 49 32N 119 41W
Summerside 107 46 24N 63 47W
Summerville, Ga., U.S.A. 115 34 30N 85 20W
Summerville, S.C., U.S.A. 115 33 2N 80 11W
Summit Lake 108 54 20N 122 40W
Summit Pk. 119 37 20N 106 48W
Sumner 116 42 49N 92 7W
Sumperk 27 49 59N 17 0 E
Sumter 115 33 55N 80 22W
Sumy 54 50 57N 34 50 E
Sunart, L. 14 56 42N 5 43W
Sunburst 118 48 56N 111 59W
Sunbury, Austral. 99 37 35 S 144 44 E
Sunbury, U.S.A. 114 40 50N 76 46W
Sunchales 124 30 58 S 61 35W
Suncho Corral 124 27 55 S 63 27W
Sunchon 77 34 52N 127 31 E
Suncook 113 43 8N 71 27W
Sunda Is. 94 5 0 S 105 0 E
Sunda Kecil, Kepulauan 72 7 30 S 117 0 E
Sunda, Selat 72 6 20 S 105 30 E
Sundance 116 44 27N 104 27W
Sundarbans, The 69 22 0N 89 0 E
Sundargarh 69 22 4N 84 5 E
Sundays = Sondags → 92 33 44 S 25 51 E
Sundbyberg 48 59 22N 17 58 E
Sunderland, Can. 112 44 16N 79 4W
Sunderland, U.K. 12 54 54N 1 22W
Sunderland, U.S.A. 113 42 27N 72 36W
Sundre 108 51 49N 114 38W
Sundridge 106 45 45N 79 25W
Sunds 49 56 13N 9 1 E
Sundsjö 48 62 59N 15 9 E
Sundsvall 48 62 23N 17 17 E
Sungaigerong 72 2 59 S 104 52 E
Sungailiat 72 1 51 S 106 8 E
Sungaipakning 72 1 19N 102 0 E
Sungaipenuh 72 2 1 S 101 20 E
Sungaitiram 72 0 45 S 117 8 E
Sungari = Songhua Jiang → 76 47 45N 132 30 E
Sungei Patani 71 5 38N 100 29 E
Sungei Siput 71 4 51N 101 6 E
Sungguminasa 73 5 17 S 119 30 E
Sunghua Chiang = Songhua Jiang → 76 47 45N 132 30 E
Sungikai 87 12 20N 29 51 E
Sungtao Hu 77 19 20N 109 35 E
Sungurlu 56 40 12N 34 21 E
Sunja 39 45 21N 16 35 E
Sunndalsøra 47 62 40N 8 33 E
Sunne 48 59 52N 13 5 E
Sunnfjord 47 61 25N 5 18 E
Sunnyside, Utah, U.S.A. 118 39 34N 110 24W
Sunnyside, Wash., U.S.A. 118 46 24N 120 2W
Sunray 117 36 1N 101 47W
Sunshine 100 37 48 S 144 52 E
Suntar 59 62 15N 117 30 E
Sunyani 84 7 21N 2 22W
Suoyarvi 52 62 12N 32 23 E
Supai 119 36 14N 112 44W
Supaul 69 26 10N 86 40 E
Superior, Ariz., U.S.A. 119 33 19N 111 9W
Superior, Mont., U.S.A. 118 47 15N 114 57W
Superior, Nebr., U.S.A. 116 40 3N 98 2W
Superior, Wis., U.S.A. 116 46 45N 92 5W
Superior, L. 111 47 40N 87 0W
Supetar 39 43 25N 16 32 E
Suphan Buri 71 14 14N 100 10 E
Suphan Daği 64 38 54N 42 48 E
Supraśl 28 53 13N 23 19 E
Suq al Jum'ah 83 32 58N 13 12 E
Sūq ash Shūyukh 64 30 53N 46 28 E
Suqian 77 33 54N 118 8 E
Sūr, Leb. 62 33 19N 35 16 E
Sūr, Oman 65 22 34N 59 32 E
Sur, Pt. 119 36 18N 121 54W
Sura → 55 56 6N 46 0 E
Surabaja = Surabaya 73 7 17 S 112 45 E
Surabaya 73 7 17 S 112 45 E
Surahammar 48 59 43N 16 13 E
Suraia 46 45 40N 27 25 E
Surakarta 73 7 35 S 110 48 E
Surakhany 57 40 25N 50 1 E
Šurandai 70 8 58N 77 26 E
Šurany 27 48 6N 18 10 E
Surat, Austral. 99 27 10 S 149 6 E
Surat, India 68 21 12N 72 55 E
Surat Thani 71 9 6N 99 20 E
Suratgarh 68 29 18N 73 55 E
Suraz 28 52 57N 22 57 E
Surazh, Byelorussia, U.S.S.R. 54 55 25N 30 44 E
Surazh, R.S.F.S.R., U.S.S.R. 54 53 5N 32 27 E
Surduc 46 47 15N 23 25 E
Surduc Pasul 46 45 21N 23 23 E
Surdulica 42 42 41N 22 11 E
Sûre → 16 49 44N 6 31 E
Surendranagar 68 22 45N 71 40 E
Surgères 20 46 7N 0 47W
Surgut 58 61 14N 73 20 E
Suri 69 23 50N 87 34 E
Surianu 46 45 33N 23 31 E
Suriapet 70 17 10N 79 40 E
Şūrīf 62 31 40N 35 4 E
Surigao 73 9 47N 125 29 E
Surin 71 14 50N 103 34 E
Surinam ■ 127 4 0N 56 0W
Suriname → 127 5 50N 55 15W
Surmene 57 41 0N 40 1 E
Surovikino 57 48 32N 42 55 E
Surprise L. 108 59 40N 133 15W
Surrey □ 13 51 16N 0 30W
Sursee 25 47 11N 8 6 E
Sursk 55 53 3N 45 40 E
Surt 83 31 11N 16 39 E
Surt, Al Hammadah al 83 30 0N 17 50 E
Surt, Khalīj 83 31 40N 18 30 E
Surtsey 50 63 20N 20 30W
Suruga-Wan 74 34 45N 138 30 E
Susa 38 45 8N 7 3 E
Suså → 49 55 20N 11 42 E
Sušac 39 42 46N 16 30 E
Susak 39 44 30N 14 18 E
Süsangerd 64 31 35N 48 6 E
Susanino 59 52 50N 140 14 E
Susanville 118 40 28N 120 40W
Sušice 26 49 17N 13 30 E
Susquehanna → 114 39 33N 76 5W
Susquehanna Depot 113 41 55N 75 36W
Susques 124 23 35 S 66 25W
Sussex, Can. 107 45 45N 65 37W
Sussex, U.S.A. 113 41 12N 74 38W
Sussex, E. □ 13 51 0N 0 20 E
Sussex, W. □ 13 51 0N 0 30W
Sustut → 108 56 20N 127 30W
Susuman 59 62 47N 148 10 E
Susunu 73 3 20 S 133 25 E
Susz 28 53 44N 19 20 E
Şuţeşti 46 45 13N 27 27 E
Sutherland, S. Afr. 92 32 33 S 20 40 E
Sutherland, U.S.A. 116 41 12N 101 11W
Sutherland Falls 101 44 48 S 167 46 E
Sutherland Pt. 97 28 15 S 153 35 E
Sutherlin 118 43 28N 123 16W
Sutivan 39 43 23N 16 30 E
Sutlej → 68 29 23N 71 3 E
Sutton, Can. 113 45 6N 72 37W
Sutton, U.S.A. 116 40 40N 97 50W
Sutton → 106 55 15N 83 45W
Sutton-in-Ashfield 12 53 7N 1 20W
Suttor → 98 21 36 S 147 2 E
Suva 94 18 6 S 178 30 E
Suva Gora 42 41 45N 21 3 E
Suva Planina 42 43 10N 22 5 E
Suva Reka 42 42 21N 20 50 E
Suvo Rudište 42 43 17N 20 49 E
Suvorov 55 54 7N 36 30 E
Suvorov Is. = Suwarrow Is. 95 13 15 S 163 30W
Suvorovo 43 43 20N 27 35 E
Suwałki 28 54 8N 22 59 E
Suwałki □ 28 54 0N 22 30 E
Suwannee → 115 29 18N 83 9W
Suwanose Jima 74 29 26N 129 30 E
Suwarrow Is. 95 15 0 S 163 0W
Suweis, Khalîg el 86 28 40N 33 0 E
Suweis, Qanâl es 86 31 0N 32 20 E
Suwŏn 76 37 17N 127 1 E
Suzdal 55 56 29N 40 26 E
Suze, La 18 47 54N 0 2 E
Suzhou 75 31 19N 120 38 E
Suzu-Misaki 74 37 31N 137 21 E
Suzuka 74 34 55N 136 36 E
Suzzara 38 45 0N 10 45 E
Svalbard 4 78 0N 17 0 E
Svalbarð 50 66 12N 15 43W
Svalöv 49 55 57N 13 8 E
Svanvik 50 69 25N 30 3 E
Svappavaara 50 67 40N 21 03 E
Svarstad 47 59 27N 9 56 E
Svartisen 50 66 40N 13 50 E
Svartvik 48 62 19N 17 24 E
Svatovo 56 49 35N 38 11 E
Svay Rieng 71 11 9N 105 45 E
Sveio 47 59 33N 5 23 E
Svendborg 49 55 4N 10 35 E
Svene 47 59 45N 9 31 E
Svenljunga 49 57 29N 13 5 E
Svenstrup 49 56 58N 9 50 E
Sverdlovsk, R.S.F.S.R., U.S.S.R. 52 56 50N 60 30 E
Sverdlovsk, Ukraine S.S.R., U.S.S.R. 57 48 5N 39 37 E
Sverdrup Is. 4 79 0N 97 0W
Svetac 39 43 3N 15 43 E
Sveti Ivan Zelina 39 45 57N 16 16 E
Sveti Jurij 39 46 14N 15 24 E
Sveti Lenart 39 46 36N 15 48 E
Sveti Nikola, Prokhad 42 43 27N 22 6 E
Sveti Nikole 42 41 51N 21 56 E
Sveti Rok 39 40 1N 9 6 E
Sveti Trojica 39 46 37N 15 50 E
Svetlogorsk 54 52 38N 29 46 E
Svetlograd 57 45 25N 42 58 E
Svetlovodsk 54 49 2N 33 13 E
Svetozarevo 42 44 5N 21 15 E
Svidník 27 49 20N 21 37 E
Svilaja Pl. 39 43 49N 16 31 E
Svilajnac 42 44 15N 21 11 E
Svilengrad 43 41 49N 26 12 E
Svir → 52 60 30N 32 48 E
Svishtov 43 43 36N 25 23 E
Svisloch 54 53 3N 24 2 E
Svitava → 27 49 30N 16 37 E
Svitavy 27 49 47N 16 28 E
Svobodnyy 59 51 20N 128 0 E
Svoge 43 42 59N 23 23 E
Svolvær 50 68 15N 14 34 E
Svratka → 27 49 11N 16 38 E
Svrljig 42 43 25N 22 6 E
Swabian Alps = Schäbischer Alb 25 48 30N 9 30 E
Swain Reefs 97 21 45 S 152 20 E
Swainsboro 115 32 38N 82 22W
Swakopmund 92 22 37 S 14 30 E
Swale → 12 54 5N 1 20W
Swan → 96 32 3 S 115 45 E
Swan Hill 97 35 20 S 143 33 E
Swan Hills 108 54 42N 115 24W
Swan Islands 121 17 22N 83 57W
Swan L. 109 52 30N 100 40W
Swan River 109 52 10N 101 16W
Swanage 13 50 36N 1 59W
Swansea, Austral. 99 33 3 S 151 35 E
Swansea, U.K. 13 51 37N 3 57W
Swartberge 92 33 20 S 22 0 E
Swartruggens 92 25 39 S 26 42 E
Swarzędz 28 52 25N 17 4 E
Swastika 106 48 7N 80 6W
Swatow = Shantou 76 23 18N 116 40 E
Swaziland ■ 93 26 30 S 31 30 E
Sweden ■ 50 67 0N 15 0 E
Swedru 85 5 32N 0 41W
Sweet Home 118 44 26N 122 25W
Sweetwater 117 32 30N 100 28W
Sweetwater → 118 42 31N 107 2W
Swellendam 92 34 1 S 20 26 E
Świder → 28 52 6N 21 14 E
Świdnica 28 50 50N 16 30 E
Świdnik 28 51 13N 22 39 E
Świdwin 28 53 47N 15 49 E
Świebodzice 28 50 51N 16 20 E
Świebodzin 28 52 15N 15 31 E
Świecie 28 53 25N 18 30 E
Świętokrzyskie, Góry 28 51 0N 20 30 E
Swift Current 109 50 20N 107 45W
Swiftcurrent → 109 50 38N 107 44W
Swilly, L. 15 55 12N 7 35W
Swindle, I. 108 52 30N 128 35W
Swindon 13 51 33N 1 47W
Swinemünde = Świnoujście 28 53 54N 14 16 E
Świnoujście 28 53 54N 14 16 E
Switzerland ■ 25 46 30N 8 0 E
Swords 15 53 27N 6 15W
Syasstroy 54 60 5N 32 15 E
Sychevka 54 55 59N 34 16 E
Syców 28 51 19N 17 40 E
Sydney, Austral. 97 33 53 S 151 10 E
Sydney, Can. 107 46 7N 60 7W
Sydney, U.S.A. 116 41 12N 103 0W
Sydney Mines 107 46 18N 60 15W
Sydprøven 4 60 30N 45 35W
Sydra G. of = Surt, Khalīj 35 31 40N 18 30 E
Syke 24 52 55N 8 50 E
Syktyvkar 52 61 45N 50 40 E
Sylacauga 115 33 10N 86 15W
Sylarna 50 63 2N 12 13 E
Sylhet 67 24 54N 91 52 E
Sylt 24 54 50N 8 20 E
Sylvan Lake 108 52 20N 114 03W
Sylvania 115 32 45N 81 37W
Sylvester 115 31 31N 83 50W
Sym 58 60 20N 88 18 E
Syracuse, Kans., U.S.A. 117 38 0N 101 46W
Syracuse, N.Y., U.S.A. 114 43 4N 76 11W
Syrdarya → 58 46 3N 61 0 E
Syria ■ 64 35 0N 38 0 E
Syriam 69 16 44N 96 19 E
Syrian Desert 60 31 0N 40 0 E
Syul'dzhyukyor 59 63 14N 113 32 E
Syutkya 43 41 50N 24 16 E
Syzran 55 53 12N 48 30 E
Szabolcs-Szatmár □ 27 48 2N 21 45 E
Szamocin 28 53 2N 17 7 E
Szamos → 27 48 7N 22 20 E
Szaraz → 27 46 28N 20 44 E
Szarvas 27 46 50N 20 38 E
Százhalombatta 27 47 20N 18 58 E
Szczawnica 27 49 26N 20 30 E
Szczebrzeszyn 28 50 42N 22 59 E
Szczecin 28 53 27N 14 27 E
Szczecin □ 28 53 25N 14 32 E
Szczecinek 28 53 43N 16 41 E
Szczekocimy 28 50 38N 19 48 E
Szczucin 28 50 18N 21 4 E
Szczuczyn 28 53 36N 22 19 E
Szczytno 28 53 33N 21 0 E
Szechwan = Sichuan □ 75 31 0N 104 0 E
Szécsény 27 48 7N 19 30 E
Szeged 27 46 16N 20 10 E
Szeghalom 27 47 1N 21 10 E
Székesfehérvár 27 47 15N 18 25 E
Szekszárd 27 46 22N 18 42 E
Szendrö 27 48 24N 20 41 E
Szentendre 27 47 39N 19 4 E
Szentes 27 46 39N 20 21 E
Szentgotthárd 27 46 58N 16 19 E
Szentlörinc 27 46 3N 18 1 E
Szerencs 27 48 10N 21 12 E
Szigetvár 27 46 3N 17 46 E
Szikszó 27 48 12N 20 56 E
Szkwa → 28 53 11N 21 43 E
Szlichtyngowa 28 51 42N 16 15 E
Szob 27 47 48N 18 53 E
Szolnok 27 47 10N 20 15 E
Szolnok □ 27 47 15N 20 30 E
Szombathely 27 47 14N 16 38 E
Szprotawa 28 51 33N 15 35 E
Sztum 28 53 55N 19 1 E
Sztutowo 28 54 20N 19 15 E
Szubin 28 53 1N 17 45 E
Szydłowiec 28 51 15N 20 51 E
Szypliszki 28 54 17N 23 2 E

T

Tabacal 124 23 15 S 64 15W
Tabaco 73 13 22N 123 44 E
Tabagné 84 7 59N 3 4W
Ţābah 64 26 55N 42 38 E
Tabar Is. 98 2 50 S 152 0 E
Tabarca, Isla de 33 38 17N 0 30W
Tabarka 83 36 56N 8 46 E
Ţabas, Khorāsān, Iran 65 33 35N 56 55 E
Ţabas, Khorāsān, Iran 65 32 48N 60 12 E
Tabasará, Serranía de 121 8 35N 81 40W
Tabasco □ 120 17 45N 93 30W
Tabatinga, Serra da 127 10 30 S 44 0W

Tabelbala, Kahal de	**82**	28 47N	2 0W
Tabelkaza	**80**	29 50N	0 55 E
Taber	**108**	49 47N	112 8W
Tabernas	**33**	37 4N	2 26W
Tabernes de Valldigna	**33**	39 5N	0 13W
Tablas	**73**	12 25N	122 2 E
Table B.	**107**	53 40N	56 25W
Table Mt.	**92**	34 0 S	18 22 E
Table Top, Mt.	**98**	23 24 S	147 11 E
Tábor	**26**	49 25N	14 39 E
Tabor	**62**	32 42N	35 24 E
Tabora	**90**	5 2 S	32 50 E
Tabora □	**90**	5 0 S	33 0 E
Tabou	**84**	4 30N	7 20W
Tabrīz	**64**	38 7N	46 20 E
Tabuenca	**32**	41 42N	1 33W
Tabūk	**64**	28 23N	36 36 E
Tacheng	**75**	46 40N	82 58 E
Tach'ing Shan = Daqing Shan	**76**	40 40N	111 0 E
Tachov	**26**	49 47N	12 39 E
Tácina →	**41**	38 57N	16 55 E
Tacloban	**73**	11 15N	124 58 E
Tacna	**126**	18 0 S	70 20W
Tacoma	**118**	47 15N	122 30W
Tacuarembó	**125**	31 45 S	56 0W
Tademaït, Plateau du	**82**	28 30N	2 30 E
Tadent, O. →	**83**	22 25N	6 40 E
Tadjerdjeri, O. →	**83**	26 0N	8 0W
Tadjerouna	**82**	33 31N	2 3 E
Tadjettaret, O. →	**83**	21 20N	7 22 E
Tadjmout, Atlas, Alg.	**82**	33 52N	2 30 E
Tadjmout, Sahara, Alg.	**82**	25 37N	3 48 E
Tadjoura	**87**	11 50N	42 55 E
Tadjoura, Golfe de	**87**	11 50N	43 0 E
Tadmor	**101**	41 27 S	172 45 E
Tadoule, L.	**109**	58 36N	98 20W
Tadoussac	**107**	48 11N	69 42W
Tadzhik S.S.R. □	**58**	35 30N	70 0 E
Taegu	**76**	35 50N	128 37 E
Taejŏn	**76**	36 20N	127 28 E
Tafalla	**32**	42 30N	1 41W
Tafar	**87**	6 52N	28 15 E
Ţafas	**62**	32 44N	36 5 E
Tafassasset, O. →	**83**	22 0N	9 57 E
Tafelbaai	**92**	33 35 S	18 25 E
Tafelney, C.	**82**	31 3N	9 51W
Tafermaar	**73**	6 47 S	134 10 E
Taffermit	**82**	29 37N	9 15W
Tafí Viejo	**124**	26 43 S	65 17W
Tafiré	**84**	9 4N	5 4W
Tafnidilt	**82**	28 47N	10 58W
Tafraoute	**82**	29 50N	8 58W
Taft, Phil.	**73**	11 57N	125 30 E
Taft, Calif., U.S.A.	**119**	35 9N	119 28W
Taft, Tex., U.S.A.	**117**	27 58N	97 23W
Taga Dzong	**69**	27 5N	89 55 E
Taganrog	**57**	47 12N	38 50 E
Taganrogskiy Zaliv	**56**	47 0N	38 30 E
Tagânt	**84**	18 20N	11 0W
Tagbilaran	**73**	9 39N	123 51 E
Tággia	**38**	43 52N	7 50 E
Taghrīfat	**83**	29 5N	17 26 E
Taghzout	**82**	33 30N	4 49W
Tagish	**108**	60 19N	134 16W
Tagish L.	**104**	60 10N	134 20W
Tagliacozzo	**39**	42 4N	13 13 E
Tagliamento →	**39**	45 38N	13 5 E
Táglio di Po	**39**	45 0N	12 12 E
Tagomago, I. de	**33**	39 2N	1 39 E
Taguatinga	**127**	12 16 S	42 26W
Tagula I.	**98**	11 30 S	153 30 E
Tagum (Hijo)	**73**	7 33N	125 53 E
Tagus = Tajo →	**29**	39 44N	5 50W
Tahakopa	**101**	46 30 S	169 23 E
Tahala	**82**	34 0N	4 28W
Tahan, Gunong	**71**	4 34N	102 17 E
Tahat	**83**	23 18N	5 33 E
Tāherī	**65**	27 43N	52 20 E
Tahiti	**95**	17 37 S	149 27W
Tahoe City	**118**	39 12N	120 9W
Tahoe, L.	**118**	39 0N	120 9W
Tahoua	**85**	14 57N	5 16 E
Tahta	**86**	26 44N	31 32 E
Tahulandang	**73**	2 27N	125 23 E
Tahuna	**73**	3 38N	125 30 E
Taï	**84**	5 55N	7 30W
Tai Hu	**75**	31 5N	120 10 E
Tai Shan	**76**	36 25N	117 20 E
Tai'an	**76**	36 12N	117 8 E
Taibei	**75**	25 4N	121 29 E
Taibus Qi	**76**	41 54N	115 22 E
T'aichung = Taizhong	**75**	24 10N	120 38 E
Taidong	**75**	22 43N	121 9 E
Taieri →	**101**	46 3 S	170 12 E
Taiga Madema	**83**	23 46N	15 25 E
Taigu	**76**	37 28N	112 30 E
Taihang Shan	**76**	36 0N	113 30 E
Taihape	**101**	39 41 S	175 48 E
Taihe	**77**	26 47N	114 52 E
Taihu	**77**	30 22N	116 20 E
Taijiang	**77**	26 39N	108 21 E
Taikang, Heilongjiang, China	**76**	46 50N	124 25 E
Taikang, Henan, China	**77**	34 5N	114 50 E
Taikkyi	**69**	17 20N	96 0 E
Tailai	**76**	46 23N	123 24 E
Tailem Bend	**99**	35 12 S	139 29 E
Tailfingen	**25**	48 15N	9 1 E
Taimyr = Taymyr	**59**	75 0N	100 0 E
Taimyr, Oz.	**59**	74 20N	102 0 E
Tain	**14**	57 49N	4 4W
Tainan	**77**	23 17N	120 18 E
Taínaron, Ákra	**45**	36 22N	22 27 E
Taining	**77**	26 54N	117 9 E
T'aipei = Taibei	**75**	25 4N	121 29 E
Taiping	**71**	4 51N	100 44 E
Taishan	**77**	22 14N	112 41 E
Taishun	**77**	27 30N	119 42 E
Taita □	**90**	4 0 S	38 30 E
Taita Hills	**90**	3 25 S	38 15 E
Taitao, Pen. de	**128**	46 30 S	75 0W
Taivalkoski	**50**	65 33N	28 12 E
Taiwan ■	**75**	24 0N	121 0 E
Taïyetos Óros	**45**	37 0N	22 23 E
Taiyib →	**62**	31 55N	35 17 E
Taiyiba	**62**	32 36N	35 27 E
Taiyuan	**76**	37 52N	112 33 E
Taizhong	**77**	24 12N	120 35 E
Taizhou	**77**	32 28N	119 55 E
Ta'izz	**63**	13 35N	44 2 E
Tajarḩī	**83**	24 21N	14 28 E
Tajo →	**31**	38 40N	9 24W
Tajumulco, Volcán de	**120**	15 2N	91 50W
Tājūrā	**83**	32 51N	13 21 E
Tak	**71**	16 52N	99 8 E
Takada	**74**	37 7N	138 15 E
Takaka	**101**	40 51 S	172 50 E
Takamatsu	**74**	34 20N	134 5 E
Takanabe	**74**	32 8N	131 30 E
Takaoka	**74**	36 47N	137 0 E
Takapuna	**101**	36 47 S	174 47 E
Takasaki	**74**	36 20N	139 0 E
Takatsuki	**74**	34 51N	135 37 E
Takaungu	**90**	3 38 S	39 52 E
Takayama	**74**	36 18N	137 11 E
Takefu	**74**	35 50N	136 10 E
Takengeun	**72**	4 45N	96 50 E
Takeo	**71**	10 59N	104 47 E
Tåkern	**49**	58 22N	14 45 E
Tākestān	**64**	36 0N	49 40 E
Takhar □	**65**	36 40N	70 0 E
Takla L.	**108**	55 15N	125 45W
Takla Landing	**108**	55 30N	125 50W
Takla Makan	**60**	39 0N	83 0 E
Takla Makan = Taklimakan Shamo	**75**	38 0N	83 0 E
Taklimakan Shamo	**75**	38 0N	83 0 E
Taku →	**108**	58 30N	133 50W
Takua Pa	**71**	7 18N	9 59 E
Takum	**85**	7 18N	9 36 E
Tala	**125**	34 21 S	55 46W
Talagante	**124**	33 40 S	70 50W
Talaïnt	**82**	29 41N	9 40W
Talak	**85**	18 0N	5 0 E
Talamanca, Cordillera de	**121**	9 20N	83 20W
Talara	**126**	4 38 S	81 18 E
Talas	**58**	42 30N	72 13 E
Talasea	**98**	5 20 S	150 2 E
Talata Mafara	**85**	12 38N	6 4 E
Talaud, Kepulauan	**73**	4 30N	127 10 E
Talavera de la Reina	**30**	39 55N	4 46W
Talayan	**73**	6 52N	124 24 E
Talbert, Sillon de	**18**	48 53N	3 5W
Talbot, C.	**96**	13 48 S	126 43 E
Talbragar →	**99**	32 12 S	148 37 E
Talca	**124**	35 28 S	71 40W
Talca □	**124**	35 20 S	71 46W
Talcahuano	**124**	36 40 S	73 10W
Talcher	**69**	21 0N	85 18 E
Talcho	**85**	14 44N	3 28 E
Taldy Kurgan	**58**	45 10N	78 45 E
Ţalesh, Kūhhā-ye	**64**	39 0N	48 30 E
Talfīt	**62**	32 5N	35 17 E
Talguharai	**86**	18 19N	35 56 E
Tali Post	**87**	5 55N	30 44 E
Taliabu	**73**	1 45 S	125 0 E
Talibon	**73**	10 9N	124 20 E
Talihina	**117**	34 45N	95 1W
Talikoti	**70**	16 29N	76 17 E
Taling Sung	**71**	15 5N	99 11 E
Taliwang	**72**	8 50 S	116 55 E
Talkeetna	**104**	62 20N	150 9W
Tall	**62**	33 0N	35 6 E
Tall 'Afar	**64**	36 22N	42 27 E
Tall 'Asūr	**62**	31 59N	35 17 E
Talla	**86**	28 5N	30 43 E
Talladega	**115**	33 28N	86 2W
Tallahassee	**115**	30 25N	84 15W
Tallangatta	**99**	36 15 S	147 19 E
Tallarook	**99**	37 5 S	145 6 E
Tällberg	**48**	60 51N	15 2 E
Tallering Pk.	**96**	28 6 S	115 37 E
Tallinn	**54**	59 22N	24 48 E
Tallulah	**117**	32 25N	91 12W
Ţallūzā	**62**	32 17N	35 18 E
Tălmaciu	**46**	45 38N	24 19 E
Talmest	**82**	31 48N	9 21W
Talmont	**20**	46 27N	1 37W
Talnoye	**56**	48 50N	30 44 E
Taloda	**68**	21 34N	74 11 E
Talodi	**87**	10 35N	30 22 E
Talovaya	**55**	51 6N	40 45 E
Talsi	**54**	57 10N	22 30 E
Talsinnt	**82**	32 33N	3 27W
Taltal	**124**	25 23 S	70 33W
Taltson →	**108**	61 24N	112 46W
Taltson L.	**109**	61 30N	110 15W
Talwood	**99**	28 29 S	149 29 E
Talyawalka Cr. →	**99**	32 28 S	142 22 E
Tama	**116**	41 56N	92 37W
Tamale	**85**	9 22N	0 50W
Taman	**56**	45 14N	36 41 E
Tamanar	**82**	31 1N	9 46W
Tamano	**74**	34 29N	133 59 E
Tamanrasset	**83**	22 50N	5 30 E
Tamanrasset, O. →	**82**	22 0N	2 0 E
Tamaqua	**113**	40 46N	75 58W
Tamar →	**13**	50 33N	4 15W
Tamarite de Litera	**32**	41 52N	0 25 E
Tamási	**27**	46 40N	18 18 E
Tamaské	**85**	14 49N	5 43 E
Tamaulipas □	**120**	24 0N	99 0W
Tamaulipas, Sierra de	**120**	23 30N	98 20W
Tamazula	**120**	24 55N	106 58W
Tamba-Dabatou	**84**	11 50N	10 40W
Tambacounda	**84**	13 45N	13 40W
Tambelan, Kepulauan	**72**	1 0N	107 30 E
Tambo	**98**	24 54 S	146 14 E
Tambo de Mora	**126**	13 30 S	76 8W
Tambohorano	**93**	17 30 S	43 58 E
Tambora	**72**	8 12 S	118 5 E
Tambov	**55**	52 45N	41 28 E
Tambre →	**30**	42 49N	8 53W
Tambuku	**73**	7 8 S	113 40 E
Tamburâ	**87**	5 40N	27 25 E
Tâmchekket	**84**	17 25N	10 40W
Tamega →	**30**	41 5N	8 21W
Tamelelt	**82**	31 50N	7 32W
Tamenglong	**67**	25 0N	93 35 E
Tamerza	**83**	34 23N	7 58 E
Tamgak, Mts.	**80**	19 12N	8 35 E
Tamiahua, Laguna de	**120**	21 30N	97 30W
Tamil Nadu □	**70**	11 0N	77 0 E
Tamluk	**69**	22 18N	87 58 E
Tammerfors = Tampere	**51**	61 30N	23 50 E
Tammisaari	**51**	60 0N	23 26 E
Ţammūn	**62**	32 18N	35 23 E
Tämnaren	**48**	60 10N	17 25 E
Tamo Abu, Pegunungan	**72**	3 10N	115 0 E
Tampa	**115**	27 57N	82 38W
Tampa B.	**115**	27 40N	82 40W
Tampere	**51**	61 30N	23 50 E
Tampico	**120**	22 20N	97 50W
Tampin	**71**	2 28N	102 13 E
Tamri	**82**	30 49N	9 50W
Tamrida = Hadibu	**63**	12 35N	54 2 E
Tamsagbulag	**75**	47 14N	117 21 E
Tamsalu	**54**	59 11N	26 8 E
Tamsweg	**26**	47 7N	13 49 E
Tamu	**67**	24 13N	94 12 E
Tamuja →	**31**	39 38N	6 29W
Tamworth, Austral.	**97**	31 7 S	150 58 E
Tamworth, U.K.	**13**	52 38N	1 41W
Tan-tan	**82**	28 29N	11 1W
Tana	**50**	70 26N	28 14 E
Tana →, Kenya	**90**	2 32 S	40 31 E
Tana →, Norway	**50**	70 30N	28 23 E
Tana, L.	**87**	13 5N	37 30 E
Tana River	**90**	2 0 S	39 30 E
Tanafjorden	**50**	70 45N	28 25 E
Tanagro →	**41**	40 35N	15 25 E
Tanahbala	**72**	0 30 S	98 30 E
Tanahgrogot	**72**	1 55 S	116 15 E
Tanahjampea	**73**	7 10 S	120 35 E
Tanahmasa	**72**	0 12 S	98 39 E
Tanahmerah	**73**	6 5 S	140 16 E
Tanakura	**74**	37 10N	140 20 E
Tanami Des.	**96**	18 50 S	132 0 E
Tanana	**104**	65 10N	152 15W
Tanana →	**104**	65 9N	151 55W
Tananarive = Antananarivo	**93**	18 55 S	47 35 E
Tanannt	**82**	31 54N	6 56W
Tánaro →	**38**	45 1N	8 47 E
Tanaunella	**40**	40 42N	9 45 E
Tancarville	**18**	49 29N	0 28 E
Tanchŏn	**76**	40 27N	128 54 E
Tanda, U.P., India	**68**	28 57N	78 56 E
Tanda, U.P., India	**69**	26 33N	82 35 E
Tanda, Ivory C.	**84**	7 48N	3 10W
Tandag	**73**	9 4N	126 9 E
Tandaia	**91**	9 25 S	34 15 E
Tăndărei	**46**	44 39N	27 40 E
Tandaué	**92**	16 58 S	18 5 E
Tandil	**124**	37 15 S	59 6W
Tandil, Sa. del	**124**	37 30 S	59 0W
Tandlianwala	**68**	31 3N	73 9 E
Tando Adam	**68**	25 45N	68 40 E
Tandou L.	**99**	32 40 S	142 5 E
Tandsbyn	**48**	63 0N	14 45 E
Tandur	**70**	19 11N	79 30 E
Tane-ga-Shima	**74**	30 30N	131 0 E
Taneatua	**101**	38 4 S	177 1 E
Tanen Tong Dan	**67**	16 30N	98 30 E
Tanew →	**28**	50 29N	22 16 E
Tanezrouft	**82**	23 9N	0 11 E
Tanga	**88**	5 5 S	39 2 E
Tanga □	**90**	5 20 S	38 0 E
Tanga Is.	**98**	3 20 S	153 15 E
Tangail	**69**	24 15N	89 55 E
Tanganyika, L.	**90**	6 40 S	30 0 E
Tanger	**82**	35 50N	5 49W
Tangerang	**73**	6 12 S	106 39 E
Tangerhütte	**24**	52 26N	11 50 E
Tangermünde	**24**	52 32N	11 57 E
Tanggu	**76**	39 2N	117 40 E
Tanggula Shan	**75**	32 40N	92 10 E
Tanghe	**77**	32 47N	112 50 E
Tangier = Tanger	**82**	35 50N	5 49W
Tangkak	**71**	2 18N	102 34 E
Tangorin P.O.	**98**	21 47 S	144 12 E
Tangshan	**76**	39 38N	118 10 E
Tanguiéta	**85**	10 35N	1 21 E
Tanimbar, Kepulauan	**73**	7 30 S	131 30 E
Taninges	**21**	46 7N	6 36 E
Tanjay	**73**	9 30N	123 5 E
Tanjore = Thanjavur	**70**	10 48N	79 12 E
Tanjung	**72**	2 10 S	115 25 E
Tanjungbalai	**72**	2 55N	99 44 E
Tanjungbatu	**72**	2 23N	118 3 E
Tanjungkarang	**72**	5 20 S	105 10 E
Tanjungpandan	**72**	2 43 S	107 38 E
Tanjungpinang	**72**	1 5N	104 30 E
Tanjungpriok	**73**	6 8 S	106 55 E
Tanjungredeb	**72**	2 9N	117 29 E
Tanjungselor	**72**	2 55N	117 25 E
Tank	**68**	32 14N	70 25 E
Tänndalen	**48**	62 33N	12 18 E
Tannis Bugt	**49**	57 40N	10 15 E
Tannu-Ola	**59**	51 0N	94 0 E
Tano →	**84**	5 7N	2 56W
Tanout	**85**	14 50N	8 55 E
Tanta	**86**	30 45N	30 57 E
Tantoyuca	**120**	21 21N	98 10W
Tantung = Dandong	**76**	40 10N	124 20 E
Tantūra = Dor	**62**	32 37N	34 55 E
Tanuku	**70**	16 45N	81 44 E
Tanumshede	**49**	58 42N	11 20 E
Tanunda	**99**	34 30 S	139 0 E
Tanur	**70**	11 1N	75 52 E
Tanus	**20**	44 8N	2 19 E
Tanzania ■	**90**	6 40 S	34 0 E
Tanzilla →	**108**	58 8N	130 43W
Tao'an	**76**	45 22N	122 40 E
Taormina	**41**	37 52N	15 16 E
Taos	**119**	36 28N	105 35W
Taoudenni	**82**	22 40N	3 55W
Taoudrart, Adrar	**82**	24 25N	2 24 E
Taounate	**82**	34 25N	4 41W
Taourirt, Alg.	**82**	26 37N	0 20 E
Taourirt, Moroc.	**82**	34 25N	2 53W
Taouz	**82**	30 53N	4 0W
Taoyuan, China	**77**	28 55N	111 16 E
Taoyuan, Taiwan	**77**	25 0N	121 13 E
Tapa	**54**	59 15N	25 50 E
Tapa Shan = Daba Shan	**75**	31 50N	109 20 E
Tapachula	**120**	14 54N	92 17W
Tapah	**71**	4 12N	101 15 E
Tapajós →	**127**	2 24 S	54 41W
Tapaktuan	**72**	3 15N	97 10 E
Tapanui	**101**	45 56 S	169 18 E
Tapauá →	**126**	5 40 S	64 21W
Tapeta	**84**	6 29N	8 52W
Tapia	**30**	43 34N	6 56W
Tápiószele	**27**	47 25N	19 55 E
Tapirapecó, Serra	**126**	1 10N	65 0W
Tapolca	**27**	46 53N	17 29 E
Tappahannock	**114**	37 56N	76 50W
Tapti →	**68**	21 8N	72 41 E
Tapuaenuku, Mt.	**101**	42 0 S	173 39 E
Tapul Group	**73**	5 35N	120 50 E
Taquara	**125**	29 36 S	50 46W
Taquari →	**126**	19 15 S	57 17W
Tar Island	**108**	57 03N	111 40W
Tara, Austral.	**99**	27 17 S	150 31 E
Tara, Can.	**112**	44 28N	81 9W
Tara, U.S.S.R.	**58**	56 55N	74 24 E
Tara, Zambia	**91**	16 58 S	26 45 E
Tara →, U.S.S.R.	**58**	56 42N	74 36 E
Tara →, Yugo.	**42**	43 21N	18 51 E
Tarabagatay, Khrebet	**58**	48 0N	83 0 E
Tarābulus, Leb.	**64**	34 31N	35 50 E
Tarābulus, Libya	**83**	32 49N	13 7 E
Tarahouahout	**83**	22 41N	5 59 E
Tarakan	**72**	3 20N	117 35 E
Tarakit, Mt.	**90**	2 2N	35 10 E
Taralga	**99**	34 26 S	149 52 E
Taranagar	**68**	28 43N	74 50 E
Taranaki □	**101**	39 5 S	174 51 E
Tarancón	**32**	40 1N	3 1W
Taranga	**68**	23 56N	72 43 E
Taranga Hill	**68**	24 0N	72 40 E
Táranto	**41**	40 30N	17 11 E
Táranto, G. di	**41**	40 0N	17 15 E
Tarapacá	**126**	2 56 S	69 46W
Tarapacá □	**124**	20 45 S	69 30W
Tarare	**21**	45 54N	4 26 E
Tararua Range	**101**	40 45 S	175 25 E
Tarascon, Ariège, France	**20**	42 50N	1 37 E
Tarascon, Bouches-du-Rhône, France	**21**	43 48N	4 39 E
Tarashcha	**56**	49 30N	30 31 E
Tarat	**80**	25 55N	9 3 E
Tarat, Bj.	**83**	26 13N	9 18 E
Tarauacá	**126**	8 6 S	70 48W
Tarauacá →	**126**	6 42 S	69 48W
Taravo →	**21**	41 42N	8 49 E
Tarawera	**101**	39 2 S	176 36 E
Tarawera L.	**101**	38 13 S	176 27 E
Tarazona	**32**	41 55N	1 43W
Tarazona de la Mancha	**33**	39 16N	1 55W
Tarbat Ness	**14**	57 52N	3 48W
Tarbert, Strathclyde, U.K.	**14**	55 55N	5 25W
Tarbert, W. Isles, U.K.	**14**	57 54N	6 49W
Tarbes	**20**	43 15N	0 3 E
Tarboro	**115**	35 55N	77 30W
Tarbrax	**98**	21 7 S	142 26 E
Tarbū	**83**	26 0N	15 5 E
Tarcento	**39**	46 12N	13 12 E
Tarcoola	**96**	30 44 S	134 36 E
Tarcoon	**99**	30 15 S	146 43 E
Tardets-Sorholus	**20**	43 8N	0 52W
Tardoire →	**20**	45 52N	0 14 E
Taree	**97**	31 50 S	152 30 E
Tarentaise	**21**	45 30N	6 35 E
Tarf, Ras	**82**	35 40N	5 11W
Tarf Shaqq al Abd	**86**	26 50N	36 6 E
Tarfa, Wadi el →	**86**	28 25N	30 50 E
Tarfaya	**80**	27 55N	12 55W
Targon	**20**	44 44N	0 16W
Targuist	**82**	34 59N	4 14W
Tărhăus	**46**	46 40N	26 8 E
Tărhăus, Munţii	**46**	46 39N	26 7 E
Tarhbalt	**82**	30 39N	5 20W
Tarhit	**82**	30 58N	2 0W
Tarhūnah	**83**	32 27N	13 36 E
Tarib, Wadi →	**86**	18 30N	43 23 E
Tarifa	**31**	36 1N	5 36W
Tarija	**124**	21 30 S	64 40W
Tarija □	**124**	21 30 S	63 30W
Tariku →	**73**	2 55 S	138 26 E
Tarim He →	**75**	39 30N	88 30 E
Tarim Pendi	**75**	40 0N	84 0 E
Tarime □	**90**	1 15 S	34 0 E
Taritatu →	**73**	2 54 S	138 27 E
Tarka →	**92**	32 10 S	26 0 E
Tarkastad	**92**	32 0 S	26 16 E
Tarkhankut, Mys	**56**	45 25N	32 30 E
Tarko Sale	**58**	64 55N	77 50 E
Tarkwa	**84**	5 20N	2 0W
Tarlac	**73**	15 29N	120 35 E
Tarm	**49**	55 56N	8 31 E
Tarma	**126**	11 25 S	75 45W
Tarn □	**20**	43 49N	2 8 E
Tarn →	**20**	44 5N	1 6 E
Tarn-et-Garonne □	**20**	44 8N	1 20 E
Tarna →	**27**	47 31N	19 59 E
Tårnby	**49**	55 37N	12 36 E
Tarnica	**27**	49 4N	22 44 E
Tarnobrzeg	**28**	50 35N	21 41 E
Tarnobrzeg □	**28**	50 40N	22 0 E
Tarnogród	**28**	50 22N	22 45 E
Tarnów	**27**	50 3N	21 0 E
Tarnów □	**27**	50 0N	21 0 E
Tarnowskie Góry	**28**	50 27N	18 54 E
Táro →	**38**	45 0N	10 15 E
Tarong	**99**	26 47 S	151 51 E
Taroom	**97**	25 36 S	149 48 E
Taroudannt	**82**	30 30N	8 52W
Tarp	**24**	54 40N	9 25 E

Tarpon Springs 115 28 8N 82 42W
Tarquínia 39 42 15N 11 45 E
Tarqūmiyah 62 31 35N 35 1 E
Tarragona 32 41 5N 1 17 E
Tarragona □ 32 41 0N 1 0 E
Tarrasa 32 41 34N 2 1 E
Tárrega 32 41 39N 1 9 E
Tarrytown 113 41 5N 73 52W
Tarshiha = Me'ona 62 33 1N 35 15 E
Tarso Emissi 83 21 27N 18 36 E
Tarso Ourari 83 21 27N 17 27 E
Tarsus 64 36 58N 34 55 E
Tartagal 124 22 30 S 63 50W
Tartas 20 43 50N 0 49W
Tartna Point 99 32 54 S 142 24 E
Tartu 54 58 20N 26 44 E
Tarṭūs 64 34 55N 35 55 E
Tarussa 55 54 44N 37 10 E
Tarutao, Ko 71 6 33N 99 40 E
Tarutung 72 2 0N 98 54 E
Tarvisio 39 46 31N 13 35 E
Tarz Ulli 83 25 32N 10 8 E
Tasāwah 83 26 0N 13 30 E
Taschereau 106 48 40N 78 40W
Taseko → 108 52 4N 123 9W
Tasgaon 70 17 2N 74 39 E
Tash-Kumyr 58 41 40N 72 10 E
Ta'shan 87 16 31N 42 33 E
Tashauz 58 41 49N 59 58 E
Tashi Chho Dzong = Thimphu 69 27 31N 89 45 E
Tashkent 58 41 20N 69 10 E
Tashtagol 58 52 47N 87 53 E
Tasikmalaya 73 7 18 S 108 12 E
Tåsjön 50 64 15N 16 0 E
Taskan 59 62 59N 150 20 E
Taskopru 56 41 30N 34 15 E
Tasman B. 101 40 59 S 173 25 E
Tasman Mts. 101 41 3 S 172 25 E
Tasman Pen. 97 43 10 S 148 0 E
Tasman Sea 94 36 0 S 160 0 E
Tasmania □ 97 42 0 S 146 30 E
Tăşnad 46 47 30N 22 33 E
Tassil Tin-Rerhoh 82 20 5N 3 55 E
Tassili n-Ajjer 83 25 47N 8 1 E
Tassili-Oua-n-Ahaggar 83 20 41N 5 30 E
Tasu Sd. 108 52 47N 132 2W
Tata, Hung. 27 47 37N 18 19 E
Tata, Moroc. 82 29 46N 7 56W
Tatabánya 27 47 32N 18 25 E
Tatahouine 83 32 57N 10 29 E
Tatar A.S.S.R. □ 52 55 30N 51 30 E
Tatarbunary 56 45 50N 29 39 E
Tatarsk 58 55 14N 76 0 E
Tatarskiy Proliv 59 54 0N 141 0 E
Tateyama 74 35 0N 139 50 E
Tathlina L. 108 60 33N 117 39W
Tathra 99 36 44 S 149 59 E
Tatinnai L. 109 60 55N 97 40W
Tatnam, C. 109 57 16N 91 0W
Tatra = Tatry 27 49 20N 20 0 E
Tatry 27 49 20N 20 0 E
Tatta 68 24 42N 67 55 E
Tatuí 125 23 25 S 47 53W
Tatum 117 33 16N 103 16W
Tat'ung = Datong 76 40 6N 113 12 E
Tatura 100 36 29 S 145 16 E
Tatvan 64 38 31N 42 15 E
Taubaté 125 23 0 S 45 36W
Tauberbischofsheim 25 49 37N 9 40 E
Taucha 24 51 22N 12 31 E
Tauern 26 47 15N 12 40 E
Tauern-tunnel 26 47 0N 13 12 E
Taufikia 87 9 24N 31 37 E
Taumarunui 101 38 53 S 175 15 E
Taumaturgo 126 8 54 S 72 51W
Taung 92 27 33 S 24 47 E
Taungdwingyi 67 20 1N 95 40 E
Taunggyi 67 20 50N 97 0 E
Taungup 67 18 51N 94 14 E
Taungup Pass 67 18 40N 94 45 E
Taunsa Barrage 68 30 42N 70 50 E
Taunton, U.K. 13 51 1N 3 7W
Taunton, U.S.A. 114 41 54N 71 6W
Taunus 25 50 15N 8 20 E
Taupo 101 38 41 S 176 7 E
Taupo, L. 101 38 46 S 175 55 E
Taurage 54 55 14N 22 16 E
Tauranga 101 37 42 S 176 11 E
Tauranga Harb. 101 37 30 S 176 5 E
Taurianova 41 38 22N 16 1 E
Taurus Mts. = Toros Dağlari 64 37 0N 35 0 E
Tauste 32 41 58N 1 18W
Tauz 57 41 0N 45 40 E
Tavda 58 58 7N 65 8 E
Tavda → 58 59 20N 63 28 E
Taverny 19 49 2N 2 13 E
Taveta 90 3 23 S 37 37 E
Taveuni 101 16 51 S 179 58W
Tavignano → 21 42 7N 9 33 E
Tavira 31 37 8N 7 40W
Tavistock, Can. 112 43 19N 80 50W
Tavistock, U.K. 13 50 33N 4 9W
Tavolara 40 40 55N 9 40 E
Távora → 30 41 8N 7 35W
Tavoy 71 14 2N 98 12 E
Taw → 13 17 37 S 177 55 E
Tawas City 114 44 16N 83 31W
Tawau 72 4 20N 117 55 E
Tawitawi 73 5 10N 120 0 E
Tāwurgha' 83 32 1N 15 2 E
Tay → 14 56 37N 3 38W
Tay, Firth of 14 56 25N 3 8W
Tay, L. 14 56 30N 4 10W
Tay Ninh 71 11 20N 106 5 E
Tayabamba 126 8 15 S 77 16W
Taylakovy 58 59 13N 74 0 E
Taylor, Can. 108 56 13N 120 40W
Taylor, Ariz., U.S.A. 119 34 28N 110 5W
Taylor, Nebr., U.S.A. 116 41 46N 99 23W
Taylor, Pa., U.S.A. 113 41 23N 75 43W
Taylor, Tex., U.S.A. 117 30 30N 97 30W
Taylor Mt. 119 35 16N 107 36W
Taylorville 116 39 32N 89 20W
Taymā' 64 27 35N 38 45 E
Taymyr, P-ov. 59 75 0N 100 0 E
Tayport 14 56 27N 2 52W
Ṭayr Zibnā 62 33 14N 35 23 E
Tayshet 59 55 58N 98 1 E
Tayside □ 14 56 25N 3 30W
Taytay 73 10 45N 119 30 E
Taz → 58 67 32N 78 40 E
Taza 82 34 16N 4 6W
Tazenakht 82 30 35N 7 12W
Tazin → 109 60 26N 110 45W
Tazin L. 109 59 44N 108 42W
Tazoult 83 35 29N 6 11 E
Tazovskiy 58 67 30N 78 44 E
Tbilisi (Tiflis) 57 41 43N 44 50 E
Tchad (Chad) ■ 81 12 30N 17 15 E
Tchad, L. 81 13 30N 14 30 E
Tch'ang-k'ing = Changqing 75 29 35N 106 35 E
Tchaourou 85 8 58N 2 40 E
Tch'eng-tou = Chengdu 75 30 38N 104 2 E
Tchentlo L. 108 55 15N 125 0W
Tchibanga 88 2 45 S 11 0 E
Tchin Tabaraden 85 15 58N 5 56 E
Tczew 28 54 8N 18 50 E
Te Anau, L. 101 45 15 S 167 45 E
Te Aroha 101 37 32 S 175 44 E
Te Awamutu 101 38 1 S 175 20 E
Te Kuiti 101 38 20 S 175 11 E
Te Puke 101 37 46 S 176 22 E
Te Waewae B. 101 46 13 S 167 33 E
Teaca 46 46 55N 24 30 E
Teague 117 31 40N 96 20W
Teano 41 41 15N 14 1 E
Teapa 120 18 35N 92 56W
Teba 31 36 59N 4 55W
Tebakang 72 1 6N 110 30 E
Teberda 57 43 30N 41 46 E
Tébessa 83 35 22N 8 8 E
Tebicuary → 124 26 36 S 58 16W
Tebingtinggi, Bengkulu, Indon. 72 3 38 S 103 9 E
Tebingtinggi, Sumatera Utara, Indon. 72 3 20N 99 9 E
Tébourba 83 36 49N 9 51 E
Téboursouk 83 36 29N 9 10 E
Tebulos 57 42 36N 45 17 E
Tech → 20 42 36N 3 3 E
Techiman 84 7 35N 1 58W
Techirghiol 46 44 4N 28 32 E
Tecuala 120 22 23N 105 27W
Tecuci 46 45 51N 27 27 E
Tecumseh 114 42 1N 83 59W
Tedzhen 58 37 23N 60 31 E
Tees → 12 54 36N 1 25W
Teesside 12 54 37N 1 13W
Teeswater 112 43 59N 81 17W
Tefé 126 3 25 S 64 50W
Tegal 73 6 52 S 109 8 E
Tegelen 16 51 20N 6 9 E
Tegernsee 25 47 43N 11 46 E
Teggiano 41 40 24N 15 32 E
Teghra 69 25 30N 85 34 E
Tegid, L. 12 52 53N 3 38W
Tegina 85 10 5N 6 11 E
Tegucigalpa 121 14 5N 87 14W
Tehachapi 119 35 11N 118 29W
Tehachapi Mts. 119 35 0N 118 40W
Tehamiyam 86 18 20N 36 32 E
Tehilla 86 17 42N 36 6 E
Téhini 84 9 39N 3 40W
Tehrān 65 35 44N 51 30 E
Tehrān □ 65 35 0N 49 30 E
Tehuacán 120 18 30N 97 30W
Tehuantepec 120 16 21N 95 13W
Tehuantepec, Golfo de 120 15 50N 95 0W
Tehuantepec, Istmo de 120 17 0N 94 30W
Teich, Le 20 44 38N 0 59W
Teifi → 13 52 4N 4 14W
Teign → 13 50 41N 3 42W
Teignmouth 13 50 33N 3 30W
Teil, Le 21 44 33N 4 40 E
Teilleul, Le 18 48 32N 0 53W
Teiuş 46 46 12N 23 40 E
Teixeira Pinto 84 12 3N 16 0W
Tejo → 31 38 40N 9 24W
Tekamah 116 41 48N 96 22W
Tekapo, L. 101 43 53 S 170 33 E
Tekax 120 20 11N 89 18W
Tekeli 58 44 50N 79 0 E
Tekeze → 87 14 20N 35 50 E
Tekija 42 44 42N 22 26 E
Tekirdağ 64 40 58N 27 30 E
Tekkali 70 18 37N 84 15 E
Tekoa 118 47 19N 117 4W
Tekouiât, O. → 82 22 25N 2 35 E
Tel Adashim 62 32 30N 35 17 E
Tel Aviv-Yafo 62 32 4N 34 48 E
Tel Lakhish 62 31 34N 34 51 E
Tel Megiddo 62 32 35N 35 11 E
Tel Mond 62 32 15N 34 56 E
Tela 120 15 40N 87 28W
Télagh 82 34 51N 0 32W
Telanaipura = Jambi 72 1 38 S 103 37 E
Telavi 57 42 0N 45 30 E
Telciu 46 47 25N 24 24 E
Telegraph Cr. 108 58 0N 131 10W
Telekhany 54 52 30N 25 46 E
Telemark fylke □ 47 59 25N 8 30 E
Telén 124 36 15 S 65 31W
Teleneshty 46 47 35N 28 24 E
Teleño 30 42 23N 6 22W
Teleorman □ 46 44 0N 25 0 E
Teleorman → 46 44 15N 25 20 E
Teles Pires → 126 7 21 S 58 3W
Telescope Peak 119 36 6N 117 7W
Teletaye 85 16 31N 1 30 E
Telford 12 52 42N 2 31W
Telfs 26 47 19N 11 4 E
Telgte 24 51 59N 7 46 E
Télimélé 84 10 54N 13 2W
Telkwa 108 54 41N 127 5W
Tell City 114 38 0N 86 44W
Tellicherry 70 11 45N 75 30 E
Telluride 119 37 58N 107 48W
Telok Anson 71 4 3N 101 0 E
Telom → 71 4 20N 101 46 E
Telpos Iz 52 63 35N 57 30 E
Telsen 128 42 30 S 66 50W
Telšiai 54 55 59N 22 14 E
Teltow 24 52 24N 13 15 E
Telukbetung 72 5 29 S 105 17 E
Telukbutun 72 4 13N 108 12 E
Telukdalem 72 0 33N 97 50 E
Tema 85 5 41N 0 0 E
Temanggung 73 7 18 S 110 10 E
Temax 120 21 10N 88 50W
Tembe 90 0 16 S 28 14 E
Tembeling → 71 4 20N 102 23 E
Tembleque 32 39 41N 3 30W
Tembuland 93 31 35 S 28 0 E
Teme → 13 52 23N 2 15W
Temecula 119 33 26N 117 6W
Temerloh 71 3 27N 102 25 E
Temir 58 49 21N 57 3 E
Temirtau, Kazakh, U.S.S.R. 58 50 5N 72 56 E
Temirtau, R.S.F.S.R., U.S.S.R. 58 53 10N 87 30 E
Témiscaming 106 46 44N 79 5W
Temma 99 41 12 S 144 48 E
Temnikov 55 54 40N 43 11 E
Temo → 40 40 20N 8 30 E
Temora 99 34 30 S 147 30 E
Temosachic 120 28 58N 107 50W
Tempe 119 33 26N 111 59W
Tempino 72 1 42 S 103 30 E
Tèmpio Pausania 40 40 53N 9 6 E
Temple 117 31 5N 97 22W
Temple B. 97 12 15 S 143 3 E
Templemore 15 52 48N 7 50W
Templeton → 98 21 0 S 138 40 E
Templin 24 53 8N 13 31 E
Temryuk 56 45 15N 37 24 E
Temska → 42 43 17N 22 33 E
Temuco 128 38 45 S 72 40W
Temuka 101 44 14 S 171 17 E
Tenabo 120 20 2N 90 12W
Tenaha 117 31 57N 94 25W
Tenali 70 16 15N 80 35 E
Tenancingo 120 19 0N 99 33W
Tenango 120 19 7N 99 33W
Tenasserim 71 12 6N 99 3 E
Tenasserim □ 71 14 0N 98 30 E
Tenay 21 45 55N 5 30 E
Tenby 13 51 40N 4 42W
Tendaho 87 11 48N 40 54 E
Tende 21 44 5N 7 35 E
Tende, Col de 21 44 9N 7 32 E
Tendelti 87 13 1N 31 55 E
Tendjedi, Adrar 83 23 41N 7 32 E
Tendrara 82 33 3N 1 58W
Teneida 86 25 30N 29 19 E
Ténéré 85 19 0N 10 30 E
Tenerife 80 28 15N 16 35W
Ténès 82 36 31N 1 14 E
Teng → 71 20 30N 98 10 E
Teng Xian, Guangxi Zhuangzu, China 77 23 21N 110 56 E
Teng Xian, Shandong, China 77 35 5N 117 10 E
Tengah □ 73 2 0 S 122 0 E
Tengah Kepulauan 72 7 5 S 118 15 E
Tengchong 75 25 0N 98 28 E
Tenggara □ 73 3 0 S 122 0 E
Tenggarong 72 0 24 S 116 58 E
Tengiz, Ozero 58 50 30N 69 0 E
Tenille 115 32 58N 82 50W
Tenkasi 70 8 55N 77 20 E
Tenke, Congo 91 11 22 S 26 40 E
Tenke, Zaïre 91 10 32 S 26 7 E
Tenkodogo 85 11 54N 0 19W
Tenna → 39 43 12N 13 47 E
Tennant Creek 96 19 30 S 134 15 E
Tennessee □ 111 36 0N 86 30W
Tennessee → 114 34 30N 86 20W
Tennsift, Oued → 82 32 3N 9 28W
Tenom 72 5 4N 115 57 E
Tenosique 120 17 30N 91 24W
Tenryū-Gawa → 74 35 39N 137 48 E
Tent L. 109 62 25N 107 54W
Tenterfield 97 29 0 S 152 0 E
Teófilo Otoni 127 17 50 S 41 30W
Teotihuacán 120 19 44N 98 50W
Tepa 73 7 52 S 129 31 E
Tepalcatepec → 120 18 35N 101 59W
Tepelena 44 40 17N 20 2 E
Tepic 120 21 30N 104 54W
Teplice 26 50 40N 13 48 E
Tepoca, C. 120 30 20N 112 25W
Tequila 120 20 54N 103 47W
Ter → 32 42 0N 3 12 E
Ter Apel 16 52 53N 7 5 E
Téra 85 14 0N 0 45 E
Tera → 30 41 54N 5 44W
Téramo 39 42 40N 13 40 E
Terang 99 38 15 S 142 55 E
Terazit, Massif de 83 20 2N 8 30 E
Terceira 8 38 43N 27 13W
Tercero → 124 32 58 S 61 47W
Terdal 70 16 33N 75 3 E
Terebovlya 54 49 18N 25 44 E
Teregova 46 45 10N 22 16 E
Terek →, U.S.S.R. 56 43 55N 47 30 E
Terek →, U.S.S.R. 57 44 0N 47 30 E
Terembone Cr. → 99 30 25 S 148 50 E
Terengganu □ 71 4 55N 103 0 E
Tereshka → 55 51 48N 46 26 E
Teresina 127 5 9 S 42 45W
Terespol 28 52 5N 23 37 E
Terewah L. 99 29 52 S 147 35 E
Terges → 31 37 49N 7 41W
Tergnier 19 49 40N 3 17 E
Terhazza 82 23 38N 5 22W
Terlizzi 41 41 8N 16 32 E
Terme 56 41 11N 37 0 E
Termez 58 37 15N 67 15 E
Términi Imerese 40 37 58N 13 42 E
Términos, Laguna de 120 18 35N 91 30W
Térmoli 39 42 0N 15 0 E
Ternate 73 0 45N 127 25 E
Terneuzen 16 51 20N 3 50 E
Terney 59 45 3N 136 37 E
Terni 39 42 34N 12 38 E
Ternitz 26 47 43N 16 2 E
Ternopol 54 49 30N 25 40 E
Terra Nova B. 5 74 50 S 164 40 E
Terrace 108 54 30N 128 35W
Terrace Bay 106 48 47N 87 5W
Terracina 40 41 17N 13 12 E
Terralba 40 39 42N 8 38 E
Terranuova Bracciolini 39 43 31N 11 35 E
Terrasini Favarotta 40 38 10N 13 4 E
Terrasson 20 45 7N 1 19 E
Terre Haute 114 39 28N 87 24W
Terrebonne B. 117 29 15N 90 28W
Terrecht 82 20 10N 0 10W
Terrell 117 32 44N 96 19W
Terrenceville 107 47 40N 54 44W
Terrick Terrick 98 24 44 S 145 5 E
Terry 116 46 47N 105 20W
Terschelling 16 53 25N 5 20 E
Terter → 57 40 35N 47 22 E
Teruel 32 40 22N 1 8W
Teruel □ 32 40 48N 1 0W
Tervel 43 43 45N 27 28 E
Tervola 50 66 6N 24 49 E
Teryaweyna L. 99 32 18 S 143 22 E
Tešanj 42 44 38N 17 59 E
Teseney 87 15 5N 36 42 E
Tesha → 55 55 38N 42 9 E
Teshio-Gawa → 74 44 53N 141 45 E
Tešica 42 43 27N 21 45 E
Tesiyn Gol → 75 50 40N 93 20 E
Teslić 42 44 37N 17 54 E
Teslin 104 60 10N 132 43W
Teslin → 108 61 34N 134 35W
Teslin L. 108 60 15N 132 57W
Tessalit 85 20 12N 1 0 E
Tessaoua 85 13 47N 7 56 E
Tessin 24 54 2N 12 28 E
Tessit 85 15 13N 0 18 E
Test → 13 51 7N 1 30W
Testa del Gargano 41 41 50N 16 10 E
Teste, La 20 44 37N 1 8W
Têt 27 47 30N 17 33 E
Têt → 20 42 44N 3 2 E
Tetachuck L. 108 53 18N 125 55W
Tetas, Pta. 124 23 31 S 70 38W
Tete 91 16 13 S 33 33 E
Tete □ 91 15 15 S 32 40 E
Teterev → 54 51 1N 30 5 E
Teterow 24 53 45N 12 34 E
Teteven 43 42 58N 24 17 E
Tethul → 108 60 35N 112 12W
Tetiyev 56 49 22N 29 38 E
Teton → 118 47 58N 111 0W
Tétouan 82 35 35N 5 21W
Tetovo 42 42 1N 21 2 E
Tetuán = Tétouan 82 35 30N 5 25W
Tetyushi 55 54 55N 48 49 E
Teuco → 124 25 35 S 60 11W
Teulada 40 38 59N 8 47 E
Teulon 109 50 23N 97 16W
Teun 73 6 59 S 129 8 E
Teutoburger Wald 22 52 5N 8 20 E
Tevere → 39 41 44N 12 14 E
Teverya 62 32 47N 35 32 E
Teviot → 14 55 21N 2 51W
Tewantin 99 26 27 S 153 3 E
Tewkesbury 13 51 59N 2 8W
Texada I. 108 49 40N 124 25W
Texarkana, Ark., U.S.A. 117 33 25N 94 0W
Texarkana, Tex., U.S.A. 117 33 25N 94 3W
Texas 99 28 49 S 151 9 E
Texas □ 117 31 40N 98 30W
Texas City 117 29 20N 94 55W
Texel 16 53 5N 4 50 E
Texhoma 117 36 32N 101 47W
Texline 117 36 26N 103 0W
Texoma L. 117 34 0N 96 38W
Teykovo 55 56 55N 40 30 E
Teyvareh 65 33 30N 64 24 E
Teza → 55 56 32N 41 53 E
Teziutlán 120 19 50N 97 22W
Tezpur 67 26 40N 92 45 E
Tezzeron L. 108 54 43N 124 30W
Tha-anne → 109 60 31N 94 37W
Tha Nun 71 8 12N 98 17 E
Thaba Putsoa 93 29 45 S 28 0 E
Thabana Ntlenyana 93 29 30 S 29 16 E
Thabazimbi 93 24 40 S 27 21 E
Thabor, Mt. 21 45 7N 6 34 E
Thai Nguyen 71 21 35N 105 55 E
Thailand (Siam) ■ 71 16 0N 102 0 E
Thakhek 71 17 25N 104 45 E
Thal 66 33 28N 70 33 E
Thal Desert 68 31 10N 71 30 E
Thala 83 35 35N 8 40 E
Thala La 67 28 25N 97 23 E
Thallon 99 28 39 S 148 49 E
Thalwil 25 47 17N 8 35 E
Thame → 13 51 35N 1 8W
Thames 101 37 7 S 175 34 E
Thames →, Can. 106 42 20N 82 25W
Thames →, U.K. 13 51 30N 0 35 E
Thames →, U.S.A. 113 41 18N 72 9W
Thamesford 112 43 4N 81 0W
Thamesville 112 42 33N 81 59W
Thāmit, W. 83 30 51N 16 14 E
Thana 70 19 12N 72 59 E
Thanesar 68 30 1N 76 52 E
Thanet, I. of 13 51 21N 1 20 E
Thang Binh 71 15 50N 108 20 E
Thangool 98 24 38 S 150 42 E
Thanh Hoa 71 19 48N 105 46 E
Thanjavur (Tanjore) 70 10 48N 79 12 E
Thanlwin Myit → 67 20 0N 98 0 E
Thann 19 47 48N 7 5 E
Thaon 19 48 15N 6 25 E

Place	Page	Lat.	Long.
Thar (Great Indian) Desert	**68**	28 0N	72 0 E
Tharad	**68**	24 30N	71 44 E
Thargomindah	**97**	27 58 S	143 46 E
Tharrawaddy	**67**	17 38N	95 48 E
Thasopoúla	**44**	40 49N	24 45 E
Thásos, Greece	**44**	40 50N	24 42 E
Thásos, Greece	**44**	40 40N	24 40 E
Thatcher, Ariz., U.S.A.	**119**	32 54N	109 46W
Thatcher, Colo., U.S.A.	**117**	37 38N	104 6W
Thaton	**67**	16 55N	97 22 E
Thau, Étang de	**20**	43 23N	3 36 E
Thaungdut	**67**	24 30N	94 40 E
Thayer	**117**	36 34N	91 34W
Thayetmyo	**67**	19 20N	95 10 E
Thazi	**67**	21 0N	96 5 E
The Bight	**121**	24 19N	75 24W
The Dalles	**118**	45 40N	121 11W
The English Company's Is.	**97**	11 50 S	136 32 E
The Flatts	**121**	32 16N	64 45W
The Frome →	**99**	29 8 S	137 54 E
The Granites	**96**	20 35 S	130 21 E
The Grenadines, Is.	**121**	12 40N	61 20W
The Hague = s'-Gravenhage	**16**	52 7N	4 14 E
The Hamilton →	**96**	26 40 S	135 19 E
The Johnston Lakes	**96**	32 25 S	120 30 E
The Macumba →	**97**	27 52 S	137 12 E
The Pas	**109**	53 45N	101 15W
The Range	**91**	19 2 S	31 2 E
The Rock	**99**	35 15 S	147 2 E
The Salt Lake	**99**	30 6 S	142 8 E
The Warburton →	**99**	28 4 S	137 28 E
Thebes	**86**	25 40N	32 35 E
Thebes = Thívai	**45**	38 19N	23 19 E
Thedford, Can.	**112**	43 9N	81 51W
Thedford, U.S.A.	**116**	41 59N	100 31W
Theebine	**99**	25 57 S	152 34 E
Theil, Le	**18**	48 16N	0 42 E
Thekulthili L.	**109**	61 3N	110 0W
Thelon →	**109**	62 35N	104 3W
Thénezay	**18**	46 44N	0 2W
Thenia	**83**	36 44N	3 33 E
Thenon	**20**	45 9N	1 4 E
Theodore	**97**	24 55 S	150 3 E
Thérain →	**19**	49 15N	2 27 E
Theresa	**113**	44 13N	75 50W
Thermaïkos Kólpos	**44**	40 15N	22 45 E
Thermopolis	**118**	43 35N	108 10W
Thermopylae P.	**45**	38 48N	22 35 E
Thesprotía □	**44**	39 27N	20 22 E
Thessalía □	**44**	39 30N	22 0 E
Thessalon	**106**	46 20N	83 30W
Thessaloníki	**44**	40 38N	22 58 E
Thessaloníki □	**44**	40 45N	23 0 E
Thessaly = Thessalía	**44**	39 30N	22 0 E
Thetford	**13**	52 25N	0 44 E
Thetford Mines	**107**	46 8N	71 18W
Theunissen	**92**	28 26 S	26 43 E
Thiámis →	**44**	39 15N	20 6 E
Thiberville	**18**	49 8N	0 27 E
Thibodaux	**117**	29 48N	90 49W
Thicket Portage	**109**	55 19N	97 42W
Thief River Falls	**116**	48 15N	96 48W
Thiel Mts.	**5**	85 15 S	91 0W
Thiene	**39**	45 42N	11 29 E
Thiérache	**19**	49 51N	3 45 E
Thiers	**20**	45 52N	3 33 E
Thies	**84**	14 50N	16 51W
Thiet	**87**	7 37N	28 49 E
Thika	**90**	1 1 S	37 5 E
Thikombia	**101**	15 44 S	179 55W
Thille-Boubacar	**84**	16 31N	15 5W
Thillot, Le	**19**	47 53N	6 46 E
Thimphu (Tashi Chho Dzong)	**69**	27 31N	89 45 E
Þingvallavatn	**50**	64 11N	21 9W
Thionville	**19**	49 20N	6 10 E
Thíra	**45**	36 23N	25 27 E
Thirasía	**45**	36 26N	25 21 E
Thirsk	**12**	54 15N	1 20W
Thistle I.	**96**	35 0 S	136 8 E
Thívai	**45**	38 19N	23 19 E
Thiviers	**20**	45 25N	0 54 E
Thizy	**21**	46 2N	4 18 E
Þjórsá →	**50**	63 47N	20 48W
Thlewiaza →, Man., Can.	**109**	59 43N	100 5W
Thlewiaza →, N.W.T., Can.	**109**	60 29N	94 40W
Thoa →	**109**	60 31N	109 47W
Thoissey	**21**	46 12N	4 48 E
Thomas, Okla., U.S.A.	**117**	35 48N	98 48W
Thomas, W. Va., U.S.A.	**114**	39 10N	79 30W
Thomas, L.	**99**	26 4 S	137 58 E
Thomaston	**115**	32 54N	84 20W
Thomasville, Ala., U.S.A.	**115**	31 55N	87 42W
Thomasville, Ga., U.S.A.	**115**	30 50N	84 0W
Thomasville, N.C., U.S.A.	**115**	35 55N	80 4W
Thompson	**109**	55 45N	97 52W
Thompson →, Can.	**108**	50 15N	121 24W
Thompson →, U.S.A.	**116**	39 46N	93 37W
Thompson Falls	**118**	47 37N	115 20W
Thompson Landing	**109**	62 56N	110 40W
Thompson Pk.	**118**	41 0N	123 3W
Thompsons	**119**	39 0N	109 50W
Thompsonville	**113**	42 0N	72 37W
Thomson →	**97**	25 11 S	142 53 E
Thomson's Falls = Nyahururu	**90**	0 2N	36 27 E
Thon Buri	**71**	13 43N	100 29 E
Thônes	**21**	45 54N	6 18 E
Thonon-les-Bains	**21**	46 22N	6 29 E
Thorez	**57**	48 4N	38 34 E
Þórisvatn	**50**	64 20N	18 55W
Þorlákshöfn	**50**	63 51N	21 22W
Thornaby on Tees	**12**	54 36N	1 19W
Thornbury	**112**	44 34N	80 26W
Thorne Glacier	**5**	87 30 S	150 0W
Thorold	**112**	43 7N	79 12W
Þórshöfn	**50**	66 12N	15 20W
Thouarcé	**18**	47 17N	0 30W
Thouars	**18**	46 58N	0 15W
Thrace = Thráki □	**44**	41 10N	25 30 E
Thráki □	**44**	41 9N	25 30 E
Thrakikón Pélagos	**44**	40 30N	25 0 E
Three Forks	**118**	45 55N	111 32W
Three Hills	**108**	51 43N	113 15W
Three Hummock I.	**99**	40 25 S	144 55 E
Three Lakes	**116**	45 48N	89 10W
Three Points, C.	**84**	4 42N	2 6W
Three Rivers	**117**	28 30N	98 10W
Three Sisters, Mt.	**118**	44 10N	121 46W
Throssell Ra.	**96**	22 3 S	121 43 E
Thrun Pass	**26**	47 20N	12 25 E
Thubun Lakes	**109**	61 30N	112 0W
Thuddungra	**100**	34 8 S	148 8 E
Thueyts	**21**	44 41N	4 9 E
Thuin	**16**	50 20N	4 17 E
Thuir	**20**	42 38N	2 45 E
Thule, Antarct.	**5**	59 27 S	27 19W
Thule, Greenl.	**4**	77 40N	69 0W
Thun	**25**	46 45N	7 38 E
Thunder B.	**114**	45 0N	83 20W
Thunder Bay	**106**	48 20N	89 15W
Thunersee	**25**	46 43N	7 39 E
Thung Song	**71**	8 10N	99 40 E
Thunkar	**69**	27 55N	91 0 E
Thur →	**25**	47 32N	9 10 E
Thurgau □	**25**	47 34N	9 10 E
Thüringer Wald	**24**	50 35N	11 0 E
Thurles	**15**	52 40N	7 53W
Thurloo Downs	**99**	29 15 S	143 30 E
Thurn P.	**25**	47 20N	12 25 E
Thursday I.	**97**	10 30 S	142 3 E
Thurso, Can.	**106**	45 36N	75 15W
Thurso, U.K.	**14**	58 34N	3 31W
Thurston I.	**5**	72 0 S	100 0W
Thury-Harcourt	**18**	49 0N	0 30W
Thutade L.	**108**	57 0N	126 55W
Thyborøn	**49**	56 42N	8 12 E
Thylungra	**99**	26 4 S	143 28 E
Thyolo	**91**	16 7 S	35 5 E
Thysville = Mbanza Ngungu	**88**	5 12 S	14 53 E
Ti-n-Barraouene, O. →	**85**	18 40N	4 5 E
Ti-n-Medjerdam, O. →	**82**	25 45N	1 30 E
Ti-n-Tarabine, O. →	**83**	21 0N	7 25 E
Ti-n-Zaouatène	**82**	20 0N	2 55 E
Tia	**99**	31 10 S	150 34 E
Tian Shan	**75**	43 0N	84 0 E
Tiandu	**77**	18 18N	109 36 E
Tian'e	**77**	25 1N	107 9 E
Tianhe	**77**	24 48N	108 40 E
Tianjin	**76**	39 8N	117 10 E
Tiankoura	**84**	10 47N	3 17W
Tianshui	**77**	34 32N	105 40 E
Tianyang	**77**	23 42N	106 53 E
Tianzhen	**76**	40 24N	114 5 E
Tiaret	**82**	35 20N	1 21 E
Tiassalé	**84**	5 58N	4 57W
Tibagi	**125**	24 30 S	50 24W
Tibagi →	**125**	22 47 S	51 1W
Tibati	**85**	6 22N	12 30 E
Tiber = Tevere →	**39**	41 44N	12 14 E
Tiber Res.	**118**	48 20N	111 15W
Tiberias, L. = Kinneret, Yam	**62**	32 45N	35 35 E
Tibesti	**83**	21 0N	17 30 E
Tibet = Xizang □	**75**	32 0N	88 0 E
Tibiri	**85**	13 34N	7 4 E
Ţibleş	**46**	47 32N	24 15 E
Tibnīn	**62**	33 12N	35 24 E
Tibooburra	**97**	29 26 S	142 1 E
Tibro	**49**	58 28N	14 10 E
Tiburón	**120**	29 0N	112 30W
Tîchît	**84**	18 21N	9 29W
Ticho	**87**	7 50N	39 32 E
Ticino □	**25**	46 20N	8 45 E
Ticino →	**38**	45 9N	9 14 E
Ticonderoga	**114**	43 50N	73 28W
Ticul	**120**	20 20N	89 31W
Tidaholm	**49**	58 12N	13 55 E
Tiddim	**67**	23 28N	93 45 E
Tideridjaouine, Adrar	**82**	23 0N	2 15 E
Tidikelt	**82**	26 58N	1 30 E
Tidjikja	**84**	18 29N	11 35W
Tidore	**73**	0 40N	127 25 E
Tiébissou	**84**	7 9N	5 10W
Tiéboro	**83**	21 20N	17 7 E
Tiel, Neth.	**16**	51 53N	5 26 E
Tiel, Senegal	**84**	14 55N	15 5W
Tieling	**76**	42 20N	123 55 E
Tielt	**16**	51 0N	3 20 E
Tien Shan = Tian Shan	**65**	42 0N	80 0 E
Tien-tsin = Tianjin	**75**	39 8N	117 10 E
T'ienching = Tianjin	**76**	39 8N	117 10 E
Tienen	**16**	50 48N	4 57 E
Tiénigbé	**84**	8 11N	5 43W
Tientsin = Tianjin	**76**	39 8N	117 10 E
Tierp	**48**	60 20N	17 30 E
Tierra Amarilla, Chile	**124**	27 28 S	70 18W
Tierra Amarilla, U.S.A.	**119**	36 42N	106 33W
Tierra de Barros	**31**	38 40N	6 30W
Tierra de Campos	**30**	42 10N	4 50W
Tierra del Fuego, I. Gr. de	**128**	54 0 S	69 0W
Tiétar →	**30**	39 50N	6 1W
Tieté →	**125**	20 40 S	51 35W
Tifarit	**82**	26 9N	10 33W
Tiffin	**114**	41 8N	83 10W
Tiflèt	**82**	33 54N	6 20W
Tiflis = Tbilisi	**57**	41 43N	44 50 E
Tifrah	**62**	31 19N	34 42 E
Tifton	**115**	31 28N	83 32W
Tifu	**73**	3 39 S	126 24 E
Tigil	**59**	57 49N	158 40 E
Tignish	**107**	46 58N	64 2W
Tigre □	**87**	13 35N	39 15 E
Tigre →	**126**	4 30 S	74 10W
Tigris = Dijlah, Nahr →	**64**	31 0N	47 25 E
Tiguentourine	**83**	27 52N	9 8 E
Tigveni	**46**	45 10N	24 31 E
Tigyaing	**67**	23 45N	96 10 E
Tigzerte, O. →	**82**	28 10N	9 37W
Tîh, Gebel el	**86**	29 32N	33 26 E
Tihama	**64**	22 0N	39 0 E
Tihodaine, Dunes de	**83**	25 15N	7 15 E
Tijesno	**39**	43 48N	15 39 E
Tījī	**83**	32 0N	11 18 E
Tijuana	**120**	32 30N	117 10W
Tikal	**120**	17 13N	89 24W
Tikamgarh	**68**	24 44N	78 50 E
Tikhoretsk	**57**	45 56N	40 5 E
Tikhvin	**54**	59 35N	33 30 E
Tikkadouine, Adrar	**82**	24 28N	1 30 E
Tiko	**85**	4 4N	9 20 E
Tikrīt	**64**	34 35N	43 37 E
Tiksi	**59**	71 40N	128 45 E
Tilamuta	**73**	0 32N	122 23 E
Tilburg	**16**	51 31N	5 6 E
Tilbury, Can.	**106**	42 17N	82 23W
Tilbury, U.K.	**13**	51 27N	0 24 E
Tilcara	**124**	23 36 S	65 23W
Tilden, Nebr., U.S.A.	**116**	42 3N	97 45W
Tilden, Tex., U.S.A.	**117**	28 28N	98 33W
Tilemses	**85**	15 37N	4 44 E
Tilemsi, Vallée du	**85**	17 42N	0 15 E
Tilhar	**69**	28 0N	79 45 E
Tilia, O. →	**82**	27 32N	0 55 E
Tilichiki	**59**	60 27N	166 5 E
Tiligul →	**56**	47 4N	30 57 E
Tililane	**82**	27 49N	0 6W
Tílissos	**45**	35 2N	25 0 E
Till →	**12**	55 35N	2 3W
Tillabéri	**85**	14 28N	1 28 E
Tillamook	**118**	45 29N	123 55W
Tillberga	**48**	59 52N	16 39 E
Tillia	**85**	16 8N	4 47 E
Tillsonburg	**106**	42 53N	80 44W
Tílos	**45**	36 27N	27 27 E
Tilpa	**99**	30 57 S	144 24 E
Tilrhemt	**82**	33 9N	3 22 E
Tilsit = Sovetsk	**54**	55 6N	21 50 E
Tilt →	**14**	56 50N	3 50W
Tilton	**113**	43 25N	71 36W
Timagami L.	**106**	47 0N	80 10W
Timanskiy Kryazh	**52**	65 58N	50 5 E
Timaru	**101**	44 23 S	171 14 E
Timashevsk	**57**	45 35N	39 0 E
Timau, Italy	**39**	46 35N	13 0 E
Timau, Kenya	**90**	0 4N	37 15 E
Timbákion	**45**	35 4N	24 45 E
Timbedgha	**84**	16 17N	8 16W
Timber Lake	**116**	45 29N	101 6W
Timboon	**99**	38 30 S	142 58 E
Timbuktu = Tombouctou	**84**	16 50N	3 0W
Timdjaouine	**82**	21 37N	4 30 E
Timellouline	**83**	29 22N	8 55 E
Timétrine Montagnes	**85**	19 25N	1 0W
Timfi Óros	**44**	39 59N	20 45 E
Timfristós, Óros	**45**	38 57N	21 50 E
Timhadit	**82**	33 15N	5 4W
Timia	**85**	18 4N	8 40 E
Timimoun	**82**	29 14N	0 16 E
Timimoun, Sebkha de	**82**	28 50N	0 46 E
Timiş □	**42**	45 40N	21 30 E
Timiş →	**46**	45 30N	21 0 E
Timişoara	**42**	45 43N	21 15 E
Timmins	**106**	48 28N	81 25W
Timok →	**42**	44 10N	22 40 E
Timon	**127**	5 8 S	42 52W
Timor	**73**	9 0 S	125 0 E
Timor □	**73**	9 0 S	125 0 E
Timor Sea	**97**	10 0 S	127 0 E
Tin Alkoum	**83**	24 42N	10 17 E
Tin Gornai	**85**	16 38N	0 38W
Tin Gornaï →	**85**	20 30N	4 35 E
Tîna, Khalîg el	**86**	31 20N	32 42 E
Tinaca Pt.	**73**	5 30N	125 25 E
Tinafak, O. →	**83**	27 10N	7 0 E
Tinca	**46**	46 46N	21 58 E
Tinchebray	**18**	48 47N	0 45W
Tindivanam	**70**	12 15N	79 41 E
Tindouf	**82**	27 42N	8 10W
Tinee →	**21**	43 55N	7 11 E
Tineo	**30**	43 21N	6 27W
Tinerhir	**82**	31 29N	5 31W
Tinfouchi	**82**	28 52N	5 49W
Tinglev	**49**	54 57N	9 13 E
Tingo Maria	**126**	9 10 S	75 54W
Tingsryd	**49**	56 31N	15 0 E
Tinjoub	**82**	29 45N	5 40W
Tinnoset	**47**	59 55N	9 3 E
Tinnsjø	**47**	59 55N	8 54 E
Tinogasta	**124**	28 5 S	67 32W
Tínos	**45**	37 33N	25 8 E
Tiñoso, C.	**33**	37 32N	1 6W
Tintina	**124**	27 2 S	62 45W
Tintinara	**99**	35 48 S	140 2 E
Tinto →	**31**	37 12N	6 55W
Tioga	**112**	41 54N	77 9W
Tioman, Pulau	**71**	2 50N	104 10 E
Tione di Trento	**38**	46 3N	10 44 E
Tionesta	**112**	41 29N	79 28W
Tior	**87**	6 26N	31 11 E
Tioulilin	**82**	27 1N	0 2W
Tipongpani	**67**	27 20N	95 55 E
Tipperary	**15**	52 28N	8 10W
Tipperary □	**15**	52 37N	7 55W
Tipton, U.K.	**13**	52 32N	2 4W
Tipton, Calif., U.S.A.	**119**	36 3N	119 19W
Tipton, Ind., U.S.A.	**114**	40 17N	86 0W
Tipton, Iowa, U.S.A.	**116**	41 45N	91 12W
Tiptonville	**117**	36 22N	89 30W
Tiptur	**70**	13 15N	76 26 E
Tirahart, O.	**82**	23 45N	3 10 E
Tirân	**65**	32 45N	51 8 E
Tirân	**86**	27 56N	34 45 E
Tirana	**44**	41 18N	19 49 E
Tirana-Durrësi □	**44**	41 35N	20 0 E
Tirano	**38**	46 13N	10 11 E
Tiraspol	**56**	46 55N	29 35 E
Tirat Karmel	**62**	32 46N	34 58 E
Tirat Yehuda	**62**	32 1N	34 56 E
Tirat Zevi	**62**	32 26N	35 31 E
Tiratimine	**82**	25 56N	3 37 E
Tirdout	**85**	16 7N	1 5W
Tire	**64**	38 5N	27 50 E
Tirebolu	**64**	40 58N	38 45 E
Tiree	**14**	56 31N	6 55W
Tîrgovişte	**46**	44 55N	25 27 E
Tîrgu Frumos	**46**	47 12N	27 2 E
Tîrgu-Jiu	**46**	45 5N	23 19 E
Tîrgu Mureş	**46**	46 31N	24 38 E
Tîrgu Neamţ	**46**	47 12N	26 25 E
Tîrgu Ocna	**46**	46 16N	26 39 E
Tîrgu Secuiesc	**46**	46 0N	26 10 E
Tirich Mir	**66**	36 15N	71 55 E
Tiriola	**41**	38 57N	16 32 E
Tirna →	**70**	18 4N	76 57 E
Tîrnava Mare →	**46**	46 15N	24 30 E
Tîrnava Mică →	**46**	46 17N	24 30 E
Tîrnăveni	**46**	46 19N	24 13 E
Tírnavos	**44**	39 45N	22 18 E
Tîrnova	**46**	45 23N	22 1 E
Tirodi	**69**	21 40N	79 44 E
Tirol □	**26**	47 3N	10 43 E
Tirschenreuth	**25**	49 51N	12 20 E
Tirso →	**40**	39 52N	8 33 E
Tirso, L. del	**40**	40 8N	8 56 E
Tiruchchirappalli	**70**	10 45N	78 45 E
Tiruchendur	**70**	8 30N	78 11 E
Tiruchengodu	**70**	11 23N	77 56 E
Tirumangalam	**70**	9 49N	77 58 E
Tirunelveli (Tinnevelly)	**70**	8 45N	77 45 E
Tirupati	**70**	13 39N	79 25 E
Tiruppattur	**70**	12 30N	78 30 E
Tiruppur	**70**	11 5N	77 22 E
Tiruturaipundi	**70**	10 32N	79 41 E
Tiruvadaimarudur	**70**	11 2N	79 27 E
Tiruvallar	**70**	13 9N	79 57 E
Tiruvannamalai	**70**	12 15N	79 5 E
Tiruvarur	**70**	10 46N	79 38 E
Tiruvatipuram	**70**	12 39N	79 33 E
Tiruvottiyur	**70**	13 10N	80 22 E
Tisa →	**42**	45 15N	20 17 E
Tisdale	**109**	52 50N	104 0W
Tishomingo	**117**	34 14N	96 38W
Tisjön	**48**	60 56N	13 0 E
Tisnaren	**48**	58 58N	15 56 E
Tišnov	**27**	49 21N	16 25 E
Tisovec	**27**	48 41N	19 56 E
Tissemsilt	**82**	35 35N	1 50 E
Tissint	**82**	29 57N	7 16W
Tissø	**49**	55 35N	11 18 E
Tista →	**69**	25 23N	89 43 E
Tisza →	**27**	46 8N	20 2 E
Tiszaföldvár	**27**	47 0N	20 14 E
Tiszafüred	**27**	47 38N	20 50 E
Tiszalök	**27**	48 0N	21 10 E
Tiszavasvári	**27**	47 58N	21 18 E
Tit, Ahaggar, Alg.	**83**	23 0N	5 10 E
Tit, Tademait, Alg.	**82**	27 0N	1 29 E
Tit-Ary	**59**	71 55N	127 2 E
Titaguas	**32**	39 53N	1 6W
Titel	**42**	45 10N	20 18 E
Titicaca, L.	**126**	15 30 S	69 30W
Titilagarh	**70**	20 15N	83 11 E
Titiwa	**85**	12 14N	12 53 E
Titograd	**42**	42 30N	19 19 E
Titov Veles	**42**	41 46N	21 47 E
Titova Korenica	**39**	44 45N	15 41 E
Titovo Užice	**42**	43 55N	19 50 E
Titule	**90**	3 15N	25 31 E
Titusville, Fla., U.S.A.	**115**	28 37N	80 49W
Titusville, Pa., U.S.A.	**114**	41 35N	79 39W
Tivaouane	**84**	14 56N	16 45W
Tivat	**42**	42 28N	18 43 E
Tiveden	**49**	58 50N	14 30 E
Tiverton	**13**	50 54N	3 30W
Tivoli	**39**	41 58N	12 45 E
Tiwī	**65**	22 45N	59 12 E
Tiyo	**87**	14 41N	40 15 E
Tizga	**82**	32 1N	5 9W
Ti'zi N'Isli	**82**	32 28N	5 47W
Tizi-Ouzou	**83**	36 42N	4 3 E
Tizimín	**120**	21 0N	88 1W
Tiznit	**82**	29 48N	9 45W
Tjeggelvas	**50**	66 37N	17 45 E
Tjirebon = Cirebon	**73**	6 45 S	108 32 E
Tjöme	**47**	59 8N	10 26 E
Tjörn	**49**	58 0N	11 35 E
Tkibuli	**57**	42 26N	43 0 E
Tkvarcheli	**57**	42 47N	41 42 E
Tlahualilo	**120**	26 20N	103 30W
Tlaxcala	**120**	19 20N	98 14W
Tlaxcala □	**120**	19 30N	98 20W
Tlaxiaco	**120**	17 18N	97 40W
Tlell	**108**	53 34N	131 56W
Tlemcen	**82**	34 52N	1 21W
Tleta Sidi Bouguedra	**82**	32 16N	9 59W
Tlumach, U.S.S.R.	**54**	48 46N	25 0 E
Tlumach, U.S.S.R.	**56**	48 51N	25 0 E
Tłuszcz	**28**	52 25N	21 25 E
Tlyarata	**57**	42 9N	46 26 E
Tmassah	**83**	26 19N	15 51 E
Tnine d'Anglou	**82**	29 50N	9 50W
Toad →	**108**	59 25N	124 57W
Toala	**73**	1 30 S	121 40 E
Toamasina	**93**	18 10 S	49 25 E
Toamasina □	**93**	18 0 S	49 0 E
Toay	**124**	36 43 S	64 38W
Toba	**74**	34 30N	136 51 E
Toba, Danau	**72**	2 40N	98 50 E
Toba Kakar	**68**	31 30N	69 0 E
Toba Tek Singh	**68**	30 55N	72 25 E
Tobago	**121**	11 10N	60 30W
Tobarra	**33**	38 37N	1 44W
Tobelo	**73**	1 45N	127 56 E
Tobermorey	**98**	22 12 S	137 51 E
Tobermory, Can.	**106**	45 12N	81 40W
Tobermory, U.K.	**14**	56 37N	6 4W
Tobin L.	**109**	53 35N	103 30W
Toboali	**72**	3 0 S	106 25 E
Tobol	**58**	52 40N	62 39 E
Toboli	**73**	0 38 S	120 5 E
Tobolsk	**58**	58 15N	68 10 E
Tobruk = Tubruq	**81**	32 7N	23 55 E
Tobyhanna	**113**	41 10N	75 25W
Tocantinópolis	**127**	6 20 S	47 25W
Tocantins →	**127**	1 45 S	49 10W
Toccoa	**115**	34 32N	83 17W
Toce →	**38**	45 56N	8 29 E
Tochigi	**74**	36 25N	139 45 E
Tochigi □	**74**	36 45N	139 45 E
Tocina	**31**	37 37N	5 44W

Tocopilla 124 22 5 S 70 10W
Tocumwal 99 35 51 S 145 31 E
Tocuyo → 126 11 3N 68 23W
Todeli 73 1 38 S 124 34 E
Todenyang 90 4 35N 35 56 E
Todi 39 42 47N 12 24 E
Todos os Santos, Baía de 127 12 48 S 38 38W
Todos Santos 120 23 27N 110 13W
Todtnau 25 47 50N 7 56 E
Toecé 85 11 50N 1 16W
Tofield 108 53 25N 112 40W
Tofino 108 49 11N 125 55W
Töfsingdalens nationalpark 48 62 15N 12 44 E
Toftlund 49 55 11N 9 2 E
Tofua 101 19 45 S 175 05W
Togba 84 17 26N 10 12W
Togian, Kepulauan 73 0 20 S 121 50 E
Togliatti 55 53 32N 49 24 E
Togo ■ 85 6 15N 1 35 E
Togtoh 76 40 15N 111 10 E
Toinya 87 6 17N 29 46 E
Tojo 73 1 20 S 121 15 E
Tokaj 27 48 8N 21 27 E
Tōkamachi 74 37 8N 138 43 E
Tokanui 101 46 34 S 168 56 E
Tokar 81 18 27N 37 56 E
Tokara Kaikyō 74 30 0N 130 0 E
Tokarahi 101 44 56 S 170 39 E
Tokat 64 40 22N 36 35 E
Tokelau Is. ■ 94 9 0 S 171 45W
Tokmak 58 42 49N 75 15 E
Toko Ra. 98 23 5 S 138 20 E
Tokong 71 5 27N 100 23 E
Tokushima 74 34 4N 134 34 E
Tokushima □ 74 34 15N 134 0 E
Tokuyama 74 34 3N 131 50 E
Tōkyō 74 35 45N 139 45 E
Tōkyō □ 74 35 40N 139 30 E
Tolbukhin 43 43 37N 27 49 E
Toledo, Spain 30 39 50N 4 2W
Toledo, Ohio, U.S.A. 114 41 37N 83 33W
Toledo, Oreg., U.S.A. 118 44 40N 123 59W
Toledo, Wash., U.S.A. 118 46 29N 122 51W
Toledo, Montes de 31 39 33N 4 20W
Tolentino 39 43 12N 13 17 E
Tolga, Alg. 83 34 40N 5 22 E
Tolga, Norway 47 62 26N 11 1 E
Toliary 93 23 21 S 43 40 E
Toliary □ 93 21 0 S 45 0 E
Tolima, Vol. 126 4 40N 75 19W
Tolitoli 73 1 5N 120 50 E
Tolkmicko 28 54 19N 19 31 E
Tollarp 49 55 55N 13 58 E
Tolleson 119 33 29N 112 10W
Tolmachevo 54 58 56N 29 51 E
Tolmezzo 39 46 23N 13 0 E
Tolmin 39 46 11N 13 45 E
Tolna 27 46 25N 18 48 E
Tolna □ 27 46 30N 18 30 E
Tolo 88 2 55 S 18 34 E
Tolo, Teluk 73 2 20 S 122 10 E
Tolochin 54 54 25N 29 42 E
Tolosa 32 43 8N 2 5W
Tolox 31 36 41N 4 54W
Toluca 120 19 20N 99 40W
Tom Burke 93 23 5 S 28 4 E
Tom Price 96 22 40 S 117 48 E
Tomah 116 43 59N 90 30W
Tomahawk 116 45 28N 89 40W
Tomar 31 39 36N 8 25W
Tómaros Óros 44 39 29N 20 48 E
Tomaszów Mazowiecki 28 51 30N 19 57 E
Tombé 87 5 53N 31 40 E
Tombigbee → 115 31 4N 87 58W
Tombouctou 84 16 50N 3 0W
Tombstone 119 31 40N 110 4W
Tomé 124 36 36 S 72 57W
Tomelilla 49 55 33N 13 58 E
Tomelloso 33 39 10N 3 2W
Tomingley 99 32 6 S 148 16 E
Tomini 73 0 30N 120 30 E
Tomini, Teluk 73 0 10 S 122 0 E
Tominian 84 13 17N 4 35W
Tomiño 30 41 59N 8 46W
Tommot 59 59 4N 126 20 E
Tomnavoulin 14 57 19N 3 18W
Toms River 113 39 59N 74 12W
Tomsk 58 56 30N 85 5 E
Tomtabacken 49 57 30N 14 30 E
Tonalá 120 16 8N 93 41W
Tonale, Passo del 38 46 15N 10 34 E
Tonalea 119 36 17N 110 58W
Tonantins 126 2 45 S 67 45W
Tonasket 118 48 45N 119 30W
Tonawanda 114 43 0N 78 54W
Tonbridge 13 51 12N 0 18 E
Tondano 73 1 35N 124 54 E
Tondela 30 40 31N 8 5W
Tønder 49 54 58N 8 50 E
Tondi 70 9 45N 79 4 E
Tondi Kiwindi 85 14 28N 2 02 E
Tondibi 85 16 39N 0 14W
Tong Xian 76 39 55N 116 35 E
Tonga ■ 101 19 50 S 174 30W
Tonga Trench 94 18 0 S 175 0W
Tongaat 93 29 33 S 31 9 E
Tongaland 93 27 0 S 32 0 E
Tongareva 95 9 0 S 158 0W
Tongatapu 101 21 10 S 174 0W
Tongcheng 77 31 4N 116 56 E
Tongchuan 77 35 6N 109 3 E
Tongdao 77 26 10N 109 42 E
Tongeren 16 50 47N 5 28 E
Tongguan 77 34 40N 110 25 E
Tonghua 76 41 42N 125 58 E
Tongio 99 37 14 S 147 44 E
Tongjiang, Heilongjiang, China 75 47 40N 132 27 E
Tongjiang, Sichuan, China 77 31 58N 107 11 E
Tongking = Tonkin, G. of 71 20 0N 108 0 E
Tongliao 76 43 38N 122 18 E
Tongling 77 30 55N 117 48 E
Tonglu 77 29 45N 119 37 E
Tongnan 77 30 9N 105 50 E
Tongobory 93 23 32 S 44 20 E
Tongoy 124 30 16 S 71 31W
Tongren 75 27 43N 109 11 E
Tongres = Tongeren 16 50 47N 5 28 E
Tongue 14 58 29N 4 25W
Tongue → 116 46 24N 105 52W
Tongyu 76 44 45N 123 4 E
Tongzi 77 28 9N 106 49 E
Tonj 87 7 20N 28 44 E
Tonk 68 26 6N 75 54 E
Tonkawa 117 36 44N 97 22W
Tonkin = Bac-Phan 71 22 0N 105 0 E
Tonlé Sap 71 13 0N 104 0 E
Tonnay-Charente 20 45 56N 0 55W
Tonneins 20 44 23N 0 19 E
Tonnerre 19 47 51N 3 59 E
Tönning 24 54 18N 8 57 E
Tonopah 119 38 4N 117 12W
Tønsberg 47 59 19N 10 25 E
Tonstad 47 58 40N 6 45 E
Tonto Basin 119 33 56N 111 27W
Tooele 118 40 30N 112 20W
Toompine 99 27 15 S 144 19 E
Toonpan 98 19 28 S 146 48 E
Toora 99 38 39 S 146 23 E
Toora-Khem 59 52 28N 96 17 E
Toowoomba 97 27 32 S 151 56 E
Top-ozero 52 65 35N 32 0 E
Topalu 46 44 31N 28 3 E
Topeka 116 39 3N 95 40W
Topki 58 55 20N 85 35 E
Topl'a → 27 48 45N 21 45 E
Topley 108 54 49N 126 18W
Toplica → 42 43 15N 21 49 E
Toplița 46 46 55N 25 20 E
Topocalma, Pta. 124 34 10 S 72 2W
Topock 119 34 46N 114 29W
Topola 42 44 17N 20 41 E
Topolčani 42 41 14N 21 56 E
Topoľčany 27 48 35N 18 12 E
Topoli 57 47 59N 51 38 E
Topolnitsa → 43 42 11N 24 18 E
Topolobampo 120 25 40N 109 4W
Topolovgrad 43 42 5N 26 20 E
Topolvățu Mare 42 45 46N 21 41 E
Toppenish 118 46 27N 120 16W
Topusko 39 45 18N 15 59 E
Tor Bay 96 35 5 S 117 50 E
Torá 32 41 49N 1 25 E
Tora Kit 87 11 2N 32 36 E
Toraka Vestale 93 16 20 S 43 58 E
Torata 126 17 23 S 70 1W
Torbat-e Ḥeydārīyeh 65 35 15N 59 12 E
Torbat-e Jām 65 35 16N 60 35 E
Torbay, Can. 107 47 40N 52 42W
Torbay, U.K. 13 50 26N 3 31W
Tørdal 47 59 10N 8 45 E
Tordesillas 30 41 30N 5 0W
Tordoya 30 43 6N 8 36W
Töreboda 49 58 41N 14 7 E
Torey 59 50 33N 104 50 E
Torfajökull 50 63 54N 19 0W
Torgau 24 51 32N 13 0 E
Torgelow 24 53 40N 13 59 E
Torhout 16 51 5N 3 7 E
Tori 87 7 53N 33 35 E
Torigni-sur-Vire 18 49 3N 0 58W
Torija 32 40 44N 3 2W
Torin 120 27 33N 110 15W
Toriñana, C. 30 43 3N 9 17W
Torino 38 45 4N 7 40 E
Torit 87 4 27N 32 31 E
Torkovichi 54 58 51N 30 21 E
Tormac 42 45 30N 21 30 E
Tormentine 107 46 6N 63 46W
Tormes → 30 41 18N 6 29W
Tornado Mt. 108 49 55N 114 40W
Torne älv → 50 65 50N 24 12 E
Torneträsk. 50 68 24N 19 15 E
Tornio 50 65 50N 24 12 E
Tornionjoki → 50 65 50N 24 12 E
Tornquist 124 38 8 S 62 15W
Toro 30 41 35N 5 24W
Torö 49 58 48N 17 50 E
Toro, Cerro del 124 29 10 S 69 50W
Toro, Pta. 120 9 22N 79 57W
Törökszentmiklós 27 47 11N 20 27 E
Toroníïos Kólpos 44 40 5N 23 30 E
Toronto, Austral. 99 33 0 S 151 30 E
Toronto, Can. 106 43 39N 79 20W
Toronto, U.S.A. 114 40 27N 80 36W
Toronto, L. 120 27 40N 105 30W
Toropets 54 56 30N 31 40 E
Tororo 90 0 45N 34 12 E
Toros Dağlari 64 37 0N 35 0 E
Torpshammar 48 62 29N 16 20 E
Torquay, Can. 109 49 9N 103 30W
Torquay, U.K. 13 50 27N 3 31W
Torquemada 30 42 2N 4 19W
Torralba de Calatrava 31 39 1N 3 44W
Torrão 31 38 16N 8 11W
Torre Annunziata 41 40 45N 14 26 E
Tôrre de Moncorvo 30 41 12N 7 8W
Torre del Greco 41 40 47N 14 22 E
Torre del Mar 31 36 44N 4 6W
Torre-Pacheco 33 37 44N 0 57W
Torre Pellice 38 44 49N 7 13 E
Torreblanca 32 40 14N 0 12 E
Torrecampo 31 38 29N 4 41W
Torrecilla en Cameros 32 42 15N 2 38W
Torredembarra 32 41 9N 1 24 E
Torredonjimeno 31 37 46N 3 57W
Torrejoncillo 30 39 54N 6 28W
Torrelaguna 32 40 50N 3 38W
Torrelavega 30 43 20N 4 5W
Torremaggiore 41 41 42N 15 17 E
Torremolinos 31 36 38N 4 30W
Torrens Cr. → 98 22 23 S 145 9 E
Torrens Creek 98 20 48 S 145 3 E
Torrens, L. 97 31 0 S 137 50 E
Torrente 33 39 27N 0 28W
Torrenueva 33 38 38N 3 22W
Torréon 120 25 33N 103 25W
Torreperogil 33 38 2N 3 17W
Torres 120 28 46N 110 47W
Torres Novas 31 39 27N 8 33W
Torres Strait 97 9 50 S 142 20 E
Torres Vedras 31 39 5N 9 15W
Torrevieja 33 37 59N 0 42W
Torrey 119 38 18N 111 25W
Torridge → 13 50 51N 4 10W
Torridon, L. 14 57 35N 5 50W
Torrijos 30 39 59N 4 18W
Torrington, Conn., U.S.A. 114 41 50N 73 9W
Torrington, Wyo., U.S.A. 116 42 5N 104 8W
Torroella de Montgri 32 42 2N 3 8 E
Torrox 31 36 46N 3 57W
Torsås 49 56 24N 16 0 E
Torsby 48 60 7N 13 0 E
Torsö 49 58 48N 13 45 E
Tortola 121 18 19N 65 0W
Tórtoles de Esgueva 30 41 49N 4 2W
Tortona 38 44 53N 8 54 E
Tortoreto 39 42 50N 13 55 E
Tortorici 41 38 2N 14 48 E
Tortosa 32 40 49N 0 31 E
Tortosa, C. 32 40 41N 0 52 E
Tortosendo 30 40 15N 7 31W
Tortue, Î. de la 121 20 5N 72 57W
Tortuga, La 126 11 0N 65 22W
Ţorūd 65 35 25N 55 5 E
Toruń 28 53 0N 18 39 E
Toruń □ 28 53 20N 19 0 E
Torup, Denmark 49 57 5N 9 5 E
Torup, Sweden 49 56 57N 13 5 E
Tory I. 15 55 17N 8 12W
Torysa → 27 48 39N 21 21 E
Torzhok 54 57 5N 34 55 E
Tosa-Wan 74 33 15N 133 30 E
Toscana 38 43 30N 11 5 E
Toscano, Arcipelago 38 42 30N 10 30 E
Tosno 54 59 38N 30 46 E
Tossa 32 41 43N 2 56 E
Tostado 124 29 15 S 61 50W
Tostedt 24 53 17N 9 42 E
Tosya 64 41 1N 34 2 E
Toszek 28 50 27N 18 32 E
Totak 47 59 40N 7 45 E
Totana 33 37 45N 1 30W
Toten 47 60 37N 10 53 E
Toteng 92 20 22 S 22 58 E
Tôtes 18 49 41N 1 3 E
Tótkomlós 27 46 24N 20 45 E
Totma 55 60 0N 42 40 E
Totnes 13 50 26N 3 41W
Totonicapán 120 14 58N 91 12W
Totten Glacier 5 66 45 S 116 10 E
Tottenham, Austral. 99 32 14 S 147 21 E
Tottenham, Can. 112 44 1N 79 49W
Tottori 74 35 30N 134 15 E
Tottori □ 74 35 30N 134 12 E
Touat 82 27 27N 0 30 E
Touba 84 8 22N 7 40W
Toubkal, Djebel 82 31 0N 8 0W
Toucy 19 47 44N 3 15 E
Tougan 84 13 11N 2 58W
Touggourt 83 33 10N 6 0 E
Tougué 84 11 25N 11 50W
Toukmatine 83 24 49N 7 11 E
Toul 19 48 40N 5 53 E
Toulepleu 84 6 32N 8 24W
Toulon 21 43 10N 5 55 E
Toulouse 20 43 37N 1 27 E
Toummo 83 22 45N 14 8 E
Toummo Dhoba 83 22 30N 14 31 E
Toumodi 84 6 32N 5 4W
Tounassine, Hamada 82 28 48N 5 0W
Toungoo 67 19 0N 96 30 E
Touques → 18 49 22N 0 8 E
Touquet-Paris-Plage, Le 19 50 30N 1 36 E
Tour-du-Pin, La 21 45 33N 5 27 E
Touraine 18 47 20N 0 30 E
Tourcoing 19 50 42N 3 10 E
Tournai 16 50 35N 3 25 E
Tournan-en-Brie 19 48 44N 2 46 E
Tournay 20 43 13N 0 13 E
Tournon 21 45 4N 4 50 E
Tournon-St-Martin 18 46 45N 0 58 E
Tournus 21 46 35N 4 54 E
Tours 18 47 22N 0 40 E
Touside, Pic 83 21 1N 16 29 E
Touwsrivier 92 33 20 S 20 0 E
Tovarkovskiy 55 53 40N 38 14 E
Tovdal 47 58 47N 8 10 E
Tovdalselva → 47 58 15N 8 5 E
Towamba 99 37 6 S 149 43 E
Towanda 114 41 46N 76 30W
Towang 67 27 37N 91 50 E
Tower 116 47 49N 92 17W
Towerhill Cr. → 98 22 28 S 144 35 E
Towner 116 48 25N 100 26W
Townsend 118 46 25N 111 32W
Townshend, C. 97 22 18 S 150 30 E
Townshend I. 97 22 10 S 150 31 E
Townsville 97 19 15 S 146 45 E
Towson 114 39 26N 76 34W
Towyn 13 52 36N 4 5W
Toyah 117 31 20N 103 48W
Toyahvale 117 30 58N 103 45W
Toyama 74 36 40N 137 15 E
Toyama □ 74 36 45N 137 30 E
Toyama-Wan 74 37 0N 137 30 E
Toyohashi 74 34 45N 137 25 E
Toyokawa 74 34 48N 137 27 E
Toyonaka 74 34 50N 135 28 E
Toyooka 74 35 35N 134 48 E
Toyota 74 35 3N 137 7 E
Tozeur 83 33 56N 8 8 E
Trabancos → 30 41 36N 5 15W
Traben Trarbach 25 49 57N 7 7 E
Trabzon 64 41 0N 39 45 E
Tracadie 107 47 30N 64 55W
Tracy, Calif., U.S.A. 119 37 46N 121 27W
Tracy, Minn., U.S.A. 116 44 12N 95 38W
Tradate 38 45 43N 8 54 E
Trafalgar 100 38 14 S 146 12 E
Trafalgar, C. 31 36 10N 6 2W
Trăghân 83 26 0N 14 30 E
Traian 46 45 2N 28 15 E
Trail 108 49 5N 117 40W
Trainor L. 108 60 24N 120 17W
Tralee 15 52 16N 9 42W
Tralee B. 15 52 17N 9 55W
Tramore 15 52 10N 7 10W
Tran Ninh, Cao Nguyen 71 19 30N 103 10 E
Tranås 49 58 3N 14 59 E
Trancas 124 26 11 S 65 20W
Tranche, La 20 46 20N 1 26W
Tranche-sur-Mer, La 18 46 20N 1 27W
Trancoso 30 40 49N 7 21W
Tranebjerg 49 55 51N 10 36 E
Tranemo 49 57 30N 13 20 E
Trang 71 7 33N 99 38 E
Trangahy 93 19 7 S 44 31 E
Trangan 73 6 40 S 134 20 E
Trangie 99 32 4 S 148 0 E
Trångsviken 48 63 19N 14 0 E
Trani 41 41 17N 16 24 E
Tranoroa 93 24 42 S 45 4 E
Tranquebar 70 11 1N 79 54 E
Tranqueras 125 31 13 S 55 45W
Trans Nzoia □ 90 1 0N 35 0 E
Transcona 109 49 55N 97 0W
Transilvania 46 46 19N 25 0 E
Transkei □ 93 32 15 S 28 15 E
Transtrand 48 61 6N 13 20 E
Transvaal □ 92 25 0 S 29 0 E
Transylvania = Transilvania 46 46 19N 25 0 E
Transylvanian Alps 46 45 30N 25 0 E
Trápani 40 38 1N 12 30 E
Trapper Peak 118 45 56N 114 29W
Traralgon 97 38 12 S 146 34 E
Traryd 49 56 35N 13 45 E
Trarza □ 84 17 30N 15 0W
Trasacco 39 41 58N 13 30 E
Trăscău, Munţii 46 46 14N 23 14 E
Trasimeno, L. 39 43 10N 12 5 E
Trat 71 12 14N 102 33 E
Traun 26 48 14N 14 15 E
Traunsee 26 47 55N 13 50 E
Traunstein 25 47 52N 12 40 E
Tråvad 49 58 15N 13 5 E
Traveller's L. 99 33 20 S 142 0 E
Travemünde 24 53 58N 10 52 E
Travers, Mt. 101 42 1 S 172 45 E
Traverse City 114 44 45N 85 39W
Traverse Is. 5 57 0 S 28 0W
Travnik 42 44 17N 17 39 E
Trazo 30 43 0N 8 30W
Trbovlje 39 46 12N 15 5 E
Trébbia → 38 45 4N 9 41 E
Trebel → 24 53 55N 13 1 E
Třebíč 26 49 14N 15 55 E
Trebinje 42 42 44N 18 22 E
Trebisacce 41 39 52N 16 32 E
Trebišnica → 42 42 47N 18 8 E
Trebišov 27 48 38N 21 41 E
Trebižat → 42 43 15N 17 30 E
Trebnje 39 45 54N 15 1 E
Třeboň 26 48 59N 14 48 E
Trebujena 31 36 52N 6 11W
Trecate 38 45 26N 8 42 E
Tredegar 13 51 47N 3 16W
Tregaron 13 52 14N 3 56W
Trégastel-Plage 18 48 49N 3 31W
Tregnago 39 45 31N 11 10 E
Tréguier 18 48 47N 3 16W
Trégune 18 47 51N 3 51W
Treherne 109 49 38N 98 42W
Tréia 39 43 20N 13 20 E
Treignac 20 45 32N 1 48 E
Treinta y Tres 125 33 16 S 54 17W
Treis 25 50 9N 7 19 E
Treklyano 42 42 33N 22 36 E
Trekveld 92 30 35 S 19 45 E
Trelde Næs 49 55 38N 9 53 E
Trelew 128 43 10 S 65 20W
Trelissac 20 45 11N 0 47 E
Trelleborg 49 55 20N 13 10 E
Trélon 19 50 5N 4 6 E
Tremblade, La 20 45 46N 1 8W
Tremiti 39 42 8N 15 30 E
Tremonton 118 41 45N 112 10W
Tremp 32 42 10N 0 52 E
Trenary 114 46 12N 86 59W
Trenche → 106 47 46N 72 53W
Trenčín 27 48 52N 18 4 E
Trenggalek 73 8 5 S 111 38 E
Trenque Lauquen 124 36 5 S 62 45W
Trent → 12 53 33N 0 44W
Trentino-Alto Adige □ 38 46 30N 11 0 E
Trento 38 46 5N 11 8 E
Trenton, Can. 106 44 10N 77 34W
Trenton, Mo., U.S.A. 116 40 5N 93 37W
Trenton, N.J., U.S.A. 114 40 15N 74 41W
Trenton, Nebr., U.S.A. 116 40 14N 101 4W
Trenton, Tenn., U.S.A. 117 35 58N 88 57W
Trepassey 107 46 43N 53 25W
Tréport, Le 18 50 3N 1 20 E
Trepuzzi 41 40 26N 18 4 E
Tres Arroyos 124 38 26 S 60 20W
Três Corações 125 21 44 S 45 15W
Três Lagoas 127 20 50 S 51 43W
Tres Marías 120 21 25N 106 28W
Tres Montes, C. 128 46 50 S 75 30W
Três Pontas 125 21 23 S 45 29W
Tres Puentes 124 27 50 S 70 15W
Tres Puntas, C. 128 47 0 S 66 0W
Três Rios 125 22 6 S 43 15W
Treska → 42 42 0N 21 20 E
Treskavika Planina 42 43 40N 18 20 E
Trespaderne 32 42 47N 3 24W
Trets 21 43 27N 5 41 E
Treuchtlingen 25 48 58N 10 55 E
Treuenbrietzen 24 52 6N 12 51 E

Trevíglio 38 45 31N 9 35 E
Trevínca, Peña 30 42 15N 6 46W
Treviso 39 45 40N 12 15 E
Trévoux 21 45 57N 4 47 E
Treysa 24 50 55N 9 12 E
Trgovište 42 42 20N 22 10 E
Triabunna 99 42 30S 147 55 E
Triánda 45 36 25N 28 10 E
Triaucourt-en-Argonne 19 48 59N 5 2 E
Tribsees 24 54 4N 12 46 E
Tribulation, C. 97 16 5S 145 29 E
Tribune 116 38 30N 101 45W
Tricárico 41 40 37N 16 9 E
Tricase 41 39 56N 18 20 E
Trichinopoly = Tiruchchirappalli 70 10 45N 78 45 E
Trichur 70 10 30N 76 18 E
Trida 99 33 1S 145 1 E
Trier 25 49 45N 6 37 E
Trieste 39 45 39N 13 45 E
Trieste, G. di 39 45 37N 13 40 E
Trieux → 18 48 50N 3 3W
Triggiano 41 41 4N 16 58 E
Triglav 39 46 21N 13 50 E
Trigno → 39 42 4N 14 48 E
Trigueros 31 37 24N 6 50W
Tríkeri 45 39 6N 23 5 E
Trikhonis, Límni 45 38 34N 21 30 E
Tríkkala 44 39 34N 21 47 E
Tríkkala □ 44 39 41N 21 30 E
Trikora, Puncak 73 4 15S 138 45 E
Trilj 39 43 38N 16 42 E
Trillo 32 40 42N 2 35W
Trim 15 53 34N 6 48W
Trincomalee 70 8 38N 81 15 E
Trindade, I. 7 20 20S 29 50W
Trinidad, Boliv. 126 14 46S 64 50W
Trinidad, Colomb. 126 5 25N 71 40W
Trinidad, Cuba 121 21 48N 80 0W
Trinidad, Uruguay 124 33 30S 56 50W
Trinidad, U.S.A. 117 37 15N 104 30W
Trinidad, W. Indies 121 10 30N 61 15W
Trinidad & Tobago ■ 121 10 30N 61 20W
Trinidad → 120 17 49N 95 9W
Trinidad, I. 128 39 10S 62 0W
Trinitápoli 41 41 22N 16 5 E
Trinity, Can. 107 48 59N 53 55W
Trinity, U.S.A. 117 30 59N 95 25W
Trinity →, Calif., U.S.A. 118 41 11N 123 42W
Trinity →, Tex., U.S.A. 117 30 30N 95 0W
Trinity B., Austral. 97 16 30S 146 0 E
Trinity B., Can. 107 48 20N 53 10W
Trinity Mts. 118 40 20N 118 50W
Trinkitat 81 18 45N 37 51 E
Trino 38 45 10N 8 18 E
Trion 115 34 35N 85 18W
Trionto C. 41 39 38N 16 47 E
Triora 38 44 0N 7 46 E
Tripoli = Tarābulus, Leb. 64 34 31N 35 50 E
Tripoli = Tarābulus, Libya 83 32 58N 13 12 E
Trípolis 45 37 31N 22 25 E
Tripp 116 43 16N 97 58W
Tripura □ 67 24 0N 92 0 E
Trischen 24 54 3N 8 32 E
Tristan da Cunha 7 37 6S 12 20W
Trivandrum 70 8 41N 77 0 E
Trivento 41 41 48N 14 31 E
Trnava 27 48 23N 17 35 E
Trobriand Is. 98 8 30S 151 0 E
Trochu 108 51 50N 113 13W
Trodely I. 106 52 15N 79 26W
Troezen 45 37 25N 23 15 E
Trogir 39 43 32N 16 15 E
Troglav 39 43 56N 16 36 E
Trøgstad 47 59 37N 11 16 E
Tróia 41 41 22N 15 19 E
Troilus, L. 106 50 50N 74 35W
Troina 41 37 47N 14 34 E
Trois Fourches, Cap des 82 35 26N 2 58W
Trois-Pistoles 107 48 5N 69 10W
Trois-Riviéres 106 46 25N 72 34W
Troitsk 58 54 10N 61 35 E
Troitsko Pechorsk 52 62 40N 56 10 E
Trölladyngja 50 64 54N 17 16W
Trollhättan 49 58 17N 12 20 E
Trollheimen 47 62 46N 9 1 E
Troms fylke □ 50 68 56N 19 0 E
Tromsø 50 69 40N 18 56 E
Tronador 128 41 10S 71 50W
Trondheim 47 63 36N 10 25 E
Trondheimsfjorden 47 63 35N 10 30 E
Trönninge 49 56 37N 12 51 E
Trönö 48 61 22N 16 54 E
Tronto → 39 42 54N 13 55 E
Troon 14 55 33N 4 40W
Tropea 41 38 40N 15 53 E
Tropic 119 37 36N 112 4W
Tropoja 44 42 23N 20 10 E
Trossachs, The 14 56 14N 4 24W
Trostan 15 55 4N 6 10W
Trostberg 25 48 2N 12 33 E
Trostyanets 54 50 33N 34 59 E
Trotternish 14 57 32N 6 15W
Troup 117 32 10N 95 3W
Trout → 108 61 19N 119 51W
Trout L., N.W.T., Can. 108 60 40N 121 40W
Trout L., Ont., Can. 109 51 20N 93 15W
Trout Lake 106 46 10N 85 2W
Trout River 107 49 29N 58 8W
Trouville 18 49 21N 0 5 E
Trowbridge 13 51 18N 2 12W
Troy, Turkey 44 39 57N 26 12 E
Troy, Turkey 64 39 55N 26 20 E
Troy, Ala., U.S.A. 115 31 50N 85 58W
Troy, Idaho, U.S.A. 118 46 44N 116 46W
Troy, Kans., U.S.A. 116 39 47N 95 2W
Troy, Mo., U.S.A. 116 38 56N 90 59W
Troy, Montana, U.S.A. 118 48 30N 115 58W
Troy, N.Y., U.S.A. 114 42 45N 73 39W
Troy, Ohio, U.S.A. 114 40 0N 84 10W
Troyan 43 42 57N 24 43 E
Troyes 19 48 19N 4 3 E
Trpanj 42 43 1N 17 15 E
Trstena 27 49 21N 19 37 E
Trstenik 42 43 36N 21 0 E
Trubchevsk 54 52 33N 33 47 E
Trucial States = United Arab Emirates ■ 65 24 0N 54 30 E
Truckee 118 39 20N 120 11W
Trujillo, Hond. 121 16 0N 86 0W
Trujillo, Peru 126 8 6S 79 0W
Trujillo, Spain 31 39 28N 5 55W
Trujillo, U.S.A. 117 35 34N 104 44W
Trujillo, Venez. 126 9 22N 70 38W
Truk 94 7 25N 151 46 E
Trumann 117 35 42N 90 32W
Trumbull, Mt. 119 36 25N 113 8W
Trun 42 42 51N 22 38 E
Trun 18 48 50N 0 2 E
Trundle 99 32 53S 147 35 E
Trung-Phan 72 16 0N 108 0 E
Truro, Can. 107 45 21N 63 14W
Truro, U.K. 13 50 17N 5 2W
Trustrup 49 56 20N 10 46 E
Truth or Consequences 119 33 9N 107 16W
Trutnov 26 50 37N 15 54 E
Truyère → 20 44 38N 2 34 E
Tryavna 43 42 54N 25 25 E
Tryon 115 35 15N 82 16W
Tryonville 112 41 42N 79 48W
Trzcianka 28 53 3N 16 25 E
Trzciel 28 52 23N 15 50 E
Trzcińsko Zdrój 28 52 58N 14 35 E
Trzebiatów 28 54 3N 15 18 E
Trzebiez 28 53 38N 14 31 E
Trzebinia-Siersza 27 50 11N 19 18 E
Trzebnica 28 51 20N 17 1 E
Trzemeszno 28 52 33N 17 48 E
Tržič 39 46 22N 14 18 E
Tsageri 57 42 39N 42 46 E
Tsamandás 44 39 46N 20 21 E
Tsaratanana 93 16 47S 47 39 E
Tsaratanana, Mt. de 93 14 0S 49 0 E
Tsarevo = Michurin 43 42 9N 27 51 E
Tsarichanka 56 48 55N 34 30 E
Tsaritsáni 44 39 53N 22 14 E
Tsau 92 20 8S 22 22 E
Tsebrikovo 56 47 9N 30 10 E
Tselinograd 58 51 10N 71 30 E
Tsetserleg 75 47 36N 101 32 E
Tshabong 92 26 2S 22 29 E
Tshane 92 24 5S 21 54 E
Tshela 88 4 57S 13 4 E
Tshesebe 93 21 51S 27 32 E
Tshibeke 90 2 40S 28 35 E
Tshibinda 90 2 23S 28 43 E
Tshikapa 88 6 28S 20 48 E
Tshilenge 90 6 17S 23 48 E
Tshinsenda 91 12 20S 28 0 E
Tshofa 90 5 13S 25 16 E
Tshwane 92 22 24S 22 1 E
Tsigara 92 20 22S 25 54 E
Tsihombe 93 25 18S 45 29 E
Tsimlyansk 57 47 40N 42 6 E
Tsimlyanskoye Vdkhr. 57 48 0N 43 0 E
Tsinan = Jinan 76 36 38N 117 1 E
Tsineng 92 27 05S 23 05 E
Tsinga 44 41 23N 24 44 E
Tsinghai = Qinghai □ 75 36 0N 98 0 E
Tsingtao = Qingdao 76 36 5N 120 20 E
Tsinjomitondraka 93 15 40S 47 8 E
Tsiroanomandidy 93 18 46S 46 2 E
Tsivilsk 55 55 50N 47 25 E
Tsivory 93 24 4S 46 5 E
Tskhinali 53 42 22N 43 52 E
Tskhinvali 57 42 14N 44 1 E
Tsna → 55 54 55N 41 58 E
Tsodilo Hill 92 18 49S 21 43 E
Tsu 74 34 45N 136 25 E
Tsu L. 108 60 40N 111 52W
Tsuchiura 74 36 5N 140 15 E
Tsugaru-Kaikyō 74 41 35N 141 0 E
Tsumeb 92 19 9S 17 44 E
Tsumis 92 23 39S 17 29 E
Tsuruga 74 35 45N 136 2 E
Tsushima 74 34 20N 129 20 E
Tsvetkovo 56 49 8N 31 33 E
Tua → 30 41 13N 7 26W
Tual 73 5 38S 132 44 E
Tuam 15 53 30N 8 50W
Tuamotu Arch. 95 17 0S 144 0W
Tuamotu Ridge 95 20 0S 138 0W
Tuao 73 17 55N 122 22 E
Tuapse 57 44 5N 39 10 E
Tuatapere 101 46 8S 167 41 E
Tuba City 119 36 8N 111 18W
Tubac 119 31 37N 111 20W
Tuban 73 6 54S 112 3 E
Tubarão 125 28 30S 49 0W
Tūbās 62 32 20N 35 22 E
Tubau 72 3 10N 113 40 E
Tübingen 25 48 31N 9 4 E
Tubja, W. → 86 25 27N 38 45 E
Tubruq 81 32 7N 23 55 E
Tubuai Is. 95 25 0S 150 0W
Tucacas 126 10 48N 68 19W
Tuchodi → 108 58 17N 123 42W
Tuchola 28 53 33N 17 52 E
Tuchów 27 49 54N 21 1 E
Tucker's Town 121 32 17N 64 43W
Tucson 119 32 14N 110 59W
Tucumán □ 124 26 48S 66 2W
Tucumcari 117 35 12N 103 45W
Tucupita 126 9 2N 62 3W
Tucuruí 127 3 42S 49 44W
Tuczno 28 53 13N 16 10 E
Tudela 32 42 4N 1 39W
Tudela de Duero 30 41 37N 4 39W
Tudmur 64 34 36N 38 15 E
Tudor, Lac 107 55 50N 65 25W
Tudora 46 47 31N 26 45 E
Tuella → 30 41 30N 7 12W
Tufi 98 9 8S 149 19 E
Tuguegarao 73 17 35N 121 42 E
Tugur 59 53 44N 136 45 E
Tukangbesi, Kepulauan 73 6 0S 124 0 E
Tukarak I. 106 56 15N 78 45W
Tūkh 86 30 21N 31 12 E
Tukobo 84 5 1N 2 47W
Tūkrah 83 32 30N 20 37 E
Tuktoyaktuk 104 69 27N 133 2W
Tukums 54 57 2N 23 10 E
Tukuyu 91 9 17S 33 35 E
Tula, Hidalgo, Mexico 120 20 0N 99 20W
Tula, Tamaulipas, Mexico 120 23 0N 99 40W
Tula, Nigeria 85 9 51N 11 27 E
Tula, U.S.S.R. 55 54 13N 37 38 E
Tulak 65 33 55N 63 40 E
Tulancingo 120 20 5N 99 22W
Tulare 119 36 15N 119 26W
Tulare Lake 119 36 0N 119 53W
Tularosa 119 33 4N 106 1W
Tulbagh 92 33 16S 19 6 E
Tulcán 126 0 48N 77 43W
Tulcea 46 45 13N 28 46 E
Tulcea □ 46 45 0N 29 0 E
Tulchin 56 48 41N 28 49 E
Tulemalu L. 109 62 58N 99 25W
Tulgheş 46 46 58N 25 45 E
Tuli, Indon. 73 1 24S 122 26 E
Tuli, Zimb. 91 21 58S 29 13 E
Ţūlkarm 62 32 19N 35 2 E
Tulla 117 34 35N 101 44W
Tullahoma 115 35 23N 86 12W
Tullamore, Austral. 99 32 39S 147 36 E
Tullamore, Ireland 15 53 17N 7 30W
Tulle 20 45 16N 1 46 E
Tullibigeal 99 33 25S 146 44 E
Tullins 21 45 18N 5 29 E
Tulln 26 48 20N 16 4 E
Tullow 15 52 48N 6 45W
Tullus 87 11 7N 24 31 E
Tully 98 17 56S 145 55 E
Ţulmaythah 81 32 40N 20 55 E
Tulmur 98 22 40S 142 20 E
Tulnici 46 45 51N 26 38 E
Tulovo 43 42 33N 25 32 E
Tulsa 117 36 10N 96 0W
Tulsequah 108 58 39N 133 35W
Tulu Milki 87 9 55N 38 20 E
Tulu Welel 87 8 56N 34 47 E
Tulua 126 4 6N 76 11W
Tulun 59 54 32N 100 35 E
Tulungagung 72 8 5S 111 54 E
Tum 73 3 36S 130 21 E
Tuma 55 55 10N 40 30 E
Tuma → 121 13 6N 84 35W
Tumaco 126 1 50N 78 45W
Tumatumari 126 5 20N 58 55W
Tumba 48 59 12N 17 48 E
Tumba, L. 88 0 50S 18 0 E
Tumbarumba 99 35 44S 148 0 E
Tumbaya 124 23 50S 65 26W
Túmbes 126 3 37S 80 27W
Tumbwe 91 11 25S 27 15 E
Tumen 76 43 0N 129 50 E
Tumen Jiang → 76 42 20N 130 35 E
Tumeremo 126 7 18N 61 30W
Tumkur 70 13 18N 77 6 E
Tummel, L. 14 56 43N 3 55W
Tump 66 26 7N 62 16 E
Tumpat 71 6 11N 102 10 E
Tumsar 69 21 26N 79 45 E
Tumu 84 10 56N 1 56W
Tumucumaque, Serra 127 2 0N 55 0W
Tumut 97 35 16S 148 13 E
Tumwater 118 47 0N 122 58W
Tunas de Zaza 121 21 39N 79 34W
Tunbridge Wells 13 51 7N 0 16 E
Tuncurry 99 32 17S 152 29 E
Tunduru 91 11 8S 37 25 E
Tunduru □ 91 11 5S 37 22 E
Tundzha → 43 41 40N 26 35 E
Tune 47 59 16N 11 2 E
Tunga → 70 15 0N 75 50 E
Tunga Pass 67 29 0N 94 14 E
Tungabhadra → 70 15 57N 78 15 E
Tungabhadra Dam 70 15 0N 75 50 E
Tungaru 81 10 9N 30 52 E
Tungla 121 13 24N 84 21W
Tungnafellsjökull 50 64 45N 17 55W
Tungsten, Can. 108 61 57N 128 16W
Tungsten, U.S.A. 118 40 50N 118 10W
Tunguska, Nizhnyaya → 59 65 48N 88 4 E
Tunguska, Podkamennaya → 59 61 36N 90 18 E
Tuni 70 17 22N 82 36 E
Tunica 117 34 43N 90 23W
Tunis 83 36 50N 10 11 E
Tunis, Golfe de 83 37 0N 10 30 E
Tunisia ■ 83 33 30N 9 10 E
Tunja 126 5 33N 73 25W
Tunkhannock 113 41 32N 75 46W
Tunliu 76 36 13N 112 52 E
Tunnsjøen 50 64 45N 13 25 E
Tunungayualok I. 107 56 0N 61 0W
Tunuyán 124 33 35S 69 0W
Tunuyán → 124 33 33S 67 30W
Tunxi 75 29 42N 118 25 E
Tuolumne 119 37 59N 120 16W
Tuoy-Khaya 59 62 32N 111 25 E
Tupã 125 21 57S 50 28W
Tupelo 115 34 15N 88 42W
Tupik, U.S.S.R. 54 55 42N 33 22 E
Tupik, U.S.S.R. 59 54 26N 119 57 E
Tupinambaranas 126 3 0S 58 0W
Tupiza 124 21 30S 65 40W
Tupižnica 42 43 43N 22 10 E
Tupper 108 55 32N 120 1W
Tupper L. 114 44 18N 74 30W
Tupungato, Cerro 124 33 15S 69 50W
Tuquan 76 45 18N 121 38 E
Tuque, La 106 47 30N 72 50W
Túquerres 126 1 5N 77 37W
Tura, India 69 25 30N 90 16 E
Tura, U.S.S.R. 59 64 20N 100 17 E
Turaba, Wadi → 86 21 15N 41 32 E
Turabah 64 28 20N 43 15 E
Turaiyur 70 11 9N 78 38 E
Tūrān 65 35 39N 56 42 E
Turan 59 51 55N 95 0 E
Turayf 64 31 41N 38 39 E
Turbacz 27 49 30N 20 8 E
Turbe 42 44 15N 17 35 E
Turda 46 46 34N 23 47 E
Turégano 30 41 9N 4 1W
Turek 28 52 3N 18 30 E
Turfan = Turpan 75 43 58N 89 10 E
Turfan Depression = Turpan Hami 75 42 40N 89 25 E
Tŭrgovishte 43 43 17N 26 38 E
Turgutlu 64 38 30N 27 48 E
Turhal 56 40 24N 36 5 E
Turia → 33 39 27N 0 19W
Turiaçu 127 1 40S 45 19W
Turiaçu → 127 1 36S 45 19W
Turiec → 27 49 07N 18 55 E
Turin 108 49 47N 112 24W
Turin = Torino 38 45 3N 7 40 E
Turka 54 49 10N 23 2 E
Turkana □ 90 3 0N 35 30 E
Turkana, L. 90 3 30N 36 5 E
Turkestan 58 43 17N 68 16 E
Túrkeve 27 47 6N 20 44 E
Turkey ■ 64 39 0N 36 0 E
Turki 55 52 0N 43 15 E
Turkmen S.S.R. □ 58 39 0N 59 0 E
Turks Is. 121 21 20N 71 20W
Turks Island Passage 121 21 30N 71 30W
Turku 51 60 30N 22 19 E
Turkwe → 90 3 6N 36 6 E
Turlock 119 37 30N 120 55W
Turnagain → 108 59 12N 127 35W
Turnagain, C. 101 40 28S 176 38 E
Turneffe Is. 120 17 20N 87 50W
Turner 118 48 52N 108 25W
Turner Valley 108 50 40N 114 17W
Turners Falls 113 42 36N 72 34W
Turnhout 16 51 19N 4 57 E
Türnitz 26 47 55N 15 29 E
Turnor L. 109 56 35N 108 35W
Turnov 26 50 34N 15 10 E
Tŭrnovo 43 43 5N 25 41 E
Turnovo 43 43 5N 25 41 E
Turnu Măgurele 46 43 46N 24 56 E
Turnu Rosu Pasul 46 45 33N 24 17 E
Turnu-Severin 46 44 39N 22 41 E
Turobin 28 50 50N 22 44 E
Turon 117 37 48N 98 27W
Turpan 75 43 58N 89 10 E
Turpan Hami 75 42 40N 89 25 E
Turrës, Kalaja e 44 41 10N 19 28 E
Turriff 14 57 32N 2 28W
Tursha 55 56 55N 47 36 E
Tursi 41 40 15N 16 27 E
Turtle Hd. I. 98 10 56S 142 37 E
Turtle L., Can. 109 53 36N 108 38W
Turtle L., U.S.A. 116 45 22N 92 10W
Turtle Lake 116 47 30N 100 55W
Turtleford 109 53 23N 108 57W
Turukhansk 59 65 21N 88 5 E
Turun ja Porin lääni □ 51 60 27N 22 15 E
Turzovka 27 49 25N 18 35 E
Tuscaloosa 115 33 13N 87 31W
Tuscánia 39 42 25N 11 53 E
Tuscany = Toscana 38 43 28N 11 15 E
Tuscola, Ill., U.S.A. 114 39 48N 88 15W
Tuscola, Tex., U.S.A. 117 32 15N 99 48W
Tuscumbia 115 34 42N 87 42W
Tuskar Rock 15 52 12N 6 10W
Tuskegee 115 32 24N 85 39W
Tustna 47 63 10N 8 5 E
Tuszyn 28 51 36N 19 33 E
Tutayev 55 57 53N 39 32 E
Tuticorin 70 8 50N 78 12 E
Tutin 42 43 0N 20 20 E
Tutóia 127 2 45S 42 20W
Tutong 72 4 47N 114 40 E
Tutova → 46 46 20N 27 30 E
Tutrakan 43 44 2N 26 40 E
Tutshi L. 108 59 56N 134°30W
Tuttle 116 47 9N 100 00W
Tuttlingen 25 47 59N 8 50 E
Tutuala 73 8 25S 127 15 E
Tutuila 101 14 19S 170 50W
Tuva A.S.S.R. □ 59 51 30N 95 0 E
Tuvalu ■ 94 8 0S 178 0 E
Tuxpan 120 20 58N 97 23W
Tuxtla Gutiérrez 120 16 50N 93 10W
Tuy 30 42 3N 8 39W
Tuy Hoa 71 13 5N 109 10 E
Tuya L. 108 59 7N 130 35W
Tuyen Hoa 71 17 50N 106 10 E
Tuz Gölü 64 38 45N 33 30 E
Ţūz Khurmātū 64 34 56N 44 38 E
Tuzla 42 44 34N 18 41 E
Tuzlov → 57 47 28N 39 45 E
Tvååker 49 57 4N 12 25 E
Tvedestrand 47 58 38N 8 58 E
Tvŭrditsa 43 42 42N 25 53 E
Twardogóra 28 51 23N 17 28 E
Tweed 112 44 29N 77 19W
Tweed → 14 55 42N 2 10W
Tweedsmuir Prov. Park 108 53 0N 126 20W
Twentynine Palms 119 34 10N 116 4W
Twillingate 107 49 42N 54 45W
Twin Bridges 118 45 33N 112 23W
Twin Falls 118 42 30N 114 30W
Twin Valley 116 47 18N 96 15W
Twisp 118 48 21N 120 5W
Twistringen 24 52 48N 8 38 E
Two Harbors 116 47 1N 91 40W
Two Hills 108 53 43N 111 52W
Two Rivers 114 44 10N 87 31W
Twofold B. 97 37 8S 149 59 E
Tychy 27 50 9N 18 59 E
Tyczyn 27 49 58N 22 2 E
Tydal 47 63 4N 11 34 E
Tykocin 28 53 13N 22 46 E
Tyldal 47 62 8N 10 48 E

Tyler, Minn., U.S.A. **116** 44 18N 96 8W
Tyler, Tex., U.S.A. **117** 32 18N 95 18W
Týn nad Vltavou **26** 49 13N 14 26 E
Tynda **59** 55 10N 124 43 E
Tyne & Wear □ **12** 54 55N 1 35W
Tyne → **12** 54 58N 1 28W
Tynemouth **12** 55 1N 1 27W
Tynset **47** 62 17N 10 47 E
Tyre = Sūr **62** 33 12N 35 11 E
Tyrifjorden **47** 60 2N 10 8 E
Tyringe **49** 56 9N 13 35 E
Tyristrand **47** 60 5N 10 5 E
Tyrnyauz **57** 43 21N 42 45 E
Tyrol = Tirol **26** 47 3N 10 43 E
Tyrone **112** 40 39N 78 10W
Tyrrell → **100** 35 26 S 142 51 E
Tyrrell Arm **109** 62 27N 97 30W
Tyrrell, L. **99** 35 20 S 142 50 E
Tyrrell L. **109** 63 7N 105 27W
Tyrrhenian Sea **34** 40 0N 12 30 E
Tysfjorden **50** 68 7N 16 25 E
Tysnes **47** 60 1N 5 30 E
Tysnesøy **47** 60 0N 5 35 E
Tyssedal **47** 60 7N 6 35 E
Tystberga **49** 58 51N 17 15 E
Tyub Karagan, M. **57** 44 40N 50 19 E
Tyuleniy **57** 44 28N 47 30 E
Tyulgan **52** 52 22N 56 12 E
Tyumen **58** 57 11N 65 29 E
Tywi → **13** 51 48N 4 20W
Tzaneen **93** 23 47 S 30 9 E
Tzermíadhes Neápolis **46** 35 11N 25 29 E
Tzoumérka, Óros **44** 39 30N 21 26 E
Tzukong = Zigong **75** 29 15N 104 48 E

U

Uad Erni, O. → **82** 26 45N 10 47W
Uanda **98** 21 37 S 144 55 E
Uarsciek **63** 2 28N 45 55 E
Uasin □ **90** 0 30N 35 20 E
Uato-Udo **73** 9 7 S 125 36 E
Uatumã → **126** 2 26 S 57 37W
Uaupés **126** 0 8 S 67 5W
Ub **42** 44 28N 20 6 E
Ubá **125** 21 8 S 43 0W
Ubaitaba **127** 14 18 S 39 20W
Ubangi = Oubangi → **88** 1 0N 17 50 E
Ubauro **68** 28 15N 69 45 E
Ubaye → **21** 44 28N 6 18 E
Ube **74** 33 56N 131 15 E
Ubeda **33** 38 3N 3 23W
Uberaba **127** 19 50 S 47 55W
Uberlândia **127** 19 0 S 48 20W
Überlingen **25** 47 46N 9 10 E
Ubiaja **85** 6 41N 6 22 E
Ubombo **93** 27 31 S 32 4 E
Ubon Ratchathani **71** 15 15N 104 50 E
Ubondo **90** 0 55 S 25 42 E
Ubort → **54** 52 6N 28 30 E
Ubrique **31** 36 41N 5 27W
Ubundu **90** 0 22 S 25 30 E
Ucayali → **126** 4 30 S 73 30W
Uchi Lake **109** 51 5N 92 35W
Uchiura-Wan **74** 42 25N 140 40 E
Uchte **24** 52 29N 8 52 E
Uchur → **59** 58 48N 130 35 E
Ucluelet **108** 48 57N 125 32W
Ucuriş **46** 46 41N 21 58 E
Uda → **59** 54 42N 135 14 E
Udaipur **68** 24 36N 73 44 E
Udaipur Garhi **69** 27 0N 86 35 E
Udamalpet **70** 10 35N 77 15 E
Udbina **39** 44 31N 15 47 E
Uddeholm **48** 60 1N 13 38 E
Uddevalla **49** 58 21N 11 55 E
Uddjaur **50** 65 25N 21 15 E
Udgir **70** 18 25N 77 5 E
Udi **85** 6 23N 7 21 E
Údine **39** 46 5N 13 10 E
Udipi **70** 13 25N 74 42 E
Udmurt A.S.S.R. □ **52** 57 30N 52 30 E
Udon Thani **71** 17 29N 102 46 E
Udvoy Balkan **43** 42 50N 26 50 E
Udzungwa Range **91** 9 30 S 35 10 E
Ueckermünde **24** 53 45N 14 1 E
Ueda **74** 36 24N 138 16 E
Uedineniya, Os. **4** 78 0N 85 0 E
Uelen **59** 66 10N 170 0W
Uelzen **24** 53 0N 10 33 E
Uere → **88** 3 45N 24 45 E
Ufa **52** 54 45N 55 55 E
Ufa → **52** 54 40N 56 0 E
Uffenheim **25** 49 32N 10 15 E
Ugalla → **90** 5 8 S 30 42 E
Uganda ■ **90** 2 0N 32 0 E
Ugento **41** 39 55N 18 10 E
Ugep **85** 5 53N 8 2 E
Ugie **93** 31 10 S 28 13 E
Ugijar **33** 36 58N 3 7W
Ugine **21** 45 45N 6 25 E
Ugla **86** 25 40N 37 42 E
Uglegorsk **59** 49 5N 142 2 E
Uglich **55** 57 33N 38 20 E
Ugljane **39** 43 35N 16 46 E
Ugolyak **59** 64 33N 120 30 E
Ugra → **54** 54 30N 36 7 E
Ugŭrchin **43** 43 6N 24 26 E
Uh → **27** 48 7N 21 25 E
Uherske Hradiště **27** 49 4N 17 30 E
Uhersky Brod **27** 49 1N 17 40 E
Úhlava → **26** 49 45N 13 24 E
Uhrichsville **114** 40 23N 81 22W
Uíge **88** 7 30 S 14 40 E
Ŭiju **76** 40 15N 124 35 E
Uinta Mts. **118** 40 45N 110 30W
Uitenhage **92** 33 40 S 25 28 E
Uithuizen **16** 53 24N 6 41 E
Újfehértó **27** 47 49N 21 41 E
Ujhani **68** 28 0N 79 6 E
Ujjain **68** 23 9N 75 43 E
Újpest **27** 47 32N 19 6 E
Újszász **27** 47 19N 20 7 E
Ujung Pandang **73** 5 10 S 119 20 E
Uka **59** 57 50N 162 0 E
Ukara I. **90** 1 50 S 33 0 E
Ukerewe □ **90** 2 0 S 32 30 E
Ukerewe I. **90** 2 0 S 33 0 E
Ukholovo **55** 53 47N 40 30 E
Ukhrul **67** 25 10N 94 25 E
Ukhta **52** 63 55N 54 0 E
Ukiah **118** 39 10N 123 9W
Ukmerge **54** 55 15N 24 45 E
Ukrainian S.S.R. □ **56** 49 0N 32 0 E
Ukwi **92** 23 29 S 20 30 E
Ulaanbaatar **75** 47 54N 106 52 E
Ulaangom **75** 50 0N 92 10 E
Ulamba **91** 9 3 S 23 38 E
Ulan Bator = Ulaanbaatar **75** 47 54N 106 52 E
Ulan Ude **59** 51 45N 107 40 E
Ulanga □ **91** 8 40 S 36 50 E
Ulanów **28** 50 30N 22 16 E
Ulaya, Morogoro, Tanz. **90** 7 3 S 36 55 E
Ulaya, Tabora, Tanz. **90** 4 25 S 33 30 E
Ulcinj **42** 41 58N 19 10 E
Ulco **92** 28 21 S 24 15 E
Ulefoss **47** 59 17N 9 16 E
Ulëza **44** 41 46N 19 57 E
Ulfborg **49** 56 16N 8 20 E
Ulhasnagar **70** 19 15N 73 10 E
Uljma **42** 45 2N 21 10 E
Ulla → **30** 42 39N [illegible] 44W
Ulladulla **99** 35 21 S 150 29 E
Ullånger **48** 62 58N 18 10 E
Ullapool **14** 57 54N 5 10W
Ullared **49** 57 8N 12 42 E
Ulldecona **32** 40 36N 0 20 E
Ullswater **12** 54 35N 2 52W
Ullung-do **76** 37 30N 130 30 E
Ulm **25** 48 23N 10 0 E
Ulmarra **99** 29 37 S 153 4 E
Ulmeni **46** 45 4N 26 40 E
Ulricehamn **49** 57 46N 13 26 E
Ulsberg **47** 62 45N 9 59 E
Ulsteinvik **47** 62 21N 5 53 E
Ulster □ **15** 54 35N 6 30W
Ulstrem **43** 42 1N 26 27 E
Ulubaria **69** 22 31N 88 4 E
Uluguru Mts. **90** 7 15 S 37 40 E
Ulungur He **75** 47 1N 87 24 E
Ulutau **58** 48 39N 67 1 E
Ulverston **12** 54 13N 3 7W
Ulverstone **97** 41 11 S 146 11 E
Ulvik **47** 60 35N 6 54 E
Ulya **59** 59 10N 142 0 E
Ulyanovsk **55** 54 20N 48 25 E
Ulyasutay (Javhlant) **75** 47 56N 97 28 E
Ulysses **117** 37 39N 101 25W
Umag **39** 45 26N 13 31 E
Umala **126** 17 25 S 68 5W
Uman **56** 48 40N 30 12 E
Umarkhed **70** 19 37N 77 46 E
Umatilla **118** 45 58N 119 17W
Umba **52** 66 50N 34 20 E
Umbertide **39** 43 18N 12 20 E
Umboi I. **98** 5 40 S 148 0 E
Umbrella Mts. **101** 45 35 S 169 5 E
Umbria □ **39** 42 53N 12 30 E
Ume älv → **50** 63 45N 20 20 E
Umeå **50** 63 45N 20 20 E
Umera **73** 0 12 S 129 37 E
Umfuli → **91** 17 30 S 29 23 E
Umgusa **91** 19 29 S 27 52 E
Umka **42** 44 40N 20 19 E
Umkomaas **93** 30 13 S 30 48 E
Umm al Arānib **83** 26 10N 14 43 E
Umm al Qaywayn **65** 25 30N 55 35 E
Umm Arda **87** 15 17N 32 31 E
Umm az Zamul **65** 22 42N 55 18 E
Umm Bel **87** 13 35N 28 0 E
Umm Dubban **87** 15 23N 32 52 E
Umm el Fahm **62** 32 31N 35 9 E
Umm Koweika **87** 13 10N 32 16 E
Umm Lajj **64** 25 0N 37 23 E
Umm Merwa **86** 18 4N 32 30 E
Umm Qays **62** 32 40N 35 41 E
Umm Rumah **86** 25 50N 36 30 E
Umm Ruwaba **87** 12 50N 31 20 E
Umm Sidr **87** 14 29N 25 10 E
Ummanz **24** 54 29N 13 9 E
Umnak **104** 53 20N 168 20W
Umniati → **91** 16 49 S 28 45 E
Umpang **71** 16 3N 98 54 E
Umpqua → **118** 43 42N 124 3W
Umrer **68** 20 51N 79 18 E
Umreth **68** 22 41N 73 4 E
Umshandige Dam **91** 20 10 S 30 40 E
Umtali **91** 18 58 S 32 38 E
Umtata **93** 31 36 S 28 49 E
Umuahia **85** 5 33N 7 29 E
Umvukwe Ra. **91** 16 45 S 30 45 E
Umvukwes **91** 17 0 S 30 57 E
Umvuma **91** 19 16 S 30 30 E
Umzimvubu **93** 31 38 S 29 33 E
Umzingwane → **91** 22 12 S 29 56 E
Umzinto **93** 30 15 S 30 45 E
Una **68** 20 46N 71 8 E
Una → **39** 45 16N 16 55 E
Unac → **39** 44 30N 16 9 E
Unadilla **113** 42 20N 75 17W
Unalaska **104** 53 40N 166 40W
Uncastillo **32** 42 21N 1 8W
Uncía **126** 18 25 S 66 40W
Uncompahgre Pk. **119** 38 5N 107 32W
Unden **49** 58 45N 14 25 E
Underbool **99** 35 10 S 141 51 E
Undersaker **48** 63 19N 13 21 E
Undersvik **48** 61 36N 16 20 E
Undredal **47** 60 57N 7 6 E
Unecha **54** 52 50N 32 37 E
Ungarie **99** 33 38 S 146 56 E
Ungava B. **105** 59 30N 67 30W
Ungeny **56** 47 11N 27 51 E
Unggi **76** 42 16N 130 28 E
Ungwatiri **87** 16 52N 36 10 E
Uni **55** 56 44N 51 47 E
União da Vitória **125** 26 13 S 51 5W
Uniejów **28** 51 59N 18 46 E
Unije **39** 44 40N 14 15 E
Unimak **104** 55 0N 164 0W
Unimak Pass. **104** 53 30N 165 15W
Union, Miss, U.S.A. **117** 32 34N 89 14W
Union, Mo., U.S.A. **116** 38 25N 91 0W
Union, S.C., U.S.A. **115** 34 43N 81 39W
Union City, N.J., U.S.A. **113** 40 47N 74 5W
Union City, Ohio, U.S.A. **114** 40 11N 84 49W
Union City, Pa., U.S.A. **114** 41 53N 79 50W
Union City, Tenn., U.S.A. **117** 36 25N 89 0W
Union Gap **118** 46 38N 120 29W
Unión, La, Chile **128** 40 10 S 73 0W
Unión, La, El Sal. **120** 13 20N 87 50W
Unión, La, Spain **33** 37 38N 0 53W
Union, Mt. **119** 34 34N 112 21W
Union of Soviet Socialist Republics ■ **59** 60 0N 100 0 E
Union Springs **115** 32 9N 85 44W
Uniondale **92** 33 39 S 23 7 E
Uniontown **114** 39 54N 79 45W
Unionville **116** 40 29N 93 1W
Unirea **46** 44 15N 27 35 E
United Arab Emirates ■ **65** 23 50N 54 0 E
United Kingdom ■ **11** 55 0N 3 0W
United States of America ■ **111** 37 0N 96 0W
United States Trust Terr. of the Pacific Is. **94** 10 0N 160 0 E
Unity **109** 52 30N 109 5W
Universales, Mtes. **32** 40 18N 1 33W
Unjha **68** 23 46N 72 24 E
Unnao **69** 26 35N 80 30 E
Uno, Ilha **84** 11 15N 16 13W
Unst **14** 60 50N 0 55W
Unstrut → **24** 51 10N 11 48 E
Unuk → **108** 56 5N 131 3W
Ünye **56** 41 5N 37 15 E
Unzha **55** 58 0N 44 0 E
Unzha → **55** 57 30N 43 40 E
Upa → **27** 50 35N 16 15 E
Upata **126** 8 1N 62 24W
Upemba, L. **91** 8 30 S 26 20 E
Upernavik **4** 72 49N 56 20W
Upington **92** 28 25 S 21 15 E
Upleta **68** 21 46N 70 16 E
Upolu **101** 13 58 S 172 0W
Upper Alkali Lake **118** 41 47N 120 8W
Upper Arrow L. **108** 50 30N 117 50W
Upper Austria = Oberösterreich **26** 48 10N 14 0 E
Upper Foster L. **109** 56 47N 105 20W
Upper Hutt **101** 41 8 S 175 5 E
Upper Klamath L. **118** 42 16N 121 55W
Upper L. Erne **15** 54 14N 7 22W
Upper Lake **118** 39 10N 122 55W
Upper Musquodoboit **107** 45 10N 62 58W
Upper Red L. **116** 48 0N 95 0W
Upper Sandusky **114** 40 50N 83 17W
Upper Taimyr → **59** 74 15N 99 48 E
Upper Volta ■ **84** 12 0N 1 0W
Upphärad **49** 58 9N 12 19 E
Uppsala **48** 59 53N 17 38 E
Uppsala län □ **48** 60 0N 17 30 E
Upstart, C. **98** 19 41 S 147 45 E
Upton **116** 44 8N 104 35W
Ur **64** 30 55N 46 25 E
Uracara **126** 2 20 S 57 50W
Urach **25** 48 29N 9 25 E
Urad Qianqi **76** 40 40N 108 30 E
Ural → **58** 47 0N 51 48 E
Ural, Mt. **99** 33 21 S 146 12 E
Ural Mts. = Uralskie Gory **52** 60 0N 59 0 E
Uralla **99** 30 37 S 151 29 E
Uralsk **52** 51 20N 51 20 E
Uralskie Gory **52** 60 0N 59 0 E
Urambo **90** 5 4 S 32 0 E
Urambo □ **90** 5 0 S 32 0 E
Urana **100** 35 15 S 146 21 E
Urandangie **97** 21 32 S 138 14 E
Uranium City **109** 59 34N 108 37W
Uravakonda **70** 14 57N 77 12 E
Urawa **74** 35 50N 139 40 E
Uray **58** 60 5N 65 15 E
Urbana, Ill., U.S.A. **114** 40 7N 88 12W
Urbana, Ohio, U.S.A. **114** 40 9N 83 44W
Urbana, La **126** 7 8N 66 56W
Urbánia **39** 43 40N 12 31 E
Urbel → **32** 42 21N 3 40W
Urbino **39** 43 43N 12 38 E
Urbión, Picos de **32** 42 1N 2 52W
Urcos **126** 13 40 S 71 38W
Urda, Spain **31** 39 25N 3 43W
Urda, U.S.S.R. **57** 48 52N 47 23 E
Urdinarrain **124** 32 37 S 58 52W
Urdos **20** 42 51N 0 35W
Urdzhar **58** 47 5N 81 38 E
Ure → **12** 54 20N 1 25W
Uren **55** 57 35N 45 55 E
Urengoy **58** 65 58N 28 25 E
Ures **120** 29 30N 110 30W
Urfa **64** 37 12N 38 50 E
Urfahr **26** 48 19N 14 17 E
Urgench **58** 41 40N 60 41 E
Uri □ **25** 46 43N 8 35 E
Uribia **126** 11 43N 72 16W
Urim **62** 31 18N 34 32 E
Uriondo **124** 21 41 S 64 41W
Urique → **120** 26 29N 107 58W
Urk **16** 52 39N 5 36 E
Urla **64** 38 20N 26 47 E
Urlati **46** 44 59N 26 15 E
Urmia = Rezā'īyeh **64** 37 40N 45 0 E
Urmia, L. = Rezā'īyeh, Daryācheh-ye **64** 37 30N 45 30 E
Uroševac **42** 42 23N 21 10 E
Urshult **49** 56 31N 14 50 E
Ursus **28** 52 12N 20 53 E
Uruana **127** 15 30 S 49 41W
Uruapan **120** 19 30N 102 0W
Urubamba **126** 13 20 S 72 10W
Urubamba → **126** 10 43 S 73 48W
Uruçuí **127** 7 20 S 44 28W
Uruguai → **125** 26 0 S 53 30W
Uruguaiana **124** 29 50 S 57 0W
Uruguay ■ **124** 32 30 S 56 30W
Uruguay → **124** 34 12 S 58 18W
Urumchi = Ürümqi **75** 43 45N 87 45 E
Ürümqi **75** 43 45N 87 45 E
Urup → **57** 46 0N 41 10 E
Urup, Os. **59** 46 0N 151 0 E
Uryung-Khaya **59** 72 48N 113 23 E
Uryupinsk **55** 50 45N 41 58 E
Urzhum **55** 57 10N 49 56 E
Urziceni **46** 44 40N 26 42 E
Usa → **52** 65 67N 56 55 E
Uşak **64** 38 43N 29 28 E
Usakos **92** 22 0 S 15 31 E
Ušće **42** 43 30N 20 39 E
Usedom **24** 53 50N 13 55 E
Usfan **86** 21 58N 39 27 E
Ush-Tobe **58** 45 16N 78 0 E
Ushakova, O. **4** 82 0N 80 0 E
Ushant = Ouessant, Île d' **18** 48 25N 5 5W
Ushashi **90** 1 59 S 33 57 E
Ushat **87** 7 59N 29 28 E
Ushuaia **128** 54 50 S 68 23W
Ushumun **59** 52 47N 126 32 E
Usk → **13** 51 37N 2 56W
Uskedal **47** 59 56N 5 53 E
Üsküdar **64** 41 0N 29 5 E
Uslar **24** 51 39N 9 39 E
Usman **55** 52 5N 39 48 E
Usoke **90** 5 7 S 32 19 E
Usolye Sibirskoye **59** 52 48N 103 40 E
Usoro **85** 5 33N 6 11 E
Uspallata, P. de **124** 32 37 S 69 22W
Uspenskiy **58** 48 41N 72 43 E
Ussel **20** 45 32N 2 18 E
Ussuriysk **59** 43 48N 131 59 E
Ust-Aldan = Batamay **59** 63 30N 129 15 E
Ust Amginskoye = Khandyga **59** 62 42N 135 0 E
Ust-Bolsheretsk **59** 52 50N 156 15 E
Ust Buzulukskaya **55** 50 8N 42 11 E
Ust chaun **59** 68 47N 170 30 E
Ust-Donetskiy **57** 47 35N 40 55 E
Ust'-Ilga **59** 55 5N 104 55 E
Ust Ilimpeya = Yukti **59** 63 20N 105 0 E
Ust-Ilimsk **59** 58 3N 102 39 E
Ust Ishim **58** 57 45N 71 10 E
Ust-Kamchatsk **59** 56 10N 162 28 E
Ust-Kamenogorsk **58** 50 0N 82 36 E
Ust-Karenga **59** 54 25N 116 30 E
Ust Khayryuzova **59** 57 15N 156 45 E
Ust-Kut **59** 56 50N 105 42 E
Ust Kuyga **59** 70 1N 135 43 E
Ust-Labinsk **57** 45 15N 39 41 E
Ust Luga **54** 59 35N 28 20 E
Ust Maya **59** 60 30N 134 28 E
Ust-Mil **59** 59 40N 133 11 E
Ust-Nera **59** 64 35N 143 15 E
Ust-Nyukzha **59** 56 34N 121 37 E
Ust Olenek **59** 73 0N 119 48 E
Ust-Omchug **59** 61 9N 149 38 E
Ust Port **58** 69 40N 84 26 E
Ust Tsilma **52** 65 25N 52 0 E
Ust-Tungir **59** 55 25N 120 36 E
Ust Urt = Ustyurt, Plato **58** 44 0N 55 0 E
Ust Usa **52** 66 0N 56 30 E
Ust Vorkuta **58** 67 24N 64 0 E
Ustaoset **47** 60 30N 8 2 E
Ustaritz **20** 43 24N 1 27W
Uste **55** 59 35N 39 40 E
Ústí nad Labem **26** 50 41N 14 3 E
Ústí nad Orlicí **27** 49 58N 16 24 E
Ustica **40** 38 42N 13 10 E
Ustka **28** 54 35N 16 55 E
Ustroń **27** 49 43N 18 48 E
Ustrzyki Dolne **27** 49 27N 22 40 E
Ustye **59** 57 46N 94 37 E
Ustyurt, Plato **58** 44 0N 55 0 E
Ustyuzhna **55** 58 50N 36 32 E
Usu **75** 44 27N 84 40 E
Usuki **74** 33 8N 131 49 E
Usulután **120** 13 25N 88 28W
Usumacinta → **120** 17 0N 91 0W
Usure **90** 4 40 S 34 22 E
Uta **73** 4 33 S 136 0 E
Utah □ **118** 39 30N 111 30W
Utah, L. **118** 40 10N 111 58W
Ute Cr. **117** 35 21N 103 45W
Utena **54** 55 27N 25 40 E
Ütersen **24** 53 40N 9 40 E
Utete **90** 8 0 S 38 45 E
Uthai Thani **71** 15 22N 100 3 E
Utiariti **126** 13 0 S 58 10W
Utica, N.Y., U.S.A. **114** 43 5N 75 18W
Utica, Ohio, U.S.A. **112** 40 13N 82 26W
Utiel **32** 39 37N 1 11W
Utik L. **109** 55 15N 96 0W
Utikuma L. **108** 55 50N 115 30W
Utrecht, Neth. **16** 52 5N 5 8 E
Utrecht, S. Afr. **93** 27 38 S 30 20 E
Utrecht □ **16** 52 6N 5 7 E
Utrera **31** 37 12N 5 48W
Utsjoki **50** 69 51N 26 59 E
Utsunomiya **74** 36 30N 139 50 E
Uttar Pradesh □ **69** 27 0N 80 0 E
Uttaradit **71** 17 36N 100 5 E
Uttoxeter **12** 52 53N 1 50W
Ützе **24** 52 28N 10 11 E
Uusikaarlepyy **50** 63 32N 22 31 E
Uusikaupunki **51** 60 47N 21 25 E
Uva **52** 56 59N 52 13 E
Uvac → **42** 43 35N 19 40 E
Uvalde **117** 29 15N 99 48W
Uvarovo **55** 51 59N 42 14 E
Uvat **58** 59 5N 68 50 E
Uvinza **90** 5 5 S 30 24 E
Uvira **90** 3 22 S 29 3 E

Uvs Nuur **75** 50 20N 92 30 E
Uwajima **74** 33 10N 132 35 E
Uweinat, Jebel **86** 21 54N 24 58 E
Uxbridge **112** 44 6N 79 7W
Uxin Qi **76** 38 50N 109 5 E
Uxmal **120** 20 22N 89 46W
Uyandi **59** 69 19N 141 0 E
Uyo **85** 5 1N 7 53 E
Uyuni **126** 20 28 S 66 47W
Uzbek S.S.R. □ **58** 41 30N 65 0 E
Uzen **53** 43 27N 53 10 E
Uzen, Bol. ⤳ **55** 50 0N 49 30 E
Uzen, Mal. ⤳ **55** 50 0N 48 30 E
Uzerche **20** 45 25N 1 34 E
Uzès **21** 44 1N 4 26 E
Uzh ⤳ **54** 51 15N 30 12 E
Uzhgorod **54** 48 36N 22 18 E
Uzlovaya **55** 54 0N 38 5 E
Uzunköprü **43** 41 16N 26 43 E

V

Vaal ⤳ **92** 29 4 S 23 38 E
Vaaldam **93** 27 0 S 28 14 E
Vaalwater **93** 24 15 S 28 8 E
Vaasa **50** 63 6N 21 38 E
Vaasan lääni □ **50** 63 2N 22 50 E
Vabre **20** 43 42N 2 24 E
Vác **27** 47 49N 19 10 E
Vacaria **125** 28 31 S 50 52W
Vacaville **118** 38 21N 122 0W
Vaccarès, Étang de **21** 43 32N 4 34 E
Vach ⤳ **58** 60 45N 76 45 E
Vache, Î.-à- **121** 18 2N 73 35W
Väddö **48** 59 55N 18 50 E
Vadnagar **68** 23 47N 72 40 E
Vado Lígure **38** 44 16N 8 26 E
Vadodara **68** 22 20N 73 10 E
Vadsø **50** 70 3N 29 50 E
Vadstena **49** 58 28N 14 54 E
Vaduz **25** 47 8N 9 31 E
Værøy **50** 67 40N 12 40 E
Vagney **19** 48 1N 6 43 E
Vagnhärad **48** 58 57N 17 33 E
Vagos **30** 40 33N 8 42W
Váh ⤳ **27** 47 55N 18 0 E
Vahsel B. **5** 75 0 S 35 0W
Vaigach **58** 70 10N 59 0 E
Vaigai ⤳ **70** 9 15N 79 10 E
Vaiges **18** 48 2N 0 30W
Vaihingen **25** 48 55N 8 58 E
Vaijapur **70** 19 58N 74 45 E
Vaikam **70** 9 45N 76 25 E
Vailly Aisne **19** 49 25N 3 30 E
Vaippar ⤳ **70** 9 0N 78 25 E
Vaison **21** 44 14N 5 4 E
Vajpur **68** 21 24N 73 17 E
Vakarel **43** 42 35N 23 40 E
Vaksdal **47** 60 29N 5 45 E
Vál **27** 47 22N 18 40 E
Val-d'Ajol, Le **19** 47 55N 6 30 E
Val-de-Marne □ **19** 48 45N 2 28 E
Val-d'Oise □ **19** 49 5N 2 10 E
Val d'Or **106** 48 7N 77 47W
Val Marie **109** 49 15N 107 45W
Valadares **30** 41 5N 8 38W
Valahia **46** 44 35N 25 0 E
Valais □ **25** 46 12N 7 45 E
Valandovo **42** 41 19N 22 34 E
Valašské Meziříčí **27** 49 29N 17 59 E
Valáxa **45** 38 50N 24 29 E
Vălcani **42** 46 0N 20 26 E
Valcheta **128** 40 40 S 66 8W
Valdagno **39** 45 38N 11 18 E
Valdahon, Le **19** 47 8N 6 20 E
Valday **54** 57 58N 33 9 E
Valdayskaya Vozvyshennost **54** 57 0N 33 30 E
Valdeazogues ⤳ **31** 38 45N 4 55W
Valdemarsvik **49** 58 14N 16 40 E
Valdepeñas, Ciudad Real, Spain **31** 38 43N 3 25W
Valdepeñas, Jaén, Spain **31** 37 33N 3 47W
Valderaduey ⤳ **30** 41 31N 5 42W
Valderrobres **32** 40 53N 0 9 E
Valdés, Pen. **128** 42 30 S 63 45W
Valdez **104** 61 14N 76 17W
Valdivia **128** 39 50 S 73 14W
Valdobbiádene **39** 45 53N 12 0 E
Valdosta **115** 30 50N 83 20W
Valdoviño **30** 43 36N 8 8W
Valdres **47** 60 55N 9 28 E
Vale, U.S.A. **118** 44 0N 117 15W
Vale, U.S.S.R. **57** 41 30N 42 58 E
Valea lui Mihai **46** 47 32N 22 11 E
Valença, Brazil **127** 13 20 S 39 5W
Valença, Port. **30** 42 1N 8 34W
Valença do Piauí **127** 6 20 S 41 45W
Valençay **19** 47 9N 1 34 E
Valence **21** 44 57N 4 54 E
Valence-d'Agen **20** 44 8N 0 54 E
Valencia, Spain **33** 39 27N 0 23W
Valencia, Venez. **126** 10 11N 68 0W
Valencia □ **33** 39 20N 0 40W
Valencia, Albufera de **33** 39 20N 0 27W
Valencia de Alcántara **31** 39 25N 7 14W
Valencia de Don Juan **30** 42 17N 5 31W
Valencia del Ventoso **31** 38 15N 6 29W
Valencia, G. de **33** 39 30N 0 20 E
Valenciennes **19** 50 20N 3 34 E
Văleni **46** 44 15N 24 45 E
Valensole **21** 43 50N 5 59 E
Valentia Hr. **15** 51 56N 10 17W
Valentia I. **15** 51 54N 10 22W
Valentim, Sa. do **127** 6 0 S 43 30W
Valentine, Nebr., U.S.A. **116** 42 50N 100 35W
Valentine, Tex., U.S.A. **117** 30 36N 104 28W
Valenza **38** 45 2N 8 39 E
Våler **47** 60 41N 11 50 E
Valera **126** 9 19N 70 37W
Valga **54** 57 44N 26 0 E
Valguarnera Caropepe **41** 37 30N 14 22 E
Valier **118** 48 25N 112 9W
Valinco, G. de **21** 41 40N 8 52 E
Valjevo **42** 44 18N 19 53 E
Valkenswaard **16** 51 21N 5 29 E
Vall de Uxó **32** 39 49N 0 15W
Valla **48** 59 2N 16 20 E
Valladolid, Mexico **120** 20 40N 88 11W
Valladolid, Spain **30** 41 38N 4 43W
Valladolid □ **30** 41 38N 4 43W
Vallata **41** 41 3N 15 16 E
Valldemosa **32** 39 43N 2 37 E
Valle **47** 59 13N 7 33 E
Valle d'Aosta □ **38** 45 45N 7 22 E
Valle de Arán **32** 42 50N 0 55 E
Valle de Cabuérniga **30** 43 14N 4 18W
Valle de la Pascua **126** 9 13N 66 0W
Valle de Santiago **120** 20 25N 101 15W
Valle Fértil, Sierra del **124** 30 20 S 68 0W
Valle Hermoso **120** 25 35N 97 40W
Vallecas **30** 40 23N 3 41W
Vallejo **118** 38 12N 122 15W
Vallenar **124** 28 30 S 70 50W
Valleraugue **20** 44 6N 3 39 E
Vallet **18** 47 10N 1 15W
Valletta **36** 35 54N 14 30 E
Valley City **116** 46 57N 98 0W
Valley Falls **118** 42 33N 120 16W
Valleyview **108** 55 5N 117 17W
Valli di Comácchio **39** 44 40N 12 15 E
Vallimanca, Arroyo **124** 35 40 S 59 10W
Vallo della Lucánia **41** 40 14N 15 16 E
Vallon **21** 44 25N 4 23 E
Vallorbe **25** 46 42N 6 20 E
Valls **32** 41 18N 1 15 E
Vallsta **48** 61 31N 16 22 E
Valmaseda **32** 43 11N 3 12W
Valmiera **54** 57 37N 25 29 E
Valmont **18** 49 45N 0 30 E
Valmontone **40** 41 48N 12 55 E
Valmy **19** 49 5N 4 45 E
Valnera, Mte. **32** 43 9N 3 40W
Valognes **18** 49 30N 1 28W
Valona = Vlóra **44** 40 32N 19 28 E
Valongo **30** 41 8N 8 30W
Valpaços **30** 41 36N 7 17W
Valparaíso, Chile **124** 33 2 S 71 40W
Valparaíso, Mexico **120** 22 50N 103 32W
Valparaiso **114** 41 27N 87 2W
Valparaíso □ **124** 33 2 S 71 40W
Valpovo **42** 45 39N 18 25 E
Valréas **21** 44 24N 5 0 E
Vals **25** 46 39N 9 11 E
Vals ⤳ **92** 27 23 S 26 30 E
Vals-les-Bains **21** 44 42N 4 24 E
Vals, Tanjung **73** 8 26 S 137 25 E
Valsbaai **92** 34 15 S 18 40 E
Valskog **48** 59 27N 15 57 E
Válta **44** 40 3N 23 25 E
Valtellina **38** 46 9N 9 55 E
Valuyki **55** 50 10N 38 5 E
Valverde del Camino **31** 37 35N 6 47W
Valverde del Fresno **30** 40 15N 6 51W
Vama **46** 47 34N 25 42 E
Vámos **45** 35 24N 24 13 E
Vamsadhara ⤳ **70** 18 21N 84 8 E
Van **64** 38 30N 43 20 E
Van Alstyne **117** 33 25N 96 36W
Van Bruyssel **107** 47 56N 72 9W
Van Buren, Can. **107** 47 10N 67 55W
Van Buren, Ark., U.S.A. **117** 35 28N 94 18W
Van Buren, Me., U.S.A. **115** 47 10N 68 1W
Van Buren, Mo., U.S.A. **117** 37 0N 91 0W
Van der Kloof Dam **92** 30 04 S 24 40 E
Van Diemen, C. **97** 16 30 S 139 46 E
Van Diemen G. **96** 11 45 S 132 0 E
Van Gölü **64** 38 30N 43 0 E
Van Horn **117** 31 3N 104 55W
Van Reenen P. **93** 28 22 S 29 27 E
Van Rees, Pegunungan **73** 2 35 S 138 15 E
Van Tassell **116** 42 40N 104 3W
Van Tivu **70** 8 51N 78 15 E
Van Wert **114** 40 52N 84 31W
Vanavara **59** 60 22N 102 16 E
Vancouver, Can. **108** 49 15N 123 10W
Vancouver, U.S.A. **118** 45 44N 122 41W
Vancouver I. **108** 49 50N 126 0W
Vandalia, Ill., U.S.A. **116** 38 57N 89 4W
Vandalia, Mo., U.S.A. **116** 39 18N 91 30W
Vandeloos Bay **70** 8 0N 81 45 E
Vanderbijlpark **93** 26 42 S 27 54 E
Vandergrift **114** 40 36N 79 33W
Vanderhoof **108** 54 0N 124 0W
Vanderlin I. **97** 15 44 S 137 2 E
Vandyke **98** 24 10 S 147 51 E
Vänern **49** 58 47N 13 30 E
Vänersborg **49** 58 26N 12 19 E
Vang Vieng **71** 18 58N 102 32 E
Vanga **90** 4 35 S 39 12 E
Vangaindrano **93** 23 21 S 47 36 E
Vanguard **109** 49 55N 107 20W
Vanier **106** 45 27N 75 40W
Vanimo **98** 2 42 S 141 21 E
Vanivilasa Sagara **70** 13 45N 76 30 E
Vaniyambadi **70** 12 46N 78 44 E
Vankarem **59** 67 51N 175 50 E
Vankleek Hill **106** 45 32N 74 40W
Vanna **50** 70 6N 19 50 E
Vännäs **50** 63 58N 19 48 E
Vannes **18** 47 40N 2 47W
Vanoise, Massif de la **21** 45 25N 6 40 E
Vanrhynsdorp **92** 31 36 S 18 44 E
Vanrook **98** 16 57 S 141 57 E
Vans, Les **21** 44 25N 4 7 E
Vansbro **48** 60 32N 14 15 E
Vanse **47** 58 6N 6 41 E
Vansittart B. **96** 14 3 S 126 17 E
Vanthli **68** 21 28N 70 25 E
Vanua Levu **101** 16 33 S 179 15 E
Vanua Mbalavu **101** 17 40 S 178 57W
Vanwyksvlei **92** 30 18 S 21 49 E
Vanylven **47** 62 5N 5 33 E
Vapnyarka **56** 48 32N 28 45 E
Var □ **21** 43 27N 6 18 E
Var ⤳ **21** 43 39N 7 12 E
Vara **49** 58 16N 12 55 E
Varada ⤳ **70** 15 0N 75 40 E
Varades **18** 47 25N 1 1W
Varaita ⤳ **38** 44 49N 7 36 E
Varaldsoøy **47** 60 6N 5 59 E
Varallo **38** 45 50N 8 13 E
Varanasi (Benares) **69** 25 22N 83 0 E
Varangerfjorden **50** 70 3N 29 25 E
Varazdin **39** 46 20N 16 20 E
Varazze **38** 44 21N 8 36 E
Varberg **49** 57 6N 12 20 E
Vardar ⤳ **42** 40 35N 22 50 E
Varde **49** 55 38N 8 29 E
Varde Å **49** 55 35N 8 19 E
Varel **24** 53 23N 8 9 E
Varena **54** 54 12N 24 30 E
Varennes-sur-Allier **20** 46 19N 3 24 E
Vareš **42** 44 12N 18 23 E
Varese **38** 45 49N 8 50 E
Varese Ligure **38** 44 22N 9 33 E
Vårgårda **49** 58 2N 12 49 E
Varginha **125** 21 33 S 45 25W
Vargön **49** 58 22N 12 20 E
Varhaug **47** 58 37N 5 41 E
Variadero **117** 35 43N 104 17W
Varillas **124** 24 0 S 70 10W
Väring **49** 58 30N 14 0 E
Värmeln **48** 59 35N 12 54 E
Värmlands län □ **48** 60 0N 13 20 E
Varna **43** 43 13N 27 56 E
Varna ⤳ **70** 16 48N 74 32 E
Värnamo **49** 57 10N 14 3 E
Varnsdorf **26** 50 55N 14 35 E
Värö **49** 57 16N 12 11 E
Vars **113** 45 21N 75 21W
Varteig **47** 59 23N 11 12 E
Varvarin **42** 43 43N 21 20 E
Varzaneh **65** 32 25N 52 40 E
Varzi **38** 44 50N 9 12 E
Varzo **38** 46 12N 8 15 E
Varzy **19** 47 22N 3 20 E
Vas □ **27** 47 10N 16 55 E
Vasa **50** 63 6N 21 38 E
Vasa Barris ⤳ **127** 11 10 S 37 10W
Vásárosnamény **27** 48 9N 22 19 E
Vascâo ⤳ **31** 37 31N 7 31W
Vaşcău **46** 46 28N 22 30 E
Vascongadas **32** 42 50N 2 45W
Väse **48** 59 23N 13 52 E
Vasht = Khāsh **65** 28 14N 61 14 E
Vasilevichi **54** 52 15N 29 50 E
Vasilikón **45** 38 25N 23 40 E
Vasilkov **54** 50 7N 30 15 E
Vaslui **46** 46 38N 27 42 E
Vaslui □ **46** 46 30N 27 45 E
Väsman **48** 60 9N 15 5 E
Vassar, Can. **109** 49 10N 95 55W
Vassar, U.S.A. **114** 43 23N 83 33W
Västerås **49** 59 37N 16 38 E
Västerbottens län □ **50** 64 58N 18 0 E
Västernorrlands län □ **48** 63 30N 17 30 E
Västervik **49** 57 43N 16 43 E
Västmanlands län □ **48** 59 45N 16 20 E
Vasto **39** 42 8N 14 40 E
Vasvár **27** 47 3N 16 47 E
Vatan **19** 47 4N 1 50 E
Vathí, Itháki, Greece **45** 38 18N 20 40 E
Vathí, Sámos, Greece **45** 37 46N 27 1 E
Váthia **45** 36 29N 22 29 E
Vatican City ■ **39** 41 54N 12 27 E
Vaticano, C. **40** 38 40N 15 48 E
Vatin **42** 45 12N 21 20 E
Vatnajökull **50** 64 30N 16 48W
Vatnås **47** 59 58N 9 37 E
Vatne **47** 62 33N 6 38 E
Vatneyri **50** 65 35N 24 0W
Vatoa **101** 19 50 S 178 13W
Vatoloha, Mt. **93** 17 52 S 47 48 E
Vatomandry **93** 19 20 S 48 59 E
Vatra-Dornei **46** 47 22N 25 22 E
Vättern **49** 58 25N 14 30 E
Vaucluse □ **21** 44 3N 5 10 E
Vaucouleurs **19** 48 37N 5 40 E
Vaud □ **25** 46 35N 6 30 E
Vaughan **119** 34 37N 105 12W
Vaughn **118** 47 37N 111 36W
Vaupés ⤳ **126** 0 2N 67 16W
Vauvert **21** 43 42N 4 17 E
Vauxhall **108** 50 5N 112 9W
Vava'u **101** 18 36 S 174 0W
Vavincourt **19** 48 49N 5 12 E
Vavoua **84** 7 23N 6 29W
Vaxholm **48** 59 25N 18 20 E
Växjö **49** 56 52N 14 50 E
Vaygach, Ostrov **58** 70 0N 60 0 E
Vazovgrad **43** 42 39N 24 45 E
Vechta **24** 52 47N 8 18 E
Vechte ⤳ **16** 52 34N 6 6 E
Vecilla, La **30** 42 51N 5 27W
Vecsés **27** 47 26N 19 19 E
Vedaraniam **70** 10 25N 79 50 E
Veddige **49** 57 17N 12 20 E
Vedea ⤳ **46** 44 0N 25 20 E
Vedia **124** 34 30 S 61 31W
Vedra, I. del **33** 38 52N 1 12 E
Veendam **16** 53 5N 6 52 E
Veenendaal **16** 52 2N 5 34 E
Vefsna ⤳ **50** 65 48N 13 10 E
Vega, Norway **50** 65 40N 11 55 E
Vega, U.S.A. **117** 35 18N 102 26W
Vega, La **121** 19 20N 70 30W
Vegadeo **30** 43 27N 7 4W
Vegafjorden **50** 65 37N 12 0 E
Vegesack **24** 53 10N 8 38 E
Veggli **47** 60 3N 9 9 E
Veghel **16** 51 37N 5 32 E
Vegorritis, Límni **44** 40 45N 21 45 E
Vegreville **108** 53 30N 112 5W
Vegusdal **47** 58 32N 8 10 E
Veii **39** 42 0N 12 24 E
Vejen **49** 55 30N 9 9 E
Vejer de la Frontera **31** 36 15N 5 59W
Vejle **49** 55 43N 9 30 E
Vejle Fjord **49** 55 40N 9 50 E
Vela Luka **39** 42 59N 16 44 E
Velanai I. **70** 9 45N 79 45 E
Velarde **119** 36 11N 106 1W
Velasco **117** 29 0N 95 20W
Velasco, Sierra de. **124** 29 20 S 67 10W
Velay, Mts. du **20** 45 0N 3 40 E
Velddrif **92** 32 42 S 18 11 E
Velebit Planina **39** 44 50N 15 20 E
Velebitski Kanal **39** 44 45N 14 55 E
Veleka ⤳ **43** 42 4N 27 58 E
Velenje **39** 46 23N 15 8 E
Velestínon **44** 39 23N 22 43 E
Veleta, La **31** 37 1N 3 22W
Vélez **126** 6 1N 73 41W
Velež **42** 43 19N 18 2 E
Vélez Blanco **33** 37 41N 2 5W
Vélez Málaga **31** 36 48N 4 5W
Vélez Rubio **33** 37 41N 2 5W
Velhas ⤳ **127** 17 13 S 44 49W
Velika **42** 45 27N 17 40 E
Velika Gorica **39** 45 44N 16 5 E
Velika Gradište **42** 44 46N 21 29 E
Velika Kapela **39** 45 10N 15 5 E
Velika Kladuša **39** 45 11N 15 48 E
Velika Morava ⤳ **42** 44 43N 21 3 E
Velika Plana **42** 44 20N 21 1 E
Velikaya ⤳ **54** 57 48N 28 20 E
Velikaya Lepetikha **56** 47 2N 33 58 E
Veliké Kapušany **27** 48 34N 22 5 E
Velike Lašče **39** 45 49N 14 45 E
Veliki Backa Kanal **42** 45 45N 19 15 E
Veliki Jastrebac **42** 43 25N 21 30 E
Veliki Popović **42** 44 8N 21 18 E
Veliki Ustyug **52** 60 47N 46 20 E
Velikiye Luki **54** 56 25N 30 32 E
Velikonda Range **70** 14 45N 79 10 E
Velikoye, Oz. **55** 55 15N 40 10 E
Velingrad **43** 42 4N 23 58 E
Velino, Mte. **39** 42 10N 13 20 E
Velizh **54** 55 36N 31 11 E
Velké Karlovice **27** 49 20N 18 17 E
Velke Meziřici **26** 49 21N 16 1 E
Vel'ký ostrov Žitný **27** 48 5N 17 20 E
Vellar ⤳ **70** 11 30N 79 36 E
Velletri **40** 41 43N 12 43 E
Vellinge **49** 55 29N 13 0 E
Vellore **70** 12 57N 79 10 E
Velsen-Noord **16** 52 27N 4 40 E
Velsk **52** 61 10N 42 5 E
Velten **24** 52 40N 13 11 E
Velva **116** 48 6N 100 56W
Velvendós **44** 40 15N 22 6 E
Vembanad Lake **70** 9 36N 76 15 E
Veme **47** 60 14N 10 7 E
Ven **49** 55 55N 12 45 E
Vena **49** 57 31N 16 0 E
Venado **120** 22 56N 101 10W
Venado Tuerto **124** 33 50 S 62 0W
Venafro **41** 41 28N 14 3 E
Venarey-les-Laumes **19** 47 32N 4 26 E
Venaria **38** 45 6N 7 39 E
Venčane **42** 44 24N 20 28 E
Vence **21** 43 43N 7 6 E
Vendas Novas **31** 38 39N 8 27W
Vendée □ **18** 46 50N 1 35W
Vendée ⤳ **18** 46 20N 1 10W
Vendée, Collines de **18** 46 35N 0 45W
Vendeuvre-sur-Barse **19** 48 14N 4 28 E
Vendôme **18** 47 47N 1 3 E
Vendrell **32** 41 10N 1 30 E
Vendsyssel **49** 57 22N 10 0 E
Véneta, Laguna **39** 45 23N 12 25 E
Véneto □ **39** 45 40N 12 0 E
Venev **55** 54 22N 38 17 E
Venézia **39** 45 27N 12 20 E
Venézia, Golfo di **39** 45 20N 13 0 E
Venezuela ■ **126** 8 0N 65 0W
Venezuela, Golfo de **126** 11 30N 71 0W
Vengurla **70** 15 53N 73 45 E
Vengurla Rocks **70** 15 55N 73 22 E
Venice = Venézia **39** 45 27N 12 20 E
Vénissieux **21** 45 43N 4 53 E
Venkatagiri **70** 14 0N 79 35 E
Venkatapuram **70** 18 20N 80 30 E
Venlo **16** 51 22N 6 11 E
Vennesla **47** 58 15N 8 0 E
Venraij **16** 51 31N 6 0 E
Venta de Cardeña **31** 38 16N 4 20W
Venta de San Rafael **30** 40 42N 4 12W
Ventana, Punta de la **120** 24 4N 109 48W
Ventana, Sa. de la **124** 38 0 S 62 30W
Ventersburg **92** 28 7 S 27 9 E
Ventimíglia **38** 43 50N 7 39 E
Ventnor **13** 50 35N 1 12W
Ventotene **40** 40 48N 13 25 E
Ventoux **21** 44 10N 5 17 E
Ventspils **54** 57 25N 21 32 E
Ventuarí ⤳ **126** 3 58N 67 2W
Ventura **119** 34 16N 119 18W
Vera, Argent. **124** 29 30 S 60 20W
Vera, Spain **33** 37 15N 1 51W
Veracruz **120** 19 10N 96 10W
Veracruz □ **120** 19 0N 96 15W
Veraval **68** 20 53N 70 27 E
Verbánia **38** 45 56N 8 43 E
Verbicaro **41** 39 46N 15 54 E
Vercelli **38** 45 19N 8 25 E
Verchovchevo **56** 48 32N 34 10 E
Verdalsøra **50** 63 48N 11 30 E
Verde ⤳, Argent. **128** 41 56 S 65 5W
Verde ⤳, Chihuahua, Mexico **120** 26 29N 107 58W
Verde ⤳, Oaxaca, Mexico **120** 15 59N 97 50W
Verde ⤳, Veracruz, Mexico **120** 21 10N 102 50W
Verde ⤳, Parag. **124** 23 9 S 57 37W
Verde, Cay **121** 23 0N 75 5W
Verden **24** 52 58N 9 18 E
Verdhikoúsa **44** 39 47N 21 59 E
Verdigre **116** 42 38N 98 0W

Verdon → 21 43 43N 5 46 E
Verdon-sur-Mer, Le 20 45 33N 1 4W
Verdun 19 49 12N 5 24 E
Verdun-sur-le Doubs 19 46 54N 5 0 E
Vereeniging 93 26 38 S 27 57 E
Vérendrye, Parc Prov. de la 106 47 20N 76 40W
Verga, C. 84 10 30N 14 10W
Vergara 32 43 9N 2 28W
Vergato 38 44 18N 11 8 E
Vergemont 98 23 33 S 143 1 E
Vergemont Cr. → 98 24 16 S 143 16 E
Vergennes 113 44 9N 73 15W
Vergt 20 45 2N 0 43 E
Verín 30 41 57N 7 27W
Veriña 30 43 32N 5 43W
Verkhnedvinsk 54 55 45N 27 58 E
Verkhnevilyuysk 59 63 27N 120 18 E
Verkhneye Kalinino 59 59 54N 108 8 E
Verkhniy Baskunchak 57 48 14N 46 44 E
Verkhovye 55 52 55N 37 15 E
Verkhoyansk 59 67 35N 133 25 E
Verkhoyanskiy Khrebet 59 66 0N 129 0 E
Verlo 109 50 19N 108 35W
Verma 47 62 21N 8 3 E
Vermenton 19 47 40N 3 42 E
Vermilion 109 53 20N 110 50W
Vermilion →, Alta., Can. 109 53 22N 110 51W
Vermilion →, Qué., Can. 106 47 38N 72 56W
Vermilion, B. 117 29 45N 91 55W
Vermilion Bay 109 49 51N 93 34W
Vermilion Chutes 108 58 22N 114 51W
Vermilion L. 116 47 53N 92 25W
Vermillion 116 42 50N 96 56W
Vermont □ 114 43 40N 72 50W
Vernal 118 40 28N 109 35W
Verner 106 46 25N 80 8W
Verneuil-sur-Avre 18 48 45N 0 55 E
Vernon, Can. 108 50 20N 119 15W
Vernon, France 18 49 5N 1 30 E
Vernon, U.S.A. 117 34 10N 99 20W
Vero Beach 115 27 39N 80 23W
Véroia 44 40 34N 22 12 E
Verolanuova 38 45 20N 10 5 E
Véroli 40 41 43N 13 24 E
Verona 38 45 27N 11 0 E
Veropol 59 65 15N 168 40 E
Versailles 19 48 48N 2 8 E
Vert, C. 84 14 45N 17 30W
Vertou 18 47 10N 1 28W
Vertus 19 48 54N 4 0 E
Verulam 93 29 38 S 31 2 E
Verviers 16 50 37N 5 52 E
Vervins 19 49 50N 3 53 E
Verwood 109 49 30N 105 40W
Verzej 39 46 34N 16 13 E
Veselí nad Lužnicí 26 49 12N 14 43 E
Veseliye 43 42 18N 27 38 E
Veselovskoye Vdkhr. 57 47 0N 41 0 E
Veshenskaya 57 49 35N 41 44 E
Vesle → 19 49 23N 3 38 E
Vesoul 19 47 40N 6 11 E
Vessigebro 49 56 58N 12 40 E
Vest-Agder fylke □ 47 58 30N 7 15 E
Vestby 47 59 37N 10 45 E
Vestfjorden 50 67 55N 14 0 E
Vestfold fylke □ 47 59 15N 10 0 E
Vestmannaeyjar 50 63 27N 20 15W
Vestmarka 47 59 56N 11 59 E
Vestnes 47 62 39N 7 5 E
Vestone 38 45 43N 10 25 E
Vestsjællands Amtskommune □ 49 55 30N 11 20 E
Vestspitsbergen 4 78 40N 17 0 E
Vestvågøy 50 68 18N 13 50 E
Vesuvio 41 40 50N 14 22 E
Vesuvius, Mt. = Vesuvio 41 40 50N 14 22 E
Vesyegonsk 55 58 40N 37 16 E
Veszprém 27 47 8N 17 57 E
Veszprém □ 27 47 5N 17 55 E
Vésztő 27 46 55N 21 16 E
Vetapalem 70 15 47N 80 18 E
Vetlanda 49 57 24N 15 3 E
Vetluga 55 57 53N 45 45 E
Vetluzhskiy 55 57 17N 45 12 E
Vetovo 43 43 42N 26 16 E
Vetralla 39 42 20N 12 2 E
Vetren 43 42 15N 24 3 E
Vettore, Monte 39 42 49N 13 16 E
Veurne 16 51 5N 2 40 E
Vevey 25 46 28N 6 51 E
Vévi 44 40 47N 21 38 E
Veynes 21 44 32N 5 49 E
Veys 64 31 30N 49 0 E
Vézelise 19 48 30N 6 5 E
Vézère → 20 44 53N 0 53 E
Vezhen 43 42 50N 24 20 E
Viacha 126 16 39 S 68 18W
Viadana 38 44 55N 10 30 E
Viana, Brazil 127 3 13 S 45 0W
Viana, Spain 32 42 31N 2 22W
Viana del Bollo 30 42 11N 7 6W
Viana do Alentejo 31 38 17N 7 59W
Viana do Castelo 30 41 42N 8 50W
Vianna do Castelo □ 30 41 50N 8 30W
Vianópolis 127 16 40 S 48 35W
Viar → 31 37 36N 5 50W
Viaréggio 38 43 52N 10 13 E
Viaur → 20 44 8N 1 58 E
Vibank 109 50 20N 103 56W
Vibo Valéntia 41 38 40N 16 5 E
Viborg 49 56 27N 9 23 E
Vibraye 18 48 3N 0 44 E
Vic-en-Bigorre 20 43 24N 0 3 E
Vic-Fézensac 20 43 47N 0 19 E
Vic-sur-Cère 20 44 59N 2 38 E
Vic-sur-Seille 19 48 45N 6 33 E
Vicenza 39 45 32N 11 31 E
Vich 32 41 58N 2 19 E
Vichuga 55 57 12N 41 55 E
Vichy 20 46 9N 3 26 E
Vicksburg, Mich., U.S.A. 114 42 10N 85 30W
Vicksburg, Miss., U.S.A. 117 32 22N 90 56W
Vico del Gargaro 41 41 54N 15 57 E
Vico, L. di 39 42 20N 12 10 E
Viçosa 127 9 28 S 36 14W
Victor, Colo., U.S.A. 116 38 43N 105 7W
Victor, N.Y., U.S.A. 112 42 58N 77 24W
Victor Harbour 97 35 30 S 138 37 E
Victoria, Argent. 124 32 40 S 60 10W
Victoria, Camer. 88 4 1N 9 10 E
Victoria, Can. 108 48 30N 123 25W
Victoria, Chile 128 38 13 S 72 20W
Victoria, Guin. 84 10 50N 14 32W
Victoria, H. K. 75 22 16N 114 15 E
Victoria, Malay. 72 5 20N 115 14 E
Victoria, Kans., U.S.A. 116 38 52N 99 8W
Victoria, Tex., U.S.A. 117 28 50N 97 0W
Victoria □, Austral. 97 37 0 S 144 0 E
Victoria □, Zimb. 91 21 0 S 31 30 E
Victoria → 96 15 10 S 129 40 E
Victoria Beach 109 50 40N 96 35W
Victoria de las Tunas 121 20 58N 76 59W
Victoria Falls 91 17 58 S 25 52 E
Victoria, Grand L. 106 47 31N 77 30W
Victoria Harbour 106 44 45N 79 45W
Victoria I. 104 71 0N 111 0W
Victoria, L. 90 1 0 S 33 0 E
Victoria Ld. 5 75 0 S 160 0 E
Victoria, Mt. 98 8 55 S 147 32 E
Victoria Nile → 90 2 14N 31 26 E
Victoria Res. 107 48 20N 57 27W
Victoria River Downs 96 16 25 S 131 0 E
Victoria Taungdeik 67 21 15N 93 55 E
Victoria West 92 31 25 S 23 4 E
Victoriaville 107 46 4N 71 56W
Victorica 124 36 20 S 65 30W
Victorville 119 34 32N 117 18W
Vicuña 124 30 0 S 70 50W
Vicuña Mackenna 124 33 53 S 64 25W
Vidalia 115 32 13N 82 25W
Vidauban 21 43 25N 6 27 E
Vidigueira 31 38 12N 7 48W
Vidin 42 43 59N 22 50 E
Vidio, Cabo 30 43 35N 6 14W
Vidisha (Bhilsa) 68 23 28N 77 53 E
Vidöstern 49 57 5N 14 0 E
Vidra 46 45 56N 26 55 E
Viduša 42 42 55N 18 21 E
Vidzy 54 55 23N 26 37 E
Viechtach 25 49 5N 12 53 E
Viedma 128 40 50 S 63 0W
Viedma, L. 128 49 30 S 72 30W
Vieira 30 41 38N 8 8W
Viella 32 42 43N 0 44 E
Vien Pou Kha 71 20 45N 101 5 E
Vienenburg 24 51 57N 10 35 E
Vienna 117 37 29N 88 54W
Vienna = Wien 27 48 12N 16 22 E
Vienne 21 45 31N 4 53 E
Vienne □ 20 46 30N 0 42 E
Vienne → 18 47 13N 0 5 E
Vientiane 71 17 58N 102 36 E
Vientos, Paso de los 121 20 0N 74 0W
Viersen 24 51 15N 6 23 E
Vierwaldstättersee 25 47 0N 8 30 E
Vierzon 19 47 13N 2 5 E
Vieste 40 41 52N 16 14 E
Vietnam ■ 71 19 0N 106 0 E
Vieux-Boucau-les-Bains 20 43 48N 1 23W
Vif 21 45 5N 5 41 E
Vigan 73 17 35N 120 28 E
Vigan, Le 20 44 0N 3 36 E
Vigévano 38 45 18N 8 50 E
Vigia 127 0 50 S 48 5W
Vignacourt 19 50 1N 2 15 E
Vignemale, Pic du 20 42 47N 0 10W
Vigneulles 19 48 59N 5 40 E
Vignola 38 44 29N 11 0 E
Vigo 30 42 12N 8 41W
Vigo, Ría de 30 42 15N 8 45W
Vihiers 18 47 10N 0 30W
Vijayadurg 70 16 30N 73 25 E
Vijayawada (Bezwada) 70 16 31N 80 39 E
Vikedal 47 59 30N 5 55 E
Viken 49 58 39N 14 20 E
Vikersund 47 59 58N 10 2 E
Viking 108 53 7N 111 50W
Vikna 50 64 55N 10 58 E
Vikramasingapuram 70 8 40N 76 47 E
Viksjö 48 62 45N 17 26 E
Vikulovo 58 56 50N 70 40 E
Vila Aiferes Chamusca 93 24 27 S 33 0 E
Vila Caldas Xavier 91 14 28 S 33 0 E
Vila Coutinho 91 14 37 S 34 19 E
Vila da Maganja 91 17 18 S 37 30 E
Vila de João Belo = Xai-Xai 93 25 6 S 33 31 E
Vila de Junqueiro 91 15 25 S 36 58 E
Vila de Manica 91 18 58 S 32 59 E
Vila de Rei 31 39 41N 8 9W
Vila do Bispo 31 37 5N 8 53W
Vila do Chibuto 93 24 40 S 33 33 E
Vila do Conde 30 41 21N 8 45W
Vila Fontes 91 17 51 S 35 24 E
Vila Franca de Xira 31 38 57N 8 59W
Vila Gamito 91 14 12 S 33 0 E
Vila Gomes da Costa 93 24 20 S 33 37 E
Vila Luisa 93 25 45 S 32 35 E
Vila Machado 91 19 15 S 34 14 E
Vila Mouzinho 91 14 48 S 34 25 E
Vila Nova de Foscôa 30 41 5N 7 9W
Vila Nova de Ourém 31 39 40N 8 35W
Vila Novo de Gaia 30 41 4N 8 40W
Vila Paiva de Andrada 91 18 44 S 34 2 E
Vila Pouca de Aguiar 30 41 30N 7 38W
Vila Real 30 41 17N 7 48W
Vila Real de Santo António 31 37 10N 7 28W
Vila Vasco da Gama 91 14 54 S 32 14 E
Vila Velha 125 20 20 S 40 17W
Vila Veríssimo Sarmento 88 8 7 S 20 38 E
Vila Viçosa 31 38 45N 7 27W
Vilaboa 30 42 21N 8 39W
Vilaine → 18 47 30N 2 27W
Vilanculos 93 22 1 S 35 17 E
Vilar Formosa 30 40 38N 6 45W
Vilareal □ 30 41 36N 7 35W
Vilaseca-Salou 32 41 7N 1 9 E
Vîlcea □ 46 45 0N 24 10 E
Vileyka 54 54 30N 26 53 E
Vilhelmina 50 64 35N 16 39 E
Vilhena 126 12 40 S 60 5W
Viliga 59 61 36N 156 56 E
Viliya → 54 55 54N 23 53 E
Viljandi 54 58 28N 25 30 E
Vilkovo 56 45 28N 29 32 E
Villa Abecia 124 21 0 S 68 18W
Villa Ahumada 120 30 38N 106 30W
Villa Ana 124 28 28 S 59 40W
Villa Ángela 124 27 34 S 60 45W
Villa Bella 126 10 25 S 65 22W
Villa Bens = Tarfaya 80 27 55N 12 55W
Villa Cañás 124 34 0 S 61 35W
Villa Cisneros = Dakhla 80 23 50N 15 53W
Villa Colón 124 31 38 S 68 20W
Villa Constitución 124 33 15 S 60 20W
Villa de María 124 29 55 S 63 43W
Villa Dolores 124 31 58 S 65 15W
Villa Guillermina 124 28 15 S 59 29W
Villa Hayes 124 25 0 S 57 20W
Villa Iris 124 38 12 S 63 12W
Villa María 124 32 20 S 63 10W
Villa Mazán 124 28 40 S 66 30W
Villa Minozzo 38 44 21N 10 30 E
Villa Montes 124 21 10 S 63 30W
Villa Ocampo 124 28 30 S 59 20W
Villa Ojo de Agua 124 29 30 S 63 44W
Villa San Giovanni 41 38 13N 15 38 E
Villa San José 124 32 12 S 58 15W
Villa San Martín 124 28 15 S 64 9W
Villa Santina 39 46 25N 12 55 E
Villablino 30 42 57N 6 19W
Villacañas 32 39 38N 3 20W
Villacarlos 32 39 53N 4 17 E
Villacarriedo 32 43 14N 3 48W
Villacarrillo 33 38 7N 3 3W
Villacastín 30 40 46N 4 25W
Villach 26 46 37N 13 51 E
Villaciado 40 39 27N 8 45 E
Villada 30 42 15N 4 59W
Villadiego 30 42 31N 4 1W
Villadóssola 38 46 4N 8 16 E
Villafeliche 32 41 10N 1 30W
Villafranca 32 42 17N 1 46W
Villafranca de los Barros 31 38 35N 6 18W
Villafranca de los Caballeros 33 39 26N 3 21W
Villafranca del Bierzo 30 42 38N 6 50W
Villafranca del Cid 32 40 26N 0 16W
Villafranca del Panadés 32 41 21N 1 40 E
Villafranca di Verona 38 45 20N 10 51 E
Villagarcía de Arosa 30 42 34N 8 46W
Villagrán 120 24 29N 99 29W
Villaguay 124 32 0 S 59 0W
Villaharta 31 38 9N 4 54W
Villahermosa, Mexico 120 18 0N 92 50W
Villahermosa, Spain 33 38 46N 2 52W
Villaines-la-Juhel 18 48 21N 0 20W
Villajoyosa 33 38 30N 0 12W
Villalba 30 43 26N 7 40W
Villalba de Guardo 30 42 42N 4 49W
Villalcampo, Pantano de 30 41 31N 6 0W
Villalón de Campos 30 42 5N 5 4W
Villalpando 30 41 51N 5 25W
Villaluenga 30 40 2N 3 54W
Villamanán 30 42 19N 5 35W
Villamartín 31 36 52N 5 38W
Villamayor 32 39 50N 2 59W
Villamblard 20 45 2N 0 32 E
Villanova Monteleone 40 40 30N 8 28 E
Villanueva 119 35 16N 105 23W
Villanueva de Castellón 33 39 5N 0 31W
Villanueva de Córdoba 31 38 20N 4 38W
Villanueva de la Fuente 33 38 42N 2 42W
Villanueva de la Serena 31 38 59N 5 50W
Villanueva de la Sierra 30 40 12N 6 24W
Villanueva de los Castillejos 31 37 30N 7 15W
Villanueva del Arzobispo 33 38 10N 3 0W
Villanueva del Duque 31 38 20N 5 0W
Villanueva del Fresno 31 38 23N 7 10W
Villanueva y Geltrú 32 41 13N 1 40 E
Villaodrid 30 43 20N 7 11W
Villaputzu 40 39 28N 9 33 E
Villar del Arzobispo 32 39 44N 0 50W
Villar del Rey 31 39 7N 6 50W
Villarcayo 32 42 56N 3 34W
Villard-Bonnet 21 45 14N 5 53 E
Villard-de-Lans 21 45 3N 5 33 E
Villarino de los Aires 30 41 18N 6 23W
Villarosa 41 37 36N 14 9 E
Villarramiel 30 42 2N 4 55W
Villarreal 32 39 55N 0 3W
Villarrica, Chile 128 39 15 S 72 15W
Villarrica, Parag. 124 25 40 S 56 30W
Villarrobledo 33 39 18N 2 36W
Villarroya de la Sierra 32 41 27N 1 46W
Villarrubia de los Ojos 33 39 14N 3 36W
Villars 21 46 0N 5 2 E
Villarta de San Juan 33 39 15N 3 25W
Villasayas 32 41 24N 2 39W
Villaseca de los Gamitos 30 41 2N 6 7W
Villastar 32 40 17N 1 9W
Villatobas 32 39 54N 3 20W
Villavicencio, Argent. 124 32 28 S 69 0W
Villavicencio, Colomb. 126 4 9N 73 37W
Villaviciosa 30 43 32N 5 27W
Villazón 124 22 0 S 65 35W
Ville-Marie 106 47 20N 79 30W
Ville Platte 117 30 45N 92 17W
Villedieu 18 48 50N 1 12W
Villefort 20 44 28N 3 56 E
Villefranche 19 47 19N 1 46 E
Villefranche-de-Lauragais 20 43 25N 1 44 E
Villefranche-de-Rouergue 20 44 21N 2 2 E
Villefranche-du-Périgord 20 44 38N 1 5 E
Villefranche-sur-Saône 21 45 59N 4 43 E
Villel 32 40 14N 1 12W
Villemaur 19 48 14N 3 40 E
Villemur-sur-Tarn 20 43 51N 1 31 E
Villena 33 38 39N 0 52W
Villenauxe 19 48 36N 3 30 E
Villenave 20 44 46N 0 33W
Villeneuve, France 19 48 42N 2 25 E
Villeneuve, Italy 38 45 40N 7 10 E
Villeneuve-l'Archevêque 19 48 14N 3 32 E
Villeneuve-lès-Avignon 21 43 57N 4 49 E
Villeneuve-sur-Allier 20 46 40N 3 13 E
Villeneuve-sur-Lot 20 44 24N 0 42 E
Villeréal 20 44 38N 0 45 E
Villers-Bocage 18 49 3N 0 40W
Villers-Bretonneux 19 49 50N 2 30 E
Villers-Cotterêts 19 49 15N 3 4 E
Villers-Outreaux 19 50 2N 3 18 E
Villers-sur-Mer 18 49 21N 0 2W
Villersexel 19 47 33N 6 26 E
Villerupt 19 49 28N 5 55 E
Villerville 18 49 26N 0 5 E
Villiers 93 27 2 S 28 36 E
Villingen 25 48 4N 8 28 E
Villingen-Schwenningen 25 48 3N 8 29 E
Villisca 116 40 55N 94 59W
Villupuram 70 11 59N 79 31 E
Vilna 108 54 7N 111 55W
Vilnius 54 54 38N 25 19 E
Vils 26 47 33N 10 37 E
Vils → 25 48 38N 13 11 E
Vilsbiburg 25 48 27N 12 23 E
Vilshofen 25 48 38N 13 11 E
Vilskutskogo, Proliv 59 78 0N 103 0 E
Vilusi 42 42 44N 18 34 E
Vilvoorde 16 50 56N 4 26 E
Vilyuy → 59 64 24N 126 26 E
Vilyuysk 59 63 40N 121 35 E
Vimercate 38 45 38N 9 25 E
Vimioso 30 41 35N 6 31W
Vimmerby 49 57 40N 15 55 E
Vimoutiers 18 48 57N 0 10 E
Vimperk 26 49 3N 13 46 E
Viña del Mar 124 33 0 S 71 30W
Vinaroz 32 40 30N 0 27 E
Vincennes 114 38 42N 87 29W
Vinchina 124 28 45 S 68 15W
Vindel älven → 50 63 55N 19 50 E
Vindeln 50 64 12N 19 43 E
Vinderup 49 56 29N 8 45 E
Vindhya Ra. 68 22 50N 77 0 E
Vineland 114 39 30N 75 0W
Vinga 42 46 0N 21 14 E
Vingnes 47 61 7N 10 26 E
Vinh 71 18 45N 105 38 E
Vinhais 30 41 50N 7 0W
Vinica, Hrvatska, Yugo. 39 46 20N 16 9 E
Vinica, Slovenija, Yugo. 39 45 28N 15 16 E
Vinita 117 36 40N 95 12W
Vinkovci 42 45 19N 18 48 E
Vinnitsa 56 49 15N 28 30 E
Vinson Massif 5 78 35 S 85 25W
Vinstra 47 61 37N 9 44 E
Vinton, Iowa, U.S.A. 116 42 8N 92 1W
Vinton, La., U.S.A. 117 30 13N 93 35W
Vinţu de Jos 46 46 0N 23 30 E
Viöl 24 54 32N 9 12 E
Vipava 39 45 51N 13 58 E
Vipiteno 39 46 55N 11 25 E
Viqueque 73 8 52 S 126 23 E
Vir 39 44 17N 15 3 E
Virac 73 13 30N 124 20 E
Virago Sd. 108 54 0N 132 30W
Virajpet 70 12 10N 75 50 E
Viramgam 68 23 5N 72 0 E
Viranşehir 64 37 13N 39 45 E
Virarajendrapet = Virajpet 70 12 10N 75 50 E
Viravanallur 70 8 40N 77 30 E
Virden 109 49 50N 100 56W
Vire 18 48 50N 0 53W
Vire → 18 49 20N 1 7W
Vírgenes, C. 128 52 19 S 68 21W
Virgin →, Can. 109 57 2N 108 17W
Virgin →, U.S.A. 119 36 50N 114 10W
Virgin Gorda 121 18 30N 64 26W
Virgin Is. 121 18 40N 64 30W
Virginia, S. Afr. 92 28 8 S 26 55 E
Virginia, U.S.A. 116 47 30N 92 32W
Virginia □ 114 37 45N 78 0W
Virginia Beach 114 36 54N 75 58W
Virginia City, Mont., U.S.A. 118 45 18N 111 58W
Virginia City, Nev., U.S.A. 118 39 19N 119 39W
Virginia Falls 108 61 38N 125 42W
Virginiatown 106 48 9N 79 36W
Virieu-le-Grand 21 45 51N 5 39 E
Virje 42 46 4N 16 59 E
Viroqua 116 43 33N 90 57W
Virovitica 42 45 51N 17 21 E
Virpazar 42 42 14N 19 6 E
Virserum 49 57 20N 15 35 E
Virton 16 49 35N 5 32 E
Virtsu 54 58 32N 23 33 E
Virudunagar 70 9 30N 78 0 E
Vis 39 43 0N 16 10 E
Vis Kanal 39 43 4N 16 5 E
Visalia 119 36 25N 119 18W
Visayan Sea 73 11 30N 123 30 E
Visby 49 57 37N 18 18 E
Viscount Melville Sd. 4 74 10N 108 0W
Visé 16 50 44N 5 41 E
Višegrad 42 43 47N 19 17 E
Viseu, Brazil 127 1 10 S 46 5W
Viseu, Port. 30 40 40N 7 55W
Viseu □ 30 40 40N 7 55W
Vişeu de Sus 46 47 45N 24 25 E
Vishakhapatnam 70 17 45N 83 20 E
Vishnupur 69 23 8N 87 20 E
Visikoi I. 5 56 43 S 27 15W
Visingsö 49 58 2N 14 20 E
Viskafors 49 57 37N 12 50 E
Vislanda 49 56 46N 14 30 E
Vislinskil Zaliv (Zalew Wislany) 28 54 20N 19 50 E
Visnagar 68 23 45N 72 32 E
Višnja Gora 39 45 58N 14 45 E
Viso del Marqués 33 38 32N 3 34W
Viso, Mte. 38 44 38N 7 5 E
Visoko 42 43 58N 18 10 E

Visp	25	46 17N	7 52 E
Visselhövede	24	52 59N	9 36 E
Vistonikos, Ormos	44	41 0N	25 7 E
Vistula = Wisła →	28	54 22N	18 55 E
Vit →	43	43 30N	24 30 E
Vitanje	39	46 25N	15 18 E
Vitebsk	54	55 10N	30 15 E
Viterbo	39	42 25N	12 8 E
Viti Levu	101	17 30 S	177 30 E
Vitiaz Str.	98	5 40 S	147 10 E
Vitigudino	30	41 1N	6 26W
Vitim	59	59 28N	112 35 E
Vitim →	59	59 26N	112 34 E
Vitína	45	37 40N	22 10 E
Vitina	42	43 17N	17 29 E
Vitória	127	20 20 S	40 22W
Vitoria	32	42 50N	2 41W
Vitória da Conquista	127	14 51 S	40 51W
Vitória de São Antão	127	8 10 S	35 20W
Vitré	18	48 8N	1 12W
Vitry-le-François	19	48 43N	4 33 E
Vitsi, Óros	44	40 40N	21 25 E
Vitteaux	19	47 24N	4 30 E
Vittel	19	48 12N	5 57 E
Vittória	41	36 58N	14 30 E
Vittório Véneto	39	45 59N	12 18 E
Vitu Is.	98	4 50 S	149 25 E
Viver	32	39 55N	0 36W
Vivero	30	43 39N	7 38W
Viviers	21	44 30N	4 40 E
Vivonne	20	46 25N	0 15 E
Vizcaíno, Desierto de	120	27 40N	113 50W
Vizcaíno, Sierra	120	27 30N	114 0W
Vizcaya □	32	43 15N	2 45W
Vizianagaram	70	18 6N	83 30 E
Vizille	21	45 5N	5 46 E
Vizinada	39	45 20N	13 46 E
Viziru	46	45 0N	27 43 E
Vizovice	27	49 12N	17 56 E
Vizzini	41	37 9N	14 43 E
Vjosa →	44	40 37N	19 42 E
Vlaardingen	16	51 55N	4 21 E
Vlădeasa	46	46 47N	22 50 E
Vladicin Han	42	42 42N	22 1 E
Vladimir	55	56 15N	40 30 E
Vladimir Volynskiy	54	50 50N	24 18 E
Vladimirci	42	44 36N	19 45 E
Vladimirovac	42	45 1N	20 53 E
Vladimirovka, R.S.F.S.R., U.S.S.R.	57	48 27N	46 10 E
Vladimirovka, R.S.F.S.R., U.S.S.R.	57	44 45N	44 41 E
Vladimirovo	43	43 32N	23 22 E
Vladislavovka	56	45 15N	35 15 E
Vladivostok	59	43 10N	131 53 E
Vlasenica	42	44 11N	18 59 E
Vlašić	42	44 19N	17 37 E
Vlašim	26	49 40N	14 53 E
Vlasinsko Jezero	42	42 44N	22 22 E
Vlasotinci	42	42 59N	22 7 E
Vlieland	16	53 16N	4 55 E
Vlissingen	16	51 26N	3 34 E
Vlóra	44	40 32N	19 28 E
Vlóra □	44	40 12N	20 0 E
Vlorës, Gjiri i	44	40 29N	19 27 E
Vltava →	26	50 21N	14 30 E
Vobarno	38	45 38N	10 30 E
Voćin	42	45 37N	17 33 E
Vöcklabruck	26	48 1N	13 39 E
Vodice	39	43 47N	15 47 E
Vodňany	26	49 9N	14 11 E
Vodnjan	39	44 59N	13 52 E
Vogelkop = Doberai, Jazirah	73	1 25 S	133 0 E
Vogelsberg	24	50 37N	9 15 E
Voghera	38	44 59N	9 1 E
Vohibinany	93	18 49 S	49 4 E
Vohimarina	93	13 25 S	50 0 E
Vohimena, Tanjon' i	93	25 36 S	45 8 E
Vohipeno	93	22 22 S	47 51 E
Voi	90	3 25 S	38 32 E
Void	19	48 40N	5 36 E
Voineşti, Iaşi, Romania	46	47 5N	27 27 E
Voineşti, Prahova, Romania	46	45 5N	25 14 E
Voiotía □	45	38 20N	23 0 E
Voiron	21	45 22N	5 35 E
Voisey B.	107	56 15N	61 50W
Voitsberg	26	47 3N	15 9 E
Voiviïs Límni	44	39 30N	22 45 E
Vojens	49	55 16N	9 18 E
Vojmsjön	50	64 55N	16 40 E
Vojnik	38	46 18N	15 19 E
Vojnió	39	45 19N	15 43 E
Vojvodina, Auton. Pokrajina □	42	45 20N	20 0 E
Vokhma	55	59 0N	46 45 E
Vokhma →	55	56 20N	46 20 E
Vokhtoga	55	58 46N	41 8 E
Volary	26	48 54N	13 52 E
Volborg	116	45 50N	105 44W
Volcano Is.	94	25 0N	141 0 E
Volchansk	55	50 17N	36 58 E
Volchayevka	59	48 40N	134 30 E
Volchya →	56	48 0N	37 0 E
Volda	47	62 9N	6 5 E
Volga	55	57 58N	38 16 E
Volga →	57	48 30N	46 0 E
Volga Hts. = Privolzhskaya V. S.	53	51 0N	46 0 E
Volgodonsk	57	47 33N	42 5 E
Volgograd	57	48 40N	44 25 E
Volgogradskoye Vdkhr.	55	50 0N	45 20 E
Volgorechensk	55	57 28N	41 14 E
Volissós	45	38 29N	25 54 E
Volkach	25	49 52N	10 14 E
Völkermarkt	26	46 39N	14 39 E
Volkhov	54	59 55N	32 15 E
Volkhov →	54	60 8N	32 20 E
Völklingen	25	49 15N	6 50 E
Volkovysk	54	53 9N	24 30 E
Volksrust	93	27 24 S	29 53 E
Vollenhove	16	52 40N	5 58 E
Vol'n'ansk	56	47 55N	35 29 E
Volnovakha	56	47 35N	37 30 E
Volochanka	59	71 0N	94 28 E
Volodarsk	55	56 12N	43 15 E
Vologda	55	59 10N	40 0 E
Volokolamsk	55	56 5N	35 57 E
Volokonovka	55	50 33N	37 52 E
Vólos	44	39 24N	22 59 E
Volosovo	54	59 27N	29 32 E
Volozhin	54	54 3N	26 30 E
Volsk	55	52 5N	47 22 E
Volta →	85	5 46N	0 41 E
Volta, L.	85	7 30N	0 15 E
Volta Redonda	125	22 31 S	44 5W
Volterra	38	43 24N	10 50 E
Voltri	38	44 25N	8 43 E
Volturara Áppula	41	41 30N	15 2 E
Volturno →	41	41 1N	13 55 E
Volubilis	82	34 2N	5 33W
Volujak	42	43 53N	17 47 E
Vólvi, L.	44	40 40N	23 34 E
Volzhsk	55	55 57N	48 23 E
Volzhskiy	57	48 56N	44 46 E
Vondrozo	93	22 49 S	47 20 E
Vónitsa	45	38 53N	20 58 E
Voorburg	16	52 5N	4 24 E
Vopnafjörður	50	65 45N	14 40W
Vorarlberg □	26	47 20N	10 0 E
Vóras Óros	44	40 57N	21 45 E
Vorbasse	49	55 39N	9 6 E
Vorderrhein →	25	46 49N	9 25 E
Vordingborg	49	55 0N	11 54 E
Voreppe	21	45 18N	5 39 E
Voríai Sporádhes	45	39 15N	23 30 E
Vórios Evvoïkos Kólpos	45	38 45N	23 15 E
Vorkuta	52	67 48N	64 20 E
Vorma →	47	60 9N	11 27 E
Vorona →	55	51 22N	42 3 E
Voronezh, R.S.F.S.R., U.S.S.R.	55	51 40N	39 10 E
Voronezh, Ukraine, U.S.S.R.	54	51 47N	33 28 E
Voronezh →	55	51 56N	37 17 E
Vorontsovo-Aleksandrovskoye = Zelenokumsk	57	44 30N	44 1 E
Voroshilovgrad	57	48 38N	39 15 E
Vorovskoye	59	54 30N	155 50 E
Vorskla →	56	48 50N	34 10 E
Vöru	54	57 48N	26 54 E
Vorupør	49	56 58N	8 22 E
Vosges	19	48 20N	7 10 E
Vosges □	19	48 12N	6 20 E
Voskopoja	44	40 40N	20 33 E
Voskresensk	55	55 19N	38 43 E
Voskresenskoye	55	56 51N	45 30 E
Voss	47	60 38N	6 26 E
Vostochnyy Sayan	59	54 0N	96 0 E
Vostok I.	95	10 5 S	152 23W
Votice	26	49 38N	14 39 E
Votkinsk	52	57 0N	53 55 E
Votkinskoye Vdkhr.	52	57 30N	55 0 E
Vouga →	30	40 41N	8 40W
Vouillé	18	46 38N	0 10 E
Voulte-sur-Rhône, La	21	44 48N	4 46 E
Vouvray	18	47 25N	0 48 E
Voúxa, Ákra	45	35 37N	23 32 E
Vouzela	30	40 43N	8 7W
Vouziers	19	49 22N	4 40 E
Voves	19	48 15N	1 38 E
Voxna	48	61 20N	15 40 E
Vozhe Oz.	52	60 45N	39 0 E
Vozhgaly	55	58 9N	50 11 E
Voznesenka	59	56 40N	95 3 E
Voznesensk	56	47 35N	31 21 E
Voznesenye	52	61 0N	35 45 E
Vráble	27	48 15N	18 16 E
Vraćevšnica	42	44 2N	20 34 E
Vrådal	47	59 20N	8 25 E
Vraka	44	42 8N	19 28 E
Vrakhnéïka	45	38 10N	21 40 E
Vrancea □	46	45 50N	26 45 E
Vrancei, Munţii	46	46 0N	26 30 E
Vrangelya, Ostrov	59	71 0N	180 0 E
Vranica	42	43 55N	17 50 E
Vranje	42	42 34N	21 54 E
Vranjska Banja	42	42 34N	22 1 E
Vranov	27	48 53N	21 40 E
Vransko	39	46 17N	14 58 E
Vratsa	43	43 13N	23 30 E
Vrbas	42	45 40N	19 40 E
Vrbas →	42	45 8N	17 29 E
Vrbnik	39	45 4N	14 40 E
Vrbovec	39	45 53N	16 28 E
Vrbovsko	39	45 24N	15 5 E
Vrchlabí	26	50 38N	15 37 E
Vrede	93	27 24 S	29 6 E
Vredefort	92	27 0 S	26 22 E
Vredenburg	92	32 51 S	18 0 E
Vredendal	92	31 41 S	18 35 E
Vrena	49	58 54N	16 41 E
Vrgorac	42	43 12N	17 20 E
Vrhnika	39	45 58N	14 15 E
Vriddhachalam	70	11 30N	79 20 E
Vridi	84	5 15N	4 3W
Vrindaban	68	27 37N	77 40 E
Vrnograč	39	45 10N	15 57 E
Vrondádhes	45	38 25N	26 7 E
Vrpolje	42	45 13N	18 24 E
Vršac	42	45 8N	21 18 E
Vrsacki Kanal	42	45 15N	21 0 E
Vryburg	92	26 55 S	24 45 E
Vryheid	93	27 45 S	30 47 E
Vsetin	27	49 20N	18 0 E
Vucha →	43	42 10N	24 26 E
Vučitrn	42	42 49N	20 59 E
Vught	16	51 38N	5 20 E
Vukovar	42	45 21N	18 59 E
Vulcan, Can.	108	50 25N	113 15W
Vulcan, Romania	46	45 23N	23 17 E
Vulcan, U.S.A.	114	45 46N	87 51W
Vulcano	41	38 25N	14 58 E
Vŭlchedruma	43	43 42N	23 27 E
Vulci	39	42 23N	11 37 E
Vulkaneshty	56	45 35N	28 30 E
Vunduzi →	91	18 56 S	34 1 E
Vung Tau	71	10 21N	107 4 E
Vŭrbitsa	43	42 59N	26 40 E
Vurshets	43	43 15N	23 23 E
Vutcani	46	46 26N	27 59 E
Vuyyuru	70	16 28N	80 50 E
Vyara	68	21 8N	73 28 E
Vyasniki	55	56 10N	42 10 E
Vyatka →	52	56 30N	51 0 E
Vyatskiye Polyany	52	56 5N	51 0 E
Vyazemskiy	59	47 32N	134 45 E
Vyazma	54	55 10N	34 15 E
Vyborg	52	60 43N	28 47 E
Vychegda →	52	61 18N	46 36 E
Vychodné Beskydy	27	49 30N	22 0 E
Východočeský □	26	50 20N	15 45 E
Východoslovenský □	27	48 50N	21 0 E
Vyg-ozero	52	63 30N	34 0 E
Vyksa	55	55 19N	42 11 E
Vypin	70	10 10N	76 15 E
Vyrnwy, L.	12	52 48N	3 30W
Vyshniy Volochek	54	57 30N	34 30 E
Vyškov	27	49 17N	17 0 E
Vysoké Mýto	27	49 58N	16 10 E
Vysokovsk	55	56 22N	36 30 E
Vysotsk	54	51 43N	26 32 E
Vyšší Brod	26	48 37N	14 19 E
Vytegra	52	61 0N	36 27 E

W

W.A.C. Bennett Dam	108	56 2N	122 6W
Wa	84	10 7N	2 25W
Waal →	16	51 59N	4 30 E
Wabakimi L.	106	50 38N	89 45W
Wabana	107	47 40N	53 0W
Wabasca	108	55 57N	113 56W
Wabash	114	40 48N	85 46W
Wabash →	114	37 46N	88 2W
Wabeno	114	45 25N	88 40W
Wabi →	87	7 45N	40 50 E
Wabigoon L.	109	49 44N	92 44W
Wabowden	109	54 55N	98 38W
Wąbrzeźno	28	53 16N	18 57 E
Wabuk Pt.	106	55 20N	85 5W
Wabush	107	52 55N	66 52W
Wabuska	118	39 9N	119 13W
Wächtersbach	25	50 16N	9 18 E
Waco	117	31 33N	97 5W
Waconichi, L.	106	50 8N	74 0W
Wad Ban Naqa	87	16 32N	33 9 E
Wad Banda	87	13 10N	27 56 E
Wad el Haddad	87	13 50N	33 30 E
Wad en Nau	87	14 10N	33 34 E
Wad Hamid	87	16 30N	32 45 E
Wâd Medanî	87	14 28N	33 30 E
Waddān	83	29 9N	16 10 E
Waddān, Jabal	83	29 0N	16 15 E
Waddeneilanden	16	53 25N	5 10 E
Waddenzee	16	53 6N	5 10 E
Waddington	113	44 51N	75 12W
Waddington, Mt.	108	51 23N	125 15W
Waddy Pt.	99	24 58 S	153 21 E
Wadena, Can.	109	51 57N	103 47W
Wadena, U.S.A.	116	46 25N	95 8W
Wädenswil	25	47 14N	8 40 E
Wadesboro	115	35 2N	80 2W
Wadhams	108	51 30N	127 30W
Wādī ash Shāţi'	83	27 30N	15 0 E
Wādī Banī Walīd	83	31 49N	14 0 E
Wadi Gemâl	86	24 35N	35 10 E
Wadi Halfa	86	21 53N	31 19 E
Wadi Masila	63	16 30N	49 0 E
Wadi Şabāḩ	64	23 50N	48 30 E
Wadlew	28	51 31N	19 23 E
Wadowice	27	49 52N	19 30 E
Wadsworth	118	39 38N	119 22W
Wafrah	64	28 33N	47 56 E
Wageningen	16	51 58N	5 40 E
Wager B.	105	65 26N	88 40W
Wager Bay	105	65 56N	90 49W
Wagga Wagga	97	35 7 S	147 24 E
Waghete	73	4 10 S	135 50 E
Wagin	96	33 17 S	117 25 E
Wagon Mound	117	36 1N	104 44W
Wagoner	117	36 0N	95 20W
Wagrowiec	28	52 48N	17 11 E
Wahai	73	2 48 S	129 35 E
Wahiawa	110	21 30N	158 2W
Wahoo	116	41 15N	96 35W
Wahpeton	116	46 20N	96 35W
Wai	70	17 56N	73 57 E
Waiau →	101	42 47 S	173 22 E
Waiawe Ganga →	70	6 15N	81 0 E
Waibeem	73	0 30 S	132 59 E
Waiblingen	25	48 49N	9 20 E
Waidhofen, Niederösterreich, Austria	26	48 49N	15 17 E
Waidhofen, Niederösterreich, Austria	26	47 57N	14 46 E
Waigeo	73	0 20 S	130 40 E
Waihi	101	37 23 S	175 52 E
Waihou →	101	37 15 S	175 40 E
Waika	90	2 22 S	25 42 E
Waikabubak	73	9 45 S	119 25 E
Waikaremoana	101	38 42 S	177 12 E
Waikari	101	42 58 S	172 41 E
Waikato →	101	37 23 S	174 43 E
Waikerie	99	34 9 S	140 0 E
Waikokopu	101	39 3 S	177 52 E
Waikouaiti	101	45 36 S	170 41 E
Waimate	101	44 45 S	171 3 E
Wainganga →	69	18 50N	79 55 E
Waingapu	73	9 35 S	120 11 E
Wainwright, Can.	109	52 50N	110 50W
Wainwright, U.S.A.	104	70 39N	160 1W
Waiouru	101	39 28 S	175 41 E
Waipara	101	43 3 S	172 46 E
Waipawa	101	39 56 S	176 38 E
Waipiro	101	38 2 S	178 22 E
Waipu	101	35 59 S	174 29 E
Waipukurau	101	40 1 S	176 33 E
Wairakei	101	38 37 S	176 6 E
Wairarapa, L.	101	41 14 S	175 15 E
Wairoa	101	39 3 S	177 25 E
Waitaki →	101	44 56 S	171 7 E
Waitara	101	38 59 S	174 15 E
Waitsburg	118	46 15N	118 0W
Waiuku	101	37 15 S	174 45 E
Wajima	74	37 30N	137 0 E
Wajir	90	1 42N	40 5 E
Wajir □	90	1 42N	40 20 E
Wakasa-Wan	74	35 40N	135 30 E
Wakatipu, L.	101	45 5 S	168 33 E
Wakaw	109	52 39N	105 44W
Wakayama	74	34 15N	135 15 E
Wakayama-ken □	74	33 50N	135 30 E
Wake Forest	115	35 58N	78 30W
Wake I.	94	19 18N	166 36 E
Wakefield, N.Z.	101	41 24 S	173 5 E
Wakefield, U.K.	12	53 41N	1 31W
Wakefield, Mass., U.S.A.	113	42 30N	71 3W
Wakefield, Mich., U.S.A.	116	46 28N	89 53W
Wakema	67	16 30N	95 11 E
Wakkanai	74	45 28N	141 35 E
Wakkerstroom	93	27 24 S	30 10 E
Wakool	99	35 28 S	144 23 E
Wakool →	99	35 5 S	143 33 E
Wakre	73	0 19 S	131 5 E
Wakuach L.	107	55 34N	67 32W
Walamba	91	13 30 S	28 42 E
Wałbrzych	28	50 45N	16 18 E
Walbury Hill	13	51 22N	1 28W
Walcha	99	30 55 S	151 31 E
Walcheren	16	51 30N	3 35 E
Walcott	118	41 50N	106 55W
Wałcz	28	53 17N	16 27 E
Wald	25	47 17N	8 56 E
Waldbröl	24	50 52N	7 36 E
Waldeck	24	51 12N	9 4 E
Walden, Colo., U.S.A.	118	40 47N	106 20W
Walden, N.Y., U.S.A.	113	41 32N	74 13W
Waldport	118	44 30N	124 2W
Waldron, Can.	109	50 53N	102 35W
Waldron, U.S.A.	117	34 52N	94 4W
Waldshut	25	47 37N	8 12 E
Walembele	84	10 30N	1 58W
Wales □	11	52 30N	3 30W
Walewale	85	10 21N	0 50W
Walgett	97	30 0 S	148 5 E
Walgreen Coast	5	75 15 S	105 0W
Walhalla, Austral.	99	37 56 S	146 29 E
Walhalla, U.S.A.	109	48 55N	97 55W
Walker	116	47 4N	94 35W
Walker L., Man., Can.	109	54 42N	95 57W
Walker L., Qué., Can.	107	50 20N	67 11W
Walker L., U.S.A.	118	38 56N	118 46W
Walkerston	98	21 11 S	149 8 E
Walkerton	112	44 10N	81 10W
Wall	116	44 0N	102 14W
Walla Walla	118	46 3N	118 25W
Wallabadah	98	17 57 S	142 15 E
Wallace, Idaho, U.S.A.	118	47 30N	116 0W
Wallace, N.C., U.S.A.	115	34 44N	77 59W
Wallace, Nebr., U.S.A.	116	40 51N	101 12W
Wallaceburg	106	42 34N	82 23W
Wallachia = Valahia	46	44 35N	25 0 E
Wallal	99	26 32 S	146 7 E
Wallaroo	97	33 56 S	137 39 E
Wallasey	12	53 26N	3 2W
Walldürn	25	49 34N	9 23 E
Wallerawang	99	33 25 S	150 4 E
Wallingford, U.K.	12	51 40N	1 15W
Wallingford, U.S.A.	113	41 27N	72 50W
Wallis Arch.	94	13 18 S	176 10W
Wallowa	118	45 40N	117 35W
Wallowa, Mts.	118	45 20N	117 30W
Wallsend, Austral.	99	32 55 S	151 40 E
Wallsend, U.K.	12	54 59N	1 30W
Wallula	118	46 3N	118 59W
Wallumbilla	99	26 33 S	149 9 E
Walmer	92	33 57 S	25 35 E
Walmsley, L.	109	63 25N	108 36W
Walney, Isle of	12	54 5N	3 15W
Walnut Ridge	117	36 7N	90 58W
Walsall	13	52 36N	1 59W
Walsenburg	117	37 42N	104 45W
Walsh	117	37 28N	102 15W
Walsh →	98	16 31 S	143 42 E
Walsh P.O.	98	16 40 S	144 0 E
Walsrode	24	52 51N	9 37 E
Waltair	70	17 44N	83 23 E
Walterboro	115	32 53N	80 40W
Walters	117	34 25N	98 20W
Waltershausen	24	50 53N	10 33 E
Waltham	113	42 22N	71 12W
Waltham Sta.	106	45 57N	76 57W
Waltman	118	43 8N	107 15W
Walton	113	42 12N	75 9W
Walvisbaai	92	23 0 S	14 28 E
Wamba, Kenya	90	0 58N	37 19 E
Wamba, Zaïre	90	2 10N	27 57 E
Wamego	116	39 14N	96 22W
Wamena	73	4 4 S	138 57 E
Wampsville	113	43 4N	75 42W
Wamsasi	73	3 27 S	126 7 E
Wana	68	32 20N	69 32 E
Wanaaring	99	29 38 S	144 9 E
Wanaka L.	101	44 33 S	169 7 E
Wan'an	77	26 26N	114 49 E
Wanapiri	73	4 30 S	135 59 E
Wanapitei L.	106	46 45N	80 40W
Wanbi	99	34 46 S	140 17 E
Wanda Shan	76	46 0N	132 0 E
Wanderer	91	19 36 S	30 1 E
Wandiwash	70	12 30N	79 30 E
Wandoan	97	26 5 S	149 55 E
Wang Kai (Ghâbat el Arab)	87	9 3N	29 23 E
Wang Saphung	71	17 18N	101 46 E
Wanga	90	2 58N	29 12 E
Wangal	73	6 8 S	134 9 E
Wanganella	99	35 6 S	144 49 E
Wanganui	101	39 56 S	175 3 E
Wangaratta	97	36 21 S	146 19 E
Wangdu	76	38 40N	115 7 E

Wangerooge **24** 53 47N 7 52 E
Wangi **90** 1 58 S 40 58 E
Wangiwangi **73** 5 22 S 123 37 E
Wangjiang **77** 30 10N 116 42 E
Wangqing **76** 43 12N 129 42 E
Wankaner **68** 22 35N 71 0 E
Wankie **91** 18 18 S 26 30 E
Wankie Nat. Park **92** 19 0 S 26 30 E
Wanless **109** 54 11N 101 21W
Wanning **77** 18 48N 110 22 E
Wannon → **100** 37 38 S 141 25 E
Wanquan **76** 40 50N 114 40 E
Wanxian **75** 30 42N 108 20 E
Wanyuan **77** 32 4N 108 3 E
Wanzai **77** 28 7N 114 30 E
Wapakoneta **114** 40 35N 84 10W
Wapato **118** 46 30N 120 25W
Wapawekka L. **109** 54 55N 104 40W
Wappingers Falls **113** 41 35N 73 56W
Wapsipinicon → **116** 41 44N 90 19W
Waranga Res. **100** 36 32 S 145 5 E
Warangal **70** 17 58N 79 35 E
Waratah **99** 41 30 S 145 30 E
Waratah B. **99** 38 54 S 146 5 E
Warburg **24** 51 29N 9 10 E
Warburton **99** 37 47 S 145 42 E
Warburton → **97** 28 4 S 137 28 E
Ward **101** 41 49 S 174 11 E
Ward → **99** 26 28 S 146 6 E
Ward Cove **108** 55 25N 132 43W
Ward Hunt, C. **98** 8 2 S 148 10 E
Wardak □ **65** 34 0N 68 0 E
Warden **93** 27 50 S 29 0 E
Wardha **68** 20 45N 78 39 E
Wardlow **108** 50 56N 111 31W
Ware, Can. **108** 57 26N 125 41W
Ware, U.S.A. **113** 42 16N 72 15W
Wareham **113** 41 45N 70 44W
Waren **24** 53 30N 12 41 E
Warendorf **24** 51 57N 8 0 E
Warialda **97** 29 29 S 150 33 E
Wariap **73** 1 30 S 134 5 E
Warka **28** 51 47N 21 12 E
Warkopi **73** 1 12 S 134 9 E
Warley **13** 52 30N 2 0W
Warm Springs, Mont., U.S.A. **118** 46 11N 112 48W
Warm Springs, Nev., U.S.A. **119** 38 16N 116 32W
Warman **109** 52 19N 106 30W
Warmbad, Namibia **92** 28 25 S 18 42 E
Warmbad, S. Afr. **93** 24 51 S 28 19 E
Warmeriville **19** 49 20N 4 13 E
Warnambool Downs **98** 22 48 S 142 52 E
Warnemünde **24** 54 9N 12 5 E
Warner **108** 49 17N 112 12W
Warner Range, Mts. **118** 41 30 S 120 20W
Warner Robins **115** 32 41N 83 36W
Warnow → **24** 54 6N 12 9 E
Warora **70** 20 14N 79 1 E
Warracknabeal **100** 36 9 S 142 26 E
Warragul **99** 38 10 S 145 58 E
Warrego → **97** 30 24 S 145 21 E
Warrego Ra. **97** 24 58 S 146 0 E
Warren, Austral. **99** 31 42 S 147 51 E
Warren, Ark., U.S.A. **117** 33 35N 92 3W
Warren, Minn., U.S.A. **116** 48 12N 96 46W
Warren, Ohio, U.S.A. **114** 41 18N 80 52W
Warren, Pa., U.S.A. **114** 41 52N 79 10W
Warrenpoint **15** 54 7N 6 15W
Warrensburg **116** 38 45N 93 45W
Warrenton, S. Afr. **92** 28 9 S 24 47 E
Warrenton, U.S.A. **118** 46 11N 123 59W
Warrenville **99** 25 48 S 147 22 E
Warri **85** 5 30N 5 41 E
Warrina **96** 28 12 S 135 50 E
Warrington, U.K. **12** 53 25N 2 38W
Warrington, U.S.A. **115** 30 22N 87 16W
Warrnambool **97** 38 25 S 142 30 E
Warroad **116** 48 54N 95 19W
Warsa **73** 0 47 S 135 55 E
Warsaw, Ind., U.S.A. **114** 41 14N 85 50W
Warsaw, N.Y., U.S.A. **112** 42 46N 78 10W
Warsaw, Ohio, U.S.A. **112** 40 20N 82 0W
Warsaw = Warszawa **28** 52 13N 21 0 E
Warstein **24** 51 26N 8 20 E
Warszawa **28** 52 13N 21 0 E
Warszawa □ **28** 52 30N 21 0 E
Warta **28** 51 43N 18 38 E
Warta → **28** 52 35N 14 39 E
Waru **73** 3 30 S 130 36 E
Warud **68** 21 30N 78 16 E
Warwick, Austral. **97** 28 10 S 152 1 E
Warwick, U.K. **13** 52 17N 1 36W
Warwick, U.S.A. **114** 41 43N 71 25W
Warwick □ **13** 52 20N 1 30W
Wasa **108** 49 45N 115 50W
Wasaga Beach **112** 44 31N 80 1W
Wasatch, Ra. **118** 40 30N 111 15W
Wasbank **93** 28 15 S 30 9 E
Wasco, Calif., U.S.A. **119** 35 37N 119 16W
Wasco, Oreg., U.S.A. **118** 45 36N 120 46W
Waseca **116** 44 3N 93 31W
Wasekamio L. **109** 56 45N 108 45W
Wash, The **12** 52 58N 0 20 E
Washago **112** 44 45N 79 20W
Washburn, N.D., U.S.A. **116** 47 17N 101 0W
Washburn, Wis., U.S.A. **116** 46 38N 90 55W
Washington, D.C., U.S.A. **114** 38 52N 77 0W
Washington, Ga., U.S.A. **115** 33 45N 82 45W
Washington, Ind., U.S.A. **114** 38 40N 87 8W
Washington, Iowa, U.S.A. **116** 41 20N 91 45W
Washington, Mo, U.S.A. **116** 38 35N 91 1W
Washington, N.C., U.S.A. **115** 35 35N 77 1W
Washington, N.J., U.S.A. **113** 40 45N 74 59W
Washington, Pa., U.S.A. **114** 40 10N 80 20W
Washington, Utah, U.S.A. **119** 37 10N 113 30W
Washington □ **118** 47 45N 120 30W
Washington I., Pac. Oc. **95** 4 43N 160 25W
Washington I., U.S.A. **114** 45 24N 86 54W
Washington Mt. **114** 44 15N 71 18W
Wasian **73** 1 47 S 133 19 E
Wasilków **28** 53 12N 23 13 E
Wasior **73** 2 43 S 134 30 E
Waskaiowaka, L. **109** 56 33N 96 23W
Waskesiu Lake **109** 53 55N 106 5W
Wasm **86** 18 2N 41 32 E
Wassenaar **16** 52 8N 4 24 E
Wasserburg **25** 48 4N 12 15 E
Wasserkuppe **24** 50 30N 9 56 E
Wassy **19** 48 30N 4 58 E
Waswanipi **106** 49 40N 76 29W
Waswanipi, L. **106** 49 35N 76 40W
Watangpone **73** 4 29 S 120 25 E
Water Park Pt. **98** 22 56 S 150 47 E
Water Valley **117** 34 9N 89 38W
Waterberg, Namibia **92** 20 30 S 17 18 E
Waterberg, S. Afr. **93** 24 14 S 28 0 E
Waterbury, Conn., U.S.A. **114** 41 32N 73 0W
Waterbury, Vt., U.S.A. **113** 44 22N 72 44W
Waterbury L. **109** 58 10N 104 22W
Waterdown **112** 43 20N 79 53W
Waterford, Can. **112** 42 56N 80 17W
Waterford, Ireland **15** 52 16N 7 8W
Waterford □ **15** 52 10N 7 40W
Waterford Harb. **15** 52 10N 6 58W
Waterhen L., Man., Can. **109** 52 10N 99 40W
Waterhen L., Sask., Can. **109** 54 28N 108 25W
Waterloo, Belg. **16** 50 43N 4 25 E
Waterloo, Ont., Can. **106** 43 30N 80 32W
Waterloo, Qué., Can. **113** 45 22N 72 32W
Waterloo, S. Leone **84** 8 26N 13 8W
Waterloo, Ill., U.S.A. **116** 38 22N 90 6W
Waterloo, Iowa, U.S.A. **116** 42 27N 92 20W
Waterloo, N.Y., U.S.A. **112** 42 54N 76 53W
Watersmeet **116** 46 15N 89 12W
Waterton Lakes Nat. Park **108** 49 5N 114 15W
Watertown, Conn., U.S.A. **113** 41 36N 73 7W
Watertown, N.Y., U.S.A. **114** 43 58N 75 57W
Watertown, S.D., U.S.A. **116** 44 57N 97 5W
Watertown, Wis., U.S.A. **116** 43 15N 88 45W
Waterval-Boven **93** 25 40 S 30 18 E
Waterville, Can. **113** 45 16N 71 54W
Waterville, Me., U.S.A. **107** 44 35N 69 40W
Waterville, N.Y., U.S.A. **113** 42 56N 75 23W
Waterville, Pa., U.S.A. **112** 41 19N 77 21W
Waterville, Wash., U.S.A. **118** 47 38N 120 1W
Watervliet **114** 42 46N 73 43W
Wates **73** 7 53 S 110 6 E
Watford, Can. **112** 42 57N 81 53W
Watford, U.K. **13** 51 38N 0 23W
Watford City **116** 47 50N 103 23W
Wathaman → **109** 57 16N 102 59W
Watkins Glen **114** 42 25N 76 55W
Watling I. = San Salvador **121** 24 0N 74 40W
Watonga **117** 35 51N 98 24W
Watrous, Can. **109** 51 40N 105 25W
Watrous, U.S.A. **117** 35 50N 104 55W
Watsa **90** 3 4N 29 30 E
Watseka **114** 40 45N 87 45W
Watson **109** 52 10N 104 30W
Watson Lake **104** 60 6N 128 49W
Watsonville **119** 36 55N 121 49W
Wattwil **25** 47 18N 9 6 E
Watuata = Batuata **73** 6 12 S 122 42 E
Watubela, Kepulauan **73** 4 28 S 131 35 E
Wau **98** 7 21 S 146 47 E
Waubamik **112** 45 27N 80 1W
Waubay **116** 45 22N 97 17W
Waubra **99** 37 21 S 143 39 E
Wauchope **99** 31 28 S 152 45 E
Wauchula **115** 27 35N 81 50W
Waugh **109** 49 40N 95 11W
Waukegan **114** 42 22N 87 54W
Waukesha **114** 43 0N 88 15W
Waukon **116** 43 14N 91 33W
Wauneta **116** 40 27N 101 25W
Waupaca **116** 44 22N 89 8W
Waupun **116** 43 38N 88 44W
Waurika **117** 34 12N 98 0W
Wausau **116** 44 57N 89 40W
Wautoma **116** 44 3N 89 20W
Wauwatosa **114** 43 6N 87 59W
Wave Hill **96** 17 32 S 131 0 E
Waveney → **13** 52 24N 1 20 E
Waverley **101** 39 46 S 174 37 E
Waverly, Iowa, U.S.A. **116** 42 40N 92 30W
Waverly, N.Y., U.S.A. **114** 42 0N 76 33W
Wavre **16** 50 43N 4 38 E
Wâw **87** 7 45N 28 1 E
Waw al Kabir **81** 25 20N 17 20 E
Wāw al Kabīr **83** 25 20N 16 43 E
Wāw an Nāmūs **83** 24 55N 17 46 E
Wawa, Can. **106** 47 59N 84 47W
Wawa, Nigeria **85** 9 54N 4 27 E
Wawa, Sudan **86** 20 30N 30 22 E
Wawanesa **109** 49 36N 99 40W
Wawoi → **98** 7 48 S 143 16 E
Waxahachie **117** 32 22N 96 53W
Waxweiler **25** 50 6N 6 22 E
Wayabula Rau **73** 2 29N 128 17 E
Wayatinah **99** 42 19 S 146 27 E
Waycross **115** 31 12N 82 25W
Wayi **87** 5 8N 30 10 E
Wayne, Nebr., U.S.A. **116** 42 16N 97 0W
Wayne, W. Va., U.S.A. **114** 38 15N 82 27W
Waynesboro, Ga., U.S.A. **115** 33 6N 82 1W
Waynesboro, Miss., U.S.A. **115** 31 40N 88 39W
Waynesboro, Pa., U.S.A. **114** 39 46N 77 32W
Waynesboro, Va., U.S.A. **114** 38 4N 78 57W
Waynesburg **114** 39 54N 80 12W
Waynesville **115** 35 31N 83 0W
Waynoka **117** 36 38N 98 53W
Wāzin **83** 31 58N 10 40 E
Wazirabad **68** 32 30N 74 8 E
Wda → **28** 53 25N 18 29 E
We **72** 5 51N 95 18 E
Weald, The **13** 51 7N 0 9 E
Wear → **12** 54 55N 1 22W
Weatherford, Okla., U.S.A. **117** 35 30N 98 45W
Weatherford, Tex., U.S.A. **117** 32 45N 97 48W
Weaverville **118** 40 44N 122 56W
Webb City **117** 37 9N 94 30W
Webster, Mass., U.S.A. **113** 42 4N 71 54W
Webster, N.Y., U.S.A. **112** 43 11N 77 27W
Webster, S.D., U.S.A. **116** 45 24N 97 33W
Webster, Wis., U.S.A. **116** 45 53N 92 25W
Webster City **116** 42 30N 93 50W
Webster Green **116** 38 38N 90 20W
Webster Springs **114** 38 30N 80 25W
Weda **73** 0 21N 127 50 E
Weda, Teluk **73** 0 30N 127 50 E
Weddell I. **128** 51 50 S 61 0W
Weddell Sea **5** 72 30 S 40 0W
Wedderburn **99** 36 26 S 143 33 E
Wedge I. **96** 30 50 S 115 11 E
Wedgeport **107** 43 44N 65 59W
Wedza **91** 18 40 S 31 33 E
Wee Waa **99** 30 11 S 149 26 E
Weed **118** 41 29N 122 22W
Weedsport **113** 43 3N 76 35W
Weedville **112** 41 17N 78 28W
Weemelah **99** 29 2 S 149 15 E
Weenen **93** 28 48 S 30 7 E
Weener **24** 53 10N 7 23 E
Weert **16** 51 15N 5 43 E
Wegierska-Gorka **27** 49 36N 19 7 E
Wegliniec **28** 51 18N 15 10 E
Węgorzewo **28** 54 13N 21 43 E
Węgrów **28** 52 24N 22 0 E
Wei He →, Hebei, China **76** 36 10N 115 45 E
Wei He →, Shaanxi, China **77** 34 38N 110 15 E
Weida **24** 50 47N 12 3 E
Weiden **25** 49 40N 12 10 E
Weifang **76** 36 44N 119 7 E
Weihai **76** 37 30N 122 6 E
Weilburg **24** 50 28N 8 17 E
Weilheim **25** 47 50N 11 9 E
Weimar **24** 51 0N 11 20 E
Weinan **77** 34 31N 109 29 E
Weingarten **25** 47 49N 9 39 E
Weinheim **25** 49 33N 8 40 E
Weipa **97** 12 40 S 141 50 E
Weir →, Austral. **99** 28 20 S 149 50 E
Weir →, Can. **109** 56 54N 93 21W
Weir River **109** 56 49N 94 6W
Weirton **112** 40 23N 80 35W
Weiser **118** 44 10N 117 0W
Weishan **77** 34 47N 117 5 E
Weissenburg **25** 49 2N 10 58 E
Weissenfels **24** 51 11N 12 0 E
Weisswasser **24** 51 30N 14 36 E
Wéitra **26** 48 41N 14 54 E
Weiyuan **76** 35 7N 104 10 E
Weiz **26** 47 13N 15 39 E
Weizhou Dao **77** 21 0N 109 5 E
Wejherowo **28** 54 35N 18 12 E
Wekusko **109** 54 30N 99 45W
Wekusko L. **109** 54 40N 99 50W
Welby **109** 50 33N 101 29W
Welch **114** 37 29N 81 36W
Weldya **87** 11 50N 39 34 E
Welega □ **87** 9 25N 34 20 E
Welkite **87** 8 15N 37 42 E
Welkom **92** 28 0 S 26 50 E
Welland **106** 43 0N 79 15W
Welland → **12** 52 43N 0 10W
Wellesley Is. **97** 16 42 S 139 30 E
Wellin **16** 50 5N 5 6 E
Wellingborough **13** 52 18N 0 41W
Wellington, Austral. **97** 32 35 S 148 59 E
Wellington, Can. **106** 43 57N 77 20W
Wellington, N.Z. **101** 41 19 S 174 46 E
Wellington, S. Afr. **92** 33 38 S 18 57 E
Wellington, U.K. **13** 50 58N 3 13W
Wellington, Col., U.S.A. **116** 40 43N 105 0W
Wellington, Kans., U.S.A. **117** 37 15N 97 25W
Wellington, Nev., U.S.A. **118** 38 47N 119 28W
Wellington, Ohio, U.S.A. **112** 41 9N 82 12W
Wellington, Tex., U.S.A. **117** 34 55N 100 13W
Wellington □ **101** 40 8 S 175 36 E
Wellington, I. **128** 49 30 S 75 0W
Wellington, L. **99** 38 6 S 147 20 E
Wellington (Telford) **12** 52 42N 2 31W
Wells, Norfolk, U.K. **12** 52 57N 0 51 E
Wells, Somerset, U.K. **13** 51 12N 2 39W
Wells, Me., U.S.A. **113** 43 18N 70 35W
Wells, Minn., U.S.A. **116** 43 44N 93 45W
Wells, Nev., U.S.A. **118** 41 8N 115 0W
Wells Gray Prov. Park **108** 52 30N 120 15W
Wells L. **96** 26 44 S 123 15 E
Wells River **113** 44 9N 72 4W
Wellsboro **114** 41 45N 77 20W
Wellsburg **112** 40 15N 80 36W
Wellsville, Mo., U.S.A. **116** 39 4N 91 30W
Wellsville, N.Y., U.S.A. **114** 42 9N 77 53W
Wellsville, Ohio, U.S.A. **114** 40 36N 80 40W
Wellsville, Utah, U.S.A. **118** 41 35N 111 59W
Wellton **119** 32 39N 114 6W
Welmel, Wabi → **87** 5 38N 40 47 E
Wełna → **28** 52 46N 17 32 E
Welo □ **87** 11 50N 39 48 E
Wels **26** 48 9N 14 1 E
Welshpool **13** 52 40N 3 9W
Welwyn **109** 50 20N 101 30W
Wem **12** 52 52N 2 45W
Wembere → **90** 4 10 S 34 15 E
Wen Xian **77** 32 43N 104 36 E
Wenatchee **118** 47 30N 120 17W
Wenchang **77** 19 38N 110 42 E
Wenchi **84** 7 46N 2 8W
Wenchow = Wenzhou **75** 28 0N 120 38 E
Wendell **118** 42 50N 114 42W
Wendeng **76** 37 15N 122 5 E
Wendesi **73** 2 30 S 134 17 E
Wendo **87** 6 40N 38 27 E
Wendover **118** 40 49N 114 1W
Wengcheng **77** 24 22N 113 50 E
Wenlock **98** 13 6 S 142 58 E
Wenlock → **97** 12 2 S 141 55 E
Wensu **75** 41 15N 80 10 E
Wentworth **97** 34 2 S 141 54 E
Wenut **73** 3 11 S 133 19 E
Wenxi **77** 35 20N 111 10 E
Wenzhou **75** 28 0N 120 38 E
Weott **118** 40 19N 123 56W
Wepener **92** 29 42 S 27 3 E
Werda **92** 25 24 S 23 15 E
Werdau **24** 50 45N 12 20 E
Werder, Ethiopia **63** 6 58N 45 1 E
Werder, Ger. **24** 52 23N 12 56 E
Werdohl **24** 51 15N 7 47 E
Wereilu **87** 10 40N 39 28 E
Weri **73** 3 10 S 132 38 E
Werne **24** 51 38N 7 38 E
Werneck **25** 49 59N 10 6 E
Wernigerode **24** 51 49N 10 45 E
Werra → **24** 51 26N 9 39 E
Werribee **99** 37 54 S 144 40 E
Werrimull **99** 34 25 S 141 38 E
Werris Creek **99** 31 18 S 150 38 E
Wersar **73** 1 30 S 131 55 E
Wertach → **25** 48 24N 10 53 E
Wertheim **25** 49 44N 9 32 E
Wertingen **25** 48 33N 10 41 E
Wesel **24** 51 39N 6 34 E
Weser → **24** 53 33N 8 30 E
Wesiri **73** 7 30 S 126 30 E
Wesleyville, Can. **107** 49 8N 53 36W
Wesleyville, U.S.A. **112** 42 9N 80 1W
Wessel Is. **97** 11 10 S 136 45 E
Wesselburen **24** 54 11N 8 53 E
Wessington **116** 44 30N 98 40W
Wessington Springs **116** 44 10N 98 35W
West **117** 31 50N 97 5W
West B. **117** 29 5N 89 27W
West Bend **114** 43 25N 88 10W
West Bengal □ **69** 23 0N 88 0 E
West Branch **114** 44 16N 84 13W
West Bromwich **13** 52 32N 2 1W
West Chazy **113** 44 49N 73 28W
West Chester **114** 39 58N 75 36W
West Columbia **117** 29 10N 95 38W
West Des Moines **116** 41 30N 93 45W
West Falkland **128** 51 40 S 60 0W
West Frankfurt **116** 37 56N 89 0W
West Germany ■ **24** 52 0N 9 0 E
West Glamorgan □ **13** 51 40N 3 55W
West Hartford **113** 41 45N 72 45W
West Haven **113** 41 18N 72 57W
West Helena **117** 34 30N 90 40W
West Ice Shelf **5** 67 0 S 85 0 E
West Indies **121** 15 0N 70 0W
West Looe **13** 50 21N 4 29W
West Lorne **112** 42 36N 81 36W
West Lunga → **91** 13 6 S 24 39 E
West Magpie → **107** 51 2N 64 42W
West Memphis **117** 35 5N 90 11W
West Midlands □ **13** 52 30N 1 55W
West Monroe **117** 32 32N 92 7W
West Moors **12** 50 49N 1 50W
West Newton **112** 40 14N 79 46W
West Nicholson **91** 21 2 S 29 20 E
West Palm Beach **115** 26 44N 80 3W
West Pittston **113** 41 19N 75 49W
West Plains **117** 36 45N 91 50W
West Point, Ga., U.S.A. **115** 32 54N 85 10W
West Point, Miss., U.S.A. **115** 33 36N 88 38W
West Point, Nebr., U.S.A. **116** 41 50N 96 43W
West Point, Va., U.S.A. **114** 37 35N 76 47W
West Pokot □ **90** 1 30N 35 15 E
West Road → **108** 53 18N 122 53W
West Rutland **114** 43 38N 73 0W
West Schelde → = Westerschelde **16** 51 25N 3 25 E
West Siberian Plain **60** 62 0N 75 0 E
West Sussex □ **13** 50 55N 0 30W
West-Terschelling **16** 53 22N 5 13 E
West Virginia □ **114** 39 0N 81 0W
West-Vlaanderen □ **16** 51 0N 3 0 E
West Wyalong **100** 33 56 S 147 10 E
West Yellowstone **118** 44 47N 111 4W
West Yorkshire □ **12** 53 45N 1 40W
Westbrook, Maine, U.S.A. **115** 43 40N 70 22W
Westbrook, Tex., U.S.A. **117** 32 25N 101 0W
Westbury **99** 41 30 S 146 51 E
Westby **116** 48 52N 104 3W
Westerland **24** 54 51N 8 20 E
Western □, Kenya **90** 0 30N 34 30 E
Western □, Uganda **90** 1 45N 31 30 E
Western □, Zambia **91** 15 15 S 24 30 E
Western Australia □ **96** 25 0 S 118 0 E
Western Ghats **70** 14 0N 75 0 E
Western Isles □ **14** 57 30N 7 10W
Western Samoa ■ **101** 14 0 S 172 0W
Westernport **114** 39 30N 79 5W
Westerschelde → **16** 51 25N 3 25 E
Westerstede **24** 53 15N 7 55 E
Westerwald **24** 50 39N 8 0 E
Westfield, Mass., U.S.A. **113** 42 9N 72 49W
Westfield, N.Y., U.S.A. **112** 42 20N 79 38W
Westfield, Pa., U.S.A. **112** 41 54N 77 32W
Westhope **116** 48 55N 101 0W
Westland □ **101** 43 33 S 169 59 E
Westland Bight **101** 42 55 S 170 5 E
Westlock **108** 54 9N 113 55W
Westmeath □ **15** 53 30N 7 30W
Westminster **114** 39 34N 77 1W
Westmorland **119** 33 2N 115 42W
Weston, Malay. **72** 5 10N 115 35 E
Weston, Oreg., U.S.A. **118** 45 50N 118 30W
Weston, W. Va., U.S.A. **114** 39 3N 80 29W
Weston I. **106** 52 33N 79 36W
Weston-super-Mare **13** 51 20N 2 59W
Westport, Can. **113** 44 40N 76 25W
Westport, Ireland **15** 53 44N 9 31W
Westport, N.Z. **101** 41 46 S 171 37 E
Westport, U.S.A. **118** 46 48N 124 4W
Westray, Can. **109** 53 36N 101 24W
Westray, U.K. **14** 59 18N 3 0W
Westree **106** 47 26N 81 34W
Westview **108** 49 50N 124 31W
Westville, Ill., U.S.A. **114** 40 3N 87 36W
Westville, Okla., U.S.A. **117** 36 0N 94 33W
Westwood **118** 40 26N 121 0W
Wetar **73** 7 30 S 126 30 E
Wetaskiwin **108** 52 55N 113 24W
Wethersfield **113** 41 43N 72 40W
Wetteren **16** 51 0N 3 53 E
Wetzlar **24** 50 33N 8 30 E

Wewak **98** 3 38 S 143 41 E
Wewaka **117** 35 10N 96 35W
Wexford □ **15** 52 20N 6 28W
Wexford □ **15** 52 20N 6 25W
Wexford Harb. **15** 52 20N 6 25W
Weyburn **109** 49 40N 103 50W
Weyburn L. **108** 63 0N 117 59W
Weyer **26** 47 51N 14 40 E
Weyib → **87** 7 15N 40 15 E
Weymouth, Can. **107** 44 30N 66 1W
Weymouth, U.K. **13** 50 36N 2 28W
Weymouth, U.S.A. **113** 42 13N 70 53W
Weymouth, C. **97** 12 37 S 143 27 E
Whakatane **101** 37 57 S 177 1 E
Whale → **107** 58 15N 67 40W
Whale Cove **104** 62 11N 92 36W
Whales, B. of **5** 78 0 S 165 0W
Whalsay **14** 60 22N 1 0W
Whangamomona **101** 39 8 S 174 44 E
Whangarei **101** 35 43 S 174 21 E
Whangarei Harbour **101** 35 45 S 174 28 E
Wharfe → **12** 53 55N 1 30W
Wharfedale **12** 54 7N 2 4W
Wharton, N.J., U.S.A. **113** 40 53N 74 36W
Wharton, Pa., U.S.A. **112** 41 31N 78 1W
Wharton, Tex., U.S.A. **117** 29 20N 96 6W
Wheatland **116** 42 4N 104 58W
Wheatley **112** 42 6N 82 27W
Wheaton **116** 45 50N 96 29W
Wheeler, Oreg., U.S.A. **118** 45 50N 123 57W
Wheeler, Tex., U.S.A. **117** 35 29N 100 15W
Wheeler → **109** 57 25N 105 30W
Wheeler Pk., N. Mex., U.S.A. **119** 36 34N 105 25W
Wheeler Pk., Nev., U.S.A. **119** 38 57N 114 15W
Wheeling **114** 40 2N 80 41W
Whernside **12** 54 14N 2 24W
Whidbey I. **108** 48 15N 122 40W
Whidbey Is. **96** 34 30 S 135 3 E
Whiskey Gap **108** 49 0N 113 3W
Whiskey Jack L. **109** 58 23N 101 55W
Whistler **115** 30 50N 88 10W
Whitby, Can. **112** 43 52N 78 56W
Whitby, U.K. **12** 54 29N 0 37W
White →, Ark., U.S.A. **117** 33 53N 91 3W
White →, Colo., U.S.A. **118** 40 8N 109 41W
White →, Ind., U.S.A. **114** 38 25N 87 44W
White →, S.D., U.S.A. **116** 43 45N 99 30W
White B. **107** 50 0N 56 35W
White Bear Res. **107** 48 10N 57 5W
White Bird **118** 45 46N 116 21W
White Butte **116** 46 23N 103 19W
White City **116** 38 50N 96 45W
White Cliffs **99** 30 50 S 143 10 E
White Deer **117** 35 30N 101 8W
White Hall **116** 39 25N 90 27W
White Haven **113** 41 3N 75 47W
White I. **101** 37 30 S 177 13 E
White L., Can. **113** 45 18N 76 31W
White L., U.S.A. **117** 29 45N 92 30W
White Mts., Calif., U.S.A. **119** 37 30N 118 15W
White Mts., N.H., U.S.A. **113** 44 15N 71 15W
White Nile = Nîl el Abyad → **87** 15 38N 32 31 E
White Nile Dam **87** 15 24N 32 30 E
White Otter L. **106** 49 5N 91 55W
White Pass **104** 59 40N 135 3W
White Plains **113** 41 2N 73 44W
White River, Can. **106** 48 35N 85 20W
White River, S. Afr. **93** 25 20 S 31 00 E
White River, U.S.A. **116** 43 34N 100 45W
White River Junc. **113** 43 38N 72 20W
White Russia = Byelorussian S.S.R. □ **54** 53 30N 27 0 E
White Sea = Beloye More **52** 66 30N 38 0 E
White Sulphur Springs, Mont., U.S.A. **118** 46 35N 110 54W
White Sulphur Springs, W. Va., U.S.A. **114** 37 50N 80 16W
White Volta (Volta Blanche) → **85** 9 10N 1 15W
Whitecliffs **101** 43 26 S 171 55 E
Whitecourt **108** 54 10N 115 45W
Whiteface **117** 33 35N 102 40W
Whitefield **113** 44 23N 71 37W
Whitefish **118** 48 25N 114 22W
Whitefish L. **109** 62 41N 106 48W
Whitefish Pt. **114** 46 45N 85 0W
Whitegull, L. **107** 55 27N 64 17W
Whitehall, Mich., U.S.A. **114** 43 21N 86 20W
Whitehall, Mont., U.S.A. **118** 45 52N 112 4W
Whitehall, N.Y., U.S.A. **114** 43 32N 73 28W
Whitehall, Wis., U.S.A. **116** 44 20N 91 19W
Whitehaven **12** 54 33N 3 35W
Whitehorse **104** 60 43N 135 3W
Whitehorse, Vale of **13** 51 37N 1 30W
Whiteman Ra. **98** 5 55 S 150 0 E
Whitemark **99** 40 7 S 148 3 E
Whitemouth **109** 49 57N 95 58W
Whiteplains **84** 6 28N 10 40W
Whitesail, L. **108** 53 35N 127 45W
Whitesboro, N.Y., U.S.A. **113** 43 8N 75 20W
Whitesboro, Tex., U.S.A. **117** 33 40N 96 58W
Whiteshell Prov. Park **109** 50 0N 95 40W
Whitetail **116** 48 54N 105 15W
Whiteville **115** 34 20N 78 40W
Whitewater **114** 42 50N 88 45W
Whitewater Baldy, Mt. **119** 33 20N 108 44W
Whitewater L. **106** 50 50N 89 10W
Whitewood, Austral. **98** 21 28 S 143 30 E
Whitewood, Can. **109** 50 20N 102 20W
Whitfield **99** 36 42 S 146 24 E
Whithorn **14** 54 44N 4 25W
Whitianga **101** 36 47 S 175 41 E
Whitman **113** 42 4N 70 55W
Whitmire **115** 34 33N 81 40W
Whitney **106** 45 31N 78 14W
Whitney, Mt. **119** 36 35N 118 14W
Whitney Pt. **113** 42 19N 75 59W
Whitstable **13** 51 21N 1 2 E
Whitsunday I. **97** 20 15 S 149 4 E
Whittier **104** 60 46N 148 48W
Whittlesea **99** 37 27 S 145 9 E
Whitwell **115** 35 15N 85 30W
Wholdaia L. **109** 60 43N 104 20W
Whyalla **97** 33 2 S 137 30 E
Whyjonta **99** 29 41 S 142 28 E
Wiarton **106** 44 40N 81 10W
Wiawso **84** 6 10N 2 25W
Wiazów **28** 50 50N 17 10 E
Wibaux **116** 47 0N 104 13W
Wichita **117** 37 40N 97 20W
Wichita Falls **117** 33 57N 98 30W
Wick **14** 58 26N 3 5W
Wickenburg **119** 33 58N 112 45W
Wickett **117** 31 37N 102 58W
Wickham, C. **99** 39 35 S 143 57 E
Wickliffe **112** 41 36N 81 29W
Wicklow **15** 53 0N 6 2W
Wicklow □ **15** 52 59N 6 25W
Wicklow Hd. **15** 52 59N 6 3W
Wicklow Mts. **15** 53 0N 6 30W
Widawa **28** 51 27N 18 51 E
Widawka **28** 51 7N 19 36 E
Widnes **12** 53 22N 2 44W
Więcbork **28** 53 21N 17 30 E
Wiedenbrück **24** 51 52N 8 15 E
Wiek **24** 54 37N 13 17 E
Wielbark **28** 53 24N 20 55 E
Wieleń **28** 52 53N 16 9 E
Wieliczka **27** 50 0N 20 5 E
Wieluń **28** 51 15N 18 34 E
Wien **27** 48 12N 16 22 E
Wiener Neustadt **27** 47 49N 16 16 E
Wieprz →, Koszalin, Poland **28** 54 26N 16 35 E
Wieprz →, Lublin, Poland **28** 51 34N 21 49 E
Wierden **16** 52 22N 6 35 E
Wieruszów **28** 51 19N 18 9 E
Wiesbaden **25** 50 7N 8 17 E
Wiesental **25** 49 15N 8 30 E
Wigan **12** 53 33N 2 38W
Wiggins, Colo., U.S.A. **116** 40 16N 104 3W
Wiggins, Miss., U.S.A. **117** 30 53N 89 9W
Wight, I. of **13** 50 40N 1 20W
Wigry, Jezioro **28** 54 2N 23 8 E
Wigtown **14** 54 52N 4 27W
Wigtown B. **14** 54 46N 4 15W
Wil **25** 47 28N 9 3 E
Wilamowice **27** 49 55N 19 9 E
Wilber **116** 40 34N 96 59W
Wilberforce **112** 45 2N 78 13W
Wilberforce, C. **97** 11 54 S 136 35 E
Wilburton **117** 34 55N 95 15W
Wilcannia **97** 31 30 S 143 26 E
Wilcox **112** 41 34N 78 43W
Wildbad **25** 48 44N 8 32 E
Wildeshausen **24** 52 54N 8 25 E
Wildon **26** 46 52N 15 31 E
Wildrose **116** 48 36N 103 11W
Wildspitze **26** 46 53N 10 53 E
Wildwood **114** 38 59N 74 46W
Wilga → **28** 51 52N 21 18 E
Wilhelm II Coast **5** 68 0 S 90 0 E
Wilhelm Mt. **98** 5 50 S 145 1 E
Wilhelm-Pieck-Stadt Guben **24** 51 59N 14 48 E
Wilhelmsburg, Austria **26** 48 6N 15 36 E
Wilhelmsburg, Ger. **24** 53 28N 10 1 E
Wilhelmshaven **24** 53 30N 8 9 E
Wilhelmstal **92** 21 58 S 16 21 E
Wilkes Barre **114** 41 15N 75 52W
Wilkes Land **5** 69 0 S 120 0 E
Wilkes Sub-Glacial Basin **5** 75 0 S 130 0 E
Wilkesboro **115** 36 10N 81 9W
Wilkie **109** 52 27N 108 42W
Wilkinsburg **112** 40 26N 79 50W
Willamina **118** 45 9N 123 32W
Willandra Billabong Creek → **99** 33 22 S 145 52 E
Willapa, B. **118** 46 44N 124 0W
Willard, N. Mex., U.S.A. **119** 34 35N 106 1W
Willard, Utah, U.S.A. **118** 41 28N 112 1W
Willcox **119** 32 13N 109 53W
Willemstad **121** 12 5N 69 0W
William → **109** 59 8N 109 19W
Williams **119** 35 16N 112 11W
Williams Lake **108** 52 10N 122 10W
Williamsburg, Ky., U.S.A. **115** 36 45N 84 10W
Williamsburg, Pa., U.S.A. **112** 40 27N 78 14W
Williamsburg, Va., U.S.A. **114** 37 17N 76 44W
Williamson, N.Y., U.S.A. **112** 43 14N 77 15W
Williamson, W. Va., U.S.A. **114** 37 46N 82 17W
Williamsport **114** 41 18N 77 1W
Williamston **115** 35 50N 77 5W
Williamstown, Austral. **99** 37 51 S 144 52 E
Williamstown, Mass., U.S.A. **113** 42 41N 73 12W
Williamstown, N.Y., U.S.A. **113** 43 25N 75 54W
Williamsville **117** 37 0N 90 33W
Willimantic **113** 41 45N 72 12W
Williston, S. Afr. **92** 31 20 S 20 53 E
Williston, Fla., U.S.A. **115** 29 25N 82 28W
Williston, N.D., U.S.A. **116** 48 10N 103 35W
Williston L. **108** 56 0N 124 0W
Willits **118** 39 28N 123 17W
Willmar **116** 45 5N 95 0W
Willoughby **112** 41 38N 81 26W
Willow Bunch **109** 49 20N 105 35W
Willow L. **108** 62 10N 119 8W
Willow Lake **116** 44 40N 97 40W
Willow River **108** 54 6N 122 28W
Willow Springs **117** 37 0N 92 0W
Willowlake → **108** 62 42N 123 8W
Willowmore **92** 33 15 S 23 30 E
Willows, Austral. **98** 23 39 S 147 25 E
Willows, U.S.A. **118** 39 30N 122 10W
Wills Cr. → **98** 22 43 S 140 2 E
Wills Pt. **117** 32 42N 95 57W
Willunga **99** 35 15 S 138 30 E
Wilmette **114** 42 6N 87 44W
Wilmington, Austral. **99** 32 39 S 138 7 E
Wilmington, Del., U.S.A. **114** 39 45N 75 32W
Wilmington, Ill., U.S.A. **114** 41 19N 88 10W
Wilmington, N.C., U.S.A. **115** 34 14N 77 54W
Wilmington, Ohio, U.S.A. **114** 39 27N 83 50W
Wilpena Cr. → **99** 31 25 S 139 29 E
Wilsall **118** 45 59N 110 40W
Wilson **115** 35 44N 77 54W
Wilson → **99** 27 38 S 141 24 E
Wilson, Mt. **119** 37 55N 108 3W
Wilson's Promontory **97** 38 55 S 146 25 E
Wilster **24** 53 55N 9 23 E
Wilton, U.K. **13** 51 5N 1 52W
Wilton, U.S.A. **116** 47 12N 100 47W
Wiltshire □ **13** 51 20N 2 0W
Wiltz **16** 49 57N 5 55 E
Wiluna **96** 26 36 S 120 14 E
Wimereux **19** 50 45N 1 37 E
Wimmera **97** 36 30 S 142 0 E
Wimmera → **99** 36 8 S 141 56 E
Winam G. **90** 0 20 S 34 15 E
Winburg **92** 28 30 S 27 2 E
Winchendon **113** 42 40N 72 3W
Winchester, U.K. **13** 51 4N 1 19W
Winchester, Conn., U.S.A. **113** 41 53N 73 9W
Winchester, Idaho, U.S.A. **118** 46 11N 116 32W
Winchester, Ind., U.S.A. **114** 40 10N 84 56W
Winchester, Ky., U.S.A. **114** 38 0N 84 8W
Winchester, Mass., U.S.A. **113** 42 28N 71 10W
Winchester, N.H., U.S.A. **113** 42 47N 72 22W
Winchester, Tenn., U.S.A. **115** 35 11N 86 8W
Winchester, Va., U.S.A. **114** 39 14N 78 8W
Wind → **118** 43 8N 108 12W
Wind River Range **118** 43 0N 109 30W
Windber **114** 40 14N 78 50W
Windermere, L. **12** 54 20N 2 57W
Windfall **108** 54 12N 116 13W
Windflower L. **108** 62 52N 118 30W
Windhoek **92** 22 35 S 17 4 E
Windischgarsten **26** 47 42N 14 21 E
Windom **116** 43 48N 95 3W
Windorah **97** 25 24 S 142 36 E
Window Rock **119** 35 47N 109 4W
Windrush → **13** 51 48N 1 35W
Windsor, Austral. **99** 33 37 S 150 50 E
Windsor, N.S., Can. **107** 44 59N 64 5W
Windsor, Newf., Can. **107** 48 57N 55 40W
Windsor, Ont., Can. **106** 42 18N 83 0W
Windsor, U.K. **13** 51 28N 0 36W
Windsor, Col., U.S.A. **116** 40 33N 104 45W
Windsor, Conn., U.S.A. **113** 41 50N 72 40W
Windsor, Mo., U.S.A. **116** 38 32N 93 31W
Windsor, N.Y., U.S.A. **113** 42 5N 75 37W
Windsor, Vt., U.S.A. **114** 43 30N 72 25W
Windsorton **92** 28 16 S 24 44 E
Windward Is., Atl. Oc. **121** 13 0N 63 0W
Windward Is., Pac. Oc. **95** 18 0 S 149 0W
Windward Passage = Vientos, Paso de los **121** 20 0N 74 0W
Windy L. **109** 60 20N 100 2W
Winefred L. **109** 55 30N 110 30W
Winejok **87** 9 1N 27 30 E
Winfield **117** 37 15N 97 0W
Wingen **99** 31 54 S 150 54 E
Wingham, Austral. **99** 31 48 S 152 22 E
Wingham, Can. **106** 43 55N 81 20W
Winifred **118** 47 30N 109 28W
Winisk **106** 55 20N 85 15W
Winisk → **106** 55 17N 85 5W
Winisk L. **106** 52 55N 87 22W
Wink **117** 31 49N 103 9W
Winkler **109** 49 10N 97 56W
Winklern **26** 46 52N 12 52 E
Winlock **118** 46 29N 122 56W
Winneba **85** 5 25N 0 36W
Winnebago **116** 43 43N 94 8W
Winnebago L. **114** 44 0N 88 20W
Winnemucca **118** 41 0N 117 45W
Winnemucca, L. **118** 40 25N 119 21W
Winner **116** 43 23N 99 52W
Winnetka **114** 42 8N 87 46W
Winnett **118** 47 2N 108 21W
Winnfield **117** 31 57N 92 38W
Winnibigoshish L. **116** 47 25N 94 12W
Winnipeg **109** 49 54N 97 9W
Winnipeg → **109** 50 38N 96 19W
Winnipeg Beach **109** 50 30N 96 58W
Winnipeg, L. **109** 52 0N 97 0W
Winnipegosis **109** 51 39N 99 55W
Winnipegosis L. **109** 52 30N 100 0W
Winnipesaukee, L. **113** 43 38N 71 21W
Winnsboro, La., U.S.A. **117** 32 10N 91 41W
Winnsboro, S.C., U.S.A. **115** 34 23N 81 5W
Winnsboro, Tex., U.S.A. **117** 32 56N 95 15W
Winokapau, L. **107** 53 15N 62 50W
Winona, Miss., U.S.A. **117** 33 30N 89 42W
Winona, Wis., U.S.A. **116** 44 2N 91 39W
Winooski **114** 44 31N 73 11W
Winschoten **16** 53 9N 7 3 E
Winsen **24** 53 21N 10 11 E
Winslow **119** 35 2N 110 41W
Winsted **113** 41 55N 73 5W
Winston-Salem **115** 36 7N 80 15W
Winter Garden **115** 28 33N 81 35W
Winter Haven **115** 28 0N 81 42W
Winter Park **115** 28 34N 81 19W
Winterberg **24** 51 12N 8 30 E
Winters **117** 31 58N 99 58W
Winterset **116** 41 18N 94 0W
Wintersville **112** 40 22N 80 38W
Winterswijk **16** 51 58N 6 43 E
Winterthur **25** 47 30N 8 44 E
Winthrop, Minn., U.S.A. **116** 44 31N 94 25W
Winthrop, Wash., U.S.A. **118** 48 27N 120 6W
Winton, Austral. **97** 22 24 S 143 3 E
Winton, N.Z. **101** 46 8 S 168 20 E
Winton, N.C., U.S.A. **115** 36 25N 76 58W
Winton, Pa., U.S.A. **113** 41 27N 75 33W
Wintzenheim **19** 48 4N 7 17 E
Wipper → **24** 51 17N 11 10 E
Wirral **12** 53 25N 3 0W
Wisbech **12** 52 39N 0 10 E
Wisconsin □ **116** 44 30N 90 0W
Wisconsin → **116** 43 0N 91 15W
Wisconsin Dells **116** 43 38N 89 45W
Wisconsin Rapids **116** 44 25N 89 50W
Wisdom **118** 45 37N 113 27W
Wishaw **14** 55 46N 3 55W
Wishek **116** 46 20N 99 35W
Wisła **27** 49 38N 18 53 E
Wisła → **28** 54 22N 18 55 E
Wisłok → **27** 50 13N 22 32 E
Wisłoka → **27** 50 27N 21 23 E
Wismar **24** 53 53N 11 23 E
Wisner **116** 42 0N 96 46W
Wissant **19** 50 52N 1 40 E
Wissembourg **19** 49 2N 7 57 E
Wistoka → **27** 49 50N 21 28 E
Wisznice **28** 51 48N 23 13 E
Witbank **93** 25 51 S 29 14 E
Witdraai **92** 26 58 S 20 48 E
Witham → **12** 53 3N 0 8W
Withernsea **12** 53 43N 0 2 E
Witkowo **28** 52 26N 17 45 E
Witney **13** 51 47N 1 29W
Witnossob → **92** 26 55 S 20 37 E
Wittdün **24** 54 38N 8 23 E
Witten **24** 51 26N 7 19 E
Wittenberg **24** 51 51N 12 39 E
Wittenberge **24** 53 0N 11 44 E
Wittenburg **24** 53 30N 11 4 E
Wittenoom **96** 22 15 S 118 20 E
Wittingen **24** 52 43N 10 43 E
Wittlich **25** 50 0N 6 54 E
Wittmund **24** 53 39N 7 45 E
Wittow **24** 54 37N 13 21 E
Wittstock **24** 53 10N 12 30 E
Witzenhausen **24** 51 20N 9 50 E
Wkra → **28** 52 27N 20 44 E
Władysławowo **28** 54 48N 18 25 E
Wlen **28** 51 0N 15 39 E
Wlingi **73** 8 5 S 112 25 E
Włocławek □ **28** 52 50N 19 10 E
Włocławek **28** 52 40N 19 3 E
Włodawa **28** 51 33N 23 31 E
Włoszczowa **28** 50 50N 19 55 E
Woburn **113** 42 31N 71 7W
Wodonga **99** 36 5 S 146 50 E
Wodzisław Śląski **27** 50 1N 18 26 E
Woerth **19** 48 57N 7 45 E
Woëvre, Plaine de la **19** 49 15N 5 45 E
Wokam **73** 5 45 S 134 28 E
Woking **108** 55 35N 118 50W
Wolbrom **28** 50 24N 19 45 E
Wołczyn **28** 51 1N 18 3 E
Woldegk **24** 53 27N 13 35 E
Wolf → **108** 60 17N 132 33W
Wolf Creek **118** 47 1N 112 2W
Wolf L. **108** 60 24N 131 40W
Wolf Point **116** 48 6N 105 40W
Wolfe I. **106** 44 7N 76 20W
Wolfenbüttel **24** 52 10N 10 33 E
Wolfenden **108** 52 0N 119 25W
Wolfsberg **26** 46 50N 14 52 E
Wolfsburg **24** 52 27N 10 49 E
Wolgast **24** 54 3N 13 46 E
Wolhusen **25** 47 4N 8 4 E
Wolin, Poland **28** 53 50N 14 37 E
Wolin, Poland **28** 54 0N 14 40 E
Wollaston, Islas **128** 55 40 S 67 30W
Wollaston L. **109** 58 7N 103 10W
Wollaston Pen. **104** 69 30N 115 0W
Wollondilly → **100** 34 12 S 150 18 E
Wollongong **97** 34 25 S 150 54 E
Wolmaransstad **92** 27 12 S 26 13 E
Wolmirstedt **24** 52 15N 11 35 E
Wołomin **28** 52 19N 21 15 E
Wołów **28** 51 20N 16 38 E
Wolseley, Austral. **99** 36 23 S 140 54 E
Wolseley, Can. **109** 50 25N 103 15W
Wolseley, S. Afr. **92** 33 26 S 19 7 E
Wolstenholme Fjord **4** 76 0N 70 0W
Wolsztyn **28** 52 8N 16 5 E
Wolvega **16** 52 52N 6 0 E
Wolverhampton **13** 52 35N 2 6W
Wondai **97** 26 20 S 151 49 E
Wonder Gorge **91** 14 40 S 29 0 E
Wongalarroo L. **99** 31 32 S 144 0 E
Wŏnju **76** 37 22N 127 58 E
Wonosari **73** 7 58 S 110 36 E
Wŏnsan **76** 39 11N 127 27 E
Wonthaggi **97** 38 37 S 145 37 E
Woocalla **99** 31 42 S 137 12 E
Wood Buffalo Nat. Park **108** 59 0N 113 41W
Wood L. **109** 55 17N 103 17W
Wood Lake **116** 42 38N 100 14W
Woodbridge **112** 43 47N 79 36W
Woodburn **99** 29 6 S 153 23 E
Woodend **99** 37 20 S 144 33 E
Woodland **118** 38 40N 121 50W
Woodlark I. **98** 9 10 S 152 50 E
Woodpecker **108** 53 30N 122 40W
Woodridge **109** 49 20N 96 9W
Woodroffe, Mt. **96** 26 20 S 131 45 E
Woodruff, Ariz., U.S.A. **119** 34 51N 110 1W
Woodruff, Utah, U.S.A. **118** 41 30N 111 4W
Woods, L., Austral. **96** 17 50 S 133 30 E
Woods, L., Can. **107** 54 30N 65 13W
Woods, L. of the **109** 49 15N 94 45W
Woodside **100** 38 31 S 146 52 E
Woodstock, Austral. **98** 19 35 S 146 50 E
Woodstock, N.B., Can. **107** 46 11N 67 37W
Woodstock, Ont., Can. **106** 43 10N 80 45W
Woodstock, U.K. **13** 51 51N 1 20W
Woodstock, Ill., U.S.A. **116** 42 17N 88 30W
Woodstock, Vt., U.S.A. **113** 43 37N 72 31W
Woodsville **114** 44 10N 72 0W
Woodville, N.Z. **101** 40 20 S 175 53 E
Woodville, U.S.A. **117** 30 45N 94 25W
Woodward **117** 36 24N 99 28W
Woolamai, C. **99** 38 30 S 145 23 E
Woombye **99** 26 40 S 152 55 E
Woomera **97** 31 30 S 137 10 E
Woonona **100** 34 21 S 150 54 E
Woonsocket **114** 42 0N 71 30W
Woonsockett **116** 44 5N 98 15W
Wooramel → **96** 25 47 S 114 10 E
Wooster **114** 40 48N 81 55W
Worcester, S. Afr. **92** 33 39 S 19 27 E
Worcester, U.K. **13** 52 12N 2 12W
Worcester, Mass., U.S.A. **114** 42 14N 71 49W
Worcester, N.Y., U.S.A. **113** 42 35N 74 45W
Wörgl **26** 47 29N 12 3 E
Workington **12** 54 39N 3 34W

Worksop 12 53 19N 1 9W
Workum 16 52 59N 5 26 E
Worland 118 44 0N 107 59W
Wormhoudt 19 50 52N 2 28 E
Worms 25 49 37N 8 21 E
Wörth 25 49 1N 12 24 E
Wortham 117 31 48N 96 27W
Wörther See 26 46 37N 14 10 E
Worthing 13 50 49N 0 21W
Worthington 116 43 35N 95 36W
Wosi 73 0 15 S 128 0 E
Wou-han = Wuhan 75 30 31N 114 18 E
Wour 83 21 14N 16 0 E
Wowoni 73 4 5 S 123 5 E
Wozniki 28 50 35N 19 4 E
Wrangell 104 56 30N 132 25W
Wrangell, I. 108 56 20N 132 10W
Wrangell Mts. 104 61 40N 143 30W
Wrath, C. 14 58 38N 5 0W
Wray 116 40 8N 102 18W
Wrekin, The 12 52 41N 2 35W
Wrens 115 33 13N 82 23W
Wrexham 12 53 5N 3 0W
Wriezen 24 52 43N 14 9 E
Wright, Can. 108 51 52N 121 40W
Wright, Phil. 73 11 42N 125 2 E
Wrightson, Mt. 119 31 43N 110 56W
Wrigley 104 63 16N 123 37W
Wrocław 28 51 5N 17 5 E
Wrocław □ 28 51 0N 17 0 E
Wronki 28 52 41N 16 21 E
Września 28 52 21N 17 36 E
Wschowa 28 51 48N 16 20 E
Wu Jiang → 75 29 40N 107 20 E
Wuchang 76 44 55N 127 5 E
Wuchuan 77 28 25N 108 3 E
Wuding He → 76 37 2N 110 23 E
Wugang 77 26 44N 110 35 E
Wugong Shan 77 27 30N 114 0 E
Wuhan 75 30 31N 114 18 E
Wuhsi = Wuxi 75 31 33N 120 18 E
Wuhu 75 31 22N 118 21 E
Wukari 85 7 51N 9 42 E
Wulehe 85 8 39N 0 0
Wuliaru 73 7 27 S 131 0 E
Wulumuchi = Ürümqi 75 43 45N 87 45 E
Wum 85 6 24N 10 2 E
Wuning 77 29 17N 115 5 E
Wunnummin L. 106 52 55N 89 10W
Wunsiedel 25 50 2N 12 0 E
Wunstorf 24 52 26N 9 29 E
Wuntho 67 23 55N 95 45 E
Wuping 77 25 5N 116 5 E
Wuppertal, Ger. 24 51 15N 7 8 E
Wuppertal, S. Afr. 92 32 13 S 19 12 E
Wuqing 76 39 23N 117 4 E
Wurung 98 19 13 S 140 38 E
Würzburg 25 49 46N 9 55 E
Wurzen 24 51 21N 12 45 E
Wushan 77 31 7N 109 54 E
Wustrow 24 54 4N 11 33 E
Wutach → 25 47 37N 8 15 E
Wutongqiao 75 29 22N 103 50 E
Wuwei, Anhui, China 77 31 18N 117 54 E
Wuwei, Gansu, China 75 37 57N 102 34 E
Wuxi, Jiangsu, China 75 31 33N 120 18 E
Wuxi, Sichuan, China 77 31 23N 109 35 E
Wuxing 77 30 51N 120 8 E
Wuyi, Hebei, China 76 37 46N 115 56 E
Wuyi, Zhejiang, China 77 28 52N 119 50 E
Wuyi Shan 75 27 0N 117 0 E
Wuying 76 47 53N 129 56 E
Wuyo 85 10 23N 11 50 E
Wuyuan 76 41 2N 108 20 E
Wuzhai 76 38 54N 111 48 E
Wuzhi Shan 75 18 45N 109 45 E
Wuzhong 76 38 2N 106 12 E
Wuzhou 75 23 30N 111 18 E
Wyaaba Cr. → 98 16 27 S 141 35 E
Wyalusing 113 41 40N 76 16W
Wyandotte 114 42 14N 83 13W
Wyandra 97 27 12 S 145 56 E
Wyangala Res. 100 33 54 S 149 0 E
Wyara, L. 99 28 42 S 144 14 E
Wycheproof 99 36 0 S 143 17 E
Wye → 13 51 36N 2 40W
Wyk 24 54 41N 8 33 E
Wymondham 13 52 45N 0 42W
Wymore 116 40 10N 96 40W
Wynberg 92 34 2 S 18 28 E
Wyndham, Austral. 96 15 33 S 128 3 E
Wyndham, N.Z. 101 46 20 S 168 51 E
Wyndmere 116 46 23N 97 7W
Wynne 117 35 15N 90 50W
Wynnum 99 27 27 S 153 9 E
Wynyard 109 51 45N 104 10W
Wyoming □ 110 42 48N 109 0W
Wyong 99 33 14 S 151 24 E
Wyrzysk 28 53 10N 17 17 E
Wysoka 28 53 13N 17 2 E
Wysokie 28 50 55N 22 40 E
Wysokie Mazowieckie 28 52 55N 22 30 E
Wyszków 28 52 36N 21 25 E
Wyszogród 28 52 23N 20 9 E
Wytheville 114 37 0N 81 3W

X

Xai-Xai 93 25 6 S 33 31 E
Xainza 75 30 58N 88 35 E
Xangongo 92 16 45 S 15 0 E
Xanten 24 51 40N 6 27 E
Xánthi 44 41 10N 24 58 E
Xánthi □ 44 41 10N 24 58 E
Xapuri 126 10 35 S 68 35W
Xau, L. 92 21 15 S 24 44 E
Xavantina 125 21 15 S 52 48W
Xenia 114 39 42N 83 57W
Xi Jiang → 75 22 5N 113 20 E
Xi Xian 76 36 41N 110 58 E
Xiachengzi 76 44 40N 130 18 E
Xiachuan Dao 77 21 40N 112 40 E
Xiaguan 75 25 32N 100 16 E
Xiajiang 77 27 30N 115 10 E
Xiamen 75 24 25N 118 4 E
Xi'an 77 34 15N 109 0 E
Xianfeng 77 29 40N 109 8 E
Xiang Jiang → 75 28 55N 112 50 E
Xiangfan 75 32 2N 112 8 E
Xiangning 76 35 58N 110 50 E
Xiangtan 75 27 51N 112 54 E
Xiangxiang 77 27 43N 112 28 E
Xiangyang 75 32 1N 112 8 E
Xiangyin 77 28 38N 112 54 E
Xiangzhou 77 23 58N 109 40 E
Xianju 77 28 51N 120 44 E
Xianyang 77 34 20N 108 40 E
Xiao Hinggan Ling 75 49 0N 127 0 E
Xiaogan 77 30 52N 113 55 E
Xiapu 75 26 54N 119 59 E
Xichang 75 27 51N 102 19 E
Xichuan 77 33 0N 111 30 E
Xieng Khouang 71 19 17N 103 25 E
Xifeng 77 27 7N 106 42 E
Xigazê 75 29 5N 88 45 E
Xihe 77 34 2N 105 20 E
Xiliao He → 76 43 32N 123 35 E
Xilin 77 24 30N 105 6 E
Xilókastron 45 38 4N 22 43 E
Xin Xian 76 38 22N 112 46 E
Xinavane 93 25 2 S 32 47 E
Xinbin 76 41 40N 125 2 E
Xincheng 77 24 5N 108 39 E
Xinfeng 77 25 27N 114 58 E
Xing'an 75 25 38N 110 40 E
Xingan 77 27 46N 115 20 E
Xingcheng 76 40 40N 120 45 E
Xingguo 77 26 21N 115 21 E
Xinghua 77 32 58N 119 48 E
Xinghua Wan 77 25 15N 119 20 E
Xingning 77 24 3N 115 42 E
Xingren 75 25 24N 105 11 E
Xingshan 77 31 15N 110 45 E
Xingtai 76 37 3N 114 32 E
Xingu → 127 1 30 S 51 53W
Xingyang 77 34 45N 112 52 E
Xinhua 77 27 42N 111 13 E
Xiniás, L. 45 39 2N 22 12 E
Xining 75 36 34N 101 40 E
Xinjiang 76 35 34N 111 11 E
Xinjiang Uygur Zizhiqu □ 75 42 0N 86 0 E
Xinjin 76 39 25N 121 58 E
Xinle 76 38 25N 114 40 E
Xinmin 76 41 59N 122 50 E
Xinning 77 26 28N 110 50 E
Xinxiang 77 35 18N 113 50 E
Xinyang 75 32 6N 114 3 E
Xinzheng 77 34 20N 113 45 E
Xinzhou 77 19 43N 109 17 E
Xinzhu 75 24 49N 120 57 E
Xiongyuecheng 76 40 12N 122 5 E
Xiping 77 33 22N 114 0 E
Xique-Xique 127 10 50 S 42 40W
Xiuyan 76 40 18N 123 11 E
Xixabangma Feng 67 28 20N 85 40 E
Xixiang 77 33 0N 107 44 E
Xizang □ 75 32 0N 88 0 E
Xuancheng 77 30 56N 118 43 E
Xuan'en 77 30 0N 109 30 E
Xuanhan 77 31 18N 107 38 E
Xuanhua 76 40 40N 115 2 E
Xuchang 77 34 2N 113 48 E
Xuguit Qi 76 49 17N 120 44 E
Xunke 76 49 35N 128 27 E
Xupu 77 27 53N 110 32 E
Xuwen 77 20 20N 110 10 E
Xuyong 77 28 10N 105 22 E
Xuzhou 77 34 18N 117 10 E

Y

Ya 'Bad 62 32 27N 35 10 E
Yaamba 98 23 8 S 150 22 E
Ya'an 75 29 58N 103 5 E
Yaapeet 99 35 45 S 142 3 E
Yabassi 85 4 30N 9 57 E
Yabelo 87 4 50N 38 8 E
Yablanitsa 43 43 2N 24 5 E
Yablonovy Khrebet 59 53 0N 114 0 E
Yabrīn 64 23 17N 48 58 E
Yacheng 77 18 22N 109 6 E
Yacuiba 124 22 0 S 63 43W
Yadgir 70 16 45N 77 5 E
Yadkin → 115 35 23N 80 3W
Yadrin 55 55 57N 46 12 E
Yagaba 85 10 14N 1 20W
Yagodnoye 59 62 33N 149 40 E
Yagoua 88 10 20N 15 13 E
Yagur 62 32 45N 35 4 E
Yahila 90 0 13N 24 28 E
Yahk 108 49 6N 116 10W
Yahuma 88 1 0N 23 10 E
Yajua 85 11 27N 12 49 E
Yakima 118 46 42N 120 30W
Yakima → 118 47 0N 120 30W
Yako 84 12 59N 2 15W
Yakoruda 43 42 1N 23 39 E
Yakut A.S.S.R. □ 59 62 0N 130 0 E
Yakutat 104 59 29N 139 44W
Yakutsk 59 62 5N 129 50 E
Yala 71 6 33N 101 18 E
Yalabusha → 117 33 30N 90 12W
Yalboroo 98 20 50 S 148 40 E
Yale 112 43 9N 82 47W
Yalgoo 96 28 16 S 116 39 E
Yalinga 88 6 33N 23 10 E
Yalkubul, Punta 120 21 32N 88 37W
Yalleroi 98 24 3 S 145 42 E
Yallourn 97 38 10 S 146 18 E
Yalong Jiang → 75 26 40N 101 55 E
Yalpukh, Oz. 46 45 30N 28 41 E
Yalta 56 44 30N 34 10 E
Yalu Chiang → 76 41 30N 126 30 E
Yalu He → 76 46 56N 123 30 E
Yalu Jiang → 76 40 0N 124 22 E
Yalutorovsk 58 56 41N 66 12 E
Yam Kinneret 62 32 45N 35 35 E
Yamagata 74 38 15N 140 15 E
Yamagata □ 74 38 30N 140 0 E
Yamaguchi 74 34 10N 131 32 E
Yamaguchi □ 74 34 20N 131 40 E
Yamal, Poluostrov 58 71 0N 70 0 E
Yamama 64 24 5N 47 30 E
Yamanashi □ 74 35 40N 138 40 E
Yamantau 52 54 20N 57 40 E
Yamantau, Gora 52 54 15N 58 6 E
Yamba 99 29 26 S 153 23 E
Yâmbiô 87 4 35N 28 16 E
Yambol 43 42 30N 26 36 E
Yamdena 73 7 45 S 131 20 E
Yamil 85 12 53N 8 4 E
Yamma-Yamma, L. 97 26 16 S 141 20 E
Yampa → 118 40 37N 108 59W
Yampi Sd. 96 16 8 S 123 38 E
Yampol 56 48 15N 28 15 E
Yamrat 85 10 11N 9 55 E
Yamrukchal 43 42 44N 24 52 E
Yamuna (Jumna) → 68 25 30N 81 53 E
Yamzho Yumco 75 28 48N 90 35 E
Yan 85 10 5N 12 11 E
Yan → 70 9 0N 81 10 E
Yana → 59 71 30N 136 0 E
Yanac 99 36 8 S 141 25 E
Yanai 74 33 58N 132 7 E
Yanam 70 16 47N 82 15 E
Yan'an 76 36 35N 109 26 E
Yanaul 52 56 25N 55 0 E
Yanbu 'al Baḩr 64 24 0N 38 5 E
Yancannia 99 30 12 S 142 35 E
Yanchang 76 36 43N 110 1 E
Yancheng, Henan, China 77 33 35N 114 0 E
Yancheng, Jiangsu, China 77 33 23N 120 8 E
Yanchi 76 37 48N 107 20 E
Yanchuan 76 36 51N 110 10 E
Yanco 100 34 38 S 146 27 E
Yandaran 98 24 43 S 152 6 E
Yanfolila 84 11 11N 8 9W
Yangambi 90 0 47N 24 20 E
Yangch'ü = Taiyuan 76 37 52N 112 33 E
Yangchun 75 22 11N 111 48 E
Yanggao 76 40 21N 113 55 E
Yangi-Yer 58 40 17N 68 48 E
Yangjiang 75 21 50N 110 59 E
Yangquan 76 37 58N 113 31 E
Yangshan 77 24 30N 112 40 E
Yangshuo 77 24 48N 110 29 E
Yangtze Kiang = Chang Jiang → 75 31 20N 121 52 E
Yangxin 77 29 50N 115 12 E
Yangzhou 77 32 21N 119 26 E
Yanhee Res. 71 17 30N 98 45 E
Yanji 76 42 59N 129 30 E
Yankton 116 42 55N 97 25W
Yanna 99 26 58 S 146 0 E
Yanonge 90 0 35N 24 38 E
Yanqi 75 42 5N 86 35 E
Yanqing 76 40 30N 115 58 E
Yanshan 77 28 15N 117 41 E
Yantabulla 99 29 21 S 145 0 E
Yantai 76 37 34N 121 22 E
Yanting 77 31 11N 105 24 E
Yantra → 43 43 40N 25 37 E
Yanzhou 76 35 35N 116 49 E
Yao 81 12 56N 17 33 E
Yaoundé 88 3 50N 11 35 E
Yap 94 9 31N 138 6 E
Yapen 73 1 50 S 136 0 E
Yapen, Selat 73 1 20 S 136 10 E
Yappar → 98 18 22 S 141 16 E
Yaqui → 120 27 37N 110 39W
Yar 55 58 14N 52 5 E
Yar-Sale 58 66 50N 70 50 E
Yaraka 97 24 53 S 144 3 E
Yarangüme 64 37 35N 29 8 E
Yaransk 55 57 22N 47 49 E
Yaratishky 54 54 3N 26 0 E
Yare → 13 52 36N 1 28 E
Yarensk 52 61 10N 49 8 E
Yarfa 86 24 40N 38 35 E
Yarí → 126 0 20 S 72 20W
Yarkand = Shache 75 38 20N 77 10 E
Yarker 113 44 23N 76 46W
Yarkhun → 69 36 17N 72 30 E
Yarmouth 107 43 50N 66 7W
Yarmuk → 62 32 38N 35 34 E
Yarmūk → 62 32 42N 35 40 E
Yaroslavl 55 57 35N 39 55 E
Yarra → 100 37 50 S 144 53 E
Yarram 99 38 29 S 146 9 E
Yarraman 99 26 50 S 152 0 E
Yarranvale 99 26 50 S 145 20 E
Yarras 99 31 25 S 152 20 E
Yarrawonga 100 36 0 S 146 0 E
Yartsevo, R.S.F.S.R., U.S.S.R. 54 55 6N 32 43 E
Yartsevo, R.S.F.S.R., U.S.S.R. 59 60 20N 90 0 E
Yasawa Group 101 17 00 S 177 23 E
Yaselda → 54 52 7N 26 28 E
Yashi 85 12 23N 7 54 E
Yasinovataya 56 48 7N 37 57 E
Yasinski, L. 106 53 16N 77 35W
Yasothon 71 15 50N 104 10 E
Yass 97 34 49 S 148 54 E
Yas'ur 62 32 54N 35 10 E
Yatağn 45 37 20N 28 10 E
Yates Center 117 37 53N 95 45W
Yathkyed L. 109 62 40N 98 0W
Yatsushiro 74 32 30N 130 40 E
Yatta Plateau 90 2 0 S 38 0 E
Yaṭṭah 62 31 27N 35 6 E
Yauyos 126 12 19 S 75 50W
Yaval 68 21 10N 75 42 E
Yavari → 126 4 21 S 70 2W
Yavne 62 31 52N 34 45 E
Yavorov 54 49 55N 23 20 E
Yawatahama 74 33 27N 132 24 E
Yawri B. 84 8 22N 13 0W
Yazd (Yezd) 65 31 55N 54 27 E
Yazdān 65 33 30N 60 50 E
Yazoo → 117 32 35N 90 50W
Yazoo City 117 32 48N 90 28W
Ybbs 26 48 12N 15 4 E
Ye Xian 76 37 8N 119 57 E
Yebbi-Souma 83 21 7N 17 54 E
Yebyu 67 14 15N 98 13 E
Yecla 33 38 35N 1 5W
Yedintsy 56 48 9N 27 18 E
Yefremov 55 53 8N 38 3 E
Yegorlyk → 57 46 33N 41 40 E
Yegorlykskaya 57 46 35N 40 35 E
Yegoryevsk 55 55 27N 38 55 E
Yegros 124 26 20 S 56 25W
Yehuda, Midbar 62 31 35N 35 15 E
Yei 87 4 9N 30 40 E
Yei, Nahr → 87 6 15N 30 13 E
Yelabuga 52 55 45N 52 4 E
Yelan 55 50 55N 43 43 E
Yelan-Kolenovski 55 51 16N 41 4 E
Yelandur 70 12 6N 77 0 E
Yelanskoye 59 61 25N 128 0 E
Yelarbon 99 28 33 S 150 38 E
Yelatma 55 55 0N 41 45 E
Yelets 55 52 40N 38 30 E
Yélimané 84 15 9N 10 34W
Yell 14 60 35N 1 5W
Yell Sd. 14 60 33N 1 15W
Yellamanchilli (Elamanchili) 70 17 33N 82 50 E
Yellow Mt. 100 32 31 S 146 52 E
Yellow Sea 76 35 0N 123 0 E
Yellowhead P. 108 52 53N 118 25W
Yellowknife 108 62 27N 114 29W
Yellowknife → 104 62 31N 114 19W
Yellowstone → 116 47 58N 103 59W
Yellowstone L. 118 44 30N 110 20W
Yellowstone National Park 118 44 35N 110 0W
Yellowtail Res. 118 45 6N 108 8W
Yelnya 54 54 35N 33 15 E
Yelsk 54 51 50N 29 10 E
Yelvertoft 98 20 13 S 138 45 E
Yelwa 85 10 49N 4 41 E
Yemen ■ 63 15 0N 44 0 E
Yenakiyevo 56 48 15N 38 15 E
Yenangyaung 67 20 30N 95 0 E
Yenda 99 34 13 S 146 14 E
Yendéré 84 10 12N 4 59W
Yendi 85 9 29N 0 1W
Yenisaía 44 41 1N 24 57 E
Yenisey → 58 71 50N 82 40 E
Yeniseysk 59 58 27N 92 13 E
Yeniseyskiy Zaliv 58 72 20N 81 0 E
Yenne 21 45 43N 5 44 E
Yenotayevka 57 47 15N 47 0 E
Yenyuka 59 57 57N 121 15 E
Yeo, L. 96 28 0 S 124 30 E
Yeola 70 20 0N 74 30 E
Yeotmal 70 20 20N 78 15 E
Yeovil 13 50 57N 2 38W
Yepes 32 39 55N 3 39W
Yeppoon 97 23 5 S 150 47 E
Yeráki 45 37 0N 22 42 E
Yerbent 58 39 30N 58 50 E
Yerbogachen 59 61 16N 108 0 E
Yerevan 57 40 10N 44 31 E
Yerla → 70 16 50N 74 30 E
Yermak 58 52 2N 76 55 E
Yermakovo 59 52 25N 126 20 E
Yermo 119 34 58N 116 50W
Yerofey Pavlovich 59 54 0N 122 0 E
Yershov 55 51 22N 48 16 E
Yerushalayim 62 31 47N 35 10 E
Yerville 18 49 40N 0 53 E
Yes Tor 13 50 41N 3 59W
Yesnogorsk 55 54 32N 37 38 E
Yeso 117 34 29N 104 37W
Yessentuki 57 44 0N 42 53 E
Yessey 59 68 29N 102 10 E
Yeste 33 38 22N 2 19W
Yeu, I. d' 18 46 42N 2 20W
Yevlakh 57 40 39N 47 7 E
Yevpatoriya 56 45 15N 33 20 E
Yevstratovskiy 55 50 11N 39 45 E
Yeya → 57 46 40N 38 40 E
Yeysk 56 46 40N 38 12 E
Yhati 124 25 45 S 56 35W
Yhú 125 25 0 S 56 0W
Yi → 124 33 7 S 57 8W
Yi Xian 76 41 30N 121 22 E
Yiali 45 36 41N 27 11 E
Yi'allaq, G. 86 30 21N 33 31 E
Yiáltra 45 38 51N 22 59 E
Yianisádhes 45 35 20N 26 10 E
Yiannitsa 44 40 46N 22 24 E
Yibin 75 28 45N 104 32 E
Yichang 75 30 40N 111 20 E
Yicheng 76 35 42N 111 40 E
Yichuan 76 36 2N 110 10 E
Yichun, Heilongjiang, China 75 47 44N 128 52 E
Yichun, Jiangxi, China 77 27 48N 114 22 E
Yidhá 44 40 35N 22 53 E
Yidu 76 36 43N 118 28 E
Yihuang 77 27 30N 116 12 E
Yijun 76 35 28N 109 8 E
Yilan, China 76 46 19N 129 34 E
Yilan, Taiwan 75 24 51N 121 44 E
Yilehuli Shan 76 51 20N 124 20 E
Yimianpo 76 45 7N 128 2 E
Yinchuan 76 38 30N 106 15 E
Ying He → 77 32 30N 116 30 E
Ying Xian 76 39 32N 113 10 E
Yingcheng 77 30 56N 113 35 E
Yingde 77 24 10N 113 25 E
Yingkou 76 40 37N 122 18 E
Yingshan 77 30 41N 115 32 E
Yingshang 77 32 38N 116 12 E
Yingtan 75 28 12N 117 0 E
Yining 75 43 58N 81 10 E

Yinjiang 77 28 1N 108 21 E
Yinkanie 99 34 22 S 140 17 E
Yinnietharra 96 24 39 S 116 12 E
Yioúra, Greece 44 39 23N 24 10 E
Yioúra, Greece 45 37 32N 24 40 E
Yipinglang 75 25 10N 101 52 E
Yirga Alem 87 6 48N 38 22 E
Yirshi 76 47 18N 119 49 E
Yishan 75 24 28N 108 38 E
Yíthion 45 36 46N 22 34 E
Yitong 76 43 13N 125 20 E
Yitulihe 76 50 38N 121 34 E
Yixing 77 31 21N 119 48 E
Yiyang, Henan, China 77 34 27N 112 10 E
Yiyang, Hunan, China 75 28 35N 112 18 E
Yizhang 77 25 27N 112 57 E
Yizre'el 62 32 34N 35 19 E
Ylitornio 50 66 19N 23 39 E
Ylivieska 50 64 4N 24 28 E
Yngaren 49 58 50N 16 35 E
Ynykchanskiy 59 60 15N 137 35 E
Yoakum 117 29 20N 97 20W
Yog Pt. 73 14 6N 124 12 E
Yogan 85 6 23N 1 30 E
Yogyakarta 73 7 49 S 110 22 E
Yoho Nat. Park 108 51 25N 116 30W
Yojoa, L. de 120 14 53N 88 0W
Yokadouma 88 3 26N 15 6 E
Yokkaichi 74 35 0N 136 38 E
Yoko 85 5 32N 12 20 E
Yokohama 74 35 27N 139 28 E
Yokosuka 74 35 20N 139 40 E
Yola 85 9 10N 12 29 E
Yolaina, Cordillera de 121 11 30N 84 0W
Yonago 74 35 25N 133 19 E
Yong Peng 71 2 0N 103 3 E
Yong'an 77 25 59N 117 25 E
Yongchun 77 25 16N 118 20 E
Yongding 77 24 43N 116 45 E
Yongfeng 77 27 20N 115 22 E
Yongfu 77 24 59N 109 59 E
Yonghe 76 36 46N 110 38 E
Yongji 77 34 52N 110 28 E
Yongshun 77 29 2N 109 51 E
Yongxin 77 26 58N 114 15 E
Yongxing 77 26 9N 113 8 E
Yongxiu 77 29 2N 115 42 E
Yonibana 84 8 30N 12 19W
Yonkers 114 40 57N 73 51W
Yonne □ 19 47 50N 3 40 E
Yonne → 19 48 23N 2 58 E
Yoqne'am 62 32 40N 35 6 E
York, Austral. 96 31 52 S 116 47 E
York, U.K. 12 53 58N 1 7W
York, Ala., U.S.A. 115 32 30N 88 18W
York, Nebr., U.S.A. 116 40 55N 97 35W
York, Pa., U.S.A. 114 39 57N 76 43W
York, C. 97 10 42 S 142 31 E
York, Kap 4 75 55N 66 25W
York Sd. 96 14 50 S 125 5 E
Yorke Pen. 97 34 50 S 137 40 E
Yorkshire Wolds 12 54 0N 0 30W
Yorkton 109 51 11N 102 28W
Yorktown 117 29 0N 97 29W
Yosemite National Park 119 38 0N 119 30W
Yoshkar Ola 55 56 38N 47 55 E
Yŏsu 77 34 47N 127 45 E
Yotvata 62 29 55N 35 2 E
You Jiang → 75 23 22N 110 3 E
Youbou 108 48 53N 124 13W
Youghal 15 51 58N 7 51W
Youghal B. 15 51 55N 7 50W
Youkounkoun 84 12 35N 13 11W
Young, Austral. 97 34 19 S 148 18 E
Young, Can. 109 51 47N 105 45W
Young, Uruguay 124 32 44 S 57 36W
Young, U.S.A. 119 34 9N 110 56W
Younghusband Pen. 99 36 0 S 139 25 E
Youngstown, Can. 109 51 35N 111 10W
Youngstown, N.Y., U.S.A. 112 43 16N 79 2W
Youngstown, Ohio, U.S.A. 114 41 7N 80 41W
Youngsville 112 41 51N 79 21W
Youssoufia 82 32 16N 8 31W
Youyang 77 28 47N 108 42 E
Youyu 76 40 10N 112 20 E
Yozgat 64 39 51N 34 47 E
Ypané → 124 23 29 S 57 19W
Yport 18 49 45N 0 15 E
Ypres = Ieper 16 50 51N 2 53 E
Ypsilanti 114 42 18N 83 40W
Yreka 118 41 44N 122 40W
Ysleta 119 31 45N 106 24W
Yssingeaux 21 45 9N 4 8 E
Ystad 49 55 26N 13 50 E
Ythan → 14 57 26N 2 12W
Ytterhogdal 48 62 12N 14 56 E
Ytyk-Kel 59 62 30N 133 45 E
Yu Shan 75 23 30N 120 58 E
Yu Xian, Hebei, China 76 39 50N 114 35 E
Yu Xian, Henan, China 77 34 10N 113 28 E
Yuan Jiang → 75 28 55N 111 50 E
Yuanling 75 28 29N 110 22 E
Yuanyang 75 23 10N 102 43 E
Yuba City 118 39 12N 121 37W
Yucatán □ 120 21 30N 86 30W
Yucatán, Canal de 121 22 0N 86 30W
Yucca 119 34 56N 114 6W
Yucheng 76 36 55N 116 32 E
Yuci 76 37 42N 112 46 E
Yudino, R.S.F.S.R., U.S.S.R. 55 55 51N 48 55 E
Yudino, R.S.F.S.R., U.S.S.R. 58 55 10N 67 55 E
Yudu 77 25 59N 115 30 E
Yueqing 77 28 9N 120 59 E
Yueyang 77 29 21N 113 5 E
Yugan 77 28 43N 116 37 E
Yugoslavia ■ 37 44 0N 20 0 E
Yuhuan 77 28 9N 121 12 E
Yujiang 77 28 10N 116 43 E
Yukhnov 54 54 44N 35 15 E
Yukon Territory □ 104 63 0N 135 0W
Yukti 59 63 26N 105 42 E
Yule → 96 20 41 S 118 17 E
Yuli 85 9 44N 10 12 E
Yülin 77 18 10N 109 31 E
Yulin, Guangxi Zhuangzu, China 77 22 40N 110 8 E
Yulin, Shaanxi, China 76 38 20N 109 30 E
Yuma, Ariz., U.S.A. 119 32 45N 114 37W
Yuma, Colo., U.S.A. 116 40 10N 102 43W
Yuma, B. de 121 18 20N 68 35W
Yumbe 90 3 28N 31 15 E
Yumbi 90 1 12 S 26 15 E
Yumen 75 39 50N 97 30 E
Yun Xian 75 32 50N 110 46 E
Yungas 126 17 0 S 66 0W
Yungay 124 37 10 S 72 5W
Yunhe 77 28 8N 119 33 E
Yunlin 77 23 42N 120 30 E
Yunnan □ 75 25 0N 102 0 E
Yunquera de Henares 32 40 47N 3 11W
Yunta 99 32 34 S 139 36 E
Yunxiao 77 23 59N 117 18 E
Yur 59 59 52N 137 41 E
Yurgao 58 55 42N 84 51 E
Yuribei 58 71 8N 76 58 E
Yurimaguas 126 5 55 S 76 7W
Yurya 55 59 1N 49 13 E
Yuryev-Polskiy 55 56 30N 39 40 E
Yuryevets 55 57 25N 43 2 E
Yuscarán 121 13 58N 86 45W
Yushu, Jilin, China 76 44 43N 126 38 E
Yushu, Qinghai, China 75 33 5N 96 55 E
Yuyao 77 30 3N 121 10 E
Yuzha 55 56 34N 42 1 E
Yuzhno-Sakhalinsk 59 46 58N 142 45 E
Yvelines □ 19 48 40N 1 45 E
Yverdon 25 46 47N 6 39 E
Yvetot 18 49 37N 0 44 E

Z

Zaandam 16 52 26N 4 49 E
Zab, Monts du 83 34 55N 5 0 E
Žabalj 42 45 21N 20 5 E
Žabari 42 44 22N 21 15 E
Zabarjad 86 23 40N 36 12 E
Zabaykalskiy 59 49 40N 117 25 E
Zabid 63 14 0N 43 10 E
Ząbkowice Śląskie 28 50 35N 16 50 E
Žabljak 42 43 18N 19 7 E
Zabłudów 28 53 0N 23 19 E
Žabno 27 50 9N 20 53 E
Zābol 65 31 0N 61 32 E
Zābolī 65 27 10N 61 35 E
Zabré 85 11 12N 0 36W
Zabrze 28 50 18N 18 50 E
Zabul □ 65 32 0N 67 0 E
Zacapa 120 14 59N 89 31W
Zacatecas 120 22 49N 102 34W
Zacatecas □ 120 23 30N 103 0W
Zacatecoluca 120 13 29N 88 51W
Zacoalco 120 20 14N 103 33W
Zadar 39 44 8N 15 14 E
Zadawa 85 11 33N 10 19 E
Zadetkyi Kyun 72 10 0N 98 25 E
Zadonsk 55 52 25N 38 56 E
Zafora 45 36 5N 26 24 E
Zafra 31 38 26N 6 30W
Zafriya 62 31 59N 34 51 E
Żagań 28 51 39N 15 22 E
Zagazig 86 30 40N 31 30 E
Zaghouan 83 36 23N 10 10 E
Zaglivérion 44 40 36N 23 15 E
Zaglou 82 27 17N 0 3W
Zagnanado 85 7 18N 2 28 E
Zagorá 44 39 27N 23 6 E
Zagora 82 30 22N 5 51W
Zagórów 28 52 10N 17 54 E
Zagorsk 55 56 20N 38 10 E
Zagórz 27 49 30N 22 14 E
Zagreb 39 45 50N 16 0 E
Zāgros, Kudhā-ye 65 33 45N 47 0 E
Žagubica 42 44 15N 21 47 E
Zaguinaso 84 10 1N 6 14W
Zagyva → 27 47 5N 20 4 E
Zāhedān 65 29 30N 60 50 E
Zahirabad 70 17 43N 77 37 E
Zahlah 64 33 52N 35 50 E
Zahna 24 51 54N 12 47 E
Zahrez Chergui 82 35 0N 3 30 E
Zahrez Rharbi 82 34 50N 2 55 E
Zaïr 82 29 47N 5 51W
Zaïre → 88 6 4 S 12 24 E
Zaïre, Rep. of ■ 88 3 0 S 23 0 E
Zaječar 42 43 53N 22 18 E
Zakamensk 59 50 23N 103 17 E
Zakataly 57 41 38N 46 35 E
Zakavkazye 57 42 0N 44 0 E
Zākhū 64 37 10N 42 50 E
Zákinthos 45 37 47N 20 57 E
Zaklików 28 50 46N 22 7 E
Zakopane 27 49 18N 19 57 E
Zakroczym 28 52 26N 20 38 E
Zala □ 27 46 42N 16 50 E
Zala → 27 46 43N 17 16 E
Zalaegerszeg 27 46 53N 16 47 E
Zalakomár 27 46 33N 17 10 E
Zalalövö 27 46 51N 16 35 E
Zalamea de la Serena 31 38 40N 5 38W
Zalamea la Real 31 37 41N 6 38W
Zalău 46 47 12N 23 3 E
Zalazna 55 58 39N 52 31 E
Žalec 39 46 16N 15 10 E
Zaleshchiki 56 48 45N 25 45 E
Zalewo 28 53 50N 19 41 E
Zalingei 81 12 51N 23 29 E
Zalțan, Jabal 83 28 46N 19 45 E
Zambeke 90 2 8N 25 17 E
Zambeze → 91 18 55 S 36 4 E
Zambezi 89 13 30 S 23 15 E
Zambezi = Zambeze → 91 18 55 S 36 4 E
Zambezia □ 91 16 15 S 37 30 E
Zambia ■ 89 15 0 S 28 0 E
Zamboanga 73 6 59N 122 3 E
Zambrów 28 52 59N 22 14 E
Zametchino 55 53 30N 42 30 E
Zamora, Mexico 120 20 0N 102 21W
Zamora, Spain 30 41 30N 5 45W
Zamora □ 30 41 30N 5 46W
Zamość 28 50 43N 23 15 E
Zamość □ 28 50 40N 23 10 E
Zamzam, W. 83 31 0N 14 30 E
Zan 85 9 26N 0 17W
Zanaga 88 2 48 S 13 48 E
Záncara → 33 39 18N 3 18W
Zandvoort 16 52 22N 4 32 E
Zanesville 114 39 56N 82 2W
Zangue → 91 17 50 S 35 21 E
Zanjan 64 36 40N 48 35 E
Zannone 40 40 58N 13 2 E
Zante = Zákinthos 45 37 47N 20 54 E
Zanthus 96 31 2 S 123 34 E
Zanzibar 90 6 12 S 39 12 E
Zanzūr 83 32 55N 13 1 E
Zaouiet El-Kala = Bordj Omar Driss 83 28 4N 6 40 E
Zaouiet Reggane 82 26 32N 0 3 E
Zapadna Morava → 42 43 38N 21 30 E
Zapadnaya Dvina 54 56 15N 32 3 E
Zapadnaya Dvina → 54 57 4N 24 3 E
Západné Beskydy 27 49 30N 19 0 E
Zapadni Rodopi 43 41 50N 24 0 E
Západočeský □ 26 49 35N 13 0 E
Západoslovenský □ 27 48 30N 17 30 E
Zapala 128 39 0 S 70 5W
Zapaleri, Cerro 124 22 49 S 67 11W
Zapata 117 26 56N 99 17W
Zapatón → 31 39 0N 6 49W
Zapodnyy Sayan 59 52 30N 94 0 E
Zapolyarnyy 52 69 26N 30 51 E
Zaporozhye 56 47 50N 35 10 E
Zapponeta 41 41 27N 15 57 E
Zara 64 39 58N 37 43 E
Zaragoza, Coahuila, Mexico 120 28 30N 101 0W
Zaragoza, Nuevo León, Mexico 120 24 0N 99 46W
Zaragoza, Spain 32 41 39N 0 53W
Zaragoza □ 32 41 35N 1 0W
Zarand 65 30 46N 56 34 E
Zărandului, Munții 46 46 14N 22 7 E
Zaranj 65 30 55N 61 55 E
Zarasai 54 55 40N 26 20 E
Zarate 124 34 7 S 59 0W
Zaraysk 55 54 48N 38 53 E
Zarembo I. 108 56 20N 132 50W
Zaria 85 11 0N 7 40 E
Zarisberge 92 24 30 S 16 15 E
Zárkon 44 39 38N 22 6 E
Żarów 28 50 56N 16 29 E
Zarqā' → 62 32 10N 35 37 E
Zaruma 126 3 40 S 79 38W
Żary 28 51 37N 15 10 E
Zarza de Alange 31 38 49N 6 13W
Zarza de Granadilla 30 40 14N 6 3W
Zarza, La 31 37 42N 6 51W
Zarzaïtine 83 28 15N 9 34 E
Zarzis 83 33 31N 11 2 E
Zas 30 43 4N 8 53W
Zashiversk 59 67 25N 142 40 E
Zaskar Mountains 69 33 15N 77 30 E
Zastron 92 30 18 S 27 7 E
Žatec 26 50 20N 13 32 E
Zator 27 49 59N 19 28 E
Zavala 42 42 50N 17 59 E
Zavarāh 65 33 29N 52 28 E
Zavetnoye 57 47 13N 43 50 E
Zavidovići 42 44 27N 18 13 E
Zavitinsk 59 50 10N 129 20 E
Zavodoski 5 56 0 S 27 45W
Zavolzhsk 55 57 30N 42 10 E
Zavolzhye 55 56 37N 43 26 E
Zawadzkie 28 50 37N 18 28 E
Zawichost 28 50 48N 21 51 E
Zawidów 28 51 1N 15 1 E
Zawiercie 28 50 30N 19 24 E
Zāwiyat al Bayḍā 81 32 30N 21 40 E
Zawyet Shammâs 86 31 30N 26 37 E
Zâwyet Um el Rakham 86 31 18N 27 1 E
Zâwyet Ungeîla 86 31 23N 26 42 E
Zāyandeh → 65 32 35N 52 0 E
Zayarsk 59 56 12N 102 55 E
Zaysan 58 47 28N 84 52 E
Zaysan, Oz. 58 48 0N 83 0 E
Zaytā 62 32 23N 35 2 E
Zāzamt, W. 83 30 29N 14 30 E
Zazir, O. → 83 22 0N 5 40 E
Zázrivá 27 49 16N 19 7 E
Zbarazh 54 49 43N 25 44 E
Zbąszyń 28 52 14N 15 56 E
Zbąszynek 28 52 16N 15 51 E
Zblewo 28 53 56N 18 19 E
Zdolbunov 54 50 30N 26 15 E
Ždrelo 42 44 16N 21 28 E
Zduńska Wola 28 51 37N 18 59 E
Zduny 28 51 39N 17 21 E
Zeballos 108 49 59N 126 50W
Zebediela 93 24 20 S 19 7 E
Zeebrugge 16 51 19N 3 12 E
Zeehan 97 41 52 S 145 25 E
Zeeland □ 16 51 30N 3 50 E
Ze'elim 62 31 13N 34 32 E
Zeerust 92 25 31 S 26 4 E
Zefat 62 32 58N 35 29 E
Zegdou 82 29 51N 4 45W
Zege 87 11 43N 37 18 E
Zégoua 84 10 32N 5 35W
Zehdenick 24 52 59N 13 20 E
Zeila 63 11 21N 43 30 E
Zeist 16 52 5N 5 15 E
Zeitz 24 51 3N 12 9 E
Żelechów 28 51 49N 21 54 E
Zelengora 42 43 22N 18 30 E
Zelenika 42 42 27N 18 37 E
Zelenodolsk 55 55 55N 48 30 E
Zelenogradsk 54 54 53N 20 29 E
Zelenokumsk 57 44 24N 43 53 E
Zelënyy 57 48 6N 50 45 E
Zeleznik 42 44 43N 20 23 E
Zell, Baden, Ger. 25 47 42N 7 50 E
Zell, Rhld-Pfz., Ger. 25 50 2N 7 11 E
Zell am See 26 47 19N 12 47 E
Zella Mehlis 24 50 40N 10 41 E
Zelów 28 51 28N 19 14 E
Zelzate 16 51 13N 3 47 E
Zembra, I. 83 37 5N 10 56 E
Zémio 90 5 2N 25 5 E
Zemlya Frantsa Iosifa 4 81 0N 55 0 E
Zemmora 82 35 44N 0 51 E
Zemoul, O. → 82 29 15N 7 0W
Zemun 42 44 51N 20 25 E
Zengbe 85 5 46N 13 4 E
Zenica 42 44 10N 17 57 E
Zenina 82 34 30N 2 37 E
Žepče 42 44 28N 18 2 E
Zeraf, Bahr ez → 87 9 42N 30 52 E
Zerbst 24 51 59N 12 8 E
Zerhamra 82 29 58N 2 30W
Żerków 28 52 4N 17 32 E
Zermatt 25 46 2N 7 46 E
Zernez 25 46 42N 10 7 E
Zernograd 57 46 52N 40 19 E
Zerqani 44 41 30N 20 20 E
Zestafoni 57 42 6N 43 0 E
Zetel 24 53 25N 7 57 E
Zeulenroda 24 50 39N 12 0 E
Zeven 24 53 17N 9 19 E
Zévio 38 45 23N 11 10 E
Zeya 59 53 48N 127 14 E
Zeya → 59 53 13N 127 35 E
Zêzere → 31 39 28N 8 20W
Zgierz 28 51 50N 19 27 E
Zgorzelec 28 51 10N 15 0 E
Zhabinka 54 52 13N 24 2 E
Zhailma 58 51 37N 61 33 E
Zhangguangcai Ling 76 45 0N 129 0 E
Zhanghua 75 24 6N 120 29 E
Zhangjiakou 76 40 48N 114 55 E
Zhangping 77 25 17N 117 23 E
Zhangpu 77 24 8N 117 35 E
Zhangwu 76 42 43N 123 52 E
Zhangye 75 38 50N 100 23 E
Zhangzhou 75 24 30N 117 35 E
Zhanhua 76 37 40N 118 8 E
Zhanjiang 75 21 15N 110 20 E
Zhanyi 75 25 38N 103 48 E
Zhanyu 76 44 30N 122 30 E
Zhao Xian 76 37 43N 114 45 E
Zhao'an 77 23 41N 117 10 E
Zhaoping 77 24 11N 110 48 E
Zhaoqing 77 23 0N 112 20 E
Zhaotong 75 27 20N 103 44 E
Zhaoyuan 76 37 20N 120 23 E
Zharkovskiy 54 55 56N 32 19 E
Zhashkov 56 49 15N 30 5 E
Zhdanov 56 47 5N 37 31 E
Zhecheng 77 34 7N 115 20 E
Zhejiang □ 75 29 0N 120 0 E
Zheleznodorozhny 52 62 35N 50 55 E
Zheleznogorsk 54 52 22N 35 23 E
Zheleznogorsk-Ilimskiy 59 56 34N 104 8 E
Zheltyye Vody 56 48 21N 33 31 E
Zhen'an 77 33 27N 109 9 E
Zhenfeng 77 25 22N 105 40 E
Zheng'an 77 28 32N 107 27 E
Zhengding 76 38 8N 114 32 E
Zhenghe 77 27 20N 118 50 E
Zhengyang 77 32 37N 114 22 E
Zhengyangguan 77 32 30N 116 29 E
Zhengzhou 77 34 45N 113 34 E
Zhenjiang 75 32 11N 119 26 E
Zhenlai 76 45 50N 123 5 E
Zhenning 77 26 4N 105 45 E
Zhenyuan, Gansu, China 76 35 35N 107 30 E
Zhenyuan, Guizhou, China 75 27 4N 108 21 E
Zherdevka 55 51 56N 41 29 E
Zhigansk 59 66 48N 123 27 E
Zhigulevsk 55 53 28N 49 30 E
Zhijiang 75 27 27N 109 42 E
Zhirnovsk 55 50 57N 44 49 E
Zhitomir 54 50 20N 28 40 E
Zhizdra 54 53 45N 34 40 E
Zhlobin 54 52 55N 30 0 E
Zhmerinka 56 49 2N 28 2 E
Zhodino 54 54 5N 28 17 E
Zhokhova, Ostrov 59 76 4N 152 40 E
Zhong Xian 77 30 21N 108 1 E
Zhongdian 75 27 48N 99 42 E
Zhongshan 77 22 26N 113 20 E
Zhongwei 76 37 30N 105 12 E
Zhongxiang 77 31 12N 112 34 E
Zhoushan Dao 77 28 5N 122 10 E
Zhouzhi 77 34 10N 108 12 E
Zhovtnevoye 56 46 54N 32 3 E
Zhuanghe 76 39 40N 123 0 E
Zhucheng 76 36 0N 119 27 E
Zhugqu 77 33 40N 104 30 E
Zhuji 77 29 40N 120 10 E
Zhukovka 54 53 35N 33 50 E
Zhumadian 75 32 59N 114 2 E
Zhuo Xian 76 39 28N 115 58 E
Zhupanovo 59 53 40N 159 52 E
Zhushan 77 32 15N 110 13 E
Zhuxi 77 32 25N 109 40 E
Zhuzhou 75 27 49N 113 12 E
Ziarat 68 30 25N 67 49 E
Zibo 76 36 47N 118 3 E
Zidarovo 43 42 20N 27 24 E
Ziębice 28 50 37N 17 2 E
Zielona Góra 28 51 57N 15 31 E
Zielona Góra □ 28 51 57N 15 30 E
Zierikzee 16 51 40N 3 55 E
Ziesar 24 52 16N 12 19 E
Zifta 86 30 43N 31 14 E
Zigey 81 14 43N 15 50 E
Zigong 75 29 15N 104 48 E
Zigui 75 31 0N 110 40 E
Ziguinchor 84 12 35N 16 20W
Zikhron Ya'Aqov 62 32 34N 34 56 E

Zile **64** 40 15N 35 52 E
Žilina **27** 49 12N 18 42 E
Zillah **83** 28 30N 17 33 E
Zillertaler Alpen **26** 47 6N 11 45 E
Zima **59** 54 0N 102 5 E
Zimane, Adrar in **82** 22 10N 4 30 E
Zimapán **120** 20 54N 99 20W
Zimba **91** 17 20 S 26 11 E
Zimbabwe **91** 20 16 S 30 54 E
Zimbabwe ■ **91** 20 0 S 30 0 E
Zimnicea **46** 43 40N 25 22 E
Zimovniki **57** 47 10N 42 25 E
Zinder **85** 13 48N 9 0 E
Zinga **91** 9 16 S 38 49 E
Zingst **24** 54 24N 12 45 E
Ziniaré **85** 12 35N 1 18W
Zinjibār **63** 13 5N 45 23 E
Zinkgruvan **49** 58 50N 15 6 E
Zinnowitz **24** 54 5N 13 54 E
Zion Nat. Park **119** 37 25N 112 50W
Zipaquirá **126** 5 0N 74 0W
Zippori **62** 32 45N 35 16 E
Zirc **27** 47 17N 17 42 E
Žiri **39** 46 5N 14 5 E
Žirje **39** 43 39N 15 42 E
Zirko **65** 25 0N 53 40 E
Zirl **26** 47 17N 11 14 E
Zisterdorf **27** 48 33N 16 45 E
Zitácuaro **120** 19 28N 100 21W
Zitava ⤳ **27** 48 14N 18 21 E
Žitište **42** 45 30N 20 32 E
Zítsa **44** 39 47N 20 40 E
Zittau **24** 50 54N 14 47 E
Zitundo **93** 26 48 S 32 47 E
Živinice **42** 44 27N 18 36 E
Ziway, L. **87** 8 0N 38 50 E
Zixi **77** 27 45N 117 4 E
Ziyang **77** 32 32N 108 31 E
Ziz, Oued ⤳ **82** 31 40N 4 15W
Zizhong **77** 29 48N 104 47 E
Zlarin **39** 43 42N 15 49 E
Zlatar, Hrvatska, Yugo. **39** 46 5N 16 3 E
Zlatar, Srbija, Yugo. **42** 43 25N 19 47 E
Zlataritsa **43** 43 2N 25 55 E
Zlatibor **42** 43 45N 19 43 E
Zlatitsa **43** 42 41N 24 7 E
Zlatna **46** 46 8N 23 11 E
Zlatograd **43** 41 22N 25 7 E
Zlatoust **52** 55 10N 59 40 E
Zletovo **42** 41 59N 22 17 E
Ẓlītan **83** 32 32N 14 35 E
Złocieniec **28** 53 30N 16 1 E
Złoczew **28** 51 24N 18 35 E
Zlot **42** 44 1N 22 0 E
Złotoryja **28** 51 8N 15 55 E
Złotów **28** 53 22N 17 2 E
Złoty Stok **28** 50 27N 16 53 E
Zmeinogorsk **58** 51 10N 82 13 E
Żmigród **28** 51 28N 16 53 E
Zmiyev **56** 49 39N 36 27 E
Znamenka **56** 48 45N 32 30 E
Znamensk **54** 54 37N 21 17 E
Żnin **28** 52 51N 17 44 E
Znojmo **26** 48 50N 16 2 E
Zoar **92** 33 30 S 21 26 E
Zobia **90** 3 0N 25 59 E
Zogno **38** 45 49N 9 41 E
Zolochev **54** 49 45N 24 51 E
Zolotonosha **56** 49 39N 32 5 E
Zomba **91** 15 22 S 35 19 E
Zongo **88** 4 20N 18 35 E
Zonguldak **56** 41 28N 31 50 E
Zorgo **85** 12 15N 0 35W
Zorita **31** 39 17N 5 39W
Zorleni **46** 46 14N 27 44 E
Zornitsa **43** 42 23N 26 58 E
Zorra Island **120** 9 18N 79 52W
Zorritos **126** 3 43 S 80 40W
Zory **27** 50 3N 18 44 E
Zorzor **84** 7 46N 9 28W
Zossen **24** 52 13N 13 28 E
Zou Xiang **77** 35 30N 116 58 E
Zouar **83** 20 30N 16 32 E
Zouérate **80** 22 44N 12 21W
Zousfana, O. ⤳ **82** 31 28N 2 17W
Zoutkamp **16** 53 20N 6 18 E
Zrenjanin **42** 45 22N 20 23 E
Zuarungu **85** 10 49N 0 46W
Zuba **85** 9 11N 7 12 E
Zubair, Jazāir **87** 15 0N 42 10 E
Zubia **31** 37 8N 3 33W
Zubtsov **54** 56 10N 34 34 E
Zuénoula **84** 7 34N 6 3W
Zuera **32** 41 51N 0 49W
Zuetina **83** 30 58N 20 7 E
Zufar **63** 17 40N 54 0 E
Zug **25** 47 10N 8 31 E
Zugdidi **57** 42 30N 41 55 E
Zugersee **25** 47 7N 8 35 E
Zugspitze **25** 47 25N 10 59 E
Zuid-Holland □ **16** 52 0N 4 35 E
Zuidhorn **16** 53 15N 6 23 E
Zújar **33** 37 34N 2 50W
Zújar ⤳ **31** 39 1N 5 47W
Zújar, Pantano del **31** 38 55N 5 35W
Zula **87** 15 17N 39 40 E
Zulpich **24** 50 41N 6 38 E
Zululand **93** 43 19N 2 15 E
Zumaya **32** 43 19N 2 15W
Zumbo **91** 15 35 S 30 26 E
Zummo **85** 9 51N 12 59 E
Zungeru **85** 9 48N 6 8 E
Zunhua **76** 40 18N 117 58 E
Zuni **119** 35 7N 108 57W
Zunyi **75** 27 42N 106 53 E
Županja **42** 45 4N 18 43 E
Zuqar **87** 14 0N 42 40 E
Žur **42** 42 13N 20 34 E
Zürich **25** 47 22N 8 32 E
Zürich □ **25** 47 26N 8 40 E
Zürichsee **25** 47 18N 8 40 E
Zuromin **28** 53 4N 19 51 E
Zuru **85** 11 20N 5 11 E
Žut **39** 43 52N 15 17 E
Zutphen **16** 52 9N 6 12 E
Zuwārah **83** 32 58N 12 1 E
Zuyevka **55** 58 25N 51 10 E
Žužemberk **39** 45 52N 14 56 E
Zvenigorodka **56** 49 4N 30 56 E
Zverinogolovskoye **58** 54 23N 64 40 E
Zvezdets **43** 42 6N 27 26 E
Zvolen **27** 48 33N 19 10 E
Zvonce **42** 42 57N 22 34 E
Zvornik **42** 44 26N 19 7 E
Zwedru (Tchien) **84** 5 59N 8 15W
Zweibrücken **25** 49 15N 7 20 E
Zwenkau **24** 51 13N 12 19 E
Zwettl **26** 48 35N 15 9 E
Zwickau **24** 50 43N 12 30 E
Zwiesel **25** 49 1N 13 14 E
Zwischenahn **24** 53 12N 8 1 E
Zwoleń **28** 51 21N 21 36 E
Zwolle, Neth. **16** 52 31N 6 6 E
Zwolle, U.S.A. **117** 31 38N 93 38W
Żychlin **28** 52 15N 19 37 E
Zymoetz ⤳ **108** 54 33N 128 31W
Żyrardów **28** 52 3N 20 28 E
Zyrya **57** 40 20N 50 15 E
Zyryanka **59** 65 45N 150 51 E
Zyryanovsk **58** 49 43N 84 20 E
Żywiec **27** 49 42N 19 10 E

Maps, Illustrations and Index printed in Great Britain by George Philip Printers Ltd., London